Contemporary Sociology

In memory of Rob Moore

Contemporary Sociology

Edited by Martin Holborn

Contributions by

Mary Daly
Mark Erikson
Martyn Hamersley
Paul Heelas
Siniša Malešević
David Miller
Darren O'Byrne
Greg Philo
Robert Reiner
Sasha Scambler
Beverley Skeggs
Philip W. Sutton
Kath Woodward

Michael S. Drake
Lorraine Green
Catherine Happer
Paul Hopper
Vanessa May
Rob Moore
William Outhwaite
Andrew Pilkington
Graham Scambler
Sheila Scraton
Tim Strangleman
Beccy Watson

polity

CONTENTS

PREFACE

This book was conceived as a way of moving beyond both general sociological textbooks and books of readings.

Sociology textbooks, even those with quite large teams of contributors, inevitably suffer from the limited expertise of the authors. Sociology is a vast discipline in which it is difficult to keep fully abreast of developments in a single area of specialism, never mind the subject as a whole. In this book, the combined expertise of the twenty-five contributors across the twenty-one chapters is phenomenal. It enables the volume to address the most recent theoretical and empirical developments in the areas covered and gives the reader a sense of the innovation and excitement in each subdiscipline. Textbooks tend to provide ostensibly balanced and comprehensive accounts of the different areas of sociology, systematically examining the main approaches and most significant research in the area. Conventional textbooks also tend to offer some explanation of the historical development of different parts of the discipline – to work their way through the classics before looking at more recent material. This book is different.

The brief for the chapter authors was to pick out the most interesting and significant *contemporary* empirical and theoretical developments in the field and to adopt a position in relation to them rather than merely to report on them as an overview. Thus, each chapter develops distinct arguments about issues of particular interest and relevance. As well as offering an insight into contemporary sociological thinking in different areas and into contemporary social issues, each chapter is a substantial contribution to the field in its own right. Unlike books of readings, where each reading was written for a different purpose, at different times, all the chapters here were written specifically for this project; they are therefore equally contemporary, and there is a continuity of style and purpose across the chapters.

Contemporary Sociology is not intended to be an introduction for those entirely new to the subject but, rather, to engage those who already have some understanding of the subject and experience of studying it. It is particularly suitable for undergraduates in sociology and related social sciences in the later stages of first-year study or going on to second and third years, though it is also for anyone who would find accessible but sociologically sophisticated chapters on contemporary sociology valuable. As well as sociology undergraduates seeking sources for assignments, this might include teachers and lecturers wishing quickly to update their knowledge of contemporary developments in particular areas of sociology, students on professional courses and those studying other social sciences, and sociology students who want a flavour of different subject areas before choosing which options to study.

Although the contributors generally work in the British Isles, and Britain is featured more than anywhere else, there is extensive coverage both of international and global issues and of individual societies worldwide. *Contemporary Sociology* should therefore be an important resource for those interested in sociology anywhere in the world.

The chapters are self-contained and can be read in any order, but they are also linked together in sections. You may find it helpful to read all the chapters in a particular section in order to compare the way linked issues have been addressed. If you use the book in this way, you may wish to read the section introductions before doing this in order to put the diverse but connected chapters in context. The academics who wrote the chapters are all from (or closely connected to) sociology or other social science departments. Different institutions tend to have different takes on sociological issues (and departments are sometimes identified with particular schools of thought). There was no intention in the selection of contributors to choose sociologists with similar political or theoretical perspectives and, in fact, they represent a wide range of sociological viewpoints and approaches. While there are many overlaps between the views and theoretical starting points of the contributors, there is no overarching framework which unites them, and the different chapters reflect the rich diversity of contemporary sociology where theoretical influences can be quite eclectic.

A number of pedagogical features are included in the book so that it can be easily used as a teaching resource or as a resource for independent study. Among these are 'Seminar questions' which can be used for active learning, and chapters can readily be employed as readings for seminars. Each chapter finishes with suggestions for further readings so that students can use the text as a springboard as they begin to explore the topic in greater depth. Boxes provide case studies, give key definitions, or highlight some of the contemporary issues which are particularly pertinent to the theme.

Whatever the reasons that that led you to use this book, and wherever you are, we hope that it convinces you of the essential contribution that sociology can make, both to understanding and to changing social worlds.

Martin Holborn

CONTRIBUTORS

Mary Daly is Professor of Sociology and Social Policy, and Fellow of Green Templeton College, at the University of Oxford.

Michael S. Drake is Lecturer in Sociology at the University of Hull.

Mark Erickson is Reader in Sociology at the University of Brighton.

Lorraine Green is Assistant Professor in Social Work at the University of Nottingham.

Martyn Hammersley is Emeritus Professor in Educational and Social Research at The Open University.

Catherine Happer is a Research Associate in the Glasgow University Media Group at the University of Glasgow.

Paul Heelas is an independent researcher, formerly Professor in Religion and Modernity at Lancaster University and Senior Research Professor in the Sociology of Contemporary Spirituality at Erasmus University Rotterdam.

Paul Hopper is Senior Lecturer in the School of Humanities at the University of Brighton.

Siniša Malešević is Professor and Head of the School of Sociology at University College Dublin.

Vanessa May is Senior Lecturer in Sociology at the University of Manchester.

David Miller is Professor of Sociology at the University of Bath.

Rob Moore was University Senior Lecturer in Education, and Fellow of Homerton College, at the University of Cambridge.

Darren O'Byrne is Reader in Sociology and Human Rights at the University of Roehampton.

William Outhwaite is Professor of Sociology at Newcastle University.

Greg Philo is Professor of Communications and Social Change and Director of the Glasgow University Media Group at the University of Glasgow.

Andrew Pilkington is Professor of Sociology at the University of Northampton.

Robert Reiner is Emeritus Professor of Criminology at the London School of Economics and Political Science.

Graham Scambler is Visiting Professor of Sociology at Surrey University.

Sasha Scambler is Senior Lecturer in Sociology at King's College London.

Sheila Scraton is Emeritus Professor of Leisure and Feminist Studies at Leeds Beckett University.

Beverley Skeggs is Professor of Sociology at Goldsmiths, University of London.

Tim Strangleman is Professor of Sociology at the University of Kent.

Philip W. Sutton is an independent researcher, formerly of the University of Leeds and Robert Gordon University, Aberdeen.

Beccy Watson is Principal Lecturer in Leisure and Sport Studies at Leeds Beckett University.

Kath Woodward is Professor of Sociology at The Open University.

Section A
Social Divisions

It should come as no surprise to students of sociology that, despite its status as a social science, sociology is still influenced by the whims and the vagaries of fashion. Theories, topics, issues and styles of sociology come into and go out of fashion, with some sociology being relegated to historical footnotes and other types enjoying periodic revivals or even pre-eminence. The issues surrounding social divisions have never disappeared from the sociological agenda, but there have been times when they have become less central to sociological thinking. In many ways, the concept of class, the subject of chapter 1, was integral to the early development of sociology in twentieth-century Britain, with discussions of social class being very prominent in empirical sociology in the 1950s, 1960s and 1970s. Social class divisions were seen by many sociologists in this period as absolutely central to understanding power, differences in opportunity and life chances, with the work of both Marx and Weber enjoying prominent places in sociological theorizing. However, it soon became apparent that an exclusive focus on class inequality left significant gaps in the understanding of other forms of inequality, such as those relating to race and ethnicity (chapter 3), sex, gender and sexuality (chapter 2) and age and the life course (chapter 4). Some attempts were made to link these latter types of inequality to class divisions, but it was evident that they could not be reduced to class and that new empirical work and different theoretical approaches were required. Much of the early work in these three areas questioned the dominant essentialist views which saw race, sex differences and age as biological phenomena – inherent in nature and immutable. These issues are taken up by Andrew Pilkington, Kath Woodward and Lorraine Green in examining the nature of sex and gender, 'race' and age, respectively. All reach broadly social constructionist conclusions, although Lorraine Green acknowledges the reality of biological ageing and Kath Woodward the corporeality of bodies (albeit bodies that are shaped by performativity (Butler 1990)).

Sociological concern with sex/gender and race/ethnicity grew in the 1970s, with an increasing emphasis on empirical studies of gender inequality and racial and ethnic inequalities stemming from racism and other sources. Rather later in the twentieth century, interest in age and the life course grew, but it has remained a relative backwater in sociological analysis. In the later part of the twentieth century and the early part of the twenty-first century, studies of class, gender and ethnic inequality became somewhat less fashionable and were seen as less theoretically interesting than they had been in earlier decades. Partly, this was because, in affluent societies, with apparently rising living standards, issues of inequality seemed less pressing. The expanding middle class, increasing employment rates among married women, rising female educational achievement, and the relative success of some minority ethnic groups in the labour market and in education appeared to offer the promise that the significance of social divisions would decline. Theoretically, the rise of postmodernism and something of a cultural turn (Steinmetz 1999) within sociology increased the focus on issues of identity and consumption. In a consumer-orientated society, in which people, it was believed, could freely choose their identities (e.g., Crook, Pakulski and Waters 1992), an obsession with inequalities and social differences stemming from them seem slightly old-fashioned. There was no shortage of theories willing to question the salience of older approaches which were focused on inequality. For example, Ulrich Beck declared class a 'zombie category', which refused to go away but had entirely lost its life force as a genuinely useful way of understanding society (Beck [1995] 2002). There were those too who thought that multiculturalism had rendered an emphasis on racism outdated. Cultural changes in minority ethnic communities were far more relevant and interesting than a focus upon inequalities. Similarly, some post-feminists argued that, with many of the major battles fought by second-wave feminists effectively won (for example, with equal rights and equal pay legislation), the focus of sociological investigation should turn to more subtle differences in cultural aspects of femininity and masculinity (Brooks 1997). Differences between groups of women were more important than any fundamental inequality between males and females. A similar trend has been evident in the study of the life course. Lorraine Green (chapter 4) examines the de-standardization thesis (Bauman 2001; Beck 1992), which claims that the social significance of age has declined significantly as people's pathways through life become more a matter of agentic personal choice than biologically and socially constrained. However, she finds little evidence to support wholesale de-standardization, and the other chapters in this section are also sceptical of theoretical developments which minimize the significance of inequality.

In all these chapters, the turn away from a focus on inequality is challenged, although the importance of new research on cultural differences is fully acknowledged. All the authors identify continuing inequalities, whether in limited working-class opportunities for upward social mobility, continuing ethnic divisions in employment and education, or global gender inequalities in relation to issues such as education, health and employment. Nevertheless, some reductions in gender inequalities and ethnic inequalities are acknowledged by Woodward and Pilkington, but Skeggs suggests that economic inequality has grown very significantly over recent decades. All these three writers acknowledge that the position of less advantaged groups in society has changed and in some cases, but by no means all, has improved. (It is somewhat ironic that the importance attached to class within sociology declined in an era when class inequalities in income and wealth grew very significantly (Lansley, 2006, 2012; Hills, 2010; ONS 2012b).)

The sociological study of age and the life course has generally been focused less on intergroup inequality than on the issues addressed in other chapters in this section. In part this may be because it is not immediately evident who the oppressed and the oppressors might be (children, youth, the middle aged, the old?), although some identify children as a group with little power and few rights (Cunningham 2006). But Lorraine Green (chapter 4) does discuss ageism and the interconnections between other social divisions (particularly social class and gender) and the life course.

The insistence by all these writers that inequality remains crucial to an understanding of social divisions does not mean that they ignore the cultural turn or deny that it has enriched these areas of sociology. Beverley Skeggs (chapter 1) makes extensive use of the theories of Pierre Bourdieu, who has perhaps done as much as any other sociologist to integrate the dual concerns of inequality and culture. Cultural issues are integral to Andrew Pilkington's discussion of ethnic group formation in chapter 3 and to Kath Woodward's discussion of pornification in chapter 2. In their different ways Skeggs, Pilkington and Woodward all move beyond the dualism of objective inequality versus cultural difference and examine the complex interplay of the two in relation to different social divisions. More broadly, other dualisms are challenged in all these chapters as well, including nature/culture and agency/structure, and all three authors acknowledge the intersectionality of particular social divisions which may be treated as analytically separate but which are always indivisibly combined in individuals. The intersectionality of class, sex/gender, race/ethnicity and age/the life course is an integral feature of all the chapters. Thus it is particularly useful to see this section as more than a collection of chapters. Read as a whole, the section provides a very valuable guide to the diverse but complementary ways in which contemporary sociology has theorized, researched and offered new insights into what are probably the most significant social divisions which shape social worlds.

THE IDEA OF CLASS

a measure of value

BEVERLEY SKEGGS

CONTENTS

INTRODUCTION

WHY IS IT THAT societies such as the USA (the richest country in the world by GDP) and the UK (the eighth richest country in the world by GDP) (Aneki 2014) have such high numbers of people experiencing inequality and poverty? Why are the top 10 percent of households in the UK now 850 times wealthier than the bottom 10 percent (ONS 2012b)? Why has inequality rapidly increased since 1979?

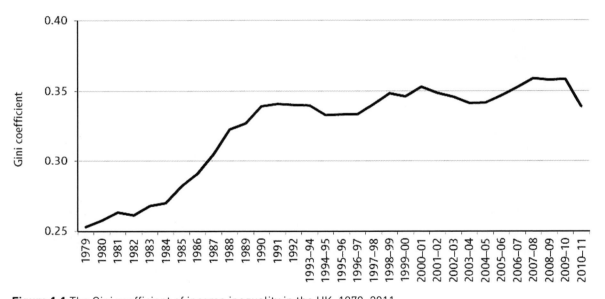

Figure 1.1 The Gini coefficient of income inequality in the UK, 1979–2011

Note: The Gini coeffcient has been calculated using incomes before housing costs have been deducted.

Source: Cribb, Joyce and Phillips (2012: 36)

The higher the Gini coefficient, the greater the degree of income inequality. A value of 0 corresponds to the absence of inequality, so that, having adjusted for household size and composition, all individuals have the same household income. In contrast, a value of 1 corresponds to inequality in its most extreme form, with a single individual having all the income in the economy.

Why are over 93 percent of new housing benefit claims from people who have a job? And why is child poverty in the UK projected to rise from 2.6 million in 2009 to 2.9 million in 2015, with some areas, such as Tower Hamlets in London, having over 42 percent of children living in poverty, closely followed by Manchester, with 38 percent (see Ramesh 2011 for an interactive map of child poverty). Between April and September 2012, over 100,000 people used food banks in the UK. Poverty and inequality are likely to increase further rapidly with the changes to the welfare state announced by the government on 1 April 2013 (see Butler 2013 for all the details). How can it be that millions of children are living in poverty and people are close to starving in the eighth richest country in the world?

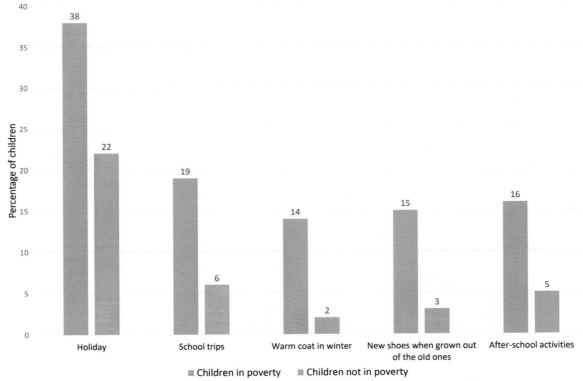

Figure 1.2 Percentage of children in poverty and not in poverty, indicating they are missing out on certain items and experiences

Source: Whitham (2012: 9).

To accompany these vast inequalities we also have the promotion of the idea of meritocracy, namely that anybody can be rich if they try. Yet the promotion of this idea is not matched at all by statistical evidence, which shows that social mobility in the USA and the UK is static (Blanden, Gregg and Machin 2005; Beller and Hout 2006). Moreover, it is predicted that, in the UK, changes to higher education policy, such as the introduction of tuition fees, may result in downward mobility (in comparison to their parents) for thousands of young people (Rampino and Taylor 2012). Careers formerly open to those with only A-levels are now accessible only to candidates with postgraduate qualifications, resulting in what has been described as credential inflation, namely having to increase one's qualifications just to prevent falling in the social hierarchy (Lindley and Machin 2013).

The concept of class has been developed as a way to approach these issues. Class is a sociological concept devised to explain a lived experience. Class shapes who we can be and how we understand others. It is one little word with a massive history and huge significance that impacts upon how we relate to others and ourselves. It is a powerful idea because it is one of the main ways through which we speak and understand injustice, inequality and value. Class itself is a classed idea, which came into speech through the struggles between groups to consolidate and represent interests. This chapter will explore the development of contesting ideas about class. It will then focus on contemporary understandings and lived experience.

How do you know what class you belong to? I begin with an example taken from a survey by the *Daily Mirror* (9 February 1997, with a readership of 2.5 million). In this survey, readers were asked to classify themselves by completing a questionnaire comprising of a list of twenty questions, of which only three relate directly to economic issues (owning/renting a house, employed/unemployed, pension plan). All the other questions are about culture and attitudes, such as 'I own a large dog', 'I regularly eat out in restaurants', 'I go to Tuscany for my holidays' (agree or disagree to be ticked). The highest scores are given to the most expensive middle-class pursuits and low scores to (im)moral behaviour such as owning a big (fighting) dog and having 'excess' sex. This symbolically equates the classification 'working class' with immoral activities. I'll explore other surveys which raise odd points about class, but as you continue to read remember how the scoring worked – which activities were given the highest and lowest values – and how these were loaded with moral judgement.

When opinion polls in the UK ask people what class they are, we usually see a high proportion of identification with the category working class (unlike in the USA, where nearly everybody thinks of themselves as middle class). A MORI poll in 2005 showed that 60 percent, a substantial proportion of the UK population, identify as working class; nearly 50 percent of people polled believed that Britain was more divided by class today than it was in 1979, and 70 percent said they believed 'the class system is harmful to us and those around us'. Strangely, a 2002 poll also found that 55 percent of those who would be categorized as middle class by occupation claimed to have 'working-class feelings'. How do we make sense of these public and popular representations of class? A YouGov poll in April 2011 found 48 percent of people perceive themselves as working class (36 percent working class, 12 percent upper working class) and 42 percent as middle class (17 percent lower middle class, 23 percent middle class, 2 percent upper middle class). But they also note that people's perceptions don't tally particularly well with the occupation-based social class classifications used by the government, as shown in table 1.1, which suggests that a substantive proportion (38 percent) of the middle class are likely to identify as working class and 28 percent of those classified as working class

Table 1.1: **Disparity between 'objective' measures and self-identification of class**			
		Self-identified class	
		Working class	Middle class
Class according to government classifications	Working class	62%	28%
	Middle class	38%	55%

Source: Data from YouGov poll, April 2011.

are likely to identify themselves as middle class. This gap between 'objective' measures and self-identification is one of the issues that has kept sociologists of class busy for a long time.

Class as an idea spans a huge spectrum, from the large-scale quantitative measures used for government classifications to qualitative psycho-social understandings of self-making. We are also kept busy because there are so many different ways of understanding class, ranging from media speak to highly complex and abstract understandings of the global economy.

Speaking and denying class

One important issue to remember is that how we use definitions and speak class tells us a great deal about the person who is speaking and making the classification. As Pierre Bourdieu ([1979] 1984: 6), a French sociologist of class, notes in relation to attempts to assert one's distinction: 'Taste classifies, and it classifies the classifier.' It is unlikely that the current UK prime minister, David Cameron, who went to the most elite, aristocratic, expensive (at approx. £35,000 per year) school in the UK – Eton – would call himself an 'arrogant posh boy', a term sometimes used by the non-right-wing media. Using that term reveals the critique made by the speaker of Cameron's social position. Likewise, as we will see later, using the term 'chav' alerts us to a judgement that is being made by the speaker about the person described.

It is for this reason that it is worth pointing to the numerous attempts by politicians (Margaret Thatcher and John Major, for instance) to deny the existence of class or to deflect

As demonstrated at these recent protests against austerity measures introduced by the majority Conservative coalition government, class is still brought up in political debate, here focusing on the perceived privileged background of the prime minister, David Cameron, and chancellor of the exchequer, George Osborne. (© MrsEds/Flickr)

attention away from class to other terms, such as 'social exclusion' or 'underclass'. We therefore need to ask what speaking of class and decrying its existence does sociologically. Rosemary Crompton (2008) notes how the 'death' of class has been announced at regular intervals from the 1960s, always by those with power: the media, governments, and some sociologists.

Although it is easy to understand why politicians would deny the existence of class relations, it is more difficult to understand why some sociologists – surrounded by the evidence of inequality – deny the significance of class. Class, claim Holton and Turner (1994), is 'an increasingly redundant issue'. Pakulski and Waters (1996) claim class is 'notoriously vague and tenuously stretched', a point to which I'd reply, 'Yes, but only if you do not work at defining it.' It is the business of sociologists to conceptualize social matter in order to make it understandable. Ulrich Beck (1992), a German sociologist, calls class a 'zombie' category that no longer has relevance, but then he contradicts himself by noting that individuals are unable to escape structural forces (such as the organization of the global economy). More recently (Beck 2013), he has argued (while performing the sociological cardinal sin of not defining what he means by class) that class cannot help us explain major risks such as the financial crisis, climate change, the euro crisis or nuclear disasters such as that at Chernobyl – but can that argument be maintained when one examines the workings of capitalism? As Mike Savage (2000) has pointed out, Beck speaks from his social position as a member of the secure, cosmopolitan Western (German) elite, unaffected by the sharp end of inequality.

But writers such as Beck should be alert to the rhetorical function of class, of how it works as 'performative speech', bringing into our vision particular ways of understanding the world. We can always speak of general inequality, but if we use the word 'class' we point to *specific inequalities between groups* on the basis of economic and social organization, showing also which groups benefit at the expense of others.

Likewise, Anthony Giddens (1991) in the UK, who was influential to the New Labour government project, also proposed that class has less significance in today's culture of individualization. He promoted the idea that individualization was now the main way in which personhood (the possibilities for becoming a particular sort of person) was experienced. But, as many of us have pointed out, the resources to pursue individualization are based on one's class position. Giddens has since agreed (following a debate at the 'Identities' research programme in 2005) that class may have more significance than he previously suggested.

We therefore need to tread carefully when defining class, taking into account what the idea of class *does* when it is spoken and used. Already we can note that it may be a shortcut to defining the moral value of people through their behaviour (such as the *Daily Mirror* survey above), understanding one's position in the world in relation to others, claiming authority for one's own social location, speaking about inequality and/or making inequality invisible, and we have only just started.

SEMINAR QUESTIONS

Most people think they know what class is. But spend a minute trying to define it and you will see it is not straightforward.

1 What is class?
2 What class do you think you occupy? Why?

Save your answers and return to them after reading the chapter to see if they change.

DIFFERENT TRADITIONS IN THE DEFINITION OF CLASS

There are three major trajectories to the development of class as an idea. The first – Marxism – prioritizes the role of exploitation and struggle in the making of classes and social relations more generally; the second, called 'political arithmetic', focuses on class hierarchies and status without reference to struggle and exploitation; and the third – Weberian – draws attention to a range of these factors and includes religion, status and social closure.

Key tradition 1: Marxism

For Marxists, class has a number of distinctive features. Firstly, class is a relationship. Marxists maintain that we can only understand one class through an understanding of the other – the middle class establishes the terms by which we can know and identify the working class. Secondly, this relationship is antagonistic because it is always based on the exploitation of one group by the other: 'oppressor and oppressed stand in opposition to one another' (Marx and Engels [1848] 1968: 41). Marx and Engels maintain that there are 'two great hostile camps facing each other' – bourgeoisie and proletariat. The bourgeoisie (middle class) owns capital (the resources to invest in factories and make money through the labour of others) and the members of the proletariat (working class) have only their labour, which they are forced to sell daily in order to survive. Therefore class is always about the struggle between groups, in which the bourgeoisie tries to make as much money as possible out of the workers (proletariat) and the workers try and resist their exploitation. (There is a great cartoon on YouTube which visualizes this relationship: www.youtube.com/watch?v=0KUl4yfABE4.)

It is important to remember that, for Marx and Engels, their analysis was not of specific individual workers but of labour and capital as a whole, about the whole organization of society

BOX 1.1 SOCIAL CLASS STRUGGLE

Marx developed the 'labour theory of value' to show, for instance, how a worker will produce commodities that are worth a great deal more than they are paid. When all the worker's labour is added together (say, 100 workers in a factory) and the costs (such as machinery) are deducted and the commodity is sold, the capitalist is left with a healthy profit (what Marx calls surplus value) = capital for further investment and more exploitation. For Marxists, the extraction of value from the worker by the capitalist is the basis for all social relations. The worker will try to protect their time and pay while the capitalist will try to make more capital through the labour of the worker. Extracting surplus value from the worker and resistance to it is the fundamental basis of class struggle. The working class is a 'class of labourers who live only so long as they can find work and who find work only so long as their labour increases capital' (Marx and Engels [1848] 1968: 51).

As for the capitalists – the bourgeoisie – they too are locked into competition with each other whereby they have to keep finding new sources of profit in order to keep generating capital. They have to keep producing commodities to sell to the workers in order to keep alive the circuit of profit. The only reason the bourgeoisie exists according to Marx is to produce wealth (from the labour of others). For Marx, the bourgeoisie brings the proletariat into effect: without the capitalists' desire for capital there would be no need for the labourers to labour and to buy commodities.

and the economy. This is why it is called the objective structure of society because it is beyond the singular subjectivity of the individual and hence why Marxists offer a structural (organizational) analysis. Because capital–labour relationships shape all social relations, this is also seen to be an 'abstract' theory: it abstracts from what happens in practice between groups to the whole of social organization.

Therefore, for Marxists, it does not matter what people think about their location (subjective class position, identity, as shown through opinion polls above); rather, it is about the location of people in structural economic relationships. Just because somebody believes they are middle class does not mean that they stop being exploited. So, class is not an identity for Marx and Engels; it is instead an *objective description of the conditions of existence of labour under capitalism*.

Marx and Engels map out the fundamental social architecture, the building blocks, that underpin all social relationships, showing how people have to act within circumstances and structures they cannot choose as individuals. Marxism can explain why the middle class wanted access to parliament and law to protect their property interests (the capital made from the profit from colonialism) and why workers rebel against their unjust conditions, but it is less powerful when explaining the complex role of religion, welfare and culture, as we will see later.

Nineteenth-century Marxist understandings of abstract structural social relations offer us a package of useful concepts for understanding class, including exploitation, conflict, struggle, inequality and injustice. Marxism is an explanation which has recently been revived to explain the current economic crisis, as it offers considerable power to analyse our present social situation. For instance, the episode on Marx in the BBC series *Masters of Money* includes interviews with Wall Street bankers who think Marx was correct in his analysis. They note the problems of stagnation in the global economy when people (labourers – through unemployment) do not have enough money to buy the consumer goods produced by capitalists to allow them to increase their capital. There have also been some excellent understandings of financialization and the banking crisis offered by Marxists (see the journal *Historical Materialism*).

Key tradition 2: Political arithmetic

The second major historical perspective for understanding class is radically different. This perspective is concerned with the precise nature of measurement for classification purposes.

Political arithmetic emerged in 1665 with William Petty, who set out to calculate the value of the 'people' of England for taxation purposes. The king needed to know how much money he could extract from the population. Petty is credited with devising what is now known as the 'political arithmetic' tradition of class analysis, one that counts what people own, earn, spend, etc., in order to provide a bigger picture of the state of the nation. In this tradition the person is conceptualized as a *measurable quantity of value*, linked to national concerns and formation. The measured individual becomes a key unit of difference between people.

The processes of calculation became institutionalized in the eighteenth century through the 'New Poor Law' (1834), which generated new information about the population and mandated more and more far-reaching fact gathering, inspection and legislation. This emphasis on measurement and calculation, however, deflects attention away from the *reasons for* inequality, focusing instead on a debate about how best to measure – a debate that continues in sociology to this day.

BOX 1.2 WEBERIAN CONTRIBUTIONS TO VALUE SYSTEMS AND SOCIAL CLOSURE

Like Marx, Weber was interested in the cause of class formation, but he moved his centre of attention away from the economy, pointing to the significance of power more generally beyond the capital–labour relation. He argued for an abstract analysis of class (like Marx) but added in *status* (which focused on hierarchy and is a measure of prestige rather than an antagonistic relationship), *party* (a term he used to define political power to command others) and different forms of *authority* (such as religious authority). Weber was concerned to show the unintended consequences of *value systems* and how different forms of religion either enabled or thwarted capitalism. His example of how the 'Protestant work ethic' operates by encouraging the worker to view his or her work as a matter of morality is still significant today and informs all the debates on the deserving and undeserving poor, slackers and scroungers.

Moreover, Weber's analysis of social closure is important and has been influential with a range of different contemporary sociologists (as we will see later). Weber was the first to identify the processes by which social collectives seek to maximize rewards by restricting access to resources and opportunities to a limited group of those defined as eligible to be members (Parkin 1979). He demonstrated how this process of defining group membership entailed identifying certain social or physical attributes as the justificatory basis of exclusion. This analysis of closure and exclusion is central to understandings not just of class but of how systems of colonialism, built through capitalism, were premised on social closure and the power to define the exploited (e.g., slaves were defined by their racialized physical attributes in order to legitimate their horrific treatment). Defining mechanisms of social closure is key to how power is maintained and used.

These very different traditions become modified as history progresses, and the third major tradition is based on the influence of Weber ([1905] 1985), who, in a critique and modification of Marx, introduced some new elements.

Key tradition 3: Weber

Weber was interested more in individual motivation, culture and power than in the objective, structural, economic conditions that people inhabit. As Parkin (1979) notes, Weber's dimensions of stratification were never regarded as aggregates of individual attributes but rather as phenomena of the distribution of power. His perspective focused on the ideas that led people to social action and the meanings that they gave to their own actions and those of others. A key difference from Marx's approach is that Weber did not believe that classes existed until we interpreted them to be so; hence he was interested in the subjective dimensions of class. Weber emphasized the importance of religious ideas as a means for understanding the genesis of capitalism. His perspective is a reversal of Marx in that he believed it is ideas, *not* economy, that determine people's life chances. For Weber, religion predated capitalism. It was specific aspects of Protestantism, such as 'the work ethic', 'predestination' and 'salvation', that encouraged a form of individualized wealth creation and led to capitalism being successful in predominantly Protestant countries

Just as Marxism has been put to many uses, so has Weber. As Rosemary Crompton (2008) noted, in the 1980s in the UK, some Weberians became obsessed with the political arithmetic tradition of calibrated measurement based solely on employment and occupation, such as the 'Goldthorpe schema', which categorized jobs into different classes. David Rose, Eric Harrison and their colleagues at the Institute for Social and Economic Research at Essex reformulated the Goldthorpe schema, based on SEGs (socio-economic groupings), in 2005 and 2010. They merged the UK government's registrar general's traditional occupational classification with Goldthorpe's SEG to produce eight social class classifications, now known as the National Statistics Socio-Economic Classification (NS-SEC). They are now working on refining the European social classification schemes. These are the classifications used in all official data.

Other Marxists and Weberians went in a more cultural direction, showing how status, exclusion and exploitation work through matters of cultural taste, beyond just occupations.

These three different perspectives inform how we understand class today. The significant difference between the perspectives is cause and effect: one attempts to explain why we have specific classes (Marxist), another (Weberian) is a more general analysis of social organization, while the third (political arithmetic) measures what exists. One advocates for changing the world, one to understand how the world is reproduced in its current form, while the third is about measurement and governance. But central to all is *value*: Marx looks to the extraction of value from the proletariat by the capitalists, the political arithmetic tradition measures how much value each person is worth, and the Weberian tradition understands how religion helps to lubricate value extraction from every aspect of people's lives. The way to spot the difference between the trajectories in the contemporary is usually through the use of the term 'stratification' (which belongs to the political arithmetic tradition) and those who see 'class' as a relationship by which one class benefits at the expense of another (neo-Marxist).

At the beginning of this chapter I used examples from a political arithmetic tradition to 'evidence' the questions I wanted to ask about the form inequality takes in the UK. We need political arithmetic data *with* explanations (theory) so we can understand how and why class exists as *measure of value* and discern a *way to speak inequality*. However, we always need to know how the measurement is made. For instance, there are substantial sociological debates over what makes up a person's wealth: their assets, their property ownership, their disposable income and their poverty. These debates inform the important information that is collected at CASE (the Centre for Analysis of Social Exclusion, http://sticerd.lse.ac.uk/case/), which provides very detailed quantitative research on the forms that inequality takes. But it is very difficult to collect reliable information about the distribution of wealth because the wealthy do not declare their assets, and a whole occupational group – accountants – is used to help them hide their wealth so that they will not be subject to taxation (think of the Amazon, Starbucks and Vodafone tax exposés and protests by the UK Uncut groups).

SEMINAR QUESTIONS

1 What are the most significant differences between the three main traditions for understanding class outlined above?

2 What are the strengths of each tradition?

3 What aspects of class are neglected by each tradition?

GENDER, RACE AND MORAL VALUE

Gender and race

It is also worth noting that, in these different traditional perspectives, gender and race are completely missing from the original analysis. Marx argued that capital does not care whether the worker who can be exploited for profit is a man or a woman, black or white. He insisted that the logic of capital is to make a profit from whomever and whatever it can. However, Marxist feminists such as Maria Dalla Costa and Selma James (1972) have asked what Marx's theory of labour–capital would look like if the largest group of workers in Britain at the time when he developed his analysis – domestic servants – were included. This criticism led in the 1980s to 'the domestic labour debate', where feminists tried to work out what exactly was the value of women's labour. They are still making the same arguments today (see Federici 2004). One of the side effects of this debate was that some European governments set out to measure the value of women's labour for calculating the general wealth (GDP) of a nation (see, for example, Giannelli, Mangiavacchi and Piccoli 2010).

The political arithmetic class theorists also found women complicated their categorizations. Like Marxists, they were subject to substantial criticism from feminist sociologists (Stanworth 1984). Finally, after much resistance, in order to take women into account they based their basic unit of calculation on 'the family household', with the man positioned as the head of the family (see the debates in the *British Journal of Sociology* between Goldthorpe and Crompton). There has been a long Marxist tradition of understanding race and class (the journal *Race and Class* has consistently related race to class through issues of imperialism and empire).

There is, however, one element – morality – that we need to add to our analysis so far in order to understand how class is *always* connected to race and gender. Even though Weber pointed to the significance for the development of capitalism of making work a moral duty in Protestantism, and Engels (Marx's co-writer) notes the significance of biological reproduction for replenishing the workforce, the significance of morality to understanding class moves in and out of understandings. For instance, during the 1850s and 1860s, there was less talk of working class and middle class and more religion-informed speech (discourse) about deserving and undeserving poor, of 'respectable' artisans and 'gentlemen', where emphasis was placed on moral rather than economic criteria (Crossick 1991). There have been certain periods when class was definable primarily by economic value while at others it was defined through moral behaviour. In my own excavation into definitions of class (Skeggs 2004), I found there were often implicit ideas about a group's or a person's moral worth: Marx talks with disdain about a 'lumpenproletariat' (Thoburn 2002), right-wing commentators and governments have tried to introduce ideas of an 'under' class (Morris 1994), classes and races have often been lumped together and associated with uncivilized primitivism (Kahn 2001), and the urban working class are often referred to as a 'dangerous class' (Stedman Jones 1971). I think therefore that we need to account for this dimension in our understandings, especially because moral judgements add in another dimension of value – moral value.

Moral value

In an analysis of British imperialism, Ann McClintock (1995) shows how the concept of class has a historical link to more generalizable 'degenerate others'. She puts an emphasis on how the newly emerging middle class wanted to define their *distance and distinction* from others (remember Weber's social closure). Class as a term, she argues, was applied as much to classifying racial 'types' as to the urban poor. The 'degenerate classes', defined as departures from the normal human type, were as necessary to the self-definition of the middle class as 'the idea of degeneration was to the idea of progress, for the distance along the path of progress travelled by some portions of humanity could be measured only by the distance others lagged behind' (1995: 46).

Domestic servants, for instance, were often depicted through fears of contagion, promiscuity and savagery. As Engels ([1845] 1987: 33) notes of the working class: 'a physically degenerate race, robbed of all humanity, degraded, reduced morally and intellectually to bestiality'. Although Engels makes this claim in order to advocate for social justice, he speaks the generalized middle-class perspective of the time on the morally degraded working class. Domestic servants, in both popular culture and political documents, were associated with the double meaning of hidden labour, the care of back passages. Yeo (1993), for instance, shows how middle-class women used working-class servants to clean the dirty parts of their houses, children and bodies, enabling the middle class to appear as hygienic. And the generalized poor came to be represented as excrement. Osbourne's pamphlet 'Excremental Sewage' in 1852 represents the working class as a problem for civilization, as sewage that contaminates and drains the nation (Yeo 1993). Dirt, sexuality and contagion, danger and disorder, degeneracy and pathology, became the moral evaluations by which the black and white working class were coded in the representations of the day (Nead 1988).

This moral evaluation continues to the present day, as we will see. What is interesting is that the black working class was not subject to the rough/respectable 'internal' division. They were always located with the dangerous, the sexual and the rough – a social position that has now been turned into an effective form of marketing within popular music: a clever way of extracting value from morally degraded groups – which would support Marx's argument that capital does not care about who it exploits as long as it can create value. But the long fight for 'anti-racism' in the UK has led to some protection from the symbolic violence that we will see below.

I will now explain some contemporary ideas about class to examine their usefulness for us as sociologists.

SEMINAR QUESTIONS

1 Why is class a measure of value?

2 How does an analysis of gender and race complicate our understandings of class?

CAPITAL, VALUE AND THEORIES OF SOCIAL POWER

Pierre Bourdieu: capitals or not

One of the most important contemporary contributions is made by Pierre Bourdieu, who combines elements from Marx (capital) and Weber (status and social closure) to develop his 'theory of social reproduction' (how social life proceeds). Bourdieu has been associated with the 'turn to culture' in contemporary class analysis through his important study of taste and distinction in 1970s France. Before Bourdieu studied taste he developed a model for understanding class in social space, based on metaphors of capitals.

BOX 1.3 BOURDIEU AND TYPES OF CAPITAL

Bourdieu identifies four main types of capital: economic, cultural, symbolic and social.

- **Economic capital**: this includes income, wealth, financial inheritances and monetary assets – what one owns.
- **Cultural capital**: this can exist in three forms: embodied in long-lasting dispositions of the mind and the body; in the objectified state, in the form of cultural goods; and in the institutionalized state, resulting in such things as educational qualifications. An essential point here is that Bourdieu defines cultural capital as high-status culture.
- **Symbolic capital**: the form the different types of capital take once they are perceived and recognized as legitimate. Legitimation (e.g., approval of authority) is the key mechanism in the conversion to power.
- **Social capital**: based on social networks, and group membership: whom you know and can use in pursuit of advancement.

People are distributed in social space according to the volume of capital they possess and the composition of their capital (the combination of the different types). How people acquire capitals over time – the evolution of the volume and composition – will influence how they can move through social space: their life trajectory.

Bourdieu is interested not in the subjective meanings people give to social class but rather to their overall position in social space through their composition of capitals. His analysis is a 'multidimensional' space analysis because it includes the different dimensions of volume, the structure of capital, and the trajectory that capital takes as it moves through social space in a person/group. This is very different from the flat hierarchical models used by political arithmetic theorists. It is a relational construct, not a gradational one.

Think about the different forms of capital to which you have had access over time. It is useful initially to think about your body as a case that you fill. This will enable you to inspect its contents.

1   Do you have plenty of economic capital that can enhance your value and enable you to access restricted social goods, such as elite education and health? Does your capital enable you to access even more capital?
2   Let's add to this. Do you have plenty of cultural capital? Can you talk to people about high-cultural activities such as art, classical music and global culture? Bourdieu argues that the feelings generated from accessing high-culture capitals transfer into the body – they become embodied – and influence how we feel about entering into space and social encounters. Confidence and entitlement are dispositions developed over time. Your local culture may give you value in your local space, but is it convertible into value outside of your locality? You have to think about what culture travels and enables you to connect to others who have power and economic capital.
3   Can your cultural capital be converted into symbolic capital? Is it legitimated by the high-cultural forms of the media (the dominant symbolic)?

Let's put these capitals together. An example of this could be if you wanted to get a job at the BBC. To begin with you would need to be able to live in London and pay rent when only on short-term contracts (can be as short as two weeks). Do you have an extensive knowledge of a variety of cultures that would enable you to speak with ease to other people about matters of global concern? You would be expected to know about which films to watch, where to go on holiday and where not. Can you speak with confidence and inhabit any social event with comfort? Or are you likely to feel anxiety and worry at meeting people unlike yourself? Knowing what is and is not 'worth' knowing is crucial to the accrual of cultural capital. As Bourdieu notes: 'In matters of taste, more than anywhere else, any determination is negation; and tastes are no doubt first and foremost distastes, disgust provoked by horror or visceral intolerance ("sick-making") of the taste of others' ([1979] 1984: 56).

More recently, sociologists such as Peterson and Kern (1996) have suggested that it is not just high culture that has to be put into one's case but an extensive knowledge of a variety of cultures. This idea is called the 'cultural omnivore thesis', based on the idea that an omnivore will eat anything. Warde, Tomlinson and McMeekin (2000) show that this extension of accessing other forms of culture alongside high culture works as a value only if one has in the first place the traditional high culture to which popular and less valued cultures can be added. Warde and his colleagues argue that the idea of the cultural omnivore enables the middle class to refashion and retool itself by also operating social closure as they decide which cultures are worth collecting and which are not. There would be no point in stuffing your case with rubbish, so only certain forms of popular music are worth collecting: boy and girl bands are not considered to be worth knowing, for instance.

Bennett et al. (2009), in a survey of 1,791 people in the UK, demonstrate the existence of systematic patterns of cultural taste and practice. They note how few activities are now monopolized by the working class. Those which had a monopoly in the past – some forms of sport, spectatorship and gambling, tastes in popular music and membership of social clubs – have been encroached upon by the middle class trying out their omnivorous tastes.

Recently a group of sociologists (Savage, Devine et al. 2013), working with the BBC on what they call the 'The Great British Class Survey Experiment', tried mixing Bourdieu's analysis of culture with political arithmetic traditions. From this they have come up with descriptions of the UK stratified into seven classes. Their categories are produced from a very specific calibration of different capitals (e.g., social activities, geographical location, higher education, property value, social network, savings, high-cultural activity participation, etc.). From this they identify a flat hierarchy with the elite at the top and the precariat (the most deprived group, with an insecure, precarious economic position and a lack of social and political capital) at the bottom, and within each class they identify factions such as traditional and emergent. However, unlike Bourdieu's, this is not a dynamic model, as the authors do not discuss the time dimensions of space, which we will interrogate further below. It is not a relational model in the Marxist sense because it does not have any understanding of exploitation, power, closure and the advantages one class can gain from another. Instead it is a mapping of micro-social differences that adds culture into traditional political arithmetic measures. It does not offer us an explanation of the cause of these classes and how they emerge as they do.

To understand how class differences are maintained we need to understand how and

This is a publicity still for the BBC series *Snog, Marry, Avoid*. The programme emphasizes stereotypical working-class representations in its recruits, who undergo a thoroughly classed makeover to be 'improved' into middle-class representations. (BBC)

why some culture is valued and some is not. Why is watching a theatre performance a high-cultural activity, worth more than watching reality television, for instance? This process of giving value (legitimating as a form of capital) to some activities relies on one class having access to 'the dominant symbolic' (e.g., the media), which will credit some activities and discredit, devalue and delegitimize others through its images and representations. We can see it in Weberian terms as symbolic closure or in Marxist terms as ideology – how the ideas of those with power reinforce the ideas of those with power. If we chart the history of the media (from novels, art, theatre and newspapers) we can see that the owners, the writers and those who can influence the media always represented themselves as the good moral people, usually against the mass, the urban unwashed, the immoral working class, those whom they define as lacking in value – remember McClintock's 'degenerate others'. They operate social closure, in Weber's terms. Rarely do those depicted symbolically as working class get a chance to access the sites of dominant representation and challenge the representations of themselves.

For example, if we focus on self-transformation reality television, on which Skeggs and Wood conducted a large Economic and Social Research Council (ESRC) research project that examined both the programmes and the audiences, published as *Reacting to Reality Television: Performance, Audience and Value* (2012), we can see that, when working-class people are invited to take part in programmes, it is to tell and perform their lack of value, in particular their lack of cultural capital. Working-class participants are purposefully recruited to these programmes as a form of entertainment, to expose their 'bad culture' as something we should laugh at, as they reveal their need for transformation. In the project we applied Bourdieu's capitals to reality TV. This illuminated how participants were usually depicted as lacking and excessive in many ways – they eat and drink too much, are too loud, appear overtly sexualized in their choice of clothing, and paradoxically watch too much television. We charted this process of devaluation across forty-two series and found it to be so extensive that we called the process of devaluation '*metonymic morality*'.

Metonymic morality occurs when each element of a person's body and behaviour is given a moral value – e.g., cellulite on the legs was seen to be a sign of irresponsible eating; allowing children to eat and watch TV from the sofa rather than sitting at a dining table was considered a sign of a bad parenting; badly styled furniture in make-over programmes was presented as a sign of lack of progress; wrinkles, we were told, were symptoms of the morally illicit excessive sunbathing and not taking care of oneself; speaking loudly was presented as a sign of lack of control of the uncivilized. In short, each form of behaviour or body part was given a negative value so that each part metonymically represents the 'whole' bad person. It is what we call a 'moral economy of person production', based on making visible different forms of capital value as they attach to or are embodied by a person (Skeggs 2009).

This, together with Hage's work on national belonging featured in box 1.4, details some of the social closure involved in cultural and symbolic capital. Social capital, just like the other forms of capital, also operates as a form of closure, often protected by those who have it to make sure that 'the wrong sort' does not enter 'the right circles'. Local networks may enable connections to others, but it is only when these networks connect cultural and social capital to the dominant symbolic (legitimate value) that they are a source of power. Think about whom you know and what networks can you put into your case that will offer you entry and movement into dominant legitimate culture.

However, generating all these capitals can be a source of great anxiety. For instance, parents spend a huge amount of time taking children to activities to enhance their cultural and social capital – more than one in twenty parents drive their children over 100 miles per week to extra educational activities (Bradford 2011). Again, economic capital and time are required to invest in social, cultural and symbolic capital. There are even handbooks to help, such as the '*How to*' guides. But, as Bourdieu notes, it takes years to learn 'how to' access and perform capitals as if they were naturally embodied dispositions.

In our reality television project (*Reacting to Reality TV*) we noticed a huge class difference between the people who were concerned constantly to add value to themselves through enhancing their volume and compositions of capitals (filling their case) and those who were not even anxious about making all their social activities count. For the purposes of the research we defined class using Bourdieu's model, recording the research respondent's capital volume and composition. A question we initially asked was 'How much television do you watch?', to which working-class respondents straightforwardly said, '24/7'. This was a very different

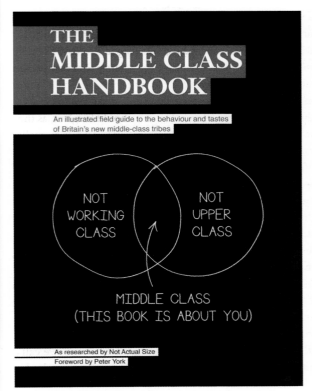

Example resources – in this case satirical and comic – for being middle class and coping with middle-class anxieties. As the middle class grows, is there increasing insecurity about 'fitting in' and knowing exactly what one's class position is? (© Not Actual Size)

BOX 1.4 SYMBOLIC CAPITAL: NATIONAL BELONGING

Ghassan Hage (1998) applied Bourdieu's model to an analysis to racial belonging in Australia to demonstrate the significance of symbolic capital. He shows how it is not just the volume and composition of the right sort of cultural capital, such as speaking the national language, wearing acceptable national clothes, eating certain food, practising a certain religion, having a particular morality, or attending particular schools, but also whether these activities *carry* authority (hence symbolic capital) and are considered to be important to dominant Australian national culture. Hage details how, no matter what he collects in his case – his economic and cultural capital – he will never be considered legitimate because he is a Lebanese person in Australia with Lebanese culture. He demonstrates how the nation determines the legitimacy of its subjects, and the Australian nation will not recognize a Lebanese person as a 'true' Australian. Symbolic capital is therefore about the formal recognition of one's value by national institutions. National belonging is a form of symbolic capital, and a person's overall capital value is always shaped by the amount of legitimate national capital that they can accumulate in order to enhance their other values.

response from that of our middle-class respondents, who went to great pains to deny their TV viewing – some had even hidden their TV or did not have one. As the research progressed over thirty months we came to realize that '24/7' meant the television was turned on but was rarely watched. It was an object of little concern. However, our middle-class participants considered the television to be a matter of great concern, even dangerous, describing it as 'addictive', 'hypnotic' – 'a bad habit' to which they might succumb, becoming 'hooked', 'sucked in', 'pulled in' or 'taken over'. They considered TV to distract them from other more worthwhile pursuits. Take Ruby2, for instance:

> I just think there's a lot more to life than TV . . . and there's other things that I'm doing with regards to my work and things that require me to focus . . . I try to go out as much as I possibly can, I mean part of my occupation what I do, when I go to the theatre sometimes it's not free time, I'm going there to catch a show or network a bit. But I go out, I see friends, I go to the gym, I work out, sometimes I do dance classes, sometimes I do singing classes, which is kind a spare time thing, but it also helps, you know, my profession . . . I'm trying to get into watching live music more, I read a lot, I do write in my spare time. (Skeggs and Wood 2011)

Ruby2 can be considered to be desperately filling her case with capitals. All her time is taken up with events and activity that will advance her profession as a theatre playwright. She networks (social capital), adds cultural capital (through shows, music, reading and dancing classes), converts her leisure pursuits into work outputs (symbolic capital) and as a result will hopefully gain more economic capital (via employment) in the future, although she needs plenty of economic capital in the first place to fund her pursuits. She is a perfect example of what Bourdieu describes. The working-class women in the research, by comparison, appear to be doing nothing – they certainly do not talk about TV 'wasting time'; instead they spend a lot of time with family and friends, just being together with the TV on, watching only intermittently or when something 'grips them'. They do not consider themselves to be wasting time, because *time was not considered to be a valuable resource*.

This difference reveals how class is constantly made but how it begins from very different starting points that generate orientations to space and time, to the present and the future. Ruby2 is totally future facing – everything is for her future value. Our other respondents dwell in the present. What we also know from other research is that, when Ruby2 and people like her become occupationally established, they will use other people's labour to protect and expand their time use. Cleaners, nannies and a whole host of service workers will enable time to be used and understood differently: as a resource that can be used and preserved for the middle class and as labour for the working class. This is why we have popular terms such as 'time poor, cash rich' and 'time rich, cash poor' that epitomize this class difference. 'Quality time' is used as an expression about time free from labour. Yet one person's labour, such as cleaning, can generate reduced labour and increased quality time for another. Marxist feminists would see this as a relationship of exploitation. Research on global service workers such as nannies and cleaners has shown how Filipina women are employed to 'free up' Western mothers' time for career advancement, but that this employment for the nannies means they have to leave their own children behind in the Philippines (Anderson 2000). Quality time for one group is deprivation and exploitation for another.

BOX 1.5 SOCIAL CAPITAL: IT'S WHO YOU KNOW

Social capital is made from the networks that can be used to increase one's value in the future. Parents who can often use their economic capital to buy the way for their children to enter 'the right circles' – that is, to increase their chance to meet people who can offer them jobs in the future – develop further connections and ease their way through social space (remember the £35k per year needed to enter Eton). Ultimately it enables one's economic capital to be enhanced. Public schools, for instance, are often seen to offer more social capital (access to networks of value) than educational or cultural capital. Social capital enables access to the national institutions that define symbolic capital, as Hage (1998) shows. For instance, over one-third (35 percent) of the 649 MPs elected in 2010 attended independent schools, which educate just 7 percent of the population. Fewer than half attended comprehensive state schools (the remainder were educated at state grammar schools); 54 percent of Conservative MPs, 40 percent of Liberal Democrats and 15 percent of Labour MPs attended a fee-paying school.

There are twenty Etonians in Parliament, the total cost of whose individual education (based on Eton school fees and fees at the prep (feeder) schools which most Etonians have attended) can be calculated at around £400,000, and that is before paying for university (even after recent fee rises, relatively cheap at £9,000 per year) – and most (nine in ten) MPs attended university (three in ten went to Oxbridge) (Sutton Trust 2010). Logically, if the capital circuit works, economic capital is used to purchase cultural, social and symbolic capital in order to increase economic capital. It should therefore not surprise us that twenty-three of the twenty-nine members of the 2012 cabinet in the UK are millionaires who are currently passing laws, such as a reduction in the 50 percent tax rate, that will enhance their economic capital even further.

These differences point to a very different way of being that moves us beyond 'what is in our case' to what we have as people that shapes the things we can do and/or relationships to others. I will develop this idea below. But before I do so I want to draw attention to how Bourdieu's model is based upon the idea of the 'subject of value'. That is, a subject such as Ruby2 who can continually add value to herself has become *the* model of personhood that is encouraged by governments across the world (Skeggs 2004).

The subject of value

In the UK, sociologists such as Nikolas Rose (1989) and Paul du Gay (1986) have drawn attention to how people have to learn to become 'the enterprising self' (that is, the person who constantly adds value to themselves) in order to secure employment. As noted above in relation to working at the BBC, it is likely that a substantial amount of employment will be precarious (temporary). In order to keep getting work one must continually enterprise 'up' by learning new skills (e.g., digital manipulation of websites) or new culture (e.g., new forms of music, travel, etc.). It is now very rare to receive training on the job for which the employer pays, so the person has to bear the cost of making themselves employable (and possibly more exploitable) even when not employed, which Marx would consider to be a very clever move by capital. Such self-enterprising is even generally referred to as 'human capital'. Research by Granovetter (1995) demonstrates how, with the expansion of service work and the decline of manufacturing, social skills based on cultural and social capital are as necessary as requirements for entry to the labour market as specific skills. Moreover, as more people gain similar-level qualifications, employers use cultural knowledge to differentiate between them. But how do you get access to, pay for and know which is the 'right' culture by which to enterprise yourself?

To complete the analysis of Bourdieu, I want to argue that he offers us (like Marx and Weber) *a theory of social power*. This is because he details how social positions and the relations between these positions are forms of power, enabling some bodies to move through social space and some not. Social mobility is not just a matter of improving one's birth class position (as has been traditionally understood) but also a matter of accessing or not different areas of social space (e.g., global, political, cultural) beyond the local. All theories of class are theories of power – who can and who cannot have power. Unlike Marx, who focuses on the exploitation of workers through the use of their time and energy (labour), Bourdieu puts the emphasis on the different combination of capitals *and* closure – a process that begins from birth and which is very hard to change precisely because it is embodied over time.

But as with other traditional theorists of class, as we have seen, Bourdieu, too, has a problem with understanding gender. Bourdieu argues that it is women's role to convert economic capital into symbolic capital for their families! And because Bourdieu's is a theory of how power works, who has it and what they do with it (e.g., closure, legitimacy, authority), we can see that, unsurprisingly, he is good on understanding the middle class and masculinity (Bourdieu 2001). But those he has difficulty understanding are groups without power, those lacking in capitals: women and the working class (Adkins and Skeggs 2004). If we accept Bourdieu's model above about the accumulation of capitals in different compositions and volume over time, then what we see is a perfect account of how the middle class come into existence, have power and live (think of Ruby2). They use capital to accrue more capitals, symbolically define what is the 'right culture', and operate social closure by denigrating all other cultures and people. For Bourdieu, the working class is the baseline zero sum of cultural value, who suffer by their proximity to necessity (Bourdieu 1999).

The different histories by which class emerged – the middle class to consolidate political and property interests and the working class to protect and defend conditions – can be seen to influence how they are lived in the present.

SEMINAR QUESTIONS

1 Why does Bourdieu think it is important to think about capitals in the plural?
2 Why is an understanding of time important to Bourdieu?
3 What is a cultural omnivore? How does this help us to understand class?
4 How does the use of time distinguish the middle from the working class?
5 What are the problems with Bourdieu's analysis of class?
6 How does Bourdieu's theory of power apply differently to the working and middle class?

MIDDLE-CLASS SOCIAL REPRODUCTION

When we are born we acquire a class position inhabited by our parents: we inherit their positioning in the social order, including their history of movement through social space and accumulation (or not) of capitals. Inheritance is significant to an understanding of social reproduction, class and power. Imagine if we changed the inheritance laws in the UK: we would see a radical shift in the resources to which people have access. The middle class would not have any capital to begin with. We would all enter a level playing field, instead of some groups being born with a massive advantage, with the potential to accumulate value, and others not.

Just as, in the world of banking, capital begets capital, in the social world capitals enable one to access and accrue more capitals. If you start with an advantage you should be able to keep it through investing in the right things, especially if your class has been able to define what the 'right things' actually are. Many studies of the middle class – and there are plenty (Featherstone 2007; Lamont 1991; Savage, Barlow et al. 1992) – draw attention to two main processes:

1   continual accumulation – just like Ruby2 above, who keeps engaging in activities that will 'pay off' in the future in terms of jobs, money and security, becoming a 'subject of value';
2   social closure. The middle class works to draw boundaries around their capitals so that others cannot have access. Most studies on consumption and taste show how the middle class use their access to symbolic capital to legitimate their tastes and denigrate others. And the law, as an institution used formally to protect that which has been accrued, symbolically justifies cultural and social capital.

Accumulation and closure

Stephen Ball (2003) studied how these processes occur through the link between education and the housing market. His research focuses on the 'micro-practices' of social life, on the enactment of class skills, resources, disposition, attitudes and expectations in order to build patterns and explanations.

Ball paints a picture of a middle class beset with insecurities and anxieties about how they are going to protect what they already have. His perspective is Weberian-Bourdieusian in that his focus is on the market (not, like Marx, on economic production) and forms of market exchange where assets are traded. He examines the ways in which the middle class maintain and improve their social advantages in and through education. One of the key mechanisms that he identifies is how they buy a house in an area with a good state school to avoid paying for expensive private schooling. But they need economic capital to purchase the house and cultural capital to know which are the good schools – this means reading and knowing how to interpret Ofsted reports. These initial economic capital investments in housing are made to produce a return on all capitals in the long term – so the child will have the right knowledge (cultural and symbolic capital) and connect to legitimate social networks (social capital) to enhance their economic capital.

Ball drew on his earlier work (Gewirtz, Ball and Bowe 1995) which studied what happened when the government introduced 'choice' into schooling, which argued that 'choice' emerges as a major new factor in maintaining and reinforcing social-class divisions and inequalities, repositioning education not as a service for the national good but as a private good (a property that can be bought by some but not others). Educational choice enables alternative and indirect routes to buying advantage. But it also makes the cultural aspect (the knowledge required) important. It would be impossible to make the 'right' choice without the right knowledge.

Overall, Ball and his colleagues' research shows how social advantage is gained through the activation of cultural resources, initially premised upon economic capital.

Emotional inheritances and 'special cases'

Diane Reay (1998, 2004) extensively documents another form of capital, 'emotional capital'. Emotional support and security will enable the child to move around the world with confidence; in this sense it is a form of embodied cultural capital. Reay defines emotional capital as 'knowledge, contacts and relations as well as access to emotionally valued skills and assets'. The form of emotional capital that is valued is the one historically associated with rationality and distancing. She uses Illouz's (1997: 56) analysis to argue that 'the ability to distance oneself from one's immediate emotional experience is the prerogative of those who have readily available a range of emotional options, who are not overwhelmed by emotional necessity and intensity, and can therefore approach their own self and emotions with the same detached mode that comes from accumulated emotional competence.' For emotion to operate as a form of capital it must be based on distancing oneself from the immediacy of one's experience, a classed skill historically associated with masculinity and the middle classes. Reay's research projects (from 1993 to 2001, with white, black, middle- and working-class mothers) offer an extensive study of mothers' involvement in their children's futures. She found that it was very difficult for working-class mothers to operate this valued form of distance and detachment, as it was something that they had never experienced, inherited or accumulated. Instead, for working-class mothers, deep emotional involvement was more likely. Reay notes: 'Working-class mothers found it much more difficult to supply their children with resources of emotional capital than their middle-class counterparts because they were frequently hampered by poverty, negative personal experiences of schooling, insufficient educational knowledge and lack of confidence' (2004: 62).

As Reay observes, emotional capital, like all others, is inherited and built up in families over time. It is displayed in bodily dispositions such as confidence, and it is unlikely that a mother who has a negative experience of schooling over a long period of time (ages five to sixteen) will suddenly be able to suspend those embodied dispositions and display confidence in schooling. One of Reay's respondents, Dawn, expresses how her own inherited fears are re-experienced through that of her child, and she realizes her inadequacy. Reay compares a middle-class mother, Linsey, who was always certain that all her daughters could do anything they set their minds to. Reay concludes: 'Middle-class emotional investments in education generate higher, more secure returns for the same level of investment compared to that of working-class parents for whom any level of emotional investment is relatively risky and insecure' (2004: 65).

Valerie Walkerdine (2012) notes how emotions such as anxiety and insecurity are transmitted across generations, making the fears of the mother significant in shaping the fears of the child. In a study of the differences between the upbringing of middle- and working-class girls she notes how the greatest fear for middle-class girls was anything that interfered with their future success, such as pregnancy (Walkerdine and Lucey 2001). She highlights the fragility and the fiction of the post-feminist 'I can have everything' girls, suggesting that the pressure on middle-class girls to perform constantly as 'subjects of value' generates huge amounts of anxiety over every aspect of their performance. Emotional capital can be seen as the lubricant that oils other capitals – enabling and disabling people from optimizing what they have inherited. Inheriting anxiety creates an entirely different disposition towards the world than does inheriting confidence.

bell hooks (2000: 3), a major black feminist sociologist from the USA, notes of her neighbours in Greenwich Village, New York:

They may believe in recognizing multiculturalism and celebrating diversity . . . but when it comes to money and class they want to protect what they have, to perpetuate and reproduce it – they want more. The fact that they have so much while others have so little does not cause moral anguish, for they see their good fortune as a sign they are chosen, special, deserving.

Andrew Sayer (2005) would argue that the positioning of themselves as special is one of the ways by which the inherited injustice is justified. He maintains that class is an embarrassing and unsettling subject, precisely because class position is an accident of birth. His book *The Moral Significance of Class* draws attention to how, in many social situations, it would be considered insensitive to refer to class because class is a measure of value that distributes people unequally. In order to justify this inequality a variety of explanations are developed.

In another project, on white urban middle-class children's schooling, Reay, Crozier and James (2011) detail how middle-class parents repeatedly refer to their children as exceptional and special. Chris, an investment manager, describes his son as having 'extraness'. If inequality can be individualized, then it can be seen to be about talent rather than about structural (capital) advantage. By focusing on 'exceptional' individuals, attention is drawn away from classed inequality.

This, Valerie Walkerdine (2012) argues, is why psychology is so popular with the middle classes, for it enables them to be seen to be unique and special rather than just the product of inherited advantage. The grammar of psychology – individualism – has replaced the grammar of exploitation to become the favoured language of those who benefit from what it hides.

However, we must not forget that underpinning these processes is the movement (or not) through social space and the use of time. The ability to access space (schooling, property) and use somebody else's time (labour) to extend one's own time is a form of exploitation that extends Marx's analysis of how one class can generate benefits from their use of another.

SEMINAR QUESTIONS

1 How might the three main processes of middle-class social power – inheritance, accumulation and closure – work through education?
2 Why is 'choice' another means for protecting middle-class advantage?
3 How does emotional capital work as a form of capital? What advantages and disadvantages does it produce?
4 How does inheritance work through emotions alongside other forms of capital?
5 How do the middle class justify their inherited inequality?

A DIFFERENT INHERITANCE: WORKING-CLASS LIVES, MISRECOGNIZED, JUDGED AND WORRIED

If we work with the definition of class as a measure of value, we need to remember the problems with Bourdieu, who describes the working class as the zero sum of culture. Let us explore some research in more detail.

An accident of birth

In a research project entitled 'Contingencies of Value' (CoV), conducted in 2006 with two groups (elderly working class and ex-offenders) purposefully chosen because they were excluded from accruing capitals and the dominant symbolic value systems (Skeggs and Loveday 2012), the injustice of inheritance was a matter of considerable concern. The research participants referred to 'an accident of birth':

> As far as I'm concerned I'll never be middle-class. I will always be a working-class man. I'm a working-class man with an education . . . it's not saying I'm proud of it but it's also something I'm not ashamed of, you know what I mean? It's an incident of birth, where I'm come from or who I am is an accident of birth. (Joe)
>
> I think to myself, what is the difference between the people who are sitting there (in the student union café) and the people who I grew up with? And the only difference is an accident of birth. (Peter)
>
> It's – it's an accident of birth, it's not something I've achieved. I'm proud of some of the things my family have done and as – as a group of people, the things that we've actually achieved, but to me, I'm no better than some of these middle class. (Mike)
>
> Why should my son, 'cause they happen to be born in – from my background . . . why should they have to work three times harder than anyone else? Why should their opportunities be limited just by the fact of where he was born? (Jack)

To which Bill replies: 'Because they're statistically nine times more likely to be arrested, more likely to go in prison . . . all that statistically just because of where he was born' (Skeggs and Loveday 2012: 481).

It is the consequences that spring from this accident of birth that are notable. We know that, statistically, this accident of birth has a powerful impact on how people can move through social space: a 2012 report from the Higher Education Funding Council for England (HEFCE 2012: 6) states that, 'For cohorts from the late 2000s, typically fewer than one in five people from the most disadvantaged 20 percent of areas enter higher education, compared to more than one in two from the most advantaged 20 percent of areas.' There are also differences in participation levels according to the type of higher education institution students enter. The Cabinet Office (2011) strategy for social mobility notes that 'Almost one in five children receive free school meals, yet this group accounts for fewer than one in a hundred Oxbridge students.' The report notes how 'The most advantaged 20 percent of young people are seven times more likely to enter the most selective institutions than the most disadvantaged 40 percent.' Thus, the middle class comprise a larger percentage of the general HE population, as well as a significantly larger proportion of the student body in elite institutions, highlighting the heavily classed nature of higher education. The accident of birth will determine not only whether you will enter higher education but also which university you are likely to attend. This is clearly apparent to Bill and, not surprisingly, outrages Joe, Peter and Mike.

A 2012 report by the Organization for Economic Co-operation and Development (OECD) noted how inequality became ingrained in children as young as three. The accident of birth has powerful effects.

To make matters worse, the people who suffer inequality as a result of this accident of birth are also judged to be inadequate rather than as victims of injustice created by inheritance. Back to Joe and Jack again:

> I think most working-class people they just want a decent quality of life . . . It can just be surrounded by family, and being . . . not bursting into tears when the car breaks down or you get another bill come in. But then you get this accusation that you're all completely un-ambitious when really you're just struggling to get by. (Joe)
>
> In fact anyone has to feed his or her children, what's so working-class about that? But there is a more major concern if it's made impossible to do. And then you're judged for that impossibility. (Jack) (Skeggs and Loveday 2012: 482)

Being judged by others as lacking through conditions over which one has no control upsets and outrages these research participants. In fact, in all the research projects I have conducted since the 1980s, the issue of being judged for something over which one has no control is central to how people live their daily lives. This is glaringly apparent in another ethnographic research project featured in box 1.6, on class and gender.

Symbolic violence

It is not just judgement by individuals in social encounters but its combination with the symbolic power that circulates through media images and government rhetoric that decrees the working-class as a problem. This analysis shows how different forms of capital are not just about value accrual but also about loss and devaluation promoted through moral judgement.

For example, there is a long history of making the 'fallen woman' a subject of public debate about morality. This debate continues especially during times of crisis, when working-class women are regularly condemned for all social problems (Rose 1999). They are repeatedly used to deflect attention away from structural inequality. For instance, the current prime minister, David Cameron, blamed 'chaotic families' for the 2012 riots. Kim Allen and Yvette Taylor (2012) note how the immediate public responses to the riots was a strident blaming of 'poor parenting' within poor communities, which spoke almost exclusively against *mothers*. These debates were permeated by a long-standing narrative of troubled mothers – single mothers blamed for failing to bring up their children properly – fuelling public discourses of welfare dependency and the (un)deserving poor. As Chris Haylett (2001)

Popular culture abounds with demeaning and demonizing representations of 'chavs', a label increasingly applied to working-class groups. (© Kevin Friery/Flickr)

BOX 1.6 FORMATIONS OF CLASS AND GENDER

In this research I studied eighty-three white working-class women in the northwest of England over a period of eleven years (Skeggs 1997). The young women research participants put a huge amount of effort into appearing 'respectable' to others. This was because they felt that they were constantly misrecognized and judged as lacking in value. They performed respectability across many areas of their lives, over time, not only in order to defend against judgements and devaluation but also to claim value for themselves. The judgements that they experienced daily came from encounters with middle-class people in positions of authority (school teachers, social workers, health visitors), who assumed they would 'just have babies' and be a 'burden on the state'. They were even judged (by health visitors) for minor infringements such as leaving a vacuum cleaner out of the cupboard and not drying the dishes after washing up. Just like the bodies of the working-class reality television participants described above, they felt that every element of their lives was subject to a 'metonymic morality' judgement. This was why they did not want to identify with the term 'working class'. For them the term represented a judgement of value-lack. They knew (quite accurately) that working-class women were represented in the media as excessive, slutty, fecund, welfare-state burdens, and they wanted to disassociate themselves from these symbolic accusations. However, just because they dis-identified from the term 'working class', because they felt it misrecognized their value, did not mean that class was insignificant in their lives. Rather it structured almost every moment of how they related to others and to themselves.

From this research we can see how class as a structure (the organization of inequality), an inheritance (the accident of birth) and a relationship (the social encounters they experienced daily) intervened in every aspect of their lives. If this were not the case, they would not have put so much effort into proving they had value through respectability. They lived with a constant sense of emotional anxiety that they would be judged lacking and as a result tried to remove themselves from any social encounter in which the judgement could take place. Interestingly they were training to become nannies, nursery nurses and care workers, precisely the women workers whose labour enables middle-class women to have more 'quality time'. They were also judged (mainly) by middle-class women who had made their careers from occupations based on institutionalized judgement (e.g., social work, welfare institutions, policing, law).

details, the white working class in Britain is now coded by the media and governments as 'dirty white', atavistic, holding back modernity.

Moral judgement is often expressed as symbolic contempt, devaluing groups of people and enabling social closure. The current circulation of symbolic hatred shocks even Ferdinand Mount (a former head of Margaret Thatcher's Number 10 Policy Unit): 'What I do not think many people have yet woken up to is that the (white) working class has been subjected to a sustained programme of social contempt and institutional erosion, which has persisted through many different governments and several political fashions' (Mount 2004: 273). Mount is surprised by the 'bad manners' and vulgarity of the middle class, who now feel it is legitimate to display their hatred of the working class so blatantly. The word 'chav', used as a shorthand to describe the working class as pathological, became an Oxford English Dictionary (most used) new word in 2004, and is now ubiquitous in everyday parlance. The term 'white trash' has been used for some time in the USA (Hartigan 1997). This is what Bourdieu would describe as 'symbolic violence', when one class uses its power via access to symbolic legitimation to denigrate another in order that the powerful class can uphold its right to power. This symbolic violence is complicated by race and gender: for instance, different symbolic value is attributed by the media to different groups. Young Muslim men have been represented as a dangerous threat 'from without' to the nation, whereas black men have been represented as dangerous and irresponsible within the nation. However, apart from the right-wing press that indulges these representations, most middle-class people do not want to be seen to be racist – hence the target of class violence is directed to the white working class.

It is the compound effects of inheriting inequality as an accident of birth over which one can do very little, the symbolic judgement experienced as a result of classed social encounters, the misrecognition of one's value by others, and the constant worry about surviving that shape very different orientations to time and space (future or present). Therefore I want to suggest that we should think of class not just through the language, ideas and concepts we use (an epistemology – a theory of knowledge) but also as a very different way of being (an ontology – a different way of inhabiting the world). As we have seen, the middle class are constantly anxious about how to move into the future loaded with value, while the working class are concerned to put a floor on their circumstances to survive in the present (see box 1.7, pp. 32–3) These are very different ways of living with very different possibilities for what it means to be a person. It is for this reason I developed the idea of 'person value' to explore how class is lived, an idea that works alongside how our conditions of existence are framed by capitalism (through Marxist understandings of class and exploitation) and government (the political arithmetic tradition) (Skeggs 2011).

SEMINAR QUESTIONS

1 Why does class have moral significance?
2 How are justifications of privilege made?
3 Why does Skeggs argue that class is a different 'ontology' (a different way of being)?
4 How does access to money shape how we can live class?

CONCLUSION

Different measures of value enable us to understand different class formations and speak of inequality. To recap, I therefore want to argue that class is an inherited measure of value that distributes people unequally, a category for understanding the unequal distribution of value. For instance, the political arithmetic tradition enables us to know that, since 1979, income inequality has been growing faster in the UK than in any other rich country. The mobility that many young people are likely to experience is downward and many parents are struggling to feed their families. Four million children in the UK – one in three – are currently living in poverty, one of the highest rates in the industrialized world (www.endchildpoverty.org.uk/), and this is predicted to get worse.

The Marxist tradition enables us to know that competition between capitalists leads to the globalization of class, as capitalists move around the world trying to find the cheapest and most compliant workers – it is called a 'race to the bottom'. As soon as the 'cheaper' workers fight to preserve and protect themselves, the capitalists are likely to move on, creating poverty and deprivation as they do so. The workers themselves will also likely try to move (economic migration) in order to find work, because only if they work will they stay alive.

But border controls and law will make their movement so much more difficult. We need Marxism to explain how we live in a capitalist society based on exploitation and power and Bourdieu to show how capital can take forms beyond the economic to increase and justify the advantages of some over the disadvantages of others. Marx, Weber and Bourdieu draw attention to the power of the symbolic as a means by which social closure can be achieved and contempt activated.

Including gender and race in the analysis of class drew our attention to how morality is deployed not only to make people work harder for capital as a duty but also to deflect attention away from structural inequality, so that some groups are repeatedly targeted and blamed for social problems, making morality legitimate inequality. Class is therefore integral to understanding not just value and inequality but also how power works. We have seen the mechanisms by which different classes reproduce themselves: the middle class can protect and represent their interests, exclude others, justify and benefit from inheritance and propel themselves into the future as a 'subject of value', while the working class is subject to judgement, a 'subject of survival'.

All the different theories demonstrate how class affects the kind of life we can lead, and many research projects show that we do indeed lead very different lives, a different ontology, different ways of being. When people are born into and inhabit different material conditions, shaped on the capitals which they can access, they will use their time, energy and emotions differently. If we think about a definition of class as a measure of value and a way of speaking inequality, that includes both *what is done to people* and *how people make and do class* over time and space, we have a dynamic definition of how class is made in the present.

Class is dynamic: it is in constant formation, as one group attempts to extract profit from another as the other tries to defend itself, while one group attempts to move forward through social space and time by accruing capital value and operating social closure. To ensure the security of their position they deploy their power within the symbolic realm to block access to others to the social goods that have value and to justify their own privilege and advantage. This is a relational power-play.

As Sayer (2005) notes, we are shamed by class because inequality is shameful, but this does not seem to worry some people. Warren Buffett (one of the richest men in the world) notes: 'There's class war, all right, but it's my class, the rich class, that's making war, and we're winning' (Stein 2006). He's right. As the rich get richer and the poor get poorer, class becomes an ever more important issue.

BOX 1.7 FROM 'SUBJECT OF VALUE' TO 'SUBJECT OF SURVIVAL'

Will Atkinson (2012), in a study of twenty-nine households in Bristol in 2010–11, documents the strategies used by families (usually mothers) to deal with reduced income. These include cutting back on food, using 'cheaper' supermarkets, making food last longer with smaller portions (e.g., one chicken for three meals for a family of four), taking in lodgers (making them feel 'it's not our home any more'), selling possessions to pay for food, stopping treats and 'nice things', and taking on extra jobs when possible. Ms Jeffers (one of his research respondents) notes: 'I've had to take on more jobs which is why I've increased my hours . . . the bills have gone up about forty percent so my hours I work have gone up forty percent.' Ms Jeffers has to do 40 percent more just to stay where she is. This is especially the case with the mothers above cited by the government as responsible for the riots: 23 percent of British households with dependent children are single-parent households; only 8 percent of single parents are fathers. There are 1.9 million single parents in Britain, caring for 3 million children. They have a disproportionate number of disabled children (34 percent) and a disproportionate number of disabilities and illnesses of their own (33 percent). They are also disproportionately poor. Some 46 percent of single-parent families are below the poverty line, compared with 24 percent of families with two parents; 57 percent of single parents work. As soon as their children reach the age of twelve, this figure rises to 71 percent, which is the also the national average for mothers in relationships (Gold 2011). And these inequalities will become even more intense following the 1 April 2012 welfare cuts to the disabled. But most people think that people on welfare are scroungers, as table 1.2 demonstrates.

Table 1.2: **Misconceptions about welfare**		
On average what people think		**Actual figure**
41%	Proportion of the entire welfare budget that goes on benefits to unemployed people	3%
27%	Proportion of the welfare budget that is claimed fraudulently	0.7%
48%	Proportion of those claiming Jobseeker's Allowance who go on to claim it for more than a year	27.8%

Source: Data from TUC, cited Grice (2013).

In contrast to the middle-class investment in the future where the capitals loaded into children can be exchanged for more capitals, Ms Jeffers tries not to lose what she has. This is not about making future investments, as do the middle class, but what I called in *Formations of Class and Gender* 'putting a floor on the circumstances' (Skeggs 1997). Ms Jeffers is racing on her treadmill of work just to keep in a steady state. Remember from the introduction the number of people experiencing in-work poverty rose by a fifth in a decade to 6.1 million, meaning that work is no longer a route out of poverty, and over 93 percent of new housing benefit claims are from people who have a job. Ms Jeffers is not a slacker or a scrounger, as she is likely to be depicted by those with symbolic capital who are trying to protect their own interests.

This is not future investment but protection from falling – a 'subject of survival' rather than a 'subject of value'. We can see this again through understandings of space and time, of different orientations: one looks forward, the other fears going backwards. The working-class respondents in all of my research projects were never in a position to disregard money, which Michèle Lamont (1991) and Bourdieu ([1979] 1984) define as a major feature of the middle class. Nor could they ever construct distance from necessity, which Bourdieu (ibid.) defines as a means of constructing distinctions in social space.

Now go back to your initial answers from the beginning of the chapter. Would you answer them any differently now?

SEMINAR QUESTIONS
1 How is an understanding of class based upon class struggles?
2 How does morality help us to understand how class is spoken and lived?
3 How do the middle class protect their interests?
4 How do the working class live class relations?

5 What is symbolic violence and how is it linked to social class?

6 Would you agree that, whatever our class backgrounds and class trajectories, we cannot avoid class shaping our way of being or ontology?

FURTHER READING

▶ Bourdieu, P. (1987) 'What makes a social class? On the theoretical and practical existence of groups', *Berkeley Journal of Sociology*, 32. This is the classic outline of Bourdieu's theory. It is the reference source used by all Bourdieu-influenced scholarship.

▶ Federici, S. (2004) *Caliban and the Witch: Woman, the Body and Primitive Accumulation* (Autonomedia). A radical analysis of class and gender from the Middle Ages. It shows how witches were a class as well as a gender problem.

▶ Haylett, C. (2001) 'Illegitimate subjects? Abject whites, neoliberal modernisation and middle class multiculturalism', *Environment and Planning D: Society and Space*, 19. Used newspaper and government reports to show how the white working class has been coded as 'dirty white'.

▶ hooks, b. (2000) *Where We Stand: Class Matters* (Routledge). A popular analysis of how and why class still matters.

▶ McClintock, A. (1995) *Imperial Leather: Race, Gender and Sexuality in the Colonial Context* (Routledge). Probably one of the most important books written on class, gender, race and sexuality with great examples, such as how a commodity 'soap' was sold to assuage the fears associated with proximity to the 'other'.

▶ Skeggs, B. (1997) *Formations of Class and Gender: Becoming Respectable* (Sage). A detailed empirical study of how we learn to fit into the positions ascribed to us by class and gender.

▶ Skeggs, B. (2009) 'The moral economy of person production: the class relations of self-performance on "reality" television', *Sociological Review*, 57(4). Reports on the reseaarch project on reality television to detail how people are expected to perform their lack of value.

2

SEX, GENDER AND SEXUALITY

the case for critical analysis

KATH WOODWARD

CONTENTS

INTRODUCTION

SEX IS EVERYWHERE IN large parts of contemporary Western culture. Sexual images dominate media representations, and sex is so often the main theme in advertising, comedy, drama, music and all forms of popular culture. What do we mean by sex in this context?

Sex includes sexual activity, which is closely linked to sexuality – that is, a person's sexual orientation – most usually assumed in Western culture to be heterosexuality, with different possibilities being categorized as 'other'. Sex involves desire and pleasurable practices too, of course, which are likely to be attractive to the field of culture. Further still, sex is also a category to which people are assigned, usually as female or male, largely on the basis of physical characteristics.

It may seem as if battles for sexual equality between women and men have been won. Access to contraception and a changing moral climate have given many young women choices in the expression of their own sexuality, albeit within the context of standard sexualized discourses. Activities which may in the past have been seen as exploitative, such as pole dancing, have in recent times been called a matter of choice for those who participate. The question of gender is relevant here, too, since there are social and cultural rules about what is deemed appropriate behaviour for women and for men.

This chapter looks at some of the connections between sex, gender and sexuality and why all three are important as subjects of inquiry for sociologists. What sort of questions do sociologists and scholars of women's and gender studies ask about sex, gender and sexuality, and why do they matter?

The continuing trouble with sex, gender and sexuality

Equal opportunities policies and practices, together with equality legislation, might be seen both to have eliminated some of the unequal treatment of women and those in same-sex relationships and to suggest that it is no longer a social issue worthy of sociological inquiry. However, the saturation of culture with sex also presents its own problems, especially in relation to questions about who benefits and who suffers in this new social world. Some have described this world as post-feminist, arguing that battles have been won. In the twenty-first century people can make choices: but can they? Sex has become gratifying for most people: but has it? The mass coverage of sex has generated an industry of sex counselling and therapy to deal with the troubles of those for whom this explosion of sex is far from gratifying, and people may not feel they have genuine choices open to them.

The SlutWalk movement began in 2011 in Toronto, Canada, after a police officer suggested women should not dress like 'sluts' if they wanted to avoid rape. Globally, people began marches to reclaim the right to dress freely without fear of violence or male oppression. The SlutWalk phenomenon shows how issues of sex, gender and sexuality are still intimately tied together, often in contentious ways. (© David Shankbone/Flickr)

The contemporary obsession with sex, gender and sexuality, where images connoting sexuality, sexual attraction and sexual activity saturate the media, might be construed as providing a more honest understanding of human sexuality and some equality both for those who have been marginalized and excluded in the past and for women, who are now permitted to express their sexuality freely within the public sphere of representation. On the other hand, the form which these sexualized images and activities take might not be so liberating, both because sexual freedom seems permissible only for the young, able bodied and attractive and because contemporary Western societies' obsession with sex raises questions about whose definition of sex and sexuality is in circulation. Is this really such a level playing field? Can people express their own sexuality or do they have to conform to a sexualized stereotype or socially accepted norm of heterosexuality and of heightened sexual activity?

In the UK at the time of writing, far from the battle of sex equality having been won, news stories proliferate about sexual harassment in parliament and by senior politicians of younger women seeking a political career in politics. Even where equal rights have been granted they have not always materialized, as in the case of equal pay. National governments across the world are involved in contentious debates about who is to be allowed to marry. Even the governing body of the Anglican Church is devoting a great deal of time to ascertaining what is and what is not acceptable sexual behaviour in private. Sex may be everywhere but this ubiquity is not necessarily liberatory, and a sociology of sex, gender and sexuality is just as crucial as it was in previous struggles for equal rights – for example, over votes for women and reproductive rights in the first-wave of feminism and the political programmes of second-wave feminism, which led to much of today's equality legislation. Now the situation is more complicated. Sex is not hidden: it is everywhere, but the relationship between sex, gender and sexuality needs to be disentangled and explored in relation to other aspects of power and social inequalities. What sort of sex is it that dominates culture? Who benefits and who doesn't?

Sex, gender and sexuality have been pivotal to feminist critiques of power and have increasingly been recognized as important to theoretical and methodological developments in understanding social relations and divisions and infrastructures of inequality within sociology. Those engaged in gender studies, queer theory and feminism have consistently worked towards putting sex, gender and sexuality onto the agenda as social forces and cultural processes involving the exercise of power, in order to give voice to those on the margins as well as to deconstruct patriarchal and heteronormative assumptions.

This chapter traces some of the ways in which sex and gender, along with and in relation to sexuality, have been explored and critiqued and, in effect, 'put into discourse' (Foucault 1978: 11) in the academy and in intellectual and political life, notably in gender studies and sociology and by feminist theories and politics. In this chapter I seek to reconsider theories which engage with the connections and disconnections between sex and gender as well as the relationship and boundaries between sex, gender and sexuality as key concepts in the understanding of social relations and divisions, especially within sociology. What is the relevance of sex, gender and sexuality to sociological critiques and ways of understanding the world? Does gender provide a category into which people can be allocated for classificatory purposes or is it something more? Does gender provide an explanation for social patterns and divisions as well?

Continuing inequality at the global level

While the proliferation of sexualized images and media obsession with sex and sexuality are largely Western phenomena, sex and gender remain central to global inequalities and are forces which shape social divisions across the world, for example in unequal access to resources and in influencing the opportunities people have to make choices and determine what they do in their lives.

Statistical evidence from the United Nations provides empirical support for my argument that sex, gender and sexuality matter to sociologists because they are explanatory concepts as well as descriptions and classifications of people. Sex, gender and sexuality are structures through which social relations are made, and an understanding of these concepts can provide some explanation of social relations, processes and, often, social inequalities.

The empirical evidence is particularly apparent in the massive range of data on global inequalities which focuses upon women's lives and experience (World Bank data; UN World's Women series and Human Development Reports; see also Woodward 2011). Even in a relatively advanced neoliberal democracy such as the UK, wide discrepancies persist between women and men, for example in terms of pay (see table 2.1) and type of paid work undertaken. Women earned on average 19.7 percent less than men in 2012 and earned £423,000 less than men in a lifetime; they were also far less likely than men to occupy senior management

Table 2.1: Median gross annual earnings for full-time employees, UK

	2009	2010	2011	2012
Male	£28,264	£28,080	£28,376	£28,713
Female	£22,118	£22,492	£22,619	£23,074
Difference	£6,146	£5,588	£5,757	£5,639

Source: ONS *Annual Survey of Hours and Earnings* (ASHE).

positions, for instance, in the FTSE top 250 companies (BBC 2013). Furthermore, although men are more likely to experience violent attack on the streets, in the case of domestic violence requiring hospital treatment, women are far more likely than men to be victims.

UN data on inequalities at the global level are even more striking. Table 2.2 gives figures on regional inequalities in terms of representation in parliaments, education and labour force participation (UNDP 2013). Only about one in five seats in national parliaments worldwide are held by women, and in every region the figure is less than 25 percent. Although more girls now go to school, in parts of the world, such as North Africa, a third of all girls still do not attend school, a figure which rises to 60 percent in the poorest households. In all regions, females

Table 2.2: Global gender inequality by region

	Maternal mortality rate (deaths per 100,000 live births), 2010	Percentage of seats in national parliament held by women, 2012	Percentage of females aged 25 and over with at least secondary education, 2006–10	Percentage of males aged 25 and over with at least secondary education, 2006–10	Labour force participation rates, females aged 15 and over, 2011	Labour force participation rates, males aged 15 and over, 2011
Arab states	176	13	31.8	44.7	22.8	74.1
East Asia and the Pacific	73	17.7	49.6	63	65.2	80.6
Europe and Central Asia	28	16.7	81.4	85.8	49.6	69
Latin America and the Caribbean	74	24.4	49.8	51.1	53.7	79.9
South Asia	203	18.5	28.3	49.7	31.3	81
Sub-Saharan Africa	475	20.9	23.7	35.1	64.7	76.2
World	145	20.3	52.3	62.9	51.3	77.2

Source: Selected data from UNDP (2013).

are less likely to have received secondary education than males. There is a similar picture with regard to labour force participation, with particularly low rates among females in Arab states and South Asia. 79 percent of the victims of human trafficking are women. Sexual violence against women is a well-known military weapon which has become systematic, for example, in the eastern Democratic Republic of Congo.

Economic inequalities between countries often show up most dramatically in statistics related to sex and gender. Outside Europe and Central Asia, maternal mortality rates remain very high: for example, in Malawi it is 1,100 per 100,000 births, whereas in the UK it is seven per 100,000. Women do not die in childbirth or from HIV/AIDs solely because they have female bodies, but because health support and treatment are not provided. The evidence of women's unequal position illustrates the unequal power relations which operate in the allocation of resources, with pregnancy, childbirth and women's sexual health, for example, being grossly under-resourced.

'Normality', diversity and biology – speaking from the periphery

The inclusion of women as a category of person with particular experiences situated within the wider social world leads to the recognition of diversity, as well as the possibility of breaking silence around inequality and of speaking from the periphery. Importantly, it also informs policy. In many areas of paid work, such as the public-sector workforce, it is no longer possible for the white, male, middle-class, heterosexual norm to pass entirely unchallenged. One of the perhaps unexpected and certainly unintended outcomes of the relatively recent inclusion of women and women's experience in empirical work has been the assumption that it is only women who are marked by gender and that somehow men are an unmarked category – the norm in a similar way to some of the taken-for-granted claims that whiteness is not ethnicized or racialized and race is somehow about black, migrant and minority ethnic people. In spite of work on critical whiteness, such as that of Les Back and Vron Ware (Back and Ware 2001), and the ever-expanding field of masculinity in gender studies (Connell 1995, 2002; Robinson and Hockey 2011), there is still some way to go before it is acknowledged that men are gendered and that white people are marked by race and ethnicity.

The feminist politics and activism which have been so closely enmeshed with feminist theories have always focused upon the promise and possibilities of change, which has been seen as more likely if gender is socially constructed. Conversely, sex has been construed as an immutable, biological category. Sexuality has been drawn into the political discussion because of the powerful ideological and social links between sex and sexuality. Sexuality has so often been assumed to be heterosexuality, and this assumption persists in the sexualized and pornified, 'raunch' culture of the twenty-first century (Levy 2005; Woodward and Woodward 2009). The use of sex and sexuality as a means of promoting products is ubiquitous, and sexual activity has become a criterion by which autonomy and personal satisfaction, and what has been called 'empowerment', are measured.

This chapter offers a discussion of sex, gender and sexuality as connected concepts in relation to questions about the politics of sex. To what extent does sexual difference still matter in relation to life choices and opportunities? The debate also focuses upon what is natural and what is social and cultural. Another key question for this chapter is how far sex and gender, for example as categories of men and women, or sexuality as sexual orientation are normative – that is, are they prescribed and preferred as 'normal' and thus morally preferable?

SEMINAR QUESTIONS

Go to the UN Decade of Women site and find the UN Women page: www.unwomen.org/2012/04/un-women-welcomes-a-landmark-action-plan-to-measure-gender-equality-across-the-un-system/.

1   List the areas of life which are included.
2   How are these categories of areas of experience influenced by biological, anatomical sex and gender and sexuality?
3   Are sex and gender more influential in women's than in men's lives?
4   How far are the areas of inequality between women and men which are identified dependent upon or shaped by biological sex or social and cultural factors?

DISENTANGLING SEX, GENDER AND SEXUALITY? THEORIES, ASSUMPTIONS AND THEIR CONSEQUENCES.

Sex, gender and inequality

The explosion of interest in sex and gender in sociology as categories to be interrogated and discussed rather than assumed, especially in second-wave feminism, led to the beginnings of the inclusion of women as a marked empirical category in critical sociological research (for example, Chanter 2006; Dworkin 1981; Greer 1970; MacKinnon 1987; Mitchell 1971; Oakley 1972, 1980; Rowbotham 1973, 1974; Segal 1994, 2007). In sociological work in the 1950s and 1960s, the only site where women were named as such – if at all – was within work on 'the family', for instance. Hitherto the norm for whatever category of person or social institution had been set by the standard of the white, heterosexual male, from the deviant young person on the street corner to judges, the police and the judiciary: work was a masculine activity in which participants engaged outside the home and in the public arena. Feminists challenged the intellectual and theoretical boundaries between public and private spheres (Elshtain 1993; Fraser 1990; Nicholson 1986a, 1986b). For example, Ann Oakley's pioneering work on housework (1974a, 1974b) and childbirth (1980, 1981) contributed to rethinking what areas of life were suitable as sites of social research.

The recognition of the distinctions between sex and gender arising from second-wave feminist critiques is a good starting point from which to explore the importance of sex, gender and sexuality in sociology and more widely in social, political and cultural theories. Ann Oakley classifies the sex/gender distinction as follows: '"Sex" is a word that refers to the biological differences between male and female', whereas '"gender" . . . is a matter of culture; it refers to the social classification into "masculine" and "feminine"' (Oakley 1972: 16). Although it might appear that Oakley was endorsing the fixities of sex (something which we will see challenged later in this chapter), what is more significant here is the challenge to the causal and universal link between anatomy (sex) and social cultural practices (gender), notably those embedded in the social institutions of patriarchy, in which men have dominance over women in all situations. Women's role in societies, unlike men's, was seen to be adversely determined by their biological sex. Second-wave feminists such as Oakley argued that sex and gender were frequently elided to women's disadvantage, whereby cultural expectations of what was appropriate or possible for women were attributed to some immutable biological law (Birke 1986) and what women did was devalued (notably childbearing and rearing and domestic labour (Oakley 1972)).

The notion that women should be relegated to second-class citizenship, or even accorded no citizenship status, because of anatomical difference from men (in particular, the possession of a uterus) has a long history. Similarly, certain attributes of physical and intellectual prowess, confidence, strength and courage have been defined as masculine and attributed to men as 'natural' qualities. The inevitability of such gendered qualities is often rehearsed by parents, who suggest that a small child's behaviour, notably bad behaviour, is 'only natural' because 'he is a real boy', in an invocation of biology as an excuse, because it is uncontrollable.

Women have been excluded from activities ranging from sport (Hargreaves 1994; Woodward 2009a, 2009b, 2012a) to paid work in the public arena and membership of the professions and posts in the military, purportedly because of their sex. The imperatives of sex were under-theorized, and within this paradigm it was women rather than men who were at the mercy of their hormones and reproductive capacities (Ortner 1974). Women have been barred from participating in certain sports and continue to run shorter distances, play bouts of shorter duration and comply with different regimes from men in sport. Examples include playing off different tees in golf or fighting fewer rounds in boxing (a sport in which women were allowed to participate competitively only in the Olympic Games in 2012) (Woodward 2014), in each case on the basis of physical difference (Woodward 2006, 2009a, 2009b). Claims that anatomy is destiny for women result in dire outcomes. The ancient Greek philosopher Aristotle suggested that the possession of a uterus made women subordinate to men. He argued that women experienced the biological and anatomical phenomenon of the 'wandering womb', which rendered them incapable of rational thought because the womb would wander around the body. However absurd the 'wandering womb' might appear in the twenty-first century, it is not far removed from the psychoanalytic figure of the 'hysterical woman' (Foucault 1978), whereby displays of anxiety are attributed to the possession of a uterus (*hyster* in Greek), which renders women more emotional than men. Women who engage in elite sport are still seen as impairing their reproductive capacities, and it is their reproductive capacities which are claimed to make women emotional and unstable. This is an asserted aspect of gender difference which has excluded women from public life and continues to exclude them in many parts of the world. Anatomical and biological explanations have been given for the cultural, economic, political and social inequalities which have been manifest in most forms of social organization.

The move to separate biology from social organization and contingent cultural practices provided a significant challenge to some of these claims. Feminists sought to make a distinction between the biological characteristics of the body and gender as a cultural construct, pointing out that many of the negative, constraining aspects of gender for women are social, specific and contingent and not fixed by biology. Debates about the sex–gender relationship within feminist theory and the social sciences have addressed the problem of binary logic in relation to the hierarchical nature of the relationship between them when the two are presented as separate concepts. While the mind and the soul might be rated above the body in soul/body, mind/body dualisms, in the sex/gender debate, embodied, anatomical sex carried greater weighting as a determinant of gender. Stanley and Wise (1984) described the argument as being one between biological essentialism, which prioritizes biological, embodied sex as the determinant of femininity or of masculinity, and social constructionism, which focuses on gender as a social, cultural category. Stanley's argument suggests the separation between the two concepts, with sex being associated with biology and embodiment and gender with social and cultural practices. This discussion highlights two issues. Firstly, sex and gender have been combined, but there is still the assumption that sex (as a biological classification) is privileged over gender (as covering social attributes) in terms of the certainty it affords in relation to sexual difference and the differences of the lived experience of gender. Secondly, where sex and gender have been explicitly disentangled, the influence of sex upon gender has been awarded priority and higher status than any influence gender as a cultural and social construct might have. There is also a normative claim involved in this hierarchy, namely that sex *should* determine gender. This normativity extends to the privileging of male over female and, as later critics pointed out (Butler 1990, 1993), of heterosexuality over lesbian, gay, bi-, queer and transsexualities, often on the basis of its 'natural' claims, which derive from the binary logic of sex as distinct from gender. The separation of sex and gender lends itself to social inequalities and has been so deployed in the social and political institution of patriarchy. Gender seems to offer the possibility of change that holding onto the corporeality of sex cannot deliver. Gender has thus been enthusiastically embraced by feminists and activists.

Essentialism and non-essentialism

The distinction that has been made between sex and gender has been very productive for critical thinking within sociology, critiquing patriarchal systems and institutions which appear to rely heavily upon assumptions about the fixity of sex as the foundation of difference and, most importantly, inequality. However, later criticisms point to an essentialist overemphasis on the homogeneous category of 'woman' which such approaches might have implied (Stanley and Wise 1984; Woodward 1997; Gillis, Howie and Munford 2007).

Essentialism is marked by determinism and reductionism, whereby transformations are limited and all aspects of social situation are attenuated to a single determining factor, suggesting that people can be reduced to core properties which determine how they behave, such as those associated with femininity and masculinity. Essentialism is closely tied to biology in that such qualities are seen not only as core but inevitable as part of nature (Woodward 1997). It is, however, the women's movement of the 1970s and 1980s which became subject to accusations of essentialism because the movement, and much feminist activism and theory of the time, asserted the singularity and bounded nature of women's experience, as if all women, by virtue of being women, might share a universal experience and situation, regardless of differences such as those of class, race, ethnicity and disability. For example, women who were anti-war activists in the 1980s mobilized essentialist notions of nurturing and caring on the part of women as counterposed to the bellicosity and aggression of men, as if these qualities were essential. Thus feminist arguments appeared to be overtaken by the very reductionism that the sex/gender distinction sought to erase. Some of these criticisms, however, do overemphasize particular aspects of second-wave feminism and do not always note the diversity of identity politics and the women's movement's own recognition of the risks of essentialism (ibid.).

Some of the criticism of second-wave feminist movements focused upon class- and race-based universalism, however. Elizabeth Spelman's classic text *Inessential Woman* castigates feminists of the 1980s and 1990s for privileging the experiences of white middle-class women in the developed, Western world as the norm (Spelman 1988). These are fair assertions, especially given the empirical evidence, for example in the UN data above on global inequalities. Inequalities between women are also strongly inflected by social class, race, ethnicity, generation and disability, although there are particular dimensions to women's experiences which, as the UN data show, are influenced by the specific embodied experiences of women and the low cultural value accorded to, for example, reproductive health and domestic labour. Focusing too much on the homogeneity of the category 'woman' and failing to acknowledge or to be attentive enough to the ubiquity of gender inequalities also has limitations of course. It is possible to argue that some groups have dominance over other groups and to point to widespread political, economic and social inequalities (such as those of poverty, racism, ethnocentricism and patriarchy) without necessarily suggesting that these categories or qualities of difference are immutable and determined. Later theorists of intersectionality argued that these different axes of power intersect to produce inequalities (Davis 2008; Taylor and Hines 2012; Lykke 2012). Criticisms of essentialist approaches have been very productive in opening up possibilities for engaging with the complex interrelationship between diverse aspects of social exclusion and marginalization and drawing attention to the complexity of forces in the assemblage of social inequities and injustices.

Non-essentialism stresses fluidity and the possibility of change: nothing is fixed and it all depends on the situation and the circumstances. Whereas essentialist approaches have often been expressed as binary opposites (Cixous 1980; Woodward 1997), recent work has challenged the oversimplification of dichotomous thinking, especially in what have been called postmodernist approaches (Braidotti 1994; Butler 1990, 1993; Gatens 1991, 1996; Grosz 1994; Haraway 1985, 1989, 1991, 2000). Third-wave feminism has taken up the anti-essentialist cause and points to the philosophical limitations of essentialism, while acknowledging the strategic possibilities and even necessity of being able to retain a political category 'woman' (Gillis, Howie and Munford 2007). There is still a dilemma which the debate about essentialism demonstrates: without identifiable shared qualities (even essential shared characteristics based on sex) the political project of feminism might seem in jeopardy. The third wave has been concerned with engaging with these challenges through a range of theoretical critiques which we will explore in the remainder of this chapter, including the phenomenology of experience in the ways in which sex and gender are experienced within particular social worlds (Beauvoir [1949] 1989; Young 2005), Judith Butler's work on social and cultural influences on (rather than the fixity of) sex (Butler 1990, 1993), and the politics of difference which marks much of what has been called French feminism (Irigaray 1985a, 1985b; Marks and Courtviron 1981; also discussed in Woodward and Woodward 2009).

SEMINAR QUESTIONS

1 Make a list of ten attributes which you associate with the category man and ten with the category woman.
2 In an approach which differentiated between sex as biological, embodied and genetic, how many of the attributes on your list could be classified as sex and how many as gender?
3 How do you differentiate between the two?
4 What difficulties are there in making these distinctions?

CHALLENGING THE SEX/GENDER BINARY

Sex and gender: social and historical meanings

Challenges to the binary logic of sex and gender have come from both post-structural and phenomenological perspectives. These approaches shared concerns about the fixity of sex as a deterministic, biological category.

Post-structuralist theorists of sex and gender were troubled by second-wave accounts from the late 1960s and the 1970s in which sex appeared to be ahistorical and divorced from social-historical meanings. Critiques of the sex/gender distinction aimed firstly to avoid biological determinism and secondly to develop a non-essentialist, historically specific understanding of sex and of the body. Post-structuralist theorists were not entirely successful in achieving these aims, it can be argued (Moi 1999), because their reconceptualizations of sex were curiously disembodied (Nussbaum 2000) and insufficiently attentive to material, enfleshed bodies (Segal 1999; Woodward 2009a, 2012a). Furthermore, the stress on theory generated more complicated problems than it solved and became too abstract (Nussbaum 2000) and completely separated from experience and the actualities of sex, gender and embodiment (Moi 1999).

This is not to say that all post-structuralist feminist accounts necessarily place sex and gender together as two equal parts of the equation. For example, Joan Scott argues that the term gender 'denoted a rejection of the biological determinism implicit in the use of such terms as "sex" and "sexual difference"' (Scott 1988: 29). Scott focused upon the historical and social effects of sexual difference and opts for gender rather than sex because of the biological implications of sex, in the tradition of second-wave feminist critiques of the sex/gender binary. Scott's account reduces the significance of sex in the sex/gender binary and focuses upon gender as a more useful concept. This preference for gender as a more useful descriptor of sexual difference demonstrates the strengths of second-wave feminist theoretical critiques, whatever the limitations of their implied presentation of sex in terms of fixity and biological capacities and the potential of fluid and hybrid interpretations of gender to underestimate the consistencies of the lived experience and social organization of gender-differentiated lives and systems.

Women's experiences and lived bodies

Feminist phenomenological accounts have been particularly productive in merging the specificities of experience with a critique which avoids the pitfalls of essentialism. Given the association of sex with biology and anatomy, an exploration of bodies and embodiment can provide a useful route into challenging the rigidity of the sex/gender binary. Bodies are more complicated than binary thinking suggests and are of key interest to sociologists. One example of such an approach (albeit one that is not without its own limitations) is the work of Simone de Beauvoir ([1949] 1989), especially in its focus upon bodies as situated and as situation. The concept of the body as situation overcomes some of the difficulties of separating sex and gender and some of the problems of essentialism (Woodward 1997, 2012a). De Beauvoir's work has also been used to develop a critique of gendered embodiment that bridges the sex/gender divide with a culturally inscribed body which – crucially – retains its bodily materiality (Moi 1999).

The meanings of bodies are not written on the surface, nor will the experience of bodies be the same for everyone. Simone de Beauvoir suggests that the human body is ambiguous, subject to natural laws and to the human production of meaning:

> It is not merely as a body, but rather as a body subject to taboos, to laws, that the subject becomes conscious of himself [sic] and attains fulfillment – it is with reference to certain values that he valorizes himself. To repeat once more: physiology cannot ground any values; rather, the facts of biology take on the values that the existent bestows upon them. (De Beauvoir [1949] 1989: 76)

This approach provides a way of bringing together what can be called the natural, material body, the experiences of embodied selves and the situations (including representations, practices and policies) which re-create the lived body (Battersby 1998). Bodies are not just 'in a situation', nor are they just objects of empirical inquiry; bodies are more than this. De Beauvoir's analysis of the 'lived body' provides a means of enabling 'a situated way of seeing the subject based on the understanding that the most important location or situation is the roots of the subject in the spatial frame of the body' (Braidotti 1994: 161). Bodies are situated on the margins through structural factors such as economic inequalities, racialization, ethnicization and discrimination on grounds of gender and of physical or mental impairment, but bodies are also themselves situations through which people experience themselves, both negatively and positively (Fraser and Greco 2005): 'The body is not a thing, it is a *situation* . . . it is the instrument of our grasp upon the world, a limiting factor for projects' (de Beauvoir 1989: 66). As Toril Moi argues, 'To claim that the body *is* a situation is not the same as to say that it is placed *within* some other situation. The body is both a situation and is placed within other situations' (Moi 1999: 65).

Thinking in terms of embodied selves and lived bodies accords individuals greater agency and possibility for transformation and avoids the reduction of the self to the body by acknowledging both the situations which bodies inhabit and the interrelationship between bodies and situations. De Beauvoir argues that to claim that the body is a situation is to acknowledge that having a woman's body is bound up with the exercise of freedom. The body-in-the-world is in an intentional relationship with the world, although, as Iris Marion Young argues, women do often end up living their bodies as things (Young 2005). Laura Mulvey, for example, offers an important critique of the semiotic of cinema to illustrate the process of seeing and being seen, in which she argues that, when women look, they always see women's bodies, and especially their own bodies and themselves, through men's eyes in the mediated gaze (Mulvey 1975). The concept of the gaze has been extensively developed to explore both various forms of oppression (notably the racialized, ethnicized gaze) and, more positively, the possibilities of a democratic gaze. Lived embodiment disrupts dichotomies of mind and body, nature and culture, public and private, and thereby foregrounds experience (Young 2005).

Young offers the example of 'throwing like a girl' to demonstrate how bodies are lived and gender is not simply learned.

Thus, drawing upon de Beauvoir's idea of bodies as situated both by social and cultural forces and by themselves as situations, Moi suggests the 'lived body' as an alternative to the categories of sex and gender (Moi 1999; de Beauvoir 1989). This concept provides a non-essentialist synthesis of corporeality by situating the physical body and its experiences in the

BOX 2.1 THROWING LIKE A GIRL

'The girl of five does not make any use of lateral space. She does not stretch her arm sideward; she does not twist her trunk; she does not move her legs, which remain by her side. All she does in preparation for throwing is to lift her right arm forward to the horizontal and to bend her forearm backward … the ball is released without force, speed or accurate aim …' (Strauss quoted in Young, 2005: 27). This is contrasted to the movement of a boy of the same age. Strauss claims support for biological difference but these differences are not anatomical. The children have similar bodies. The different practices are lived. Each child has already acquired a gendered state of being through comportment, that is the way in which the body moves and its dispositions. This example is particularly useful in showing how what looks like biology is practice and a way of being; it is the lived body.

Young goes on to develop a critique of how such practices are used to support biologically determinist view of gender; they seem to be embodied and thus 'natural'.

social world around it. The embodied self can initiate action in different situations. Bodies do not exist out of time and place (the exceptionality of out-of-body experiences notwithstanding). Even in the transcendence of experiences that are 'in the zone' (Csikszentmihalyi 1975), the material body is still temporally and spatially located. In the same way, sex and gender are also temporally and spatially situated. Bodies are born, they breathe, eat, sleep and reproduce and are classified, usually as either female or male in the vast majority of known societies, in a binary paradigm which so classifies people and provides a blueprint for how they should live their lives in that society. Most significantly, the division of societies into male and female is marked by inequalities and value systems which vastly over-privilege men and their activities over women and their capacities (Connell 2002; Woodward 2011). There are some acknowledged departures within the life course of individuals and in relation to intersex which are recognized more in some societies than others (Kessler 1998), such as the *hijras* in India, Pakistan and Bangladesh, but social processes and systems are largely dominated by the gender binary, and those who do not fit neatly into the gender binary, even if they gain legal status like the hijras, are largely classified as a third sex.

These value systems also impact upon bodies, for example in relation to nutrition, constraining cultural practices or the management of childbearing, so that it becomes impossible to disentangle sex as embodied and anatomical and gender as social and cultural: we need both terms. The anatomical body is shaped by social forces, such as the climate, what we eat, and policies and practices which govern reproduction. Even our bones are socially influenced (Fausto-Sterling 2005), and two sexes are insufficient to classify the diversity of sex (Fausto-Sterling 1992, 2001). Fausto-Sterling rejects the idea of intersex as a third sex or 'hermaphrodite' and suggests that there is a range of possibilities each of which has embodied authenticity and validity. The body is always located in a given environment, as a 'situation' incorporating the physical facts of its materiality, such as size, age, health, reproductive capacity, skin, hair and the social context. Moi's 'lived body' is not biologistic – that is, it is not reducible to its corporeal parts, subject only to general laws of physiology and divided into two categories of gender. This eliminates the constraints of other binaries too, such as nature/culture; the body is always part of culture, inculcated with habits, acting according to social and cultural rules, but it retains the possibilities of addressing what is enfleshed (Woodward 2009a, 2012a).

'*Hijra*' is a term used in South Asia to refer to transsexuals and transgender people. They have a long history as a social category within South Asian societies and are one example that challenges a male/female gender binary. (© Def Ref/Flickr)

> To consider the body as a situation . . . is to consider both the fact of being a specific kind of body and the meaning that concrete body has for the situated individual. This is not the equivalent of either sex or gender. The same is true of 'lived experience' which encompasses our experience of all kinds of situations (race, class, nationality, etc.) and is a far more wide-ranging concept than the highly psychologizing concept of gender identity. (Moi 1999: 81)

The idea of the 'lived body' provides one route into addressing difference and othering without reductionism. However, as Iris Marion Young (2005) points out, although the lived body avoids the binary logic of sex/gender, it may pay insufficient attention to the structural constraints which shape experience. Consequently, she argues for the retention of the concept of gender, which is a term that has been taken up with some enthusiasm by a range of regulatory bodies and institutions of governance. The term 'gender' may suggest more possibilities of transformation, but it is also the currently preferred term in the practices of sports regulating bodies, which seek to achieve some degree of certainty in ascertaining the sex or – as they currently describe it – gender of individual athletes (which we explore in the next section). Although the range of post-structuralist and phenomenological approaches express different ideas about sex, gender and sexuality, there is some consensus about the complexity of the relationship between each of the three as well as

BOX 2.2 BODIES AS SITUATIONS: SITUATED BODIES

Childbirth, which is one of the most specifically gendered, embodied experiences, offers a good example of the situated body within a particular spatial and temporal context, as well as being subject to social and cultural forces. The activity takes place in the home or hospital according to social policies and customs and is subject to various technological interventions which categorize the experience. Those who give birth are also subject to the influences of social class, poverty or affluence, ethnicity and cultural practices, as well as personal, community and kinship investments in the outcome. The vast majority of those who give birth are classified as women (Woodward 2011), but the possibility of those who classify themselves as men giving birth also illustrates the body as situation.

The labouring body is also a situation, as the corporeal and subjective dimensions of the experience such as pain, fear, participation in decision-making about techniques to be used and place of birth are all experienced in the subject body. The enfleshed body is the site of pain, elation and anxiety as well as the nature of the outcome – the baby or babies – all of which are located within the body as situation. In the rare cases of men 'giving birth', the body as situation is usually a body with a uterus, having been born female but then identifying as male. The medical interventions are more transformative than those customary in the management of childbirth but illustrate how the body becomes a situation.

agreement about the impossibility of disentangling material bodies from social and cultural situations.

SEMINAR QUESTIONS

1 What kind of examples can you come up with of interventions into bodies which, possibly through technological or pharmaceutical processes and medical science, transform the subjects of the interventions and create a new social position for the people involved?
2 Are some bodies more valued than others?
3 Which bodies do you think are most valued in contemporary Western society and why?
4 What are the links between social and cultural forces and the most valued bodies?

GENDER VERIFICATION: A SPORTING EXAMPLE

The assumption of a sex/gender binary

Whatever arguments there may be about the insufficiency of the sex binary, suggestions that there should be five sexes (Fausto-Sterling 1992, 2001) or claims that the duality of female and male is fluid and can be transgressed (Butler 1990, 1993), in the field of sport there are two sexes. It is particularly important to be certain about the category to which participants belong. Regimes of truth in the world of sport are much less fluid and mobile in relation to sex and gender than in many other social worlds. Sport is premised upon a sex/gender binary which informs its regulatory framework and the embodied practices of athletes, a clear dichotomy of difference which also privileges one aspect of the binary, notably that of the male and the attributes of masculinity (Cixous 1980). There are women's competitions and men's competitions and very few that are mixed, especially at the highest levels. Mixed doubles in tennis is one of the few competitive mixed sports with public recognition, unlike foursomes in golf, which are low-status leisure activities; the high prizes and kudos go especially to top male golfers. Mixed competitions are still based upon the supposed balance of the female/male binary and take on board difference in all its dimensions – enfleshed difference and that of cultural practice and recognition – which means that male athletes top the table in terms of rewards and mixed activities are mostly relegated to the lower echelons of both status and reward. Bodies matter in sport, and the characteristics of male bodies in terms of size, weight and upper-body strength, for example, are particularly celebrated. The impact of sport resonates far beyond the pitch, field, ring, pool and track (Woodward 2012a, 2012b, 2012c, 2009a, 2009b) and is particularly a field in which hegemonic masculinity is enacted and circulates (Connell 1995, 2002). An exploration of gender-verification testing demonstrates some of the key features of sex, gender and sexuality which have wider resonance than sport itself.

Sporting bodies and testing

The International Olympics Committee (IOC) introduced sex testing, as it was then called, in 1968 at the Olympic Games in Mexico City, apparently after claims about the masculine appearance of some competitors. The development of broad shoulders, flat chests and muscular bodies among women athletes is very likely to have been inevitable as women's events became more competitive and with the subsequent increased participation of women in elite sport. Sex and gender cannot be easily separated into artificially constructed terrains of material, anatomical bodies in cultural practices. Enfleshed selves are always both. 'The gender polarities long sustained through competitive sport became blurred as female athletes generally became bigger and stronger' (Wamsley and Pfister, 2005).

The debate about the masculinization of women athletes had been raging for several decades in the twentieth century, both before and after the institution of gender-verification testing, and it persists in different forms in the twenty-first. Instances of gender ambiguity are framed within ethical discourses with the implication of cheating and moral transgression. They usually involve either a reassertion of the masculinity to which women, mistakenly, aspire in sport, because they cannot attain it without being masculinized, or a sense of pity. Sport also offers a field in which pharmaceutical, legal and illegal interventions in the body clearly have a range of impacts, suggesting close interconnections between bodies and cultural practices where the former can themselves be reconstituted through the latter. Women's bodies can become the target of organized deception and corruption, as sex becomes a tool for the manipulation of sporting success in a process in which women's bodies are deeply implicated.

This debate was greatly intensified and took on an explicit political aspect during the Cold War. On the one hand, women in Eastern bloc countries had greater freedom to compete in sport and sport was a catalyst for social change (Guttmann 1992) but, on the other, they were vehicles for communist ideology, which was antithetical to neoliberal politics. Women played a key role in the making of the Eastern bloc's sporting success story. Female athletes thus became political tools as a means of enhancing the role of Eastern bloc countries in world sport.

The stated aim of gender-verification testing was to prevent any man from masquerading as a woman in order to gain advantage in women-only athletic competitions. Gender-determination tests run by doctors as medical experts involved humiliating and invasive physical examinations. Certainty was to be achieved through the common sense of visible difference, based on a simplistic definition of sex. Later the IOC used genetic tests, based

BOX 2.3 BODIES AS SITUATIONS: A SPORTING EXAMPLE

Before the unification of Germany, in the former East Germany it is estimated that as many as 10,000 athletes were caught up in the attempt to build a race of superhuman communist sports heroes using steroids and other performance-enhancing drugs. Shot-putter Heidi Krieger was given steroids and contraceptive pills from the age of sixteen and became European champion by the age of twenty. Her overdeveloped physique had put a huge amount of pressure on her frame, causing medical problems, while the drugs had caused mood swings and depression and resulted in at least one suicide attempt. Later Krieger underwent gender-reassignment surgery, claiming that she had been confused about her gender but felt that the drugs had pushed her over the edge.

This example illustrates some of the complex connections between social forces and gendered, sexed bodies, where pharmaceutical interventions impact upon bodies and generate expectations about sex/gender.

on chromosomes. Geneticists criticized the tests, saying that sex is not as simple as X and Y chromosomes, and it is not always simple to ascertain. It is thought that around one in 1,600 babies are born with an intersex condition, the general term for people with chromosomal abnormalities (Blackless et al. 2000). It may be physically obvious from birth – babies may have ambiguous reproductive organs, for instance – or it may remain unknown to people all their lives.

Far from being a simple response, as in the childbirth narratives where the arrival of the infant is universally greeted by a cry labelling its gender – 'It's a girl!' or 'It's a boy!' – things are more complicated. Human beings may exhibit a variety of chromosomal and physiological characteristics, such as androgen insensitivity syndrome (AIS), when a child is born with XY chromosomes but feminine genitalia, or those with congenital adrenal hyperplasia, who have XX chromosomes but masculine genitals.

This complexity is demonstrated by the actual experience of gender-verification testing. At the Atlanta games in 1996, eight female athletes failed sex tests but were all cleared on appeal; seven were found to have an intersex condition. Athletes, just like everyone else, might have a more complex sexual identity, whether as intersex or involving trans-sex or a whole range of sexual identities which have become muddled up in sport's search for binary simplicity and certainty.

There was considerable resistance to gender-verification testing from different constituencies, which included medical scientists and doctors, all of whom challenged the reliability and validity of such tests. They were also, of course, strongly criticized by the women athletes who had been subjected to the tests and on ethical grounds. The processes through which the tests were carried out were humiliating. As a result, by the time of the Sydney games in 2000, the IOC had abolished universal sex testing, but, as has continued to happen, some women still have to prove they really are women. The IOC, however, was slow to make the decision to abandon the tests.

In 1990, the International Federation of Athletics Associations (IAAF) became the first major international sports body to recommend allowing transsexuals to compete, with some restrictions, which were agreed in 2004. Athletes who have sex-reassignment surgery before puberty are automatically accepted as their new sex provided that all surgical changes are completed, they are legally recognized as their new sex in the country they represent, and they have had hormone therapy for an extended period of time. For male-to-female transsexuals, this generally means a minimum of two years. Transsexuals who have had a sex change from male to female can compete in women's events in the Olympics as long they wait for two years after the operation. The reasons for the timescale are not entirely clear, and the possible explanations range from the assertion that athletes have to prove that they have learned to be real women, to women having to show they have the necessary stamina and can survive in the world and pass as women, before they can compete. Another element in this mix which relates to the materialities of enfleshed sex is the period of time it takes for the balance of 'male' and 'female' hormones to settle in order to secure an authentic female make-up.

Inequality, ethics and gender verification

This discussion raises questions about self-identification and lived experience. Are you the sex you say you are? What relevance is the testing to those who have lived their entire lives as the sex they say they are, whatever the genetic testing suggests? The humiliation of gender testing is evident in several of the high-profile cases of recent years. For example, Santhi Soundarajan, a 27-year-old Indian athlete, was stripped of her silver medal for the 800 m at the Asian Games in 2006. Soundarajan, who has lived her entire life as a woman, failed a gender test, which included examinations by a gynaecologist, an endocrinologist, a psychologist and a genetic expert. It appeared likely that she has androgen insensitivity syndrome, where a person has the physical characteristics of a woman but the genetic make-up includes a male chromosome; the trauma of the testing led her to attempt suicide while awaiting the results.

The IAAF set out its approach in a paper in 2006 in order to establish a policy and mechanism for managing the issue of gender among participants in women's events. According to this paper, if there is any 'suspicion', or if there is a 'challenge', then the athlete concerned can be asked to attend a medical evaluation before a panel, comprising gynaecologist, endocrinologist, psychologist, internal medicine specialists and experts on gender/transgender issues. The medical delegate can do an initial check, which could be construed as a pragmatic strategy or a reprise of the focus on visible difference and gendered corporeal characteristics (IAAF 2006).

What creates suspicion is a woman who does not conform to stereotypical female, feminine behaviour and appearance. This was the case with Caster Semenya, the South African 800 m runner who was subjected to a series of tests and public humiliation based largely on her strong athletic appearance as well as later some chromosomal complexities (Woodward 2009a, 2009b, 2012a). Although not specifically about sexuality, the norms attached to masculinity and femininity are all constitutive of heteronormativity which attributes prescribed masculine qualities to men and feminine ones to women in this normalized relationship. Semenya, as a strong black woman who comes from a poor rural community in South Africa, challenged this norm.

Appearance and cultural practices are part of the story; athletic prowess is another. Semenya was not the fastest athlete in her class, but in one competition she left her rivals standing. Ye Shiwen the Chinese swimmer was challenged in 2012 at the London Olympics *solely* on grounds of her speed. She was subjected to questioning, if not gender testing, because at times her speeds equalled those of male gold medalist Michael Phelps (Woodward 2012c). This case was not about gender testing, but it does illustrate one of the elements in the gendered process.

In what ways does the investigation into Caster Semenya's gender demonstrate continuing prejudice against women and expectations of male–female hierarchies in the world of sport? (© Chell Hill/Wikimedia Commons)

In sport, if women go too fast they are taking on successful (male) attributes and might be accused of cheating.

Gender-verification tests present a mix of cultural, social and political inequalities which intersect with embodied, enfleshed materialities. Masculinity has not been subject to the same doubts, perhaps because men and masculinity have been seen as the yardstick of normality by which standards and classification of sex are judged. Also women would be unlikely to want to masquerade as men in athletic competition because of material differences in performance outcomes. If there are two sexes there can be no obfuscation. Establishing criteria by which a person's sex can be incontrovertibly ascertained also suggests that finding certainty and the truth is the morally superior route. The IOC has always insisted that gender-verification tests were designed not to differentiate between the sexes but to prevent men pretending to be women and winning unfairly. Ethical questions may have appeared to be paramount, but control of women's gender and sexuality also informs these claims.

Gender-verification testing has largely failed to recognize the possibility of women's athletic achievement; if they are any good they must be men. Gender verification shows that sex is far from simple, and different social, cultural and political forces are in play and intersect in shaping the relationship between anatomy and culture.

SEMINAR QUESTIONS

1 How successful have sporting governing bodies been in securing and proving the existence of two sexes?
2 What are the different social elements involved in the process of gender verification?
3 Sports regulatory bodies draw upon the expertise of psychologists in gender-verification testing; what could be the role of sociologists in these processes?
4 What light can sociologists shed on these debates?

REVISITING 'SEX'

Performing sex?

Judith Butler has developed one of the most influential theories and contributions to the sex/gender distinction debate: her powerful and innovative argument that it is not only gender but also sex that is socially constructed; the sex/gender distinction is no distinction at all (Butler 1990). Butler's work has also most usefully engaged with the points of connection between sex and sexuality and the political dimensions and impact of sex and gender.

In *Gender Trouble* (1990), Butler offers a radical rethinking of the sex/gender binary which also contests the presumption of heterosexuality that renders all other sexual and gendered practices illegitimate. She does not simply make the point that sex is gendered: sex is, 'from the start, normative[, operating as] what Foucault has called a "regulatory ideal" producing the bodies it governs' (Butler 1990: 1). Butler draws upon Foucauldian notions of discursive productions of knowledge (Foucault 1972) in her critique of both sex and gender. Sex is discursive in that it brings into being the material bodies it claims to describe. Sex thus serves to pathologize those bodies which do not conform to the normative parameters of masculinity and the male body. Sex is performative as well as a performance.

BOX 2.4 PERFORMATIVITY

Gender categories are not only performed: they *are* that performance. It is through the everyday acts, the clothes we wear, the way we talk and move, and what we do that gender is made and remade. When a baby is born and the midwife announces the sex (of which there is a choice of only two) and wraps it in a pink or a blue blanket, the sex of the infant as well as its gender is *created*. Even before it can perform any of the actions associated with a particular sex, the infant is labelled, which generates ways of being in the world. Sex, like gender, is the result of these actions through the processes of performativity. The physical body can only be sexed through gender. By doing certain things we become female or male. This is just the start.

Butler's (1990) main example of performativity is drag, whereby established gender categories are disrupted by a person wearing the clothes and performing in ways associated with the other sex. Butler, like Garfinkel (1967), argues that you can understand what is performed only by reference to what is prohibited, but drag, rather than being a conscious choice, is also tied up in the making of sex and gender. Performativity is the process through which social and cultural identities and subjects are constituted and experienced.

Butler argues that one way to challenge the heteronormativity (discussed in more detail in the next section of this chapter) which is an outcome of the binary logic of sex is through transgression – for example, in the parodic performances of drag and through transsexualities. Drag is important to Butler because it is a practice which sheds light on how heteronormativity naturalizes the relation between sex, gender and desire and thus challenges the law of heterosexual coherence. By looking at what is *not* the norm, it is possible to explain what that norm is, rather in the manner of Garfinkel's ethnomethodological sociology. Garfinkel used breaching experiments to demonstrate the rules of everyday life by doing the wrong thing, by not following the rules (Garfinkel 1967). Examples of exploring what the rules are by showing what happens when we break them include haggling over the price of goods in a supermarket or students behaving like lodgers in their own home. Appropriate behaviour among one's own family is very different from the polite and more distant interactions of lodgers, and what is quite acceptable in the latter situation is most inappropriate and even insulting when addressing one's own family. Similarly, men wearing conventional women's clothes and moving in ways associated with women demonstrate dramatically the rules by which we identify gender categories. Butler's work has been informed by theatrical direct action politics, which has contributed to the development of queer theory (Lloyd 2007). *Gender Trouble* became a foundational text of queer theory, with all its capacities to disrupt and subvert normative thinking and established rules about sex, gender and sexuality.

Sex in everyday practices

The meaning of 'sex' is strongly mediated by cultural understandings that, it is argued, make it impossible to differentiate between sex and gender, and it is increasingly recognized that they are mutually constitutive. The use of gender permits an acknowledgement of this powerful cultural and social mediation (Price and Shildrick 1999). Gender may provide a satisfying theoretical account of difference which fails, however, to accommodate the everyday experience of sex and lived contradictions of sex. The contradictions and ambivalences are all too evident in some of the routine practices of everyday life as well as in more public, visible phenomena. Mandy Merck argues that experience is distorted by the social insistence upon and persistence of the dichotomous categories of female and male (Merck 2010). The feminist writer Shulamith Firestone claimed in the early years of the second wave that liberation for women would never be possible until not only male privilege but also the sex distinction itself is eliminated (Firestone 1970). More recent, much more complex arguments echo the spirit of this challenge to the rigidity of the sex/gender binary. There are strengths in this argument, except that it remains premised largely upon the philosophical categories of sex and its corporeality, rather than on the empirical experience which combines lived experience and situatedness with the enfleshed actualities of the body as a situation (de Beauvoir 1989).

Stella Sandford argues for an understanding of sex which can be critical of the routines of everyday life and engages with the complexities of the relationship between sex, gender and sexuality (Sandford 2011). The routine experiences which are the subject of phenomenological accounts (de Beauvoir 1989; Merleau-Ponty 1962; Moi 1999; Young 2005) inform and are informed by the visible representations of media-transmitted public displays (Woodward 2009a, 2009b, 2012a). To focus upon the capacities of bodies and embodiment may not involve a reduction to entrenched binaries, but it may afford possibilities to challenge the rigidity and inflexibility of an ontology in which sex is said not to exist and is dismissed as a discursive fiction.

Sandford traces the genesis of sex through its philosophical and empirical narratives and argues that the recent preference for gender, some of which derives from the sex/gender distinction that is assumed to have been made in de Beauvoir's *The Second Sex* (1989), is based largely upon a misunderstanding. Sandford suggests that the idea that de Beauvoir is separating sex as biological from gender as cultural is a misrepresentation of the latter's exposition of women as the second sex arising from a problem in translation, especially from French into English. The issue is one of how de Beauvoir has been read in the Anglophone world and, because of the endurance of these interpretations, which are part of a wider intellectual movement, it seems unlikely that the more recent translation of the entire original text of *The Second Sex* (2010) makes a great deal of difference to this aspect of the debate. Although in French *sexe* signifies the sexual life, and sex and sexual difference are synonymous, in English sex and sexual difference refer to the material reality of the human (Sandford 2011). This is more than a matter of language, although translation explains some of the misunderstandings.

Embodied difference is not only a constituent of subjectivity and the formation of the self and part of the explanatory framework through which gendered and sexual identities can be understood; it is also part of the sexual division of labour and requires the possibility of collective action – for example, in challenging social exclusion and its embodied consequences. The possibility of collective action is, however, further subverted by Butler's assertion that the category 'woman' is itself unsustainable and serves only to limit feminist projects. The feminist subject is generated by its representation. Gender identity is unstable because it relies upon performativity, which involves repetition through acts and gestures. Thus Butler has challenged the idea that gender is predicated upon sex. Sex, gender and desire are all effects: none of them is natural or essential. This has some purchase in an interrogation of the performativity of heteronormativity in everyday life, although it is problematic in the political project of feminism if there is no category 'women', not even one based on a strategic essentialism, as advocated by Gayatri Spivak (1988). It is also problematic because material, empirical, enfleshed sex is absent. This raises some important issues for theorizing difference and sex/gender.

SEMINAR QUESTIONS

Think about the occasions when you have been asked to classify yourself as female or male – for example, to tick a box as either 'f' or 'm'. You may have to think about it as these things are so routine you might not even notice – the census and forms from the Office of National Statistics, university entrance, examination registration, accommodation, health information, passport. Have you filled in any questionnaires recently?

1 Why does the agency responsible for the form need to know your sex?
2 Can you decline and what would happen if you did?
3 How can these examples illustrate Butler's view that sex is produced through performance?

BRINGING IN SEXUALITY

The connections between sex, gender and sexuality

Sexuality is not the same as sex or gender (Taylor and Hines 2012), but in the history of ideas these areas of study have often merged and overlapped, not least because of sexual politics and earlier silences about sex, gender and sexuality in the social sciences. Some of the overlap between sex and sexuality has also evolved from the associations of sexual activity with reproduction which have fuelled the idea that heterosexuality is the normal, default position. Despite the feminist challenges to this normative essentialism, sexuality remains closely entwined with sex and gender in contemporary society.

BOX 2.5 PORNIFICATION

Pornification, or pornogrification (Levy 2005), describes how practices and techniques of pornography have filtered into the mainstream. Models for a range of consumer products in the pages of up-market fashion magazines, from clothes to perfumes, adopt poses hitherto associated with top-shelf pornography. Scenes of sexual violence are frequently presented in mainstream television programmes, and the web is a largely unregulated site for the display of pornography. Not only are images and representations of women sexualized in terms of visible appearance and personal details, but the nature of the detail amounts to pornography. Sexuality and sex are displayed and represented for the titillation of the voyeuristic spectator, however irrelevant such information might be in the particular instance, which could range from the reporting of road traffic accidents to political news. In spite of the somewhat awkward terminology, the concept of pornification remains a useful tool for understanding the tensions between sexuality as an expression of autonomy and control over one's self and one's body and the danger which can underlie the deployment of sex and sexuality as exploitative and compulsive forces; far from being 'empowering' to women, pornification is disempowering. Volubility about sex and sexuality does not in itself make for liberation, as Michel Foucault (1978) argued. Pornification is a new version of this volubility and visibility, with the particular features of visibility and public display of sex masquerading as liberation for women.

The saturation of contemporary Western popular culture and, indeed, everyday life with the visibility of sex has been called *pornification* (Levy 2005). It is no longer confined to the top shelf of the newsagent's shop or the back room.

There have been different responses to the rise of pornification. For example, the adoption of masculine, heterosexual models of sexual expression in the pornification of culture might suggest that young women in neoliberal democracies have been empowered by sexual freedom of expression. On the other hand, far from creating opportunities, such cultural developments can be said to have created even greater oppressions for women by imposing a pornified heteronormative culture and denying them the opportunity to express their own sexuality (Levy 2005; Woodward and Woodward 2009). Pornification can be seen as more oppressive than Western patriarchal discourses of domesticity and the idealized motherhood of the 1950s. Pornified cultural practices can be illustrated by the debate about pole dancing and lap dancing. Both of these activities involve mimicking pornographic practices which provide the representation of sexual practices rather than its experience for women. The practices have been defined by pornography, but young women may engage in them as ironic practices which they are claiming. Nonetheless, the activity is one framed and underpinned by male desire within a tradition of heteronormative pornified culture. Sociocultural change is not all progressive, and using sex/gender as a conceptualization rather than a description permits some understanding of power relations and the legacy of binary logic.

Pornification demonstrates, firstly, that, although they are not the same, sex, gender and sexuality are connected, especially in relation to sexual politics, and, secondly, that these are strongly debated topics because of the normative elements that are involved. In terms of sexuality (that is, people's sexual orientation and the sexual practices in which they engage and from which they derive pleasure), people are often assumed to be heterosexual. This is statistically the norm, but statistically normal merges with morally normal, so that what most people *are* becomes what everyone *ought to be*. Judith Butler calls this assumption of heterosexuality heteronormative (Butler 1990, 1993). This means that, rather than being natural and what everyone ought to be, heterosexuality is socially and culturally constructed and even imposed; people have to be persuaded to be heterosexual.

The historical diversity of sexuality, as sets of sexual practices, at different times and in different places, signposts the possibilities of fluidity and further challenges the assumption that sex is fixed and biological. Norms of sex and sexuality which purport to be natural, however, are also generated by powerful social imperatives that make them appear 'normal'.

BOX 2.6 HETERONORMATIVITY

Heteronormativity involves the assumption that heterosexuality is the norm – that it is normal and that it should be the norm – so much so that social and cultural forces are in place to impose heterosexuality as desirable. Thus heterosexuality is taken for granted and imposed as part of a regulatory framework. The heteronormative discourse can be imposed through such social institutions as marriage and through legislative structures, such as the benefit and taxation systems, whereby only heterosexual partners receive state support through the welfare system. Heteronormativity is also reiterated through everyday practices whereby people assert their own conformity – for example, in routine encounters ('My wife likes those television programmes', 'My husband and I enjoy going to concerts') or in media coverage, as in the case of sports celebrities whose heterosexual partners are reported as 'watching every game' and whose (heterosexual) intimate lives are covered in every detail in the popular media as part of the reassurance that, however colourful their lifestyles, they are secure in their heterosexuality.

Heteronormativity is part of what Butler refers to as the *heterosexual matrix*, which is a system, or a series of networks and practices, through which heterosexuality is secured. These include public rituals and legal processes, public policies, and cultural representations and stories through which we make sense of the world as well as routine everyday exchanges. Heteronormativity and Butler's concept of the heterosexual matrix also contribute specifically to the sexual politics of sexuality and of campaigns and movements which seek more freedom to express sexuality and to challenge the particular constraints of heterosexuality. This politics has been called queer politics, thereby avoiding the limitations of further categorization (as, for example, 'gay' or 'lesbian' or 'bi') and to open up different possibilities for the expression of sexuality. The concept of queer, which denies that individuals possess a stable or essential sexuality, has generated a way of challenging heteronormativity and escaping from the rigid boundaries of sex/gender or categories of person defined by sexual feelings and practices. The emphasis of this approach is that, far from being fixed and innate, heterosexuality has to be established and secured through iterative practices and regimes. This approach has application to and overlap with thinking about sex and gender, too, since it raises some big questions about what people take for granted as being natural and normal and challenges the essentialist views of sex and sexuality.

Sexuality is powerfully driven by desire, which seems absent from many sociological

As the photographer of this picture noted: 'I don't remember ordering white supremacist heteronormative patriarchy with my tea, but whatevs [*sic*].' Heteronormativity is everywhere, sometimes without us realizing it. (© sarah-ji/Flickr)

accounts of sex and gender. Butler's attempts to marry Foucauldian discursive approaches with those of psychoanalysis, which incorporate the role of unconscious forces in the making of sex, gender and sexuality, have been productive and significant, especially in acknowledging the unconscious forces at play in sexual relationships and expressions of desire. Categories of sexuality, such as 'the homosexual' (a figure which Foucault identified as being created historically through legal and medical discourses rather than as an essential type of person), demonstrate the power of social institutions. However, such categories may not fit people's own perception of their sexuality or adequately explain cultural change. Moira Gatens argues that the sex/gender distinction is incompatible with a psychoanalytical account of sexual differences and fails to engage with the psychic as well as the social dimensions of sex and sexuality (Gatens 1996). Butler notes that a limited focus on social institutions is insufficient to explain the strength of feelings and, notably, the irrationality of sexual desire. We may fall in love with the 'wrong' person; whatever the social forces challenging the authenticity of sexual identities, people feel that this is really who they are, whether it is bi, gay, lesbian, straight, trans or, what has now come to be associated with Butler's work, queer. Foucault's social constructionism can be seen as unable to accommodate the intensities of sexual desire and expressions of sexuality.

The politics of difference

As is clear in debates over pornification, bodies are central to an explanation of sex and gender not only in sport. The role of the body or, more commonly, bodies in the language of the corporeal turn (Howson 2005; Fraser and Greco 2005; Witz 2000) highlights the problem of gender, the interconnections between sex and gender, and how sexuality is incorporated into this mix. The materiality of embodiment and the capacities and specific properties of the flesh offer a challenge to some of the excesses of social constructionism which the concept of gender as fluid and malleable might suggest. There is a tension between, on the one hand, acknowledging women's bodies as situated by the properties of the material body and social circumstances (de Beauvoir 1989) that require different provision of care and, on the other, the subordination and devaluing of women justified on such biological grounds (Pateman 1988; Phillips 1998). Recognition of the body and its particular demands and needs which are specific to sex, notably in relation of childbearing and lactation, have generated political difficulties, which have been well recorded in feminist theory and activism but which nonetheless persist, especially in the search for equality in the labour market.

Irigaray's politics of difference challenges the patriarchal claims of Freudian psychoanalysis which suggest that women are defined only in terms of not being men and thus women are largely absent from history. For example, Western history is about fathers and sons and not about mothers and daughters. In Western culture, one of the most dominant representations of women is Mary, the mother of Christ, who is both a mother and a virgin, which Irigaray argues is a strong denial of women's sexuality. Women are represented only as Madonnas or whores in many cultural traditions. Irigaray argues that Western culture rests on the death of the mother and that sexual difference is both embodied in its specificities and cultural in its manifestations and impact. She argues for more representations of the mother–daughter relationship and of women in Western thought, which offers a dynamic and powerful assertion of difference and of female sexuality based upon the actualities of women's bodies rather than their sexualized images or as asexual (Irigaray 1985a, 1985b; Whitford 1991). Irigaray transforms the relationship between bodies and culture in a politics of difference that has enormous resonance with the politics of sex/gender as played out through bodies and discursive regimes, regulatory bodies and bodies of regulation.

Women, and especially the mother–daughter relationship, are absent from much of Western culture, for example in psychoanalysis, which draws on Classical mythology for its tropes and metaphors, and in the regimes of truth which circulate in the field of heroic narratives of the state, public life and the military. Such absences are also startling in sport, where so many heroic legends are based on male kinship networks and the father–son relationship (Woodward 2006) – rarely that of mother and daughter. Motherhood may be an absent presence (Woodward 1997) or tied up with the mechanisms of control of women's sexuality and reproductive capacities – for example, where participation in competitive sport might be construed as dangerous and deleterious to women's capacity for childbearing. Motherhood is not only an empirical category here, but a construction which impacts upon all women, whether or not they are mothers. Women's sexuality is configured around the idealized conceptualization of maternity, embodied in the Madonna, which thus excludes all alternatives to the heterosexual matrix and reinforces heteronormativity.

SEMINAR QUESTIONS

1 When exploring the importance of sex, gender and sexuality, what are the main differences between people which matter?

2 What is the relevance of material bodies in the making of sexual difference?

3 Does sexual difference, for example between women and men, create unequal divisions, or can difference be used as a political tool to gain greater equality? Should we stress difference or equality?

4 How does motherhood and the representation of motherhood impact upon sex, gender and sexuality?

5 How does motherhood illustrate the need for material sex and socially constructed gender in a sociological account of sex, gender and sexuality?

CONCLUSION

The idea of an oppositional distinction between sex and gender has been challenged and, for many, the term 'gender' is largely preferred. The use of gender permits an acknowledgement of this powerful cultural and social mediation (see Price and Shildrick 1999). Hence gender has frequently been the preferred term for feminists and policy-makers and practitioners with a commitment to the promotion of equal opportunities and diversity.

This binary has been challenged, however, and this chapter makes the case for '*sex gender*' as a conceptualization which engages with material, enfleshed inequalities and provides a route into understanding as well as describing social forces and cultural differences. Sex is usually linked to biology, which sometimes gets confused with bodies (Rose 1998). Sex, as linked to biology, flesh, genetic make-up and anatomy, however, has the advantage of allowing both the material capacities of flesh and embodied properties. This understanding of sex may be set in opposition to gender as entirely and distinctively socially constructed, which I suggest is a distortion of the complex and inextricable interaction between sex and gender. There is not a simple one-way force between sex and gender but a two-way dynamic. I use 'sex gender' in order to include the material and physical properties of sex and sexuality as experienced and embodied in the flesh and their interaction with the social and cultural forces which also constitute gender and categories of sexuality. It's not a matter of one or the other – sex or gender. They are co-constitutive. 'Sex gender' permits understanding of the material actualities of sex as well as the fluidity and contingency of gender and historically situated sexuality within a theoretical framework which acknowledges how sexuality fits into and departs from the discussion of sex and gender.

This chapter has demonstrated some of the contributions which the concepts of sex and gender, and particularly sex gender – which encompass the materialities of sex with the social, cultural dimensions of gender – have made to the understanding of social relations and especially to social inequalities. Second-wave feminist critiques which offered an explanatory framework that put gender onto the agenda opened up new ways of theorizing social relations and divisions and the possibilities of deconstruction.

Sex gender is a relational concept which subverts the binary logic of sex/gender and challenges some of the social constructionist excesses of post-structuralist approaches which overemphasize the social construction of sex or marginalize the material properties and particular characteristics of sexed bodies, and is thus more supportive of a politics of difference which can accommodate the specificities of lived bodies and situated experience.

One of the major contributions which a focus upon sex, gender and sexuality offers is, firstly, to draw attention to inequalities and the processes through which they are forged, especially in the routine practices of everyday life in which the discursive regimes and arguments are invoked to support particular systems of power and relations of inequality. Secondly, looking at sex gender and how sex, gender and sexuality interrelate suggests the need to explore the specific operation of different power structures and processes. Feminist critiques of sex, gender and sexuality have not only put the subjects onto the agenda in the academy and in the development of theoretical explanations, they have also linked these concepts to the possibilities of change and to political action with a much wider application than solely in the empirical field of gender.

There has been some reluctance within feminism and sociology to engage with the materialities of enfleshed selves and to prioritize the social forces through which sex and gender and meanings and classifications of sexuality are made. Although Butler argues that sex is also socially constructed (in spite of the focus of some of her later work), she says less about the relevance of flesh and embodiment and the ways in which gender is also material in ways which include bodies. There have, however, been serious attempts to engage with the materialities of sex as well as the discursive dimensions of gender, all of which impact upon sexuality, using a variety of interdisciplinary approaches which reflect the diversity of contemporary sociology and sociology's engagement with a range of material inequalities and the uneven and unequal operation of power.

SEMINAR QUESTIONS

1 What are the links between sex, gender and sexuality?
2 What is the role of bodies and material enfleshed capacities in the making of sex, gender and sexuality? Is this fixed? How could we change it?
3 Who wins in the differentiation of sex and gender – and who loses?
4 How do inequalities such as class, race and ethnicity relate to sex and gender?

FURTHER READING

The following texts engage with some of the key debates and questions which emerge from the above discussion.

▶ Howson, A. (2012) *The Body in Society* (2nd edn, Polity). A very useful discussion of the bodies in social contexts.
▶ Lloyd, M. (2007) *Judith Butler* (Polity). Examines the work of one of the most influential feminists of recent times.
▶ Price, J., and M. Shildrick (eds) (1999) *Feminist Theory and the Body: A Reader* (Edinburgh University Press). A series of key readings which are central to understanding the connections between sex, gender and sexuality and the body or bodies.
▶ Richardson, D., and V. Robinson (eds) (2014) *Introducing Gender and Women's Studies* (4th edn, Palgrave). Provides an accessible interdisciplinary collection of texts on the most important themes in feminist and gender theory.

▶ Woodward, K. (2011) *The Short Guide to Gender* (Policy Press). A short introduction to the key concepts in gender studies with illustrations and case studies of how sex gender and sexuality are understood and experienced in contemporary life.

▶ Woodward, K., and S. Woodward (2009) *Why Feminism Matters: Feminisms Lost and Found* (Palgrave Macmillan). An accessible conversation between feminist theories across generations which identifies some of the continuities as well as disconnections in feminist thought and different approaches to gender.

RACE, ETHNICITY AND NATIONALITY

the future of multiculturalism in a global age

ANDREW PILKINGTON

CONTENTS

INTRODUCTION

THE QUESTION OF IDENTITY lies at the heart of sociological accounts of race, ethnicity and nationality. 'Identity is about belonging, about what we have in common with some people and what differentiates us from others' (Bloch and Solomos 2010: 6). Throughout human history, human beings have distinguished between those who are deemed to be members of their community and those who are not. While for long periods people have felt secure in their collective identities, there have been times when these have been brought into question. The attention currently being paid to the question of collective identity, evident in discussions of race, ethnicity and nationality, suggests that we are living through such a period when settled identities have been challenged and there is widespread unease about who we are.

In the modern world, we are typically aware of having a range of identities which compete for our attention. These may be based on various intersecting attributes, including gender, age, sexuality, disability and class. They may also be based on attributes central to this chapter: race, ethnicity and nationality. These are highly contested concepts, as we shall see, but they nonetheless denote phenomena of critical importance to a sociological understanding of the modern world. We live in a global age where the boundaries between communities are porous and where people increasingly live in proximity with others deemed to belong to a different race or those who see themselves as belonging to a different ethnic group or, indeed, nationality. This development may be represented as a positive one, inaugurating a convivial multicultural society, or a negative one, signalling the erosion of cherished values and increasing conflict. This chapter will focus in particular on Britain to explore the debate between these competing positions.

In the first section, the central concepts that form the focus of this chapter are delineated. Race, ethnicity and nationality comprise categories which entail drawing boundaries between people. People who share a common racial or ethnic or national identity often consider one or other of these communal affiliations to be of critical importance and as overriding other identities based on, for example, gender or class. The persistence and salience of such identities across the world, coupled with the intractable conflicts they engender, may suggest that, in some sense, race, ethnicity and nationality signal natural and fundamental divisions between people. While it is tempting to make this leap, sociologists argue that race, ethnicity and nationality are socially constructed and that the importance given to these identities changes over time and space and is dependent on the social context.

In the second section, the central significance of the first two of these concepts to an understanding of the modern world is illustrated by taking the case of Britain. Two central issues are explored – post-war migration and ethnic diversity; racism and racial disadvantage – which provide evidence of both continuity and change.

In the third section, the focus switches to nationality and Britain in a global and European context. Western European societies have to varying degrees all experienced considerable inward migration since the war, but their approaches have differed. Three ideal-typical approaches are distinguished: differential exclusion (e.g., Germany), assimilationism (e.g., France) and pluralism (e.g., Britain).

In the fourth section, we examine recent critiques of multiculturalism, paying particular attention to a speech by the prime minister in 2011. It is argued that the speech draws on old arguments, which have been effectively rebutted, and that Britain should continue to embrace pluralism.

THE SOCIAL CONSTRUCTION OF RACE, ETHNICITY AND NATIONALITY

Race, ethnicity and nationality are categories which involve drawing boundaries between people (Walters, 2012). Racial boundaries are normally drawn on the basis of physical markers, such as skin pigmentation, hair texture and facial features, while ethnic and national boundaries are normally drawn on the basis of cultural markers such as language, religion and shared customs. While members of a purported race may not identify themselves as sharing a common racial identity, members of an ethnic or national group necessarily recognize that they share a common identity with other members of their group. Contrary to the expectations of the founders of sociology, the force of race, ethnicity and nationality shows no signs of diminishing. Indeed, given the persistence and power of racial/ethnic/national ties and identities across the globe, and the conflicts which they can engender, we may be tempted to believe that the division of people into racial, ethnic and national groups is in some sense natural or 'primordial'. What we need to recognize, however, is that the strength of racial/ethnic/national ties and identities changes over time and varies across the globe. This suggests that such divisions can only be understood when located in their social and historical context. Sociologists take this position and argue that race, ethnicity and nationality are socially constructed. Let us deal with each in turn.

The social construction of race and the importance of an empty concept

There have always been physical differences between groups of human beings as a result of 'population inbreeding' (Giddens and Sutton 2013: 676), but it is only since the seventeenth century that these differences have been conceptualized as racial (Pilkington 2003). In other words, the idea of race is distinctively modern and emerged in a fully fledged form only in the nineteenth century.

The idea of race developed in the course of European imperialism to account for the manifest physical and cultural differences between people (Garner 2010). By the end of the nineteenth century, the idea of race had fully crystallized. The truth of its central tenets seemed to many Europeans to be self-evident: a limited number of fixed and discrete races could be distinguished on the basis of clear physical differences between people; these races were not only physically different but also different in terms of their intellectual capacities and cultural achievements; as a result, they formed a hierarchy whereby some were inherently superior to others. The idea of race could thus be routinely drawn upon to account for the observed physical and cultural differences between people and the assumed superiority of the West. The idea of race continued to hold many people in thrall in the twentieth century. Indeed it underpinned one of the world's greatest atrocities, the extermination of Jews in Nazi Germany. Disquiet with the idea did, however, grow, culminating after the Second World War in its complete repudiation by most scholars, morally appalled by the use to which it was put in justifying the Holocaust. Intellectually, two arguments were compelling.

Firstly, the essential condition for race is that populations remain insulated from one another so that interbreeding does not occur. This condition, however, has not been met for centuries, especially since the expansion of Europe from the sixteenth century onwards. As a result the possibility for distinct subspecies to consolidate has not materialized. Indeed, popular television programmes have illustrated how most of us have a mixed ancestry. People who define themselves as mixed constitute one of the fastest-growing populations in Britain, and 'this growth refutes the idea that there exist distinct natural races among people in multiethnic societies such as Britain' (Song 2008: 265). Secondly, the focus on visible or 'phenotypical' differences has been shown to be misplaced since the discovery by Mendel of the unit – the gene – upon which natural selection operates. A new specialism, genetics, has resulted in the realization that visible differences between people are biologically trivial and that there is far greater genetic variation within rather than between groups previously defined as races (Younge 2010). Indeed 'some 85% of human genetic diversity occurs within rather than between populations' (Rose and Rose 2005).

While the idea of race has been in 'retreat', the concept of race has not been abandoned by all biologists (Schaffer 2008). The rationale for continuing to employ the concept is that it is possible to distinguish populations with significant differences in gene frequencies. There are indeed genetic differences in susceptibility to particular diseases, and people can trace their own ancestral roots through DNA analysis. It is important to recognize, however, that 'such genetic differences are . . . not the same as racial differences' (Malik 2008: 3). The more genetic diversity is discovered, the smaller become the subpopulations that can be described as races, and these subpopulations do not match the populations *socially* defined as races. The consequence is that, 'as a scientific concept, race is well past its sell by date' (Rose and Rose 2005).

This raises a paradox. On the one hand, we now have good scientific evidence that there is no such thing as race. On the other hand, we know that classifying people in racial terms has real effects. The paradox is solved once we realize that, as W. I. Thomas put it, 'if men (*sic*) define things as real, they are real in their consequences' (Thomas, quoted in Pilkington

2003: 14). This means that physical differences such as skin colour can become significant because of the importance attached to them by people's beliefs.

We must not assume, however, that historically skin colour has been the only indicator of race. During the nineteenth century, the combination of a rising population and bad harvests encouraged a major movement of population from Ireland. The Irish who came to Britain – though white – moved to a society in which they were already seen as an inferior race. And the same fate awaited a later immigrant group at the turn of the century – Jews – who were seeking to escape violent anti-Semitism in Eastern Europe.

The concept of an inferior race was not, however, restricted to people in the colonies or to immigrants. During the nineteenth century, an analogy was often drawn between sexual differences and race, so that white indigenous women were also represented as an inferior race. As one writer (Stepan 1990: 39–41) puts it:

> Women it was observed, shared with Negroes a narrow childlike and delicate skull, so different from the robust and rounded heads characteristic of males of 'superior' races. . . . Women and lower races were called innately impulsive, emotional, imitative rather than original, and incapable of the abstract reasoning found in white men . . . in short, lower races represented the female type of the human species, and females the lower race of gender.

And, indeed, the concept of inferior race was extended even further:

> By analogy with the so called lower races, [not only] women [but also] the sexually deviate, the criminal, the urban poor, and the insane were . . . constructed as biological 'races apart' whose differences from the white male, and likeness to each other, explained their different and lower position in the social hierarchy.

The idea of race entails a particular representation of the One and the Other, us and them. What above all marks the difference are certain (alleged or real) biological features which signify inherent superiority and inferiority. Races themselves do not exist; rather, during a particular period, groups have been represented as races. It is revealing to note what the vast range of groups represented above as inferior races have in common: they are all groups who are disadvantaged in various ways. Representing these Others in racial terms – 'both the "lower orders" in European society and non-European peoples' (Malik 1996: 99) – justifies the inferiority of both. The justification takes a particular form. In a society purportedly valuing equality, inequalities are pictured as fixed by nature and therefore unalterable. The idea of race therefore provides 'a means of reconciling the conflict between the ideology of equality and the reality of the persistence of inequality. Race account[s] for social inequalities by attributing them to nature' (ibid.: 6).

The idea of race has been thoroughly discredited. In view of this, the question arises as to whether we should continue to employ the term in sociology on the grounds that many people continue to believe that race is real and that belief has real consequences. Is it still legitimate to define a race as 'a group of human beings socially defined on the basis of physical characteristics' (Cornell and Hartmann 2007: 25)? Typically, the answer has been, yes. Recently, however, this answer has met with vigorous opposition.

One highly influential view has been put forward by Robert Miles. The continued employment of the term, he stresses, is misleading, since it seems to refer, and thus give credibility, to the notion of naturally occurring populations, when in fact it constitutes a false representation of reality. Instead, he enjoins us to abandon the term and utilize the concept of 'racialization' to refer to the 'process of defining an Other' in terms of (alleged and real) biological characteristics (Miles 1989: 75). There is some merit in this view. Take, for example, the implicit assumptions underlying legislation on 'race relations' law. 'By incorporating into the law . . . the idea that there are "races" whose relations . . . must be regulated' (Miles 1993: 6), the law (however helpful it is in combating discrimination) reifies the concept of race. It implies that there really are races to which people belong. To acknowledge this danger in the use of the term does not, however, mean that we can banish it. The concept of racialization itself presupposes a concept of race (Anthias 1990) and, given this, it is perhaps not surprising that the term continues to appear in sociology books.

To acknowledge a debate about whether and, if so, how to employ the term race should not blind us to the more fundamental points of agreement between sociologists. Whether we seek to banish the term, problematize it or refer to *socially* defined groups, there is widespread consensus that the idea of race, which came to fruition in the nineteenth century, has been thoroughly discredited and that we are talking about a phenomenon which is socially constructed. 'Racial categories are created, inhabited, transformed, and destroyed' by human action and therefore are a product of society and not nature (Omi and Winant 1994: 55).

The social construction of ethnicity

Although the concept of race has by no means disappeared from the lexicon of sociologists and policy-makers, the concept of ethnicity is now more readily employed. The widespread use of the term stems at least in part from the realization that 'it does not suffer from the historical association of error in the way that the concept of race does' (Fenton 2010: 6). It avoids biological determinism and identifies groups primarily in terms of the self-definitions of their members (Mason 2000).

Ethnicity is a term with a longer ancestry than race. Deriving from the Greek word *ethnos*, meaning people, it still retains in its contemporary usage the sense of belonging to a particular group. What distinguishes an ethnic group from most other groups is the 'belief' shared by its members 'in their common descent' (Weber 1997: 18; Smith 1986). The crucial issue here is not whether members actually do have a common ancestry but that they believe that they do and share common memories and on that basis claim a common identity.

Ethnic groups are not dissimilar in this respect to nations and, indeed, on occasions they may become nations. There are differences as well as similarities, however. In contrast to nations, which are – as we see in box 3.1 – modern groupings with a distinctively political agenda concerned above all with the establishment of political sovereignty over a territory, ethnic groups are a recurrent feature of human history, comprise subpopulations within a larger society and have multifarious concerns. At the same time they share with nations the fact that they are more extensive than kinship groups or even neighbourhood groups and consequently are 'imagined communities' – imagined because members 'will never know most of their fellow members . . . yet in the minds of each lives the image of their communion' (Anderson 1983: 15).

Crucial to the formation of ethnic groups as imagined communities is socialization into a distinct subculture, whereby members learn to differentiate themselves from others and recognize which cultural features symbolize their difference. The degree to which ethnic groups are in fact culturally distinctive varies enormously, but typically particular cultural practices are highlighted to signify a group's identity. Different imaginings are of course possible, with the result that the boundaries between ethnic groups may change over time or be drawn differently on different occasions. Although ethnic groups entail a sense of belonging in their members, we should not assume that the boundaries between one group and another depend wholly on processes internal to a particular group and result purely from the power of some members to persuade other members of their imagining. Ethnic groups always coexist with other ethnic groups. Some groups are more powerful than others and therefore are in a strong position to exert an external influence on where group boundaries are drawn.

BOX 3.1 ETHNIC GROUP FORMATION

The position of black people in the United States can serve to illustrate the process of ethnic group formation. Black people were forcibly taken from diverse ethnic groups in West Africa to become slaves in America. Their previous ethnic identities counted for nothing and instead they were assigned a common racial identity. Over time, however, black people formed themselves into an ethnic group and asserted their own identity. Members therefore typically identify themselves as sharing a common descent (an African ancestry) and common memories (slavery and continuing racial disadvantage); and, despite often not being very culturally distinctive from the wider society, they draw upon a variety of cultural features (from language to music) to signal their difference and common identity. Within this group different imaginings have been evident. The term 'black', which at one stage had negative connotations and was a term of abuse, was subverted in the 1960s and made into a positive source of identity: 'Black is beautiful'. For many this is still the favoured identity; hence the use of the term 'black' above to identify a group previously described as Negro or coloured. Different names, however, have been preferred at different times. 'African-American' is now a preferred term for some to signal the fact that black people are in a comparable position to other groups which migrated to the United States, such as the Irish. They are American but, like other Americans, are proud of their roots in another country and thus have a hyphenated identity. 'People of colour' is a preferred term for others to signal the fact that black people share a disadvantaged position with other non-white groups and to point to the need for a wider grouping to combat such disadvantage. Although continuing racial discrimination limits possible imaginings, the choice of these different names to describe the group's self-identity indicates that different imaginings and different group boundaries do exist.

Contrary to the expectations of the founding fathers of sociology and many of their successors, ethnic attachments show no signs of erosion. Cornell and Hartmann's constructionist approach provides a persuasive account for both the changing nature of ethnic ties and their remarkable persistence. While they accept that circumstances play a critical role in the construction of ethnic groups, they emphasize the creative role of people in fashioning their own identities. Ethnic identities therefore are the products of an ongoing and continuous interaction between, on the one hand, the circumstances groups encounter – including the conceptions and actions of outsiders – and, on the other, the actions and conceptions of group members – of insiders. The power of ethnic ties derives not from the fact that they really are primordial but from a discourse of primordialism that is so often attached to them (Cornell and Hartmann 2007). In some contexts, individuals may internalize an ethnic identity in the course of 'primary socialization, along with many of the markers of ethnicity such as language, religion, non-verbal behaviour, etc.'. As a result, ethnicity may be experienced as fundamental and therefore 'be characterizable as a *primary*, although not a primordial, dimension of individual identity' (Jenkins 1997: 47). Where this is prevalent, ethnicity may indeed exhibit a stubborn persistence, especially when it is embedded in established relationships and institutions, cultural practices, and ways of seeing the world (Cornell and Hartmann 2007).

Recognition of the social construction of ethnicity makes it easier to avoid the pitfall of reification. When we study ethnic groups, there is the very real danger that the boundaries between them will be overdrawn and the cultural distinctiveness of each exaggerated. The very language we use – for example, our reference above to people's 'membership' of ethnic groups – tends to imply that ethnic groups are distinct things. As a result of such reification, it is often believed that 'ethnicity [is] typically – or even only – an attribute of the Other' (Jenkins 1997: 14). This failure to recognize the ethnicity of the majority group implicitly assumes that the latter comprises the norm from which minority groups deviate. And the consequence all too often is that minority ethnic groups in turn are represented as distinct, static and 'distinguished by a social and cultural essence' (Eade 1996: 61). By alerting us to the social processes by which ethnic identities are born, persist, change and disappear, the constructionist approach sensitizes us to the danger of such reification.

The social construction of nationality

National identities can be characterized by five features which together distinguish them from other collective identities: a shared belief that members 'belong together'; a perception that this association stems from a long history of living together which, it is envisaged, will continue into the future; a recognition that the community is 'active' and takes decisions; an acknowledgement that it is 'connected to a particular territory'; and the existence of a 'common public culture' which marks it off from other communities (Miller 1995a: 23–7). Although nations typically aspire to be politically self-determining, we cannot equate nations with states: some states (including the United Kingdom) are multinational and some people who share a common national identity (for example, the Kurds) are scattered in a number of states. Somewhat 'confusingly, the term nationality has a double everyday meaning' (Roberts 2012: 75). It refers to a person's membership of a community which shares a common national identity, but it also refers to the state of which a person is a citizen. For the sake of clarity, I shall follow Roberts in using the term 'nationality' in the first sense and using the term 'citizenship' to refer to the second sense.

Most people feel some attachment to a particular nation (and in some cases nations), with loyalty to the wider community being exhibited at times in a willingness to sacrifice personal gain to promote its interests. While national sentiment has historically sometimes degenerated into chauvinism, this is not inevitable. The pervasiveness of national identities in the modern world suggests in fact that they meet certain needs. As one writer argues, such identities enable us, firstly, to see ourselves as part of some larger social whole and thus provide a framework for us 'to make sense of' our lives and, secondly, to foster 'bonds of mutual trust' which facilitate social solidarity and 'make successful democratic politics possible' (Miller 1995b: 153).

Although nations typically purport to have a long ancestry and trace their roots back to time immemorial, national identities cannot be seen in any way as primordial. While they may in some cases bear the imprint of a more ancient ethnic group (itself, as we have seen above, not a primordial phenomenon) which was dominant when the nation first took shape (Smith 1995), the idea of a nation as a community which demands people's loyalty and aspires to exercise control over a particular territory is distinctly modern (Gellner 1983). For most of human history people have lived in small communities, seeing themselves as belonging to kinship groups and neighbourhood networks and in some cases a wider religious community. Nations emerged as mass phenomena only in the eighteenth and nineteenth centuries, when a series of complex economic, political and cultural changes encouraged their formation and made it possible for national identities to be widely disseminated (Hutchinson and Smith 1994). The new media of communication, especially print, facilitated this process by standardizing vernacular languages and enabling 'the mass of people within a particular state to understand each other through a common print language' (Barker 1997: 189). This allowed people for the first time to feel part of what Anderson has called the 'imagined community' of the nation (Anderson 1983: 15).

BOX 3.2 THE NARRATIVE OF THE NATION

Recognizing that nations are modern inventions and comprise imagined communities entails an acknowledgement that national identities are socially constructed. Of critical importance to the reproduction, and indeed transformation, of national identities is the process of representation, the way members of a culture use language and other symbolic systems to 'produce meanings through which we can make sense of our experience and who we are' (Woodward 1997: 14).

National identities are reproduced through 'the *narrative of the nation*, as it is told and retold in national histories, literatures, the media and popular culture' (Hall 1992a: 293). A variety of stories, images, symbols and rituals thereby produce meanings about the nation with which we are invited to identify. Such representations typically emphasize the continuity of the nation, which is portrayed as 'rooted in the remotest antiquity', and the ancient nature of its traditions. On inspection, however, 'traditions which appear or claim to be old are often quite recent in origin and sometimes invented' (Hobsbawm and Ranger 1983: 1). Thus the rituals and pageantry associated with the British monarchy originated in the late nineteenth century and, 'until recently, the British royal family was overwhelmingly German in blood and often in preferred language as well' (Colley 1999: 27). However mythical the narrative may be, reminders of our shared nationhood are evident in the institutions which surround us and not least in the way *we* are daily addressed as members of the nation by the media. The result is that our national identities are often deeply ingrained, a phenomenon which has been described by one writer as 'banal nationalism' (Billig 1995).

When we actually examine contemporary nations, we discover that they are generally multi-ethnic. They have never in fact been culturally homogeneous or comprised unified cultural communities but 'are without exception ethnically hybrid – the product of conquests, absorptions of one people by another' (Hall 1992b: 6), with the British, for example, the product of a series of such conquests – Celtic, Roman, Saxon, Viking and Norman – and various waves of immigration. While people who share a national identity necessarily also share to some extent a common public culture which distinguishes them from other communities, we should not assume that the latter is inevitably monolithic. The development of a British national identity, for example, did not eradicate pre-existing ethnic identities and allegiances. It is possible

The recent case of the referendum for Scotland to become an independent sovereign state has brought the issue of nationality and nationhood to the fore, as both sides tried to appeal to a sense of national belonging. (© Màrtainn MacDhòmhnaill/Flickr)

therefore for people to have a common national identity and at the same time acknowledge differing identities of other kinds. The British, for instance, continue to have an overarching identity which recognizes the legitimacy of people having not only other national identities (English, Scottish, Welsh) but also ethnic identities. Nonetheless it has to be acknowledged that 'national cultures are not simple repositories of shared symbols to which the entire population stands in identical relation. Rather they [need] to be approached as sites of contestation in which competition over definitions takes place' (Schlesinger 1991: 174). In multi-ethnic nations there is often a tension between the competing demands of unity and diversity: the need, on the one hand, for 'cohesion and a sense of common belonging' and the wish, on the other hand, of minority communities to 'preserve and transmit their ways of life' (Parekh 1998: 1). In practice it has often proved difficult to reconcile this tension. National cultures historically reflect the values of the dominant ethnic group who wish to uphold their vision of the nation. Since nations are imagined communities, other imaginings are of course possible and put forward, often by subordinate groups, in the light of social changes. The result, however, is that alternative and competing definitions of the nation vie for our attention. While therefore some seek 'to represent what is in fact the ethnic hotchpotch of modern nationality as the primordial unity of "one people", see no need for changes in the national culture and demand complete assimilation from minorities' (Hall 1992b: 6), others put forward an alternative pluralist vision which entails public recognition of minority cultures and some modification of the national culture to reflect its multicultural character.

Nationality, like race and ethnicity, is socially constructed. The constructionist approach encourages us to explore the possibility that national identities are contested, dynamic and fluid.

SEMINAR QUESTIONS

1 Why is race sometimes still seen as a very real phenomenon despite scientific research questioning the validity of the concept?

2 Is it possible to talk about race and not fall into the trap of perpetuating myths?

3 Do 'white British' people constitute a distinct ethnic group?

4 Find two different definitions or representations in the media of the nation in which you live. What are the differences and similarities in the representations that you have found? To what extent (if any) do you believe that these portrayals of national identity are misleading?

THE INTERACTING DYNAMICS OF RACE AND ETHNICITY: THE CASE OF BRITAIN

In this section, I shall illustrate how race and ethnicity are socially constructed in Britain. I will begin by looking at migration in the post-war period, which has entailed significant growth in ethnic diversity and given birth to multi-ethnic Britain. I will then move on to demonstrate how people from some ethnic groups but not others are subject to racial discrimination and experience racial disadvantage. In the next section I shall then explore the implications ethnic diversity and racial disadvantage entail for Britishness.

Migration and ethnic diversity

Population movements have always been part of human history. There is little doubt, however, that 'migration took on a new character with the beginnings of European expansion from the sixteenth century' and that European colonialism accelerated such population movements (Castles and Miller 2007: 2). Colonialism entailed in turn the migration of European colonizers to the colonies; the transfer of slaves from Africa to the Caribbean and the Americas; the employment of indentured servants from India and China in other colonies; and, in the period 1850–1914, the mass migration of Europeans to North America and Australasia and considerable migration within Europe.

In the interwar period, migration slowed down in tandem with economic stagnation, but since 1945 it has accelerated again. 'The movements that started after 1945 and expanded sharply from the 1980s involve all regions of the world' (Castles and Miller 2007: 2). Two main phases can be distinguished. The first, which lasted until the 1970s, involved significant migration to Western European countries and North America. These societies faced a labour shortage after the Second World War and recruited labour either from former colonies or from neighbouring countries to allow significant economic growth to occur. A serious recession in the early 1970s, however, entailed – especially in Europe – a reduced demand for labour and therefore falling recruitment of new migrant workers. But migration did not slow down; rather, a second phase began. It involved not only the permanent settlement of earlier migrants as they were joined by family members and had children in the countries to which they had migrated but also new forms of migration (Castles and Miller 2007). Migration increased in volume initially in response to upheavals in the former Soviet bloc and elsewhere but has steadily involved all regions of the world. Indeed, the hallmark of what has been labelled 'the age of migration is the global character of international migration', which 'in most instances' has entailed increasing 'diversity within a society' (ibid.: 15). The result is that virtually all countries are becoming more ethnically diverse.

We need to be careful to contextualize post-war migration to Britain and acknowledge continuities with previous phases of migration. There have been significant waves of immigration before. Thus, in the nineteenth century, the combination of a rising population and bad harvests encouraged a major movement of the population from Ireland, and around the turn of the century virulent anti-Semitism prompted the movement of Jews from Eastern Europe. What is more, population movements have not been one way. Millions of people have emigrated from Britain in the last two centuries to settle in new lands; indeed, except for relatively short periods, emigration exceeded immigration. Migration, therefore, is nothing new. Nor is the presence of Asian and black communities in Britain. Asian people came to Britain, both as servants or 'ayahs' and 'lascar' seamen, as early as the seventeenth century (Visram 2002), while black people, who first arrived during Roman times, have been a continuous presence since the sixteenth century (Fryer 1984).

To recognize continuity should not, however, blind us to change. While migration to Britain has a long history, 'the appearance in most major towns and cities [in] Britain of permanently settled, substantial minorities – clearly distinguishable by appearance, traditions and customs and practice from the very large majority of the population – is a development of the very recent past, of the late 1950s and succeeding decades' (Spencer 1997: 4). It is a consequence in fact of a series of migrations from Britain's former colonies since the Second World War.

We can distinguish two main phases of post-war migration. The first phase, from the late 1940s to the early 1970s, involved the primary migration of people from Britain's former colonies to work and settle in the country. This is the phase Spencer is referring to in the previous paragraph. The second phase gained momentum from the 1980s and has brought about various forms of migration, including the secondary migration of dependants of those who migrated to work in the first phase, a rise in asylum-seekers and, with the expansion of the European Union in the last decade, significant economic migration.

Although 'in most years until 1993, fewer people came to live in the UK than left', net migration has consequently grown, with migration since the 1990s becoming the main engine of population growth (Spencer 2011: 30). Of the 3.7 million increase in the population between 2001 and 2011, 2.1 million is attributable to immigration (Jivraj 2012). The combination of significantly greater net inward migration (generated in large part by economic growth and the enlargement of the European Union) and a falling birth rate has thus increased the proportion of the British population born overseas (Somerville 2007). While the majority of people migrating to the United Kingdom neither seek nor are granted permanent settlement, 'Britain's foreign-born population has . . . become more diverse in terms of religion, language, socio-economic status, immigration status, transnational connections and location in the UK' (Spencer 2011: 33–4). This second phase of migration has entailed what one writer has called 'super-diversity', a 'level and kind of complexity surpassing anything the country has previously experienced' (Vertovec 2007: 1024). At the same time the number of people accepted for settlement since 1997 has increased, albeit with variations from year to year, with the vast majority comprising people who initially came to the UK for work or family reasons rather than as asylum-seekers.

To give a sense of the magnitude of change, we can compare successive censuses. The decennial UK census has asked a question on ethnicity since 1991. The question, however, has changed both in terms of how it is framed and in the form of the predefined response categories people are asked to complete. In 1991, the census asked, 'Which ethnic group do you descend from: White, Black-Caribbean, Black-African, Black – Other, Indian, Pakistani, Bangladeshi, Chinese?' In 2001, it asked about 'your ethnic group in terms of your cultural background' and added further categories: Mixed, and White Irish, as well as 'Other' for each broad category of White, Black, Asian and Mixed. In 2011 (see figure 3.1), the most recent census simply asked about 'your ethnic group or background', with additional categories created for White Gypsy or Irish Traveller and Arab. While these changes signal a concern to be sensitive to the way in which people define themselves, it is noticeable that the groups from which respondents are asked to choose have been distinguished in terms of a broad range of criteria, typically skin colour and geographical/national origin. Whether these criteria enable significant ethnic groups to be identified is debateable. The White category (which is by far the largest) certainly is not representative here of an ethnic group and, indeed, conflates a range of groups which

BOX 3.3 ETHNIC DIVERSITY IN BRITAIN

Table 3.1: Britain's growing ethnic diversity: percentage of total population of England and Wales by ethnicity

	1991	2001	2011
White	94.1	91.3	86.0
Mixed	N/A	1.3	2.2
Asian	3.3	4.4	6.8
Black	1.9	2.2	3.3
Chinese	0.3	0.4	0.7
Other	0.6	0.4	1.0

Source: Abridged from Jivraj (2012: fig. 2).

Table 3.1 shows clearly the increasing ethnic diversity in England and Wales. The population other than White doubled in size between 2001 and 2011, from 3 to 7 million, and now comprises 14 percent of the population, as opposed to 8.7 percent a decade earlier. The White population encompasses not only the White British but also White Irish and White Other. The population other than White British now comprises 20 percent of the population, as opposed to 13 percent a decade earlier. If we survey a longer period, the nature of the change is even more graphically brought out, with one estimate of sixty years earlier calculating that the non-White population amounted to fewer than 80,000 (Spencer 1997).

Another way to emphasize the change is to look at the proportion of foreign-born people in England and Wales. This increased between 2001 and 2011 from 4.6 million (9 percent of the population) to 7.5 million (13 percent). In 2011, a third were born in other EU member states, among them Poland (579,000), Ireland (407,000) and Germany (274,000), while a fifth were born in South Asia, including India (694,000), Pakistan (482,000) and Bangladesh (212,000), and a sixth were born in Africa (Jivraj 2013).

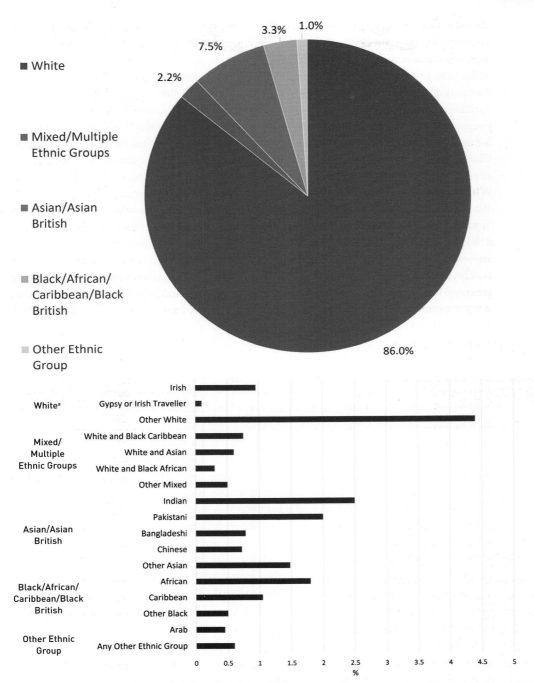

Figure 3.1 Ethnic groups, England and Wales, 2011 census

Note: ª Excludes White British (80.5 percent).

Source: ONS (2012a).

do believe they have a distinct ancestry and so comprise ethnic groups, and the same applies to the Mixed group and Others, which both contain a disparate range of groups. The ethnic question clearly is not subtle enough to do justice to people's fluid and sometimes overlapping ethnic identities. It is nonetheless helpful in conveying some sense of the magnitude of ethnic diversity and importantly enables us to monitor how 'non-White' groups are faring.

The evidence from successive censuses clearly demonstrates that inward migration since the war has made Britain not only a significantly more ethnically diverse society but also one that contains substantial minority ethnic groups, distinguishable by colour as well as culture, who are permanently settled. The question which we need now to address is how these communities are faring.

Racial discrimination and racial disadvantage

There is considerable evidence that the first generation of people who migrated to Britain from the New Commonwealth faced considerable racial prejudice and racial discrimination (Pilkington 1984, 2003). Few recent studies have considered these issues. What they reveal, however, are both continuities and changes.

The British Social Attitudes (BSA) surveys have asked a question on respondents' self-reported level of prejudice virtually every year from 1983 to 2006. These reveal in each year a significant minority of the population describing themselves as prejudiced in some way. At the same time they indicate 'some decline in prejudice' over time. Each year before 1996, the proportion describing 'themselves as prejudiced lay between 30 and 40 percent', while subsequently 'the figures were between 25 and 30 percent' (Heath, Rothon and Ali 2010: 195). Further analysis of BSA surveys between 1983 and 1996, focusing 'on two items dealing with how respondents feel about social contact with ethnic minorities', confirms an overall decline in racial prejudice (Ford 2008: 616). The most important driver of this trend is 'a generational shift in white attitudes towards ethnic minorities', with younger respondents who have grown up alongside minorities much more 'at ease with racial diversity' than older respondents (ibid.: 630). It is conceivable that this trend reflects the increasing unacceptability of admitting racial prejudice rather than a genuine reduction in prejudice, but declining residential segregation and increasing intermarriage suggest that racial prejudice is indeed declining. Despite this positive trend, it has to be acknowledged that 'the generational decline in racial prejudices is not evenly spread', with less qualified working-class young men much more likely to exhibit hostility towards minority ethnic groups than other young people (ibid.: 632).

In moving from racial prejudice to racial discrimination, we move from the realm of attitudes to that of behaviour. While there is a relationship between prejudice and discrimination, we cannot assume that one leads ineluctably to the other. The relationship of 'generalised prejudice to employer discrimination can only be oblique – only those in a position to appoint or refuse a job can do so' (Platt 2011: 91).

One way of approaching racial discrimination is through an examination of whether people from different ethnic origins, with the same educational qualifications, have equal chances of attaining the most desirable occupational destinations, for example managerial and professional occupations (the salariat), and avoiding the least desirable occupational destinations, for example unemployment. If members of minority ethnic groups with the same educational qualifications as native-born Whites do not have the same opportunities, we can conclude that they face an ethnic penalty. An ethnic penalty is 'a broader concept than that of discrimination', since it refers to 'all the sources of disadvantage that might lead an ethnic

BOX 3.4 RACIAL DISCRIMINATION IN BRITAIN

The most recent systematic study of racial discrimination in Britain comprises a correspondence test, where written applications were submitted for advertised vacancies in seven major cities. The applications were matched in terms of education, skills and work history but differentiated in terms of ethnicity, with ethnic identity being conveyed using names associated with the ethnic groups that were the focus of the study (Black African, Black Caribbean, Chinese, Indian, Pakistani/Bangladeshi, White British). These names were randomly assigned to each application and three applications were submitted for each vacancy (one of the three was White British, the other two from different minority ethnic groups). Sixteen percent of applications received a positive response from an employer and were analysed. While 68 percent of White British applications received a positive response, only 39 percent of minority ethnic applications did so. This points to 'net discrimination in favour of white British names over equivalent applications from ethnic minority candidates [of] 29 percent' (Wood et al. 2009). The level of discrimination did not vary significantly across the minority ethnic groups, although there was considerably less discrimination by public-sector employers than their private-sector counterparts. While the level discovered is lower than that found in earlier studies (Pilkington 2003), it is disturbing to discover racial discrimination still evident at the early stage of the recruitment process.

group to fare less well in the labour market than do similarly qualified Whites' (Heath and McMahon 1997, quoted in Pilkington 2003: 89). Pooling the data from the annual General Household Surveys conducted between 1991 and 2001, a major study discovered that both first-generation and second-generation 'members of visible minorities . . . experienced significant ethnic penalties . . . in gaining employment', but, whereas first-generation members experienced significant ethnic penalties in gaining access to the salariat and non-manual work more generally, second-generation members appeared 'to obtain the same kind of jobs as people of British ancestry with the same qualifications' (Cheung and Heath 2007: 541). While this study does point to some progress, the persistence of ethnic penalties for the second generation in gaining employment is disturbing. We cannot infer that racial discrimination is the sole explanation for this, but 'discrimination . . . must clearly be a rather likely explanation for the disadvantages experienced by visible minorities in the second generation', especially when we bear in mind 'the fact that ethnic penalties with respect to unemployment are not present for any of the white ethnic groups' such as the Irish and West Europeans (ibid.: 542).

What we have examined so far is only one form of discrimination – direct discrimination. There is, however, a more subtle form of discrimination, sometimes labelled 'institutional racism', but which we shall call here indirect discrimination. This refers to institutional practices which, however unintentionally, have the consequence of systematically operating to the disadvantage of groups seen as racially different. Here are a few examples:

- immigration rules which do not give British citizens the automatic right to be joined by their wives/husbands and children;
- using behavioural as well as academic criteria to allocate pupils to streams, a practice which (if, for instance, teachers stereotype Caribbean pupils as less well behaved) may disadvantage a group seen as racially different;

- recruitment to a workforce via old universities, which have disproportionate numbers of white graduates, or through informal networks to which minority groups may have less access;
- the routine use by the police of 'stop and search' powers within areas of high minority ethnic settlement.

These are only a few examples from the research literature, but they do indicate that indirect discrimination is pervasive and that both direct and indirect racial discrimination, despite legislation outlawing it, is still evident.

For most of the post-war period, sociologists concerned with explicating the position of minority ethnic groups in the labour market have emphasized racial disadvantage. For some, the extent of such disadvantage signified the emergence of a racially defined underclass. Since all minority ethnic groups face racial discrimination, it seemed reasonable to infer that

The disproportionate rate of 'stop and search' measures being used with members of black ethnic groups in particular continues to charge the political agenda and cause ill feeling in minority ethnic groups across the UK. Is the use of stop and search powers justified? (© Chris Schmidt/iStock)

members shared a common position at the bottom of the class structure. Drawing upon a range of national surveys conducted in the 1990s, one analysis of the labour market position of minority ethnic groups in Britain shed serious doubt on the thesis that minority ethnic groups are concentrated in an underclass (Pilkington 2003). Minority ethnic groups continued to encounter racial discrimination and did indeed face some common disadvantages in comparison to the majority ethnic group – for example, a higher risk of unemployment and long-term unemployment and a glass ceiling in relation to elite positions. A recent analysis of unemployment by ethnicity and age conducted for the House of Commons provided evidence of marked inequality, as shown in table 3.2. Particularly significant was the very high level of youth unemployment among black ethnic groups aged sixteen to twenty-four, which stood as high as 47 percent.

Table 3.2: **Unemployment by ethnic background and age, UK, July 2011 to June 2012, based on Annual Population Survey microdata**

	16–24	25–49	50+	Total (16+)
White	20%	6%	4%	7%
Black	47%	15%	12%	18%
Asian	29%	10%	9%	12%
Other ethnic background	28%	10%	7%	13%
All ethnic backgrounds	21%	6%	5%	8%

Source: Hough (2013).

At the same time, however, the evidence indicated considerable diversity in the socio-economic position of different minority ethnic groups. While the patterns here depend partly on which ethnic groups are distinguished and what indicators are used for comparative purposes, the most systematic survey conducted in Britain demonstrated that a contrast could be drawn between African Asians and the Chinese, on the one hand, and Pakistanis and Bangladeshis, on the other (Modood et al. 1997). While the former tended to be performing above or at much the same level as whites, the latter tended to be severely disadvantaged across the board. Indians, who were catching up fast, were closer to the former, while Caribbeans (especially the men) were closer to the latter. What is more, and again contrary to the predictions of the underclass thesis, there was 'an overall trend of progress in the job levels and earnings of ethnic minorities and a narrowing of the differentials between the ethnic majority and the minorities' (Modood 1998: 62). In short, examination of the (changing) position of minority ethnic groups in the labour market provided scant support for the notion of an ethnically distinguishable underclass. What was evident instead was racial disadvantage and ethnic diversity.

An anatomy of economic inequality in the UK constitutes the most recent systematic examination of the position of minority ethnic groups in the labour market (Hills 2010). It broadly confirms the findings of earlier studies. After surveying the evidence, the report concludes that 'the central problem in relation to racial inequality and the labour market is now unequal levels of unemployment and the employment sectors which some people are constrained to enter' (ibid.: 234). There is considerable evidence that members of minority groups continue to have a higher risk of unemployment and an increased chance, when employed, of being in a sector characterized by low-paying jobs. Minority ethnic groups are more likely to be unemployed even after controlling for education and age, with 'significant increases in unemployment rates for Black African, Black Caribbean, Pakistani/Bangladeshi and (to a lesser extent) Indian men and women' (ibid.: 225). And when we turn to those in employment we find 'clear pay differences relative to majority group men . . . for men and women from most minority groups, with only Indian and Chinese not experiencing pay disadvantage' (Platt 2011: 85). When further analysis is undertaken to compare groups with similar qualifications, ethnic penalties in pay are evident for most minority groups, including those groups such as the Chinese, who were seemingly not disadvantaged. What is more, the pay gap between white workers and minorities actually worsened in the fifteen years to 2008, a function to a large extent of the clustering of minorities in particular sectors comprising low-paid jobs (Brynin and Guveli 2012).

While minority ethnic groups continue to experience racial disadvantage, we should note that 'there are wide variations in the labour market achievements of different ethnic minority groups', and that Indians and Chinese 'are on average doing well and often outperforming Whites' in the labour market (Cabinet Office 2003). Theorists who focus exclusively on racial discrimination and racial disadvantage share a tendency to emphasize the way external structural forces impact on us and thus underplay the role of agency. In the process they tend to neglect the way minority ethnic groups draw on the cultural capital of their own communities to resist discriminatory practices and exclusionary processes, in some cases with considerable success. Minority ethnic groups invest a great deal in education, and this has to some extent paid off. While the persistence of ethnic penalties indicates that 'education and qualifications . . . are not sufficient to equalise chances across groups', they have clearly been 'critical to reducing employment inequalities among minority groups' (Platt 2011: 89).

When we turn to examine trends over time, we find a somewhat complex picture. On the negative side, we have already noted that second-generation minority groups face similar ethnic penalties to first-generation groups in gaining access to employment and that the pay gap over a fifteen-year period more than doubled. In addition, there is evidence 'that ethnic minorities find it difficult to obtain high-ranking executive positions' (Clark and Drinkwater 2007). On the positive side, we should note that the second generation 'made considerable progress in relation to job levels and now has, if in work, similar chances of accessing professional and managerial jobs as the White British population' (Hills 2010: 234). Studies of intergenerational social mobility concur in discovering that 'ethnic minorities . . . tend to have higher rates of upward mobility than the British-born Whites' (Heath and McMahon 2005; see also Platt 2005). In addition, and despite a growing pay gap, researchers have discovered that the ethnic penalty in pay 'was much less in the second generation than the first' (Hills 2010: 230). It is difficult drawing up a balance sheet, but the overall conclusion from a recent study seems apposite: 'Ethnic minority groups still experience labour market disadvantage but the differential between White and ethnic minority groups has been narrowing', and 'the position of some ethnic minority groups is now approaching equality with that of White people' (Hogarth et al. 2009: xiii, 97).

SEMINAR QUESTIONS

1 In surveying the evidence on ethnic diversity and racial disadvantage, are you more impressed by the continuities over time or the changes?

2 What factors apart from racism could contribute to continuing inequality between ethnic groups?

3 What factors might help to explain reductions in inequality (where they have taken place) between ethnic groups?

BRITAIN IN A EUROPEAN AND GLOBALIZING CONTEXT

Globalization and Britishness

Britishness, like other national identities, is a relatively recent construction. When the Act of Union in 1707 between England and Wales and Scotland was passed, creating the British nation-state, almost nobody defined themselves as British. One hundred years later this had changed. Crucial in developing a sense of nationhood was the existence of some Other against which Britishness could be formed. In this particular case, central to the shaping of a (Protestant) British identity was the existence of (Catholic) France. As Colley puts it:

> Great Britain was an invention forged above all by war. Time and time again, war with France brought Britons into confrontation with an obviously hostile Other and encouraged them to define themselves collectively against it. They defined themselves as Protestants struggling for survival against the world's foremost Catholic power . . . And, increasingly as the wars went on, they defined themselves in contrast to the colonial peoples they conquered, peoples who were manifestly alien in terms of culture, religion and colour . . . Britishness was super-imposed over an array of internal differences in response to contact with the Other, and above all in response to conflict with the Other. (Colley 1992: 5–6)

While 'Britishness was, initially, primarily an elite identity, dominated by Englishness . . . it became a more secure mass national identity with the advent of industrialisation and mass literacy' (Guibernau and Goldblatt 2000: 133).

To appreciate the social construction of national identities is to acknowledge their malleability and recognize that they are not fixed but change over time. For a long time the British felt confidence in their identity. Even when, during the nineteenth century, Protestantism became a less central ingredient to their identity, continuing economic success, pride in constitutional government and leadership of a large empire allowed the British to see themselves as belonging to a unique nation and as a civilizing force in the wider world. In the course of the twentieth century, and especially after the Second World War, such confidence dissipated and attention began to be paid to the question of British identity. Economic decline, increasing criticism of its constitutional arrangements and the loss of empire precipitated a crisis of identity.

Arguably, it is globalization which has entailed the biggest challenge to Britishness. While globalization, in the sense of the interconnectedness of societies, has been a feature of modernity since the sixteenth century, a number of social theorists have suggested that in the last three decades it has entered a qualitatively new phase. One of its main features has been described as 'time–space compression', in recognition of the fact that our lives are increasingly and remarkably quickly influenced by distant events (Harvey 1989). Globalization is a dialectical process in the sense that it does not bring about 'a generalized set of changes acting in a uniform direction, but consists of mutually opposed tendencies' (Giddens 1990: 64), for example the conflicting pressures of centralization and decentralization. Globalization does make it more possible for organizations to develop which transcend national boundaries; for example, transnational corporations seek to exploit markets on a world scale, and the European Union seeks through some pooling of sovereignty to enable nation-states which individually are incapable of resisting global forces to recover jointly some control. At the same time globalization generates a powerful decentralizing dynamic as communities, feeling that the 'world' has become 'too large to be controlled, . . . aim at shrinking it back to their size and reach' (Castells 1997: 66). Examples include the 'resurgence of various forms of nationalism and calls for a return to the pure (if mythic) certainties of the "old traditions"' (Morley and Robins 1995: 8). The resurgence of nationalism in Eastern Europe, in the wake of the disintegration of the Soviet Union and its European satellites, and the advent of religious fundamentalism, including both Islamic and American Christian forms, represent cases in point.

In the case of Britain, centralization has entailed pressures from above in the growing powers of the European Union, while decentralization has created pressures from below in the form of demands in some quarters for national independence in Scotland (and Wales) and the strengthening of ethnic identities. Membership of the European Union, the devolution of powers to Scotland and to a lesser extent Wales, and the 'very presence' of 'postcolonial peoples' in Britain serve to symbolize the changing nature of Britain and disrupt the narrative of the nation (Bhabha 1990: 218). In this context, new narratives are fashioned and alternative visions of the nation compete for our attention. The opening ceremony of the Olympics, for example, arguably represented Britain in an inclusive way (Katwala 2012; Werbner 2013), while media representations of immigrants and Muslims frequently represent the country in a more exclusive fashion (Morey and Yaqin 2011).

Globalization tends to undermine the power of tradition and custom on our lives by making us aware of alternative ways of living. Increasing reflexivity in turn has significant implications for our collective identities. For established identities are destabilized as alternative representations compete for our attention 'in a world of dissolving boundaries and disrupted continuities' (Morley and Robins 1995: 122).

Britain in a European context

Britain is often seen as having a better record on race and ethnicity than its partners in Europe. This is for two main reasons. The first concerns its approach to racial equality, while the second concerns its approach to ethnic diversity.

What is notable in relation to the first (Britain's approach to racial equality) is its recourse to race relations legislation. There have been four Acts, in 1965, 1968, 1976 and, most recently, 2000. This legislation started earlier than elsewhere in Europe and has gone much further. While EU directives may have been significant in pushing us on some equality strands, they have been of little importance in driving the agenda in Britain in relation to race and ethnicity.

The legislation outlaws indirect discrimination as well as direct discrimination, covers a wide range of organizations, places a statutory duty on public bodies to promote racial equality, and grants an independent commission significant powers of enforcement. Such wide-ranging and comprehensive legislation arguably reflects to some extent a greater readiness to be accommodating to the concerns of minorities.

What is notable in relation to Britain's approach to ethnic diversity is its greater sympathy towards multiculturalism. This is evident when we distinguish three ideal-type approaches to citizenship, nationality and migration in Western Europe (Castles 1995), discussed in box 3.5.

BOX 3.5 APPROACHES TO CITIZENSHIP, NATIONALITY AND MIGRATION

- The first approach is that of **differential exclusion**, where migrants are granted limited rights in delimited spheres. Here the nation is envisaged as consisting of those who share a common ancestry or ethnicity. Since migrants are seen as temporary, they will not be granted full citizenship rights and the nation cannot by definition be multi-ethnic.
- The second approach is that of **assimilationism**, where immigrants are eligible for full citizenship rights but must give up any distinctive values, at least in the public sphere. Here the nation is envisaged as consisting of those who share a common culture. The nation cannot by definition be multicultural.
- The third approach is that of **pluralism**, where immigrants can gain full citizenship rights without having to give up their cultural distinctiveness. A process of mutual adaptation is possible because the nation is envisaged as consisting of those who share a common residence. Here multiculturalism can thrive.

These are ideal types and as such cannot be found in their pure form. The approaches of different states epitomize in all cases an amalgam that draws upon a mix of these ideal types. What is more, the approaches of different states have exhibited significant changes over time. Nonetheless, there is widespread agreement that Germany approximates closest to the first, France to the second and Britain to the third.

Germany was particularly close to the first model in the 1980s, when, in marked contrast to the favourable treatment of ethnic Germans in Central and Eastern Europe, there was extreme reluctance to grant full citizenship rights to foreign migrants and their children who had settled in Germany. Germany has subsequently, despite significant opposition, relaxed its citizenship rules by permitting citizenship on the basis of residence and granting it automatically to children of foreign migrants born in the country. Even so, the continuing reluctance to tolerate dual citizenship and the lack of protection for religious rights prevents the full inclusion of many Turkish residents.

France continues to be close to the second model. The dominant conception of the nation – a conception which emerged after the establishment of the state and has its origins in the Revolution of 1789 – is one which visualizes France not as a community of descent but as a territorial community in which citizenship is granted not only to all who are born in France but also to many who migrate there. The expectation, however, is that all will

The ban on wearing the veil in France has led to protests not only in France but in other European countries with Muslim populations. Is the banning of the veil forced assimilation? (© REX)

assimilate to French cultural norms, with the presumption of *la France, une et indivisible*, entailing an intolerance of diverse cultural identities. France has, if anything, moved even closer of late to assimilationism, with a new decade witnessing legislation both banning ostentatious religious symbols in public schools and outlawing the wearing of the burka in public.

Of the three countries, Britain is still closest to the third model. The Act of Union between England and Wales and Scotland 300 years ago created a British state comprising three nations. Britishness was never thereby an exclusive identity, and there has therefore always been an acknowledgement that it is legitimate for there to be different ways of being British. This may have facilitated a greater respect for diversity and mutual accommodation. We must not overstate Britain's commitment to multiculturalism, however, which is significantly more tentative than that of Canada and is not institutionalized in the same way. And we should not forget the trajectory of its immigration policy, which in the post-war period became more exclusionary and racially biased. The state's approach in Britain may be closer than that of the state in Germany and France to pluralism, but its commitment to multicultural citizenship is hesitant and by no means without contradiction (Kymlicka 2003).

Despite these reservations, the example of the nation-state's approach to the headscarf (*hijab*) epitomizes Britain's greater willingness to be more accommodating to minority concerns. British schools have generally adapted uniforms to respond to Muslim concerns, drawing the line only at the *jilbab* (for pupils) and *niqab* (for language teachers). By contrast, the states in Germany are empowered to prohibit Muslim teachers wearing headscarves, and many, including those where the majority of Muslims live, do; in France school children are expressly forbidden under the law to wear them, and in 2011 the wearing of the burka in public was outlawed. While it is important not to exaggerate the point, there is some evidence that, in the area of race and ethnicity, though not other equality strands, Britain is comparatively progressive.

SEMINAR QUESTIONS

1 How different do you think are the approaches of Germany, Britain and France to migration, integration and citizenship?

2 Research the approach of a nation-state other than Britain. Is it closer to differential exclusion, assimilationism or pluralism?

3 Is there any justification for the French ban on the wearing of the burka in public?

IS MULTICULTURALISM IN RETREAT?

Confronting institutional racism

The dominant discourse on race and ethnicity in Britain has undergone a significant shift in the last twelve years. The advent of a New Labour government in 1997 apparently signalled a renewed concern with egalitarianism and for a short period promised to inaugurate a new era whereby Britain was at last prepared to take serious steps to combat racism and promote race equality. In its first year of government, New Labour commissioned an official inquiry, chaired by a senior judge, Sir William Macpherson, into the police investigation into the murder of Stephen Lawrence, a black teenager, by five white youths in 1993. Although the primary focus of the inquiry was on the police, the report suggested that all major organizations in British society were characterized by institutional racism. The Macpherson Report (1999), and its charge that major organizations were infused with institutional racism, was at first widely accepted across the political spectrum and led, among other things, to a much more proactive approach to promoting race equality, the Race Relations (Amendment) Act 2000 (Pilkington 2011). The same year saw the publication of the Parekh Report, a major report of an independent commission on the future of multi-ethnic Britain, chaired by Lord Parekh, which highlighted the importance of creating a multicultural society that struck a balance between the need to treat people equally, the need to respect differences and the need to maintain social cohesion, and which argued that this needed to be done within a human rights framework (Parekh 2000).

While there were always some dissenting voices, throughout 1999 and much of 2000 the dominant discourse was a progressive one. There was an explicit commitment to egalitarianism, a genuine concern to combat racism, an espousal of multiculturalism, and a concern to create a more inclusive representation of the nation. What I have called the radical hour did not, however, last long (Pilkington 2008a).

Fears of extremism and the rise of nationalism

The backlash, already evident in the media reaction to the Parekh Report, has steadily gained strength. The concept of institutional racism has been cast into the dustbin and multiculturalism has been castigated rather than celebrated as concerns over Islamic terrorism and rising net migration have taken precedence over issues to do with racism. Fast forward from February 1999, when the Macpherson Report was published and its recommendations fully accepted by the government, to February 2011. Here is David Cameron, the British prime minister at the time, speaking in Munich:

> Under the doctrine of state multiculturalism we have encouraged different cultures to live separate lives, apart from each other and the mainstream . . . We have failed to provide a vision of society to which they feel they want to belong. We have even tolerated these segregated communities behaving in ways that run counter to our values. All this leaves some young Muslims feeling rootless. And the search for something to belong to and believe in can lead them to extremist ideology [which in turn can lead to terrorism] . . . When a white person holds objectionable views – racism for example – we rightly condemn them but when equally unacceptable views or practices have come from someone who isn't white we've been too cautious, frankly too fearful, to stand up to them . . . This has led to the failure of some to confront the horrors of forced marriage. (Cameron 2011a)

This speech was heralded as a radical departure from the orthodoxy of previous post-war governments. This can be gleaned from the headlines of most British newspapers the day after his speech:

> Muslims must embrace core British values, says Cameron. The days of doing deals with Muslim extremists are over (*Daily Telegraph*)
> PM: Tougher stand on extremism (*Daily Mirror*)
> Cameron: My war on multiculturalism (*The Independent*)
> Softies stoked terrorism. Zero tolerance for Muslim extremists (*The Sun*)
> Cameron: It's time to stop tolerating the Islamic extremists (*Daily Mail*)
> Multiculturalism has failed us: It's time for muscular liberalism says Cameron (*The Times*)
> Cameron tells Muslim Britain: Stop tolerating extremists. PM says those who don't hold British values will be shunned by government (*The Guardian*)

A number of themes are evident in this coverage: the failure of multiculturalism; the danger of Islamic extremism; and the need to reassert Britishness. In most cases, a series of binary oppositions are repeated: us/them; British/Muslim; moderate/extremist. Most newspapers presented Cameron's speech in a sympathetic light, with the only critical editorial and commentary being in *The Guardian*. The coverage drew upon old themes evident, for example, in the media reaction to the Parekh Report, when multiculturalism was questioned and nationalism promoted (Pilkington 2009); the refrain of political correctness gone mad was repeated (Pilkington 2008b), and there was also a focus on British Muslims being a threat (in relation to terrorism) or a problem (in terms of differences in values), or both (Muslim extremism in general) (Moore, Mason and Lewis 2008).

But how radical was Cameron's position on multiculturalism? And how valid are the arguments marshalled against multiculturalism?

The first point that needs to be made is that Cameron's intervention draws upon earlier critiques of multiculturalism, especially those mounted in the previous decade. Multiculturalism in the UK has been an integral ingredient in the dominant discourse on race and ethnicity only at particular points in time in the post-war period and has been steadily on the retreat since 2001. While Cameron's speech was presented as a radical departure from the dominant discourse on race and ethnicity, he was in fact reproducing elements of it which have developed since 2001.

The co-ordinated attacks on the World Trade Center in New York and the Pentagon in Washington on 11 September 2001 helped to consolidate an emerging discourse, evident earlier in the official response to the riots in northern British cities in 2001, that saw institutional racism as less significant than the threat of Muslim disorder/terrorism and identified the central issue as that of cultural integration. If the responses to terrorism and disorder in 2001 signalled a de-prioritization of equality as a central policy objective, mounting attacks on multiculturalism since that time indicate that diversity is no longer something to be celebrated. By 2004, it was already common to read or hear that the cultural separatism and self-segregation of Muslim migrants represented a challenge to Britishness and that a 'politically correct' multiculturalism had fostered fragmentation rather than integration (Modood 2005).

In the post-war period, Britain has been more sympathetic, as we argued above, to the notion of multicultural citizenship than its European neighbours, Germany and France, and thus more accommodating to the concerns of minority ethnic communities (Castles 1995). Nonetheless, multiculturalism has always been highly contested in Britain (Pilkington 2003, 2005). While proponents have highlighted the importance of publicly recognizing and respecting identities that are important to people, critics from the left have tended to identify it as a mode of social control which neglects racism and wider social inequality, and critics on the right have tended to worry about its purported threat to national culture. The onslaught on multiculturalism since 2004 has taken on a somewhat different form, with those who would describe themselves as progressive social democrats not only taking the lead but also mounting arguments that resonated across the political spectrum, arguments that Cameron regurgitates.

Two highly influential critiques were put forward by David Goodhart (2004), the editor of *Prospect*, and Trevor Phillips (2004), the chair at the time of the Commission for Racial Equality. For Goodhart, what is problematic is the multicultural itself, notably ethnic diversity. Since too much diversity erodes solidarity, it is important to control the rate of immigration and require the integration of immigrant communities – especially Muslim ones (Goodhart 2004). Cameron's focus in his February speech is not on the multicultural, but in a subsequent speech in April he highlighted the importance of 'controlling immigration and bringing it down' and warned that immigrants unable to speak English or to integrate have created 'a kind of discomfort and disjointedness' which has disrupted communities (Cameron 2011b). The multicultural is here seen as problematic in exactly the same way as was identified by Goodhart.

For Phillips, by contrast, what is problematic is not the multicultural itself but multiculturalism, the (or at least some of the) policies that entail 'some level of public recognition and support for . . . minorities to maintain and express their distinct identities and practices' (Banting and Kymlicka 2006: 1). We are in danger, as he puts it in a famous sound bite, of 'sleep walking to segregation'. We must wake up and reject multiculturalism, which he depicts as involving separateness between communities. What is needed instead is race equality and the adoption of common values (Phillips 2004).

What is noticeable is that the same two arguments are typically marshalled to challenge multiculturalism. O'Donnell (2007: 253–4) outlines them well when he presents the case that multiculturalism threatens social solidarity. The first criticism of multiculturalism is that it overemphasizes differences between people and thus obscures communalities. It is, in short, divisive and thus corrosive of social cohesion. The second criticism of multiculturalism is its valorization of political correctness. Political correctness has stifled freedom of expression, inhibited open cross-cultural dialogue and made us reluctant to defend our values. This situation entails a 'threat to social solidarity'. These are of course exactly the same two arguments presented by Cameron.

Let me address the critiques of both the multicultural and multiculturalism. I shall deal with the first very quickly. A comprehensive survey of twenty-one European countries indicated that rising ethnic diversity did not have a detrimental effect on social cohesion. 'In short, there is no evidence that diversity is undermining social cohesion and European welfare states' (Legrain 2011). But what about multiculturalism, the focus of Cameron's February speech?

Let me deal with each of his criticisms in turn (see also Pilkington 2007). We can distinguish, following Miller (2006), a moderate and radical conception of multiculturalism. A moderate conception sees policies that recognize and accommodate minority identities (for example, being Muslim) as working in tandem with policies that promote a national identity that embraces these distinct identities (for example, being British). A radical conception, by contrast, believes that it is unnecessary for policies that acknowledge different identities to be accompanied by others that seek to inculcate an overarching national identity. While multiculturalism does of course have divergent meanings and takes different forms, the vast majority of its proponents advocate that respect for difference be complemented by adherence to some common values, and indeed 'no country in the West has adopted radical multiculturalism' (Banting and Kymlicka 2006: 40). What is being attacked here is a straw man.

It is difficult not to resist the temptation to see multiculturalism as an easy scapegoat for concerns about disorder and terrorism. Multiculturalism cannot seriously be seen as causing segregation, since segregation predates the heyday of multiculturalism and is in fact declining (Finney and Simpson 2009). And multiculturalism cannot seriously be seen as responsible for Islamic radicalism since the latter can also be found in France, which has expressly rejected multiculturalism.

Let us turn to the other criticism Cameron makes of multiculturalism – the purported association of multiculturalism with political correctness. It is true that legislative changes have been accompanied by normative changes about what it is acceptable to say and publish. This is on the whole, as I am sure Cameron would agree, a positive development. Muslims and other minority ethnic groups can scarcely be expected to pursue integration while being subject to verbal insults and abuse from other groups in the population. For Cameron, however, these normative changes have gone too far and have resulted in political correctness, with images conjured up of the 'thought police' cajoling us to stay in tune with the latest party line. Labelling attempts to be sensitive in the way we address and represent people as political correctness ('PC'), however, is to fall prey to a right-wing discourse which turns the world upside down and 'becomes a coded shorthand for an attack on equality and diversity' (Younge 2010: 60). According to this view, the problem is not the stereotyping, stigmatizing and marginalizing of vulnerable groups but PC zealots, who threaten freedom of speech. It is remarkable that this discourse has become so pervasive. The vitriol thrown at multiculturalism, and indeed the current demonization of Muslims, by large sections of the media scarcely indicate an intimidated press. I would suggest that what such coverage indicates instead is the hegemonic position of a right-wing anti-PC discourse (Pilkington 2008b). The purported dominance of political correctness, and the accompanying moral relativism that inhibits criticism of practices such as forced marriage or female genital mutilation, is clearly contradicted by the fact that people are not reluctant to make moral judgements about these practices (Parekh 2000). Cameron, in short, criticizes a version of multiculturalism that has not been seriously proposed and certainly has little or no influence. Contrary to Cameron's view that multiculturalism undermines social cohesion, I concur with Modood (2005) when he argues that multiculturalism is still an attractive and worthwhile political project; and, indeed, we need more of it rather than less. Multiculturalism for Modood is a form of integration. It entails changes on the part of established institutions as well as minority groups in a process of mutual accommodation. What is crucial in the current context is that British Muslims are represented in the public sphere, that there is genuine dialogue, that pragmatic and mutual adjustments are made, and that over time we move towards a situation where, irrespective of difference, people experience equal respect. Especially damaging to multiculturalism are ideologies that represent the social world in terms of a simple binary opposition of the West/Islam, whereby people are divided into two mutually exclusive categories. While Islamophobia and Islamist ideologies comprise mirror images of each other, neither is 'conducive to fostering dialogue, respect for difference, to seeking common ground and negotiated accommodation, in short to citizenship in general and above all to multicultural citizenship' (Modood 2013: 120).

The media may have presented Cameron's speech as radical. But a discourse celebrating Britain's multicultural society has been on the retreat since 2001 and in its stead a nationalist discourse from different sides of the political spectrum has been revived (West 2005; Goodhart 2006), a discourse which highlights community cohesion, emphasizes Britishness and urges Muslims to integrate (Modood 2013). This discourse is not unique to Britain, and indeed Cameron's speech bore an uncanny resemblance to an earlier speech by the German chancellor, Angela Merkel, in October 2010 and a later speech by the French president, Nicolas Sarkozy, in February 2011. There seems little doubt that centre-right politicians are trying to shore up support on the right at a time of declining popularity, increasing concern over immigration and the rising appeal of far-right parties. Multiculturalism here comprises a free-floating signifier, signalling unease with immigrants and Muslims.

Anxiety about Islamic terrorism (and increased net migration) has led to multiculturalism being attacked. The recent attacks epitomized by Cameron's speech, however, draw on old arguments and are aimed at a straw man. These arguments find fault with a radical conception of multiculturalism which is neither advocated by proponents nor institutionalized in policies (Vertovec

and Wessendorf 2010). The danger of these attacks is that we cease to value diversity and do not engage Muslims in dialogue, and Britain's incorporation policies shift away from pluralism and multicultural citizenship towards assimilationism and differential exclusion (Castles 1995). We need to find an appropriate balance, as the Parekh Report argued, between equality, diversity and social cohesion. That means in the current political context, contrary to Cameron, placing more rather than less stress on equality and diversity.

Graffiti in Brick Lane, London: the hope of multiculturalism and inter-ethnic solidarity. (© Martin Pettit/Flickr)

SEMINAR QUESTIONS

1   How persuasive do you find the critique of Cameron's speech mounted in this section?
2   Are you more impressed by the continuities or changes in the dominant discourse in Britain with respect to race, ethnicity and nationality over the last fifteen years?

CONCLUSION

We have a range of shifting identities. In this chapter, we have focused on those related to race, ethnicity and nationality. A perusal of news on any day across the world confirms the salience of these identities, which in some cases engender bitter and intractable conflicts.

We have seen that Britain is an ethnically more diverse society than it was fifty years ago, but that minority ethnic groups still face racial disadvantage and are not seen as truly British by some members of the indigenous population. On the other hand, racial prejudice and discrimination have declined considerably, minority groups have made significant progress in the labour market, and the dominant representation of Britishness is an inclusive and multicultural one. While contemporary anxieties over the economic impacts of current immigration and the growing threat of home-grown extremism demonstrate how easily public debate falls back onto old fears and old arguments, this chapter has sought to show that the concept of multiculturalism stands strong and that Britain should continue to embrace pluralism.

SEMINAR QUESTIONS

1 In the light of what you have read in this chapter, do you believe migration is inaugurating a convivial multicultural society in Britain or signalling the erosion of cherished values and increasing conflict?

2 In a country of your choice, suggest what types of policy changes would you like to see with respect to the issues addressed in this chapter. Justify your suggestions.

FURTHER READING

▶ A useful reader which surveys a range of theories pertinent to race, ethnicity and nationality is Back, L., and J. Solomos (2009) *Theories of Race and Racism* (Routledge).

▶ Useful edited collections exploring race, ethnicity and nationality in Britain include Bloch, A., and J. Solomos (2010) *Race and Ethnicity in the 21st Century* (Palgrave), and Modood, T., and J. Salt (2011) *Global Migration, Ethnicity and Britishness* (Palgrave).

▶ An interesting American textbook which explicitly adopts a social constructionist approach to race and ethnicity and illustrates its case with examples from across the world is Cornell, S., and D. Hartmann (2007) *Ethnicity and Race: Making Identities in a Changing World* (2nd edn, Pine Forge Press).

▶ For a clear and compelling defence of multiculturalism, see Modood, T. (2013) *Multiculturalism* (2nd edn, Polity).

▶ If you wish to explore the utility of the concept of institutional racism to an understanding of the police and higher education, you will find the following case study of interest: Pilkington, A. (2011) *Institutional Racism in the Academy* (Trentham Books).

AGE AND THE LIFE COURSE

continuity, change and the modern mirage of infinite choice

LORRAINE GREEN

CONTENTS

INTRODUCTION

THIS CHAPTER INTRODUCES AN embryonic but fascinating subdivision of sociology, the life course, which emphasizes changing and multifaceted understandings of age, life pathways and intergenerational relations. It therefore considers whether common perceptions of older people as doddery and confused and of children as carefree and protected are accurate and whether prevalent markers of adulthood, such as full-time work and independent living, are becoming outmoded as young adulthood becomes a very different experience from what it was thirty or forty years ago. The chapter also covers ageism, age segregation and age stereotyping, which often intersect with discriminatory racist, sexist, sexual, gendered or classed assumptions. These include pervasive images of the asexual and innocent child, the anti-social council-estate 'chav', the irresponsible working-class teenage mum, the primordial, hypersexual black youth, the unattractive middle-aged spinster and the predatory older gay man.

Until the late 1980s the terms 'life cycle' and 'life course' were interchangeable in sociology (Bryman et al. 1987), 'life cycle' also being common to medicine and demography and psychology adopting the term 'life span'. Psychology originally concentrated on lifelong, sequential human development, privileging the de-contextualized, biologically preordained individual over structure and, ironically (since psychology has always concentrated more on the individual than the social), *individual* agency. The term *life span* is therefore typically associated with psychological, positivist and biological approaches and assumes a fixed series of stages through which all individuals pass. *Life cycle* has similar connotations but often includes assumptions about the circularity of birth, reproduction and death passing from one generation to the next. In contrast, sociology views the *life course* as a dynamic, multi-level process, whereby people's heterogeneous passages through life vary considerably both within and across different societies. Individuals' life courses therefore are not subsumed within or funnelled through fixed developmental stages but, rather, are a complex product of both individual choice and wider social circumstances, with sociology placing less emphasis on the biological and more on cultural and global influences. Life course sometimes also refers to a broader multidisciplinary paradigm, but it is used here sociologically to refer exclusively to people's navigation through life across time and cultural and spatial location, a praxis considering the interplay between history, individual agency, social forces and related institutional constraints.

The interest in life course sociology was propelled by rapid social, political and economic global change from the 1960s on. This included:

1 growing financial affluence and the development of Western welfare states in the 1940s to 1960s;
2 the impact of recurrent economic crises from 1973 onwards;
3 the effects of 1960s/1970s civil rights/social movements – feminist, black power, disability, anti-war and gay rights movements; and
4 the demise of the Eastern communist bloc and the 'Cold War' from the 1980s onwards.

Also relevant was the linked accelerated spread of a monolithic yet diffused and culturally sensitive global capitalism (involving the rise of multinational companies such as Disney and Coca-Cola alongside the escalating power of transnational organizations such as the International Monetary Fund (IMF), the European Union (EU) and the United Nations (UN)). The maturation of some early longitudinal studies (e.g., Glen Elder's *Children of the Great Depression*, 1974), also showed the profound importance of studying people's lives from birth to death, with the next section illustrating the importance of timing and context and showing how profound disadvantage in childhood can be neutralized or even reversed, given certain conditions or opportunities.

BOX 4.1 CHILDREN OF THE GREAT DEPRESSION

Elder studied children born in the USA in the late 1930s, during the worst of the Great Depression (a time of prolonged mass unemployment and hardship), through to young adulthood and beyond. Many endured extreme poverty, and the community and the familial/marital stress this engendered therefore seemed to present them with poor prospects as young adults. However, military conscription, through offering these young adults responsibility, a structured environment, skills and new opportunities, then acted as a great leveller for past disadvantage. Conversely, later military mobilization, when people had reached their thirties, lifted them out of established adult roles and responsibilities and so led to disruption and disadvantage (Elder 1974, 1986).

The chapter commences with a key terminology and methods section. Socially constructed notions of age, age segregation and age discrimination are then analysed and illustrated. Following this, claims are evaluated that a once relatively structured, linear life course has now, in the late twentieth and early twenty-first century, an era of late modernity, become de-standardized. Advocates of de-standardization claim that people's contemporary life courses have been transformed into less predictable but more risky and choice-orientated processes, but this hypothesis pays insufficient attention to considerable structural, institutional and biological constraints that indicate we may not all have the same opportunities to exercise choice.

The latter part of the chapter critically evaluates selected but roughly hewn age categories such as childhood, young adulthood and midlife, thereby extending and illustrating concepts previously examined. These later sections draw largely on five key themes: (i) agency, autonomy and choice-making; (ii) consumption; (iii) work and living arrangements; (iv) new technology; and (v) ageism and age segregation.

KEY TERMS, PROCESSES AND METHODOLOGY

Key life course principles

Elder, Kirkpatrick Johnson and Crosnoe (2003) advocate five key life course principles: (i) 'human development' and ageing as lifelong processes; (ii) the interplay of human lives in historical time and place; (iii) the timing of lives; (iv) linked or interdependent lives; and (v) human agency in choice-making. Mayer (2003), in contrast, emphasizes three fundamental life course mechanisms: (i) institutions; (ii) transitions and trajectories; and (iii) cohort effects. He asserts that institutions greatly structure our lives – for example, mandatory education in the UK until the age of sixteen (soon to be eighteen) or being accorded certain rights, benefits or responsibilities at specific ages. Although Elder can be criticized for neglecting wider social structures and institutions, it is now generally accepted that a life course perspective assumes our lives are:

1   profoundly influenced by timing and socio-historical and geographical location – i.e., when and where we are born and key events preceding and after our birth;
2   interlinked with and interdependent on others in many ways and at different societal levels – 'linked lives';
3   constructed through both chosen and inadvertent actions within the constraints of the socio-economic and historical context; and that
4   heterogeneity or variability are very important.

However, debates ensue as to whether life course sociology should always exclude biological, evolutionary and genetic factors (Mayer 2003) and whether the unit of analysis should be the individual or a collective (for example, a population or cohort) (Dannefer 2012).

Cohorts and generations

Two common, often conflated life course terms, which confusingly also possess multiple meanings, are *cohort* and *generation*. A *generation* commonly refers to kinship and genealogical descent, such as parent, child and grandparent generation. It covers a period of twenty to thirty years but is methodologically and analytically problematic and may become even more so if the trend towards late childbearing continues. If one five-year-old child has parents in their early twenties, another parents in their forties, and a third has a mother of twenty-two and a fifty-year-old father, the parents are clearly not all of the same generation. This creates problems for comparative kinship analysis, particularly as the most common intergenerational research design involves sampling different people of similar ages interviewed alongside at least one parent. The term *(social) generation* has also been used synonymously with *cohort* to describe a generation which self-identifies or is other-identified as different from preceding and future generations, particularly in relation to political and cultural values, activism and/

or social behaviour (Braungart and Braungart 1986; Pilcher 1994). Much debate, however, ensues about the specific characteristics of different generations and dividing lines between them. A *cohort* refers to a shorter period and people born within a few years of each other who share some common experiences, such as going to school or experiencing a war together. Cohorts, generally statistically grouped five to ten years apart, are easier to measure statistically than kinship generations. Cohort analysis is therefore more prevalent in life course research, and a generation can comprise many cohorts or cohorts may bridge generations.

Being a five-year-old is not the same for all cohorts and generations: varying social phenomena and contexts will have affected – and continue to affect – the people shown in these nursery photos. (© ann_t/Flickr, © Colin J. Campbell/Flickr, © David Tett/Flickr)

The 'hippie generation' of young adults in the 1960s campaigned for equality and justice and challenged unnecessary wars, thereby fitting the definition of both a generation and a social generation, although not everyone identified as a peace-loving flower child. Mannheim (1952) contends that a lifelong generational consciousness is acquired in youth, linked to the prevailing socio-economic and political climate, a claim partially evidenced by the enduring activism and politics of young people in the USA in the 1960s (McAdams 1989). The Baby Boomers, born after the Second World War, between 1946 and 1964, were the first generation to experience full welfare-state benefits, greater individual affluence and mass consumerism – major cultural and socio-economic changes – although they would not necessarily see themselves as politically similar. Confusingly, some older Baby Boomers also inhabited the hippie generation, as blurring often occurs at the margins of different generations (Alwin and McCammon 2003). Being part of such a large generation, some Baby Boomer cohorts – although these varied significantly in size and birth timing in different countries (Phillipson 2007; Phillipson et al. 2008) – suffered significant socio-economic disadvantage because of intense competition for resources such as university places (Easterlin 1987). They have also been portrayed as a selfish, unjustifiably affluent generation, or sometimes ironically the opposite, as a social justice generation, although the first-wave Boomers (1946–55) were more affluent and visibly political than the second wave (1955–64).

Those born between 1964 and the mid-1980s, now in their thirties and early to mid-forties, the X or 'slacker' generation, were initially depicted in Douglas Coupland's (1991) novel *Generation X* as media and technologically savvy, aimless, overeducated and underemployed young people from broken families. Sociologists have, furthermore, represented Xers as angry, nihilistic and culturally and politically unanchored, being forced to take on a succession of unfulfilling McJobs but simultaneously being inventive in their consumption-driven activities (Osgerby 2004). Others, however, have depicted contemporary Xers in a much more positive pro-family and career-successful light (Neate 2007). The succeeding Y, millennial, digital, net, IPOD (Insecure, Pressured, Overtaxed and Debt-ridden) or echo-boomer generation, born between the mid-1980s and the late 1990s, are even more immersed within sophisticated consumer and hi-technology cultures and suffer increasing job insecurity. They also express more neoliberal, individualistic and less egalitarian attitudes (Konstam 2010; Stainton Rogers et al. 2004) and much cynicism about the government and partisan politics. Like the Xers, they barely question brand labels and global capitalism and are more accepting of diversity than previous generations, as well as being less debt cautious, having never experienced (or perhaps have never even heard second-hand of) the dire poverty of pre-Boomer generations. The political values or lifestyles of newer generations may, however, change with age and socio-economic or political shifts. *Turning points* or 'fateful moments' (Giddens 1991) in young adulthood involving significant, often unexpected and negative, personal events, such as experiencing unplanned pregnancies or developing serious disabilities, may fundamentally alter or disrupt future plans (Shirani and Henwood 2011), thereby potentially overriding any particular generational or political consciousness acquired (Denzin 1989).

A *cohort effect* relates to individuals born at a similar time and sharing comparable experiences, such as similar schooling, and an *age effect* refers to differences linked to chronological age and/or life stage. A *period effect* refers to the impact of a specific historical period, such as a war followed by a recession, and may affect many cohorts or generations. Cohorts' experiences are formed not only by historical events and conditions at one point in time but also by the cumulative effects of past historical conditions (Hareven 1994). Consequently, one cohort is affected by both preceding and succeeding cohorts as well as by individual choice and the changing social context (Macunevich 1999). The knock-on effect of one cohort's behaviour on others was illustrated in a rather sexist Australian newspaper article entitled 'Cougars Ready to Pounce'. This cited statistical data showing that many middle-aged women, more likely to be single than their male equivalents, were initiating relationships with men in their twenties whom they met in bars. Women in their twenties had often opted for relationships with older men in their thirties, leaving a surplus of available single men in their twenties (Ganska 2010), who presumably did not want to date teenage girls still at school. One's ability to find a partner therefore may depend on many past and present cohorts and on the numbers, preferences and communication networks of those simultaneously searching. Until the early 1990s most people met their partners at work, through personal networks (Hearn et al. 1990) or, clandestinely, via the then stigmatized lonely hearts newspaper columns. Today many people source possible relationships through internet dating sites and other internet mediums such as Facebook and Twitter and initially email each other (Hardey, 2002), thereby communicating differently with and instigating relationships with those they would have been unlikely to meet in earlier epochs.

Transitions, trajectories and research methodology

A *transition* is a shift from one status or role to another – for example, from being single to being married or from being a student to being a full-time worker. A *trajectory* is a long-term themed pathway through one's life, which may or may not be linear or have an intended endpoint but often assumes an overall direction, such as trajectories of work, school and parenthood. Trajectories may encompass many transitions which become longer or shorter at different time periods. Educational trajectories, for example, have become extended for many with the mass expansion of tertiary education, alongside de-industrialization and economic recessions. These combined have led to greater youth unemployment and intermittent education in between periods of working. Longitudinal research is useful for understanding *transitions* and *trajectories* over long periods in relation to different cohorts and generations, but different research designs and methods may be useful for understanding different aspects of ageing and the life course and how these interact, diverge, complement or conflict with each other. Figure 4.1 shows changing trajectories for women in England and Wales in terms of when they marry and have children, with marriage now typically following the birth of children.

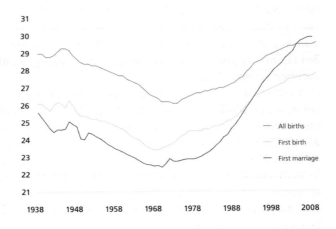

Figure 4.1 Age at first marriage, at birth of first child, and average age for all births for women in England and Wales, 1938–2008

Source: Thompson et al. 2012: 18.

BOX 4.2 METHODOLOGICAL NOTES

The most effective research designs for studying ageing are longitudinal studies of the same individuals researched over long time periods – *panel designs*. *Cross-sectional designs* involve people of different of ages, often a random population sample at one snapshot in time, and can be repeated. The *cohort sequential* design follows a number of cohorts over time, and *cross-sequential* research combines panel designs and repeated cross-sectional designs, thereby sampling the same individuals but also adding in new ones each time. *Event history analysis* studies the length of time between different transitions, such as employed to unemployed. Analyses of life course patterns have generally relied on 'both a discrete "transition" and a "holistic" trajectory [and although] single events should not be isolated from each other . . . most . . . insights in quantitative life course sociology gained thus far are based on the analysis of the timing and comparison of transitions' (Aisenbrey and Fasang 2010: 421), unfortunately obscuring close observation of a trajectory.

Socio-historic changes may also impact on research techniques and other life course terminology. Between the early 1960s and the 1990s it was unlikely one would simultaneously be a university student and a full-time employee, but this is now a distinct possibility, rendering the study of the transition from student to full-time employee hugely problematic. Similarly, previously we might have measured the transition time from people being single to when they married. Today, however, we engage in many different types of living arrangements. These include solo living, living with friends, civil partnerships, cohabitation and non-residential relationships – known as *LATS* (living alone togethers) or *commuter marriages*, where both parties are committed but live in geographically disparate locations (Haskey 2005; Holmes 2006). The age and generation of the researchers (generally young or middle-aged adults) vis-à-vis the study participants may also impact problematically upon research design, questions and findings, particularly if everyday interaction is rare and discriminatory unthought-through stereotypes are invoked (Grenier 2007).

Agency in sociology is often generically used to refer to the micro-context, a person's or group's ability to make (semi-)autonomous decisions, whereas *structure* relates to macro, broader overriding social forces. These include politics, culture and social norms, embedded in legislation, institutions, everyday social practices, beliefs and ideologies. Structure thus influences and constrains envisaged and actual possibilities, choices and actions. People's actions therefore often reproduce structure over time, for example gender or social class divisions and inequalities. This occurs sometimes purposively but at other times unconsciously (for example, being highly likely to select a partner from a similar culture or class while thinking one has randomly 'fallen in love'). Agency should also be considered in its different manifestations, since in many past and some present societies strong collectivities such as families or communities are the decision-making bodies, not individuals (Kok 2007). And agency may manifest itself through seeming inertia – *passive agency* – as opposed to *active agency*. That apparently deferred or 'non'-decision-making may be carefully deliberated (ibid.) but is difficult to discern in large statistical data sets. It is therefore important to consider both biographic approaches (generally characterized by qualitative data such as life history interviews) and the cohort or life event approach (often predicated on standardized quantitative data) (Heinz and Kruger 2001) in order to understand interactions between self-directed behaviour, institutional constraints and wider social structure.

SEMINAR QUESTIONS

1 Evaluate the claim that different cohorts and generations are likely to have very different experiences of the life course, using examples from your own family, novels, films, television series or sociological literature.

2 'The social construction of age tends to constrain behaviour more than biological ageing.' Discuss.

AGE: GRADING, STAGES, NORMS, DISCRIMINATION AND SEGREGATION

Different perceptions of age

Although late modern societies tend to view age one-dimensionally as *chronological age* – how many years a person has lived – other less dominant definitions of age utilize different criteria. *Self-perceived/felt age, subjective age* or *age identity* refers to how old an individual sees themselves, and *other-perceived/social age* is concerned with how old you are considered by others or by society. *Biological age*, in contrast, refers to the biological maturity or deterioration of your body in comparison to general ageing processes (for example, the infirm could be seen as having an older biological than chronological age). *Functional age* is judged by comparing your physical and mental functioning with others of the same chronological age (so an elderly person with a sharp brain may have a lower functional age than chronological age).

Expectations linked to chronological age profoundly influence our life experiences, with institutions often operating age criteria in terms of benefits, rights and responsibilities. When people have not assumed certain roles or achieved specific goals by a certain age they are often seen as being 'off time' (Neugarten 1968), suggesting a socially age-appropriate time span for certain activities. Although age or stage assumptions may today be less rigid, we still see children and the elderly as more vulnerable and less purposive than those of other ages (Pahl 2000), referring to obsolete stereotypes such as grandmothers with blue-rinse perms sitting passively knitting on their rocking chairs. One ironic example involved a psychiatrist diagnosing a middle-aged male as mentally ill because of his incessant boasting about his multiple sexual conquests – behaviour apparently appropriate and sane only for teenage males (Holstein 1990). Biology is also important, although little engaged with sociologically, because often it is applied crudely to justify socially constructed inequalities (Freese, Li and Wade 2003; Newton 2003). We do, however, need to acknowledge how our bodies age over time and impact on our activities and past and future time perspectives (Adam 1990). Receiving a substantial inheritance will thus be very different for a healthy young adult and an eighty-year-old with mobility problems.

Traditional developmental psychology arguably has arbitrarily created 'universal' age-graded biological, cognitive and psychosocial life-span stages, remaining relatively silent about cross-cultural or historical variability (Green 2010). Some social scientists additionally uncritically impose normative Eurocentric understandings of chronological age on their research as they paradoxically claim to be trying to comprehend their respondents' indigenous vernacular and how they construct and navigate notions of age and stage (Janssen 2009). In one cross-cultural study of adolescence in linguistically diverse communities, the researchers asked respondents questions about late and early adolescence and its duration (Chaterjee, Bailey and Aronoff 2001). They therefore assumed not *only* that these other cultures would have a model of adolescence but that their model would mimic Western conceptualizations.

Although chronological age is a key categorizer in Western societies (Nikander 2009), it assumes less salience in non-Western societies (Keith 1990). There, family descent, social role or characteristics such as wisdom may be more important. An aunt may therefore possess more seniority than her same-aged niece. Some UK asylum-seekers do not know when they were born, casting bureaucratic asylum procedures into disarray, especially when it is unclear if such individuals are adults or children. This often leads to discriminatory, arbitrary forms of age evaluation (Crawford 2007). Most elderly people self-perceive as younger, women are more sensitive to negative old-age stereotypes, and those of a higher social class or with more education often perceive themselves as younger and are less traditional. Loss of status and changing social roles can also impact on subjective age (Barak and Schiffman 1981). A national random sample of British people aged sixty-five and over found 'felt' rather than chronological age was a more sensitive indicator of health and social and psychological characteristics (Bowling et al. 2005). Family turbulence, such as maternal death during childhood, linked to decreased psychosocial resources and stress, also leads to higher/older adult age identity (Schafer 2009;

Schafer and Shippee 2010). The salient point, however, is that other ways of judging ages are only understood in relation to the baseline of chronological age in the West.

Age segregation and discrimination

Age segregation – the often enforced separation of people of different ages – and *ageism* or *age discrimination* – treating an individual or a group differentially on the basis of age or stereo-types – are two different but often related and mutually reinforcing processes. While ageism and age segregation have been applied disproportionately to older people (Bytheway 1995; Filinson 2008), they *can* apply to most ages and stages, including children, young people and midlifers. Ageism is often seen as an individualized prejudice which ignores the effects of wider social forces and norms and the impact of age segregation (Hagestad and Uhlenberg 2006). Ageism may either be caused by, or be the consequence of, age segregation, which is minimized by sustained familiarity among individuals of different ages (Hagestad and Uhlenberg 2005, 2006).

Macnicol (2010) claims age discrimination often occurs in three different spheres. It can occur in social relations and attitudes, whereby lower social standing is linked to chronological age. This can operate from the interpersonal to the institutional level and be most damaging when seen as justified or inevitable – one example might be older people receiving substandard medical treatment because it is assumed they have lived their life and will probably die soon anyway. Age discrimination is also evident in influencing who is hired, at what level, and who is demoted, trained or retired. Age discrimination and sexism can intersect in employment in relation to young women not being hired or promoted because it is assumed they will soon have children and resign or take long periods of maternity leave. Paradoxically, young men are more likely to move companies and jobs more frequently and thereby actually cost employers proportionally more than women who go on maternity leave but are more likely to stay with the same employer (Green, Parkin and Hearn 2001). The third sphere identified by Macnicol relates to how goods and services are distributed, for example holiday or car insurance. Older people may be routinely charged higher premiums for travel insurance purely because of their age and not necessarily because they have any specific health problem. In modern societies our lives are structured in a tripartite manner, whereby schooling, work and retirement represent the three main institutional 'acts' for our life scripts (Kohli 1986), and these involve age seg-regation. For example, children's education in Western countries excludes them mostly from working, and they spend their days with similar-aged peers and teachers, in schools or under-taking structured activities. In many Western countries, until recently, retirement at a specific age was mandatory, eradicating older people from employment structures within which most 'working-age' adults spend the vast majority of their days.

Institutional age segregation occurs when chronological age precludes participation in institutional activities (such as being on a jury) or reception of services. It can work overtly through direct discrimination or be covert and less intentional. *Spatial age segregation* occurs when differently aged individuals rarely occupy the same space, such as university campuses with separate living accommodation and retirement villages. *Cultural age segregation* con-cerns lifestyle differences – for example, in language and social activities which then reduce familiarity and social interaction (Hagestad and Uhlenberg 2005). A recent English survey showed significant gendered, generational and socio-economic differences in consumption were linked to cultural practices. Older people were less likely to engage in activities outside

Retirement can be a severe form of age segregation as older people transition away from a core arena of adult life. Many individuals thus choose not to retire as early as they could, which, with youth unemployment currently so high, is increasingly creating intergenerational conflict. (© stockstudioX/iStock)

the home and cohort; period and age effects were evident in relation to cultural activities such as food, TV, cinema, live music and crafts (Scherger 2009). For example, older white British people are likely to prepare traditional British food conventionally and adhere to set mealtimes. Conversely, for younger people set mealtimes are rare, and purchasing convenience pre-prepared microwaveable food and 'ethnic' takeaways is common. People of different ages therefore rarely meaningfully interact today except in the family context (Hagestad and Uhlenberg 2005, 2006) and the periods of both 'growing up' and 'growing old' have become extended. Because the different generations have experienced such significant differences in their lives, such as wars and the proliferation of global capitalism and hi-technology, they have become increasingly more culturally differentiated. At the same time, less regular face-to-face intergenerational familial contact occurs on account of greater family mobility (Pooley, Turnbull and Adams 2005) and nucleically smaller but generationally wider families having become the norm (Brannen 2003; Settersen 2007). Adults today also have fewer informal interactions with children outside family or work settings because children now have diminished 'freedom to roam' (Cunningham 2006), which can lead to different generations becoming alienated from and hostile towards one another. In a questionnaire study of 2,000 children and 500 adults, only a minority of children experienced most adults being friendly; 33 percent of the adults worryingly agreed with the statement 'The English love their dogs more than their children', with only 42 percent disagreeing (Madge 2005).

That is not to say age-differentiated behaviour is always discriminatory. It may be benevolent but simultaneously over-accommodating in that unnecessary or unwanted support may be foisted upon or offered to elderly people, potentially adversely affecting their autonomy, dignity and self-esteem (Minichiello, Browne and Kendig 2000). An interesting study examining age perceptions reported that, paradoxically, those who initially seemed to have the most positive views of older people actually saw them through a dependent 'pity' lens and were therefore unlikely to advocate for increased numbers of older people in representatory spheres (Tornstam 2006). Similarly, 'paternalistic' reduced costs for public transport and discounts for goods and services would be unnecessary if most elderly people received a 'living' income (Krekula 2007). Age is therefore a dynamic, multifaceted phenomenon which cannot be understood only in relation to chronological age and associated age grading, staging and expectations but in many other ways.

SEMINAR QUESTIONS

1 In what ways do institutions shape people's life courses and how do they impact at different ages?
2 Illustrate and discuss some examples of cohort, period and age effects.
3 How could greater interaction between older and younger people be encouraged?

DE-STANDARDIZATION OF THE LIFE COURSE?

The rise of individualization and changing life patterns

For many years, events such as marrying and bearing children often followed each other or co-occurred and were statistically far more likely to cluster around certain ages. These configurations were highly influenced by the stable nuclear family, education and work trajectories and the relative economic prosperity evident between the 1950s and the mid-1970s. This differed from the nineteenth century, when family obligations linked to financial security, particularly in poorer families, superseded strict age norms and made transitions erratic (Hareven 1994). This could lead to a daughter delaying marriage and childrearing potentially indefinitely if her economic work-based contribution was vital for her family to survive. Sociologists in the 1970s and the 1980s argued that individuals' lives had become more predictable and institutionalized as Western welfare states now buffered people from historically normative major deprivations (such as absolute poverty caused by cyclical unemployment, illness or incapacity). This occurred through universal health and welfare services, such as the NHS in the UK, public housing, civic services and various forms of universal, targeted or contributory social insurances. Institutions also structured transitions and trajectories through educational, work, marriage and retirement legislation, directives and supports (Brückner and Mayer 2005). For example, for many years married couples were given preferential tax allowances and were eligible for state or council housing, whereas those couples 'just' living together were not.

Recently, however, some sociologists have argued that an *individualization, de-standardization, de-linearization* or *yo-yoization* of the life course has occurred (e.g., Beck 1992; Bauman 2001; Brannen and Nilsen 2005). Although these terms are often multiply interpreted, they suggest our 'lives have become less predictable, less collectively determined, less stable, less orderly, more flexible and more individualized' (Brückner and Mayer 2005: 28). The de-standardization perspective therefore suggests a greater variety of paths taken through life by individuals than in the past and that both the timing and the sequence of transitions in life (such as cohabiting with a partner, getting married, having children, starting work, retiring, etc.) are no longer predictable. Indeed, many people may opt out of some transitions – for example, by staying single, living on their own or choosing not to retire. Major transformations in living arrangements and gender roles therefore have occurred since the 1970s, but do they support the de-standardization hypothesis? The ideological foundations supporting the 1950s idealized model of the traditional, heterosexual, monogamous, nuclear family seemed to be crumbling by the 1990s, in conjunction with more 'liberalized' attitudes and 'no fault' divorce laws. Cohabitation, both as a precursor and an alternative to marriage, became popular (Jamieson et al. 2002) and the divorce rate increased, although 'reconstituted families' and friendships became recognized as important interpersonal relationships (Budgeon 2006). Some people became serial monogamists, moving from one relationship to another. Solo living became more popular, and gay relationships slowly became less stigmatized with the removal of criminal sanctions and psychiatric labels (Green and Grant 2008). There thus exists more choice and diversity in family formation today, particularly with new reproductive technology for infertile couples (Friese, Becker and Nachtigall 2008), gay couples visibly producing different family structures (Smart 2007b; Weeks, Heaphy and Donovan 2001), and single parenthood and serial monogamy increasing, although the nuclear family ideologically and statistically remains highly popular. Greater longevity has also led to people today being more likely to have living parents who may require significant support (Bures 2009).

Giddens (1991) arguably captured the spirit of the times with 'the pure relationship', enduring only when both parties are satisfied. This implies both greater instability and greater gender equality in relationships, since both partners can choose whether a relationship still works for them and whether or not to 'move on'. The 'pure relationship' seemed to be reflected in changing attitudes from the 1970s onwards, which included increasing symbolic sexual equality in all spheres. Women were no longer seen as housewife adjuncts, and men correspondingly were encouraged to engage more emotionally. A 1980s Athena picture of an attractive half-naked man tenderly holding a baby (the best-selling poster ever) arguably symbolized the emergence of the egalitarian, caring 'new' man (Bruzzi 2005). Some, however, claim he was an ephemeral by-product of a cynical, consumerist marketing campaign targeting men, and he was rapidly superseded by the sexist 'beer, boobs and football' 'laddish' backlash images popular in the late 1980s and early 1990s and still prominent in men's magazines today (Braddock 2010). Others have asserted that many relationships are less equal and more tradition-bound than Giddens claimed, particularly in relation to sustained sexual and gender inequalities (Wilson 2007; Jamieson 1999; Pilcher 2000). This suggests the new man may indeed have been at least partly illusory and that gay couples and heterosexual men and women may not be able to make choices to follow a non-standard life course on an equal footing.

Counter-narratives and the persistent role of institutions in shaping the life course

Although full employment, clear career trajectories and 'a job for life' seemed enduring in the 1960s, the 1973 OPEC oil crisis and successive economic downturns, including the UK's current recession (from 2008 and ongoing in 2014), eroded such hopes and ideals. These financial crises, alongside de-industrialization (factories and mines being replaced by fast-food outlets and shopping malls and the manufacturing bases and often the service industries of Western countries, such as call centres, shifting to 'cheaper' developing countries), have resulted in a casualized labour force and increasing un/underemployment. This has affected particularly young and middle-aged people. Jobs therefore have become less secure and more fragmented, and it often takes years before young people settle into a career trajectory (Furlong and Cartmel 2007). Mass higher education and the demise of grants have also led to young adults depending on their families financially and in other ways for increasingly longer periods. Young people leave the family home later and often return afterwards or live there while attending university, meaning that debates circulate around what markers or transitions should indicate full adulthood.

There are also differences across Western countries. Many still follow a fairly linear, normative pattern, but others reveal extended transitions to adulthood, in large part because of considerable institutional constraints and significant changes in role occupations and family and work patterns.

BOX 4.3 INTERNATIONAL CASE STUDIES

Brückner and Mayer (2005), using the German Life History Study and assessing transitions to adulthood for cohorts born between 1920 and 1971, found marriage and childbearing had decoupled and that labour market entry occurred later, often as a result of longer educational trajectories. Furthermore, both gender convergence regarding men and women's education and work pathways and pronounced changes in family formation were evident. However, the school–training/higher education–work continuum was still highly structured by institutions.

Macmillan (2005) similarly shows that, although normative sequences were never that normal in the USA, since the 1970s people's life courses have become increasingly timetabled through age-graded institutions, although working, attending university and parenthood, previously characterizing disparate life stages, are now more likely to co-occur. In addition, Macmillan identified a general extension of the transition into adulthood alongside major transformations in work and living arrangements and more reversibility and instability of roles, such as being a parent or worker. Like others, Macmillan stresses how claims of individualization, de-standardization and choice biographies underplay 'geographies of disadvantage' and significant variations in life course pathways linked to divisions such as social class.

A Belgian study of 4,666 individuals aged eighteen to thirty-six conversely found little evidence of de-standardization, either in respondents' expectations of when certain events should occur or their actual occurrence, although parenthood and full-time work often commenced slightly later because of extended education and cohabitation prior to marriage (Elchardus and Smits 2006).

A European project also found that most respondents' expectations in terms of transitions and trajectories to and through adulthood were fairly normative and linear (Biggart 2003). In Switzerland, since the late 1960s individuals comprised of younger cohorts have experienced increasingly diverse living and work situations, but unlike the situation in Germany, Swiss men experience more stable, linear, occupational trajectories through to retirement than women, largely because women still shoulder the familial caring burdens (Widmer and Ritschard 2009).

Biological constraints also require acknowledgement. The menopause, for example, prevents women giving birth with their natural eggs after a certain age, and both men and women's declining strength and stamina from the age of thirty onwards precludes competing in top athletic events. Therefore (although major changes in living and family arrangements, gender roles, work and education have taken place, often linked with shifting socio-economic and global situations), it provisionally seems that a wholesale de-standardization of the life course has not occurred. People's pathways through life are becoming increasingly structured by institutions, as well as being impacted upon by inequality and diversity related to gender, 'race'/ethnicity, sexuality and social class/socio-economic status. However, the epistemological fallacy in late modernity conveys a false but dazzling illusion of individual choice and, with that, an individualized blame for failure, alongside an ignorance of structural barriers and collective risks (Furlong and Cartmel 2007).

The final sections in this chapter will therefore deal with some age stages critically, giving illustration and substance to some key concepts. Age stages are often debated, fluid and changing. Sometimes childhood is seen to extend until the age of sixteen or eighteen or is divided into three or four substages, such as infancy, young and middle childhood and teenagedom. Alternatively, the teenage years are often encompassed by the very amorphous term 'youth', which can last until the mid-twenties, thereby also including early young adulthood. In the early 1980s, the later part of what today is called young adulthood (the thirties) was viewed for some as the new middle age (Featherstone and Hepworth 1983). Conversely, today some healthy, energetic (often affluent) adults in their sixties and seventies are seen to inhabit the new middle age (Laslett 1989), pushing old age further forward into the future chronologically as average life expectancy and retirement ages also increase. Childhood is now seen to be a feature of young adulthood, with many young adults remaining multifariously dependent on parents until their mid-twenties.

Because this chapter obviously cannot cover every age stage or the debates about them in detail, childhood up until the teen years, youth from the teen years to the early twenties, and midlife ranging from forty-to sixty-five have been the age periods selected, since they are closer to the age range of most likely readers of this book. However, it could be contended that old age is the most important life stage because of its potential length, from sixty to 120 years, rapidly expanding greying populations in most post-industrial nations, and the health and care burdens potentially associated with them. These are sometimes seen as scaremongering (Vincent 2003) but at other times as realistic concerns.

CAPTIVE 'ADULTS IN WAITING' OR AGENTIC CHILDREN?

Changing paradigms and discourses and their impact

In classical sociology and psychology the socialization and age/stage paradigms depicted children as malleable and in deficit mode, traversing an unfinished journey to completed development – adulthood! This deflected attention away from the conditions in which children live now and their current accomplishments, instead projecting forward to their future adult 'worker' incarnation (Lister 2003; Green 2006; 2010). It also universalized childhood, ignoring global, cross-national, cohort, generational and structural inequalities and justified significant adult control because of children's assumed immaturity and apprenticeship status. The 'new social studies of childhood' movement, visible from the late 1980s onwards, contested this view, proposing a knowing, agentic child. They also exposed the divisive, disempowering and controlling way in which adults customarily treat children – it being legal to 'reasonably' physically chastise (i.e., assault) your children in the UK but not your pets and no longer your wife!

In the 1960s Ariès (1960) challenged ahistorical, universalist notions of childhood through analysis of medieval artefacts which depicted children as mini-adults, although not until the 1980s did the social construction of childhood really take hold. Sociologists then began to identify the contradictory ways in which children were eclipsed through the discourses of innocence, evil, immaturity and sacralization (Zelizer 1985; Gittins 1998; Meyer 2007), different discourses assuming prevalence at different times and influencing each other. According to Judaeo-Christian doctrine, the belief that children are born blemished by original sin has a long history, stemming from Adam and Eve. Beliefs about children's 'wickedness' then solidified in the sixteenth century with the creation of the Protestant Church, strengthened by philosophers such as Hobbes (1588–1679), who viewed mankind as amoral. Other philosophers conversely saw children as innately pure, a quality enhanced or diminished by upbringing, and some Romantic poets even imbued children with qualities of profound aestheticism, wisdom, morality and sensitivity (Heywood 2001). In Victorian England children were seen as licentious beings, redeemable only through strict discipline, hence ubiquitous phrases such as 'Spare the rod, spoil the child' and 'Children should be seen and not heard'. In contemporary society, on the one hand, in accordance with developmental psychology, the functionalist socialization paradigm and the Romantic poets, we see children as immature innocents who require nurturance and protection. On the other hand, deviant and violent children, such as the ten-year-old boys who killed two-year-old Jamie Bulger and joyriding hoodie burglars, are typecast as the embodiment of evil (Franklin and Horwath 1996). Stereotyping childhood as a time of carefree innocence and protection metaphorically robs both deviant and violated children, such as those who have been sexually abused and those who commit crimes, not only of the status of being a child but of childhood itself (Kitzinger 1997). Abused children who then abuse others, violent or criminal children, or those labelled sexually or intellectually 'precocious' correspondingly create a quandary for the dominant paradigm of childhood.

Terms such as 'the protection of children' and 'children's needs' therefore require rigorous interrogation (Woodhead 1997). Whose needs are we referring to, what might be the possibly variable result of not fulfilling them, might they be met in different ways, and what vested agendas might underlie them? Our apparent concern about children's welfare has also led to middle-class children in particular being 'over-protected' by adults. This prevents them from cumulatively building up knowledge and repertoires to manage uncertain situations. Western children's spatial and geographical freedom has been restricted considerably in the late twentieth and early twenty-first century (Rosier and Kinney 2005; Cunningham 2006) because of over-elevated concerns about 'stranger danger' and road traffic accidents. These adversely shape children's own fears too (Wells 2005). Many children's activities are closely supervised by adults (Lee 2001), and it is predominantly disadvantaged working-class children who now roam and are depicted as being 'out of place' and threatening. Children have few rights that are not delegated to adults, and they are not allowed to work, vote, sit on juries or receive benefits. Paradoxically, although in the UK the age of criminal responsibility is ten, it is sixteen when children can legally consent to sex or marry with parental consent. The purchase of alcohol or cigarettes and the right to vote or marry without parental consent occurs at eighteen, although one can join the armed forces at sixteen and apply for a provisional driving licence at seventeen. The school leaving age rose from fourteen to sixteen in 1972 but now most children are not only encouraged to stay on at school until eighteen but to engage in tertiary education until the early twenties. It was only around a hundred years ago that predominantly young working-class children worked long hours as chimney sweeps or machine operatives in factories. Although we might not wish to subject children to such arduous and dangerous activities today, the cogent point is that young children were largely *competent* enough to do such jobs (Cunningham 2006).

Societal proclamations of valuing children also conflict with current statistics. These show that, in the UK, an affluent post-industrial country, 4 million children (one-third of all children) currently live in relative poverty (defined as living in families with less than 60 percent of average income) – one of the highest rates in the Western world and one subject to significant regional disparities (End Child Poverty 2012). The new sociologists of childhood draw attention to these contradictions and to associated socio-economic and structural inequities related to disability, gender, social class and 'race'/ethnicity. They also advocate studying children with children as co-researchers rather than using proxy measures (such as parents' understandings of what *their* children do, and why, and statistical studies locating children as units of family expenditure or dependants rather than creative actors (Qvortrup 1997)). A strong argument therefore could be made that we are artificially extending childhood, segregating children and adults and denying children not only an acceptable standard of living but the right to make decisions and to learn how to evaluate risks.

Agency and structure in interaction

Three areas in which children's agency in action is clearly visible are (i) sibling relationships, (ii) new technology, and (iii) consumption. Settersen's term 'agency within structures' (2007), suggesting agency is nested within and profoundly influenced by context and power, is useful here. However, agency may not only be constrained by structure but on occasions may challenge structure or prevailing social norms. This suggests we should have an awareness of traditional conceptions of power as force and threat (which directly involve the powerful forcing the less powerful to do things they would not otherwise have chosen to do) as well as more subtle and ideological understandings of power. From a Foucauldian perspective, for example, resistance is always possible and power is not monolithic and unidirectional, from top down, but is multidirectional, and the micro-politics of power require study alongside wider societal discourses and norms. Foucault therefore sees power not as a possession but as something that is observable only in its exercise, which infiltrates everything. It resides in the smallest seemingly trivial paternal pat on the back an adult gives a child or a manager an employee, in a teenager claiming they are exercising individual choice by choosing to wear a branded jacket or purchase a particular android or smart phone, and in the physical power of mighty armies.

In a study of sibling interactions with children in Scotland aged between five and seventeen, the older children managed to threaten, hoodwink, bribe or exchange resources, such as money or sweets, with younger siblings (McIntosh and Punch 2009). They often procured the best deal because of their larger size and more extensive life experience/knowledge, gained largely through evaluating their own parents' attempts to control them. However, much negotiation took place and sometimes younger siblings negotiated the best deal. Some middle children also perceived their position as advantageous, as they had both someone older to 'look up' to and learn from, who would take care of them, and someone younger whom they could 'look down' upon and cajole or threaten into doing things for them, such as tidying their room. Older children, anticipating the difficulties with babysitting younger siblings, skilfully doled out treats and allowed otherwise forbidden activities to occur in order to ensure peace reigned. Children therefore manifested as accomplished and skilled actors (Garfinkel 1967)

Children's growing competency with new technologies can often outstrip that of their parents or grandparents, problematizing the adult–child relationship of dependence. (© Lucelia Ribeiro/Flickr)

in ways that are rarely observed in adult–child relationships. In this study, age hierarchies were contested and negotiated, although birth order/age conferred some advantages and was more influential than gender.

Another example of where age hierarchies and children's agency interacted was in ethnographic research in Sweden focused on new technology, particularly computer and video games. Because children were more digitally literate than their parents, a generational digital divide occurred which children exploited (Aarsand 2007). Here, children were illuminated as both actors and as agents. They not only taught adults to use the technology but manipulated temporal disciplinary rules. In one scenario the boy wins the console game because he deliberately teaches his father how to play only during the game, not how to select prior options such as strength and speed which confer additional advantages. In another scenario, a ten-year-old boy deflects a linear clock time request that he finishes the game now and goes to bed by arguing he has a 'few more things' to do before he can finish. His grandfather, confused by what 'a few things' might mean in clock time, agrees, although his grandmother correctly interprets the deception.

Children's consumption not only illuminates their skills in persuading parents to buy expensive items through 'pester power' and subtler persuasion but also demonstrates their simultaneous manipulation by the market, thereby again illustrating 'agency within structures' (Settersen 2009). Consuming within the context of an arguably all-pervasive global capitalism sets the 'new sociology' ideal-type image of the agentic child against the not-yet-complete, still-at-risk child who can be manipulated. Children are intensively researched by corporate capitalism, which must get them to appeal to adults to purchase the goods they desire (Mintel 2003). Boden's research, utilizing focus groups with parents and children and ethnographic work, focuses on clothing consumption. She shows agency is exercised by children but simultaneously influenced by nuanced marketing strategies, which skilfully manoeuvre 'wants' into essential 'needs' by linking them to identity, belonging, peer acceptance and respect. Parents understood how consumer culture pervaded their children's thoughts and were concerned about cost, a label culture and age appropriateness, such as the skimpy sexualized clothing marketed to prepubescent girls. However, market power not only impacted on children's peer relations but tapped into parental anxiety about their own comparative social standing, sometimes leading to conspicuous proxy compensation for their own childhood disadvantage. Parents did, despite this, try (mostly unsuccessfully) to impart to their children some perspective to counter 'a commercial culture of abundance, choice and instant gratification' (Boden 2006: 5). Children under eleven were more likely just to ask for the desired clothing, whereas older children deployed flexible and subtle persuasion strategies. They were also very knowledgeable about brands and could easily discuss why some were ranked higher and were 'cooler' than others and therefore more desirable and status enhancing.

This section therefore has briefly analysed the sociology of childhood literature within the context of a life course perspective, focusing on three key areas to examine the agency/structure or micro/macro debate – new technology, sibling relationships and clothing consumption. The main conclusion drawn is that, although children may be creative, accomplished actors, they operate within the constraints of considerable adult/child power, divisive social structures and an all-pervasive and inegalitarian global corporate capitalism which contributes to deep-rooted cultural and socio-economic disparities through manufacturing dynamic, neversated 'needs' and desires.

SEMINAR QUESTIONS

1 Are current beliefs and practices in relation to children protective, disabling or empowering?
2 Discuss the different ways in which children have been stereotyped and represented in different cultures and time periods and the impact this may have had on their treatment and self-perceptions.
3 In this section, computer games, sibling interactions and clothing consumption were used as exemplars of the interplay between structure and agency. What other examples can you think of where children are both constrained by structure but exercise choice and show initiative?

FERAL YOUTH AND FOREVER EMERGING ADULTHOOD

Demonized or demonic youth?

Those aged from about the mid-teens to the mid-twenties will be the focus here. Youth is perceived sociologically as a blurred, transitional, but often demonized period, set between the mythical polarities of dependence/childhood and independence/adulthood. Public understandings, however, have been greatly influenced by ongoing psychological notions of adolescence as a universal time of 'biologically preordained' storm and stress, influenced by Hall's work at the turn of the century (Hall 1904). Later psychologists strongly contested Hall's claims of universal adolescent turbulence (e.g., Coleman and Hendry 1999; Arnett 1999; Herbert 2008). Others questioned the validity of adolescence as a developmental stage at all because of its unclear biological (pubertal) beginning and even less clear social (rights and responsibility) end, but Hall's representations have persisted and remain influential (Kelly 2003; Stephen and Squires 2004).

Media representations have consequently depicted young people as feral, amoral and out of control, 'a risk', or alternatively vulnerable, 'at risk' – suggesting individualized, often punitive responses and youth rarely being represented as competent, altruistic and successful (Bolzan 2005). 'Contemporary moral panics about youth [therefore] centre around young people's sexual behaviour, "binge drinking" and drug consumption, young people being represented as irresponsible, disrespectful to adults, easily addicted and involved in ever increasing street violence and unsafe sex while intoxicated' (Green 2010: 106). However, girls are seen as more at risk sexually (Jackson and Tinkler 2007) and working-class and disadvantaged white and black young men as more threatening than 'respectable' white middle-class males (Griffin 2001). Some disadvantaged young men's lives are so poverty-stricken and meaningless that they admittedly retreat into consuming much alcohol and habitually engage in alcohol-driven rituals of petty violence (Winlow and Hall 2006). Alternatively, they combine legitimate but alienating, poorly paid, insecure jobs with illicit entrepreneurial enterprises, such as selling drugs or unlicensed alcohol and cigarettes (McAuley 2007). However, such behaviour needs to be understood within its socio-historical context.

BOX 4.4 THE 2011 RIOTS

The 2011 August riots took place in a number of British cities, during which there was not only violence and killing but millions of pounds' worth of property was damaged and goods were stolen. Right-wing politicians attributed the rioters' actions to individualized greed, 'broken communities' or 'poor parenting', whereas left-wing explanations conceded the part played by poverty but still held individuals responsible.

Birch and Allen (2011) analysed opinion polls and survey and focus group data relating to the riots, concluding they were integrally linked to *both* socio-economic *and* personal deprivation, those taking part constituting largely a young disenfranchised underclass (McKee and Raine 2011). Complex links emerge between relative deprivation and social unrest when expectations and reality diverge during an economic downturn occurring after sustained relative prosperity (Gurr 1970), as befits the contemporary UK situation. Young people were particularly vulnerable because of increasing unemployment and cuts in youth services, leading to them becoming poor, unoccupied and alienated, and from May 2010 the poor lost far more income proportionally than did the rich.

When these events are contextualized within ongoing scandals concerning the moral degeneracy of the rich and powerful, pertinent from 2008 onwards (when the financial crisis coincided with reports of bankers' monumental bonuses, the MPs' tax expenses scandals and tax evasion by the rich), Birch and Allen's research shows trust in the political realm diminishes. This leads to the most disadvantaged (even if they are unable to articulate this clearly) feeling that, if democratically elected accountable politicians fail to curb others' corruption and may even benefit from it, then they may also 'help themselves'.

Although this contemporary example comes at the beginning of the section, other literature will be examined which deepens understandings both of why the riots occurred and of social class divisions.

Historical changes and social class divisions

Traditionally three important transitions characterized the journey to adulthood (Coles 1995):

1 from full-time education to full-time work;
2 from family of origin to family of destination; and
3 from residing in the family home to independent living.

Recurrent recessions, the transfer of both industrial and much service-sector work to the cheaper developing countries, technology replacing many labour-intensive jobs, the expansion of higher education, and significant changes in living arrangements have, however, impacted on the significance and formation of these transitions. In the 1970s the UK was a labour-intensive, industrialized society with full employment. Since then, the quantity, quality and types of jobs available for young people have declined. Even posts disproportionately occupied by graduates are often part-time, are poorly paid and have no career structure. In 2012 a major media scandal erupted. Hugely profitable multinational companies (MNCs), such as Tesco supermarkets, were, in conjunction with the government, exposed as forcing young people receiving jobseekers' allowance to work thirty hours a week for up to two months doing menial work with no additional benefits or employment guarantees (Malik, Wintour and Ball 2012). Had protests not forced the government to rethink, might predominantly working-class young people's exploited labour and taxpayer-funded benefits continue to have been used to generate profits for MNCs?

These young people's transitions are strongly influenced by educational achievement and opportunity, which, in turn, continue to be closely related to class of origin. Good GCSE and A-level passes, furthermore, are still disproportionately gained by students from affluent families (Curtis 2008; Shepherd 2009) who disproportionately attend prestigious universities, benefiting from parental financial, practical and moral support and the mobilization of private schools, tutors and social networking to ensure maximum educational advantage (Reay 2005). Putnam's (2000) *bridging capital*, which draws on outward-looking, heterogeneous and geographically differentiated resources to 'get ahead' rather than 'get by', also pertains more to middle-class youth. Working-class youth depend more on inward-looking *bonding capital* (which results in people socializing predominantly with those from a similar background). They are more likely to leave school at the minimum age and converge in the less prestigious post-1992 universities (Davis 2010). In one study, a young black man turned down a sports degree scholarship at a top university, attending his local college instead because he feared leaving his familiar working-class neighbourhood. Another young woman, with excellent A-level grades, studied nursing locally because she was a single parent and neither she nor her family had higher aspirations (Holland, Reynolds and Weller 2007). Even after university, unpaid internships, offering valuable networks and work experience, are occupied predominantly by middle- and upper-class young people.

Transitions into and markers of adulthood

Accompanying the de-standardization thesis, many claims now centre on the changing nature of young adulthood. Arnett (2000, 2004) posited a new developmental stage, taking place between the late teens and the mid-twenties, which he named *emerging adulthood*. Arnett claimed this stage was characterized by extended education, greater career and identity exploration, and postponing family formation. Despite valid criticism of Arnett's neglect of structural inequalities (e.g., Bynner 2005), much US and European research shows many young people stay in education longer than in previous generations and delay marriage, childbearing and career trajectories (Buchman and Kriesi 2011; Andrew et al. 2007; Macmillan 2007). There are, however, significant cross-national heterogeneities, often influenced by different cultural norms and welfare regimes, as shown in figure 4.2. In the social-democratic Nordic countries, where benefits are universalistic and often generous, encouraging autonomous behaviour, young adults leave home at earlier ages than in such neoliberal countries as the UK, where minimalist means-tested benefits predominate. The conservative European welfare regimes, such as in Spain and Greece, channel benefits and status through the family; often leaving home occurs later there because of this and cultural norms (Billari and Liefbroer 2010).

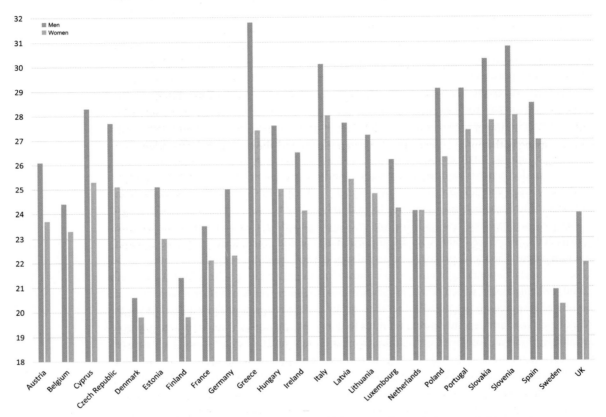

Figure 4.2 Age by which 50 percent of all young people are living away from their parental home, by sex, 2007

Source: Compiled with data from Iacovou and Skew (2010).

The young people in Arnett's research (2000, 2004) were ambivalent about whether they perceived themselves as adults, viewing adulthood more in terms of mature behaviour than predefined historical markers such as a wage packet. Other research shows many young people regard personal characteristics as crucial but still judge adulthood according to conventional markers (e.g., Molgat 2007). Shanahan, Porfeli and Mortimer (2005) found those living independently who were married and had become parents were twice as likely to regard themselves as adults as others who had not experienced all three transitions and that financial independence was an important subjective marker too. In another US focus-group study of sixty-one college students and graduates, financial independence, responsibility for oneself and others, giving advice, and undertaking parenthood and intimate relationships with maturity were crucial. University was also an important conduit to adulthood, allowing experimentation with different roles and experiences (Andrew et al. 2007). Hartmann and Swartz's (2007) interviewees, likewise, conceived of adulthood as multidimensional, including roles, personal qualities, transitions, agency and subjectivity. Similarly, longitudinal English research with one hundred fifteen- to 24-year-olds uncovered temporally shifting understandings of adulthood. Among these were chronological age, legal rights and responsibilities, completing education and occupying a full-time job, alongside personal characteristics such as caring for others and exercising autonomy (Holland, Reynolds and Weller 2007).

Blatterer's (2007) research with young Australian men questions the traditional markers of adulthood and contests negative views of young people as increasingly infantile, interested only in playing computer games and reading *Harry Potter* (e.g., Furedi 2003; Blacker 2006; Collinson 2009). Blatterer argues for new conceptions of adulthood to be forged that accommodate the increasing occupational fragmentation and financial insecurity confronted by contemporary young people. He may be right, but a postponement of adulthood does seem to be occurring with some young adults that extends over and above financial dependence on parents and living at home for longer periods. For some years there have been media reports of 'helicopter parenting' emanating from universities or employers (Hilpern 2008a, 2008b). These often middle-class parents are arguably over-involved with their adult children's education, relationships and employment, intervening when their children receive poor university grades and controlling and arranging their bank accounts and job interviews. Another variant, black hawk parents, engage in unethical and illegal activity, including bribery, threats and plagiarism, to further their children's progress (Macleod 2008; Gumbel 2011).

New technology

Today's youth inhabit a society where screen-based communication, game-playing and information access and exchange prevail, with the rise of social-oriented technologies such as blogs, wikis and social networking sites, including Facebook, Bebo and Twitter. These allow friendships to be made and remade on the internet and people to publicize their activities and share personal news, information and photos with selected others. When first developed in the 1980s, mobile phones were heavy, brick-sized and prohibitively expensive, generally exclusive to rich businessmen. They are now like a customized umbilical cord for many young people (Williams and Williams 2005; Green and Singleton 2007) and, aside from being used for texting and phone calls, smart and android phones enable email and internet access and downloading and playing apps, music and films. Communication mediums are now more diverse, with synchronous communication possible. Games are played with people on other continents, and computer-mediated relationships are often initiated through internet dating websites and continued through email contact and Skype before any face-to-face meeting occurs (Chayko 2002; Hardey 2002).

This technology has therefore changed the way young adults socialize, search for romantic relationships, communicate, and structure their lives, although a class-based digital divide still exists. While middle-class youth use the internet more to access information and enhance their social, education and financial capital, working-class young people use it more for entertainment and socializing (Bonnaert and Vettenburg 2011). Views are also divided between cyber-optimists and cyber-pessimists as to whether the new 'social' technology is a good thing, but there are clearly both disadvantages and advantages (Kraut et al. 1998; Pallet, Roberts and Dunbar 2011). Teenage girls report feeling more confident with mobile phones in unfamiliar locations (Foley, Holzman and Wearing 2007), but are they actually safer? Those suffering social anxiety report social networking sites provide a less anxiety-provoking environment for communication (Pierce 2009), but could this merely be avoiding confronting their difficulties as it does not enhance social communication offline? Furthermore, many young people have difficulty judging the validity of internet sources, and information overload and confusion between propaganda and reputable research may ensue. Socially disadvantaged young people are also more at risk of being duped and bullied on the internet and subjected to aggressive online sexual solicitation (Wells and Mitchell 2008). This can be more threatening and insidious than face-to-face bullying because the harassers often retain anonymity. 'Internet trolls', for example, deliberately post inflammatory messages – 'flaming' – on online discussion or bereavement tribute sites, but are rarely identified and punished.

Agency, structure, autonomy and changes in the teenage and young adulthood years

The literature analysed above suggests that significant global, socio-economic and political changes have fundamentally changed the nature, experience and markers of youth and young adulthood, with both becoming less linear and more revisable. Relationships have diversified, and in some cases romance and relationships have even become separated from sex (England, Schafer and Fogarty 2007) – hence the contemporary terms 'fuck buddies' and 'friends with benefits'. The job market is characterized by fragmentation and insecurity and is particularly precarious for those least qualified. With the demise of state support for university attendance, young people often depend on their parents and live at home for longer, except for the most disadvantaged – dispossessed individuals leaving care and deprived working-class youth – whose transitions are more risky and who are likely to live independently and reproduce earlier (Webster et al. 2004; Osgood et al. 2005). Social divisions, therefore, appear highly relevant to the life chances, behaviour and educational and occupational opportunities of young adults, although social class has been the main emphasis in this section. Many young people seem unaware that 'choice biographies' are not available equally to everyone (Schwartz 2004). Although most practise individual reflexivity (the ability to think through and consider one's actions and choices and their potential consequences), some have more skills and resources to exercise it successfully (Hendry, Kloep and Olsson 1998; Threadgold 2011).

SEMINAR QUESTIONS

1   Are teenagers always 'naturally' rebellious and impetuous?
2   Are the current protracted transitions to adulthood experienced by many young people today beneficial and, if so, for whom?
3   How might 'race'/ethnicity, religion or sexuality impact upon one's experience of young adulthood?
4   Do young adults today have more choices than previous generations about whom they live with, where they live and what jobs they do?

MIDLIFE: CRISIS, STAGNATION OR MAGICAL TRANSFORMATION?

Midlife, the least researched age span, encompasses the years between forty and sixty-five. Some midlifers engage in activities previously associated with younger age groups, such as childbearing, affected by new reproductive technology, reconstituted families and dual-career couples delaying having a family. Affluent midlifers may also retire, an activity associated more with old age. So, what typifies midlife and are any ascertainable characteristics universal features? Psychologists have found moderate physical senescence, alongside peaking in one's confidence and career (Green 2010). Sociology, however, has had little to say, although some research exists on the Boomers, now middle-aged or entering early old age. Lay images of the midlife crisis were initially associated with unattractive depictions of 1950s 'empty nest' females, 'left on the shelf' spinsters and paunchy middle-aged men driving fast sports cars and pursuing younger females. The film *Hall Pass* (2011) revolves around two family men given licence by their exasperated wives to do whatever they want over one week, including sleeping with other women, the humour deriving from the humiliations befalling them when they unsuccessfully attempt to relive their youth. The 'empty nest' 1950s full-time housewife, depicted as bereft and role-redundant after her children have left, if ever relevant is less so today, since bringing up children is rarely women's sole occupation and women have much more control and choice over fertility than ever before. New terms such as 'the swollen nest' and the 'pivot' or 'sandwich' generation, however, do suggest that midlifers experience significant stress when working and supporting both dependent young and adult children and elderly parents, thereby challenging lay beliefs that claim midlife is a relatively sedentary period.

Many methodological problems are associated with assessing if the midlife crisis is an urban myth, a universal phenomenon, or culture, period, cohort, class or gender specific. The term 'midlife crisis' is difficult to define and measure but suggests not only significant re-evaluation of life's meaning and structure but also considerable distress. Some commentators in the 1980s claimed, according to different indicators and measures, that the midlife crisis did not exist. Recent rigorous cross-national statistical research, however, shows that, in most European countries, overall wellbeing dips during midlife (between the ages of forty-two and fifty-eight) (Blanchflower and Oswald 2009), although this does not necessarily signify a midlife crisis. Some change during midlife does seem inevitable, including acknowledging our restricted possibilities and impending mortality, and we tend to shift focus from time lived to time left to live (Jacques 1965). Strenger (2009) proposes that a midpoint between accepting our limitations, shaped by age, past choices and circumstances (without succumbing to either 'happy' or 'discontented' stagnation), and capitalizing on our strengths is the best way to tackle midlife. However, midlife is often seen as a time where we confront work, family pressures and ageist narratives, which fetishize youth. The following subsections will therefore deal with ageing, self-perception and body image and then issues during midlife associated with work, family and lifestyle, briefly examining the cumulative advantage/disadvantage (CAD) hypothesis.

Ageing, self-perception and body image

Biggs (1999) views the key task in midlife as negotiating secure subjectivity in the face of an age-hostile culture where the progressively ageing body may be experienced as a cage.

Gullette's (2008) radical social constructionist analysis clearly illuminates our cultural terrorization into ageing as a decline narrative, which, taken to its ultimate conclusion, suggests that older people are a burden and have a duty to die. *The mask of ageing* relates to how ageing individuals often perform Cartesian mind/body dualism, thus separating out body from mind and privileging the mind. Midlifers and older people therefore often dis-identify with their external mirror image, which shows wrinkles, grey hair and lost teeth, and embrace a youthful psychic identity as more genuine (Featherstone and Hepworth 1994). Such behaviour occurs within a sexist society that breeds a precocious, endemic dread of ageing and paranoiac self-surveillance, to the extent that even teenage girls invest in anti-ageing products (Gullette 2008). A cross-over can occur in women as young as twenty-five, where they want to be seen as younger than their chronological age (Galambos, Turner and Tilton-Weaver 2005). The middle-aged female body is particularly marked by ambiguity and lack (Schwaiger 2006) because the gendered attributes valued most in women, such as 'youthful' beauty and fertility, decline. Conversely, those qualities most prized traditionally in men, such as power, status and financial acumen, often accrue, although, for men, old age rather than middle age may be more precarious on account of a considerable loss of autonomy and status.

In one American study, the younger people felt subjectively in comparison to their actual chronological age, the more likely they were to see middle age beginning and ending later. Women were disproportionately more likely both to feel younger and to judge middle age as starting and ending later than men, possibly because age devalues women so much. Those who felt older were additionally more likely to foresee a foreshortened life span (Toothman and Barrett 2011). In the USA, where minimal state support for the elderly is available and status is linked to work and money, more people reported feeling younger than in countries which proffered more generous welfare provision (Westerhof, Barrett and Steverink 2003). In a US qualitative interview study of successful career women, all feared age discrimination and reproduced the master narrative of decline in their accounts. Some tried to resist by acting younger or were seriously considering plastic surgery. Others found it liberating to be no longer considered sex objects and felt they were taken more seriously at work (Trethewey 2001). Anti-ageing products and cosmetic surgery are consequently and rather unsurprisingly 'big business' for middle-aged women. Unfortunately for those who 'buy into' them, they do not re-create a youthful appearance but rather invoke a haunting apparition of 'stretched middle age'. Botox paralyses the facial muscles, restricting open emotional expression, and most anti-ageing surgery involves pulling the skin back, creating an immobile doll-like demeanour (Cooke 2008). Botox can also be conceptualized as a *pharmakon*, which 'cures' old age socially as it 'poisons' physically. The 2005 figures for cosmetic plastic surgeons found anti-ageing procedures were the most popular after breast augmentation for women, but men conversely tended to change a feature with which they had always been unhappy (Mackay 2006).

During midlife one's senses and bodily fitness decline more noticeably. This is poignant for manual workers, competing for ever-decreasing jobs against fitter, younger men (Gilbert and Constantine 2005). Athletes also possess a heightened awareness of their declining prowess but respond in ambivalent and contradictory ways (Partington et al. 2005; Tulle 2008). Boomers often report concern with bodily maintenance and physical health, some taking up fitness regimes which lapsed during young adulthood or doing sport with their children (Biggs et al. 2007). Recent research has shown that Boomers are more likely than young adults to drink alcohol every day (Burn-Murdoch 2012) and that their drug use has increased

(Laurance 2012). This might suggest greater interest in the aesthetic aspects of bodily preservation rather than overall health, indicate the entrenched acceptability of habitual drinking and drug use for this generation, or be a form of stress management. However, other research has conversely shown women's weight loss and bodily preservation strategies become healthier as they traverse midlife (Johnston, Reilly and Kremer 2004).

Although old age has been associated with muted colours and plainer ampler clothing, suggesting increasing desexualization and toning down – women in particular risk negative labelling as 'mutton dressed as lamb' (Fairhurst 1998; Twigg 2007) – the current Baby Boomer generation is the first to embrace a consumption-saturated, more youthful, individualist and lifestyle-oriented society (Bywater 2006). They largely dis-identify with older generations, mostly analogizing their outlook and lifestyle to those younger than themselves (Frith 2004; Harkin and Huber 2004; Gilleard and Higgs 2007). In a UK study of first-wave Baby Boomers (1945–55), alongside some acceptance of the 'mature self', midlifers drew similarities between their and their children's lives (Biggs et al. 2007). They conceded a less slavish following of fashion and more stable discerning tastes than when young, although a closure of age tastes sometimes occurred, with some midlife females reporting they and their daughter might shop together or swap clothes. Others reported they would look ridiculous in their daughter's clothes, but both sexes stressed they would not dress like 'fuddy duddies' as their parents had.

Work, finance, family and lifestyle

Media and political coverage has often depicted midlifers and older people as extravagantly plundering their children's inheritances and wantonly becoming an increasing liability to younger generations where future social care and health costs are concerned (e.g., Glasgow 2003; Robine, Michel and Herrmann 2007; Willetts 2010). Counter-claims represent midlifers as a pressurized generation, desperately trying to support younger and older generations (Hill 2007; Bennett 2008) and showing more concern with social justice and reform than any cohort or generation since (Harkin 2006) – but what evidence supports either of these claims?

Considerable research has documented midlifers' multifaceted commitment to younger and older generations (Brannen 2003; Grundy 2005; Hillcoat-Nalletamby and Dharmalingam 2003). Midlife could also be more traumatic for women because of the dual burden of work and familial caring responsibilities, and some suffer stress-related sleep disorders (Hislop and Arber 2003; Chatzitheochari and Arber 2009). Much care work is done unpaid by families and neighbours, predominantly midlife females: one study estimated over 2 million out of 6 million informal carers were over fifty (Buckner and Yeandle 2007). One German ageing study, using a narrow definition of the sandwich generation, argues that midlife multiple-role overload is a rare phenomenon, particularly as both older and younger generations may offer as well as need support from midlifers (Kunemund 2006), although even supporting one generation of relatives may be highly stressful. Midlife working females caring for elderly relatives, for example, documented high stress levels and reported their employers as being unsympathetic and unaccommodating (Ward 2005), although more work and welfare support and flexibility is available in the Nordic social democratic welfare regimes (Gornick and Meyers 2003; Anxo and Boulin 2006). Changing family structures, which are shifting from a pyramidal shape to a beanpole structure, with more generations of kin alive but increasingly smaller numbers in the younger generations, also means there are now fewer family members available to offer informal care to older generations, particularly as most women now undertake paid work. The widespread dissolution, fragmentation and reconstitution of families also produce more complex, unstable relationships (Settersen 2007). A middle-aged woman whose marriage has endured may, for instance, be more likely to care for her mother-in-law than a newly married woman or a divorced ex-daughter-in-law.

Midlifers are an increasingly pressurized generation, caught between responsibilities for both younger and older generations. (© Blend_Images/iStock)

BOX 4.5 ITALIAN MIDLIFERS

In the face of recurrent economic recessions and increasing employment and relationship insecurity, one qualitative Italian study of thirty, mostly married people aged fifty-five to sixty-five showed their myriad commitment to both their children and older generations financially, emotionally and practically (Facchini and Rampazi 2009). At the same time, in the face of biographical uncertainty, these midlifers negotiated new lifestyles which embraced innovative and traditional perspectives, reflecting both the standardization and de-standardization perspectives. Some respondents did voluntary work or took up new interests or resumed those abandoned in their youth. Others reported starting working again to support their children financially, although they would have preferred to retire.

Boomers were the first generation to experience welfare states, now being eroded in Europe with the rise of global capitalism, neoliberal governments, and a financial squeeze as a result of recessions, greater longevity, earlier retirements and the expansion of higher education (Frericks, Harvey and Maier 2010). Little evidence, however, suggests that Boomers exhibit an irresponsible attitude to money. Many focus on supporting their children, saving for retirement and not accruing debt (a trait they share with the older generations), in stark comparison to younger generations. Many would also like to retire early but, because of the collapse of many pension schemes or their declining value, are unable to do so (Glasgow 2003). In comparison, more affluent Boomers form a prime market for expensive cars, motorbikes, mobile phones and audiovisual systems (Kotarba 2005). A compression of morbidity is also evident with today's older people, which relates not just to greater longevity but to a shorter, less debilitating period of ill heath before death (Settersen 2007). This suggests that projected health and social care costs for midlifers may have been overstated, although poverty and lower social class have significant cumulative mal-effects on health in both middle and old age (Blane, Netuvelli and Bartley 2007). Vincent (2003) also argues that the media and politicians, heavily influenced by capitalist interests, have amplified 'the problem' of social and health care for the elderly so much that it has caused a moral panic which could pit generations against one another.

For those who choose or have no choice economically but to work in middle and old age, employment ageism becomes an unwelcome barrier and a significant challenge. A life-course longitudinal panel study in the USA involving 7,225 working women, followed between 1972 and 1989, found perceived age discrimination was high in the twenties, dropped in the thirties but then peaked in the fifties, factors exacerbated by high unemployment, economic restructuring and global pressures (Roscigno et al. 2007). In the USA and the UK, those between their forties and sixties (even if age discrimination has not caused their initial job loss) struggle to find jobs and often end up underemployed, with lower wages, or long-term unemployed (Allen 2012). There is also a link with high death rates for those in the USA between the ages of fifty-five and sixty-four without heath insurance (Gullette 2011). In England statistics show that almost 25 percent of the 400,000 people unemployed for more than two years in 2011 were over fifty. Women were disproportionately affected because of their locations in more part-time jobs (agediscrimination.info 2011; Allen 2012). The potent intersection of age and sex discrimination, for which higher social class status and full-time work fails to compensate, is also clear when observing a succession of female panel-show hosts and newsreaders being unceremoniously 'fired' after reaching a certain age. This stands in stark contrast to midlife men, who are often seen as wise and distinguished and rarely viewed as 'eye candy' or dismissed from media jobs because of their age or ageing appearance (L. Holmwood 2007; Green 2010; Plunkett 2012). Those around fifty undertaking unskilled or semi-skilled work are particularly vulnerable to downward occupational mobility influenced by explicit and implicitly ageist stereotypes, often falsely justified on the basis of corporate costs (Roscigno et al. 2007). This ageist discrimination, sometimes entwined with sexism, seems ironic, as those between forty and sixty-eight outperform those of other ages on a range of cognitive skills important in work situations, among them emotion management and the ability to generate concrete solutions to intricate complex problems, to draw connections, and to appreciate and accommodate context, subtlety and ambiguity (Strauch 2010). Other research shows that a decision-making peak in financial and political matters occurs in midlife (Cohen 2012).

Cumulative (dis)advantage (CAD)

CAD describes a process with many direct and indirect mechanisms at the individual, cultural and structural level. It results in cohorts becoming increasingly heterogeneous and unequal in various aspects, such as health, educational and occupational attainment and wealth and pension rights, as they age across the life course. Although little research has been conducted on the intersection between midlife and social divisions, Phillipson (2007: 8) claims the Boomer generation is 'likely to carry forward cumulative processes of advantage and disadvantage, with distinctive class, ethnic and gender divisions being maintained'. The CAD hypothesis therefore focuses on the additive nature of (dis)advantage, resulting in inequalities at the beginning of life having an increasingly greater effect the more or the longer they are experienced, the worse they are and the more they intersect and co-occur, with institutions having a significant effect. 'Structural or institutional arrangements [therefore] operate to stratify cohorts as they allocate differential opportunities for the accumulation of value and reward . . . [and] the temporal characteristics of individuals' behaviours and attainments across these institutional domains have additional influence' (O'Rand 1996: 230).

BOX 4.6 CAD CASE STUDIES – FROM CHILDHOOD TO MIDDLE AGE

The Whitehall II Study, which tracked 10,309 civil servants of different grades aged between thirty-five and fifty-five from 1985 onwards, when the study commenced, until the present day found low socio-economic positions, measured at three life course points, resulted in significantly increased risks for coronary heart disease (CHD), poor physical functioning for both sexes, and poor mental functioning for men (Singh-Manoux et al. 2004). Even after controlling for those in the lower grades being more likely to have high blood pressure, to smoke, and to have less leisure time and lower weight-to-height ratio, they still had more CHD risk factors, suggesting stress and social status were also important (Marmot 2004).

Bäckman and Nilsson (2011) used a Swedish cohort study, following 14,294 individuals from birth (1953) to age forty-eight (2001). Those suffering multiple family problems and persistent poverty throughout the life course were at highest risk of being excluded from paid work and of receiving welfare benefits in midlife, particularly in times of economic recession.

Analysing data from the British National Child Development Study, Jackson (2010) also detected strong links between child health, social class, mother's health behaviours, educational disadvantage and adult occupational qualifications in mid-adulthood. Those from the poorest socio-economic backgrounds, in persistent poor health, were at highest risk of educational disadvantage and hence of lower midlife occupational qualifications.

In addition, an American study, utilizing data from the National Longitudinal Study of Youth, found that educational disadvantages in youth, exacerbated by class inequalities, were linked to accumulating educational and health disadvantages by midlife (Walsemann, Geronimus and Gee 2008).

Different welfare-state regimes, however, can mediate. Anglo-Saxon neoliberal welfare regimes such as in the USA, Australia and the UK, with minimal welfare benefits and means-testing, are the least successful at counteracting the demoralizing effects of poverty, but the more generous Nordic and Bismarckian (Germanic) regimes are more successful not only at preventing long-term and short-term poverty but sometimes in reversing its effects (Levecque et al. 2011).

In examining midlife, particularly in relation to the Boomers, some features seem to characterize the period, such as introspection, stocktaking and recognizing how our past experiences and limited time mean no magical transformations are likely. However, if economic recessions and cumulative disadvantage do not intervene, midlife may also be a time of competence and confidence. Midlife appears stressful for many because of competing, often cross-generational demands for resources such as time and money. Disadvantages and stressors throughout the life course additionally begin to have a significant cumulative effect by midlife. Boomers seem more fixated on lifestyle, leisure and 'performing' youthfulness than previous generations. Furthermore, there is no clear evidence that a midlife crisis is a universal phenomenon and even less evidence for the universality of the empty nest housewife or sandwich-generation phenomena. These phenomena seem strongly linked to historical points in time, linked lives, and cohort and period effects (life course ideas discussed in the first section of the chapter).

Brief notes on old age

Although old age is not covered in detail here, it is still hugely important but, as with the other stages, immensely variable and ragged around its boundaries. Therefore, this section will end by briefly noting some pertinent characteristics associated with contemporary old age.

Old age today in most Western nations generally commences around the age of sixty-five, with the oldest humans recorded as living until about 120. It is the norm rather than the exception now for people in the UK to survive until at least young old age in comparison to over 100 years ago and the situation with some poorer countries today. This is largely because of better nutrition and environmental conditions, greater control over infectious diseases and fertility, and less likelihood of females or their offspring dying during childbirth. The large number of people surviving well into old age, with average life expectancy now being calculated at around seventy-seven years for men and eighty-five years for women (ONS 2008), has resulted in old age being broken down into two subdivisions. The young old, or *the third age*, extends from about sixty-five to eighty or eighty-five years of age. Most third-agers enjoy good health and wellbeing and relatively high levels of social engagement, although clearly one's past life trajectory and concepts such as CAD are important. The *fourth age* of the oldest old pertains to those over eighty or eighty-five who possess some unique demographic features. There are more women in this subdivision, levels of social engagement are lower, and the likelihood of suffering from a serious disability or of becoming significantly depressed rise sharply. Consequently, this group are more likely to be institutionalized and consume significantly more health and social care resources than the young old.

The over eighties are the fastest growing population group in the UK, with the Audit Commission (2008) estimating that they will almost double in size between 2009 and 2029, from 2.4 million to 4.3 million. Older people are also subject to both paternalistic ageism (others making decisions or doing things for them because of 'kindly' but inaccurate assumptions they are not capable) and more aggressive or discriminatory individualized or institutionalized ageism. This occurs, for example, in relation to the provision of substandard health care for the elderly, or when the old are spuriously represented as a demographic time bomb, greedily devouring all the nation's finances and resources because of their health and care needs. These forms of ageism fail to consider the contribution older people have already made to society, with many still significantly contributing via unpaid or paid work or caring for younger or older family members. And, as Vincent has previously argued, this irresponsible but well-targeted scaremongering in relation to older people needs to be seen in the context of sectional financial interests which have socially constructed a moral panic for their own benefit.

SEMINAR QUESTIONS

1 Why might some commentators depict the Baby Boomers as a selfish generation and how realistic is this representation?
2 Discuss why middle age might be a particularly stressful time for women today.
3 Does the midlife crisis exist?
4 Discuss different forms of ageism in respect of older people and evaluate their potential impact on both older people themselves and the wider society.

CONCLUSION

This chapter has hopefully offered an enticing invitation to the sociology of the life course, a perspective relatively neglected in UK sociology. It initially explained focal influences, defining key terminology and themes and discussing common research methodology. Different attributions of age were then explored alongside the effects of ageism, age segregation, age grading and age staging, which strongly influence lay perceptions and institutional structures. The latter part of the chapter analysed three broadly drawn age categories – childhood, youth merging into early young adulthood and middle age – in order to show how age and age stages are socially constructed and historically and culturally influenced. A specific emphasis was placed on the agency/structure debate (particularly in the section on childhood) and the intersection of age or generation with other social divisions (particularly social class in the section on youth and gender in the section on midlife). It is therefore hoped that students will not only find this chapter thought-provoking and relevant to their own lives but will be spurred on to integrate concepts of age and the life course and associated social divisions with/into whatever area of sociology they are currently studying.

SEMINAR QUESTIONS

1 In what ways does life course sociology help us to appreciate the complex interplay between agency and structure over time?
2 Discuss the usefulness of the concept of cumulative advantage/disadvantage and elaborate on how it might contribute to understanding the life course trajectories of two very different groups, such as those brought up in state care and those who had a public/private-school education.
3 How might life course sociology enhance our knowledge about intergenerational relationships and inequalities?

FURTHER READING

▶ Green, L. (2010) *Understanding the Life Course: Sociological and Psychological Perspectives* (Polity). A clearly written introductory textbook which contrasts and compares psychological and sociological theory and research on the life course.

▶ Phillipson, C. (2013) *Ageing* (Polity). An accessible and contemporary text, written by one of Britain's leading sociologists of age, which examines different understandings of ageing and their impact, setting these within the context of a rapidly aging society.

▶ Settersten, R. A. (ed.) (2003) *Invitation to the Life Course: Towards an Understanding of Later Life* (Bayville). Although it is focused more on later life as opposed to the early life course and is written from a US perspective, many of the concepts and ideas it draws upon are relevant and transferable to a UK context.

▶ *Advances in Life Course Research.* An international and multi-disciplinary journal concerned with life course theory and research. It is a wide-ranging and up-to-date resource for students and academics interested in the life course, and the quality of the articles within it is mostly excellent.

Section B
Opportunities and Inequalities

Section B follows on from the opening section because it too has a strong (though not exclusive) emphasis on inequalities and social divisions. Poverty, which is discussed in chapter 8, for example, is clearly very closely related to inequality, and the difference between those who are in poverty and those who are not is a form of social division. Social divisions and inequalities are often manifested through health and illness, education, and work or unemployment. Social divisions based on class, gender, ethnicity, sexuality and age are all significant in the topics covered by the chapters in this section, and there is coverage of at least some of these social divisions in all of them. For example, Tim Strangleman (chapter 5) examines changes in opportunities for gaining employment, particularly secure and well-paid employment, for workers with different skills. Graham and Sasha Scambler (chapter 6) consider changing patterns of mortality and morbidity particularly in relation to socio-economic groups. Rob Moore (chapter 7) discusses the complex relationships between class, gender, ethnicity and educational attainment, and Mary Daly (chapter 8) examines the relationship between social class, welfare and poverty.

The section is broadly concerned with life chances – the opportunity to obtain socially desirable outcomes and avoid undesirable ones. Avoiding poverty is an obvious example, but there is also a recognition that wellbeing involves much more than simply material success. Thus Daly discusses broader conceptions of deprivation and social inclusion/exclusion. Moore is concerned with more than the marketability of qualifications and concludes that education can enrich individuals' lives by 'opening up new realms of possibility as people'. Graham and Sasha Scambler discuss how biomedical definitions of health can have a negative impact on the wellbeing of some social groups, and they have been challenged not just by disability activists but also by 'new' social and health movements pressing for a demedicalization of society. Similarly, Strangleman is just as concerned with the experience of work, autonomy and control, and the work–life balance as with issues such as pay and unemployment. Of course, none of these differences in life chances can be understood simply in relation to any one of the topics examined in these chapters – there are strong interrelationships between them. For example, Graham and Sasha Scambler examine how material and psychosocial factors are connected to work and these in turn influence the distribution of ill health. The interplay of poverty, illness, educational opportunity and access to employment are addressed in Daly's chapter.

Despite the strong affinity between the chapters in the first two sections, the social divisions covered in section A are not the primary focus of section B. Instead, the emphasis is more on the ways in which opportunities and inequalities are structured at an institutional level and how institutions shape experience as well as affecting opportunities. Health care, education, welfare and the labour market are central to particular chapters. As such, the chapters appear to concentrate more on a meso-level of analysis, being centrally concerned neither with macro-social processes nor with the minutiae of everyday life at a micro-level. However, all the authors are anxious to make strong links with other levels of analysis. Strangleman discusses the effects of globalization, modernization and deindustrialization on changes in the nature of work. Daly emphasizes that poverty cannot be understood without reference to macro-economic processes. Graham and Sasha Scambler stress the importance of the 'constraining/enabling input of social structure' and consider broad changes in the nature of capitalism. Moore contrasts the 'logic of industrialism' and the 'logic of capitalism' approaches to understanding educational inequality.

However, none of the authors neglects more micro-processes either. Some chapters look at how changes in particular spheres affect the experience of social life. There is a discussion of ways in which people cope with poverty and the experience of 'disrespect' and 'humiliation' which can accompany it. Meaning (or lack of it) at work is extensively addressed. Most chapters pay some attention to the role of agency in moving beyond structural understanding of inequalities and opportunities, but none claim that individualistic explanations alone are credible. Meritocratic theories of education, cultural theories of poverty, and ideas on 'personal responsibility' and health are all critiqued. However critically some of these theories are evaluated, though, there is an implicit or explicit recognition of the importance of both agency and structure. Daly addresses this directly, making some insightful observations (based on the work of Sen) that access to resources affects the ability to exercise agency, an argument which is relevant to all the chapters in section B. Similarly, Moore stresses that access to knowledge is important in providing opportunities for the exercise of agency and that the habitus of the school can be an enabling resource for pupils.

Agency is not just constrained by individual differences in access to resources. Wider patterns of power are also very significant and their impact can be highlighted in different ways. One factor is the way in which issues are defined, social problems are identified, and, in some cases, social groups are stigmatized. Strangleman discusses the ways in which the social definitions of work and unemployment are problematic and some 'work' (especially paid work) is valued above other types (especially unpaid work). Graham and Sasha Scambler consider how definitions of illness and health and discourses about the body are related to power relationships and stigmatize some people as deviant. The definition of poverty, deprivation and social exclusion are extensively covered by Daly, and a central concern of Moore's chapter is the way that knowledge is defined and valued or devalued. But definitions of health, education, poverty and valuable work are not just imposed by the powerful on powerless individuals. Agency is exercised when dominant definitions are challenged – for example, by 'New' sociologists of education, social movements in the health domain, anti-poverty campaigners, or feminists campaigning for greater recognition for unpaid care work. Of course work itself is also a site of struggle with organized resistance from trade unions.

In addition, power relationships are examined in relation to social policies. The 'Work' chapter has some discussion of social policies in relationship to unemployment, but there is a stronger emphasis in the other chapters, which examine important institutions of the welfare state. Daly is concerned most broadly with welfare, while Moore and Graham and Sasha Scambler concentrate, appropriately enough, on education and health care respectively. Daly is clear that welfare policies, and indeed the distribution of poverty, are closely related to the distribution of power. She argues that welfare states are a product of capitalism and have never been designed to eliminate poverty, although they may aim to reduce it. Graham and Sasha Scambler are equally vehement that power relations stand behind the social policies and the distribution of opportunities and inequalities in relationship to health and illness. Their discussion of the 'greedy bastards hypothesis' and the recommodification of the NHS strikes a pessimistic note about the future direction of social policy in this area, but this is balanced by an upbeat assessment of the potential impact of social movements. Moore reports only limited progress in increasing opportunity in education and notes how the senior ranks of top professions remain solidly elitist, having members drawn largely from the privately educated. Social class differences in achievement remain stubbornly persistent despite decades of policies ostensibly designed to promote meritocracy. Moore concludes that this may be explained partly by the priority given to the 'knowledge of the powerful' rather than the teaching of 'powerful knowledge'.

Despite the apparent focus on the meso-level of analysis, then, the chapters integrate the meso with the macro with the micro. They explore how complex social processes in particular spheres of social life operate to define social issues and social problems, how they reflect power relationships, social change and resistance, and how they empower and facilitate agency and opportunity but also constrain and create inequality while limiting opportunities. As such they connect personal troubles and public issues in the way advocated by C. Wright Mills in his classic expression of the project of sociology, *The Sociological Imagination* (1959).

WORK

experience, identities and meanings

TIM STRANGLEMAN

CONTENTS

INTRODUCTION

WORK IS ONE OF the most interesting and dynamic areas of sociology. Issues of employment, industry, recession and the work–life balance are rarely out of the news headlines. But what is work and how do we understand it sociologically? This chapter aims to answer these two seemingly simple questions. When we think of work in a commonsense way it is easy to define it: work is what we do when we are not enjoying ourselves, when we are doing a task that needs to be done. We do work in order to earn a living, which in turn enables us to do the things we really want to do. Work is labour, a drudge, something we would rather avoid – simple? However, we could also see work as something that defines us, which confirms our identity and gives meaning to life. It bestows on us status in our own eyes and in those of others. Work embeds us in community, it is a major aspect of social life; it gives us hope, a life narrative, and to be without it can cause deep despair. We can see straight away that our commonsense definitions of work are too simple (see Anthony 1978; Budd 2011).

Let's set up some simple ways to define what we mean by work. We can begin by making a distinction between *paid* and *unpaid* work. Paid work, or employment, is marked by the exchange of labour (physical or mental) for payment, usually in modern societies in the form of money. Unpaid work, by contrast, is marked by no monetary or other exchange taking place. Simple! Well even this definition needs to be refined even further. While employment, the exchange of work for money, is pretty straightforward, work in its unpaid form can take many different guises. Recently there has been a lot of media coverage about the use (and abuse) of interns – people who volunteer to work for nothing in return for gaining experience in an industry or sector (Perlin 2011). Work can be done for love in a domestic setting. So we can imagine this as household chores or caring for children, elder relatives or a partner. These chores could be done by any member of the household, but often there is a strongly gendered nature to the way such jobs are allocated and done. This same type of work could be done in a slightly different way. It could be a neighbour who pops into the house to offer a small or large amount of their effort to help out a friend – so unpaid work could be voluntary. There is also a darker side to unpaid work, namely slavery, where work is forced from a person for no compensation. Slavery has existed almost as long as human beings, and it would be a mistake to see it as a form of labour that belongs to the past – slavery is very much still with us all over the world. Often the nature of slavery is highly gendered and racialized; it can be thought of in domestic settings as well as on industrial scales in the past (see Bales 1999, 2005; Bales, Trodd and Kent 2009).

So the 'simple' idea of work is more complex, but in turn we understand it better. We are starting to think about it sociologically. The most important thing to note here is that work is a *social relationship*. Work, in other words, takes place in relations with one or more other human beings. Therefore knowing the social context of work is vital in order to understand it, as is illustrated in figure 5.1.

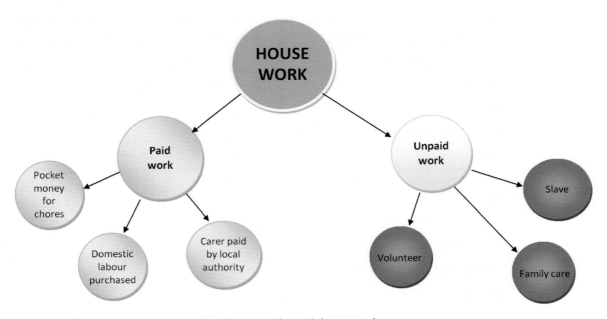

Figure 5.1 Thinking about work and employment through housework

We can see in figure 5.1 many different forms of labour just around domestic work. The most obvious division is between paid and unpaid labour, but even here we can see that understanding the form labour takes and the social relations in which work is embedded is vital if we are to understand work fully. Another thing to note here is the way sociology combines abstract theory (in terms of the models it may develop to understand a phenomenon) and empirical observation. We can populate the theoretical abstraction such as that represented in figure 5.1 with real-life examples through conducting research.

Work and social relationships

Social relationships around work are themselves far from simple. They can entail connections of kin, family; they can be based on friendship or love and caring; they can be straightforward relationships of employer–employee. But they can also be forced relationships, as in slavery. Understanding the social contexts of work involves addressing questions of gender, age, skill, education, race and ethnicity. But whenever we look at work we also need to understand the power one set of humans can exercise over another. So far, then, we have begun to understand the way work is both structured by, and structuring of, everyday life. By this we mean that who gets to do certain types of work is socially structured and determined by a range of forces and influences. To return to figure 5.1 for a moment, we can see the potential to employ another person to do work for you is based on your ability to pay. Equally the likelihood is that those who undertake paid domestic caring often do so because of a lack of other job opportunities or educational qualifications, and they could well be on zero-hours contracts.

We have so far discussed work in terms of the divide between paid and unpaid work. We have also begun to think of other ways in which work is divided up and allocated. Sociologists call this the division of labour. This division of labour can be thought about in a number of ways. It can be seen in the most basic completion of tasks – in a domestic setting it could be one person washes dishes while the other dries them. In early societies there was little need for a highly differentiated division of labour, but as societies became more complex so too did the work undertaken in them. Tasks in more modern societies become increasingly specialized. We may become more skilled or knowledgeable, but often we are less broad in our knowledge of how we do things.

Before we move on, it is worth looking at other ways in which sociologists might understand work. We have seen the way we must always understand the social relationships and contexts of work, but it is also important to understand the way people are attached to and think about the work they do. Again think about the relationships in figure 5.1 for a moment. In each of these instances we need to consider what work might mean to the person doing it. The most common assumption is that people seek employment only for the money, but a person might choose caring work because they find it more fulfilling than another type. Equally, unpaid caring work of, say, a parent can be done for love or there could be a real resentment informing the way people think about work. The point to make here is that we cannot simply read off attitudes and assumptions based on someone's place in the division of labour.

Sociologists often begin talking about any subject by returning to classical sociology. This period, from the mid-nineteenth century through to the early twentieth century, is associated particularly with the writings of Karl Marx, Émile Durkheim and Max Weber. Work and economic life were central to the writings and research of each of these so-called founding fathers. All of them, for instance, discussed the increasing division of labour in modern industrial societies. In different ways each was interested in the process of rationalization where organizational structure and the detail of work process were subject to greater design and control by employers. They worried about the consequences of modern industry on community and the individual. This can be seen in Marx's ideas on alienation, Weber's thoughts on estrangement and disenchantment, and Durkheim's notion of anomie. Modern work is positive – it is efficient and more productive – but it also comes at a cost – industrial work is often repetitive and uncreative. These themes are still central to any analysis of contemporary patterns of work, and we will return to them throughout the chapter.

Work and how we understand it is very complex and at times contradictory. It is something we may want to avoid or embrace, love or hate, something to live for or die by. This is illustrated in the variety of ways in which it is possible to think about work (Budd 2011).

BOX 5.1 TEN WAYS OF THINKING ABOUT WORK

Work as Curse
Work as Commodity
Work as Occupational Citizenship
Work as Freedom
Work as Disutility
Work as Personal Fulfilment
Work as Identity
Work as Caring for Others
Work as Service
Work as a Social Relationship

Source: Budd (2011).

The job of the sociologist is to problematize work, to reveal the hidden structures shaping economic life and to show that the way we organize work and who gets to work is the product of complex social and economic forces created by humans. Equally, if humans have created an unfair and unequal distribution of employment, we collectively have the power to shape it differently. Sociologists of work should always ask difficult questions which challenge taken-for-granted assumptions about why things are as they are.

SEMINAR QUESTIONS

1 Refer to figure 5.1 and think about the place where you live. How does the labour that surrounds you fit into this model?
2 What is the value of theory when we look at work and what does it add to our understanding of the subject?
3 Find any passage of writing about work and see how many of Budd's ideas you can find.

CONTROL, SKILL AND LABOUR

The labour process

One of the enduring legacies of classical sociology on the study of work has been a set of debates about how labour is controlled, managed and organized. Once again these themes were prominent in the writing of Marx, Durkheim and Weber, but it is Marx's ideas on what he described as the labour process where it is most keenly felt (Marx [1867] 1954; Marx and Engels [1848] 1968,

[1845] 1970). For Marx, the capitalist system of production was essentially a dynamic one in which the owners of the means of production were under constant pressure to reduce their costs and increase production. He suggested that this would mean that, increasingly, machines would be substituted for human labour, as they were more productive. But this capital equipment was dead capital in that it was assumed that it would be worked to its maximum efficiency and that eventually all manufacturers would adopt similar technology. Capitalists could not squeeze extra profit from their plant and machinery but instead had to focus on their labour costs or variable costs, since it was only here that they could gain more surplus value. Now Marx believed that this situation would inevitably lead to ever greater pressure to realize extra surplus value from workers, and this could be achieved by lowering wages, by making employees work harder or longer, or by some combination of these. This pressure would increase as greater amounts of fixed capital (machines) were introduced (Edgell 2012; Thompson and McHugh 1995).

Control of labour was vital for modern capitalist industry in a way it had not been before. In the pre-industrial era, workers had more control over their working lives or their labour was governed by seasons, the weather or simply the amount of daylight available. The tools and the infrastructure needed for production was far more limited than in later industrial societies. Also employers had a more direct relationship with their employees, as illustrated in figure 5.2.

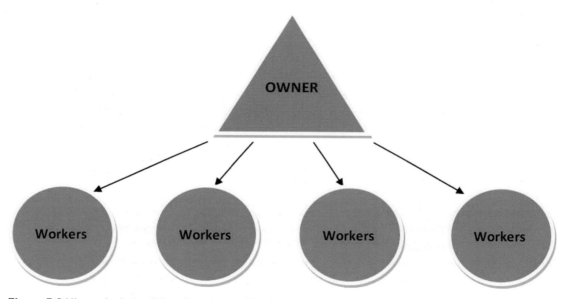

Figure 5.2 Hierarchy in traditional work organizations

Once larger amounts of money were invested in fixed capital – plant and machinery – investors wanted to see a return on their capital. Organizations became more complex because of the increased divisions of labour and larger workforces, and, with it, management itself became more specialist, as shown in figure 5.3.

The large labour forces necessary in this system had to be reliable in order to turn up when and where they were needed – an idle machine was a waste of money. This meant that there was a greater imperative to control aspects of workers' lives and how they worked. Marx

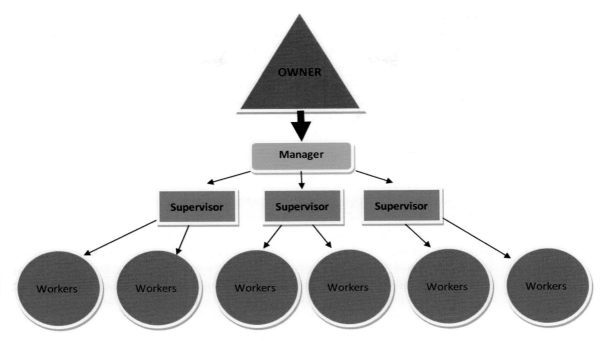

Figure 5.3 Hierarchy in modern work organizations

conceptualized this problem in abstract terms by arguing that what an employer purchased when they paid wages was not an *amount* of labour but, rather, the *potential* for labour. This was because labour has an ambiguous quality about it. If we think about this problem, it is very difficult to specify how hard someone has worked or to know if someone is working to their full capacity. Work involves both physical exertion and mental activity. So the basic question is: How do you ensure that someone is working hard, and who decides what working hard is? Marx understood the need for management and supervision in the new industries in order to maximize the workers' efforts (see Brown 1992).

This gets us to one of the fundamental conceptions within a Marxist sociology of work: the employment relationship. Marx saw all societies historically as underpinned by class struggle, and modern capitalist industrial societies were no different. The fundamental tension at the heart of capitalist society could be expressed as the fact that, for employers, the wages they paid were a *cost* and therefore had to be minimized as far as possible. However, for the workers, the wages they received were their *income* and therefore something they wanted to maximize. So employers wanted as much labour as possible for as little cost, while the workers wanted as much money as possible for as little as effort as possible. Importantly this is an abstraction, but nonetheless it helps us understand the contradiction at the heart of the system. The interests of employers and employees are not the same for Marx; indeed, they are fundamentally opposite. There is therefore a contradiction right at the centre of capitalism.

Deskilling, scientific management and Fordism
One of the ways in which labour costs could be reduced was through the process of *deskilling*. Deskilling involves looking at any work process and attempting to remove as much skilled

labour as possible from the process. In doing this an owner is reducing their wage bill – skilled labour is more expensive than semi-skilled or unskilled labour. Unskilled labour is more plentiful and can more easily be substituted. The highpoint of this drive to deskill work came around the turn of the twentieth century, and there are two main figures who were very influential in this process – Fredrick Winslow Taylor and Henry Ford.

F. W. Taylor is known as the father of 'scientific management', best described as the systematic examination of work processes in order to rationalize them to reduce costs and make them more efficient. Taylor studied individual parts of work processes in such detail that he was able to shave fractions of seconds from individual movements. He was interested in the tools workers used, the position in which they stood, the distance they travelled in performing certain tasks. Once he understood a process he then set about designing the optimum way in which that task could be done efficiently. He thought that it was the job of management to do this design and conception of work. The workers, on the other hand, were simply there to carry out the designated task as instructed. At the heart of Taylor's philosophy was an understanding that, if workers were left to their own devices, they would perform work suboptimally. Indeed, they would collectively decide the pace of any particular task and then enforce this pace on the group through workplace norms. They were able to do this, he believed, through their greater knowledge of the workplace and the tasks they did. The point Taylor made was that it was the object of management to separate out the *conception* of a task and its *execution*. Taylor believed that management must assume the right to design and implement how, where and when a task was to be carried out. The execution, the *doing* of the task, was what the worker did. Needless to say, Taylor's ideas were not popular with workers and were difficult to realize fully because of the sheer complexity of most work tasks. Fundamentally, Taylor's system had flaws in that the advantage of having human beings doing work was that they could exercise their own judgement and discretion over what they did. This means that workers can adapt and evolve as things change; in other words, they do not have to be told to do something by management or supervisors. By attempting to remove all discretion from workers, businesses had to employ greater levels of supervisory and management staff when trusting workers to some extent might have been a lot cheaper. What Taylor's system also did was remove some or all of the intrinsic rewards of tasks from workers by not allowing them actively to engage their minds in judgement (see Braverman 1974; Kanigel 1997).

Our second influential figure in the early part of the twentieth century is Henry Ford, founder of the Ford Motor Company, the first automotive firm really to embrace mass-production techniques. Ford was not the inventor of the technology he used, but he was the first to see how various features such as moving production lines, the use of highly standardized parts, and the employment of semi-skilled and unskilled labour rather than craftsmen could all be combined to produce highly standardized products very quickly and cheaply. In doing so, Ford dramatically cut the cost of labour, raw materials and, ultimately, the price of the cars so that increasing numbers of people could afford one of their own. As was the case with Taylor, Ford set about designing out skill and discretion from the tasks he expected of his workers. The point of his system was that, with minimal training, virtually any employee could be taught in a matter of hours to work on one of his production lines. Initially workers resisted these new forms of practice, and Ford experienced huge turnover in staff who were not willing to accept these conditions. They objected to the pace of production and the boredom involved in doing the same routine task over and over again hundreds of times in a shift (see box 5.2). Ford responded to this problem by introducing his famous $5 per day pay rates, which cut labour turnover at a stroke. Effectively what Ford was doing was compensating his workers for the lack of *intrinsic* reward by giving them greater *extrinsic* reward – more money. Ford's system – named Fordist production – was widely copied in the automotive sector and beyond. Its strength was that it was able to enjoy huge economies of scale by mass-producing large numbers of identical units. Some plants, such as Ford's River Rouge factory, were like vast citadels in their own right, with virtually every aspect of production carried out on site: raw materials (iron, glass and rubber) came in at one end of the plant and finished cars came out at the other end.

BOX 5.2 THE EXPERIENCE OF FORDIST PRODUCTION

Ben Hamper describes in his book *Rivethead* the experience as a child of being taken around the car plant where his father worked:

> I was seven years old the first time I ever set foot inside an automobile factory. . . . After a hundred wrong turns and dead ends, we found my old man down on the trim line. His job was to install windshields using this goofy apparatus with large suction cups that resembled an octopus being crucified. A car would nuzzle up to the old man's work area and he would be waiting for it, a cigarette dangling from his lip, his arms wrapped around the windshield contraption as if it might suddenly rebel and bolt off for the ocean. Car, windshield. Car, windshield. Car, windshield. No wonder my father preferred playin' hopscotch with barmaids. This kind of repetition didn't look like any fun at all. (Hamper 1992: 1–2)

The Fordist system of mass production was highly successful and for some period very profitable. It was not, however, without its weaknesses. One problem for Ford and the others who followed his example was the rigidity of the production regime he created: its advantage was it had huge economies of scale but equally it was inflexible and slow to change. American consumers quickly developed new wants, and these included product differentiation – they wanted cars in colours other than black (Gartman 1994). In addition to shifts in consumer demand, mass-production plants were vulnerable to swings in demand, especially in times of economic depression. Ford's factories had also created fertile breeding grounds for a strong mass labour movement. The new industrial colossus was a perfect arena in which workers could organize for better pay and conditions. Unions grew and increasingly challenged management's absolute authority over aspects of working life (see Brody 1993; Green 1998).

Rationalization

Deskilling of work is most obvious in factories like those build by Ford, but these ideas have found favour in many other types of work both in the past and in contemporary society. While much of the writing on deskilling has been within the Marxist tradition – most notably by Harry Braverman (1974) – we can see that such ideas transcend a purely Marxian framework. Clearly, subjecting work to ever greater levels of critical scrutiny in order to make it more efficient is part of a wider process of rationalization and therefore could be looked at from a Weberian perspective. Most recently Weberian ideas on work organization have had a revival, with George Ritzer's (2000) idea of the so-called McDonaldization of society thesis. This is the idea that all work and organizational processes are increasingly subject to being structured along the lines McDonald's use in their fast-food restaurants. What this means is that virtually any work process can be designed to minimize the amount of discretion that workers need to apply to their tasks. We can see this in shop work, where modern electronic tills need little skill to operate and workers simply scan in products using bar codes; indeed, increasingly customers are expected and being encouraged to scan their own shopping.

The endpoint of rationalization and deskilling? The self-scan checkout, where a combination of machine and customer do the work. (© fiahless/Flickr)

There are always contradictions in these developments. The increasing use of technology may deskill or even remove jobs altogether, but it also creates new jobs in terms of those who design, install, maintain and repair that same technology. Equally, while technology and job design may minimize and restrict skill and discretion, there nonetheless remains scope for and the need to have employees able to exercise discretion over their work. Management need to trust workers to some degree, however limited that space may be. Theorists of organizations have been considering this question for a long time. One way of thinking about the issue is to see it in terms of a continuum, a position adopted by Andrew Friedman (1977) and illustrated in figure 5.4.

Figure 5.4 suggests that a worker's ability to enjoy control over their work can vary considerably. Supervisors and management have choices over how much autonomy they give their

BOX 5.3 MCDONALDIZATION

George Ritzer describes the ongoing deskilling process in fast-food preparation. He sees this as part of a wider process of rationalization common to many types of work, not just fast-food 'restaurants'. Ritzer says:

> Much of the food prepared at McDonaldized restaurants arrives preformed, precut, presliced, and 'preprepared.' All employees need to do is, where necessary, cook or often merely heat the food and pass it on to the customer. At Taco Bell, workers used to spend hours cooking meat and shredding vegetables. Now, the workers simply drop bags of frozen ready-cooked beef into boiling water. They have used preshredded lettuce for some time, and now preshredded cheese and prediced tomatoes have appeared. The more that is done by nonhuman technology before the food arrives at the restaurant, the less workers need to do and the less room they have to exercise their own judgement and skill. (Ritzer 2000: 105–6)

Furthermore, even the human interaction is rationalization, with workers sometimes using prepared scripts in interaction with customers to encourage them to buy more.

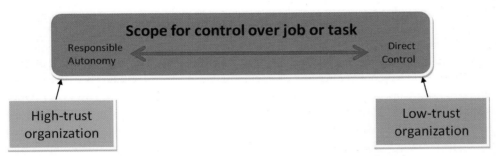

Figure 5.4 The management/supervision continuum after Friedmann (1977)

staff or the amount of control they exercise over what is done. In low-trust organizations, workers will usually be subject to greater levels of scrutiny over what they do. At the extreme end of the continuum workers may be monitored virtually all the time – this is known as *direct control*. Over the last decade or so there has been an explosion of interest in call centre work, in part because of the close management techniques to which call centre workers are subject.

By contrast, at the other end of this continuum, in high-trust organizations workers may be given tremendous amounts of trust and granted what has been labelled as *responsible autonomy*. It doesn't always follow, but often high-trust/responsible autonomy settings are associated with skilled and technical labour, whereas low-trust/direct control settings are associated with unskilled labour. This way of thinking about trust and the role it plays in management and supervision strategies was developed by Andrew Friedman (1977), in part as a response to simplistic interpretations of Marx's writings on the labour process. Levels of autonomy and trust can vary both between and within companies and other organizations. However, it should be kept in mind that this is an abstract ideal model and that the mix of

BOX 5.4 EMOTIONAL EXHAUSTION AND TELEPHONE CALL CENTRES

Stephen Deery, Roderick Iverson and Janet Walsh (2002) studied 480 workers in call centres in five Australian telecommunications companies. All the workers were phone operatives who spent much of their time talking to members of the public, but it was found that there was little variety in the tasks they were given, they were subject to close surveillance and they had little opportunity to use their discretion. When they did, they could be criticized by their managers. For example, one operator said, 'The emphasis on wrap-time affects me greatly, as at times I feel like I have done an excellent job and have been complimented by the customer for the effort put in, only to be told that my wrap-time is bad. This destroys any job satisfaction for me' (ibid.: 490). Another observed that 'There are at least two to three calls per week that require a lot of time and patience for a solution – these customers are often at their wit's end . . . I believe in customer service and I dislike being punished for attempting to fulfil the obligation of service to customers' (ibid.). Deery, Iverson and Walsh concluded that such factors, along with others such as abuse from customers, could lead to 'emotional exhaustion' as well as high rates of absenteeism.

autonomy and control can vary considerably even for an individual worker during a working week.

While Braverman (1974) argued that there was a tendency within capitalist organizations to deskill and exert more direct forms of control, others have suggested that all jobs involve varying levels of control and discretion or direct control will be very expensive to enforce; essentially at some point you have to trust the workforce (see Fox 1974). Work sociologists have suggested other forms of control may hold the key to understanding how managers and supervisors ensure work is done and conflict at work is contained. Edwards (1979), for example, suggested a three-stage progression, from *direct* control through *technical* control to *bureaucratic* control. Edwards thought that management systems had evolved historically from direct control, where small firms with owner managers could know very effectively what was being done in the workplace. Here employees and owners may well have worked alongside each other. With the increasing size of organizations this simple control was no longer possible, and managers started to rely on what has been labelled as technical control. This is where workers are paced by the rate of the machines they tend. Finally, control can be exercised through bureaucratic structures. This is where conflict is defused by reference to workplace rules and procedures. In essence workers are enrolled in norms of behaviour by way of workplace custom, law, and the terms and conditions of their employment, including pay for seniority and the prospect of pensions. Thus control is exercised through all sorts of cues, prompts, norms and values rather than by direct coercion by supervisors or managers. An excellent example of this latter control strategy can be seen in Michael Burawoy's (1979) classic workplace ethnography *Manufacturing Consent*, where supervision, direct or otherwise, seems almost entirely absent and workers largely self-manage.

The 'contested terrain' of management control

This is not to say that workers are passive in the workplace and simply go along with whatever new management style is adopted. Rather we have to view the workplace as what one theorist described as a 'contested terrain' (Edwards 1979). Workers always have some degree of agency over their work which allows them a little ability to exercise control, even in extreme cases refusing to do work altogether. We can see the way management control strategies have dialectically evolved down the years, reflecting the ongoing conflict between capital and labour. Management, therefore, may design new strategies to control tasks more effectively, while workers find novel ways to exploit weaknesses in them. In his classic essay on management's attempt to control work, Richard Hyman (1987) argued that any attempt to impose control was ultimately doomed, as workers would find ways to subvert any strategy imposed on them. It is easy to think that capital is all powerful. Employers after all have the power to hire and fire workers. They can discipline employees and they can decide what work is done. Workers, by contrast, need wages to live. However, in reality workers do exercise all sorts of power over the tasks they do. To comprehend fully the strengths and weakness of either side we also need to grasp the power relationships both inside and outside the workplace – for example, the state of the local labour market, labour law and rates of unemployment are important factors. Sociologists talk about worker resistance, and such opposition can take many forms. Rather than power lying solely in the hands of management, we can conceptualize all workers as being able to offer some form of resistance, and we could see work as a 'negotiated order' wherein this power and resistance is subject to debate or bargaining. This negotiated order can be seen occurring at the level of the firm or organization or as a day-to-day process. In short, capital is not all powerful, and nor is labour powerless. However, this negotiated order takes place within a setting of unequal power.

So how do we think about this resistance and how does it manifest itself? Again it helps if we think about worker resistance as taking a variety of forms across time and space. Ackroyd and Thompson (1999) proposed the description 'organizational misbehaviour' rather than 'resistance', and they produced a continuum of misbehaviour which is shown in figure 5.5. Here we see a spectrum of resistance strategies, ranging from leaving work early through strikes to industrial sabotage. We can see the way pilferage from one's workplace could be a relatively minor offence, such as stealing small amounts of stationery, through to massive fraud or theft. The point is that all these behaviours could be seen as resistance to workplace authority and management control strategies.

We have already touched on issues of workplace norms and values, and in the next section we will look at them in more detail. We will return to control and resistance later on in the chapter when we explore issues such as emotional labour.

Figure 5.5 Organizational misbehaviour/resistance after Ackroyd and Thompson (1999)

SEMINAR QUESTIONS

1 Think about the model in figure 5.5. In your own experience, what sort of resistance have you offered in the jobs you have carried out?
2 Think about the model in figure 5.4. What sort of management control have you been subject to or seen?
3 In what ways can workers exercise power at work?
4 What factors might affect the amount of power workers can exercise compared to owners and managers?

CULTURE, IDENTITY AND MEANING AT WORK

Alienation and workplace ethnography

The themes of culture, meaning and identity have in many ways framed the sociological understanding of work, industrialization and capitalism. The sociological project is built on attempts to gauge the effects of industrial development on work identity and meaning. Often this impact has been understood as a negative one, with industrial processes and management regimes restricting the ability of workers to exercise autonomy over what they do and how they do it. As the division of labour becomes more complex, people's idea of how their role fits into a wider schema is reduced and their work routine becomes increasingly repetitive and narrow. Marx saw this in terms of alienation and suggested that in modern industrial work intrinsic rewards would be replaced by extrinsic ones – workers are compensated for a lack of interest in their work by their wages, much as we saw in the case of Henry Ford's $5 per day.

As one of the keenest observers of the new capitalist system, Marx believed that the greater division of labour cruelly distorted an individual's humanity. He wrote in the first volume of *Capital*: 'It converts the labourer into a crippled monstrosity, by forcing his detail dexterity at the expense of a world of productive capabilities . . . Intelligence in production expands in one direction, because it vanishes in many others' (Marx [1867] 1954: 340–1). Compare this with Ben Hamper's account of working on a car assembly line:

> We had been able to conquer the other annoyances. We adjusted to the heat and grew accustomed to the noise. After a while, we even got used to the claustrophobia of the wheel wells. The idea that we were being paid handsome wages to mimic a bunch of overachieving simians suited us just dandy. . . . The one thing that was impossible to escape was the monotony of our new jobs. Every minute, every hour, every truck and every movement was a plodding replica of the one that had gone before. (Hamper 1992: 40–1)

In their different ways, all of the classical theorists saw the potential danger in modern work of eroding any sense of meaning in jobs. This assumption was based on a sense of what was being lost from the type of work that went on in traditional societies. Often older types of work are portrayed as meaningful, fulfilling and paced in a more humane way. While it is certainly true that traditional pre-industrial societies did manage work in a different way, we should not run away with the idea that agricultural or extractive labour were not hard, heavy and monotonous – anyone who doubts this should spend a day weeding a field! More recently, in another factory halfway round the world, we can see that some workers in China are faced with very similar conditions to those described by Hamper (see box 5.5).

BOX 5.5 MANUFACTURING APPLE PRODUCTS IN CHINA

Foxconn is the world's largest electronics contractor manufacturer and assembles products for Apple and other leading electronics firms. The Dutch Center for Research on Multinational Corporations (SOMO) and Students & Scholars Against Corporate Misbehavior (SACOM) published a report on Foxconn's Chengdu factory, which produces iPads and other products solely for Apple. The factory became notorious after a spate of suicides and suicide attempts that took place there in summer 2010:

> According to the report, workers are routinely overworked, given only scarce breaks for food amidst abysmal living conditions. It found that employees work 174 regular hours each month, in addition to overtime: while the legal limit for overtime is 36 hours a month, workers routinely work 80 to 100 hours overtime in continuous shifts that do not allow for meal breaks. (Lee 2011)

Issues around workplace culture continue to interest those studying work from various perspectives. As we saw above, early management scientists such as Taylor viewed workplace culture as a problem in that the independence and autonomy workers enjoyed meant that they could control their own work and the pace at which they did it. A little later the so-called Hawthorne experiments carried out by early industrial anthropologists likewise recognized that the shared values and meanings of workers were important factors that had to be taken in to account in understanding how work got done (Gillespie 1991). It could be argued that this type of approach to understanding work groups in order to increase productivity gave birth both to the modern disciplines of management and to industrial sociology, especially during and just after the Second World War (see Brown 1992).

In terms of sociological understanding of culture, it is important to recognize workplace ethnography as an approach for tapping into norms, values and meanings. A central tenet of ethnographic approaches to any social setting is understanding culture in a natural setting, and clearly the workplace is an important environment for this type of study. There is a long tradition of workplace ethnography stretching back to the post-Second World War era if not before, with classic studies such as Donald Roy's (1973) study of a Chicago machine shop in various papers, including his memorably entitled 'Banana Time'. Since Roy, other ethnographers have studied various places of work, among them car plants, steel works, shipyards, shops, bars and restaurants, and theme parks. All of these have the aim of understanding the internal dynamics of the work group. How do they function, what are their norms and values, how do they interact with management, etc.? The ethnographic eye is then skilled in identifying what work means to individuals and groups and the nature of identity around work.

BOX 5.6 BEN FINCHAM TALKS TO CYCLE COURIERS

One of the best examples of workplace ethnography from the UK in recent years can be found in Ben Fincham's participant observation of cycle couriers in London. His research found that, for this group of workers, the distinction between work and leisure was far from clear-cut. Cycle couriers are low paid and their work is very dangerous, carrying a significant risk of their being injured or even killed in a road accident. However, many were committed to their work because of its links to cycling subcultures and the possibility of symbolic rewards through wearing fashionable clothes and being seen riding appealing bikes. One courier said he took his job because:

> It looked cool. Yeah. And nutcases. They looked like a cross between Mad Max and a road warrior, something like that, you know. And still, you know, you're out on the road you can still see them. You can see the freedom. You know like surfers or skateboarders. You know, you can see the freedom. (Cargo Chris, 5 June 2003) (Fincham 2008: 622)

Another commented:

> It is a kind of cool image. Earning money cycling is cool, no doubt about that. I love being outdoors and being paid to ride my bike is a good thing and it's definitely a bonus that it's kind of perceived as quite a good job . . . erm my girlfriend likes it. (Slam, 18 March 2003) (Ibid.)

A third courier emphasized the social relationships involved in the job:

> [There] was something of a community. That wherever I worked I jumped into a place and there was a unit that you felt was part of you. You were part of it. (Simon Eastcoast, 19 March 2003) (Ibid.)

Fincham concluded that, for cycle couriers, their work was so closely entwined with their leisure and lifestyle that it made little sense to see work as separate from other parts of their lives.

Work identity and workplace culture

During the 1960s in the UK, issues of work identity came to the fore in the so-called affluent worker debate associated with John Goldthorpe, David Lockwood and their colleagues (Goldthorpe et al. 1969). Their interest was in the impact of rising levels of affluence in post-war Britain and the effect this was having on employees' attitudes to work and their class position. Through various publications the group studied workers in Luton (Bedfordshire) and were interested in what they called their orientations to work. This was a position derived from a Weberian approach to understanding social action and was effectively testing the idea that growing prosperity would see the embourgeoisement of workers. In other words, affluent workers were likely to take on the values of the middle classes as their material conditions improved. The affluent worker team developed typologies of worker orientation, including 'traditional proletarian', 'deferential proletarian' and a new group of 'instrumentally orientated workers'. The finding of the study was that these new affluent workers were not so different from other members of the working class, and they certainly were not becoming middle

Cycle couriers reflect a contemporary example of the blurring between work and leisure identity. Indeed, it could be said that cycle couriers have formed their own subculture, organizing races such as the one pictured here. (© hairyeggg/Flickr)

class: they were increasingly instrumental in their attitudes and outlook. Another aspect of the orientations to work approach to culture and identity can be seen in the spin-off from the research of Goldthorpe and his colleagues (1969) in later debates about occupational communities, where sociologists tried to understand the relationship between place, work and community. Researchers were particularly interested in isolated or concentrated workgroups, where attitude, orientations and assumptions about work and its impact could be studied in detail. Classic research was carried out into coalmining, railway settlements and other traditional industries (see, for example, Dennis, Henriques and Slaughter 1956; Salaman 1974; Tunstall 1962). The key point is that worker identity had been discussed and had a central place in British and American sociology long before the so-called cultural turn of the 1980s, although this intellectual shift has produced important cultural readings of work and identity (see Halford and Leonard 2006; Webb 2006).

During the 1980s and 1990s, issues of workplace culture and identity came to the fore more explicitly for arguably two main reasons. Firstly, there was an important series of debates about culture change within organizations, which was often instigated by management schools, and, secondly, identity was seen to be under threat from the changing nature of the economy. (We will pick up on this latter issue in the next section.) The interest in culture in management literature stemmed from changes in the way managers and management theorists started to think about organizations and the people that worked in them. There was a sense that organizations had become too bureaucratic and slow moving to respond to the large-scale changes in the economy, particularly the impact of globalization. One reaction to these changes was to put stress on creating new cultures within organizations which would be more flexible and quicker to respond to change. One of the buzzwords was 'entrepreneurial', or, more precisely, the attempt to create a more entrepreneurial culture within organizations (du Gay 1996). As part of this move, management scientists identified the culture of traditional workplaces as being somehow lacking and that it was the role of management to design or change the culture of their organizations. In the process, some of these writers borrowed ideas from sociology, anthropology and other social sciences and twisted them to fit their own purposes better. As organizational anthropologist Susan Wright noted, management theorists had turned culture 'from being something an organization *is* into something an organization *has*, and from being a process embedded in context to an objectified tool of management control. The use of the term culture itself becomes ideological' (Wright 1994: 4). The point being made here is that, whereas critical social scientists would see culture as an emergent property of a group within organizations, many management writers saw it as something that could and should be manipulated by management for their own purposes. At the same time as some organizations were paying more attention to workplace culture, a few academic writers were suggesting that we were entering a period when it was possible to see the end of work identity, and we discuss this in greater detail below. As sociologists, we think of culture as something to be studied and understood, whereas management consider that their role is to form and manipulate culture.

SEMINAR QUESTIONS

1   Why is work identity and meaning important to sociologists?

2   With reference to Ben Hamper's account of working on a car assembly line, do you think that he has a strong work identity?

3   Is work central to Ben Fincham's cyclists? How are their views on work different from Hamper's?

4   Is work identity being eroded in modern employment?

UNEMPLOYMENT, DEINDUSTRIALIZATION AND GLOBALIZATION

Unemployment and deindustrialization

Unemployment is a central issue within work sociology. This may seem strange, as when we study unemployment we are studying the exact opposite of work. But what is increasingly clear is that the absence of work, either individually or collectively, can tell us a lot about work, its meaning and the identity people derive from it. This is why we are linking here unemployment, deindustrialization and globalization, which is a major driver of industrial and social change. Marx was interested in unemployment and thought it was an integral part of the capitalist system. He saw the role of the unemployed as acting as a check on wages within a labour market, where employers could draw on a ready supply of desperate potential workers when they needed them. The unemployed therefore formed part of what he labelled as the 'reserve army of labour' (Marx and Engels [1845] 1970).

Unemployment has figured at various points in work sociology since Marx's day but was to really come to the fore only in discussions from the late 1970s onwards in Western countries as they experienced large-scale industrial change, and especially the loss of significant traditional industries such as coal, engineering, shipbuilding and other forms of manufacturing. This presented an interesting challenge for work sociologists for two related reasons. Firstly, much of post-war *industrial* sociology (this was the usual description for sociological interest in work before the 1980s) had focused on male manual workers in the industries now in decline, so researchers faced the question of what their subject was to be in contemporary society. Secondly, the heyday of work sociology had been in an era of high and sustained employment, so the discipline was forced to consider the absence of work more directly. What also flowed from these two points was that *industrial* change brought about *social* change in terms of the make-up of the workforce and the new forms of work which were emerging. This shift in academic focus also reflected pressure from feminist scholars as well as those interested in race and ethnicity (Allen 1971; Bradley 1989; Oakley 1972; Rex 1973; Walby 1986).

The sustained loss of jobs in countries such as the UK, the USA and Canada, as well as Western and later Eastern Europe, began to be known as deindustrialization. In the USA, two economists, Bluestone and Harrison, wrote a highly influential book, *The Deindustrialization of America* (1982), in which they referred to the systematic reduction in industrial capacity in formally industrially developed areas. What was so central to Bluestone and Harrison's contribution was the way it sought to place social and community factors alongside economic and political considerations of industrial change. What has followed, especially in the USA, is a rich range of studies of the process of industrial decline and its impact on North American cities and towns. While the work that was once so central to these communities is of course discussed, the central focus of these studies is the impact of loss viewed through the lens of gender, race and ethnicity, and place. Crucially for us, such studies beg many important questions about the status and meaning of work for ordinary people. An American sociologist, Tom Juravich, captures the quality of working life in a quote from a laid-off machinist called Boden:

> My godmother's brother was a foreman over here for years. My next door neighbour when I was little, little kid worked there . . . my oldest boy is named after a toolmaker that I worked for when I first got here. My godchild, who I gave away last summer at her wedding, was one of the guys I worked with's daughter, and he passed away at a young age . . . and I gave her away. And it goes on and on and on. I mean, the girl in the office in personnel, she and I went through kindergarten and through all of school together. In this plant, everybody had those interactions. These weren't just people you worked with. They were sometimes your relatives, they were mostly your friends. (Juravich 2009: 152)

This quotation speaks to a whole different way in which people engage and position themselves in terms of work; it shows the way people see themselves as formally, at least, being embedded in their work. We see here and in many of the other oral histories from deindustrialized workers the interpenetration of economic, social and cultural forces. What these insights reveal about deindustrialization is the way in which the process inspires complex reflection on industrial work and its meanings. We can see the consideration of loss, of nostalgia and of critique, as the industrial past is continually subject to forms of emphasis, erasure and contestations. Many of the studies used here that look at the experience of deindustrialization deploy powerful testimony from the workers caught up in the process, capturing the sense of outrage, regret, confusion, anger and loss. Here Steven High interviews General Motors (GM) worker Gabriel Solano:

> To watch the people go to work. To watch my Dad get up. To see this just was mesmerizing because this was what America was about. This was what we all worked for, to make corporations their money so we could get on with our lives. People tended to their houses. Everyone was part of the community. Community was whole and it was wholesome. . . . This was what we live for. And I enjoyed it. I enjoyed going to work. I enjoyed being with my co-workers because this is what we lived for . . . And this was taken away. To see the abandoned houses popping up, to see the storefronts closing, to see the devastation of the joblessness because the small shops fed the big shops. It was like a domino effect. (High and Lewis 2007: 122)

Through this often moving testimony we start to unpack some really important ideas about work more generally. One way to think about deindustrialization is to extend Douglas Ezzy's (2001) ideas on the role played by redundancy and unemployment. He examined the way the experience of unemployment was narrated by those he studied and conceptualized the event of losing one's job in terms of a 'breaching experiment'. This notion of the breaching experiment, coined by ethnomethodologist Harold Garfinkel (1967), is where the object is to disorientate an actor in order to disrupt the normal or conventional patterns of social life – picking an item out of another person's shopping trolley at a supermarket, for example. The point was that this disruption of the expected flow of social interaction breached everyday norms and values and thus exposed the taken-for-granted social structures and understanding underpinning everyday life. Ezzy used this idea in theorizing the event of unemployment and the way individuals self-narrated the experience. While Ezzy examines this sense of breach at the level of the individual, we could and should see the process of deindustrialization at the level of the community or even the nation-state as a gigantic breaching experiment in itself, wherein the taken-for-granted assumptions about the present, the future and indeed the past come into question at a societal level. We can see this reflection on work and what it meant in a quote from a redundant automotive worker recorded by US industrial anthropologist Kate Dudley:

> When they start tearing [the plant] down, I'm going to go get a brick. I would just keep it. My kids know Mama spent fifteen years of her life [in the plant] working, and to tell my future grandkids about it. You know, tell them that it was a place where we worked, and that when they tore the building down, Grandma went and got herself a brick. For all that I put in there. I figure at least I deserve a brick. (Quoted in Dudley 1994: 173)

Globalization

It is impossible to understand fully these related issues of unemployment and deindustrialization without addressing the question of globalization. Globalization is a widespread term or concept which seeks to explain or describe the way in which events occur because of macro world patterns or events. There is a direct, if not always clear, link between the global and the local. It is important that we recognize that world trade has been occurring for five hundred years or more, and Marx saw capitalism in the mid-nineteenth century as a world system. However, in its modern incarnation globalization really refers to the increasing use of new technology (especially ICT and the internet), new production techniques and the new international division of labour (see Ray 2007; Waters 2001). All of these combined during the 1970s and the 1980s to speed up shifts in global capital. So steel plant closures in the North American 'rustbelt' are the direct consequences of multinational corporations' strategic decisions to relocate production to the newly industrializing parts of the world. It is vital that we place these industrial changes in the context of wider political changes such as the fall of communism in Eastern and Central Europe during the 1980s and 1990s and the opening up of the Chinese economy in the 1990s and 2000s. These geopolitical changes allow capital to seek out new markets and supplies of cheaper labour. Important as the changes of the last thirty years have undoubtedly been, some scholars of work suggest that these shifts themselves build on earlier international restructuring, such as the investment in the so-called dragon economies of Korea, Taiwan, Singapore and Hong Kong from the 1950s onwards (Bello and Rosenfeld 1990).

Even in the heyday of United States industry, companies sought out cheap labour within the country or just over the border in Mexico (Cowie 1999). All of these developments have direct and indirect consequences for workers in the West. Directly, work and industry may be 'off-shored', moved across the world, where labour costs may be a fraction of those in the West. But also, indirectly, the simple threat of off-shoring or out-sourcing work is a powerful disciplinary device that organizations can use to lower costs. The image promoted by some is that capital is footloose and global, whereas labour is tied to the local. The reality is far more complex, with some industry and work being tied directly to place and, equally, some labour being very mobile. The critical questions sociologists of work need to ask are around whether it is acceptable for big business to treat workers and whole communities in the ways they often do. Is it right that perfectly viable factories and plant are destroyed because labour costs are cheaper elsewhere in the world? We will explore some of these issues in more detail below.

SEMINAR QUESTIONS

1 What can unemployment tell us about work?
2 Is deindustrialization new?
3 Why should we care about the loss of industrial employment?
4 What is the relationship between the global and the local? Think in terms of your own experience of workplaces.

EMOTION, EMBODIMENT AND AESTHETICS AT WORK

Emotional labour

One of the features of classical sociological understandings of work, especially in Max Weber's writing, was the idea that the emotional content of work was gradually squeezed out of organizations as they became increasingly subject to the process of rationalization. Organizational structures, work processes and relationships within employment were depersonalized, stripped of emotion, as actors were expected to conform to relationships based on workplace rules, qualification and hierarchy (Albrow 1997; Fineman 1993; Ray and Reed 1994). One of the major developments in work sociology over the last three decades has been the pioneering work of American sociologist Arlie Russell Hochschild and her concept of 'emotional labour'. In her book the *Managed Heart* (1983), Hochschild suggested that, with the decline in the West of traditional manufacturing and extractive industries, the content and management of jobs and tasks was likely to change. She suggested that one way to understand these new forms of control was through ideas of the way in which an employee managed their emotions or, as part of their job, helped to manage or form the emotions of those they served. She studied two groups of workers – airline stewardesses and debt collectors – coining the labels 'toe' and 'heel' emotion management. The former was where positive reassurance was offered to customers, while in the latter the point was to intimidate people.

What was original was the way Hochschild recognized that service-sector jobs relied on workers being able to manage their own emotions and those of customers during the transaction. Workers might heighten their mood or suppress their rage at customer behaviour in an attempt to impart a positive and professional experience. To some extent, workers in these types of employment have always had to do this type of emotional labour. However, Hochschild argued that there was evidence that managers were taking more of an interest in how their staff behaved and that they were increasing specifying, or scripting, the inter-action between staff and customers. Such scripting could be seen as the further rationaliza-tion of the employment relationship, as we saw above. In Fordist-type work, management simply wanted docile, pliant bodies in their workplaces. Car manufacturing, for example, did not demand happy workers but simply workers prepared to put in a shift on the line. In this new development of emotional management, employees were subject to control of what they did and how they did it, as well as their emotional attachment and deportment. Hochschild made further differentiations between what she called surface acting and deep acting. Surface acting was where a worker superficially adopted a particular deportment – smiling without really meaning it. Deep acting, on the other hand, demanded more emotionally and psychologically of the workers. They needed to commit far more deeply to what they were being asked to do, almost act into a role. The danger in all this was that workers would come under greater pressure at work and suffer more intense stress as they suppressed or heightened their feelings. This is captured in the following quote from a worker at a Disney theme park:

> I sometimes find myself smiling at people. They're like, 'What are you smiling at me for?' I know they're thinking that, but it's because I still feel like I am constantly this character. I have to say, 'Oh, no one notices me, no one recognizes me. It's okay.' It's strange sometimes. I'll smile at people or if a child falls down. I go to pick him up, and people probably don't under-stand that, but I forget. (Quoted in Klugman 1995: 138)

Hochschild suggested that, as the nature of the economy shifted, increasing numbers of work-ers were likely to experience emotional management and emotional labour as part of their day-to-day duties. Inevitably this type of requirement would remove more autonomy from workers over how they decided to respond to a given situation and, to some extent, reduce their ability to control their work (see Sosteric 1996).

Embodiment

Emotional labour shifted attention to the embodiment of labour, or, to put it another way, the way in which we need to understand how the body is implicated in the work we do. In some ways work sociology has been slow to adopt some of the ideas that come out of the sociology of the body (see Shilling 2012). However, recently there has been a considerable amount of interest in the area (McDowell 2009; Wolkowitz 2006). Firstly, and most obviously, there has been attention paid to what is known as 'body work', where workers work on the bodies of others – medical and social care, beauty treatment or tattooists, for example. Here sociologists are interested in issues of touch and feel, how skills and knowledge are exercised through touch. More broadly, research and writing on embodied work can capture a whole range of important features of employment or labour which, though vital, are often neglected – touch, feel, smell and even taste. For example, sociologists of work are often interested in issues of skills and knowledge and how workers learn to do the things they do. Often these insights provide ideas on tacit skill and knowledge which we can't observe or get workers to express clearly in interviews (see, for example, Lyon and Back 2012).

Another aspect of embodiment is the way we can include in a discussion the long-standing issue of industrial injury and accidents at work, as well as issues of fatigue and strain. The classic text for understanding industrial injury is Theo Nichols's ground-breaking *The Sociology of Industrial Injury* (1997). A far older contribution to work and the body comes from Baldamus's *Efficiency and Effort* (1961), where the attempt is made to understand sociologically the effort expended in particular tasks and how it is experienced by the individual worker. Deindustrialization has also been a spur to writing about work and the body, in particular the consequences on the body of *not* working. US cultural anthropologist David Kideckel (2008) studied the effects of deindustrialization through the notion of the body in his research on Romanian chemical workers and coal miners. Where once these groups had held a privileged position in a workers' state, the loss of employment had seen them experience depression, stress and mental health problems, as well as alcohol and drug issues.

Finally, work sociology has increasingly been interested in the portrayal and representation of labour and work over the years. At times the working body has been the object of pity, and we could think of the social investigations into sweated labour or industrial accidents (Sampsell-Willmann 2009). But labour has also been portrayed as dignified or even heroic (Rogovin and Frisch 1993). This brings into the sociology of work approaches and literature from a host of other disciplines, such as fine art, photography or even sculpture (Dabakis 1999). There is interest, too, in so-called aesthetic labour, where goods and services are sold in part through the aesthetic appearance of those providing them. For example, up-market hotels, restaurants, bars or shops may put a premium on good-looking employees, insisting staff dress in particular ways or deport themselves to particular standards imposed by the company (Witz, Warhurst and Nickson 2003; Nickson, Warhurst and Dutton 2005; Warhurst and Nickson 2007). We could see this interest in the way employees look and present themselves as nothing new – think of domestic servants in country houses, for example. The critical point is to what extent employers can dictate how their employees look and behave. Where is the boundary between acceptable requests and unacceptable demands? Understanding work sociologically through visual methods, approaches and evidence has a long-standing pedigree, but arguably it has often been neglected by mainstream writers, whether by design or accident (see Strangleman 2004, 2008). However, to comprehend fully some of the exciting developments within and beyond the workplace, sociologists need to develop a visual literacy of work.

A recent trend in the embodiment of labour is represented by the clothing shop Abercrombie and Fitch, which goes further than using sexualized imagery to market its products and employs staff who can sell the brand identity through their bodies, on display as 'greeters'. (© Victoria Pickering/Flickr)

SEMINAR QUESTIONS

1 Have you ever had to manage your emotions at work?
2 Have you ever had to change the way you look at work?
3 Find an image of work. Think about what it tells us about society's attitude to work.
4 Using the same image, think about why it was produced and what was the intention in its creation. What do you think about it?

THE FUTURE OF WORK/THE END OF WORK?

The end of work and the loss of identity? Too much work or too little work?

In this section we explore some further contemporary debates about work. Interestingly, we can see the way in which discussions and themes from the past constantly re-emerge in the way people think about work now and what it may be like in the future. In the post-Second World War period, and especially during the late 1960s and early 1970s, there was a sense in Western economies that growing prosperity and increasing automation would allow more and more people to reduce the hours they worked and even shorten their working life as they chose. There was then a clear sense that work could be better for everyone, with shorter hours, longer periods of leisure and more holidays. Society and the work that occurred in it could and should be continually improved. This positive and hopeful projection into the future was, however, short-lived (see Bell 1973; Kumar 2005). As we saw when we discussed unemployment and deindustrialization, the period of the long post-war boom in the West came to a dramatic and shuddering halt doing the 1970s, and the result was wide-scale job losses, wage stagnation for many American blue-collar workers, and the process of deindustrialization described above (Harvey 1989).

During the 1990s, many sociologists and other commentators started to speculate on the nature of work being created (or destroyed) in what some labelled as the 'new capitalism'. US journalist Jeremy Rifkin wrote an influential book entitled *The End of Work* (1995), in which he argued that work was being squeezed in two distinct but related ways. Jobs were rapidly being abolished by mechanization and the adoption of information technology. At the same time the ability of national politicians to do anything to preserve or protect jobs was progressively reduced as a result of globalization, international trade agreements and neoliberalism. The argument Rifkin and others made was that the modern globalized, networked world was having a profound effect on the nature and quality of work. In Rifkin's wake many academics started to extrapolate from this a wholesale shift in the nature of work. One of the best examples is Richard Sennett's book *The Corrosion of Character* (1998). Sennett suggested that the 'new capitalism' was different from older varieties in that its time horizons became shorter: shareholders demanded that greater levels of profit were returned more quickly than had been achieved in the past, and CEOs were judged not over years but over financial quarters. Sennett was interested in the effect this had on the social relations in workplaces between employees and the way this new atmosphere bred greater competition between them rather than cooperation. He suggested that, as part of this process, workers themselves increasingly started to mirror in their own behaviour that of the organizations they joined and worked for – they became more individualized, and they tended to move between companies rather than stay with the same one. Sennett argued that the danger was that what was being created was a set of loose ties between people at work rather than relationships embedded over years. While this had profound effects for collective social relations, there were two further concerns for Sennett. Firstly, these new workers themselves were not rounded in the way previous generations had been – the lack of engagement with co-workers corroded their individual character. Secondly, Sennett suggested that these new workers had very fugitive ties with their local communities; they failed to put down roots, as they saw connection to community as a potential tie that would prevent them from moving onwards and upwards in their career. This was disastrous for society, as people became more and more isolated from one another.

This pessimistic tone was repeated time and again by other leading sociologists and social theorists. Zygmunt Bauman, for example, suggested that, whereas in the past work had been one of the main anchors of a person's life, now: 'A steady, durable and continuous, logically coherent and tightly-structured working career is . . . no longer a widely available option. Only in relatively rare cases can a permanent identity be defined, let alone secured, through the job performed' (Bauman 1998b: 27). Ulrich Beck suggested that 'Paid employment is becoming precarious; the foundations of the social-welfare state are collapsing; normal life-stories are breaking up into fragments' (Beck 2000a: 3). There were a number of others whose writing echoed these gloomy assessments. To summarize their position, essentially what was suggested was that in the past work had been stable and that it had afforded working people an opportunity to create and maintain an individual and social identity. It had allowed the emergence of vibrant working-class cultures linked to particular workplaces and industries. By contrast, the new capitalism undermined this by not allowing individuals and groups to put down roots and form social bonds and networks. In a dramatic summing-up of the situation, Catherine Casey suggested that 'The industrial legacy of the centrality of production and work in social and self formation hovers precipitously with the post-industrial condition in which work is declining in social primacy. *Social meaning and solidarity must, eventually, be found elsewhere*' (Casey 1995: 2).

This type of account of the way we work now has not gone unchallenged. Some scholars, for example, have argued that, far from the *end* of work being the big problem facing contemporary workers, it is in fact the issue of *too much* work and that consequently they experience stress and fatigue (Basso 2003; Schor 1991). Indeed, with modern information technology, some have suggested that the boundaries between work and home or leisure have become too porous, in that work can spill over into what would traditionally have been seen as non-work time. Mobile communications technology and laptop PCs and tablets allow employees to work both outside the traditional workplace and outside standard work time (Felstead, Jewson and Walters 2005; Fraser 2001). Another aspect of this criticism of the end of work literature is that the real problem is the low wages paid for the majority of unskilled jobs, and this has led to calls for living wages in the USA and Europe (Ehrenreich 2001; Shulman 2003; Toynbee 2003).

Insecurity at work

Another strand of the opposition comes from scholars who argue that the empirical evidence for the end of work and in particular greater job insecurity simply doesn't stack up. Kevin Doogan (2009), for example, using a variety of statistical material, suggests that job tenure has actually risen in recent years and therefore that there is less turbulence in the labour market, not more. Doogan and others such as Fevre (2007) point to several reasons for the popularity of the account given by the end of work theorists. For the left, many of whom would fall into the category of the end of work theorists, the ability to talk of constant change is in line with traditional Marxist views about work and its continual decline. For those on the liberal right, the message of flux and chaos feeds into an account of the inevitability of market forces and globalization and the futility of opposing the market (see Strangleman 2007).

More recently still, this debate has reignited around questions of insecurity and particularly the idea put forward by the British sociologist Guy Standing in his book *The Precariat* (2011). In many ways *The Precariat* rehearses many of the ideas we have discussed immediately above and, arguably, draws on far older Marxist ideas about the proletariat and the reserve army of labour that Marx himself wrote about. What is new about what Standing is suggesting is that he sees the coming together of distinct but differentiated groups of people with little or no security or long-term stake in the labour market. All of them are united in their inability to access 'good jobs' – namely those with reasonable pay and prospects, that offer pensions or other welfare benefits, and where there is an expectation that the post is secure. Standing's precariat, on the other hand, have few if any of these attributes. They are the unskilled, the young, the old, sometimes women, who for various reasons are unable to secure a place in the 'good' labour market. Standing's thesis is controversial and has created a lot of debate, both directly about his ideas and more generally about the changing nature of work. Interestingly, Standing has created a class schema which links labour market position with a class hierarchy (see figure 5.6). At the apex of the triangle are the rich global elite, and underneath them come what Standing calls the salariat, a group concentrated in large corporations or government agencies. These workers enjoy good terms and conditions, pensions and levels of pay. Alongside them comes another group labelled the proficians – a combination of professional workers and technicians. Below these two relatively well-off groups comes the old working class, who may still enjoy reasonable labour market status because of their marketable skills. Finally, at the bottom of the pyramid we

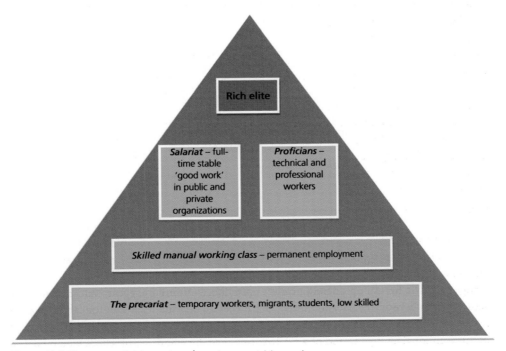

Figure 5.6 The precariat in a class/employment hierarchy

find the precariat, those in some type of work, however temporary or contingent. This is a very disparate group with little or nothing in common but for their precariousness.

As with Sennett's book, the question Standing poses for society generally and for politicians is: Are we content to create this type of labour market and are we willing to live with its consequences? Some might say that this is simply the logic of market forces. Critical sociologists, on the other hand, would argue strongly that the creation of a large number of precariously employed fellow citizens does nobody any good, and that we should adopt policies which create better opportunities for all citizens.

BOX 5.7 *A COMPANY OF ONE*

A slightly different account of the labour market from that put forward by Standing can be found in a recent book by the anthropologist Carrie Lane called *A Company of One* (2011). Lane looks at workers in the US software industry in places usually seen as part of the modern 'good' part of the economy. What she found in her ethnography of these highly educated people were high levels of insecurity in terms of employment. What is most original about *A Company of One* is that her interviewees did not seek to blame anyone for their predicament – neither government nor employers; instead they saw the labour market as something to which they had to constantly adapt by retraining, by constantly networking and by enhancing their CVs. As the title suggests, this was a highly individualized set of people who did not look to collective solutions for their troubles, rather considering it as their business alone to look after their careers. A flavour of this type of attitude can be seen in the following quotation from Ed, an IT worker, discussing job insecurity:

> One of the things they preached over and over and over again to us, through management, through memos, whatever, was to be loyal to yourself, not to Exalt [an IT company]. They're right. No one but you is going to look out for you as well as you can. You have to decide for yourself what you want and where you can get it. Yeah, Exalt will do what they have to to keep employees, so long as they need employees, but you have to decide for yourself what you want . . . .. It's the only perspective that makes sense these days. The old days of cradle-to-grave employment are long gone. I'd say they first started dying in the eighties, maybe in the early nineties, and it's taken this long for a lot of people to realize, but realize it they have. (Quoted in Lane 2011: 113)

Importantly here, workers don't blame anyone or any institution for their plight but feel fully responsible for their situation and for finding the means to escape it. They seemingly ignore the wider, deeper structural forces in US society of the long-term process of globalization.

Visions of the future

Sociology's role is to make visible the link between the position in which individuals find themselves and the larger social structures in which they are embedded. Furthermore, in doing so, sociologists have the responsibility to ask critical questions about that society and those very structures and the inequalities that flow from them.

How then do we think sociologically about the contemporary and future nature of work? In the past sociologists and other commentators have always held out the prospect of a positive future. These views are often rooted in the vision of more equal societies and are frequently seen as being driven by technological advances. While such visions could be criticized for being utopian or completely unrealistic, it is important that society does not simply accept that work needs to be as it is. At various points social theorists have suggested the need for the introduction of a social wage that would give all people in a society a decent standard of living, regardless of whether they were in work, were unemployed or were engaged in caring full time. Ulrich Beck (2000a), for example, suggested this in his book *The Brave New World of Work*, and likewise Andre Gorz (1999) proposed a radical rethink of society's relationship with economic life. Where these visions founder is in terms of the current economic system based on capitalism. Attempts to soften the impact of capitalism often fail, as it has proved impossible to protect working conditions from global market forces. For example, the European Union has, and could try to produce, all sorts of social and economic protection for its citizens, but, in an era of free trade, products can be made more cheaply in other parts of the world where employers don't need to pay a social wage. We can see this in the USA, where car manufacturing used to pay large wages and provide good health care. The last two or more decades in North America have seen the flight of manufacturing or the erosion of these conditions of service for the workers who remain in the sector.

As we saw right at the beginning of the chapter, Marx viewed capitalism as a restless system constantly seeking to revolutionize the productive processes, to seek out new markets for its products and to obtain ever cheaper inputs, including labour. These current debates about the end of work, the precariat and general labour market conditions take us right back to the beginning of our story.

SEMINAR QUESTIONS

1 Do you think you are part of Standing's precariat?
2 Has work lost its meaning?
3 What do you think work in the future is likely to look like?

CONCLUSION

Work, as we have seen in the course of this chapter, is far from a simple phenomenon. It is something almost all of us do at some point in our life. Some of us do too much, others too little. For many people it defines the way we are viewed by ourselves and others. Work is an essential part of one's identity; it has been claimed that this was the way in which men in particular in the past were defined and found meaning in their communities. We saw that work has been at the heart of the sociological project right from the nineteenth century and the subject's classical roots. Marx, Durkheim and Weber all wrote about work and industrial society. They were interested in how the shift from traditional to industrial societies witnessed changes in work and the social relations that surrounded employment and organization. All of the founding fathers saw work as both structured by society and in turn as helping to structure society – class, gender, race, ethnicity and age all played a part in structuring work.

Since the classical era, sociologists of work have researched and written within and beyond these themes. They are still centrally concerned with social relations at work and how these are shaped by and define work. Sociologists are interested in how people interact in organizations, how they cooperate, how conflict is managed. They are also concerned with how people look at their work and understand it. They ask some basic but fundamental questions about work: What do people draw from their work? What meaning do they gain from it and how that has changed over time? Work and workplaces have changed radically over the last century or two, but in many ways the questions sociology asks about work remain the same. We also need always to ask critical questions about the society we live in. Is work fair? How could it be more evenly distributed? Can we afford a work–life balance? Is there a viable alternative to capitalism? A vital sociology of work is fundamentally humanistic in the type of questions it asks as well as the solutions it can offer.

SEMINAR QUESTIONS

1 What do you expect your working life to look like? In what ways does it differ from those of your parents and grandparents?

2 Can all work be meaningful and interesting?

3 Take an occupation or profession. Think about how it is socially structured in terms of who does what. What sorts of people occupy the lowest and highest parts of the organization? Why is this so?

4 Write a short reflection on an aspect of the work you have experienced in your life.

FURTHER READING

For a really great read from an autobiographical account of work, take a look at Ben Hamper's (1991) *Rivethead: Tales from the Assembly Line* (Warner Books).

▶ Guy Standing's book is an important renewal of interest in the changing nature of work and its links to the class structure: Standing, G. (2011) *The Precariat: The New Dangerous Class* (Bloomsbury).

▶ My own book with Tracey Warren is an excellent introduction to all the themes covered here: Strangleman, T., and T. Warren (2008) *Work and Society: Sociological Approaches, Themes and Methods* (Routledge).

▶ For issues around the body and work, the standout book is Wolkowitz, C. (2006) *Bodies at Work* (Sage).

HEALTH, ILLNESS AND THE BODY

what lies beneath

GRAHAM SCAMBLER AND
SASHA SCAMBLER

CONTENTS

INTRODUCTION

HEALTH PROVIDES AN EXCELLENT lens through which may be seen the social structures and forces that shape so many facets of our lives. In a multitude of ways the societies in which people live leave their mark on what are understandably seen as very *individual* values, decisions and outcomes. It is the mission of this chapter to show how and why this is. On the face of it, health and illness make for mundane inquiry, but what is more basic to an individual's sense of who he or she is, or of embodiment, worth or the 'meaning of life', than the experience of health or wellbeing and a realistic estimate of total life span?

Variation by time and place is an uncontroversial starting point. It can be readily accepted that notions of the body and self and health and sickness have differed in Neolithic, Aztec, French medieval and contemporary Western communities. Moreover, this applies as much to recognized 'healers' as to 'lay' people. This is not simply a matter of 'knowledges' being culture-specific. Cultures, like the agency of their members, are always 'structured', *if never structurally determined*. In other words, cultures show biases towards the privileged and powerful. It has long been sociology's task to chart changes to and to examine and 'expose' hierarchies of privilege. This study of social *stratification* has documented the role of enduring systems such as caste in India or class in modern industrial societies, as well as that of institutions such as slavery, serfdom and colonialism. More recently, a Weberian concern with the staples of stratification – class, status/honour and party/power – has been complemented by a more rigorous focus on gender, ethnicity, sexuality, ageing, and so on, all of which will be visited in this chapter.

By way of illustration of the salience of stratification for health in modern Western societies, reference might be made to Parsons's (1951) classic delineation of the 'sick role'. People in the USA in the post-war era could not simply define themselves as sick and take time out to recover. Although it was accepted that sickness afforded grounds for release from normal obligations, including time off work, this process, Parsons argued, was 'policed' by the healers of the day, namely, qualified medical practitioners licensed by the state. It was doctors who decided who was 'really' sick and who not (and, Freidson (1970) was later to add, what sickness 'really' was). Moreover sickness brought obligations as well as rights, notably to be motivated to get well as expeditiously as possible and, when necessary, to seek counsel and therapy from a doctor. It was not that American doctors wanted or were even reflexive about policing the health of the workforce and underwriting and reinforcing a capitalist 'imperative to work'; but their contributions in this respect echoed the stratified interests of the privileged and the management of the workers.

So, as this example suggests, a sociology of health, illness and the body, extending to a sociology of medicine and health care systems, necessarily involves looking 'beneath the surface' to explain patterns of events discernible 'on the surface'. Stratification has to be inferred from the study of events: as Schutz (1967) phrased it, it is not a 'first-order construct' but a sociological or 'second-order construct'. This concern with second-order constructs runs like a thread through the discussions below.

The chapter is divided for convenience into six sections. The first of these elaborates on variations in *health and illness by time and place*. What emerges here is a set of parameters within which sociological questions might be asked. There is no doubt, for example, that expectation of life at birth has increased dramatically over time, albeit not always in a linear fashion and always with some countries or communities bucking the trend; nor are there any guarantees for the future. Associated with this increase in longevity has been a dramatic change in the dominant causes of death, and not only in developed societies.

The second section picks up on this change by concentrating on *long-term and disabling conditions*. These are not just characteristic of modern – for some, postmodern – Western societies but figure also in developing societies. Statistics on prevalence are fleshed out via studies of the impact of long-term and disabling illness on the lives of those affected.

The third section, on *modern and postmodern bodies*, takes off from rival interpretations of 'disability'. The very concept of disability, it was argued with force and effect within 'disability studies', implies an unacceptable binary involving acceptable, normal or able-bodied people and unacceptable, abnormal or disabled people. This normative judgement justified what was essentially the oppression of the latter by the former. As we shall see, there have been many twists and turns in this lively and heated debate.

Fourthly, we consider the *delivery of health care* using the framework of what the American anthropologist Kleinman (1985) helpfully terms 'local health care systems'. Kleinman identifies 'popular' and 'folk' as well as 'professional' sectors within any local health care system. Health care systems, in other words, extend well beyond the state-sanctioned and monitored provision of 'expert' interventions by medical practitioners. A sociological analysis of the passing of the Health and Social Care Act in England in 2012 affords an opportunity to revisit the sociology of health care provision in the prevailing neoliberal climate.

Common sense tells us that the nature or type of health care system must impact crucially on levels of health inequalities; but it is not as simple as this. *Tackling health inequalities* involves more than securing universal and ready access to doctors. Health status and life expectancy are primarily functions of the lives people lead and the circumstances that release or constrain their choices. Statistically, poorer citizens die sooner after coping with more than their share of acute and long-term assaults on their health. Why is this? Competing approaches, models and theories, and sociology's distinctive input, are presented and assessed.

The chapter concludes with reflections on the role of *social movements in the health domain*. As should be clear long before these paragraphs, health and health care are not simply matters for government pronouncement. The latter may hold sway, as has been the case with the Health and Social Care Act, which promises a controversial 'recommodification' of the National Health Service in England and Wales, but there remains a popular, public or lay voice. This is often heard indistinctly via the collective agency of social movements, which vary by constituency, commitment, organization and effectiveness.

SEMINAR QUESTIONS

1   What might the study of health, illness and the body tell us about the nature of our society?
2   How might it be claimed that in modern societies doctors 'police' the behaviour of the workforce?
3   How might a case be made that macro-social structures such as class and gender impact on the health, wellbeing and life spans of individuals?
4   Is a sociology of health, illness and the body necessarily critical of existing institutions?

HEALTH AND ILLNESS BY TIME AND PLACE

Concepts of health

Historians and anthropologists have documented multiple variations in human understandings and behaviour around health and sickness or illness. The 'falling sickness', now routinely recognized in modern Western cultures under the 'umbrella' diagnosis of epilepsy, was no less routinely, and is elsewhere still, regarded as a spiritual visitation – and one that can deliver benefits as opposed to stigma to those experiencing 'seizures', for example by revealing their links with the gods. What we now regard as symptoms to be treated, in short, has been, and in some parts of the world continues to be, interpreted very differently (Temkin 1945). It may be less obvious, however, that this complexity or lack of uniformity in making sense of health problems persists within modern developed as well as between developed and developing societies.

In a much cited early study of people's ideas of health and illness, Herzlich (1973) identified three metaphors for illness detectable in the accounts offered by eighty largely middle-class French adults:

- *illness as destroyer*: involving loss, isolation and incapacity;
- *illness as liberator*: referring to a lessening of burdens;
- *illness as occupation*: meaning freedom from responsibility, excepting a primary need to combat the disease.

She also found that illness was typically seen as 'external' and a product of a largely urban way of life. Health, on the other hand, was seen as 'internal' to the individual. People's accounts suggested three discernible dimensions: (1) an absence of illness ('health in a vacuum'); (2) a 'reserve of health', fashioned by constitution and environment; and (3) a positive state of wellbeing or 'equilibrium'.

Attention deficit hyperactivity disorder (ADHD) is a psychiatric disorder with symptoms including inattentiveness, hyperactivity and impulsiveness. Its diagnosis and treatment has long been controversial, since its symptoms are explained by others as simply poor behaviour. The medical status of ADHD is an example of how understandings vary and change around particular behaviours and conditions. (© Pete Quily/Flickr)

Herzlich's findings have been echoed in subsequent studies. In her review of these, Blaxter (1990) noted that health can be defined 'negatively', as the absence of illness; 'functionally', as the ability to cope with everyday activities; or 'positively', as fitness and wellbeing. She went on to observe that health can also have moral connotations, as if people feel they have a duty to be well and associate illness with failure. Unsurprisingly, people from low-income families, for whom life is more of a struggle, are most likely to define health in negative and functional ways, and it is the well-to-do who lean towards more positive definitions.

Bury (2005) makes a useful distinction between health as an *attribute* and health as a *relation*. The former is associated with the medical profession. Doctors tend to assume that illness or disease is an attribute of an individual, an 'it' that an individual 'has' or harbours. The notion of health as a relation, however, as the contributions of Herzlich and Blaxter imply, is more often associated with lay thinking. The focus here is less on biological mechanisms at work in the individual body and more on social and psychological processes that influence the pattern and expression of illness. As we shall see later, long-standing conditions, involving episodic breathing difficulties, intermittent blackouts or daily pill-taking, for example, become part and parcel of people's lives. Bury is insistent, however, that he is presenting ideal types and that there is often a considerable overlap between the perspectives or orientations of doctors and patients. Indeed, sometimes it is 'would-be patients' who adopt a health-as-attribute approach, as when they claim that their illness results from an underlying biological mechanism – for example, in the cases of contentious disorders such as myalgic encephalomyelitis (ME) or chronic fatigue syndrome (CFS).

Illness and disease

Freidson (1970) helpfully distinguishes between 'illness' and 'disease'. He sees illness as an essentially lay or 'subjective' sense of a health problem, while disease is defined as a professional or 'objective' acknowledgement of a health problem that can be *scientifically* diagnosed by means of signs and symptoms. It is a distinction that opens up the possibility of someone being ill without having a disease and of having a disease without being ill. If the medical profession holds jurisdiction over disease, it certainly does not control lay notions of illness. It might be said of recent campaigns in relation to ME and CFS that lay groups have sought to have (their) illnesses legitimated as diseases.

Mechanic and Volkart's (1960) concept of *illness behaviour* refers to how and why people come to define themselves as ill and what if anything they do about it. Going to a doctor is of course only one option, and one exercised fairly rarely. The term *illness iceberg* captures the common research finding that the majority of illness episodes do not lead to a medical appointment but are dealt with in Kleinman's popular sector of local health care systems – that is, by deploying unpaid labour, overwhelmingly that of women. Feminists and others have rightly pointed out that the NHS would rapidly sink without trace without this 'invisible' gendered input, and a generation ago some called for appropriate remuneration. Retrospective studies in the UK suggest that only one in five symptom episodes precipitates a visit to the doctor (Wadsworth, Butterfield and Blaney 1971), while some prospective studies put this ratio at one in eighteen (Scambler, Scambler and Craig 1981). That more people are also using the folk sector of their local health care system, consulting acupuncturists, osteopaths, herbalists, and so on, is another phenomenon worthy of note.

Most illness is attended to in and around private households and, setting aside for the moment the unpaid and gendered investment in caring that this implies, two further comments might be made. Firstly, most episodes of illness are minor and self-limiting; and secondly, professionals offering treatment and care through systems such as the NHS would be swamped if most, or even more, illness was brought to doctors' attention. Of concern, however, is the evidence of what might be called a *disease iceberg*. It is not just lay-identified illness that goes without professional scrutiny. Some significant, treatable and even life-threatening disease also falls short of medical examination. A classic London study by Epsom (1978), whose team took a mobile health clinic into a London neighbourhood, discovered people with serious long-term and occasionally terminal conditions who were not receiving any kind of ongoing professional help. The existence of a disease iceberg lends urgency to inquiries into illness behaviour.

There are countless factors that are known to play on people's decision-making when they sense disruptions to their health. Some of these are unsurprising: problems manifesting dramatically, through severe pain, high fevers, and so on, are more likely to lead to requests for professional help than those that present less obtrusively (although some major diseases typically have mild onsets, and dramatic symptoms do not always presage serious disease). Help-seeking can also turn on ease of appointment-making and distance from a GP's surgery.

BOX 6.1 ZOLA – TRIGGERS FOR MEDICAL CONSULTATIONS

Zola (1973) produced a revealing study of circumstances most likely to 'trigger' a consultation, some of which are far from obvious. He identified five triggers:

1 the occurrence of an interpersonal crisis (e.g., a death in the family);
2 perceived interference with social or personal relations;
3 'sanctioning', or pressure from others to consult;
4 perceived interference with vocational or physical activity;
5 a 'temporalizing of symptomatology', or setting of a deadline – e.g., 'If it's the same on Monday . . .'.

Source: Zola (1973).

Two features of Zola's study warrant attention: firstly, it is often not the symptoms per se but the way in which health problems impact that is decisive for seeking help; and secondly, it matters whether or not physicians pay attention to just why people decide to become patients. Listening to patients can be decisive for their taking medication, heeding advice and turning up for follow-up appointments.

Whether or not individuals frame their problems as assaults on their health, the actions they take, and whether or not they see a doctor, involve a multiplicity of social processes; and, clearly, doctors' responses to people who become patients also matter. It should not be assumed, however, that consulting a doctor is always positive. Moreover, recognition of disease via diagnosis itself reflects social processes. What counts as disease, as with people's behaviour around illness, varies by time and place. This is a matter to which we return later when considering social constructionist analyses of disease. For now it should be acknowledged that the Western professionalization of medicine is a relatively recent phenomenon. In Britain it was in fact the Medical Act of 1858 that created the medical profession as we understand it today.

Medicalization and social control

At the core of Freidson's (1970) influential analysis is the notion that disease is a form of social 'deviance'. To have a disease, in other words, is to fall short. After all, to have a disease – acknowledged and legitimated by a doctor – is to have a fault that needs correcting, a problem requiring a solution. Moreover, and here Parsons's (1951) positing of the sick role is relevant, it is a problem that one has a social, *and moral*, duty to solve, using state-sanctioned and licensed expertise if and when necessary. Freidson's argument may seem unobjectionable when diseases such as lung cancer and multiple sclerosis are in the frame; but what about 'being gay'? Arguably the identity of the male 'homosexual' emerged in the West only in the late nineteenth century, but the historical trajectory of 'men who have sex with men' (MSM) took some interesting turns. There is evidence that sexual relations between older 'mentoring' males and aspiring youths in the ancient Greek world were at least *culturally tolerated*. When Christianity was introduced to the Roman Empire, however, these same relations were redefined as deeply *sinful*. What was for many centuries sinful then eventually became a *crime*: it was only in 1967 in England and Wales that sexual relations between men were de-criminalized. What had been a crime subsequently came to be considered a *disease*. Only from the 1970s on, at least within the confines of Britain, were MSM gradually reassimilated into *mainstream culture*. Already the notion that MSM have a diagnosable disease seems distinctly 'historical', yet at the time many people understandably judged the transition from crime to disease to be progressive. Freidson's point, of course, is that categorizations in terms of disease are as negative as those in terms of crime: both signal forms of social deviance.

The linking of disease with deviance encouraged the development of notions of *medicalization* and *social control*. Zola (1972) seminally emphasized medicine's social control function. At the core of his thesis was the claim that the doctor had displaced the cleric and become Western communities' fount of homely wisdom. This shift was part and parcel of a broad 'medicalization' of people's everyday problems or quandaries. More and more of these were being translated into medical problems requiring formal health care consultations.

Illich (1975) offered a hard-hitting polemic, citing the (American) medical profession for three forms of 'iatrogenesis' – preventable harm brought about by the medical profession, summarized in box 6.2. Illich charged medicine, as he charged other putative expert and 'monopolistic' professions such as law and education, with cultivating and exploiting its publics. He wrote of 'medical imperialism', advocating a (utopian) return to a genuine marketplace in which wares and outcomes might be compared on a 'sink or swim' basis. It is a charge from which sociologists came to distance themselves.

BOX 6.2 ILLICH AND IATROGENESIS

Clinical iatrogenesis: Doctor-induced disease (e.g., when one clinical intervention leads to another, too often leaving the patient worse off, or even dead);
Social iatrogenesis: A growing public or lay dependency on the doctor as a professional expert;
Cultural iatrogenesis: The loss of individual autonomy, or problem-solving capacity, consequent upon social iatrogenesis.

Clearly medicine delivers benefits as well as problems of its own devising. Processes of medicalization are more complex than Illich allowed for. Ballard and Elston (2005) make a case that writing of medical dominance can be as misleading as it remains illuminating. While we think it entirely appropriate to continue to analyse medicalization, even to suggest a continuing 'medicalization of society' (Conrad 2007), a more nuanced analysis is required. Strong (1979) was quick off the mark to warn of the risk of hubris and of overlooking sociology's own pretensions, or of the tendency to think all phenomena essentially social and therefore answerable first and foremost to sociological interpretation. Thus against any charge of medical imperialism must be considered a counter-charge of 'sociological imperialism'. Moreover, even if medicalization remains a core issue for medical sociology, it is not always the product of medicine's imperialistic aspirations. Often, it is *lay pressure* for recognition and legitimacy that triggers processes leading to the medicalization of personal or social problems (see Bury above on ME and CFS, for example).

So the debate about medicalization has become subtler. It has also taken on new guises over the last generation. It is helpful in this context to consider Conrad's (2005) account of the 'shifting engines of medicalization'. He discerns three major drivers of this change.

1   ***Biotechnology*** Conrad highlights the roles in particular of the pharmaceutical industry and genetics.

   (a)   *Big pharma* While doctors remain the 'gatekeepers' for many drugs, in the less-regulated, post-Prozac world, 'big pharma' has become more aggressive in its marketing, targeting the public as well as doctors. The marketing of diseases, then selling drugs to treat those diseases, has grown more commonplace, and not only in the USA, Conrad's major source of data (see Goldacre 2012).

   (b)   *Genomic medicine* The Human Genome Project (the draft of the human genome was completed in 2000) heralds a new dawn, although as yet genomic medicine is more about potential than practice: knowledge about specific genes for cystic fibrosis and Huntington's disease has been available for nearly two decades without significant improvements in treatment. What Conrad calls 'biomedical enhancement' (for children, our bodies, or our mental or social abilities) offers another field for medical and commercial development.

2   ***Consumerism*** Having survived the rationing and shortages of the post-war era, it is often said we now live in a post-scarcity 'consumer society'. Medical care has in consequence become more like other products or services. Cosmetic surgery provides a paradigmatic example, although the growing public habit of 'shopping' in Kleinman's popular and folk sectors might also be cited. Individuals as consumers rather than as patients now help shape the scope, and maybe the demand, for professional-sector help.

3   ***Managed care*** The concept of managed care is more familiar in the USA than the UK. It is a device for containing escalating costs by (a) requiring pre-approval for medical treatment and (b) setting limits on some types of care. It can be both an incentive and a constraint as far as medicalization is concerned (e.g., it pays out more readily for drug therapy for mental health problems than it does for psychotherapy). It gives third-party payers more leverage.

Conrad's analysis outlines some key twenty-first-century influences on medicalization. Ignaas and Hoyweghen (2011) pick up on this but stress that medical consultations have become activities of consumption and transaction. Patients are no longer passive. Medicine and commercialization have co-evolved. Rose (2007: 700–2) puts it well:

> Marketing techniques, since the 1950s, have not regarded the consumer as a passive object to be manipulated by advertisers, but as someone to be known in detail, whose needs are to be charted, for whom consumption was an activity bound into a form of life that must be understood. Marketing does not so much invent false needs, as suggested by cultural critics, but rather seeks to understand the desires of potential consumers, to affiliate those with their products, and to link these with the habits needed to use those products.

'Desire' is the concept that Ignaas and Hoyweghen emphasize. They write of 'wish-fulfilling medicine' and what has been termed 'technoluxe' – that is, a view of the body as something to shape and of life as the process of this shaping as realized through acts of consumption. We return to these issues later in the chapter, notably when addressing postmodern bodies and the delivery of contemporary health care.

The changing pattern of disease

So, when the prevalence and incidence of various diseases is recounted in contemporary text-books, the fact that dynamic social processes are involved needs to be factored in. In fact, two sets of processes are implicated. The first has to do with the institutionalization of concepts of disease, the second with the ever shifting health problems that this reflects *and* shapes. Disease may be socially constructed, but people suffer and die from different assaults on their health in the USA and Britain now than they did in these countries in past eras and do elsewhere at the present time. As we shall see, this is pivotal for the delivery of cost-effective professional-sector health care within many local health care systems.

What is beyond dispute is that people worldwide have a greater expectation of life at birth now that in any previous epoch, and this should be registered early in this contribution. A contemporary cross-national life expectancy at birth of sixty-eight by far exceeds the mid-twenties of the Neolithic age, the mid-thirties of medieval Europe or the mid-forties of early Victorian England. In Britain, expectation of life at birth has risen by approximately forty years in a century and a half. Why is this? It was McKeown (1979) who alerted us to the possibility that expectation of life at birth *is not simply a function of the kind of healing or health care on offer*. The evidence he mustered that it was *public health/social* rather than *scientific/medical* inter-ventions that secured an 'epidemiological transition' from a majority of deaths at the hands of infectious diseases to a majority at the hands of chronic or long-term and degenerative dis-eases has survived the test of time. When Queen Victoria ascended the British throne in 1837, the main causes of mortality (and infant mortality comprised nearly a quarter of the total) were infectious diseases such as scarlet fever, diphtheria, whooping cough, tuberculosis, polio, and so on; when she died, at the dawn of the twentieth century, these were being displaced by long-term and degenerative conditions, diseases of the heart and the cancers, complaints we associate with survival into old age.

Not all infectious diseases had the same timeline or followed the same trajectory of decline. Tuberculosis (TB), the most common cause of death in the nineteenth century, started to decline in the first half of that century (significantly, it has been estimated that the availability of BCG vaccination 'late in the day', in the 1950s, accounted for only 3 percent of the total decline). The decline in deaths from airborne diseases such as pneumonia occurred later. In the case of both TB and pneumonia, however, much emphasis is placed on the salience of factors associated with enhanced resistance, such as the improvement in nutritional intake as technologies of agriculture improved, alongside those of the transportation of its produce. The nineteenth century was also witness to unprecedented increases in real wages and the standard of living in Britain, which at least partially underwrote the epidemiological transition (Fitzpatrick 2008).

There has been a global increase in life expectancy at birth *and* continuing inequal-ities between and within continents and countries. At the time of writing, life expec-tancy at birth across the globe stands at seventy, an increase of six years since 1990. The figure for high-income countries is eighty, that for low-income countries sixty. Europe stagnated during the 1990s, largely because of adverse mortality trends in the former Soviet countries. In Africa, however, life expectancy actually decreased, largely because of HIV/AIDS (it stood at fifty-one in 2000, although it picked up after 2005 as antiretroviral therapy became more widely available). Health inequalities within the UK are discussed below.

Table 6.1: **Life expectancy at birth by WHO region**			
	1990	**2000**	**2011**
Africa	50	50	56
Americas	71	74	76
Eastern Mediterranean	61	65	68
Europe	72	73	76
South-East Asia	59	63	67
Western Pacific	70	72	76
GLOBAL	**64**	**66**	**70**

Source: World Health Organization (WHO), Global Health Observatory, Data Report

SEMINAR QUESTIONS

1 In what ways is the distinction between 'illness' and 'disease' of significance?
2 Why is the sociological understanding of 'illness behaviour' important for the delivery of effective health care?
3 Does the concept of 'medicalization' still have applicability in contemporary society?
4 How did social interventions contribute to the 'epidemiological transition'?

LONG-TERM AND DISABLING CONDITIONS

Biographical disruption and identity

In the wake of the epidemiological transition there were increases in rates of mortality from long-term and degenerative disorders. In fact, long-term conditions show a high prevalence in contemporary developing as well as developed societies. In 2010, Stuckler and Basu (2011) claim, four chronic diseases – heart disease, respiratory disease, common cancers and type 2 diabetes – accounted for more than 35 million lives, or about three out of every five deaths in the world. If current trends continue, the number of premature deaths and lives lived with disability caused by chronic disease will triple by 2030.

The King's Fund (2012) has estimated that 15.4 million people in England, almost one in three of the total population, suffer from a long-term condition such as diabetes, asthma and heart disease. Moreover, it is more than likely that many more remain undiagnosed (witness the earlier discussion of the illness and disease icebergs). Three out of every five people over sixty in England are known to suffer from a long-term condition; and it is commonly accepted that the pressure on the health services will grow as the proportion of older people in the population continues to rise.

Independently of the medical diagnosis of long-term conditions, the 'stretching' of the experience of illness has brought its own challenges. The onset of a long-term condition such as rheumatoid arthritis, diabetes or ulcerative colitis can, as Bury (1982) showed, result in 'biographical disruption'. It can, in other words, turn an individual's life upside down, requiring a total rethink of everything from personal aspirations to the mundane routines comprising day-to-day living. Charmaz (1983) graphically describes how this disruption can result in a 'loss of self'; and Gareth Williams (1984) has written of a common need for 'narrative reconstruction' as a new sense of identity displaces the old. Sometimes, particularly if the condition carries stigmatizing connotations, the making and passing on of an authoritative medical diagnosis represents an important turning point in people's lives. Scambler and Hopkins (1986) showed how a doctor's authoritative communication of a diagnosis of epilepsy can turn a 'person' into an 'epileptic'. Moreover, the *label* can become a 'master status' for self or others: the 'epileptic identity' becomes paramount and the driver in personal and social interaction. These authors also found, interestingly, that because people with epilepsy have an disorder which is 'invisible' – in other words they are 'discreditable' rather than 'discredited' (Goffman 1969) – and because they tend not to disclose their condition/diagnosis, the primary cause of biographical disruption for most was 'felt stigma' (i.e., a sense of shame and fear of stigmatization) and not 'enacted stigma' (i.e., actual stigmatization on the part of others). People with epilepsy typically 'internalized' what they understood to be the beliefs and attitudes of what Mead (1934) called the 'generalized other' and as a result *took defensive or self-limiting decisions about themselves and their futures.*

Defining and interpreting disability

A systematic way of thinking through the impact of long-term conditions on people's lives emerged courtesy of the International Classification of Impairments, Disabilities and Handicaps (ICIDH) (Wood 1980). This model was premised on an uncritical acceptance of medical concepts of disease. It defined impairment in terms of abnormalities in the structure or functioning of the body or its parts; disabilities in terms of the performance of activities; and handicap in terms of the broader psychosocial consequences of living with impairment and/or disability. The merit of this classification seemed to be that, by separating out these three 'dimensions', it was possible to say, for example, that a minor impairment/disability could lead to a major handicap (as when a concert pianist lost a finger as a result of an accident), or that a major impairment impairment/disability could end up as a minor handicap (as when a website designer had a leg amputated but carried on working and socializing as usual).

This ICIDH model attracted criticism, not least around the word 'handicap'. Some preferred words such as 'disadvantage' or 'deprivation'. A more informed critique was mounted by activists intent on securing basic civil rights for people with disabilities. The 'social model of disability' pointed the finger at those who label and treat people as 'dis-abled', 'abnormal', 'deviant', 'outsiders', and so on. In other words, the focus was on *oppression*. What medical sociologists had uncritically addressed as *personal tragedy*, it was argued, was in fact an unacceptable form of oppression against people stereotyped as undesirably different, and therefore subject to systematic neglect and discrimination. In a book entitled *End of Stigma?* Green (2009) implied a need to 'go beyond' the implicit individualism of medical sociology's 'victim-based' approach.

People with disabilities were consulted before the ICIDH was displaced by the International Classification of Functioning, Disability and Health (ICF) in 2001. Over time the ICF has evolved: human functioning is assessed by the body's – impaired or non-impaired – interrelationship with, and freedom to participate in, given contexts or environments. Environmental factors are physical *and* social, embracing:

1   aspects of the physical environment such as climate and population density;
2   features of the human-built environment such as homes, streets and public buildings;
3   people's attitudes, values and beliefs;
4   the prevailing social, cultural and political institutions and systems (Thomas 2012: 214).

Thomas (2012) is among those who advocate a coming together of medical sociology and disability studies over notions of the body. She rejects what she calls medical sociology's 'social deviance paradigm' in favour of a 'social oppression paradigm', but she acknowledges that medical sociologists have been on a learning curve since the personal tragedy studies characteristic of the 1980s. She notes, for example, how Bury (2008) now uses politico-structural and discursive frameworks to examine how contemporary medical treatment and care is managed and delivered. He strongly critiques the so-called *self-management* and *expert patient programmes* now deployed in the NHS. These are considered by many to be driven by a political aspiration to cut health care costs and to shift responsibility for treatment and care onto patients (see below).

Thomas uses the term *impairment effects* to acknowledge that bodies have non-social properties regardless of how they are 'socially constructed' by the discourses of the day. She also refers to *disablism*, or the social imposition of avoidable restrictions on the life activities, aspirations and psycho-emotional wellbeing of people categorized as 'impaired' by those deemed 'normal'. She is currently arguing for a new, mature sociology of disability encompassing studies of impairment effects and disablism.

SEMINAR QUESTIONS

1 Distinguish between and assess the rival merits of the 'deviance' and 'oppression' paradigms of disability.
2 Analyse the challenges long-term conditions pose for health practitioners.
3 How might long-term conditions occasion 'biographical disruption'?
4 'The principal problem confronting people with disabilities is 'disablism'. To what extent is this statement true?

MODERN AND POSTMODERN BODIES

From the biomedical 'body-with-organs' to the postmodern 'body-without-organs'

The active intervention of disability theorists helped occasion a rethink not only of medical sociology's under-examined premises but also of orthodox, authoritative, 'biomedical' notions of the body. This was associated too with the gradual emergence of what came to be known as post-1970s 'postmodern' culture. The Cartesian duality of mind and body – the distinction bequeathed us by the philosopher Descartes that has led us to regard our mental and corporeal natures as separate, with the former holding sway over the latter – was called into question. Using the phraseology of Lyotard (1971), the settled 'grand narratives' of oldthink, rooted in Western Enlightenment ideas of universalism, science and progress, were displaced by the 'petit narratives' of newthink. Medicine found itself representing oldthink against a quite unexpected head of steam. The postmodern newthink can be characterized as follows: (1) the abandonment of a sense that *any* particular – in fact Western, Enlightenment – narrative or discourse can command universal, cross-cultural assent; and (2) the acceptance of epistemological relativism, or a newfound freedom to abandon a false prospectus offering time- and culture-free truths (and values) in favour of a multiplicity of options.

Along with Cartesian dualism, all sorts of other binaries were rejected. This meant that the epistemological (i.e., knowledgeable) and normative (i.e., moral) privileging of *normal, able-bodied* persons was consigned to a passing historical phase. Not only did this *cultural turn* or *shift* threaten the near monopolistic authority of biomedicine, reducing it to one of many rival *petit* narratives, it raised questions about the lenses through which bodies are viewed. Foucault was much cited in this connection. For Foucault (1980), 'discourses', the vehicles of 'knowledge-power', come and go; and the present has witnessed the usurping of biomedicine as the dominant discourse. The modern biomedical body is ceding ground to a plethora of postmodern bodies. People unequivocally defined as 'impaired', 'disabled' and/or 'handicapped' in the pre-modern and modern eras are, some claim, now on level terms: bodies have been freed from the chains of biomedicine.

Natalie Du Toit is a South African swimmer and Paralympic champion. Prostheses have greatly improved the racing capacities of single- and double-leg amputees, and Du Toit even competed in the Beijing 2008 summer Olympics against able-bodied athletes. Is the postmodern body levelling the playing field that biomedicine defined as uneven? (© REX/Mark Pain)

Fox (1998) has drawn on the theories of Deleuze and Guattari to take this line of argument further. He is encouraged by the postmodern emphasis on open-mindedness, diversity and taken-for-granted and ritualized forms of categorization and behaviour. Following Foucault (1980), he characterizes this emphasis in terms of the 'micro-politics' of the interplay of power/knowledge texts, with 'texts' here reaching beyond writing to refer to 'any kinds of meaningful systems of communication or behaviour' (Fox 1998: 10). For Deleuze and Guatarri (1984), biomedicine and its kindred discourses have *territorialized* humans as organisms, as 'bodies with organs'. But the body can be grasped in other ways. They present the body as a 'philosophical' surface upon which are inscribed a range of *knowledgeabilities* (texts of power/knowledge), only one of which is called biomedicine. So, while biomedicine constructs the body as a 'natural' organism, whose functioning is defined as 'health' and dysfunctioning as 'illness/disease', the body might be, and actually is, differently situated in other – less celebrated – discourses. Deleuze and Guatarri term the philosophical surface the 'body-without-organs'.

Freeing bodies from time, space and discourse

Unlike the biomedical body, the body-with-organs that typifies modernity, the postmodern body-without-organs is free from time and space, becoming subject to temporal and spatial constraints only as the outcome of inscription. According to Fox, Foucault does not admit of resistance to power/knowledge, while Deleuze and Guatarri (1986) claim to do so via their project of *nomadology*. For them, the body-without-organs is highly contested, with a variety of distinct knowledgeabilities inside as well as outside the medical profession, for example between medicine and surgery. Differentiation and rivalry create possibilities for 'breaking free from discourse altogether, if only for a moment', a moment of 'nomadic subjectivity' (Fox 1998: 15). Nomadology for Deleuze and Guattari is the riposte of the repressed to those who exercise power through their discourses on the human predicament. 'Nomads', it seems, are warriors without strategy or goals, 'at war' with those who would territorialize them. Strictly speaking, however, there are no nomads; 'nomad*ism*' is a process, not an identity. Nomadism is about becoming other, and one never finally becomes other; rather, one lurches from one identity to another. Deleuze and Guatarri see nomadism as *rhizomatic*, a growth that is branching and diversifying, refusing to allow a single line of development (Scambler 2002).

In an echo of Derrida (1976) on 'arche-writing', Fox develops a concept of *arche-health*. This refers to a 'becoming other', a freeing of the body-without-organs from discourse, a nomadic subjectivity. While health and illness constrain or territorialize the body-without-organs, arche-health represents a refusal of, extending to resistance to, these discourses. Thus the ethics and politics of arche-health are 'deconstructive'. It reminds us, in Fox's (1998: 36) words, 'to ask hard questions of the modernist disciplines which inscribe us into subjectivity through their conceptions of, and preoccupations with, health and illness.' In a more recent contribution Fox (2012: 165) writes:

> health is processual, and both at the level of the individual and the wider public health this is a process that encompasses natural and social science disciplines. For health care (as for education, citizenship and every aspect of social action), the analysis developed from the work of Deleuze and Guattari suggests an agenda for its practitioners that fosters deterritorialisation in the bodies of those for whom they care, and generates a politics of health that transcends economic and management perspectives. To engage productively with such agendas collapses disciplinary boundaries and establishes a pressing need for collaboration between medical and caring professions, social and political scientists, social activists, indeed everyone with a body.

While a 'rhetoric' of integration in the education and praxis of health professionals has become increasingly common of late, it is doubtful whether this is likely to meet Fox's aspirations in the delivery of health care. What writings on the postmodern body call for is a recognition *and appreciation* (a) of the extent of historical and cultural variations in conceptualizations of the 'sick body' that we mentioned at the start of this chapter; and (b) that current Western biomedical conceptualizations are neither compelling nor sacrosanct (i.e., it is open to us to reclaim our bodies).

SEMINAR QUESTIONS

1 How would you characterize the distinction between 'modern' and 'postmodern' bodies?

2 Is the biomedical concept of the body past its sell-by date?

3 Are postmodern conceptions of the body genuinely emancipatory?

4 How would you assess Fox's ideas of 'arche-health' and 'nomadic subjectivity'?

DELIVERY OF HEALTH CARE

Health care in Britain before the NHS

Concepts of health and sickness have, as we have seen, varied by time and place and, if Fox is right, are now in a state of flux in Western nations; but, as historians and anthropologists have documented, *healers* have always been part and parcel of human settlements. The emergence of the modern medical profession in Britain has already been alluded to but can now be described more fully. The Medical Act of 1858 formally created the profession of medicine with which readers will be familiar. The *gentlemen*, the hospital-based 'physicians' and 'surgeons', were prevailed upon by a government under pressure from its electorate to deliver better health care to submit to a deal with the *traders*, the community-based 'apothecaries' (shortly to be known as general practitioners, or GPs). They acquiesced because they relied on the latter for referrals; and an informal system of referral from GP to specialist was in place by the end of the nineteenth century.

The brief account of health care before the NHS that follows draws on the work of Mays (2008). In the nineteenth century, hospitals were dangerous resources used mostly by the poor. It was only at the century's close, with developments in anaesthesia and antiseptic surgery, that the corner was slowly turned. The more affluent had access to fee-for-service treatment either in the surgery or at home. A variety of insurance schemes, organized by friendly societies and trade unions, gradually enabled less affluent groups to use GPs. By the end of the nineteenth century, however, only approximately half the working class was covered by these schemes of contributory insurance. In 1911 a National Health Insurance (NHI) scheme was introduced by the Lloyd George administration, in large part because of fears that males of working age were (a) unfit to fight for their country should the need arise (the Boer War had been a wake-up call in this connection) and (b) unfit to sustain work performance. This legislation covered manual workers aged sixteen to sixty-five whose earnings were below the threshold for payment of income tax. It afforded funds for sickness, accident and disability benefits in cash and access to GP services free of charge (hospital services were not covered). It was an Act as notable for its exclusions as for its inclusions.

NHI improved GPs' remuneration because it provided public funds to subsidize the treatment of many more poorer patients while still allowing them to work for other insurers on a fee-for-service basis. By 1939, approximately 40 percent of the working population enjoyed some coverage through the NHI scheme, while about two-thirds of GPs were involved in NHI work.

Hospital care was provided by (a) voluntary hospitals and (b) municipal or local authority hospitals. The former were charitable institutions and treated just over a third of all hospital patients by 1939. Their consultants treated poor patients without payment but also saw more 'interesting' or complex cases. They earned their incomes from private practice outside the hospitals. With developments in medical science through the early decades of the twentieth century, however, most voluntary hospitals were in financial difficulty by 1939. The nineteenth-century Poor Law system incorporated long-term hospital care for society's poorest. In 1929 these Poor Law hospitals were taken over by local government. They continued thereafter to provide mainly means-tested care for those chronically sick who were unable to obtain care from either the voluntary hospitals or private practice.

The significance of public health legislation between the years 1848 and 1875 was noted earlier. This had led to major improvements in water supplies and the treatment of sewage, leading ultimately to the control of a number of infectious diseases. By the end of the nineteenth century each local authority was charged by law to have a medical officer for health (MOH) responsible for environmental health, the control of infectious disease, the certification of causes of death, and a broad range of preventive services. By 1939 an MOH led a department in every local authority that extended to services not provided by NHI, including maternity care, child health and welfare (health visiting), a school medical service, and services and support for the elderly in their own homes (district nursing).

BOX 6.3 DEFICIENCIES IN HEALTH CARE AT THE OUTBREAK OF THE SECOND WORLD WAR

- Financial barriers to health service usage: National Health Insurance did not cover more than half the population, including the dependants of insured workers.
- National Health Insurance did not cover hospital care.
- GPs, specialists and hospital beds were unevenly distributed across the country.
- Wide variations in quality existed across all services.
- Financial problems were accumulating, especially in voluntary hospitals, leading to staff and equipment shortages.
- Local authority, GP and voluntary hospital services were uncoordinated.

Source: Mays (2008).

The birth of the NHS

At the outbreak of the Second World War there was a general awareness of the need for improvement, but it took the disjuncture occasioned by the war to propel change. Three contributory factors should be mentioned: (a) the Emergency Medical Service, (b) the Beveridge Report and (c) the sanction of the wartime coalition government headed by Churchill with Atlee as his deputy prime minister.

The Emergency Medical Service was established to ensure comprehensive medical cover throughout an embattled nation, stretching out from the cities and towns of urban Britain to its outermost rural areas. This involved a 'direction of labour' inconceivable in

BOX 6.4 THE GOVERNMENT'S COMMITMENT TO AN NHS, 1944

The following quotations demonstrate the strength of government commitment to making proposals for an NHS a reality and on making it universally and freely available.

To ensure that everybody in the country – irrespective of means, age, sex and occupation – shall have equal opportunity to benefit from the best and most up-to-date medical and allied services available. To provide, therefore, for all who want it, a comprehensive service covering every branch of medical and allied activity.

To divorce the case of health from questions of personal means or other factors irrelevant to it; to provide the service free of charge (apart from certain possible charges in respect of appliances) and to encourage a new attitude to health – the easier obtaining of advice early, the promotion of good health rather than only the treatment of bad.

Source: Ministry of Health (1944: 47).

peacetime: London's hospital consultants were dispatched to all parts of the domain to provide organization and cover. In short, the Emergency Medical Service offered the kind of comprehensive health care that had been inconceivable before the war. The Beveridge Report was published in 1942 and advanced a blueprint for a post-war 'welfare state'. A dry and lengthy tome, it nevertheless caught the popular imagination at home and abroad, translating into a vision of a future worth fighting for. A central plank in the report was the concept of a ubiquitous and comprehensive health service. In 1944 the wartime coalition government signed up to the Beveridge aspiration for health care. The commitment was unambiguous.

It fell to the post-war Labour administration under Atlee to negotiate the details with the medical profession. Perhaps inevitably there were compromises. The GPs wanted to retain their professional autonomy rather than become salaried employees, while the hospital consultants resisted the proposal that they be subject to local authority control. The resultant National Health Service Act of 1946, vigorously negotiated by Aneurin Bevan, represented a compromise between the interests of traditional medical authority and rational public administration (Klein 2006). GPs remained independent contractors; hospital doctors were paid for the hospital work they had been doing for free; consultants were permitted to work part-time for the NHS on salaries while keeping their private practice; beds for private patients ('pay beds') were allowed in NHS hospitals; a system of distinction or 'merit awards' at the behest of the profession was established for hospital consultants, but not GPs; doctors were integrated into policy-making; and hospitals were not to be controlled by local authorities but 'nationalized' under local, appointed bodies. For all the compromises, however, the NHS represented a radical departure. It was open to the whole population based on need, free at the point of use, and was funded almost entirely from general tax revenues.

Changes in the NHS and recommodification

The NHS was launched in 1948. It has been subjected to a number of 'reforms' since, most of which need not delay us here. In 1974 it was reformed in favour of more integration, and in the early Thatcher years, 1982–7, efforts were made to introduce innovative and more 'corporate' management structures, leading commentators to write of a 'new managerialism'. Thatcher's orientation to *markets*, however, led to a National Health Service and Community Care Act in 1990 which resulted, in 1991, in the introduction of an 'internal market'. This separated the roles of 'purchaser' and 'provider' and was designed to encourage competition between suppliers, including those from the private sector. Often decried as a 'pseudo-market', it sat on a spectrum between a private free market and a bureaucratic 'command and control' economy. If it was closer to the latter, it also broke with precedents. It was a portent of what was to come.

Thatcher's displacement by Major in 1990 precipitated the introduction in 1992 of the Private Finance Initiative (PFI), the significance of which is now more routinely acknowledged. The PFI delegated the building of new hospitals and other health care facilities to the private sector, which then leased them back to the NHS, often at 'exorbitant rates', on the back of twenty- to thirty-year deals. The advantage to government was that the rebuilding programme did not appear on its books (i.e., it represented an investment of private as opposed to public monies). It proved an expensive way to get new buildings on the cheap, and the chickens have since come home to roost. 'New Labour' under Blair and Brown pursued PFIs with a vengeance between 1997 and 2010. At the time of writing – that is, after the global financial crisis of 2008–9 – we are seeing an increasing number of health care facilities under threat because of the levels of debt occasioned by PFI commitments.

It was the formation of the Conservative–Liberal Democrat coalition government in 2010 that was to prove the real turning point. Notwithstanding a pre-election commitment not to reform the NHS 'from above', Prime Minister David Cameron's first health minister, Andrew Lansley, put together a Health and Social Care Bill that included a root-and-branch privatization, or *recommodification*, of health care. The medical profession, a reluctant recruit to the concept of an NHS in the 1940s, fatally hesitated. In March of 2012 the Bill became law, and the consequences are already becoming apparent. Trusts in both primary and secondary health care, already overstretched by PFI deals and committed to making significant savings from 2011 to 2014 under a New Labour initiative in 2009, are facing challenges from acquisitive and often foreign-owned for-profit businesses.

Public health academic and physician Scott-Samuel (2012) has offered some evidence-based predictions:

- the NHS will become a publicly funded budget and a brand name for a subcontracting operation for competing private organizations, subject to European competition laws which will allow private companies to predominate over other – third-sector – providers;
- the post-credit-crash NHS has a more or less fixed budget, so services of 'low clinical priority' will cease to be free;
- this will lead to a market for health insurance, affordable for the affluent, which will drive up costs (administrative, fees, private profits);
- personal health budgets will lead to personal charges, as commissioning groups will operate on an individual basis in order to be compatible with the insurance companies (*no more population-based pooling of risk*).

Scott-Samuel's predictions are, it seems, rapidly being realized.

This full-frontal assault on the NHS has not been publicized in the traditional media, although opponents using new social media such as Twitter and blogs have been active. It is an assault born of sustained and careful planning and not, as many health professionals and journalists assumed, one born of incompetence. For Scambler (2012) it is an illustration of a new, post-1970s *class/command dynamic*. Drawing on historian David Landes's (1998) observation that those with wealth have always bought those with power, Scambler's argument is that, in this present phase of financial capitalism, those comprising largely transnational financial and business elites hold greater sway over a more national political elite than was the case in the immediate post-war period. More sociologically, *class relations* have assumed a new authority relative to the *command relations* of the state: those with wealth get more for their money now than previously. Hence the programmes of privatization energetically pursued at their behest by New Labour as well as by Conservative or Conservative-led regimes. There is a great deal of money to be made out of the break-up of the public sector, perhaps most dramatically in relation to the iconic 'socialist' achievement, the NHS. This is an argument revisited and developed further in the next section on health inequalities.

SEMINAR QUESTIONS

1 What combination of factors led to the formation of the National Health Service?

2 How and why are we witnessing a recommodification of health care in England and Wales?

3 What is meant by the 'new class/command dynamic', and is this a credible basis for a sociology of health care transition?

4 What are the likely consequences of the Health and Social Care Act of 2012?

TACKLING HEALTH INEQUALITIES

Class and inequality

There is strong historical evidence that living in poverty diminishes people's chances for long and healthy lives. The 'haves' live longer than the 'have-nots'. In the early 1840s two commentators, Engels and Virchow, put forward theories that went beyond the mere noting and documenting of this social patterning to morbidity and mortality. Engels argued that class exploitation was the overriding cause of premature death in England. Moreover, he added, those guilty of exploiting are murderers:

> when society places hundreds of proletarians in such a position that they inevitably meet a too early and unnatural death, one which is quite as much a death by violence as that by the sword or bullet; when it deprives thousands of the necessities of life, places them under conditions in which they cannot live – forces them . . . to remain in such conditions until that death ensues which is the inevitable consequence – knows that these thousands of victims must perish, and yet permits these conditions to remain, its deed is murder. (Engels [1845] 1987: 127)

Engels refers to 'inequity', which is now understood to denote inequality that is avoidable, unnecessary or unfair. Virchow, like Engels, was in favour of revolutionary change. A Prussian physician, his report on an outbreak of typhus in Upper Silesia bears comparison with Meillassoux's (1981) classic analysis of industrial England. It was the poor, he insisted, who bore the brunt of the epidemic. 'Disease', he pronounced, 'is not something personal and special, but only a manifestation of life under (pathological) conditions . . . Medicine is a social science and politics is nothing else but medicine on a large scale' (Virchow [1848] 1985, quoted in de Maio 2010: 20).

At the same time that Engels and Virchow were protesting against the production and repro-duction of social disadvantage, *and its health sequelae*, a form of social accounting was emerg-ing in the UK that gave substance to their arguments. Positive associations between absolute and relative poverty and reductions in health status and longevity were being documented. Socio-economic classifications (SECs), sometimes interpreted as proxies for the more theo-retical ideas of class in the work of Marx and Engels, featured in many influential reports. The SEC currently favoured is the National Statistics Socio-Economic Classification (NS-SEC), derived from the neo-Weberian research of Goldthorpe and his associates (Rose and Pevalin 2003). This instrument classifies occupations according to the structure of employment rela-tions operating in modern economies like that of the UK. Occupations are differentiated in terms of reward mechanisms, promotion prospects, autonomy and job security. The most advantaged NS-SEC 'classes' typically exhibit personalized reward structures, have positive opportunities for promotion, and enjoy high levels of autonomy and security relative to those least advantaged. SECs such as the NS-SEC are of interest independently of their status as 'operationalizations' of classical sociological concepts of social class.

As far as England and Wales are concerned, the changes captured by a succession of SECs, on the one hand, and health status/longevity, on the other, are unambiguous (ONS 2011) (see box 6.5).

As occupations shift from most to least advantaged, so the prospects for health and lon-gevity decline. More than this, there would seem to be a discernible 'social gradient'. It is not just a matter of the contrasting fortunes of those at the 'top' and those at the 'bottom'. Rather, as the Whitehall studies of Marmot and his colleagues (1991) showed, there are fine-tuned differences even between occupational grades within the middle ranks of the civil service: astonishingly, each and every elevation of grade brings a positive return for health status and longevity. But *statistical* associations between SECs and health/longevity need not also be *causal*. Maybe, for example, poor health leads to downward social mobility? It certainly can do, but only relatively rarely it seems. Reviewing research contributions in the round, epidemiol-ogists Wilkinson and Marmot (2003: 10) conclude:

> Both material and psychosocial factors contribute to these differences and their effects extend to most diseases and causes of death. Disadvantage has many forms and may be abso-lute or relative. It can include having few family assets, having a poorer education during adolescence, having insecure employment, becoming stuck in a hazardous or dead-end job, living in poor housing, trying to bring up a family in difficult circumstances and living on an inadequate retirement pension. These disadvantages tend to concentrate among the same people, and their effects on health accumulate during life. The longer people live in stressful economic and social circumstances, the greater the physiological wear and tear they suffer, and the less likely they are to enjoy a healthy old age.

Sociologists have contributed to three principal attempts to *explain* the plethora of findings represented in Wilkinson and Marmot's summary. These are generally known as the *behav-ioural*, *material* and *psychosocial* models and are defined briefly in table 6.2. It is not simply a matter of choosing *between* these models of course: there is truth and falsity in each. Nor are they the only models on offer: one 'outlier model' maintains that IQ is the most important explanatory factor for health and longevity, for example.

BOX 6.5 LIFE EXPECTANCY BY SOCIO-ECONOMIC CLASSIFICATIONS

MEN

- Inequalities in male life expectancy by SEC increased across most of the period 1982–2006, despite improvements over time for all classes.
- The difference in male life expectancy at birth between the most and least disadvantaged classes rose from 4.9 years in 1982–6 to 6.2 years in 1997–2001. A slight fall to 5.8 years in 2002–6 was not statistically significantly different from the previous figure.
- In the period 2002–6, life expectancy at birth for males whose parent(s) had an occupation which was classified as 'higher managers and professionals', such as directors of major organizations, doctors and lawyers, was 80.4 years compared with those born to parents classified as 'routine' occupations, such as labourers and cleaners, whose life expectancy was 74.6 years.
- The greatest growth in life expectancy at birth for males between 1982–6 and 2002–6 was experienced by those in the lower managerial and professional class, such as school teachers and social workers, at 5.3 years.
- The least growth in life expectancy at birth was experienced by those in the two least advantaged classes, 'semi-routine' and 'routine' occupations, at 3.8 and 3.9 years respectively.
- In the period 2002–6, the life expectancy of men at age sixty-five classified by occupation as 'higher managerial and professional' was 18.8 years compared with 15.3 years for those assigned to the 'routine' occupations class.

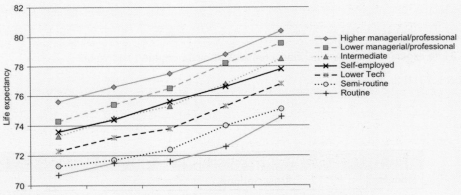

Figure 6.1 Life expectancy by NS-SEC class, males at birth, England and Wales

Source: ONS (2011: 2).

WOMEN

- Inequalities in female life expectancy by SEC persisted across the period 1982–2006, despite improvements over time in all classes.

- The difference in female life expectancy at birth between the most and the least advantaged classes rose slightly, from 3.8 years in 1982–6 to 4.2 years in 2002–6. There was no statistically significant pattern over time.
- For females at birth in the period 2002–6, those whose parents had an occupation which was classified as 'higher managerial and professional' had a life expectancy of 83.9 years compared with 79.7 years for those in the 'routine' class.
- For females, the greatest growth in life expectancy was experienced by those in 'lower managerial and professional' occupations (3.7 years) and the least by those in 'lower supervisory and technical' occupations, such as supervising sales assistants and catering supervisors.
- In 2002–6, life expectancy for women at age sixty-five classified by occupation as 'higher managerial and professional' was 21.7 years compared with 18.5 years for those assigned to the 'routine' occupations class.

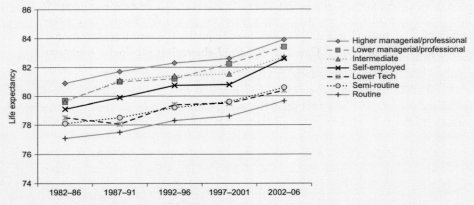

Figure 6.2 Life expectancy by NS-SEC class, females at birth, England and Wales

Source: ONS (2011: 3).

Table 6.2: **Three models to account for health inequalities**	
Models	Descriptions
1 Behavioural	Emphasizes SEC-related differences in rates of 'risk behaviours' for health
2 Material	Focuses on SEC-related differences in material 'standard of living' for health
3 Psychosocial	Accents SEC-related differences in levels of social inclusion, support, autonomy and recognition for health

Recently there has been an emphasis on the concept of the *life course*. This is a useful concept in that it can provide a 'frame' or context for understanding and explaining health inequalities. Factors disadvantageous for health tend both to cluster and to accumulate over time. It seems also that there are 'critical junctures', most notably childhood. This was acknowledged in the Marmot Review on health inequalities in the UK in 2010. Problems experienced in infancy and childhood, stretching into adolescence, cast long shadows: what happens early in the life course, in other words, can quite literally circumscribe individuals' futures.

Wealth, power and health inequality

While there is clearly merit in each of the behavioural, material and psychosocial models, and in a life-course orientation, they are often more socio-epidemiological than sociological. Coburn (2000) mounted a challenge by interrogating Wilkinson's (1996) thesis that income inequality precipitates the psychosocial factors – social fragmentation, leading to a breakdown in trust and relations of reciprocity – that ultimately undermine health and life expectancy among the disadvantaged. What are the causes of income inequality?, he asked. His answer was a 'neoliberal ideology' that had become ubiquitous in the post-1970s era of a globalized financial capitalism. This, indeed, was the ideology used to justify the recommodification of health care via the Health and Social Care Act discussed above. But ideologies bear testimony to vested interests – so which vested interests? Scambler (2012) reasserted the class/command dynamic, arguing that it was this dynamic that underwrote the rapid increase in income inequality in the UK, *and its health sequelae.*

To develop a comprehensive sociology of health inequalities, Scambler maintained, it was necessary to study the advantaged: after all, it is the wealthy and powerful who, by defending their privileges, produce and reproduce disadvantage. His 'greedy bastards hypothesis' (GBH) asserts that our widening health inequalities are a largely unintended consequence of the strategic behaviour of (1) a rapidly globalizing cabal of financiers, CEOs and directors of FTSE100 companies and rentiers, operating on and through (2) a more weakly globalized power elite running the state. The personnel who comprise (1) and (2) are of less significance than the social structures that allow them to behave in these ways; and this takes us back to the class/command dynamic. When the CEOs and directors of large transnational companies decide to downsize their workforces, substitute part-time for full-time workers, undermine working conditions, sidestep health and safety regulations, reduce work autonomy, outsource work, end final salary pension schemes, and so on, often in return for huge pay packages, pension pots and 'honours', they in effect attack the health, wellbeing and lifespan of their (ex-)employees. There is more than an echo of Engels and Virchow here.

As these last paragraphs suggest, it is no simple task to 'tackle health inequalities'. The recommendations of the Marmot Review (Marmot 2010) in the UK are very much in line with those of the 'global' Marmot-led WHO Commission on Social Determinants of Health published in 2008. Six policy objectives are outlined:

1 give every child the best start in life;
2 enable all children, young people and adults to maximize their capabilities and have control over their lives;
3 create fair employment and good work for all;

4   ensure healthy standards of living for all;

5   create and develop healthy and sustainable places and communities;

6   strengthen the role and impact of ill health prevention.

This will require coordinated action by central and local government, the NHS, and the third and private sectors and community groups, plus participatory local decision-making (which in turn depends on empowering individuals and communities).

The omens for securing such action are not good: health inequalities are currently increasing, not decreasing. Moreover, there has been a strong political impulse to deflect the blame for this from government onto the individual. Notwithstanding differences in rhetoric, and to some limited extent policy, governments of all complexions since Thatcher's election victory in 1979 have emphasized 'personal responsibility'. We each have a personal responsibility, governments insist, not only (a) to eschew risk behaviours, such as smoking, consuming alcohol or eating to excess and settling into sedentary life-styles, but also (b) to pursue any and every opportunity to earn an income and support our families. That there might be a fundamental incompatibility between accomplishing (a) and (b) is conveniently glossed over. If this message was leavened by some compassion on the part of New Labour before the global financial crisis of 2008–9, it has been vigor-ously reasserted by the Conservative-dominated coalition post-2010 under the aegis of deficit reduction. One way or another, the poor are culpable for the circumstances in which they find themselves. More than this, invoking a principle of 'behavioural conditionality', it has been suggested that the 'feckless' poor – those who continue smoking, for example – should slip down the list for priority treatment in a more explicitly rationed health care service.

For some sociologists this is another example of the class/command dynamic. While the Marmot and WHO reports appear to take a strong line on the need for urgent and radical action, for example, they make no mention of capitalism's contradictions, including the strug-gle between classes. Coburn (2009) counters that sociologists must see beyond SECs and focus on more classical notions of class as a social structure. People with a high SEC status do live longer than those with a low SEC status, he acknowledges, but SEC is itself a product of class forces:

> the nature of the capitalist class structure, and the outcome of class struggles, determine the extent and type of socioeconomic inequalities in a given society, and the socioeconomic inequalities in turn shape the pattern of health – and health care. But while many theorists of the social determinants of health proclaim an interest in the basic determinants of health and health inequalities, much of their literature omits any consideration whatsoever of the political and class causes of SES (socio-economic status) and the SES–health relationship. When they speak of analyzing the 'causes of disease', they seldom go far enough up the causal chain to confront the class forces and class struggles that are ultimately determinant. (Coburn 2009: 44)

While many agree with Coburn, the pertinence of research utilizing SECs such as the NS-SEC should not be underestimated: factors such as degree of work autonomy are clearly influen-tial. While health inequalities undoubtedly reflect deep structural inequalities in society, any comprehensive sociology of health inequalities must also address meso- and micro-factors affecting lifestyles and choices over the full stretch of the life course. In other words, ways must be found to trace the effects of social structures on individual decision-making via middle-range theories that expose the linkages between the two – a tall order, admittedly.

SEMINAR QUESTIONS

1 Outline the requirements for a specifically 'sociological' theory of health inequalities.
2 What are the benefits of adopting a 'life-course' perspective on health inequalities?
3 Evaluate Coburn's theory of health inequalities.
4 Does the 'greedy bastards hypothesis' (GBH) represent a disrespectful, counter-productive contribution to the understanding of health inequity?

SOCIAL MOVEMENTS IN THE HEALTH DOMAIN

Enough has been said in this chapter to indicate that the concepts of health, illness and medicine are highly contested. As the continuing debates about medicalization testify, whichever bodies secure jurisdiction over terms such as these also gain political and commercial power and influence. This impacts on population control and surveillance and the nature of health care systems and extends to – collectivist versus individualistic – approaches to tackling health inequalities.

There is growing resistance by 'lay' representatives or communities to 'professional' – often politically and/or commercially expedient – *presumption*. We noted earlier how disability activists challenged ubiquitous biomedical definitions they considered injurious and amounting to a form of oppression. Some have referred in this context to the emergence of a disability *movement*, and others have claimed that there now exist a number of active social or health movements. Della Porta and Diani (1999) define social movements in terms of four elements. They can be said to be (a) *informal networks*, based on (b) *shared beliefs and solidarity*, which (c) *mobilize around conflictual issues* and (d) *deploy frequent and varying forms of protest*.

Mobilizing potentials for health-related movements

Scambler and Kelleher (2006) have utilized Habermas's (1986, 1989a) distinctions between 'system' and 'lifeworld' and 'strategic' and 'communicative rationality' to analyse social movements in the health domain. The system comprises the subsystems of economy and state and the lifeworld those of the private sphere (that is, the household) and the public sphere (that is, the domain of open debate). The economy and state operate according to strategic rationality (oriented to outcome), while the private and public spheres operate according to communicative rationality (oriented to shared understanding and consensus). Habermas argues that in modern Western societies like ours the economy (via its steering medium of money) and the state (via power) have come to dominate or 'colonize' the lifeworld. In short, people's capacity to take their own decisions about their lives has been usurped.

Scambler and Kelleher contend that 'new' social and health movements have emerged as a way of opposing or fighting back against lifeworld colonization. They suggest a 'culture of challenge' is developing in the context of health, illness and disease, pitting lay knowledge and expertise against that of medicine. These initiatives might be characterized as the potential drivers or engines of a de-colonization of society in general and a de-medicalization of society in particular, but it would be foolish to make extravagant predictions on their behalf. These authors go on to draw up a typology of 'mobilizing potentials', which are outlined with examples in table 6.3.

Table 6.3: **Mobilizing potentials for social movements**	
Mobilizing potentials	**Examples**
Rights	Disability activists
User	Mental health users
Campaign	Anti-smoking initiatives
Identity	'Third-wave' feminism
Politics	Ecology movement

Source: Scambler and Kelleher (2006).

Rights as mobilizing potentials focus on cultural and civil rights. As we have already seen, disability activists reject medical definitions of normal and abnormal or pathological and the oppression they announce. By promoting a social over a biomedical model of disability, many have sought to 'rewrite' difference through communicative rationality, challenging not just the expert discourse of medicine but also political agents of the wider society.

The mobilizing potentials realized through *users* frequently originate in patient dissatisfaction. Mental health users afford a paradigmatic example. Pilgrim and Rogers (1993) adopt users' own terminology and write of 'survivors', suggesting that mental health users may even constitute a new social movement in their own right (see also Crossley 2006). With the recent increase in the prevalence and interest in Alzheimer's, it might be anticipated that this is likely to give rise to more specific vehicles of lifeworld representation. It might be further contended that users of self-help groups are particularly innovative because they encourage a collective sense of identity independent of medical and other professionals.

Campaigning as a mobilizing potential incorporates specific interventions in civil society and Habermas's public sphere. Anti-smoking campaigns provide an obvious instance, although the series of protests against the Health and Social Care Bill in 2011–12 afford a more dramatic example. Other examples are campaigns against local pollution threats, the siting of masts for mobile phone users, and landmines. Campaign groups should be distinguished from (colonizing) corporate penetrations of the lifeworld that promise health-bestowing lifestyle choices.

Identity potentials are typically associated with segments of society differentiated by gender, ethnic affiliation, age, sexual preference, and the like. Unlike second-wave feminism, which focused on gender equality, the third-wave feminism of the 1980s and 1990s emphasized the role of 'choice': resistance to the medicalization of childbirth was displaced by a demand for access to elective caesarians. In short, the foci for movements realizing this mobilizing potential are less to do with productivist redistribution and opportunity than with consumerist celebrations of difference and identity formation.

Finally, *politics* as a mobilizing potential refers to resistance to the subsystems of the economy and state and is often linked with environmental concerns, although material and other forms of psychosocial deprivation also feature. These movements can be defined in terms of their long-term resistance to the corporative exploitation of our natural and social environments, whether state-sanctioned or not. Protests against agribusiness in general and genetically modified crops in particular fall into this category.

At the time of writing, resistance to 'corporate greed' and the emergence of an extremely wealthy 'superclass' under neoliberalism would seem to be growing. Moreover, as Castells (2012) has documented, it is taking radically new forms in the internet age. There is a volatility and fluidity about protests now. While the mobilizing potentials outlined by Scambler and Kelleher rarely address strategies of social structural transformation, there is evidence – in relation to the Occupy movement, for example – that they can 'coalesce' in the guise of loose alliances of interests: their looseness is both a strength (otherwise heterogeneous activists have a common understanding of what they are *against*) and a weakness (there is no consensus on what they are *for*). Nor should 'old' class-based movements be neglected. The conditions for class-based resistance to phenomena such as the Health and Social Care Act and the increase in income and health inequalities clearly exist, even if 'class consciousness' has diminished in financial capitalism.

Recent years have seen an increase in protests and campaigns against legislation such as the Health and Social Care Act and to protect the NHS. (Flickr)

SEMINAR QUESTIONS

1 What potential do 'new social movements' have for achieving social change relevant to the distribution of health?
2 Are 'loose' alliances a strength or weakness in relation to the health of Western populations such as that of the UK?
3 Evaluate the potential of new social (digital) media for accomplishing health-enhancing change.

CONCLUSION

We have of necessity covered a lot of ground in a hurry while still being selective in terms of issues broached: this is intrinsic to the formatting of an introductory chapter. Hopefully appetites have been whetted. Certainly the length and quality of the life span is pivotal for any society and those who comprise it. We close the chapter by pulling some threads together and hinting at future agendas for medical sociologists. The first point to note is that health, illness, disease and medicine are undeniably social phenomena, although they are of course not *only* social phenomena (they are, for example, biological and psychological phenomena too). If there are 'real', causal social (as well as biological and psychological) mechanisms at work, there is no denying that our understandings and explanations of these are bounded by time and place, and therefore socially constructed.

A second point is that we are living through a period of considerable social change. While it is true that this is a historically routine claim, almost a cliché, the present phase of financial capitalism seems notably unpredictable. 'Solid modernity' has been succeeded by 'liquid modernity', in Bauman's (2000) graphic language. While some trends in morbidity and mortality seem clear – the increase in life expectancy at birth and the switch in the major causes of death, the increase in health inequalities and the recommodification of health care – others are less certain. What of the changing demography of the UK, novel patterns of migration within and without the European Union, changes in household composition, the fragmentation of schooling, 'flexible work', the implosion of the security enjoyed by the post-war 'Baby Boomers', and the new dynamics of identity formation in our post-productivist consumer society? How will these seismic shifts play out for differential health and longevity? It is too early to say, and understandable speculation should and will yield to painstaking empirical inquiry.

There has been a discernible tension throughout this chapter, our third point, between the constraining/enabling input of *social structures* into people's circumstances and decision-making in the health field *and agency*. The culture and social institutions within which they define themselves and their actions are arguably structured without being structurally determined. This 'tension' can only be relieved via empirical investigation. And this investigation must occur at each of (a) macro-sociological, (b) meso-sociological and (c) micro-sociological levels. In other words, what a credible sociology of health, illness and the body requires is an intensive examination of the relative inputs of structure and agency via ethnographic/qualitative to quantitative enquiry. If macro-social structures leave their traces on individual choices and behaviours, it is perhaps meso-sociological or 'middle-range' theory that is most lacking. An example of this 'genre' is Seigrist's (2009) theory of 'effort–reward imbalance'. It is, he maintains, when we put the effort in and yet perceive ourselves to be unappreciated and unrewarded, in or out of work, that our health is deleteriously affected.

Fourth, and finally, innovative agendas are unfolding. Some concern what people who define themselves as ill want; others, the more pertinent in financial capitalism, concern what they can have. 'Self-management' is a rubric that covers for efficiency savings. And what of the future of *ehealth* in its multifarious guises and of *genetic screening* and *genetic engineering*? If the first has been slower to make an impact than many anticipated, the latter two stand to make their mark long before they are able to deliver on their promises. It is perhaps in the multi-billion-dollar field of genetics that medical sociology's input will be of special salience. If the natural world has long since lent itself to human intervention and manipulation, probably with the direst of consequences, so too is the world of human nature yielding itself to exploitation. In a far more literal sense than Sartre and the existentialists ever intended, *who we are* is shifting ineluctably towards *who we choose to be* – and therein lies a challenge for the discipline as well as for society and the species.

SEMINAR QUESTIONS

1 Is capitalism bad for most people's health?

2 What are the prospects for health inequality in the future?

3 Discuss the view that science provides some potential for greater control over our own bodies but the social world controls our bodies more than ever.

FURTHER READING

▶ Blaxter, M. (2010) *Health*, 2nd edn (Polity). A short and readable introduction to the diverse meaning of 'health'.

▶ Conrad, P. (2007) *The Medicalization of Society* (Johns Hopkins University Press). A good introduction to medicalization and its contested impacts.

▶ Green, G. (2009) *The End of Stigma? Changes in the Social Experience of Long-Term Illness* (Routledge). A good guide to the changing social experience of long-term illness.

▶ Fox, N. (2012) *The Body* (Polity). A short introduction to classic and contemporary debates about the body as a biological and social construct.

▶ Marmot, M. (2010) *Fair Society, Healthy Lives: Strategic Review of Health Inequalities in England Post-2010* (The Marmot Review). The key contemporary publication of the state of health inequality in the UK and recommendations for how to alleviate it.

EDUCATION

beyond meritocracy and reproduction

ROB MOORE

CONTENTS

INTRODUCTION

THIS CHAPTER IS CONCERNED with the sociology of education. It will not, however, review in detail the wide range of issues in education in relation to the various theories in the conventional way – how issues a, b, c, are approached in turn through theories x, y, z, etc. Rather, it will in a deeper way explore the *logics of explanation* within the dominant approaches to the linkage between education and the wider society and how particular ways of understanding education and what it does relate to more general models of social order. It is concerned with problems and explanations rather than issues and approaches. This is a broad-brushstroke method that allows the identification of a set of underlying deep problems that different perspectives (functionalist, liberal, Marxist, feminist, postmodernist, etc.) need to take account of and adequately accommodate if they are to be convincing. However, this approach is distanced from the intricacies of the fine detail *within* the various issues. There is considerable debate about social mobility, for instance, over its extent, whether it is increasing, declining or remaining constant, and how education relates to these things. In the area of ethnicity there are complexities relating to the great diversity of ethnic groups and class and gender differences within them.

It is well established that there are class, gender and ethnic differences in achievement. For example, in relation to social class, table 7.1 shows the attainment gap between those nineteen-year-olds who were eligible for free school meals (fsm) (because of low income) and their peers who did not get free school meals (non-fsm). (This difference is sometimes used as a crude proxy measure for class.) Attainment is measured in terms of achieving A-levels or other equivalent qualifications. There was a 22.7 percentage point gap in 2005 between the higher performing non-fsm group and the lower performing fsm group, and a 24.2 percentage point gap in 2012.

Table 7.1: Percentage point gap in attainment at age nineteen in England between those eligible and those not eligible for free school meals			
Cohort	% level 3 at 19 through 2+ A-levels	% level 3 at 19 through other qualifications	% level 3 at 19 total
19 in 2005	22.7	3.8	**26.4**
19 in 2006	21.9	4.3	**26.3**
19 in 2007	21.8	3.9	**25.7**
19 in 2008	21.3	3.9	**25.2**
19 in 2009	20.9	3.7	**24.6**
19 in 2010	20.8	3.4	**24.2**
19 in 2011	21.7	3.1	**24.8**
19 in 2012	21.9	2.3	**24.2**

Source: Department for Education, 'Attainment gap at ages 11, 16 and 19: Impact indicator 9', www.gov.uk/government/publications.

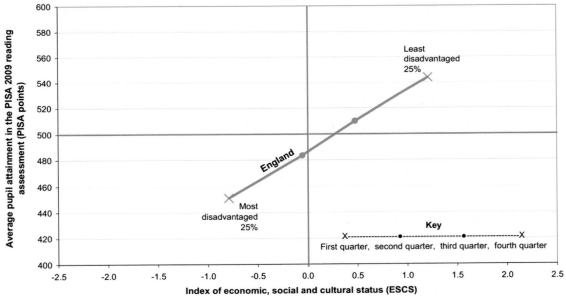

Figure 7.1 Average pupil performance in reading, by index of economic, social and cultural status, England, 2009

Source: Knowles and Evans (2012: 9).

A recent study of performance in the reading skills of fifteen-year-olds compared four quartiles of the population ranked by economic, social and cultural status. The results showed a clear relationship: the higher your economic, social and cultural status, the better your performance in reading tests, as shown in figure 7.1. Similar relationships between reading skills and economic, social and cultural status were found in all the OECD countries studied, although the strength of the relationship and the actual reading abilities of the different groups varied in different countries (Knowles and Evans 2012: 16).

Apparently consistent relationships between variables such as class (and gender and ethnicity) have sometimes led sociologists to neglect intricacies within issues. Some of these intricacies are highlighted in the boxes in the chapter as a counterpoint to the broad brushstrokes of the text. For example, a review of factors associated with low achievement in school is the Joseph Rowntree Foundation's report entitled *Tackling Low Educational Achievement* (2007). Box 7.1 lists four of the key findings that give a good sense of the complexities *within* issues.

BOX 7.1 THE JOSEPH ROWNTREE FOUNDATION REPORT TACKLING LOW EDUCATIONAL ACHIEVEMENT

- Nearly half of all low achievers are White British males. White British students on average – boys and girls – are more likely than other ethnic groups to persist in low achievement. If they start in the lowest categories of achievement in primary school, they are more likely than other ethnic groups to remain there at the end of secondary school.
- Boys outnumber girls as low achievers by three to two. But the gender gap is larger for some ethnic groups – Bangladeshi, Pakistani and Black African – among those not achieving any passes above D. Eligibility for free school meals does not affect boys and girls differently, other things being equal.
- Chinese and Indian pupils, as is well known, are the most successful in avoiding low achievement; Afro-Caribbean pupils are the least successful on average, though their results have been improving, and when compared with White British pupils of similar economic backgrounds, they do no worse.
- Schools do make a difference to outcomes. While students' social and economic circumstances are the most important factors explaining their educational results, we find that about 14 percent of the incidence of low achievement is attributable to school quality.

(Cassen and Kingdon 2007: xi)

The points in box 7.1 indicate the problems of producing general explanations of social differences in education. The problem is multifaceted and it is difficult to determine a single overriding factor – and 86 percent concern things other than the school! Consider this further observation: 'Our evidence as well as that of the DfES and of other researchers is that disadvantaged students and minority ethnic students are likely to attend worse performing schools' (Cassen and Kingdon 2007: viii). But then: 'Good schools – those that are particularly effective in helping students to avoid low achievement – are not uniformly distributed across local authorities; they are concentrated in some local authorities more than others. There is considerable variability in school quality between local authorities' (ibid.: p. xii). So, there are complex and varying interactions between class, gender, ethnicity, the school and where you live.

The 'logics of explanation' approach being adopted here enables an analysis that shows how models that are, in certain respects, very different are in other, deeper ways assuming things in common. A central argument to be developed below is that, although the 'liberal meritocratic' model and the 'critical reproduction' model are opposed both ideologically and in their theoretical analyses of the relationship between education and society, they nevertheless share a deeper level commitment to the principle of 'strong linkage'. What I mean by this is that the meritocractic paradigm is organized by a logic of explanation along the dimension of a strong *technical* linkage between education and the economy, whereas the reproduction paradigm is organized along the dimension of strong *cultural* linkage between family and school. It will be argued below that both of these approaches are limited in explanatory power, in that neither is totally wrong but each is only partly right. Each provides a part of what is needed to understand properly what is happening in the relationship between education and society. They will be contrasted with another way of looking at things in terms of *weak* linkage. The influential ideas of Pierre Bourdieu will be examined in relation to the reproduction paradigm, those of Raymond Boudon in relation to 'weak linkage', and those of Basil Bernstein as representing a sociology of 'interruption' rather than reproduction. Finally, it will be argued that the technical dimension of the meritocratic paradigm and the cultural dimension of the reproduction paradigm need to be complemented by a *knowledge* dimension that each, in its own way, obscures. Hence, this chapter is both an exposition and an argument.

SEMINAR QUESTIONS

1 Are there any findings of the Joseph Rowntree Foundation report that are surprising?
2 What common assumptions about differential educational achievement are challenged by these findings?
3 Do the findings suggest problems that need to be addressed more fully by sociologists of education?

EDUCATION AND SOCIOLOGY

Education and society

In order to address the question 'What is the sociology of education?' it is first necessary to ask some questions about education itself: What is it? These questions range from the most general one about education in the broadest sense to more specific ones relating to the particular concerns of the sociology of education in contemporary society.

Emile Durkheim, in addition to being a founding father of sociology of education, was the world's first professor of sociology. In his pioneering analysis, when societies reach a certain level of development in terms of *complexity* ('organic solidarity'), a new social form of education is required – the modern education system (Durkheim 1956). This kind of education must do two different things: it must prepare children as full members of society, but at the same time it must foster individuality and capacity for change. These two things can pull in opposite directions and a balance must be struck between them. It is in terms of these complexities that the sociology of education is concerned with the ways in which education is *social* in four different ways. Firstly, it is concerned with the social character of the education system and the processes that occur within it in schools and classrooms. Secondly, it is concerned with the links between it and other major institutions such as the economy, the state and the family. A third concern is with the interaction between those links in terms how the wider society affects education and how education affects the wider society. A final concern is with the deep sense in which education is the way that human beings become social beings.

The key term in all of this is *system*: the education system. The need for education systems arises when (a) children can no longer be socialized simply for the particular milieu into which they are born because of the rapidity of social change and of mobility in society and (b) where this is a requirement for all: *mass* education. The 'education' that is the primary concern of the contemporary sociology of education is that of the modern education system and its role in complex modern societies. Indeed, the development of such an education system is often seen as the driver of modernization, and developing nations are encouraged to construct such systems in order to facilitate economic growth and social change.

Education systems as we know them come into being with modernity and are intrinsically connected with it. This is so in a number of ways. Modern education systems are associated with Western Enlightenment views about knowledge and the transformative power of Reason both socially and for the self (implying a particular model of the self). This becomes associated politically with the individual's right to such knowledge. The mass education system is the means of securing that right.

Less idealistically, modern societies are driven by economic growth, and this requires an increasing level of skill in the population, beginning with mass literacy and numeracy and then increasingly reflecting developments in science and technology. These skills are also required within another characteristic institution of modern societies – the state, with its demand for administrators, from filing clerks to mandarins. Schools formalize and transmit these capacities.

Mass education can impart knowledge and teach specialized skills, as well as foster a sense of citizenship and deference to society, its organization and authority. (© Stefan Krasowski/Flickr)

These bureaucracies are those of nation-states, and the education system provides not only skills but also the elements of a national culture and identity, of citizenship. Within liberal democracies the further point is that this culture and identity be a democratic one and supportive of the democratic process. This implies an important distinction between critical liberal education and indoctrination – is the latter in fact 'education' at all and, if not, what is the difference?

All of this makes for a complex and complicated field of study! Today, the processes of globalization are challenging many of these historically formative features within education and modernity.

The meritocratic model of education in advanced industrial society

Order can be brought into this diversity of issues and areas by suggesting that the sociology of education has a central focus and core set of concerns – with the relationship between education and social inequality. The points above suggest the reason for this: the relationship between education and democracy. This is a quintessential concern not just for the sociology of education but for society and politics as well. Since the end of the Second World War, educational reforms have invariably had as their central justification the claim that they will make a fairer society. By 'fairer' is meant one in which there are more opportunities for all, as represented, for instance, in chances for social mobility. This appealing principle fits with the other overriding objective of reform: to foster economic growth and development. The reason for this lies in the logic of how modern societies are understood in this *meritocratic model*. The origins of this logic can be found in two influential theories: human capital theory and technical-functionalism. The former is the theory in economics that education should be viewed as a form of collective investment rather than individual consumption. Investing in education benefits the whole society because it produces better-skilled workers who are more productive and can adapt to technological change – they can 'learn how to learn' and participate in the 'knowledge society' of 'lifelong learning' in the contemporary rhetoric. This is essential if we are to maintain growth and international competitiveness. Technical functionalism provides the idea that, within such an economy, employers, in order to maximize profitability, will rationally select the person best suited for the job, regardless of their class, sex, race or religion, and pay them the appropriate price for their labour. The key link is the credential – the level of educational qualification. This was known as the 'tightening bond thesis'. The idea is that success in society will depend increasingly on possessing qualifications (achieved status) and decreasingly on social background characteristics (ascribed status). On the condition that we have a free, fair and open education system for all, then where we as individuals eventually end up will depend purely on our qualifications, and these in turn upon our abilities plus our efforts (the 'meritocratic' principle).

Behind this is the belief that 'ability' is randomly distributed in society and not directly inherited within classes or related to sex or race. The role of the education system is (a) to identify ability wherever it can be found, (b) to develop it to its full potential, and (c) to endorse appropriately that development in the form of a qualification that can be used effectively by employers to allocate the most suitable people to the most suitable jobs. This presupposes a certain orthodox economic model of a 'rational' labour market and of a fit between educationally developed capacities and occupationally required ones. This meritocratic model of education also has an important political aspect: provided that all conditions are met, then all citizens can feel that they have been fairly treated and given equal opportunities to succeed. Consequently, the emerging structure of social inequality is a 'just' one, reflecting the meritocratic principle of ability plus effort in education and the rational workings of the market in determining income differentials relative to the technical demands of the occupational structure. In this way the model legitimizes social inequality or, from another point of view, 'blames the victim' for failure.

Mediated by a modern education system, the relationship between the structure of social inequality and social groups reflects the distribution of abilities and skills across groups and the demand for the technical requirements for those abilities and skills in the economy. This entails two processes: (a) credentialization, whereby jobs have a credential attached to them as the condition of entry, and (b) the same credential comes to be treated equally for all who hold it, regardless of other personal attributes. However, historically another process can be identified: that of credential inflation, which is the process whereby as more people acquire a credential its value in the job market declines. Successive generations require higher qualifications for the same job. This factor is central to understanding the dynamic of the relationship between educational change and expansion in modern societies and factors such as class differentials and social mobility. It will be returned to below, but at this point it can be noted that the technical part of 'technical functionalism' assumes a strong link between educationally developed capacities and the actual requirements of particular kinds of jobs. But credential inflation sheds doubt upon this principle. In many occupational areas the linkage appears much weaker, and people with higher and lower qualification levels perform the same job at different times just as well. This is the Achilles heel of the meritocractic model and of increasingly shifting tuition costs onto students!

Problems with the meritocratic model

There are, however, a number of problems with this model, the biggest of which is that it does not work! What was expected to happen failed to do so in the way it should have done, and it is still failing to happen today. Since the 1980s, social mobility has slowed and social inequalities have increased (Brown and Lauder 2009) – and this despite expansion within the education system, especially at the university level. This points to problems to be explored below in terms of assumptions about causality in the interrelationships between the education system and society and in educational processes within the school and social groups. It is important to note that these problems are not uniquely British; they are present in many other places, especially within the Anglo sphere, where neoliberal market approaches have significantly displaced social democratic welfarist ones.

The expectation was that the education system could do two things at once through the same mechanism: promote economic development *and* social mobility, leading to a society that is both increasingly prosperous and more open, democratic and meritocratic and, so, more socially cohesive. This optimistic vision sustained investment in educational development in modern societies until the 1970s. But, in that decade, difficult problems began to emerge. The most important of these was evidence that educational reforms and the expansion of the education system had not resulted in increased social mobility and meritocracy. Although it was and continued to be the case that overall levels of educational attainment increased year on year, class differences in attainment levels remained roughly the same. This is strange: the average level for all groups was improving, but in a proportionate way, such that the differential between the classes remained unchanged. Bourdieu and Passeron (1977) refer to this process as the 'upward translation' of educational inequality whereby the positions of different classes change but the overall shape in terms of relationships between them is maintained. From a sociological point of view this state of affairs raises fundamental problems in terms of explanatory models of causality and linkage between the education system and others, especially the economy. The dominant approach, which is still powerfully influential today, assumes a *strong* link between educational change and social change. However, what we actually see is strong *educational* change but, in these respects, weak *social* change.

Educational policy and social change: class and gender

The education system of England and Wales can be seen as a historical educational laboratory in that, since the 1944 Education Act that laid the foundations of the contemporary education system, it has gone through a wide spectrum of reforms. Firstly, it went from being a decentralized system, largely under the control of local education authorities (LEAs), with weak central government coordination, to, in the 1980s, a highly centralized system with strong central government control – e.g., through the National Curriculum and weakened LEA powers. In the first period, from the 1944 Act until roughly the 1960s, it moved from a selective 'tripartite' school system of grammar schools, secondary modern schools and (a few) technical schools towards a non-selective and 'progressive' comprehensive school system based on the American community high school. However, because of the weak coordinating powers of the central government and a dependency upon the willingness of LEAs to implement them, these reforms tended to be piecemeal. These modifications (from both left and right) were within a broadly social democratic consensus. This changed in the 1980s when the New Right Conservative governments of Margaret Thatcher employed a combination of neoconservative and neoliberal policies to bring the education system under direct central state control while, paradoxically, promoting a market model of schooling (Ball 2011). The New Labour governments of Tony Blair after 1997 began to relax this system of central control and allow both new kinds of schools and more flexibility in the curriculum. This trend was continued by the subsequent coalition (Conservative–Liberal Democrat) government. Hence, we can see the history of education in England and Wales as consisting of four distinctive educational reform episodes of radically different kinds. But these episodes did not unambiguously correlate with major national trends in attainment, nor did they have obvious impacts upon class differentials. We cannot look back over this period and clearly say, 'The evidence shows that this model was better than that.'

There are a number of reasons why the issue of *class* is central to the sociology of education. In the first place it remains a strong predictor of educational attainment. Secondly, social inequalities associated with sex and race manifest themselves largely *through* class disadvantages (e.g., an ethnic minority group suffering discrimination will find its members confined to low-paid jobs, and similarly with women facing sex discrimination). Thirdly, successive educational reforms directed at reducing class differences in education had remarkably little impact. The problem presented by class is further problematized by another striking development in the last quarter of the twentieth century – what has been called the 'gender revolution' (Arnot 2007). In the 1980s it became increasingly obvious that girls were beginning to outperform boys in education. This was happening at all levels and across the entire curriculum, albeit in some places faster and more fully than in others. There are two significant aspects to this. Firstly, it was *not* the intended product of educational reform; it happened without being deliberately engineered. Secondly, girls' success was not confined to so-called female subjects – girls were succeeding in many so-called male subjects too (see box 7.2). This second point requires further elaboration because it directs attention to another important dimension of the sociology of education: the *social effects* of school knowledge and learning.

BOX 7.2 THE GENDER REVOLUTION

The 'gender revolution' as a general phenomenon is a major event both in society and for the sociology of education. However, as indicated above, it is not a *uniform* event. The following information is from a report by the Institute of Physics on girls and physics education.

- 49% of [state] maintained co-ed schools sent no girls on to take A-level physics in 2011. The figure for all secondary schools is 46%.
- Girls were almost two and a half times more likely to go on to do A-level physics if they came from a girls' school rather than a co-ed school (for all types of maintained schools in England).
- Twice the percentage of girls who went on to do A-level physics came from schools with a sixth form, compared to schools that only teach up to age 16 (for co-ed maintained schools in England).
- For maintained schools in England, the positive effect of single-sex education on girls' choice of physics post-16 is not replicated in the other sciences.
- The variation in the experience of physics between school types is not gender-neutral: *it's different for girls.*

(Institute of Physics 2012: 7)

So far the emphasis has been on the macro-dimensions of educational and social differences, but attention now must shift to the educational *process*, to what actually happens in schools and classrooms. The gender revolution raises the problem of policy because it occurred *without* a policy – indeed, feminists record significant official opposition from the authorities towards feminist-inspired 'girl-friendly' initiatives within education (Weiner 1985). But there is another problem, because, in a sense, the gender revolution should never have happened – the reason being that, for many researchers working in this area, one of the key and enduring functions of schooling is reproducing and reinforcing *conventional* sex roles and gender differences. This function is fulfilled through the ways in which school knowledge, pedagogy and organization are male-centred and patriarchal. So, logically, the gender revolution in educational attainment should reflect radical changes in these things. But there were no such systematic changes across the education system of sufficient scale to account for the gender revolution in these terms. There is a further complication: the girls who were in the vanguard of the revolution tended to be from 'traditional' schools – the very ones which most obviously institutionalized these 'patriarchal' forms of knowledge and pedagogy, evidenced by the finding that girls from 'traditional' schools are more likely to do physics A-level. The 'gender revolution' in education presents a further problem. Why has it not proceeded at the same pace in the wider society and especially in the economy? According to the meritocratic model, if it is the qualification that counts, there should be a smoothing out of gender differences in things such as income

Increasing numbers of girls and young women are studying and succeeding at traditionally 'male' subjects such as physical and chemical sciences. (© George Joch/courtesy Argonne National Laboratory/Flickr)

and occupational mobility. But it remains the case that income inequalities between the sexes remain and that females, however well qualified, still come up against a 'glass ceiling' in promotion in many areas. Females frequently need more education than males to get the same occupational opportunities. Again, though, it is the case that these features are not uniform, and in some areas females are not only achieving equality with males but pulling ahead (Hakim 2000).

How can we consistently account for the following facts?

1   Despite sustained systematic and system-wide reforms of radically different types aimed at reducing class differentials, there has been strikingly little change.
2   Nevertheless, significant changes have occurred in the gender area without a sustained reform programme.
3   However, that change was largely driven from the 'wrong' place – the traditional rather than the progressive sites within the education system.
4   The gender revolution in education has not in a commensurate way translated into a 'gender revolution' in the labour market.

It should be emphasized, though, that these issues are as much a problem for the meritocratic model's major rival – i.e., the reproduction paradigm (below).

If ethnic differences in educational attainment are also considered, then the problems are compounded because no valid overall generalization is possible. Some non-white ethnic minority groups in the UK are among the highest achieving (above the mean for the white British population) but others are among the lowest, and this is further compounded by gender differences within communities.

BOX 7.3 ETHNICITY, ACHIEVEMENT AND COMPLEXITY

To return to the intricacies indicated in the relationship between social groups and educational achievement discussed above, consider the following conclusion based upon an analysis of Ethnic Minority Attainment Grant (EMAG) data:

The most interesting fact to emerge from the EMAG data is that for each of the main ethnic groups we studied there is at least one LEA where *that* group is the highest attaining. Potentially this is very encouraging news, although it must be remembered that this is a measure of their attainment *relative* to other groups. It suggests that even for the groups with the most serious inequalities of attainment nationally, there are places where that trend is being bucked. This view must be tempered by an awareness of the small numbers involved in some areas. Nevertheless, the significance of this finding should not be overlooked and is a reminder of the variability of attainment and the lack of any necessary or pre-determined ethnic ordering. (Gillborn and Mirza 2000: 9)

Taken together, the problems of class, gender and ethnicity provide the sociology of education with its own problem because they indicate significant shortfalls in the explanatory power of the dominant theories in the field.

SEMINAR QUESTIONS

1   Discuss the contention that the meritocratic model 'does not work'.

2   In physics it is still 'different for girls', but it is also different for different girls – in which ways for which ones? Why should the kinds of differences between schools and school types make the kinds of differences they do?

3   With reference to some of the data presented here, suggest why it might be impossible to suggest any simple explanations of differences in achievement by class, gender and ethnicity.

4   What does this complexity suggest about the sorts of theories and models that should be developed in the sociology of education?

REPRODUCTION THEORY

The reproduction of inequality

Within the sociology of education, the dominant response to the meritocratic model has been to argue that its basic logic was mistaken to begin with. In fact, what the education system does is *reproduce* the relations of social inequality and those of power and economic interests: the class relations of capitalism entwined with the inequalities of gender and race. The persistence of class differentials in educational attainment is what is meant to happen.

Such theories comprise the 'reproduction' paradigm, which has assumed a diversity of forms. However, its most influential and sophisticated version is in the work of Pierre Bourdieu (discussed below).

A contrast can be made between two competing models – what John Goldthorpe (2000: 22) calls that between the 'logic of industrialism' and the 'logic of capitalism' – between liberal and Marxist models of modern society. The key point about the liberal logic is that it presents itself as politically and ideologically neutral: as a technical or 'objective' description of the character of advanced industrial societies. The key point about the Marxist logic is that it re-presents the liberal account as being an ideological legitimation of what are in fact the social relations and inequalities intrinsic to capitalist society (Bowles and Gintis 1976; Althusser 1972). The basic Marxist paradigm was later rewritten by feminists to show that this society was also patriarchal and then by race theorists to show how it was racist.

The construction of knowledge in the classroom

How did this 'logic' translate into a theory of education in terms of how it actually works in the classroom? The origins of the approach at the level of the educational process, still active today in the form of postmodernist and post-structuralist perspectives, is a formative movement in the early 1970s: the New Sociology of Education (NSOE). It adopted a 'constructionist' (sometimes called 'constructivist') approach to educational knowledge – i.e., it took knowledge as the key factor in education. It shifted attention to educational processes in the classroom itself and thus to cultural factors within the school. It had its origins in the American school of symbolic interactionism (Collins 1979). Today, this approach can be identified with 'postmodernism', including post-structuralism. Its basic premise is that knowledge is always humanly constructed under particular socio-historical conditions, and it represents the standpoint of those constructing the knowledge and their particular interests. In this manner, knowledge is always ideologically involved, always politically implicated and always entwined with power relations. This position is then typically pitted against what is commonly, though often inaccurately, called 'positivism', which, it is held, presents an objectivist or scientific view of knowledge as corresponding with that which simply *is*, which is therefore *given* as truth, and 'discovered' as such by human beings. For constructionists, knowledge is not 'discovered' but *created*.

The constructionist approach does a number of things:

- Firstly, it calls into question taken-for-granted assumptions about the status of school knowledge. Rather than being 'given', school knowledge is always open to contestation and critique because it has no special epistemological privilege; it is simply the 'knowledge of the powerful' – those with the power to impose their particular constructs (Young 1971).
- Secondly, it raises the question, *Whose* knowledge is being represented in the school? This shifts the curriculum debate from 'What is the *best* knowledge for children to learn?' to '*Whose* knowledge are they being required to learn?'
- Thirdly, it delegitimizes received knowledge claims by critically deconstructing them in terms of the standpoints and interests they represent.
- Finally, it translates questions of knowledge into questions of *learning* by arguing that what pupils are required to learn affects *how* they learn – pupils from non-dominant social

groups are alienated by school knowledge and from the culture of the school and so 'under-achieve'. In this manner the school becomes a 'reproducer' of social inequality rather than a promoter of social equality.

Social constructionism is thus an argument about the socially differentiating *effects* of knowledge in terms of learning. Social constructionism in its newer forms is still active under the heading of postmodernism, especially in relation to 'identities'. It also assumed feminist forms and was influential in the areas of race, sexuality and disability, and its basic logic is being repeated today in Southern Theory and in relation to 'indigenous knowledge' (Connell 2007).

The high priest of reproduction theory, however, is Pierre Bourdieu, who is neither a constructionist nor a postmodernist and, indeed, is scathingly dismissive of both. There are two interrelated issues here: What is distinctive about Bourdieu's theory of reproduction and how does his approach also signal certain general problems for the reproduction paradigm? His ideas have had a major influence in the sociology of education but have remained largely uncriticized (Chan and Goldthorpe 2010). His system incorporates education within a wider theory of society and of social reproduction.

Bourdieu, capital and reproduction

In the first place, it is necessary to outline Bourdieu's theory of reproduction and the key concepts employed (see Bourdieu 2006; Bourdieu and Passeron 1977; Grenfell 2012). Bourdieu's terminology can be confusing at first. His well-known theory of 'capitals' is part of a more general theory of society that can be approached in terms of three levels.

1 Habitus and capital   (a) Success in education is determined by the congruence between the primary habitus of the home and the secondary habitus of the school. Habitus is an underlying structure of cognitive and cultural dispositions formed in the first instance in the home and then further reinforced (for some) in the school. These dispositions are both enduring and transportable, giving rise to a distinctive style of life represented in things such as speech, cultural tastes, patterns of consumption and political allegiances, and modes of bodily deportment (they are 'embodied' and appear like a 'second nature'). These things are 'cultural capital' with varying degrees of social value. Habitus is not individual personality but what/who we socially are.

(b) Habitus is class-based and the habituses of different classes are ranked invidiously from the 'distinction' of upper-class taste to the 'vulgarity' of lower-class taste. The education system represents and endorses the habitus ('tastes') of the upper class and devalues those of lower classes. Consequently the education system is the major reproducer of cultural capital because different groups are disproportionally endowed with the dispositions, capacities and skills inscribed within the school and the capacity to cope with them.

All this is, in a sense, a version of a familiar kind of 'cultural distance' account in the sociology of education – of the disparities between home and school and the kinds of cultures schools value. The theory begins to assume greater distinctiveness if we start to further unpack other key terms.

2 Capital and fields   Why does Bourdieu talk about cultural capital rather than simply 'cultural values'? The reason lies in a deeper level of the theory. For Bourdieu, 'cultural capital' is what he refers to as a 'transubstantiation' of economic capital. What he means by this is that society is made up of a number of 'fields': the economic field, the cultural field, the field of consumption, etc. Each field is a set of positions that are defined relative to one another in terms of high and low status and power and define symbolic 'capitals' of different kinds. The economic field is primary and all other fields are representations of its structure, especially its relations of power and inequality (they are homologic to it). In this respect, the relations of the cultural field are transformations of those of the economic field (the 'transubstantiation' of economic into cultural capital).

However, the legitimating principle of the economic field is transparently instrumental: it is simply to do with material gains. But in the cultural field the principle is that of 'disinterestedness': art is for its own sake; aesthetic value resides in the art object in itself. However, Bourdieu rejects this principle in favour of a 'relationalist' one, where the value of any cultural 'object' lies in its relationships to others of higher or lower cultural capital – or 'distinction' – positioned in the field.

In that the dominant class is able to inscribe its taste within the secondary habitus of the school, it can secure intergenerational transmission of its dominance through cultural as well as economic means. Basically, the school simply endorses upper-class students in doing what they are already equipped to do. Hence, upper-class students appear to succeed effortlessly, having an 'aristocratic' relation to the school's habitus, and this gains them superior *social* opportunities. Key players within the cultural field are that subordinate fraction of the dominant class delegated to create the cultural capital that transforms economic capital into the habitus that gives the dominant class its apparent 'distinction'. The principles of the cultural and the educational fields create an illusion of independence from the economic field through the apparent disinterestedness of judgements.

3 Fields, the arbitrary and objective probability   Because the cultural field is no more than the economic field reversed, the relationships within it are arbitrary in that they reflect no more than the differences in taste between the upper and lower classes. There is no basis for authentic or autonomous distinction on aesthetic or on any other grounds between those things preferred by one class rather than another. Because the taste of the dominant class is enshrined within education and presented as disinterested, it produces misrecognition and, also, symbolic violence (in that it is an imposition without intrinsic authority). Educational knowledge is simply the knowledge of the powerful rather than powerful knowledge in its own right.

However, the educational system is continually evolving, though the relationship between the educational field and the economic field is maintained over time through a process of adjustment that ensures that the aggregate effect of the choices made by people of different classes reproduces the established structure of social inequality (within the 'objective probability structure'). This process of upward translation is mediated by habitus that reproduces the underlying relationship between fields, akin to the credential inflation mentioned earlier, and discussed further below. Change takes place, but only that which ensures that no *real* change actually occurs.

Bourdieu's model is complex, and it is necessary to understand the lot, not just bits, because each bit is dependent on the others. But the complexity and obscurity of his ideas can obscure the fact that there is much wrong with it, and this applies to the reproduction paradigm in general.

Problems with the reproduction paradigm

To begin with Bourdieu: in effect, his system of 'transubstantiation' is a system of miracles – How on earth could any of this actually be secured? To say that 'habitus' does it is rather like saying that the 'fairies' do it. There is also a more prosaic problem: How could any of this be tested? Bourdieu's propositions are essentially non-falsifiable tautologies, because it is impossible to specify in advance just how much social change (say, in social mobility through education) can be 'allowed' to occur that is compatible with preserving the established regime of social inequality. The statistical analyses (such as those in Bourdieu [1979] 1984) are retrospective and have no predictive potential because they describe only the outcomes of habitus, not its generative principles. We don't know whether the system is being 'reproduced' because we can't determine at any point in time what the forthcoming reproduction of the system should look like. How would we recognize a changing or changed system? Bourdieu provides no criteria as to what would count as 'change' rather than as simply more of the same, because the theory assumes axiomatically that what looks like change is in fact no more than the same.

Accounting for social change is an endemic problem for reproduction theory in general. A common approach is to argue that periodically the relationship between fields gets out of joint: there is then a period of adjustment in which they are brought back into alignment through educational 'reforms' or changes in habitus. Bourdieu terms this 'hysteresis' (Hardy 2012). It is important to note the contingent and episodic nature of these change moments.

Bourdieu aside, we can identify several more straightforward problems with the general reproduction paradigm in the sociology of education. There are two substantive areas here. The first is the fact that, historically, trends in educational attainment have consistently improved, albeit proportionally, for all classes. The second is to do with variance in attainments *within* classes. Hence, there are two key issues: firstly, inter-class differences *between* classes (in mean attainment levels) over time and, secondly, intra-class variance *within* classes (dispersion around the means) at points in time. These two issues can be seen as relating to the problems of both the liberal meritocratic and the critical reproduction paradigms. They indicate shared problems and underlying similarities between them despite their ideological differences.

Inter-class differences and the problem of change over time

One of the biggest problems in the sociology of education is in explaining why it is that, while class differentials in attainment have remained largely constant, average levels of attainment have improved for all over time. Reproduction theory might seem to do this, but the problem comes with '*how?*'. This is what is problematic about the 'cultural turn', as it is often called. Whereas the meritocratic model assumes that the link between the education system and the economy is a technical one in which educationally acquired skills match occupationally required ones, the reproduction paradigm argues that the real link is between the cultures of social groups and that of the school (between primary and secondary habitus: cultural factors associated with class, with gender and with ethnicity). This general thesis has commonsense plausibility.

The problem arises when the principle is applied to changes over time rather than just to differences at a point in time. Imagine for the sake of simplicity a society with three classes: upper, middle and lower. At a point in time (T1) the upper group has the highest average level of educational attainment, the middle group the medium average level, and the lower group the lowest average level – a simple three-tiered hierarchy. The culturalist principle may well look like a plausible explanation in terms of the relative cultural distances between the three groups and the culture of the school (between primary/family and secondary/school habitus) at T1.

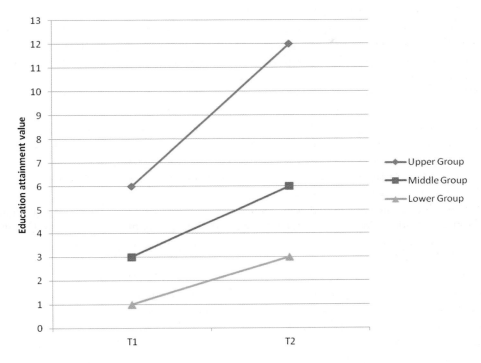

Figure 7.2 Educational attainment in a simple three-tiered society over time

However, the education system is expanding and all groups are gaining higher levels over time such that, at a later point (T2), the lower-class group's attainment average is the same as that of the middle group's at T1, and the middle group's that of the higher group's at T1. Can the cultural distance principle accommodate this? Taking the case of the relationship between the lower and the middle groups, it would have to be established that either:

1 between T1 and T2 the primary habitus of the lower group came to resemble that of the middle group at T1; or
2 at T2, the typical secondary habitus of the school for the middle group at T1 came to resemble that of the typical secondary habitus of the school for the lower group at T1.

For this to be demonstrated rigorously, it is necessary that habitus can be defined in terms of its *effective* characteristics – that is, the characteristics that make it that *particular* habitus producing the substantive effects attributed to it – and that these characteristics can be demonstrated to be present and active in the same ways at both times: the T2 secondary habitus of the school is *effectively* the T1 secondary habitus of the school as far as lower-group children are concerned. Given the way in which habitus is defined (as a deeply ingrained, enduring and transportable structuring of consciousness and culture), this would have to be a *substantive* similarity – the school would have had to have changed radically.

The basic problem is that, if the cultural distance principle is to be applied consistently over time, then it must be the case that the 'distance' between primary and secondary habitus is somehow maintained despite the fact that the children from the lower class are in successive generations encountering in the same school a secondary habitus increasingly distanced from their primary one (in which case, their relative attainment levels would logically decline rather than remain constant – which empirically they don't). It is not good enough to say that the fact that the lower-class group achieves the T2 level of attainment proves that the habitus has changed, because this would be an axiomatic assertion.

The cultural distance principle that might plausibly account for class differences at one point in time cannot consistently account for changes in differences over time unless it can be demonstrated that radical constitutive changes of a substantive kind have been orchestrated in a synchronized way between primary (family) and secondary (school) habitus across the time period that stabilizes the cultural distance effect – but given how habitus is defined this could not be possible. Remember that educational careers extend over many years, and so the secondary habitus of the school would have to be inscribed in an enduring way within class-specific educational career pathways that inculcate habitus over time, not simply represented in a school culture at a particular time.

To avoid any possible confusion here, it should be noted that, if it were the case that average lower-group income at T2 had risen to that of the middle group at T1, this would not affect the argument because, as income levels rise, the lower group can consume more, but within the same logic of habitus. The explanatory principle is in terms of *cultural* not *economic* capital.

Intra-class differences and the problem of variance

The problem that emerges here is that there is always a considerable degree of dispersion around the mean: large numbers of lower-class pupils succeed in education beyond the attainments of large numbers of middle-class ones. From a sociological point of view, the really interesting question could be 'What does the category of high achievers (and the schools that produce them) have in common regardless of the ways in which they otherwise differ in terms of class, sex and ethnicity and school social demographics?' By and large the sociology of education has signally failed to address the issue of what makes for educational success (Power and Whitty 2006). But it might be that the answer to why on average working-class pupils have lower levels of attainment than middle-class ones lies in understanding how it is that many of them do *not*. This issue becomes even more pertinent when applied between and within ethnic groups and their gendered and class differences. The general question is: How might education compensate for deficiencies in primary cultural capital, and why for some but not others?

The variance problem can be approached by taking the simple model above and rewriting it in terms of educational rather than social classes. If we think of such educational classes, within each one there will be representatives from each of the classes (and social groups defined in other ways) in varying proportions. Also, the socially 'atypical' representatives are numerous and not, as Bourdieu and Passeron (1977) suggest, rare exceptions. The relationship between educational differences *between* social classes and those between social differences *within* educational classes must be treated in a systematically holistic way.

The culturalist logic of explanation in the reproduction paradigm appears at first glance to account for mean differences but cannot with theoretical consistency account for the variance – it has to make up ad hoc explanations of 'anomalies'. Cultural distance, however measured, cannot explain how it is that significant numbers of pupils who are 'far' in terms of distance (deficient in cultural capital) nevertheless succeed to the highest levels – and that significant numbers who are 'near' in distance (high in cultural capital) fail to do so.

There is an extremely important implication in the above: schools not only reproduce cultural capital, they create it, as shown in the 1970s by the Oxford Mobility Study. Halsey, Heath and Ridge (1980: 199) conclude an analysis of class and boys in grammar schools by saying that 'education, therefore, gave "superior" education to vast numbers of boys from "uneducated" homes. It is the dissemination rather than the reproduction of cultural capital that is more apparent here.' They summarize their findings as follows:

> In other words, the educational system has undoubtedly offered chances of securing cultural capital to large numbers of boys to whom the ethos of the grammar and technical schools was new. . . . [Furthermore], as we have noted, two-thirds of our respondents at grammar school were 'first generation', and two-thirds of these went on to secure some kind of academic credential. Moreover, their chances of success were very little different from those of second-generation grammar-school boys. (Ibid.)

A very important issue here is that, although class differences might be significant at the point of entry into educational institutions of different types (especially elite ones), they are not so at the point of exit in terms of differences in the qualification levels attained. Pupils and students of different classes, though represented in different proportions, achieve similar levels of success. Early evidence for this was found in the Oxford Mobility Study. A more recent study of higher education found that, in Cambridge University,

> The two-way tests of association showed that three variables were significantly related to class of degree, subject studied, gender, and ethnicity; and that two variables, social class and type of school attended, were not significantly related to class of degree.
>
> The fact that social class and type of school are not directly related to class of degree is both significant and interesting. It shows that students from state schools, whether comprehensive or selective, perform just as well in examinations as those from independent schools. Thus attendance at an independent school does not advantage students as is often assumed. It is also clear that the minority of students from working-class backgrounds perform just as well as the majority of students who come from middle-class backgrounds. (Whitehead 2003)

Differences at point of entry transform into similarities at point of exit, and these transformations translate as meaningful acquisitions of cultural capital, qualifications and life chances for significant numbers of relatively disadvantaged pupils. The key point here is the explanatory one of understanding just what it is that accounts for differential educational attainments, but also what enables them to be equalized. Education *can* work, and understanding *how* it does is key to the justice issue.

Differences in cultural capital at one's entry into an education system can be transformed into equality at the point of exit, as students graduate with the same qualifications. However, it is potentially short sighted to think that differences in people's backgrounds are cancelled out by educational qualifications and that their opportunities and life outcomes will match those of others from more 'mainstream' backgrounds. (© Nottingham Trent University/Flickr)

For most, but by no means all, members of all groups in society, education does not present an unsurpassable internal barrier to advancement (as secondary habitus), instead, for many, presenting the opportunity to progress. This implies that 'cultural capital'-type effects might apply at entry conditions into different sites within the education system, but not within those sites. However, this should not lead to complacency – there is a significant proportion of the school population who do not achieve a basic qualification level and who remain significantly disadvantaged both in the labour market and socially.

The school can, then, for significant numbers of 'atypical' pupils, interrupt the relation between primary and secondary habitus and enable academic success for those who *prima facie* lack the required cultural resources as predicated by reproduction theory. The major gap within the field of the sociology of education concerns how education can effectively operate as an interrupter agency rather than as just a reproducing one. What is it within education that makes this possible? Identifying this is especially pertinent to teachers who *want* to be interrupters! We want an optimistic sociology of education rather than the deterministic pessimism of reproduction theory.

When children enter schools or students universities they are encountering something more than simply forms of cultural capital and habitus at different degrees of cultural distance. And this variable potential to engage with the 'something more' enables them either to compensate for cultural deficits by meeting its demands or fail through their inability to meet its demands despite their cultural advantages. It might seem rather obvious to suggest that this 'something other' in education is knowledge because, surely, knowledge is what education is all about! Maybe we should be looking at an interaction effect in education between external cultural factors outside of the education system and internal knowledge factors within it. The implication of this is that culturalist approaches tell a part of the story, but the reproduction paradigm cannot tell the whole of the story. This is not to suggest that the reproduction paradigm is wholly wrong, rather that its logic is limited in its explanatory power. It explains some parts of the data but cannot explain other parts. It is not so much that the reproduction paradigm needs to be displaced as that it needs to be complemented in other ways by an additional logic of explanation and a synthesizing theory that can read between these logics.

We can say that the meritocratic model of the relationship between education and society describes its *technical* relation and the constructionist model describes its *cultural* relation, but we are lacking a model that describes the *knowledge* relation and an overarching sociological theory that can integrate the three. Therefore, we need to consider a third model of the relationship between education and society: a 'structural dynamic' model that can incorporate a 'knowledge effect'.

SEMINAR QUESTIONS

1 What are the main weaknesses of Bourdieu's theory?
2 Why has Bourdieu's theory proved so influential despite its weaknesses?
3 Is credential inflation inevitably bad for disadvantaged groups?
4 How much opportunity do teachers have to be interrupters? How can they best succeed in becoming interrupters?

BEYOND MERITOCRATIC AND REPRODUCTION PARADIGMS

From strong to weak linkage

Rather than enumerating the ways in which they differ, we need to ask what the meritocratic and reproduction paradigms have in *common*. They share the principle of strong linkage between the education system and different aspects of the wider social system. In the meritocratic model that linkage is through the technical relationship between educationally developed capacities and the requirements of the occupational system, and in the case of the reproduction model it is between the cultures of social groups and that of the school. But neither paradigm can consistently accommodate the facts. Both are half right but also half wrong. Both are 'underdetermined' by the empirical data: there is too much social mobility through education to support the reproduction paradigm and too little to support the meritocratic paradigm (Goldthorpe 2000). So, let us look at approaches that question the principle of strong linkage in favour of a principle of weak linkage.

The phenomenon that is central to the idea of weak linkage is that of *credential inflation*:

the process whereby over time the same type of job demands an increasingly higher level of qualification – that is, over time, the same educational career paths terminate with occupational placements of decreasing social status and earning power. Credential inflation, the increasing numbers gaining the qualification, devalues the worth of the qualification in terms of its market returns. This challenges the assumptions of both technicist and culturalist models of strong linkage because it demonstrates that a wide range of credentials is technically compatible with performing a wide range of jobs and that a wide range of educational career paths is compatible with a wide range of social origins and destinations.

Boudon and credential inflation

In complex modern societies the principle of strong linkage is not viable, because such societies, by virtue of their complexity and rapidity of social change, require workers and citizens who are technically flexible and culturally adaptable. An education system that functioned to overspecialize students in terms of either their skills or their cultural values, or both, would quickly seize up. To the degree that the education system mediates between origins and destinations, it must do so through weak linkages. Modern societies demand degrees of indeterminacy or 'tolerance' between family, educational career paths and occupation.

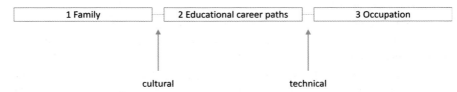

Figure 7.3 Linkages mediated by education systems

Strong linkage between either 1 and 2 (cultural) or between 2 and 3 (technical) in figure 7.3 simply does not work: there must be 'quantum spaces' between each – the space of the *possible* beyond that of the merely 'probable'. This space is that of *knowledge* as an effective category in addition to the cultural and the technical. The knowledge effect in education is, as it were, the 'lubricant' between the joints of the social mechanism.

What does credential inflation entail and imply? The most systematic treatment of the issues is to be found in the seminal work of Raymond Boudon (1974), who has received rather less attention than Bourdieu. Boudon's concern is with the key issue: How is it that educational expansion and reductions in educational inequality does not result in decreasing levels of social inequality? What is the relationship between inequality of educational opportunity (IEO) and inequality of social opportunity (ISO)? Boudon employs a 'logical simulation model' (Boudon 1977; Hamlin 2002: 43) that attempts to reproduce in a systematic theoretical form the kinds of trends that are empirically observable in the world. The basic conclusions are:

1   in a class-stratified education system, where
2   the system is expanding and
3   consequently, over time, members of all classes acquire more credentials of increasingly higher levels, then

4   educational inequalities will decrease at successively lower levels, but without resulting either in any reductions in the overall structure of educational inequalities or in decreases in social inequalities because they are reproduced at successively higher levels;

5   at the lower levels of the system different classes reach 'saturation point' at different times. The highest class group will have a majority of its children achieving to the lowest level before the middle group and then the lower group. As the system expands at the lower levels, the majority of new entrants will be from the lower-class groups because the higher groups will already have reached their saturation point and will be taking up places at the higher levels;

6   hence educational inequalities are continually decreasing at the lower levels while remaining, and in certain periods temporarily expanding, at successively higher levels.

Pupils/students from different classes are, as it were, 'squeezed' higher and higher up the educational system simply in order to maintain their existing social position. Boudon's logical model simulates empirically observable trend data (Halsey, Heath and Ridge 1980). Declining educational inequalities at the lower levels of the system do not generate declining social inequalities in opportunities. Unlike Bourdieu, with his 'upward translation' model, though, Boudon is not making any metaphysical assumptions about a need for and capacity of the system to secure its own reproduction.

Boudon argues as follows: there is a distinction between primary and secondary effects in the relationship between education and social stratification. Primary effects are mainly to do with material inequalities between classes. These differences certainly have an impact upon educational chances but historically, because of increasing prosperity, their influence declines (though social inequalities have increased in many countries since Boudon was first writing). Secondary effects are to do with educational decision-making processes and how they differ between social groups. The key concept here is that of the 'educational decision field'.

There are two aspects to this: the first is that of 'aspirations' and the second that of 'costs'. Aspirations are to do with what pupils and students in education are aspiring to in relation to the acquiring of credentials – the jobs (and social status and opportunities) they want and the expectations they hold. Importantly, Boudon notes that it is often argued that higher-class pupils have higher levels of aspiration than lower-class ones. But, he points out, this mistakenly assumes a common baseline against which all are being measured. Aspiration levels are relative to where people are coming from in the first place: the son of a doctor who aspires to be a doctor has the same level of aspiration as the son of a garbage collector who aspires to be a garbage collector. In general, the majority of people choose to maintain their social position (with some improvement over their parents) rather than strive for high levels of social mobility, and upper-class groups have strategies for protecting their educationally unsuccessful children from downward mobility. The 'cost' aspect involves two things: the straightforward economic costs of acquiring more education and the personal (social/cultural) costs of an education significantly different from the norms of your social group – a cultural 'outsider'. Of course, significant numbers of lower-class people *do* aspire to and pursue high upward mobility, and established upper-class families have a range of means of guarding against downward mobility; in the main, however, people aspire to be much what they began as, albeit with a rising intergenerational and then a life-cycle improvement in relative prosperity and security.

The 'weak linkage' aspect of Boudon's model lies in its structural dynamic. The general principle is that people will aspire to acquire the amount of education commensurate with their social aspirations as determined by prevailing labour market demands. The secondary principle is that, in an expanding education system associated with credential inflation, these 'amounts of education' (qualification levels) will become higher and higher over time. For each generation: more work, more cost for the same rewards.

It could be said that the class/credential 'escalator' is an upward one whereas the credential/job 'escalator' is a downward one. In successive generations, people have to travel further up the credential escalator in order to get off at the same floor of the occupational structure. So why do different groups tend to get off the educational escalator when and where they do? The simple answer is that, in general, they do so when and where they choose. But this is rather too simple, because in different situations complex sets of differing factors and pressures come into play to influence choices. But as a general principle it provides entry to some important considerations. Firstly, it highlights the fact that, in general, pupils tend to exit themselves from the education system: large numbers with qualifications sufficient to progress to the next level do not do so. Secondly, it suggests that, potentially, pupils at an earlier time could have achieved the attainment levels of similar pupils at a later time – but they did not need to do so in order to acquire the jobs commensurate with their aspirations and cost evaluations.

Educational attainment levels and the differentials between them are 'pulled' by the dynamic of the interaction between educational expansion and credential inflation rather than 'pushed' by the cultural determinism of primary and secondary habitus, that between educationally developed capacities and technical occupational demands, or that of educational policy and reform. Educational decision-making processes are contingent upon the prevailing set of relationships between the credential system and the occupational system for each generation in its particular time, and pupils and students of all classes and groups adjust their educational attainments to their social aspirations under those conditions and relative to their evaluations of the economic and social costs involved in pursuing those aspirations through education.

As opposed to Bourdieu's 'objective probability structure', Boudon's 'educational decision field' opens the space for non-determined agency. But it remains, as it were, 'anthropologically poor'. We gain little sense of the means and processes whereby individuals come to make their decisions. Goldthorpe (2000) endorses Boudon's general position but argues that his Rational Action Theory (RAT) approach be 'modified'. The question is *how* should it be modified? A major criticism of the RAT model is that it is too economistic and individualistic. It takes as its exemplar a rational individual consumer making informed market choices. But this orthodox economic model falls far short of the 'messy' and 'fuzzy' complexities of real life (Reay, David and Ball 2005). Social groups are significantly unequal as 'rational decision-makers' in terms of the amounts of knowledge they possess in their decision-making processes and individuals are pushed and pulled by all manner of personal circumstances (Hatcher 1998). Boudon's decision field needs to be made 'anthropologically rich' through detailed qualitative studies of how educational decision-making processes actually enact in people's lives and their embeddings in family, community and network relationships rather than being left individualistically uncontextualized (Dyke, Johnston and Fuller 2012).

Bernstein and the pedagogy of interruption

We need an approach that can engage more directly with the educational process itself – what happens (or could happen) in schools. The work of Basil Bernstein is such an approach and, unlike reproduction theory, it constitutes a sociology of interruption. Johan Muller says that

> the task is always not only to map an existing state of affairs, but to understand that state as an actualized possibility, with determinate features of variation, alongside other virtual possible worlds with equally determinate features of variation. It is these possible worlds, when delineated, which offer themselves up for political choice and action. (Muller 2004: 3)

Bernstein himself puts it thus:

> Under these conditions there is a potential discursive 'gap', a 'space' which can become the site of alternative possibilities, for alternative realizations of the relation between the material and the immaterial. This potential 'gap', 'space', the site of the 'unthinkable' . . . is the meeting point of order and disorder, of coherence and incoherence; it is the crucial site of the 'yet to be thought' . . . Any distribution of power attempts to regulate the realization of that potential, in the interests of the social ordering it creates, maintains, and legitimates. (Bernstein 2009: 182)

There is an elective affinity between Boudon's approach and Bernstein's. As Hamlin comments on the role of agency in Boudon's work: 'It is in fact the "creative" aspects of human agency that allow Boudon to break with structural determinism without altogether disregarding the social structure's effects' (Hamlin 2002: 44). This could apply equally to Bernstein. As the critical realist theorist Margaret Archer has put it: 'People are indeed perfectly uninteresting if they possess no personal powers which can make a difference to shaping their own lives or their own societies' (Archer 2003: 18). On this basis, pedagogy must be understood in terms of 'powers' or potentials, both actualized and unactualized, and within which individuals can realize possibilities according to their own powers and visions.

What does all of this mean? It is best explained through considering Bernstein's theory of the 'structure of pedagogic discourse' and his concepts of 'classification' and 'framing' (Moore 2013).

The structure of pedagogic discourse

The argument develops as follows.

1   The basic form of any pedagogic act of any kind is a relationship between a transmitter and an acquirer.
2   This is simultaneously a relationship of a person to a 'meaning'.
3   This relationship is intrinsically hierarchical in that you cannot teach someone something they already know or can already do. The transmitter has to 'know' more than the acquirer.

Hence Bernstein begins from the basic pedagogic relation. The 'transmitter' is not necessarily a person; neither need it be a formal educational situation. Bernstein's 'pedagogy' applies to any act of learning. However, this basic relationship is always a structured relationship: pedagogy is realized and enacted through distinctive 'codes'. The structures of pedagogic discourse are expressed in the relations between three fundamental dimensions of the pedagogic relation.

1   *The curriculum relation*: that is, essentially the organization of knowledge/skill. In some cases bodies of knowledge ('meanings') are strongly demarcated and different things kept apart (e.g., in the relation between formal educational knowledge and everyday knowledge), but in other cases the boundaries may blur and things flow into each other. (This distinction is reflected in the contrast between 'traditionalism' and child-centred education.)
2   *The temporal relation*: there must be principles (more or less explicit) that regulate both the sequence in which meanings should be acquired and the pacing of the time periods of acquisition (e.g., in formal education, the structure of modules and how long pupils can study them).
3   *The evaluative relation*: if the purpose of the pedagogic relation is to transmit knowledge of different kinds, then there must be a 'test' of how successful the process has been. Again these criteria can be more or less formal, explicit or tacit.

Identifying these principles enables Bernstein to conceptually model the different structural modalities of pedagogic discourse. He begins with 'classification' and 'framing'. By classification, he means the boundaries between categories – e.g., between subjects in the school curriculum. Classification can vary in strength from strong to weak. By framing, Bernstein means the pedagogical relationship between the teacher and the taught, and the power/control each has over the other. Classification and framing coordinate the relationships between the three dimensions of pedagogy: curriculum, sequencing/pacing and evaluation. Classification can be seen as shaping the relations of *what* is taught, and framing the relations of *how* it is taught. Classification relates to relations of power in society (what gets taught) and framing to relations of control (who decides the *how* and the criteria of success). These two principles can each vary in terms of 'strength' and do so independently, in combination giving rise to four basic structures: $+C+F$, $+C-F$, $-C+F$, $-C-F$. The most obvious forms are those of $+C+F$ and $-C-F$ – expressions of 'traditional' education (where a strongly defined subject is taught by a teacher who identifies as an expert) and 'progressive' education (with a stronger emphasis on teaching *people* rather than teaching *subjects*, taking cues from what the person being taught responds to). The two can be expressed in different 'strengths', from strong to weak classification and from strong to weak framing. Bernstein conceptualizes these clines in terms of 'visibility', from 'visible' to 'invisible' pedagogies.

Another basic distinction Bernstein discusses is between visible and invisible pedagogies: how far the rules of the educational transmission code are explicit or implicit. The difference between these two modes of pedagogic discourse is not to do with more or fewer rules, but with 'visibility' of the rules, their explicitness and hence their public availability. This enables a disconnection between the ideological 'voice' of pedagogy and its 'message' as a structure (or 'relay', as Bernstein liked to say). In visible pedagogies (typically $+C+F$), looked at sociologically, the point is the explicit (visible) character of the rules. Invisible pedagogies (typically $-C-F$) often deny that they have rules. They are based upon the principle that the 'pedagogy' unfurls from within 'the child' as the self-actualization of an authentic self. In England this approach was strongly endorsed by the influential Plowden Report on primary education (CACE 1967). The teacher is seen as a facilitator of the child's autonomous learning/realization, but in fact the teacher is 'reading' the child in terms of rules and criteria that may often be unavailable to the child and its parents (Bernstein 1975). The rules of the pedagogy are 'invisible' but nevertheless present as an essentialist idealization of 'the child' that the progressive teacher possesses.

In this way Bernstein is able to conceptualize the underlying structures, the social 'grammar', of pedagogy – as distinct from any particular content. He argues that the sociology of education has too often concerned itself with the 'what' (which comes into education from the outside) but has ignored the internal structure of educational transmission. It is this internal structure that is fundamental because of the ways in which it relates to the structures of family types, modes of socialization and their wider social relations.

The discretionary gap

The theory of the structure of pedagogic discourse enables the systematic conceptualization of the modes of pedagogic discourse regardless of whether all of them are empirically known to us. The theory enables us to envisage a range of possibilities beyond the given. It opens up the more substantive sociological issue: Why some modalities rather than others? Why are they socially distributed as they are? and What are their differential social effects?

But there is a deeper principle to do with the potential of pedagogy:

> In a fundamental sense, pedagogic communication, of both transmitter and acquirer, cannot be programmed (and therefore has some autonomy) . . . it is not possible for that communication to be effectively policed and made uniform. Further, the basis of the hierarchy of pedagogic (school/university) discourse cannot always be derived from class hierarchies or their dominant cultures except with reference to a simple mental/manual division. In these two senses there is a potential discretionary space. (Bernstein 2009: 174)

What does the 'potential discretionary space' – this gap between what *is* and what *could be* – mean? For Bernstein, this means that pedagogy has an intrinsic power to transform and interrupt. The key purpose of education is to realize this potential. Hence there is a tension at the very heart of pedagogy and, in that this tension has to be continually managed, it can also be continually contested.

There is a final 'discretionary space' that is located where school knowledge is *created* before it is transmitted in the curriculum. The key term here is that of 'recontextualization'. Bernstein argues that school knowledge is always a recontextualization that selects aspects of knowledge in one place (e.g., in universities where new knowledge is created) and transfers and reassembles it in another. School physics is not university physics. It is a selectively reassembling and re-presenting of 'physics' endorsed by things such as textbooks, syllabi and examinations. But this recontextualization would be as true for, say, the ways in which everyday knowledge is brought into the curriculum. This process is inherently political and ideological in that, in the first instance, *how* knowledge gets recontextualized is the result of power struggles between contending agencies in various sites. How these conflicts resolve and stabilize determines how knowledge is recontextualized and re-presented as school knowledge. A striking episode of this kind can be seen in the 1980s when the New Right Conservative governments shifted educational power away from teachers and local education authorities towards central government (the National Curriculum) and parents were constructed as consumers in an education marketplace. Crucially this episode saw a significant reduction in

Various forms of 'progressive' education are susceptible to Bernstein's critique that they are set up in a way which favours children from middle-class backgrounds with high levels of cultural and social capital. In this classroom of individualized teaching, children with confidence will thrive, but what of a pupil entering this classroom who is not self-assured? (© woodleywonderworks/Flickr)

the relative autonomy of education and of the teaching profession (J. Beck 1999). Bernstein calls this recontextualizing mechanism the 'pedagogic device' – a device for regulating the construction of school knowledge. But these struggles are always open to contestation and challenge.

Bernstein's approach is distinctive in that it systematically identifies at a number of levels, from the macro to the micro, spaces that represent the quantum of the possible where we can potentially think the unthinkable. It is this potential of pedagogy that lies behind the reality of weak linkage and signals the transformative rather than merely the reproductive powers of education in society – an optimistic sociology of education.

Bernstein's critique

Bernstein's analysis also provides a critique of the underlying ideological position that has prevailed for many decades in the sociology of education and that has been supportive of a range of 'progressive' forms of education, from those of the Plowden model of the 1960s, through feminist and multiculturalist and anti-racist forms, to postmodernist 'voice' theories (Moore and Muller 2002). The underlying logic of reproduction theory is a reductive principle that presents educational knowledge as being 'constructed' by dominant social groups in a way that reflects their standpoints and interests. To the degree that this is seen as represented by 'traditional', subject-based education, it follows that any educational ideology that opposes this 'progressivism' of one kind or another represents the interests of the dominated and marginalized. However, by showing how progressivism is an 'invisible pedagogy', Bernstein was

able to demonstrate its real cultural and discursive base – within the 'new middle class' – not a marginalized group! 'Progressivism' tends to legitimate itself as acting for disadvantaged groups by opposing the educational knowledge and pedagogy of the dominant. But as an invisible pedagogic code it actually requires a highly specialized set of cultural skills for pupils to succeed in it. These skills are most developed in the new middle class, located in the fields of symbolic production and control such as the welfare state and the culture industries.

Bernstein's theory identifies differences within classes as well as between them. It identifies a radical dislocation between the ideological 'voice' of progressivism and its 'message' as particular structuring of pedagogic discourse, and it is the latter that really counts. The move to progressivism marked a struggle between fractions of the middle class. In Bernsteinian terms, working-class pupils are more likely to be advantaged by 'visible pedagogies' where the rules and criteria of the pedagogy are made explicit and hence available. Further research (e.g., Morais and Neves 2006) identified pedagogic practices in the classroom that bring educational advantages to lower-class pupils. Their findings suggest that teachers should transmit well-defined bodies of knowledge in which they are experts in order to structure the sequencing of knowledge (strong classification of knowledge). The pacing of the transmission of knowledge should be flexible so that pupils can work at their own pace through the sequencing (weak framing). The relationship between teacher and pupil should be open in that pupils can feel confident to ask questions and seek advice from the teacher. The relationship between pupils should be open so that they can engage in cooperative learning. Furthermore, teachers should make explicit the rules and criteria of the learning process, and in order to do this they require a reflexive relationship to their own practice. This entails a theoretical rather than simply a technical mastery of 'teaching methods'.

We need to recognize that, in the first instance, Bernstein's theory is one of pedagogy, not knowledge. The theory of the structure of pedagogic discourse does not prescribe what should be taught. A key absence in Bernstein's theory is that of a systematic engagement with epistemology in two major respects: firstly, he strongly resisted any attempt to 'pigeonhole' his own theory within any particular 'paradigm' and, secondly, he did not address the issue of the epistemological status of what should count as 'school knowledge'. However, his approach does imply a particular epistemological position. I have suggested elsewhere that he was a Realist without a theory of Realism (Moore 2013). It is also the case that his later writings on 'knowledge structures' (Bernstein 2000: ch. 9) have strong epistemological implications, also of a Realist character. Since his death a number of people taking on his ideas have been exploring these issues, especially within the school of Social Realism (Young 2008; Maton and Moore 2010; Moore 2012).

Making weak linkage work

There is another important implication for an optimistic sociology of education – important because it is ultimately political, and hence subject to popular choice and control. In general the historical and comparative evidence indicates that, the more equal societies are economically, the more equal they tend to be in terms of educational differences and chances of social mobility. Crucial factors here are both the maintenance of high employment levels and opportunities for the young and progressive reductions in levels of economic inequality in society. The conclusion must be that, for many, though not for all, the 'secondary habitus' of the school does not act as an insurmountable barrier to potential educational achievement but, rather, can be an enabling condition. However, the degree to which that potential is realized is contingent upon complex factors beyond the school and how individuals feel themselves positioned within them and their life chances and choices, and it requires theoretically informed understandings of the pedagogic process and its social relations.

The report discussed in box 7.4 indicates the complex range of factors involved in producing educational inequality, many of which have already been referred to in this chapter. It found that:

> Private schools, which educate only 7% of all pupils, continue to have a stranglehold on our country's top jobs. . . . But it is not just in schools that the sources of Britain's low levels of social mobility can be found. There are many contributory factors. It is as much about family networks as it is careers advice, individual aspirations as it is early years education, career development opportunities as it is university admissions processes. It is also about the fact that too often the professions close their doors to a wider social spectrum of talent instead of opening them. (Millburn 2012: 3–4)

The report concludes with a wide range of recommendations – educational ones and others. Education alone cannot do the job, but it can do some things and, perhaps, do even better the things it is already doing best. The most fundamental conclusion to be drawn from structural dynamic models of weak linkage is that equality of educational opportunity does not automatically generate equality of social opportunity. Rather, it is the social opportunity structure and degrees of economic inequality in the first instance that crucially influence the educational opportunity structure, and these issues are political ones. It is also the case that we need a rigorous theory of pedagogy, and this is different from simply models of teaching methods.

BOX 7.4 EDUCATION AND THE SOCIAL ELITE

Box 7.1 at the beginning of the chapter highlighted the conditions of the 'low achievers'. The research here provides another sense of perspective from the opposite direction – that of the social elite. An extract from a report by Alan Millburn tells us that,

> Across the professions as a whole, the glass ceiling has been scratched but not broken. The professions still lag way behind the social curve. If anything . . . since 2009, . . . the professions – despite some pockets of considerable progress – have done too little to catch up. The general picture seems to be of mainly minor changes in the social composition of the professions. At the top especially, the professions remain dominated by a social elite. (2012: 3)

In more detail the report finds the following:

- the judiciary remains solidly socially elitist, with fifteen of the seventeen Supreme Court judges and heads of division all educated at private schools before going on to study at Oxford or Cambridge;
- of thirty-eight justices of appeal, twenty-six attended private schools, eight attended grammar schools, just two attended state comprehensive schools, and two were schooled overseas;
- 43 percent of barristers attended a fee-paying secondary school, with almost a third going on to study at Oxbridge;
- of the country's top journalists, 54 percent were privately educated, with a third graduating from Oxbridge;
- privately educated MPs comprised 30 percent of the total in 1997 but since the 2010 election now comprise 35 percent, with just thirteen private schools providing 10 percent of all MPs;
- 62 percent of all members of the House of Lords were privately educated, with 43 percent of the total having attended just twelve private schools.

This is social engineering on a grand scale: the senior ranks of the professions are a closed shop. Unfortunately, the evidence here suggests that there is, at best, limited progress being made.

SEMINAR QUESTIONS

1 Does evidence suggest that agency needs to be incorporated into sociological paradigms on education?
2 What are the main insights provided by Boudon and Bernstein which go beyond theories of strong linkage (reproduction and meritocracy theories)?
3 Why might we 'need a rigorous model of pedagogy' and how is this 'different from models of teaching methods'?

CONCLUSION: THE PROBLEM OF KNOWLEDGE

There are two major problems within the reproduction paradigm: whether in its constructionist/ postmodernist reductionist forms or in Bourdieu's relationalism, the reproduction paradigm expunges knowledge as an *effective* category. Both constructionism and relationalism are concerned primarily with deconstructing and delegitimizing knowledge claims rather than exploring ways of warranting them. They show how 'knowledge' is not really knowledge rather than how it *might be* knowledge. The problem is that the reproduction paradigm has no theory of knowledge in itself as 'powerful knowledge' as distinct from simply the 'knowledge of the powerful'. In its constructionist version knowledge is reduced to the standpoints of those constructing the knowledge, and in the relational version it is an arbitrary transubstantiation of the structure of the economic field. Secondly, as indicated above, as an intellectual field the reproduction problematic is fragmented into a proliferation of incommensurable paradigms inhibiting the formation of general theory and synthesis. Hence the sociology of education has had great difficulties in building a wealth of empirical data into a general theory of how education works in society. We could say that the field is in a certain sense 'theory rich' in that there are many contending paradigms (the 'isms') and 'data rich' in that there is a great body of data, but that the theory and the data are too far distanced from each other for there to be effective synthesis. This is principally because the constructionist approach treats theories as 'paradigms' and hence as incommensurable (Bernstein 2000; Kettley 2006; Moore 2009). It reduces knowledge to the standpoints of those producing the knowledge – their experience, perspectives and interests.

It has been suggested above that the missing element in the sociology of education is that of *knowledge*. It has been argued that a strong theory of knowledge is necessary in order to complement and complete the technicist dimension of the meritocratic model and the culturalist dimension of the reproduction model. What is the relationship between the 'weak linkage' model of the relationship between the education system and the wider society and the 'strong theory' of knowledge, and why, if the strong theory of knowledge is so important, is it consigned to the conclusion of this chapter? Basically because the sociology of education does not yet have a strong theory of knowledge! It is important always to remember that there is more to liberal education than instrumental concerns. Ultimately the purpose of education is to enrich people's lives and open to them new realms of possibility as people – as the philosopher Charles Bailey put it: 'to free us from the tyranny of the present and the particular' (1984). This returns us to the question of knowledge: what it is *worth* teaching rather than simply what it is *useful* to teach. There is more to 'culture' than 'capital' – powerful knowledge as an entitlement, not merely the knowledge of the powerful.

SEMINAR QUESTIONS

1 Based on the theories discussed in this chapter, how could the sociology of education help to tackle the inequalities detailed in Alan Millburn's report on social mobility?

2 What important types of knowledge are largely absent from the education system?

3 What would you change about educational knowledge and for what purpose(s)?

4 If theories were no longer considered as paradigms, could a useful synthesis of competing theories of education be possible and desirable?

FURTHER READING

Since 1961, A.H. Halsey has with various others produced an authoritative collection of readings on the sociology of education each decade. These volumes provide a rich review of thinking and research in the field and also a series of snapshots of the changing issues over time and the approaches to them. Reading the introductions to each volume provides a comprehensive history of the field of sociology of education and also of social and educational change over this period.

- ▶ I have used the most recent collection, Lauder, H., P. Brown, J. Dillabough and A. H. Halsey (eds) (2006) *Education, Globalization, and Social Change* (Oxford University Press), as a core reference in order to provide readers and teachers with an accessible, affordable single authoritative source.
- ▶ I offer my own book from 2004, *Education and Society: Issues and Explanations in the Sociology of Education* (Polity), as a general introduction to the field and its debates and, more recently, Gewirtz, S. and A. Cribb (2009) *Understanding Education: A Sociological Perspective* (Polity).
- ▶ Jones, K. (2003) *Education in Britain: 1944 to the Present* (Polity) provides a historical perspective.
- ▶ For developing contemporary debates in relation to Social Realism and the critique of constructionism and postmodernism, see Maton, K., and R. Moore (eds) (2010) *Social Realism, Knowledge and the Sociology of Education* (Continuum) and also, in relation to 'Southern Theory', Rata, E. (2012) *The Politics of Knowledge in Education* (Routledge), from New Zealand, and Wheelahan, L. (2010) *Why Knowledge Matters in Curriculum: A Social Realist Argument* (Routledge), from Australia (2010).

POVERTY AND THE WELFARE STATE

economic, social and political intersections

MARY DALY

CONTENTS

INTRODUCTION

POVERTY IS ONE OF the most important concepts in this textbook. Consider for a moment its extent. The World Bank has estimated that some 1.3 billion people were living on less than $1.25 a day in 2008 (World Bank 2012a). Moreover, nearly a billion people are undernourished and some 22,000 children die from poverty-related causes every day (You et al. 2012, cited in Wisor 2012: 3). In the European Union (EU) as a whole, 23 percent of the population was at risk of income poverty or social exclusion in 2010 (Eurostat 2012a); to put this into numbers, it involves some 115 million people. Closer to home, in the UK in 2010–11 there were 9.8 million individuals (16.1 percent of the population) in relative poverty, measuring incomes before housing costs, and 13.0 million (21.3 percent) measuring them after housing costs using a poverty line equal to 60 percent of median income (Cribb, Joyce and Phillips 2012). In terms of the identity of those who are poor, children make up a large proportion, as do sixteen- to nineteen-year-olds, people who are unemployed, lone-parent families and those with an illness or disability (see box 8.1). Poverty is highly patterned in terms of which sectors of the population it hits – for example, six out of every ten of the world's poorest people are women. As well as gender, other forms of inequality along social class, generational and ethnicity lines are closely intertwined with poverty.

Poverty is important not only because it is a feature of every known society but also for how it reveals core aspects of society. One cannot explain poverty without taking account of such factors as the welfare state, the organization of family life, the economy and the labour market. Poverty is not just a lens on the structure of societies, though; it is also a concept that is heavily imbued with everyday meaning, symbolism and relational resonance. Exploring the experiences of the people affected, the prevailing attitudes towards 'the poor' and the representations of poverty is highly insightful from a sociological perspective. Moreover, as Alcock (2006) points out, poverty is a political concept – what people mean by it depends to some extent on what they intend or expect to do about it. Hence, the way the concept of poverty is used tells us something about the connections between poverty and broader systems of power and dominance. This is as true of academic and/or policy debates as it is of everyday discourse.

BOX 8.1 SOME FACTS ABOUT POVERTY IN THE UK IN 2011–12

- 3.5 million children, equivalent to one in every four, are living in poverty.
- Two-thirds (66 percent) of children growing up in poverty live in a family where at least one member works.
- Working-age adults with no reported educational qualification were almost twice as likely to live in poverty as those who reported a qualification below degree level.
- In general, the older the age of the pensioner, the greater the likelihood of poverty.
- 6 percent of working-age adults in households with all adults in work were in poverty.

For the purposes of these data, someone is considered to be in poverty if they have less than 60 percent of the average income in the year in question. This and other issues of measurement are discussed later in this chapter.

Source: Department for Work and Pensions (2013).

One might think that such an old concept as poverty would be settled by now in terms of conceptualization and constituent features; this is far from the case. Poverty is the source of active debate, ongoing research and, in some cases, strong disagreement. This means that the student of poverty must live with considerable uncertainty and accept that there is no one correct way of conceiving of the subject. That said, the fact that the concept is disputed means that the idea, understanding and knowledge of poverty keep evolving.

The complex and contested economic, political and social patterns of poverty are also institutionalized in the welfare state. While in the first and major part of this chapter the discussion proceeds through the conceptualization of poverty, its definition, the setting of a poverty threshold and experiences of poverty, the second part moves on to focus on the welfare state, as a decisive political and social institution and its role in relation to poverty. In the third part, different explanations for poverty are considered. The most developed Western countries, especially in Europe, are the main focus, although the discussion is also informed by considerations relating to other parts of the world.

CONCEPTUALIZING POVERTY: CHALLENGES AND DISPUTES

Two questions get to the heart of disputes about poverty:

- Should it be conceived in absolute or relative terms?
- Is poverty just about income or should it be viewed more broadly?

Absolute or relative?

One of the classic ways of distinguishing approaches to the definition of poverty is the absolute/relative differentiation. The absolute approach is built around the view that there are certain conditions essential for human survival and that these do not change substantially over time. Poverty, then, is the condition of not being able to meet such basic needs. The idea of subsistence – as the minimum necessary to sustain life – is close to the core set of ideas here. Hunger and being unable to afford basic foodstuffs are benchmarks for an absolute approach, as are minimum standards around being clothed, sheltered and free from disease. This approach is associated with the early work of Charles Booth in London (1889) and Seebohm Rowntree in York (1901, 1941). It has also been informed by scholarship attempting to define a set of basic needs that are universal (Doyal and Gough 1991; Nussbaum 2000). Absolute or subsistence understandings of poverty tend to be most widely used in the less-developed world, where resources are scarcer and the standard of living closer to a minimum.

A relative approach, in contrast, identifies poverty on the basis of the standards that are typical or average for the society or group as a whole at the time. Rather than positing the existence of a definitive set of needs that must be unmet for poverty to be said to exist, a relative approach locates those who are poor as being deprived or in need relative to the situation of the rest of the population in the group or society being compared at the time. A relative approach is in principle limitless in terms of what it could focus on, especially in comparison to an absolute approach, which has to posit a particular set of needs and conditions for human survival. It always involves a reference group, however, so as to identify the societal norm or usual standard of living. The approach, which unlike the absolute view does not necessarily claim to be objective, focuses on inadequacy or deprivation in relation to socially perceived or widely prevailing standards. The classic reference works are those of Townsend (1979) and Abel-Smith and Townsend (1965). The relative approach involves a number of crucial assumptions, such as, for example, that it is possible to identify an average or 'normal' standard and that a relative standard is meaningful for all in society. This in turn raises issues about which 'society' is being referred to, especially in an increasingly diverse and globalized world.

These two ways of thinking coexist in the field of poverty research today, although they tend not to be used together. Efforts have been made to link them. Some have suggested the use of a continuum bounded at one end by an absolute conceptualization and at the other by a relative approach. The continuum suggested by George and Howards (1991), for example, ranges from starvation or hunger, through subsistence and social coping, to social participation. The work of Amartya Sen – which will be discussed below – also bridges the two perspectives.

Who is poor? Some can afford a holiday to Martinique, some cannot. Some have a home to sleep in, others do not. (© phillipe leroyer/Flickr)

We can proceed with the following set of insights in mind: essentially, absolute and relative views of poverty describe different conditions – physical poverty and poverty vis-à-vis the resources available to fellow members of society. If we wish to retain poverty as a concept, we should be conscious of the strengths and weaknesses of different understandings and capitalize on the strengths of the particular approach adopted (Pinker 1999; Alcock 2006).

Is poverty just about income?

Poverty is usually conceived of in terms of scarce material resources. This is true of both absolute and relative approaches. One can easily see why income is most widely taken as a proxy for material scarcity or abundance: it is a universal metric; people can think it through with relative ease; and it seems reasonable to assume a strong association between low income and poverty in countries where money is the most important medium of exchange. Theoretically, reliance on income lays the emphasis on poverty as an economic condition, one produced in and realized by the system of economic exchange. Viewing poverty in terms of income alone runs three risks: of neglecting a broader series of factors, of 'materializing' poverty, and of seeing it as an exclusively economic phenomenon.

Let us think of poverty in broader terms. There are different ways in which this line of thinking can be developed, but questioning to what extent poverty and those who experience it are linked to the institutions of society gets to the heart of the matter.

One way of broadening the perspective is to view poverty as a form of relative deprivation. This has a closer link than income to investigating how people actually live. It is focused more on consumption and outcomes, measured by people's lack of or constrained access to items relating to housing, food consumption, clothing and consumer durables, as well as social and cultural activities. The potential offered by the concept of deprivation to conceive of poverty in more complex and multidimensional terms and to study it in regard to how people actually live has galvanized the field of poverty research in Europe (and elsewhere) (Gordon and Townsend 2000). Factors such as social isolation and lack of social support may be encapsulated in a conception of social deprivation. But they are core to another relevant concept: social exclusion. While it is broader than poverty, social exclusion as an approach seeks to understand structures and processes associated with the continuation of low income and disadvantage over time. It conceptualizes these in terms of (degrees of) exclusion from society – effected by processes such as dissociation, polarization and separation. It is interested in how people become excluded but also why. In the latter regard it is especially interested in the factors at work – whether at the micro- or the macro-level – which act to distance individuals and/or groups from the broader society (Levitas 1998; Daly and Silver 2008). In this and other ways, the perspective focuses on factors leading to weakening or even closure of the linkages between individuals and society at large.

One interesting theorization of how this occurs is to be found in the work of the early German sociologist Georg Simmel (1965). According to Simmel, those who are poor may be excluded by means of ostracism, misrecognition, contempt or lack of respect; they are rendered 'different'. This is akin to what Lister (2004: 100) calls 'othering'. She uses this term to denote a dual process of differentiation and demarcation. In the first instance, 'the poor' are distanced and represented as different from 'the rest of us' and, in the second, negative value judgements are applied to label and stigmatize and often stereotype people who are 'poor'. 'Strangers in our midst', is how Katz puts it (1989: 7, cited in Lister 2004: 116). The social reactions that people's situations evoke in others and in society at large are therefore crucial to poverty as a sociological phenomenon and as a corrosive social relation (Jones and Novak 1999). Simmel also suggested that society's responses to those who are in need have played a key role in creating and perpetuating a category of 'the poor'. Think of the process that has to be gone through to receive welfare benefits – tests of means, which are widespread, serve not just to establish whether people merit help but also lump those who receive help into a particular category of 'poor' separate from the rest of us. Analysis of the organization and operation of state benefits and services (undertaken below) is very revealing.

There are other ways also of broadening the focus. The work of Amartya Sen (1983, 1985, 1992, *inter alia*) centres on the link between resources and people's capacity for agency (conceived in terms of a whole range of human actions). For Sen, material and other resources are important not in their own right but as means to achieve ends. People's capabilities – the freedom they have to do and be what they have reason to value – is at the core of his framework. Capabilities imply the opportunities and resources to make choices – for those who are poor or in disadvantaged situations it is vital that they have the possibility to convert their resources into conditions that lead to improved functioning, just like the rest of us. Poverty is interpreted as a lack of resources impeding people from engaging in whatever they regard as valuable for them. The factors that might impair this 'conversion' include illness, low educa-tion or knowledge and discrimination. In a major challenge to the concept of poverty and the reliance on income, Sen has claimed that it is not resources or command over commodities per se that matter in determining quality of life but rather opportunities. Sen's perspective invests heavily in people's agency but also has a sense of state or condition – the former relates to 'doing' and the latter to 'being'. Both doing and being are connected in the concept of 'functionings' (the illustrative examples of which include healthfulness, longevity, literacy). The critical element, though, is capabilities. It is these that confer the freedom or opportunity for people to achieve what it is they value. Capabilities are absolute and universal in Sen's view. He has refused to define a list of such capabilities and, rather than specifying desired outcomes, prefers an expansive conception of what is valuable in human life. He, therefore, does not subscribe to the view that universal basic needs exist (although note that Nussbaum (2000) has used Sen's approach to devise a list of essential capabilities to live at a minimum decent level with dignity). Among other things, this makes the concept of capabilities difficult to operationalize and interpret.

All of these perspectives raise valid considerations. Taken as a whole, they suggest that poverty has different components and layers. Hence, there are social and political as well as economic dimensions to poverty. That said, there is a strong set of arguments for not going too broad with the conceptualization of poverty and retaining a view of it as being at its core about absence or scarcity of key resources. If it is viewed too broadly it becomes impossible to separate out poverty from other situations or conditions, such as lack of wellbeing or inequal-ity. There is also an argument not to dismiss money and material resources too readily because they have huge actual and symbolic significance in market-based societies (Lister 2004: 9). Roll (1992: 18) cautions against going too broad with the definition of poverty for another set of reasons: the more widely the boundaries of the definition of poverty are drawn, the more the abolition of poverty merges into broader social goals. This might mean that poverty loses its distinctiveness as a phenomenon and as a 'problem' for policy to address.

By way of overview the following should be borne in mind:

- It is important not to view the different debates about conceptualization and focus in polarized terms or, indeed, to regard poverty conceptualization in a dichotomized fashion. Each tends to highlight different elements, processes and experiences.
- While the concept of poverty is contested, none of the debate should be read to suggest that poverty does not exist.

Definitions of poverty

Another way of learning about the concept – and a crucial part of being able to critically assess the evidence on poverty – is to explore the ways in which it has been researched. Poverty has fuelled a large body of research and a sizeable research community. Since a lot of the pioneer-ing work was carried out in England, an outline of the development of research there serves as an example of the complexities of poverty definition. It also showcases the particular tradition of micro-level studies of poverty which is a characteristic of the field of poverty research.

One of the original and founding approaches to the study of poverty was that of Charles Booth. He commenced his studies in London in 1886 and did not consider them finished until nearly twenty years later (in 1903), mainly because of the complexities and level of detail required. As a positivist believing that 'facts' could be discovered through social research, Booth guided his empirical investigations towards the living conditions of those who could be said to be poor relative to others who were better off. His work was qualitative and micro-level in that he focused on comparing how people in different circumstances lived and spent their money. On this basis, he developed a number of indicative household budgets for people in different situations. He was the first to use a poverty line to distinguish poor people from non-poor people, which he set at 18 to 21 shillings a week, making clear that the line was an estimate of the levels of income at which people are likely to become poor rather than a strict cut-off point (Spicker 1993: 30).

The next link in the English chain of poverty research is provided by Seebohm Rowntree, who, in his study of 11,560 working-class families in the regional city of York in 1899, distinguished different types of poverty – what he called primary and secondary poverty. Rowntree saw the former as occurring when people had too little income to meet basic or subsistence needs; secondary poverty was something quite different in that it occurred when, despite sufficient resources, people's (mis)use of their resources brought them below a minimum standard. With primary poverty, Rowntree was interested in setting a floor or threshold and in demonstrating that, no matter how well they managed their money, people could not avoid poverty if their income was too low. One of his main contributions was to analyse poverty on the basis of different household types. Rowntree identified six 'causes' of poverty: low wages, high numbers of children, death, old age, irregular employment or unemployment of the main earner. With secondary poverty, Rowntree raised the very contentious question of whether people are poor because of lack of resources or because they do not use the resources they have properly. The latter figures prominently in popular discourse.

One could capture much of the transformation since the classic early studies by observing that poverty conceptualization is becoming more and more 'socialized'. Of signature importance was the work of Peter Townsend, in the UK from the 1960s on and internationally from the 1980s on. Townsend's approach was heavily sociological – he saw poverty as relative to the income situation of others and held that the experience, meaning and political significance of poverty could not be conceived of apart from social context. For Townsend, the touchstone for poverty was 'the normal life of society'. One of his driving interests was to establish the connection between income and other assets and material and social deprivation – the extent to which people could not gain access to patterns of life, resources and opportunities that were considered normal in society. The idea of poverty as exclusion from the customary lifestyle of one's peers was born, and it has been influential especially in the EU understanding of poverty: 'People are said to be in poverty if their income and resources are so inadequate as to preclude them from having a standard of living considered acceptable in the society in which they live' (EU Council of Ministers 1975).

The picture painted thus far holds closely to the situation in the highly developed world. For other parts of the world, one sees a close focusing on poverty as malnutrition, ill health, illiteracy, lack of shelter and lack of basic security, not just around income but also around access to such resources as safe water: 'Absolute poverty is a condition characterized by severe deprivation of basic human needs, including food, safe drinking water, sanitation facilities, health, shelter, education and information' (United Nations 1995). The UN has sought through its Multidimensional Poverty Index (MPI) to develop a composite measure that can apply universally. It shows the number of people who are multidimensionally poor (suffering deprivations in 33.33 percent of weighted indicators) and the number of deprivations with which poor households typically contend. The MPI centres on the same three dimensions as the UN's Human Development Index – health, education and living standards. The actual indicators of poverty for each are measured by child mortality and nutrition, years of schooling and enrolment rates for children, and availability of cooking fuel, a toilet, water, electricity, a floor and assets.

The work to reframe the definition and understanding of poverty is ongoing and, as Lister (2004) has pointed out, the push for broader conceptions of poverty has come in particular from the developing world, or at least the development discipline. One example is the sustainable livelihoods framework, developed by the UK's Department for International Development and others. Oriented especially to improve NGOs' efforts to eliminate poverty, the framework lays emphasis on what it calls 'livelihood assets': human capital (i.e., the amount and quality of knowledge and labour available in a household); natural capital (i.e., the quality and quantity of natural resources, ranging from fisheries to air quality); financial capital (i.e., savings and regular inflows of money); physical capital (i.e., the infrastructure, tools and equipment used for increasing productivity); and social capital (i.e., social resources, including networks for cooperation, mutual trust and support). It would be wrong to see this just in terms of definition, though. It is a political discourse, focused on denial of rights, full citizenship, access to power and voice (Narayan et al. 2000; Lister 2004).

SEMINAR QUESTIONS

1   Is a common definition of poverty for the world as a whole possible?
2   How good is income level as an indicator of poverty or wealth?
3   Should poverty be conceived of in terms of what people have or what they can do?
4   Compare the Human Development Index for two very high, high, medium and low human development countries (available at http://hdr.undp.org/en/statistics/).
5   Compile your own index of statistical indicators relevant to poverty in three countries of your choice using the UN 'build your own index' tool (http://hdr.undp.org/en/data/build/). Use the OECD's 'Better Life Index' to design an index of wellbeing for three countries of your choice (available at www.oecdbetterlifeindex.org/about/better-life-initiative/).

MEASURING AND RESEARCHING POVERTY

Poverty lines, budget standards and lifestyle/participation thresholds

Poverty research and anti-poverty policy are constantly beset by the challenge of separating the people who are living in poverty from those who are not. To capture the differentiation, one must decide not only on the yardsticks or set of indicators that will be used to measure poverty but also whether one is going to use a cut-off point to differentiate between them (Nolan and Whelan 1996).

There are many disputes associated with a poverty threshold; and such disputes exist whether this threshold is income based or derived on the basis of assets and activities (as in the deprivation studies). One dispute is about whether such a threshold can be identified at all – it is problematic because it assumes a discontinuity of resources at a particular point which acts like a rupture between those above and those below the threshold. Another problem is that poverty lines are subject to systematic biases in application and interpretation (Spicker 1993: 51). For example, in order to draw an income poverty line, one has to adjust for household size and composition – through equivalence scales – without actually knowing how resources are utilized inside the particular household or family. Those studying the gender dimensions of poverty are especially critical of this because of the likelihood that the assumption of equal sharing underestimates poverty among women (Chant 2010). There is also the matter of degrees of distance above and below the cut-off – in the case of income poverty this is called the poverty gap. The depth or severity of poverty is not necessarily taken into account by a poverty threshold. These reservations notwithstanding, the search for the poverty threshold or line is the centre of gravity for much poverty research.

Concentrating on the highly developed countries, there are basically four main ways in which poverty is measured in practice. These draw from different theoretical or conceptual perspectives and follow different methodologies.

One of the best known – and a leading measure used to count the number of people living in poverty globally – is the International Poverty Line, set by the World Bank. Currently, this designates the poverty threshold as living on less than $1.25 Purchasing Power Parities (PPP) a day. PPP, as defined by the World Bank, is a method of measuring the relative purchasing power of different countries' currencies over the same types of goods and services. Because goods and services may cost more in one country than in another, PPP allows us to make more accurate comparisons of standards of living across countries. The figures according to this measure for selected countries are given in table 8.1. The $1.25 cut-off is in many ways a notional threshold, though, used because of its intuitive appeal as a universally applicable metric rather than because it has been systematically worked out. Most countries and international research take as the poverty line a cut-off point of average income in the country being examined. In European countries the line is typically set at 50 percent or 60 percent of median income (Gordon and Townsend 2000). While such cut-offs are arbitrary, their advantages include simplicity, comparability, and the fact that they yield results that can be immediately understood by different sections of the population (Nolan and Whelan 1996: 20). However, since the cut-off point is relative, there are grounds to claim that it is a measure of low income and inequality rather than poverty. There are also technical problems, not least that any improvement or deterioration in living standards which is shared by the rest of the population will not be detected (Sen 1983). There is also the matter of taking account of households' costs – such as those for housing – and whether the poverty rates should be calculated before or after housing costs. In a general sensitivity to the critique of the approach, researchers often use more than one cut-off – 40 percent, 50 percent and 60 percent of median income thresholds, for example. Measures of poverty depth or gap are also widely used – calculating how far below the poverty line people's incomes actually fall. The poverty gap measure is a response to the criticism that the cut-off lumps together those who are just around the poverty line with those who fall far below it. It also gives a better indication of how policy and other changes affect people below the poverty line (Brady 2009: 41–2).

Table 8.1: **Percentage of the population living on less than $1.25 a day in 2009, at 2005 international prices (PPP measure)**	
Country	Percentage of population living on less than $1.25
Angola	43.4
Argentina	2.0
Brazil	6.1
Burkina Faso	44.6
Cambodia	18.6
China	11.8
Colombia	9.7
Fiji	5.9
Georgia	15.2
Indonesia	20.4
Kazakhstan	0.1
Latvia	0.2
Moldova	0.4
Philippines	18.4
Romania	0.4
Slovak Republic	0.1
South Africa	13.8
Sudan	19.8
Thailand	0.4
Turkey	0.6
Uganda	38.0

Source: Compiled with data from World Bank (2013).

A second method – closer to an absolute approach than the relative income cut-off – is the budget standards approach, which is based on the specification of a nutritionally adequate diet and the costing of the basket of goods to meet that standard. One example of this method is the official poverty line in the USA, adopted in 1965. A 'food basket' of essential items was put together, costed and multiplied by three – on the assumption that people were poor if they spend more than a third of their cash income on what is considered a minimally acceptable diet. As this approach has been applied and developed in the UK and Europe, the intention has been to establish thresholds concerned less with physical necessities and more about low cost and modest but adequate budgets (Bradshaw 1993; Veit-Wilson 1998; Bradshaw et al. 2008; see the Minimum Income Standard website at www.lboro.ac.uk/research/crsp/mis/). Budget standards involve drawing up a list of commodities, employing normative judgements supported by a combination of scientific and behavioural evidence. The budget is then priced and used as an income or expenditure standard – anyone living at or below that standard is considered to be in poverty. There are advantages to this approach. In particular, budget standards are very concrete and indicate exactly what standard of living an income level corresponds to (Van den Bosch 2001: 8). They are also derived in relation to real life. But they are time consuming to derive and need to be worked out for many different household types. In addition, they can be difficult to update and there is no agreement about how subsistence needs change as incomes rise or fall. For example, because it is updated on the basis of prices rather than standard of living, the poverty threshold in the USA fell from 48 percent of median family income in 1960 to 29 percent in 2000 (Le Grand, Propper and Smith 2008: 160).

A third approach measures poverty on the basis of people's views about minimum standards. Such an approach, known as the consensual poverty line approach, has been developed especially in the Netherlands (Hagenaars 1986). People are asked either to rate particular income levels for a list of hypothetical families of different types or to specify the income they consider to be the minimum they themselves would need. The difference between asking individuals about hypothetical families and their own family should be noted. While the former has the advantage of getting feedback on a range of family types, it runs the risk that people's opinions may be based on quite limited knowledge. In any case, drawing a poverty line from this kind of information involves a complex weighting structure and a number of far-reaching assumptions (Nolan and Whelan 1996: 19). It may also be the case that there is no consensus on minimum needs (Piachaud 1987).

The fourth approach is a combination one, also known as a triangulation of methods. Most commonly, an income poverty line and a threshold derived from patterns of lifestyle and participation (which measure deprivation) are used together. This is inspired by Townsend's approach to poverty, which has led scholarship to move beyond the use of either a single indicator or income alone. It also gets beyond the anomaly whereby poverty tends to be conceived in terms of living standards but measured in terms of income – a criticism of the conventional poverty line approach made by both Atkinson (1985) and Ringen (1988). Townsend (1979) used deprivation indicators in an attempt to validate an income poverty line. This provoked considerable criticism (Piachaud 1987). Mack and Lansley (1985) used such indicators directly to identify the poor. Aiming to supersede the criticisms that Townsend's list of items and activities was arbitrary and that people might choose to do without some of the 'necessities' even if they could afford them, they defined poverty as 'an enforced lack of socially perceived necessities'. Hence they not only introduced a subjective element into the measurement, by asking people about their attitude towards necessities, but also investigated whether people were without these by choice. Households are defined as being in poverty if they lack three or more socially perceived necessities, and according to this measure poverty has been increasing in Britain (see table 8.2).

Table 8.2: **The rise in multi-deprived households in Britain**		
	1983	2012
Percentage lacking three or more necessities	14	33

Source: Gordon et al. (2013: 16).

Some of the necessities lacked by households detailed in table 8.2 included adequate food and housing as shown in tables 8.3 and 8.4.

However, this approach, too, has its difficulties. One is the challenge of selecting and

Table 8.3: **Percentage of households unable to afford a warm, damp-free home**

	1983	1990	1999	2012
Heating to keep home adequately warm	5	5	3	9
Damp-free home	6	2	7	10

Source: Gordon et al. (2013: 16).

Table 8.4: **Percentage of households unable to afford food basics**

	1983	1990	1999	2012
Fresh fruit and vegetables	n/a	6	5	7
Meat, fish or vegetarian equivalent every other day	8	3	2	5
Two meals a day	4	1	(1)[a]	3

[a] 1999 figure was under 1 percent and fewer than twenty unweighted cases.
Source: Gordon et al. (2013: 16).

aggregating items which can be said to represent deprivation if people are forced to do without them; a second is how to take account of the role of tastes or preferences vs. resource constraints in determining whether absence of an item is in fact 'enforced' (Nolan and Whelan 1996: 21). This method is not used officially by any country, but both the UK and the EU could be said to be moving towards it in their use of a multidimensional approach to poverty. In its most recent iteration of poverty measurement, for example, the EU uses a combination of income poverty, severe material deprivation and the proportion of jobless households (defined as households where no more than 20 percent of the labour capacity is in employment). People are considered 'severely materially deprived' if they experience at least four out of the following nine deprivations: they cannot afford to i) pay their rent or utility bills, ii) keep their home adequately warm, iii) face unexpected expenses, iv) eat meat, fish or a protein equivalent every second day, v) enjoy a week of holiday away from home once a year, vi) have a car, vii) have a washing machine, viii) have a colour TV, or ix) have a telephone (Eurostat 2012b).

How to adjudicate between these different approaches? To some extent the method selected depends on the intended purpose – to compare material resources within and across populations, to get a comprehensive view of how income co-varies with other aspects of life, or to get at the values of the population and the common views and lifestyles (Roll 1992). As well as being mindful of the intent or purpose, one should be conscious of the underlying assumptions and the compromises involved in each approach. In relation to many of the measures used, for example, a long chain of factors has to go right in the research: income, assets and activities have to be reported accurately; the right weightings or equivalences have to be applied to capture variations in household or family circumstances; correct decisions have to be made about how to take account of assets other than income and how to estimate the value of these over time. Given this, poverty rates should be regarded as estimates and poverty measurement as a work in progress.

Experiencing poverty

There is a strong argument to make that a quantitative perspective is best at providing a snapshot of poverty whereas, if one wants to get to the core of poverty and especially to examine poverty as dynamic and diverse rather than fixed, qualitative methods – including interviews and focus groups as well as more experiential and creative methods along the lines of diary keeping, life histories and mapping – are to be preferred. These seek to reveal what it means to be poor.

While it is not the largest seam of work on poverty, there is a significant body of research that sets out to allow people living in poverty to tell their own story (Beresford et al. 1999; Narayan et al. 2000; Daly and Leonard 2002). This may be for epistemological reasons, such as better to investigate the experiences associated with poverty – the texture of real life in poverty. It may also be political in origin – to allow people in this situation to be heard in the belief that their voice is usually silenced. First-hand accounts are valued in their own right in this work, challenging the tendency for researchers and other experts to 'know' without personal experience. One operationalization of a participatory approach is in research and other work carried on under the auspices of the World Bank, which has employed Participatory Poverty Assessments. These examine poverty not as a pre-defined problem but in the terms in which those living in poverty themselves identify and understand the situation (Norton et al. 2001).

When people are asked about living in poverty, what do they say? There tend to be two dominant narratives in individuals' accounts of everyday of life in poverty. One focuses on money and its management and the other on the way people feel they are treated by others (Kempson, Bryson and Rowlingson 1994; Daly and Leonard 2002; Flint 2010). Daily life is described as living constantly from hand to mouth – going without, putting off even small expenditures, not celebrating family-related or other events. Sacrifice and compromise are commonplace. Budgeting becomes almost a survival skill. Exploring how they manage suggests that people living in poverty not only have diverse coping skills but also strategies to make money and resources stretch as far as possible (Flint 2010). Because many would not qualify for or are outside the orbit of formal credit, a key element of their lives is a constant round of short-term credit and long-term debt (Dearden et al. 2010). There is a strong sense of an alternative or underground economy – moneylending, short-term informal loans from private sources, swapping goods, favours and skills, and buying goods and services at knock-down prices and in used condition. People also try to hide their circumstances, especially if they have children, to keep up appearances and retain a sense of pride and avoid feelings of embarrassment and shame (Chase and Walker 2013).

A second dominant theme in people's accounts is how they are treated. Poverty is for many people an experience of disrespect, humiliation, powerlessness and denial of rights (Lister 2004: 7). Those who are living in poverty report stigma as part of their everyday experience (Chase and Walker 2013). They probably already feel on the defensive or shameful about needing help and yet on a regular basis have to open themselves up to probing questions and ultimately judgements from others on whether they deserve assistance or not. This kind of experience may also extend into contacts with employers or potential employers. It is a powerful reason why poverty affects people on the inside as well. It is not uncommon to encounter a discourse of personal failure in the narratives of people living in poverty (Narayan et al. 2000; Chouhan, Speeden and Qazi 2011).

However, there is no one-way depiction of people living in poverty – they may and commonly do have access to other 'resources' or protective factors. They often have very firm

As well as material hardships and deprivation, people living in poverty can experience social, personal and emotional hardship. This billboard relates to Glasgow Housing Association, which promotes itself on its website as 'providing better homes and better lives to thousands'. However, the billboard paints a picture of social housing tenants as worn-down, miserable and gender stereotyped, and warns prominently that they shouldn't shirk their responsibilities. (© the justified sinner/Flickr)

friendships and family relationships, for example, as well as support from their community, especially if their living situation is similar to that of those with whom they closely interact. As Pemberton, Sutton and Fahmy (2013) put it, the presence of family, friends, neighbours and community can all serve to soften the harsh realities of life on a low income. However, such networks can also be fragile because they are often overstretched, something that can easily happen given that the people called upon to help tend to be in a similar low-resource situation. And there are also many people who have no one to call upon.

Exploring people's experiences alerts us to the fact that there are also trajectories into poverty. Among precipitating factors are job loss, marriage or family break-up (which can lead also to homelessness), illness and disability. If there is a way in, then it follows that there should also be a way out. Exits from poverty are hard to pinpoint in practice, although they are very easily imagined in public discourse. According to Stephen Smith (2005: 3), on a worldwide basis, about three-quarters as many people fall into poverty as escape from it. This leads him to suggest that the struggle against poverty may be one of four steps forward and three steps back.

Listening to the accounts of people who are living in poverty conveys a strong sense of being trapped (Lister 2004: 140). Entrapment comes about not just because of lack of money but via the vicious circle created by being under-resourced or even negatively resourced. Consider how difficult it is for someone who has low education and skills, poor work experience and lack of access to opportunities to change their situation. Evidence suggests that the route out of poverty can be frustrated by several factors. The first is a lack of genuine opportunities for lifelong learning and adult education that would act as a pathway to higher-paid and rewarding jobs (Scott, London and Edin 2000). Secondly, there is the fact that people in poverty situations often lack the networks (of support, information and influence) that are so important for getting on. They may also lack the necessary social skills – the 'know-how' – to make a good impression and capitalize on situations. Thirdly, those living in poverty tend to have poor and disjointed work histories. Their employment patterns are typically characterized by low-paying, low-skilled and short-term jobs which lead nowhere. Pemberton, Sutton and Fahmy (2013) speak of a revolving door of the labour market which shuttles certain people in and out.

Poverty affects the person on the inside. It is not uncommon to encounter a discourse of personal failure, for example, in the narratives of people living in poverty (Narayan et al. 2000; Chouhan, Speeden and Qazi 2011). People voice worries especially about their children's future and whether it is compromised by their growing up in a situation of low income and/or poverty (Daly and Leonard 2002). They frequently voice feelings of guilt about their children. While their offspring tend to be the source of their greatest hope, they are also the focus of their greatest fears.

We should not assume that negative feelings emerge spontaneously. There is a vast repertoire of negative depictions or labels for those who are poor: 'feckless', 'dependent', 'scroungers', 'untrustworthy', 'stupid'. These and other terms arouse feelings of shame and worthlessness among those who are exposed to them. In a more positive vein but a rendering that still distances, poor people may be represented as 'to be pitied', pathetic, passive, hopeless, victims (Lister 2004: 116). We know that sections of the media regularly use both types of image to represent the poorer sections of society; but government agencies too may be engaged in processes of distancing those who live in poverty (as we shall see below when we discuss the causes of poverty). While it may not be the intention, 'othering' serves to blame the poor and perpetuate and justify existing distinctions and inequalities (ibid.: 102). It also acts to affirm the identities and power of those who do the labelling, just as it denies those labelled an opportunity to create or retain an identity worthy of respect – How are they to think of themselves other than as failures? Jones and Novak (1999) point out that the negative depictions of those living in poverty tend to be more prevalent when poverty and unemployment rates are high. According to Lister, 'othering' as an exercise of power draws from a profound history of morally censoring those who live in poverty (2004: 103–4). All of this underlines the importance of hearing what people who are poor have to say – in the absence of voice they tend to be depicted as 'others' and granted no agency – and of according them respect for who they are.

The following are the key points to be taken forward from considering the experience of what it is like to live in poverty.

- The situation of people living in poverty should never be seen in static terms – they utilize their agency for the purpose of coping (and in extreme cases even for surviving). However, agency is constrained by lack of resources and so, while people living in poverty are not passive in their situation, they do not have the same range of choices as others.

- Poverty is no single situation or experience – it is a condition which means, among other things, that it is a bundle of related factors and experiences (Jones and Novak 1999).
- People who are poor encounter relatively fixed and often negative views and expectations. There is a sense in which poverty sets up a negative dynamic whereby people who are poor are almost always forced to defend themselves against negative expectations and are hampered by a lack of authority, power, influence and respect.

SEMINAR QUESTIONS

1 Does it really matter how poverty is measured? Why/why not?
2 Compile a list of essentials that should be in the basket of goods for: a) a child up to twelve years of age; b) a teenager between the ages of thirteen and eighteen; c) an adult aged twenty-five to forty; d) an adult aged forty-one to sixty; e) an adult over sixty years. Identify the assumptions you are making here with regard to the unit of analysis, the needs of people by age, and how resources are shared between people. Reflect on the difficulties involved.
3 What are the costs of poverty to those affected and how do these connect to costs for society at large?
4 Is it possible to understand poverty without taking account of the views and experiences of those who live in poverty? What are some innovative ways in which the experiences of people living in poverty could be researched?

THE WELFARE STATE

Introduction to the welfare state

All analyses of poverty lead in one way or another to the welfare state, for where it exists it is a key social institution in the fight against poverty, hardship and insecurity. The term 'welfare state' has a broad set of meanings. Firstly, it is a theoretical term, invoking theories of power and how authority is vested in the state and utilized by it to both control and protect. Secondly, the welfare-state concept incorporates the idea of a comprehensive model oriented to social planning and the use of public resources to improve the welfare of the society at large. While welfare states emerge and change over time, they are usually conceived as decisive interventions whereby public resources are used to combat existing ills, including poverty. The notion of regime, which has become a popular way of thinking comparatively about welfare states, especially since Gösta Esping-Andersen used it in his book *The Three Worlds of Welfare Capitalism* (1990), conveys the sense of system implied here.

One can conceptualize the welfare state narrowly and broadly. Most narrowly, the term refers to the aims and objectives of publicly funded actions concerning social needs and the social programmes and social services put in place to meet such needs. Conceived somewhat more broadly, the welfare state is a particular state form in which power, authority and resources are deliberately used (through politics and administration) in an effort to modify economic, political and social relations and practices. The goals here may encompass improving standards in and the functioning of the labour market, guaranteeing people a minimum income irrespective of their employment situation, narrowing the extent of insecurity so that people are taken care of in situations such as childhood, sickness, old age and unemployment, and ensuring that all citizens can avail themselves of a range of social services (Briggs 1961). In other words, the welfare state is situated between the individual and economic and social life. The notion of citizenship entitlements and rights is a helpful way of appreciating that the welfare state institutionalizes certain guarantees, especially around income and services. Those who can afford to pay taxes will be compelled to do so, and some of the monies collected will be recirculated via income support when people are less well-off and through public services such as health, education, training and housing.

The welfare state embodies a commitment to transfer some responsibility for welfare from individuals, families and communities to the public authorities. Classically, welfare states were oriented to the welfare of workers and the less well-off. At their most aspirational (mainly in Europe), they sought to generalize this concern and build a common set of life chances above sectional interests but favouring those with fewer resources and less power. This oversaw the growth of a vast conglomerate of nationwide, compulsory and collective arrangements (De Swaan 1988: 218). Welfare-related programmes in Europe and other parts of the developed world were, in fact, a relatively long time in the making, and so the term 'evolution' better

Some have referred to the situation in China as a ticking time bomb: an ageing population caused by increasing longevity as a result of rapid economic development and by the one-child policy, which has limited the working population now able to support their elders. The welfare system will face tough challenges in the coming decades. (© Richard.Asia/Flickr)

captures their emergence than does 'revolution'. The development of social programmes in some parts of the less developed world has occurred much faster, especially if one takes as the starting point the period when broad economic development set in. It is said, for example, that China will have a window of only twenty or thirty years to deal with the social problems that took nearly 100 years to emerge and be addressed in Europe.

The welfare state's association with equality does not end with equality from a social class perspective. Gender equality has also been an important social policy consideration, especially from the 1970s on. Think of the moves towards providing benefits and services for women (such as provision for lone mothers, maternity leave, widows' pensions, and so forth) and towards granting women and men equal access to benefits and services (Daly and Rake 2003). Much of this is now being rethought though – as the costs of the welfare state escalate, there is a questioning of how widely welfare measures should range in ambition and coverage, with many claiming that social expenditure should be tightly reined in. This kind of thinking has led to some withdrawal of public services and benefits in favour of market-based and other providers, or indeed to let people fend more for themselves. The form and nature of the welfare state is therefore changing.

Welfare states today and historically vary considerably from one another. Indeed, variation is so widespread that it renders discussion of 'the welfare state' in generic terms imprecise. Nowadays, it is very common to speak of welfare-state types or regimes. The academic work of recent years makes a strong claim that European welfare states can be grouped into a number of base types or models (Esping-Andersen 1990; Daly and Rake 2003). While there is dispute, most analysts would agree that the differences and similarities among welfare states in Europe are such that one can speak of a liberal model (typically found in the UK), a Nordic social democratic model (in the Scandinavian countries), a continental European (conservative) model (in Germany, Austria and a number of other countries) and a Mediterranean model (see box 8.2). The models are differentiated from one another in key respects, especially in regard to the range and generosity of benefits and services.

Poverty and welfare states

Welfare states engage in a number of activities that affect poverty. First, they seek to prevent poverty by managing and protecting against risk. In most countries social insurance is core to the classic welfare-state design, with people paying social insurance contributions (which are usually automatically deducted through wages) to cover themselves against four main risks of income loss: illness or accident, unemployment, old-age and maternity. It is obvious that all of these are risks that derive from an inability to be employed. Second, welfare states try to deal with poverty or too low income when it occurs. For this purpose, welfare states put in place income and other supports for people should they encounter inadequate income or poverty. These operate not to a principle of legal entitlement but on the basis of a discretionary judgement of a welfare official. Third, welfare states seek to address poverty indirectly by putting in place measures to get people into employment. These are the so-called activation measures, which are long-standing in some countries but increasingly favoured throughout Europe as well as elsewhere. Such measures reinforce and seek to realize the conviction that people should support themselves through paid work rather than be supported wholly by the state. Hence, as a social policy reform project, activation proceeds by reining in the generosity of benefits, attaching greater conditionality to their receipt (especially for the unemployed and

BOX 8.2 WELFARE-STATE TYPES

Liberal welfare-state model This kind of welfare state – to be found in the UK and the USA especially – is more individualistic than collective in orientation and tends to support the market as the main means of resource allocation. Social policies strongly encourage participation in paid employment for all by offering mainly low-level welfare payments and attaching strong conditions to their receipt. The latter makes for widespread use of means tests. Within the universe of different types of welfare state, this model looks residual in that, rather than to security and protection for all, it is oriented to poverty alleviation through minimum income support.

Social democratic welfare-state model In the Nordic countries, universalism is a strong principle, with benefits extended to the whole population rather than just for wage earners and a wide network of social services in place. Hence, poverty alleviation is a relatively minor part of the welfare state's activities because poverty tends to be low. A commitment to equality, including gender equality, is deeply embedded in these mostly tax-financed welfare states, where the idea of a benefit system that covers all citizens is well established.

Continental European (conservative) model This model, to be found to a varying extent in Austria, Germany, Belgium and Luxembourg, and partly in France and the Netherlands, is oriented to employment and the preservation of status and other differences between different occupational groups. By and large, benefits have to be earned through employment, but when they are the benefits are generous, although how much one gets by way of pension or sickness benefit is largely dependent on one's salary level. There are relatively strong safety nets in place to alleviate poverty.

Mediterranean model Although it is in some ways a mix of other models (in particular the conservative and the liberal), a characteristic Mediterranean welfare-state model has been said to exist as well (Ferrera 1996). Social insurance benefits are limited mainly to public-sector workers. This, together with the fact that social service provision is patchy, has led to a characterization of the Mediterranean welfare state as 'dualistic' and 'underdeveloped'. The family plays a major role in welfare provision. The prevailing family model is traditional (especially from a gender sense) and also multi-generational.

those who do not or cannot work) and increasing efforts by the public authorities to prepare recipients for employment and actually to place them into employment or training.

Different welfare states go about addressing poverty in different ways and to differing degrees. This is because they have different philosophies and different programmes and systems of provision (Daly 2011). Variation is also a function of differing goals that may be in tension with one another – e.g., encouraging employment, protecting the most vulnerable. But, in Europe, most welfare states alleviate poverty quite substantially. While we have no exact way of measuring this, we can compare income levels before and after welfare-state benefits have been received to give an indication of how much poverty there would be if people got no benefits. As table 8.5 shows, in most countries social transfers reduce poverty by anything up to a half. Welfare states clearly therefore have an impact on the extent of poverty and must be taken into account in explaining it, but failures of the welfare state are by no means the only cause of poverty.

Table 8.5: **Poverty rate (measured on 60 percent of median income) before and after social transfers in a selection of European countries and in the EU as a whole, 2010 (%)**

	Before	After
France	25.0	13.5
Germany	24.2	15.6
Sweden	26.7	12.9
UK	31.0	17.1
EU (estimate)	25.7	16.4

Source: Eurostat (2012a).

SEMINAR QUESTIONS

1 Why is poverty not the first priority of welfare states?
2 Who (if anyone) would support people if the welfare state did not?
3 What is likely to be the effect of recession on welfare-state variation? Are they all likely to become more similar?
4 Using the OECD Social Expenditure Database, analyse the trends in public and private social expenditures in three countries of your choice over the last ten years (available at www.oecd.org/social/expenditure.htm). On the basis of a sample of websites of your choice, identify the main actors who are in favour of public services and those who favour private provision.

EXPLAINING POVERTY

Individualistic and structural explanations

Miller (1996: 569) sounds a useful note of caution when he says that poverty is under-theorized and yet has too many explanations. What he means is that explanations of poverty are frequently unconnected to a larger body of thought that explains the processes leading to particular outcomes and links these to how social structures and institutions operate. Townsend's (1993) observations about the field of poverty explanation are helpful in understanding why this might be the case. He charts a dichotomized theoretical picture wherein exchanges about the nature of poverty are dominated by, on the one hand, individualistic perspectives and, on the other, structural explanations. It is important that we pause to ensure that we understand the difference between these approaches before proceeding further.

Individualistic approaches locate their explanation in the characteristics and behaviour of people and their beliefs and culture. In regard to poverty, the classic procedure here is to pinpoint the characteristics of those who are poor as the causes of their poverty (Miller 1996: 570). They are shiftless, lack a work ethic, have no proper role models, live in communities where benefit dependency is widely accepted, etc. On the other hand, structural approaches seek to explain poverty by virtue of the structure and organization of the economy, political system and society as a whole. Some examples of theoretical perspectives from which structural approaches draw are Marxist theory, dependency theories of development, theories of stratification and feminist approaches (all of which are considered elsewhere in this book). A structural approach to poverty especially treats the functioning of the economic and political systems, both national and international, as complicit in poverty.

There are two main versions of individualistic explanations. A first is to take the individual and situational characteristics of people living in poverty – such as their assumed attitude to the labour market, their lifestyles and family backgrounds – to make the case that if we know the distribution and incidence of these factors we can explain poverty. But these are not real explanations – they are at best proximate causes and at worst little more than descriptors of people's situations. There is certainly some explanatory merit in having an overview of the factors that appear to be common among those who are experiencing poverty, but they themselves require explanation and so are at best intermediate points in a chain of explanation rather than endpoints. Another type of individualistic explanation is behaviouralist. People's choices (around education, work, personal life or whatever) are seen to cause their poverty. This kind of view gives people 'agency' but it does so mainly to be critical of the choices they make and blame their subsequent situation on these choices (e.g., Centre for Social Justice 2012). Favoured lines of criticism are girls getting pregnant at a young age, young people dropping out of school, people choosing to get divorced, to have more than the average number of children, and so forth – all are depicted as self-destructive behaviours which are freely chosen. These are arguments about people rather than poverty in that they lay the emphasis on their culture, their practices, their outlooks and their dispositions (Miller 1996).

The classic work here is that of Oscar Lewis (1959, 1961), an American anthropologist who is famous especially for his 'culture of poverty' concept, which evolved from his work researching poor families in Mexico. The basic idea is that some people have a culture of poverty which in effect keeps them poor. Others have used cultural or subcultural arguments to suggest that 'the poor' form an underclass. This is an argument that has been developed strongly in the USA, associated especially with the work of Charles Murray (1984) and Herrnstein and Murray (1994). The underclass theorists suggest that there is a class of people – with all the sense of permanence and coherence implied by the use of the term 'class' – who are set apart from the rest of society. The underclass hypothesis dispenses with the definitional and measurement intricacies that we have discussed earlier, identifying 'the poor' as those who live in areas impacted by such factors as large-scale unemployment, housing degradation, and extensive 'dependency' on benefits (Wilson 1987). It is an argument that categorizes and objectifies 'the poor'.

To move beyond personal characteristics and individualistic explanations and towards an approach that merges agency with structure, it is helpful to think in terms of different domains or institutions of social and economic life and how these operate and interconnect at the micro- and the macro-level. The economy is one vital domain. One can see its impact at an everyday level in the way that economic factors in the person's immediate situation or environment may lead to poverty. This is true in terms of people's access to resources such as money and material assets and also other forms of capital (e.g., physical strength and endurance, human capital such as skills and education, and social capital in the form of networks that provide support, know-how and also potential influence). There is an argument – favoured by neoclassical economists and many political figures – that poverty results from low human capital among certain sectors of the population. Among the widely used versions of this argument is that those who are poor do not have enough of the right skills or motivation to do well in employment or even to become employed. The opportunities are there but 'the poor' cannot or will not avail themselves of them. This kind of view informs the strong focus on labour-market preparation and 'activation' for the unemployed in current policy in Europe and elsewhere. As Miller (1996: 575), among others, points out, though, it assumes that if people were to improve their skills then jobs would somehow materialize – an eventuality for which there is a dearth of evidence, especially given how the recent recession has swept away so many jobs.

Thinking about why massive job loss occurred alerts us to the fact that the economy is as much a macro- as it is a micro-phenomenon. Hence, individual or group circumstances cannot be treated as given – they did not just happen but are connected to features of the macro-economic environment and the policy choices made to manage it. The general level or stage of national or regional development, for example, the historical pattern of development and the policies pursued are just some factors of relevance to poverty. But some macro-level economic arrangements are associated with greater poverty than others. A global perspective on poverty – whether we understand that as taking a worldview or moving beyond local or national conditions to see the broader picture – helps us to recognize the impact of processes and structures such as business cycles, the capitalist economic structure, the different corporate and other players and their interests, and politics at national and international levels. Globalization – the term given to the latest phase of capitalist development – depicts a form of economic development that is autonomous of individual countries and governments, driven by the search after profit in the interests of shareholders in the biggest companies and corporations which trade everywhere but belong nowhere. The last three decades have not only vastly increased the returns to capital but have channelled the gains more and more to a relatively small sector of the population located towards the top of the income spectrum (OECD 2008). As Novak (1996: 48) points out, it is not individuals' inability to adapt to global economic changes that should be considered as poverty's prime cause but, rather, these processes themselves act to impoverish some sections of the community and regions of the world. This did not just happen, though – it was facilitated by public policy, whether on the part of national governments or international institutions.

Poverty, power and politics

And this brings us to politics – a second domain that is integral to explaining poverty. Thinking of poverty as caused by political factors opens a number of possible lines of explanation. One is that people are poor because they lack a political voice or influence; a second is about how policy and the distribution of public resources function and who most benefits from this. Both are closely related.

The possibility that people are poor if and when they lack political voice and influence is a vital clue to the explanation puzzle. They may not or cannot take part in the democratic process, for example. One concept that is foundational here is that of power. A political understanding of poverty sees it as mapping on to the distribution of power – power and influence are concentrated in the hands of particular sectors and groups in most societies, and those most distant from the centres of power have a greater likelihood of living in poverty. A political explanation such as this resonates with a number of emphases in the poverty struggle. The global poverty debate, which is often set in a context of human development and human progress, holds that the levels of world poverty will not change without a profound shift in the world's power structure. This is one reason why UN definitions of poverty emphasize decision-making or being heard for the purposes of defining and combatting poverty. Other actors – for example, global NGOs such as Oxfam and wider alliances such as Make Poverty History – echo this, suggesting that it is not only as regards the definition of poverty that those living in poverty should be heard but also in the measures devised to address poverty and foster economic growth.

This brings us to policies and the policy process. While it is possible to link the existence or continuation of poverty to inadequacies in policy provision – such as inefficiencies associated with means-testing, for example, benefits that are too meagre to meet need, inefficiencies between different benefits, support systems not being in touch with changing circumstances, poor administration and inappropriate attitudes on the part of staff and/or clients – it is highly unlikely that these factors cause the welfare state to fail to address poverty. A more profound and critical explanation is called for. As part of this, we must probe the assumption that welfare-state policies and provisions are intended to eliminate poverty. In fact, no known welfare state explicitly aims to eliminate poverty; usually governments target a reduction. The current EU poverty target, for example, aims to reduce the numbers of people at risk of poverty and/or social exclusion by 20 million; but that will leave nearly 100 million people still in this situation in the EU (see http://ec.europa.eu/social/). Jones and Novak (1999: 20) claim that policy has sought the relief but not the abolition of poverty. Many governments tolerate poverty and many more ignore it. Why is this the case?

Public policy is subject to contestation by different political interests and groupings. Indeed, the welfare state is both a product of social conflict and shaped by ongoing contestation between different interest groups and their representatives. The development of the welfare state was closely linked to the development of democracy – most of the advanced welfare states flourished once people started to use their ballot strategically and vote for parties that would act in their interests (the development of the welfare state is most closely associated with labour-oriented parties). The welfare state is not necessarily the product of working-class interests, though, and the relationship between low-income sectors and the welfare state was never straightforward. It has been argued that the welfare state would not exist were the middle and upper classes not benefiting from it also (Goodin and Le Grand 1987). One cannot divorce social class interests from economic interests. The welfare state is in many ways a product of capitalism and continues to exist only to the extent that it can strike an accommodation with capitalist interests (which lie in controlling the costs of waged labour, market expansion and profit-taking). Hence one can see why poverty is just one of many considerations for policy and why it might not be high on the list of priorities.

When we look at the process of policy-making and also the process of policy administration at the everyday level, we have to see them as involving political contestation. The discussion above has elucidated the macro-elements of this. But there are also micro-level elements. Recalling Simmel, think of what is happening through particular benefits and services and the procedures for adjudicating on 'claims' from different individuals and groups and the way in which different situations are recognized as meriting support while others are not. Up to about ten years ago, for example, it was considered proper that lone mothers in the UK be supported by the state, whereas now it is thought that they should support themselves through employment once their child reaches school age. This kind of consideration reveals public policies as one of the major sites within which needs of different sectors of the population are interpreted and adjudicated upon (Fraser 1989). In this view, the welfare state is engaged in a micro-politics of power; it is part of a system of 'power/knowledge' (along the lines suggested by the perspective of Michel Foucault (1991)). This kind of perspective debunks the idea of the welfare state as a straightforward response to poverty and other social problems; rather it is implicated in processes that both define and legitimize poverty, valuing some people and groups while systematically devaluing others. Looking through this lens also reveals the power and significance of bureaucrats as mediators between people and the state system of resource distribution.

The following are among the most important points to bear in mind about explaining poverty:

- Rather than reproducing dichotomized framings, it is best to view different causal explanations as having application at different levels. It is also important to link individualistic with structural explanations. Miller's term 'the great chain of poverty explanations' (1996: 569) is helpful in appreciating that one must speak of explanations rather than explanation and that explaining poverty should be approached as a many-layered endeavour.
- The explanations for poverty vary in popularity from place to place and time to time. This is one reason why there is nothing fixed about explanations. Therefore, one should not decouple explanations from prevalent conceptualizations and discourses. As Lister (2004: 3) puts it, there is no single concept of poverty that stands outside history and culture.
- Poverty is reproduced in numerous ways. Public policy and the broad edifice in which it is located plays a key role in, on the one hand, combatting poverty but, on the other, reproducing it.

SEMINAR QUESTIONS

1 Can we explain poverty without theory?
2 What is the difference between explanations that focus on people living in poverty and those that focus on poverty?
3 What are the key considerations for state policy to address in relation to poverty today?
4 Why would the welfare state perpetuate poverty?

CONCLUSION

Poverty is a complex bundle of images, values, theories and experiences which are not easy to pin down (Roll 1992). Poverty does not describe a particular kind of attribute which people do or do not have, nor does it describe a particular person; rather, it is a cluster of conditions (Spicker 1993: 10). The probability of being poor is not distributed randomly. The most common pattern of poverty in developed societies is not that a person living in poverty lacks every kind of good but that some people lack some things in combination for much of the time (ibid.: 17). It is therefore part of the pattern of poverty for people in that situation individually, or as members of their family or larger group, to experience a combination of negative conditions (Daly and Leonard 2002). This can be thought of, in a structural sense, as due to factors that are embedded in the structure of society, whether in the economy, the polity, or key elements of social life itself. Along with structure, agency is a key part of the story of poverty. At an individual level, one might think of this, following Sen, in terms of people's capabilities, what people can do or be, the choices open to them, and the role and significance of different types of resources for freedom of agency. Collective agency is also a key part of the explanation for poverty. In this chapter, the welfare state as one of the key domains and expressions of collective agency in regard to poverty, at least in the highly developed societies, has been given a central explanatory role. The welfare state is active in determining the resources and opportunities available to people, interacting with the economy, the family and other institutions to privilege some sectors at the expense of others.

Most of the academic energy around poverty is devoted to its measurement. Having looked at the various measures, we saw that each was a compromise in key respects, so much so that one can really speak of the resulting numbers only as estimates. While we should not give up on the idea that each of the existing measures cannot be improved, we should abandon the notion of a single, unitary measure or conceptualization. Poverty can, then, be recognized as a phenomenon and experience which has different degrees and dimensions. However, some fundamentals also need to be accepted: that no measure should be developed or applied without reference to its theoretical or philosophical underpinning; that a measure should be relative to and meaningful for the people, place and context in which it is being applied; that it is impossible to understand poverty without taking account of what it is like as an experience in real life; and that researchers and students should adopt a critical stance to their own approach as well as to the approaches of others.

SEMINAR QUESTIONS

1 Construct an anti-poverty policy. What should be the goals? To eliminate it? To stabilize it? To reduce it to a manageable level? What should be the content? How widely should it extend in terms of policy areas or domains?

2 How can anti-poverty campaigners in the developed and developing countries work together?

3 Substantiate an argument with evidence that the government cares about poverty and that it does not.

FURTHER READING

▶ Brady, D. (2009) *Rich Democracies, Poor People: How Politics Explain Poverty* (Oxford University Press). This book interrogates different understandings of poverty and critiques different approaches to understanding it and addressing it. It locates poverty especially in the widespread inequalities that exist in society and demonstrates how poverty varies significantly according to aspects of the aims, design and generosity of the welfare state.

▶ Lister, R. (2004) *Poverty* (Polity). This offers a broad-ranging but at the same time detailed discussion of debates about the meaning of poverty, its measurement and associated politics. Global in orientation, it brings together insights from different bodies of scholarship, including the experience and wishes of people who are themselves affected by poverty, to offer an understanding of poverty that is grounded in real life and the need for political change.

▶ Scott, J. (1994) *Poverty and Wealth: Citizenship, Deprivation and Privilege* (Longman). This locates poverty in long-standing historical patterns of wealth and status distribution. With a focus on the UK, it traces the evidence on poverty and develops poverty as a phenomenon that is inextricably related to the distribution of privilege and the maintenance of the status quo.

▶ Smith, S. C. (2005) *Ending Global Poverty: A Guide to What Works* (Palgrave Macmillan).

The book is quite micro-level in focus, identifying and exploring the traps that keep people in poverty, analysing different policy and other approaches and pointing to examples of programmes and activities that have successfully helped people escape poverty.

▶ World Bank PovcalNet, an online poverty analysis tool, is available at http://iresearch. worldbank.org/PovcalNet/index.htm.

▶ The Luxembourg Income Study offers self-teaching materials and sample databases of income and other quantitative data for some thirty countries at www.lisdatacenter.org/ resources/self-teaching.

▶ Unicef has lesson plans and teaching resources, geared to school pupils, available at http:// teachunicef.org/explore/topic/poverty.

▶ The OECD offers an online interactive resource – Better Life Index – which can be used to design, visualize and compare countries on some of the key factors – such as education, housing, environment, income – that contribute to wellbeing in OECD countries. It is an interactive tool that allows one to see how countries perform according to the importance *the user* gives to each of the eleven topics of wellbeing that make for a better life. See www. oecdbetterlifeindex.org/about/better-life-initiative/.

▶ The University of Illinois runs poverty simulations with students and the public (see video at www.youtube.com/watch?v=z8AXy_bULo0) which is a role-playing exercise – one is randomly assigned to a type of family living in poverty and has to work out how to live and function, and so forth.

▶ In the UK, the site of the poverty and social exclusion research project offers a wide range of research, data and other resources, information and news relevant to poverty in the UK and elsewhere. Among its aims are to provide independent assessment of the impact of government policy on poverty and social exclusion and to engage a wide audience in the debate on poverty and social exclusion. See www.poverty.ac.uk.

Acknowledgement: The detailed and very helpful comments of my Oxford colleague Fran Bennett on an earlier draft of this chapter are gratefully acknowledged.

Section C
Globalization and Social Change

If the previous section concentrated on the meso-level of analysis, this section starts by looking at the macro-level with a discussion of globalization (chapter 9). The concept of globalization remains contested, with a few sociologists (notably Hirst and Thompson 1999) questioning whether it has really taken place, or whether instead there has merely been internationalization on a regional basis. Nevertheless, it is one of the most influential concepts in contemporary sociology, and globalization is a theme which runs through the chapters both in this section and in many other chapters. Globalization is not just significant because it (allegedly) describes processes of social change, but also because it changes the primary object of sociological study away from the (relatively) self-contained society towards the world as a whole. This makes some forms of social theorizing (for example, looking at the culture of a single society) seem outdated and theoretically flawed and challenges sociologists to examine the interconnectedness of everything. By implication, then, nothing can be satisfactorily understood purely at the micro- or even the meso-level: the macro has always to be brought in, even when considering the local. If theories of globalization are to be believed, then drawing boundaries around particular spaces for the purposes of analysis is problematic, and it may be better to analyse the world in terms of flows or networks which cut across national and even continental boundaries.

These issues are taken up by Darren O'Byrne in his chapter on globalization, but they are also embedded elsewhere in this section, whether in examining global warming (chapter 10), global influences on development (chapter 12) or the consequences of globalizing technology (chapter 11). That does not of course mean that smaller-scale social processes can be ignored or marginalized. In this section the counterpoint to the macro is perhaps better conceived as the local rather than the micro. O'Byrne directly addresses the global and the local and the relationship between them (glocalization). He says that 'we need always to take this complex, one might say symbiotic, relationship between the global and the local into consideration.' Despite the global connections in scientific communities and the global influence of technology, as Mark Erickson (chapter 11) points out, scientists come together in local settings such as laboratories and other sites where scientific knowledge is produced. Investigating the social processes in such localized sites is an important focus for sociologists of science. This is particularly true of ANT (Actor-Network Theory) – one of the most influential sociologies of science. In Paul Hopper's chapter (chapter 12) the local features in relation to the advocacy of sustainable development, an issue which overlaps with the environmental problems addressed in chapter 10.

As well as a concern with globalization, there is a strong emphasis on social changes in the chapters in this section. Of course social change is a major issue in all subdisciplines within sociology, but this section addresses some of the most significant and wide-ranging contemporary social changes. If sociology was born in the nineteenth century out of a concern with changes resulting from processes of industrialization and urbanization, it is partly sustained in the twenty-first century through concern with processes of globalization, technological change, environmental degradation and development in 'a globalizing world'. Globalization, almost by definition, has some impact almost everywhere, leading, according to Hopper, to a blurring of patterns of development and underdevelopment. Some societies which were previously among the LEDCs (less economically developed countries) have experienced rapid development and change. In some cases, this has involved speedy industrialization and urbanization, which has some similarities with the industrial revolution of the eighteenth and nineteenth centuries. But, of course, these changes are being experienced in circumstances very different to those in earlier centuries.

One significant difference is the existence of science and technology which facilitates global economic, cultural and political networks. Certainly, tremendously significant social changes are discussed in O'Byrne's chapter, and Hopper's chapter goes as far as suggesting that the social world may be shifting on its axis (from North–South towards East–West). Phillip W. Sutton's chapter (chapter 10) is, ostensibly, focused more on changes in the natural world than in the social world, but of course the two may be inseparable, especially in the future. Social changes which have been made in response to environmental problems may thus far have been significant, but not perhaps revolutionary. Beck's idea of 'risk society' (1992) does suggest important changes have taken place, and environmental sociologists (particularly environmental realists) have also postulated that there have been fundamental changes in the relationship between humans and the natural world. However, it is perhaps in the discussion of possible futures that the most striking claims about social change are made by environmental sociologists. Unsurprisingly, much of this discussion concerns the impact of climate change, although resource depletion might also have far-reaching consequences. Any such changes will affect sociology itself, which explains why John Urry (2011) urges that a 'post-carbon sociology' will have to be developed. Climate change also figures prominently in Erickson's chapter, linked to discussions of technoscience and scientific determinism.

Sutton's and Erickson's chapters have a particular focus on the relationship between social worlds and nature. This raises issues about the status of sociology as a discipline and ontological and epistemological issues about scientific and social scientific knowledge. The relatively high status of natural sciences and relatively low status of social sciences is discussed by both Sutton and Erickson, and both are concerned with what niche sociologists can occupy in fields dominated by natural scientists. Sutton raises the question of what the environment has to do with sociologists, and Erickson addresses attacks by scientists on the relativistic nature of social science. However, both argue convincingly that sociology has a vital role, whether it is in examining how socially and politically realistic policies can be developed to tackle the causes and consequences of climate change or in 'showing the capacities and capabilities of experts and guiding the public towards making better judgements about experts and their statements'.

The status of sociology in relation to science is not an issue in O'Byrne's and Hopper's chapters, but its status in relationship to other academic disciplines is. The study of development tends to be dominated by economics, while geographers, economists and political scientists may all think of globalization as 'their' issue. But in all the chapters the short-sightedness, even futility, of trying to maintain strict disciplinary boundaries and the arrogance of disciplinary imperialism are exposed. None of the contributors here believe that sociology *alone* can explain all the phenomena being discussed, but all, quite rightly, suggest that a full understanding cannot be achieved without a significant contribution from sociology.

The strongest denials of the value of sociology tend to come from natural scientists. Both Sutton and Erickson discuss these issues in some detail, with Erickson including a very useful section on scientism. Neither wishes to challenge the basic assumptions of scientism that science is concerned with real processes and that it can produce invaluable knowledge and very useful technology. Indeed, in studying climate change, natural science may be identifying a process that threatens the future wellbeing of the whole of humanity. However, scientific knowledge is produced through social practices, and its reception and the uses to which it is put are, of course, social phenomena. The objective nature of science and the rational use of technology and science can never be assumed. Just as in other areas of social life, the interests of the powerful are always likely to be in play. This is connected to a final theme which links the chapters here – the pervasive influence of neoliberalism.

The influence of neoliberalism is evident in the championing of (supposedly) free trade, the lack of urgency in tackling climate change, resource depletion, the influence of 'big pharma' in the drugs industry, the global spread of technology, the continuing low incomes in some parts of the world, and so on. However, the interests of the powerful have not remained unopposed, and this is illustrated in these chapters through discussions of anti-science, movements for sustainable development, the global justice movement and ecological campaigns. Hopefully, then, this section provides further evidence that sociology is essential for understanding many of the most pressing issues of the twenty-first century and that it has expanded its areas of concern well beyond the preoccupations of earlier centuries.

9

GLOBALIZATION

experiencing social change on a global scale

DARREN O'BYRNE

CONTENTS

INTRODUCTION

I
T'S NOT ENTIRELY CLEAR when sociologists first used the term 'globalization', and there is considerable debate about when they first began to recognize and address the *idea* of it, regardless of whether the exact term was used. Some could argue that many of the nineteenth-century pioneers of the discipline *implicitly* recognized the globalizing potential of their respective projects, whether it was Comte's quest to uncover the universal laws of social development or Marx's recognition of the ever expansive nature of capitalism and his call for international solidarity. In any case, it is probably fair to say that, throughout its early history, most significant contributors to the discipline repeated the same mistake, namely, the tendency to conflate *society* with the *nation-state*. If sociology as a body of knowledge is designed to help us better understand the concept of *society*, and if this 'society' is even implicitly assumed to be synonymous with the society of the nation-state within which the knowledge is generated, then necessarily that knowledge is in itself problematic. It is for precisely this reason that Immanuel Wallerstein (1991), one of the most radically outspoken critics of methodological nationalism, has demanded that we 'unthink social science'.

Perhaps, though, it is too radical a move in a textbook designed to cover the width and breadth of what sociology can offer to begin this chapter by asking you to disregard everything you currently think you know! More modestly, let's ask instead that you keep an open mind about it, and bear in mind the possibility that some of it might be problematic for precisely the reason outlined above, that it fails to deal adequately with the influence of factors beyond the nation-state. The purpose of this chapter is not solely to introduce you to what sociologists have had to say about the subject of globalization, but to help you think about what it might mean to 'globalize' your own sociological imagination.

DEFINING GLOBALIZATION

Some definitions of globalization

According to Anthony Giddens, globalization can be defined as 'the intensification of world-wide social relations which link distant localities in such a way that local happenings are shaped by events occurring many miles away and vice versa' (Giddens 1990: 64). Or, to put it another way (as Giddens does, in the preceding paragraph), it refers 'to that stretching process, in so far as the modes of connection between different social contexts or regions become networked across the earth's surface as a whole' (ibid.). Ulrich Beck, another prominent scholar who has much to say on the subject (and particularly on the environment), provides a similar definition with a slightly different emphasis, when he describes globalization as 'the *process* through which sovereign nation-states are criss-crossed and undermined by transnational actors with varying prospects of power, orientations, identities and networks' (Beck 2000b: 11; emphasis in original).

Note the similarities and differences between the definitions. Giddens focuses on linkages or modes of connection between localities, forming a worldwide *network*. Beck also invokes the image of an interconnected network or grid with his use of the term 'criss-crossed', but he adds an additional dimension to the definition which emphasizes *power* dimensions (note, especially, the reference to nation-states being undermined by 'transnational actors'). Now compare both to the snappy definition provided by Roland Robertson: 'Globalization as a concept refers to both the compression of the world and the intensification of consciousness of the world as a whole' (Robertson 1992: 8). If Giddens and Beck both to some degree reference increasing interconnectedness (and to an extent interdependence, even if that is within uneven power relations), Robertson asks us first to imagine that the world is shrinking (not literally, obviously, but nonetheless compression does refer to the way the whole world is more accessible to us than before) but, more significantly, he also emphasizes a subjective dimension, a consciousness of the world as a whole.

All of these dimensions – and more besides – find their way into Martin Albrow's (1996) thorough, but rather wordy, definition:

1   Making or being made global:
    (a)   In individual instances
        (i)   By the active dissemination of practices, values, technology and other human products throughout the globe
        (ii)   When global practices and so on exercise an increasing influence over people's lives
        (iii)   When the globe serves as a focus for, or a premise in shaping, human activities
        (iv)   In the incremental change occasioned by the interaction of any such instances;
    (b)   Seen as the generality of such instances;
    (c)   Such instances being viewed abstractly.
2   A process of making or being made global in any or all of the senses in (1).
3   The historical transformation constituted by the sum of particular forms and instances of (1)

(Albrow 1996: 88)

Eight models of global change

One strategy for navigating through this minefield of competing definitions is provided in a recent publication by O'Byrne and Hensby (2011). The authors suggest that, rather than arbitrarily using the term 'globalization' to refer to such a diversity of different and often competing processes, it makes more sense to define 'globalization' solely as the process of becoming global and so distinguish it from other processes with which it has become entangled. Such other processes as 'liberalization', 'polarization', 'Americanization', 'McDonaldization', 'creolization', 'transnationalization' and 'balkanization' indicate dynamics which may not necessarily be globalizing in their reach. The outcome is to accept that such processes are mutually present and absent, that they are both happening and not happening at the same time.

For O'Byrne and Hensby, it is appropriate to use 'globalization' when referring specifically to the process of *becoming global*. Of course, this is to some extent an open-ended definition because, while the term certainly denotes a process, the endpoint of that process is uncertain: What might it be to actually *be* global? As with Albrow's definition, O'Byrne and Hensby suggest that this might refer to the extent to which something becomes global in its reach (i.e., spans the whole world) but it might also refer to the extent to which something engages with the world as a whole. An example of the former might be to imagine that the globalization of the political state, as a completed project, would require the presence of a single world government, while an example of the latter might be a corporation's advertising campaign which is clearly directed to a global audience.

However, according to O'Byrne and Hensby, there are plenty of instances when the term 'globalization' is used to refer to processes that do not actually relate to any processing of becoming global. Rather, they relate in one or another way to the process of becoming something else! Liberalization is a better way of describing the process by which borders between nation-states are apparently becoming relaxed so as to enable freer exchange of goods and people – although commonly referred to as globalization, there is nothing inherently 'global' about the outcome of such a process. Similarly, the suggestion commonly made by critics and activists that 'globalization' results in increasing exploitation of the Global South by the North is actually counter-intuitive unless one replaces the reference to 'globalization' with something like polarization.

The authors present five other models which are similar to globalization and sometimes used interchangeably with it but do not necessarily result in anything 'global': these are Americanization (the suggestion that cultural and military imperialism has expanded American influence far and wide); McDonaldization (the suggestion that, from country to country, certain practices are becoming increasingly standardized); creolization (the suggestion that new hybrid cultures are constantly emerging around the world); transnationalization (the suggestion that power and influence now resides at a level above that of the nation-state, albeit not necessarily one that is fully global); and balkanization (the suggestion that the world today is not only more divided but also increasingly prone to conflict).

SEMINAR QUESTIONS

1 How does the 'global' differ from the 'international'? Provide examples of each.
2 How, if at all, might 'globalization' differ from 'liberalization' or 'Americanization'?

3   In your further reading on the subject, keep a notebook record of all the different defini-
    tions of globalization you come across. Keep a separate notebook recording how the term
    is used in the media or by politicians. How do these definitions and uses differ from one
    another?

4   Read O'Byrne and Hensby's *Theorizing Global Studies* and make a note of the differences
    between the eight models discussed therein. Each is intended to represent a *process* that
    reflects a reality, at least in some part of the world. Think of an example of each process that
    is not mentioned in the book.

EXPERIENCING GLOBALIZATION

If globalization is a process, it can be experienced in a number of forms. Sociologists have long
been fond of dividing up the various forms of social activity into three categories: economic,
political and cultural. Of course, these are merely useful heuristic devices and make no absolute sense in reality, but they do provide a convenient framework within which to assess the
'extent' of globalization in real terms.

   When assessing the extent of globalization in each of these categories, we should constantly remind ourselves that it is not a totality but a process. Like all processes, then, it can
be read as a journey but, to measure the progress of anything on any journey, one has to
have an idea of what the actual indicators of such process might be. In other words, rather
than just speak of, for example, the global economy, we need, as good critical sociologists,
to interrogate the criteria used to make the claim that the economy actually *is* global.
Maybe it is – maybe we can accept that there are sufficient reasons for us to concede that
economic processes do indeed operate on a global level. But maybe it isn't – maybe, if
we look carefully enough, we will find that the indicators we use to measure the extent of
globalization in this field are not sufficiently met for us to make such a claim. There are no
easy answers. Highly knowledgeable commentators have gone to great lengths, and provided convincing arguments, to champion one side of the debate or the other. In any case,
any such 'evidence' of globalization in one field does not automatically suggest the same
in another. The world we are discussing is complex, and we might come to the conclusion
that the process of globalization is occurring in any meaningful way only in the economic
field, and not at all in the political or cultural ones, or we may accept that there is very little
that is globalized about the economy, but that cultural globalization is a lived reality, or any
other such variation.

Globalization in the economic field

It has become somewhat commonplace for commentators of a certain disposition to refer
uncritically to the 'global market'. Underpinning this is an assumption that 'free trade' across
borders has become a reality. In the same vein, activists frequently take to the streets to protest
against the perceived injustices of the 'global' economy, 'global' capitalism. In either case, it is
presumed that there is something historically distinctive about the capitalist economy of the
late twentieth and early twenty-first centuries.

   Of course, any claim for historical distinctiveness on such a scale demands closer investigation. At the heart of this claim are certain presumptions concerning this 'new global

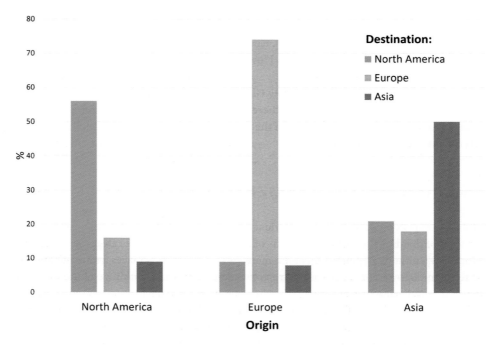

Figure 9.1 International vs. regional trade – share of interregional merchandise export flows in each region as a percentage of total merchandise exports, 2004

Source: Based on data from Hirst, Thompson and Bromley (2009: 164).

economy' of 'free' trade which present us with three distinct but interlinked questions: Is it 'new'? Is it 'global'? Is it 'free'? In an important contribution published in 1999, tellingly titled *Globalization in Question*, Paul Hirst and Graham Thompson sought to debunk the claim that there was anything new or really global about this 'new global economy', or that trade within it was carried out in anything like a free way on an even playing field. The vast majority of trade, the writers suggested, remains heavily regional rather than global in its scope (see figure 9.1, for example). At the same time, some of the world's most powerful economies have remained heavily protectionist, encouraging investment outwards while closing their borders to any reciprocity. In other words, 'globalization' is not an appropriate way of describing what is happening in the modern economy. In fact, Hirst and Thompson suggest, the modern economy is *less* globalized that it was a hundred or so years earlier, during the height of the British Empire, when a considerable amount of trade really did span the world. However, even if these authors are correct and most international trade is regional rather than global, there are surely other aspects of the economic system which *do* span the globe: the very suggestion that the current financial crisis which has been so destructive to many national economies is a *global* crisis, the solutions to which cannot be found at the level of the nation-state, is surely a testament to that.

In order better to understand the current state of the economy, we need to take a historical journey through changing ways of thinking about the dynamics of capitalism, beginning with a short trip back in time to the nineteenth century. Writing as they were during a period most presume to be the genesis of the modern capitalist system, the 'founding fathers' of the study of political economy, Adam Smith and Karl Marx, both defined the nature of capitalism in ways

BOX 9.1 THE GLOBAL FINANCIAL CRISIS

It is a widely held belief that nobody – not least economists, bankers and politicians – truly understands the causes of the 2007–8 global financial crisis and the ensuing ongoing recession. For many, the principal factors were a collapse in the US property market, resulting in a severe drying up of liquidity, and a subsequent banking crisis tied closely to hedge-fund investments. As commodity prices plummeted and unemployment and poverty levels rose, around the world governments struggled to deal with the effects of the recession: many introduced 'austerity' measures to curb public spending significantly, banks were bailed out and in some cases nationalized, and drastic measures were put into place to rescue entire national economies. As more and more people came to experience the full consequences of the crisis, public confidence in financial institutions and the economic system collapsed and worldwide protest movements sprang up.

that presupposed the later writings on globalization. In his definitive *Wealth of Nations* (Smith [1776] 1999), to this day considered a sacred text by liberals championing an unregulated capitalism, Adam Smith argued against attempts by governments to try to control the direction of the economy, insisting instead that it should be left to its own devices, to be regulated by its own logic, its 'invisible hand'. If left alone, Smith believed, it would generate sufficient wealth and prosperity for all. Marx accepted the basis of Smith's account of capitalism while inverting his outcomes: capitalism, for Marx, is like a hungry tiger, seeking out new markets wherever it can find them to satisfy its insatiable appetite, effectively exploiting more and more resources until it is has exhausted the supply. In either case, capitalism is inherently globalizing.

During the early to mid-twentieth century, though, alternative economic theories rose to prominence which suggested that capitalism could, and should, be regulated so as best to generate wealth without surrendering to rampant exploitation. In the years following the end of the Second World War, the ideas of John Maynard Keynes came into vogue. With the formation of the United Nations in 1945, political elites began to consider how best to tackle the problem of underdevelopment in much of the world. Already, following the Bretton Woods conference of 1944, transnational institutions later brought under the auspices of the United Nations had been established to help regulate economic activity and assist with economic development. The marriage of Keynesian economics with functionalist social theory produced an approach to the problem of underdevelopment which became known as 'modernization theory' (e.g., Rostow 1960). In a nutshell, modernization theory proposed that, through economic regulation at the level of the nation-state and an injection of investment into the social infrastructure of a particular underdeveloped country, it would be possible in the long run for that country to attain a particular standard of living akin to that enjoyed by the stronger economies.

There were clear problems with this approach. For one thing, the whole concept of 'modernization' was deemed flawed, for it presented the 'modern' economies (the stronger economies of the West) as some kind of 'ideal state' to which others should aspire. At the same time, it presumed infinite growth. Nation-state economies were dealt with largely in isolation from the rest of the world, the assumption being that each could successfully 'develop' or 'modernize' to a particular standard. Such an assumption was subjected to a trenchant critique by the school of 'dependency theory', of which the most vociferous spokesperson was Andre Gunder Frank (e.g., Frank 1967), and by advocates of 'world-systems theory' such as Immanuel Wallerstein

(1979). Adopting a more structural approach to economics, these critics pointed out that, at the global level, wealth was a finite resource, and so, for some to have it, the implication is that others do not. In other words, some countries are poor *because* some countries are rich, and vice versa. One cannot tackle the problem of underdevelopment or poverty in one part of the world without considering the excess of wealth elsewhere. Wallerstein took this basic claim and from it devised a structural and relational theory of the world as an interdependent system of unequal power relations between rich and poor, or 'core' and 'periphery'.

If modernization theory had focused primarily at the level of the nation-state, the contributions of the dependency and world-systems theorists helped to steer the debate over the dynamics of the capitalist economy more into the global domain. However, even otherwise sympathetic fellow travellers equally inspired by the Marxian project came to identify some serious flaws in their analysis. Chief among these is the sociologist Leslie Sklair (2002). One of the main problems with the Wallersteinian account, according to Sklair, is that it remains committed to treating the nation-state as the primary unit of analysis in studying the economy. Sklair has suggested that, in the current phase of capitalism, it is not nation-states but *transnational* forces that dictate the direction of the economy and account for the primary exploiter–exploited dialectic. Wallerstein's 'world-system' has given way to what Sklair calls a 'global system' characterized by the presence of transnational corporations, transnational practices, and even a transnational capitalist class. Effectively, this means the end of the earlier phase of political economy: the market is separated from the state, the economy freed from government interference. Transnational corporations exercise far more power to exploit an international division of labour, operating post-Fordist production practices, disembedding and relocating their centres of operation at will, no longer reliant on government endorsement in return for taxes and tariffs, and are run by powerful individuals capable of influencing policy while able to change citizenship to suit business interests.

For Sklair, then, there *is* something new, and something global, about the modern capitalist economy. However, unsurprisingly, given that Sklair is a neo-Marxist in orientation, this is characterized not by the triumph of free trade and the so-called borderless world but by a new set of unequal power relations that transcend nation-state boundaries. Sklair's concerns about unequal power relations are echoed by the many activists as well as academics who target their attacks on the claim that any trade in this new global economy is in any way 'free'. The neoliberal shift in the 1980s resulted in a significant policy change in respect of global poverty. For a country to be in receipt of a World Bank loan, particular conditions now have to be satisfied, primarily that the receiving country open up its borders (and thus its resources) to foreign investment. Rather than being an indicator of free trade, critics suggest, this results in a situation where the natural resources of a country can more easily be exploited by already powerful economies, making it harder for such a country to escape poverty. The result of this economic 'globalization', such that it is, is the increased polarization of the world into rich and poor.

So, are we in a position to judge whether this 'new global economy' is myth or reality? Or, if we accept some truth to the claims that there is indeed something distinct about this phase in capitalism, can we assess whether it is a potential force for good or a source of increasing polarization and inequality? Actual free trade across borders would surely be an indicator of some degree of globalization, but evidence indicating that most trade remains regional, coupled with accusations of the one-directional nature of many such trade agreements, seems to suggest this is not yet a reality. On the other hand, it is hard to deny that many large corporations do operate beyond the level of the nation-state, particularly in respect of their transnational production practices, or that, in the field of consumption, particular brands are immediately recognizable worldwide and are deliberately marketed to a global audience. Financial markets, meanwhile, are probably best described as remaining distinct but interlinked: there may be no standardized world currency, but global financial institutions such as the International Monetary Fund, the World Trade Organization and the World Bank do exist to coordinate finance and trade beyond local markets. The financial crisis of the early twenty-first century is clearly a *global* crisis. So perhaps, as ever, there is no simple answer. The economy of the twenty-first century may not be a fully globalized economy, but there are certainly globalizing processes at work within it.

Globalization in the political field

On one level, the question of whether we can identify a process of globalization taking place within the political field seems more clear-cut: surely a fully globalized polity would require a single global state? We clearly do not live in such a world. Rather, the world we occupy remains divided into numerous states, each operating according to its own laws and governed by its own political machinery, which claims sovereignty over its territory.

But, as ever, the real answer is not so simple. As with the economy, we can clearly identify globalizing processes at work within the political field. A useful starting point to this discussion might be to consider a very basic question: What is the point of government? To this end, we may wish to revisit the classic contributions of the seventeenth-century English philosophers Thomas Hobbes and John Locke, whose legacies remain with us in the 'realist' and 'liberal' theories of government. In his famous work *Leviathan*, Hobbes ([1651] 1968) asked us to imagine a world *without* government, without laws to which we must be obedient. Dissatisfied with attempts to justify the right of the monarch to rule over his (or her) subjects according to some mystical 'divine right', Hobbes turned instead to philosophical anthropology. Presuming that humans are by nature self-serving, he suggested that, without laws to regulate our behaviour, we would be free to do as we please, but in enjoying such freedoms we would also be at the mercy of the freedoms of others to do as they please to us, thus threatening our security. It is thus for the preservation of our security that people act rationally to surrender many of their freedoms to an overarching authority, the machinery of the state, which Max Weber (1946) later so beautifully described as the centralized means of violence. Following Hobbes, then, the primary purpose of government is to protect its citizens from threats, both internal and external, and it remains in the interests of each individual to be subject to this authority. Locke, by contrast, imagined a natural state to be one of relatively benign interdependence. Following Locke's view of human nature rather than Hobbes's, we do not *need* government to exercise power *over* us in order to keep us safe; rather, we invent it to serve as an objective source of arbitration to be called upon where necessary, to facilitate (and thus be subservient to) our private exchanges.

There is a point to this detour into early modern political philosophy. If we follow Hobbes, we may wish to consider whether the modern nation-state, caught up as it allegedly is in a set of power relations that rarely respect its borders, is suitably equipped to satisfy the primary function of government. Can the government of any single nation-state honestly protect its citizens from the threats of environmental destruction or modern warfare? The question of political globalization requires us to look beyond the obvious fact that we continue to live in a world of states and to consider the challenges that may serve to undermine the authority of the nation-state in the first place.

The underlying question, then, is straightforward: Who has *power* in the world today? It is this very question that first gave rise to the time-honoured field of *international relations*. International relations is the (clearly misnamed) study of how states *relate* to one another. Two early attempts to answer this question were provided by the heirs to the legacies of Hobbes and Locke. On one side were the *realists* (e.g., Morgenthau 1948, 1951), who maintained that each state has the right of sovereignty over its own territory and, in the absence of any superior authority carrying out the parallel role of maintaining order in the international realm, should be obedient solely to its prime directive of national self-interest. While such a position largely advocated non-interference by one state in the sovereign affairs of another unless its own security was threatened, it did posit the realm of international affairs as an anarchic one, in which the interests of the stronger states would naturally take precedence over those of the weaker ones. On the other side were the *liberals* (e.g., Angell 1914), for whom the international arena was an extension of the original state of nature, with the state, as facilitator of private exchange, necessarily empowered to interact with other states and related actors so as to further promote the cause of peaceful coexistence.

Naturally, the realist–liberal distinction was always an oversimplification of the reality of international relations, and complex attempts were made to blend aspects of the two, as well as new emergent theories which sought better to capture the complexity of the subject matter. Marxists drew attention to the way states are locked into a world capitalist system, constructivists suggested that states relate to each other in a way that reflects the perception each has of the other – for example, as a threat or a potential ally – and functionalists began to identify the gradual process of integration of hitherto autonomous states into interdependent networks. As a field of study, international relations shifted from being the study of states as rational actors operating within an arena of other states to a concern with the role such a state plays within the much broader system of states, the international political community.

It is within this framework that debates concerning political globalization began to take hold. Towards the end of the twentieth century it became apparent that the study of how states relate to one another in the international political community could no longer focus primarily on the motivations and role of the state itself. The formation of the United Nations in 1945 – out of the ashes of the defunct and largely impotent League of Nations – sent out a clear message, that political events in one part of the world could have worldwide implications and thus require a global response. The sovereign nation-state in isolation would not be enough. Before too long, a variety of different challenges emerged to nation-state sovereignty, including multinational companies and global financial markets in the global economy; transnational bodies such as the World Bank, WTO, UN and EU; internationally binding conventions and charters in international law; and NATO and other power blocs (Holton 1998: 106).

But what might political globalization actually *mean* in real terms? As with all things discussed in this chapter, there is no easy single answer to that question. We can, however, identify various *forms* of political globalization, various distinct processes that in some way indicate how an aspect of political activity might be shifting in focus towards the global stage. I am going to identify four such forms, which, for the sake of convenience, I am going to call the processes of *unification*, *standardization*, *interdependence* and *postmodernization*.

By *unification*, I mean the globalization of political institutions, specifically, the state itself.

To what degree is the UN a platform for multinational cooperation and for countries to have their voice heard? To what degree is it a tool of key powerful nation-states to direct international agendas? (© United Nations Photo/Flickr)

The process of global unification would, by definition, be one of increasing interstate federation, integration and, ultimately, as the 'endpoint' of the process, the formation of a single world state. Such a denouement is clearly not a reality at present, so the process is far from complete. However, the formative stages of such a journey clearly are a reality in our lifetimes: we have regional federations and alliances of various shapes and sizes, including the European Union, NATO and, most significantly, the United Nations itself.

By *standardization*, I am referring to the globalization of political processes. This is an altogether different form of globalization than unification – the process of unification necessarily weakens the sovereignty of the nation-state, and its endpoint demands its dissolution entirely. With standardization, there is no necessary suggestion that the nation-state is so weakened, only that the processes of government adopted by each nation-state is becoming increasingly homogenized, such that there are fewer distinctions between states in respect of how politics is performed. In the 1950s, such a view underpinned the 'convergence theory' of liberal academics such as Clark Kerr et al. (1960) and Daniel Bell (1973), for whom technological change and modernization processes (remember the brief discussion we had about modernization theory in the previous section) would inevitably result in a coming together of nation-states under the shared banner of 'modern' Western society. Shades of this view resurfaced in the 1990s, when Francis Fukuyama (1991) declared that the end of the Cold

War and the fall of the Berlin Wall represented the 'end of history', the ultimate triumph of Western liberal democracy as a political form. From an entirely different perspective, in the 1960s neo-Marxists such as Herbert Marcuse (1964) attempted to show how Western liberal democracies, Soviet-style socialism and European fascism as forms of government were all similarly driven by an ideology of oppression and a denial of basic human freedoms, and more recently it has become commonplace for commentators to bemoan the lack of alternatives to mainstream centrist political parties, suggesting that in many democratic countries, so similar are the competing parties in many respects, the 'choice' between them is really no choice at all. The UK is a clear example of this. In any case, what is being suggested is that politics is becoming increasingly driven by a process akin to what Ritzer (2000) calls 'McDonaldization'. In the 1990s it was entirely appropriate for writers such as Diamond

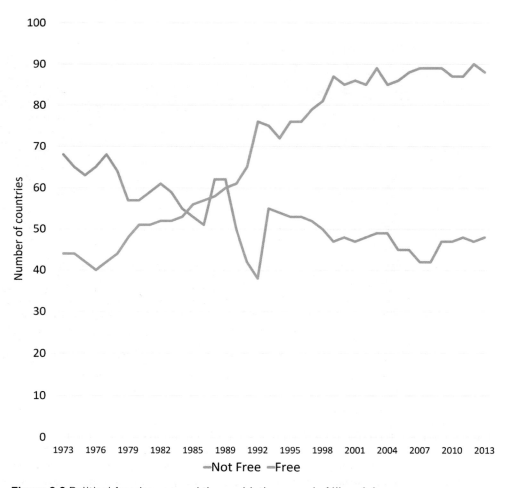

Figure 9.2 Political freedom around the world: the spread of liberal democracy

Note: The terminology 'Free' and 'Not Free' is used by Freedom House and is based on political rights and civil liberties. There is also a middle-ground category, 'Partly Free'.

Source: Compiled with data from Freedomhouse.org.

BOX 9.2 THE ARAB SPRING

On 18 December 2010 – the day after merchant Mohamed al Bouazizi set himself on fire following police and government harassment – public protests erupted in Tunisia. Such was the ferocity of this unrest that, in January 2011, the country's president of twenty-three years, Zine El Abidine Ben Ali, fled the country. The protests in Tunisia were quickly followed by a wave of similar protests in other Arab countries, notably Algeria, Jordan, Egypt and Yemen. On 11 February, Egyptian president Hosni Mubarak stepped down after thirty years. On 23 August, Muammar Gaddafi, the long-standing ruler of Libya, was overthrown. In February 2012, public unrest forced President Ali Abdullah Saleh of Yemen to call an election which resulted in his removal from office. The revolutionary wave continued and spread to Iraq, Sudan, Kuwait, Oman, Lebanon, Morocco, Mauritania, Syria, Israel, Palestine, and more countries besides, resulting in sweeping political changes in many cases. Commentators dubbed this period of intense unrest in the Arab world the 'Arab Spring'.

The trajectory of political globalization is not necessarily towards the global spread of liberal democracy. The toppling of the Egyptian government in 2011 has left a contested field in which Islamist parties such as the Muslim Brotherhood have sought power, and some international hostilities (such as against Israel and the USA) have been inflamed, as shown in this Cairo protest. (© Hossam el-Hamalawy/Flickr)

Many such commentators viewed these events with tremendous optimism, seeing them as heralding a new process of democratization in the region, particularly given the despotic reputations of some of those removed from power. But it soon became clear that the transformations taking place could not be reduced to some traditional model of 'democratization' – namely, the establishment of a primarily Western-style liberal democracy in place of an autocratic regime. The revival of Islamist groups in the wake of the revolutions has in some cases brought to the fore concerns over human rights, gender equality and religious inclusion.

(1993), and also Meyer and his colleagues at Stanford University (e.g., Meyer 1980), to suggest that constitutional liberal democracy had become *the* form of government in the world, such that any aspiring new state, seeking as it must recognition from other states to achieve legitimacy, would feel compelled to adopt such a system in order to receive such recognition. Perhaps, then, at the time, there was considerable mileage in the political-globalization-as-standardization argument. But, from our vantage point in the early twenty-first century, the world looks somewhat different. Appearances seem to suggest that the tide has turned somewhat. The full implications of the so-called Arab Spring have yet to be revealed, but early suggestions indicate that the transition to liberal democracy is not so inevitable, or desirable, as earlier commentators may have believed. Time will tell.

My third form of political globalization is *interdependence*. By this I mean the globalization of political problems. While the sovereignty of the nation-state may not be challenged per se, and there is no necessary requirement for it to result in the formation of interstate federations of any kind, interdependence suggests a challenge to the role of the nation-state in carrying out its duties, due to the fact that the problems it increasingly has to deal with are not particular to it but rather global in reach. Interdependence suggests a loose rather than a fixed or formal integration of states into a larger system, driven primarily by necessity. As I've already suggested, a problem in one part of the world might indeed have serious implications for other states across the globe, so this necessarily has an impact on how states respond to such problems.

My fourth form of political globalization, *postmodernization*, is slightly different from the other three, but it is important because it reminds us that political activity does not *just* take place at the level of the state. Politics is not just a formal process executed at the level of the institutional machinery of the state but is also a form of social action performed by people as an articulation of their values. Postmodernization, then, is the globalization of political values – of the things that matter to us as political actors. At the level of the nation-state, a lot of political activity in democratic societies was articulated through movements that operated at that level, namely, political parties or trade unions. Political parties are usually formed to represent the interests of a particular group in society, and historically in the UK and elsewhere these have been class-based. However, as the things that directly impact upon the lives of people take on an increasingly transnational shape, so have the responses to those things become increasingly transnational. Personal security is clearly not something one can easily entrust to the machinery of the state to safeguard when the things that threaten it, such as bio-hazards, environmental damage, nuclear war, and so on, do not do so through the medium of the state. The sociologist Anthony Giddens (1991) speaks of a shift from 'class politics' to 'life politics' to refer to this transformation in values and the impact it has on an individual's political identity. If there has been a decline in many countries in political 'participation', measured in terms of party membership or voting figures, this is surely representative not of any political apathy as such among the current generation but of a pragmatic realization that such nation-state politics no longer addresses the things that matter. If my concern is for the protection of the global environment, I do not necessarily articulate this concern through these more traditional forms of political participation; rather, I seek to tackle them head-on by joining global social movements, including non-governmental organizations (NGOs).

All of this, of course, leaves us more questions than answers. Who has 'real' power in the world today? Does the nation-state have a future if it can no longer perform its central function, which, from Hobbes and Weber onwards, is to ensure security by acting as a centralized means of violence? If it does still have a role to play, what might that role be? And, if we consider the four examples outlined in this section, how far down the road of political globalization might we reasonably say we are?

Globalization in the cultural field

During the 1990s, when the term 'globalization' was becoming the buzzword for an era, its popular usage was dominated by those addressing economic processes. Against this prevailing wind, much of the sociological discourse on the subject turned instead to addressing the question of culture. Roland Robertson's definitive book *Globalization* (1992) bore the subtitle *Social Theory and Global Culture*, and was one of a number of publications on this theme produced in association with the academic journal *Theory, Culture and Society* (*TCS*). Leading the way for this new approach to globalization was the collection of articles taken from *TCS* reproduced in 1990 as *Global Culture*, edited by Mike Featherstone.

The 'cultural turn' was not without controversy: for some critics, it rode on the back of the growing influence of 'postmodernism' in sociology, influenced largely by the writings of Jean-François Lyotard and Jean Baudrillard, which seemed to be celebrating the ultimate 'triumph' of culture, emphasizing style over substance, image over content and (echoing Marshal McLuhan's (1964) famous comment) the medium over the message. As a subject matter for sociologists, culture has always been somewhat complex, not least because it often seems like an amorphous term, an umbrella for so many different things of interest to social scientists, from religion to food and from ethics to art and music. Among the 'founding fathers' of the nineteenth century, it was Durkheim who prioritized culture above all others. Developing a broad definition that would remain central to anthropological understandings of the term for generations to come, Durkheim saw culture as the glue that binds a society together, a shared

Among younger people in particular, there is a trend to 'do' politics outside of the traditional mainstream of political parties within nation-states and, instead, to campaign with international pressure groups and non-governmental organizations, such as Amnesty International. (© Jas n/Flickr)

Table 9.1: **Four forms of political globalization**	
Unification	Globalization of political institutions
Standardization	Globalization of political processes
Interdependence	Globalization of political problems
Postmodernization	Globalization of political values

set of norms and values which manifests itself in the practices and rituals of everyday life. For Durkheim, religious rituals, acceptable tastes in food or fashion, artistic styles, and moral conventions were all expressions of a *conscience collective* existing outside of the individual, which serve to unite an individual with the collective group and thus maintain order in society. Durkheim's definition of the role of culture was not without its critics: Marx had already paved the way for an understanding of culture as ideology, reflecting the interests of the economic base, the mode of production, while a separate literary tradition emerged in the twentieth century that saw culture in more elitist terms, the 'best' of what a society can offer. By the later twentieth century, the new field of cultural studies had emerged to challenge the elitist assumptions of the literary tradition and to celebrate the distinctiveness of 'working-class culture' or, more recently, 'popular culture'. To their credit, journals such as *TCS* sought to reconcile the populist, postmodernist celebrations of popular culture with the more traditional Durkheimian view.

So much for culture itself: more to the point, what might it mean to speak of a *global* culture? It is easy to be sceptical about the Durkheimian emphasis on shared norms and values, particularly when trying to apply such a model to a world clearly defined by diversity. But one does not need to dwell under the illusion that we share a single global cultural system to take seriously the concept of cultural globalization. Influenced heavily by Durkheim, Roland Robertson (1992) sees the history of globalization as the history of a global consciousness building, the evolution of an orientation towards the world as one place. *Globality* thus becomes a globalized form of *conscience collective*. Equally, the perceived spread of globalist values, from human rights to consumerism, can be seen as a cultural process. More specifically, research carried out on the increasingly global reach of the media as transmitters of culture, as well as on diasporic communities and intercultural or multicultural ways of life within localities, comes under the broader heading of global culture.

So, as students of the social sciences, we need at this point clearly to abandon the idea that cultural globalization must refer to the emergence of a single global cultural system in the Durkheimian sense, just as we have moved beyond any assumption that political globalization must ultimately entail a single world state. Globalization processes *make possible* transformations in our understanding of culture which demand our attention. Our focus need not be on the problematic idea of a global culture, but rather on the possible forms that a process of cultural globalization might take. In the crudest possible way, to simplify this extremely complex area as much as possible, we can divide these forms into two broad camps: on the one hand, those which fall under such banners as 'Americanization' or 'McDonaldization' and which focus on the *erosion* of cultural diversity and the imposition of standardized dominant practices worldwide; on the other hand, those associated with such terms as 'creolization' or 'hybridization' which focus on the *expansion* of cultural diversity and the ever dynamic nature of culture itself. Naturally, the reality is a bit of both.

It is easy to see the return to Marx, and to some extent also Weber, as a reaction to the perceived populism of the postmodernist invasion, an attempt to restore some politics to the field of culture. Rekindling the spirit of Marx's own economic determinism, Immanuel Wallerstein (1990) refers to culture as the 'ideological battleground of the modern world-system', while neo-Marxists such as Leslie Sklair (2002), David Harvey (1989) and

Frederick Jameson (1991) see global consumerism and/or postmodern cultural styles as comprising the culture-ideology of late capitalism, and George Ritzer (2000) has resurrected Weber's theory of rationalization to fuel his own model of global transformation as 'McDonaldization'. One characteristic of late capitalism is that, as Theodor Adorno (2001) famously pointed out over half a century ago, culture is no longer merely subservient to the economy, as suggested by Marx in his famous base–superstructure distinction, but has become collapsed *into* the economy, and so to speak of global culture is in effect to speak of a global *cultural economy* that is based on symbolic as well as material value. If, in its classical sense, *commodification* was the process through which a product is placed on the market and thus receives an exchange value beyond the actual cost of its own production which then results in profit for the capitalist (and, of course, exploitation), then, in late capitalism, cultural forms, ideas, images, sounds, and so on, have equally become commodified. In other words, in late capitalism, commodities are not just material products but also *brands*. The global cultural economy is an economy of such brands or, as Scott Lash and John Urry (1994) put it, an economy of 'signs and space'. And if consumption *is* the culture-ideology of late capitalism (in so far as it has become a source of identity), then the global media are crucial in transmitting and reproducing this global consumer culture. As Anthony Giddens (1990, 1991) and others have pointed out, today's media reaches everywhere, such that specific events become 'global moments' and information itself becomes an item of consumption. Whoever controls the media wields tremendous power in the world. So, the 'triumph' of culture can easily be seen as a triumph of a media machinery dominated by Western corporations, promoting Western values and reflecting Western interests. At the same time, old-fashioned class analysis can still be useful in understanding the unequal power dynamics of this new information age. Those without access to the new technologies become increasingly disenfranchised – what Scott Lash refers to as a new 'information underclass' (Beck, Giddens and Lash 1994) – while, as Darren O'Byrne (1997) suggests, this inequality in access to the material 'means of compression' coincides with unequal access to the 'means of globality', in so far as cosmopolitanism as a worldview remains identifiably bourgeois.

But, of course, it is by no means such a simple process as all this would suggest. Where there is power, after all, there is always resistance! No culture has ever been truly static, and cultures have been produced and reproduced through the constant interplay of global and local flows. To speak of cultural globalization solely as a one-directional process spreading from the core to the periphery, shaping and reshaping the world in its image, is to miss the point entirely (Hannerz 1996: 67–8). New identities, or 'new ethnicities', as Stuart Hall (1991) and others tell us, emerge from the separation of nation from state and challenge the assimilationist model of culture hitherto dominant. Such hybrid, multiple identities make use of various labels to define themselves and form part of a broader ideological struggle associated with postcolonialism which is often situated in the localized environments of 'multicultural' global cities, hubs of cultural globalization. Not that this is necessarily a new phenomenon: from Paul Gilroy's (1993) majestic *The Black Atlantic*, we come to understand the emergence of a transnational black identity uniting Europe, West Africa and the Americas in a shared history of slavery and segregation. It is, therefore, in the interplay that Hannerz and others speak of that new cultural practices emerge, blending traditions, old and new, core and periphery, and, if the periphery is transformed, so is the core: how else can one explain why in modern Britain, once the centre of a great empire, the most popular food dish is the chicken tikka masala, while the quintessentially British drink is the cup of tea, neither of which are truly 'native'? There is clearly much to be said for understanding cultural globalization as a form of creolization or hybridization. John Tomlinson (1999: 141) sums it up neatly: 'the increasing traffic between cultures that the globalization process brings suggests that the dissolution of the link between culture and place is accompanied by an intermingling of these disembedded cultural practices producing new complex hybrid forms of culture.'

Globalization in everyday life: the global and the local

All of this means we *experience* globalization in a wide variety of ways. The global interconnectedness of the economic system means we feel first-hand the effects of a financial crisis. The interdependence of political problems connects us directly to people in every corner of the world, citizens though they might be of other nation-states. The stirring of tensions between the United States and parts of the Middle East, drawing in wider concerns about global terrorism and counter-terrorism as well as real military interventions, reaches out to us through the increasing use of surveillance in our everyday lives, slower queues at airport security gates, and, perhaps for some of us, the likelihood of being arrested and detained without charge based on little more than our demographic profile.

There is little escape from the reality of globalization in our lives. But this is not just a question of impact – that phrase seems to suggest, wrongly, that globalization happens *out there* and has a far-reaching and transformative effect *upon* our lives. In fact, we *act out* globalization processes through our personal and local lives. Most serious commentators on the subject steer well clear of making any such oversimplification as the crude polarization of global and local; this is certainly the case with Roland Robertson (1992), who, to avoid any such misunderstanding, has frequently used the term 'glocalization' to refer to precisely what in his view globalization means. It is also the case with Anthony Giddens (1990), for whom the current project of globalization results from the emerging *reflexivity* of agents within late modernity.

Part of the problem here is that sociologists have too often been confused in their use of the term 'local'. As such, the relationship between 'local' and 'global' has been treated as one of polar opposites, akin to the old sociological chestnut 'structure' and 'agency'. In classical sociological theory, 'structure' was always taken to refer to some kind of social determinism, whereby human action was somehow shaped by forces outside the actor, by society itself. 'Agency', by contrast, was used to define the way those actors intentionally shaped the world around them through their perceptions of it and by their actions. What started off as a methodological distinction, with Durkheim hailed as the champion of structure and Weber the advocate of agency, unhelpfully became an attempt to define some kind of social reality. If, then, 'agency' theorists could be accused of ignoring external power relations that influence our everyday lives, 'structural' theorists were guilty of presuming that the human actor is merely a passive puppet of those wider forces. In the context of globalization, the 'global' came to represent the tidal wave of structure, a force from beyond overwhelming us and reshaping our lives, while the 'local' came to be viewed as the familiar territory over which we have some control.

But the reality has always been somewhat different. Marx knew this well enough when he rightly pointed out that, while we do indeed have the capacity to act, and thus to shape our surroundings and our futures, the world we live in is defined by conditions we did not create and which do therefore influence the extent to which we can realize that capacity. Just as structure and agency are interminably intertwined, so are 'local' and 'global'. To see the 'global' as the enemy, and to mount some defence of the 'local' as some kind of pure, untainted utopia, is to commit a grave intellectual error.

Research into globalization is, at the end of the day, the latest expression of intellectual curiosity about the processes of social change. It inherits the mantle of those classical theorists whose sociological imaginations were piqued by the onset of what we now call 'modernity': those historic transformations centred around the nineteenth century in Western Europe which included urbanization, industrialization, the shift from feudalism to capitalism, the centralization of power into the modern nation-state, and the emergence of new, more tightly specified family structures and forms of social solidarity. For many classical theorists, particularly the German scholar Ferdinand Tönnies ([1887] 1957), a significant aspect of this period of change was the decline in traditional forms of 'community', to be replaced with more impersonal social relationships. A tradition emerged, not just in sociology but in the arts, in politics and in public discourse, that sought to defend the 'old ways of life' against the threat of the new by *romanticizing* the past. 'Community' became a byword for some idealized lifestyle lost in the new world. A tendency then developed in twentieth-century sociology to conflate two otherwise distinct terms – 'community' and 'locality' – thus confusing questions of how people live with those of where people live. Thus, the concept of the 'local community' became somehow essentialized in the groundbreaking studies of the Chicago School in the 1920s and the 'community studies' tradition that reached its peak in the UK in the 1950s, much of which added the concept of social class to the equation, thus presupposing the significance of this 'local community' in the formation of class-based identities. What was missing from much of this research was any serious interrogation of what these terms 'community' and 'locality' actually mean, and whether communities have to be 'local'.

But, as Benedict Anderson (1983) famously tells us, such 'communities' are always 'imagined'. They are mythologies, narratives constructed in the present to apply to the past. Similarly, 'localities' are never fixed. They are indexical points of reference which have to be understood in context. My definition of what is 'local' to me depends on who I am speaking to: on holiday abroad, 'London' is usually local enough, but in my nearest high street a more particular description is required. Within London, but outside the nearby vicinity of the house where I live, I may make use of the name given to the village, suburb or district of the city, but that label may not coincide with how politicians define where I live, because official constituency, ward or borough boundaries are rarely synonymous with the everyday definitions of those parts of the city (and I have never met a Londoner who consciously defines her or his 'local' space by the name of the actual borough it is located in!).

The romantic belief is that these 'local communities' are bound by solidarity, consensus and belonging. The reality is that they are exclusive spaces defined in the dialectic between who 'does' and who 'doesn't' belong: as the urban sociologist Ray Pahl brilliantly said: 'conflict from without creates consensus within' (Pahl 1970: 102). Far from being idealized spaces free from the overwhelming forces of the outside world, localities are heavily politicized constructs, sites of struggle between 'insiders' and 'outsiders'. As the anthropologist

Arjun Appadurai (1990) says, localities are themselves social constructs produced by global communications and communities, and global processes are actually capable of liberating such local identities from these exclusivist limitations. In other words, globalization can encourage local identity by breaking down the walls of nationalism. Local voices emerge within transnational settings. In Europe, Scottish, Catalan, Breton, Basque, Cornish or Welsh voices are empowered by transnational challenges to the nation-state, not overwhelmed or silenced.

In researching globalization, we need always to take this complex, one might say symbiotic, relationship between the global and the local into consideration, and not fall prey to the expedient temptation to treat them as polar opposites. Globalization does not, it seems, entail the breakdown of local identities: indeed, it may have the opposite effect! Similarly, globalization cannot entail the breakdown of local communities, because these are always derived from convenient fictions. If globalizing processes do somehow challenge local solidarities, then we should bear in mind that these solidarities are themselves forged as strategies for exclusion of 'the other'. And, when such communities are always imagined, globalization certainly cannot be a threat to the concept of 'community'. In reality, we *live out* the global in our everyday lives, which we *live* locally.

BOX 9.3 EVERYDAY LIFE IN THE GLOBAL CITY

The following is one academic's account of a stroll down Kilburn High Road, London:

It is a pretty ordinary place, north-west of the centre of London. Under the railway bridge the newspaper stand sells papers from every county of what my neighbours, many of whom come from there, still often call the Irish Free State . . . At the local theatre Eamon Morrisey has a one-man show; the National Club has the Wolfe Tones on, and at the Black Lion, there's Finnegan's Wake. In two shops I notice this week's lottery winners: in one the name is Teresa Gleeson, in the other, Chouman Hassan.

Thread your way through the almost stationary traffic diagonally across the road from the newsstand and there's a big shop which as long as I can remember has displayed saris in the window. Four life-sized models of Indian women, and reams of cloth . . . On another ad, for the end of the month, is written, 'All Hindus are cordially invited'. In another newsagents I chat with the man who keeps it, a Muslim unutterably depressed by events in the Gulf . . . Overhead there is at least one aeroplane – we seem to be on a flight path to Heathrow and by the time they're over Kilburn you can see them clearly enough to tell the airline and wonder as you struggle with your shopping where they're coming from. (Massey 1994: 152–3)

A strikingly similar account is given on an altogether different location – the African township of Sophiatown:

There is indeed a sense of the global ecumene here, of the simultaneous presence within one's field of experience of ancestral gods, Western philosophy, and the jazz of black America, and it is all being worked on right there, in the township. Distinctive cultural currents are coming together, having been separated by oceans and continents, working their way into one another over time, developing new ways of shaping human beings. (Hannerz 1996: 167)

SEMINAR QUESTIONS

1 The presence of *transnational* corporations as defined by Sklair would be one indicator that there is some substance to the claim that there is now a global economic system. A single global currency would be another, but this is clearly less of a reality at present. What other such indicators can you think of?

2 Carry out a little research to find out more about the origins, purposes, structure and operations of the United Nations. In particular, look at where, and in what way, the UN has involved itself in world affairs. Think about how the UN – and in particular its Security Council – might be improved? Consider to what extent the UN has *power* in the world today.

3 Take a walk down *your* high street or local shopping centre. Make a note of all the global influences you encounter. Speak to a selection of people and ask them how *they* define their 'local' space. Compare the responses and write up a short report considering the *contexts* in which those different definitions are appropriately used.

4 Discuss the extent to which the 'new global economy' is at all 'new' or 'global'.

5 Who has power in the world today?

6 Can there be such a thing as a 'global culture'?

NEGOTIATING GLOBALIZATION: GLOBAL CIVIL SOCIETY

Ethical globalization and civil society

In the 1990s, as the economic form of globalization discussed above reached its highest point and public unrest grew over the perceived injustices and increasing polarization of rich and poor it brought with it, a new kind of social movement emerged as people took to the streets in Seattle, USA, and Genoa, Italy, and elsewhere to protest against the power, influence and ideology of the World Bank, the World Trade Organization, the International Monetary Fund, and other such agents of what was increasingly being seen as a transnational project of imposing 'globalization from above'. For reasons that soon became apparent to all concerned were counter-intuitive, this movement became known as the 'anti-globalization movement', the sentiment (and irony) of this summed up in one famous banner from the Seattle protests, which championed the 'worldwide movement against globalization'.

It is far more commonplace now to refer to this movement as either the 'global justice movement' or the movement for 'global civil society'. With this simple act of redefining the movement came a renewed intellectual interest in the idea of civil society, largely left dormant for decades, and the concept of justice took centre-stage in sociological debates for possibly the first time since the high point of critical theory in the 1960s. It was clear that a new intellectual space was opening up within the wider discourse on globalization, one which would not easily be captured within the traditional conceptual frameworks of economics, politics or culture. What was being discussed, not merely in normative terms but in substantive ones as well, was the idea of an *ethical* globalization.

Not that the concept of civil society, which we may now comfortably use to refer precisely to this ethical domain, detached from state and market, politics and economics, as well as from culture, has always been used in such a way. Its classical definition comes from Hegel, for whom it mediates between the private realm of the individual and the public realm of the state, and thus embraces all forms of social relations, how people engage with society, including economic and formal-legal as well as ethical relations. Writing in the early twentieth century, the Italian Marxist Antonio Gramsci did define civil society in ethical terms, but as the 'ethical content of the state' (1966: 164), ethics here equating to political and cultural hegemony. The more contemporary usage of the term is best defined by the eminent American sociologist Jeffrey Alexander, in which it becomes 'the realm of interaction, institutions and solidarity that sustains the public life of societies outside the worlds of economy and state' (Alexander 1993: 797).

By treating civil society as this ethical space outside the worlds of economy and state, Alexander invites us to take seriously another form of social action not reducible to the logics of the economic, political or even cultural fields. This is action directed not to the pursuit of power, which is a pragmatic, one could say instrumentalist, pursuit, any more than it is to the pursuit of wealth or the pursuit of knowledge (in the narrower culturalist sense), but rather to the pursuit of justice. While such action is political in the wider sense of the term, it is a different form of politics, its goals defined not by the expedient demands of problem-solving – 'how best to get the job done' – but by the more normative demands of 'what ought to be done'.

Global citizenship

There is, of course, an obvious overlap with one of the forms of political globalization discussed earlier. Using a broader definition, politics is not just about the power and role of political institutions but about the orientations and actions of individuals who *act* politically. The apparent shift in such political allegiances over the last thirty years or so from nation-state-bound political parties to transnational campaigning or protest movements seems to illustrate a shift in values, which in turn can be seen to reflect a shift in the basic needs of people and at what level those needs can be best protected. A term has entered into popular usage to describe such people who operate transnationally to champion such causes as human rights or environmental protection: we call them global citizens.

On the one hand, this is itself a deeply problematic expression. How can they be citizens if there is no global state to which they are contracted? This is an interesting, and a relevant, question, although it derives from yet another common misunderstanding. It presumes that citizenship must be a formal political contract between a state and an individual, which allows the individual to enjoy the benefits of certain protected rights in return for the accomplishment of certain duties. This is a very legalistic and formal definition of citizenship which came into prominence with the rise of the modern nation-state, and which we can call the 'liberal' definition. But citizenship itself is not reducible merely to an exchange of rights and duties: in its classical usage, from the ancient Greek philosophers onwards, it also involves membership of a political community and active participation in the affairs of that community. Such a 'communitarian' definition of citizenship is precisely that which is embraced by those who claim that acting politically as part of a global community of people constitutes global citizenship.

Even so, it is a vague definition, and for many centuries little more than a normative one, an aspiration rather than a reflection of reality. It is easy to debunk the idea of a one-world community, given the huge diversity of cultures, values and practices involved. While such expressions of 'cosmopolitanism' (another term that has enjoyed something of a renaissance recently precisely within this context) have over the years yielded attempts to formalize the nature of this kind of citizenship through the introduction of the language of human rights, these were by and large abstract, ill-defined and substantively meaningless articulations of what 'ought to be' rather than what 'is'. Sociologists had little interest in such vague abstractions (Turner 1993). But, since the end of the Second World War, that situation has changed. The first attempt to agree a (legally non-binding but nonetheless significant) framework for formalizing these rights came with the signing of the Universal Declaration of Human Rights in 1948. Since then we have seen the growth of international law as an authoritative space above the nation-state, incorporating acts and conventions designed to protect not only human rights but also other 'global' concerns. And with the realization that the nation-state is not equipped to handle the problems faced by the world at this point in history, and that the international institutions remain insufficiently armed to follow through on their own promises, we have seen the simultaneous emergence of these non-governmental organizations (NGOs) campaigning on precisely such issues, not by seeking political power in the formal sense but by campaigning for what they believe needs to be done.

BOX 9.4 WORLD GOVERNMENT OF WORLD CITIZENS

Most civil society organizations would define themselves as NGOs – specifically, non-governmental organizations. However, one particular organization based in the United States takes a very distinctive position on this: non-governmental equates to no power! In 1948, a former US fighter pilot named Garry Davis publicly renounced his US citizenship while in Paris and declared himself a 'citizen of the world'. His philosophy for doing so was thus: citizenship is about empowerment, but how can one be empowered if one subscribes to the nation-state model, given that wars are fought primarily between nation-states? As the problems facing us in the nuclear age are global, so must true empowerment recognize our agency on a global scale. For Davis, the logical extension of this philosophy was actually to announce the formation of world government, which he did in 1953 when he launched the World Government of World Citizens. Government, after all, is the servant of the people, and, if the people have declared their citizenship to be of the world, world government is born. Davis's take on world government is very different from those of the many cosmopolitan advocates of such an idea throughout history. They call for a world government to emerge on the transnational plane, possibly through the UN. For Davis, world government already exists, the offspring not of states but of people exercising their fundamental rights to political sovereignty. The administrative arm of this body, the World Service Authority, works to help individuals, such as refugees, who are caught up in the quicksand of the nation-state system, by effectively undermining that system through its promotion of global documents, such as its famous world passport.

It is also possible to argue, as O'Byrne (2003) does, that, in the context of globalization, global citizenship does take on a distinct and very real meaning, far more than just a vague aspiration. It involves individuals engaging directly with the forces that most impact upon their lives, and each dimension of citizenship is suitably 'transformed', as table 9.2, summarized from the original text, illustrates.

This, then, is the space of global civil society, a space that is consciously set up to provide an alternative direction for global transformations to those presented by the dominant forms of a global marketplace, a global system of rival nation-states competing for power, or a single overarching global state. It is a model that has become prominent in the writings not only of

Table 9.2: **Nation-state citizenship and global citizenship**

Dimension of citizenship	Nation-state model	Global model
Rights	Citizens' rights, enshrined in national law and exclusive	Human rights, enshrined in international law and inclusive
Duties	To the nation-state, such as national service or taxation	To the world, such as environmental protection
Membership	Of the nation-state, defined in exclusive terms using the 'assimilationist' framework	Of the global community, defined in inclusive terms as reflecting cultural diversity
Participation	Via formal institutions of government, e.g., political parties, voting at elections, etc. (liberal democracy)	Via non-governmental campaigning organizations facilitated through communications technology (radical democracy)

Source: Adapted from O'Byrne (2003).

left-leaning activist-academics such as Richard Falk and Jeremy Brecher but also of communitarians such as Michael Walzer, whose collected volume *Toward a Global Civil Society* (1995) is worth reading (even if it is a bit challenging at first). Rather than seeing itself as a movement *against* globalization (in the narrow sense), the global civil society movement has increasingly come to recognize the perceived need to contrast the dominant *form* of globalization (often presented as 'globalization-from-above') with an alternative model, globalization-from-below: 'Globalization-from-below . . . aims to restore to communities the power to nurture their environments; to enhance the access of ordinary people to the resources they need; to democratize local, national, and transnational political institutions; and to impose pacification on conflicting power centers' (Brecher, Childs and Cutler 1993: xv).

A number of important questions, though, do arise from the current usage of the term 'civil society' in a global context. While it is commonly associated with a particular kind of campaign, promoting 'left-leaning' or 'progressive' values such as human rights or economic development, there is nothing inherent in the idea of ethics that demands such a classification. To act in the context of civil society, and thus in global civil society, is to act in a manner informed by ethics, not politics, and the ethics may also be articulated through more moderate, conservative or even reactionary campaigns. Similarly, in treating civil society as a space beyond state and market, we are necessarily limiting the involvement of more directly political or economic actors. In other words, while campaigning NGOs, the global justice movement, and even transnational friendship networks may reasonably be seen to occupy this space, can the same be said of corporations or political parties, or are their motivations entirely incompatible with the goals of civil society? Such questions, which are addressed in a more recent collection on the subject (Eade and O'Byrne 2005), become particularly significant when governments commit themselves to 'ethical foreign policies' or transnational corporations speak of 'ethical capitalism' and 'corporate social responsibility'.

SEMINAR QUESTIONS

1 With reference to two or three relevant organizations, discuss the ways in which various civil society movements might operate on a global level.

2 Does the idea of global citizenship really make sense?

3 Is the idea of ethical capitalism an oxymoron?

THEORIZING GLOBALIZATION

So far, I have tried to show how difficult it is defining 'globalization', because the term carries so many diverse and even contradictory meanings. I have also tried to show how we might experience globalization, in one or another of its forms, in various aspects of our lives. The final important issue I want to address in this chapter is how we make sense of globalization, or what theoretical tools we might use to explain it. Naturally, this is a problematic endeavour, given how slippery a concept globalization is, and particularly if we have taken seriously the warning not to think that 'it' as a thing in itself exists at all! Nonetheless, most of the literature accepts that the globalizing processes we encounter are in some way interconnected and reflective of a particular set of historical conditions, and so we can, at least, develop theories to make sense of those conditions.

When attempting to 'theorize globalization', though, we need to be extra cautious, because, for reasons already alluded to, many of the standard theoretical perspectives commonly used in sociology do not apply here, at least in any familiar sense. Take Marxism as an example. A simplistic application of sociological theory would ask us to look for a Marxist explanation of globalization, one which no doubt would locate its driver in the dynamics of the capitalist system. However, in the sociology of globalization there is no single such account, but rather a multiplicity of Marxian-inspired accounts of globalization. While each may owe a debt to Marx for its concern with capitalism and economic inequality, so diverse are the views on what globalization even means, if it means anything at all, that the differences between such authors as Hirst and Thompson (1999), Wallerstein (1979), Sklair (2002) and Harvey (1989) are probably more significant than their similarities!

Phases of globalization and globalization theory

One schema we might usefully employ to help us understand the dynamics of global change is to contrast different perspectives on what the contemporary phase of globalization might represent. With this in mind, 'globalization theory' exists as a loose body of knowledge bound together within a framework that treats globalization as a historical phase in human social development (for all sorts of reasons, 'development' is not an ideal choice of word here, but far preferable to alternatives such as 'evolution', 'progress' or 'modernization'). Globalization theory – major contributors to which include Roland Robertson (1992), Anthony Giddens (1990) and Martin Albrow (1996) – thus stands in opposition to perspectives such as world-systems theory, 'new times' theory, neoliberalism and international relations, which see it primarily as the product of some other transformation. For Robertson (1992), globalization is the gradual historical process through which the world comes to be recognized as a single place, originating (roughly) in Europe in the fifteenth century. The process has undergone various phases (see table 9.3) before 'taking off' from the 1870s to the 1920s and finally (to the time of writing) reaching a heightened 'uncertainty phase' from the 1960s. If Robertson treats the latest (heightened) phase of globalization as a natural extension of the previous stages, Giddens (1990) clearly identifies globalization as a relatively recent historical process, emanating from post-Second World War globalism and the rise of communications and information technology, defined by a 'speeding-up' of the logic that defined the earlier phase of modernity. Albrow (1996) goes even further to distance the current phase of globalization from the earlier project of modernization, by claiming that the process of globalization does not merely radically transform the modern project but brings to an end the entire modern age and ushers in a new logic for a new, 'global' age.

Table 9.3: **Five phases of globalization**		
Phase	**Approximate dates**	**Defining events**
Germinal phase	Early 15th–mid-18th centuries	Expanding scope of Catholic Church; idea of 'humanity' takes hold; heliocentric theory of the world; Gregorian calendar
Incipient phase	Mid-18th century–1870s	International relations; international exhibitions; crystallization of the concept of the nation-state
Take-off phase	1870s–1920s	Idea of 'international society' takes hold; immigration restriction; developments in communication; global competitions, e.g., Olympics; world time; First World War
Struggle-for-hegemony phase	1920s–1960s	League of Nations and United Nations; Second World War; threat of global nuclear destruction; Cold War; Third World
Uncertainty phase	1960s–1990s	Moon landing; post-materialist values; end of Cold War; legalization of human rights; global institutions and movements; acceleration of global communications; multi-ethnic societies; identity politics; environmentalism; global civil society; globalizing Islam

Source: Compiled from Robertson (1992: 58–9).

The emergence of globalization theory came partly as a response to the perceived inadequacies not only of existing sociological perspectives, which continued to privilege the centrality of the nation-state, but also of more overtly internationalist perspectives. The discipline of international relations had in any case challenged the assumption that society was reducible to the level of the nation-state, yet it continued to see the nation-state (and the competition between nation-states) as the defining characteristic of the world, a position incompatible with that of the globalization theorists. Another perspective challenged by globalization theory for continuing to prioritize relations between states rather than the world as a single place is the 'world-systems theory' developed primarily by Immanuel Wallerstein (1979) and his colleagues at the State University of New York at Binghamton. For scholars in the world-systems tradition, the current phase of 'globalization' is in fact the most recent stage of the development of the modern world-system of capitalism. According to such a perspective, capitalism can be treated as a system of exchange originating in Europe in the early seventeenth century (a significant departure from a Marxist analysis, which sees capitalism as a system of production originating in the Industrial Revolution). The history of capitalism has always been a history of unequal power relationships – between what Wallerstein calls the 'core' and the 'periphery' countries – so the most recent phase of 'globalization' is merely the core–periphery dynamic on a worldwide scale (effectively, the polarization of the world into the rich North/West and the poor South). Scholars working within the tradition of 'new times theory' also seek to understand the current phase of globalization within a broadly Marxian theoretical framework, but in a more conventional sense, identifying as the driving factor a shift in the process of production, from an earlier phase of 'organized' industrial capitalism utilizing Fordist practices to a new, post-Fordist, post-industrial, disorganized and decentred capitalism (in this tradition, see Hall and Jacques 1989; Harvey 1989; and, for a similar but non-Marxist version, Lash and Urry 1987). Also treating globalization as a consequence of a shift in the dynamics of capitalism – albeit from a more sympathetic perspective – is neoliberalism. Neoliberal theories of globalization tend to dominate much of the popular debate on the subject, treating it as they do as the process which facilitates the 'ultimate' stage of capitalism, a 'global marketplace' or 'borderless' world of free trade (Ohmae 1990).

In recent years, more distinct approaches have emerged which challenge some of the core assumptions of globalization theory while retaining its globalist (or at best transnational) emphasis, of which the traditions of cultural studies, cosmopolitanism and critical globalization studies stand out. Scholars within the cultural studies tradition sought to move the debate beyond relatively abstract and simplistic historical accounts of global transformation towards its everyday experience, highlighting the ever changing nature of culture (see the discussion above on cultural globalization and 'creolization') within the context of postcolonial and core–periphery relations. More recently, the tradition of critical globalization studies (Appelbaum and Robinson 2005) has drawn on critical theory more generally in the social sciences to treat the current phase of globalization not only in historical but also in dialectical terms, as represented by a 'dominant' form ('capitalist globalization' or 'globalization-from-above') against which can be posited a counter-hegemonic alternative ('globalization-from-below'). Leslie Sklair's (2002) work is a superb example of this kind of approach: modifying ideas derived from Gramsci, Sklair suggests that the dominant 'capitalist globalization' is sustained by a culture-ideology of consumerism, against which can be posited a 'socialist globalization' sustained by a culture-ideology of human rights. Another good example of critical globalization studies can be found in one of the popular slogans of the global justice movement: 'Another world is possible'. Finally, cosmopolitanism (see Beck 2006) has undergone a recent revival in suggestions that the current phase of globalization not only undermines the primacy of the nation-state but paves the way for an era of transnational governance, human rights and respect for international law.

Table 9.4 **Eight theories of globalization**	
	The current phase of globalization is . . .
Globalization theory	. . . the most recent stage in human social development characterized by social relationships spanning the globe and social actions oriented towards it.
International relations	. . . the articulation of new forms of interdependence and conflict between states.
World-systems theory	. . . the further extension of the historical dynamic between the rich 'core' and the exploited 'periphery'.
New times theory	. . . a new stage in capitalism, exemplified by a new international system of production.
Neoliberalism	. . . the facilitator of an ultimate form of unrestricted capitalism defined by free trade regardless of national borders.
Cultural studies	. . . the most recent stage in cultural hybridization in the context of postcolonial core–periphery relations.
Critical globalization studies	. . . represented by a dominant form of capitalist globalization contrasted dialectically with the possibility of an alternative grassroots form.
Cosmopolitanism	. . . the revitalization and realization of the timeless cosmopolitan ideal symbolized by the centrality of transnational institutions.

SEMINAR QUESTIONS

1 What are the key factors and defining moments that have facilitated the acceleration of globalizing processes since the end of the Second World War?
2 Are these factors likely to be as important in the future?

CONCLUSION

'Globalization' signifies the key 'problem' of our age because, rather like 'industrialization' or 'modernization' for previous generations of scholars, it has become something of an umbrella term for all sorts of radical transformations in the organization and experience of society. Like them, it also suffers from a lack of clarity as to what might constitute the culmination of the process, and that is why the term is so contested: few people even agree on what it means!

Nonetheless, it is an essential concept for today's generation of sociologists to grasp, because its relevance is far-reaching indeed. Its tentacles find their way into almost every other chapter of this book – it affects how we engage with health, with education, with politics, with development, with the environment, with work, and so on. I have tried, in this chapter, to refrain from looking at the specifics of such applications and to keep my analysis of 'globalization' at a rather conceptual level. However, it is certainly worth your reading this chapter in conjunction with each of those others that deal with more substantive objects of sociological inquiry.

Remember, when you do so, to keep an open mind: globalization is all things to all people, so try not to fall into the trap many casual commentators make by using it as short-hand for a far more specific concern (more often than not, the global economy). To do so would not only be rather lazy but also quietly dangerous because, by treating globalization as a *thing* rather than a *process*, we subject it to what earlier scholars have called 'reification'. The problem with reification is that it results in our taking something for granted, not engaging with it in a critical way, and thus serves to close down debate. The good sociologist will always be prepared to open up debate.

SEMINAR QUESTIONS

1   Compare and contrast any two theories of contemporary global change presented in this chapter.
2   Give arguments why one of these theories could be seen as stronger than the other.
3   Write your own definition of globalization. Does your definition have any weaknesses?

FURTHER READING

▶ Appelbaum, R., and W. I. Robinson (eds) (2005) *Critical Globalization Studies* (Routledge). Useful not only because it contains digestible chapters from some of the leading scholars in the field, including Leslie Sklair, David Harvey, Walden Bello, Saskia Sassen and Richard Falk, or even because it also contains contributions from celebrated activists such as Susan George and Anita Roddick, or even because it provides the framework for a distinctive critical approach to globalization, but also because of its inclusion of voices from the Global South, often neglected in academic debates in the West.

▶ Giddens, A. (1990) *The Consequences of Modernity* (Polity). This is a pretty small book, but don't let that fool you because, as you would expect from Giddens, it is full of complex ideas and demands reading from beginning to end. Make sure you are clear about the following: How does Giddens define the key dimensions of modernity? What has happened to those? How does he define the key dimensions of *late* modernity? What does he mean by 'time–space distanciation'? What does he mean by 'disembedding'? What does he mean by 'reflexivity'?

▶ Martell, L. (2010) *The Sociology of Globalization* (Polity). This is without a doubt the best of the many student-focused textbooks embracing the breadth of sociological work in this area. Martell covers the 'usual suspects' – economy, culture and politics – but he takes time to interrogate some of the key themes in the current literature, including migration, technology, poverty, the global justice movement, and even war. There's also a decent section on theory. One to purchase and keep with you for the duration!

▶ O'Byrne, D. J., and A. Hensby (2011) *Theorizing Global Studies* (Palgrave Macmillan). In this book, O'Byrne and Hensby distinguish the process of becoming global from seven other coexisting but often conflicting processes. Make sure you can distinguish clearly between the eight processes defined and what each one might mean for the nation-state.

▶ Robertson, R. (1992) *Globalization: Social Theory and Global Culture* (Sage). This book really establishes the debate around globalization within sociology. Core chapters outline Robertson's long-term historical approach, his concept of 'globality', and his diagrammatic rendition of what's distinct about the current phase of globalization – what he calls the 'global field'. Make sure you understand what each of these means.

▶ Sklair, L. (2002) *Globalization: Capitalism and its Alternatives* (Oxford University Press). In my experience, students of globalization who make the effort to read Sklair are rewarded with a conceptual framework that addresses much of what matters to them, as academics and as people. Make sure you understand what Sklair means by the 'global system', what he means by transnational corporations and practices, and what the key features of capitalist globalization and its alternative, socialist globalization, are.

THE ENVIRONMENT

sociology at its (natural) limits

PHILIP W. SUTTON

CONTENTS

INTRODUCTION

S TUDENTS OFTEN ASK a simple yet fundamental question about environmental issues – What do they have to do with sociology? When a small number of sociologists began studying environmental matters in the 1970s and 1980s, many of their peers posed the same query. Sociology, the self-styled 'science of society', studied families, crime, gender relations, social class and work. Natural environments were surely the province of environmental and other natural sciences, as sociologists are just not competent in this area, having received no institutional training in the 'hard' sciences. As a result, distinctive sociological perspectives on environmental issues developed much later than in human geography, economics, political science and even psychology.

The field of environmental sociology is very broad indeed, and it is quite impossible to do it justice in a single chapter. In order to produce a coherent narrative, this chapter picks out a small number of key ideas and issues that have shaped or are shaping the field. But there is no room to discuss environmental movements, green politics, ecological modernization, ecotourism, political ecology, animal–human relations, biotechnology and much more. Instead, the chapter provides sketches of risk theory and global environmental problems before covering the central methodological divide between constructionism and realism. It then debates climate change or, more specifically, global warming, as an extended case study of a global environmental issue *par excellence*. Finally, the range of policies and practices which come under the general umbrella of 'sustainable development' are included. Readers wishing to expand their knowledge of environmental sociology should consult some of the suggestions in the 'Further reading' section.

Until very recently, the discipline of economics has been the dominant social scientific contributor to the study of environmental matters (Urry 2011: 2). However, this chapter shows why a comprehensive understanding of environmental issues has to embrace a sociological perspective. In a nutshell, sociology explains the underlying social *causes* of environmental problems, helps us to understand the *consequences* of those problems for societies, and is essential for evaluating the *policies* aimed at mitigating environmental damage. However, sociology does not have all the answers. To anticipate my conclusion, I will argue throughout that studying environmental issues ought to lead sociologists in the direction of multi- or interdisciplinarity. That is, environment–society relations cannot be properly understood by any single scientific discipline, and sociologists must be prepared to engage with and learn from the natural sciences. However, the converse is also true, that the natural sciences also need to engage with and learn from sociology and other social sciences. Such collaboration should, of course, not be pursued in an uncritical, naïve fashion, but finding ways of working with other scientific disciplines is essential for any environmental sociology worth the name and which remains true to the best traditions of sociological inquiry.

SEMINAR QUESTIONS

1   Suggest a possible sociological explanation for any one environmental problem.

2   Suggest a possible social effect of any one environmental problem.

3   Suggest a social policy that might help to deal with an environmental problem.

SOCIAL THEORY AND THE ENVIRONMENT

One reason why sociologists arrived late to the study of environmental issues lies in the unpromising theoretical legacy left by the discipline's classical traditions. It is not that sociology's founders entirely ignored the natural environment. Marx, Durkheim and Weber all had things to say about society–environment relations, but what we now call 'environmental issues' just did not exist as such during their lifetimes. When environmental issues did rise to prominence in the 1970s and 1980s, some sociologists looked to the key ideas of Marx (Parsons 1977; Grundmann 1991; Dickens [1992] 2004, 1996, 2002; Benton 1996a, 1996b; O'Connor 1998; Foster 2000), Durkheim (Turner 1996, 1999; Catton 1998, 2002) and Weber (West 1985; Murphy 1994a, 1994b, 1997, 2002) as guides. However, it cannot be fairly said that the environment was central to these theorists' work. Similarly, nineteenth-century sociological theory used the existing stock of biological knowledge of the time which, by contemporary standards, was limited and flawed. This means simply returning to the classics could be a fruitless enterprise.

Classical social theory was never devised to explore and understand how environmental problems are generated. In fact, it tried to explain how modern societies had broken with the natural obstacles that had restricted the development chances of traditional societies (Goldblatt 1996: 4; Urry 2011). Indeed, one of the founding arguments of environmental sociology was that we must break with sociology's existing Human Exemptionalist Paradigm (HEP), which implied that societies were exempt from natural laws and limits, and move over to a New Ecological Paradigm (NEP), which accepts that societies do not exist apart from the natural environment on which they depend (Catton and Dunlap 1978).

Given this assessment, many consider that sociology has to be creative and devise new theories which build in society–environment relations from the outset. Examples of these are theories of reflexivity and de-traditionalization (Giddens 1990, 1991, 1994a, 1999), theories of the 'risk society' (Beck 1992, 1994, [1995] 2002, 1999), post-industrial socialism (Gorz 1980, 1985, 1989, 1994), environmental movements as resistances to the 'colonization of the lifeworld' (Habermas 1981, 1986, 1989a, 1989b, 1990) and the transformation of the dominant cultural paradigms of modernity (Eder 1982, 1985, 1990, 1993, 1996). Although the classical traditions have not been abandoned wholesale in these approaches, their motivations and 'central problems' are significantly divergent, inspired to varying degrees by substantive environmental issues. We cannot cover all of these theories in this short chapter but will focus on arguably the most productive and widely cited perspective, which is Ulrich Beck's theory of the risk society.

The risky environment

When environmental issues began to make headway in sociology in the 1990s, Beck's theory of the 'risk society' dominated theoretical debates (Beck 1992, 1999). This theory locates society–environment relations in the context of the fundamental transformation of the industrialized societies. Paradoxically, it is the normal functioning of the latter which has brought about a series of environmental problems which now threaten their own existence. As they spread around the globe, continual economic growth, industrialization and modern consumerism produce more environmental problems (such as pollution and the destruction of 'natural' environments), higher consequence risks (including the proliferation of nuclear weapons and risks associated with nuclear power) and global environmental changes (atmospheric ozone depletion and climate change). The side effects of the push for growth and industrial development begin to pile up, and we see industrial societies and cultures gradually dissolving. By the end of the twentieth and into the twenty-first century, Beck argued that we were moving rapidly towards a global or 'world risk society' (1999, 2008). As a result, a general risk consciousness and risk avoidance have become increasingly central to social life and politics.

It is important to note that the 'post-industrial', service-based societies of the global northern hemisphere are not immune from industrial pollution and global environmental damage. Industrial processes have always produced pollution, but today's environmental risks are in many ways 'higher consequence risks', with the potential to affect people far away from the site of their production. Giddens (1999) also argues that the production of high-consequence risks is a novel development – evidence of a 'runaway world' where governments are clearly not in control, social life becomes less certain and citizens become fearful for the future. For both Beck and Giddens, the natural environment and environmental issues have moved from the margin to the centre of politics. A good example of a global, high-consequence, manufactured risk is the 1980s environmental issue of a dangerous thinning of the ozone layer. The Earth has a protective layer consisting mainly of ozone that blocks ultraviolet radiation from the Sun, thus helping to prevent skin cancers in people and animals. The stratospheric ozone layer is instrumental in helping to maintain safe levels of radiation for the continuation of life. Yet just one or two generations ago the vast majority of human populations across the world did not know such a thing as an 'ozone layer' even existed. However, the cumulative observations of chemists, climate scientists and meteorologists and reporting of these in mass media led to a growing awareness of the risk and pressure for governments to act.

The issue of ozone layer depletion illustrates important aspects of Beck's risk thesis. Industrial societies produce risks that most people are not even aware exist. Who would have guessed that everyday consumer products such as aerosol cans could have had such devastating

BOX 10.1 OZONE LAYER DEPLETION

In the 1970s, plans for supersonic aircraft that would fly within the stratosphere were announced in the former Soviet Union, in America and in the British–French collaborative venture, Concorde, raising fears of damage to the ozone layer. At the same time, scientists in the USA reported that certain aerosol propellants might also damage the ozone layer, and in 1978 chlorofluorocarbons (CFCs) were banned in the USA. CFCs are human-made gases used as propellants in aerosol cans and other applications. But when released they rise into the stratosphere and, once they are there, radiation from the Sun causes them to decompose and release chlorine compounds, which then destroys ozone, thus depleting ozone levels (Yearley 1991). In 1987, scientists conducting an Airborne Antarctic Ozone Experiment definitively identified CFCs as the main cause of ozone depletion. The risk of continuing production and use was a potential increase in skin cancers but the solution was obvious: stop using CFCs in aerosols, refrigerators and freezers and replace them with less damaging alternatives. International agreement on phasing out CFCs was reached quickly, and in 1989 the Montreal Protocol came into force. Through a range of national and local measures, CFC use was rapidly reduced, though replenishing the ozone layer would take much longer. Current estimates suggest that by 2050 the ozone layer will have all but recovered.

If environmental risks were entirely the product of natural forces, they would not impinge on political life too much, but, as the ozone layer issue illustrates, the more serious environmental risks are 'manufactured' or human-made, quite unlike the natural disasters of pre-modern times. And, as products of human activity, they are inevitably subjects of political debate and decision-making and often centre on our apparently innocuous everyday actions.

effects on the global environment and human health? Secondly, the scientific knowledge necessary for the manufacture of aerosols, freezers and refrigerators helped to produce the ozone layer problem, but it was also scientific research which confirmed the causal link to CFCs, thereby paving the way for a solution. In the modern world, scientists perform essential functions that no other group within society can. Thirdly, it was quite easy to damage the ozone layer in a short time period, but the timescale for recovery was far longer. This is why some green activists argue for a 'precautionary principle' that restricts technological developments until their environmental impact can be shown to be benign. This is, after all, how regulatory bodies in medicine and the pharmaceutical industry operate. On the other hand, it simply is not possible to avoid risks altogether, and they will always have to be weighed against the potential benefits.

As the state of the natural environment becomes a political issue, the previous polarization between 'nature' and 'society' is eroded, and it is less easy to talk of 'nature' as something untouched and free of human influence (Evernden 1992). As Giddens (1994a: 77) argues, 'Nature has become socialised. Today, among all the other endings, we may speak in a real sense of the end of nature – a way of referring to its thoroughgoing socialization.' Something as taken for granted as the natural seasons can no longer be accepted as 'natural', especially when global warming is changing natural cycles. Today, human activity partially shapes those cycles, so that 'A child born now will never know a natural summer, a natural autumn, winter or spring. Summer is going extinct, replaced by something else that will be called "summer"' (McKibben 1990: 55). For Beck, the uncertainty, anxieties and fear this realization produces are yet another sign of the emerging risk society.

Risk and vulnerabilities

The risk society thesis is certainly provocative and has stimulated a good deal of research. As a theory of social change which foregrounds the environmental consequences of globalizing industrialism, it also helps to explain the emergence of environmental sociology and green politics in the 1980s. However, the concept of 'risk' may not be the most appropriate or realistic way of theorizing environmental problems. An alternative is to shift the focus from risks to 'vulnerabilities' and to think of the emerging global society as producing higher level vulnerabilities (de Vries 2002). This shift marks a different way of thinking about social development and change. Increasing human control over the natural environment is always gained at a price: increasing dependence on the social relations and technological means which enable that control to be established (McNeill 1979; Goudsblom 1989, 1992). As human interdependencies extend over geographically larger areas, so vulnerabilities are created at higher levels. If we consider the vulnerability of our increasing reliance on information technologies in routine administration, international banking, air traffic control systems, and so on, it becomes easier to see the force of such a proposition.

Similarly, cities depend on enormously complex and extensive infrastructural networks. Even the apparently environmentally benign technology of the internet is completely

Our current age could be typified as one of increasing vulnerability, as we place more and more reliance, for example, on information technologies to run and organize society. The speed with which financial transactions take place in automated stock exchanges means that one minor error can quickly multiply into a bigger problem. (© Baron Visuals/Flickr)

dependent on energy systems, many of which produce large quantities of pollution. The world wide web is an increasingly heavy user of electricity, which makes it dependent on fossil fuel extraction, refinement, transportation and use. Some estimates suggest that Google alone owns up to 1 million servers, and its Dalles plant in Oregon, USA, was expected to demand around 103 megawatts of electricity, similar in size to the power demand of 82,000 homes (Strand 2008). In many developing countries, where the urban infrastructure can be unreliable at best, the vulnerability to disruption of all the 'invisible' networks of pipes, cables, generating plants and workers is in the foreground of city life. However, in the industrialized countries, precisely because these systems are more reliable, people give them little thought and may not even be aware of their existence (Graham 2010). Only when disasters such as earthquakes and floods, or more prosaic disruptions such as urgent transport maintenance, strike is the vulnerability of modern infrastructure brought into the open.

Introducing the idea of shifts in the level of vulnerability provides a useful alternative to risk. Modern societies are certainly producing higher level vulnerabilities, but this does not mean they are 'high risk' societies. Vulnerability acknowledges that the increasing scale of human life produces both gains and new problems and that these always go hand in hand. For instance, while information technologies enable easier and safer travel systems, they also make such systems vulnerable to breakdowns that affect large parts or even the entire system. However, recognizing that the system is more vulnerable to a general disruption does not make travel more 'risky'. Modern travel systems are generally much safer for the vast majority of the people who use them. Our global society may not be increasingly risky, but it is rather more vulnerable than we previously thought.

SEMINAR QUESTIONS

1 Read Beck's (1992) *Risk Society*. What are the main features of the risk society and do they apply beyond the advanced industrial societies?

2 In what ways could it be argued that global warming provides strong evidence for Beck's risk society thesis?

ENVIRONMENTAL ISSUES, REAL AND CONSTRUCTED

Constructionism versus critical realism

As the environmental problematic developed in the 1980s, so too did a methodological divide in sociological studies of environmental issues between social constructionists and critical realists. The debates between these two groups were often heated and acrimonious, and a brief outline of the terms of this divide will show why. However, more recent approaches have tried to bridge or circumvent this divide, and examples are discussed towards the end of the section.

In general terms, social contructionists have tended to develop a 'sociology of the environment'. That is, environmental issues are studied, from the perspective of sociology, as *social* problems that can be analysed in similar ways to other types of social problem (Sutton 2004). Constructionists investigate the way that some environmental issues are taken more seriously or gain more urgent attention than others. The approach poses a series of important questions about the claims made for environmental issues, such as who is making the claim, how they articulate that claim, who (if anyone) challenges the claim, and the reasons for their challenge.

In short, environmental issues are, in part, social constructions that can be deconstructed. Doing so may help to explain why the problems perceived as most urgent tend to shift over time, even without resolution. Exploring the process of construction may help us to decide whether an environmental problem really is as serious as the claims-makers say it is. There are at least two broad forms of constructionism outlined in box 10.2.

BOX 10.2 'STRICT' AND 'CONTEXTUAL CONSTRUCTIONISM'

A helpful distinction is that between strict and contextual approaches to social constructionism (Hannigan 2006). Strict constructionists (the minority) point out that the natural environment can never speak to us directly and always needs people to speak for it. Ideas, theories and concepts within society therefore shape the way the natural environment is perceived, appreciated and thought about. Some argue that 'natural' things can be said to exist only if they are either amenable to investigation or useful to human societies. For example, Tester (1991: 46) says that 'A fish is only a fish if it is socially classified as one, and that classification is only concerned with fish to the extent that scaly things living in the sea help society define itself.' Fish certainly are scaly creatures that swim in water, but they are also food, an object of sport (angling), pets (kept in fish tanks), part of home decoration schemes and creatures with inalienable rights. 'Fish' are social constructions and they are constructed in different ways. And, if fish are socially constructed, then the rest of nature must be too.

We can accept all of the uses of fish above, but have we really learned anything about fish? If we apply the same approach to the natural environment, then we might learn how people make use of it, but we will not learn much about the natural environment itself or the impact of human activity on it. Hence, contextual constructionists begin from the premise that environmental problems may well be very real and pressing. However, there are many environmental problems and they do seem to be ranked in order of their perceived significance in society. Currently, global warming seems more urgent than ozone depletion, which is more serious than river pollution, which is more serious than street litter. Yet it is this social ranking that is of interest, because environmental problem claims exist within a changing social context and are influenced by prevailing scientific and political ideas, economic circumstances and cultural attitudes. It is at exactly this point that social constructionism performs a useful function by investigating *all* environmental problem claims, whoever makes or denies them. That way, it may be possible to add something to public understanding of the seriousness of contested environmental issues.

We can see three stages in the process of construction: assembling, presenting and contesting the claim (Hannigan 2006). Every claim has to be assembled to turn a *possible* environmental problem into a *real* one that people believe. This stage requires evidence to be presented which justifies the claim. For instance, in the 1980s the issue of biodiversity loss came to the fore in international politics as the human impact on flora and fauna and species extinctions became a key environmental issue. Species extinctions were already known about, but these were localized in particular countries. Only when an international political infrastructure was created did biodiversity loss start to be seen as more urgent. A legal and organizational infrastructure developed within the United Nations from the 1970s and new agreements, such as the World Cultural and Natural Heritage Convention (1972) and the Convention on International Trade in Endangered Species (known as CITES), gave political credibility and legitimacy to the biodiversity claim. In the 1980s a new subdiscipline, conservation biology,

combined biological evidence with a desire for conservation. Conservation biologists identified endangered species and habitats across the world, lending scientific credibility to the
claim. Linking biodiversity to extinctions also gave it an urgency that other claims did not
have. Naming a claim can have an impact on its success or failure. 'Biodiversity loss' was a
useful label because it tied the problem to something generally understood – the extinction of
dinosaurs in popular science and children's educational programmes.

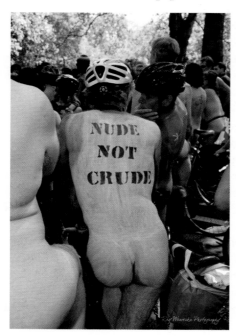

Environmental activists often
use symbolic direct actions as a
way of dramatically presenting
environmental issues which helps
them to construct a particular version
of reality. (© Ray Wewerka/Flickr)

Secondly, the claim has to be *presented*, and this means
grabbing people's attention or otherwise persuading them.
Environmental activists have become specialists in grabbing the public's attention with set-piece demonstrations and
direct actions geared to presentation in the visual mass media.
Greenpeace direct actions, anti-GM and anti-roads protests,
and campaigns targeting airport expansion plans aim to move
people by gaining media attention. They shake people into
action by showing them things they did not know, making an
emotional appeal that might legitimize their claim morally as
well as scientifically. Biodiversity loss was a tough claim to make
because the main losses were in developing countries rather than
in the industrialized world. Why should the latter care about
what happens in the former? One powerful way of presenting
the claim was to argue that tropical rainforests were planetary
resources with unique reserves of biodiversity that may be used
in the advanced medicines of the developed countries too. This
presentation brought biodiversity loss into an understandable
and relevant framework for the general public.

Having assembled and presented a claim, the third stage is
when environmental problem-claims are *contested*. Claims-
makers always upset people. Governments may not find it easy
to face the implications of environmental claims and try to limit
them or deny them. Businesses may not want to hear that their
activities are polluting the environment, and cleaning up will
reduce their profits. Contesting biodiversity loss involved the
relationship between the developing South and industrialized
North. Western companies sought agreement on their right to
patent genetic material from their bioprospecting efforts that would allow them to exploit
natural resources for profit. Environmental activists and national governments in developing
countries rejected these arguments, opposing the legal rights of companies to 'own' genetic
material. The contest in this case was not about the science and of biodiversity loss. Rather
it was about who owns biodiversity and what rights they have over it. The contest actually
helped to popularize the claim in a relatively simple and easily understandable way and, in that
sense, contestation often brings welcome publicity for the claims-makers. By the mid-1990s,
biodiversity loss had become an environmental priority alongside global warming as the most
pressing problem, while other issues such as acid rain, marine pollution and air quality fell
down the ranking order.

The constructionist approach tells us a lot about the various attempts to understand biodiversity loss and how those making the claim managed to get it widely accepted. However, constructionism is agnostic about the issue itself. Is biodiversity loss really a serious environmental problem that requires our urgent attention? Is it more serious than other environmental issues? The analysis of claims-making and claims-denying tells us much we did not know before, but it cannot tell us what to do about biodiversity loss, and this, for some, is the frustrating aspect of the approach. Of what use is constructionism to policy-makers, governments or the general public? One response is that making decisions about which problems should be tackled is a political act, not something that can be left to sociologists. The great virtue of constructionism is that it can facilitate a wider and better informed public engagement with environmental issues. But not everyone agrees, and realists of various kinds take issue with the constructionist approach.

Critical realism

Critics of social constructionism have generally been unhappy with what they see as its failure to accept or acknowledge the reality of the active natural environment. They argue that ways must be found to bring the reality of the natural environment into sociological research. The most widely advocated alternative has been critical realism, sometimes referred to as 'environmental realism' in this field (Benton 1994; Martell 1994; Dickens [1992] 2004; Bell 2011). I will use both terms interchangeably. For most realists, a 'sociology of the environment' is not enough. Environmental issues demand an *environmental sociology* – a sociology that takes into account the reality of the natural world within which societies exist and on which they depend. Their starting point is that human societies are part of the natural environment and should be studied together using the same method, which should be capable of uncovering the underlying causes of events.

The best way to understand critical realism is to look at some examples that demonstrate some of the key points and arguments. Modern agriculture is a good place to begin. Commercial crop production yields outputs that are literally impossible using traditional methods, while the widespread application of pesticides and fertilizers have allowed industrialized societies to remove some natural obstacles to food production. Farmed animals are commercial products, with cattle selectively bred and scientifically 'improved' to produce rapid muscle-growth. Cows can be continuously pregnant to facilitate the continuous supply of milk for human consumption. For human beings the industrialization of agriculture has been of immense significance. Yet in the process the natural capacities and abilities of plants and animals have been pushed to their natural limits and beyond. Cattle suffer because of their large size and weight, which puts strain on the bones, and in the forced pregnancies of cows whose calves are so large that the natural act of giving birth is too risky without human intervention. Pigs, naturally intelligent animals requiring stimulation and activity, can become so bored in factory farms they will bite off each other's tails and ears, while respiratory disease is widespread in such environments. Industrial crop production has led to quite staggering amounts of chemical pesticides and fertilizers being used on land, which leeches into watercourses, polluting rivers, seas and lakes. Crops become overly standardized, reducing biodiversity and leading to the effective extinction of some species through loss of habitat.

For environmental realists, the consequences of industrial farming tell us something sociologically significant. Animals and plants, indeed the natural environment as a whole, are so much more than just the ways in which human societies use them. The natural environment has a reality over and above all human constructions. Arguably, one of the most striking examples of this 'intransigence of nature' – the natural limitation of human manipulation of natural things – was the British epidemic of Bovine Spongiform Encephalopathy (BSE) – commonly known as mad-cow disease – discussed in box 10.3.

BOX 10.3 BSE CROSSES THE SPECIES BARRIER

In cattle, BSE is a fatal neurodegenerative disease, with symptoms similar to scrapie in sheep and Creutzfeldt–Jakob Disease (CJD) in human beings: loss of coordination and memory, nervousness, and aggression (hence 'mad' cows). Scrapie has never interfered with sheep-farming and the consumption of meat from sheep because the disease has not crossed the species barrier into humans; nor had CJD ever been previously related to BSE. But, in 1996, the British government admitted the theoretical possibility that at least ten recent human deaths had been caused by a new variant of CJD in humans (vCJD), which may have developed as a result of people eating BSE-infected beef during the 1980s.

The subsequent UK BSE Inquiry Report highlighted 'the recycling of animal protein in ruminant feed' – a long-standing practice that had continued in spite of previous warnings of the possible dangers of feeding animal protein to cattle, which are naturally herbivorous. In effect, the spread of BSE among cattle was explained by the cattle being fed BSE-infected offal (Macnaghten and Urry 1998: 253–65). Before the 1980s, the scrapie agent had been destroyed by chemicals and high temperatures in the production of animal feed but, once temperatures were lowered in the process, the scrapie prion survived, leading to the spread of BSE in cattle, which then made its way into the food chain. The inquiry noted that the link between BSE and the human vCJD 'was now clearly established'.

Although the BSE episode led to changes in meat-rendering practices and the implementation of other safeguards to avoid its happening again, this did not completely stem growing public mistrust in science, politics, regulatory bodies and the meat industry. In 2013 the discovery of horsemeat in processed food products labelled as 'beef' across Europe again drew attention to food production. The food production and distribution system is one of those 'abstract systems' (Giddens 1990) which are largely hidden from view or taken for granted by most citizens and in which they invest their trust. Only when problems emerge does the reality of modern food production methods become evident and that trust is challenged. Yet food production systems now stretch across nation-states and regions as processes of globalization reshape modern life, and it seems unlikely that romantic ideals of self-sufficiency could ever support current population levels across the world.

BSE may seem at first glance like a naturally occurring problem of disease in animals that was identified by science and resolved through the political process. But on closer examination we see that the crisis was caused by decisions made in the animal feed production system.

A critical realist approach would suggest that, to understand this event properly . . ., we need to know what kind of creatures cows are: what are their natural capacities? We also need to understand human beings to know why the disease had such devastating effects on people. What happens when infected foodstuff finds its way into the human body? We also need to know how the animal food production system operates and what political and economic decisions were made that allowed dead animals to be fed to others. And we need culturally specific knowledge – just why do so many people eat so much beef in the UK? (Giddens and Sutton 2013: 161)

Sociology cannot answer all of these questions. We need findings from biology, zoology, history, sociology, political science and more. Like social constructionists, realists agree that cows are social as well as natural creatures, but there is a reality to cattle that has to be understood if we are to arrive at a satisfactory explanation as to why BSE and vCJD developed. Taking into account the objective reality of natural objects and environments means rethinking sociological theories and concepts so that the discipline can accommodate natural processes.

Beyond polarization

Given the entrenched positions of the realism vs. constructionism debate, some sociologists have tried to move beyond both to develop new ways of studying environmental issues. What is needed are ways of connecting 'the social' and 'the natural' within a single framework that would enable a new research programme for environmental sociologists. One example is Macnaghten and Urry's *Contested Natures* (1995, 1998). Macnaghten and Urry argue that sociologists should concentrate on 'embedded social practices' that are constituted in several ways. Examples are through discourse: in the way that people in social groups speak of, write about and construct models of nature and the environment; through embodiment: the way that people sense or experience nature and natural objects; through space: via differing conceptualizations of local, national and global forms of nature; through time: in changing ideas around the immediacy or longevity of environmental problems; and, finally, through models of human activity, including theories of human nature and what the specifically human natural capabilities might be. Taken together, these elements generate particular social practices that are amenable to analysis. The focus on social practices is intended to open up new questions that realism and social constructionism have not considered and to explore a sociology of the environment after the society/nature dualism has been dissolved.

In Britain, the Lake District is seen as an area of natural beauty and national heritage. It is also a national park governed by the Lake District National Park Authority (LDNPA). One reason why the Lake District is valued in this way is the social discourse that sees 'unspoiled' natural areas as inherently beautiful. A host of writers, poets and novelists have spoken of the Lakes in this way, from Wordsworth to Ruskin. Yet, at the start of the eighteenth century, Daniel Defoe had seen this same landscape as 'the wildest, most barren and frightful' he had ever seen (Macnaghten and Urry 1998: 114). In this period, wild nature was widely seen as unproductive, untamed and containing all manners of hidden dangers that were best avoided (Thomas 1984). 'Development' was necessary and beneficial. The discursive construction of the Lake District has clearly changed. Not only has the discourse on the Lakes changed, but so too has people's sensual experience of it. Viewing this landscape is experienced as pleasant and satisfying rather than frightening. Hearing the sound of rivers and waterfalls, smelling the woods and flowers, touching the bark of old trees, all are involved in the reconfiguration of 'the nature experience'. Instead of interpreting these things as dirty, obnoxious and uncivilized, many natural objects are now routinely experienced as positive and life-affirming (Elias [1939] 2000). The concept of space also enters Macnaghten and Urry's analysis in the form of a discussion of 'walking practices'. In the Lake District the practice of hill or 'fell' walking has become very popular with tourists. Such spatial practices help to shape the experience of people in such environments. To climb the Lake District fells is to commune with traditional and 'timeless' natural forces and, in this way, the concept of time is brought into people's experience of nature. The relatively new social practices of the mass tourist industry have helped to change the way that such landscapes are now appreciated and experienced.

All the elements in Macnaghten and Urry's model come together not just through discourse or textual meanings, but via changing social practices that alter dominant meanings and sensual experience, together with understandings and experiences of time, space and human nature. The benefit of focusing on social practices is that it effectively bypasses both realism and constructionism as *distinct* approaches. We do not have to accept that nature speaks directly to society, but nor is it necessary to claim that nature has no causal powers of its own. Rather, the natural and the social are closely bound together within the same social practices.

A second example comes from Alan Irwin's *Sociology and the Environment* (2001). Irwin adopts a sociology of scientific knowledge (SSK) perspective, arguing that most environmental problems are neither self-evidently 'problems' nor entirely social constructions. Environmental issues are *hybrids* of the social and the natural that are co-constructed. The concept of co-construction promises to avoid the criticisms levelled at strict constructionism, referring to the way that, to the extent that environmental issues are constructed, this is always a co-construction involving both the social and the natural within the same 'nature–culture nexus' (Irwin 2001: 174). It is not simply that 'the social' constructs 'the natural', but the social also constructs the social. Hence a co-constructionist analysis bypasses the nature/society dualism (Demeritt 1998). In the analysis of environmental problems, a co-constructionist approach asks some basic constructionist questions to do with how nature is being discussed, written about and experienced, but it also draws attention to the way that the social is being written about, experienced and discussed. In this way Irwin believes that the tired old dualism can be circumvented.

In cases such as BSE, pesticide use, nuclear energy and many others, we have to accept that the taken-for-granted separation of nature and society does not apply. Environmental issues are, at root, hybrids of nature, science and society, which call into question not just the legitimate role of sociologists but also the disciplinary boundaries of science and the ability of specialized disciplines to understand environmental issues. It is unlikely that any single discipline will have enough expertise to arrive at a comprehensive explanation. However, in practice, it is not clear how 'the natural' plays any significant part in co-constructionist studies. What comes through more clearly is the way that 'the social' constructs *both* the social and the natural, making it very difficult to see how 'nature' plays any active role. What we see much more clearly are 'contested natures', which are produced through the activities of social and political processes. Despite their laudable aim, it seems that both Irwin and Macnaghten and Urry's approaches remain quite close to mainstream constructionist studies.

Nonetheless, over time the constructionist–realist divide has become a little less sharp, and more scholars are interested in moving away from or beyond it. This is probably a 'good thing', though it will always be the case that critically minded sociologists (aren't we all?) will treat all natural science claims of an unambiguous 'reality', about which we should all be concerned, with a healthy scepticism. This should not mean that we do not engage with other disciplines, though. One of the founders of North American environmental sociology, Riley Dunlap (2011: 23–5), recently argued that constructivism–realism is giving way to a broader difference between 'agnosticism–pragmatism'. Pragmatist studies make use of a range of data sources and indicators, both quantitative and qualitative, drawn from a diversity of scientific disciplines in order to address the relationships between social and environmental factors. For instance, research on environmental justice and inequality has made use of both government statistics and indicators of environmental quality, as well as original research into the quality of life for differently positioned (both geographically and socially) groups. The pragmatic use of data based on the evidence that research questions demand offers one promising possibility for interdisciplinary working in environmental sociology.

SEMINAR QUESTIONS

1 Choose one environmental issue and analyse the claims made for it using the three stages of a constructionist approach: assembling, presenting and contesting. How successful is this approach?

2 'Given that the "natural environment" is culturally determined, realist social theory is based on a false premise.' Critically discuss this statement.

GLOBAL WARMING: SCIENCE, SCEPTICS AND SOCIOLOGY

The scientific case for anthropogenic climate change

In the present period, one environmental issue has come to dominate all others: global warming, the gradual increase in the average surface temperature on planet Earth. On this measure, the years 1998, 2005 and 2010 were the warmest years on record since reliable measurements began in the late nineteenth century; according to NASA data, nine of the ten warmest years ever recorded have occurred since 2000 (NASA 2012). The effects of very hot weather can be catastrophic, and an increasing average temperature may have a severe impact on regions that already have high temperatures. In 2003, a serious heat wave in Europe was estimated by the Earth Policy Institute (an environmental think-tank) to have killed almost 40,000 people in Europe (14,802 in France, where the crisis was most severe), who died from causes attributable to the extreme temperatures (Bhattacharya 2003).

Climate change will have an impact on every society on the planet (albeit to varying degrees), and in this sense it is the clearest example of a genuinely global environmental problem. Global warming is perhaps the ultimate test case for sociology. What role is there for social scientists in understanding, explaining and resolving the issue of planetary warming? It has taken quite some time, but at last some sociologists are making a very strong case that a sociological perspective is an urgent necessity if we are properly to understand the underlying causes of global warming, its social consequences and its possible solutions. Before we explore this claim, we need a brief guide to the science of climate change, contained in box 10.4.

A majority of climate scientists argue that a large part of the increase in levels of CO_2 in the atmosphere can be attributed to the burning of fossil fuels, industrial production, large-scale agriculture, deforestation, mining, and landfill and vehicle emissions. The spread of industrialization around the globe has produced major, world-historical environmental change. The Intergovernmental Panel on Climate Change (IPCC 2007) – an international

BOX 10.4 THE SCIENCE OF GLOBAL WARMING

The gradual rise in the Earth's average surface temperature is due to changes in the chemical composition of the atmosphere. The current scientific consensus is that what we are currently witnessing is in large part 'anthropogenic global warming' – i.e., caused by humans – since the composition of the Earth's atmosphere is being caused by the build-up of the very gases that are produced in immense quantities by industrial processes and modern life. Although this section will necessarily outline key findings from climate science, bear in mind that the causes of anthropogenic warming are essentially social and that the experts in understanding the development and consequences of capitalism, industrialization and modern forms of organization, for example, are sociologists. There is no reason for sociologists to avoid the conclusion that understanding, explaining and mitigating global warming (and other environmental problems) must be an interdisciplinary endeavour.

The build-up of heat-trapping gases within the Earth's atmosphere contributes to the greenhouse effect: while most energy from the Sun is absorbed directly by the Earth, with some of it being reflected back, greenhouse gases act as a barrier to the outgoing energy and, in a similar way to the glass panels in a greenhouse, trap heat within the atmosphere. This natural greenhouse effect is what keeps the Earth at an average surface temperature of about 15.5° Celsius, as opposed to the −17° Celsius it would be if greenhouse gases didn't play this important role. With rising concentrations of greenhouse gases there is an intensification of this natural greenhouse effect, which results in even warmer temperatures. The concentration of greenhouse gases has risen significantly since the start of industrialization, and this continued apace from the 1970s (see figure 10.1): a 30 percent rise in carbon dioxide – the main greenhouse gas – since 1880, a doubling of methane concentrations, a 15 percent rise in nitrous oxide concentrations, and rises in other greenhouse gases that do not occur naturally.

The principal greenhouse gases that enter the atmosphere because of human activities are:

Carbon dioxide (CO_2) Carbon dioxide enters the atmosphere through the burning of fossil fuels (oil, natural gas and coal), solid waste, trees and wood products, and also as a result of other chemical reactions (e.g., manufacture of cement). Carbon dioxide is also removed from the atmosphere (or 'sequestered') when it is absorbed by plants as part of the biological carbon cycle.

Methane (CH_4) Methane is emitted during the production and transport of coal, natural gas and oil. Methane emissions also result from livestock and other agricultural practices and by the decay of organic waste in municipal solid waste landfills.

Nitrous oxide (N_2O) Nitrous oxide is emitted during agricultural and industrial activities, as well as during combustion of fossil fuels and solid waste.

Fluorinated gases Hydrofluorocarbons, perfluorocarbons and sulfur hexafluoride are synthetic, powerful greenhouse gases that are emitted from a variety of industrial processes. Fluorinated gases are sometimes used as substitutes for ozone-depleting substances (i.e., CFCs, HCFCs and halons). These gases are typically emitted in smaller quantities but, because they are potent greenhouse gases, are sometimes referred to as High Global Warming Potential gases ('High GWP gases').

Source: www.epa.gov/climatechange/ghgemissions/.

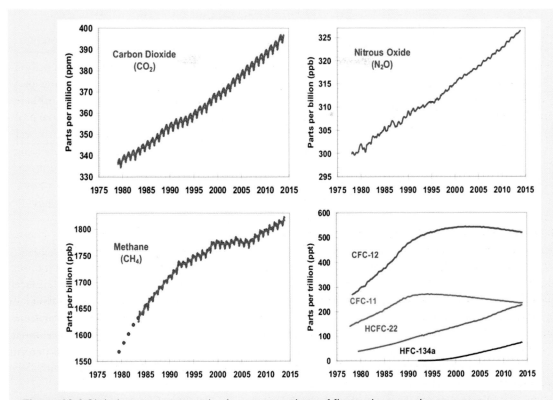

Figure 10.1 Global average atmospheric concentrations of five major greenhouse gases

Source: US Department of Commerce, National Oceanic and Atmospheric Administration, 2009.

body set up in 1988 by the United Nations Environment Programme (UNEP) and the World Meteorological Organization (WMO) – evaluates evidence on climate change from across the world. When comparing a model based on only 'natural forcings' ('natural' climate change) and a model based on natural *and* anthropogenic forcings, in conjunction with actual observations of global warming and climate change, their report states that it is 'very likely' that the increase in observed temperatures since the mid-twentieth century is due to increasing anthropogenic greenhouse gas emissions (see figure 10.2). The language used by the IPCC is necessarily cautious, but this conclusion is stronger than that arrived at six years earlier, which suggests that the evidence for human-induced climate change is becoming stronger over time.

The social impacts of global warming

The impacts of global warming are likely to be experienced to uneven degrees across the world: there will be devastating consequences for some regions and countries, but not for all. The following is a selection of social impacts suggested by the IPCC's Fourth Assessment Report (2007: 50–2):

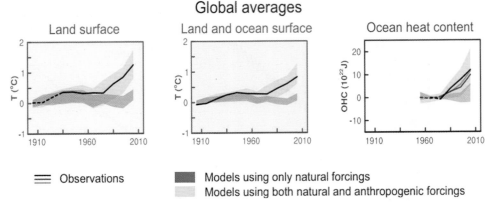

Figure 10.2 Global and continental temperature change: natural forcing and natural plus anthropogenic forcing

Source: IPCC (2013: 18).

1 By 2020, some 75 to 250 million people across Africa will experience greater stress on water supplies, and agricultural yields may fall by as much as 50 percent, severely compromising access to adequate levels of food and increasing levels of undernourishment. The IPCC also forecasts an increase in arid land by 2080 of between 5 and 8 percent in Africa, while a rise in sea levels would affect the low-lying coastal areas with large populations.

2 In Central, East, South and South-East Asia, availability of freshwater is forecast to be reduced by 2050, leading to increasing problems with water security. Coastal areas are likely to be subject to flooding, both from rivers and from the sea. Sickness and deaths from diarrhoeal diseases will rise as global warming changes the hydrological cycle, making floods and drought more common.

3 In Latin America, eastern Amazonia is likely to see tropical forests becoming savannah as soils dry out, and semi-arid vegetation will be lost. Food security will be reduced as the productivity of crops and livestock declines, resulting in more people at risk of undernourishment and chronic hunger. Shifting rainfall patterns will lead to uncertain water supplies for drinking water and agriculture.

4 In Australia and New Zealand the forecast is for a loss of biodiversity in some important sites, including the Great Barrier Reef. Water insecurity will increase in southern and eastern Australia and parts of New Zealand. Agricultural production will decline in much of southern and eastern Australia and eastern New Zealand because of increasing droughts and fires.

5 In Europe, more frequent coastal flooding and coastal erosion are expected due to sea level rises and more severe storms. Southern Europe will see more drought and higher temperatures that will reduce the availability of water and crop productivity, and higher temperatures will worsen health problems arising from heat waves.

6 North America will experience more intense and frequent heat waves in cities that already have problems, bringing increasing health problems. Warming in the western mountains is likely to cause more flooding in winter and reduced flows in the summer months.

7   Rising sea levels are likely to present major challenges for many small island communities in the Pacific and Caribbean. Storm surges will be higher and erosion exacerbated, threatening communities and infrastructure. By the mid-twenty-first century, water resources are likely to be reduced to the point that they will not be sufficient to meet demand during times of low rainfall.

(Giddens and Sutton 2013: 179–80)

Questioning climate change science

Some sceptics argue that global warming is not actually occurring at all. One of the most prominent of these climate change deniers has been the former chancellor of the exchequer Nigel Lawson, who, though he accepts that there has been 'mild warming' in the last quarter of the twentieth century, argues that there has been a 'lull' in global warming in the twenty-first century (2009: 1) and charges climate scientists with cherry-picking their evidence. The position held by Lord Lawson has been challenged, however, by the UK government's chief scientific adviser, Sir John Beddington, who argued that Lawson was 'making "incorrect" and "misleading" claims' based on short-term trends which 'are meaningless in the context of global warming', and that scientific evidence from multiple sources shows that 'the risks are real' (Boffey 2011). However, this all points to the way the 'science' of climate change is now under scrutiny as never before, particularly following some potentially damaging allegations.

In 2009, in an affair which has become known as 'ClimateGate', the Climatic Research Unit (CRU) at the University of East Anglia in the UK had its email system hacked and around 1,000 emails were published online. Sceptics saw clear signs of the 'cherry-picking' of evidence and even possible falsification of data in some of the email exchanges. This related to emails in which the CRU director, Professor Phil Jones, spoke of performing 'a trick' with climate data and 'hiding the decline' in temperature for one data series, as well as admitting to refusing repeated requests to share data with critics. For sceptics, this was proof that many climate change scientists were prepared to sacrifice key principles in order to further and protect their careers and reputations, which were tightly bound up with proving anthropogenic global warming. The following year, the vice-chair of the IPCC, faced with criticisms from glaciologists, was forced to retract a claim in the 2007 report that Himalayan glaciers 'could disappear by 2035'. How many other IPCC predictions are incorrect?

Professor Jones argued that his email comments were taken out of context. By speaking of a 'trick' he was referring to an innovative way of joining two data sets; by speaking of 'hiding the decline' he was referring to correcting a false impression in one data set by including extra instrumental data (BBC 2010). Three independent inquiries were set up to investigate 'ClimateGate', and none found any evidence of scientific malpractice, falsification of data or attempts to subvert the peer review process. A further review commissioned by the Dutch government in 2010 also upheld the IPCC's main forecasts, finding no errors that might call into question the central finding that anthropogenic climate change was real. However, the affairs have allowed sceptics to cast more doubt on the conclusions of climate science.

A second line of criticism is that global warming *is* real but that it has nothing to do with human activity, as global warming is a natural phenomenon related to the fluctuating activity of the Sun. While the majority scientific view accepts that fluctuations in solar activity affect the Earth's surface temperature, the suggestion that present global warming could be caused naturally is challenged by the fact that there is no evidence to point to an increase in solar activity since the 1960s that would be needed to produce it. Even accepting the reality of anthropogenic global warming, a third criticism posed by sceptics is that our response is wrongheaded. Given the unreliability of the computer modelling of the kind used by the IPCC (particularly when extrapolating current trends far into the future), the predicted consequences are highly speculative at best and grossly exaggerated at worst. Therefore valuable resources, along with political, economic and social efforts, should be directed to other more urgent social problems, such as poverty in developing countries (Lomborg 2001).

However, the ongoing IPCC research programme remains the most reliable, evidence-based assessment currently available, though some argue that it actually tends to be quite conservative in its conclusions (McGuire 2008). 'The Fourth Assessment Report notes that, since 1990, IPCC forecast values have averaged 0.15 to 0.3° increase per decade, which compares favourably with the observed increase between 1990 and 2005 of 0.2° Celsius per decade. Such evidence suggests that the IPCC modelling is, in fact, quite realistic' (Giddens and Sutton 2013: 182).

Responding to global warming

Governments have tried to reach international agreement on stabilizing and reducing greenhouse gas emissions, the most notable attempt being the Kyoto Protocol created in 1997 in Kyoto, Japan. Agreement was reached to cut greenhouse gas emissions significantly by 2012, with different targets for different countries, ranging from an average 8 percent cut for most of Europe to a maximum 10 percent increase for Iceland. In recent years there have been some success stories where large greenhouse-gas-producing states have cut emissions, including the UK, Germany, China and Russia. However, the effectiveness of these efforts can be questioned. The USA – one of the largest emitters of CO_2 – has not ratified the agreement (having originally committed to a 7 percent cut). According to many climate scientists the targets are in any case too modest and stronger action would be needed, particularly when one considers that CO_2 will remain in the atmosphere for a century after emission.

There are also claims that the Kyoto Protocol favours industrialized countries, since it bases a country's target on their greenhouse emission levels as they stood in 1990, thereby ignoring industrialized countries' 'historical responsibility' for the problem of global warming (Najam, Huq and Sokona 2003: 223). Most greenhouse gases are produced by industrialized countries, though emissions from the developing world are increasing rapidly as these countries undergo industrialization. It is this industrialization which is helping countries to develop and improve the lives of huge numbers of people across the world. As such some argue that these 'survival' emissions cannot be considered in the same way as the 'luxury' emissions of the already rich countries, arguing that it is reducing the latter which is most urgent while developing countries must be allowed to 'pollute to catch up'. Any international agreement which does not take into account the inevitably higher emissions of developing countries as they seek to catch up will be seen as unfair and unworkable (Najam, Huq and Sokona 2003).

Following a 'Washington Declaration' in 2007 (approved by the G8 countries along with China, India, Brazil, Mexico and South Africa), the 2009 Copenhagen talks failed to secure a binding agreement amid acrimonious disagreements. It was not until the 2010 Cancun meeting that progress was widely seen as being made among the 190 countries who agreed to the voluntary targets set out in Copenhagen and to limit temperature rises to 2° Celsius.

Importantly, a commitment worth US$100 billion was made to help developing countries grow economically without putting such pressure on the atmosphere. There are still critics, however, who argue that the measures in place are not radical enough to prevent a 2 degree warming.

In responding to global warming as sociologists, we recognize that an understanding not only of basic climate science but also of social processes is needed to grasp the underlying anthropogenic causes of climate change, and that there is a clear role for sociological theories and research. John Urry (2011: 15–16) argues that sociology was founded in the 'carbonized' era of modernity and was essentially unconcerned with the resource base of modern life. But what is now needed is a 'post-carbon sociology' for the post-carbon world into which we are moving. However, convincing people and businesses in the developed world to change their behaviour has proved to be extraordinarily difficult. 'There is a disjunction between the widespread acceptance of global warming and people being prepared to change their routine behaviour to help tackle it' (Giddens and Sutton 2013: 183).

Giddens (2011) argues that, because the dangers of unchecked global warming have no tangible effects on their everyday lives, people will not change their behaviour. For instance, as the price of petrol and diesel has risen rapidly over recent years, it is striking how people have remained committed to using their private vehicles. Some routines are clearly much harder to break than others. But if everyone waits until global warming *does* interfere with their lives, it will be too late to do anything about it – a 'catch 22' situation. Hence, ways have to be found to 'embed a concern with climate change into people's everyday lives, while recognizing the formidable problems involved in doing so' (Giddens 2011: 12). And yet, social practices *do* and *have* changed quite significantly in relatively short periods of time. The best example is perhaps the spread of recycling among households, which may have started as a grudging acceptance of government initiatives but over time has developed into a strong environmental commitment for many individuals, who now push for an expansion of the process. Without the positive involvement of the critical mass of individual citizens it is unrealistic to think that state policies alone can succeed.

Like Giddens, Urry argues that there is much that states can do to promote a low-carbon future. However, he is keen to stress that environmentally damaging social practices must also change. It is likely that the latter will prove very difficult as systems of resource use and the routines of social life tend to be sedimented over long periods, thereby becoming normalized. Shove (2003) argues that sociology is unlikely to make real progress in this area if it focuses merely on 'green consumption' and ecologically benign technologies. Many of the most energy-rich or 'wasteful' behaviours, such as frequent showering, heavy use of domestic hot water and constant central heating, are actually embedded within the routines of daily life. They have become normalized as aspects of the 'comfort, cleanliness and convenience' that modern life affords and are therefore largely invisible. Shove suggests that exploring how such energy uses become normalized in the first place is a more productive avenue for sociological research (Shove and Spurling 2013).

It is true that, faced with a manufactured risk we have not experienced before, many questions remain as to what the effects of global warming will be. 'Would a "high" emissions scenario truly result in widespread natural disasters? Will stabilizing the level of carbon dioxide emissions protect most people from the negative effects of climate change? Is it possible that global warming has already triggered a series of further climatic disturbances?' (Giddens and

Sutton 2013: 184). While the answers to these and many other questions are uncertain, the combination of international scientific collaboration, political agreements and positive building of 'lower-carbon' social practices and everyday routines offers the most viable ways of dealing with the problem.

SEMINAR QUESTIONS

1 In what ways, if any, are sociologists better equipped than the 'intelligent layperson' to assess the evidence on global warming?

2 Review the sceptical arguments against the global warming thesis. What evidence is there that the IPCC case has been overstated?

SUSTAINABLE DEVELOPMENT: THEORIES AND PRACTICES

The concept of sustainable development

The concept of sustainable development is politically contested, flexible and open to conflicting interpretations. It is also not entirely novel and 'had been espoused by German and Indian foresters, and by Roosevelt and [Gifford] Pinchot', among others (McCormick 1992: 149). Nonetheless, some version of it underpins the thinking of many environmentalists, governments and international agencies concerned with how environmental problems can adequately be dealt with. The combination of the idea of *sustainability*, with its focus on maintaining the natural environment, and *development*, with the emphasis on economic and social progress, gives the sustainable development concept a particularly inclusive content. While this is a possible strength of 'sustainability talk', it can also make the public discourse of sustainability appear incoherent and discordant, meaning all things to all people.

The seminal report *Our Common Future* (1987) (known as the Brundtland Report, after its President, Gro Harlem Brundtland) produced by the World Commission on Environment and Development (WCED), defined sustainable development as 'development which meets the needs of the present without compromising the ability of future generations to meet their own needs'. This definition brings together the global conservation of resources and economic development in poorer countries and, as such, appeals to northern environmentalists *and* activists in developing countries. However, it is premised on the questionable idea that we could know today what the needs of future generations might be. The report also linked sustainable development to the elimination of gross inequalities between the Global North and South, raising questions about resource distribution and international power relations (Baker et al. 1997). Yet some see sustainable development as ultimately dominated by Western ideals. For instance, Jacobs (1999: 35) argues that 'There can be little doubt that protecting the environment is the dominant motivation for and idea within sustainable development.'

Sustainable development initiatives cover the whole range of human activity and social development, and it is not possible to cover anything close to this range here. However, a flavour of what is involved can be gleaned from the eight Millennium Development Goals set by the UN in 2000 for achievement by 2015. These are to:

1 *eradicate extreme poverty and hunger* – reduce by half the 1.3 billion people living on less than $1 a day and the 815 million without enough food to meet daily energy needs;

2 *achieve universal primary education* – 115 million children, most in sub-Saharan Africa and Southern Asia, do not go to school. Reduce this number;

3 *promote gender equality and empower women* – in three main areas – education, employment and political decision-making;

4 *reduce child mortality* – 11 million children die before the age of five, most from treatable diseases. The aim is to cut this by two-thirds;

5 *improve maternal health* – particularly in sub-Saharan Africa, by investing in health facilities, birth attendants and education;

6 *combat HIV/AIDS, malaria and other diseases* – an estimated 39.4 million people are living with HIV, and malaria kills more than 1 million people per year. The aim is to reduce these numbers significantly;

7 *ensure environmental sustainability* – reverse the loss of environmental resources (forests, biological diversity, the ozone layer), provide safe water and adequate sanitation and affordable housing;

8 *develop a global partnership for development* – encourage the North to increase aid to developing countries, to move to fairer trade and to cancel the debts of struggling developing countries (in June 2005, it was agreed to cancel $40 billion debt of eighteen countries to the World Bank, International Monetary Fund and African Development Bank).

Is it realistic or fair to expect developing countries to prioritize environmental sustainability over economic development? (© Oxfam International/Flickr)

This is a mixture of clear targets and vague objectives, some of which seem achievable, some well nigh impossible. There is also a mixture of social and environmental issues to be tackled, with a strong focus on improving the conditions of life for millions of people in the developing world. It may well be possible to get more children into primary schools and reduce child mortality in some developing countries, but will there really be environmental sustainability by 2015? That flies in the face of all the available evidence. In fact, the Millennium Report itself describes the outlook for achieving this goal as 'grim'.

The body charged with monitoring the implementation of initiatives aimed at achieving these goals is the Commission on Sustainable Development (CSD), which looks for good examples and best practice across the world, reporting these back in the form of case studies. An interesting area to consider is energy production and use, because this clearly links economic and social development with environmental protection. The long-term goal is to move towards energy production systems that can produce sustainable and reliable energy in developing countries and yet also be sustainable in terms of their consequences for the natural environment. If sustainability can be demonstrated in this key area, then it would go a long way towards answering the critics of such a consensus-seeking international political process.

Energy production and use are fundamental elements of any policy aiming at sustainable forms of development, though debates on the way forward can be extremely confusing and conflictual. In the relatively rich countries of the northern hemisphere, governments and businesses are experimenting with renewable energy sources while continuing to rely on coal, oil, gas and nuclear power for the bulk of their generation needs. In developing countries, forms of social organization and the urban–rural population balance may be very different, but energy generation remains a thorny problem for a genuinely sustainable policy. Developing countries with large natural reserves of fossil fuels, such as China and India, are likely to use them simply because they are available and comparatively cheap to extract and use. However, if this happens in relatively unregulated ways, then all of the efforts to restrict greenhouse gases through the terms of the Kyoto Protocol may be called into question. We have space here for only one example from the developing world, and that is the energy situation in India, in box 10.5.

The case of Indian energy production illustrates the problem of sustainable development quite well. In principle there are renewable energy resources available to replace coal burning and the use of gas and oil, but these alternatives are expensive and currently unattractive. The urban–rural population balance in India and elsewhere means that small-scale energy production systems such as domestic bio-gas plants and energy-efficient wood-burning stoves are more likely to fit local energy production practices than attempting simply to eliminate the national coal-fired thermal power stations and replace these with solar and wind power. But if, as seems likely, the vast coal reserves available to India (and China) are to be used for energy generation in the future, then the country will continue to be an overall contributor to global warming. The current pace of change to energy generation patterns will just not be rapid enough to make a significant difference to the global situation. What we see here is certainly very welcome economic 'development', but is it 'sustainable' in environmental terms?

Towards global sustainability?

In 2000, the United Nations secretary-general, Kofi Annan, called for a *Millennium Ecosystem Assessment* (MEA) that would involve experts from around the world to produce an overall evaluation of the state of the global ecosystem in light of the pressures placed on it by human activity. This resulted in a board statement in March 2005 entitled *Living Beyond Our Means* (a highly provocative title), which begins with the 'stark warning' that 'Human activity is putting such strain on the natural functions of Earth that the ability of the planet's ecosystems to sustain future generations can no longer be taken for granted.' It suggests that, in the quest to satisfy their growing demands, human societies have now 'taken the planet to the edge of a massive wave of species extinctions, further threatening our own well-being'. In one sense, this is something of an indictment of the concept and practice of sustainable development.

BOX 10.5 SUSTAINABLE ENERGY IN DEVELOPING COUNTRIES

India is the second most populous country on Earth (behind China). It remains heavily dependent on coal reserves, which supply around 60 percent of its energy generation. Coal is a non-renewable fossil fuel which, when burned, releases carbon dioxide, a greenhouse gas that most scientists accept makes a major contribution to continuing and worsening the problem of global warming. India also generates 24 percent from hydro power and imports a large amount of crude oil for domestic use. Nuclear power and energy from renewable sources are minimal, and one reason for this is the high start-up costs involved, which are beyond not just India but much of the developing world. However, there is excellent potential for solar energy production, as it is estimated that India receives some 5,000 trillion kilowatt hours (Kwh) of solar radiation per annum. But the cost involved in producing and installing the necessary photovoltaic cells is prohibitive, and switching away from existing fossil fuels may be perceived as putting at risk the economic and social progress achieved so far. This is a good example of how a more systematic policy of North–South technology-sharing could speed up the move towards sustainable development in developing countries and, in the process, help to tackle global warming. In India's rural areas, electrification has now reached almost 90 percent of villages and more efficient wood-burning stoves for cooking have been introduced and widely spread. The Indian government is also making efforts at energy conservation, including moving public transport away from diesel to compressed natural gas (CNG).

In rural areas, where wood-burning is the norm, the issue of deforestation is recognized as a serious problem, partially remediable perhaps by programmes of afforestation to create so-called carbon sinks. Carbon sinks are new forests created specifically to counteract the CO_2 production from fossil fuel use. Trees remove carbon dioxide from the atmosphere, and more trees means less CO_2 in the atmosphere, which therefore means a reduction in global greenhouse gases. In this way, carbon sinks may help to provide a better balance against harmful emissions.

However, in January 2006 the UK Royal Society of Chemistry reported on some recent research which shows that trees and other plants actually give off millions of tonnes of methane – another greenhouse gas – every year. Therefore, planting more forests to remove carbon dioxide may not be the straightforward environmental gain previously thought. Even if the net balance of emissions would support more carbon sinks, these will still do nothing to solve the problem of rapidly diminishing natural resources, including fossil fuels. As Urry (2011) has argued, we do seem to be heading inexorably towards a post-carbon world, which will also mean a rethinking of some of sociology's (and economists') long-established assumptions about what modern life will look like in the future.

The MEA also ran a series of future scenarios. Four 'plausible futures' for the next fifty years were constructed, based on differing international approaches. In all four future scenarios, some similar themes and increasing pressures on the natural environment came to the fore. Firstly, human population: global human population is forecast to rise from just over 7 billion today to between 8 and 10 billion by 2050, and much of the increase will be among already poor urban populations in the Middle East, sub-Saharan Africa and South Asia. Population of this magnitude will add increasingly heavy pressure onto the natural environment for energy, food, shelter and consumer goods. Secondly, there is an increasing conversion of land to agricultural use, leading to a reduction of biodiversity and the possibility of large-scale animal and plant extinctions. Thirdly, climate change has a larger impact on economic development, leading to more floods and droughts and making species extinctions more likely.

The report makes three broad suggestions for change that should be more likely to work than any alternative courses of action or those that rely on a single solution. The MEA says that *nature* must be placed at the centre of all efforts and activities. This is an important assessment because it effectively privileges the 'sustainable' side of sustainable development and is likely to appeal more to northern environmentalists than to southern governments. Making nature central to sustainable development is also not very likely unless the real costs of using up natural resources are built in to all economic calculations. This would mean businesses and governments moving away from treating the natural environment simply as the backdrop to human life.

But what would such a change mean in practice? Firstly, an end to agricultural, fishing and energy subsidies that damage the environment, but payment for landowners who manage natural resources, provided they improve water quality and carbon storage (as in afforestation, for instance). Secondly, encouraging local communities to take up conservation activities by making sure they play a proper part in decision-making and share in the benefits that result from their actions. Thirdly, instead of assuming that state environment departments can tackle sustainable development initiatives by themselves, these should be included within *all* of central government's decision-making processes so that nature would really be at the heart of government. Fourthly, businesses should be encouraged and financially enabled to pilot new resource-saving initiatives. Although such suggestions may well be eminently sensible and have some impact on changing the way that governments, business and the public deal with environmental issues, they do seem quite timid when compared to the report's conclusion that we are already 'living beyond our means'.

SEMINAR QUESTIONS

1   Sustainable development is 'development which meets the needs of the present without compromising the ability of future generations to meet their own needs'. How might we forecast what the 'needs' of future generations might be?
2   Read the Millennium Ecosystem Assessment's report (2005), which reaches the conclusion that, as a global humanity, we are 'living beyond our means'. Why do some believe that democratic societies are incapable of taking the measures needed to change people's environmentally damaging behaviour?
3   'The aims of global environmental sustainability and economic development for poorer countries are not compatible.' Using evidence and specific examples, assess the validity of this assertion.

CONCLUSION

It is evident that sociological studies of environmental issues have an extremely broad scope, now constituting a sociological specialism in its own right. Some of the central problems in social theory and in society itself are debated within this field, which brings together academics and political activists, social and natural science findings, and theories of the social and the natural. Environmental sociology may not yet be as established as other sociological specialisms, but it is far from the marginalized 'outsider' it once was. Studying society–environment relations is slowly emerging as one of the most urgent tasks for twenty-first-century sociology.

As I have argued, this task must push sociologists towards interdisciplinary collaboration in order to make use of research from a variety of disciplines from both the social and the natural sciences. Yet the practicality of interdisciplinary working remains a difficult problem, especially when collaboration is across the natural and social sciences with their very different starting points, research methods and disciplinary traditions. Why is this?

We have to acknowledge the fact that there is a hierarchy of scientific disciplines, with the natural sciences generally in relatively more powerful positions than the social sciences (Elias 1982). This relative power difference partly accounts for the defensive strategies of sociologists and their strong reaction to any perceived intrusion by the natural sciences. Acknowledging these broader issues throws the dispute between constructionists and realists into relief. What might appear from the outside as a small local dispute is actually framed by long-standing concerns about the scientific status of sociology and its attempt to demonstrate the existence of a social level of reality.

It is not surprising that most sociological approaches to environmental issues are still closer to constructionism, as this avoids the need to engage with our higher status neighbours. Constructionist research within the tradition of the 'sociology of the environment' is both interesting and produces useful knowledge, and I expect this to continue long into the future. However, it seems likely that, for many interested sociologists, the agnosticism of this body of work risks leaving the discipline open to the charge of irrelevance. Attempts by critical realists and others adopting a pragmatic approach to data collection and testing show that environmental sociologists do not need to become agnostics. Today's pressing global environmental issues can no longer be studied in isolation from the natural world, which means that the disciplinary boundaries of the social and the natural sciences must become much more permeable.

SEMINAR QUESTIONS

1 What could sociologists contribute to interdisciplinary research on climate change?

2 What types of useful knowledge can constructionist approaches produce?

3 What disadvantages and advantages might there be in weakening the disciplinary boundaries between sociology and the natural science?

FURTHER READING

▶ A good place to start is with a genuine introductory text which covers all of the key issues but assumes no expert knowledge of environmental matters. My own book, Sutton, P. W. (2007) *The Environment: A Sociological Introduction* (Polity), is one good example. But then I would say that, wouldn't I?

▶ A reliable guide to theoretical perspectives in this field is indispensable if you intend to study environmental sociology. John Barry is a very good guide, and he writes in a clear and jargon-free style covering important social and political theories of the environment: Barry, J. (2007) *Environment and Social Theory* (2nd edn, Routledge).

▶ The dominant environmental issue of our time is global warming, and it is good to see some of sociology's 'big names' now making a contribution. One of the most interesting and thought-provoking of the latter is John Urry's discussion of a possible 'post-carbon sociology': Urry, J. (2011) *Climate Change and Society* (Polity). Highly recommended.

▶ For simple reasons of space, ecological modernization is not covered in this chapter. However, the perspective has generated many fascinating empirical studies of practical ways of continuing the modernization process but in ecologically benign ways.

I suggest a good collection of recent essays that will help to fill this gap: Mol, A. P. J., D. A. Sonnenfeld and G. Spaargaren (eds) (2009) *The Ecological Modernization Reader: Environmental Reform in Theory and Practice* (Routledge).

▶ Environmental sociology is a very broad enterprise and, to get an idea of how this field has developed and what is new today, try: Redclift, M. R and M. Woodgate (eds) (2011) *The International Handbook of Environmental Sociology* (2nd edn, Edward Elgar). This book contains some excellent articles that illustrate the scope of the specialism.

▶ Finally, readers will have noted that I am strongly in favour of interdisciplinary collaboration. However, they may also wonder what that might look like. It is still quite early days, but an inspiring example of how this could work is: De Vries, B., and J. Goudsblom (eds) (2002) *Mappae Mundi: Humans and their Habitats in a Long-Term Socio-Ecological Perspective – Myths, Maps and Models* (Amsterdam University Press). Contributors include a biologist, a physicist, a sociologist, a social anthropologist, an archaeologist, a historian and a mathematician. Admit it, now you're interested?

11

SCIENCE, TECHNOLOGY AND SOCIAL CHANGE

knowledge, expertise and practices

MARK ERICKSON

CONTENTS

INTRODUCTION

Sociology, science and technology

SOCIOLOGY DOES NOT HAVE a particularly good track record when it comes to questions of science and technology in society, and this may be one reason why these topics receive fairly scant attention in contemporary textbooks. But the topics themselves, the things that we call science and technology, are very significant in our society, and have been for a considerable period of time. Our society needs technology to function, we are surrounded by technologies and representations of technology, we

BOX 11.1 BIG SCIENCE

The sheer scale of science in contemporary society is difficult to imagine. Science got much 'bigger' in the decades immediately following the Second World War, and it did this in a number of ways. The first was through the construction and execution of large science experiments and projects funded by national governments or even international collaborations between governments. CERN, the home of the Large Hadron Collider (LHC), is one such big science project. Founded in 1954 by twelve European states, the European Organization for Nuclear Research was set up to operate large-particle physics experiments, and it opened its first particle accelerator in 1957. CERN employs about 2,500 staff, most of whom are at its main site near Geneva, and it hosts around 10,000 visiting scientists per year. CERN's budget for 2012 was 1,165.9 million Swiss francs (£783 bn) (www.cern.ch).

The scale of the Large Hadron Collider experiment is quite staggering. Located 100 metres below ground, the LHC is a 27 kilometre ring tunnel which accelerates particles to near-light speed and then smashes them together. Detectors are placed through the tunnel to identify the products of these collisions. The largest detector is the Compact Muon Solenoid (CMS), composed of 5,000 magnets joined together in pieces weighing some 2,000 tons each. Simply manoeuvring these into place was a major feat of engineering. The LHC experiment is the most expensive scientific instrument ever built, costing about €7.5 billion. 'Big science' is an apt term for this kind of activity and facility.

Of course, vast quantities of 'small science' experiments are still carried out across the globe. The amount of scientific knowledge produced has expanded dramatically in recent decades as more countries around the world produce more and more scientific research. This increase can be seen in the number of journal articles published. Predictions made in the early 1960s that the number of scientific papers published in journals would double every ten to fifteen years have proved correct, although there is variation between disciplines. For example, chemistry doubles over a twenty-year period and maths over a twenty-two-year period, but technology-oriented papers double in a nine-year period (Larsen and von Ins 2010). Older, well-established disciplines such as mathematics and physics tend to have slower growth rates than new disciplines including computer science and engineering, but the overall growth rate for science has been at least 4.7 percent per year, which gives a doubling time of fifteen years (ibid: 600).

value scientific knowledge above other forms of knowledge, and we use science to explain the world around us. Our world is infused with science and technology and it is difficult to imagine our society without the degree of technology or prevalence of science it has.

BOX 11.2 THE 'BRIAN COX EFFECT'

'Brian Cox effect' leads to surge in demand for physics. One of Britain's top universities has been forced to dramatically raise entrance requirements for its physics course after being flooded with applicants on the back of the popularity of Brian Cox. – *Daily Telegraph*, 11 January 2013 (Paton 2013)
Physics geeks Brianwashed. – *The Sun*, 13 January 2013 (Faulkner 2013)

Physics professor and TV presenter Brian Cox has done much to reinvigorate the popularity among young people of studying science. Cox's advocacy of cosmic wonderment, informal but informed presentational style, and use of spectacular images and special effects is a sure-fire success on TV. BBC programmes such as *Wonders of the Universe* (2011) and *Wonders of Life* (2012) remind us that science can be, and is, popular with general audiences.

Cox does more than just inspire people to study science subjects. His programmes, originally focusing just on astronomy but now covering much wider areas of the natural world, express the assumed unity of the project of science. They also illustrate the hierarchy of science disciplines, with physics at the apex and the applied and life sciences much further down; it is unlikely that a microbiologist, say, would get to present a TV programme about physics or astronomy.

Watching TV programmes like this we learn how to approach science as a whole: Cox visibly expresses a sense of awe and deep respect for nature and the achievements of science.

We know that we need technology to facilitate our lifestyles and we know that we need science to provide us with knowledge of what the world is and to produce more technologies for us. In our everyday lives we tell ourselves this story of science and technology in many different ways and places – from courts of law to science fiction films, from TV nature programmes to mobile phone adverts, from doctors' surgeries to health food stores. And the story we tell ourselves about science and technology is one that we learn from an early age as we are socialized (see box 11.2). It is a complex, shifting story that takes on different forms in different places and is at times contradictory. But at heart the story we tell ourselves about science and technology has two main components: that scientific knowledge is better than other sorts of knowledge, and that technology is powerful and changes our lives. These two elements to our societal story of science and technology – we can call them scientism and technological determinism – are deeply embedded in practices and discourses, and for this reason they make the examination of science and technology, and their role in society, a difficult enterprise. And, unlike other enterprises in sociology, the examination of science and technology is doubly difficult because sociology itself has internalized both of these stories and finds it difficult to come to terms with this. Yet another layer of difficulty attaches itself to these problems: simply stated, it is that we don't really know what we are talking about. What do we mean by science? While most people 'know' what science is – the experimental/observational work done by scientists in special places (e.g., laboratories) – this kind of definition doesn't even begin to address the complexity, diversity and sheer massiveness of what 'science' in society is. Similarly with technology: we have a widespread societal understanding of what technology is – mobile phones, iPads, MP3 players, DVD recorders, and so on. But some of the most significant technologies in our lives are hidden from us (think of, say, water purification systems) or are so mundane (e.g., writing implements, cutlery, spectacles) that we don't consider them to be technologies, thus rendering our societal definition rather unhelpful. Not knowing what it is we are considering makes it difficult to ascertain in what ways these things are significant in explaining social change. So why is it that we find thinking and examining science and technology in society, even from a sociological perspective, so difficult?

Scientism

> What we 'lay people' (as we are significantly called) mostly notice about the sciences is simply their power. Technology impresses us so deeply that we are not much surprised by the claim that scientific methods ought to be extended to cover the rest of our thought.
> (Midgley 2001: 59)

We think of science in society in a certain way because there are some very powerful and dominant ideas about what science is. Throughout any investigation of science and technology we have to bear in mind that our understanding of the world is conditioned, at the very least in part, by our social experiences, and in our society we are socialized into thinking in a particular way about science. This social understanding of science is reinforced in many ways: our everyday experience of science through contact with technology, our contact with health and medical professions, media representations – factual and fictional – of science, scientific knowledge and scientists, and so on. We are surrounded by deeply entrenched pictures and understandings of what science is, and we will find it both difficult and necessary to challenge these deeply held understandings if we are to begin to make sense of how science, technology and society are connected.

The idea that science is a superior form of knowledge, or at least of a different form to other types of knowledge, is at the centre of the public understanding of science. We tell ourselves that science has had a role in transforming society by making us understand the natural world better and by providing technologies that improve and change our lives. In addition, as a society we are often asking for more science – in education, in workplaces, in providing new technologies, in solving problems in the natural world such as climate change or foot and mouth disease, even in curing social problems such as crime. Our societies, and our understanding of knowledge in society, are often based on the idea that science is the best mode of explanation for things in the world, that it is good at getting things done, that it provides progress and technological innovation – that it is powerful. This way of understanding science, of seeing it as superior, pervasive, dominant and powerful, we can call scientism: the belief or general feeling that science is the best mode of explanation for things in the world. Elsewhere I have described scientism as something that *infects* our ways of thinking (Erickson 2005: 22), and many social theorists see similar processes taking place (especially Midgley 2001, 2010). But we don't need to overstate this – it is enough just to recognize how prevalent and significant science is in our lives for us as social researchers to understand how important it is to come to grips with it.

Scientism delivers to us a powerful story of science in society. It tells us that much of what we take for granted around us is the result of scientific endeavour and the application of scientific knowledge. It tells us that much of the technology that surrounds us is a spin-off from scientific work. It reminds us that commonsense knowledge is of a second order to superior scientific knowledge, based as it is on its regular and standardized method of experimentation and systematic investigation. Scientism colonizes and expands in our everyday lives such that all of us become responsible for creating a story of science in society where science is seen as being separate, different, special and superior, a story of science *and* society. Many people don't like this, and we can see all sorts of challenges to the hegemony of science and dissent in terms of anti-science movements, New Age mysticism, religious fundamentalism promoting reactionary and specious views such as creationism and intelligent design, the articulation of negative stereotypical representations of scientists, and the hostility with which some new scientific breakthroughs are received (e.g., stem-cell research and genetic modification of organisms) (see box 11.3). But, despite this, we are still surrounded by scientism and its relentless message of 'science first'. Scientism does not confine itself to pervading public understandings – it is also a powerful mode of explanation in the formal sciences and the social sciences. Indeed, despite its perhaps weakening hold on exoteric thought communities (the widespread communities

BOX 11.3 ANTI-SCIENCE IN THE USA

In his final book *The Demon-Haunted World: Science as a Candle in the Dark*, the eminent American astronomer and science communicator Carl Sagan railed against what he saw as the climate of pseudoscience, New Age mysticism, Ufology and fundamentalist zealotry that characterized contemporary popular culture (Sagan 1996). He felt that science and the scepticism that modern science engenders were being overshadowed by scientific illiteracy. 'Spurious accounts that snare the gullible are readily available. Skeptical treatments are much harder to find. Skepticism does not sell well' (ibid: 5). (It is worth noting that such statements from self-selected representatives of the scientific community are often rather wild exaggerations. Apart from anything else, Sagan's suggestion that popular culture is crammed full of pseudoscience and mysticism is simply wrong; after all, Sagan himself was the presenter of one of the most popular TV shows in the history of the world, the popular science series *Cosmos*, which, by his own reckoning, had been seen by 500 million people in sixty countries by 1996 – about 15 percent of the *world's* adult population at the time (Erickson 2005: 148). Scepticism, in this case, seems to sell pretty well.)

Voices opposed to, or distant from, a scientific worldview are not confined to popular culture. The 2012 US presidential election campaign often featured heated debates and strong statements about science, many at odds with the views of the mainstream scientific community. For example, the governor of Texas, Rick Perry, a candidate for the Republican Party nomination for president, claimed that evolution is 'a theory that's out there. It's got some gaps in it. In Texas we teach both creationism and evolution' (*Washington Post*, 18 August 2011). A 2009 Gallup poll found that 'only 39% of Americans say they "believe in the theory of evolution," while a quarter say they do not believe in the theory, and another 36% don't have an opinion either way. These attitudes are strongly related to education and, to an even greater degree, religiosity' (Gallup 2009). Turning his attention to climate change, Perry said that 'the science is not settled', and he refused to sign Texas up to federal regulation of greenhouse gas emissions, the only US state to do so (*The Guardian*, 14 October 2011). Perry is in good company: 'Ninety-six of newly elected Republican members of Congress either deny climate change is real or have signed pledges vowing to oppose its mitigation' (Otto 2011: 39). Scientists, and even social scientists, who draw the public's attention to the problems of anthropogenic climate change are often the subject of unpleasant personal attacks in the right-wing US media.

throughout society of which we are all members – in contrast to the esoteric thought communities that scientists in their working environments inhabit) (Fleck [1935] 1979; Erickson 2005: 19–22), scientism seems to be taking a stronger grip on academic disciplines such as criminology, psychology and education, all of which are increasing in their tendency to reach for organic, genetic and quantifiable explanations of social behaviour and problems.

Scientism creates particular problems for sociology. Firstly, the founders of the discipline of sociology did not identify scientism as a problem or even as a social phenomenon. They tacitly accepted it and internalized it in their sociological theory. Spencer's science of society (Spencer 1874; Spencer and Andreski 1972) and Durkheim's positive method (Durkheim [1895] 1964) are based directly on adopting the methods and aims of the natural sciences as being both appropriate and better ways of understanding the social world. Marxism makes a similar move: the science of historical materialism is an avowedly realist approach to making sense of society, and it, too, adopts the philosophy and methods of the natural sciences (Engels, Dutt and Haldane 1940; Lenin [1908] 1967). These sociological approaches start from the assumption that science and the scientific method are better than other ways of making sense of the social world. Not surprisingly, they produced uncritical accounts of science, scientists, scientific institutions and scientific knowledge. There is an obvious problem here: a social science that wants to look at science in society is trying to do so using the tools and assumptions that are inherent in the object under inquiry. To draw a parallel, it would be as if sociology of religion assumed the mantle of mysticism that religion requires its adherents to adopt; clearly, such an inquiry would take us in a quite peculiar direction. And yet sociology of science, from its inception in the early twentieth century, has tried to do just this.

SEMINAR QUESTIONS

1 Is science a good thing for society? If it is, why does it attract so much controversy?

2 Do you believe science stories in the media?

3 What is scientism?

SOCIOLOGY OF SCIENCE

Standard accounts of science

The first specifically sociological examinations of science tried to shift away from the story of science *and* society to a picture of science *in* society. Max Weber's seminal essay 'Science as a Vocation' ([1919] 2007) looked at the institution of science in society, the role of scientific knowledge in wider patterns of social knowledge and the career or vocation of scientists. Weber's essay, quite remarkably, still provides an accurate account of what it is that scientists think they are doing and why they are doing it: the inner drive and passion that scientific workers have to extend their and, by extension, our knowledge of the natural world (Erickson 2002). As Paul Rabinow notes: 'the scientific vocation retains its actuality, despite the melodramatic, neoromantic cast of Weber's prose' (Rabinow 1996: 16).

This focus on the people who do science, rather than simply the institution or the product of scientific work, did not prevail in sociology of science, superseded almost immediately by a very dominant, and domineering, functionalist account produced by Robert K. Merton ([1942] 1973). Using historical and contemporary sociological analysis of Western science, Merton distilled the ethos of science into four institutional imperatives, norms that defined and governed the operation of scientific institutions, regulated scientific communities and underpinned, and were expressed in, scientific knowledge itself.

1 ***Universalism*** Truth claims are to be subjected to pre-established impersonal criteria. All claims are approached using similar methods (universal methods) – and all claims are as likely as others until proven otherwise. For Merton, this expands to give the ethos of science a view of careers – these should be open to talents, not prejudice. Universalism rejects versions of science that are particular, such as the science of Nazi Germany which was based on Aryan science.

2 ***Communism*** (here Merton means the common ownership of goods) The substantive findings of science are a product of social collaboration and are assigned to the community. Property rights in science are whittled down to a bare minimum by the ethics of the scientific community. Secrecy is the antithesis of this norm – communication of findings is a must. The only thing the scientist owns is the esteem and recognition due to him by the wider scientific community.

3 ***Disinterestedness*** There is competition in the field of science, but this is not at a level of falsifying others' findings without good reason. Disinterestedness relates to the ways that scientists scrutinize their peers in such a way that the main winner is 'the truth'.

4 ***Organized scepticism*** The suspension of judgement until the facts are at hand. The scientist suspends their common sense – thus allowing the hidden truth to appear.

(Merton [1942] 1957: 550–61)

Merton's work became the cornerstone of sociology of science from the 1950s to the 1970s, and studies of scientific institutions and communities were the staple of sociology of science (e.g., Hagstrom 1965; Barber and Hirsch 1962). But what object was sociology looking at when it produced these accounts? These sociological accounts identified 'science' in a way that mirrors what scientific institutions, communities and individual scientists consider their project to be – a 'standard' account of science that still dominates in contemporary society and which received very little critical attention until the 1980s. It is worth considering this account in some detail given its dominance and its co-emergence in scientific communities *and* sociological communities.

The standard account of scientific knowledge can be summed up as:

- science is a form of knowledge that produces facts and fact-like statements.

It goes on:

- science is not metaphysics, where metaphysics is a range of sweeping generalizations. Science is a series of factual propositions. These factual propositions are connected to each other by a common subject matter (the natural world) and a project (the extension and completion of knowledge of the natural world);
- science connects factual propositions through the use of theories. Scientific theories

describe what is known about the world and extend science to make predictions about what is not known about the world;

- science is empirical. It is based upon experience – i.e., actually perceiving things rather than just creating theories about them;
- scientific knowledge is applied rationality: it is produced using concrete and rigorous methods;
- scientific knowledge is a direct refutation of religious experience. Religion relies upon faith, science upon facts;
- scientific knowledge is based upon objectivity and seeks to remove subjectivity from analysis of the world;
- scientific knowledge has definite outcomes, it makes science 'work'. It transforms our lives through producing technological breakthroughs, cures for illnesses, new ways of understanding our environment, etc.;
- scientific knowledge is cumulative and progressive, through theories coming together and supporting each other. We know more about the natural world than we did in the past and we build our knowledge on foundations that have been laid down in the past.

(Erickson 2005: 55–6)

This standard account of the knowledge and theories of science makes a strong, and widely held, claim about the methods of science: that they are shared across science disciplines and by practitioners, objective, rigorous and empirical. As we have already seen, sociology has attempted (as have other social sciences) to emulate this scientific method, in part because of the power attached to it.

The standard account of science is widely distributed in society, but it is most closely associated with two social objects: the scientific community and scientific institutions. As with the standard account, we are very familiar with both of these things: we know what the scientific community is (we have a popular construction of who and what 'scientists' are) and we know what counts as a scientific institution (again, we have a popular construct of labs, research institutes, universities). More recent sociological studies of science have presented a strong challenge to these beliefs.

Yet when we reflect on the standard account we can see that it is doing something in addition to presenting a story of science, scientists and scientific places. It is taking science away from other things in society, separating science from society by claiming that scientific knowledge is different and better, that scientists are a separate community and that scientific institutions are not like other institutions. Despite the strength of this account, we can challenge it, and in quite profound ways.

Challenges to the standard accounts

Challenges to the status, and nature, of scientific knowledge began to emerge in the 1960s following the publication of Thomas Kuhn's *The Structure of Scientific Revolutions* (1962). Kuhn's relativist approach brought together history and philosophy of science to present a radical alternative to the standard account of the inexorable progression of science through the cumulative amassing of facts and theories. In marked contrast, Kuhn's analysis of the history and conduct of physics showed a discontinuous history, where progress could not be measured outside of individual, and mutually exclusive, paradigms. Inside each paradigm activities constitute normal science, with scientific communities working to solve puzzles set by an overarching theory (such as those provided by Newton or Einstein). However, as anomalies begin to accrue, a discipline may enter a crisis phase where the underlying theory is called into question. The result is a scientific revolution – a social process – where scientists will shift from one paradigm to another, adopting a new, core theory and restarting the normal science of puzzle-solving.

Kuhn's introduction of social factors into the 'progress' of science is very significant. If science proceeds through social processes, rather than through the accumulation of facts and theories, then we need to rethink our understanding of what facts and theories – scientific knowledge – actually are: 'Perhaps science does not develop by the accumulation of individual discoveries and inventions' (Kuhn 1962: 2). Kuhn's work opened the door to allowing a relativist understanding of scientific knowledge. Although by no means the first relativist account of scientific knowledge, and even though much of the core argument of *The Structure of Scientific Revolutions* was borrowed from the work of Ludwik Fleck ([1935] 1979), it was certainly the most influential in terms of epistemology of science and has become the basis for the critical appraisal of scientific activity that is now termed 'social constructionism'.

The roots of social constructionism are contested, and in the sociology of science they are also diverse. One of the key voices contributing to early social constructionist accounts of science in society was the philosopher Paul Feyerabend, whose 'anarchist' theory of knowledge sought to reveal the 'myths' and 'fairy tales' that attended science:

> The image of twentieth-century science in the minds of scientists and laymen is determined by technological miracles such as colour television, the moon shots, the infra-red oven, as well as by a somewhat vague but still quite influential rumour, or fairy-tale, concerning the manner in which these miracles are produced. According to the fairy-tale the success of science is the result of a subtle, but carefully balanced combination of inventiveness and control. Scientists have *ideas*. And they have special *methods* for improving ideas. The theories of science have passed the test of method. They give a better account of the world than ideas which have not passed the test. The fairy-tale explains which modern society treats science in a special way and why it grants it privileges not enjoyed by other institutions. (Feyerabend 1978: 300)

Feyerabend is not against science, but he is against dogma, particularly the dogma that there is a unified, objective scientific method. As relativist accounts of science became more prominent in the 1970s, sociological attention turned from scientific institutions and communities (structures) to scientific method and practice (actions and meanings) – the site of the production of scientific knowledge. Particularly significant was the Strong Programme, with its core tenet of symmetricality: if we are to explain beliefs, we should explain true and false beliefs in the same way (Bloor [1976] 1991). This is a compelling move. Why should we explain truth and falsehoods in different ways if we consider that all knowledge has a social origin? But, once this move is made, it is difficult to maintain the idea of factual scientific knowledge being 'better' than other forms of knowledge other than having a status ascribed to it by social convention. Not only that, the object that we are investigating – science – comes under a different form of scrutiny: How are scientists coming together to make their knowledge? What are the conditions of its social construction?

If true and false beliefs are to be treated in the same way, then we are not merely talking about distortions of the picture of knowledge which is painted. What is being claimed is that *many pictures* can be painted, and furthermore, that the sociologist cannot say that any picture is a better representation of Nature than any other. Scientists can socially construct many different versions of the natural world. (Pinch 1986: 8)

When sociologists followed this line of inquiry into laboratories and other sites of the production of scientific knowledge, they did, indeed, find groups of scientists joining together to construct scientific knowledge. Rather than seeing scientists as uncovering the hidden truths of nature, they found scientists constructing facts and generating a discourse of truth through their practical activities. Scientific activity is not about nature, it is a 'fierce fight to *construct reality*' (Latour and Woolgar 1979: 243).

So the laboratory or the observatory are sites where different agents come together to manufacture something we call the truth. But these sites of construction retain characteristics that are determined by external factors, notably their gendered character. While not a primary concern for the first wave of social constructionists and subsequent actor-network theorists (see box 11.4), the gender dimension of the production of scientific knowledge and the feminist critique of science is the third element (after Kuhn's relativism and the principal of symmetry) of the comprehensive critique of the standard account that sociology produced.

As well as the innumerable component parts, or actants, a huge number of actors are involved in the production and launch of a NASA spacecraft, including not just scientists, researchers and manufacturers but also government officials who allocate money for such projects, the media who report on the projects and, ultimately, the public whose taxes fund NASA. (© NASA HQ PHOTO/Flickr)

BOX 11.4 ACTOR-NETWORK THEORY

Actor-Network Theory (ANT) was devised in the 1980s by the French anthropologist Bruno Latour (1987) and collaborators. In marked contrast to earlier sociology of science, ANT sought to collapse the divide between the production of science and its use in society. To do this it proposes seeing the parties involved in the construction of science as taking positions in a network that has specific outcomes. These nodes in a network are 'actors' (humans) and 'actants' (non-humans). All can have similar agency and all are involved in construction of each other and the network. The process of constructing these networks is what is of interest to ANT, and the network itself is responsible for constructing the boundaries and categories of the world – nature, the social, politics, science, technology. For example, a biochemist working on a specific biological molecule will enrol other biochemists, funding agencies and actants (PCR machines, spectrophotometers, bacteria) to construct a solid network that can produce theories, experimental results and technologies. Subsequent to carrying out experiments, further actors and actants can be enrolled (or disenrolled) in the network – the media, for example, can be enrolled to disseminate the experimental findings or to display technological outcomes.

ANT relies on the principle of symmetry – there is no purpose in trying to identify the 'truthfulness' of what emerges from the network. Instead, it encourages the researcher to investigate what actors are actually doing rather than examining the product of the endeavours of scientists. Latour has put this approach to good use in a number of detailed studies, including an examination of a biochemistry laboratory (Latour and Woolgar 1979), the failed construction of a high-tech rapid transit system for Paris (Project Aramis; Latour 1996) and, most recently, the Conseil d'État (one of the French supreme courts; Latour 2010).

Sexism and science

We live in a sexist and patriarchal society: women are systematically discriminated against in society and particularly in workplaces, and women's experiences and knowledge are consistently derided or downgraded. While our dominant story of science tells us that scientific knowledge and scientific institutions are gender neutral, and that scientific communities are meritocracies open to all as long as they have sufficient ability, in practice this is simply not the case. Our sexist and patriarchal society is mirrored in androcentric, sexist and patriarchal science and, until fairly recently, androcentric, sexist and patriarchal sociology of science.

Robert Merton's identification of the 'institutional imperatives' of science provides a good example of this. While Merton correctly identifies what the majority of scientists considered to be the norms and values around which they organized their work and their community, he fails to notice that these imperatives were being applied in quite biased ways. The history of science, particularly nineteenth- and twentieth-century science, is replete with examples of women whose major contributions to scientific knowledge have been ignored or whitewashed out of the official record (see box 11.5).

The neglect of women's contribution begs the question: Just how 'universal' or 'disinterested' can science be when it is systematically undervaluing the contribution made by such a large group of participants? It also should make us question the kind of sociology that can investigate scientific communities as rationally and fairly organized institutions without noticing the gender divides inside them: although many sociologists looked at scientific communities, no significant study of gender and science was carried out until the 1970s, when Zuckerman and Cole explained the lack of representation of women in the higher echelons of the US scientific community by reference to the 'triple penalty':

BOX 11.5 JOCELYN BELL BURNELL, THE DISCOVERER OF THE PULSAR

In 1967 a graduate student at Cambridge University – Jocelyn Bell Burnell – was completing her PhD on radio telescopes. She worked with her supervisor, Anthony Hewish, to build a radio telescope, which she then pointed at the constellation Cygnus and measured the radio waves coming from it. She found a peculiar signal, rhythmically pulsing radio waves. No known astronomical object pulsed so regularly, and this discovery was anomalous. At first her supervisor dubbed this phenomenon LGM-1 (Little Green Men), thinking that Bell must have made an error. In contrast, Bell worked out that the pulsing came from a star and realized it must be a neutron star. Neutron stars are leftovers from supernova explosions, and the pulsations arise because the stars are spinning very rapidly

The discovery of proof of the existence of neutron stars, an idea that was first proposed in the 1930s, was so important that the physics committee of the Nobel Institute awarded its prize for physics and astronomy in 1974 to the discoverer of pulsars: Anthony Hewish and his collaborator Martine Ryle. The Nobel committee made no mention of Bell Burnell, despite her being a co-author of the original paper and the person who made the discovery and analysed the data. There was considerable controversy attached to this, and some astronomers dubbed the award the 'No-Bell Prize'. Bell went back to doing postdoctoral work, gradually working her way up through the ranks of the astronomy community, and finally received wider recognition in the 1990s.

> First, science is culturally defined as an inappropriate career for women; the number of women recruited to science is thereby reduced below the level of which would obtain were this definition not prevalent. Second, those women who have surmounted the first barrier and have become scientists continue to be hampered by the belief that women are less competent than men. Whatever the validity of this belief, it contributes to women's ambivalence towards their work and thereby reduces their motivation and commitment to scientific careers. And third . . . there is some evidence for actual discrimination against women in the scientific community. To the extent that women scientists suffer from these disadvantages, they are victims of one or more components of the triple penalty. (Zuckerman and Cole 1975: 84)

This triple penalty persists to the present day. Sociological research into the structure of scientific communities reveals deep, structural gender divides, where women in science get less money, status and prestige and fewer prizes. While the picture is slightly better in the twenty-first century than it was in the twentieth, the levels of discrimination are still stark. We often consider universities to be liberal institutions which are more meritocratic than other employers in society, but women academics in STEM (science, technology, engineering, mathematics) departments are getting a raw deal. As figure 11.1 shows, in 2007–8, 5,375 women worked full-time as researchers, accounting for 30.3 percent of all full-time researchers. There were also 2,065 female lecturers (26.1 percent), 1,790 female senior researchers/lecturers (18.3 percent), and only 540 female professors (9.3 percent) in STEM full-time employment. Women were much more likely to be in part-time and insecure positions in these departments, and, of course, women receive lower pay than men (UKRC 2010).

It isn't just institutional discrimination that faces women: scientific knowledge itself is gendered: 'Never was what counts as general social knowledge generated by asking

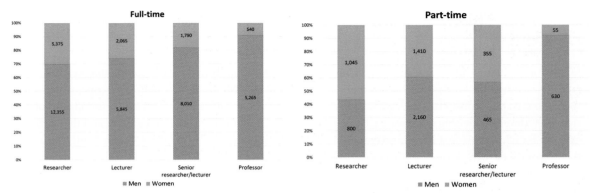

Figure 11.1 STEM academic staff by gender, grade and mode of employment at UK HE institutions, 2007–8

Source: Compiled with data from UKRC (2010: 65).

questions from the perspective of women's lives' (Harding 1991: 106). The work of Sandra Harding is useful here in examining how science that is gender aware and attempts to challenge sexism and discrimination would benefit us all. The systematic exclusion of women from and the devaluing of women's perspectives in science have negative consequences for scientific knowledge. Knowledge is based upon experience, and, with different experiences, different knowledges can emerge. Women's positions as outsiders can allow them to have an edge, as researchers, finding things that male scientists may not; they can access an alternative starting point to much androcentric science. Harding's 'standpoint epistemology' is seen as a threat to the 'standard' project of science in that it is challenging the fundamental assumptions of that project, yet it need not be seen in this way. The 'objectivity' of androcentric science is weak in that it is exclusionary, partial and directed by interests that do not represent those of the vast majority of science. Harding proposes a 'strong' objectivity that seeks to gain less false and less partial knowledge, but, of course, not absolute truth or impartial knowledge. In doing so, she points out that the standard account of science is not just a myth, it is a smokescreen behind which sexism, androcentrism and patriarchal attitudes persist.

Cyborgs and technofeminism

Once we begin to become aware of the gendered aspects of science and technology in society, then a whole range of possibilities begin to open up. Donna Haraway's cyborg theory extended the challenge to another of the central ideas of the standard account – that nature is an external, fixed object to which science can apply its universal method such that it will reveal its hidden truths. In stark contrast, Haraway asks us to recognize that we are not humans now, we are cyborgs; cyborgs see the world differently and can see that, like themselves, nature is an artefact, something that is made of both fiction and fact: 'A cyborg is a cybernetic organism, a hybrid of machine and organism, a creature of social reality as well as a creature of fiction' (Haraway 1991: 149). For Haraway – as a second-generation feminist – it is not enough simply to challenge the social inequalities experienced by women. It is also necessary to

How far have we become cyborgs, so as to be able to reconstruct gender relations in society? Will this Cambodian woman and the people around her be likely to reappraise the nature of being human, and gender's part in that? What might be required for this break to happen? (© World Bank Photo Collection/Flickr)

construct a new language, law and mythology through challenging the gender bias in existing language, law and mythology. In her construction of the cyborg, Haraway clearly challenges the gender bias in scientific discourse but also constructs a new mythology, one that is not dependent upon the past or transcendental, essentialist categories. Our interactions with, use of and penetration by technology have made us into different sorts of beings. For Haraway, a way of reappropriating and reconstructing science such that it loses its androcentric character and oppressive practices is to begin to understand that human beings no longer exist, having been replaced in technoscience by cyborgs.

This idea is taken further by Judy Wajcman in her construction of technofeminism. While embracing some aspects of Haraway's cyberfeminism, Wajcman proposes a more thoroughgoing materialist analysis of the socio-technical networks that women inhabit. Technofeminism looks at gender relations in our technoscientific society as materializing in technology, which is always a socio-technical product – i.e., exhibiting both social and technical characteristics. Not only that, we need to see how sexualities acquire their meaning from being embedded in working machines (2004: 107).

Technofeminism is a critical approach to understanding science and technology as gendered objects in a technoscientific society. But it is also a refreshingly reflexive approach in that it offers a strong critique of contemporary science and technology studies (STS) and sociology of science's failure to consider the social conditions surrounding *their* construction of knowledge:

One of the ironies of mainstream science and technology studies is that, while its central premise holds that technoscience is socially shaped and inherently political, there has been a reluctance to consider the implications of its own methodologies. Practitioners act as if their own methodologies are not affected by the social context and have no politics. They do not reflect on how the preponderance of white, privileged, heterosexual men might have framed the field. (Wajcman 2004: 128)

Wajcman is reminding us that knowledge is a social product, and that includes *our* sociological theories and knowledge.

SEMINAR QUESTIONS

1 Why is the standard account of science so prevalent and persistent?

2 Is science a social construction?

3 What factors contributed to your decision to study (or avoid) science subjects at school, college or university?

4 Is science sexist?

5 Does the technology you use in your everyday life change you? Your social relationships?

TECHNOLOGY AND SOCIAL CHANGE

Defining technology

While we may not feel ourselves to be fully up to speed with what science, scientists and scientific institutions are up to, we can at least identify generally what science is. Technology is much more difficult to pin down, and we have a similar range of difficulties as researchers facing us when we begin to examine technology in society.

Again, as with science, we 'know' what technology is: the mobile phone, MP3 player, smart bomb or hybrid car are all technology. But then so are spectacles, knives and forks, bicycles and beach balls. In general, our social definition of technology is synonymous with 'innovation': we think technology is what is newly innovated. Yet this is somewhat misleading: vast amounts of technological innovation are hidden from us, often physically hidden by virtue of being underground (fibre-optic cables), elsewhere (robot fabricators in Chinese factories) or invisible (mobile phone signals or CCTV cameras we have learned to ignore). We will find that defining technology will prove to be even more difficult than defining science. Indeed, the eminent philosopher of science Joseph Agassi noted that 'technology in general is not definable in any narrow clear-cut definition. . . . This disturbs quite a number of people when they begin to think about it' (Agassi 1985: 23–4).

Agassi is probably right, and perhaps we should not try to define technology so much as to consider why it is that we have particular understandings of it, and where these come from. Central to this is another powerful mode of explanation that pervades much social thinking, a way of describing social change and even society as a whole as a product of technological change and improvement. We can call this mode of explanation technological determinism. As with scientism, it is a trend that is prevalent in general social thought but also in formal academic theories.

Technological determinism

Technological determinism is used to explain the world around us a lot of the time. Why do children get obese? Because they spend their time in front of computers rather than running around, thus computers have changed the world around us. Why is our society 'superior' to other societies? Because we have higher levels of technological development. How do we explain the rise of our industrial society in history? Through the innovations brought about in the late eighteenth century, notably the steam engine and other technologies that allowed industrialization to take place.

Technology of course does have significant effects on our society: just think about how our society has been transformed by the invention of antibiotics, contraception and anaesthesia. However, there is a fundamental problem with technological deterministic explanations, and this problem connects us very strongly to scientism. It is that technological determinism cannot explain or account for technological change itself: it shows technologies as emerging seamlessly through some hidden logic of their own, or through being a by-product of science which, in turn, is then represented as having an inexorable, and hidden, inner logic of emergence. Technological determinism hides all human social contributions to innovation and, equally significantly, gives us an often inaccurate understanding of what technology means to us. Finally, the idea of a relentless logic of technological innovation, with discovery piling on top of discovery and social change resulting from this, is wrong in a large number of specific cases. Here are two examples.

The fax machine, an almost ubiquitous item of office furniture from its emergence in the 1980s onwards, can scan and transmit images (facsimiles – hence the name) of documents electronically. This technology, now largely superseded by email and other internet-based means of transmitting documents, was very popular through the 1980s and 1990s, and was initially seen as cutting edge. Yet the first patent for an electronic document scanner was granted as far back as 1843, and fax machines were already being mass produced in the 1920s (www. technikum29.de/en/communication/fax).

The invention of the compact disc (CD) and its emergence onto the market in 1982 marked the start of the decline of vinyl record sales and record turntables. A technological determinist account would almost certainly see that vinyl LPs would go the way of shellac 78 rpm records before them and disappear in the face of the 'improved' technology of digital music. Indeed, LP sales plummeted, and at a certain point in the early 1990s many record companies simply stopped producing vinyl records, having given their production over entirely to new digital formats (as well as CDs there were also minidisks and a few other transitory formats). However, LPs and 7" singles have staged a remarkable comeback due almost wholly to the realization that the technology used to listen (passively) to vinyl records could also be used (actively) to create music in a way that the inventors, producers and marketers of record players never imagined. DJ-ing and scratching not only resulted in the creation of remarkable new forms, genres and sounds (including jungle – possibly the only popular music genre created wholly in the UK) but also meant that music began to be produced on vinyl records again, and record turntables became must-have items for many people.

The above discussion of technological determinism and scientism needs to be placed in some context if we are to avoid the charge that we are also applying a kind of deficit model where people appear to be foolish for adopting these frames of reference. This would be quite wrong. Scientism is, at least to some extent, an appropriate response for people to adopt given the importance and intrusion of science into people's lives. Not only that, we must also recognize that large amounts of social scientific thought deploy forms of scientism: psychology is particularly prone to this mode of explanation. Similarly, technological determinism asks good and sensible questions of society, particularly in terms of questioning our individual relationship to specific technologies (e.g., how mobile phone technology has changed our society and our identities; see box 11.6).

However, where these theories fall short is in their oversimplification of the issues surrounding science and technology and in their construction of science and technology as essentially separate and neutral forms of knowledge that are impervious to human agency. They are very meagre theories to explain the complexity, richness and importance of science and technology, as McKenzie and Wajcman argue:

BOX 11.6 MOBILE PHONE TECHNOLOGY IN A GLOBAL CONTEXT

The pace at which mobile phone technology has spread across the globe is unparalleled in the history of technology. About three-quarters of the world's population now have access to a mobile phone. In 2000 there were about 1 billion mobile phone subscriptions; by 2012 that number had risen to 6 billion (World Bank 2012b: 3). Ninety percent of the world's population can receive a mobile phone signal, and it is the developing world that is utilizing the technology in greatest numbers: most phones are owned by people living in low-income regions (ibid.: 9). This dramatic rise in the availability of mobile phone technology is coupled to significant changes in how such technologies are used. Thirty billion mobile phone apps were downloaded in 2011, signalling a change in how mobile phones are being used. Not surprisingly, the World Bank sees vast potential for economic development based on this technology: 'Mobile applications not only empower individual users, they enrich their lifestyles and livelihoods, and boost the economy as a whole' (ibid: 3).

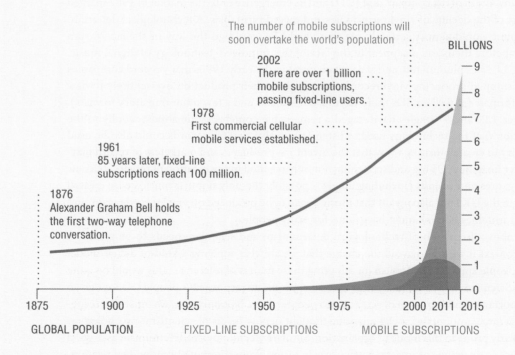

Figure 11.2 The global spread of mobile phones

Source: World Bank (2012b: 8).

The view that technology just changes, either following science or of its own accord, promotes a passive attitude to technological change. It focuses our minds on how to *adapt* to technological change, not on how to *shape* it. It removes a vital aspect of how we live from the sphere of public discussion, choice, and politics. Precisely because technological determinism is partly right as a theory of society (technology matters not just physically and biologically, but also to our human relations to each other) its deficiency as a theory of technology impoverishes the political life of our societies. . . . As a vitally important part of 'progress', technological change is a key aspect of what our societies need to actively shape, rather than passively respond to. (MacKenzie and Wajcman 1999: 5–6)

For this reason we need to bear in mind that scientism and technological determinism are significant factors in the thought style of many people in our society, and this thought style has not emerged in a vacuum: it has been formed through experience and culture, both of which, in our technoscientific society, are themselves suffused with ideas of science and technology.

SEMINAR QUESTIONS

1 Does technology change the world?
2 Is technological change a good measure of societal progress?
3 Why do new technologies emerge?
4 Can you define 'technology'? How have sociologists tried to do this?

SCIENCE BATTLEGROUNDS

Science versus relativism

The widening gap between the account of science that was offered by scientists and that offered by social scientists was indicative of a number of changes in society, not least the phenomenal rise in the sheer amount of science being done and the shift in emphasis of importance of different disciplines inside higher education institutions. The result, in the mid-1990s, was what became known colloquially as the 'science wars'. This was a disparate collection of arguments surrounding a number of polemical texts written by academics largely to antagonize other academics. Simplifying greatly, the science wars were 'started' by US-based natural scientists who wanted to defend their version of what science was and to denounce the relativist trends in social scientific studies of science. En route, a great many topics were thrown into the fray, including the idea of 'political correctness' and postcolonial thought. The reason for this is quite plain if you think about the title of the main text that started this battle: *Higher Superstition: The Academic Left and its Quarrels with Science* (Gross and Levitt 1994). Gross and Levitt attack 'postmodern' sociologists and philosophers of science, claiming that they do not understand science and are disparaging of the work of scientists. They argue that social constructionist theories claim that scientific theories are just social constructions with no more claim to truth than any other socially constructed idea. But those being attacked felt aggrieved that Gross and Levitt were denigrating their work, not taking them seriously and acting in an imperious way. The arguments raged between both sides, and still do to some extent.

The charge, from these self-appointed spokespeople for the natural sciences, was that social constructionists and postmodernists were 'anti-science'. This is a strong charge and, given the dominant scientism of our times, one that makes not only a specific claim but also a general claim – that a group of academic investigators of science are out of touch with reality. Not only did some scientists object to how social scientists had poked their noses into their affairs and, we may conjecture, undermined the project of science by applying relativism to it, they also objected to how social theory and social science had 'borrowed' their language – i.e., had taken specific pieces of scientific terminology and apparently misapplied them to objects that were simply not analysable in this way.

BOX 11.7 FASHIONABLE NONSENSE OR BOUNDARY WORK?

One point of controversy in the science wars has been the use by philosophers and social scientists of 'scientific' concepts and terminology. In an excoriating attack on, mainly, French social and philosophical thought of the 1990s, Alan Sokal and Jean Bricmont (1998) catalogue the errors, as they see it, of leading thinkers in using scientific concepts to explain the social world, resulting in 'fashionable nonsense'. For example, they argue that Latour misunderstands Einstein's theory of relativity, that Deleuze and Guatarri's interpretation of what chaos can be understood to be is incompatible with how physics defines it, that Virilio mistakes space and time for 'space–time', and so on. While Sokal and Bricmont may be technically correct in their identification of these different usages, they display a very strong form of boundary work: the process by which those claiming epistemic authority assert their sole right to make pronouncement on certain matters. In this case Sokal and Bricmont are working to maintain a strict boundary between the natural sciences and the social sciences and, by extension, between science and society.

Alan Sokal, a professor of physics at New York University, published his (in)famous article 'Transgressing the Boundaries: Towards a Transformative Hermeneutics of Quantum Gravity' in 1996. It was largely a parody of postmodernists' language and theorizing. The article broadly suggests that there are parallels between postmodern theory and quantum theory, but it does this in a clichéd way that deploys nonsensical science statements. Sokal has a deliberately ironic opening section; after a quotation from Stanley Aronowitz, he goes on: 'There are many natural scientists, and especially physicists, who continue to reject the notion that the disciplines concerned with social and cultural criticism can have anything to contribute, except perhaps peripherally, to their research' (Sokal and Bricmont 1998: 199). The article proceeds by constructing a 'mélange of truths, half-truths, quarter-truths, falsehoods, non sequiturs, and syntactically correct sentences that have no meaning whatsoever', just 'like the genre it is meant to satirize' (ibid). The journal *Social Text* published it, not realizing it was a parody, and was immediately and brutally humiliated by Sokal. *Social Text*'s editor Stanley Aronowitz did not react terribly well: he saw the article as being deliberately deceptive, claimed that it was unethical to do this, and noted that his journal is not peer reviewed (perhaps it should be?). Regardless, the strong scientists won this one hands down. Sokal went on to publish a book that identifies what he calls scientific nonsense in contemporary philosophy:

> Sokal subsequently assembled a series of longer texts to illustrate these authors' handling of the natural sciences, which he circulated among his scientific colleagues. Their reaction was a mixture of hilarity and dismay: they could hardly believe that anyone – much less renowned

intellectuals – could write such nonsense. However, when non-scientists read the material, they pointed out the need to explain, in lay terms, exactly why the cited passages are absurd or meaningless. (Sokal and Bricmont 1998: 3)

Sokal and the larger group who see themselves as 'defenders' of the sciences may be right in their arguments about the use of language and terminology, although the idea that a single group can claim ownership of words seems extreme. Science is denying its position inside society, arguing instead for a position outside society where it has a superordinate view of the world. And there is, at the very least, a tendency in this kind of critique to restate the situation where science has absolute hegemony as the only legitimate form of description of the world, and that it remains the ultimate arbiter of rules. Stephen Hawking, the most renowned natural scientist in contemporary society, makes this quite clear in his most recent book, *The Grand Design* (2011). Speculative questions of life and its meaning used to be the province of philosophers: 'but philosophy is dead. Philosophy has not kept up with modern developments in science, particularly physics. Scientists have become the bearers of the torch of discovery in our quest for knowledge' (Hawking and Mlodinow 2011: 13).

This takes us to the crux of the argument, and also to the rather sad ending to this episode. Science has become removed not from society – this is simply not possible; all and everything in the world is a part of society and we cannot move outside of that – but from social and, crucially, democratic control of its institutions and actions. Scientific institutions, scientific research and scientific communities had, by the 1990s, become increasingly isolated from other social institutions and social groups, and this was the culmination of a long trend.

University science

The natural sciences, from the late nineteenth through the twentieth century, had assumed a much higher prominence in universities across the world. From being excluded in early modernity, natural science subjects had become the main elements of the modern university, with high levels of funding, at least when compared with arts and humanities. There are two things worth considering here from a sociological perspective. The first is that institutions that contained and legitimated knowledge – universities – changed their idea about what counted as being 'good' knowledge. From early modernity, when the subjects that received this status were philosophy, divinity, rhetoric and aesthetics, we move to a situation in late modernity where it is the natural sciences that are legitimated by universities. This situation has been compounded in UK higher education establishments in very recent times, with the government removing all subsidies to arts- and humanities-based subjects taught at undergraduate level in universities; now the only undergraduate teaching programmes that receive government subsidy are STEM (science, technology, engineering and mathematics) subjects and medicine.

The second thing to note is that it was the natural sciences that became the template for how knowledge should be discovered, analysed and explained, and the value system that apparently underpinned scientific endeavours – broadly speaking that identified by Merton – was the thing that allowed science to achieve its goals. Thus, as Immanuel Wallerstein points out, the separation between arts, humanities and social sciences, and the natural sciences became entrenched, and uncrossable. An uneasy truce was drawn up in the mid-twentieth century. The sciences were given the role of discovering and asserting legitimate truths (and in the eyes of society seen as having exclusive control over these), and the arts and humanities the role of asserting what was good and beautiful. 'Never before in the history of the world had there been a sharp division between the search for the true and the search for the good and the beautiful. Now it was inscribed in the structures of knowledge and the world university system' (Wallerstein 2006: 63).

Why did this happen? It is a reflection of society, and the imperatives of society, particularly those in power. Technical questions and technical solutions became much more important in late modernity – as ways of making money, increasing efficiency, controlling populations. The consequences of this are far reaching. In essence, the ways that a democratic society would and could debate with itself narrowed as more and more decision-making passed into the hands of those in power. Decisions about planning, education, the environment became the purview of specialists who were working for governments, themselves increasingly separate from populations.

The consequence, by the late 1990s in many industrial societies, was a situation where the public was becoming increasingly distrustful of politicians and even scientists. Large-scale public campaigns against genetic modification of organisms, stem-cell research, nuclear power programmes, even cell phone masts received extensive media coverage, and these issues were often presented as the public versus scientists (Gregory and Miller 1998). But it is in the realm of education – the realm where decisions are made about how we socialize our young people – that the battle between science and 'non-science' (for want of a better term) really took off.

Conflicts with religion and politics

> The intellectualistic conception of science, underlying positivism, is itself rooted in a definite *Weltanschauung* [worldview] and has progressed in close connection with definite political interests. (Mannheim [1936] 1960: 148)

The account provided so far, of scientism as a dominant mode of thinking in contemporary society, needs to be understood in a wider, more political context. While it is fair to say that much of the form of social organization, particularly in terms of education, welfare and care systems, relies on science and technology, we can also identify strong currents in contemporary social thought that challenge scientism and rationalism. These include the claims of alternative health movements, conspiracy theorists, nutritionists and others who consider that scientific evidence for some phenomena is fabricated, exaggerated or simply misplaced. However, the biggest challenge comes from organized religions, and particularly fundamentalist tendencies in organized religions.

The dominant story in society is that science and religion are quite separate things. For example, the American Association for the Advancement of Science offers this position statement: 'Science is about causes, religion about meaning. Science deals with how things happen in nature, religion with why there is anything rather than nothing. Science addresses specific questions about the workings of nature, religion addresses the ultimate ground of nature' (cited in Nelkin 2004: 144). This is an optimistic story – one where there is a clear demarcation between what science does and what religion does (it is worth noting that this is quite a narrow conception of religion – see chapter 14 in this book on sociology of religion). The AAAS is attempting to find some reconciliation between religious and scientific communities, but this reconciliationist story is, despite this strong backing from a powerful institution, contradicted in many ways in contemporary society.

Firstly, social science has contradicted the story by challenging the truth claims of religion. Religion is understood as, variously, an ideological smokescreen, a mechanism to enforce dominant values, a means to maintain traditions, or simply a way of bringing disparate people together to share interests. More critical social science perspectives see religion as simply wrong and an impediment to human social progress or happiness. If this critique of religion were confined to the social sciences there would be little problem, but it isn't. A further challenge to the reconciliation story comes from scientists who are becoming increasingly vocal in their denunciations and are calling for religion to be banished, or at least to stop receiving state support. Richard Dawkins, whose book *The God Delusion* (2006) was a bestseller, is a good example of this. A prime mover behind the recent decades of genetic reductionism, Dawkins now vociferously campaigns against religion being taught in schools, against perceived religious interference in the project of science and against religion in general. Many of the themes of older science wars are revisited in his work, and his criticism of all aspects of religion (and, by extension, non-scientific thought) is scathing. It is noteworthy that, in all his writings on religion in society, Dawkins never considers sociological understandings of religion and its role in society. For him there is a simple equation to be made: religion = ignorance and credulity.

But the reconciliation story is also contradicted by the contemporary practices of scientists and religionists. As the sociologist Dorothy Nelkin points out, 'God talk' is pervasive among American biologists these days. 'In popular writings, they are using spiritual constructs and religious rhetoric to describe their work and to convey its significance' (Nelkin 2004: 139). Why is this happening?

1   It is a reflection of an ethos that has long driven scientific pursuits.
2   It reflects an enthusiasm about science that is often expressed in excessive hyperbole.
3   It reflects the wider prevalence of God talk that pervades political rhetoric in the United States.
4   It appears to be an instrumental response to public concerns about the social and ethical implications of contemporary biology.

(Ibid.: 140–1)

Point 4 is most pertinent here, and it is a new point – to many observers science is treading on theological turf: genetics and evolutionary biology are touching on cosmological and essentialist questions and producing technologies that challenge understandings of what life is and how it can be brought into being.

Nelkin shows how DNA has taken on an almost mystical significance, and biologists have bought into the language that promotes this idea. 'DNA has taken on the social and cultural meaning of the soul' (Nelkin 2004: 145). The reductionist approach that sees everything as explainable by genes and DNA has led to the position where DNA is seen as being immortal (like the soul) and has led to bitter conflicts between religion and biology. The gene is a powerful deterministic agent: this meets the needs of people for having a grounded understanding of what contemporary life is: I am my genes. We define ourselves through the genome – it is, in Nelkin's words, a solid and immutable structure. But, if this is the case, then any tampering with genes must be a bad – sacrilegious – thing. This has led to campaigns against and restrictions on cloning research, stem-cell research and genetic modification of organisms. It has also led to some scientists being cautious about how they describe their work to other people, particularly those who would see their work as 'morally contestable' (Erickson 2002: 51, n. 20).

Rather than there being a reconciliation between science and religion, the opposite transpires: science and religion attack each other. A good case in point is the debate about the teaching of the theory of evolution in schools – particularly US and, increasingly, UK schools. Should Darwin's theory be presented alongside religious explanations of the emergence of life on earth? Or should Darwin's theory be confined to science classes and creationist, and other religious explanations be reserved for religious education classes?

Why can't some religionists just come to terms with or accommodate scientific findings? After all, many physicists say 'we cannot explain the cause of the moment of creation, the big bang', as a way of gesturing to faith groups that they are not trying to dismiss ideas of a divine creator completely. And many religionists will also adopt this kind of account that is based on a demarcation of territory to be explained. The Catholic Church, for example, has taken this stance with respect to most, although not all, aspects of natural science research, having earlier in its history been responsible for repressing, often quite brutally, scientific understandings of the natural world. But the same doesn't happen with discussions about evolution for many religionists (although they did in the past): no accommodation can be made. Why not? Because to accommodate Darwin's theory of evolution into a religious framework of understanding would, for many religionists, requires them to assert that human beings are no different to other living organisms, that the emergence of human beings was simply part of a random process of evolution, and that therefore there is nothing special about human beings, despite the claims made in religious books that a supreme being has chosen people for a special purpose.

Creationism is, in its pure form, the belief that the Christian Bible's representation of the creation of life on Earth is a true and accurate account: any other account (such as, say, evolution) is a crude lie that not only presents a falsehood but also is a sacrilegious position that insults Christianity and maligns the role of faith. This is a difficult, but not impossible, position to hold in contemporary society given the mass of evidence to the contrary, not least the discovery of the age of the planet we inhabit, the mechanism by which the Sun works, the geological and fossil record and the theory of evolution. Given the mass of this evidence, creationism has declined as a popular account of the origin of life, but it is worth noting that eminent scientists such as Sir Isaac Newton strongly adhered to the tenets of creationism as the dominant, and only plausible, account of the origin of life on Earth.

In recent years a number of attempts have been made to reconcile creationism with contemporary scientific evidence and practices. The most successful of these is Intelligent Design theory (ID or IDT), which has been rather rudely called 'creationism with a web site'. IDT is the project of establishing 'by the usual scientific appeals to reason and evidence' that the world and life in it were purposefully designed by an intelligent agency competent to the task of creating a universe. ID looks for points of 'irreducible complexity' in biological systems and uses these as evidence that a standard evolutionary account cannot explain their emergence: complexity implies deliberate design. Leading ID theorist Michael Behe uses the example of a mousetrap as an irreducibly complex system which could not have arisen without the intervening hand of a designer (Behe 2003: 294). Needless to say, molecular biologists disagree very strongly and are scathing of IDT 'experiments'.

Perhaps surprisingly, IDT has been lent support by a leading STS scholar, Professor Steve Fuller of Warwick University (Fuller 2007). Fuller describes himself as a secular humanist who is not trying to promote, or denigrate for that matter, any religious cause or position. His main thesis is that IDT should be allowed the same position in science as any other theory – i.e., it should be allowed to work towards proving that some kind of intelligent designer was responsible for the generation of life on Earth. This should be visible in experiments and observations. For Fuller, IDT and evolutionism should be discussed at the same level – i.e., the general. Fuller thinks that evolution at the general level has no more explanatory power than IDT. Perhaps this is the case – evolution can't be 'proved' in the way that the theory of gravity can be. But IDT can't be proved either. For Fuller this makes them equivalent. However, when you look at examples of IDT science writing – reports of experiments and formal observations – they are quite strange objects, almost a simulacra of what other scientists get up to. Interestingly, almost all IDT studies are funded by US-based fundamentalist Christian churches, which does suggest some wider public engagement with science, although perhaps not the kind of public engagement that many STS commentators have called for. Fuller's point, that IDT and Darwin's theory can be treated in the same way, is debatable, but his underlying concern about science in society is worthy of further analysis. As far as he is concerned, a scientific paradigm that places the randomness of evolution at its centre serves a social purpose of reducing the value of human life to that equal to all other living things; this paradigm is a necessary consequence of new practices in the life sciences, particularly cloning, genetic testing, stem-cell research and genetic modification of organisms. There's nothing special about us from the perspective of evolutionary theory, according to Fuller, a position shared with many religionists. However, Fuller takes this in a different direction, using it as a critique of the social sciences and an indication of the decadence of sociology in the early twenty-first century:

> I call this emergent sensibility, associated with the new 'third culture' and toward which even sociologists are gradually moving, *bioliberalism*. Bioliberalism consists of a politically devolved eugenics policy that encourages the *casualization of the human condition*, by which I mean the tendency to make it easier for humans to come in and out of existence, especially in terms that do not presume the human condition to be an unmitigated good. Bioliberalism is the biggest threat to the social sciences, as both a disciplinary and a political project: that is, *sociology* and *socialism*. The two italicized concepts are more intimately intertwined than many wish to admit. Indeed, were another reason needed to believe that social scientists constitute the Academic Undead, it would be the ease with which we dissociate the incontrovertible decline of socialism from the sustainability of sociology as a field that retains an intuitive appeal to students and operational purchase on researchers. (Fuller 2006: 12)

This is a serious charge, but one that has a certain resonance to it. Sociology of science and, more recently, science and technology studies have moved towards much more speculative and circumspect forms of analysis and, through the deployment of Actor-Network Theory (Latour 1987), have become much more descriptive and less prescriptive. This is neither a good nor a bad thing, but it does alter considerably the project of sociology as a whole, and it also changes the status of social scientists. If we cannot make more or less definitive statements about the world, if we are simply describing the world, as we are advised to do by STS theorists such as Bruno Latour, then what are we doing? In what ways are we experts?

SEMINAR QUESTIONS

1 Do the 'science wars' indicate an unbreachable gap between different disciplines?

2 What can scientists learn from social science or philosophy?

3 Is ownership of specific 'science' concepts – e.g., relativity or chaos theory – a form of boundary defence on the part of the scientific community?

4 Is it acceptable to teach intelligent design theory in schools?

5 Can science and religion be reconciled?

THE CASE OF CLIMATE CHANGE

Authority and expertise

This question – of who has the authority to represent knowledge – ushers in a whole slew of questions about science in society, questions that have a particular urgency in the current context of anthropogenic climate change (see chapter 10 on the environment for more details on global warming). The Intergovernmental Panel on Climate Change was set up in 1988 to monitor and assess the risks of climate change. It has issued four reports, each one producing more and more evidence for human-made climate change. It also makes predictions for where climate change will go. By 2100 there is a 20 percent risk of a more than 5°C increase in temperatures – this would be catastrophic for humanity and a massive physical change in the planet. 'Even a worldwide temperature increase of 3°C overall is beyond known human experience and would totally change temperature patterns, rainfall, crops, animals and human life worldwide' (Urry 2011: 5). Climate change is, undoubtedly now, the biggest threat facing humankind at the present time. However, unlike the other global catastrophes that have loomed on humanity's horizon (a nuclear Third World War being the most obvious one), global warming and climate change are known to us only through the work and actions of scientists: without their work we would simply not be aware that changes in weather patterns were indicative of a *global* condition that, if unchecked, will lead to a global catastrophe.

What can sociology of science and technology tell us about climate change? And does sociology of science undermine the voice of scientists as experts warning and advising on how to cope with climate change? It could be that, following from the science wars of the 1990s, the relativism of science and technology studies, with their emphasis on the contingent nature of scientific knowledge, weakens the message that climate change science is presenting to society. Given the level of opposition to this message that is emerging from pressure groups and lobbies that are opposed, for example, to carbon-trading schemes and other attempts to reduce fossil fuel consumption, such a situation could be perilous. However, recent STS work on understanding expertise in questions of science and technology may be helpful here.

Harry Collins and Robert Evans's *Rethinking Expertise* (2007: 15) presents an extensive and detailed account of what expertise is and how we can classify and understand different sorts of expertise. Starting from the observation that 'ordinary people are talented and skilful almost beyond comprehension', they identify, firstly, the ubiquitous expertises that most people possess (general and basic knowledge – what Collins and Evans call beer-mat knowledge – through to knowledge gained from primary sources and experiences), then move on to look at the specialist expertises that, for example, scientists and technologists possess and deploy. The central point here is that *all* human expertise touches on tacit knowledge, but some expertise requires the acquisition of specialist tacit knowledge which can only be gained from immersion in a specialist domain (e.g., a scientific community).

Acquiring specialist tacit knowledge requires experience, and experts gain experience through their practices. This leads to higher levels of specialist expertise – firstly, interactional expertise (knowing how to interact in the specialist domain) and, subsequently, contributory expertise (knowing how to do something). Standing above these forms of expertise we find 'meta-expertises', which allow people to make judgements and to discriminate between different experts and forms of knowledge. These range from the ubiquitous expertise of discrimination into which we are socialized by living in a democratic society (i.e., making decisions about political choices) to the specialized forms of expertise one acquires from being a specialist and which allow an expert to make judgements about other experts. These judgements aren't made solely on the basis of personal experiences, however. A final layer of meta-criteria – credentials, experience and track record – are used by people to judge experts and expertise.

Given this analysis, social science can have a role in showing the capacities and capabilities of experts and guiding the public towards making better judgements about experts and their statements, through identifying and explaining the types of expertise involved in particular cases. The academic study of expertise and experience (SEE) (Collins and Evans 2007: 139) could be brought to bear in debates about climate change science, helping to assess the credibility, or otherwise, of statements made by participants in ongoing arguments about the causes, or even existence, of global warming. Showing the origins of the knowledge being deployed by experts would clarify which voices are expressing knowledge based on reliable results and which are expressing 'beer-mat knowledge', which have suitable credentials and which have unproven, or non-existent, track records.

This approach, however, does not imply that the public have a simple deficit of scientific knowledge that needs to be filled. Concerns about the lack of public understanding of science (a 'moral panic', according to Steve Fuller (1997)) have been expressed for many decades in many Western industrial societies, and much time, effort and money has been thrown at this alleged problem. However, Collins and Evans show, and most sociologists of science and technology would agree, that the problem here is not a lack of knowledge about science but a lack of communication and engagement between different parts of society, notably the scientific community and the 'lay' public. The deficit model of the public understanding of science (PUS) is a red herring, one that serves to reinforce the status of science as a superior form of knowledge, but also one that is used to excuse the scientific community for poor communication of its work by blaming non-scientists for a lack of understanding. The more robust and appropriate idea of public engagement with science and technology (PEST) has been adopted in recent years to try to investigate the relationship between science and its publics and to attempt to foster a more mutually aware relationship. This has been reflected, at least in part, in recent years in UK science research councils' insistence that publicly funded scientific research should be disseminated to the public; after all, it is the public who are paying for this. But this is not much of a two-way street, and much dissemination is done in a top-down way, rather than inviting the public into the sites of scientific research (Toumey 2006). Perhaps what is needed is CUSP – critical understanding of science in public – where the public are involved

Recent years have seen an increase in the number of science festivals, aimed at engaging the public more with science, scientists and their world. This can be particularly important in some cases where public perceptions of scientific advances may be negative – for example, surrounding genetically modified crops. (© CambPlants University of Cambridge/Flickr)

in, and aware of, the negotiation and construction of the meaning of science in public (Broks 2006: 94).

In the case of climate change, despite the large amount of scientific knowledge concerning the topic and the huge amount of media coverage it has received, there has been almost no significant action taken by any national or international agency that has served to reduce greenhouse gas emissions. It could be argued that the PUS model – climate change scientists telling the public about a great and imminent danger – needs to be replaced with a PEST model – climate change scientists, members of the public, agents of the state and the media joining together to consider what the evidence is and how it should best be disseminated to society. Given the high levels of apparent controversy concerning global warming, despite a situation where there is almost total unanimity in the scientific community on its causes and consequences, it would appear that more efforts must be made in this direction.

Beyond knowledge and expertise

However, a lack of knowledge of the science of climate change may not be the reason for a general lack of public action. Kari Marie Norgaard's ethnographic study of a Norwegian ski resort's response to the palpable effects of climate change on their weather and, consequently, livelihoods showed, alarmingly, that most members of this community knew a large amount about climate change science and were not sceptical about global warming (Norgaard 2011). Yet, despite this, they were not committed to taking any form of political action on the issue or even changing their own practices. Is what we need more science, or something else?

There are lots of ways of explaining inaction on climate change, from political inertia and the actions of fossil fuel companies lobbying governments and publics to mistrust climate change science to the idea that the way that climate change is represented to us serves to make it something that is remote, and therefore irrelevant to us (Doyle 2011). It may be that all of these things come together to create a perfect storm of inaction and, as both Giddens and Urry point out, the only thing that will really spur us into taking action is catastrophic climate change itself, by which time our actions will be too late (Giddens 2011; Urry 2011).

There are other factors at work here. As I noted above, we live in a society that is infused with scientism and where technological determinism is a standard mode of explanation of social change. Our technoscientific society asks constantly for more science and technology and expects more technology to address human needs, wants, desires and, of course, problems. A recent article in the journal *Nature*, the most prestigious and widely read academic journal of the scientific community, called for states to abandon using coal, start taxing carbon, and invest in technologies to address climate change and global warming (Helm 2012). These technologies range from electric cars to geoengineering on a global scale, such as pumping SO_2 into the upper atmosphere or seeding the oceans with iron oxide to promote algal blooms. Applying Collins and Evans's schema, we can appraise these technoscientific experts' proposals according to clear criteria and considerations of their reliability and track record, although doing this may make us miss the wider point that it was the rapid expansion of capitalism and consumerism that has largely got us into the present situation – capitalism has created a problem for which capitalism will now sell us a solution. And one final irony pertains here: if

BOX 11.8 BIG SCIENCE TO THE RESCUE?

Geoengineering – using technology to alter the climate of the planet – is one possible solution to the problem of climate change that is receiving considerable attention. Despite some scepticism from the IPCC, which concluded that geoengineering options were largely unproven, research in this direction has continued. There are two main groups of geoengineering proposals: carbon dioxide capture and removal and the deflection or management of solar radiation. Some proposals are relatively mundane – adding iron to oceans to promote the growth of algae that will take up CO_2 and release oxygen, for example. Others are wildly ambitious, such as constructing mirrors or sunshades in space. In recent years a large number of patents have been taken out over methods to engineer the world's climate, something that causes concern among some climate change scientists (Hamilton 2013).

Microsoft founder Bill Gates, the world's richest man, 'has provided at least $4.5 million of his own money over 3 years for the study of methods that could alter the stratosphere to reflect solar energy, techniques to filter carbon dioxide directly from the atmosphere, and brighten ocean clouds' (Kintisch 2010).

technology could and did solve the global problem of climate change then, yes, technology would indeed be the thing that changes our society.

SEMINAR QUESTIONS

1 PUS, PEST or CUSP?

2 What makes an expert?

3 Is technology the solution to anthropogenic climate change?

CONCLUSION: WHAT SHOULD SOCIOLOGY OF SCIENCE AND TECHNOLOGY DO?

Distilling the last century or so of sociology of science and technology is difficult. We have moved from a situation of almost consensus as to what sociology of science should concern itself with (the institution of science) to a remarkable diversity of topics, approaches and theories. The account presented here has focused on a major theme in the sociology of science: the construction and articulation of structures of thought and practice in society and the effect these have on the execution and perception of science and technology. But much sociology of science has focused, particularly following the work of the Edinburgh school in the sociology of scientific knowledge, on clarifying how science is done, what happens in laboratories and research sites, and how scientific communities come together to carry out shared projects or construct knowledge networks. Sociology of science has produced acute analyses of how scientific institutions and funding regimes come about (Webster 1991; Fuller 2000; Nowotny, Scott and Gibbons 2001) and have consequences for the production of knowledge. And the subdiscipline of scientometrics, the measurement of scientific outputs and using these measurements to map scientific networks (Garfield 1979) – a Cinderella subject in the 1970s and 1980s – has grown hugely in significance with the rise, particularly in the UK and the USA, of institutional quantitative measurement of research outputs as signifiers of research activity and even quality. From narrow beginnings, sociology of science has become a very broad range of research sites, topics, concerns and theories. However, sociology of science is becoming eclipsed by its recent offspring, science and technology studies (STS).

STS is more coherent in terms of a core set of theoretical concerns and orientations, as ANT has become the main way of making sense of objects of inquiry, but there is still a wide diversity of topics under consideration (from big pharma as an actor in the construction of state policies to social networking technologies as contributory to personal identity constructions). However, much of what these disciplines are doing is trying to make sense of science and technologies as *practices*, and it is very likely that this trajectory for studying the social world will continue. Rather than concerning itself with examining the epistemology of scientific knowledge as an object to be emulated or contextualized, sociology of science can look at scientific knowledge (the product of the endeavours of science) as a set of practices (Mol 2003: 5). From this perspective, knowledge is not about facts, it is about manipulation, and the question we can ask is 'How is knowledge being practised, being done?' This connects squarely to Collins and Evans's recent work on expertise and the role of the social sciences in understanding expertises. Knowledge as practice presents a new set of questions for sociologists, ones that cut across more traditional socio-logical concerns and bring into focus new objects of inquiry, particularly technological objects. We need to recognize that knowledge is assembled from different things: Who are the distinctive subjects, in what specific sites are they operating, and what objects are they using?

Sociology still struggles with questions of science and technology; this is not surprising given the amount and variety of these things. Despite many decades of work, sociology is still not even sure what these things actually are. The prevalence of scientism and technological determinism has hampered the project of the social analysis of science and technology, and these are still significant things to address. While this can be quite frustrating, it is what makes sociology such an exciting discipline. Not only that, it may be that sociology of science and technology will have an important role in helping society understand the science, challenges and possible adaptations and solutions to climate change.

SEMINAR QUESTIONS

1 How should sociology approach the topic of science and technology in society?

2 What should sociology of science and technology study?

3 Is classical sociological theory (e.g., Marx, Durkheim, Weber) still of use in understanding science, technology and social change?

4 How do *you* acquire knowledge and deploy knowledge? Is this a useful starting point for a sociology of knowledge?

FURTHER READING

▶ MacKenzie, D., and J. Wajcman (eds) (1999) *The Social Shaping of Technology* (2nd edn, Open University Press). A very good general introduction to understanding technology in society. This edited collection includes classic and contemporary writers on technology and society as well as a comprehensive theoretical overview from the editors.

▶ Latour, B. (1987) *Science in Action* (Harvard University Press) and (2005) *Reassembling the Social: An Introduction to Actor-Network Theory* (Oxford University Press). Two clas-sic texts by the leading theorist in science and technology studies. The first presents a detailed account of how science and technology are produced, the second a theoretical treatise on Actor-Network Theory, the main theory in contemporary STS, now making significant inroads into other areas of sociological interest.

▶ Erickson, M. (2005) *Science, Culture and Society: Understanding Science in the 21st Century* (Polity); Sismondo, S. (2004) *An Introduction to Science and Technology Studies* (Blackwell); Yearley, S. (2004) *Making Sense of Science: Understanding the Social Study of Science* (Sage). These three books present general introductions to science and technology in society. The first approaches the topic from a sociology of science perspective, the second uses STS, and the third connects contemporary social theory to the study of science with more of an emphasis on the environment.

▶ To find out more about emergent technologies and current scientific research there are two UK-based publications that are invaluable. The first – *New Scientist* – takes a more news-based format but also includes extended features on science research topics. *New Scientist* is aimed at a general audience who are either working or have a background in science, engineering, technology or mathematics. The second – *Nature* – is a much more heavyweight publication. While still presenting news and comment on science and technology, *Nature* publishes cutting-edge science research in the same format as science journals. It is one of the most prestigious journals for scientists to have their work published in, and as such it is a very useful resource for social scientists interested in what is happening in the communities inhabited by academic scientists and leading technology researchers. Both publications are available online and in print form.

12

DEVELOPMENT AND UNDERDEVELOPMENT

rethinking the shape of a globalizing world

PAUL HOPPER

CONTENTS

INTRODUCTION

DEVELOPMENT AND UNDERDEVELOPMENT HAVE long been important themes within sociology (e.g., Worsley 1964). The concern of this chapter is to examine these issues in relation to contemporary sociology as well as the wider global context. In the case of the latter, it will be contended that development is increasingly determined by globalization and global environmental decline. Quite simply, development is taking place within a period of unprecedented global interconnectedness – whether in the form of trade, finance, communication or governance (to cite but a few forms of human activity) – that informs the nature of development but also has profound consequences for the environment.

However, the central claim of this chapter is that there are now compelling reasons to rethink the nature and role of development, a move that will have considerable consequences for future sociological approaches to this subject area. To begin with, the economic rise of Asia and Latin America, as well as some African states, disrupts the traditional geographical focus of development upon the Global South (UNDP 2013). This is compounded by the relative economic decline of some Northern countries, a shift that goes beyond the recent difficulties that they are experiencing as a result of the global economic crisis. At the same time, states and regions outside of the North are deepening their links in terms of trade and investment, such as China's growing relationship with Africa (Kaplinsky, McCormick and Morris 2010) – see box 12.1. In this regard, Jan Nederveen Pieterse (2012) believes we are witnessing an East–South turn which is challenging the North–South axis that has dominated development thinking in the post-war period. Similarly, the economic rise of the BRICS (Brazil, Russia, India, China and South Africa) – by 2020 they are expected to contribute nearly half of all global gross domestic product (GDP) growth – leads others to emphasize South–South cooperation (e.g., Cabral 2013) – see figures 12.1 and 12.2. In addition, the globalization of information and communication technologies (ICTs), such as mobile phones, the internet and satellite telecommunications, is aiding business development in the South by ensuring that more citizens can participate in the global network society. All of this is contributing to more complex patterns of global poverty and inequality and blurring patterns of development and underdevelopment. For example, gated communities surrounded by deprivation can be found in both the North and the South. Finally, and most significantly, environmental decline raises major difficulties for the economic growth model that has underpinned development in the post-war period.

BOX 12.1 CHINA'S DEEPENING ENGAGEMENT WITH AFRICA

China's bilateral trade with Africa grew from $10 billion (£6 billion) in 2000 to $150 billion in 2011 (Branigan 2012). But China has also been fostering its soft power or influence within Africa through such measures as helping to fund the new African Union headquarters, which opened in Addis Ababa, Ethiopia, in January 2012. In addition it is estimated that, between 2001 and 2011, Beijing committed $75 billion (£48 billion) to aid and development projects in Africa, including debt relief and infrastructural works, but also the provision of medical support and education and training programmes. It has entailed China sending thousands of doctors and teachers to work in Africa (Provost and Harris 2013).

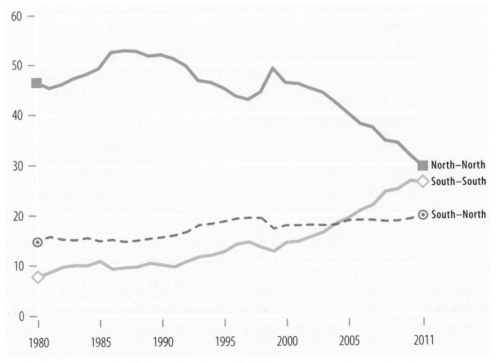

Figure 12.1 Share of world merchandise trade (%)

Source: UNDP (2013).

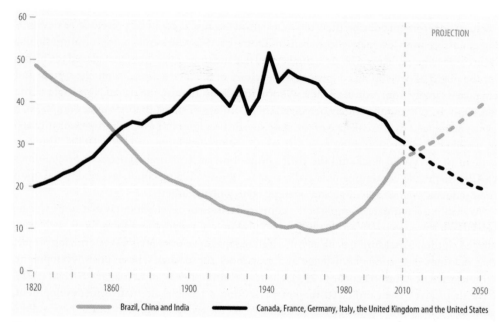

PROJECTION

Brazil, China and India — Canada, France, Germany, Italy, the United Kingdom and the United States

Figure 12.2 Share of global output (%)

Source: UNDP (2013).

WHAT IS DEVELOPMENT?

Contested theories, contested politics

In order to examine the sociological debates about development and underdevelopment, we need to understand the concept of development. The origins of development are disputed, but for many writers on this subject its intellectual roots can be traced to eighteenth-century European Enlightenment notions of progress, rationalism and modernity. Indeed, the idea of becoming modern and modernizing is often viewed as both the goal and the process of development. Development in its contemporary guise emerged after the Second World War with the creation of the UN and, in particular, the international financial institutions the World Bank and the International Monetary Fund (IMF). While development is something that all countries and regions experience, the traditional focus within development studies has been upon countries in the South and their perceived underdevelopment. However, as will be returned to in the conclusion to this chapter, this approach to development may need to be revised in the light of contemporary transformations.

More broadly, development is a complex and contested area of study, something that is evident in the different disciplinary and theoretical approaches to the subject as well as the divergent explanations of underdevelopment. In addition, development is inextricably bound up with issues of power and politics and competing conceptions of how societies should be organized. This is especially evident in relation to development theories that have come to form an integral part of the sociology of development (see Graaff 2003). Thus, modernization theory, the dominant development approach in the 1950s, was politically expedient for

Western governments during the Cold War period because it could be presented to developing countries as an alternative to socialism. From the 1960s onwards, modernization theory itself came to be challenged by structuralist and dependency approaches that placed the blame for the plight of developing countries on the nature of the international capitalist system and emanated largely from radical and left political traditions. In turn, the rise of New Right in the USA and the UK and the widely perceived shortcomings of statist theories of development, a view encouraged by the collapse of the state socialist regimes in Eastern Europe, contributed to neoliberalism becoming the new orthodoxy within development in the 1980s. This was evident in the World Bank and the IMF's promotion of structural adjustment programmes (SAPs) that made continuing financial assistance for developing countries conditional upon their reducing welfare spending and opening up to global markets.

Arguably, the ultimate example of the contested nature of development is that some writers working in this area maintain that we should give up on development for reasons such as its alleged cultural bias. More specifically, it is claimed that development is a Westernizing project that devalues indigenous knowledge and grassroots approaches. These 'post-development' writers, such as Arturo Escobar (1995), Gustavo Esteva (1992) and Wolfgang Sachs (1992), have themselves been criticized for not presenting a feasible alternative to development, although they would challenge this contention. As for today, at the start of the new millennium, the contested nature of development has never been more apparent as neoliberalism, participatory approaches, post-development perspectives and sustainable development all compete to define contemporary development theory and practice.

Another notable feature of development is that it is an evolving concept. It has evolved from a concept concerned primarily with economic growth to one which pays more attention to the quality of human life, a shift that has entailed attaching greater weight to the attainment of political freedom and social welfare targets. This pattern reflects the post-war dominance of development by economics but also how other academic disciplines such as sociology have come to exert greater influence upon the subject in the recent period. Furthermore, there have been other areas and issues, such as debt, the international terms of trade, the role of aid, conditionality, 'good governance', human security and the environment, that have come to shape the development agenda. For critics, however, if development is forever evolving and continuing to incorporate new areas, it makes it difficult to think outside or beyond development and even to critique it.

Conceptualizing development

Despite its contested and evolving nature, there have been numerous attempts to conceptualize development. At a basic level, development has been defined simply as 'good change' (Chambers 1997). But, given that post-development writers would dispute such an assertion, Cowen and Shenton's contention that our focus should be upon 'What is intended by development?' rather than with 'What is development?' is perhaps apposite (1996: viii). In this spirit, in the late 1980s the United Nations Development Programme (UNDP) began to employ the Human Development Index (HDI) as an alternative measurement of development to the purely economic GDP. The HDI stresses the importance of people having a range of opportunities in order to lead productive and creative lives and to develop their human capabilities. Development from this perspective is about 'expanding the choices people have to lead lives that they value' (UNDP 2001: 9). Hence the HDI acknowledges that the most basic of human capabilities are to lead a long and healthy life, to be knowledgeable through access to education, and to have the

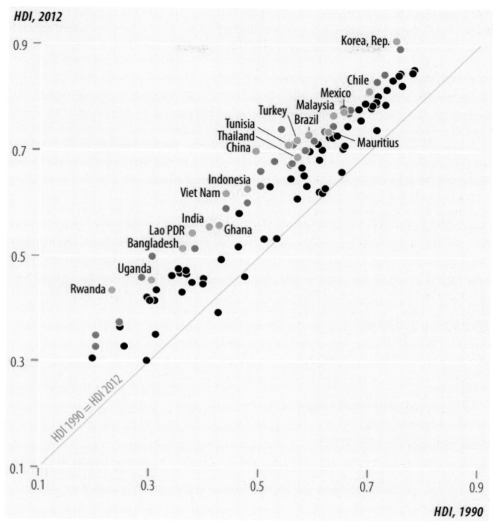

Figure 12.3 Selected Southern countries' growth in the HDI, 1990 and 2012

Source: UNDP (2013).

necessary resources to achieve a decent standard of living. Interestingly, as well as enjoying GDP growth, many Southern countries are experiencing gains in relation to the HDI (see figure 12.3).

The focus of the HDI is therefore upon human wellbeing. But, for many people working within development, this goal also entails the ability to participate in the life of the community, human security and empowerment. Of course, economic growth continues to be an important determinant of development and, indeed, helps to provide the resources necessary to attain human wellbeing, a point acknowledged within the HDI, which continues to factor in an economic measurement in the form of per capita income. In addition, this broader conception of development can be found in Amartya Sen's influential work *Development as Freedom* (2001), in which he makes the case for development being oriented towards enhancing human freedom and the provision of choice and opportunity for people, employing the vocabulary of 'entitlements' and 'capabilities'. It also reflects the increased prominence of human rights, as well as ethical and moral agendas, within development over the last decade or so (Corbridge 1998; Elliott 2002).

The UN Millennium Development Goals

Finally, the UN Millennium Development Goals (MDGs) are perhaps the clearest statement by the international community to date about the nature and purpose of development. They were adopted in September 2000 and synthesized the various declarations and targets from the numerous international summits and conferences held during the 1990s. The eight goals with their respective targets were to be achieved by 2015 (see box 12.2). The MDGs followed the United Nations Millennium Declaration and, taken together, formed a universal framework for pursuing

BOX 12.2 THE MILLENNIUM DEVELOPMENT GOALS AND TARGETS

The UN adopted the MDGs in September 2000, which consist of eight goals that were to be achieved by 2015:

1   Eradicate extreme poverty and hunger.
2   Achieve universal primary education.
3   Promote gender equality and empower women.
4   Reduce child mortality.
5   Improve maternal health.
6   Combat HIV/AIDS, malaria and other diseases.
7   Ensure environmental sustainability.
8   Develop a global partnership for development.

Source: UNMDG (2005)

In order to meet the MDGs, specific targets were established for each goal; notable among them were the following:

Goal 1: Reduce by half the proportion of people living on less than $1 a day and the proportion of people who suffer from hunger.
Goal 2: Ensure that all boys and girls complete a full course of primary schooling.
Goal 3: Eliminate gender disparity in primary and secondary education, preferably by 2005, and at all levels by 2015.
Goal 4: Reduce by two-thirds the mortality rate among children under five.
Goal 5: Reduce by three-quarters the maternal mortality rate.
Goal 6: Halt and begin to reverse the spread of HIV/AIDS and the incidence of malaria and other major diseases.
Goal 7: Reduce by half the proportion of people without sustainable access to safe drinking water.
Goal 8: Develop further an open trading and financial system that is rule-based, predictable and non-discriminatory.

Source: UNMDG (2005).

development and eradicating extreme poverty, notably halving the number of people living on less than $1 per day between 1990 and 2015. From the perspective of the UN, creating a common agenda would encourage joined-up thinking and action within international development.

However, the UN Millennium Development Goals have attracted criticism. Some critics believe the time frame for achieving such ambitious goals is unrealistic (Black and White 2006). Moreover, Ashwani Saith (2006) contends that the MDGs both neglect poverty and deprivation within advanced industrial economies and fail to address the persistence of high levels of global inequality. From a sociological perspective, Alan Thomas (2000) has expressed concern that the shift to target-setting within development diminishes the notion of it as a historical process of social change and ignores the fact that dealing with such complex issues as poverty invariably requires deeper structural changes to societies and even social transformation.

GLOBALIZATION AND DEVELOPMENT

As was mentioned in the introduction to this chapter, development and underdevelopment now need to be understood in the context of a period of unprecedented global interconnectedness that we have come to call globalization. Sociology has contributed significantly to the study of globalization (e.g., Giddens 1990; Robertson 1992), and different schools of thought have emerged to account for it. For instance, globalists consider that globalization marks a new phase in human history that entails the emergence of a global economy based upon open markets and the breaking-down of national borders, a development that has been aided by advances in transportation and the spread of information and communication technologies (ICTs) (Ohmae 1990; Wriston 1992). They see evidence of globalization in the increased volume of international trade, in the greater mobility of capital, information and people, in the growing power of multinational corporations (MNCs), and in rising levels of foreign direct investment (FDI). In relation to development, increasing global economic interdependence is the overarching context in which less economically developed countries (LEDCs) must operate. From a globalist perspective, such interdependence makes it more difficult for states to pursue national economic management and, in particular, undermines the developmental state that played such a prominent role in development from the end of the Second World War until the rise of neoliberalism in the 1980s. From a sociological perspective, Scott Lash and John Urry (1987, 1994) similarly maintain that these conditions have implications for all states and their ability to act autonomously. More specifically, capitalism has departed from its organized national/societal form to become both disorganized and global, characterized by highly mobile and complex economies (of signs and people).

Determining the impact of globalization upon development is complicated by the fact that writers such as Paul Hirst and Grahame Thompson (1999) dispute its existence. Based upon their research, Hirst and Thompson maintain that the world economy is far from being genuinely 'global'. Trade, investment and financial flows are concentrated in a triad of Europe, Japan and North America and look likely to remain so; they therefore contend it is more appropriate to talk of 'triadization' than of globalization. Hirst and Thompson acknowledge certain contemporary developments in the flows of trade, people, finance and capital investment across societies but point to historical precedents such as the period 1870–1914, when they claim the world economy was even more internationalized than it is in our own time. Hirst and

Thompson therefore conclude that contemporary trends can best be described as a process of economic internationalization rather than as fully developed globalization.

Nevertheless, since the publication of Hirst and Thompson's book, regions and countries such as Latin America and China have become more deeply embedded in the global economy and taken off economically, and a growing number of African states are displaying signs of global engagement and economic prosperity. Hirst and Thompson have also been accused of focusing overly upon the economic aspects of globalization and underplaying its other dimensions, such as the cultural and technological, which critics argue display clear signs of globalization.

Advocates of globalization emphasize its range of contributions to development. In considering the merits of this contention, three aspects of globalization will be considered here in relation to development: firstly, economic globalization; secondly, global communication; and, thirdly, global migration.

Economic globalization

For advocates of globalization, there are many aspects of economic globalization that both facilitate and shape development. For example, it is claimed that the expansion of world trade that is an integral part of economic globalization has contributed to a rise in average incomes and material living standards, including within the Global South (Bhagwati 2004; Wolf 2004). In particular, states that have participated fully in this trade, for example China and South Korea, have enjoyed considerable economic growth. China is set to overtake the USA as the world's largest economy in 2018, although it will still be behind America in per capita terms (Jacques 2012). Likewise, India has pursued export-led growth, and this has contributed to the transformation of the Indian economy, which by 2008 was growing at more than 9 percent per annum. Indeed, the extent of India's economic growth led the British government to announce in November 2012 that it will end financial aid to the country by 2015.

Another claim made in relation to economic globalization is that a feature of growing economic interdependence has been the tendency for production to shift to the developing world. This movement is a consequence of higher wage levels in more economically developed countries (MEDCs) and hence higher production costs, and the fact that ICTs make it relatively easy for MNCs to relocate much of their production to developing societies where labour costs are cheaper. At the same time, MNCs are able to maintain their communication links with offices, branches and outlets in the industrialized North. MNCs have therefore become truly global enterprises and production has been globalized in the process. Globalists argue that this is reflected not only in the massive migration of capital from major OECD (Organization for Economic Cooperation and Development) countries to low-cost production sites in the developing world but also in the emergence of a new international division of labour, involving the transfer of manufacturing industry from the North to the newly industrializing countries (NICs) of East Asia and Latin America. This transformation presents obvious challenges for existing industries in the developed world and helps to explain the shift to the 'service economy' in parts of the North, with some countries focusing on areas such as banking, insurance, software development and accountancy. However, the rise in outsourcing means Northern domination of the service sector is also vulnerable; many global companies are choosing to go to India, for example (Schifferes 2007).

In short, according to its advocates, economic globalization has contributed significantly to development in the South and, in the process, has served to blur the North–South division

(Kiely 1998). In particular, it has aided the economic development of countries such as China and India. Indeed, both are now investing some of their growing wealth overseas, including purchasing Western companies.

Global communication

Beyond the expansion of world trade and the evolution of the global economy, there are additional globalizing processes that have implications for development, notably the telecommunications revolution. Technological advances such as the internet, mobile phones, fibre-optic cables, and satellite and digital technologies facilitate global communication and the exchange of data and in doing so potentially allow LEDCs to accelerate their development. This is because information (knowledge) and communication (networking) are increasingly viewed in the contemporary period as important sources of wealth-generation (see Castells 1996). Indeed, some Latin American governments consider a post-industrial mode of development, one which is based upon information technology, the service sector and a knowledge-based economy, to be a way of breaking free from their role as producers of commodities. In particular, there have been some interesting innovations in relation to mobile phones in recent years, such as in mobile banking and micro-financing. For example, M-PESA is a branchless banking service that is widely used in Kenya and Tanzania (see box 12.3). Even war-torn Somalia has a well-developed mobile phone and internet sector that has been aided by the advanced money transfer business.

BOX 12.3 KENYA, ICTS AND DEVELOPMENT

ICTs have contributed significantly to development within Kenya, especially aiding the formation of small businesses. Kenya has the fastest broadband connections on the continent, and the Kenyan government is seeking to build Africa's 'Silicon Savannah', a $7 billion (£4.36 billion), 5,000-acre technology city. Mobile phone usage has also spread dramatically within the country and has encouraged the growth in the number of mobile phone apps built by local designers that are geared to local needs. For example, M-Farm allows farmers to get information about market prices and weather conditions as well as helping sell their products. In short, Kenya is now widely perceived as the regional centre for communication and financial services (Gatehouse 2012). However, additional factors have contributed to Kenya's economic development, such as an economy that is open to foreign investment and a labour force containing a relatively high number of university-educated professionals.

However, critics contend that the impact of ICTs upon development in the South is reduced by the persistence of a 'global digital divide'. In other words, many Southern countries still have limited access to ICTs, thereby reducing the capacity of such technology to act as a catalyst for development. In this regard, Africa is less endowed with both ICTs and supporting telecommunication infrastructure compared to industrialized regions in the North, meaning that African citizens and states are not as integrated into global information and communication networks as their Northern counterparts. Internet usage is also uneven in Africa, with the majority of users based in South Africa. By the end of 2010, internet user penetration in Africa had reached 9.6 percent, which was some way behind the developing country average of 21 percent – the global average was 30 percent (ITU 2010). More broadly, 71 percent of the population in MEDCs were online in 2010 compared to only 21 percent of the population in LEDCs (ibid.).

Nevertheless there are signs of the diminution of the global digital divide. The dramatic rise in GSM (Global System for Mobile Communications) connections, especially in the South, means that mobile phones are the first communication technology to have more users in the developing world than the developed world. According to the International Telecommunication Union (ITU), the developing world increased its share of total mobile subscriptions from 53 percent in 2005 to 73 percent in 2010 (ITU 2010). Most importantly, third- and fourth-generation (3G and 4G) mobile telecommunications provide internet access, enabling the less well-off to make wireless connections to the Web without having to purchase PCs. Furthermore, access to mobile networks has grown to the extent that at the end of 2010 it was available to 90 percent of the world's population (ibid.). In addition, a number of practical measures are being implemented in order to narrow the global digital divide. For example, the construction of an undersea fibre-optic cable around the continent is intended to transform high-speed communications within Africa and ensure integration into the international telecommunications network. More broadly, the UN is attempting to connect every village in the world to the internet by 2015.

Development takes place via many routes and at various levels. Migration contributes to the development of sending countries as migrants can remit money back home, and can do so increasingly thanks to global communications technologies such as money transfer services, as advertised here in Mogadishu, Somalia. (© Albany Associates/Flickr)

Global migration

Global migration is another aspect of globalization that arguably contributes to development. More specifically, the contribution is from the remittances that millions of migrant workers transfer to family back home (or to family in third countries) annually. According to the World Bank, in 2012 these money transfers topped £335 billion, which was three times larger than the global aid budget and constituted a threefold increase since 2002 (Provost 2013). Moreover, the World Bank believes the figure could be much higher, as globally there were more than 214 million migrants in 2012 and many of them bypass the banks and big money transfer companies that are its main source of data.

For some LEDCs, remittances account for a major proportion of national income. For example, Tajikistan receives the equivalent of 47 percent of its GDP from its workers abroad (Buckley, Haidar and Provost 2013). Indeed, for many LEDCs, remittances are worth more than the aid they receive: in 2011, Bangladesh received over £472 million in remittances from migrants in the UK compared to UK aid of £236 million. And it is not only LEDCs but also rising economic powers that benefit from cash being sent from overseas: China and India were the biggest beneficiaries of remittances in 2012, with each receiving over £38 billion (Provost 2013).

In short, many diaspora communities are making a significant contribution to development (see box 12.4). This method also has the additional advantage of money being sent directly to families, whereas a substantial proportion of bilateral aid can often be absorbed by bureaucratic governments. Furthermore, for LEDCs this is generally a more reliable source of income than aid, with the latter susceptible to fluctuation especially during periods of economic downturn, when governments are looking for ways to tighten budgets. All of this means that any attempt to resist this form of globalization – such as Northern governments seeking to limit or reduce migrant labour – can have a major impact upon the incomes of LEDCs. Commentators have long noted that global poverty reduction strategies need to be geared more towards facilitating this important source of development income. For instance, addressing the interest rates charged for remittances by banks and wire transfer firms – the average fee in 2012 was 9 percent – would help to ensure that migrants' families receive more money (Provost 2013). In addition, the harsh way in which migrant workers are treated in many parts of the world requires serious international attention leading to concerted action.

BOX 12.4 SOMALIA, MIGRATION AND DEVELOPMENT

Around 1.5 million Somalis live abroad, and it is estimated that they send back remittances of up to $2 billion a year to their relatives, which has been vital in the context of the collapse of direct bilateral assistance for Somalia. Moreover, a UNDP-sponsored report found that, in 2011, the Somali diaspora was also heavily involved in development and post-conflict reconstruction through the promotion of education, health care, public infrastructure and private enterprise. In addition, people from the diaspora were returning temporarily to provide technical skills, advice and leadership (Hammond 2011). Interestingly, the researchers found evidence of tensions between local and diaspora Somalis, with the former believing the latter lacked real knowledge of present-day Somalia, while some diaspora returnees complained that their efforts were unappreciated by local people.

Cumulatively, global migration, global communication and the other processes associated with globalization have implications for sociology. For example, John Urry (2000) maintains that the daily permeation of national borders by global processes and flows presents a major challenge for sociology, which has traditionally been centred upon an examination of national societies. For Urry, it necessitates developing sociology beyond societies: a 'sociology of mobilities' that is able to go beyond the borders of the nation-state. However, Urry's focus upon mobility, as well as more generally the emphasis within the globalization literature upon metaphors such as scapes, networks and flows, has been criticized for being light on empirical data and research (e.g., Favell 2001).

Critics of globalization

The linkages between globalization and development made by advocates of globalization have provoked a variety of critical responses. For critics of globalization, claims about its processes contributing to development and blurring the North–South division ignore the persistence of underdevelopment in many LEDCs, particularly in Africa, where some states are displaying signs of fragility and economic decline. In addition, many within the anti-globalization movement condemn what they regard as the lack of international regulation and control of globalization. This is leading, they argue, to developing countries being exposed to the often unfair and unethical practices of MNCs, with their workers having to endure poor labour standards and working conditions – a state of affairs not helped by the fact that the International Labour Organization (ILO) lacks substantive enforcement powers (Amoore 2005). Indeed, the greater mobility of capital has not been matched by the greater mobility of labour. Furthermore, the lack of effective governance of world capital and financial markets means that LEDCs are vulnerable to any downturns in commodity prices for their products as well as to economic recessions in our more globally connected world. In contrast, from the perspective of advocates of globalization, greater regulation of the world economy will serve to reduce world trade, and this in turn will reduce average incomes in the developing world.

Sceptics also contest the notion that we are witnessing a new international division of labour facilitated by global technologies and processes. They note that many poorer countries in the developing world simply lack the productive capacity and infrastructure to diversify and shift to manufacturing and service sectors, and hence continue to be reliant upon the export of primary products. Nor can they rely upon MNCs moving into their countries and regions and providing this productive capacity and infrastructure. This is because, according to Hirst and Thompson (1999), genuinely global or transnational companies are relatively rare. Based upon their research, they argue that most companies are nationally based, if for no other reason than it is costly to relocate. From their perspective, this in turn raises doubts about the extent to which production has been globalized.

Finally, from the perspective of sceptics, if globalization does not exist, then it follows that states, including developmental states, retain the capacity to pursue independent economic and political management. Indeed, sceptics argue that globalization can be politically expedient for governments, with political leaders citing it as a way of deflecting attention away from their own performance for their country's lack of economic growth.

In summary, the nature of the impact of globalization upon development is contested. But on balance this relationship is likely to be more complex than both advocates and critics of globalization allow for. For instance, their respective positions on the issue of whether globalization is leading to greater convergence between the North and the South neglect the extent of the economic disparities that exist within these blocs, both between countries and within them. Moreover, determining whether this diversity is because of globalization or other factors, will require a contextualizing approach that examines what is taking place within particular countries and societies and the nature of the engagement with globalizing processes (Hay and Marsh 2001; Hopper 2006). It is here where there is a particular need for a sociological approach to globalization and development.

Adding to the complexity, what is arguably underpinning many of the disputes surrounding globalization is a basic disagreement over whether it is a process or a specific (neoliberal capitalist) project (Nederveen Pieterse 2001: 152). In reality, it is likely to be a combination of both. While neoliberalism has undoubtedly facilitated the global spread of trade and finance, many writers on globalization maintain that, as a phenomenon, it both predates neoliberalism and includes important non-economic dimensions. Finally, the broader changes discussed here have implications for the future trajectory of development and, in turn, sociological approaches to it, a point which is returned to at the end of this chapter. More specifically, the rapid economic growth of a number of countries and regions traditionally located in the Global South disrupts the conventional North–South territorial or spatial conception of development.

SEMINAR QUESTIONS

1 Is globalization helping or hindering development?
2 To what extent, if at all, does globalization undermine the Global North–South divide?
3 Are migration policies more important than overseas aid for development in LEDCs?

POVERTY, INEQUALITY AND DEVELOPMENT

Trends in poverty and inequality

Sociology has a long-held interest in poverty and inequality (e.g., Townsend 1979), and in the present day these issues are increasingly considered as global phenomena, especially in relation to globalization (e.g., Martell 2010). For many people working in development, dealing with underdevelopment is the most effective way of achieving poverty reduction and in turn addressing global poverty and inequality. However, there remains a dispute about whether levels of world poverty and income inequality have risen or fallen in the recent period. For instance, Martin Wolf (2000) maintains that global inequality and the proportion of the world's population in extreme poverty declined in the 1980s and 1990s. This view is contested by Robert Hunter Wade (2003), who is critical of how institutions such as the World Bank determine and measure poverty and income inequality. More broadly, the nature of the interrelationships between poverty, inequality, development and globalization is the source of much debate (e.g., Held and Kaya 2007; Kaplinsky 2005). But, as will now be shown, what can be stated with greater certainty is that patterns of global poverty and inequality have become increasingly complex, and this forms the broader context for contemporary international development as well as a sociological approach to this subject area.

At the beginning of the new millennium, according to the UNDP (2001), approximately

1.2 billion people lived on less than US$1 a day and 2.8 billion people on less than US$2 a day. Of the 1.2 billion, 800 million were located in South Asia and sub-Saharan Africa. Yet the number of people living in absolute poverty declined from 33 percent in 1981 to 18 percent in 2001. This reduction is largely down to the rapid economic growth of such countries as China and India. Indeed, the fast economic growth of the two most populous nations not only impacts upon the global poverty rate but is also disguising the divergence between rich and low-income countries (World Bank 2005: 7).

A more recent World Bank report by Shaohua Chen and Martin Ravallion (2008) confirmed that there has been strong progress towards reducing overall poverty: 1.4 billion people in the developing world were living on less than US$1.25 a day in 2005 compared with 1.9 billion in 1981. However, new cost-of-living data suggests poverty has been more widespread across the developing world over the past twenty-five years than previously estimated, with up to 400 million more people living in poverty than earlier thought. Moreover, regional differences in poverty reduction trends persist. For example, poverty in East Asia has fallen, from nearly 80 percent of the population living on less than $1.25 a day in 1981 to less than 20 percent in 2005, whereas, in Sub-Saharan Africa, the $1.25-a-day poverty rate has shown no sustained decline over the whole period since 1981, starting and ending at 50 percent (ibid.). Current trajectories suggest that about 1 billion people will still live on less than $1.25 a day in 2015, and this is without factoring in the impact that rising food and fuel prices since 2005 and the global financial crisis will have had upon poor people and poverty reduction.

Numerous studies of poverty and inequality reinforce this complex picture. Based on his research of household surveys for 1988, 1993 and 1998, Branko Milanović (2005) detects an uneven pattern: global inequality increased strongly between 1988 and 1993 but then displayed a minor decline in the subsequent five years. As he puts it: 'inequality among people in the world today is extremely high, though its direction of change is unclear' (ibid.: 32). Likewise, Glenn Firebaugh (2003) contends that, while income inequality between nations has declined, it has risen within nations. In particular, there has been the rise in inequality within China, India, Russia, Sweden, the UK and the United States. The UNU/WIDER study on the links between poverty, inequality and growth confirms the view that within-country income inequality has risen in most countries since the early 1980s (Cornia and Court 2001). Much of Latin America (notably Brazil), the former Soviet bloc and Southern Africa, as well as countries such as Pakistan, have levels of inequality that undermine attempts at poverty reduction (ibid.: 24). While China's rapid economic growth has reduced absolute poverty within the country, it has also contributed to a sharp increase in inequality that threatens future poverty reduction, with some of its citizens accumulating considerable wealth in the new economy (ibid.: 8–9). There have also been notable increases in inequality within Malaysia, Thailand and Hong Kong as they too have advanced economically. Likewise, the economic benefits of India's rapid development have been unevenly shared. A wealthy elite has emerged in the country – in 2005, India had forty-seven billionaires compared with ten in France – while more than three-quarters of its 1.2 billion people have to get by on less than £1.30 a day, and this is despite a reduction in absolute poverty levels (Wilson 2010).

In addition, there has been a marked rise in regional and rural–urban inequality in the recent period (Cornia and Court 2001). In the case of China, patterns of inequality reflect the divide that exists between coastal provinces such as Guangdong, which are integrated into the global economy, and the underdeveloped regions in the west of the country

Mumbai is a classic example of economic development being unequally distributed even within the space of one city, as some of the world's poorest slums lie adjacent to affluent communities in new high-rise blocks. (© David Warlick/Flickr)

that are less so. However, the absolute number of poor is also increasing in urban areas worldwide, and faster than in rural areas in some countries, with writers now discussing the 'urbanization of poverty' (UN-Habitat 2003: xxvi). Even within relatively wealthy cities, for example Mumbai and Rio de Janeiro, areas of extreme poverty are often adjacent to areas of affluence, with the rich able to shelter in gated communities. Indeed, in 2003, the number of people living in slums was almost 1 billion, the majority of them in developing regions (ibid.: xxv).

Thus, the income and wealth generated by the fast economic growth of countries such as China, India and Brazil has generally not been evenly spread within those societies. Indeed, within many of them it has led to the formation of wealthy new elites, many of whom are globally connected, often with their counterparts in the developed world. At the same time the level of inequality within many Northern countries has increased significantly, and poverty remains an everyday fact of life for some citizens, especially those living in urban areas. From a global perspective, all of this is leading to a blurring of the developing and developed worlds.

Measuring global poverty and inequality

Sociology has long been preoccupied with how poverty and inequality are determined (see box 12.5). In determining levels of global poverty and inequality, much depends upon what is being measured and how averages are employed. Poverty is typically measured at the household level, but this can generate its own problems as households often contain their own inequalities and, in particular, can be highly gendered institutions. Poverty surveys often neglect differences in household composition and the number of women in paid employment.

BOX 12.5 DEFINING POVERTY

- Most approaches to poverty are economic and oriented towards quantifying it, usually by establishing a poverty line. The international poverty lines of $1.25 a day (extreme poverty), which is equivalent to the $1-per-day poverty line introduced in 1981 after adjustment for inflation, and $2-a-day (poverty) were established in 2005.
- While much attention is devoted to low income, poverty also encompasses quality of life issues such as health and access to health care, education and employment prospects, security and wellbeing, and societal participation.
- Absolute poverty describes a condition where incomes are so low that even a minimum standard of nutrition, shelter and personal necessities cannot be maintained.
- Relative poverty refers to people who do not enjoy a sense of wellbeing and/or are materially disadvantaged compared to others living in the same society.
- In recognition of the complexity of poverty, and that understanding it cannot be explained simply by economics and poverty lines, the UNDP has devised the Human Poverty Index (HPI). Under this scheme, poverty for developing countries is calculated in terms of the percentage of the population who are illiterate, are not expected to live to age forty, and do not enjoy decent standards of living (defined as access to treated water supplies and health care and by the percentage of children under five who are underweight) (UNDP 2002).
- However, the HDI has been criticized for continuing to employ a quantitative – as opposed to a qualitative – approach to poverty. In other words, it does not incorporate the actual experiences of poverty of those involved, such as forms of social exclusion.

(McIlwaine 2002)

The incidence of poverty is shaped by how poverty is defined, which can be on the basis of income, consumption or capability. Capability refers to quality of life outcomes – for example, longevity, education and health. For Sen, poverty is the deprivation of basic capabilities rather than merely low income. Capability is the substantive 'freedom to achieve various lifestyles' (2001: 75). Development should therefore be about us utilizing and expanding our capabilities, and hence our freedom, as a means of enriching our lives (ibid.: 3). Likewise, inequality is more than just divergences in income or wealth between or within countries. It also refers, for instance, to differences in consumption expenditure levels and in access to education, health care and other social services. Some commentators emphasize the political dimension to inequality, regarding it as entailing differences in levels of political participation, such as voting rights (Justino, Litchfield and Whitehead 2003). Inequality is also a plural phenomenon reflected in gender, racial, ethnic, class and age inequalities.

Lastly, determining what is happening internationally with regard to poverty and inequality is made more difficult by the fact that, while they are distinct phenomena, they are also multidimensional and interrelated concepts. For example, writers on inequality argue that achieving substantive poverty reduction requires addressing the unequal economic and social conditions that serve to perpetuate poverty. Persistent inequalities lead to poverty traps because it becomes virtually impossible for certain population groups to be economically and socially mobile, which undermines efforts to reduce poverty (Justino, Litchfield and Whitehead 2003).

BOX 12.6 LEVELS OF INEQUALITY

- **National inequality** refers to the distribution of income among people within each country.
- **International inequality** is the economic disparity that exists between countries.
- **Global inequality** refers to income differences between all individual people in the world, and includes intercountry as well as intra-country inequalities.

Sources: Cornia and Court (2001); Held and Kaya (2007).

Explaining global poverty and inequality

Numerous explanations have been postulated to account for patterns of global poverty and inequality, and they will be considered here in the form of three broad approaches.

Sociology of development accounts of global poverty and inequality tend to prioritize either internal or external factors. In the case of the latter, the role of the international capitalist economy is highlighted in theories of underdevelopment, such as structuralism and dependency theory, mentioned above. In the case of the former, the focus is upon how societies are organized in accounting for poverty and inequality. Support for this position can be found in the *World Development Report 2006*. It contends a major obstacle to equality is that the predetermined circumstances of human beings and the social groups into which a person is born (race, gender, place of birth, family origins) continue to determine whether they succeed economically, socially and politically (World Bank 2006: 19). The report estimates that between one-third and one-half of the inequalities within countries can be explained by 'between-groups' differences, with the poor, people in rural areas, women, and those of low caste or status generally having reduced access to education, land and credit. Other explanations for the high incidence of poverty and inequality include the level of debt in poor countries; legacies of colonialism; the failure of aid programmes; the impact of technological change upon levels and types of employment; the social division created by an abundance of natural resources (the 'resource curse thesis'); internal misman-agement and inappropriate development strategies; and politically unstable and corrupt states.

As regards economic perspectives, Simon Kuznets provides a classic economic account of how inequality emerges in societies (see box 12.7). However, there is also criticism of ortho-dox economic approaches to development. For Cornia and Court, the rise of within-country

The 'resource curse thesis' postulates that countries rich in natural resources, for a variety of reasons, tend to suffer poor economic development. Conflicts and tensions over diamond mining in the Democratic Republic of Congo (among other issues) have meant that the country's abundance of this globally prized commodity has not translated into wealth for the people – and perhaps has even undermined it. (© James Oatway/ Panos Pictures)

income inequality since the early 1980s is because of the 'excessively liberal economic policy regimes' and the way in which economic reform policies such as structural adjustment have been carried out (2001: 1). Thus, reduced employment protection and wage flexibility have been more significant than traditional causes of inequality, such as the nature of land ownership, urban bias, and inequality in education (ibid.: 6). The greater emphasis upon flexibility in the workplace has enabled some skilled workers to enjoy higher earnings but has also diminished the bargaining power of trade unions, resulting in an erosion of minimum wages (Cornia 2005). Likewise, the SAPRI (2004) investigation into the impact of structural adjustment maintains that poverty has been increased through privatization programmes and cuts in public goods and services. The effects were felt especially in Africa because of the high level of public-sector employment. In Nigeria, around 60 percent of jobs were in the public sector, and it is estimated that up to 1 million workers were made redundant because of structural adjustment programmes between 1984 and 1989 (Mohan et al. 2000: 64).

Critics of globalization maintain that trade openness and worldwide production processes are exacerbating levels of poverty and inequality. Thus, while the poor lack the financial resources to adapt readily to the greater competition which results from opening up economies to global markets, those with resources and the productive capacity can take advantage of the export opportunities that this presents (Glewwe and Hall 1998). For example, the smallholder farmers and landless labourers that make up Brazil's more than 10 million rural poor remain

BOX 12.7 THE KUZNETS CURVE

The economist Simon Kuznets (1955) maintained that, as a country experiences economic growth, inequality rises. This is because some population groups will benefit from these new economic conditions while others will not. At the higher levels of economic growth and income generation, inequality starts to decline as the wealth spreads to the rest of society. The end of the development process sees a new equilibrium of high incomes and low inequality. For Kuznets, this whole process takes the form of an inverted U-shape. However, critics argue that there is no guarantee that the increased income will spread to the poorest in society.

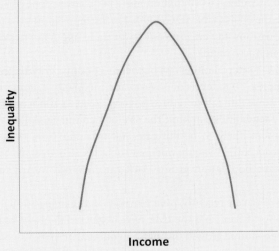

Figure 12.4 The Kuznets curve

largely outside of its growing agricultural export market, which is dominated by large commercial farms (UNDP 2005: 123). Unsurprisingly, advocates of globalization contest these claims. Martin Wolf maintains that we need to look to domestic policies rather than globalization to account for the persistence of global inequality, which is reflected in the disparities in national economic performance within the South (Wade and Wolf 2003). In this vein, globalists maintain that countries which have integrated into the global economy, such as China and India, have experienced significant increases in per capita wealth and poverty reduction (Dollar and Kraay 2002; Wolf 2004). Dollar and Kraay contend that globalizing developing countries grew at 5.0 percent per capita in the 1990s, while for rich countries and non-globalizing developing countries growth was only 2.2 percent per capita and 1.4 percent per capita, respectively (2002: 18). For Dollar and Kraay, growth generally benefits the poor as much as everyone else, and for this reason openness to international trade 'should be at the centre of successful poverty reduction strategies' (2001: 32). In response, critics note that, as mentioned above, within-country income inequality has risen since the early 1980s, and this undermines the claim that the wealth being generated by the growth of world trade is filtering down to the poor (Nayyar 2003; Stiglitz 2003). Finally, as we saw in the previous section, Grahame Thompson (2007) questions the existence of a global economy, maintaining that economic activity is conducted mainly nationally and regionally and occurs primarily between developed countries. He is therefore sceptical of discussions about the impact of globalization on global inequality and argues that inequalities should be examined on a national and regional basis.

Tackling global poverty and inequality

Numerous proposals to alleviate poverty and reduce inequality have emerged (see Collier 2007; Cornia and Court 2001), but the most concerted international effort to reduce poverty is represented by the Millennium Development Goals. However, these have been disrupted by the 2008 financial crisis. According to *The Millennium Development Goals Report*, in 2009, an estimated 55 million to 90 million more people were living in extreme poverty than anticipated before the crisis (UNMDG 2009: 4). The report notes that, as well as reducing aid from some donor nations, the crisis meant fewer trade opportunities for developing countries and a lack of economic growth.

However, the interrelationships between economic growth, inequality and poverty reduction are complex. High levels of poverty and inequality can restrict economic growth, which can make it more difficult to reduce poverty (Cornia and Court 2001: 1). For instance, persistent high inequalities can limit the size of a country's skilled workforce, as disadvantaged groups are more likely to be illiterate and to suffer from poor health (Justino, Litchfield and Whitehead 2003). Highly unequal societies also struggle to generate national demand because poorer population groups lack the financial means to buy domestic goods and services.

Yet, until relatively recently, policy-makers in the international financial institutions (IFIs) such as the World Bank and the IMF have neglected the issue of inequality, choosing instead to prioritize economic growth through a neoliberal or market-led policy approach. But, as was indicated above, rapid economic growth can exacerbate inequalities. Indeed, a major report by the UN Economic and Social Affairs Department found that, in 2005, despite considerable economic growth in many regions and improved living standards in some places, inequality between and within countries was greater than it was in 1995 and poverty remained entrenched (United Nations 2005). The report concludes that: 'Focusing exclusively on economic growth and income generation as a development strategy is ineffective, as it leads to the accumulation of wealth by a few and deepens the poverty of many' (ibid.: 1). Thus, 'Ignoring inequality in the pursuit of development is perilous' (ibid.). The World Bank's *World Development Report 2006* similarly concludes that tackling inequality is the key to development, conceding that economic growth will not be enough to end world poverty and that it will require forms of redistribution (World Bank 2006). These reports reflect a growing awareness that tackling poverty and inequality requires a mixture of policies – including government intervention, institutional reform, redistribution, and investment in education – depending on local conditions, and cannot simply be left to pro-growth policies. In other words, economic growth is not the same as development.

The reasons for the emergence of complex patterns of poverty and inequality are numerous and varied, but ultimately they will be context-specific and shaped by the intersection of global, local, regional and national factors and processes. From a wider perspective, the complex patterns of poverty and inequality delineated here serve to blur further the conventional North–South spatial conception of development. The implications of this transformation for development and sociology are explored in the conclusion to this chapter. But it may be that, in time, the notion of a North–South divide will become less relevant within development and perhaps, like the concept of a 'third world', even become obsolete.

SEMINAR QUESTIONS

1 Is global poverty and income inequality rising or diminishing?
2 Why do levels of global inequality and poverty remain so high?
3 What method (or methods) of measuring inequality and poverty are most useful for understanding development?
4 Do levels of inequality in LEDCs matter and, if so, why?

SUSTAINABLE DEVELOPMENT

John Hannigan (2006) claims that, until relatively recently, sociology can be accused of foot-dragging on environmental matters because of its close association with modernity as well as a tacit commitment to equality on the part of many sociologists, which have combined to entail an uncritical acceptance of economic growth, progress and technology. He points to the sociological literature on modernization and modernization theory as an example of how sociology became inextricably linked with economic development and technological innovation. Indeed, Hannigan even has a section in his opening chapter of *Environmental Sociology* that is entitled 'Sociologists as "hucksters" for development and progress' (ibid.: 3). This general position will be returned to at the end of this section. As for development, its engagement with environmental matters has coalesced around the concept of sustainable development. However, sustainable development remains a contested subject area, one that has generated a range of conceptualizations and perspectives from, among others, deep ecologists, eco-socialists and eco-feminists as well as sociologists, economists and politicians. For the sake of analysis, however, these different positions will be discussed in terms of two broad approaches, namely advocates and critics of sustainable development.

Advocates of sustainable development

Sustainable development is a response to the environmental harm caused by the predominant economic growth-led model of development but also to the growing body of scientific research into environmental decline. In relation to the latter, the leading international climate body, the Intergovernmental Panel on Climate Change (IPCC), produced a series of reports during 2007 highlighting how global warming was more advanced than had previously been anticipated. Similarly, Lord Stern – author of the influential UK government-commissioned review on climate change (published in 2006) – conceded in early 2013 that he had underestimated the risks posed to economies by rising temperatures (Stewart and Elliott 2013).

For its advocates, sustainable development is conceived of as a way of bridging the divide between economic growth and environmental sustainability. It acknowledges that, without economic development, the Global South will be condemned to perpetual underdevelopment, but this has to be balanced with protection of environmental resources as well as other species. Running through it, therefore, is a concern with social justice, and this is reflected in a strong interest in the plight of future generations (Adams 2001). Indeed, the influential Brundtland report published by the World Commission on Environment and Development in 1987 defines sustainable development as 'development that meets the needs of the present without compromising the ability of future generations to meet their own needs' (WCED 1987: 43). Consequently, sustainable development has been conceived of as a moral rather than a market concept (Jacobs 1990) and has even been described as marking a 'paradigm shift' (Koenig 1995: 2).

Mainstream approaches to sustainable development essentially pursue a synthesis of economic growth, the effective management of resources, and reliance upon technological innovation in addressing environmental decline (e.g., Simon 1981). There also persists a faith in market-based solutions and mechanisms. For example, David Pearce believes attaching a monetary value to the environment will help us stop treating natural resources as if they were free (Pearce, Markandya and Barbier 1989). Likewise, the free operation of the market is viewed as providing a profit incentive to encourage the development of green technologies and the selling of eco-friendly goods and services (Clapp and Dauvergne 2005). In contrast, stronger conceptions of sustainable development question the continued reliance upon the market within mainstream sustainable development. Within this tradition, sustainable development is promoted at a grassroots level, with local contexts, knowledges and participation all prioritized. Consequently, there is an emphasis in this approach upon the pursuit of autarchy (economic self-sufficiency) and the empowerment of local people.

Critics of sustainable development

With multiple definitions and models of sustainable development in existence, and states pursuing their own conceptions of it with varying degrees of rigour, there is a danger of the concept being rendered meaningless (Rogers, Jalal and Boyd 2008). One writer has gone as far as to suggest that sustainable development is effectively anything that one wants it to be (O'Riordan 1995). Above all, this pluralism makes it difficult to establish universal environmental standards or to determine progress. For this reason, sustainable development needs to be based upon more clearly defined and universally accepted principles, with common strategies for achieving it (Ben-Eli 2007). Advocates of sustainable development maintain that established and rigorous strategies do exist, and development specialists spend a great deal of time analysing and seeking to enhance them (see Dalal-Clayton and Bass 2002). In this vein, the European Union and the OECD have devised sets of sustainable development indicators in order to measure progress. Susan Baker contends that the different models of sustainable development 'share the common belief that there are ultimate, biophysical limits to growth' (2006: 212). Conversely, other advocates maintain that multiple conceptualizations of sustainable development allow for the input of local knowledge and expertise but also take into account local and national contexts and conditions (Redclift 2002). In other words, sustainable development can only ever be a guiding principle rather than a universally prescribed set of policies.

Some environmentalists contend that economic development rather than environmental sustainability is the dominant discourse within the concept of sustainable development, reflected in the continuing preoccupation with the GDP and Gross National Product (GNP) achieved by countries (Banerjee 2003). They advocate instead a Green GNP that takes into account factors such as environmental decline and resource pollution when measuring national income accounts (see Hamilton and Dixon 2003). For some green writers there is simply insufficient emphasis within the discourse of sustainable development upon reducing ecological harm by limiting growth (Jacob 1994) and even pursuing degrowth strategies (Alexander 2012).

Southern critics note that the North was freely able to pursue and enjoy the benefits of economic growth-based development, which has harmed the Earth's ecosystems and means that the South must now pursue sustainable development. Sustainable development erodes Southern autonomy because it insists that the natural resources of LEDCs are part of a common project in which all the citizens of the world have an interest (Soto 1992: 694). Moreover, the governments and peoples of developing societies are expected to nurture and protect these assets for the good of humankind (Elliott 2004: 171). At the same time, Northern consumption patterns and lifestyles continue to cause environmental harm. Northern governments respond that they are taking measures to reduce their carbon dioxide emissions through more efficient energy usage and alternative energy sources. They argue that they are facilitating sustainable development in the South in the form of technology transfers and financial aid to Southern states in recent environmental treaties. Moreover, they have accepted the common but differentiated responsibilities principle that acknowledges the varying degree to which countries have contributed to environmental harm and that states have differing capacities to safeguard the Earth's resources, although this is often a source of North–South contestation during environmental treaty negotiations.

The most serious charge raised against sustainable development is that it is an inadequate and misguided response to contemporary environmental threats. The incorporation of economic development into sustainable development negates any notion that it is an ecological concept or that it represents a paradigm shift. For ecologists, economic development is inherently harmful to the Earth's ecosystems as such activity invariably leads to resource depletion and pollution. Sustainable development ignores the fact that the Earth's natural self-regulating systems exist simply to sustain the climate and the chemistry of the planet (Richardson 1997: 57). We must therefore focus upon the pursuit of ecological sustainability and end our preoccupation with economic development. For deep ecologists, the existing economic order needs to be replaced with ecologically sustainable belief and knowledge systems (Naess 1973). In short, we need values and lifestyles that are in harmony with nature. However, this perspective is criticized as being politically impractical. Not only is there is little sign of the international economic system being replaced, but at this stage even restricting economic growth would create enormous political problems for any government.

As was mentioned in the introduction to this chapter, global environmental decline raises major difficulties for the economic growth model that has been the main way of tackling underdevelopment in the post-war period. For ecologists, climate-friendly economic growth is simply a contradiction in terms, and hence mainstream sustainable development will not suffice as a response to contemporary environmental threats. In this regard, Paul Raskin and his co-authors (2002), who are part of a global think-tank (the Great Transition Initiative), argue for a 'great transition' that would see the emergence of a 'new sustainability paradigm', one that would rethink the concept of progress. Of course, this would require rethinking development, given that its intellectual origins can almost certainly be traced to eighteenth-century European Enlightenment notions of progress, rationalism and modernity. But it also poses a challenge for sociology given its close association with modernity.

Indeed, the classical sociological theory of Marx, Weber and Durkheim constituted a profound engagement with the forces and processes of modernity, such as capitalism, rationalism and progress – although this does not mean that they were silent on the relationship between society and nature. As mentioned at the beginning of this section, a re-evaluation of sociology's relationship with the environment has been taking place in the recent period, and arguably since the early 1970s. This rethinking is evident in the emergence of risk society theory (Beck 1992) and the development of environmental sociology as a field of inquiry.

SEMINAR QUESTIONS

1   Critically assess the concept of sustainable development.
2   Is it time to give up on sustainable development on environmental grounds?
3   Will it ever be possible to have global economic growth without increasing environmental damage?

CONFLICT, SECURITY AND DEVELOPMENT

Along with sustainability, the other major growth area within development in the recent period has been in relation to conflict and security. There is increasing acceptance within development circles that development and security are inextricably linked, and this is reflected in a greater emphasis upon post-conflict development and the emergence of the concept of human security (e.g., McGrew and Poku 2007; Picciotto and Weaving 2006). In 2006, OECD member states spent approximately $6 billion on peace work through official development assistance or aid and the funding of UN peacekeeping missions (DAC 2008: 1). The specific sociological dimension of this shift within development is linked to debates about social capital that are addressed at the end of this section.

The development–security nexus

The case for merging of development and security has essentially been made on the following grounds.

> ***The failing state phenomenon***   According to the World Bank, the number of failing states rose from seventeen in 2003 to twenty-six in 2006 and is part of a trend that can be traced back to at least the early 1990s on account of factors such as the impact of the end of the Cold War, globalization, and the rise of civil or intra-state wars (BBC 2006a). Among failing states are Afghanistan, Angola, Haiti, Somalia and the Central African Republic. According to the UN, a third of the people living in poverty in the world reside in conflict-affected states (Reality of Aid 2006).
>
> ***Conflict harms development***   The conflict that helps to produce fragile states can be detrimental to development in numerous ways, including eroding communication, transport and civil (i.e., hospitals, schools) infrastructures. Civil society is also invariably damaged, as it becomes difficult for individuals and communities to organize and function under such conditions. Moreover, conflict can lead to a significant reduction in the levels of domestic consumption and FDI. Many parts of Africa are considered to be politically unstable,

and consequently the continent attracts 'less than 1 percent of annual global financial flows' (McKay 2004: 155). On average the economic growth rate of countries affected by civil war declines by 2.2 percent per year (Collier and Hoeffler 2004: 5). Conversely, states that have successfully emerged from violent conflict – e.g., Ethiopia, Mozambique and Rwanda – are making good progress towards reducing poverty (World Bank 2011).

The human cost of conflict In its *World Development Report 2011*, the World Bank estimates that more than 1.5 billion people live in countries affected by violent conflict (World Bank 2011). Civilians have increasingly been targeted in recent intra-state conflicts, leading to large numbers being killed and population displacement. Armed conflicts can also disrupt agricultural production, resulting in food shortages and hunger. A report published by the International Food Policy Research Institute (IFPRI) in 2006 revealed that the countries with the highest levels of hunger and malnutrition are plagued by civil wars and violent conflicts (Wiesmann 2006).

Declining aid Failing states are typically those with ineffective governance and high levels of corruption and crime, and under such conditions there is an increased likelihood of aid being squandered and embezzled. In some instances aid may even become an additional resource to compete over (Brown et al. 2007). More broadly, the cost of an average civil war in a low-income country – which was $54 billion (£29 billion) in 2004 – can almost wipe out the total worldwide aid budget, which amounted to $78.6 billion (£42 billion) in that year (BBC 2006b). The major consequence of aid being wasted is that donor governments and their respective citizens are inevitably less willing to continue providing this type of assistance.

Human security

The merging of development and security is most in evidence in the emergence of the concept of human security. However, it is a concept with multiple meanings and associations. Some commentators see human security approaches as contributing to improvements in health care (e.g., Takemi et al. 2008). Others consider the promotion of democracy is the most effective way of generating security within societies and achieving human dignity (Large and Et Sisk 2006). Green writers link human security to environmental decline, noting that climate change and land degradation can potentially lead to food and water shortages, population displacement and, ultimately, resource competition and conflict (Barnett and Adger 2005).

The landmark *UNDP Human Development Report* of 1994 similarly articulated a multidimensional conception of human security, one that incorporated areas ranging from environmental to personal security. Likewise, at its Millennium Summit in September 2000, the UN called upon the international community to work together to achieve not only 'freedom from want' but also 'freedom from fear'. This pronouncement was followed by the setting-up of the Commission on Human Security (CHS) in January 2001. The CHS maintains that achieving human security entails 'both shielding people from acute threats and empowering people to take charge of their own lives' (CHS 2003: iv). In practical terms, this involves recognizing that the threat to human security comes not only from armed conflict but also from disease, hunger, economic inequality, environmental pollution and natural disasters.

However, the definitional and intellectual coherence of the concept of human security has been questioned (Foong-Khong 2001). And by embracing such a wide range of concerns the concept becomes meaningless, making it difficult to establish priorities and formulate policy (Paris 2001). Moreover, the lack of a commonly accepted definition raises the prospect of powerful interests interpreting human security to further their own foreign policy objectives.

The development–security nexus: critical perspectives

Some commentators question the necessity of merging development and security. The *Human Security Report 2005: War and Peace in the 21st Century*, published by the University of British Colombia's Human Security Report Project (HSRP), detects worldwide a substantial decline in the number of armed conflicts, military coups, genocides and human rights abuses, and this is reflected in a reduction in the average number of people killed in conflicts each year. The authors of the report note that 'the number of armed conflicts around the world has declined by more than 40 percent since the early 1990s', while 'five out of six regions in the developing world saw a net decrease in core human rights abuses between 1994 and 2003' (HSRP 2005: 1, 2). They contend these developments are the result of changes that have taken place in the post-Cold War period, notably an unprecedented upsurge in international activism geared to conflict prevention, peacemaking and reconciliation. Free from the paralysis of Cold War politics, the UN Security Council has also been able to play a more active role in maintaining international security, reflected in a fourfold increase in the number of UN peacekeeping operations between 1987 and 1999 (ibid.: 8–9). For the HSRP, the lack of popular awareness of these positive developments is due to sensationalist media coverage of global security and the overstated claims made by NGOs and international organizations in relation to this area.

However, for the CHS, the reduction in armed conflict does not mean human security has been achieved, because this still leaves the threats that stem from poverty, hunger, disease and other humanitarian emergencies. In other words, by conceptualizing human security as the protection of individuals from violence, the HSRP has a narrow conception of empowerment. Moreover, some sixty wars were still being fought in 2005, and some conflicts – notably those in Afghanistan, Darfur and Somalia – show little sign of being resolved.

For some critics, Northern governments are paying closer attention to the interrelationship between development and security for reasons of self-interest. For instance, failing states harm markets, restrict access to mineral resources, provide safe havens for terrorist networks, aid transnational crime, and lead to refugees ending up on their own borders (Bøås and Jennings 2007). In addition, some donor governments are increasingly using aid to fulfil their security objectives. The US and Australian governments have even changed the mandate of their aid programmes in line with this policy goal. It helps to explain why in the recent period more than a third of aid resources have been allocated to the wars in Afghanistan and Iraq (Ibon Foundation 2007). Moreover, the rebuilding of fragile states provides a pretext for Northern governments to intervene in the internal affairs of developing societies (Duffield 2007).

Social capital

This concern with fragile states and a lack of societal cohesion has led to growing interest in the concept of social capital. 'Social capital' is essentially the social fabric that knits societies together, and the concept has been used to explain the decline in social cohesion and community values in Western societies considered by some commentators to be a by-product of globalization, notably increased geographical mobility and familial instability, greater individualism and privatization, the spread of the market, increasing commercialization, and growing inequality (see Hopper 2003). Thus, societies with good stocks of social capital are socially cohesive, with shared values and norms, a plethora of social networks and associations, and high levels of trust (Fukuyama 2001). A number of writers helped to instigate the social capital debate, although Robert Putnam's discussion of it in relation to civic decline in the USA has led the way (2000).

Many development policy-makers are attracted to the notion that countries that are socially cohesive are likely to be more stable, enjoy greater economic growth and have better functioning governments, and hence develop more rapidly. It has led to the setting up of the World Bank social capital and civil society working group to promote social capital. In practical terms, generating social capital entails encouraging civic engagement and social solidarity through local participation in networks and civic associations. These bodies are also able to contribute directly to development and poverty reduction through such schemes as micro-finance programmes. For some writers, social capital has helped to broaden development's focus by adding social and institutional factors to its traditional economic agenda (Francis 2002: 88).

However, social capital has attracted criticism. For many critics, it is simply too broad a concept to have any implications for policy-making (Fine 1999; Harriss and de Renzio 1997). As one commentator has stated, 'It explains everything and nothing' (Francis 2002: 89). In addition, social capital is difficult to measure or quantify, and the number of networks and associations tells us nothing about the nature and quality of the social connections. A criminal gang may have a high degree of interconnectedness, but its anti-social behaviour depletes rather than augments social capital. There is also a view that social capital cannot be generated through public policies because it evolves within societies over time. For example, the funding used by the World Bank to build social capital in Malawi and Zambia had relatively little effect as the nature of community participation in the projects was shaped by existing power and social relations (Vajja and White 2008). More broadly, many economists are sceptical that, at the macro-level, a clear link exists between social capital and economic growth (Field 2008).

From a sociological perspective, John Harriss (2002) contends that social capital is geared to maintaining the existing social and economic order. He argues that social capital has been used by the World Bank to 'depoliticize development' and to obscure power relations and patterns of inequality. For Harriss, social capital and related ideas such as trust, participation and civil society suit global capitalism because they 'represent problems that are rooted in differences in power and class relations as purely technical matters that can be resolved outside the political arena' (ibid.: 2).

The merging of development and security reinforces the view that development is an evolving subject area and is having to broaden its focus in response to recent events. Unstable financial markets, global terrorism, transnational crime, pandemics and environmental decline see states struggling to protect their citizens but also highlight how, in our interconnected world, insecurity afflicts people in both developing and developed societies. In other words, development can no longer be regard as primarily a Southern phenomenon. The turn to security within development also marks a further shift from its economic growth orientation and towards a greater emphasis upon quality of life issues.

SEMINAR QUESTIONS
1 Account for the merging of development and security in the recent period.
2 Is the new emphasis on security in studying development a way of prioritizing the interests of Northern governments?

3 Explain the view that 'different definitions of security lead to radically different policy implications'.

CONCLUSION

As we have seen in this chapter, traditional assumptions about development and underdevelopment are increasingly challenged by contemporary global transformations. Such changes in turn raise difficulties for sociology – or indeed any single discipline – in understanding development and suggest the need for an interdisciplinary approach to this subject area. But arguably development itself is brought into question by some of these changes. The conventional North–South territorial or spatial conception of development is challenged by the rapidly growing economies in the South and ever more complex patterns of global poverty and inequality aided in part by ICTs. East Asia, in particular, is increasingly the main beneficiary of contemporary globalization. Indeed, China became the world's biggest trading nation in goods in 2012, ending the post-war dominance of the USA in the process (Inman 2013). At the same time, development economics faces critical scrutiny because the market-driven mentality that has been preponderant since the 1980s has arguably contributed to periodic economic crises as well as environmental harm. The latter phenomenon has led to an expanding interest in sustainable development, although for a growing number of writers this is an inadequate response to contemporary environmental challenges, which require the widespread implementation of de-growth strategies. As has been shown, global environmental decline raises profound questions about the nature and purpose of development.

More broadly, global transformations demand that development must continue to evolve in order to remain relevant. As we have seen, in response to regional instability and the wider context of global terror, development has broadened its remit to incorporate the conflict and security agenda. This shift is reflected in the growing concern within development circles with fragile states, human security, peacekeeping and post-conflict development. In turn, this raises the prospect that development as a subject area starts to resemble security studies. In this vein, the potential cumulative effect of the global transformations identified here is that, in responding to them, 'development' begins to look amorphous and poorly defined and perhaps even needs to be redefined as 'global studies'.

However, a counter-view is that development has traditionally sought to enhance human wellbeing and therefore remains a valid and legitimate enterprise that should not simply be written off. If this point is accepted, then perhaps we need to modify this project and employ a new lexicon or vocabulary, one that is more attuned to our global era. Thus, rather than 'development', with its contentious history and close association with economic growth, we should instead be pursuing social and political transformation. This is a subject area of considerable interest to sociology and sociologists, and devising the nature of this transformation will require not only engagement with the classic sociological theories but also exploring new theories of society. In short, sociology will be integral to this process. Above all, such a transformation must place a high value upon empowerment and human flourishing as well as our relationship with other species and the environment, and it will have implications for all global citizens, irrespective of whether they live in the Global South or North.

SEMINAR QUESTIONS

1 Do we still need a sociology of development?
2 Should the study of development be left to economists?
3 Are there more reasons to be optimistic or pessimistic about global development in the future? Why?

FURTHER READING

▶ For a concise sociological introduction to development and underdevelopment, see Johann Graaff's (2003) *Poverty and Development* (Oxford University Press).

▶ Raphael Kaplinsky's (2005) *Globalization, Poverty and Inequality* (Polity) is an informative exploration of the complex interrelationships between globalization, poverty and inequality; see especially chapters 1, 2 and 8.

▶ John Hannigan's (2006) *Environmental Sociology* (2nd edn, Routledge) tracks the emergence of environmental sociology as a field of inquiry – see in particular chapters 1 and 2.

▶ Mark Duffield's (2007) *Development, Security and Unending War* (Polity) examines the merging of development and security in the recent period with reference to contemporary conflicts (see chapters 1 and 9).

▶ For a sociological approach to the concept of social capital, see John Field's (2008) *Social Capital* (2nd edn, Routledge), especially chapter 5, which considers its policy implications.

Section D
Culture and Personal Life

This section has a particular focus on sociological specialisms which appear to be concerned primarily with individual choices in areas of social life that are (to a greater or lesser extent) outside the public sphere. There can be little which is more private than personal and family life (chapter 16), but our leisure choices (chapter 13), personal beliefs (chapter 14) and the choices we make in terms of media consumption (chapter 15) can also be seen as private matters. Of course, sociologists do not concede that any of these areas of social life are *purely* a matter of individual choice, but a number do see them as increasingly characterized by such choices. Thus if individuals are, to a greater extent, freed from a modernist straitjacket which insists on conformity to universal ideas of progress, then they may be able to form whatever personal relationships they choose; to relax in any way they wish and express themselves through consumption; to believe, or refuse to believe, whatever they want; and to consume, produce and interpret the media at will. The idea of greater choice, the ability to construct and reconstruct identity, and to give your own meaning to social life is considered in all the chapters here. This is sometimes, but not always, in relation to postmodern or post-structuralist theory. All the authors acknowledge that there have been significant changes in culture and/or personal life, but none sees the changes as simple or as following a straightforward path towards a playful, pluralistic, postmodern society characterized by choice and lack of constraint. All are concerned with just how great the changes in culture and personal life have been, and, while all acknowledge significant change, all recognize important continuities as well.

In chapter 13, Sheila Scraton and Beccy Watson contrast post-structuralist/postmodern interpretations of leisure and consumption and the more conventional sociological accounts which place greater emphasis on inequality and constraint. They explicitly see merit in both approaches but advocate the 'middle ground', which 'retains a focus on structural inequalities while seeking ways to account for the fluidity of multiple identities'. They point out that leisure can be conceived as 'free time' when individuals are not constrained by the demands of work and unavoidable obligations. It is time when, potentially, seriousness and responsibility can be put aside and 'freedom, fun and enjoyment can take centre stage'. However, they argue that leisure is still constrained and influenced by social divisions. For example, many groups suffer social exclusion in the '24-hour city', which continues to be racialized and gendered. Disabling society often still limits the leisure opportunities of the disabled. Scraton and Watson acknowledge, though, that inequalities are not static and that it is important to examine the intersectionality of social divisions and inequalities to understand how these relationships play out. They attach considerable credence to theories of individualization but, ironically, individualization can lead to leisure being taken very seriously. Serious leisure involves the dedicated pursuit of a new and improved self. Scraton and Watson see leisure as closely linked to consumption, and therefore capitalist companies have an interest in promoting all forms of leisure that can be exploited commercially. Yet consumers do have real choices, and deviant leisure shows that these choices sometimes step outside the moral boundaries of mainstream culture. Yet, even in deviant leisure, consumption can be commercialized and mainstreamed, as in the commercialization of consensual sadomasochism in E. L. James's *Fifty Shades* books.

The authors accept there has been a move towards the individualization of leisure and a rise in sociological awareness of identity construction through leisure. They accept too that leisure is increasingly part of consumption. However, leisure it not just about difference; it also produces arenas in which social inequalities are reproduced and oppression can occur.

Paul Heelas's chapter (chapter 14) focuses on the theory of secularization, a theory which is strongly associated with theories of modernity through the work of Weber and others. The theory has been challenged, of course, partly by those who have questioned the empirical reality of secularization, and partly by those who have found evidence of a 'spiritual revolution' in individualized spiritualities expressed in New Age beliefs. Paul Heelas himself has been involved in empirical studies of New Age spirituality (most notably in the Kendal Project; Heelas and Woodhead 2005), but he does not claim that anything like a spiritual revolution has occurred (at least as yet). Nor does he argue that the evidence points away from secularization in Western societies. With detailed analysis of a wide range of evidence, he convincingly argues for an unambiguous decline in Christian belief, religious participation and affiliation as well as in the influence of Christianity on society and culture in the UK and Europe. Significantly, he also finds strong evidence to support a 'revisionist account' of Islam in Britain, which suggests that it, too, is subject to secularizing tendencies. But Heelas does not simply conclude that modernity is antithetical to all non-rational beliefs or that trends will lead to the predominance of atheism. Instead he argues that 'fuzzy transgressors' – those who transgress against secular humanism but have no engagement with formal religion or strong commitment to New Age beliefs – are becoming the most numerous group in society. People still seek sources of significance in their life that are not provided by materialism or consumerism or, for most, through traditional religion or involvement in the New Age. The continuing significance of existential questions therefore suggests that most sociological accounts of changes in belief are misleading. For many people in Western societies, their beliefs are founded upon a version of humanism which looks beyond the individual.

The extent to which social life has been individualized is also taken up by Greg Philo, David Miller and Catherine Happer (chapter 15), but they come less close to occupying the 'middle ground' than the other authors in this section. They acknowledge that some accounts do claim that the media have become more individualized, less constrained and less able to manipulate the population ideologically. Such accounts have two main strands. Firstly, active audience models emphasize that the reception of media messages depends very much on the standpoint of individuals (and social groups), which limits the ability of the media to shape or manipulate perceptions of reality. However, by studying both media content and audience reception they are able to show that most people do not read the media in idiosyncratic and individualized ways. Most are well able to identify and describe the central messages presented by the media, indicating that audience readings of media messages do largely coincide with those intended by those who produce them. The second source of claims that the media have become less 'mass' and more individualized is the growth of digital media which facilitate audience participation and blur the distinction between consumer and producer. Social networking is a key example of this. It does allow a genuine two-way relationship and creates more potential for audiences to have a public voice. However, Philo, Miller and Happer are concerned much more with the political significance of these changes than with their role in identity construction. In respect of Facebook, they argue that 'its individualized stream of "me" personalizes and de-politicizes public issues and is more likely to promote conservative ideology than to challenge it.'

This quotation gives a good flavour of this chapter, which is concerned more with power relations and institutions than are the others in this section. It acknowledges significant change in contemporary societies but sees this as resulting from a neoliberal structural transformation of the media (and indeed other parts of society) rather than from increased choice. Of course, there is greater choice of media in the digital age, with more TV channels, radio stations and online sources of information available than ever before. However, to Philo, Miller and Happer, the choice is largely illusory, with certain types of message – those reflecting the commercial and ideological interests of the most powerful – being dominant. This is discussed in relation to the influence of the public relations industry and the coverage of a range of topics, from the Arab–Israeli conflict to the financial crash. Philo, Miller and Happer develop an insightful model of the circuit of communications, in which complex interactions shape the media but, for the most part, the output of the media remains ideologically biased. In this sense, they are much more sceptical about the significance of individualization than other contributors. It is seen as a manifestation of neoliberal consumerism rather than as a significant shift in the way social lives are lived.

Vanessa May (chapter 16) is more inclined than Philo, Miller and Happer to see significant changes taking place in social life, in this case in families and personal life. Families and personal life seem to provide ample evidence of rapid and significant change in the broad direction of individualization. Theorists such as Giddens and Beck have generally supported the idea that there is increased choice. The case for the trend is supported by greater family diversity, the supposed decline of traditional families, and more acceptance and legal acknowledgement of LGBT relationships, 'new fatherhood', and so on. Perhaps the ultimate move towards choice is represented in the idea of families of choice – where the historical straitjacket of biological relationships and heterosexual norms is cast aside so that families are conceived and structured however individuals wish. From this point of view, even biological constraints can be overcome with the assistance of new reproductive technologies. However, May is unconvinced by the more one-sided claims of those who contend there is a straightforward movement towards greater choice. She says that, 'while we can see an increase in choice, our choices are still structurally shaped.' This is the case when people 'fall back into gender', or when women from poorer countries end up working as maids or nannies in the Global North as part of global chains of care. It is evident in the continuation of a breadwinner discourse (when fathers do not need to justify undertaking paid employment but mothers do). Evidence suggests that families of origin remain very important for lesbian women and that 'ideologies around "the family"' are still 'visible in the stereotyping of non-nuclear and non-white families as deficient and (dangerously) "other"'. Ideologies of 'the family' may be insensitive to the reality of different family practices (what families actually do), but they nevertheless continue to be influential.

All sociologists like to live in 'interesting times' and to attach special significance to the changes they experience in their lifetime. Indeed, arguably sociology was very much born out of unprecedented and radical changes in the social associated with the industrial revolution. But perhaps there is a danger that sociologists will sometimes engage in wishful thinking, keen to see the changes they study as epoch-making and as a radical break from the past. All the chapters in this section avoid this common pitfall and emphasize both the changes and the continuities, acknowledging the individualization of personal life and culture where the evidence supports claims that this is occurring, but questioning or rejecting claims of radical change where they are not justified. As such, and despite the different topics discussed and different theoretical concerns, they all offer nuanced accounts of social change based upon strong foundations in empirical evidence.

13

LEISURE AND CONSUMPTION

a critical analysis of 'free time'

SHEILA SCRATON AND
BECCY WATSON

CONTENTS

INTRODUCTION

EVERYONE HAS A COMMONSENSE understanding of leisure. It is 'free time', what we choose to do when our work and other obligations are over; it is non-serious, the relaxed part of our lives. So, why study it as a topic in sociology? Leisure is not as straightforward as this common-sense view suggests. It can be spontaneous, informal and freely chosen, but it can also be extremely serious, involve the support of others, entail inconspicuous or conspicuous consumption, and be a primary source of identity construction. It can take place in the home, such as video gaming or watching television, or be consumed in the public sphere in an increasingly commercialized context. We may have free choice in what we do or we may be constrained by persistent inequalities of gender, race, class or disability which impact on our ability to consume, participate in and experience leisure. Leisure can be an activity or a state of mind. It can be fun and enjoyable or more problematic for both individuals and society, as exemplified by excessive drinking or drug use.

Today the study of leisure is situated within the social, political and economic context of a consumer society. Whereas earlier analyses concentrated on the relationship of leisure to work and the provision of leisure in the public and voluntary sector, contemporary sociological analyses engage more critically with questions relating to culture and consumption. As work patterns have changed and society has shifted from production to consumption, people are seen increasingly to construct their identities through consumption practices often implicitly tied to leisure. Leisure spaces are sites of cultural consumption and leisure activities are increasingly commercialized. Much public-sector leisure provision has been replaced by the private leisure sector, offering a range of diverse activities, products and opportunities to consume. Yet, for us, the analysis of leisure is about what people can both afford and choose to do within a broader public discourse relating to what is expected and considered to be socially acceptable. Leisure cuts across public and private spheres and provides a critical lens on the complexities of varying social practices. It is about the inconspicuous aspects of people's lives as well as involving spectacular sites of consumption in the public domain. Leisure is a key social and cultural 'act' where people choose, within a context of scarcity (Rojek 2010), to do or not to do active or passive 'things', individually and collectively, and where the complexity of social life is continually played out.

This chapter provides an introduction to some of the key issues that are currently significant within the sociology of leisure. Although the issues discussed are by no means exhaustive, they have been chosen because they demonstrate how a sociological lens on leisure can contribute to our understandings of social life. Firstly, we explore contemporary questions about the relationship between work and leisure. We consider how leisure for some can be the work of others, how leisure can become a very serious pursuit with many work-like qualities, and how increasingly, in our individualized and commercialized society, we feel the need, or are urged by the media, to work on ourselves to improve both health and appearance. This links to our second issue, the body. Displaying the body and active bodies at play are key leisure experiences within contemporary consumer culture. However, some bodies are more excluded and marginalized than others, and so we include a focus on the disabled body and leisure as a relatively under-researched area. Leisure is often seen as a positive and functional aspect of everyday life, incorporating a non-problematic view of leisure as consumption. This is not always the case, and the third issue develops this through what Rojek (1995) defines as a 'darker' aspect of leisure: those activities deemed deviant, such as drugs, prostitution and pornography. We consider activities that do not seem to fit with mainstream definitions of leisure and which raise complex questions around such things as appropriateness, morality and anti-social behaviour.

As will become obvious throughout this chapter, a sociological perspective is crucial for a comprehensive understanding of leisure in the twenty-first century. Hopefully, the chapter also demonstrates the significance of taking a leisure perspective or a leisure *lens* to further our sociological understanding.

SEMINAR QUESTIONS

1 Why might the idea of leisure not be as straightforward as commonsense views might suggest?
2 To what extent do consumption and leisure overlap?
3 To what extent might 'anti-social behaviour' be seen as leisure activity?

LEISURE THEORY

The work–leisure relationship

The study of leisure has early origins stretching back to Veblen's *The Theory of the Leisure Class* (1899). However, it was not until the 1960s and 1970s that the foundations of the sociology of leisure were laid. It was during this period that the writings of the French sociologist Dumazedier were key to recognizing leisure as a valid area of study within sociology. In his book *Toward a Society of Leisure* (1967) he defined leisure as activity that is set apart from other obligations such as work and family and provides individuals with the opportunity for relaxation, the broadening of knowledge and social participation. He argued that leisure involves pleasure and freedom of choice outside or separate from paid work and everyday commitments. Leisure could be seen as *compensation*, a means of escape from the routines of daily labour, or as *residual time*, time left over when other commitments have taken place.

BOX 13.1 EXPLORING THE WORK–LEISURE RELATIONSHIP

The relationship between work and leisure was one of the earliest issues for the sociology of leisure. Parker (1971) argued that leisure is an important aspect of social life that demands rigorous sociological analysis alongside the more conventional areas of work, family, education, youth, and so on. He suggested that it was with industrialization that leisure became more clearly a separate sphere of life, as work was demarcated in terms of time and space. Leisure cannot be understood in isolation from work and is shaped by paid work and employment. Parker asserted that the relationship between work and leisure could take one of three forms and provided some examples for each.

Extension   Leisure is similar to work activities and there is no clear distinction between the two, e.g., social workers.

Opposition   Leisure is deliberately unlike work and there is a clear distinction between the two, e.g., deep-sea trawlermen.

Neutrality   Leisure activities are generally different from work but with no deliberate distinction between the two. Work and leisure are complementary aspects of people's lives, e.g., bank clerks.

A commonsense view of leisure sees it in opposition to work, but, as Parker (1971) suggests, this is by no means a straightforward relationship. There were several criticisms of Parker's early typology of the work–leisure relationship as his analysis ignored the many people who were outside the paid workforce, such as the unemployed, the retired, students, and those, primarily women, occupied as carers or as domestic home workers. However, Parker's study was a defining moment in the development of the sociology of leisure, as leisure became understood as socially situated rather than simply free time or an autonomous sphere of individual choice.

Theoretical traditions: pluralism, Marxism, feminism

Throughout the 1970s and 1980s, scholars developing social analyses of leisure introduced competing paradigms that reflected theoretical developments within sociology more broadly. In the UK the three major traditions in leisure studies were pluralism (often referred to as the 'conventional wisdom'), Marxism and feminism.

The early work of Roberts (1978) drew on a pluralist model of society to understand contemporary leisure in the 1970s. His seminal contributions to the field of leisure studies have remained consistent within this paradigm, arguing that there is a plurality of tastes and interests generated by different circumstances. Both commercial and public providers of leisure supply experiences from which individuals seek to fashion their varying lifestyles. Leisure is both a 'freedom from' and a 'freedom to' and is concerned primarily with relatively self-determined behaviour. The pluralist model does not assume that leisure is free from all influences but argues that age, gender, socio-economic status and other 'variables' operate in a multitude of configurations (Roberts 1999).

As elsewhere in sociology, in the 1970s and 1980s Marxist theorists challenged this plural-ist model of society and argued that we need to look under the surface of leisure at the eco-nomic, political and ideological processes that have produced it. Clarke and Critcher (1985) considered that leisure's domination by the market and the state, the persistence of leisure inequalities, and the drift to post-industrialism all demonstrate how leisure is part of capitalist society. Capitalism shapes leisure through hegemonic processes of both constraint and coer-cion. Their work provided a powerful critique, emphasizing the importance of history and the significance of *social* processes such as work, the family, the life cycle and the market. Leisure is about people's choices, but these choices are made within structures of constraint. Leisure needs to be understood within the dialectical relationships of structure and agency, control and choice, continuity and change. The emerging neo-Marxist analyses of leisure drew on the 'sociological imagination' of C. Wright Mills, grasping the relationship between history and biography. Leisure as 'freedom' and 'constraint' is seen as socially constructed around time and space, institutional forms and social identities. This approach was derived from cultural studies and views leisure as potentially an arena for cultural contestation between dominant and subordinate groups in society.

Further criticisms of the 'conventional wisdom' of leisure studies came from feminist sociology during the 1980s. Feminist scholars identified a male-dominated approach that had characterized much of sociology, including the study of leisure. Leisure understood as free time or freedom of choice was seen as being problematic and irrelevant to many women's lives. Women's lives cannot be neatly compartmentalized into periods of work and periods of leisure, as most women have domestic work responsibilities as well as paid work and often childcare or other caring responsibilities. For many women, family leisure is a time when they are supporting others' free time, such as transporting children to activities, preparing meals for entertaining friends, or planning and organizing family holidays. Thus their leisure often involves a *relative freedom* rather than clearly demarcated time. Feminist work identified the need to examine leisure in the context of women's lives as a whole and

BOX 13.2 WOMEN'S LEISURE IN SHEFFIELD, 1984–1987

Research by Green, Hebron and Woodward (1990) provided the UK's largest study of women's leisure and today remains the only comprehensive study to have been completed. The research in Sheffield, England, between 1984 and 1987 focused on the cultural significance of leisure in women's lives and leisure as a potential site for conflict and inequality and made a considerable contribution to how women's leisure was understood. The study concluded that:

- the concept *leisure* is extraordinarily resistant to being confined to a single, neat, definitional category. For the women in the study, leisure was a highly personal and subjective mix of experiences and was linked to, and a part of, other areas of life;
- leisure is divided by gender, class and race relations;
- women's material position and prevailing definitions of masculinity and femininity have a determining effect on how leisure is understand and experienced;
- issues of sexuality, respectability and social control are extremely important for women's leisure;
- control by men is widely practised and seen as a normal feature of everyday life.

not as a separate sphere divorced from all other areas of their lives. Consequently, the existing definitions and theories of leisure were viewed as androcentric, having meaning only in relation to men.

Post-structuralism

Both the feminist and Marxist analyses throughout the 1980s shared a predominantly materialist or structuralist approach to the sociology of leisure. Since the 1990s, sociological approaches have also drawn on postmodern and post-structuralist developments in social theory. Rojek (1985, 1995, 2000, 2005, 2010) has been the most prolific writer to have criticized the former traditions of leisure theory. In his writings he not only debates and challenges the paradigmatic traditions within leisure studies but also seeks to understand and interpret postmodern cultures and their relevance for leisure. Rojek argues for a phenomenology of leisure, with experience at the centre of analysis. Within postmodernity, the weakening and

Postmodern and post-structuralist approaches to leisure and consumption see leisure activities as increasingly becoming part of our identities, sometimes leading to the formation of subcultures, such as at sci-fi conventions. As is clear, however, this is still caught up with broader economic structures (the mass commercialization and merchandizing of films such as *Star Wars*) and, in some cases, traditional representations of gender (as in this scene). (© Bart/Flickr)

destabilizing of former structures and the blurring of social divisions such as class, race and gender have led to leisure and leisure lifestyles gaining increasing significance in the construction of individual and social identities. The development of new technologies and shifts in cultural practice are seen to find expression within postmodern leisure. These include notions of hyperreality, loss of authenticity, dissolution of cultural boundaries, depthlessness and superficiality, fragmentation, parody and pastiche. No longer are leisure places and experiences seen to be static and fixed, with theme parks, such as Disneyland, challenging the distinctions between real, imitation and fiction. Leisure becomes more individualized, with pleasure, risk and excitement centre-stage. The connections between leisure lifestyles and consumption are of increasing significance, and leisure plays an important role in the reflexive project of identity construction and definition.

The shift in emphasis from leisure being associated with work and production to its relationship to culture and consumption has produced new understandings and raised new questions. Increasingly leisure spaces are recognized as important sites of cultural consumption. Featherstone (2007: xiii) describes leisure as 'involving active lifestyle construction and bodily renewal linked to mobility: the promise of social mobility and personal transformation, along with the freedom of physical mobility, the capacity to move to search employment, leisure and new significant others'. It is not only the consumption of goods and experiences that is important but also the mass consumption of images promising style, pleasure and hedonism. Images and representations are central to understanding consumer culture, including ideas about the body, celebrity and the creation of seemingly fluid lifestyles that often blur fictions and realities. As box 13.3 demonstrates, this aspect of consumer culture can be profoundly gendered and sexualized, and gendered identities are often constructed, maintained and experienced through consumption. However, this is not simply *determined* and, as such, contemporary leisure and sport provide an interesting site to explore these shifting social relations.

BOX 13.3 CONSUMPTION, GENDER AND THE BODY

There are a number of ways of understanding and interpreting images of women's active bodies. Second-wave feminism argues that women's bodies are objectified in and through sport and active leisure; they are used to pose on cars in motor sports, and top female athletes are judged on their bodies either as heterosexual 'babes', such as the tennis star Anna Kournikova, or judged as muscular 'freaks' whose heterosexuality or identity as a woman is challenged (Hargreaves 2000).

Contemporary consumer culture focuses far more on differences between bodies, as well as empowerment through the body and the potential for the individual construction of alternative bodies and identities. Active bodies within leisure and sport provide an ideal context through which to explore questions of empowerment, difference and the construction of alternative bodies. From this perspective, women athletes are no longer judged only in relation to heterosexual, white femininity but can enjoy a powerful physicality, moving between and across identities (Heywood and Dworkin 2003).

Images of female athletes can loosen and destabilize traditional gender stereotypes. Jessica Ennis-Hill, for example, can be considered a 'perfect' contemporary role model, an athlete with powerful muscles, of mixed heritage, highly competitive and successful while at the same time firmly positioned in normative heterosexuality and able to adopt recognized symbols of femininity, for example through make-up and clothes, when posing for photographs or appearing in public life.

Thinking intersectionally

During the 1970s and 1980s, inequalities were at the centre of leisure theorizing, raising the question of the place of leisure in the production and reproduction of social inequalities. This has been explored in relation to class and gender and to a far lesser extent in relation to race, ethnicity, sexuality, age and disability. With the theoretical shift to postmodernity and post-modernism, questions of difference, identities and lifestyle have become more prominent. However, persistent inequalities at the level of the institutional and the individual remain and require analysis. Certainly theoretical advances since the 1990s ensure that we move beyond static concepts of inequality and deconstruct categories and universalisms to explain more fully contradictory, dynamic manifestations of power. Leisure theorists are now exploring the 'middle ground' between difference and inequality, which retains a focus on structural inequalities while seeking ways to account for the fluidity of multiple identities (Watson and Scraton 2013).

One way to explore this 'middle-ground' theorizing is through taking an intersectional theoretical approach. Thinking intersectionally offers the potential to engage with difference in more meaningful ways than a mere recognition of plurality and diversity. Concentrating on the messiness of accounts somewhere between modernist and post-structuralist analyses, common to intersectionality, allows us to explore inequalities *and* differences rather than one at the expense of the other. Thinking intersectionally includes giving voice to marginalized groups and individuals, but we need to go beyond this to engage with the systems and processes that produce and reproduce inequality and marginalization. The sociological study of leisure suits an intersectional approach, as leisure itself is multi-layered and more often than not is the outcome of a range of interrelated factors.

In this chapter we engage with several issues that are central to our leisure lives in the twenty-first century and which help us understand contemporary society. While we consider competing viewpoints on each of the issues, we prioritize our own perspective, which is informed by a critical, feminist leisure lens that engages with the 'middle ground' between modernist and postmodernist understandings of leisure.

SEMINAR QUESTIONS

1 Discuss Parker's three forms of the work–leisure relationship. What are the weaknesses of his approach? Think of five very different work contexts today – e.g., teacher, call-centre worker, builder, full-time carer, investment banker – and then consider how leisure may or may not be related to these work contexts.

2 Provide some examples of how leisure has become a source of gendered identities as well as a reflection of them.

3 Consider the view that leisure is now central to consumer culture. Can you think of examples from your leisure experiences?

THE WORK OF LEISURE

Leisure and paid work

As discussed earlier, leisure has traditionally been positioned and understood as secondary to paid work. While we find much to contest in this approach, it nonetheless continues to inform a commonsense view of how leisure is perceived and valued. Changing work patterns have inevitably had major consequences for leisure. The rise of the service sector and the knowledge economy, the increasing deregulation and flexibility of working time, the growth of part-time and casual work, the increasing numbers of women in the full-time and part-time workforce, and the large-scale migration of workers across national boundaries has meant that we can no longer simply understand leisure as in binary opposition to work or as 'compensation' or 'free time' (Rojek 2005). As Bramham and Spink (2009: 15) note in relation to their analysis of the postmodern city, 'Leisure in the postmodern city is as diverse, segmented and flexible as the economic, social and political context within which it exists.'

BOX 13.4 LEEDS, UK, AND SYDNEY, AUSTRALIA: 24-HOUR CITIES?

Work by Rowe and Lynch (2012) on the night-time leisure economy in Sydney, Australia, and similar work by Bramham and Spink (2009) in Leeds, England, provide useful case studies of leisure consumption and provision in Western urban environments in the twenty-first century.

The image of the 24-hour city developed in the 1990s was one of a sophisticated and democratized context, where people would experience their 'free time' and leisure. The boundaries between work, leisure, residence and shopping would become blurred as people work, live and play within the city, consuming and producing a bricolage of leisure lifestyles. Sydney and Leeds, while very different in size, location, governance and leisure provision, share certain characteristics, and the research by Rowe and Lynch (2012) and Bramham and Spink (2009) suggests that it is a far more complex scene than the one envisioned in the 1990s. Many more people now live in the city and more young people remain living in the parental home as a financial necessity. Both Sydney and Leeds have been gentrified, with inner-city areas redeveloped to become the residences of the young, predominantly white, professional middle classes. However, city centres can become 'no-go' areas dominated by young people, often fuelled by alcohol, and with a club scene that excludes many who do not fit the mould. Cities can be gendered and racialized spaces that marginalize women, minority ethnic groups and older people (Scraton and Bramham 1998; Scraton and Watson 1998). Many work *within* leisure contexts that reflect the diversity and fragmentation of leisure provision. This work in the leisure industries is marked by low pay, casualization, irregular part-time hours and lack of tenure. There is little doubt that working *in* leisure impacts on how you *experience* leisure.

Constant inducements to consume leisure create relationships that are complex and prone to conflict (Rowe and Lynch 2012). Thus there is an increasing gulf between young and old, relatively wealthy and the unemployed or low waged, able-bodied and disabled, white and minority ethnic. In this scenario, leisure becomes centrally defined as a commodity to attract further investment and leisure-sector job opportunities and, as such, is a powerful vehicle of social *exclusion* rather than social inclusion. It is important to consider who has access to the 24-hour city and whether increased opportunities to live, work and play in the city creates a 24-hour locus of fun and leisure opportunity or a space of exclusion and conflict.

Social, political and economic changes have had a major impact on leisure, but not as predicted in the 1960s and 1970s, when the coming of a 'leisure society' was hailed as the future. Any idea that leisure would become available to all and the fulcrum on which we build our lives seems an idea today far removed from the lived reality of most people. While our understandings of leisure and the experiences of paid work have become more complex and the boundaries between work and leisure increasingly blurred and permeable, it is important to acknowledge that the structure and patterns of work still impact directly on leisure provision and consumption. Paid work gives individuals not only access to financial resources but also social confidence and status. Rather than the arrival of a leisure society, we have seen an intensification of work with a growing insecurity of tenure and an escalation of control and surveillance. Work has become destandardized, with far more part-time and flexible schedules. Increasingly there are those who have resources but very little time to spend them, in contrast to those with time but very limited resources to consume. Persistent long-term unemployment has created what Rojek (2005) terms a 'new residuum' identified with extreme poverty and instability. What is leisure for this group in society? Clearly leisure choices must be contextualized in relation to scarcity, 'the unequal distribution of economic, cultural, social and political resources and your position in relation to them' (Rojek 2010: 6).

Early work on leisure and unemployment identified that poverty, isolation and powerlessness made leisure choice, autonomy and self-development an unrealizable dream for those outside the labour market (Glyptis 1989). Today, the same arguments prevail, even if our understandings of leisure have become more sophisticated and look to commodification and consumption rather than freedom and choice. Understanding unemployment and leisure, as Roberts (2010: 5) suggests, still requires a class (and we would add intersectional) analysis in that 'they are unwanted as producers and they are flawed consumers – unwanted in society's main "cathedrals" of consumption'. By 2013 there were 1.9 million NEETS (sixteen- to 24-year-olds not in education, employment or training) in the UK, a rise of 18.3 percent since 2008 (European Working Conditions Survey 2010). For these young people, leisure is a hollow concept if it relates to work, choice or consumption (see table 13.1).

Table 13.1: **Young people not in education, employment or training, UK, June 2013**

	16- to 17-year-olds	18- to 24-year-olds	16- to 24-year-olds
Number (thousands)	72	1,020	1,092
Percentage	4.9	17.7	15.1

Source: ONS (2013b).

Studies of leisure in contemporary large cities increase our understandings of the lifestyles of particular groups and individuals in an expanding consumer culture. More and more aspects of leisure are mediated by the consumption of goods (e.g., food, drink, sportswear, technology, body care products) and take place within significant sites of consumption (e.g., shopping malls, holiday resorts, sports stadia). To take part in this leisure requires financial resources and the cultural capital needed to engage in and select opportunities. The temporal and spatial aspects of the work–leisure binary have become blurred as they merge into each other, yet the 'old' questions relating to inequality remain pertinent today as the gap between those who have power to consume and those who do not gets ever wider and deeper.

The labours of leisure

Women have always disproportionately serviced the leisure of others. Women's domestic labour facilitates leisure for other members of the household, which has a significant impact on their own leisure experiences and opportunities (Green, Hebron and Woodward 1990). Early feminist critiques of women's leisure focused on all the 'hidden' work women do, such as transporting children to clubs and sporting activities, washing kit for partners or preparing family meals. Women were also seen to be constrained by their position as carers and home-makers, resulting in their leisure being shaped by family life and domestic commitments. Women provide considerable emotional work within the family, and the development of an 'ethic of care' often makes them feel guilty and selfish if they take time and space for their own leisure, thus reducing their sense of entitlement (Henderson and Bialeschki 1991). These analyses of the structural determinants of women's leisure told us a great deal about inequalities across private and public spheres.

Later feminist work argued that these approaches to understanding women's leisure concentrated too much on family labour and not enough on how individual women can make changes in their lives and the relationships between leisure and culture (Aitchison 2003; Wearing 1998). For example, a recent study of the leisure of single mothers found that, although they have dual-work commitments and their leisure is influenced by financial hardships, time, an ethic of care and gender-role expectations, they still experience new and positive leisure experiences *because* of their identity as single parents (Irving and Giles 2011). These women gain a degree of control and empowerment by being single parents and use creative strategies to ensure leisure time and space and to re-examine their perceptions of what leisure could be for them.

These more recent applications of feminist post-structuralism, while engaging with some exciting questions of identities and diversity (which we will consider in more detail in the next section on bodies), have moved the debates away from the earlier feminist concerns about the sexual divisions of labour and leisure (Scraton 1994). However, there is little evidence that there has been significant change to the division of labour within the household. Indeed, although attitudes to gender roles may be changing and becoming less traditional, the allocation of domestic tasks (including supporting children's leisure) remains very similar to that of twenty years ago (Crompton and Lyonette 2008; Walter 2010) (see figure 13.1). If this is the case, while women have made gains in the public sphere, the implications for women's leisure of unpaid servicing in the home of both the family and their leisure remain significant.

The example in box 13.5 of women climbers also relates to how many people work at their leisure by engaging in serious pursuits that challenge the notion of leisure as frivolous, fun and casual. Stebbins (1992, 2005, 2007) distinguishes between 'serious' leisure and 'casual' leisure'. For Stebbins, 'serious leisure' frees leisure from any notion that it is casual, enjoyable or hedonistic, instead emphasizing long-term commitment, goal orientation, perseverance and dedication. People work hard at their serious leisure. It is the systematic and serious pursuit of an activity that individuals find 'so substantial, interesting and fulfilling that, in the typical case, they launch themselves on a [leisure] career in acquiring and expressing a combination of its special skills, knowledge and experience' (Stebbins 2007: 5). Examples of serious leisure are as diverse as dog sports (Hultsman 2012), football fandom (Jones 2000) and barbershop singing (Stebbins 1992). What many studies of serious leisure have in common is that they focus primarily on

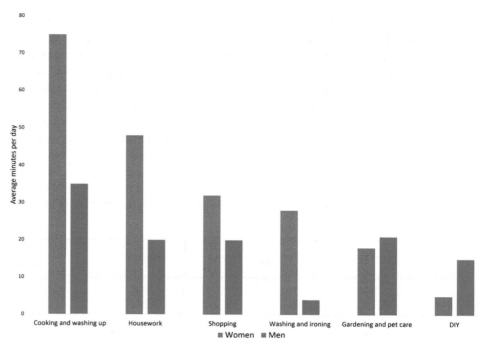

Figure 13.1 Allocation of domestic tasks by gender, UK, 2000

Source: Compiled with data from the UK Time Use Survey.

BOX 13.5 WOMEN CLIMBERS: MOTHERHOOD AND THE ETHIC OF CARE

In a study of women climbers, Dilley and Scraton (2010) found that, although they were highly committed, had acquired specialist skills and knowledge, and had created a serious leisure career out of their climbing, their climbing identities and participation were also implicitly and intricately linked to their gendered identities. Although embodied as strong, muscular and physically competent women resisting traditional notions of femininity, some of them also experienced gendered constraints of motherhood. The labour of caring greatly influenced their ability to commit to climbing and consequently influenced the 'turning points' and 'trajectories' of their serious leisure careers. This influence related not only to a restriction on their time to climb but also on their emotional ability to take risks and commit themselves to serious climbing routes. Domestic and caring responsibilities affected disproportionately the women who also had male climbers as partners. In this context the male climber continued to commit to their chosen leisure and played a secondary role in childcare and domestic labour. It would seem that domestic and caring responsibilities in the private sphere continue to impact on the leisure of many women in both private and public spaces. This is despite the fact that, at the same time, these women are constructing alternative physicalities and challenging traditional expectations of women's muscularity and their ability to develop high level skills in a risk activity.

the activity itself and the people involved and stress the value or function of the activity both for individuals and for society. However, feminist research, such as that by Dilley and Scraton (2010), highlights the fact that many studies of serious leisure fail to provide an adequate social analysis that also recognizes the significance of social relations, identities and spaces to an individual's ability to choose freely their leisure time or engage in more committed leisure careers.

People work at their leisure, and studies of volunteering and serious leisure provide further examples of how leisure is more than simply time left over after paid work is done. However, it is important to retain a critical approach to servicing leisure in the home, serious leisure or volunteering to understand the complexities of social relations, power, control and resistance.

BOX 13.6 VOLUNTEERING AS SERIOUS LEISURE

Volunteers are a major part of the work of leisure in a number of contexts, including sporting events, tourist attractions, museums, conservation projects, and so on. As the 2012 London Olympics and Paralympics demonstrate, in excess of 70,000 people gave up their time to support and facilitate a huge event that was the work and/or leisure of athletes, spectators, retail organizations, leisure industries and the media. Working at leisure in this context is seen as a vehicle of self-improvement and for civic good, and a key aspect of the 'big society'. Through their volunteering, volunteers facilitate and support the leisure of others while engaging in work-like activity in their own leisure time (Lockstone-Binney, Holmes and Baum 2010).

The Games Makers formed a key feature of the 2012 London summer Olympic and Paralympic Games and demonstrate how work, leisure and 'serious', work-like leisure were all bound up in this great sporting event. (© eltpics/Flickr)

As we discussed earlier in the chapter, in post-industrial societies people no longer construct their identities solely through their paid work (although this notion has always been problematic for those outside the labour market) but increasingly actively also through their leisure lifestyle and consumption practices. Whereas many people previously gained a sense of identity from their paid work (I *am* a teacher, miner, doctor, builder, etc.), many now associate with their consumption practices, which often overlap with their leisure (I *am* a snowboarder), identified through particular styles, clothing, equipment, holidays, and so on. This identity is constructed in what is perceived as 'free time' or leisure rather than through paid work.

Working *at* leisure, for example working on the self, also makes individuals good consumers, as is evidenced by the growth in private-sector fitness and health-related industries. As Featherstone (1991: 170) notes, 'the vast range of dietary, slimming, exercise and cosmetic body-maintenance products which are currently produced, marketed and sold point to the significance of appearance and bodily preservation within late capitalist society.' Individualization and reflexive self-production are key facets of contemporary Western societies (Giddens 1991; Bauman 1998b). The fitness industry is a primary example of leisure as self-work: 'the body is a site of work, and work on the body is also, fundamentally, self-work' (Smith Maguire 2008: 60). The selling of fitness has been a major aspect of the commercialization and commodification of leisure, epitomized by the work-out videos and fitness books developed by Jane Fonda in the late 1970s and early 1980s (Mansfield 2011) and continued today by 'celebrities' – for example, 'Jennifer Ellison's Fat Blaster DVD' (2011) and 'Davina – Ultimate Target' (2012) – and 'Infinity' fitness programmes online.

Since the 1980s there has been a continual stream of fitness fads and fashions, each requiring new 'looks', magazines, clothing and footwear. 'Working out' is about discipline and hard work, which seems to be in conflict with the ideals of leisure as freedom, fun and enjoyment. The blurring of a work ethic with a leisure ethic is part of the neoliberal discourse of individual responsibility, self-determination and market forces (McRobbie 2009; Rojek 2010). In a consumer society, this self-work becomes directly linked to the economy of social reproduction. In this context leisure is a site for producing an embodiment that epitomizes neoliberalism, suggesting that working hard on the body is an individual task, part of the culture of consumption that promises happiness, health and success by adopting a work regime for self-betterment. The marketing of commercial fitness and exercise clubs as leisure involves not only access to gym apparatus, swimming pools and exercise classes but also to cafes emphasizing healthy food, sports drinks to boost your energy, saunas, televisions, beauty therapies, and even the opportunity to purchase your next swimming costume, exercise outfit or headphones to tune into television or music. Working on the self has become a major leisure business. 'Working out' and 'working on the body' is about a discourse of responsible health and self-betterment. However, feminist scholars, in particular, articulate the importance of the body as a site also for resistance and empowerment. In the next section we consider in more detail the significance of a critical understanding of the body for the study of leisure.

SEMINAR QUESTIONS

1 Critically discuss Stebbins's notion of 'serious leisure'.
2 Consider examples of when leisure for some can become the work of others.
3 Discuss the view that the selling of fitness is a major aspect of the commercialization and commodification of leisure.

LEISURE AND THE BODY

It is only relatively recently that sociologists have shown an interest in bodies and embodiment. In the 1980s and 1990s, sociologists such as Turner (1984), Featherstone (1991) and Shilling (2012) challenged the view that the thinking subject is disembodied, emphasizing the social body as opposed to the traditional view of a 'natural' biological body. Feminist theory has also centralized the body since the 1960s and 1970s (Grosz 1994; Butler 1993). Early feminist writers were keen to emphasize and celebrate women's bodies, urging women to take control over them, particularly in relation to reproduction. Since this time different feminist positions have focused on the body as a site of gendered power relations; the performance of gender; the materiality of bodies; and the body as a site for personal empowerment. While we cannot expand on all these arguments here, we explore how the body has become a central issue for leisure, particularly active leisure, including physical culture and sport (Hargreaves and Vertinsky 2007).

Display of the body

Many people spend a great deal of time trying to achieve the 'perfect' body, which is intricately linked to expectations of gender. We are constantly bombarded by our consumer culture and the media with images and representations of bodily ideals that are hard to withstand (Walter 2010). While men have traditionally worked out to try to achieve a muscular body, a female body needs to be careful not to become too muscular; there are clear definitions of what should, or should not, constitute an ideal physicality for both men and women. It is often through consumption in leisure time and spaces that people construct their embodied identities, consuming the latest fashion trends and obsessively following the latest 'look'. Shopping, whether in the city centre, in an out-of-town shopping mall, or online, is a major leisure pursuit. Are we, therefore, all passive dupes who consume leisure goods and experiences that reproduce and re-create traditional unequal social relations? This has become a major debate within leisure studies, especially how new forms of leisure have opened up opportunities to explore alternative identities.

Sport is a crucial aspect of leisure – a pursuit, pastime or activity engaged in as leisure. The physical, moving body is central to our understandings of active leisure, sport and physical recreation. Bodybuilding is one area that has received academic attention: how we construct, sculpture or display our bodies to challenge conceptions of what constitutes a 'natural' body for men and women (Obel 1996). Bodybuilders subject their bodies to intense, strenuous disciplinary practices and work to achieve a particular muscular body. For women the development of a powerful muscularity can be viewed as positively challenging stereotypical notions of femininity and actively embodying an alternative gendered identity. However, women who are seen to embody a female masculinity (Halberstam 1998), through their participation in bodybuilding (Obel 1996), boxing (Mennesson 2000), rugby (Wright and Clarke 1999), wrestling (Sisjord and Kristiansen 2009) and other male-defined sporting activities, can also be abhorred and stigmatized to such an extent that they feel they must 'prove' their femininity. This can be seen in women's football, with most players displaying traditional femininity by growing their hair long and emphasizing their femininity when off the pitch (Scraton et al. 1999). The chapter on gender in this volume includes more discussion and examples of gender and sport, including 'gender verification'. In bodybuilding the concern about women being cast as masculine has resulted in 'femininity' now being part of the judging criteria in women's competitions. In a similar way, male bodybuilders are under pressure not to contravene traditional notions of masculinity. Although it would appear that muscles and masculinity are entirely compatible, many 'feminine' practices, of dieting, shaving body hair, applying fake tans, taking ballet classes and posing for performance, call into question gendered identity. Most theoretical understandings of gendered body images and practices draw on Foucault's use of disciplinary practices and how power works in a complex way, incorporating control *and* active resistances. Analysing such activities as bodybuilding highlights the contradictions and ambiguities surrounding body practices and gender representations. It suggests that leisure can be a crucial site where the gender order can be replayed but also where diverse and fluid gender discourses can be explored (Obel 1996).

BOX 13.7 POLE DANCING: AN EMBODIED LEISURE PRACTICE?

Holland (2010) provides a fascinating study of pole dancers. She begins by comparing the pole dancer to the gymnast. To do this she challenges her readers to imagine a female athlete on a horizontal bar. She highlights the skill, flexibility, balance and core strength required to complete gymnastic moves to music. The gymnast wears a leotard, the most appropriate clothing to be able to move and perform skilful movements. Holland then suggests we imagine the pole as vertical rather than horizontal, and we have a pole dancer not a gymnast. How does this influence our understandings of the activity and the performer?

Holland's analysis focuses on agency, pleasure, femininity, sexuality, body image and empowerment in trying to unpack and make sense of this particular activity. Fundamentally, she is interrogating pole dancing as an exercise class and therefore a leisure activity. The links with the sex industry and lap-dancing clubs are obvious; both involve exercise around a metal pole. However, her study shows that pole classes, run as exercise classes, can offer more than the objectification of the body, viewing women as passive, sexual beings. These women were rediscovering the pleasures of physical activity, feeling in control, identifying with their body and gaining pleasure from physical skill. However, although Holland's work focuses on pole dancing as exercise, can it be fully divorced from its sister activity in lap-dancing clubs? Is it control and objectification or pleasure derived from an active physicality?

Considering an activity such as pole dancing raises many questions that have been central within feminist leisure studies over the past few decades. Some post-structuralist feminists would identify pole dancing as leisure through individual choice, a freedom to develop personal physicality, bodily skill and enjoyment. It is an activity where friends can be made and pleasure and fun are absolutely central. Alternative social readings would link lap dancing, and by association pole dancing, to a consumer culture built around big business and finance. Women in these industries have little individual choice and often need the work to support themselves and families. They are objectified and controlled for the benefit of business, but more specifically men.

The display of the body is integral to leisure, be it through fashion, style, subcultural identities, physical activity or physical culture. Questions in relation to how the body is displayed are central to feminist leisure studies; people do extreme things in their leisure, *to* and *on* their bodies. We consider this further in relation to deviant leisure below.

The body at play

Lifestyle as a concept has challenged the deterministic view that sees class as the social relations of production, emphasizing how consumption has become a primary source of social identity rather than production. In consumer culture, social activities focus on the accumulation and consumption of a diverse range of experiences, activities and goods (Featherstone 1991). With the commodification of experience, any distinctions between consumption and leisure appear to be breaking down. Lifestyle is associated with consumption, taste and distinction; it is about leisure being more than an activity and more about a style of life that provides meaning and experience for the participants.

Lifestyle sports are a good example of how social analysis can help us understand and explain contemporary leisure and also how a leisure lens can contribute knowledge to the sociology of the body. Sports that fit into this category have also been called 'extreme', 'alternative', 'whiz', 'action sports', 'panic sport', 'postmodern' and 'new sports' (Wheaton 2004). Mintel (2001), in a report on extreme sports, highlights this relationship between the activity, meanings and experience. There are many activities that fit under the heading of 'lifestyle sports', from more traditional activities such as climbing, mountaineering, surfing and mountain biking to more recent, emerging activities such as kite surfing, BASE jumping (building, antenna tower, span, earth) and ski flying.

Lifestyle sports constitute alternative sports spaces which are outside the bureaucratic, competitive and regulatory aspects of traditional sport. How far they constitute an alternative is open to debate, as increasingly lifestyle sports are 'traditionalized', commercialized and commodified to fit into a competitive ethos. It is perhaps more useful to move beyond seeing a simple dichotomy between lifestyle sports and mainstream sports (Wheaton 2004). Lifestyle sports arguably involve considerable consumption of equipment and associated 'goods' linked to certain activities, including specific labels and styles and certain places and spaces, all packaged and sold to consumers. Yet they are more than activity alone. For many they constitute a style of life where identity can be constructed and maintained.

Rachel Dilley's (2007) study mentioned earlier analyses the lifestyle sport of rock climbing. She takes a gender perspective to explore the notion of empowerment through participation. As with pole dancing, this research takes the theoretical debates around the sociology of the body further by exploring lived bodily experiences. Lifestyle sports are particularly interesting sites to explore sociological questions about the body because, as alternative spaces, they have the potential to challenge the existing social order through the creation of new subversive behaviours and values (Wheaton 2004; Dilley 2007; Dilley and Scraton 2010). The climbers demonstrate a high level of commitment to their sport and develop their own subcultural communities and lifestyles. Dilley's research supports Giddens (1991) and Bauman (1998b) in demonstrating how important leisure spaces can be as sites of identity construction. However, whereas postmodern theorists argue that social structures are becoming less relevant, Dilley's research on climbers and Wheaton's on windsurfers suggest that how people are positioned in relation to gender, sexuality, class, disability and ethnicity continues to impact on their ability to engage in these alternative lifestyles. In both studies, being white, middle-class, heterosexual and able-bodied appears to be crucial in terms of the economic and cultural capital needed for participation.

Although still structured to a large extent around social relations, the women climbers and windsurfers also found that their leisure offered the possibility to challenge and explore alternative gendered expectations. Through learning how to use their bodies in different ways, they increased their strength and physicality and experienced their bodies as 'active, physically engaged, strong, skilled, capable and pleasurable' (Dilley 2007: 253). In doing this they challenged many traditional notions of femininity and developed active and empowered femininity.

Marginalized bodies

Understanding inequalities and the needs of those identified as marginal or excluded has been a central feature of the sociology of leisure (Aitchison 2009). However, there has been little work that has considered bodies that are placed outside those normalized as white, heterosexual, middle-class and able-bodied. If we take as an example disabled bodies, it becomes clear how our current understandings of leisure are at least partial and potentially discriminatory and exclusive. The United Nations Treaty on the Rights of the Disabled in 2006 concluded that leisure provision is crucial for the quality of life of the 650 million disabled people around the globe. In the UK, a study on the leisure of young people aged eleven to fifteen conducted for SCOPE, the UK's largest disability organization, found that young people with disabilities share many of the same leisure priorities as their able-bodied peers (Aitchison 2000). At this age, main leisure interests are focused on informal and electronic media, with the main differences being the amount rather than the type of participation and the social circumstances surrounding that participation; leisure is very much defined and influenced by who these young people engage and interact with during their leisure. It seems that, from the limited research that we have, relationships are the key to disabled young people having satisfactory leisure experiences (Aitchison 2000; Murray 2002). Leisure provides an important context for the development of valued relationships, vital for inclusion in mainstream culture and the breaking down of discriminatory practices and stereotyping.

Disability has traditionally been understood within a medical model which concentrates on the limitations of an individual imposed through a clinical or medical issue and then seeks to reduce or adapt these conditions in order to 'normalize' and support access and participation. Within leisure and sport, this has developed into areas such as therapeutic recreation. This approach uses leisure and sport as a tool, through assessment, treatment plans and interventions, to facilitate rehabilitation and inclusion. While no doubt some individuals benefit from this approach, the medical model has been heavily criticized for its focus on disability as the 'problem'. The social model, which developed as a challenge to the medical view of disability, emphasizes systematic barriers, stereotyping and exclusionary practices as well as the structural foundations of oppression. People are disabled by society, not their bodies (Oliver 1995).

Just as in sociology more generally, the sociology of leisure studies has begun to build on these critical social definitions to explore the complex nature of disabled bodies, resistance

BOX 13.8 LIVING WITH DISABILITY

David Howe provides an interesting vignette on his own experiences of disability and visiting the pub, an everyday leisure activity and a significant leisure space for many people. His own words describe graphically his experiences:

Movement in leisure space is negotiated carefully though not always recorded ethnographically. My body is ever present and never absent because of my impairment . . . Whether it is at work or leisure I have lived with the fact that my body is different in part because of how others react to it. The simplest of acts like a handshake or the carrying of pints from bar to table that does not conform to standards of normality often entails a judgement on the part of others. Often these judgements take the form of aversive disablism. Being a spaz is an integral part of my identity but there are times when I find myself trying to pass as able. I am increasingly uneasy about this because it is to enter the masquerade and pass off my impaired body for another that may not be better, just different. (Howe 2009: 494)

Howe recognizes that, although many people he meets in the pub would not see themselves as prejudiced or disablist in their approach to him, they are, in fact, engaging in aversive disablism. The more we have access to the lived experiences of disabled people, the more we will understand the complexities of disability and begin to recognize multiple identities and how these are lived and experienced.

and identities (Fitzgerald and Kirk 2009). Bodies have resurfaced as important for under-standing disability, recognizing the impaired body as the social body (Goodley 2012), thus deconstructing the binary between medical and social models. Exploring through sport and leisure how disabled people engage in the construction of embodied identity has helped us understand more fully issues of inequalities and exclusion as well as identities and resistances. We are beginning to have more reflexive ethnographic accounts that help make sense of disa-bility and challenge overt disablism.

As the work on disability demonstrates, leisure is an important site for social exchange and opportunities to develop shared interests. This has been shown to be the case for many marginalized in society, including minority ethnic groups (Watson and Scraton 2001; Watson and Ratna 2011) and older people (Scraton and Watson 1998). Leisure can be both a site for discrimination and a space for the construction of alternative and multiple identities.

SEMINAR QUESTIONS

1 How far do lifestyle sports contribute to alternative leisure spaces?

2 What do Dilley's work on climbers and Wheaton's work on windsurfers tell us about gender relations in sport and leisure?

3 Discuss the different theoretical approaches to disability.

4 What can the sociology of leisure contribute to our understandings of disability?

DEVIANT/DARK LEISURE

The 'dark side'

Terms that have gained more common usage among leisure scholars relatively recently are 'deviant' and 'dark' leisure (Stebbins, Rojek and Sullivan 2006; Williams 2009). The use of the term 'dark leisure' in particular calls into question a sense of leisure as a 'good' and con-structive endeavour, rooted in part, as earlier sections suggest, to its relationship to paid work, industriousness and self-improvement. As already indicated, this can be in relation to gen-erating effective consumers of products and services associated with the leisure industries and their multifarious service-sector outlets. It includes individual body projects of working out, getting fit, maintaining health, and so on (Rojek 2010). These activities are scrutinized by both participants and onlookers and often 'valued' via various elements of moral coding, social policing and related discourses of purposeful and acceptable forms of leisure. While we might seek to examine what is meant by 'dark leisure', its implicit oppositional form is so cul-turally imbued and taken for granted as the 'norm' that it is not suffixed with an adjective – it is simply 'leisure'.

Earlier in the chapter we outlined how constrained choice is one of the key ways in which leisure can be understood. Even scholars who appear to take a fairly uncritical view of leisure recognize that to regard leisure as 'free' is limited (Stebbins 2005). Stebbins offers 'uncoerced behaviour' as an alternative to leisure choice to account for human agency in the context of broader social factors and structures (and draws on classical Marxist theory in order to do so). It is intriguing that the focus here, however, remains on leisure as implicitly functional, 'good' and worthwhile. What then of leisure choices that are deemed to be 'bad'? For instance, 'doing nothing' is commonly construed negatively depending on the context within which it occurs; hanging about on street corners 'doing nothing' is dangerous, yet relaxing at home in privatized space is regarded very differently. Both can be understood as leisure, but in different ways. Some people have a choice or opportunity to 'do nothing' as their leisure, but for others 'doing nothing' may be the only option available because they lack the resources for other forms of leisure and consumption.

It is difficult to offer a clear definition for deviant or dark leisure, and highlighting some key related issues is perhaps more useful. For some scholars, such as Williams (2009), the key starting point is to widen our view of what leisure is and certainly to question how and why some aspects are regarded as 'abnormal' and deviant. He questions leisure in relation to legitimacy, criminalization and social acceptability. Leisure overall is regarded as good, positive, 'wholesome', reflecting a legacy of 'free time' as earned, to be used constructively within acceptable moral codes and frameworks. Williams questions these moral codes in relation to sexual practices, among them consensual sadomasochism, human vampirism and radical body modification. Writing twenty years earlier, Dorn and South (1989) questioned why 'guilty pleasures' were not more fully acknowledged and addressed by leisure scholars, including recreational drug-taking and sex. They drew on Rojek (1985: 177) to argue for leisure to be conceptualized as 'relations of permissible behaviour' and from this point of view to begin to critically assess leisure habits and practices of consumption beyond simplistic oppositions of 'good' or 'bad' 'behaviours'. Williams (2009: 212) therefore argues for more appropriate explanations of leisure as regards 'unusual practices' and states it is 'time for leisure scientists to embrace the many fascinating varieties of deviant leisure' (ibid.).

Young people and deviant leisure

As with many other aspects that social theory attempts to make sense of, leisure as a social phenomenon represents a challenge in dealing with complexity, in relation to meanings, perceptions, practices, locations, and so on. Young people's leisure practices arguably require analysis beyond early explanations reliant on the concept of socialization as proposed and understood by social psychologists (Hendry et al. 1993). From the outset, this assumes a set of outcomes whereby some young people will be effectively and adequately socialized and some will require 'correction', be that through formal legislative procedures or more informally through softer mechanisms of control, including family, education and social services. Social theories of youth are extensive (see, for example, Furlong 2009), and it is beyond the scope of this chapter to do justice to this work. However, it is often young people's leisure that is at the crux of much of the work on youth, young people, and behaviour and its associated consequences.

Griffin (1993) provides a useful overview of the social construction of youth and leisure as deviant and socially problematic. She outlines how policy discourse and political rhetoric regarding youth, particularly since the Second World War (but with continuities linking to previous eras too), has centred on delinquency and moral panic. Leisure for young people is perceived to require policing and control; being a youth is to be a deviant – think of the connotations, for example, of the term 'hoodie'. Griffin argues that, during the 1980s, key discourses positioned youth as deficient and/or rebellious. Education, training and leisure (particularly sport) were identified as an antidote to this assumed deficiency. If young people could be moved off the streets and into the leisure centre this would help 'resolve' deviant behaviour. Young people's 'free time' was viewed as a breeding ground for many social 'ills' and societal

Young people's 'free time' can be viewed and interpreted negatively by many in society, shaped by a broader notion and moral panic about youth with nothing to do being prone to causing trouble. Would a group of middle-aged or older adults sitting in the shadow of a medieval Norwich church be judged in the same way? (© Tim Caynes/Flickr)

problems. Leisure or 'free time' must be used constructively and in a way deemed 'appropriate'. Having too much (of the wrong sort of) time on one's hands invariably leads to unruly behaviour. Young people become deviant because they are not contributing to workforce production and/or, in a contemporary context, are labelled as NEETs (not in education, employment or training). They do not use their leisure appropriately as they are not active as consumers and have too much time with insufficient resources. We might argue that this has fed into the discourse of 'Council House and Violent', associated in contemporary Britain with the term 'chavs'.

Recently, leisure scholars have begun to re-engage with deviance and resistance, particularly in relation to changing contexts of consumption. Consumer society offers opportunities for the purchase of 'alternative' identities for young people, especially evident in phone apps, what is 'trending' via social media, and a relentless barrage of online advertising within which an increasing reliance on social networking is housed. Questions remain as to whether this is about choice or conformity:

Adolescents, it is argued, build up defence mechanisms against the continual barrage they receive to their senses through consumer culture (particularly through the mass media and advertising). One area of life where they might be able to escape is in the use of leisure time and spaces. Deviance is one activity where they can seek some sense of individual purpose for themselves free from the constraining influence of authority figures. However, with the sophistication of consumer marketing, media and advertising, this can be manipulated to provide a mechanism to repackage this resistance and resell it to those same adolescents: the outcome being a leisure that is commodified. (Wearing, McDonald and Wearing 2012: 2)

In earlier studies it is gangs of young men who are focused on as deviant in their use of 'free time' and leisure, be that 'hanging around city streets' or engaging in so-called hooligan behaviour at football matches. In the 1970s and 1980s critical analysis emphasized class conflict and resistance, drawing on Marxism and examining how leisure can be a site for cultural resistance to oppressive social and economic conditions (Hall and Jefferson 1976).

For young women, meanwhile, a primary discourse has been one of 'sexual deviance' (Griffin 2004), a focal point for examining sexual relations through leisure. Young women who are seen to be heterosexually promiscuous are represented extensively as amoral and deviant and considered irresponsible, while 'heterosexual promiscuity' is considered 'normal' for young men (Griffin 1993). This is often intensified through a racialized discourse of female black sexual promiscuity that is evident in popular cultural representations. Postmodern feminism has concentrated on consumer culture and how young women today are expected to emulate hedonistic styles of sexuality associated with young men (McRobbie 2009). Is this a sexual freedom to behave as men and pursue sexual pleasure as they wish? The discourse of sexual deviance relates either to a patriarchal notion of 'good' and 'bad' women or to a more permissive discourse that suggests equality, although this 'equality' seems to relate to white, able-bodied, middle-class, heterosexual young women (Griffin 2004).

Young people's leisure is therefore often defined as deviant because it challenges a view of how people should behave and is frequently regarded as dysfunctional both for individuals and for society. These same activities, be they displaying the body through piercing and tattoos, hanging around the streets, attending raves and the club scene, or taking recreational drugs and alcohol, can also be understood as a resistance. This resistance might be to the dominant consumer culture that expects certain ways of being and behaving based on discourses of gender, sexuality, race and class, or it might be based on challenging authority and a 'parent' culture. Deviance here suggests a temporary state of being 'off course' that is somewhat 'allowed' for young people. Young people can use their leisure after all as a site and space for the construction of alternative identities that deconstruct previous ideas about who we are and how we should behave. Cross-dressing, exploring sexualities and radical body modification may be deemed deviant, but there is an underlying assumption that normative and acceptable behaviours will prevail in the long run. Think about how rowdy student behaviour is often accommodated, taken for granted or expected, and think about the increased contexts for conspicuous consumption this now includes, from fancy dress at local pubs to 'spring breaks' in far-flung resorts such as Cancún.

When young people 'deviate' for too long or excessively, then it is questionable whether they are engaging merely in 'dark leisure' and whether their practices are 'freely' chosen at all. A contentious topic of debate in this area continues to be around recreational drug-taking. Dorn and South (1989) draw on Foucault's *History of Sexuality* to question how pleasure has come to be known only in relation to control and constraint. That is, surveillance and control, acceptability and normativity, shape leisure habits and lifestyles in ways that call further into question the notion of 'free choice'. Dorn and South argued relatively early on in leisure studies work, for example, that it is not so much examining whether or

BOX 13.9 YOUNG PEOPLE AND DRUGS: A LIFESTYLE LEISURE CHOICE?

Recent surveys have found that some young people are high risk-takers in consuming drugs, knowing little about what they might be buying on a night out and engaging in what is regarded as increasingly 'reckless behaviour'. However, many see it as a fundamental part of their leisure lives on the streets, at parties and with friends. For many young people, relationships and sociability are crucial, and drugs can give them a shared quest for pleasurable excitement (Butler, Topping and Boseley 2012). In 2011, 17 percent of young people aged eleven to fifteen had taken drugs compared with 29 percent in 2001; although the trajectory is downwards, drug use remains an important aspect of many young people's lives. The most common drug was identified as cannabis, with both boys and girls using to the same extent (Fuller 2011). Drug-taking and a central association of hippie culture with marijuana, for example, was seen to represent counter-cultural alternatives to a dominant mass cultural, meritocratic, work-oriented society. Others view illicit drug-taking as the outcome of material and structural inequalities. The use of ketamine has increased dramatically over the last few years (Griffin et al. 2008). Arguably, drug use has become normalized and is commonplace as part of people's consumption-orientated leisure (Smith, Thurston and Green 2011). However, not everyone would agree that drugs are simply a lifestyle or leisure choice. There is a complex interrelationship between 'individual choices of 15–16 year olds, their subcultural affiliations, and the material and structural situations in which they find themselves' (ibid.: 376).

not drug-taking is a leisure activity per se as what this aspect of recreational activity can tell us about wider lifestyles. We now turn to look at this type of question in relation to sex and leisure.

Sex and leisure

Sex is undoubtedly a key aspect of leisure. Everyday life is saturated by references and representations illustrating how popular culture is sexualized and how sex is commodified. Despite this, sex as a form of leisure is a relatively new topic for researchers (Williams 2009). Sex work and/or prostitution are associated with deviant leisure and, as with pole dancing (see bodies section), reminds us that analysing leisure and its consequences demands further attention be paid to different perceptions and meanings. The 'contract' of sex work between 'provider' and 'client' as a form of leisure can be scrutinized in ways that contribute to the complex and often contradictory nature of sex work as a social phenomenon. It is mostly men who are paying for sex in their leisure time or watching pornography on the internet; while that is not to suggest that men are the only consumers, they are certainly the main consumers in the sex industry. The sex industry is a major feature of the leisure industry and yet it is often left off the list because it is regarded as 'sordid'. Sex work, as a site of leisure, a set of leisure practices or activities, requires engagement across a broad spectrum of 'indulgence' (the client's demands) to acts carried out in desperation or hardship (the sex worker's lifestyle) and a whole myriad of meanings and perceptions in between.

For some commentators, sex work might be considered as mainstream and normative and fundamentally about women's oppression through men's leisure. Radical feminists argue that prostitution is a form of abuse and that sex work can never be extrapolated from acts of oppression (Jeffreys 2003). Others, taking a post-structuralist feminist perspective, argue for harm reduction strategies and a more open engagement with the nature and conditions of sex work. The sex worker is seen 'as a leisure service provider deserving of protection rather than a social problem to fix or ignore' (Mulcahy 2008: 5). Mulcahy's argument is that, until social researchers engage with the contexts and meanings of sex work beyond moralistic and normative parameters, then its significance, however troublesome people find it, will not be fully understood. Prostitution often takes place in public spaces – on streets and in public parks that are leisure spaces. Sex work is embedded and emplaced and thus a leisure lens contributes further analysis to the sociology of sex work.

Discussing sex work is complicated because it raises further questions about sexual practice and sexual norms. Williams (2009) considers the implications of consensual sadomasochism (BDSM) for leisure, stating that a serious leisure framework is one way of explaining motivation and engagement in this practice. The practice Williams refers to is assumed to be consensual, whereby boundaries and behaviours are understood by participants and is not based around a financial transaction. Yet other aspects of consumption are a key feature of leisure activity. Recently we have witnessed the 'popularization' of BDSM in E. L. James's *Fifty Shades* series of novels, for example. These international bestsellers have enlivened discussion about the parameters of erotica, which have been mainstreamed in new and prolific ways. New avenues for mass consumption of 'risky' literature, for example, require us to consider what consumer demand is based upon and how things previously kept (literally) in the 'dark' become exposed to a safe and bright marketer's 'light' telling people it is okay to read this in one's leisure time.

Examining sex and leisure interrelationships is about the construction and boundaries of people's actions and how these inform our analysis of power relationships and capital (in a very broad sense) and about complex processes of exchange. Another key feature of sex as leisure, commonly occurring in the private sphere of the home, is consumption of pornography via the internet. Is this deviant leisure? Is it dark leisure? If we were focusing on children and young people under the age of sexual consent (sixteen years in the UK), accessing online pornography would certainly be labelled as 'dark leisure'. The consumption of pornography by and involving adults, meanwhile, remains a contentious topic in considering leisure in general (it is just that not many people talk about it).

For some feminists, pornography cannot be categorized as anything other than a form of oppression and a reinforcement of male heterosexual power. For others, there are claims that women 'freely' consuming pornography is an important aspect of liberation. Pornography as a means to satiate or excite via processes of consuming sexual imagery is a form that can undoubtedly be associated with leisure. Susan Shaw is one of the few scholars to engage directly with pornography as a feature of leisure. She found that,

> Despite the fact that pornography was clearly not an enjoyable leisure activity for the women in this study, it was evident from this, and from other research studies and reports, that pornography use is a common leisure activity for at least some men. . . . Since most pornography focuses on women's bodies and depicts women in various sexual acts for the exclusive pleasure of men, pornography can be seen as the quintessential leisure activity in which women are used as the objects of men's leisure. (Shaw 1999: 209)

Further feminist analysis has gone on to establish more fully what research there has actually been on pornography and to attempt to account for the complexities of why people use 'porn'

(Attwood 2005). In an intriguing proposition, Eberstadt (2009) compares the consumption of tobacco and the smoking habits of the 1960s to the consumption of pornography in the present day. Both sites of consumption are institutionalized and commodified and rely on a public to form habitual relationships to them, usually in their leisure. This acts as a reminder that perceptions of deviant and dark leisure change over time. The smoking ban in public spaces renders smoking an act of deviance in ways that would have seemed quite fantastic only twenty years ago, while pornography, Eberstadt (2009) suggests, is now taken for granted in much the same way that tobacco was previously. The consumption of pornography may have become more mainstreamed but arguably has done little to challenge normative, particularly heteronormative, patterns of sexual relations. This suggests that, rather than its avoidance as a result of distaste towards deviant or dark leisure practices, there is a need for further debate and acceptance of how significant this form of leisure consumption is.

SEMINAR QUESTIONS

1 What can leisure that falls 'outside' normative codes tell us about complex social relations in contemporary society?
2 Outline activities that you associate with dark leisure and deviant leisure and assess some of the similarities and the differences between your lists under the two headings.

CONCLUSION

Leisure is a multidisciplinary area of study, but the sociology of leisure has been the dominant approach within the UK. Over the past fifty years, the sociology of leisure has moved from focusing on how people enjoy recreation during their free time from work to engaging with the conspicuous consumption of risk, pleasure and escapism. Processes of de-standardization and individualization have altered how we view leisure and shifted our attention to how leisure is involved in the construction of social identities and difference. Yet, in all the issues we have discussed in relation to work, bodies and deviant/dark leisure, it remains the case that, however we define leisure, it is a major part of all our lives.

Leisure does not 'exist' for people simply to discover and engage in. It is a product and constituent of complex social and cultural values that requires a more nuanced analysis of work, how people use their bodies, contexts and spaces, and what configurations of play, risk and danger they encounter in relation to this. Leisure is a mainstay of contemporary global capitalist societies and is implicitly tied to consumer culture; it is not likely to change that dramatically any time soon. Whereas the early sociology of leisure was concerned with civil society, public leisure and volunteerism, leisure is now centrally concerned with consumption and commerce. The sociology of leisure, while central to leisure studies, remains on the periphery of sociology. Yet, as this chapter has shown, practices common to leisure are intricately and inextricably linked to some of the most fundamental questions facing sociologists, including healthy bodies, risk, changing work practices, deviance, and so on. Locating social issues within a leisure context adds to our sociological imagination and provides alternative ways of seeing and understanding our everyday world.

SEMINAR QUESTIONS

1 Think about your own leisure. How has leisure altered over the past thirty or forty years? Does your leisure differ from that of your parents, your guardians or those a generation older?
2 How would you analyse the relationship between leisure and consumption?
3 Choose work, bodies or deviance and discuss how leisure can be a source of identity construction.

FURTHER READING

▶ Rojek, C., S. M. Shaw and A. J. Veal (eds) (2006) *Handbook of Leisure Studies* (Palgrave Macmillan). Leisure is a multidisciplinary field of study, and this handbook provides a good introduction to the various and diverse ways in which leisure forms and practices are situated and develop.

▶ Wearing, B. (1998) *Leisure and Feminist Theory* (Sage). This is a seminal text within feminist leisure studies and remains a key reading.

▶ Blackshaw, T. (2010) *Leisure* (Routledge). This provides an in-depth look at definitional issues and key modernist and postmodernist perspectives on leisure, as well as introducing the notion of 'liquid leisure'

▶ Pritchard, A., N. Morgan, I. Ateljevic and C. Harris (eds) (2007) *Tourism and Gender* (CABI). To extend understanding of leisure through tourism, this addresses some of the issues explored in the chapter.

▶ Carrington, B. (2010) *Race, Sport and Politics: The Sporting Black Diaspora* (Sage). This is recommended to develop further understandings on issues of race, sport and leisure.

RELIGION AND SOURCES OF SIGNIFICANCE

the dawning of a secular age?

PAUL HEELAS

CONTENTS

INTRODUCTION

THE FOLLOWING IS INSPIRED by Charles Taylor's *A Secular Age* (2007), the most significant study of religion and spirituality of recent decades. As Taylor is acutely aware, possibly for the first time in human history, certainly for the first time in the much briefer history of modernity, it could very well be the case that certain societies are entering – or have entered – a secular age. On first sight, the decline of Christianity in a great deal of Northern Europe does not bode well for the sociologist of religion. It seems that the advent of a secular condition means that there is little left to study. On second sight, the decline provides a marvellous opportunity to test two venerable schools of thought.

One school, developed by the secular wing of the Enlightenment, holds that the secular is *self-sufficient*. Once countries such as Britain (the focus of this essay) enter the secular condition, the age of the secular is set to run for the foreseeable future. It is self-sustaining. For people such as Richard Dawkins (2006a), it is perfectly possible, indeed highly desirable, to live a worthwhile, fulfilling life without Christianity, or any other form of religion or spirituality. The second school of thought holds that the secular condition is *insufficient*. There is something about the human condition which means that the secular, alone, is not enough. The argument is that the erosion of Christianity's influence means that the secular comes into greater prominence. And this means that ever more people have experiences, apprehensions, comprehensions or outlooks that transgress the secular condition itself. To a degree, the secular is self-defeating.

SECULARIZATION: FROM CHRISTIANITY TO SECULARITY

An increasing number of sociologists of religion are directing their attention to whether a secular age has dawned, or whether some kind of post-secular condition is emerging. In Northern Europe, secularization has been in evidence for a considerable time. In 1914, Durkheim observed that 'The old ideals and the divine figures that embodied them are in the process of dying' (Christiano 2007: 50). In 1917, Simmel noted: 'In our present context the essential fact is the existence of large social groups who, in pursuit of their religious needs, are turning away from Christianity', and referred to 'the widespread rejection of any fixed form of religious life' ([1917] 1976: 258–9). In 1904, Max Weber ([1905] 1985: 182) bemoaned the disappearance of religion from the workplace in no uncertain terms. The demise of the Protestant 'spirit of capitalism' had turned the workplace into a spiritless 'iron cage' – the home of 'specialists without spirit, sensualists without heart'.

Since these early days, sociologists of religion have used a battery of gauges to chart what has been happening to Christianity. There is now a formidable amount of data. The website 'British Religion in Numbers' (www.brin.ac.uk) is an invaluable resource. The three outstanding researchers today, Callum Brown, Steve Bruce and David Voas, are based in Britain. To set the scene, Bruce (1996: 273) states, 'in so far as we can measure *any* aspect of religious interest, belief or action and can compare 1995 with 1895, the only description of change between the two points is "decline".'

Evidence of decline

Tracking change from the middle of the nineteenth century in Britain, Alasdair Crockett and David Voas (2006: 567) demonstrate 'a relentless fall in church attendance since the 1851 Census of Religious Worship'. Dwelling on decline in England during recent decades, Christian Research (2005: 5) reports that 11.7 percent of the population attended church on a weekly basis in 1979, 9.9 percent in 1989, 7.5 percent in 1998 and 6.3 percent in 2005.

As the main indicator of belief in Christian theism, belief in a 'personal God' declined, in Britain, from an average of 43 percent (for the period from 1947 to 1970) to an average of 28 percent (for the years 1990 to 2000) (Field 2010a). (The last figure can be compared with the belief in God in in 2005 in Sweden, at 23 percent, and Denmark, at 31 percent (Zuckerman 2012: 18).) The category of 'strong believers', namely those who are convinced that God exists, is now at 17 percent in Britain (Smith 2012: 7). Other telling measures of decline of belief in Christianity are faith in the 'divine authority' of the New Testament, falling from 68 percent in 1960 to 49 percent in 1993 (Field 2010b), and 'belief in the divinity of Jesus Christ', falling from 71 percent in 1957 to 40 percent in 2008 (Field 2010c).

Drawing on Crockett and Voas (2006: 581), in Britain 'Religious affiliation, almost universal among those born at the start of the twentieth century, is found in less than half of those born in the 1970s.' As for the number of those who do not think of themselves as belonging to a religion, 31 percent claimed 'no religion' in 1983; in 2009 the figure was 51 percent – a significant increase of 20 percent (Voas and Ling 2010: 72). More widely, 'the dominant trend in nearly all Western countries is the rise of non-religion' (Voas and McAndrew 2012: 47). To mention the USA, in 1990, 7 percent of the adult population were 'nones' (Putnam and

BOX 14.1 INHERITANCE

Exceedingly important evidence demonstrating decline in Britain concerns what Crockett and Voas (2006: 577) describe as a 'striking pattern of inheritance':

> For the vast majority of children, the likelihood of having a religious affiliation is a function of whether neither parent, one, or both have an affiliation. As one would expect, the child's affiliation is usually to a parental denomination . . . With two religious parents, the child has just under a 50% chance of adopting a parent's affiliation; with only one, the likelihood drops to just below 25%. (Ibid.: 577–8)

Emphasizing the sheer significance of the inheritance factor, Crockett and Voas continue: 'It is evident from this pattern of transmission that religiosity has almost halved in a single generation . . . These young British adults are only a little more than half as religious as their parents, whether the measure used is affiliation, attendance, or belief' (ibid.: 578). (See also Voas and Crockett 2005: 21.)

Campbell 2010). Since 1990, the number of 'nones' increased to around 15 percent by 2007, then to around 20 percent by 2012 (Pew Research Center 2012: 1).

The influence of Christianity has patently diminished within the institutional and cultural fabric of the secular world. Whether it be the workplace, health care, education, politics or culture, Christianity has faded, or disappeared. In the Northern Europe of some 200 years ago, Christian tradition was alive and well within the domains of bureaucracy and commerce. As Weber noted (above), by the beginning of the last century, the workplace was without 'spirit'. In the Northern Europe of the past, Christianity contributed a great deal to health care. Today, the National Health Service is basically secular. Using mainstream high-street bookshops as an indicator of cultural presence, Christian publications have become marginalized.

Without going into further detail here, it suffices to make a basic point. The decline of Christian beliefs and faith means that distinctively Christian influence is likely to wither within the cultural and institutional fabric of the secular world. True, a minority can make a lot of cultural noise. In the main, though, as the number of Christians diminishes, so does the likelihood of Christian-focused public debate having a significant impact. In hospitals, the fewer the Christians, the less likely that Christian-based caring will be in evidence. The same kinds of consideration apply to specifically Christian matters in government, Christian-focused teaching in schools, Christian literature in non-specialized bookshops, and so on. Furthermore, although politically orientated Christianity has contributed to the multiculturalism debates of recent years, the contribution has not been on the scale of engagements with Thatcherism during the 1980s (Heelas and Morris 1992). Relative to the past, Christianity is not alive and well in the public life of Britain.

The secularization of Christianity and the secular condition

Does the decline in the number of those who attend church on a regular basis, and who hold beliefs with conviction, entail commensurate expansion of the number of atheists? The obvious endpoint of secularization is atheism. The expectation is that, the greater the number of those who move away from religion, the greater the number who become disbelievers. However, this is not the case. After many decades of decline, just 6 percent of the population were atheists in 1950. According to the RAMP (Religion and Moral Pluralism) survey, just 9 percent were atheists in 1997. By 2008, just 11.2 percent identified as 'strong atheists', namely those who 'Don't believe in God; never believed in God; and strongly disagree there is a personal God' (Smith 2012: 11). Given the number who have lost faith in Christianity, relatively few assert that Christianity is false, that God does not exist, that the secular is all that there is. The pervasive notion that the collapse of Christianity means that more or less everyone ends up as an atheist is erroneous.

Sitting in an extraordinarily hot and humid room in Dacca in 1988, I had a rather half-'baked' eureka moment. It belatedly dawned on me that there must be far more to the process of secularization than a straightforward shift from faith to the disbelief of the atheist. The increase in the number of atheists (and agnostics) in the UK has not kept pace with the decline in church attendance, and this has to be explained.

So what has happened to all those who are neither regular attenders of church nor atheists/agnostics? Surely, these people *have* to believe in *something*; minimally, they have to entertain the possibility or likelihood of something beyond the secular. Hence the idea of a middle ground, occupied, for example, by those holding quasi-Christian beliefs, including a 'Higher Power', or by those inclined to the 'New Age'. The middle ground has been growing. The percentage of the atheists and agnostics in Britain doubled between 1950 and 1990, to 24 percent, and that of regular attenders fell by 30 percent during the same period – entailing that the middle ground expanded by nearly 20 percent of the population.

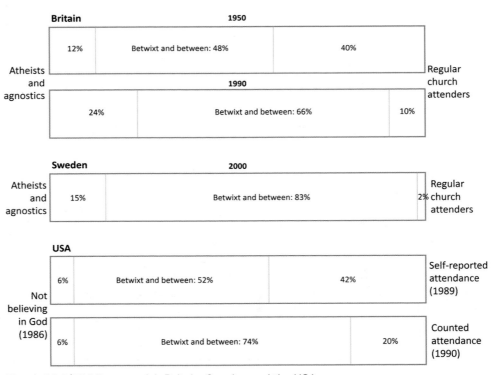

Figure 14.1 'Middle grounds': Britain, Sweden and the USA

Source: Based on Heelas (2002: 360–1).

Since my rather inadequate effort at explaining the relatively sluggish growth of atheism by thinking in terms of a zone betwixt and between the atheist and the regular attender, middle-ground studies have flourished. David Voas is the great expert. In an important article, 'The Rise and Fall of Fuzzy Fidelity in Europe' (2009: 155), he explores 'the significance of the large sub-population that is neither religious nor completely unreligious'. Deriving their fidelity from Christianity, 'fuzzies' (as they have come to be known) might be 'nominal adherents', perhaps using Christianity to symbolize fidelity to national identity (ibid.: 162). Fuzzies might show 'residual involvement' with 'Christian belief, practice, and self-identification' and 'casual loyalty to tradition' (ibid.: 161, 155). Other fuzzies are of 'New Age' inclination (ibid.: 162). In another seminal article, 'Religion in Britain: Neither Believing nor Belonging', co-authored with Alasdair Crockett, the point is made that 'beliefs' held by the fuzzies 'may consist of little more than opinions' (Voas and Crocket 2005: 14). The most pervasive belief-cum-opinion, it is claimed, is 'a vague willingness to suppose that "there's something out there"' (ibid.: 24). 'New Age' orientations also make their appearance (ibid.: 25).

Christian ideas and symbols still pervade aspects of social life in the UK, especially at times of national tragedy or remembrance, as when Lee Rigby, a British soldier, was killed on the streets of London in May 2013. (© David Holt/Flickr)

According to Voas (2009: 162), more than half the population in most European countries (including Britain) are neither secular nor especially religious. If stricter criteria are used to ascertain the number of secularists (such as Tom Smith's 'strong atheists', at 11.2 percent of Britons) and belief in God (such as Smith's 'I know God really exists and I have no doubts about it', at 16.8 percent), the percentages of the betwixt and between rise very considerably: to around 70 percent (Smith 2012: 11, 7).

Voas (2009: 167, emphasis added) argues that the zone is 'a *staging post* on the road from religious to secular *hegemony*'. The inheritance factor, introduced above, is at work. And this takes time: 'Societies do not turn away from religion overnight or even from one decade to the next; rather, secularization occurs as increasing numbers of people become nominally religious or only half-believing, before their descendants shed religious belief, practice, and identity altogether' (Voas and McAndrew 2012: 46). Since it takes a considerable length of time for the zone to empty, the relatively few number of atheists can be explained by arguing that there has not yet been enough time for all that many to leave the fuzzy zone to become disbelievers. However, fuzzies have existed ever since church attendance went into decline. The 'staging post' to the secular has long been operative. There should be more atheists. So why is this not the case? Many of those who leave the fuzzy zone have to be adopting some sort of attitude, or outlook, that differs from that of the atheists (or agnostics). Could it be indifference?

Steve Bruce (2002: 42) is the first contemporary theorist to argue that the endpoint of secularization is 'widespread indifference': the opinion that there is simply no need to think about religion – with more important things to get on with, why take any notice? The indifferent do not belong to the zone of fuzzy fidelity. They do not think in terms of fidelity. Neither do the indifferent belong to the territory of the atheist. The indifferent are secularists by default. The number of atheists is not growing as fast as one might expect largely because the indifferent are becoming more pervasive. For people to become entirely indifferent – that is, to arrive at the position of religion not being of any relevance whatsoever – all that the nominals of the fuzzy fidelity zone have to do is stop using Christianity (or another religion) as an identity badge.

Criticisms of the secularization thesis

It is fashionable to criticize the secularization thesis. Unfortunately for the critics, the long-term decline of Christianity in Northern Europe is incontestable. A favoured criticism is to point to congregations that are growing. The case is argued by contributors to a volume edited by the Anglican Priest and academic David Goodhew (2012). No one denies the congregations of some churches are expanding. However, particular congregations often expand by way of consolidation, attracting people from other churches which then close. The claim of decline, overall, is not undermined.

Linda Woodhead is among the chorus of voices that object to the secularization thesis. Although she has written on the importance of 'gendering' secularization theory, she now describes secularization as 'a crazily narrow-minded approach, which has to turn a blind eye to the luxuriantly variegated religiosity of most the world, and ignores the past. Including our own' (2013: 8). However, leading authorities – Bruce, Voas and Callum Brown (2001) – do chart the history of secularization in Britain, and are as aware as anyone else that religion is flourishing in many countries. With secularization theorists focusing on lands such as Britain, it is no more sensible for them to turn to other cultures (say the Philippines) to chart secularization than it would be for those studying delinquency in the schools of the North-West of England to address (say) Saudi Arabia.

Is decline bottoming out? This possibility does not pose a threat to contemporary secularization theorists, who do not specify that Christianity will disappear *in toto*. However, if Christianity has stabilized it will perpetuate itself, and this counts against the idea that the future lies with the imperfect of the secular alone. Thinking of church attendance, Britain's foremost authority on the subject, Peter Brierley, writes: 'the most recent figures for Anglicans and Catholics (important because these are the biggest denominations) show that while decline continues overall, the rate of decline is lessening' (2010: 2). Although attendance might gradually be 'pulling out of the nosedive', as Brierley puts it in the title of a 2006 volume, it has yet to stabilize.

It is reasonable to say that up to 25 percent of the population of Britain are (fairly) faithful religious believers. This percentage is arrived at by incorporating the 17 percent of Britons who concur with the proposition 'I know God really exists and I have no doubts about it' (as reported by Smith, above), adjusting this figure upwards to take into account both some fuzzies and a percentage of those who claim to believe in the divine authority of the New Testament or the divinity of Jesus Christ. As for how many of the 25 percent total are full-bodied religious adherents, experiencing the sacred of their Godhead as a significant force in their lives, one can make only an informed guess. Bearing in mind the importance of congregational, associational activity for nurturing a 'sense of God', the numbers could be closer to the 6.1 percent of regular church attenders than to the 25 percent of believers.

Whatever the exact percentage of full-bodied religious adherents, Christianity remains sufficiently in evidence to count against the claim that Britain has entered a secular age. According to Voas's account, though, the fuzzy zone will progressively give way to the secular of the atheist or the indifferent. If Voas is correct, the number of atheists – currently around 15 percent – will gradually increase and the number of indifferent – currently unknown – will swell (Bagg and Voas 2009).

SEMINAR QUESTIONS

1 What is the *best* evidence of secularization?
2 Why are their relatively few secularists?
3 Is indifference widespread?

ISLAM: A BULWARK AGAINST SECULARIZATION?

The secularization of Christianity in Britain is indisputable. On first sight, it is equally indisputable that Islam in Britain stands firm, has not secularized and is in fact expanding, to count against the idea of a comprehensively secular age. Is this true?

The standard account

For those who would like Britain to remain a 'Christian country', there is apprehension, even fear, that Islam is set to replace Christian values with an alien imposition. Apprehension is partly based on quantitative evidence.

BOX 14.2 THE GROWTH OF ISLAM IN BRITAIN AND EUROPE

The Muslim population of England and Wales (where the vast majority of British Muslims live) has risen from 3.0 percent of residents (approaching 1.6 million), reported by the census of 2001, to 4.8 percent (amounting to 2.7 around million), reported by the census of 2011 (ONS 2011; Field 2012). Approaching half are British Pakistanis. Peach (2007) estimates that in 1950 the Muslim population of Western Europe numbered fewer than 300,000. Today, Voas and Fleischmann (2012) report 18.3 million Muslim inhabitants. For Europe as a whole, the number adds up to 38 million (Sapsted 2010).

In Bradford, Field (2010d) estimates that some 110,000 are Muslim – a number which equates to around 20 percent of the population. With average weekly attendance of Christian services amounting to just 11,400 people (Church Statistics 2012), the number of regular mosque attendees is clearly higher, probably considerably so. A religious revolution has taken place here.

In Britain, analysis by the Office for National Statistics of the 2001 census of England and Wales shows that the median age of Muslims is twenty-five (Field 2013b: 1), far lower than the median age of churchgoing Christians. The low age profile, cultural factors bearing on family size, and immigration mean that Islam is set to continue to expand – hence articles with titles such as 'Islam Could be the Dominant UK Religion in 10 Years' (*RT News* 2013: 1). A religious revolution could well be in progress on the national front.

For the standard account, Islam is also an increasingly powerful presence. 'Surveys demonstrate a *developing* divide between Muslim and non-Muslim communities in Britain' (Field 2010d: 24, emphasis added), a divide that can readily be attributed to actual, or perceived, hardening – perhaps radicalization – of Islam in the face of actual, or perceived, hardening of the opposition. Although Voas and Fleischmann (2012) are far from being die-hard advocates of the standard account, they nevertheless provide sound sociological reasons in support of the view that the Muslim population is already 'highly religious'.

- People arrive in Europe together with their religion. Generally speaking, the countries they hail from are dominated by Islam. And, generally speaking, settlers retain close links with their ancestral homelands. Male British Pakistanis, for example, often return to Pakistan to marry. In Rotterdam, flats occupied by settlers can readily be identified by the alignment of TV satellite dishes (to receive signals beamed from Morocco, for example). The 'desire [is] to maintain the heritage culture' (Voas and Fleischmann 2012: 535).
- Voas and Fleischmann (ibid.: 538, 530) refer to the 'high residential concentration in destination countries' and use the expression 'residential segregation'. Muslims live in enclaves, environments that are fairly self-sustained. A wide range of services are available, including mosques, schools, shops, and religious/spiritual health care. Extended families, communal events such as weddings, mosque-based activities, other community groups, mutual support networks, and so on, mean that life within enclaves is intensely associational. Individuals are born into communities of (largely) shared values, the sacred canopy is mutually reinforced and relativization is avoided (ibid.: 531; and see Bruce 2011). Respectability calls for religious practice (ibid.: 529).
- Voas and Fleischmann (ibid.: 540) make the important point that 'The lack of a gender gap in Muslim religiosity – so that men are just as committed as women, although their

religious activities may be different – helps to maintain high levels of family involvement and transmission to the next generation.'

- Voas and Fleischmann (ibid.: 536) write of 'the wish to uphold a Muslim identity in the face of prejudice and social exclusion'. Intent on defending themselves against the hostilities of the outside world, it seems, Muslims assert the ascendancy of an Islamic over a British identity.

A revisionist account

The revisionist account criticizes the view that Islam serves as a bulwark against the progressive secularization of Britain and the view that it is set to conquer the future of religion. A national opinion poll commissioned by YouGov's Anthony Wells (2006), found that 48 percent of Muslims never attend a mosque, with just an additional 6 percent attending on special occasions. It could be the case that this is because of women being disinclined to enter the mosque for prayer or not being welcomed (Dyke 2009). However, there is evidence from elsewhere that mosque attendance, for prayer, is in *overall* decline.

In the Netherlands – where there is far better, systematic, national data than in Britain – the Central Bureau of Statistics (2009) reports that the decline of those who regularly go 'to a religious gathering' is greatest among the 5 percent of the population that is Muslim: from 2004 to 2008, an average of 35 percent of Muslims went to a mosque at least once a month, compared with 47 percent in 1988–9. (Protestant church attendance fell only slightly during this period.) And Maliepaard, Lubbers and Gijsberts (2010: 466) conclude that, 'although the vast majority of second-generation Turks and Moroccans living in the Netherlands still refer to themselves as Muslim, they identify less strongly with their ethnic [Moroccan or Turkish] and religious [Islamic] group and engage less in . . . religious practices [participating in Ramadan and turning to prayer].' Remaining with the Netherlands, Daniel Pipes (2010) reports research showing that an increasing number of younger Muslims say that they no longer believe in God. More widely, results from a European social survey, announced in 2010, show that, whereas 60.5 percent of Muslims go to mosque regularly on arrival from overseas, after a year in Europe the figure drops to 48.8 percent, with the remainder attending rarely or never (Pipes 2010; *Aftenposten*, 29 May 2010).

Findings from the Burnley Project (2005–7) support the revisionist account. The research included a survey of some 1,000 mid-teen students, attending five schools. (For further information and background material, see Holden (2009) and Purdam et al. (2007).) Findings from the mono-Muslim (and largely British-Pakistani) school indicate that students are not especially religious.

- In response to the question 'How often do you follow religious rules in your own daily activities?', 73 percent of students replied with 'sometimes', 21 percent with 'always', 6 percent with 'never'. In broader context, it is noteworthy that Voas and Crockett's (2005: 24) report of the (largely Muslim) minority groups of Great Britain runs, 'Although half of these young adults say that their religious beliefs make a great difference, a third say that they make only a little difference or none at all.'
- In response to the question 'Do you pray regularly?', around half of the mono-Muslim school said 'most days'. Of the remainder, 21 percent reported 'weekly', another 21 percent 'rarely', and 4 percent 'never'. Given the centrality of prayer to Islamic practice – whether at home, in the mosque or elsewhere – secular orientation is quite apparent.

- In response to a question concerning knowledge of leaders of the Islamic faith, a third of respondents did not know the name of their imam. With imams traditionally held to play a critical role in the transmission of faith, secularity is in evidence. At various points in his book (2009), Holden draws attention to failures of communication between imams and younger people and reports that imams are concerned about mosque attendance, especially among the younger generation.
- In response to the question 'If one or both your parents are religious, do you think that you are more or less religious than your parents?', 56 percent reported that they were 'less religious', with just 10 percent responding 'more religious'. In line with this finding, Voas refers to the inheritance factor (discussed above) to make the point that 'downward trends in belief and attendance [among Muslims] are similar to the rest of the [British] population' (in Pigott 2006: 7; see also Crockett and Voas 2006: 567; Berry 1997).

The revisionist account is also supported by looking at the ways values operate – in Pakistan itself, then in Britain, values which encourage at least a measure of secularization. Most of the British Pakistanis of Northern England hail from the Mirpur district of Azad Jammu and Kashmir (AJK) – not far from the capital, Islamabad – and from the Punjab (mainly to the north of the province) (Sial 2008). These are lands of (relatively) liberal Islam, lands where moderate Barelvi Islam joins hands with humanistic Sufism (exemplified by the great saint Bulleh Shah), lands where 'moderate religious trends' are well in evidence (ibid.: 22; and see Pew Research Center 2010: 3; Heelas 2013c).

The great majority of those who decide to leave these homelands to move to Britain are moderate Islamic or Sufic humanists; conservative Islamists are less inclined to travel to Western countries (Voas and Fleischmann 2012: 528). Once settled in Northern England, or elsewhere, Muslims strive to develop what they value of their ancestral homelands. As Roger Ballard (2006: 180) puts it, 'Slowly but surely, the whole panoply of popular practice in rural Punjab [and AJK] is steadily being recreated in Britain' (on Sufism in Britain, see Geaves 2013).

How does this transmission of Islamic/Sufic humanism so typical of British Pakistanis contribute to secularizing tendencies in the process? Returning to the mono-Muslim school of the Burnley Project:

- In response to the question 'Do you think that Christianity and Islam teach the same way to be a good person?', over 80 percent responded with 'yes' or 'in some ways yes', with just 4 percent saying 'very definitely not'.
- In response to the question 'Would you like to see the different faiths working together to produce a society in which people get on better?', approaching 80 percent answered in the affirmative.
- And in connection with an array of options under the question 'How important do you think are the following values?', the overall picture is of a rather extraordinary degree of tolerance and respect. Figures range from the 96 percent who judge 'Being friendly with people who are from other religious or ethnic groups' as 'important' or 'fairly important' to the 76 percent who make similar positive judgements in connection with the option 'Respecting others regardless of their gender'.

In the spirit of liberal humanism, respondents are clearly open to, and happy to engage with, cultures beyond their communal dwelling place. And the greater the extent that inclusive attitudes prevail, the greater the likelihood that the sacred canopy of the enclave will be questioned – perhaps undermined (Voas and Fleischmann 2012: 530–1, 535–6, 539). By promoting multicultural education, for example, the mono-Muslim school contributes to teaching pupils to respect, indeed value, religions other than Islam, and this can readily serve to weaken faith in Islam as *the* true way. The liberal humanism of the pupils of the mono-Muslim school – most especially the values revolving around the cornerstone of religio-liberal humanism, *ethical equality* – points to the view, formulated here as a blog message, that 'The most important thing is not how many times you go the mosque or how many times you pray. The most important thing is that you be a human being' (see essays in Cesari and McLoughlin (2005) on liberal 'humanization').

Turning to the other great cornerstone of religio-liberal humanism – the freedom of the autonomous person – arguably the most significant of all Burnley Project findings concerns responses to the questionnaire option 'Finding your own way in life rather than depending on others'. Seventy percent of respondents of the mono-Muslim school saw this as 'important' and another 25 percent 'fairly important'. Whether it is because of education, parental or grandparental influence (most especially the entrepreneurial ethos they have carried with them from Pakistan) or because of Western youth culture, in their discussion of Islam in Europe, Voas and Fleischmann (2012: 538) write: 'Instead of being constantly reminded that the future is in God's hands, people are reminded of their *own* ability to choose.' (For more on parental influence, see Voas and Doebler (2011: esp. 39, 57); and see essays in Cesari and McLoughlin (2005) on 'individualization'.)

'It is difficult to sustain tradition when individuals have a sense of autonomy', write Voas and Doebler (2011: 42). And it is even more difficult to sustain 'unsullied' tradition when younger British Pakistanis enter the pluralistic, questioning world of further or higher education, with an eye on careers which could well mean yet closer contact with the non-Muslim world.

From present trends into the future

According to the standard account, the growth in the number of Muslims means that the number of those with *faith* in Islam will continue to grow at the *same* rate. Although Voas and Fleischmann (2012: 539, emphasis added) argue that 'it seems likely that the secular, nominal, lapsed, or inactive will *ultimately* outnumber the committed', they maintain that 'Muslims in the West will *remain* highly religious into the medium term.' I think they are too cautious. There are already distinct signs of Islam adjusting to the secular of the West; of degrees of movement towards the secular condition; of some of the faithful diluting or dropping their faith – perhaps of people not acquiring faith as they grow up.

Accordingly, the expansion of the *Muslim* population does not automatically translate into the *same* expansion of faith in Islam. Based on current trends, the prediction is that an increasing number of people will think of themselves as 'Muslim' (in accord with what the 2011 census calls 'ethnic group'), with a *smaller* increase in the number of people who are committed to traditional Islam (in accord with what the census calls 'religion') – see Voas and Fleischmann (2012: 535) on ways in which identification with being Muslim alone can be divorced from Muslim identification with Islam.

So what of that great favourite of the standard account: radical Islam? Returning to the mono-Muslim school of the Burnley Project, only 15 percent of respondents thought that it is it 'unimportant' to 'show loyalty to the UK', much the same percentage found in the mono-white school, where students often have strongly patriotic parents, sometimes of far-right persuasion. Secondly, Field's (2013b: 22) research found that 58 percent of respondents affirmed that they 'very strongly belong to Britain', with another 29 percent affirming that they 'fairly strongly belong' – in total, 87 percent. The Burnley Project survey found *no* radicals among the Muslim school students. The argument is that the radicalization of 'reactive Islam' (Voas and Fleischmann 2012) can occur later in life, when Muslims, brought up as liberal Islamic humanists within their relatively sheltered enclaves, leave school to have greater contact with the outside world – to encounter racism; to feel that their humanistic faith has been *betrayed*. Not far from the mono-Muslim school, the teenager population of the mono-white school, in a desperately poor area, contains what can only be described as an appalling number of racists (75 percent thought 'that there are different races'; 41 percent that 'one race is better than another'). So long as there is white extremism among the impoverished, who use Islam/Muslims as a media-fuelled scapegoat to handle their sense of exclusion, radicalization will not disappear. However, unless Sunni–Shia tensions spill over from elsewhere in the world to generate intra-Muslim radicalization, the revisionist account predicts that the radical wing of Islam does not have a promising future.

Overall, the Islam of British Pakistanis does not serve as a bulwark against secularization, let alone a bulwark that is expanding in ever more powerful form.

SEMINAR QUESTIONS

1   Is Islam set to become the 'dominant' religion of the UK?
2   Does the 'betrayal' account of radicalization explain 7/7?
3   Blair, Blunkett, Cameron, Merkel and Sarkozy have rejected multiculturalism on the grounds that it encourages unwholesome divisiveness. Do you agree?

SACRALIZATION: THE RISE OF 'NEW AGE' SPIRITUALITIES OF LIFE

The other great objection to the idea that the secularization of Christianity leads to a secular age is that spiritualities of life, found *beyond* Christian (or Islamic) tradition, are on the rise. Could it be the case that sacralization – movement out of the imperfect of the secular towards or into the non-theistic sacrality – supports the fashionable notion of a post-secular age? Are we witnessing 'a fundamental revolution in Western civilization, one than can be compared in significance to the Renaissance, the Reformation, or the Enlightenment' (Campbell 2007: 41)?

Core themes

Writing in 1911, Simmel referred to 'the spiritual reality, that, in philosophical terms, one could call the self-consciousness of the metaphysical reality of our existence' ([1911] 1997: 18). Humans are spiritual beings by virtue of their very existence. Spirituality is inherent life-itself, sustaining and vitalizing what it is to be alive. And, as Simmel's reference to self-consciousness serves to indicate, spiritualities of life prioritize experience. Spirituality is 'not a set of claims but a certain state of being' ([1909] 1997: 6). Spirituality is about *self*-awareness, *being* aware, awareness as *being*. Essentially, as William James ([1902] 1974: 328) put it, the sacred heart of spirituality lies with first-hand encounters.

So why don't we all experience ourselves as spiritual beings? The claim is that we are 'sacred by nature, contaminated by culture'. We all have to live within the secular world – minimally, to stay alive. Secular institutions teach us how to do this. But, it is held, the secular is imperfect. Accordingly, and inevitably, socialization transfers the imperfections of the secular into the person. The person is contaminated by, say, the ways in which culture fuels conspicuous or self-indulgent consumption. Socialization means that we all lose contact with the core of our being. Socialization divides the person. On the one hand there is the perfection of the sacred self, on the other the imperfection, the unhealthy condition, of the socialized self – the 'ego' or 'lower self'. Hence spiritual teachers: all those who help liberate people from their attachments to the imperfect.

The teaching is that once people are liberated they quite naturally experience their inner being, their 'source' or 'vital force'. As spiritual teachers continually emphasize, though, inner-directed aspirations are elusive. The ego or lower self is powerful: it loves its secular attachments, for instance seeking money to be superior. Liberation from the ego is not permanent: the ego reasserts its hold. Liberation is a lifelong struggle. The utopia of an enduring 'new age' of the sacred, without the ego, does not materialize.

Those with faith in the sacred of the inner life have little truck with religion. First-hand experience matters, not tradition. Beliefs, canons, doctrines, creeds, transmitted from the past to the present, are taken to be highly suspect. Beliefs might have been distorted by translation, altered by translators, or composed and imposed by politically motivated authorities. Belief in the personal God of Christianity can readily be judged to be the personification of the ideology of the all-powerful male. In any case, beliefs fail to capture experience and traditions are judged on the basis of the test of experience. If a belief rings true, fine; if not, it is rejected as secular. In the main, beliefs of tradition are cast to the winds. The 'sense' is that religious tradition does far more to hide, or distort, the sacred than to reveal its true glory.

With 'life' taking over from tradition, spiritualities of life are beyond belief. Spiritualities of life are not experienced as depending on anything which lies beyond the flow of the inner life. The transcendent God-on-High, themes such as God's grace, gift, salvation, even the immanence of humankind created in the image of God-on-High, are rejected, 're-experienced' or simply ignored. Spiritualities *of* life can therefore be distinguished from spiritualities *for* life: those theistic spiritualities that belong to the transcendent Godhead rather than those emanating from 'life' in the here and now.

Spiritualities of life as neither religious nor secular

Voas (2009: 162) and Voas and Crockett (2005: 25) locate 'New Age' spiritualities within the fuzzy fidelity zone. So does Ingrid Storm (2009: 707), calling the 22 percent of the fuzzies that include 'New Age' the 'passively religious'. It is rather more accurate to think of 'New Age' spiritualities of life as an autonomous third option. Rather than being submerged within the fuzzy fidelity zone, this kind of spirituality (sacred at heart) occupies the third corner of a triangle, standing apart from the other two corners, namely those occupied by the Christian or Islamic (etc.) religious traditions and the secular condition (Heelas 2012a; and see Houtman and Aupers (2007: 311) on 'post-Christian spirituality as a third way beyond faith and reason'). Justice is done to the fact that spiritualities of life are distinctive. They have their own ontology of the sacred, their own teachings and practices. They stand on their own feet. Justice is also done to the fact that New Age spiritualities are becoming more popular, a fact that is obscured when participants are located among the fuzzies. Furthermore, justice is done to the consideration that, whereas fuzzies are 'religious' to some extent or another, many of those attracted by spiritualities of life are not of a religious persuasion, and never have been. Because spiritualities of life are distinctive means that to place them under the rubric of 'religion', as some do, serves only to mislead.

The most popular practices, such as acupuncture or homeopathy, are devoted to health care: preventative, remedial, curative, the enhancement of the health of the healthy. A rough guide to the numerical significance of CAM – complementary and alternative medicine – is provided by the European Information Centre for Complementary and Alternative Medicine (2008: 6):

> Utilization levels of CAM in the [EU member states] varied from 20 to 70% of the population in 1998. Analysing surveys over the past ten years the general conclusion can be made that 20% of EU-citizens have a clear preference for CAM healthcare, another 20% are regular users and another 20% are occasional users of CAM. This means more than 100 million citizens in the EU make use of CAM.

Three of the most significant findings of the Kendal Project – a locality study of the town of Kendal (and environs) located on the border of the Lake District of the North-West of England – are that 82.4 percent of those involved with CAM-orientated holistic mind–body–spirit practices maintain that there is 'some sort of spirit or life force that pervades all that lives'; that 73 percent express belief in 'subtle energy (or energy channels) in the body'; and that just 2 percent say they do not believe in spirituality (Heelas and Woodhead 2005: 25; www.lancaster.ac.uk/fss/projects/iepp/kendal/; and Aupers (2005) on very similar findings from the Netherlands). Whether it be called 'spirit,' 'sacred power,' 'life force,' 'energy,' chi, the *qi* of acupuncture, the 'vital spiritual force' of homeopathy, or the 'innate intelligence' of chiropractic, the basic message is more or less identical. (See Heelas (2013a), where particular attention is paid to the spiritual humanism of the healing power of CAM; McNeil (2000) is an excellent guide to varieties of CAM; and Eisenberg et al. (1998) charts the growth of CAM in the USA during the 1990s.)

CAM has become firmly ensconced within the mainstream. Around half the GP partnerships in England refer patients to CAM (Dobson 2003). 'Nursing spirituality' and 'hospice spirituality' are abroad, especially the latter (Heelas 2006). More generally, health and wellbeing activities and products are widely disseminated in subjective wellbeing culture: health and fitness clubs, spas, the mind–body–spirituality literature of bookshops, etc. (Heelas and Woodhead 2005: 83–94). Spiritualities of life are also present within the educational sector, where 'Ofsted spirituality' is inner-life-orientated; and there is now a very large literature on 'workplace spirituality', where the focus lies with the humanization of work (Heelas 2008: 62–73).

Table 14.1 presents outcomes of the RAMP UK survey of 1997 and the Soul of Britain survey of 2000. Around half of the respondents selected options that are neither secular nor obviously theistic: 51 percent in the case of RAMP ('God within' plus 'impersonal spirit or life force') and 44 percent in the case of the Soul of Britain ('some sort of spirit or life force' plus 'something there'). The RAMP finding, that 37 percent of Britons concur with the statement 'I believe that God is something within each person, rather than something out

Health and well-being practices with (non-religious) spiritual connections are finding their way into the mainstream in schools, where 'meditation' and 'mindfulness' sessions are increasingly part of the school day. (© Alok Sharma MP)

Table 14.1: **Comparing Soul and RAMP (%)**			
The Soul of Britain (2000)		**RAMP UK (1997)**	
There is a personal God	26	I believe in a God with whom I can have a personal relationship	23.4
There is some sort of spirit or life force	21	I believe in an impersonal spirit or life force	14.3
There is something there	23	N/A	
N/A		I believe that God is something within each person, rather than something out there	37.2
I don't really know what to think	12	I really don't know what to believe	16
I don't really think there is any sort of God, spirit or life force	15	I don't believe in any kind of God, spirit or life force	9.1
None of these	3	N/A	

there', is especially striking. Whatever else it might indicate, many of those who select this option identify spirituality with the inner-life (see Heelas and Houtman (2009) for further discussion). Respondents who selected one of the 'impersonal spirit or life force', 'some sort of spirit or life force' or 'something there' options are also likely to locate spirituality within (Houtman and Mascini 2002: 462–3). Spiritualities of life, it seems, are popular – as they are in much of Europe, where the average figure of those who 'believe there is some sort of spirit or life force', in the twenty-seven EU countries of 2010, is 28.2 percent (Eurobarometer 2010: 9).

Table 14.2: **Countries where percentages for 'God within' are higher than percentages for 'personal God'**

	Personal God	God within	% difference
Sweden	18.0	36.0	18.0
Denmark	20.1	35.2	15.1
UK	23.4	37.2	13.8
Portugal	25.9	39.1	13.2
Belgium	21.5	30.8	9.3
Netherlands	23.4	26.4	3.0
		Average difference	**12.0**

Source: Based on Heelas (2008: 73–4); and see table 14.3 below.

A primary aim of the Kendal Project (October 2000–June 2002) was to explore the popularity of New Age spiritualities of life. We tested a version of the spiritual revolution claim, namely that the decline of Christianity is of sufficient magnitude, and the growth of spiritualities of life of a sufficient scale, for Christianity to have been eclipsed by the latter. We tested the claim by ascertaining the numbers involved in the two *associational* heartlands of the town: the congregational domain of churches and chapels and the holistic milieu of mind–body–spirit healing practices of a group or person-to-person nature.

It transpired that 7.9 percent of the population were active in the congregational domain of Kendal on a typical Sunday, with 1.6 percent of the population of the town and its environs active in the holistic milieu during a typical week (Heelas and Woodhead 2005: 45; and see Heelas (2007: 67), where the 1.6 percent figure is adjusted to a more realistic 2.2 percent). Clearly, 'a spiritual revolution has not taken place' (Heelas and Woodhead 2005: 45). We also made a cautious prediction. Assuming that the congregational domain continues to decline, and assuming that the holistic milieu continues to grow, we predicted that, 'in 40 or so years' time . . . between 3 and 4% of the population will be active in each during a typical week' (ibid.: 149). The prediction was made late in 2003. It now looks as though it was along the right lines. By 2005, church attendance had declined to 6.3 percent; and Brierley (Field 2013a: 2) has recently suggested that attendance could fall by another half (or more) by 2030. Elsewhere in Europe, it is highly likely that Sweden is on the brink of a spiritual revolution of associational activities. In Dalarna – a major region of central Sweden – weekly church attendance lies at 3.4 percent, weekly participation in holistic practices at 2.7 percent (Frisk, Höllinger and Åkerbäck 2014).

BOX 14.3 SPIRITUAL REVOLUTIONS OF 'BELIEF'?

Spiritual revolutions of 'belief' appear to have occurred in a number of countries. As seen opposite, the number of those who select the 'God within' questionnaire option is higher than those who opt for 'personal God'. Or consider Russia. Just 2 percent attend religious services 'almost every week', and just 4.3 percent of the Orthodox 'know what they believe and pray often' (Levada Center 2011: 1). Yet around 25 percent are 'spiritual, not religious', and 33.8 percent hold beliefs in 'spirit/life force' (Lunkin 2012: 2; Smith 2009: 282). On the basis of a 2006 survey, Demyan Belyaev (2011: 353) reports 'that heterodox religiousness appears to have become the dominant form of religiousness in contemporary Russia and involves a larger proportion of the population than traditional Christian religiousness.'

Spiritualities of life and the secular age claim

Spiritualities of life are certainly more popular than, say, in 1960. However, it would be rash in the extreme to assume that the increased popularity of 'New Age' literature, 'beliefs' or CAM is directly linked with an increase in the extent of self-sacralization. It is highly likely, for example, that 'New Age' literature is often read for secular ends, like amusement. The popularity of resources is one thing; the popularity of *faith in the sacred* of spiritualities of life is another.

Do so-called beliefs of the 'god within, not without' variety count against the secular age thesis? Casting our minds back to table 14.1, some of the responses to the RAMP and Soul questionnaires probably owe more to the options provided than to what respondents, themselves, have in mind. RAMP provides the response option 'I believe that God is something within each of us, rather than something out there'. Instead of providing this option, the Soul of Britain includes 'There is something there'. Percentages vary accordingly. RAMP finds 37.2 percent believing in the God within; the Soul survey finds 23 percent believing in 'There is something there'. Needless to say, by not providing the 'something there' option, RAMP does not pick up data on the option ; and, by not providing the 'God within' option, the Soul survey is silent on this issue. It is perfectly clear that questionnaire options influence responses and so survey results of this variety have to be treated with extreme caution. They cannot be taken literally, at face value. They cannot be used to infer (for example) that 37 percent of adult Britons think they are gods to count against the secular age claim. Nor can they be used to support grandiose claims to do with a spiritual revolution of belief (Heelas and Woodhead 2005: 73–4).

Turning to the numerical significance of holistic practices, although a spiritual revolution of associational engagements with sources of the sacred might be under way, relative to the scale of Christianity in the past the growth of holistic, inner-life practices is far, far too small to compensate for the massive decline of church attendance. Furthermore, among holistic milieu participants are those who are not involved with the sacred to any significant extent. CAM, including yoga, might be numerically large. The number of those having full-bodied, experiential contact with the sacred power or vitality that numerous practitioners 'know' to be at the heart of their practices is smaller. Not infrequently, participants adopt a 'what works, works' attitude. Their interest lies with outcomes of CAM, like feeling better, not with the possibility that the *sacred* is the source of wellbeing. (See Voas and Bruce (2007) and Heelas (2007; 2012a) for findings and discussion.)

As things stand, research findings do not permit anything like a determinate assessment of the proportion of Britons who draw on the sacred of spiritualities of life to help source their lives. We might have a fair idea of the percentage of people who participate in holistic CAM, yoga and similar associational practices. We have nothing like a fair idea of the number of those who encounter sacred sources of significance by themselves – perhaps walking in nature; perhaps acquiring the skills of tai chi from books, videos or friends to practise alone, at home; perhaps attending a yoga class for a few weeks, never to return, while continuing practice. Neither do we have anything like a fair idea of the number of people who come to 'realize' the sacred of the inner-life by immersing themselves in books, films, music, poetry or deep conversations with friends.

However, it is doubtful that the number of those placing a fair degree of faith in the life within does much to support the idea of a post-secular age; and surely does not support Campbell's 'fundamental revolution in Western civilization' thesis.

SEMINAR QUESTIONS

1 How do spiritualities of life differ from monotheistic religion?
2 Why is it so tricky to determine the number of people who seek the spirituality of life?
3 Is a 'spiritual revolution' taking place?

THE SIGNIFICANCE OF TRANSGRESSION

I've been peppering the foregoing with notions such as 'secular' and 'sacred'. Clarification is called for.

Firstly, the notion of the secular. Those with faith in religion and/or spirituality join critical sociologists-cum-philosophers, epitomized by the immensely influential Frankfurt School, to maintain that the secular *is* the realm of the imperfect. It is a realm where things never quite work or operate very badly indeed. The secular might aspire to the perfect. It never obtains it. Things always go wrong – the 'perfect wedding', with flies alighting on the cake.

Secondly, the notion of the sacred. Many faithful (Christian, Islamic, spiritual) join hands with those studying religion to assert that the sacred exists beyond the imperfections of the secular. The Godhead, believed to lie at the heart of religious/spiritual tradition, or the life source experienced at the heart of spiritualities of life are the sacred of utopia – the absolutely perfect. Whether the Godhead or the life source, *distinctive* promises of salvation or self-actualization are taken to provide a *real* difference: distinctive precisely because promises come from beyond secular imperfection, beyond what the secular can do (Durkheim [1912] 1971: 420 *passim*).

And, thirdly, the notion of transgression. As the term is used here, transgression involves movement from the imperfect of the secular towards, perhaps 'into', the sacred-as-perfect. However, it is *not* the case that everyone moving beyond the secular encounters the perfect. Whether Islamic *jinns*, Christian angels, those contacting their ancestors in Spiritualist Churches, or ghosts, the less-than-perfect is widely abroad. Or consider all those Britons who transgress in that they apprehend 'something more': beyond the secular, but not in any obvious sense the sacred-as-perfect. The 'beyond' clearly includes an array of the less-than-perfect, the array differing from the imperfections of the secular in that it 'evades science or distinct thought in general' (Durkheim [1912] 1971: 24).

Transgressing the secular: the fuzzy transgressors

So to the 'fuzzy transgressors', as I'll call them. Unlike atheists or the indifferent, to varying degrees, and in various ways, transgressors do not accept that the secular frame provides the sum of life; that they have to remain locked into it; that there is not 'more' (to use a term favoured by William James ([1902] 1974: 484)). The notion of *fuzzy* makes the point that transgressors express their views, apprehensions, outlooks in ways that are indistinct, unclear, incoherent, perhaps confused. Their very fuzziness shows that they have not adopted the *lingua franca* of spiritualities of life (or any other language of the beyond, including those of theistic traditions or non-theistic higher powers) to express their apprehensions or experiences in an articulate, determinate, spelled-out manner. It should be emphasized, though, that lack of clarity need not entail lack of certainty about the existence of states of affairs beyond the secular. It is perfectly possible to be fuzzy with conviction.

Whereas Voas's fuzzies belong to a staging post *en route* from Christianity to the secular of indifference or atheism, fuzzy transgressors belong to a zone which lies between the secular frame and the full-bodied spiritualities of life. The zone is populated largely by those who have been brought up without Christianity – people who have realized that the secular is not *it*. So why don't fuzzy transgressors become more fully engaged with the transgressive? The argument is that the secular holds them back. People are too absorbed and taken in by everyday concerns to pay more attention. Some are held back by the secular canon of exercising critical reason on the basis of empirical evidence.

Are fuzzy transgressors numerically significant in Britain? As we have seen, percentages of the 'God within, not without' or 'some sort of spirit or life force' variety tend to vary in tune with how questionnaires are formulated. Respondents are flexible enough to fall in line with options provided by questionnaires. However, although questionnaire responses might well express relatively unclear experiences or apprehensions, it does *not* follow that questionnaire findings come out of the blue – that respondents answer at random. Findings *must* indicate something. By asking 'Which of these statements comes nearest to your own belief?', RAMP and Soul enable respondents to select the statement that is closest to what they have in mind. Respondents would not select the 'God within, not without' option, for example, unless it approximated to (in some cases, accurately reflected) their judgement. It is highly unlikely that there is anything casual about selecting the 'God within, not without' option rather than the 'personal God', for instance. Some respondents are distancing themselves from the theistic of the personal God. Some might be expressing their apprehension that the secular is not the be-all and end-all of life; that there is more to life than permitted by the secular condition; and that this lies with the heart of life. Others might select 'God within', rather than other options in order to emphasize the value of the human/humankind (see Barker (2004) and Heelas and Houtman (2009) for further discussion).

Table 14.1 (above) surely contains data that indicates the numerical significance of fuzzy transgression. David Hay provides more evidence. Summarizing a study of people who were not involved with formal religion but who nevertheless felt they were somehow spiritual or religious, Hay (2012: 364) writes that 'The phrase we most commonly heard was "I definitely believe in Something; there's Something there".' Summarizing another survey, focusing on out-of-the-ordinary experiences, he notes 'over 75% of the sample claimed that they were personally aware of a spiritual dimension to their experience' – a percentage that is considerably higher than that found by earlier surveys (ibid.: 362).

Then there is the fuzzy transgression of 'the magic of modernity'. Although only 10 percent or so of the population of Britain respond in the affirmative to the question 'Do you believe in magic?' (Field 2010e), the percentage is higher if CAM users (past and present) are included. Frequently, people turn to CAM to contact healing forces which lie beyond the imperfections of allopathic medicine. They might be unhappy with the idea that they are practising 'magic' (a term which smacks of the weird). Nevertheless, they are aware that out-of-the-ordinary power is at work – not least because many of those who turn to CAM are already spiritually inclined (Astin 1998; Heelas 2007). The 'transgressive groundswell' of countries such as Britain is also indicated by interest in 'New Age' literature, with books and articles about CAM being the main staple. It is reasonable to suppose that many readers are interested precisely because the literature chimes with their awareness of the inner beyond the secular.

Additional support from surveys

With the decline of Christianity, a growing number of people are without Christian ways of 'knowing' what lies beyond the secular. According to the fuzzy transgressive thesis, the increasing number of non-Christians should result in an increasing number of fuzzy transgressions. Comparing the scale of 'tradition' (most obviously Christianity) and 'post-Christian spirituality' (including notions of 'there is some sort of spirit or life force' variety) in a number of Western countries, research by Dick Houtman and Stef Aupers (2007) supports the contention. Data from Estonia also serve as a graphic illustration of the inverse relationship between the number of Christian believers and the number of fuzzy transgressors. According to Eurobarometer's (2010) summary of findings from EU countries, only the Czech Republic has a smaller percentage of people who 'believe there is a God' (table 14.3). And its weekly (or more) church attendance figure, at 2 percent, shares lowest place with its neighbour Finland (ibid.). Judged by these criteria, Estonia is one of the most secular of EU nations. Yet it has the

Table 14.3: EU countries where percentages of spirit/life force are higher (or the same as) belief in God

	'I believe there is some sort of spirit of life force'	'I believe there is a God'
Estonia	50	18
Latvia	48	38
Denmark	47	28
Sweden	45	18
Czech Republic	44	16
Bulgaria	43	36
Finland	42	33
Netherlands	39	28
Slovenia	36	32
France	27	27
Average	**42.1**	**27.4**

Source: Based on Eurobarometer (2010).

highest number of those who 'believe in some sort of spirit or life force' (and see Altnurme 2011). Elsewhere, surveys show that Christian countries such as Romania and Malta score highly on 'I believe there is a God', with few affirming 'I believe there is some sort of spirit or life force'. In Romania, the former lies at 92 percent; 'spirit or life force' at just 7 percent. Dwelling on the Estonian end of the list, table 14.3 indicates an inverse relationship between Christianity and spiritualities of life.

The fuzzy transgressive thesis has the advantage of circumventing two drawbacks of Voas's account of fuzzy fidelity and associated movement into the secular. One concerns the implausibility of allocating 'beliefs' more akin to 'New Age' than Christianity to the fuzzy fidelity zone. The drawback is circumvented when 'beliefs' of this variety are allocated to the zone of the transgressive. The second drawback concerns the number of the indifferent. Bearing in mind that Christianity has been in decline for a long time, bearing in mind that the fuzzy fidelity zone has presumably been around for an equally long time, bearing in mind the claim that Voas's fuzzies become secular, and bearing in mind the relatively sluggish growth of the number of atheists, one would expect to find a large number of the indifferent.

The expectation is not fulfilled. Generally speaking, questionnaires provide an option that would be selected by those who want to indicate their indifference. It is it is rarely taken. In the case of the Soul survey, for example, just 3 percent of respondents ticked the 'None of these' box (table 14.1, above). Furthermore, it is most unlikely that the 'can't be bothered with religion' mode of indifference is of any importance. Events such as 9/11 mean that it is virtually inconceivable that people are indifferent in the sense of 'being aware, could not care'. Many are horrified not just by radical religion, but also by conservative features of Christian traditions. Many have more positive concerns, perhaps drawing on Christianity to affirm their sense of identity with the nation (for further observations, see Bullivant 2012). Admittedly, engagement with the challenges and opportunities of the secular deflects attention from 'ultimate' matters of the 'what happens after death' variety. It is highly likely, though, that particular circumstances – the loss of a loved one, serious or terminal illness, feeling that life is empty – elicit reflection, even among the most dedicated of atheists.

Qualifying the secular age claim

Up to 50 percent of Britons are fuzzy transgressors. Drawing together evidence that has already been provided, and erring on the conservative side, the percentage arrived at is as follows:

- reasonably faithful or convinced Christians: say 20 percent;
- reasonably faithful or convinced Muslims: say up to 5 percent;
- reasonably faithful or convinced inner-seekers: say 10 percent;
- atheists and 'indifferents': say 20 percent.

The total (55 percent) means that 45 percent of Britons are neither obviously secular nor obviously engaged with the beyond – a percentage that is broadly in line with Houtman and Aupers's finding, based on data from fourteen countries, that 'more than 40% consider themselves neither convinced atheists, nor have confidence in the churches' (2007: 311).

Of those 45 percent of Britons, if fuzzy transgressors are predominant, the transgressive thesis is supported. If fuzzies of Voasian variety are predominant, the secular age claim is supported. With evidence presented elsewhere in this essay in mind, I'm convinced that fuzzy transgressors are the main camp. Unless transgressors are dismissed as idle pipe-dreamers, arguments for an enduring secular age do not hold water.

SEMINAR QUESTIONS

1 Characterize 'the secular' and/or 'the sacred'.
2 What is it to transgress the secular?
3 Based on your views, and/or those of friends/relatives, and/or from reading, what drives fuzzy transgression?

THE SELF-SUFFICIENCY AND INSUFFICIENCY THESES

Can the secular, alone, serve the worthwhile life, or is the 'beyond' significant to some extent or another? Are those looking beyond wasting their energy, or is this the only sensible course?

The self-sufficiency thesis

The self-sufficiency thesis maintains that, when the process of secularization has more or less come to a close, the secular time becomes an age. The secular condition is self-sufficient, self-sustaining, self-containing, self-limiting – able to roll on into the future within its own frame of endeavour. The secular is the endpoint for what lies ahead. Currently, those who place their *faith* in the secular probably do not amount to all that many. Richard Dawkins's *Unweaving the Rainbow* (2006), a paean for secular humanism, of science as poetry, as the ground of purpose in life, meaning and beauty, is rather exceptional. In time, though, the self-sufficiency thesis maintains that faith in the secular will grow. Ever more people will appreciate the extent to which *the* route to the flourishing life lies with the human of the secular order. It is not just that there is no need for religion/spirituality. More fundamentally, ever more will appreciate that they are far better off without the compensatory illusions, delusions, irrationality or non-rationality of religion/spirituality. Nothing should stand in the way of secular humanism – the cultivation of the valued life from within the secular itself.

The insufficiency thesis

This thesis maintains that the secular condition is not up to the task of serving as a self-contained home for most Britons. With the fading of Christianity in Northern Europe, ever more people realize that the secular, with all its imperfections and limitations, is not enough. Accordingly, people transgress. In Charles Taylor's (2007: 530) formulation, secular 'longing for . . . a more-than-immanent perspective remains a strong independent source of motivation in modernity'.

As well as by the evidence of fuzzy transgression that has already been provided, the insufficiency thesis is supported by the operation of dynamics, generated by the human condition of the secular, that can prompt movement beyond. Consider the 'mystery (or Hamlet) factor'. According to a survey of Britain by the think-tank Theos, 'Over three-quarters of all adults (77%) and three fifths (61%) of non-religious people believe that "there *are* things in life that we simply cannot explain through science or any other means"' (2013: 7, emphasis added). In the words of Hamlet, 'There are more things in heaven and earth, Horatio, / Than are dreamt of in your philosophy.' Some address the mysterious to make more sense of their lives. One mystery plays a major role in instilling movement beyond: the secular cannot address 'the truth of death' – that is, what the death of material existence entails for the future. Among secularists, there is fear of not knowing *what* will happen after death and fear of what *could* happen after death (annihilation, damnation). Resolutions are sought. Furthermore, transgression is impelled by the 'desire for eternity factor' (Taylor 2007: 530). In one of Taylor's illustrations, 'deep love' generates the desire by virtue of the fact that '*by its nature* [it] calls for eternity' (ibid.: 720; emphasis added; cf. Nietzsche's 'all pleasure desires eternity'). True love is too precious to die.

Transgressive momentum is also generated by the 'purpose-of-life dynamic'. If Tolstoy and Weber are anything to go by, the most important question of life is the ethical matter of ascertaining the 'right' way to live. For Tolstoy ([1882] 2008: 30), the greatest of all life questions is 'why do I live? or: what must I do?'. Citing Tolstoy with transparent approval, Weber places the question of purpose-in-life at the very core of his cultural sociology. 'The metaphysical needs of the human mind', Weber proclaims, 'is *driven* to reflect on ethical and

Is it short-sighted to think that the secular age is self-sufficient? Or will people continue to seek something more outside the secular world which increasingly dominates the twenty first-century – a calm oasis within the rush of modern life? (© chicagogeek/Flickr)

religious questions, driven not by material needs but by an *inner compulsion* to understand the world as a meaningful cosmos and *to take up a position toward it*' ([1922] 1992: 117, emphasis added). The inner compulsion derives from that most vital of matters: the desire to be at home in the world – more precisely, to sense being at home – for life – with truly worthwhile purpose.

Everybody looks to improve their sense of purpose-in-life, and for any number of reasons. Especially among those who believe that this is the only life that they will live, few would concur that their current sense of purpose-in-life is all that it could be. Life within the secular is too imperfect and impoverished not to stand in need of improvement. But, although everyone seeks progress within the secular, some – probably many – are also prompted to transgress. Sources of purpose might be felt to lack significance, any sense of ultimacy; to be too shallow, uncertain, unstable, incoherent; to be too cold; to be experienced with dismay. People might feel confused by having to face so many choices bearing on the right way to live. People might feel that options undermine one another. Certainly, from Weber's perspective, *nothing* secular can provide a sense of truly convincing purpose-in-life. *When* the value of life is *really* highlighted, *when* it hits home that secular senses of purpose simply don't suffice, *when* people ask the question, 'Is this it/Is this all there is?', *when* efforts to fulfil secular ideals or 'ideal-ologies' of progress are too assailed by the accidents, disasters, contingencies, disruptions, flaws of everyday life, *then* people might well be prompted to look beyond the confines of secularity.

Impelling this, an 'ideals dynamic' is at work. Ideals always make promises. Many an ideal implies or explicitly promises the perfect. Ideologies of human flourishing, including those embedded in consumptive and productive capitalism, call for completion, fulfilment of wholeness of being, ultimate 'satisfaction'. Accordingly, ideals readily direct people to reflect on the possibility of the utopia, the perfect itself – the step beyond the 'even better' of the secular. With ideals generating the desire to live *within a canopy of purpose*, Weber's 'inner compulsion' is at work. Given the centrality of the ideal of the purpose-suffused life, it is hardly surprising that people transgress to quest for the most perfect, worthwhile life as absolutely possible.

Of other transgressive dynamics, the 'vitality of life factor' is of particular note. For Simmel ([1909] 1997: 24), 'this emotional reality – which we can only call life – makes itself increasingly felt in its formless strength . . . claiming . . . inalienable rights as the true meaning or value of our existence.' 'Those unique impulses of life itself', he argues, yearn for 'fullness of being' (ibid.: 6, 17). In similar vein, for Edward Shils (1967: 80), vitality of life, and life in face of death, generates transgression: 'The idea of sacredness is generated by the primordial experience of being alive, of experiencing the elemental sensation of vitality and of fearing extinction.'

The insufficiency thesis and transgression to the very depths of humanism

With the demise of Christianity in mind, Durkheim wrote a marvellous passage, one that provides the basis of the argument sketched in a moment:

> there is one idea that it is necessary for us to get used to: it is that *humanity is deserted* on this earth, left to its capacities alone and able to rely upon itself to direct its fate. As one moves forward through history, this idea only gains ground; I doubt, therefore, that it will lose any in the future. At first glance, the idea can upset the man who is accustomed to depicting as extra-human the powers that he leans on. But if he comes to accept that *humanity by itself* can

provide him with the support that he needs, is there not in this perspective something highly reassuring, since the resources that he is calling for are found thus placed on his doorstep and, as it were, *right at hand*? (Quoted in Christiano 2007: 50, emphasis added)

It appears that Durkheim is advancing an exemplary formulation of the self-sufficiency argument. Christianity fades away; secular humanity takes over; being 'deserted', humanity *has* to make the very most of its *own* resources, and is set fair for the future. However, Durkheim elsewhere uses the term 'sacred' in connection with humanity, the human, the person (see his essay in Lukes 1969). Although he did not enter into the matter, he clearly thought that secular humanity somehow generates transgression – towards the absolutely human. How might this occur?

Of the numerous ethics informing various forms of humanity (including those of totalitarian racist regimes), Durkheim dwelt with the ideals of a humanist ethic. Described by Durkheim as the dominant force of his time, and even more dominant today (Heelas 1996), this is the ethic of secular humanism. The two most influential sentences of our time run: 'All human beings are born free and equal in dignity and rights. They are endowed with reason and conscience and should act towards one another in a spirit of brotherhood' (the foundational Article 1 of the UN's Universal Declaration of Human Rights, 1948). Clearly, the declaration is grounded in ideals: the importance of doing everything possible to value life on a universal compass, treating life with dignity, aspiring to freedom and equality, seeking the spirit of 'brotherhood'. And what counts as wellbeing, the life of the humanist, the flourishing of humanity, is couched accordingly.

In itself, the 'UN ethic' is too legalistic, formal, imposing, to contribute a great deal to *feeling* more alive as a humanist. It does not have much soul. The life of the ethic lies deeper. Charles Taylor writes of the widespread sense that life can be 'fuller, richer, deeper, more worthwhile, more admirable, more what it should be' (Taylor 2007: 5). This sense lies at the core of what Taylor (1991: 26) calls 'the massive subjective turn of modern culture'. Here, within psychological life, lies the 'natural goodness' of 'the best in all of us', the best that is to be drawn upon, brought out, expressed, cultivated for a fuller or richer life as a humanist. What matters is developing virtues, values, sentiments, experiences, developing trust, love, sense of fairness, in relationship with others and the environment. What matters is healing – that is, humanizing – ill-being or strife. What matters is the cultivation of love – a major theme of Martha Nussbaum's *Political Emotions*, where she writes that 'Love is what gives respect for humanity its life, making it more than a shell' (2013: 12). I have just watched, and found profoundly moving, the opening ceremony of the 2014 winter Olympics: a wonderful illustration of the orchestration of art, music, ballet, Russian romanticism, the Olympian, the speech – expanding humanistic sensibilities.

A great many (myself included) more or less automatically assume that, to some extent or another, in some way or another, 'the best' lies within humans in general – without for a moment thinking that there is anything transgressive about this. After all, the assumption is a defining mark of secular liberalism. Transgression occurs when the ideal of becoming *truly* human, in all regards, prompts movement from being content with bringing out the *best* of life within the secular to bringing out the *perfect* of human nature. Transgression occurs when people seek to ground the 'spirit of brotherhood' (as the UN puts it) in experience of ultimate spirit of life. Transgression takes place when those who are suffering, or who are well enough by secular standards, turn to spiritual CAM to 'complete' their health, to become 'entire', that is 'wholly human' (Heelas 2013a). Transgression occurs when people fulfil their humanism by moving out of themselves to experience 'oneness with all creation' – humanity as a whole, the whole of the natural. Here lies 'true' spiritual humanism.

To flesh things out, consider a life history of fuzzy transgression in Britain, one with a pronounced flavour of humanistic spirituality.

- At least on occasion, around 50 percent of younger Britons cast their feelings beyond the secular (Theos 2013). On account of a range of factors – including the cultural unpopularity of Christianity, with its perceived emphasis on regulating life from 'above' and the significance of the 'massive subjective turn' – transgression is orientated predominantly to the 'inner'. And, in accord with cultural values, transgression is humanistic: emphasizing the humankindness of relationships, for example.
- While people are consumed by secular concerns, most obviously raising families and advancing careers, their sense of 'something there – within' is unlikely to be a priority. Transgressive inclinations are mild, in a resting room.
- Some of those with transgressive inclinations, however, *taste* the deeper, more expansive, richer or fuller life of humanity by feeling the 'beyond within' of their human relationships, contacts with nature, encounters with the movement of music or other art forms, perhaps involvement with those wellbeing activities, like dedicated running, that can take people out of themselves to experience the flow of life.
- When the going gets rough – when the sense of humanness is denuded by depression, by 'half a life' at work or in a marriage, or by loss of self-esteem on retirement – fuzzy transgressors can go deeper on a more sustained, serious basis. The secular has really let them down. The aim is to address a sense of dehumanization, of feeling less than human. The aim is to experience the absolute of humanism. The quest within is pressing. Spiritual practices count: practices for health for life, vitality for activity, sentiments of equality or compassion for relationships, liberation for becoming, tranquillity or harmony for facing up to mortality (see Heelas (2013a, 2012b, 2013b) for further discussion).

SEMINAR QUESTIONS

1 How would you explain transgression in terms of the sociological study of the limitations, inadequacies, failures of the secular condition?
2 'Human existence bereft of transcendence is an impoverished and finally untenable condition' (Berger 1999: 13). Do you agree?

CONCLUSION

Is it possible that a secular age will come to reign supreme? With so much favouring the insufficiency thesis, with so many not being prepared to exclude the horizons, expectations, experiences, senses, of 'more', the answer has to be 'no'. Secularity is not exactly all-conquering. Atheism has not come to rule the roost. Secularization has not resulted in 'the long-awaited triumph of rational thought over religious orthodoxy that many expected' (Bagg and Voas 2009: 167). Neither does it appear that the indifferent are set to dominate.

The think-tank Theos (2013) reports that 'only 13% of [British] adults . . . agree with the statement "humans are purely material beings with no spiritual element"'. Taken at face value, 87 percent transgress the secular self. The transgressive cannot be ignored. And, as the following observation – composed by one of the most thoughtful sociologists – serves to indicate, neither can the existential: 'The ground of religion [and spirituality] is existential: the awareness of men [and women] of their finiteness and the inexorable limits to their powers and the consequent effort of find a coherent answer to reconcile them to that human condition' (Bell 1977: 449).

In many a country, it is high time that the designator 'sociology of religion' be relegated to history. It is high time to reactivate the perspective of the great masters, Durkheim, Simmel, Weber, Freud and James – currently, Taylor. The secular condition, the fuzzies and the fuzzy transgressors, the engagement of the theistic, those engagements with spiritualities of life: what matters is *the comparative study of sources of significance for life*. What matters is exploring the value of sources; their credibility, authority; the purposes they advance for the worthwhile life; their failures (shallowness, anomie, alienation, despair, sometimes suicidal tendencies); the expectations, hopes, fears, existential concerns that arise; the extent to which sources enter social, cultural, ethical life. What more significant inquiry could there be?

SEMINAR QUESTIONS

1 Is the 'sociology of religion' approach outdated?

2 Can a secular age ever reign supreme?

FURTHER READING

▶ Aldridge, A. (2013) *Religion in the Contemporary World: A Sociological Introduction* (3rd edn, Polity). An illuminating discussion of the sociology of religion today.

▶ Bruce, S. (2013) 'Post-secularity and religion in Britain: an empirical assessment', *Journal of Contemporary Religion*, 28(3). A concise refutation of the 'post-secularity' contention, with no punches pulled. Adopts a rather cavalier approach to deny that spiritualities of life are expanding.

▶ Clarke, P. (ed.) (2009) *The Oxford Handbook of the Sociology of Religion* (Oxford University Press). A volume of high-quality essays that address the major issues in the sociological study of religion.

▶ Field, C. (2011) 'Young British Muslims since 9/11: a composite attitudinal profile', *Religion, State & Society*, 39(2–3). A goldmine of information that tends to support the 'standard account'.

▶ Kashyap, K., and V. A. Lewis (2012) 'British Muslim youth and religious fundamentalism: a quantitative investigation', *Ethnic and Racial Studies*, 36(12). Based on new data from the ground-breaking 'Faith Matters: British Muslims', the article provides the best analysis of Islamic youth (aged between seventeen and twenty-nine) that has appeared to date. Compare J. Scourfield et al. (2013) *Muslim Childhood: Religious Nurture in a European Context* (Oxford University Press).

15

THE SOCIOLOGY OF THE MASS MEDIA

circuits of communication and structures of power

GREG PHILO, DAVID MILLER AND
CATHERINE HAPPER

CONTENTS

INTRODUCTION

ONE OF THE FIRST places that people go to find out what is happening in the world is the media. Yet most people do not devote all that much time to thinking about the way in which that content is shaped and the mechanics which lie behind it. In fact, the communications process is complex, with a diverse range of elements and agencies facilitating the flow of information. These include the interest groups that input to the production of media, the content of media products such as television news and social media, and the way in which audiences respond to media messages and any consequent outcomes. The advent of digital media complicates the situation in that it constructs audiences simultaneously as media consumers *and* content producers, allowing for a more interactive level of response while also supporting a parallel flow of information that interacts with mainstream media. A further dimension is the actions of policy-makers, who can both feed information into the range of media and, at the same time, respond to what they assume are the beliefs and attitudes of audiences. The key point is that all of these elements interact and are dynamic. While in past research each element (e.g., content or effects of media) has often been examined separately, we will explain here why it is important to analyse the interrelations of each of these different elements of the communications process simultaneously. To illustrate this we will focus on the relationship between media content and what audiences actually believe and understand. We will then go on to show the results of recent research in this area and discuss how our work relates to other approaches in mass communications studies, such as the theory of the 'active' audience. Finally we will look at the social consequences of audience beliefs and understandings and how these relate to decision-making in society.

CIRCUITS OF COMMUNICATION

Let's outline the four key elements of the communication process.

1 ***Social and political institutions and their influence on the supply of information*** These institutions include a vast range of organizations – government, business, interest or pressure groups, trade unions, universities and research institutes, scientists, think-tanks, lobbyists and PR consultancies. In this, 'lobbying' can mean the supply of information by interest groups and their attempts to influence state policy. It can also refer to the 'lobby system' by which the UK government supplies information to journalists in parliamentary groups who meet regularly to receive briefings on policy.

2 ***The media and their content*** The press, radio and television and online news, blogs and social networks, current affairs and documentary programmes, science programming, talk shows, popular and professional scientific magazines and journals, popular books on science, and women's and men's magazines; fictional forms include novels, feature films, television and radio plays, drama serials and soap operas.

3 ***The public*** Stratified in terms of class, gender, race/ethnicity, nationality, sexual identity and age as well as by professional and political commitments and social experience.

4 ***Decision-makers*** In local, national and supranational government as well as in business organizations, interest groups, universities, think-tanks and lobbyists and PR consultancies. In UK terms, government is at the local council level, the national level (the Scottish Parliament and Welsh Assembly), the state level (the UK Parliament), and the supranational and global levels (the European Parliament and European Commission, the World Trade Organization, the World Bank or the UN).

These different elements constitute a circuit and lead in some senses into one another, so 'decision-makers' (number 4) are also key figures in social and political institutions which supply information to the media (as in number 1). In formulating policy statements for public consumption, politicians and other decision-makers will consider in advance how what they release will be received and interpreted by the media and the likely public response. As we have suggested, these elements must be analysed simultaneously to show the interactions between them.

It is also important to note that the elements can interact independently and that circuits of communication are not simply linear. Many models or theories of mass media assume a linear model in which social institutions supply information, which is published in the mass media, and to which audiences respond in particular ways. Public responses then feed through to decision-making in society. Arguably this kind of linear model is embedded in both liberal and neo-Marxian accounts. For liberal or pluralist accounts, the competition of interests in society is reflected in a relatively heterogeneous media landscape from which citizens decide on their political preferences, leading to democratic decision-making. Some neo-Marxian approaches see ruling-class ideas as dominating mass media, with the result that these 'dominant' ideas are reproduced among the public. This is assumed to lead directly or indirectly to the reproduction of capitalism. Both models find it difficult to conceive that public opinion may not be a critical element in decision-making in society. Yet the interactive model we advocate hypothesizes that any element in the circuit can interact with any other directly.

For example, the model suggests that the media may have direct effects on decision-making in society and that social interests may be able to influence decision-making directly via their communicative activities. In both cases this is a kind of 'short-circuit' which leaves out the public. The research priority for us is to examine the linkages between differing nodes of the circuit empirically. In practice the relationship between elements of the circuit varies with the subject, the relative balance of forces and specific historical contexts. To illustrate this we will consider some recent developments in our society.

The neoliberal era and the structural transformation of the circuit of communication

The relationship between the elements of the circuit of communication has changed structurally in the last three decades. To understand this we need to examine changes in all elements of the circuit. The most significant changes over the last three decades in the West, and indeed most of the rest of the world, have been connected with the phenomenon known as neoliberalism. In the period before the Second World War, the effects of the Great Depression of the 1930s had led many to oppose the development of an unfettered capitalism. The Depression had followed the stock market crash of 1929, and free market capitalism was seen as inherently unstable and corrupt. After the war, new 'social democratic' societies were planned, especially in Europe, in which the state would be responsible for planning employment and welfare systems. In the UK, the NHS was established and large sections of industry were taken into public ownership. These policies required progressive taxation and were seen as moving society towards a greater equality. In the 1970s a strong reaction to these policies developed, initially in the USA and the UK, especially to the taxation of the rich and to controls on the 'free market'. This was the rise of the New Right or the neoliberals.

The neoliberal project was to roll back the priorities of the social democratic state, with its commitments to welfare and full employment and 'high' taxation to fund these. The state would shrink and its role would instead be to remove the 'restrictions' on the free market, to deregulate (as with the banks) and to produce a 'flexible' labour market (which involved removing trade union powers). This would increase the mobility of capital and allow larger units to form, making money wherever possible, which would include speculating on property or food prices or packaging up useless debts and selling them on the world markets as 'financial instruments'. The whole process would of course 'reward the wealth-makers', which in practice meant that those who owned and controlled capital could use their position in the market to multiply their wealth. This last priority was certainly achieved. A recent report from Oxfam notes that: 'Over the last thirty years inequality has grown dramatically in many countries. In the US the share of national income going to the top 1% has doubled since 1980 from 10 to 20% . . . In the UK inequality is rapidly returning to levels not seen since the time of Charles Dickens' (Oxfam Media Briefing, 18 January 2013). The neoliberal revolution over the last thirty years has transformed social institutions and their relationships both to one another and to the media of mass communication. We will now look in turn at corporations, the state, civil society and the quality of democracy.

An increase in corporate power is a widely recognized feature of the current period. One obvious way in which corporations came to have more power was the transfer of key sections of the economy from the public to the private sector via privatization. Following this there were many further waves of neoliberal reform, including the introduction of market or market-like mechanisms into what remained of the public sector – the health service, education, social services and central government. These were compounded by the rise of the Private Finance Initiative (PFI) and Public–Private Partnership (PPP) schemes: all of these gave corporations more direct control over investment decisions, as well as more involvement in what had been democratically controlled institutions and directly in the provision of government services – meaning not simply in delivery but in policy and decision-making. In other words, during the period from 1979 to 2012, the space for direct exercise of corporate power and the space for the direct influence of corporations over government policy increased very markedly.

Although neoliberal ideology suggests that the state should be reduced to a simple 'night-watchman' role, in practice under neoliberalism the state is strengthened in a number of ways, as is captured very well in the title of Andrew Gamble's (1983) early book on Thatcherism: *The Free Economy and the Strong State*. It is also true that many neoliberals recognized that the free market has all sorts of consequences which are not conducive to social order and which can, if left unchecked, develop into threats to corporate power. One response is neoconservatism – an attempt to bring moral order back in at both the international and the interpersonal level. As a result we see the undermining of civil liberties, increases in state surveillance of the poor and of dissent, and a remoralizing of politics (Miller 2006).

Neoliberalism has also meant attacks on the organized working class (Philo and Miller 2001). In the UK, which pioneered neoliberal reforms, the attack on the trade unions occurred very early in the process, most notably in relation to the defeat of the miners' strike of 1984–5 and in the breaking of the print unions by Rupert Murdoch (Miller and Dinan 2008).

While state power increased in a number of respects in the UK, there was also a hollowing out of the state in terms of its representative functions. Power was concentrated increasingly in central government, and in particular with the prime minister, while Parliament was sidelined, thus diluting the democratic potential of the political system. There were some countervailing tendencies, particularly under New Labour, which introduced devolution in Scotland, Wales and Northern Ireland and a watered-down Freedom of Information Act (Schlesinger, Miller and Dinan 2001). None of these measures significantly reversed the general decline of demo-cratic accountability, at least in the central government at Westminster.

The diminution of democratic controls on capital and on unaccountable state power led to corruption in the political system and throughout the private and public sectors. It was certainly the case that market reforms of the mass media undermined its ability to perform the watchdog function and, as the Leveson inquiry showed, corrupt practices also flourished in sections of the media. However, it is plain that many other institutions were vulnerable to corruption, including the police, the criminal justice system, the City of London, banks, large corporations, the House of Lords and the Commons, and government itself. These had not enjoyed great public trust before the recent neoliberalism, but our own research shows that the elements of the political and economic system have increasingly fallen into disrepute (Miller 2004a). Much of this was traceable to or involved in the liberalization of markets or the expanded role of the private-interest or private-sector actors in public governance, this being a signature element of neoliberalism, or 'market-driven politics', as Colin Leys put it (Leys 2003).

The trend towards global 'governance' has been boosted by the progressive dilution of democratic controls on capital as corporations have increasingly sought to buy their way into the political process. There has been a torrent of books with very similar titles on this 'cor-porate takeover' and on the 'sleaze' and 'scandals' which go with it, at the national level in

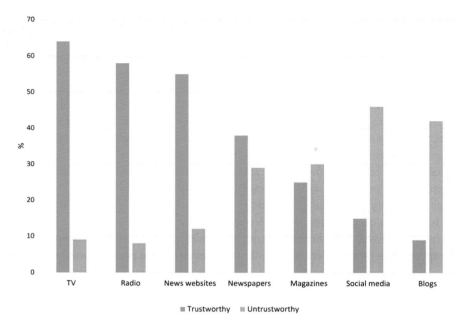

Figure 15.1 Public (dis)trust of various media forms

Note: Totals do not add up to 100 percent because of other answers ('Neither trustworthy or untrustworthy' and 'Don't know')

Source: Compiled with data from the *PBS UK Trust Report* (2011).

the USA, Canada and the UK, as well as at the EU and global levels (Balanya et al. 2000; Beder 2006a, 2006b; Carroll 2010, Derber 1998; Monbiot 2000; Sklair 2000). The increasing blurring of previously separate roles and the decreasing clarity on accountability have been described by the anthropologist Janine Wedel (2011) as presaging the emergence of a 'shadow elite' whose activities are 'beyond the traditional mechanisms of accountability' because they have multiple, overlapping and not fully disclosed roles. They work as government advisers, think-tankers and consultants to businesses. They appear in the media. As Wedel notes, 'it's very difficult for the public to know who exactly they represent' (cited in Schwartz 2010). These developments suggest a weakening of democratic controls.

We can now turn to how these transformations relate to varying elements of the circuit of communication.

Short circuits: private communication channels

The circuit of communication suggests that social institutions can communicate directly with decision-makers in pursuit of their interests. In terms of the model of the circuit of communication, lobbying is about the direct relations between social interests and decision-makers in local, national and supranational governmental agencies. This direct relationship means that, in general, lobbying bypasses media and public debate. Under neoliberalism the scope for direct attempts at influencing policy has greatly expanded, developing most significantly in the USA and the UK (Miller 2008). The British lobbying industry itself is estimated to have doubled in size since the early 1990s (Dinan and Miller 2012).

Table 15.1: Public attitudes to news media in the UK (%)

	Strongly agree	Tend to agree	Neither agree nor disagree	Tend to disagree	Strongly disagree	Don't know
I believe that UK news and media organizations always report stories accurately	2	22	28	31	11	5
I believe that UK news and media organizations are fully independent from the influence of powerful people and organizations	2	13	19	38	21	7

Source: Compiled with data from the *PBS UK Trust Report* (2011).

BOX 15.1 LOBBYING IN THE UK AND THE USA

In the USA the role of lobbyists in the political system has been a recurrent political issue. So much so that, on his inauguration as president, Barack Obama enacted in January 2009 a sweeping executive order on ethics and the so-called revolving door for members of his administration (Blumenthal 2011). The 'revolving door' analogy is used to describe the situation where personnel in various industries move between roles in private corporations and decisive roles in legislative or regulatory bodies which are meant independently to regulate the very same industries and corporations from which they have come (and often return back to). The issue of the revolving door has also been seen as a contributory factor in the financial crisis, as financial regulators often either came from or entered the industry punctuated by their spell as supposed watchdogs. In some instances members of financial regulatory bodies even remained as directors of banks or other financial corporations while they worked with the regulator (Miller and Dinan 2009).

Since 'cash for questions' in the 1980s and 'cash for access' in the 1990s, there has been a recurrent drip-drip of lobbying scandals in the UK (Dinan and Miller 2012; Leigh and Vulliamy 1997; Miller 2008) and, indeed, at the EU level (Dinan and Miller 2006; Miller and Harkins 2010). Lobbying itself is an almost completely covert business (Silverstein 1998). It trades influence for cash and generally does not attempt to influence public opinion. In its day-to-day activities it is beyond the reach of public debate. It runs the risk of undermining democracy in the sense that private interests try to influence legislation and decision-making directly, rather than democratically or by means of media or public debate.

The role of the media here is negligible, with one exception. That is when lobbying misdeeds are exposed in the media. The audience of the mass media is interested in the behaviours of the powerful, and sometimes newspapers, TV and, more recently, social media will respond to this. The banking crisis and arguments over tax evasion have focused public attention on corporate and private wealth. This can have the effect of undermining elements of corporate self-interest. However, the bulk of the mainstream media tend to side with or at

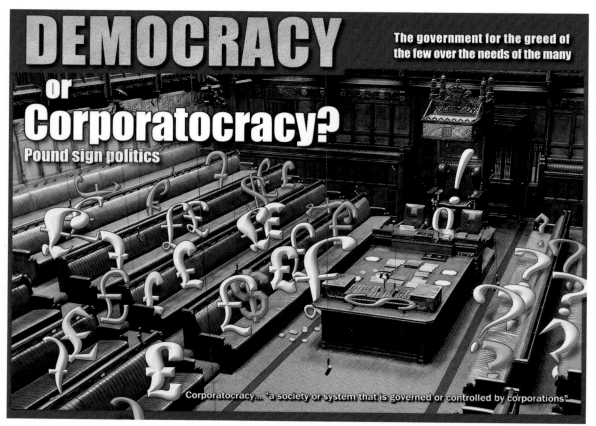

Undercover lobbying by corporations with vested interests in pushing forward particular government policies represents a democratic short circuit which needs to be publicized by various media forms in order to be tackled. (© Byzantine_K/Flickr)

least not criticize powerful corporate interests, and, whatever the faults of individuals, free market capitalism is presented as essentially the only game in town. Indeed, much of the media is owned by such interests. In practice, decision-making by corporations and governments in both the USA and the UK may go on in secret, away from the eyes of the media and with little popular involvement. While social media can raise awareness of individual cases of unethical behaviours, as witnessed by the damage done to the Starbucks brand by the recent #boycottstarbucks campaign on Twitter, 'consumers' are almost completely ignorant of all such debates. This does not suggest that they are 'dupes' of the system – it is just that they don't know.

There is also a sense in which much of what appears in even mainstream newspapers is not really for the bulk of the audience who consume the news. Private debates among the powerful can surface in the media as part of a struggle within the state apparatus or corporations, such as when opposing elite factions brief against each other in the media (Miller 1993). Indeed it is plausible to argue that many of the outbreaks of apparent dissent express, at least in part, faction fighting between closely allied fractions of the elite, as in the opposition to the

Iraq war from significant sections of the military and intelligence agencies. Much of the PR workload of large publicly listed corporations is devoted to 'investor relations', a specialism that targets the business pages and communicates directly with fund managers and others in the world of financial capital (Miller and Dinan 2000). Their successes and failures are won and lost quite outside the headline news agenda of TV news (Davis 2000). In spite of the changes digital media have made to public participation in the flow of information, there are still few ways in which we can be part of the conversation (Curran, Fenton and Freedman 2012).

SEMINAR QUESTIONS

1 How does a circuit of communications approach to the media differ from other sociological approaches?
2 What might the advantages of this approach be?
3 How does the example of lobbying demonstrate that we need to be aware of historical changes in the circuit of communications?

INFORMATION SUPPLY INSTITUTIONS AND THE MEDIA INDUSTRY

The public relations industry

Without sources of information, there would be no news. Social institutions of all types increasingly understand the value of planning media strategies to manage their image in the media and with key publics (Miller 1998). Equally, the value of keeping an organization out of the news is recognized, particularly where there is significant political controversy.

Many different organizations now have press offices and engage in public relations activities. Government departments have large information divisions responsible for protecting their image and publishing large amounts of information every day. In the last twenty years the PR industry has become more and more significant in attempting to shape the news, and a host of books have chronicled the rise of the dishonesty and deception that goes with it (e.g., Beder, 1997; Hager and Burton 1999; Nelson 1989; Rowell 1996; Stauber and Rampton 1995, 2001). The growth of the public relations industry is closely linked to corporate globalization (Miller and Dinan 2003) and to forms of neoliberal governance, including deregulation and privatization (Miller and Dinan 2000). As a result public relations has itself become big business, with the emergence of a number of mega-corporations such as Omnicom, Interpublic and WPP, each owning many global public relations consultancies and networks (Miller and Dinan 2003). There has been very strong growth in professional PR (consultancy and in-house) in the past couple of decades. For instance, in 1963 there were 'perhaps' 3,000 PR people in Britain (Tunstall 1964). In 2005 a 'conservative estimate' suggested some 47,800 were employed in public relations in the UK (Chartered Institute of Public Relations 2005: 6). A US study has estimated that in 1980 there were 1.2 PR workers for every journalist. By 2010 the ratio was four to one (Hazlehurst 2013).

Recently, the focus of much lobbying and public relations activity has shifted from the centres of power in the nation-state to international bodies as corporations increasingly move capital globally to seek higher and quicker profits. But in the wake of the globalization of capital has come the globalization of protest. The protests in Seattle in 1999 against the WTO and in Prague in 2000 against the IMF signalled the public emergence in the West of a heterogeneous assemblage of different global interests united by their opposition to the free market and the dominance of predominantly US multinationals. Anti-capitalist protests have occurred across the world as the global reach of corporations has made clear the interconnectedness of local protests and then as this was reinforced by the global financial crisis. While digital media has aided public relations in some ways – speeding up the process by which damage control can be implemented – it also allows for the public, operating en masse, to build influential global campaigns such as the Occupy movement. One key aspect of the protests is an opposition to the marketing, PR and advertising strategies of multinationals. There has also been extensive criticism of government PR activities. The propaganda campaign to sell the invasions of Afghanistan and Iraq, including the false claims about the existence of stockpiles of weapons of mass destruction, are now well known to have involved significant misinformation and have convinced many that government communications were less than accurate (Miller 2004b).

The speed with which the propaganda on Iraq was discredited in 2002–3 showed an intensified new level of resistance to the misinformation and distortion that are central to the PR

BOX 15.2 WIKILEAKS

Perhaps the greatest potential challenge to the PR industry in the twenty-first century came in the form of WikiLeaks, the global online organization which has 'leaked' classified documents, from the Afghan warfront among others, that governments sought to keep confidential. The aim of the 'leaks' was to provide the public with not only secret information but information without spin. WikiLeaks disclosures of 2010 showed real potential for the breakdown of the governmental mechanisms of controlling the release and shape of information; however, it also exposed that transparency is far from achievable, even in the digital age. For example, when it released US State Department cables in November 2010, several companies that WikiLeaks used, including Amazon and PayPal, bowed to government pressure and blocked them, which made it much more difficult for the organization to sustain its online operations. Further, as the information to be released was so dense and complex, WikiLeaks was forced to turn to major media outlets to assist in the delivery of the information – with this move it handed the information over to traditional gatekeepers to shape and sell as was deemed 'newsworthy'.

and propaganda business. Key elements of the propaganda were debunked by the use of the internet by activists rather than mainstream journalists, an illustration of the potential for the internet to be used for countervailing power.

There are increasingly possibilities for pressure groups and the powerless to intervene in the process of PR. It is also possible to plan and execute promotional strategies on behalf of the powerless which don't compromise either radical politics or a respect for truth. The key question for the future is whether the systematic distortions of promotional culture can be curbed in the interests of democratic deliberation and decision-making.

The media industry

The media operate within a complex set of pressures of ownership, editorial control and economic interest. Journalists do have some measure of autonomy in their daily work routines, but this varies across media. These variations are in part a result of variations in news values, but they also reflect the promotional networks that form around varying journalistic beats. At the pinnacle of the news values of broadcasting, of the broadsheet press and of some elements of the tabloid press is hard news. This typically revolves around the news beats of central government, which are covered by political correspondents or lobby journalists. Down a notch in terms of news value are more peripheral government departments, such as defence, education, agriculture or health, which typically have their own corps of specialist journalists.

As a result of this form of organization, the bulk of political news originates with the central bureaucracies of Whitehall and the political party's news management apparatus, although specialist correspondents have more freedom to devote their output to the intricacies of policy debates or in the activities of 'resource poor' groups (e.g., charities or activist groups) than their non-specialist colleagues on the news desk. The backdrop to all of this, however, is a media industry which is increasingly accountable to commercial imperatives. In the press, investigative journalism has declined, to be replaced by lifestyle and consumer writing. In what is now a 24-hour TV news environment, the obsession with 'liveness' and what looks like immediate on-the-spot reporting has taken precedence over clear accounts of what is happening and why (Snow 2000). On social media, where things move even faster, stories come and go in minutes, and sensationalism is paramount.

A recent trend in media reporting is towards 'liveness' and immediate on-the-spot reporting of everything from natural disasters and terrorist attacks to public scandals and celebrity gossip. How might this affect the quality of journalism, and ultimately its purposes in society? (© U.S. Department of Agriculture/ Flickr)

The media remain central to the exercise of power in society. They not only guide us in what to think, they are very good at telling us what to think *about* – in other words, at setting agendas and focusing public interest on particular subjects (McCoombs 2014). But the media can also severely limit the information with which we understand events in the world. They can remove issues from public discussion. The analysis of media content – of what we are told and not told – remains a prime concern. The method which the Glasgow Media Group (2000) has developed to analyse the content of media texts is called thematic analysis. It is based on the assumption that in any contentious area there will be competing ways of explaining events and their history. Ideas are linked to interests, and these competing interests will seek to explain the world in ways which justify their own position. So ideology (meaning an interest-linked perspective) and the struggle for legitimacy go hand in hand. The media response to the financial crisis of 2008 and its aftermath illustrates this well, as discussed in box 15.3.

We can see how various constraints affected discussions in the media of how the banking crisis and the problems it generated should be resolved. There are four key factors which structured this coverage, and these also shape media coverage in different areas.

1   Privately owned newspapers have their own political and economic preferences.
2   This has to be qualified by the fact that these are commercial organizations and have, in some way, to respond to the beliefs and desires of their readers in order to sustain sales.
3   Democratic representation in relation to publicly accountable institutions such as the BBC, which has been described above.
4   The most powerful unelected groups, such as the bankers themselves and other members of the financial class, are likely to have immediate access to the BBC and other media outlets because they are treated as 'experts' and important decision-makers.

All this means that, when the crisis develops, the people who are most likely to be asked about solutions are very likely to be those who are most supportive of the system which created the problems in the first place. These people and other key figures such as senior politicians are often referred to as 'primary definers', as they can set agendas for media coverage.

The lack of alternative systems pushed by the media made it possible in practice for the terms of the public debate to be changed. The banking crisis had caused a contraction in the world economy; in the UK, tax receipts fell, while the government continued to spend, in part to subsidize the banks. Since no transformation of the economy or the banking system was deemed possible, the solution was simply to cut spending. This was justified by arguing that welfare spending was too high. A receptive popular media highlighted stories of 'scroungers' and 'shirkers', though overwhelmingly the bulk of welfare cuts were actually felt by the elderly and those in low-paid work. But, by this sleight of ideological hand, the banking crisis and the intrinsic problems of economic systems disappear from view.

BOX 15.3 THE BANKING CRISIS

The heart of the crisis was that international banks had lent huge sums of money to inflated property markets, mainly in the USA but also in the UK and other parts of Europe. These loans were often to people and institutions that would not be able to repay them. But the risks were ignored, many argue, because the financial sector was interested only in profits and the huge bonuses that were being made from the deals that were being pushed through. As Elliot and Atkinson (2008: 11) put it: 'In January [2008], panellists at the World Economic Forum in Davos were asked how the big banks of North America and Europe had failed to spot the potential losses from sub-prime lending. The one-word answer from a group that included the chairman of Lloyds, London . . . was "greed". In the UK, the political group which would historically have been most likely to criticize such behaviour would have been the Labour Party, which for most of the twentieth century was social democratic: it believed that free market profiteering should be curbed, that the people as a whole should own key sectors of industry and commerce, and that the rights of working people should be defended. However, after election defeats in 1983, 1987 and 1992 to the Conservatives – who promoted a free market philosophy – the Labour Party rethought its approach. As a result it abandoned its traditional criticism of the free market and adopted a very supportive policy towards the financial sector (Philo 1995). New Labour was elected to power in 1997 on the slogan 'Things can only get better', which was a reference to the perceived decline in public services and of corruption and sleaze in public life. New Labour would have a bigger safety net for the poor and spend more on health and the public sector. But nonetheless its new leader, Tony Blair, was seen as continuing Thatcher's key economic policies.

The deregulation of the banks continued under Blair and his chancellor (later prime minister), Gordon Brown. The reasons for this sympathetic relation with finance were not simply electoral. This sector of the economy is very powerful and can pressure governments with the argument that it is relatively mobile and can move if the conditions in a particular country are not favourable. The City of London is an extremely powerful institution – a private corporation in its own right and perhaps the most effective lobbyist in history. It's a city government that represents one interest alone, which is the financial interest. The City still acts as a state within a state. The PM has to meet the City if it asks for it in ten days; the queen has to meet within a week if it requests it. So it has this extraordinary power within the UK's institutional framework.

So how did these social, political and commercial relationships affect the media coverage of the banking crisis when it happened? The bulk of the press is privately owned and is traditionally conservative in its support, favouring free markets and deregulation. Put simply, the bankers, private enterprise and high profits were heroes, or at least were accepted as heroes, as long as the economy appeared to be booming, house prices went up, and the New Labour government could spend increased tax revenues on health and education.

The free market approach was championed by the Murdoch press (including *The Sun* and *The Times*) plus the *Daily Telegraph* and the *Daily Mail*. The *Daily Mirror* is traditionally more left wing but tends to follow the policies of the Labour Party. *The Guardian* and *The Independent* are sometimes to the left but have relatively small readerships. However, the key suppliers of public information and news for the bulk of the population are the television services, particularly the BBC. This is important since the BBC limits the range of the political arguments which it features on the basis of its own definition of democracy. This in essence consists of the population voting for elected representatives. The BBC then features these representatives on television and radio, and what they say constitutes very largely the limits of democratic debate. In other words, TV debate is limited mostly to the views of the three main parties. But, since all of these have become wedded to free market philosophy, the discussion of alternatives to this approach is very sparse.

BOX 15.4 RESPONSES TO THE CRISIS

When the financial crisis broke in 2008, the British popular press reflected the angry mood of its readers. The *Daily Mail*, with its middle-class readership whose pensions and savings were potentially threatened, thundered from its front page:

> GREED THAT FUELLED A CRASH (14 October 2008)

The Sun put it more succinctly:

> SCUMBAG MILLIONAIRES
> Shamed Bank Bosses 'Sorry' for Crisis (11 February 2009)

But, among the sound and fury, there are no demands here for alternative solutions, such as taking back the bonuses through a wealth tax or transforming the financial sector by taking the bulk of it into public ownership. These are 'outside' acceptable media debate, so we can complain, but in the end the existing system must remain. As *The Sun* explains in an editorial, 'Many will ask if it is right that tax payers are forced to subsidise irresponsible borrowers and greedy banks. But what was the alternative? Neither America nor Britain could stand by and watch their economies disintegrate' (20 September 2008). This thought is then taken further by David Cameron who, as prime minister, argued that we must stop attacking the bankers. In the *Daily Telegraph*, under the headline 'David Cameron: stop seeking vengeance on bankers', he was reported as saying: 'Voters must stop seeking to "take revenge" on banks and accept they are vital to economic recovery' (15 January 2011).

A month later *The Independent* and *The Guardian* (9 February 2011) reported that the Conservative Party had received more than half its income from the City and property developers. In the face of such structures of power, the role of the mainstream media is largely to act as a forum for grumbles and discontent but not to explore serious alternatives.

SEMINAR QUESTIONS

1 Discuss the proposition that the PR industry is a neutral tool which can be used by a wide range of interests in society.
2 Does the rise of social media make it easier for anti-establishment voices to get a hearing?
3 Explain how the circuit of communications operates to limit alternatives and potential solutions to dominant explanations of the economic crisis.
4 How can the content of news be affected by powerful social interests?

MEDIA CONTENT AND AUDIENCE BELIEF/ UNDERSTANDING

'Preferred' views and explanations

We can now show in detail how this absence of alternatives, together with the highlighting of 'preferred' views and explanations, can influence public understanding. In our recent research we have illustrated this by analysing the content of television and the press. The

essence of our method here was first to note each of the explanations and ways of understanding which were being put forward and the range of available evidence which could
underpin different positions. We identified these from existing public debate, from published materials such as books, and from any other relevant sources. We then analysed the
content of TV news programmes and showed how all of these different explanations were
featured (or not). In practice we found that some explanations were given prominence in
news headlines or interview questions while others were downgraded or excluded. If some
explanations were present on the news and others were absent, then it seemed likely to us
that this would affect what TV audiences understood and believed. Of course people might
have access to other sources of information – for example, if they had direct experience of
what was being reported or if they read 'alternative' accounts which gave information that
was not on the news. These methods form the basis for the substantial series of content
studies which the Glasgow Media Group (2000) has undertaken. However, to investigate
how the media impacts on what people actually believe and the source of those beliefs, it is
necessary to work directly with audiences.

Further, we believe it is important to study media content and processes of audience
reception simultaneously. The impact of media on public belief depends in part on the
manner in which messages are constructed and also on what audiences 'bring' to their
understanding of what they are being told. But how well informed they are and what they
can bring in terms of prior knowledge of a subject is not the same for everyone in the audience. This means that a media message can be received differently and its potential influence
will vary between audience groups. It is not just levels of knowledge that audience members
carry with them – they also bring cultural values, preferences and levels of interest. These
can all affect how the message is received. So the impact of media is best assessed by looking
at content and processes of reception together as parts of the circuit of communication. We
can illustrate this with examples from our study of media and the Israeli–Palestinian conflict,
discussed in box 15.5.

Explaining coverage

So why does the news not give proper explanations of the history and context of events? The
crucial reason is that to explain these, or to refer to them as underlying the violence, could be
very controversial. Israel is closely allied to the United States, and there are very strong pro-
Israel lobbies in the USA and to some extent in Britain. For a journalist to delve too deeply
into controversial areas is simply to invite trouble (what Herman and Chomsky (1988) call
'flak'). It is much safer to stick with 'action' footage and simply recount the day's events. Israel
has very powerful voices to speak for it, and it combines this with a well-organized public relations apparatus which supplies 'favourable' stories and statements to the media and criticizes
those of which it disapproves. *The Independent* newspaper reported in September 2001 that
the Israeli embassy 'has mounted a huge drive to influence the British media' and that 'a senior
Israeli official [has] publicly boasted that Israel has influenced the editorial policy of the BBC'
(21 September 2001). Israel prefers to stress the attacks and bombings made upon it and the
vicious anti-Semitism of some Islamic groups rather than to have the legality of its own actions
subject to public debate. The settlement policy is widely regarded as illegal in international law,
and this has certainly been the view of the British government. Human rights organizations
have also been very critical of the conduct of Israeli forces in the occupied territories. The

BOX 15.5 CASE STUDY: BAD NEWS FROM ISRAEL

In our research we have found that people who were well informed on or who had direct experience of a subject area were more likely to be critical of what they saw on the news than people who knew very little about it. In the area of foreign coverage, for example, where direct experience is comparatively rare, audiences are more likely to rely on TV news as a key source of information. Our research showed that many people had little understanding of the reasons for the Israel–Palestine conflict and its origins. It was apparent that this lack of understanding (and indeed misunderstanding) was compounded by the news reports they had watched. A key reason for this was that explanations were rarely given on the news and, when they were, journalists often spoke obliquely, almost in a form of short-hand. For the audience to understand the significance of what they were saying would require a level of understanding and background knowledge which was simply not present in most people. For example, in a news bulletin which featured the progress of peace talks, a journalist made a series of very brief comments on the issues which underpinned the conflict: 'The basic raw disagreements remain – *the future, for example, of this city Jerusalem, the future of Jewish settlements and the returning refugees.* For all that, together with the anger and bitterness felt out in the West Bank, then I think it's clear this crisis is not about to abate' (ITN, 18.30, 16 October 2001, emphasis added).

There are several elements in this statement that require some background knowledge to be understood. 'Refugees', for example, are cited as a key issue. The journalist does not say which refugees, but he means the Palestinians. In our research, we asked an audience sample of 743 young people where the Palestinian refugees had come from and how they had become refugees. The vast majority replied that they did not know. To understand the journalist's comments, the audience would need to have the information that the refugees were forcibly displaced from their homes and land when Israel was established in 1948 and later subject to military occupation at the hands of Israeli forces – which the Israeli historian Avi Shlaim documents in detail in *The Iron Wall* (2000). In a content study of eighty-nine news bulletins, however, we found that, of 3,536 lines of text in total, only seventeen explained the history of the conflict.

Further, in our audience groups we found that many people did not understand that the Palestinians were subject to a military occupation and did not know who was 'occupying' the occupied territories. On TV news, journalists sometimes used the word 'occupied' but did not explain that the Israelis were involved in a military occupation. For example, a BBC bulletin referred to 'the settlers who have made their homes in occupied territory' (BBC1, 18.00, 9 February 2001). The reference to settlers is interesting because it speaks of 'occupied territories' without making it clear that it is the Israelis who are the 'occupiers'.

There was extensive coverage of the violence, and there was sympathy expressed for those caught up in it, but very little analysis of the nature and causes. Again Palestinian perspectives were not there in any substance, and the practical effect was to remove the rationale for Palestinian action. Much of the news implicitly assumed the status quo – as if trouble and violence 'started' with the Palestinians launching an attack to which the Israelis 'responded'.

In our work with focus groups we found many examples of how much assumptions impacted upon public understanding. As one young woman put it:

Speaker: You always think of the Palestinians as being really aggressive because of the stories you hear on the news. I always put the blame on them in my own head.
Moderator: Is it presented as if the Palestinians somehow start it and then the Israelis follow on?
Speaker: Exactly, I always think the Israelis are fighting back against the bombings that have been done to them. (Quote from 2002 in Philo and Berry 2011: 297–8)

Israeli human rights group B'Tselem wrote in1998 that 85 percent of Palestinian prisoners interrogated by the security services were tortured (about a thousand people each year, as reported in *The Observer* 13 December 1998). The United Nations human rights commission has also been severely critical, but we hear little of such matters on TV news. Our research showed that the Israeli government is normally able to present a coherent public relations perspective and to dominate news agendas with its own way of seeing the conflict.

In terms of the communications process, this shows the clear links between information supply, production and news content. Speaking with us, one veteran BBC journalist commented on the absence of the Palestinian perspective. What was missing was the view that 'It is a war of national liberation – a periodic guerrilla war, sometimes using violent means, in which a population is trying to throw off an occupying force' (Philo and Berry 2011: 335). The ideological construction of the news has a crucial impact on audience understanding. In a separate study we have shown how the media can construct audience uncertainty, and we will now go on to look at that research in detail.

Audience understanding and new information

Following the election in 2010 when the Conservatives formed the coalition government with the Liberal Democrats, the prime minister pledged to form the 'greenest government ever'. But, by October 2011, on the question of the positioning of tackling climate change in relation to this top priority, the chancellor, George Osborne, in his Conservative Party Conference speech, boldly stated: 'We're not going to save the planet by putting our country out of business'. This political reprioritization mirrors the global and national media coverage, with 2010, according to Dailyclimate.org (3 January 2011) the year that 'climate change fell off the map'. The media will not consistently prioritize an issue without the sustained commitment of primary definers, the most powerful of whom are politicians – so, if the politicians are not speaking about it, the media are not reporting it.

But news reporting was problematic before 2010, often criticized for its lack of clarity on the basic scientific arguments. Much has been written about the way in which journalistic norms, primarily the aim of 'balanced' reporting, have shaped climate change as an issue of uncertainty (Boykoff and Boykoff 2004, 2007; Boykoff 2011) in that it has allowed a range of powerful lobby groups – often referred to as the climate sceptics – an equal voice to those of the scientists. Organized climate sceptics, such as the Global Warming Policy Foundation in the UK, contribute to a range of media outlets and are instrumental in shaping the agenda on reporting, particularly newspaper reporting. In *Merchants of Doubt* (2010), Oreskes and Conway document the way in which these groups of sceptics, with close connections to key political and industrial figures, have run deliberate and effective strategic campaigns to mislead the public over this issue. In line with this, it was revealed in 2012 that George Osborne had strong personal links with the president of lobbying group British Institute of Energy Economics (BIEE), which is sponsored by Shell and BP (Merrick and Chorley 2012), indicating the closeness of front-line politicians and the sceptical groups.

In 2011 we undertook research to explore the impact of media coverage of climate change on audience understanding and engagement with the issue. This study utilized new methods which involved the creation of an information environment in which audience groups were introduced to a range of possible arguments from different and competing perspectives. We produced television news reports and newspaper articles and online content set in the future, which showed the predicted consequences of climate change, including a flood in Bangladesh which led to mass global displacement of climate refugees and severe localized flooding, as if they had actually occurred. The aim was to identify the specific triggers which lead people to accept or reject different arguments.

Perhaps not surprisingly, what we found was that the current dip in media attention was having an impact – overwhelmingly, people felt it was a less pressing subject than it had been in the past, with the economic recovery being a greater priority for most. Reflecting the wide range and diversification of voices feeding audiences on this topic, the backdrop to this was a high level of confusion around the scientific arguments concerning climate change and the need for action. While scientists were the most trusted source – 'information straight from the horse's mouth' – the vast majority of participants felt that the science was confused and inconsistent. The belief that the evidence that was available was not solid fuelled the idea that climate change could be (and is) appropriated by different interest groups, such as politicians and business leaders, to their own ends.

This left audiences with no clear idea of who to trust on this subject, a situation exacerbated further by the strongly expressed and widely felt distrust of authority figures, which led to general feelings of powerlessness. The highest number of people named politicians as the source which they trusted least, and discussions revealed that a majority believed they could not be relied upon to act in the best interests of the public in relation to climate change (or indeed on any other issue). The overall picture of current audience reception was therefore one of confusion, cynicism and distrust about public communications, as well as a sense of lessening priority, all of which led to disengagement.

We then introduced the new information in the form of our constructed news reports and newspaper articles. Of the two climate-change-related scenarios, most said that the Bangladesh refugee story affected them most. The main reason for the greater concern and urgency was that the Bangladesh scenario tapped into existing worries about issues such as immigration and the scarcity of resources such as employment and housing. The media accounts alerted participants to the potential personal impact of the causes of climate change and greatly enhanced concern. Most crucially, audience members no longer saw climate change as a vague and theoretical issue but as one that might have real and serious consequences for themselves and their communities. Once they understood that the science is solidly based, and that the potential consequences are real and severe, they saw more clearly that action has to be taken.

When asked at the end of the session about the impact of the scenarios, we found evidence of genuine attitudinal change, most notably an increase in concern in relation to climate change issues (see figure 15.2). However, when we revisited half of our sample six months later, in spite of their immediate responses, the majority claimed that the experience of taking part in the group had not changed their attitudes on climate change in the longer term. This worked both ways. Even among those who had responded during the session with greater concern about the potential effects of climate change there was evidence of original cynical attitudes persisting. Most acknowledged their earlier concern had waned. Evidently the impact of the information and discussions had not always been sustained in the intervening six months. While the new information offered the potential for attitudinal – and behavioural – change, unfortunately the research coincided with a period of low media attention. The attention that was there focused on the political debate over the impact of investment in green energies on the UK economy, widely recognized by our sample as the

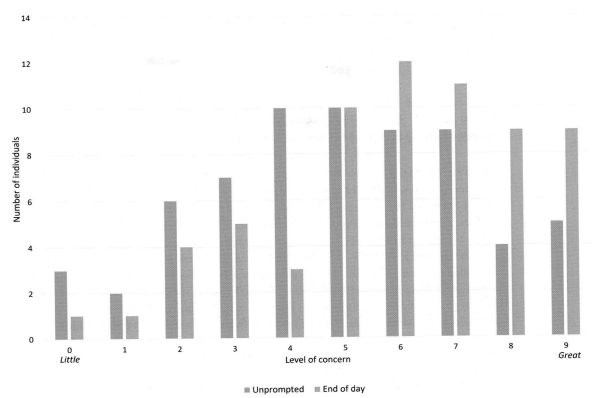

Figure 15.2 Level of individuals' concern on climate issues, before and after watching constructed news reports

Source: Compiled with data from Happer, Philo and Froggatt (2012).

current political priority – in other words, coverage which further highlights uncertainty in relation to taking action. The wider media environment to support such attitudinal change currently does not exist, and the audience engagement and interest we fostered was largely not sustained once people were exposed to the coverage which followed.

The continuing politicization of the subject in the UK media, and the prominent space given to the climate sceptics, has not only led to confusion and distrust but is a strong contributory factor in climate change dropping off the agenda, as the media take their lead from the political sphere. There is strong evidence that the current coverage has inhibited engagement on this issue. Ultimately it lies with the media to redress the balance and properly inform their audiences, but the key to this lies in the redefining of the issue as one of science rather than politics and rebuilding public trust on this basis.

SEMINAR QUESTIONS

1 What might be the benefits of studying media content and audience reception simultaneously?

2 How far would you agree that the media coverage of the Palestinian–Israeli conflict is an ideological construction?

3 Read Boykoff and Boykoff's 2004 article 'Balance as bias: global warming and the US prestige press'. What are the main reasons for the 'bias' in coverage?

4 Discuss the proposition that the coverage of climate change has effectively led to audience disengagement with the issue.

DYNAMIC AUDIENCE MODELS AND DECISION-MAKING OUTCOMES

'Active' audience models

Debates in mass communications theory can be seen to lie on a spectrum in relation to the degree of control that audiences are understood to have. At one end are theories of the 'active' audience. This tradition incorporates a convergence of a number of different schools of thought based on the fundamental premise that small groups or individuals 'actively' construct their own interpretations and the meaning of the world. Media texts are seen to be polysemic – to have many meanings. Media effects are therefore limited, because audiences interpret media messages in different ways reflecting their own background, specific contexts and positionings. This work dominated communications theory for a period, and the focus tended to be on audience pleasure, resistance, identity and fandom. These studies, largely ethnographic in nature, represent a moment in which 'audience activity' lost its grounding in the reality of what audiences actually do with texts. In its most extreme form, the suggestion is that a text will mean completely different things to different audiences. But our own work on responses to media output suggests that varied audience groups do actually have a very clear understanding of the intended message and can reproduce it very accurately. We tested this across a number of different areas of media output and formats – on coverage of Northern Ireland (Miller 1994a, 1994b, 1997), on images of mental illness (Philo 1996) and HIV/AIDS (Kitzinger 1990, 1993; Miller et al. 1998), on the reporting of the 1984–5 miners' strike (Philo 1990), on the Israel–Palestine conflict (Philo and Berry 2006, 2011) and, most recently, on disability (Briant, Philo and Watson 2011). In these studies we asked audience groups to produce their own news accounts from memory, and these consistently reflected the dominant message of typical news content.

Audience experience and the evaluation of media messages

Those who were reliant on information from the media tended to see fraudulent disability claims as a major issue, whereas disabled people themselves expressed significant anger at some of the press reporting and at the accusations linking them with scrounging and fraudulent claims. A key result of our research has been to show how people used their own direct experience or alternative sources of knowledge to evaluate media messages. A corollary of this was that, if there was no direct experience or other knowledge of an issue, then the power of the message would increase. We normally found that if people had direct experience of an issue, and that this conflicted with the media account, then they would reject the media message. However, in the disability study, we found that almost all of those to whom we spoke also had direct experience of disability either through a close family member or close friends, many of whom had tried to get benefits and had failed. One participant, for example, talked about how hard it had been for her mother to get any benefits, and another described the difficulties her partner had faced in trying to get access to the services he required. But this did

BOX 15.6 DISABILITY AND BENEFITS FRAUD

In the study of beliefs about disability and disabled people, we found that audience members' ideas on what constituted a typical newspaper story on disability coincided with the findings of our content analysis (i.e., benefit fraud, equality and services for disabled people). The audience groups were very clear on what the intended message was (i.e., in the first case, that people mainly claim disability benefits fraudulently). They did not interpret the intended meaning of the news differently, although there were differences between the different groups – not over the meaning of the message but over whether they believed it. When we asked the groups to consider what the percentage of people who were fraudulently claiming disability benefits might be, the responses varied from 'about 10 percent' right up to 70 percent. The actual figure is closer to 0.5 percent (Department for Work and Pensions, *Fraud and Error in the Benefit System, 2010/11 Estimates*). When asked to justify where they got their figures from, respondents talked about newspaper articles (for example, the 70 percent figure was said to come from an article in the *Daily Express*) but also referred to their own experiences, with almost all claiming that they knew people who were fraudulently claiming one form of disability benefit or another. Many felt that the system was too easily manipulated:

Speaker 1: It's really easy to fake symptoms. Or even bad backs.

Speaker 2: That's the biggest one isn't it, bad back.

Speaker 3: . . . people know, don't they, they know what to say and how to get round the system, so there's a big increase in people knowing how to defraud the system.

Further, there was a great deal of resentment directed at what were seen as the large numbers of people fraudulently claiming benefit:

Makes you angry for people who work full time and there are loads of people who are scamming it . . . I mean when you've been scrimping and scrapping and yer man's not too well, you know what I mean?

They get the best of everything . . . Because they're getting their rent paid . . . They've learned the system. You know there are people getting Chinese deliveries every night and you can't afford it.

not lead to a simple rejection of the media message – in fact, we found that individuals often held two potentially competing beliefs in their head simultaneously. Other research shows that direct experience does not necessarily override media coverage where great anger or fear has been generated. Our content analysis on disability showed a significant change in the way it had been reported in British newspapers since 2006, with a reduction in the proportion of articles that described disabled people in sympathetic and deserving terms, an increase in articles which focused on disability benefit and fraud, an increase in the number of articles documenting the claimed 'burden' that disabled people are alleged to place on the economy, and an increase in the use of pejorative language to describe disabled people (Briant, Philo and Watson 2011).

Our research did not show people effortlessly constructing the meaning of texts on the basis of pre-existing systems of thought, as suggested by some active audience theorists. A range of factors, including the level of direct experience, the level of fear generated by media campaigns, and the use of logic and reasoning all influenced how the message was received. We also showed that people from different perspectives concurred as to the meaning of the message and that its accuracy could be evaluated using agreed evidence. A key finding was that the media message becomes more powerful if there is no direct experience or other knowledge of an issue.

The reception model therefore should be dynamic. Media messages change and so does the flow of experience. The two are crucially related. When political ideologies are developed as political practice, they have consequences in public experience. This means that the systems of ideas which legitimize social and political power must be constantly reworked. For example, in the eighteen years after 1979, the poor really did get poorer and there were increases in interpersonal violence, unemployment and insecurity at work. These changes led in part to the election of Tony Blair and the New Labour government and forced the Conservatives to rethink how they could now justify their own position. The recession of 2008 made way for the newly elected coalition government to bring in a series of extreme and painful cuts to which very little alternative was presented, as discussed above. Each time there is such a radical change, political propaganda must be reformulated to explain, apologize for or legitimize these new relationships and events (Philo 1995). It is exactly because people are not sealed off in conceptual bubbles that there is a need to keep reworking social ideas in relation to the defence of interests. If belief systems were not constantly challenged by new experience and its contradictions, there would be no need for political debate or, indeed, for propaganda and public relations. In real societies, there are parties, class fractions and interest groups who contest how the world is to be explained and what is to be understood as necessary, possible and desirable within it. In our work we have analysed the role of the media in such struggles because of its potential power in reflecting and developing such key elements of public belief.

Digital media and audience 'activity'

By the late 1990s, 'active' audience theories had gone as far as they could go. One reason was the emphasis on ethnographies of different audience segments, which were inexhaustible and increasingly niche. This provided no theoretical grounding for the work. A further reason, however, was the advent of digital media, which allowed for a reframing of the notion of the audience as no longer simply 'active', but 'interactive'. The opportunities offered by digital media allow for a genuine two-way relationship: audiences can be understood simultaneously as media consumers and content producers – or 'produsers' (Bruns 2009) – while the text is constructed in the process of engagement. Wikipedia of course is perhaps the greatest example of this process. It is participatory and a source of collective knowledge and expertise, and each unique element is essential. Twitter meanwhile represents the full spectrum of conversations, from mass-personal to micro-personal, the integration of which has created one of the dominant sites of public communication. These and other forms of digital media simply have no equivalents in traditional media. At the same time, traditional media have not been abandoned in favour of new media. Old and new feed off each other in new and different ways in what is sometimes called 'convergence culture' (Jenkins 2006). In the case of Twitter, it can be said to support a parallel flow of information that interacts with mainstream media, both feeding off it and, in turn, feeding it. But what can be said about the activity of the audience in digital media? And is the role of creative and influential content producer the new norm for media consumption? There are also new issues of power and control that need to be addressed in the digital environment.

Firstly, we'll turn to the patterns of engagement and level of reach and/or influence that audiences actually have. There is greater potential for audiences to have a public voice in the digital arena and to give the concerns of the public a platform. However, that potential is not always realized. The majority of people are not active producers of digital content. Van Dijck (2009) argues that there are greatly varying levels of participation, from creators to 'lurkers'. Blogs, which really took off after 9/11 and the invasion of Iraq, have peaked, and statistics show that up to 80 percent are abandoned within one month (Caslon Analytics Blogging) and the others aren't regularly updated – the problem is lack of audience and, as a result, lack of influence. To most people, blogs mean the popular weblogs by high-profile individuals such as Robert Peston of the BBC or Stephen Fry. For the most part blogs operate on a very traditional media model of the few speaking to the many, and largely via their public personae, albeit in their own names. Social networking, the form of online activity that is currently most mainstream, engages audiences at a higher level. Twitter offers its millions of users the opportunity to take part in the public flow of communication but suffers from the same elitism as blog-posting – studies have shown that those with higher levels of education and income are more likely to be engaged (Kagan 2011). Similarly, studies have shown that Twitter is closely aligned with the mainstream media, with the latter shaping the agenda – and its roots in the political process – rather than the other way around.

The other major player, of course, is Facebook, which in less than ten years has become one of the most visited sites in the world. However, early techno-optimists such as Sherry Turkle (2011) have denounced the site as shallow and addictive, fostering a culture of meaningless identity play. For some it is seen simply as social life amplified online and made all the more stressful for keeping permanent records of essentially transient experiences and conversations. In terms of audience engagement, it represents the more mundane, even passive form of consumption. Its individualized stream of 'me' personalizes and depoliticizes public issues and is more likely to promote conservative ideology than to challenge it. While we should not eliminate the possibility of social media as a potential route to the mobilization of resistance in authoritarian regimes, as was arguably the case in the Arab Spring, the key offering of increased public influence offered by digital media is largely mythical thus far (Curran, Fenton and Freedman 2012).

Finally, there are some important points to be made about ownership and control of digital media. Media industries offer this potential for control within a very specific and very effective economic and business model (Bruns 2009). They not only actively encourage user-generated content but are very efficient at co-opting audience activities either for their own expansion or to feed content – or 'data' – to corporations to target consumers. Increasingly we are also seeing the promotion of 'audience as pusher', as Facebook focuses more on the connection with products such as Coca-Cola than on other potential 'friends'. In this case the audience does the advertisers' jobs for them, and such audience 'activity' is commercially rewarding, as Facebook demonstrated when it floated on the stock market in early 2012. Further media industries are increasingly effective at disciplining and shaping audience engagement. For example, Google search's reliance on algorithms reflects a move away from human beings choosing where they want to go to a computer deciding for them based on (albeit personalized) numbers (Rogers 2010). While studies correlating production, content and reception have not yet developed in relation to digital media, it is not yet looking like an arena that will necessarily encourage plurality of viewpoints or open up opportunities for anonymous members of the public as opposed to elite groups.

Much attention has been paid to the role that social media played in organizing and connecting the various protest movements that constituted the Arab Spring, the first of its kind in the twenty-first century. (© Rowan El Shimi/Flickr)

Decision-making and outcomes

The information that people are given and the judgements that they form are important in how society operates and can both limit and legitimize the actions of the powerful. However, our society is not perfectly responsive to the democratic will of the people. In fact, change comes about not simply as a reflexive response to changes in public belief but because of a further series of processes that are partially dependent on public belief, but not guaranteed by it. Outcomes in society depend on action (or inaction) by people or groups. There is a need to examine the relationship between beliefs about the world and the political conclusions drawn by the public, the relationship between political conclusions and taking political action, and that between public action or protest and political change or continuity.

There is a range of research on how public opinion is constructed, how people evaluate political debates, and how they become involved in activism or political struggles (Gamson 1992; Herbst 1998; Lewis 2001; Lichterman 1996). For us it is important that such questions are asked in relation to other elements of the circuit of communication and power. The agenda of media and communication studies is typically focused on the public and mainstream media elements of communication circuits, such as media production, content and audience reception. But it is also clear that there are potential aspects of circuits of communication that may involve private or only partly public communication. As we saw at the beginning of the chapter, it is quite possible for social institutions such as corporations or governments to pursue their interests in private communications and decision-making processes, entirely bypassing the public. In societies such as the UK, much decision-making takes place in virtual isolation from open public debate, both online and offline. So public interpretations of media messages, public belief and opinion and even political campaigning may be entirely irrelevant to the exercise of communicative power.

SEMINAR QUESTIONS

1 Can you think of a current example in which the media have successfully promoted a previously unpopular political decision?

2 How much of a platform do digital media offer the general public?

3 Can you think of an example in which social media was used effectively to curtail the activities of the powerful classes or one in which it failed to do so?

4 Discuss the view that private communications may be even more important in exercising power than public communications.

CONCLUSION

We have argued that it is important to conceive of communication as an integral part of the constitution and operation of modern societies and that we need to examine all aspects of the circuits of communication if we are properly to understand the role of the media and other private and semi-private networks of communication and power. It is not adequate either theoretically or methodologically to examine only part of the circuit. A research agenda based on the circuit of communication is more complex than that arising out of studies of production, content or audience by themselves. The added dimension of digital media, which open up opportunities for the public to take part in the process, further supports this approach. It also makes it harder to trace the connections between differing elements of communicative circuits. Nevertheless, such connections between the interests of powerful institutions, their communicative strategies, media coverage, public opinion, decision-making and outcomes do exist and can be demonstrated by an empirical approach to circuits of communication and power. We have shown in this chapter some of the connections between dominant interests, news coverage and public knowledge (or lack of it) as well as pointing to some of the ways in which decisions in society may be the outcome of undemocratic processes of private communication.

In essence we have described a class society in which the 'free market' operates to concentrate wealth while both excluding the bulk of the world's population and focusing the power to make decisions in increasingly unrepresentative elites. Such processes are not typically discussed in our media and, to the extent that the relationships that structure our world feature at all, are presented as necessary, unavoidable or even beneficial. So the manner in which media accounts function to justify and legitimize while excluding possible alternatives is crucial, and in our work we have sought to explain both class power and how ideology actually works as it is developed and reproduced.

Other theorists have also looked at how the media endorse and legitimize the values of neoliberalism. Curran, for example, argues that media endorse individualism – the 'values' of neoliberalism against collectivism (2011: 64). In some areas this is clearly true; Curran's example is the promotion of notions of self-help in reality TV rather than the analysis of the structures that limit individual development. But in practice very few media outlets or the politicians who supply them with quotes actually endorse outright individualism in the sense of the destruction of others for selfish interest. So there is a difference between the publicly expressed values of neoliberalism, which embody its legitimations, and its actual consequences in political and economic practice. No serious politician actually advocates Social Darwinism – that social groups should be left to compete with the 'survival of the fittest' – even if in practice their policies on climate change, for example, are moving the world in this direction. Arguments in the public sphere and the ideology of the right are most usually conducted in terms of the public good – thus the genesis of phrases such as 'We are all in this together'. In the USA, the anti-welfare debate is focused in part on how 'welfarism' and 'socialism' would sap the morale of the nation and damage the possibility of the individual living the American Dream. The accumulation of wealth by a few is justified as the mechanism of economic growth, and 'trickle-down economics' is the legitimation by which private accumulation is linked to public good. Much debate in the media is conducted within such a rationality, and the success or failure of policy is judged by notions of the overall good. Thus the pros and cons of the wars in Afghanistan and Iraq are discussed in the terms of the cost in human lives and money and whether they have met objectives such as improving human rights. The right-wing press will even feature criticism on these terms. Is the Afghan war a 'blood-soaked mess' and has the war actually spread the influence of al-Qaeda? ('Decade of Delusion', *Daily Mail*, 8 October 2011). But there are other rationalities which remain almost completely outside media discussion and have little to do with 'we', 'our' and the public good. Corporate and elite interests which harvest the trillions spent on war do not measure success and failure in these terms. For them the conflict has only to take place – though in the case of the Cold War the endless preparation for conflict was sufficient. From such a perspective, how would the spread of al-Qaeda be a problem, since it is now a key legitimizing component in a massive wealth-creation project which produces security and surveillance systems spread through the world and new military technology to drones and beyond. In public media debate, the left and many scientists puzzle over climate change and how the people of the world could possibly ignore such a threat. But the key decisions are not made by 'the people'. Power and wealth in the world are intensely concentrated, and international elites will extend the principle of the gated communities in which they already live to gated parts of the planet. A key area of media studies should be to analyse such absences in media debate and to develop more detailed accounts of what *is* present in the media, how this is ideologically shaped and in whose interests. It must then also go beyond what is visible to ask how elites ensure that issues are decided without recourse to public debate, and how such decisions can be brought into the public sphere and subjected to forms of democratic decision-making.

SEMINAR QUESTIONS

1 Suggest some examples of significant 'absences' in media debate.
2 Suggest examples where some of these 'absences' have been successfully highlighted and brought into the public sphere.
3 Discuss the extent to which 'new media' might have changed the circuit of communications.

FURTHER READING

▶ For a classic discussion of how the media control what is discussed in the public sphere by the process of agenda-setting, see Maxwell McCoombs (2014) *Setting the Agenda: Mass Media and Public Opinion* (2nd edn, Polity).

▶ For the conflation of media consumption and media production, see Axel Bruns (2009) *Blogs, Wikipedia, Second life, and Beyond: From Production to Produsage* (Peter Lang).

▶ For a clear introduction to the connections between media, politics and democracy, see James Curran (2011) *Media and Democracy* (Routledge).

▶ For an in-depth case analysis of media reporting, see Maxwell Boykoff (2011) *Who Speaks for the Climate? Making Sense of Media Reporting on Climate Change* (Cambridge University Press).

Acknowledgements: Thanks to Alison and Maureen Gilmour for research on the coverage of Israel/Palestine, Antony Froggatt for his work on climate change and energy security and Will Dinan for his work on PR and lobbying.

16

FAMILIES AND PERSONAL LIFE

all change?

VANESSA MAY

CONTENTS

INTRODUCTION

FAMILY LIFE IS ONE of the areas of life that is undergoing constant change. If you compare yourself to your grandparents, it is likely that your views on what is 'proper' and 'acceptable' when it comes to how you should conduct your relationships will differ. For example, while your grandparents grew up in an era when divorce was frowned upon, you are likely to have known many children growing up with divorced parents, and you might feel that living in a lone-parent family or a step-family is nothing out of the ordinary. Similarly, your grandparents' generation has experienced a time when homosexuality was illegal in many Western countries, the UK included, whereas you are now witnessing same-sex relationships gaining legal recognition, even the status of marriage, in these same countries. But what do these changes mean for your personal life and for society? The task for sociologists is to explain not only how, but why, these shifts are taking place. What has actually changed, and what has remained the same? What other social changes are these changes in attitude and behaviour linked to?

This chapter focuses on six issues concerning recent shifts in how people conduct their closest relationships and personal lives. When we think of the changes listed above, perhaps the first thought that comes to mind is that we are living in an era of increased individual choice where we get to decide how best to conduct our own lives. I begin by discussing a highly influential theoretical approach that has claimed exactly this, namely the individualization thesis. I examine why this thesis seems to have captured the sociological imagination, as well as compelling critiques against it.

Talking about family life often provokes strong feelings, the strength of which is partly explained by the existence of ideologies that prescribe how families 'should be'. Just think of the at times virulent public debates that have been sparked by same-sex marriage. The following three sections of this chapter focus on how sociologists have engaged with the ideological nature of family life. Firstly, I explore sociological debates around whether the increasing diversity in family life that Western countries have witnessed is a sign of 'family breakdown' or merely another phase in the ever changing landscape of family life. Secondly, I discuss a particular approach within family studies, namely the 'family practices' approach, the aim of which has been to move away from measuring family lives against an ideal structure (in the process of which many families are found wanting) and instead focus on how people *do* family. A third question that is connected to beliefs about what family 'should be' is whether families are 'given' (based on a genetic link) or 'created' through social relationships, issues that have been at the heart of the 'families of choice' approach and 'new kinship studies'. I use same-sex marriage and parenting to illustrate continuities and changes in how the 'givenness' of families is understood.

I then go on to examine the generally accepted notion that women have gained equality with men within opposite-sex couple relationships. I explore this question in relation to parenting and, in a final section, in relation to the management of money, looking at both changes and continuities when it comes to inequalities between men and women. Throughout the chapter, I point out the ways in which shifts in how people lead their personal lives are closely linked to wider social changes such as de-industrialization, globalization, the increasing commercialization of personal life and changes in gender relations. A focus on personal life, in other words, does not mean that we restrict ourselves to looking at what goes on in the 'private' sphere of 'home' or 'household'; rather, it encompasses also the 'public' spheres of work, politics and the economy (May 2011).

INDIVIDUALIZATION OR RELATIONALITY?

Do-it-yourself biographies

The examples provided at the start of this chapter – changes in social norms concerning sex, cohabitation and marriage – are often interpreted as signs of a more liberal normative context within which individuals have the ability to choose for themselves how they are to live their personal lives. This question of individual choice has stood at the heart of family sociology for over two decades now, as sociologists have debated the claims put forward by the so-called individualization thesis about the weakening of tradition and a concomitant increase in individual choice. As one of the main theorists of individualization, Anthony Giddens, has expressed it, we now have 'no choice but to choose' in most areas of our life (1991: 81). With regards to personal life, this thesis claims that the institution of marriage has lost much of its normative power, and that people no longer follow set paths but rather create 'do-it-yourself' biographies which are characterized by 'everyday experiments' around, for example, sexuality. The ensuing debate has been one of the most heated ones in the area of family studies.

In most Western countries, some of the central trends in family life since the end of the Second World War are a rise in divorce rates and a decrease in marriage rates (though both seem to have reached a plateau), an increase in cohabiting unions, a higher age at first marriage and childbirth, lower birth rates, and higher rates of births outside of marriage. These demographic shifts have been coupled with changing social norms: for example, sex before marriage is no longer frowned upon, and previously stigmatized family forms, such as single-parent families and step-families, have become more accepted.

As a way of trying to explain some of these changes, Giddens (1992) famously coined the term 'pure relationship'. He argued that, rather than being held together by the (unbreakable) bond that marriage traditionally presented, contemporary couple relationships are reliant on emotional reciprocity and last only as long as both parties are satisfied with their relationship. He also argued that relationships between men and women had become more equal, and one off-shoot of this was that women were now leaving unhappy relationships. Jamieson (1999: 486), however, disagreed with Giddens and proposed that we can explain higher incidences of relationship dissolution by the fact that couples find it difficult to fulfil the ideals of intimacy, equality and mutuality that they are expected to attain because their relationships continue to be unequal. To take an example that will be discussed in more detail below, women and men continue to share housework and child care unequally, while men still earn on average more than women (Eurostat 2013), thus allowing them more say in some household decisions. I will return to this question towards the end of this chapter when I discuss whether the promised 'gender revolution' has in fact stalled.

Another theorist who has contributed to the individualization thesis is Ulrich Beck, whose key concept in relation to family life was 'de-traditionalization', by which he meant that the bonds and boundaries found in 'traditional societies' have mostly disappeared. Beck sounded a more cautious note than Giddens by arguing that this increased choice was coupled with a loss of inner stability and a growing selfishness. Beck and Beck-Gernsheim (1995) further asserted that the loss of old certainties (such as 'marriage is for life') has led to new insecurities and a need to create what Beck (1992) calls a 'do-it-yourself biography'. One place where people have turned to seek stability in an insecure world, according to Beck and Beck-Gernsheim, is the romantic relationship. This, they say, explains why love has become so significant in contemporary societies. But, rather than providing the stability that people desire, love brings with it its own insecurities as couples today have to look for answers to questions such as whether they should have children, whether both should work outside the home, and whose career should come first. Thus love is likely to lead to conflict and disappointment, which in turn makes couple relationships fragile.

One of the reasons why the individualization thesis has risen to such prominence within sociology is that it seems to tap into a general sense that our lives have become increasingly free of constraints and are now under our own control. Adams (2003) and Brannen and Nilsen (2005) have pointed out that the individualization thesis merely reflects this current ethos of individuality, popular in political rhetoric, and fails to take into account that the 'new traditions' that have emerged to fill the void left by the demise of old traditions, though perhaps more flexible than the ones in the past, are not 'completely . . . subject to rationally-oriented, individual control' (Adams 2003: 230). In other words, our lives continue to be rule-governed, as Gilding (2010) points out through the example of inheritance and wills. In England and Wales, there is 'testamentary freedom', meaning that a person can freely choose to whom they wish to leave their property and belongings upon their death, be that a cats' home or a friendly neighbour rather than their spouse and children. Gilding argues that if we did indeed live in an era of individualization where family relationships had lost much of their traditional hold on us, we would see a significant number of such cases. But the fact that most people continue to bequeath their property to family members (Finch and Mason 2000) points to the continuing importance of the institution of 'family'.

The persistence of social structure

Beck (1992) would probably agree, at least to an extent, for he is careful in pointing out that our lives are shaped by new secondary institutions such as education and the welfare state, which means that most members of a society still go through the same life events, such as graduating, moving away from home and setting up a family, at roughly the same stage in their lives (Brannen and Nilsen 2005). Thus, although there may be some increased variability in how people lead their personal lives, we can still see broad patterns (Bottero 2011). This indicates that our lives continue to be shaped by structural factors, although we tend to have difficulty in identifying these in our everyday lives, while the ideology of individualization further helps to obscure such structural influences. Thus, for example, the young women in Brannen and Nilsen's (2005: 423) study believed that they had equality, ignoring 'the ways in which gender continues to structure opportunities'. For example, as shown in figure 16.1, in EU countries women earn on average 16 percent less than men do, despite advances in women's education. The gender pay gap varies from 2 percent in Slovenia to 27 percent in Estonia (Eurostat 2013).

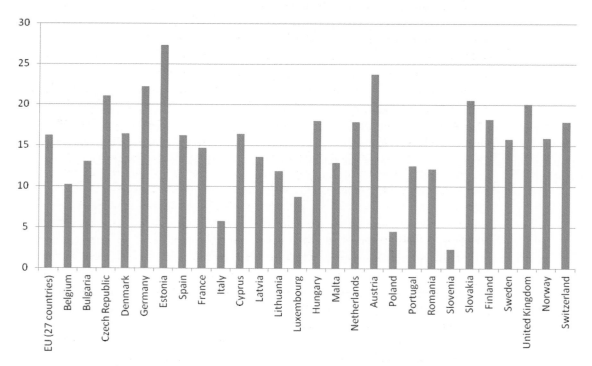

Figure 16.1 The gender pay gap in the EU, 2011 (%)

Source: Compiled with data from Eurostat (2013).

It is also important to realize that 'choice' is a privilege not available to all; it tends to be white middle-class men who have the resources and opportunities to create their own biography. Women, working-class people and ethnic minorities are perhaps more aware of the ways in which their opportunities to achieve the idealized 'do-it-yourself' biography are curtailed (Brannen and Nilsen 2005; Adkins 2002; Skeggs 2004).

The notion of 'do-it-yourself' individualized biographies in relation to personal and family life should not be taken too far so as to ignore the persistence of social structure. For example, gender will still play a large part in the choices these medical students are able and free to make in their lives. (© MAPW Australia/ Flickr)

BOX 16.1 PERSONS RATHER THAN INDIVIDUALS

Carol Smart (2007b) has taken a different tack in challenging the individualization thesis, particularly the work of Beck and Beck-Gernsheim. She argues that the focus of the individualization thesis on 'the individual' is misguided because the term points towards an autonomous being, independently making his or her own decisions on a 'rational' basis of self-interest. This, she argues, is a misunderstanding of the nature of personal life, which remains deeply embedded in webs of relationships. Our lives are, in other words, inherently relational. We are from birth connected to other people, and these other people matter when we make important life choices. The autonomous individual is a myth, but one that chimes with the current neoliberal ethos, according to which individuals make their own way in this world (as opposed to having their opportunities limited by inequalities based on social class or race, for example). Smart (ibid.) also argues that, by focusing on family relationships alone, sociologists have neglected other, at times equally significant, relationships. She urges sociologists to broaden their scope to study the connectedness and socio-cultural embeddedness of people's personal lives.

SEMINAR QUESTIONS

1 Think of examples of areas of life where the degree of choice has increased for many people.
2 On the basis of the above discussion, consider the various ways in which your choices might be constrained.

FAMILY DECLINE OR DIVERSITY?

Sociologists are also interested in determining the wider significance of the increasing diversity in and acceptance of different family forms, including step-families, lone-parent families, living-apart-together couples (LATs) and those living on their own. One of the key debates in relation to this is whether or not these demographic changes herald a downfall of 'the family'. But it is important also to understand the context-bound nature of such debates – family relationships are understood differently in different cultures – which is why I also discuss briefly some non-Western conceptions of 'family'.

Downfall of 'the family'?

A question that has been widely debated by politicians, in the media and by sociologists is whether 'the family' is experiencing its downfall, and whether this 'family breakdown' can be linked to social ill effects such as juvenile delinquency and children's reduced educational achievement. Much of this debate has been underpinned by the concept of an 'underclass' of people, who are seen to be on the ascendancy and whose values and family lives deviate from the 'norm'. The 'underclass' discourse is strongly raced (particularly in the USA) and classed: the 'dominant values' to which people are expected to adhere are clearly those of the middle-class white majority.

What such pronouncements about a downfall of 'the family' do not take into account is that the idealized nuclear family is a product of its time. In other words, 'the family' is a social construction, and what is considered ideal in family life changes over time and across cultures. This is why we cannot equate changes in family form with the impending collapse of family life (Jamieson 1998: 15). In addition, during any historical time period, the ideal family is also partly a fiction that few families are able to attain in practice (Coontz 1992). The historian John Gillis (1996) has described this as the difference between 'the families we live with' (the actual flesh and blood people with whom we form family bonds) and 'the families we live by' (the idealized family that many strive for). It is important as well to exercise caution when interpreting the meaning of demographic shifts, such as a decrease in the average number of children per family or an increase in the number of divorces. While the former are the result of small changes in the personal lives of individuals, such as having one child fewer or getting married a year later, rather than indicating major shifts in how people value family (Bottero 2011), Bengtson, Biblarz and Roberts (2002) found that, despite an increase in divorce rates, family relationships have not become any less significant in people's lives.

Given the changeable nature of family life, many argue that, rather than trying to measure the families we live with against idealized families we live by, sociologists would make better use of their time by trying to understand the complexity and richness of family life and the ways in which family ideologies can also act to constrain individuals' lives by imposing 'mythical homogeneity on the diverse means by which people organize their intimate relationships', which in effect presents a 'sentimental fictional plot' (Stacey 1991: 269–70). Stacey notes that the lament over 'family decline' deflects attention from important social inequalities of class, gender and race. 'The family' has traditionally been a patriarchal institution based on women's financial dependence on and general subordination to men. It has also been well documented that many working-class families have been unable to live up to middle-class standards of 'the family' (such as a stay-at-home mother) because of a lack of resources, while the nuclear family ideology has been used to denigrate the family practices of, for example, African Americans in the USA or African Caribbeans in the UK. I will return below to this point about the Eurocentric nature of the families we live by.

BOX 16.2 CHANGE AND CONTINUITY IN FAMILY LIFE

To find out the extent to which arguments of 'family decline' accurately describe what is going on in families, Bengtson, Biblarz and Roberts (2002) conducted the Longitudinal Study of Generations, which began in 1971 in California (Wave 1). By the time Wave 6 was conducted in 1997, the sample contained four generations, born between 1896 and 1985, and over half of the study participants lived outside of California. Bengtson and his colleagues found that, despite rising rates of divorce and maternal employment, 'family influences across generations are strong and families still matter – much more than advocates of the family decline hypothesis would admit' (ibid.: 159). They conclude that children's feelings of closeness and solidarity with their parents continue to be high, and that the effects of parental divorce on children's aspirations, self-esteem, values and self-confidence are less significant than expected. Divorce can have a negative effect on children, but this has to be understood in a broader context where other changes have had positive effects. This means that, *overall*, we cannot speak of family decline as a result of higher divorce rates. The main conclusion of Bengtson and his colleagues is that, because parents still influence their children's aspirations, self-esteem and values, family relationships continue to be central in people's lives.

Contrary to the 'family decline' thesis, dominant discourses continue to influence how people organize their family lives (Smart 2007a; Williams 2004). The nuclear family continues to be the ideal form. For example, the riots in the UK in the summer of 2011 prompted David Cameron to talk of a 'broken Britain', characterized by 'family breakdown' and 'fatherless families', both of which he blamed for the perceived moral breakdown of society. It is important not to take such pronouncements at face value, for, just as the desirability of the nuclear family is a social construction, so is the social pathology of alternative family forms (McIntosh 1996: 150). The task of sociologists is to critically examine how the families we live by get constructed, and the impact this has on the lives of individuals. It is also important for sociologists to remain mindful of the fact that their work plays a role in defining what constitutes (or should constitute) 'family' (May 2010). We can see this, for example, in the way that policy-makers make use of sociological research when they institute changes in family policy.

Cultural context

The 'family decline' thesis (and family sociology overall) can be critiqued for its Western-centredness. What is not often noted within public debates over 'family decline' is the contingent nature of any family ideal. The strength of ideology becomes apparent when we look at reactions to different cultural family practices in multicultural societies. In countries such as the UK, the USA and the Netherlands, which are home to people from a number of different cultures, we have witnessed at times virulent debates where the white majority bemoan the family practices of ethnic minorities for lacking in or being in direct opposition to 'proper' and 'acceptable' values. For example, in the African-Caribbean community in Britain, there are a relatively high proportion of families headed by a single mother – a family type that has often been highlighted as the opposite of the 'ideal' white nuclear family (Reynolds 2005). This kind of (racist) stigmatization fails to take into account the social history of the Caribbean and the historical difference between Western and Caribbean family practices. Caribbean plantation owners attempted to impose a European family ideology by, for example, encouraging Christian marriage among their slaves, leading to a particular pattern of family life that combines Caribbean and European practices and values (Chamberlain 2006). Marriages in the Caribbean tend to start as a form of 'visiting relations' that includes sex, followed by a period of cohabitation, with the couple marrying only later in middle life. Thus, in the Caribbean, Christian marriage has been seen not as the prerequisite to family formation, as in most Western countries, but as a confirmation of the couple's loyalty and fertility. In addition, there is a strong tradition of African-Caribbean women both working outside the home and being heads of household, in contrast to the patriarchal family ideal in Western countries that traditionally defined women as housewives. These differences in family formation practices have been considered a problem by whites both in the Caribbean and in the UK.

Another group of migrants who have settled in the UK comprises the Pakistani community, who also engage in family practices that differ from those of the white majority. British Asian families are often accused, for example, by politicians and the media of not 'integrating' into the white majority culture. Especially Muslim families are stereotyped as inflexibly holding on to traditional practices such as honour killings. Shaw (2000), however, argues that, in reality, the picture is more complex. Shaw points out that extreme outcomes such as honour killings are rare; in most cases conflict is resolved through negotiation, often with a solution that adapts tradition to the British context. In other words, the Pakistani kinship system is both durable and adaptive, and it would be a mistake to assume that the family practices of migrants remain 'traditional' and unchanging. While traditional ideas about gender and marriage can still be seen in operation, there is also evidence of change. For example, sons might be allowed to have romantic relationships before marriage and with non-Muslim women, while many daughters are encouraged to gain an education, because this means that they can better secure their future family's financial position if their husband becomes unemployed, while also allowing a daughter to 'stand on her own two feet' should her marriage fail.

In sum, I would argue that the continued strength of ideologies around 'the family' is visible in the stereotyping of non-nuclear and non-white families as deficient and (dangerously) 'other'.

SEMINAR QUESTIONS

1 How do you think that family ideologies are transmitted? How do we come to know what the 'ideal' family that we should strive for is?

2 Consider arguments for and against the notion that migrant families should 'assimilate' to the host culture.

FROM NORMATIVE FAMILY STRUCTURES TO EVERYDAY FAMILY PRACTICES

Families are what families do

I have above several times used the term 'family practices', a term made famous by David Morgan (1996), who urged sociologists to shift their attention away from family structure (and from ideological prescriptions of what a family 'should' be, however implicit) and pay more attention to what families *do*. He criticized the tendency of family sociologists to focus on 'the family' and to equate this with the nuclear family. In doing so, Morgan argued, family sociology was unable to capture the diversity and complexity of family life, namely that family practices do not take place merely within nuclear families and are not limited to relationships between people who are strictly kin. If we concentrate on family practices, claims of a 'decline of the family' become nonsensical, precisely because 'family' does not become equated with just one type. Morgan argued also that, while they should be careful in how they use the concept of 'family', sociologists should not abandon this altogether because it has significant purchase in everyday usage, for example in the widespread distinction between family and friends. Family practices also retain some distinctiveness that would be lost if we subsumed these under some broader term such as intimacy practices.

In focusing on family practices, Morgan directs our attention to the everyday. Many family practices are attached to regular festivities (for example, celebrating birthdays and holidays such as Eid or Christmas) while others are more mundane, such as taking the kids to school or preparing meals. Such practices have a taken-for-granted quality which means they rarely involve much conscious thought *as such*, except when they are breached or become problematic, for instance when a couple divorces. One example is considering who counts as kin, which in many families is taken for granted. But take the case of Mary, who marries Steve, whose children from a previous relationship become Mary's step-children. If Mary and Steve divorce, the family has to decide whether or not the children are still her step-children, or whether the family relationship ceases upon divorce (Mason 2011). What a family practices approach highlights is that families are fluid because the practices that define family are likely to shift over time, and so the boundary between 'family' and 'non-family' can easily become blurred. Thus we cannot view 'the family' as a thing that exists in and of itself or as a bounded unit.

Morgan (2011: 67) also points out that 'family practices' are not necessarily willingly chosen or positive. For example, many women find upon marriage that housework is a given consequence of being a wife and a mother, though they would not necessarily choose it to be so or enjoy this domestic labour. Similarly, there are many aspects of being a breadwinner that men do not choose. Family practices can also be cruel and abusive, as the sadly frequent cases of domestic violence and child abuse demonstrate. Calling such practices family practices 'is not to invest them with an aura of virtue but simply to say that they are carried out with reference to others who are defined as being family members' (ibid.: 73).

Morgan's 'family practices' approach has had a profound impact on at least British family sociology, and most of the empirical studies discussed below fall under the umbrella of 'family practices' even though not all of them necessarily use this terminology. What is crucial is that, rather than starting from family structure, these studies examine what people *do* in their family or family-like relationships.

Displaying family

Janet Finch (2007) has extended Morgan's original argument by saying that families are not only done, they also have to be displayed, not merely to those involved in the interaction but also to 'relevant others'. These 'relevant others' could be other family members, friends or neighbours, but also state officials. Indeed, for some families, engaged for example with social services, it is imperative that they are able to demonstrate that they are doing 'appropriate' family-like things with each other. Although the need to 'display' is not only relevant to 'non-conventional' families, Finch argues that there are likely to be different degrees of intensity to which display is necessary, depending on the type of family and on the particular circumstances. Finch provides the example of children moving away from home; at this point, there is a more intense need to display family relationships as they are being reconfigured.

It is when our 'doing' of family is understood as 'doing family things' that the 'family-like' nature of our relationships is acknowledged and confirmed. It is, in other words, important that the practices in which we engage, such as weekly phone calls with a parent, are interpreted by ourselves and 'relevant others' as *family* practices. For this to happen, they must be 'linked in a sufficiently clear way with the "wider systems of meaning"' (Finch 2007: 67) – in other words, they must be widely recognized as things that family members do for and with each other. Finch says that there is plenty of existing research evidence to answer the question of why family relationships must be displayed but rather less for how they do so and to whom. Her call for more research to be conducted on this has led to the publication of an edited collection of work exploring different types of family display, such as motherhood and fatherhood, and the displays of families whose home is also their workplace (Dermott and Seymour 2011).

There have also been critical voices in the mix, warning us that using a 'family display' approach does not necessarily help us escape the normative element of 'the family'. For example, Heaphy (2011) points out that displays both tend to be measured against the ideal white, middle-class nuclear family and can help reproduce norms about which displays are acceptable, as well as helping to reproduce inequalities. Those at the bottom end of class hierarchies (such as families defined as belonging to an 'underclass'), non-white families, and families that do not follow the norm (such as lone-mother families) are more likely to be closely monitored by state agencies and risk being judged as failing to display family appropriately. It is important to keep asking the question 'Who gets to "claim" family?' and 'Who is recognized as family?' because this recognition is often linked to legal, socio-cultural and economic rights and benefits (such as pension rights and immigration rights). Being recognized as 'family' is, in other words, a privilege and potentially a highly charged political issue, as will be discussed below in relation to same-sex families.

BOX 16.3 FAMILY DISPLAY IN FAMILY FOOD PRACTICES

In their study of family food practices, James and Curtis (2010) combine Finch's (2007) notion of 'family displays' and Smart's (2007b) point that personal lives (including family displays) must be understood as socially and culturally embedded and connected. Similarly to Heaphy (2011), James and Curtis critique Finch for depicting family displays as free-floating and point out that all family displays are to an extent normative. By doing family displays, people are invoking norms about what 'proper' families do and inviting affirmation from others of their family-like quality. In so doing, they help lend legitimacy to these norms. This is especially the case with family practices that take place in a public setting, where there is added pressure to do family 'properly', particularly if the display involves children. It was also important for people to convey that they eat together as a family: the family meal retains its iconic status as something that 'proper' families do. Such displays help families to locate themselves culturally by using cultural norms as a sounding board against which they work out and comprehend their own family practices.

SEMINAR QUESTIONS

1 How might the birth of a baby change the family practices of a couple?
2 Do you think that a family display must be accepted by others outside the family in order to be successful? Why/why not?

FAMILY AS GIVEN OR CREATED?

In this section, I explore an issue that has come increasingly to the fore in both sociological and public debate, namely whether families should be seen as 'given' or 'created'. This might seem like a nonsensical question because we all probably assume that we 'just know' what constitutes family. Yet recent changes in the landscape of family life, particularly the rise of LGBT families and new reproductive technologies, have challenged the traditional assumption that 'family' is based on biology and marriage. As Morgan (1996) noted, 'family' is not done merely with members of one's kin. I begin by discussing the 'families of choice' approach, which emerged out of studies into same-sex relationships and highlighted the importance of friends, thus putting into question the 'given' nature of family. This distinction between 'given' and 'created' relationships has also been the focus of 'new kinship studies', conducted in an era of new reproductive technologies when biological relatedness of parents and children can no longer be assumed. I conclude this section by discussing the most recent literature on lesbian and gay parents, which seems to indicate the continued importance of biology for how people understand 'family'. Throughout, the focus is on how people *do* family – that is, on family practices.

Families of choice

The increasing visibility and acceptance of gay, lesbian, bisexual and transgender (LGBT) people is having an impact on understandings of what constitutes a 'family', which in turn has in many countries been reflected in recent changes in legislation over equality and marriage. Weston's (1991) study of 'families of choice' in the USA is a key work within this field, and was later followed by Weeks, Heaphy and Donovan's (2001) research on same-sex intimacies in the UK. These studies were conducted after the initial impact of the Gay Liberation movement – which brought much needed visibility to LGBT lives and led to the first pieces of legislation banning discrimination on the basis of sexual orientation – but before more recent developments which have in some parts of the world brought same-sex couple relationships legal recognition.

Weston and Weeks and his colleagues found that many of the gays and lesbians they interviewed were uncomfortable with the term family because 'the family' was seen as a solely heterosexual institution. This discomfort stemmed partly from a militantly anti-family phase in the gay and lesbian movement in the 1970s and a stated wish not to conform to heterosexual norms. As Weeks, Heaphy and Donovan (2001: 10) pointed out, the term 'family' came with 'historic baggage and oppressive heterosexual connotations'. Yet both studies found that, in many cases, friends were 'spoken about as equivalent to the idealized family (*and infinitely preferable to the real one*)' (ibid.: 10, emphasis added). Because many had been shunned by their families of origin, they created their own 'families of choice' within which friends and ex-lovers played a key role. This reappropriation of the word 'family' indicates that 'the values and comforts that the family unit is supposed to embody, *even if it regularly fails to do so*', remain important (Weeks, Heaphy and Donovan 2001: 10, emphasis added). Thus the use of the language of family can be seen both as an effort to challenge and subvert conventional definitions of family and as a desire for legitimacy by identifying with existing patterns.

Weeks and his colleagues state that this use of the term 'family' to denote something broader than traditional definitions based on lineage and marriage, referring to kin-like networks of relationships based on friendship and commitments 'beyond blood', is having an impact on how 'family' is defined within our culture in general. In other words, being able to live an openly non-heterosexual life has implications beyond the LGBT community, because this is part and parcel of a broader transformation of intimacy. Here the authors refer to Giddens's reflexive project of the self: as people are being unmoored from traditions, they are forced to find new ways of life, and new narratives that promote alternative ways of doing family are important in this process.

Friendship

The literature on 'families of choice' helped fuel sociological interest in the role that friends play in people's personal lives. One question that has exercised the minds of sociologists such as Roseneil and Budgeon (2004) is whether friends are eclipsing family as the most significant relationship (their answer is 'yes'). Spencer and Pahl (2006) have in their work argued against such notions of the decreasing importance of family. While a niche population might see friends as more important (for example, some non-heterosexuals and young people), Pahl and Pevalin (2005) found that, as people get older and establish families of their own, kin relationships become more central again. There is also evidence that same-sex couples who have children can experience a similar return to the 'family fold', as it were (Almack 2008), as will be explored in more detail below. Furthermore, Spencer and Pahl (2006) suggest that this question of whether or not friends are eclipsing family is not even the most interesting question to be asking. For them, what is fascinating is the sheer diversity in people's personal communities, ranging from friend-based to family-based, and the consequences of this diversity. Taking personal communities (the networks of different types of relationship that a person has) as our starting point means that we cease to focus fixedly on the differences between 'friends' and 'family' and come to understand that both relationships can have aspects of a 'given' and 'chosen' relationship. Thus we may choose which family members we are close to, while some friendships can feel given in the sense that they are experienced as inevitable and enduring. Using Morgan's terminology, the focus is on the practices in which people are involved and on how they understand their relationships rather than on structural definitions of what constitutes a family versus a friendship relationship.

These debates reference Giddens's argument that one aspect of the 'transformation of intimacy' is that individuals are now conducting 'pure relationships' that last only as long as both parties are satisfied with the situation. Indeed, as Davies (2011) notes, friendship can be seen as best reflecting this new type of relationship that lasts only until further notice. Yet there is mounting evidence that, far from being idealized relationships of choice unfettered by obligation, friendships are not only socially structured but can also be difficult to sever, even after the relationship has ceased to bring pleasure to both parties. McPherson, Smith-Lovin and Cook (2001) found that friendship networks tend to be fairly homogeneous, for example, in terms of social class and ethnicity. As they put it, 'birds of a feather flock together' – meaning that the people with whom we become friends tend to resemble us in many important ways. This is both because we feel at ease with people with whom we share interests and a common outlook on life and because the places that are part of our everyday lives, such as schools, workplaces and leisure venues, tend to be frequented by others who are similar to us.

Smart and her colleagues (2012) found, furthermore, that friendships can be tinged with similar feelings of obligation as family relationships, which in turn means that people can find it very difficult to end a friendship even if it is proving to be a difficult one. Davies (2011) notes that this can perhaps be explained partly by people's wish to be seen as a 'moral' person – and one of the key elements of being 'moral' is being a trustworthy and dependable friend, not someone who dumps their friends when things get rough. In sum, the 'choice' that we have in forming any kind of relationship seems to have been overstated by the individualization thesis and the 'families of choice' literature.

Beyond biology?

But what about biology – are our understandings of genetic relatedness changing? While sociologists have been busy arguing over which family structure, if any, is most conducive to individual and social wellbeing, anthropologists within 'new kinship studies' have been examining connectedness and relatedness and what these mean to people, and are therefore, according to Mason (2008), better positioned to capture new developments such as the impact of new reproductive technologies (NRTs) on how people conceive 'family'. The significance of genetic relatedness has gained new attention in the wake of NRTs and other technological advancements, which have helped to trouble conventional notions of kinship but have also made it possible to ascertain who is genetically related to whom. These technologies have led to debates about the relative importance of 'genetic' and 'social' ties and to new 'family dilemmas', such as whether parents who have used gamete donations should tell their children of their genetic origins, what the relationship of the egg or sperm donor is to the child, or whether a person should take a test to ascertain whether they have inherited a genetic illness (Konrad 2005, 2003).

What is gaining increasing importance is the notion of genetic 'truth', which Smart proposes is part of a broader cultural ethos according to which 'the healthy self and the healthy relationship require truth telling' (Smart 2009: 552). It is now considered important for children to know their 'true' genetic inheritance – for example, in the case of adoption, sperm or egg donation, or 'paternity uncertainty'. We must remember, Smart notes, that this quest for a physical or genetic truth is a relatively new phenomenon. The fact that adoptive parents in the 1950s often did not tell their children of their adopted status was not at the time seen as deceitful but 'as a way of protecting the best interests of the child, and of course of preserving the respectability of the families involved' (ibid.: 559).

The above examples help demonstrate the complexity of kinship: a kin tie is not merely about biology or genetic relatedness, but 'kinship is nested in relationships which are lived and meaningful' (Smart 2009: 555). Thus both the social and the biological are mobilized in notions of kinship, because biological ties do not automatically translate into affinities; this requires also a sense of being emotionally connected (Mason 2008; Edwards 2000). In effect, we must 'do family' in order for a biological connection to mean something, and this meaning is not fixed in advance.

Same-sex marriage and parenting

Since the initial studies into same-sex relationships, LGBT people have experienced advances in terms of being able to live openly non-heterosexual and queer lives, giving rise to two further issues, namely same-sex marriage and same-sex parenting, which further complicate traditional notions of 'family' and 'relatedness' but also, to an extent, confirm these. Same-sex marriage has become an issue that few Western governments can ignore, and it continues to divide opinion both within academia and in public debate (Einarsdottir 2011). While those in favour of same-sex marriage argue that this is a simple question of equal rights (and let's not forget that marriage not only brings with it important legal rights connected to next-of-kin status; it can also lend legitimacy to a relationship), there are two types of argument against it. Firstly, opponents within the LGBT community argue that seeking the right to marry is equivalent to acquiescing to heterosexual norms. After all, marriage has traditionally been an important institution in the upholding of patriarchy, whereby men gain authority over women, as well as being a thoroughly heterosexual endeavour. Thus some LGBT people argue that, rather than aping what heterosexuals do, it is important to carve out a space for couple relationships that do not follow heterosexual norms. Another form of opposition to same-sex marriage comes from various religious organizations, such as the Catholic Church and the Anglican Church, which argue that marriage is an institution that only a man and a woman can enter.

Notwithstanding this opposition, many countries have given same-sex couples the right to register their relationships, while in a small handful of countries, such as Sweden and the Netherlands, same-sex couples have the same rights to marry as opposite-sex couples do. The debate continues, and the legislative terrain on this issue is constantly shifting in many countries. For example, during the writing of this chapter, new legislation on same-sex marriage was passed in England and Wales and in Scotland, while several states in the USA have recently held ballots on whether or not same-sex marriage should be legalized. What we can take from this is that the meaning of one of the central institutions attached to 'family', namely marriage, is undergoing a significant change, and, because of the strong ideologies attached to marriage, these changes are accompanied by emotive debates.

Non-heterosexual family lives have also been changing in relation to the question of children, an issue that helps shed light on the extent to which family relationships (at least between parents and children) are understood to be based on a biological link. Many Western countries have in recent years witnessed a so-called lesbian baby boom or gayby boom, with an increasing number of same-sex couples having children within this relationship (Taylor 2009; Ryan-Flood 2009). Recent sociological research focusing on how same-sex parent families *do* family has found that fairly normative views on 'family' influence these practices as well. For example, the couple relationship has remained central, despite earlier claims that non-heterosexual people were in the vanguard of a new type of intimacy where couple relationships would be de-centred (cf. Roseneil and Budgeon 2004). Ryan-Flood (2009) points out that the earlier concern over whether LGBT families were 'transgressing' or 'assimilating to' traditional notions of (heterosexual) 'family' oversimplified things. If we look at lesbian mothers, for example (and the sociological literature up to date has focused more on lesbian mothers than gay fathers), we can see that they are doing both: they are transgressing heterosexual norms around parenting (by having a child within a lesbian relationship), yet many also make use of the same understandings and symbols of kinship as heterosexual parents do.

Elton John and David Furnish are famous same-sex parents of two boys, born of a surrogate mother. The procedure took place in California, where sperm from both men can be mixed prior to fertilization of an egg and both partners can be listed as parents, without knowing or needing to stipulate which was the biological father. What might this tell us about the continuing importance placed by some on biological parenthood? (© Rex Features)

Ryan-Flood (2009) found that the biological mother (and father) automatically retains the important status of 'parent', while the position of the co-parent (the parent who is not biologically related to the child) could often be experienced as vulnerable and 'made-up', indicating that biology, which is one of the cornerstones of conventional notions of family, continues to be important. As a result, many of the biological mothers in Ryan-Flood's study made sure they validated the social mother's status as parent, while no social mother felt the need to do the same for the biological mother. In some families, for instance, the child was given the co-parent's surname as a way of establishing her place in the child's lineage (cf. Nordqvist 2012). What the two mothers were called by the child also reflects this perceived difference in the status of the two parents. The name 'mother' was usually reserved for the biological mother, while the co-parent was often called by her first name. These examples help illustrate the continuing normative power of 'family' and how difficult it can be to form new kinds of relatedness in a society where kinship is clearly delineated along the lines of a distinction between biological and social ties and where the heteronormative family form is still seen as the gold standard (Ryan-Flood 2009: 136).

As a further critique of the emphasis on 'choice' in much of the literature on same-sex relationships, Taylor (2009) points out that the choice to become a same-sex parent is classed. It seems

BOX 16.4 THE CONTINUING IMPORTANCE OF FAMILIES OF ORIGIN

While the 'families of choice' literature emphasized the 'everyday experiments' in which LGBT people engage when constructing their families, more recent work has demonstrated that the pendulum has not necessarily swung as far away from more traditional notions of what constitutes family as was originally thought (or hoped). For example, Almack (2008) found that lesbian couples were deeply committed to sustaining ties with family and wider kin, perhaps more so than they were with friends. The participants in her study referred to the widespread notion that 'you can choose your friends but not your family', thus emphasizing the role of kin relationships based on traditional notions of relatedness. Almack (ibid.: 1191) did encounter some narratives of 'families of choice' – one participant, Elaine, said: 'My family are my strong friendships around me and not necessarily blood relatives' – as well as lesbian couples who did 'family-like' things with friends, such as lending money, spending holidays together, and helping out practically. But the birth of children could disrupt these 'family-like' friendships, whereas the children could act as a bridge between the lesbian couple and their families of origin. Many of these couples relied on relatives for help with childcare and showed a clear commitment towards their relationships with families of origin (cf. Ryan-Flood 2009).

that it is easier for middle-class gays and lesbians to present same-sex parenting as a valid choice that can be celebrated, and they also have more financial resources to seek IVF and surrogacy. Middle-class couples are also more likely to have the cultural and social resources to present themselves 'acceptably' and to navigate the complex bureaucratic procedures involved in becoming foster or adoptive parents, and therefore stand a better chance of success. Taylor points out that similar family practices can be 'read' differently, for example, by social workers, depending on the social class background of the parents. Family practices and arrangements that in middle-class families could be seen to indicate 'a fluid and enchanting familial "mess"' could be interpreted as "chaotic and deviant" in the case of working-class families living on a council estate' (ibid.: 62–3).

SEMINAR QUESTIONS

1 How do same-sex relationships and families both reproduce and trouble traditional notions of 'family'?

2 Why is marriage such an important issue, both for advocates and opponents of same-sex marriage?

PARENTING: A STALLED GENDER REVOLUTION?

Changes have also been taking place within parenting in opposite-sex households. This section explores the shifts that have occurred in motherhood and fatherhood and how these are linked to broader social changes. The role of women within families and the labour market has changed in the UK as in many other Western countries, with an increasing number of mothers, especially mothers with young children, seeking paid employment. For example, the UK has moved from being a male-breadwinner country to a 'one-and-a-half' breadwinner country, where fathers tend to be employed full-time and mothers work part-time (Crompton 2006). There have been corresponding shifts in gender ideologies (what is acceptable behaviour for a man and a woman) as well as in social policy, whereby women are no longer seen merely as carers but also as earners. Similarly, the role of men in families has undergone changes. Below I discuss two issues in particular, namely the extent to which discourses about a 'new fatherhood' are warranted and why it is that most opposite-sex parents 'fall back into gender' in terms of who does the childcare and household work.

New fatherhood?

There has been much talk in the UK and other countries about a so-called new fatherhood that is characterized by fathers' increasing involvement in practical childcare as well as an emotionally close relationship with their children. This discursive shift is coupled with evidence from empirical studies indicating that fathers of today are indeed approaching fatherhood differently compared to previous generations, with a decreasing emphasis on 'breadwinning' and an increasing involvement in the lives of their children (Brannen and Nilsen 2006). Many contemporary fathers are keen to be involved already during pregnancy by attending prenatal screenings and classes, and indeed around 98 percent of fathers in the UK now attend the birth of their child (Dermott 2008).

Brannen and Nilsen (2006) conducted a study across four generations in the UK and found clear changes in how men approach fatherhood and work. The shifts in the labour market mentioned above were also clearly visible in this study: two-thirds of the oldest generation, but none of the current fathers, were sole breadwinners. The attitudes towards maternal employment had also changed: while the older generations felt that mothers *should* look after their children, the current fathers spoke of a 'mother's choice' and a family's financial situation as determining whether or not a mother works outside the home. Nevertheless, all of the fathers in this study thought that very young children 'need' to be looked after by their mothers – thus some traditional notions linking femininity and the care of young children persist.

So what is the difference between the so-called new fatherhood and what must then be 'old' fatherhood? For a start, current fathers are expected to have a higher degree of involvement in their children's everyday lives – for example, by taking them to and from school, spending time with them, and knowing what is going on in their lives. Fathers are also expected to develop a nurturing relationship with their children – indeed, emotional closeness is now very much part of 'good' fatherhood. The assumption, by now practically taken for granted, that fathers should be present at the birth signals this, and indeed many fathers speak of the experience as 'life changing' and as an important step in 'bonding' with their child (Dermott 2008). There has been a corresponding shift in masculinity, whereby it is now acceptable for a proud father to show photos of his children at work and to talk about them with other men (Miller 2011).

We must, however, be careful not to overstate the extent to which fathers' nurturing involvement with children is 'new'. Fathers of old were not uncaring, and many did significant amounts of housework and childcare (Smart 2011). The 'caring father' who had a loving bond with his children was a popular ideal before the early 1800s (Miller 2011). Perhaps the most significant shift that has taken place is that men's caring is becoming both more visible and more widely talked about (ibid.). We can also see classed differences in the adoption of these 'new' fatherhood practices. Both Brannen and Nilsen (2006) and Gillies (2009) suggest that working-class fathers might be in a better position to change their fathering practices because, as Western countries have de-industrialized, they are the ones who have been affected most directly by the loss of traditionally male manufacturing jobs, which means they are more likely than middle-class fathers to be at home with their children.

It is important to note that, in families with two parents of the opposite sex, motherhood and fatherhood are mutually constitutive, and thus 'new fatherhood' requires a rethinking of what motherhood is. A father's increasing involvement can, for instance, pose a challenge to the mother's status as the main carer, or it can offer her a welcome escape from traditional gender roles (Miller 2010). But, despite the 'new fatherhood' discourse, fathers do fathering in a culture that still assumes that the mother is the main hands-on parent. So, for example, public buildings have a 'mother and baby' room for changing nappies, but there are few if any equivalent spaces for fathers to do this. Most playgroups and events provided for parents of young children tend to be attended by mothers. As a result, public childcare spaces are by many fathers experienced as 'estrogen-filled worlds' where they do not belong (Doucet 2006). There is some evidence that fathers are beginning to seek each other out – playgroups for fathers and their children are springing up in cities such as London. Some childcare spaces are also becoming more accepting of fathers. Doucet notes in her study of Canadian fathers that, as they are increasingly becoming involved in caregiving, the more 'normal' and acceptable it becomes, and fathers who turn up at community playgroups are no longer necessarily treated with suspicion.

But it is also clear that, despite this 'new fatherhood' discourse, and the very real intentions of many to be hands-on fathers, a gendered division of labour continues to exist in families (Sullivan 2000). Although men are spending more time with their children, this is still considerably less than mothers, and fathers' caring work is often squeezed into evenings and weekends. The latest UK Time Use Survey in 2005 showed that women still do about two-thirds of the housework and that women with children do most of all, while men continue to have more leisure time (ONS 2006: 28, 38) (see table 16.1). A similar gendered difference in time use can be seen across the EU (Eurostat 2008). It would also appear that fathers do different things with their children than mothers, who continue to be the ones mainly responsible for the day-to-day physical care of their children. Fathers engage more in playing and in activity-based care outside the home, for example by taking their children to the park at the weekend, and are often 'debriefed' by the mother about what needs to be done and how. The fathers in Dermott's (2008) study talked of the importance of 'being there', not necessarily in the sense of interacting with their children, but physically present in case their children need them. These clear gendered patterns develop during maternity leave, which allows mothers to gain more expertise over childcare (Miller 2011). It would therefore seem that fathers can still be more 'hands-off' parents than mothers are.

The fact that mothers continue to be responsible for the majority of childcare can be explained at least partly by the economic realities that families face, such as having to pay the monthly rent or mortgage payments, as well as the cost of childcare. The demands of the labour market mean that combining work and childcare is difficult, no matter which parent

Table 16.1: **Time use (average minutes per person per day) by sex, and presence and age of children in the household, 2005**

		Age of youngest child in household			No dependent children in household
		0–4 years	5–10 years	11–15 years	
Men	Paid work, study	326	300	313	261
	Domestic work	191	126	66	92
	Free time	231	278	336	348
Women	Paid work, study	97	182	213	258
	Domestic work	376	273	209	129
	Free time	243	232	284	288

Source: Adapted from ONS (2006: 34).

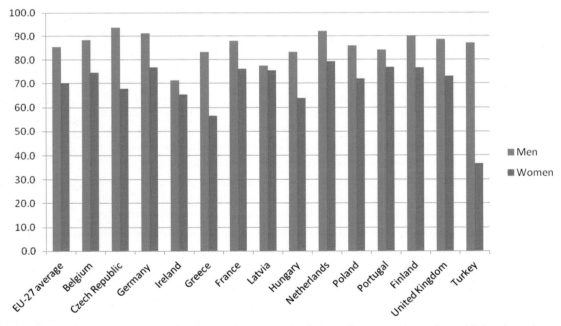

Figure 16.2 The employment rate for men and women who have at least one dependent child, selected EU-27 countries plus Turkey, 2012 (%)

Source: Compiled with data from Eurostat (2012c).

does it. The fact that men earn on average more than women do, coupled with the importance of work for men's identities, means that many new parents very soon return to a 'new normal' where the mother becomes the main carer, while the father returns to the world of work (Miller 2010). This continued gendered division of labour in the home is reflected in the differences between fathers' and mothers' employment rates, as shown in figure 16.2. In all of the EU-27 countries, fewer mothers than fathers work outside the home.

The gendered pay gap also widens when a couple has children. Dermott (2008: 30) found that women in couples earn 56 percent of what the men do, but for women with children this drops to 39 percent. While we can no longer talk of the UK being a male breadwinner country, on average 67 percent of the income in two-parent families is earned by the man (ibid.).This is explained not only by continued gender inequalities in pay but also by women's shorter working hours: 40.6 hours per week compared to men's 44.9 hours (Crompton 2006: 101). These statistics reflect the fact that some mothers with young children stay at home and that a high percentage of mothers who are employed work only part-time (OECD 2011).

BOX 16.5 FALLING BACK INTO GENDER

When and if they eventually do return to work, mothers continue to shoulder most of the housework and childcare. It would thus seem that straight couples easily 'fall back into gender' when they become parents (Miller 2011). The 'new fatherhood' discourse is therefore perhaps overstating the magnitude of change, and what is actually happening is that men are both doing and undoing gender: they are both reverting back to familiar gendered performances of worker selves and at the same time narrating gender differently, for example by talking of 'bonding' and 'instincts' when it comes to fathering. The fact remains that the pace of change regarding fathers' participation in childcare is slow and does not reflect the significant changes in women's lives. This has led to concerns over a stalled gender revolution (Hochschild 1989). Even in the Nordic countries, which have the most 'family-friendly' policies, with the specific aim of improving gender equality within families and in the labour market, gendered notions of childcare as women's responsibility continue to influence how parents divide childcare work (Haas and Hwang 2008). For example, even in families where the woman earns more than the man, the mother is more likely to take a longer break from work after the birth of a child than the father (Björnberg 2002).

Miller (2011) found that the 'breadwinner discourse' is still alive in the UK in the sense that fathers do not need to offer any justifications for why they go out to work and can articulate choice differently from mothers. Women report feeling guilty if they do *not* feel fulfilled by their role as a mother and if they yearn to return to the world of work, while fatherhood tends not to be seen as an all-consuming identity – a man's self as 'worker' remains more important (Dermott 2008; Miller 2007, 2011). Correspondingly, it can be difficult for a father to express a wish to be a primary caregiver or to take on a larger role in bringing up his children. Fathers who work part-time have to field questions and comments about this because men are expected to work full-time, while those who are primary caregivers can encounter some suspicion from others (Miller 2011; Dermott 2008; Doucet 2006). We can conclude that, although there seems to be less support nowadays for traditional gender roles, these have by no means completely disappeared.

SEMINAR QUESTIONS

1 Why might it be difficult for straight couples to 'do parenting' equally, even though they may wish to do so?
2 Why might both fathers and mothers resist changes in how parenting is organized between them?

MONEY AND THE COMMERCIALIZATION OF INTIMACY

Intimacy and money – never the twain shall meet?

This last section examines an issue that tends to be understood to be far removed from the world of intimate relationships, namely money. Zelizer (2005) has called this the 'hostile worlds paradigm', according to which money and intimacy should not mix. And, when they do, this is often considered (morally) dubious, such as in the case of prostitution, where sexual intimacy is performed in exchange for money. The roots of this paradigm lie in the distinction between the 'private' (intimate, emotional) sphere and the 'public' (economic, financial, rational) sphere.

But, if we look at this issue more closely, we can see that money is inherent in intimate relationships, from birth to dating to death. As Zelizer points out, virtually all of the most important couple and family rituals and celebrations require the spending of money and are commercialized. The archetypical Western date, for example, incurs costs in the form of restaurant bills, bar tabs and cinema tickets, while a multi-billion-pound industry has risen to provide the rings, dresses, venues and catering for engagements and weddings. Zelizer argues that money 'cohabits regularly with intimacy, and even sustains it', because 'None of these intimate interactions would long survive without their economic component' (2005: 28, 291). The things that family members do for each other, such as preparing food, maintaining clothing or the home and garden, and ferrying family members around, involve some form of consumption of goods and services. Further examples provided by Zelizer are paying someone to look after one's child or elderly relative, paying maintenance to an ex-partner, giving children pocket-money, paying for a child's education, lending a son or daughter money for a house purchase, and leaving money in wills.

There are important macro-economic consequences to such intimate transactions, which can also further strengthen class and gender inequalities. For example, wealthy families can transmit wealth from one generation to another. In addition, the gendered division of labour within families is closely connected to gendered notions of what women and men 'should' do and affect their position in the labour market, as discussed above. I now turn to explore these issues in relation to how straight couples manage their money.

Straight couples managing money

How couples manage their money says a lot about prevailing gender ideologies and power dynamics within families. Jan Pahl's (1980) landmark study indicated that the majority of couples operated a fairly traditional division, where women remained financially dependent on men. She distinguished between the housekeeping allowance model (where a woman is given a housekeeping allowance by her male partner) and the whole wage model (where the husband gives his wife his whole pay packet, a model that was found only in cases of considerable poverty). The pooling model, which at least on the surface looks more equal, has since the 1980s become the most common one. Couples in the UK seem now to be shifting to a new model of only partially pooling their finances (Pahl 2005; Vogler, Brockmann and Wiggins 2006; Vogler, Lyonette and Wiggins 2008). They may, for example, have a joint bank account for shared expenses, such as the mortgage and bills, but combine this with individual accounts for money that each can do as they like with. More and more couples are also managing their money independently.

These changes clearly reflect the fact that an increasing number of women are working and that independence is now seen as desirable for women as well. While the ostensible reason behind such practices as pooling, partial pooling and independent money management is equality, with both parties seen as contributing to the household income and having equal access to shared or independent resources, in practice these can highlight gender inequalities. Women may find that their partner expects them to pay childcare costs, which in the UK are exorbitant, thus leaving them with little or no personal spending money (Pahl 2005). And men, who tend to earn more, can have greater control over how shared resources are spent.

It would also seem that marriage, and especially the arrival of children, can shift a couple from an independent money management model to a pooling one, moving from an idea of 'my money' to 'our money', indicating that the status of the relationship is reflected in how couples approach money (Burgoyne et al. 2006). This is perhaps understandable given that most mothers go on maternity leave around the birth of the child and that many of them return to work on reduced working hours, leading to a smaller income. In such cases, the family may have to rely more on the father's income to pay shared bills such as the mortgage and mothers might become at least partially financially dependent on the father.

It is also interesting to note that there is now tentative evidence to suggest that same-sex couples are more likely to adopt a partial pooling or independent money management model than to pool their resources completely, let alone adopt a model whereby one partner is the breadwinner (Burgoyne, Clarke and Burns 2011). This indicates that *gender* continues to be important in structuring inequalities within families.

Global chains of care

So far I have discussed the impact that women's increased labour market participation has had on family relationships. But these shifts in family life in the West also have global consequences. Hochschild (2003) notes the emergence of the 'post-production family', particularly in the USA, where an increasing amount of care work is no longer performed by family members but outsourced to professional carers who do the work for money. We have to remember, though, that this is nothing new. The upper classes have traditionally given over many 'family' tasks to paid servants, such as breastfeeding, cooking, childcare, and so on – even dressing. But what is new is that outsourcing is no longer limited to the upper classes but is being done also by 'ordinary' families. An important reason why more families are outsourcing caring tasks is that growing numbers of women have entered the labour market and employees work increasingly long hours. In the Nordic states, though, in contrast to countries such as the USA and to an extent the UK, the welfare state has taken over some of the functions such as childcare, and these services need not be bought on the private market.

Thanks to globalization and the continuing 'colonization' of the Global South by the Global North, these shifts are also being felt in other parts of the world. A large number of

Childcare arrangements demonstrate the complexities of family, gender and money. The high costs of childcare can mean that some women are expected not to return to work, or at least not full time. Increasing childcare needs have also led to an increase in migrant female workers to meet this demand, perpetuating the female care-giver role for these migrant workers. (© Emily Goodstein/Flickr)

Third World women work in the West as maids, nannies, and so on – about half of the world's migrants are women, many filling the care gap created when Western mothers enter the labour market. This in effect constitutes an 'importation of care and love from poor countries to rich ones' (Hochschild 2003: 186), which in turn poses a 'care drain' on poor countries. This is part of a long imperialist pattern of 'extracting resources from the Third World in order to enrich the First World' (ibid.: 194). The irony is that many migrant women end up looking after other people's children while having to pay someone to look after their own children back home. Hochschild calls this a 'global chain of care'. Thus we can see how shifts in our personal lives can have far-reaching ramifications, not just within countries, but globally as well.

SEMINAR QUESTIONS

1 Think about instances where the way in which you have conducted your relationships in the past week has involved the consumption of goods and services. Which institutions outside the family were involved in these transactions, either directly or indirectly?

2 Why do you think that women from the Global South are migrating in such great numbers to the Global North?

CONCLUSION

I have in this chapter explored some of the central issues that are affecting personal lives today, including gender, sexuality and new reproductive technologies. Shifts in these are often in step with and linked to broader social changes, such as variations in the economy and the labour market, and should be understood and interpreted as part and parcel of these. For example, we cannot understand changes in parenting without at the same time exploring the developments in the labour market and social policy that have encouraged women's entry into waged work. I have also discussed how changes in the personal lives of Western people can be felt on a global level, such as the 'chains of care' that have developed between First and Third World countries. A further point that I wish to highlight is that, when it comes to family, it is not enough to look at what people say about their family lives; sociologists must also pay attention to what families *do*. As the example of gender and parenting has demonstrated, parents may 'talk equality' but 'do inequality' when it comes to sharing childcare and housework. Throughout this chapter, I have aimed to temper arguments according to which we are free to choose how we conduct our personal lives and that, as a consequence, we live in a new era where family relationships are being drastically reconfigured. While we can see an increase in choice, our choices are still structurally shaped, as shown, for example, by the continuing gender inequalities in the home and in the labour market. In addition, traditional notions of what family is and how families should be continue to hold considerable sway.

Where to next in the field of families and intimacies? Far from being 'dead' or tired, families and personal life constitute a vibrant, ever shifting field of study. Changes in both legislation and family practices mean that our understanding and experiences of what 'family' means never stand still. An emerging field of study is one that focuses on the impact that information and communication technologies (ICTs) are having on our relationships. Developments in ICTs mean that we are able to keep in touch with people across vast distances in real time and through ever increasing means, giving rise to new terms such as 'mediated intimacy' and 'mobile intimacy' – meaning that we can perform intimacy on the move through (increasingly portable) technological media such as mobile phones and computers (Sawchuk and Crow 2012; Hjorth and Lim 2012). Key issues under debate are whether or not ICTs are having a profound impact on how we relate to and interact with other people and whether social networking sites such as Facebook are changing our notions of what a 'friend' is (Agosto, Abbas and Naughton 2012, Livingstone 2008), while others are interested in exploring how these new ways of staying in touch are changing the experiences of transnational families (Wilding 2006), the role that technologies can play in close relationships (Lasén and Casado 2012), and how parents and children negotiate the use of new technologies such as mobile phones (Clark and Sywyj 2012).

Further likely issues that will shape our personal lives are the continuing effects of globalization. As the number of people moving from one country to another grows, transnational families are becoming increasingly prevalent and will continue to find creative ways to keep their family links going, for example with the help of ICTs. Transnational migration is also likely to have an impact on cultural understandings of what constitutes 'family', both in countries of origin and in 'host' countries. Furthermore, the recent global economic crisis has demonstrated how our lives are becoming more globally connected, and many families across the world are faced with the problem of how to support themselves as jobs are lost and austerity measures make themselves felt. There are also likely to be continued changes in gender and parenting, as the generation of children who are being brought up today under the 'new fatherhood' discourse will gain a somewhat different view of what it means to be a man and a woman than the current generation of parents did. The issue of same-sex marriage and parenting is on the ascendancy, and the fight for marriage rights is likely to continue for as long as legislation distinguishes between same-sex and opposite-sex couples. In addition future developments in new reproductive technologies will no doubt continue to influence our understandings of how families are 'made' and who counts as kin. Perhaps the one constant that we have seen throughout this chapter, and which is likely to continue, is that, despite shifts in how people do family and lead their personal lives, close family-like relationships remain important.

SEMINAR QUESTIONS

1 Explain, with reference to examples, why, 'when it comes to family, it is not enough for sociologists to look at what people say about their family lives but should also pay attention to what families *do*'.

2 Discuss the view that 'family-like' relationships are becoming as important as families related by blood and marriage.

3 What are the most significant changes and the most significant continuities in family and personal life over the last half century or so?

FURTHER READING

▶ Morgan, D. (2011) *Rethinking Family Practices* (Palgrave Macmillan). In this book, Morgan discusses in depth and extends his famous 'family practices' approach, providing examples of studies that have utilized this.

▶ Dermott, E., and J. Seymour (eds) (2011) *Displaying Families: A New Concept for the Sociology of Family Life* (Palgrave Macmillan). This edited collection builds upon Finch's influential concept of 'family display', showcasing a number of empirical studies that have used the concept.

▶ Jamieson, L., R. Simpson and R. Lewis (eds) (2011) *Researching Families and Relationships Reflections on Process* (Palgrave Macmillan). An excellent resource for students who are thinking about doing a research project on families or relationships, with a number of contributions by key researchers in the field.

▶ May, V. (ed.) (2011) *Sociology of Personal Life* (Palgrave Macmillan). This is the first textbook on the sociology of personal life, covering topics such as families, same-sex relationships, consumption, public space and politics.

▶ Ryan-Flood, R. (2009) *Lesbian Motherhood: Gender, Families and Sexual Citizenship* (Palgrave Macmillan). Ryan-Flood provides an overview of existing research into lesbian parenting and extends the debate by exploring how lesbian mothers are both doing and undoing traditional families.

Section E
The State, Violence, Crime and Control

There are strong themes linking the chapters in this section. All, to a greater or lesser extent, are concerned with the state, and all involve some discussion of violence (whether violence by states, violence against states, or acts of violent criminality committed between citizens). States and violence are connected in Weber's widely used definition of the state as 'a human community that (successfully) claims the *monopoly of the legitimate use of physical force* within a given territory' (Weber [1919] 1946). Violence is the central theme of Siniša Malešević's chapter (chapter 18), which examines several forms of organized violence, including war, genocide and terrorism. Robert Reiner (chapter 19) discusses violent (as well as non-violent) crime, and Michael S. Drake (chapter 17) considers the role of violence in state formation, violence and state legitimacy, and violence as a source of power.

The state is also a key aspect of all three chapters. The section starts with Drake's discussion of the relationship between different forms of power and the state. Organized violence, as considered by Malešević, is of course often carried out by states, and certainly states are responsible for most large-scale violence. Reiner's chapter (chapter 19) examines the concepts, causes and control of crime and shows how it is often problematized in terms of individual deviance (both in the media and in many positivistic theories of crime). However, states, of course, make crime possible by passing laws and then criminalize certain individuals by applying those laws. The efforts of states to control crime through formal social mechanisms (such as policing and imprisonment) are important for understanding crime and crime rates. Furthermore, the actions of states may be seen as criminal. States may break international law (through acts of genocide, for example). They also operate in ways that may be regarded as criminal by critical criminologists, who regard acts as criminal if they produce social harms rather than if they are against the law (see the discussion of zemiology in chapter 19). The ability of states to exercise power, secure conformity from populations, meet challenges to their authority and monopolize violence are key to all these chapters, then, although they are dealt with in quite different ways.

In chapter 17, Drake examines the claim of Zygmunt Bauman (1989) that power and politics have become separated. He points out that there has been a strong association between the state and power since medieval times in Europe, and it has until recently been widely assumed that state power would continue to grow. The development of state power has been closely related to the control of violence. Norbert Elias ([1939] 2000) saw the state as developing through a civilizing process in which warrior nobles were forced/persuaded to give up their use of violence. Charles Tilly (1992) views the state as cementing power through a form of 'protection racket' (promising protection from the violence of others in return for payments). States exercise power on many levels, from international relations to control over the bodies of its citizens (for example, through forced sterilization, mass starvation or executions). However, the power of the state has been threatened by processes of globalization, which make it more difficult to achieve loyalty from citizens (through national identity), collect taxes or monopolize violence. States are much less likely to fight wars against other states than in the past, and many states struggle to maintain international legitimacy when facing internal insurrection. The constituted (or established) power of the state can be threatened by constituent power (establishing power) in revolutions, such as those of the Arab Spring, or in social movements, such as Occupy. Furthermore, as well as facing these challenges, there is increasing awareness from social scientists (as a result of the work of Foucault) that power is diffuse and closely linked to knowledge and discourse (as much as to the use of force). At best, the state has to share power with other groups (for example professionals). However, at the same time as facing all these challenges and threats, the state is able to increase the surveillance and monitoring of its citizens. This is often justified in terms of the need for greater security in the face of terrorism. Consequently, states 'retain the ability to oppress, to monitor, to inflict violence and destruction from an individual micro-scale . . . to the macro-scale' (for example in Syria). In the face of globalization, though, the state is 'creaking at the seams, buckling under pressure, able to buttress itself only by forming transnational blocks which fundamentally change the nature of the component states.'

Malešević in chapter 18 also looks at the changing role of the state in relation to violence and agrees with Drake that, in the development of nation-states in the nineteenth and twentieth centuries, there was a growing 'interdependence of state, society and warfare'. This, along with the industrialization of warfare and the mass mobilization of civilians, allowed states to wage the two world wars of the twentieth century with unprecedented destruction. However, states have not waged war on the same scale in recent decades, nor have they monopolized the use of force. Just as Drake does not see the state as containing and monopolizing power in the way that it used to, Malešević argues that organized violence cannot be understood solely in terms of the actions of states. Methodological nationalism – treating states and the societies with which they are associated as unitary actors – is no longer credible. This is because 'wars, revolutions, genocides, insurgencies and terrorism often involve complex networks of social actors and organizations that regularly transcend or criss-cross the borders of specific nation-states.'

Unlike the study of the state and of crime and deviance, the study of organized violence is not a well-established area of sociology. Malešević argues that sociology has a crucial role to play in understanding the cultural, economic and, most of all, political factors that help to explain violence. The political embraces many non-state actors who pursue political ends through violence, such as terrorists and (some) revolutionaries. The most extreme of all forms of organized violence – genocide – often results from the actions of rival groups from different ethnic backgrounds as they fight to establish a new state and seek to establish that they represent 'the people' by wiping out their rivals. Terrorism tends to have far fewer victims than genocide but often attracts more publicity. Terrorist acts tend to be committed in opposition to states by non-state actors and can be explained, according to Malešević, by a combination of 'complex and historically contingent phenomena' and 'micro-sociological dynamics'. These dynamics make terrorism a surprisingly middle-class phenomenon. If terrorists threaten the state's monopoly over the use of force (and even of *legitimate* force if they enjoy widespread popular support) then human rights discourse challenges the state's monopoly over the protection of its citizens. Human rights are seen as transcending the social rights provided in return for responsibilities to states (such as obeying the law). The increasing importance attached to universal human rights could be linked to declining state sovereignty as well as being a response to the abuse of human rights by many states. Malešević concludes that organized violence cannot be understood without sociological perspectives, and that the understanding of organized violence is essential to a comprehension of the contemporary world (including power and the state).

Reiner's chapter (chapter 19) discusses crime in general rather than violence in particular, but serious violence, including murder, is covered as part of a more general analysis of changing crime rates. This chapter examines both the explanation of criminality and the state's role in the legal and criminal justice systems. Early positivist criminologies tended not to see the role of the state as an issue and concentrated on the motivation and causation of individual criminality. The role of social audiences who might label acts and individuals as criminal was first highlighted by labelling theory in the 1960s, but a particular focus on the state in these processes came with the development of critical and radical criminology. *Policing the Crisis* (Hall et al. 1978) was a case in point, with its emphasis on the role of the state in criminalizing young black male 'muggers' in response to a crisis of legitimation for the British state.

Over recent decades 'law and order' has been heavily politicized, and Reiner considers how 'law and order' politics has become both a party political issue and integral to the ideology of neoliberal societies. He examines how a crime-control consensus has developed in the UK that treats crime and disorder as major threats to society, justifying ever greater levels of surveillance and 'tough' punitive policies. There are close links here with Drake's discussion of 'securitization' in chapter 17 and the way many states maintain their ability to monitor and punish citizens even as other forms of power may be on the wane. Whether law and order policies have had much effect on the incidence of law- breaking is highly contested, but Reiner argues that the 'adoption of protective equipment and preventative routines by crime-conscious citizens' may have had more impact than increased incarceration and zero-tolerance policing. Despite the notoriously unreliable nature of crime statistics, Reiner does believe that there has been some drop in 'street crime' since the early 1990s, but he argues that it can only be explained with reference to social and economic change as well as changes in law and order policies and crime prevention. Reiner maintains that, since the underlying drivers of criminality (such as consumerism and inequality) have not been fundamentally addressed, it is questionable whether the state will be able to keep the lid on crime indefinitely.

Reiner's chapter gives a flavour of how macro-changes in the nature of the state and historical changes in the nature of violence are connected to the individual experience of crime (whether as victims or offenders). In addition to illuminating the relationship between the individual and structural change, these chapters all have the merit of offering a historical perspective. Long-term trends in crime, the origins and development of states, and changes in the nature of violence over time are all addressed. If at one time the state seemed to have largely succeeded in monopolizing the legitimate use of violence, it now has to address threats to its legitimacy from many directions, ranging from crime to terrorism and allegations of human rights abuses. By taking the long view, all these chapters have succeeded in putting these problems in a historical perspective and showing how trajectories of social change are essential to understanding contemporary social worlds.

17

POWER AND THE STATE

flourishing union, divorce or metamorphosis?

MICHAEL S. DRAKE

CONTENTS

INTRODUCTION

THE PHILOSOPHER AND SOCIOLOGIST Zygmunt Bauman has recently argued that power has become separated from politics (and by implication from the state) in today's world. This is a momentous claim, especially from a theorist whose previous work has included a sociological study of the Holocaust (Bauman 1989) – one of the most heinous and extreme examples of the power of the modern state, when between 1942 and 1945 the German Nazi regime, in control of the German state institutions and occupying more than half of Europe, implemented a plan to kill the continent's entire Jewish population, numbering millions. That project was, as Bauman points out, a version of the function of the state in modernity as the most effective means through which human beings could realize their notion of an ideal society. The state has been central to sociology because it has had the unique power to command life and death, to order its subjects to die for it, or to kill some of them selectively, but also to promote, enable and shape life in unprecedentedly productive and beneficial ways. The state in modern societies validates life bureaucratically, through the surveillance of its citizens from birth to death. The resulting state statistics are the empirical bedrock of sociology, thereby framing 'society' by the boundaries and jurisdiction of the nation-state. Within national state societies, politics becomes the contention of power through control of the state.

Today, however, Bauman argues that power has evaporated from the state, with 'the ever more visible divorce between power (that is, the ability to have things done) and politics (that is, the ability to decide which things need/ought to be done). The two abilities, conjoined for a few centuries in the institutions of the nation-state, inhabit now, in the result of globalization processes, two different spaces' (Bauman 2012). In this chapter I will trace the background to and the current context of Bauman's argument, explaining why it is significant, what basis there is for it in our actual globalizing world and what the implications are. Finally, I will refer both to recent events and to recent developments in sociological theory which suggest that it is a flawed claim, only part of the picture.

CLASSICAL SOCIOLOGY OF THE STATE AND POWER

Weber on the state and authority

It is difficult but necessary to discuss the state in the abstract, so that the concept covers a wide range of different regimes and ideological plans. If we refer to a particular state, such as the USA, we may develop a definition that does not apply to all modern states, because some, such as the People's Republic of China, are arranged differently. However, all modern states do share basic characteristics which a sociological, general definition of the state can attempt to identify.

> Sociologically, the state cannot be defined in terms of its ends. There is scarcely any task that some political association has not taken in hand, and there is no task that one could say has always been exclusive and peculiar to those associations which are designated as political ones: today the state, or historically, those associations which have been the predecessors of the modern state. Ultimately, one can define the modern state sociologically only in terms of the specific means peculiar to it, as to every political association, namely, the use of physical force . . . we have to say that a state is a human community that (successfully) claims the *monopoly of the legitimate use of physical force* within a given territory. Note that 'territory' is one of the characteristics of the state. (Weber [1919] 1946)

This definition has been formative for sociology and political science. However, this narrow interpretation, that the state is ultimately comprised of force (state-legitimated violence), has been taken up only by anarchists and libertarians, more usually in polemic than in rational analysis.

Weber ([1922] 1992) additionally pointed out that violence alone is an unsustainable form of domination. In order to endure, the subordination that can be produced through coercion has to become voluntary. Those subject to power have to acquiesce in their own submission, to give their obedience willingly, if the immediate domination that can be achieved through violence and coercion is to become a sustainable form of power. Weber calls this process 'legitimation'. In pointing out that power is never simply a quality of structures or institutions but results only from processes underpinning them, Weber undercuts an entire tradition of theorizing in which sovereignty, the quality of overarching power, was seen as resulting from purely political or juridical relations. That tradition can be traced back to the absolutist monarchies of early modern Europe, where the sovereign was seen as appointed by God, through Reformation arguments which replaced the will of God with the rule of law, and finally to the will of the people. However, for Weber, these formulae for power are not adequate in themselves but always the outcome of social processes of legitimation.

In contrast to the purely formal conditions traced by political science, Weber defines three *social* sources of legitimate authority: tradition, charisma and legal rationality. All three exist in tension with one another, and Weber thus provides an analytical framework for analysing power struggles. In the first case, authority is ascribed to a figure or an institution because it conforms with tradition. The resulting power is clearly circumscribed and limited, and usually socially conservative, resistant to and even repressing tendencies to change in new forms of social life. Traditional authority can be challenged by charismatic authority, where legitimation is ascribed to a figure or an institution (e.g., a revolutionary party can acquire charisma) because it successfully lays claim to extraordinary qualities. Those qualities transcend the ordinary demands of life as it is known in that society and demand a complete revision of society and the way of life of its subjects. Christianity was such a force in the ancient Roman Empire, and even today religious fundamentalisms command charismatic authority, making demands on their followers in the political sphere (traditional religion, by and large, today restricts its authority to the private sphere and is often perceived with hostility by fundamentalists, for whom religion is a source of authority ultimately transcending all others). However, Weber argues that charismatic authority rarely persists in the long term without either itself becoming tradition or else becoming the third form of legitimate authority he identifies: legal-rational authority. Legal-rational authority is legitimated by a general recognition throughout society that an overall system of laws and rules makes sense. Action which complies with law is therefore seen as legitimate. A simple example would be the way that drivers stop at red traffic lights even when there is nothing coming the other way, because they know by reason that these rules operate effectively to ensure the safety of all road users only if everyone observes them without exception. Legal-rational authority will therefore hold more strongly in individualized societies, where subjects operate on the basis of rational choice. Arguments for causes such as social justice have to be advanced in such societies in terms that emphasize the function of reforms for the whole of society, and therefore for each member, rather than on the basis of transcendent or traditional values.

The authority of the modern state is for Weber based in legal-rational authority, which legitimates the state monopoly of violence. Weber throughout his writings gives a number of alternative definitions of the modern state, which can be summarized as the durable form of political administration dominating a particular territory and its population. However, to say that the state is a form of political administration simply begs the question What is political administration? We can understand Weber to mean the administration (the organization and management) of the non-economic relations in society. It is the extensiveness of this role and the way in which it is accomplished which differentiates the modern state from earlier forms of state (e.g., patrimonial, feudal) and from other forms of political administration (such as religious organization). Only the modern state operates according to a purely instrumental rationality, concerned (at least in principle) simply with getting the assigned job done within the law, and not with people's feelings, status, reputation, wealth, poverty or anything else except where those are themselves the object of state policy.

Marxism on the state and ideology

The Marxist analysis of the state is quite different. Marx himself never developed a theory of the state as such, and it has been left to those who have developed and applied his work to infer a theory of the state from his political economy. That theorization was most influentially developed by Lenin, picking up the remark by Marx and Engels in *The Communist Manifesto* that the modern state functions as the 'executive committee' of the bourgeoisie. Like Weber, Lenin and other Bolsheviks such as Trotsky emphasized the state's repressive capacity, expressed in Lenin's formulation that the authority of the state is underpinned by 'special bodies of armed men' (Lenin [1918] 1992).

However, for the Marxist theory of the state, as for Marxism in general, a problem is posed by the apparently willing acquiescence of workers in both their own exploitation by capital and their own oppression by the state. Some Marxists resolved this problem by integrating a Weberian perspective on legitimation with Marxist ideas about ideology and class consciousness, in which the state's bureaucratic rationalization is presented as a process complementary to capitalist commodification (Lukács [1922] 1971; Adorno and Horkheimer [1947] 1997). However, later Marxist theorists took up the concept of hegemony as an alternative explanation. Hegemony is not a term used regularly by Marx but was introduced by Antonio Gramsci in his writings while imprisoned in Mussolini's Italy in the 1930s (Gramsci 1971a). Hegemony is often misunderstood as a term for dominant ideology, but Gramsci used the term to describe a more fluid and less determined situation, where ideological viewpoints compete within society. For hegemony to be achieved, it is enough that most workers accept some key elements of bourgeois ideology (most critically, the necessity of capitalism) and acquiesce to a degree that enables the system to perpetuate itself, rather than that they adopt all bourgeois ideology as 'false consciousness'.

Other Marxist explanations of the state draw upon this concept because they explain capitalism's social legitimacy, or the acquiescence of the oppressed in their own oppression, in terms of the functions of the state. These explanations seemed particularly relevant in the era when the welfare state appeared to be becoming the

What is it that makes us obey authority, such as not crossing police lines? Is it our trust in the rational organization of the state and the benefit of its rules in the long run? Or are we subject to the rules of capitalist oppressors who seek to protect their own property and interest? (© Matt S/Flickr)

normal form of state for advanced capitalist societies. The welfare state produced ideological hegemony because it made the state appear to cater to the interests of the working class, with state provision of education, health care and social insurance. However, Marxist critical thinkers (e.g., the debate between Miliband and Poulantzas 1972) variously pointed out that those provisions also served capitalism and functioned to procure an educated and healthy workforce for willing exploitation in a stable social context, as well as this expanded state providing a market for capitalist goods and services, all funded out of general taxation rather than out of profits.

That approach has most recently been developed further by Jessop (1990, 2002), who accommodates the deviation from that model by states (even the archetypal welfarist states of Scandinavia) in the late twentieth- and early twenty-first-century era of neoliberalism, where the welfarist function is marginalized. Jessop emphasizes the state as what political scientists call an 'essentially contested concept', which means its functions are not fixed but vary across cultural, political and historical context. For Jessop, the definitive permanent feature of the modern state is as a social relation, mediating between the class forces of the bourgeoisie and the proletariat, the balance of which therefore determines the actual form and function of the state at any given time. The Marxist explanation can then be extended to explain the late twentieth-century neoliberal erosion of welfare-state provision and non-Western economies where the welfare state is almost non-existent, such as India, Indonesia, Korea and Brazil. However, those explanations remain dependent on the notion of constant social forces of classes as discrete entities. In broad terms, Jessop's reformulation of Marxist state theory compromises Marxism as a total view of society, since his model has to allow that class composition may change historically, as some have argued has been the case since the post-industrialization of the late twentieth century (Crook, Pakulski and Waters 1992; Negri and Scelsi 2008). A post-industrial 'balance of class forces' will be quite alien to the Marxist notion of a society comprised essentially of the bourgeoisie and the proletariat and shaped by their struggle. Jessop can only adapt the Marxist model to contemporary conditions by incorporating some of the elements of the Weberian perspective, in which the state is fundamentally characterized as a social relation of domination in a situation of continuous and fluid competition for power by collective fractions within society, regardless of the particular class composition of society as a whole.

The Marxist perspective, even when updated to take account of historical change, lacks an analysis of power. Its strength in ideological analysis is often developed to substitute for that, with the argument that the state provides a means of ideological control, as the arbiter of meaning for society in and through its regulation of social institutions (e.g., of education, media, or public behaviour). In this analysis, ideology serves the same role in the sociological explanation of power as Weber's analysis of legitimation, since ideology is seen as providing a framework (or hegemony) of predominant ideas, defining the limits of what is possible for

BOX 17.1 WORKERS' PARTIES

The German Social Democratic Party was founded in 1875 with a revolutionary Marxist programme but came to understand the transition from capitalism to socialism in evolutionary terms, and in 1914 the party's elected representatives supported the German war effort. This resulted in the split of a minority led by Rosa Luxembourg and Karl Liebknecht, both of whom were murdered during the failed 1919 Spartacist uprising, which they had organized, by militia operating on behalf of a Social Democratic government. In their reconstruction after the Nazi era, the SPD dropped even the rhetorical claim to pursuit of a long-term replacement of capitalism.

In the UK, the Labour Party never officially endorsed a revolutionary socialist programme, although the potential to influence it in more radical directions attracted those committed to more radical politics. However, the party's historical refusal to endorse alternatives to capitalism was made officially explicit in New Labour's rejection of Clause IV of the party constitution, which had called for the ultimate goal of 'common ownership of the means of production, distribution and exchange'.

More recently, the policies of the Workers' Party in Brazil and the much vaunted socialism of Hugo Chavez in Venezuela achieved their mass support base among the working class largely by accommodation to global capitalism, in order to redistribute wealth through the state. But those policies result in the classic crisis of clientilism (securing the votes of social groups by policies favouring that group), witnessed in the recent mass riots in Brazil against the Workers' Party-led coalition government. The immediate focus of the rioters' resentment was the vast sum being spent on developing infrastructure to host the World Cup, producing the most unlikely event of Brazilians rioting against soccer!

society. Under the hegemony of bourgeois ideology, radically critical ideas of social alternatives may be formulated, but they appear incredible because the abolition of capitalism and its relations of production appears to be unrealistic and hence politically implausible. The result is that, even where working-class parties exist and generate mass support, they tend to operate policies which leave the underlying, determinant relations of production unchanged. This can be supported by manifold examples of political parties which began with radical ideological programmes but which compromised themselves the closer they came to government office.

SEMINAR QUESTIONS

1 Does political ideology determine state policy?
2 Is the welfarist state a thing of the past?
3 What are the limitations of classical sociology for analysing the state today?

GOVERNMENT, POWER AND BUREAUCRACY

Government, state and power

In a general sociological sense, the tasks of the state are assigned by *government*, which can be any variety of totalitarian or democratic regime; the essential administrative form of the state remains whatever kind of regime governs. Even the Leninist project of a 'worker's state' reverted to the same form under the internal pressures of modern society for effective political administration and external pressures of international competition.

In sociological analysis, government (or regime) is a different concept from that of the state. Unlike pre-modern forms, where the household of the ruler was not entirely distinct from the offices of state, in modern states the two are formally demarcated. Modern government refers to executive power, the decision-making process. However, radical perspectives recognize that, as with Marxism, the options of governments and the apparent feasibility of policies are determined by factors extrinsic to the formal decision-making process and even beyond the wider forces and factors which set the agenda for political action. By the 1960s, political sociology and political science were trying to come to terms with the way that the parameters of the political were being extended through the course of the twentieth century by movements for women's and minority rights. With each apparent achievement, the power to effect real change seemed to recede further, remaining out of the grasp of these movements as they progressed. Power therefore always seemed also to lie somewhere else, beyond the formal decision-making itself, producing demands for ever more extensive social change. Lukes ([1974] 2005) analysed these widening spheres of effective political factors as three 'dimensions' of power. The widest of these, which he refers to as the third face of power, sets the background understandings against which problems are formulated and solutions devised and appears similar to the Gramscian concept of hegemony, as indirect factors which delimit the perception of what is possible and what it is necessary to do.

Rather than focusing only on government or executive power and its relation to wider society, however, we also have to consider how the state as the means of government enables and constrains how societies can decide to live. For modern, complex, industrial-era societies,

BOX 17.2 LUKES'S THREE FACES OF POWER

The three faces of power identified by Lukes can be illustrated through the three phases of the women's movement. In the 'first wave' of the women's movement, the aim was to achieve formal equal rights, enabling women to participate directly in elections and thus influence the decision-making process of government. Lukes calls this the first dimension of power. However, the electoral franchise failed to achieve the goal of delivering gender equality in outcomes. 'Second-wave' feminists and women activists pointed out that, across most of the institutions of society, women's issues were simply being sidelined or not recognized as relevant at all. Lukes identifies this issue of setting the agenda for decision-making as the second face of power. The result was a wave of campaigns to ensure that 'equal opportunities' were guaranteed across society as a matter of general principle underpinned by law, so that this general issue would always be on the agenda. However, once again these measures have not resulted in equality in outcomes. For instance, comparable data across the EU, where equal opportunities legislation is mandatory for all member states, show that women statistically earn less than men, suffer more from poverty, poor housing and other indicators of social exclusion, and are less likely to achieve political office or to rise to the top of their careers.

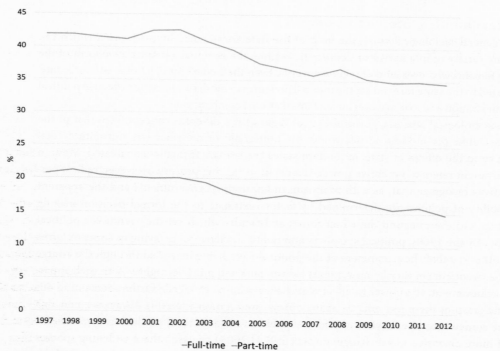

Figure 17.1 Decreasing but still present gender pay gap, UK

Source: Compiled with data from Perfect (2013: 30).

'Third-wave' feminism has identified that the source of this persistent social bias against women lies in background ideas about gender roles in ideology, culture and social structure (e.g., in the expectation that it will be women who look after children, the sick or the elderly, and the socially structuring effects of that general social expectation). Lukes calls this the third face of power – the commonly accepted background understandings and assumptions that form the cognitive and structural context in which it is decided exactly what constitutes an issue that needs to be addressed in the first place.

Table 17.1: **World and regional averages of women in parliament, situation as on 1 January 2010 (%)**		
	Single or lower house	**Upper house or senate**	**Both houses combined**
World average	**19.0**	**17.8**	**18.8**
Nordic countries	42.1	--	42.1
Americas	22.1	22.5	22
Europe (Nordic countries included)	21.8	19.8	21.4
Europe (Nordic countries not included)	19.9	19.8	19.9
Asia	18.7	16.4	18.5
Sub-Saharan Africa	18.4	20.4	18.7
Pacific	13.2	32.6	15.3
Arab states	10.1	7.6	9.5

Source: United Nations (2010).

the state appeared essential to coordinate the multifarious activities of society as a whole (see box 17.3). I will discuss later how it became apparent that the *nation*-state afforded the most effective scale for such political administration of modern social life.

BOX 17.3 WHEN STATES COLLAPSE

The apparent necessity of the state for modern societies can be illustrated by two examples. After the end of the Second World War, the de-Nazification policy applied to Germany had to be curtailed because so many officers of the state had been Nazi Party members, whether in order to keep their jobs or out of ideological commitment. These state officials had to be excused their past party affiliation in order that the Allied governments of occupation had a functioning state apparatus at their disposal. More recently, the obliteration of the Iraqi state by the 'shock and awe' strategy of the Allied invasion in 2003 created social chaos which has still to be resolved, apart from the much more widely recognized problem of the political vacuum created by the elimination of Saddam Hussein's Ba'athist Party apparatus. Not only was the government regime toppled and its executives deposed from positions of power, but the structures, resources and offices and even the archives of government were destroyed. From the invasion to this day, Baghdad, previously a modern city, suffers from chronic problems with the supply of water, electricity and sanitation because of the destruction of infrastructure and the Planning Ministry in the spectacular aerial bombardment preceding the Allied invasion in March 2003.

What is the state?

As Weber points out, the state cannot be defined by its functions or ends: some states have no health or education service but oversee those provided by private enterprise. A state may have no standing armed forces (e.g., Iceland), and one can imagine a state which does not even run its own police force but subcontracts the enforcement of law and order to private service providers. Currency and weights and measures in common use may be those of a powerful neighbour or predominant trade partner. The function of the judiciary is conventionally incorporated into the modern state, but a judiciary can exist independently of a state, and in pluralist democratic countries citizens may voluntarily subject themselves to a range of subordinate legal systems in their religious, career or political affiliation. However, it is characteristic that the modern state functions bureaucratically, as Weber said, 'without regard for persons', which is why it was already being described in the nineteenth century as 'a cold monster' by the philosopher Friedrich Nietzsche, whose work informed Weber's sociology.

The modern form of the state was analysed by Weber as characterized by ideal-type bureaucracy. For Weber ([1919] 1946: 196–240), bureaucracy in its 'ideal type', or generic form, is characterized by formal rationality, on which it depends for the legitimacy of its administration as legal-rational authority. The state's authority is supported by a particular institutional and ethical structure, organized on a continuous basis, with tasks divided into clearly demarcated functions and officials strictly separating their work from their private interests, thus ruling out corruption. Written rules and continuous monitoring within a meritocratic career structure ensure that officials follow the rules and do not pursue their own private interests to enrich or otherwise gain advantages for themselves through their work. The effect, however, is depersonalizing and even dehumanizing. The ethical effect of bureaucracy on society is contentious, with views ranging from that of du Gay (2000), who argues that bureaucracy is a necessary basis for a democratic and a fair society, instilling virtues of public service, to Bauman (1989), who points out that bureaucratic rule compliance was a necessary condition for the Holocaust, sidelining ethical considerations. Weber himself reasoned that bureaucracy was ambivalent. His analysis is presented as an ideal type, and in reality variations or alternatives to this form are widespread, but the tendencies of modern bureaucracy are always towards meritocracy (because it aims to be rationally efficient) and impersonality (because it takes decisions on the basis of rules rather than personal considerations). Bureaucracy tends to iron out differences and channel divergences.

We can therefore identify some general characteristics of modern states, even if there are frequent exceptions, as a kind of 'ideal-type' concept, a concept of the state which not only inheres in sociological jargon but forms both an ideal and an expectation in real life. Modern states are expected to be bureaucratic and therefore impartial, objective. The policies they implement may be severely biased by the ideology of government, but the state itself is expected to apply those rules 'without regard for persons'. Many modern states are corrupt, but the perception that this is the case requires the concept of the impartial bureaucratic state as its reference point, as the norm for how states *should* operate. Modern states are expected to have clear territorial borders, which they can police; states are assumed to hold a monopoly of the legitimate means of violence and to provide protection for their citizens under the laws of that state; states are assumed to regulate the conventions necessary for market transactions (e.g., coinage, time, weights and measures); and states are assumed to monitor and regulate their populations, economies, social order, culture and even religion (Scott 1998; Giddens 1985).

Not all states perform all of these functions in the same way or with the same degree of effectiveness, but the general template functions as the norm for modern societies. Confronted with almost any problem, the first reaction became 'Why doesn't the state do something about it?', a refrain that is still frequent today – although, according to critical commentators such

In the UK, immigration is a topic of heated public debate, with some people suggesting the state is not in control of immigration and failing to perform its functions as they see them. Where, in previous decades, greater international cooperation was sought through the founding of organizations such as the European Union, the latter is also under attack and vulnerable to democratic deficit. (© Ian Glover/Flickr)

as Bauman and Beck, the state has become in this regard a 'zombie' institution, still shaping the horizon of our expectations and demands, but hollowed out of power and no longer able to accomplish the functions expected of it. One result of this has been a 'democratic deficit' which has affected most modern democracies in the form of voter apathy and/or disillusionment (Crouch 2004; Hay 2007; Drake 2010). To date, no alternative object for popular demands has emerged at the national level, and the global economic crisis, which radically disempowers any political authority, also seems to affect 'postnational constellations' – such as the EU – which some saw as taking up the functions of the nation-state on a more effective scale (Habermas 2001, 2012).

Power and the state

Ever since the emergence of the state from the institutions of European medieval society, there has been an implicit association of the state with power. The state appeared to be the centre and even the generator of power in modern societies: whoever controlled the state wielded power in society and could increase their power through the state. Therefore, organizations and ideologies seeking to change society focused on gaining control of the state apparatus. Power in modern society had grown with the state, along with expertise that had developed in response to its requirements, so that, by the twentieth century, states were able to manage their territories, economies and populations on every scale, from international relations, where the state interacted as a personified entity with other similar states, right down to the micro-management of the bodies of its individual subjects – for instance, in the policies, informed by eugenic science, of forcible sterilization of selected individuals that were carried out in many countries during the first half of the twentieth century. Utilizing and informed by specialist expertise across a

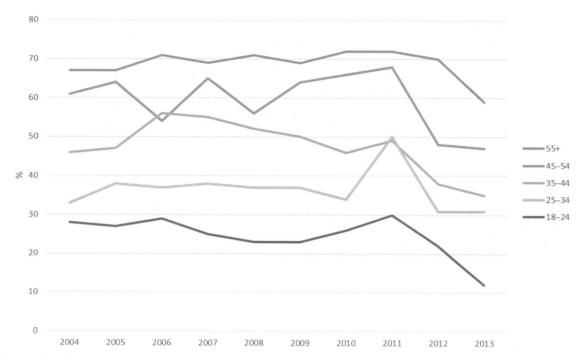

Figure 17.2 Proportion of respondents saying they would be sure to vote in the next elections, by age, 2004–2014

Source: Compiled with data from the Hansard Society (2014).

huge range of fields, from childrearing to urban planning, the modern state not only acted on the inert body but also sought to shape the consciousness of its subjects, via the media of education, propaganda, and the planning of everyday life through provision of infrastructure and regulation, and even moulding desires and hopes through its services and regulations, extending into the most intimate areas of individual life. Ultimately, the state could require its subjects to give their lives for it, and, in the most extreme instances, twentieth-century states condemned to death large sections of their populations, either by indirect means, such as the mass starvations in Stalin's Russia and Mao's China, or by actually killing them, as in Nazi Germany and the territories it occupied during the Second World War. For those states, informed by scientific expertise, such policies appeared necessary in order for the state to achieve its goals.

However, since the late twentieth century, that implicit assumption of an ever increasing growth of power in the state has been challenged in both theory and reality. Radical developments in the way that we understand power in modern societies have shifted the focus of attention in the study of power away from the state and onto what had hitherto appeared innocuous and even benign expert discourses and practices, which, by defining for us what we are and could be, were shown to operate as exercises of power in ways more subtle and invidious than the power of the state. If control of the state could always be contested politically, politics itself was limited by such expert, authoritative knowledge of what was normal and possible for human beings.

On the basis of this radical understanding of power, political activism since the 1960s has been transformed from struggles for control of the state by conspiratorial cliques into much broader, more diffuse movements, coalescing around issues such as the environment or gender inequality rather than an ideological programme. These social movements have aimed to reform society from within, by changing those ideas of what was possible, of how we could live. In the same period, the scope of any state effectively to pursue its own particular interests in relation to an external environment of other states and global market forces has declined significantly. Today, only 'rogue states' make war autonomously against other states.

SEMINAR QUESTIONS

1 What are the advantages and disadvantages of a modern bureaucratic state?
2 Think about a typical day in your life. How does the state affect your life (directly and indirectly) during the course of a single day?
3 In what ways has the power of the state been increasingly challenged in recent years?

HISTORICAL SOCIOLOGY OF THE STATE

Norbert Elias on state formation

The bureaucratic, sovereign state has become the norm for the world order today, but that norm has a history, arising from historical processes of state formation. Norbert Elias takes the most long-term view of state formation (Elias [1939] 2000), but he does not see the process as accomplished or secured in modernity. For Elias, state formation is an ongoing part of a long-term historical tendency, a 'civilizing process' originating in medieval Northern Europe. Through a narrative account which mixes cultural sources with political developments, Elias shows how a long-term historical tendency for the concentration of power and violence in a central authority is linked to the development of a pacified modern subject predisposed to recoil from violence in everyday life. Modern people tend to avoid violence because it has become dysfunctional and repulsive to them, not because they are scared of punitive sanctions, and that enables the state to exercise a successful monopoly of legitimate violence. There is a correlation rather than a disjuncture between internal pacification of the psyche and the external pacification of society (Elias and Dunning 2008).

Elias begins his narrative from about 1000 AD, when the dispersal of power in Europe was at its maximum, with monarchs in name only and each knight within their own castle holding hereditary authority over the local village. That knightly nobility engaged in a process of often violent competitive elimination, creating gradually larger territories under each remaining authority and resulting ultimately in the concentration and centralization of power in one single authority dominating a large, integrated territory, over which it held a monopoly of violence. That authority was to become the territorial sovereignty of the modern state, as the sovereign authority of the monarch was replaced in the modern era by the sovereignty of the people, represented in a government and implemented through a state.

Uniquely among historical sociologists, Elias shows how this process of state formation is related to modern national culture, society and individual subjectivity (i.e., the set of predispositions shared by members of a particular society or social location). The warrior nobility was gradually both seduced and coerced into abandoning violence as a means of dispute resolution by their acculturation in the noble courts of the late medieval and early modern eras, where the refinement of manners and self-conduct substituted for aggression as the medium of status competition. Physical violence then came to be considered vulgar, a disgraceful loss of self-control. This occurred in tandem with structural changes in which the warrior nobility were gradually transformed into the civil servants and officer caste of the monarchical state, a role which persisted in Germany into the early twentieth century, with particular consequences for the character of national identity (Elias 1997). The manners of the aristocracy were emulated by the rising class of the bourgeoisie, and theirs in turn by aspirant elements of the industrial working classes. The result of this 'civilizing process' is therefore that modern subjects of a state holding a monopoly of legitimate violence are predisposed to be repelled by physical violence.

Although it produces startling insights and usefully analyses processes of historical development neglected by other historical sociologists, Elias's study of the civilizing process is difficult to apply beyond the scope of his original formulation without adaptation which undermines some of his insights into the European cases. The most sustained application has been to the USA (Mennell 2007). This problem with Elias's work as the basis for a general sociology of the state and modern society is, to be fair, a problem facing all studies which work at the interface between sociology, which seeks general explanations, and history, which seeks to trace particularities. In historical sociology and developmental sociology, this broad issue has been formulated as the issue of 'path dependence', in which accounts of state formation depend on a singular common path. This critical reflection emerged in the context of the Cold War, as a critique of liberal-capitalist models of development that appeared to be contradicted by the development of state and society in countries such as modern China, where very different paths were taken. In the wake of globalization, the concept of modernity has become pluralized, often by tracing the particularities of regional, national or even local paths of development and how these have produced subtly but significantly different variations on modernity (Kumar 2005), a shift anticipated by Elias's interpretation of the peculiarity of the civilizing process in Germany.

From the perspective of modernity, the state appears as the most effective form of political administration, and therefore as rational. However, instrumental efficiency was not always the criterion by which the state was evaluated; it only became so under particular conditions, when the state came to depend on the acquiescence of economically powerful subjects to pay taxes. Early modern capitalists, Charles Tilly has argued, made a rational calculation that the state was the form of administration which best suited their interests, and there emerged an implicit pact between state and capital which was in some places tilted more towards coercion (the state enforcing tax payment) and in others more towards capitalist interests (so the state deliberately assisted capital to expand).

Charles Tilly on state formation

In a radical twist, Tilly points out that the state can be seen simply as a form of protection racket, in which taxation is taken by the power that controls the means of violence in exchange for declining to inflict that violence on the taxpayers while protecting them from the violence of others. In this sense, all states began as 'rogue states', or even in simple territorial warlordism. The successful powers in a process of competitive elimination simply succeeded in legitimating their violence as the defence of society and their extortion as state fiscal policy (taxation). Fundamentally, Tilly argues, there is no effective sociological distinction between the gangster with his thugs and protection racket and the state with its taxes, police and armed forces. Furthermore, just as gangsters compete violently with one another, so 'war makes states and states make war' – warfare is built into a system of nation-states in competition for control of resources and revenues. This approach has been developed further by Michael Mann (2003) in his 'war-for-oil' explanation of the twenty-first-century global struggles that are otherwise misguidedly ascribed to a 'clash of civilizations' (Huntington) between 'Islam' and 'the West', a perspective which assumes that either of these can be considered as actual entities (Huntington 1996).

Refusal to pay tax and violence against the state are more severely punished than other forms of financial wrongdoing and of violence, but Tilly's formula presupposes both that the state can effectively hold tax avoiders accountable and that it can protect its subjects from the violence of others and subject them to its own. Today, perhaps, the pact between the state and other collective social actors has begun to break down, with widespread use of tax-avoidance strategies across many countries by transnational capitalist corporations and challenges to the state's monopoly of legitimate violence from threats to citizens' security by non-state actors such as terrorists and from restrictions imposed on state violence by international human rights treaties. Given the tenacity of terrorism, even when its adherents remain a small clique, and the opportunities opened by globalization, it is unlikely that states will be able to secure the safety of their citizens completely. Indeed, the state today seems able to invoke a climate of fear, and hence demand for its function of security, more effectively than it is actually able to meet that demand. As with combatting tax avoidance, in a globalizing world, single sovereign states cannot accomplish security alone but have to work closely with other states, which requires giving up a degree of sovereignty (such as allowing the right of pursuit across borders, agreeing to extradition, sharing intelligence and even intelligence-gathering, and having joint armed forces, coordinated military procurement, and shared research and development programmes (Hirst 2001), or, in the case of tax avoidance, formulating common policies with other states). The fiscal-military functions of the state were the legitimating principles of state territorial sovereignty, and Tilly's account thus presumes the legal characteristic of sovereignty that it sets out to explain sociologically. In today's world, both those presumptions are questionable.

Where Elias tends to focus on cultural and political aspects of state and social formation, Tilly (1992) traces a symbiotic relationship between the political form of the state and the structures of emergent economic capitalism through three paths of state formation – coercion-intensive, capital-intensive and capitalized-coercion – with the three different kinds of state characterized by the emphasis they place on promoting their national commerce or developing their military force. Through these three different paths, the modern state became the primary form of political organization on a global scale.

Postcolonial states

The flexibility of Tilly's analysis, in comparison to the 'path-dependent' models of the 'modernization' narrative of state formation based on the European historical example, enables it to be applied to non-European, postcolonial state formation of the twentieth century, a process which, with the formation of new states from republics previously federated in the USSR, continued right up to the 1990s. The first wave of twentieth-century postcolonial state formation began in Europe itself with the successes of national liberation struggles dating from the nineteenth century, linking the formation of states such as Ireland (from the UK) and Iceland (from Denmark) genealogically to the national unifications of states such as Germany and Italy, which had themselves subsequently become colonial powers. The sharp break between European state formation and the successes of national liberation movements in the twentieth century is thus questionable. Those movements themselves and the postcolonial states they produced in the wake of European imperialism were shaped by intellectual elites educated in the West by the colonial powers, often as a class fraction intended to administer the imperial colony on behalf of their European overlords (Anderson 1983). Those elites led the national liberation movements of the twentieth century, and the states that resulted from their successes were modelled not on indigenous traditions but on Western ideologies, Western institutions and Western practices. Even where these were given a distinctively national presentation, as most notably in China in Mao Tse-tung's developments of Marxist–Leninist doctrine and its political programme, cultural, political and economic distinctions were applied to a basically Western model, within the form moulded on the Western nation-state and political party, and in the framework of a Western ideology. In this way, the form of the state become globally universalized, so that national sovereignty extended across almost the entire planet, at least in theory, even if the actual authority of the state sometimes failed to reach far-flung and economically and strategically insignificant corners of nation-states both new and old. The nation-state therefore provided the common unit of equivalence which has enabled the development of globalization processes.

The state and national identity

Postcolonial states were modelled on the European state form because it appeared to be the most successful and most rational way of providing political administration for complex industrializing societies, and it therefore had the strongest claim to legitimation. Giddens (1985) conceptualizes the success of the modern territorial state as a 'power-container', not only centralizing power but actively generating it by the containment of resources, enabling surveillance and specialization in the management of those resources in ways unattainable by smaller units in which people must perform multiple tasks. States are also able to supplement this with the development of an ideology of the territorial state and its population as a coherent unity – nationalism, which provides a basis for solidarity between subjects who otherwise appear to share few interests in common and which provides a subjective dimension to the territorial integrity of the modern nation-state.

This construction of a common identity was crucial to the success of the modern territorial state. Scott draws our attention to the way that nation-states tend to homogenize differences among populations, by force if necessary. Throughout the nineteenth and twentieth centuries, minority languages and cultures were actively oppressed in core, democratic nation-states such as France and Britain. Even something as benign as the 1944 Beveridge Report (the blueprint for the British welfare state) ignored regional and class differences across the national territory and its population, so that all citizens were deemed to need the same resources at the same stages in the life cycle, regardless of culture or class. This homogenization extended into the most intimate areas of life. Sexuality, for instance, required opportunity for expression, which meant that housing, infrastructure, education, health services and even the employment market were all to be managed in a way that would make this life opportunity available to all citizens of an appropriate age. However, this apparently benevolent state policy assumed everyone to want the same kind of 'normal' sexual expression, with the same outcome, results which were monitored by the state. Those who did not comply with its requirement were at best outside the structures of state support and at worst could be forced into compliance, as were homosexuals, who up to the 1960s in Britain were criminalized and could be subject to compulsory electroshock therapy in an attempt to 'cure' them of their 'deviance'. Other welfare states went even further in their drive to normalize – staunchly social democratic Sweden, an exemplary beacon of equal opportunities within the norms set out by the state, routinely sterilized its mentally disabled citizens well into the 1970s. Other forms of deviance were similarly subject to normalization or social exclusion.

The modern state sought to socially construct those who were subject to it. That is, it defined the parameters of social norms and policed them. These tendencies of the state to centralize, contain, survey, normalize and homogenize illustrate both the problems it faces in the context of globalization and its enactment of very different forms of power which rendered its authority vulnerable to challenges beyond the usual forms of politics.

SEMINAR QUESTIONS

1 What do we gain through a historical understanding of state-formation processes?
2 How important are differences in histories of nation-state formation for our contemporary world?
3 Identify some parts of the planet where national sovereignty is weak.

THE STATE AND GLOBALIZATION

Globalization has been theorized and studied empirically very extensively over the past two decades. It is conventional to break it down into analytical categories as economic, political, cultural and social globalization. All four of these dimensions of globalization (and perhaps an additional military/security dimension) present challenges to the modern state as an ideal type. Unsurprisingly, the modern state form then comes under the greatest pressure where it is least well developed and where its ideology of nationalism has weakest purchase as a form of social cement that can overcome differences of political ideology, class, ethnicity, lineage, religion, and any other markers which define potential social division. However, those challenges have affected even the most apparently powerful of states, such as the USA and the People's Republic of China.

The state and economic globalization

Economic globalization challenges the state's ability to control its own internal economy and to manage its economic relations with the outside world. Economic autarchy (complete national self-sufficiency) was always an illusory goal, leading at an extreme to such deluded paths as the Nazi Party's occupation of much of Europe and penetration into Eurasia and North Africa in the Second World War in its attempt to secure for itself the resources necessary for a self-sustaining modern economy, as well as to eliminate perceived threats to national political autonomy and cultural purity. Today, the illusion of autarchy persists as a fantasy of petty nationalists. However, economic globalization is generally recognized as unavoidable and even beneficial, and the main adjustment has been a shift in the operations of states towards management of their effects. This in itself is not new: even nineteenth-century imperial states sought to make strategic adjustments in competition with their rivals. However, the globalization of finance that has occurred as the least obvious aspect of economic globalization has perhaps the greatest effects, when, regardless of policies and (apparent) power, all national economies are vulnerable not only to international corporate capitalist enterprises but even to petty non-state actors which are relatively powerless in any conventional sense, such as credit ratings agencies (e.g., Standard & Poor's), whose pronouncements can effectively undermine even multi-state economic management.

The state and political globalization

Political globalization is to a large extent, similarly, an extension of twentieth- and even nineteenth-century trends. Ever since the early modern period, the world has seen a gradual development of a system of states, each dependent on its recognition as a state by others. The modern states system is often traced originally to the Peace of Westphalia, which ended the Wars of Religion that had devastated much of Europe after the Reformation. Since then, the states system has advanced through adoption of the form of the state as the most efficient form of political administration for modern development in all areas of life (for instance, by the postcolonial regimes that replaced imperial domination in the developing world, such as India and Indonesia). The states system also developed, however, through the process of what has been called 'internationalization', where states negotiated and signed treaties creating norms and institutions which constrained them in common. The Geneva Convention was an early example. This process can be seen as leading to the ultimate creation of a level of political action above and beyond the state – for example, in the UN and the EU, to which states have effectively devolved some of their political sovereignty.

Globalization, the state and culture

Cultural and social globalization, because relatively informal, are more difficult to assess, but their impact on everyday life may far exceed the effects of political and economic globalization. Nation-states and the ideology supporting them depended on the imaginary construction of a community in which most members remained anonymous and unknown to one another personally. In this sense, nationalism occupied a category of identity which had previously been achieved only by religion, and was indeed referred to as a form of 'civil religion' by Durkheimian scholars (Bellah 1967). The nation-state needed to be represented as culturally homogeneous, based on shared values, shared understandings and a common body of knowledge. These were never more than claims and always invoked divisions as well as asserting common identity. It is the very normalization and homogenization of identity in the nation-state which Appadurai (1998) sees as the key condition for modern genocide. Indeed, genocide was always a 'final solution' to the problems of creating national identity, from the genocide against the Armenian minority in the early twentieth century by the Ottoman Empire under pressure from modernizing nationalist 'Young Turks' who wanted a state on the European model, through the policies of the German Nazi Party from 1933 in their attempt to revitalize Germany by purging it of its minority elements, to the genocides produced by the re-creation of national identities in the break-up of Yugoslavia in the 1990s.

However, the imaginary social and cultural identity of the modern nation-state has been challenged by two interrelated developments.

Culturally, nation-states have seen the proliferation and flourishing of what is now a global melange of subcultures. Subcultures always existed within and across modern states, but from the advent of consumer society from the mid-twentieth century they have proliferated to such an extent that they have today displaced the bourgeois 'high culture' which used to provide a norm against which other cultural forms were labelled as in some way deviant. High culture today has become simply another niche market, one subculture among many. Simultaneously, minority cultures have asserted themselves within nation-states, and new cultural influences have arrived everywhere through both the migration of people on an unprecedented scale and the opening of culture to the global world of international travel and, more recently, the internet. The hope of identifying and preserving distinctive, indigenous national cultures untainted by 'outside' influences was even in the nineteenth century a fantasy, as national identities were constructed from fragments collected by anthropologists and folklorists, or actually manufactured anew in response to commercial opportunities (Hobsbawm and Ranger 1983).

Gestures at national culture today, whether those of language preservation or commercial representations for tourism, already acknowledge a degree of adjustment to or adoption of

In response to concerns that globalization might be a threat to local cultures, UNESCO now has a fund dedicated to 'Intangible Cultural Heritage', including *frevo*, a form of Brazilian music and dance shown here in Olinda, Brazil. (© Passarinho/Prefeitura de Olinda/Flickr)

global influences (Featherstone 1990), or else take a 'zombified' form such as fascism, knowingly denying the constructedness of the identity and culture with which they choose to identify. This form today is empty of the relevance it had for relatively homogeneous and isolated national populations in the nineteenth and twentieth centuries, where the idea of a given national identity had at least some grounding in common social experience. Eating, listening, looking, reading, dressing, playing, working, loving, believing, and all other aspects of life are today actually lived and experienced through influences which circulate not only at the local or national level but through global connections. Our tastes, our sense of beauty, our desires and our needs have all become irreversibly, and often happily, 'globalized'. However, this may in itself not be anything new; even Neolithic culture, millennia back in human history, is being revealed today as far more migrant across space than was hitherto thought possible. The Neolithic 'revolution' itself appears in today's archaeology as a globalization process, spreading an entirely new way of human life across the world, often connecting and even apparently networking what were hitherto assumed to be discrete, self-contained societies. Globalization has not perhaps altered what we do so much as opened our eyes to see what we do in a new way, changing our perceptions of ourselves and others (Drake 2003). However, we could observe sociologically that, as in the earlier era which discerned national histories in the relics of former times, anthropologists and archaeologists today perhaps tend to see in the past a reflection of themselves and their own globalizing society.

Globalization and the power of the state

Against this backdrop of globalization, states appear increasingly compromised in their scope to act as coherent, sovereign entities. Some have argued that, in fact, the state has become a kind of mid-level agent of globalization processes, actually necessary for globalization (Sassen 2006). In situations of state collapse, the default appears to be at best reversal to local informal organization, at worst the absence of any social order at all aside from militia gangs living off an increasingly disorganized and demoralized civil population (Münkler 2005). Somalia has seen both forms in its long period of statelessness since 1991. However, states are today compelled to comply with the requirements of global economic and political processes and can do little to affect cultural and social globalization. If the nation-state could be imagined as a ship or container afloat on the seas, providing and demanding order of its occupants, that container ship has become a sieve, afloat only because of the effects of ocean currents which buffet it this way and that, even when it ties itself to others to make a raft in the hope of increased stability.

However, even as the power of the state to affect or insulate itself from external factors declines, its power to monitor, survey and regulate its own citizens increases. We conventionally think of power in the sense of 'power over' – power by A to compel or influence B to act according to A's will (Lukes [1974] 2005). This the way the power of the state is usually understood, seeing people as generally following its regulations and orders because they seek to avoid its sanctions (which ultimately include violence as seizure of the body or of property – hence Weber's emphasis on the state monopoly of legitimate violence). In addition, as Weber pointed out, people follow the regulations of a state because they acknowledge the legitimacy of those regulations. The concept of ideology represents the furthest scope of this understanding of power, where we may be unwittingly influenced by representations which cause us to construe a situation and of ourselves in a particular way.

The theory of ideology was developed particularly by Marxist theorists in the twentieth century to explain why the working classes of industrial capitalism had not risen up and over-thrown capitalist relations of exploitation and the entire social and political edifice constructed on that 'base', as Marx and Engels had predicted in *The Communist Manifesto*. However, the analysis of ideology tended to diverge from the individualistic model of power developed by Lukes and other liberal theorists, because capitalist ideology represented the interests of a class which did not itself produce the representations that promoted its worldview as natural and universal. The sociological use of the term 'ideology' thus came to mean something more amorphous, less conspiratorial, than the political ideology of political parties. This sense of ideology as the representation of commonly held assumptions came to indicate the lines of struggle not just against capitalism but against social and cultural normalization and con-straint of all kinds (Marcuse 1964) – ideas taken further by Foucault, who connected power to knowledge, as we will see in the next section.

SEMINAR QUESTIONS
1 What does national identity mean today?
2 To what extent (if any) has the power of the nation-state declined because of globalization?
3 Is the era of the state over? Will the state disappear?

POWER BEYOND THE STATE?

Foucault and power/knowledge
For Foucault, knowledge, as authoritatively accepted definitions of situations and subjects, is already a kind of power, encapsulated in his term 'power/knowledge' (Foucault 1980). This mode of power functions by defining its subject and thereby defines what the horizons of possibility are. While not directly involved in politics as a struggle for 'power over', power/knowledge has immense effects on that struggle and penetrates deeply into everyday life in ways far more insidious than in Weber's or Luke's models of power. Power/knowledge is embedded in 'discourse' (what is written and said about something), but Foucault went beyond a literary concept of discourse to include organizational and career structures, technology, and even the arrangement of bodies and spaces. This broader scope of his concept appears most fully in his work on the origins of modern penal, military and industrial sectors (Foucault 1977), where he develops an understanding of 'disciplinary power' as the way in which power/knowledge is introduced into and structures our everyday lives. The idea was taken up most notably by Giddens (1985) in his analysis of the modern state, but there it tends to become reduced to a description of a form of 'power over', losing the sense of the more pervasive and insidious penetration of power/knowledge into our very understanding of ourselves.

Foucault (1984) first formulated the concept of 'biopower' in an essay reflecting on the his-tory of medicine in the eighteenth century in the context of public medicine, which informed the great infrastructural 'sanitation' projects of the subsequent century and which shaped the provision of health services as we still know them today. Biopower in Foucault's terms refers to an effective alliance between the state and other expert actors in modern societies, most nota-bly the medical profession. Foucault (1978) identified two phases of biopower. The first, from the eighteenth to the early twentieth century, was when the state took up the task of providing collective care for the environment of the body through regulation and surveillance of the health of the population, the condition of housing, the spread of disease, sanitation, working conditions, child development, and many other initiatives. In the second phase, the responsibility for care of the body becomes increasingly devolved to the individual.

We cannot really call medicine 'ideology' in the Marxist sense, and Foucault uses instead the concept of discourse, as a specialist body of statements in which the subject of the discourse is written about, spoken of, discussed and argued over in a particular way. The body is the subject of medical discourse which constructs it as a biological entity. That understanding of the body, and the value ascribed to its health as the ultimate value for society and its individuals, provides the subject for biopolitics in modern society. Where even Marxist perspectives accepted medical knowledge as neutral, Foucault sees it as inherently bound up with power relations, both in its alliance with the state in the modern nexus of biopower and in the sense that the biological definition of the body and the value ascribed to it by medical discourse defines the way we can think of ourselves, and therefore produces our political horizons.

Through their tacit alliance, medicine and the state both advance their own interests, but they do so not by obscuring the real interests of their subject, as the Marxist critique of ideology reasons, but by constructing that subject in the first place. For Foucault, there is no 'real' subject to be liberated, no 'truth' of the body which is repressed by medical discourse and biopower. The effects of discourse, however, do foreclose other possibilities, and Foucault's politics consist in attempting to show how even apparently benign sciences and services foreclose the possibility of thinking and enacting radical alternatives in the way we could live and perceive ourselves and others.

BOX 17.4 THE 'OBESITY EPIDEMIC'

The 'obesity epidemic' of the early twenty-first century in Britain and the USA produces power for both medicine and the state. The medical profession gains access to funding, creates research and career opportunities, and increases its status and power over areas of social life by medicalizing a phenomenon that is really nothing more than a part of the spectrum of possible shapes of the human body and could be construed in many non-pathological ways (for instance, as an indicator of a successful society that can feed all its members or as a form of beauty). The scope of the power of the state is also enhanced, though not in the way we conventionally think of it, as 'power over'. Rather, in pronouncing the individual's responsibility to ensure against obesity of the body, the state becomes a moral legislator for everyday life and self-understanding. In doing so, it also shifts responsibility from the public to the 'private' sphere, from public provision to individual choice, and, in doing that, constructs the subject of the state as a choosing individual rather than as a subject of rights and entitlements to state provision of services. That choosing subject is also told in the very definition of their status (as someone responsible for their own health) what the correct choices are. The sum of power therefore consists not only in the gains of the discursive and political forces involved but also in the production of a subject predisposed not so much to comply, as in the disciplinary society of the industrial era which Foucault had analysed in *Discipline and Punish*, as to conceive of life as a responsibility to choose responsibly.

What Foucault calls 'governmentality' involves an analysis developed and introduced into sociology by Rose and Miller (1992) as 'power beyond the state' (though much of the analysis of governmentality focuses on institutions of or dependent on their association with the modern state). Foucault extended this analysis to include sovereignty, the cornerstone of political science, because it is central to the notion of the state as a self-contained, self-determining unit. Sovereignty is of course, from a realist point of view, a fiction. No nation-state can sustain itself entirely in isolation, even if only because it shares the seas around it with other nation-states. It is therefore never entirely free to act absolutely unilaterally, just as the kings of the pre-modern era did not in reality hold the unbridled power within their realm which the concept of sovereignty was originally formulated to describe. However, this concept enabled the Peace of Westphalia and subsequently other treaties between states which established the conditions for the modern international system of nation-states (Hirst 1997). It is therefore, despite existing only as an ideal, central not only to political science and international relations theory but also to the political structure of the modern world.

Sovereignty

Because of its fictive quality, sovereignty has received little attention from sociologists, who have instead focused on exposing the structures of interest, class and organization which underpin this quality of the state – i.e., its real sources of power. In turn, however, this has predisposed sociologists to associate their endeavours with the nation-state. It is remarkable how the 'founding fathers of sociology' ardently participated in the jingoistic nationalism of the First World War, with Durkheim, Simmel, Weber and others all lending their expertise and advocacy to the war cause of their respective nation-state (Joas 2003). In addition, sociology has conventionally seen the nation-state as the primary unit of analysis, in what is known as 'methodological nationalism' (Chernilo 2007), so that we often speak unreflectively of (for instance) British, French, Moroccan, Japanese society, etc.

Today, globalization challenges the fiction of sovereignty to a hitherto unprecedented degree. The conceptual emperor of modern international world order is being stripped of his clothing, denounced not so much by those on the margins of the crowd as by those in the centre of it, such as the prominent German sociologist Ulrich Beck, who has included the sovereign nation-state in his list of 'zombie categories', units of analysis and social institutions which have become emptied of determinant, precise meaning but continue to function as categories for thought in social science as in everyday life (Beck [1995] 2002). To continue with this example, we know that the definition of the sovereign nation-state today has to be hedged around with multiple qualifications because of the multiple internal and external changes that are summarily conceptualized as 'globalization'. However, the response to this is both popular, operating at the level of everyday life and the politics of the street and online social media, and political, operating through the agencies of the state and political discourse.

On the one hand, the exposure of the ficticity of sovereignty produces as a reaction an intensification of nationalism, now, however, as a pure imaginary, in which the participants know full well that the object of their identification (national culture, institutions, traditions, racial heritage, national independence, economic autonomy, etc.) is fictional but pursue it avidly anyway for the sake of the satisfaction available in the construction of a stable identity (and what can be more stable than an imaginary, fictive identity sealed off from reality?) amid an ever more uncertain world. Such identification also provides the basis for pleasure in projecting all negative qualities onto an Other, as scapegoat and repository of resentment against the failure of reality to match up to the imaginary. This kind of analysis, applying insights from psychoanalysis to a collective subject and combining it with a realist view of the world which is able to recognize these imagined, fictive forces as real in so far as people act as though they were, was originally developed to explain phenomena such as the Rwandan genocide of 1994 (Appadurai 1998) and the wars in ex-Yugoslavia from 1991 to 1995, where people who had hitherto been friendly neighbours, and even intermarried families, became the bitterest of ethnic enemies in the wake of the collapse of the old, forcibly unifying regime of communism (Žižek 1996). This approach can also be applied to the neo-nationalisms of any nation-state and to the viciously xenophobic and often racist postings which spatter the archives of online news comments columns and social media. Very often, those posts resurrect the old prejudices of the imperial past in which both imperial identity and its Other were constructed (Said 2003), projecting them onto ethnic minority populations in contemporary society. In this realm of fantastic identifications, however, the 'markers' of Otherness are not fixed but can be almost any shared characteristic, as in the well-remarked shift of racism from a biological to a cultural referent. Similarly, sectarian markers provide points of reference for collective identification, tribal identities re-emerge from under modern national imagined identity, and entirely new points of reference are created through subcultures or other fantastic imaginings, such as in the religious right of the USA, for whom the identifier is an acceptance that America is a God-given community. Under these conditions, the formation of social identity proceeds not along structural lines but by the same process that Max Weber used to describe the formation of interest groups in a competitive labour market. Globalization, it seems, has produced a competitive market of collective identification in the realm of the imagination.

On the other hand, the political response to the 'erosion' of sovereignty is an intensification of the power of the state in the only area where it can intensify, in a tightening of control over its own populations even as its capacity to act unilaterally to affect its own fate in the world at large has been undermined. This tendency is not necessarily aligned with the popular response. Indeed, mass popular identifications are anathema to this rationalizing process in which internal sovereign power, usually in the form of a governmental executive and its agencies, becomes strengthened against perceived threats from within. The most important critiques of this development have taken their cue from Foucault. In a highly philosophical work, Agamben (2005) has been particularly influential on critical perspectives on state power in the twenty-first century, combining Foucault's analysis of biopolitics and governmentality with insights from Carl Schmitt, a right-wing critic of liberalism. Schmitt took realist analysis to its logical extreme, arguing that democracy and liberalism were effectively a sham, a form of collective self-delusion, while the realities of power and authority lay in the capacity of those in control of the state to make executive decisions. This power, the core of sovereignty, carries forward in the modern era in the form of the 'state of exception', the declaration of a state of emergency which can be issued by any ruling executive, right or left, democratic or totalitarian, in which ordinary political rules and procedures governing the use of power are suspended in order to enable executive and technical decisions and actions to proceed without constraint.

The state, legitimacy and violence

Agamben's work (2000) offers a critical perspective on the expansion of executive power that has accompanied neoliberalism. For such critics, neoliberalism is a façade beneath which power itself defines the logic of action. However, in the twenty-first-century context, that executive power becomes an attribute not only of an executive elite but also of the agencies of state concerned with security, whose scope of operation is today global. It is in this respect that the divorce between power and politics is at its widest, as the security functions of the state become more prioritized, more specialized and technical, and more separated from ideology, consensually accepted as a necessity for executive power. In part, this is a consequence of changes in what was the primary executive function of the state – war.

As the structure of organized violence has changed since the late twentieth century, so the agencies of the state have responded, and the function of the state itself has shifted in relation to its population. The state as a globalized institution has retained its hold on what, for Weber, was the defining characteristic of the sovereignty of the state – the monopoly of legitimate violence. Today that monopoly extends on a global scale. Legitimate force is deployed by states that are recognized as such within the international community. The parameters of that qualification have shifted and today include at least a formal commitment to rule of law and human rights, as well as a recognition of the sovereignty of other states. A state may therefore forfeit its legitimacy in the face of resistance which provokes or exposes faults in the commitments by which it qualifies for recognition by the international community. The Libyan regime of Muammar Gaddafi was one such example. However, an opposition has also to appear as a viable and qualifying alternative in order to garner international support. In some situations, most notoriously that of the Central African Republic, no single force is accorded such legitimacy by the international community, and the result is the dissolution of the state and a condition of continuous warfare between competing rival forces which are themselves prone to division. In such conditions, achievement of sovereign power may be a less attractive proposition for military forces and their commanders than the perpetuation of a state of war itself, in which they are relatively privileged in relation to the civilian population by virtue of their capacity to exercise force to achieve immediate objectives. That situation has been termed 'new war' (Münkler 2005; Drake 2007).

In this context, the state monopoly of violence is very rarely used unilaterally in war against other states. Today, 'war' is rather fought by coalitions of states against regimes who have forfeited the international recognition required by international hegemony or against non-state actors. This shift is expressed in terms of the 'war against terror', initiated in response to the 9/11 terrorist attacks on the USA, or in terms of a 'war against drugs' or against any other phenomenon against which states can unite. However, the effects are not only external. Even while the capacity of sovereign states to act unilaterally is curtailed, these same developments produce an intensification of the state's internal control over its own citizens. Because the state is increasingly globalized, and because all sovereign states need to comply with prevailing tendencies in order to retain international recognition of their legitimate status, so increasing internal control over the state's own citizens becomes a hegemonic norm, a global tendency.

The increased requirement for the validation of individual identity has produced DNA databases, CCTV surveillance of public spaces, facial pattern recognition programs, retinal scan recognition, and other measures enrolling new technologies in social control, all attesting to the biopolitical dimension of the twenty-first-century securitizing state. However, the critical narrative of increasing control and state securitization is positively challenged by the revolutions of the Arab Spring of 2011, just as the revolts of Eastern Europe of 1989 shattered the twentieth-century myth of totalitarian control.

BOX 17.5 SECURITIZATION

Using a Foucauldian analysis of power to supplement the idea of international hegemony, we can recognize discursive conditions to the process whereby states increase control over their citizens. International relations theorists have coined the term 'securitization' to describe the process whereby policy issues become defined as security issues (Buzan, Waever and de Wilde 1998). This has the effect of depoliticizing those issues so that they are no longer subject to ideological contention or debated through political media, but become technical matters to be dealt with by experts under the approval of executive power. The logic of this process can be illustrated by the use of UK anti-terrorism legislation for apparently unrelated purposes.

- In 2005, Walter Wolfgang was detained under the Terrorism Act when he attempted to re-enter the conference of the then ruling Labour Party, from which he had been ejected by security guards after heckling a government speaker over the party's commitment to the war in Iraq.
- In 2008, assets of the Icelandic Landsbanki were seized under anti-terrorism legislation against UK account holders' deposits in the wake of the bank's financial collapse.
- Collective street arrest ('kettling') and pre-emptive arrest under anti-terrorism legislation has been used against a range of protesters at and en route to demonstrations since 2001.
- UK and other European governments and intelligence agencies appear to have colluded in the transport through their airspace and airports of US-detained terror suspects en route to countries where they could face torture in what has become known as 'extraordinary rendition'.
- Most recently, in 2013, it has been revealed that UK intelligence services have used their close relations with US security services to access vast quantities of online and telecommunications data surveillance of UK citizens, which they themselves are not legally able to obtain.

The return of revolution

Despite its centrality to the history of modernity, revolution as a concept had all but disappeared from the sociological lexicon by the turn of the millennium. Twentieth-century analysis of revolution tended to ground itself in or against Marxist analysis, referring to class forces as the source of the overthrow of political regimes and often assuming that revolution meant, as Marx asserted, the replacement of one social (as well as political) order with another. For such analyses, power was without question vested in the state, and these approaches saw the form of the state as the vehicle through which such change could be steered. In contrast, the radical philosopher Hannah Arendt (1965, 1970) had rather analysed resistance, or protest, and revolution in terms of power. The state and its governing executive, she argued, did not hold power; they held the capacity to use force, against which protest and revolution mobilized power as the capacity for people to act spontaneously in concert or, in her terms, to engage in political life by contending how we should and can live. Arendt's distinction between force and power reiterates the dichotomy, first developed in the French Revolution of the eighteenth century, between constituted (i.e., established) power and constitutive or constituent (i.e., establishing) power. Together, these represent two moments of modern revolution – firstly the overthrow of an existing order by a constituent power that has the capacity to inaugurate a new order and then that new order in existence. As was evident from the beginning of this analysis, the two moments are not necessarily concordant or even compatible. Constituted power always encroaches on constituent power.

This tradition of analysis of power derives ultimately from the Western tradition of political thought which runs through Rousseau, Max Weber, Walter Benjamin, Hannah Arendt and, today, Giorgio Agamben. Angus Stewart develops an Anglicized version of this traditional distinction, pointing out that we can distinguish between analyses of power as domination (power over) and those which understand power as the 'expression of collective autonomy' (power to) (Stewart 2001: 35–60). This distinction is very similar to that made by Poggi (2001) between power to act and power to act upon and the distinction made in radical political theory between constituted and constituent power (Hardt and Negri 2000; Raunig 2007).

Table 17.2: **Distinctions between constitutive and constituted power**	
Constitutive (or constituent) power	**Constituted power**
Power to	Power over
To act	To act upon
Agency	Structure
Civil society	State

Source: Drake (2010: 49).

We can see this being played out in the course of the recent and ongoing revolts that have become known as the Arab Spring, though in effect these revolts, considered sociologically, both extend back across a number of years (Al Aswany 2011) and continue in the present. In Egypt, in particular, the effect of the revolution of spring 2011 proved unsatisfactory to the aspirations and hopes of many of the revolutionaries, invoking a repeat performance in spring 2013; at that point the army served as arbiter in the interests of national security in a state of uncertainty, as the sovereignty invested in the Muslim Brotherhood in post-revolutionary democratic elections had been contentiously withdrawn by popular protest.

While the uprisings of the Arab Spring and beyond have been analysed variously as rebellions of a generation, of a new middle class, of a digitized social media-literate elite, or of a latent proletariat of informational capitalism, they can perhaps more accurately be conceptualized, as were the revolts of 1989, as a revolt of civil society, a term developed from classical sources by Enlightenment thinkers to understand a public acting in what it conceives of as the general interest, distanced both from the interests of the state and from individual economic interests (Keane 1988, 1999). Just as the European revolts of 1989 followed a wave of pro-democratic defiance across Asia, including South Korea in 1987, the Burmese uprising of 1988 and the protests in Tiananmen Square and elsewhere in China in 1989, so we can understand the global manifestations of the Occupy movement of 2011–12 against the austerity produced by the collapse of the global financial bubble as an extension of the Arab Spring, as the revolt of a new civil society increasingly networked across the globe, transcending the divisions of international society and its nation-states. Conceptualizing these revolts as the expression of a new, global civil society potentially keys into the concepts of cosmopolitanism (Fine 2007; Beck 2006; Skribis and Woodward 2013) the hopes of some theorists and activists that a globalized and networked

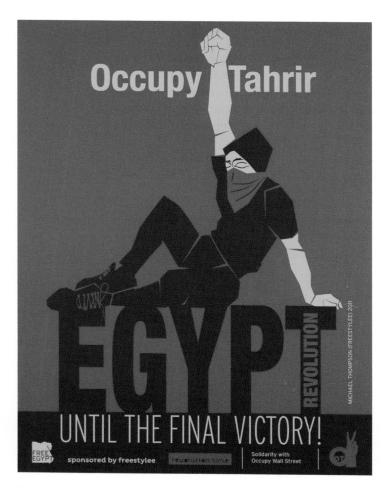

Movements such as the Arab Spring and Occupy arose at the same time, and, while separated by great distances and focused on different targets, many involved in these protests nurtured a sense of solidarity between the groups, akin to a global civil society. (© Michael Thompson/Flickr)

world will produce a global equivalent of the sense of common human purpose which swept the world in the Enlightenment, producing new political forms as vehicles for progress just as the Enlightenment produced the concept of the nation-state as the vehicle for human emancipation.

However, the abstract concept of a global civil society, like the emphasis on social media as the key factor in these revolts (Castells 2012), tends to lose the sense of embodiment and individual self-integrity that is central to contemporary movements of constituent power, the sense of individuals thinking independently but acting collectively in literally putting their bodies on the line to confront a state machinery that has at its disposal the resources of a global security industry which, like the military industrial complex in the era of the sovereign nation-state and international society (Mills 1956), is both a product and an agent of securitization. It is only when individuals risk their bodies that constituent power is realized. We could take as a guide to these new movements, to their spontaneity and almost unintentional, anti-ideological thinking, Mohamed al Bouazizi, the young man whose suicidal self-immolation led to the first revolt, in Tunisia in December 2010.

Bouazizi's death symbolizes the rebirth of the political in the movements that followed, as the ultimate act of integrity of means and ends in which millions put their lives and bodies on the line, with no further objective than the exposure of injustice and the overthrow of repression, without blueprints or programmes. Paradoxically, Bouazizi's self-immolation illustrates how constituent power requires a continuous openness, requires revolution to be kept alive rather than ossified in institutions and structures of order. In that, we also keep open the question of the political, of how we can and should live.

BOX 17.6 MOHAMED AL BOUAZIZI AND THE TUNISIAN REVOLUTION

Bouazizi was a member of the most recent and global baby-boom generation to which these revolts are sometimes traced as a generational phenomenon. He was not a part of the middle class or even, as was originally reported, a university student, but a member of the economically excluded 'surplus population' produced by globalization (Bauman 1998a). Contrary to the criminalizing stereotype of the underclass, Bouazizi worked selling fruit from a stall in order to support his family and his sister's university studies. His work was precarious, involving embodied performance of authenticity, but it seems to have enabled him to have salvaged some self-respect from a world which had denied him any value. However, semi-criminalized and abused by petty officials and blocked in his endeavours by the bureaucracy of rational state regulation, Bouazizi eventually saw no future for himself as an integral individual, and he doused himself in petrol and set his own body on fire in protest. Unlike the self-immolation of protesters against totalitarianism and imperialism in the 1960s, his was not an explicitly or even an intentionally political act; rather, it was the act of an individual, driven not by commitment to a greater collective cause but by a sense of self-integrity to expose injustice by total, fatal use of the only resource left to him, his living body.

SEMINAR QUESTIONS

1 Scanning news reports of the past year, can you find other examples of (a) governmentality, or (b) securitization?
2 Can you identify other examples of constituent power, either recently or in history?
3 Does revolution have a future?

CONCLUSION

Recent developments in the analysis of power from Foucault onwards, as well as social and political thinking about power and the state, suggest that Bauman's assertion of a current and ongoing epochal 'divorce between power and politics' is correct but also incorrect, because it is incomplete. His formulation applies only to one mode of power, that of constituted, established power. It neglects the other aspect, currently being asserted across the world in only slightly differing forms, from the revolts of the Arab Spring to the Occupy movement to the riots against the soccer World Cup in Brazil. The overview I have presented above suggests that power and politics as we used to understand them are indeed in advanced divorce proceedings, beyond the point at which each perceived their union as anything more than a means to an end rather than the end itself. However, Bauman neglects their offspring, the new modes of power, the new understandings of the political that have appeared in the world since those divorce proceedings began.

So far, those revolts appear unable to crystallize, to take a form in the way that the revolutions of modern industrial society were able to find a form for established, constituted power in the state. Meanwhile, the powers of the state are not finished; they retain the ability to oppress, to monitor, to inflict violence and destruction, from an individual micro-scale (as in the case of Bradley/Chelsea Manning, currently serving a prison sentence for leaking US military secrets) to the macro-scale (as in the ongoing destruction of the social infrastructure by the Syrian state today). But after two hegemonic centuries in which its capacities have defined the horizons of the political, the state today is creaking at the seams, buckling under pressure, able to buttress itself only by forming transnational blocs which fundamentally change the nature of the component states. The common feature seems to be that the institutional forms which have contained power and politics, in which they have been held together for the past two centuries, today no longer perform that function. The state, political parties, ideology and the other staple categories of political sociology and political practice alike simply no longer work in the way they used to.

In focusing on the institutions and practices of politics, political sociology risks losing its way, insulating itself from changes in the wider world and from changes in the discipline more broadly, becoming merely a sociology of politics, unable to grasp or even recognize the new. In order to begin to think differently, to be able to understand what is happening in the world today, and to be able to identify 'developmental tendencies' (as Max Weber once put it), we cannot rely on the categories and definitions which were developed to think about the political world in the nineteenth and twentieth centuries.

SEMINAR QUESTIONS

1 What are the 'new modes of power'?
2 In what ways is the contemporary state 'creaking at the seams'?
3 Suggest ways in which sociology will have to change to understand the political world of the twenty-first century.

FURTHER READING

▶ Giddens, A. (1985) *The Nation-State and Violence* (Polity). This critically synthetic work builds on Weber, Marx and Foucault to develop a distinctive analysis of the relations between power, authority, violence and organization which constitute the modern state. Its historical scope is extensive and the breadth of examples often fascinating. Giddens here develops his concept of the state as a 'power container'.

▶ Scott, J. C. (1998) *Seeing Like a State: How Certain Schemes to Improve the Human Condition Have Failed* (Yale University Press). Scott's book enables us to see the state around us in everyday life – in architecture, landscape, language and measurement – opening up ubiquitous and taken-for-granted features embedded in social life as examples of a grand vision which reduces everything to equivalences. Scott reminds us acutely of how the state is an artifice, a political project of a particular kind, which has ultimately, he argues, failed to deliver on its promises.

▶ Stewart, A. (2001) *Theories of Power and Domination: The Politics of Empowerment in Late Modernity* (Sage). This book provides more than a coverage of classic theories of power, drawing from them common themes which enable Stewart to undertake original synthesis and anticipating emergent developments which recognize and analyse power as more than a zero-sum game. Stewart's consideration of empowerment breaks the conventional division between the sociology of power and the state (the usual coupling) and the study of citizenship, social movements and civil society.

▶ Caygill, H. (2013) *On Resistance: A Philosophy of Defiance* (Bloomsbury). By treating ideas as a frame in which people act, Caygill embeds his exploration of the interplay of power and resistance in concrete events and sociological processes up to the inextricably globally interlinked movements of resistance of the early twenty-first century. This genealogy of the concept of resistance, traced on a global and epic scale, provides a lucid and insightful explanation of those ideas, their implications and their context.

▶ Orwell, G. (1949) *1984* (Secker & Warburg). Orwell reflects on the tendency of the modern form of the state and of all ideologies of central authority towards totalitarianism. The novel thus develops a critique of all forms of statism, including those of the post-war social-welfare state, foreseeing its moralistically judgemental penetration deep into every-day and private life. Orwell's analysis of technocracy and technocratic language anticipates later critical theories of power and discourse.

▶ Saramago, J. (1999) *All The Names* (Harvill Press). In this more recent novel, also set in an indeterminate modernity, Saramago provides us with a brilliantly insightful exploration of the effect on the individual of the bureaucratic, monumental, depersonalizing surveillance state. However, he also captures the ambivalence of the modern state, unfolding to show us another version – an organic, adaptive service state integral with the community of everyday life.

VIOLENCE, COERCION AND HUMAN RIGHTS

understanding organized brutality

SINIŠA MALEŠEVIĆ

CONTENTS

INTRODUCTION

W HAT DISTINGUISHES MOST CONTEMPORARY societies from their historical predecessors is the different perception and the organizational role that violence has in everyday life. Unlike their predecessors, who encountered some form of violence on a daily basis, to most present-day citizens of Western Europe violence remains largely invisible, confined to the images of faraway wars, revolutions or acts of terrorism seen on their TV screens or, if unlucky, to the occasional experience of mugging or domestic abuse. We live in a world where violence is generally delegitimized and proscribed by the stringent legal systems of modern nation-states. Furthermore, both popular attitudes and existing legal frameworks extol the idea that every human being has an inalienable set of human rights which have to be unconditionally protected and preserved. This situation has led some to believe that, as such, violence and coercion have little sociological relevance in contemporary world. Some authors, for example Pinker (2011) and Mueller (2004), even argue that all forms of violence are on the wane and that the discourses of human rights are gradually becoming the universally shared norms.

However, to understand fully our current condition, one needs to engage with the historical sociology of violence, coercion and rights. As will be seen in this chapter, historical sociologists convincingly show that our relatively peaceful situation is rooted in the particular historical and geopolitical arrangements established in the wake of the Second World War. They also demonstrate that periodic escalations of violence throughout history had to do less with 'the irrationality' of pre-modern humans and much more with the organizational and ideological inability of traditional polities to control their territories and populations. Most importantly, such studies emphasize that, rather than witnessing a gradual disappearance of violence and coercion, what is actually happening is the transfer of coercive power from individuals and organized groups towards the nation-states that establish and expand their monopolies on the legitimate use of force over the territories and populations they control (Malešević 2013a, 2010). Hence to understand and explain properly how societies operate, change or develop, one needs the historical sociology of violence, coercion and rights.

This chapter explores the complex relationships between organized violence, coercive power and human rights. The first part focuses on the social dynamics of violence and its impact on society. The second part provides a critical review of the three leading theoretical approaches that study this relationship. The third part analyses the principal types of organized violence, including warfare, revolutions, terrorism and genocide. The focal point of the final section is human rights.

ORGANIZED VIOLENCE AND SOCIETY

The absence of sociology

For much of the second half of twentieth century the study of violence was not at the forefront of sociological interest. Although sociologists have made important contributions in the analysis of the relationships between crime, deviance, surveillance or policing, there were very few attempts to provide a sociologically nuanced explanation of warfare, terrorism, insurgency, ethnic cleansing and genocide. In other words, the conventional view at that time was that sociology is meant to focus only on the social processes that take place within the domain of a specific society, whereas the social phenomena that involve several societies or take place at their borders, such as wars, insurgencies or genocide, are seen to be the prerogative of other academic disciplines. This neglect of organized violence was in part grounded in the deep-seated Enlightenment heritage that has historically underpinned much sociological thinking and analysis (Tiryakian 1999). The pioneering works of early social theorists – Montesquieu, Saint-Simon, Comte, Spencer and Tönnies, among others – were built on the mutually exclusive dichotomies that distinguish sharply between the traditional and modern world. In these interpretations, pre-modern orders were generally characterized by deep inequalities, rampant irrationality and superstition, widespread poverty and, most of all, violence. In contrast, modernity was conceptualized as an era defined by instrumental rationality, scientific progress, economic growth, general prosperity and, ultimately, peaceful social conduct. Hence, in this view, war and other forms of mass-scale violence were understood to be remnants of the past epochs destined eventually to vanish once modernity takes hold throughout the globe. Latter-day sociologists expressed more scepticism towards such simple dichotomies. Nevertheless much of this Enlightenment heritage remained fairly strong within sociology. The view that organized violence in all of its forms is on the wane and that sociologists should focus on other phenomena was further reinforced by the geopolitical stability and relative economic prosperity of the post-Second World War era. Thus, despite the significant differences between various sociological approaches that developed in this period, there was a near universal ignorance of the organized violence.

Secondly, the general idea that sociology is essentially the systematic study of society was regularly understood in terms of specific, nationally defined societies. In other words, a society and a nation-state were often conceptualized as if they are one and the same thing: French society was viewed as something that consists of citizens of the French Republic and

British society as being coterminous with the territory of United Kingdom of Great Britain and Northern Ireland. However, such static and restricted understandings do not distinguish between a historically specific and formalized political unit (the nation-state) and a dynamic social order that involves complex and multiple forms of social action often undertaken below and beyond one's state borders. Such a simplified understanding cannot capture the multiple allegiances, cross-border interactions, transnational networks or continental and global processes that have historically shaped and continue to form the outlooks and behaviours of millions of individuals. Such a view that makes no distinction between a society and a nation-state has been termed 'methodological nationalism'. According to Wimmer and Glick-Schiller (2002: 303–4), methodological nationalism is characterized by 'the apparent naturalness and givenness of a world divided into societies along the lines of nation-states'. Instead of problematizing and historicizing this nation-centric view of the world, much of the traditional social sciences simply took 'national discourses, agendas, loyalties and histories for granted' whereby the social science imaginary has been narrowly territorialized and analytically impoverished.

Looking beyond borders

While the rampant prevalence of methodological nationalism within twentieth-century sociology obstructed the proper development of several research areas, it had a particularly significant impact on the discipline's neglect of the study of organized violence. Since wars, revolutions, genocides, insurgencies and terrorism often involve complex networks of social actors and organizations that regularly transcend or criss-cross the borders of specific nation-states, they cannot be properly analysed and explained if one focuses exclusively on a single polity. These large-scale social phenomena often involve several nation-states as well as many non-state movements and agents, and they can generate long-term social changes in many societies. The ultimate outcomes of the French and American revolutions were not just changes in French and US society: almost the entire world was radically transformed by these two violent events.

BOX 18.1 THE IMPACT OF WORLD WARS ON THE CONTEMPORARY WORLD

The onset and outcome of the First and the Second World War have had a profound impact even on the citizens of nation-states that did not take part in them. The two world wars brought about sweeping transformation in social relations throughout the globe: the huge reliance on female labour during the war years eventually fostered greater gender equality; the mass participation of small farmers and manual workers on the battlefields was decisive in the expansion of citizenship rights and the accelerated democratization of many European states; and the enormous number of war casualties stimulated the emergence of cross-class solidarity and the gradual extension of the welfare-state model (Mann 2013, 1993; Tilly 1985).

Furthermore, the direct legacy of the Holocaust and the Rwandan genocide has been the worldwide public de-legitimization of anti-Semitism and racism and the greater elevation of the rhetoric and practice of universal human rights. More recently, with the rise of al-Qaeda ISIS and other extremist groups, it has become apparent that terrorism is a global social phenomenon that affects individuals regardless of where they live, work or travel.

However, both the Enlightenment heritage and methodological nationalism have become less pronounced in the latest sociological analyses. The globalizing trends of recent years, together with the rise of constructivist thinking in social science, have had an impact on the study of organized violence in sociology. Furthermore, the proliferation of civil wars, ethnic cleansing, revolutions, terrorism and insurgency since the end of the Cold War – from Africa, the Caucasus, the Balkans, and Central Asia to the Middle East and the Western military interventions in Iraq, Afghanistan, Libya and Mali – means that sociologists have become more interested in the study of organized violence in all its forms.

SEMINAR QUESTIONS

1 Why was the study of organized violence neglected by much of post-Second World War sociology?

2 What is methodological nationalism?

3 What impact has methodological nationalism had on the study of organized violence?

THE SOCIOLOGY OF ORGANIZED VIOLENCE: CONTEMPORARY APPROACHES

Intellectual predecessors

Although the study of organized violence was marginalized in sociology throughout the second half of the twentieth century, this was not the case at the end of the nineteenth and the beginning of the twentieth century. On the contrary, topics such as wars, revolutions, intergroup antagonism, mass killings and coercive behaviour were at the heart of classical sociology (Malešević 2010: 17–49). The early European and American sociologists, such as Ludwig Gumplowicz, Gustav Ratzenhofer, Franz Oppenheimer, Lester Ward, Gaetano Mosca, William Sumner and Otto Hintze, were fascinated by the impact organized violence had on the transformation of societies. Weber, Marx and Durkheim have also provided significant analyses of organized violence. Durkheim ([1897] 1951: 208) demonstrated empirically that the presence of a war environment leads to decreased suicide rates, arguing that such cataclysmic events as war and revolutions tend to foster greater social cohesion, where 'the individual thinks less of himself and more of the common cause'. Marx (1999: 367) understood revolutionary violence as an important social mechanism for social change, pointing out that 'force is the midwife of every old society pregnant with the new one.' For Weber ([1922] 1992), the disciplinary practice that underpins all modern rational bureaucratic systems was born in war and the military realm. Moreover, this coercive quality remains the bedrock of the modern social order, since state apparatuses worldwide derive their power from the ability to monopolize the use of force over specific territory.

Many of these ideas and insights of the classics have been revisited and developed further by the three leading contemporary approaches in the study of organized violence: culturalist, economistic and political perspectives.

Culture and violent action

Culturalist perspectives have developed persuasive explanations of organized violence. Whereas some classical sociologists, such as Sorokin (1942), invoked civilizational, cultural or religious divides as the inimitable sources of violent conflicts, more recent culturalist perspectives have tended to avoid such simplistic conclusions. Instead, contemporary culturalist approaches direct their attention to how organized violence is structured by specific cultural symbols, practices, rituals and shared meanings. John Hutchinson (2007, 2005), Jeffrey Alexander (2004) and Philip Smith (2008, 2005) have provided distinct cultural sociological interpretations of war, revolutions, terrorism and genocide. While Hutchinson has focused on the importance of collective remembrance of past wars, revolutions and rebellions in generating and institutionalizing stable national identities, Alexander and Smith have analysed the cultural practices that help articulate, code and reinforce past traumatic events. Hence, for Hutchinson, the periodic commemorations of wars, such as the American Independence Day or Remembrance Day in the UK that celebrate the sacrifice of previous generations, help anchor the shared moral universe of several generations. The reverence of 'the glorious dead' establishes a distinct sense of ethical responsibility of contemporaries towards those who have made the ultimate sacrifice and in this way reinforced one's sense of national identity. Such commemorations represent an act of national self-worship that brings to light the fact that a nation is a sacred communion of what Edmond Burke called 'the prematurely dead, the living and the yet unborn'.

This culturalist understanding of organized violence is even more explicit in the writings of Smith and Alexander, for whom violent action by itself is unlikely to generate long-term collective meanings. Instead, for the particular events to be understood as traumatic, it is crucial that they are culturally articulated and institutionalized in these terms. Thus the Pearl Harbor attack or the atomic bombings of Hiroshima and Nagasaki were not immediately experienced as national traumas but were dependent on such latter-day cultural framings. In this view, collective trauma is not a biological reflex but a cultural process that entails the social attribution of particular meanings: 'It is the meanings that provide the sense of shock and fear, not the events in themselves' (Alexander 2004: 10). This sharp differentiation between the reality of action and its cultural representation is even more visible in Smith's (2005: 212) sociology of war: 'war is not just about culture, but it is all about culture.' In other words, Smith argues that, without a distinct apocalyptic framing of the agents and events involved in conflict (such as sacred vs. profane or good vs. evil), warfare would not be possible.

Although culturalist perspectives seem very convincing, they have several shortcomings. Firstly, the focus on the shared cultural symbols, myths and ritualist practices does not really help us explain the causes and the distinctive trajectories of individual forms of organized violence. While shared practices of signification are useful in making a particular violent event meaningful or legitimate, cultural frames are not sufficient in themselves to trigger or stop a particular violent conflict. The apocalyptic narratives of imminent Armageddon or about the incessant greed of the aristocracy were fairly common throughout medieval Europe, but this in itself was not enough to galvanize the necessary mass mobilization of peasantry for large-scale violent action that would result in revolution. The study of cultural symbols that accompanied the 1789 French Revolution or 1917 Russian October Revolution would not tell us much about the origins of these unprecedented historical events (Mann 2012, 1993).

Secondly, in most culturalist interpretations of violence, human actions are perceived primarily through the prism of shared norms and values. Such understandings operate with a too consensual view of group action; no emphasis is given to internal disagreements, any

To what extent is the UK's understanding of the two world wars shaped by cultural framings of national remembrance? As time passes and fewer people have direct connections to these conflicts, will their remembrance be dictated by cultural framings? (© Ministry of Defence)

competing interpretation of the shared past and present or the different interests within a specific group. The commemorations of past wars, revolutions, insurgencies or genocides are rarely non-contested. However, not only are the interpretations of such events often challenged by different political groupings, but the dominant framing of such events also tends to change through time, as illustrated by the example of Remembrance Day celebrations.

BOX 18.2 REMEMBRANCE DAY AND THE SYMBOLISM OF THE POPPY

UK Remembrance Day commemorations, which initially memorialized British white men who died in the First World War, have gradually become more inclusive and now commemorate all men and women, regardless of their ethnicity, who served in all armed conflicts and military operations. However, since the 1930s the principal symbol of the occasion, the wearing of red poppies, has been contested by pacifist groups, who see this as a militarist symbol and advocate the use of white poppy instead. Furthermore, the red poppy has also been contested by the non-Unionist population in Northern Ireland, who see it as a Unionist symbol, and by anti-colonialist organizations that see it as an imperial symbol (Elias 2008).

Thus, although cultural framing and symbolism are indispensable ingredients of wars, revolutions, terrorism and insurgency, they are inadequate by themselves to generate organized violence. Rather than being a solely cultural phenomenon, violence is first and foremost a material event: it is something that involves physical practices – killing, dying, injuring and destroying – and entails competing economic interests, political motives or changing geopolitical realities.

The economics of violence

The view that organized violence has more to do with individual or collective self-interest than with one's culture is the leitmotiv of several economistic perspectives on violence. The idea that violence is a means that can be utilized to acquire scarce resources was already familiar to the ancient Greek philosophers such as Plato or Aristotle who conceptualized wars as a form of organized robbery. A number of classical social theorists, from Adam Smith and Herbert Spencer to Karl Marx, emphasized the economic foundations of organized violence. For the classical liberals, such as Spencer and Smith, the expansion of the free market is seen as being conducive to peace. Their argument was that when people trade they do not start rebellions, fight wars or engage in ethnic cleansing. In contrast, Marxist interpretations saw the proliferation of free market capitalism as the principal source of violence in both domestic and global contexts. Marxist perspectives insist that the capitalist principles of competitive individualism domestically foster a constant struggle for money, status, material and symbolic possessions which ultimately leads towards violent confrontations, including revolutions and rebellions. Furthermore they argue that this same principle contributes to warfare in the global arena, as coalitions of big corporations and state elites in their incessant search for cheap resources and new markets periodically embark on territorial conquests. The colonial wars of the nineteenth and early twentieth centuries, like the First World War, are seen as being typical in this respect.

The most influential recent articulations of economic-centred approaches include globalization theories of organized violence. For social theorists of globalization such as Kaldor (2007, 2004) and Bauman (2006, 2002), neoliberal capitalism has become a global force that, through its policies of ever increasing deregulation, privatization and marketization, decouples private enterprises from state control and thereby dramatically reduces the power of individual states. They argue that recent technological innovations have made transport and communication faster and cheaper, which on the one hand substantially increased global trade and on the other generated greater inequalities between the West and the rest. More specifically, Bauman and Kaldor point out that the profoundly unequal character of globalization engenders new forms of violent conflict in the less developed parts of the world. In their interpretation, neoliberal policies encourage the rise of kleptocratic governments and weak states in Africa, parts of Asia and the post-Soviet world which are ultimately unable to control their territories and prevent the emergence of civil wars, ethnic cleansing, revolutions or insurgencies. In this chaotic environment, multinational corporations prolong violence by supporting individual warlords in order to benefit from monopolistic contracts in oil, gas, gold, diamonds and other valuable minerals.

There is no doubt that economic-centred explanations contribute to our understanding of organized violence. What might appear to an uninformed observer who encounters a violent intergroup conflict as sheer madness often in fact has a very rational logic. Indeed, violence can be utilized for individual or collective gain. However, there is more to human beings than resource and profit accumulation. The causes of organized violence cannot be reduced to economics alone, as revolutions, wars, insurgencies, genocides and terrorism have often had distinctively non-instrumental origins. While the Nazi state certainly benefited from the appropriation of Jewish property and the slave labour of the concentration camp inmates, there is an abundance of historical records demonstrating that ideological motives played a much greater role in the planning and implementation of the Holocaust (Mann 2005; Kershaw 2009). There is not much instrumental rationality behind the establishment of extermination camps and the killing of millions of civilians. Similarly, economistic approaches cannot properly explain why insurgencies emerge in economically deprived areas (such as Kosovo, Chechnya or South Sudan) as much as in economically prosperous regions (such as the Basque country). Furthermore, although economic deprivation can contribute to an individual's decision to support or even join an extremist organization, most terrorist activity is conducted by middle-class professionals (Gambetta and Hertog 2009; Pape 2005; Hassan 2011). Wars too are not initiated and fought only for economic resources but can be triggered by geopolitical instability, ideological and wider political disagreements, dynastic claims, territorial disputes, status anxieties and so many other reasons.

However, the principal weakness of the economistic explanation of organized violence is its overly intentionalist and present-centred view of social change. Rather than exploring the structural and historical contingencies of violent action, most economic-focused approaches assume that violence is a direct product of individual or collective action – by interest-based collective associations, greedy CEOs of multinational corporations, corrupt political leaders or unscrupulous warlords. While globalization and neoliberalism bring another layer of complexity to workings of organized violence in the contemporary world, they do not possess such power radically to transform the constitutive features of violent action. More historically nuanced analyses show that one should not overstate the impact globalization and new technologies have had on the transformation of organized violence (Malešević 2010: 311–31; Kalyvas 2001).

The politics of belligerence

Although biology, culture and economics are all integral to violent action, it is really politics that is at the heart of most forms of organized violence. Wars, revolutions, insurgencies, genocides and terrorism are first and foremost political events through which one side aims to overpower or control the other. This link between violence and political power has been recognized and studied by classical sociologists, Weber, Hintze, Gumplowicz, Ratzenhofer, Oppenheimer and Mosca, among others. In their explanations of the origins of the nuclear family, private property, the state, law, social stratification and civilization, they all emphasize the coercive character of political life. A number of highly influential contemporary historical sociologists, including Michael Mann (2013, 2012, 1993), Charles Tilly (1992, 1985), Anthony Giddens (1985) and Randall Collins (1999, 1986), have further developed this line of analysis. More specifically, their spotlight is on the relationship between state formation, societal transformations and violence. Thus, for Mann (2012, 1986) and Tilly (1992, 1985), modern social orders owe their existence to the violent confrontations and coercive actions of previous epochs.

BOX 18.3 MICHAEL MANN AND CHARLES TILLY ON THE VIOLENCE BEHIND THE NATION-STATE

In Mann's view, the very possibility of social order is premised on the long-term historical process that he calls 'social caging', whereby individual liberties were 'exchanged' for military protection and economic security. In other words, the emergence of the first states, which were the only institutions capable of organizing large-scale agricultural production, meant that kinship ties were gradually replaced by political centralization, with populations steadily locked into compulsory administrative institutions. Once this coercive mechanism was fully in place, states utilized wars and other forms of externalized violence to preserve internal peace, to extract resources, to establish geopolitical dominance or to impose ideological hegemony. Mann (1986: 2) argues that, to understand the impact violence had on social development, it is necessary to abandon the unitary concept of society and shift attention towards 'multiple overlapping and intersecting power networks', among which four stand out: political, economic, ideological and military power. Mann also distinguishes between the despotic and infrastructural forms of state power, whereby the former is defined by the ability of state elites to use coercion without consultation with civil society groups and the latter is understood as 'the capacity of the state to actually penetrate civil society and implement its actions across its territories' (Mann 2008: 355). The key feature of state development over the past centuries has been the steady increase in the infrastructural at the expense of despotic power. Thus modern democracies are characterized by low despotic but exceptionally high infrastructural powers: unlike its predecessors, the modern democratic state is able to police its territories fully, extract taxation at source, collect and utilize information on all of its citizens, monitor flows of people and goods on its territory, and even conscript its citizens in times of war.

For Tilly (1992), these ever increasing infrastructural powers are the direct result of previous protracted wars and revolutions. In his view, the modern features of rule, such as the expansion of bureaucratic control, centralization and territorial monopoly, are all unintended consequence of long-term violent conflicts over the last three centuries. Moreover, war-making has not only enhanced state-making but has also contributed to the development of civil societies. To win protracted wars European rulers had to mobilize wider sectors of the population. The direct corollary of this transformation was the gradual expansion of civil liberties, citizenship rights, parliamentarianism, party pluralism and welfare provision, all of which were a price paid for mass participation in wars. In other words, to finance wars, which with the further development of science and technology were becoming more expensive, European ruling groups had to find a long-term solution to increase taxation, resource extraction and universal conscription, and the ultimate by-product was the constitutional, democratic nation-state.

Politically centred analyses of organized violence seem highly convincing in their attempt to trace the origins of modern life in the violent and coercive processes of past epochs. Unlike much of mainstream sociology, which is too presentist and tends to overemphasize the novelty of contemporary events such as globalization, individualization or cosmopolitanism, Mann, Tilly and other historical sociologists demonstrate more historical subtlety and awareness. Simply put, there is a greater degree of organizational continuity between this era and the last two centuries than is ordinarily assumed. The root causes of late twentieth- and early twenty-first-century terrorism, insurgencies, wars and genocides are in fact often very similar to those of the nineteenth and early twentieth centuries (Malešević 2010; Kalyvas 2001). Furthermore, despite their focus on politics, Tilly, Mann and others from this perspective acknowledge that the complexity of social actions is not reduced to one sphere of social life but takes into account economic factors and material resources, cultural and religious beliefs, military power and the potency of administrative reach. Rather than seeing violent action as being the sole product of economics, biology or culture, there is recognition that all of these aspects make a contribution to organized violence.

Notwithstanding their greater explanatory potential, political perspectives also exhibit two weaknesses. Firstly, although ideology is general acknowledged as an important variable when trying to explain the character of organized violence, there is a tendency to conceptualize ideology in very narrow and highly instrumentalist terms. No significant distinction is made between culture, religion and ideology, and secular ideologies such as liberalism, socialism or nationalism are often seen as no more than modern equivalents of religious beliefs. With the partial exception of Mann, who provides an analysis of ideological power (but still treats it as secondary force), representatives of the political perspective largely treat ideology as a weak, parasitic force that is used as a tool of elite action. There is no focus on differences in the content of particular ideologies and how they influence popular perceptions. For example, Tilly makes no room for ideological action, and, as Brubaker (2010: 380) points out, this approach is too materialist in the sense that it addresses the political aspects of 'claim-making' while 'ignoring the cultural content of . . . sense-making'.

Secondly, although political perspectives rightly insist that social organizations are crucial vehicles of social change and that 'ideas cannot do anything unless they are organized' (Mann 2006: 346–7), they focus almost exclusively on one form of social organization – the state. While there is no doubt that modern-day nation-states remain the most significant 'bordered power containers' (Giddens 1985: 120) and have historically been the main purveyors of wars, a great deal of organized violence is also generated by non-state actors. Many forms of non-state social organization – from terrorist networks, insurgency movements and revolutionary cells to professional ethnic cleansers – are at the forefront of violent conflicts throughout the world. Such social organizations have been in existence for centuries but have become more visible and prominent with the relative decline of interstate wars over the past fifty years. Let us explore in greater detail how all of these different forms of social organization operate in variety of violent contexts.

SEMINAR QUESTIONS

1 Why do we commemorate past wars?
2 What is the relationship between globalization and organized violence?
3 Is globalization fostering or preventing the expansion of warfare in the contemporary world?
4 What is social caging? Suggest some contemporary examples of social caging.

THE DOMINANT FORMS OF ORGANIZED VIOLENCE

Much of recent empirical research demonstrates that violence does not come naturally to human beings. Unlike other mammals, which are equipped with sharp teeth, strong jaws, sturdy horns or large paws, we have no biological prerequisites for inflicting violence on others (Malešević 2013b; Malešević and Ryan 2013). As Collins (2008) shows, on the inter-personal level most violent action is messy, incompetent, short and characterized by fear and tension. Hence it is only when violence is organized that it becomes prolonged, destructively efficient and socially significant. In other words, behind all 'effective' violence stand potent social organizations. As the historical record demonstrates, before the emergence of proper social organizations such as chiefdoms or pristine forms of statehood, there were no ade-quate means to inflict large-scale destruction and mass murder. However, since these com-plex social organizations became established, their coercive capacity has constantly been on the increase, often resulting in enormous human casualties. Although organized violence has historically appeared in many guises, including violent rebellions, uprisings or coups d'état, to name a few, the dominant and socially most influential forms of violent action have been and remain warfare, revolution, genocide and terrorism.

Warfare

The fact that wars are the most recognizable and most written about violent conflicts to have shaped much of recorded human history has often led to the popular perception that the institution of warfare is as old as, if not older than, the human species. Nevertheless, as archaeological and anthropological evidence indicates, most simple hunters and gatherers, which accounts for more than 98 percent of our existence on this planet, were not engaged in prolonged violent intergroup conflicts. Instead war emerges only in the early Mesolithic – that is, somewhere between 10,000 and 12,000 years ago (Otterbein 2004: 11; Ferrill 1985: 18–26). What is of particular sociological relevance is that the institution of war appears on the historical scene together with the gradual shift from the hunting and gathering towards the settled lifestyle. More specifically, the archaeological record shows that permanent human settlements, the domestication of animals, farming, and the development of complex tools and weapons, like the invention of warfare, are all products of the Neolithic revolution. There is an obvious and non-accidental parallel development of war and civilization. Moreover, as social organizations, technology, the division of labour and proto-ideological modes of rule justifica-tion have advanced in different civilizations, so has the institution of warfare.

In medieval Europe, cultured aristocratic knights, with their monopoly on military skills, access to expensive weaponry, horses and armour, and land ownership, came to dominate the rest of society. In this context, the presence of war was essential in maintaining the existing social order, as knights were considered to be the only legitimate warriors and the entire social order was defined in terms of the knight/non-knight dichotomy. However, despite their profu-sion, most feudal wars were either highly formalized ritualistic skirmishes between aristocrats that resulted in minimal casualties or simply plundering expeditions. One of the key features of wars, often initiated over mutually incompatible dynastic claims or even trivial issues such as failed marriage proposals, was the preservation of stable but highly stagnant status orders. In this environment, technological innovation was openly discouraged, while military efficiency and discipline were considered irrelevant.

All of this was to change substantially from the late sixteenth century onwards, as a combination of military, political, economic and ideological factors brought about a dramatic transformation in the relationship between war and society. The religious schism initiated by the Reformation and reinforced by the Counter Reformation fostered the greater ideological mobilization of pop-ulations throughout the European continent, the pinnacle of which was the devastating Thirty

Years' War (1618–48). This ideological change went hand in hand with significant technological and organizational developments in the military sphere, such as the invention and eventual mass use of handguns, the rise of almost impenetrable fortifications, the adoption of cannon in naval and siege operations, and the switch from highly expensive cavalry to large-scale, less costly infantry. The mass production of relatively cheap weaponry, new uniforms, food, supplies and other equipment was stimulated and also helped foster the growth of capitalism, initially throughout Europe, then, with the expansion of colonialism, all over the globe. The ever increasing size of militaries in conjunction with prolonged and more destructive warfare increased costs, which in turn led to the greater centralization of state power. The continuing development of state-wide fiscal systems with much more effective taxation, together with the growth and professionalization of state bureaucracy, brought the military under the control of a centralized authority. As both Tilly (1985) and Mann (1993) demonstrate, this centralized authority was a direct product of warfare. The late seventeenth, the eighteenth and the beginning of the nineteenth centuries witnessed the states and wider societies thoroughly transformed from being the sole 'property' of royal dynasties with little popular support into entities that legitimized their very existence through the notions of popular sovereignty and the equality of all citizens.

This interdependence of state, society and warfare further intensified in the aftermath of the French and American revolutions, which were followed by the equally significant industrial and military revolutions. The late nineteenth and early twentieth centuries were marked by the industrialization of warfare, with new scientific and technological breakthroughs being pioneered and utilized on a mass scale, firstly in the military sector and eventually finding their way into the civilian sphere too (Hirst 2001). Technological inventions came together with the further bureaucratization of both war and society. The greater division of labour, the establishment of meritocratic and impersonal hierarchies, and the reliance on technical, codified and written rules and regulations now became cornerstones of military as well as civilian institutions. In this context, the soldier's role changed too: instead of being an independent aristocrat, a mercenary who fought for those who paid more or a servant of a monarch, the solider became an employee of the state who fought out of the sense of loyalty towards his nation-state. Furthermore, the French and American revolutions, together with the Napoleonic wars that followed, soon initiated profound ideological shifts. Instead of the divine authority of a monarch or supreme royal sovereignty, the new legitimizing ideology became popular sovereignty, with nationalism becoming established as the potent mobilizing force. The impact of nationalist ideologies became even more prominent throughout the nineteenth and twentieth centuries, as different social strata such as manual labourers and small farmers were given greater citizenship rights (Malešević 2013a; Mann 1988).

The direct consequence of these organizational and ideological changes was not only a greater fusion of military and civilian spheres but also the ability and willingness to produce mass destruction and enormous human casualties. Both the First and the Second World War were the embodiment of industrialized total war, where large sectors of the population and most resources and services (including industrial production, transport, communications and trade) were mobilized for the war effort. What traditionally would be a conflict between two military apparatuses had ultimately morphed into a total war encompassing entire populations. The ultimate outcome of these big structural changes was a dramatic increase in war deaths: whereas in the twelfth and thirteenth centuries combined there were around half a million human casualties, by the nineteenth century this figure had jumped to 19 million.

However, the twentieth century outstripped anything seen before, as the total tally of human casualties in wars rose to a staggering 120 million (Eckhardt 1992; Malešević 2010: 119–20). Nevertheless, the two world wars have had another form of legacy: the mass mobilization for warfare helped extend citizenship rights, contributed to greater gender equality (with women entering the labour force en masse), established society-wide systems of welfare provision, and brought about a geopolitical stability that created preconditions for post-Second World War economic prosperity.

The decades of geopolitical stability, which were rooted in the balance of force between the two superpowers, came to an end with the worldwide collapse of state socialism and the Soviet federal state. Although during the second half of the twentieth century civil wars had already become more frequent than interstate wars, they have become much more visible in the aftermath of the communist collapse. These civil wars have been termed 'new wars' and have been seen as being generated by the processes of globalization (Kaldor 2007; Bauman 2002; Münkler 2005). For Kaldor (2007), these are predatory wars that arise in the context of failing post-Cold War states where new political elites rely on identity politics to mobilize ethnic and religious sentiments among the population. Employing paramilitaries and remnants of the collapsing state structure, they politicize cultural difference and wage genocidal wars on civilians while at the same time acquiring personal wealth and maintaining a hold on power.

BOX 18.4 SOMALIA'S NEW WARS

The ongoing violent conflict in Somalia is understood to be a typical representative of the 'new war'. Following the end of the Cold War, Somalia's pro-Soviet government of Mohamed Siad Barre was toppled in 1991 by the collation of clan- and region-based Islamic and secular armed resistance. The deep divisions between these diverse groups generated further infighting between various factions, which severely weakened the central authority of the state and its ability to keep a monopoly on the use of legitimate violence over the entire territory of Somalia. The direct outcome of this was the splintering of the state into a number of semi-independent units controlled by different factions, including Somaliland, Khatumo, the Islamic Emirate of Somalia and the very weak federal government. Furthermore, the past two decades have witnessed the expansion of externally supported and funded predatory warlords, such as Mohamed Farrah Hassan Aidid or Abdullahi Yusuf Ahmed, and armed militias including the Islamist Al-Shabaab and Islamic Courts Union, who tended to rely on fear and the use of the religious, ethnic and clan-based attachments to gain power.

In addition to 'predatory wars', the late twentieth and early twenty-first century have witnessed the emergence of high-tech risk transfer wars waged by the most technologically advanced states such as the USA and the UK (Shaw 2005). The focus here is on minimizing the risks to Western military personnel and consequently on minimizing the electoral and political risks to state leadership, which is accomplished by transferring such risks directly to the weaker enemy. From the Falklands War of 1982 to the Gulf, Kosovo, Afghanistan, Iraq and, most recently, the wars in Libya and Mali, the reliance on technologically sophisticated weapons helps create the systematic transfer of risks from elected politicians to military personnel and from them to the enemy combatants and their civilians. When the choice is between (foreign) civilian lives and the lives of Western soldiers, then the soldiers always have priority. The

An unmanned X47-B navy drone in testing for the development of drones with strike capability: drones are a controversial military tool, part of risk transfer tactics in asymmetric warfare. (© Charles McCain/Flickr)

use of highly sophisticated and expensive military technology allows wars to be fought from a distance. For example, the Kosovo War of 1999 was waged and won by NATO relying solely on airpower. More recently, the US military actions in Afghanistan and Yemen were accomplished through the use of unmanned armed drones.

Revolution

Despite their relatively rare occurrence, revolutions have received much more attention from sociologists than war and other forms of organized violence. The classics of sociology, most notably Marx and Weber, provided extensive theoretical and empirical analyses of revolutionary events and processes. For example, Marx ([1871] 1988) offered a proscriptive theory of revolution centred on the violent overthrow of capitalist state power by the proletariat. However, he also analysed the revolutionary upheavals of his own time – the 1848 European revolutions as well as the 1871 Paris Commune, occasionally referred to as the Fourth French Revolution. Weber (1995) too provided comprehensive theoretical analyses that centred on the relationship between bureaucratization, charismatic authority and revolutions. He focused in particular on the sociological implications of the 1905 and 1917 Russian revolutions and made a successful prediction that, despite its anti-bureaucratic rhetoric of class liberation, the 1917 Revolution would result in even greater expansion of administrative control. Nevertheless, the systematic sociological study of revolutions was initiated by Theda Skocpol's (1979) *States and Social Revolutions*.

The shift in focus from the class models envisaged by Marxist accounts of revolution towards more state-centred explanations was even more evident in the influential studies of Goldstone

BOX 18.5 MILITARIZATION

Militarization has been defined by the Bonn International Center for Conversion as 'the relative weight and importance of the military apparatus of one state in relation to its society as a whole' (BICC 2013). Each year the BICC produces an index on levels of militarization. This is based on a combination of expenditure (including a comparison with health spending), the proportion of the population in the military, and the number of heavy weapons compared to the size of a country's population. The index has revealed a trend towards increased militarization in some regions, particularly the Middle East. For example, military spending in that region between 2000 and 2012 rose from $80 billion to $128 billion. The top ten most militarized countries are shown in table 18.1.

Table 18.1: **Global Militarization Index (GMI) top ten, 2012**					
Rank	Country	Military expenditure index score	Military personal index score	Heavy weapons index score	GMI index
1	Israel	4.69	6.27	3.65	794
2	Singapore	4.22	6.49	3.29	752
3	Russia	4.41	5.93	3.32	729
4	Armenia	4.44	6.18	2.97	724
5	Syria	4.47	5.68	3.30	714
6	Jordan	4.28	5.66	3.22	694
7	South Korea	3.84	6.14	2.94	679
8	Azerbaijan	4.47	5.55	2.83	673
9	Cyprus	3.60	5.83	3.33	667
10	Kuwait	4.45	5.12	3.18	666

Source: BICC (2013).

BOX 18.6 SKOCPOL'S THEORY OF REVOLUTION

Theda Skocpol (1979) compares and contrasts the revolutionary experiences of France, Russia and China, arguing that, rather than being events brought about by the direct action of specific individual leaders or groups of conspirators, revolutionary situations tend to be the result of several contingent factors. Among these, two are emphasized: the profound crisis of the state, often triggered by security concerns (external threat), economic collapse, natural disasters or food shortage, and class-based upheaval from below. However, in contrast to traditional Marxist accounts, Skocpol finds peasants, not urban workers, to be the principal social agents of revolutionary action and sees structural forces such as the weakened state, unable to amass needed resources, as the root cause of successful revolution. Furthermore, she distinguishes between political and social revolutions: the outcome of the political revolution is the change of political regime while the social revolution involves a more profound change of social order: 'Social revolutions are rapid, basic transformations of a society's state and class structures . . . [they] are set apart from other sorts of conflicts and transformative processes above all by the combination of two coincidences: the coincidence of societal structural change with class upheaval, and the coincidence of political with social transformation' (Skocpol 1979: 4).

(2001, 1991), Tilly (1996) and Goodwin (2001). For Goldstone (1991), despite the inevitable diversity of revolutionary experiences, most revolutions are the consequence of three mutually intensifying processes: the fiscally and organizationally drained state, incapable of collecting revenue and other resources, the presence of deep conflict between ruling elites, and burgeoning popular discontent. Hence revolutions are more likely to happen in the context of a lost war or a natural disaster resulting in a weakened state, a dissatisfied population and a polarized political elite. However, although the presence of these three factors is conducive to revolution, it does not mean that their very existence will inevitably produce a revolutionary outcome. History is full of cases of weak, impoverished and fiscally strained states whose populations resent their unpopular and divided rulers but where there have been a very few revolutions. To account for this problem, Tilly (1994) differentiates between a revolutionary situation and a revolutionary outcome. The two differ substantially: a revolutionary situation involves collective action against the power holders (e.g., riots, demonstrations, rebellions, organized social movements and even civil wars). However, despite violent upheavals and mass mobilization, revolutionary situations rarely reach the level of a revolutionary outcome, which involves the actual transfer of power. In other words, a revolutionary outcome is likely only when the power contenders are able to mobilize coercive, material, organizational and other resources that are greater than those of the existing power holders.

State-centred perspectives also emphasize the modernity of revolutions. Although there are many examples of violent uprisings throughout history, revolution is a highly distinct phenomenon that emerged only in the sixteenth century and became prevalent during the last three centuries. The key issue here is that, if the revolution is broadly defined as the illegal seizure of state power, then there could be no revolutions without states. As Goodwin (2004) emphasizes: 'until the modern era . . . there existed no institution with sufficient infrastructural power to remake extensive social arrangements in fundamental ways: the consolidated national state, however, made it possible to do – and to think of doing – just that.' In other words, before the arrival of the nation-state model, most organized attempts to overthrow a particular government did not have transformative, revolutionary outcomes and would often end not only in removing a particular rulers but also in destroying the organizational structure of the existing polity.

Although statist approaches have been highly effective in explaining the European and North American revolutions of the eighteenth, nineteenth and twentieth centuries, the postcolonial revolutionary experience and especially the Iranian Revolution of 1979 have proved to be challenging to this research paradigm. In contrast to its French or Russian counterparts, the Iranian Revolution was not rooted in the Enlightenment tradition that emphasized secular, progress-oriented social change intent on bringing about individual autonomy, reason and egalitarian social relations. In contrast, it was spearheaded by a religious elite who advocated a return to the 'pristine' interpretation of religious texts and their implementation in the everyday life of Iranian society.

Since the statist accounts could not easily explain the Iranian and several other postcolonial cases, the sociological study of revolutions has shifted in focus towards the analysis of cultural and ideological sources of revolutionary upheavals. Hence Selbin (2010), Foran (2005) and Foran, Lane and Zivkovic (2008), among others, have argued that, instead of conceptualizing revolutions as solely material events, it is important to recognize their cultural underpinnings and ideological resonance. For Selbin (2010), revolutionary experience is often understood

BOX 18.7 THE REVOLUTION IN TUNISIA, 2010–11: THE JASMINE SPRING

The campaign of civil resistance and disobedience that started in Tunisia in December 2010 and ended with the overthrow of the authoritarian regime of Zine el Abidine Ben Ali in January 2011 represents the beginning of the Arab Spring. The Tunisian uprising was initiated by a spectacular event – police brutality towards a poor street vendor, Mohamed al Bouazizi, which ended in his suicide by setting himself on fire. This revolutionary experience was marked by a high diversity of participants, including middle-class professionals (such as solicitors and teachers – 95 percent of Tunisia's 8,000 lawyers went on strike in January 2011), work-ers, students and the unemployed. Furthermore, this revolution benefited extensively from social media, as YouTube, Facebook and Twitter instantly conveyed images of the self-immolation of Bouazizi and the police brutality towards demonstrators. The mass circulation of these images and messages stimulated further resist-ance among the outraged Tunisians. The success of this Jasmine Uprising (also referred to by Tunisians as the Dignity Revolution) sparked similar protests in Egypt, Libya, Syria, Yemen, Bahrain and other Arab coun-tries, where social discontent was also voiced through the use of new social media.

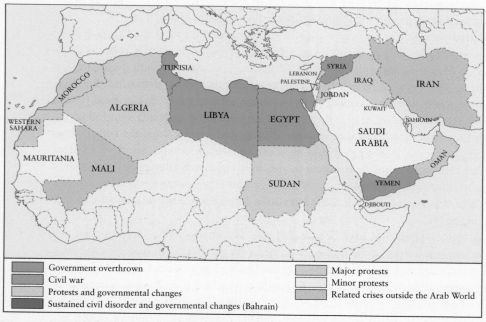

Figure 18.1 The Arab Spring and its effects, by 2014

through the prism of narratives that connect past experiences with present struggles and shared aspirations for a better future.

The collapse of communism and the phenomenon of 'velvet revolutions' – the relatively peaceful but profound transformation in Eastern Europe and the former Soviet Union – have also dented some of the traditional, statist understandings of revolutions. The post-communist revolutions emerged in the context of relatively stable state structures with little if any elite polarization and no sudden or significant change in the ability of the state to collect its revenue. Furthermore, these revolutions, with the exception of that in Romania, did not involve significant resistance on the part of ruling groups, nor were they driven by the world-transforming utopian vistas that characterized the French and Russian October revolutions.

Similarly, the 'colour revolutions' of the early 2000s, including relatively peaceful transitions of power in Serbia, Georgia, Ukraine and Kyrgyzstan, as well as the Arab Spring of 2010–11, have defied the classical statist accounts of revolutionary change. In all of these cases it was civil society groupings, social movements and ad hoc organized individuals rather than states that proved decisive for the revolutionary outcome.

The direct consequence of these historical events was a further rethinking of existing structuralist explanations of revolutions. So the new approaches have not only re-examined the cultural and ideological contexts of revolutions but have also shifted the focus from structure towards agency. More specifically, the revolutions were not seen solely as sudden and violent state breakdowns but as the long-term processes that generate societal transformation. Researchers have devoted more attention to the study of subjective motivations of different agents involved in revolutionary processes: elites, peasants, the middle classes, workers, students, minorities, etc. Foran, Lane and Zivkovic (2008) have called attention to the role that shared myths, symbols, memories and historical figures play in mobilizing civil society and wider sectors of the population. Others have emphasized the importance of new technologies and new means of communication as a powerful device for organized action. The role of social media in helping ferment the seeds of the Arab Spring is often stressed, as are demographic changes, including the dramatic growth of urban, educated and unemployed youth in the Middle East (Goldstone 2011). These new perspectives recognize that the traditional understanding, whereby the French Revolution is taken as a model of all revolutionary activity, is largely misplaced. Even the traditional interpretations of the French and Russian revolutions have been questioned and reinterpreted as cultural and social processes rooted in transnational networks, changing geopolitical relations and imperial struggle for global domination (Markoff 1996).

Genocide

Genocide is by far the most extreme form of organized violence. The term 'genocide' was coined by Raphael Lemkin in 1943, and after years of intensive campaigning it was institutionalized in a 1948 UN convention as one of most serious forms of crime. Article 2 of the Convention on the Prevention and Punishment of the Crime of Genocide defines genocide as an act 'committed with intent to destroy, in whole or in part, a national, ethnical, racial or religious group'. More specifically, it lists five different forms of action that characterize genocide:

1 killing members of a specific group;
2 causing grave bodily or mental harm to members of that group;
3 intentionally forcing on that group conditions of life calculated to cause its physical destruction in whole or in part;
4 imposing measures aimed to prevent births within that group; and
5 transferring children of that group to another group by force.

Although the legal recognition of genocide is less than seventy years old, the social processes this resolution describes are obviously much older. Instances of mass murder and forced prevention of births, deliberate collective physical and mental deprivation of entire communities, and the coercively imposed transfer of children from one group to another have been recorded throughout history. However, the key question is how systematic, organized and ideologically driven were the mass murders and other forms of large-scale violence in previous epochs. Scholars of genocide and ethnic cleansing are generally divided over questions such as: Is genocide/ethnic cleansing an ancient or modern phenomenon? Are these phenomena caused by powerful individuals and groups or by structural forces? Are genocide and ethnic cleansing the product of authoritarianism or democratization? And what is the relationship between genocide and warfare?

While no serious scholar argues that mass murder is a historically novel phenomenon, there is a pronounced disagreement among those who distinguish sharply between the pre-modern and modern mass exterminations and those who insist on their similarity. Thus Goldhagen (2009) and Kiernan (2007), among others, insist that genocide is an ancient practice, recorded in the Assyrian mass murders of Babylonians and Jews (7th century BC), the Roman destruction of Carthage (2nd century BC), various religious pogroms and killings, such as that of Jews and Muslims (Moors) in fifteenth-century Spain or of Huguenots in sixteenth-century France, and the murderous colonization of South and North America between the fifteenth and nineteenth centuries. They argue that, in all of these cases, just as in the more recent events such as the Holocaust or the Rwandan genocide, a large number of people were deliberately massacred. In contrast, while acknowledging the instances of mass killings throughout history, most contemporary sociological approaches (Mann 2005; Levene 2005; Bauman 1989) demonstrate convincingly that genocides are quintessentially modern because they are qualitatively different from pre-modern massacres. Whereas the killings in previous eras were sporadic, ad hoc, technologically ineffective and ideologically unarticulated, in the modern age organizational and technological sophistication combined with society-wide ideological commitment creates conditions for the planning and execution of fully fledged genocidal projects. In other words, while before the modern age people were killed principally for where they were (to acquire territory, resources, etc.), in modernity individuals are massacred because of who they are.

BOX 18.8 MODERNITY AND THE HOLOCAUST

Zygmunt Bauman argues that genocide is a modern phenomenon because it is premised on Enlightenment-based engineering ambitions and blueprints to mould a new, racially pure world. In contrast to pogroms, violent riots and occasional massacres of traditional eras, which entailed ritualist morbidity and expressions of ad hoc brutality, the Holocaust was underpinned by the specific grand vista of 'the Final Solution', aimed at establishing a completely new and perfected social order. The modernity of genocide stems not only from future-oriented utopian grand vistas but also from unprecedented technological and organizational advancements. The implementation of 'the Final Solution' involved a sophisticated bureaucratic apparatus, a meticulous division of labour, a clearly defined hierarchical order, and faultless technology and science, all of which are products of modernity. Thus, for Bauman, the bureaucratic, business-like routine that is associated with modern state administration, big private corporations or modern factories was just as visible in the extermination camps of Auschwitz-Birkenau, Majdanek or Sobibor: 'Rather than producing goods, the raw material was human beings and the end product was death, so many units per day marked carefully on the manager's production charts. The chimneys, the very symbol of the modern factory system, poured forth acrid smoke produced by burning human flesh. The brilliantly organized railroad grid of modern Europe carried a new kind of raw material to the factories' (Bauman 1989: 8).

There is a near universal consensus among scholars that Hitler was directly responsible for the Holocaust. However, the long-term trajectories that led to 'the Final Solution' and other genocides are less clear. Whereas some historians and political scientists insist that specific individual or group agents are indispensable for initiating and implementing genocidal policies, many sociologists point to the structural conditions that make genocide and ethnic cleansing possible. In addition to the technological, organizational and ideological know-how that is necessary for the realization of any large-scale mass killing, several specific structural processes have been identified as decisive in creating conditions for genocide. For example, as both Shaw (2007, 2003) and Mann (2005) argue, rather than being a premeditated and well-planned event, conceived and executed by a small group of extremist leaders and their close disciples, genocide is a product of complex and contingent social processes. So, whereas some historians see the Rwandan (1994) and Armenian (1915) genocides as being caused by the actions of a handful of leaders (such as Mehmed Talaat, Ismail Enver and Ahmed Djemal in the Armenian case or Agathe Habyarimana or Ferdinand Nahimana in the Rwandan case), Mann (2005) argues that genocides are usually the outcome of gradual radicalization in the context of dramatically changed geopolitical environments. Moreover, Mann contests the view that murderous ethnic cleansing originates in authoritarian societies led by dictatorial leaders. On the contrary, the empirical evidence shows that most cases of genocide transpire in the context of the flawed democratization of formerly authoritarian regimes. In Mann's own words, 'Murderous cleansing is most likely to result where powerful groups within two ethnic groups aim at legitimate and achievable rival states "in the name of the people" over the same territory, and the weaker is aided from outside' (Mann 2005: 33). Hence the genocidal outcome is often the result of two competing state-building projects, both of which attempt to justify their existence in terms of popular sovereignty. However, as there is no clear distinction between the ethnic and civic conception of 'who constitutes the people', democratization can easily slide into a project of ethnic homogenization. In this context murderous ethnic cleansing becomes 'the dark side of democratization'. Thus Mann emphasizes that the Armenian genocide would not have been possible under the old authoritarian but multi-ethnic Ottoman Empire. Rather, the systematic mass murder came about through the structures of the modern, liberalizing, democratizing and Westernizing Turkish state led by nationalist Young Turks.

Similarly, Shaw (2007, 2003) and Levene (2005) see genocides as modern events produced by several structural contingencies, including intensive state-building, ideological radicalization and the presence of warfare. For Levene (2005: 35), 'genocide occurs when a state, perceiving the integrity of its agenda to be threatened by an aggregate population – defined by the state as an organic collectivity, or series of collectivities – seeks to remedy the situation by the systematic, en masse physical elimination of that aggregate, *in toto*, or until it is no longer perceived to represent a threat.' In Shaw's view, since genocides usually take place during times of war, it is crucial to explore the connection between the state, war and genocide. He identifies the three central links that bind genocidal experience with war and the state: 1) the genocides are always organized and implemented by state apparatuses; 2) the key organizational vehicle of the state's involvement in the genocidal process is the military, often aided by police, party organizations, paramilitaries or intelligence services; and 3) the genocides tend to take place during interstate or civil wars. Nevertheless, Shaw (2007) makes clear that war by itself does not cause genocide, as there have been thousands of wars in the modern era and a very few genocides. Instead he argues that genocide is best conceptualized as a distinct form of war where it is specific social groups rather than adversary militaries that are defined and targeted as the enemy of the state. As he puts it: 'when armed military force is being extensively used against organized armed enemies, then it is easier for leaders to take the extraordinary, generally illegitimate steps towards also using armed force against social groups as such' (Shaw 2003: 44). In other words, for most sociologists, rather than being solely a product of predetermined will of powerful individuals or small groups, genocides are generally the consequence of complex and contingent social processes.

Terrorism

Unlike genocide, which usually entails an attempt to obliterate entire groups of individuals with casualties numbering in millions, the victims of terrorism are generally few and far between. However, terrorism has often received much more attention in the public eye than many genocidal episodes. For example, the assassination of Archduke Ferdinand and his wife in 1914 (which led to the outbreak of the First World War) has attracted substantially more interest than the genocide of the Herero and Nama people in South-West Africa, which took place only a few years earlier. In a similar vein, the hijacking and killing of eleven Israeli members of the Olympic team by Black September at the 1972 Munich Olympics has completely overshadowed the murderous ethnic cleansing in Burundi that took place in the same year. Why is public opinion often more scandalized by killing of several individuals than by massacres that involved over 100,000 deaths?

Leaving aside the Eurocentric and colonial legacies of these particular two cases, there are two main reasons why terrorism is often more alarming to the general public than systematic mass murders. For one thing, unlike genocide, which is ordinarily part of an ongoing war and is often conceptualized initially through the prism of war experience as something exceptionally repugnant but not wholly unexpected, terrorism thrives on unpredictability and dramatic actions that provoke instant fear. The principal aim of terrorist groups is not to defeat their military opponents but to convey a specific political message. In this process they utilize violent and provocative practices (such as assassinations, hijackings, bombings, suicide missions or rocket and mortar attacks) aimed at producing maximum shock and fear among the wider public. For another thing, although state apparatuses also rely occasionally on similar tactics, most forms of terrorism are associated with non-state groups. Whereas genocide is first and foremost a product of state actions, terrorism has often been described as the 'weapon of the weak'. It is precisely for this reason that state authorities, the mass media and legal systems all over the world deem terrorism a profoundly illegitimate form of organized violence. While there are ongoing disputes between states as to whether a particular instance of mass killing should be termed genocide or just an extremely violent episode in a specific war (e.g., the Turkish government position on the Armenian genocide or Serbia's stance on the genocidal events in Srebrenica), there seems to be unanimity among state authorities worldwide that the use of violence for political purposes within one's state is an act of terrorism. The term 'terrorism' has been heavily politicized and generally used by state authorities to delegitimize various types of dissent, even when this was not expressed in violent form. The use of such definitions has also historically oscillated, so that some representatives of the same political movement were at one point dubbed 'terrorist' and at another 'freedom fighters' or 'politicians', as was the case of Nelson Mandela and the ANC before and after the Apartheid eras and of Yasser Arafat before, during and after the First and Second Intifada (Boehmer 2005; Victoroff 2005).

In other words, it is difficult to come up with a single, widely acceptable understanding of terrorism. Nevertheless, Vertigans's (2011) definition seems most suited for a sociological analysis. He sees terrorism as 'the targeted and intentional use of violence for political purposes through actions that can range in intended impact from intimidation to loss of life'.

Although since 9/11 terrorism studies have proliferated dramatically, there is an overwhelming dominance of psychological, political and economic explanations of this phenomenon. Just as with most other forms of organized violence, until very recently there was no systematic study of terrorism by sociologists. However, over the last decade several sociologists, including Gambetta and Hertog (2009), Vertigans (2011) and Collins (2009, 2008), have developed potent explanatory frameworks based on extensive empirical research. Most of these studies challenge the dominant psychological, political science and other interpretations of the causes and functions of terrorism. Hence, whereas psychologists such as Victoroff (2005), Bandura (2004), Kobrin (2002) and Horgan (2003) focus on identifying a personality profile of a typical terrorist, the sociological analyses emphasize the social context that gives rise to terrorist activity. For example, several influential psychological and political science studies have identified paranoid delusions, personality disorders, narcissistic rage, sexual repression, shame or brainwashing as the key explanatory variables that generate terrorist behaviour. Furthermore, terrorism is often linked to uncompromising ideological vistas and doctrinal fanaticism whereby individual terrorists are understood to be highly religious or exceptionally committed to specific secular ideologies (Salib 2003; Juergensmeyer 2003; Lachkar 2002). The general problem with these non-sociological interpretations is that they wrongly assume that terrorist actions are either caused by specific personality traits or are the direct product of political or ideological manipulation. However, as empirical research demonstrates, most psychological evaluations of known terrorists show that they are not more prone to psychological disorders than the average individual (McCauley 2002). On the contrary, as Sageman (2004) shows, the majority of suicide bombers had happy childhoods and grew up in caring families. The arguments about stringent ideological commitments and manipulation also fail to convince, as they cannot explain why, among thousands exposed to 'ideological brainwashing', only a very small number embark on a terrorist career (Vertigans 2011: 3). The key point is that terrorism cannot be explained if treated as a form of mental disorder. Rather than being a form of individual madness, terrorism is a social phenomenon.

Economic-centred arguments, with their focus on relative deprivation and economic disparities between the West and the rest, seem more persuasive, as they focus on social contexts rather than on the psychological deviation of individuals. There is no question that sharp social inequalities and class polarization breed popular discontent. However, what is crucial in attempting to explain terrorism is that, despite widespread inequalities and deprivation throughout history, popular dissatisfaction has rarely translated into acts of terrorism. Why is there more terrorist activity in the Middle East than in areas with even more pronounced inequalities, such as sub-Saharan Africa and South America? There is no direct causality between social injustices, poverty and violence, and the exclusive focus on deprivation cannot explain when, why and how people become terrorists. Moreover, a number of recent empirical studies indicate that the increase in living standards is, in fact, positively correlated with involvement in or support for terrorism (Hassan 2011: 39: Maleckova 2005).

Contemporary sociological analyses seem much more successful in accounting for the rise and fall of terrorism. There is a degree of agreement that terrorism is a complex and historically contingent phenomenon that originates in a combination of different macro-structural factors, including geopolitical transformations, economic inequities, changing cultural perceptions, rising aspirations and the political instrumentality of non-state organizations (Crenshaw 2011; Vertigans 2011). However, to understand fully how terrorist cells operate, it is also important to explore their micro-sociological dynamics. Hence sociologists have demonstrated convincingly that much terrorist activity is driven less by inflexible ideological dedication and more by specific micro-concerns. The motivation to join a terrorist cell and conduct violent insurgency is often strongly rooted in the micro-universe of family, friends, neighbours, peers and one's locality. Sageman (2008) has emphasized the role that peer- and family-based networks have played in recruiting for suicide missions. Collins (2009, 2008), Hassan (2011) and Ricolfi (2005) point out that radicalization is a long-term process where one does not became a terrorist as an individual but as a member of a small, internally cohesive group: 'The relative isolation of the individual from the surrounding society beforehand appears to play an important role in creating group cohesion, solidarity and a sense of common purpose' (Hassan 2011: 40).

Furthermore, in contrast to the popular view that sees terrorism as a response of impoverished, uneducated and desperate individuals, research indicates that the majority of terrorists come from relatively privileged backgrounds. Most members of al-Qaeda are voluntarily recruited from the upper or middle classes. They are as a rule highly educated, with the majority having higher degrees in science, engineering and medicine. As clearly demonstrated in Gambetta and Hertog's (2009) study of 404 extremist Islamists involved in violent actions, the majority were engineers. Interestingly enough, many suicide bombers grew up in a profoundly secular environment, and until the start of the Iraq War in 2003 only one-third of missions had been organized by religious groups, whereas the majority were carried out by secular organizations and movements such as the Tamil Tigers, the Kurdistan Workers Party (PKK) or Chechen rebel groups (Gambetta 2005: 261–2). The fact that terrorism has been and remains largely a middle-class phenomenon is linked in part to the organizational, technical and other skills required to undertake a successful terrorist action and in part to the particular worldview associated with dissatisfied middle-class cohorts. For example, Collins (2008b: 2) argues that middle-class individuals are particularly suited to act as suicide bombers precisely because they are usually not well accustomed to direct violent confrontations:

> the secret of their tactic is not to perform it as violence at all, until the very last second when they detonate the bomb . . . There is no confrontational tension because the bomber acts as if there is no confrontation. Clandestine, confrontation avoiding violence such as suicide bombing is . . . a pathway around confrontational tension. It succeeds only because the attacker is good at pretending that he or she is not threatening at all.

Table 18.2: **Suicide bombings, 1981–2006**			
	Number of attacks	**Minimum killed**	**Maximum killed**
1981	1	31	61
1982	1	62	62
1983	6	408	447
1984	2	20	29
1985	25	224	263
1986	3	9	9
1987	3	36	56
1988	1	9	9
1989	3	4	4
1990	3	9	16
1991	7	227	253
1992	2	32	38
1993	7	33	35
1994	10	201	225
1995	24	317	358
1996	23	413	446
1997	10	57	160
1998	17	421	735
1999	19	56	102
2000	39	262	394
2001	76	3324	3420
2002	92	1004	1036
2003	75	795	889
2004	190	1931	2267
2005	306	2572	3026
2006	255	2142	2385

Source: Flinders University Suicide Terrorism Database, 2008.

SEMINAR QUESTIONS

1 How valid is the distinction between 'old' and 'new' wars? Critically assess sociological theories of 'new wars'.

2 What causes social and political revolutions?

3 Is genocide a modern or an ancient phenomenon?

4 What motivates individuals to join terrorist organizations?

HUMAN RIGHTS AND VIOLENCE

Historical roots

Even though the concept of human rights is generally understood as being the antithesis of violence, its historical origins and its sociological meaning have developed in close relation with the expansion of specific violent and coercive actions. It is not a historical accident that the starting point of human rights discourses is often traced to the decision of the Second Lateran Council in 1139 to prohibit the use of the crossbow in wars between Christians or to the Statute of Kalisz in 1264 that proscribed the use of hate speech and discrimination against the Jewish minority in the kingdom of Poland (Robertson 2002; Lewin 1985). In both of these cases, the language and legal framework of rights emerged in direct response to the proliferation of organized violence: in the first case the central issue was intensifying intra-Christian conflicts as an outcome of the Great Schism and the second emerged in the context of the invasion by the Golden Horde that devastated much of the medieval kingdom of Poland. This dialectical inter-connection between the rise of rights and the expansion of organized violence was particularly visible in the aftermath of the French and American revolutions. These two pivotal events in history were crucial in institutionalizing the idea of human rights, which became enshrined in such fundamental documents as the French Declaration of the Rights of Man and of the Citizen (1789) and the US Declaration of Independence and Virginia Declaration of Rights (1776). Nevertheless, despite their Enlightenment-inspired rhetoric of equality, justice and 'rights of man', the two revolutions were themselves instituted through profoundly violent upheavals and the mass slaughter of those deemed to be 'anti-revolutionary forces'. Furthermore, revolution-ary violence was followed by decades of incessant and brutal warfare, with the revolutionaries determined to impose the Enlightenment principles on the rest of the world by coercive means (Malešević 2010: 121). While the two revolutions were highly significant in making the notion of human rights integral to the constitutional and legal systems of many states, it was really the devastating experience of the Second World War that raised the idea of human rights to the global level. The mass casualties of the war and the deliberate targeting of civilians, including the unprecedented experience of the Holocaust, gave new, worldwide impetus to articulating a set of general principles, adopted in 1948 by the General Assembly of the UN as the Universal Declaration of Human Rights. Hence, paradoxically, it was the unparalleled proliferation of organized violence in the world that ultimately gave birth to the universally accepted concept of human rights. As Turner (2006a: 45) rightly emphasizes: 'Human rights are essentially a twentieth-century legal response to atrocities committed against civilian populations.'

The sociology of human rights

Despite their pronounced interest in the sociology of law, Marx, Durkheim, Weber and other classical theorists did not consider human rights to be of major significance in understand-ing social relations. While Durkheim understood legal norms as a form of society-imposed obligations and downplayed the importance of individual choice, Weber analysed the law through the prism of ever increasing rationality and value neutrality where there was no place for natural rights. For Marx, human rights were no more than a bourgeois façade which hides the class-based inequalities that preserve the status quo between property owners and the pro-letariat (Turner 2006b). This scepticism towards the analytical relevance of human rights still

BOX 18.9 THE UN DECLARATION OF HUMAN RIGHTS

The UN declaration conceptualizes human rights as fundamental inalienable rights to which everyone is entitled on the simple account of being a human being. They include the right to life, liberty, security, equality, the preservation of one's dignity, to own property, recognition before the law, freedom of movement and residence, nationality, freedom of thought, conscience and religion, and many more specific rights. The development of human rights theory and practice has been analysed extensively by legal scholars, historians and political scientists, but until recently most sociologists have neglected this research area.

permeates much of mainstream sociology. For some the very notion of human rights is too normative and too prescriptive to allow for detached and balanced sociological analysis. For others the emphasis on rights is counterproductive as it shifts the focus of sociological analysis from dynamic forces that are structure and action towards more formal and static entitlements that are rights. The universalist principles of a human right have also been questioned. Some sociologists argue that sociological analyses are meant to focus on exploring the diversity and difference of social experience, which the formal and universalist concept of rights inherently precludes. However, most criticisms have been levelled against the liberal, Western and individualist underpinning of the human rights discourse. For example, Žižek (2005: 120) argues that:

> liberal attitudes towards the other are characterized both by respect for otherness, openness to it, and an obsessive fear of harassment . . . My duty to be tolerant towards the other effectively means that I should not get too close to him or her, not intrude into his space – in short, that I should respect his intolerance towards my over-proximity. This is increasingly emerging as the central human right of advanced capitalist society: the right not to be 'harassed', that is, to be kept at a safe distance from others.

And 'universal human rights are effectively the right of white, male property-owners to exchange freely on the market, exploit workers and women, and exert political domination.'

However, several sociologists have attempted to develop more nuanced theories of human rights. Woodiwiss (2005) widens the traditional liberal understanding of human rights to encompass not only political and civil liberties but also economic, social and cultural rights. He argues that, from their inception, the discourses of rights have always been interweaved with power relations and especially with the liberal focus on the protection of private property and capital. The contemporary framing of human rights, shaped by powerful political actors in the USA and Europe, remains determined to constrain 'the effective meaning and the disciplinary power of international human rights within the narrow, "market friendly" limits defined by civil and political rights' (ibid.: 121). To counter this trend, Woodiwiss advocates a 'new universalism' that would go beyond the restrictive 'Western' understanding of rights and would be completely independent of the political and economic order one lives under.

Whereas Woodiwiss combines the historical sociological analysis of rights discourses with the normative prescriptive diagnosis, Bryan Turner provides a more general sociological theory of human rights. Drawing on his previous work on the sociology of the body and citizenship, Turner (2006a, 2006b) insists that, since human beings share the same ontological foundations and common bodily vulnerability, there is a need to conceptualize human rights as the universal properties of all human beings. Although collective experiences and ways of shared life are different, all human beings are inherently vulnerable creatures who can feel pain and humiliation and whose lives are finite. To protect themselves, humans require institutional safeguards, but the institutions built to protect our intrinsic vulnerability, such as the state, church or political party, are often the same ones that can endanger our very existence. States provide security for their citizens, but states are also the main threats to human rights: they initiate, implement and support genocidal projects, ethnic cleansing, wars, insurgencies and other forms of organized violence. Hence the social arrangements under which we all live remain precarious and prone to unintended consequences. This is visible particularly in the complex and contradictory relationship between citizenship and human rights. For Turner (2006a, 2001b) there is an inherent and unresolved tension between the social rights of citizens and individual human rights. Both the French and American revolutions inaugurated simultaneously the idea that all human beings have natural and inalienable rights and that 'the nation is essentially the source of all sovereignty'. Nevertheless, in Turner's view, these two principles are incompatible, as one is seen to be an inborn and absolute right and the other as a state creation. In other words, there is an irresolvable strain between citizenship and human rights. Citizenship entitlements encompass a set of specific social rights which are protected by the legal and coercive structures of the sovereign state. They include civil, political and some socio-economic rights, from the freedom of religion, expression and assembly to universal suffrage and some welfare provisions (Marshall 1950). Moreover, these entitlements are also linked to the specific responsibilities that citizens are expected to fulfil, among them their willingness to pay taxes, attain full employment, fight for or support the state in times of war, be conscientious parents and perform other civic duties. In direct contrast, human rights are individual entitlements that stem from the fact that one is member of the human race; they are universal rights that have no obvious or institutionalized connection to the contributory obligations. There is, as Turner (2006a: 46) points out, 'no corresponding system of taxation relating to the possession of human rights. There is as yet no formal declaration of human duties . . . The United Nations Declaration implies obligations, but they are not clearly or forcefully specified. While states enforce social rights, there is no sovereign power uniformly to enforce human rights at the global level.'

The consequence of this is that, historically, citizenship, meaning a set of entitlements and duties tied to a specific nation-state, was a much more effective social device for protecting one's rights. As early critics of human rights discourse such as Arendt (1951) emphasized, once state protection is taken away, human rights became abstract claims with no authority to compel their implementation. For Turner (2006b: 48), the intensification of globalization provides another layer of complexity to this relationship between national citizenship and human rights. In his view, the transformation of the nation-state model and the apparent weakening of state sovereignty are likely to undermine not only citizenship entitlements and obligations but also the organizational mechanisms for the protection of all rights. In this context, calls for flexible, multiple and global citizenship can only be deceptive, as 'to employ the notion of citizenship outside the confines of the nation state is to distort its meaning, indeed to render it meaningless.'

While both Turner and Woodiwiss aim to ground their historical analyses of rights in the corporal frailty, materiality and universality of human beings, a number of recent studies (Waters

In the recent troubles in Syria, millions of Syrians have fled the country as refugees. The state has failed to meet their rights as citizens, but, while there are refugee camps (such as Kawrgosk Refugee Camp in Irbil, Iraq, shown here) and limited support available from the international community, there is no formal system to ensure their human rights – outside the state/citizenship system, they are in part left to fend for themselves. (© IHH Humanitarian Relief Foundation/Flickr)

2001, 1996; Gregg 2011) have emphasized the socially constructed character of human rights discourses. Hence Waters argues that, rather than seeing human rights as having biological foundations in human vulnerability, the focus should shift towards the historical and cultural contexts under which such discourses emerge and proliferate. In Waters's (1996) view, 'the construction of universal human rights' is 'the product of the balance of power between political interests at a particular point in history'. The popularity of human rights interpretative frames in the aftermath of the Second World War was not seen as a logical outcome of the shared trauma of the Holocaust. Instead Waters perceives this development through the prism of victorious allies consolidating their hegemonic position and interests over the side that lost the war. Similarly Gregg (2011) questions the idea of the universality and corporality of human rights and aims to show how universalizing discourses of rights tend to rely on theological or metaphysical assumptions that are external to very diverse and localized ways of living. He insists that human rights are culturally particular and rooted in locally developed understandings. Since they are socially and locally constructed, they are also dynamic and prone to what Gregg calls 'cognitive reframing' – the changing perceptions of what constitutes a specific right. Female genital mutilation in parts of Africa and child prostitution in South-East

Asia may have their origins in local traditions and customs, but gradual cognitive reframing has helped change local understandings of what constitutes a human right.

In spite of their pronounced differences, the sociological analyses of rights have helped provide a much stronger explanatory ground for the study of human rights than that available in law, history or political science. Human rights are constituted, articulated, changed, advanced, impaired and developed through social relations and interaction. Since sociology is the discipline that studies the collective interactions and relations of human beings, it is best suited to the comprehensive exploration of human rights.

SEMINAR QUESTIONS

1 The UN declaration of human rights is officially called 'The Universal Declaration of Human Rights'. Read this declaration (www.un.org/en/documents/udhr/) and assess whether its articles are genuinely universal.

2 What is distinct about sociological approaches to the study of human rights? Critically assess the approaches of Turner and Woodiwiss.

CONCLUSION

The popular view, shared by some academics, insists that most forms of organized violence belong to past eras and as such have little relevance in understanding the contemporary world. The main aim of this chapter was to show that one cannot fully understand how social orders develop and change without engaging with the coercive and violent aspects of these processes. Even though in the contemporary world it has become less visible, violence is far from being extinct. On the contrary, the modern era has witnessed a proliferation of different types of organized violence: genocides, civil and interstate wars, revolutions and terrorism. Moreover, with the expansion of the infrastructural powers of modern social organizations, many forms of individual and group violence have been gradually converted into the coercive strength of the state, business corporations and other institutions. Similarly, to understand fully the expansion of human rights rhetoric and practice, one needs to link this historical development to wider social processes and in particular to the transformation of organized violence. As shown in this chapter, it is not a historical accident that the discourse of human rights emerges and expands together with the revolutionary upheavals and wars of the late eighteenth, the nineteenth and the twentieth centuries. Instead of focusing on the legislative context of rights, it is crucial to explore the sociological underpinning of human rights discourses. Although much of post-Second World War sociology tended to ignore the study of organized violence and human rights, this has changed significantly in recent years, and contemporary sociologists have developed comprehensive theoretical and empirical studies which demonstrate that neither organized violence nor human rights can be properly explained without sociology.

SEMINAR QUESTIONS

1 Compare and contrast the principal features of organized violence in the pre-modern and modern era.

2 What is the industrialization of war? How important were wars for development of the modern nation-state?

3 What are the social sources of violence? Critically assess economistic, culturalist and political approaches in the study of organized violence.

4 Some authors argue that the very concept of 'a human right' is overly individualist and Eurocentric. On which grounds are such arguments made?

FURTHER READING

▶ The classical and contemporary sociological theories of organized violence are extensively analysed in S. Malešević (2010) *The Sociology of War and Violence* (Cambridge University Press) and in H. Joas and W. Knöbl (2012) *War in Social Thought* (Princeton University Press). Highly accessible sociological studies of contemporary warfare include P. Hirst (2001) *War and Power in the 21st Century* (Polity), M. Kaldor (2007) *New and Old Wars* (2nd edn, Polity) and M. Shaw (2005) *The New Western Way of War* (Polity).

▶ A very good overview of different approaches to the study of revolutions is J. Foran (ed.) (2004) *Theorising Revolutions* (Routledge).

▶ The most influential recent sociological studies of genocide include M. Mann (2005) *The Dark Side of Democracy* (Cambridge University Press), Z. Bauman (1989) *Modernity and the Holocaust* (Polity) and M. Shaw (2003) *War and Genocide* (Polity). Although there are many books on terrorism, a very few develop an explicitly sociological approach. Among more sociological analyses two stand out: M. Crenshaw (2011) *Explaining Terrorism* (Routledge) and S. Vertigans (2011) *The Sociology of Terrorism* (Routledge).

▶ B. S. Turner (2006) *Vulnerability and Human Rights* (Pennsylvania University Press) remains the best sociological introduction to human rights.

19

CRIME

concepts, causes, control

ROBERT REINER

CONTENTS

INTRODUCTION

CRIME IS A PERENNIAL theme in popular culture, as all branches of the mass media indicate. Approximately 20 to 30 percent of the content of most types of mass media are news or entertainment stories about crime and criminal justice (Greer and Reiner 2012).

Crime has become a central focus of political debate and public concern. Fear of crime as measured by opinion polls has been one of the main public anxieties since the 1970s. The risks of crime as indicated by official statistics increased for some forty years after the mid-1950s, although since then they have declined (a decrease still disbelieved by most people). This has resulted in a culture and daily practices hugely shaped by the perceived threat of crime.

This chapter offers an analysis of contemporary issues of crime and control, drawing on sociological research evidence and theory. It begins by probing the problematic concept of crime, followed by a critical review of the major theoretical perspectives seeking to understand it. The core of the chapter offers an analysis of patterns and trends of crime in contemporary society and how they have been reacted to and, in turn, shaped by crime-control and criminal justice policies.

The key sources of crime lie deep in society, culture and political economy, so that even the wisest and most effective forms of prevention, policing and penality are at best salves, not solutions to the problems posed by crime. The law and order perspective that has become entrenched as a political consensus since the 1970s, reflecting the hegemony of neoliberal economic and social governance more generally, is misguided and dangerous. As the crime novelist Raymond Chandler put it sharply in *The Long Goodbye*: 'Crime isn't a disease, it's a symptom. Cops are like a doctor that gives you aspirin for a brain tumour.' Tough and smart policing and penal policy may succeed in reducing crime for a time without tackling its fundamental roots (as they have done since the mid-1990s). But this is symptom suppression – 'liddism' – holding down a lid on simmering social tensions (Rogers 2002).

WHAT IS CRIME?

The term 'crime' is usually tossed about as if its meaning is clear and unproblematic, yet most arguments about it involve people talking past each other (for more detailed discussion of the concept of crime, see Henry and Lanier 2001; Reiner 2007: ch. 2; Lacey and Zedner 2012). At least five different constructions of crime can be distinguished.

Legal constructions

If asked to define 'crime', most people would probably invoke the criminal law as its basis. And they would have the authority of the Oxford English Dictionary on their side (crime is 'an action or omission which constitutes an offence and is punishable by law'). Yet there is considerable conflict between legal, moral and social constructions of crime.

Defining the scope of criminal law itself in substantive, rather than procedural, terms is hugely problematic because of the vast, rapidly growing and shifting corpus of criminal law. Consequently, most criminal law texts define crime in a formal, essentially circular way – e.g., 'crime is an act capable of being followed by criminal proceedings having a criminal outcome, and a proceeding or its outcome is criminal if it has certain characteristics which mark it as criminal' (Williams 1955: 107).

Some critical legal theorists have sought to transcend the divide between legal and sociological conceptions of crime by the concept of 'criminalization', recognizing that 'the boundaries between legal and social constructions of crime are contingent on the environment in which they are formed' (Lacey and Zedner 2012: 159). This analysis underlines the question-begging character of attempts to define crime in purely legal terms. It points to the variety of alternative, often conflicting, conceptions of crime apart from, and often in conflict with, the legal.

Normative constructions

The formalist legal definition of crime opens itself to normative critique. On the one hand, critical criminologists have frequently argued that law fails to define as criminal very serious and wilful harm committed by powerful people, states and corporations (Green and Ward 2012; Nelken 2012). Tax 'avoidance' refers to ways of minimizing payment that are legal, but perhaps at least the more egregious tactics should be criminalized as evasion? Don't 'banksters', whose reckless practices have wrecked the lives of so many since the 2007 credit crunch, deserve criminalization alongside the most heinous gangsters?

Such arguments have developed into the recent claim that criminology should be replaced by 'zemiology', the study of serious culpable harms, making problematic whether or not they are proscribed by criminal law (Hillyard et al. 2004). The definition of 'harms' is, of course, as socially contentious as notions of 'crime', but it explicitly invites normative evaluation, not authoritative declaration.

Conversely, the law criminalizes conduct that perhaps should not be sanctioned at all, or would best be regulated without criminal penalties. Liberal political philosophers have claimed that, for both principled and pragmatic reasons, 'private (im)moral behaviour' should not be subject to criminal law. This was the subject of two famous debates, the first between John Stuart Mill and Judge Fitzjames Stephen in the nineteenth century, and the second between

H. L. A. Hart and Lord Justice Devlin in the 1960s, following the Wolfenden Report's recommendation that the criminal law regulation of homosexuality and prostitution should be liberalized (Mill [1859] 1998; Hart 1963; Devlin 1965).

The question of whether prostitution should be legalized is commonly debated. Is what some people judge 'immoral behaviour' between consensual adults being criminalized? Are vulnerable women being criminalized and at risk of not accessing the help and security they require, for fear of arrest? (© philippe leroyer/Flickr)

Social/cultural constructions

Emile Durkheim, the great French sociologist, made some seminal contributions to the study of crime. One was his influential attempt to provide a sociological definition of crime: 'Crime shocks sentiments which, for a given social system are found in all healthy consciences . . . an act is criminal when it offends strong and defined states of the collective conscience' (Durkheim [1893] 1973: 73, 80).

As Durkheim himself recognized (anticipating contemporary critical criminology's 'labelling theory'), conceptions of the criminal vary considerably between and within societies, and over time. What is socially sanctioned as deviant will vary from the formal definitions of law and is hotly contested between different groups. Jeremy Clarkson fans may complain that the police and courts harass motorists, not 'real' criminals. Are speeding or driving using a mobile phone socially deviant? They are certainly against criminal law, and sometimes prosecuted, but many people engage in them. Drink-driving is socially deviant in most circles nowadays, but was not in England until some three decades ago, although it was even then in Scandinavia. Who is 'really' criminal – the 'honest, victimized' householder or the young burglar she or he shoots in the back?

Criminal justice constructions

Who gets processed formally by the criminal justice system suggests another contrasting social construction of crime and criminality. Recorded crimes and criminals form a tiny, unrepresentative sample of all law-breaking. The overwhelming majority of those in prison are male, from economically underprivileged groups, and there is a huge disproportion of black and other ethnic minority people. And they are in prison mainly for street crimes, not suite crimes – car-theft and burglary, not insider trading or pensions mis-selling.

Mass media and policy constructions

The constructions of crime offered by the mass media indicate yet another pattern. Mass media representations follow a 'law of opposites' (Surette 2011) compared to official crime statistics.

Mass media stories ('factual' or 'fictional') focus overwhelmingly on the most serious violent and sexual offences, above all murder, even though these are thankfully rare (Greer and Reiner 2012). Victims and offenders in media accounts are disproportionately older and higher up the social scale than their counterparts in official statistics (though they share the common feature of being mainly men). The media identify criminal justice primarily with the police, who are portrayed as effective, law-abiding and morally virtuous. Negative depictions have increased but remain a minority. In news and fiction stories the police almost invariably catch the perpetrator, although in reality only a tiny proportion of crimes are cleared up.

It is this mass media picture that informs most public and policy debate. The media focus on the suffering of a (thankfully) small minority who are the massively injured, vulnerable, angelically innocent victims of sensational but rare crimes. Politicians are highly sensitive to such reporting, thus distorting policy-making.

SEMINAR QUESTIONS

1 'A crime is any act prohibited by criminal law'. Discuss.

2 What relationship, if any, is there between crime and morality?

3 How accurate are newspapers, films and television in portraying crime and criminal justice?

MODERN CRIMINOLOGY

The term 'criminology' was originally associated with a positivist attempt to explain crime by the biological characteristics of criminals: the 'science of the criminal', pioneered by Lombroso's 1876 *Criminal Man*. 'Criminology' has for most of its history been dominated by positivist approaches, biological, psychological and sociological, although these were seriously challenged by the 1960s development of critical perspectives.

Positivist analyses of crime face some fundamental problems. Crime is not a universal, objectively definable type of behaviour. So how can we aspire to objective knowledge of it?

BOX 19.1 BASIC AXES OF CRIMINOLOGICAL DEBATE

Criminological analysis has revolved around certain key dimensions of debate, reflecting broader currents of argument in social science and philosophy. Three of the recurrent tensions are between:

1 *autonomy vs. determinism* How far is human behaviour structured by causes? How much scope is there for autonomy and choice?

2 *conservatism vs. critique* How far does the analyst accept the values and purposes of criminal law and criminal justice? How far does she subject them to critique and perhaps rejection?

3 *individual vs. society as the analytic unit* How far does the explanation of human behaviour lie within the actor's own physical constitution or individual psyche? How much is it structured by the social and cultural groups and networks within which action occurs?

Positivist criminology offers deterministic analyses of supposed causal relationships between variables, leaving no scope for human consciousness, agency or values.

Historical development is never as clear-cut as in the simplistic periodizations of textbook writers. There is always a complex coexistence of competing perspectives. Nonetheless, some broad periods can be distinguished in terms of the relative dominance of particular theories.

1870–1960: varieties of positivist criminology

As noted earlier, the term 'criminology' was coined in the 1870s to refer to a new positivist 'science of the criminal', at first locating criminality in the physical constitution of the offender, but later encompassing a variety of psychological perspectives. Even during the heyday of individualistic positivism, however, some analysts offered social accounts of crime. The acknowledged pioneers of *sociological* criminology were the 'moral statisticians' Guerry and Quetelet, in 1820s France. Using new national crime statistics, Quetelet and Guerry showed that poor, unemployed, uneducated young men were more likely to commit offences – in places where there were more wealthy people to steal from. Crime was a function both of social pressures stemming from inequality *and* of the distribution of targets and temptations. Quetelet's most fundamental discovery was the relative constancy of rates and patterns of crime over substantial periods of time, which stimulated Durkheim's later development of an explicitly sociological perspective.

During the 1920s the Chicago School analysed patterns of crime in different areas of cities, seeing these as shaped by structural socio-economic pressures, mediated by interactions between people forming different cultures. In the 1930s Edwin Sutherland synthesized social ecology and symbolic interactionism in a proposed general theory of crime: differential association. He postulated that crime was generated by a predominance of deviant over conformist meanings in a person's social world. Although he accepted the association between low social class and conventionally defined crime shown by the Chicago School's spatial analyses, he certainly did not accept any implication that crime was inherently a product of poverty. On the contrary, his most significant contribution to criminology was his creation of the concept of 'white-collar' crime, which he saw as flourishing in large corporations and among the powerful and privileged, albeit largely hidden and unrecorded by official statistics.

Robert Merton's development of anomie theory in the 1930s remains the most influential broadly positivistic sociological theory of crime. Merton adapted the concept of anomie from Durkheim's 1897 book *Suicide*. How it still illuminates contemporary issues will be discussed below (see p. 579).

1960–1975: critical and radical criminologies

During the 1960s, reflecting broader ferment in culture and social relations, the sociology of crime and criminology went through an epistemological break, a fundamental reformulation of its intellectual agenda. The subject had been dominated by two interdependent projects: the (largely positivistic) explanation of criminal behaviour and the application of this to improve techniques governing deviance and disorder. There was little questioning about whose interests were served by the institutions of law and order. Why were some people (predominantly disadvantaged and powerless) deemed deviant and in need of correction or punishment, while others – who engaged in similar or even more harmful behaviours – were not? Whose law, what order? These questions came to the forefront during the 1960s and 1970s with the emergence of critical and radical criminologies.

BOX 19.2 MARXISM AND CRIME

Until the 1960s flowering of radical criminology, Marxists or others on the left seldom referred to crime or criminal justice. It is often stated that, in his mature theoretical work, Marx did not systematically address issues of law, crime or criminal justice. *Capital* does, however, contain a lengthy historical analysis of the emergence of the Factory Acts in early nineteenth-century England (Marx [1867] 1954: ch. 10). This constitutes a pioneering case study of criminalization and of what would nowadays be called corporate crime. Marx's account is very far from the economic determinism attributed to him and gives weight, in complex interaction, to both structure and action (for more detailed discussion, see Reiner 2002: 239–52; 2012: 309–10).

Willem Bonger, a Dutch professor, made the first attempt to develop a systematic Marxist analysis of crime (Bonger [1916] 1969). In Bonger's analysis, the structure of capitalism generates particular criminogenic pressures by stimulating a culture of egoism – at all levels of society. This enhanced the material aspirations of workers and the poor and weakened their internal controls against predation in times of hardship. Bonger traced a complex multiplicity of linkages between the structural conflicts of capitalism, with its general egoism, and particular forms of crime. The root causes of crime in the larger immorality and injustices of capitalism did not remove the moral accountability of offenders. Bonger introduced many ideas that were explored in later critical criminology. He recognized that legal conceptions of crime reflected disproportionately the interests of the powerful, anticipating labelling theory.

This critical break in the study of crime that occurred in the 1960s was a shift from the questions why criminal behaviour occurs, and how it can be corrected, to why behaviours and people are labelled as criminal. The subject position moved from a taken-for-granted identification with law-makers and enforcers to an appreciation of the position of those labelled as deviant.

Howard Becker pioneered the fundamental critique known as labelling theory. Building on the theoretical foundations of social constructionism and symbolic interactionism, this problematized precisely those questions that positivist 'correctionalist' criminology left unexplored.

> The same behaviour may be an infraction of the rules at one time and not at another; may be an infraction when committed by one person, but not when committed by another; some rules are broken with impunity, others are not. In short, whether a given activity is deviant or not depends in part on the nature of the act (that is whether or not it violates some rule) and in part on what other people do about it. (Becker 1963: 14)

The labelling perspective has transformed criminological theory and practice since the 1960s. Its permanently valuable contributions include the recognition of criminal law and criminal justice as problematic research areas that shape at least as much as they control crime. These developments are taken for granted and domesticated within mainstream sociological criminology.

What is questionable is the imperialistic version of labelling theory that claimed to offer a total theory of crime. This grandiose version flourished as the 1960s counter-culture's criminology and could be plausible as a general theory only in that context. Its claims are epitomized by two frequently cited quotes:

1 'deviance is not a quality of the act . . . but of the application . . . of rules and sanctions' (Becker 1963).
2 'Older sociology tended to rest heavily upon the idea that deviance leads to social control . . . the reverse idea i.e. that social control leads to deviance, is equally tenable and the potentially richer premise for studying deviance in modern society' (Lemert 1967).

While it is the case, as Lemert claims, that often 'social control leads to deviance', it is disputable whether it is the 'richer premise for studying deviance'. Lemert's assertion rests on the assumption that 'secondary deviance', which follows labelling, is more pervasive and problematic than 'primary deviance', which precedes it. But this is an empirical question that is likely to vary in different times and places, and with regard to different kinds of deviance and social reaction, not a 'premise'.

Any plausibility held by the imperialistic claims of labelling theorists derived from the limited scope of their empirical research. This concentrated on marginal or exotic forms of deviance, which could reasonably be seen as problematic only because of labelling: marijuana use, the bohemian subculture of jazz musicians (Becker 1963); 'hustlers, beats and others' (Polsky 1967); 'crimes without victims' (Schur 1965). Any early critique castigated this pithily as the 'sociology of nuts, sluts and "preverts"' (Liazos 1972).

The focus of labelling theory on the dramatic and colourful ignored the harms done by some primary deviance. Labelling theorists concentrated on the creation of crime by the labelling activities of low-level control agents, reversing the moral assessments of criminal law and justice – as explicitly advocated by Becker in his call for criminologists to ask 'Whose Side Are We On?' (1967). This bracketed out the structural determinants of control activity – law, culture, political economy, social institutions (as Gouldner argued in his 1968 riposte to Becker 'The Sociologist as Partisan'). This critique stimulated the morphing of labelling theory in the 1970s into more politically radical forms of 'new criminology' and 'deviance theory' (Cohen 1971; Taylor, Walton and Young 1973, 1975; Hall et al. 1978).

Labelling theory had a huge impact, although its influence is now largely hidden, domesticated in the proliferating analyses of policing, media and criminal justice. Although the sweeping claims of its originators are hard to sustain, its legacy lives on explicitly in contemporary cultural criminology and other qualitative and critical approaches (Hayward and Young 2012).

Macro-sociology and political economy combined with the insights of the labelling perspective in the Marxist-influenced radical criminologies that became prominent in the early 1970s. The flagship text was *The New Criminology*, with its conception of a 'fully social' theory of crime (Taylor, Walton and Young 1973: 268–80). This offered 'a political economy of criminal action, and of the reaction it excites', together with 'a politically informed social psychology of these ongoing social dynamics'.

The checklist of elements for a 'fully social theory' is a valuable reminder of the wider contexts in which deviance and control are embedded. Nonetheless, it has been criticized for not including enough. Despite its emphasis on social psychology as well as political economy, one of the co-authors of *Policing the Crisis* argues that it does not adequately probe the psychodynamics of crime and control (Jefferson 2008). It also brackets off the existentialist appreciation of 'the seductions of crime' from the perspective of offenders (Katz 1988) and downplays cultural, interpretive and symbolic dimensions (which are foregrounded in contemporary

BOX 19.3 *THE NEW CRIMINOLOGY*'S 'FULLY SOCIAL THEORY'

The New Criminology postulated that a 'fully social theory' must include analysis of:

1 the wider origins of the deviant act . . . *a political economy of crime* . . .
2 immediate origins of the deviant act . . . a *social psychology of crime* . . .
3 the actual act . . .
4 immediate origins of social reaction . . . a *social psychology of social reaction* . . .
5 wider origins of social reaction . . . a *political economy of social reaction* . . .
6 the outcome of the social reaction on deviant's further action . . .
7 the nature of the deviant process as a whole.

(Taylor, Walton and Young 1973: 270–8)

The closest attempt to incorporate all these elements was the magisterial study of mugging and the reaction to it, *Theorizing Crime Deviance* (Hall 2012). Starting from the sentencing of the perpetrators of a robbery in Birmingham, the book analysed the mass media construction of a 'moral panic' about 'mugging' and police responses to this. It then developed a wide-ranging account of British economic, political, social and cultural history since the Second World War to explain the deeper concerns that 'mugging' condensed. The later chapters offered an analysis of the impact of transformations in the political economy on black young men in particular, and how this structured the formation of specific subcultures in which robbery was more likely. *Policing the Crisis* remains a uniquely ambitious attempt to synthesize macro-, middle-range and micro-analysis of a particular offence and the reaction to it.

cultural criminology; cf. Hayward and Young 2012). Furthermore, it does not suggest practicable crime-control policies, the basis of the 'Left Realist' auto-critique (Lea and Young 1984).

1975 onwards: the 'realist' counter-revolutions

Left Realism claimed radical criminology was in an 'aetiological crisis', as the reductions in poverty and unemployment associated with the post-war Keynesian welfare state failed to stop crime from rising (Young 1986). Left Realists emphasized immediate steps to control crime by more effective policing and criminal justice, not the 'root causes' approach attributed to earlier 'left idealism'.

Nonetheless, when Left Realists considered crime causation, they incorporated earlier sociological perspectives such as relative deprivation and anomie, although the origin of these ideas was scarcely acknowledged (e.g., Lea and Young 1984: ch. 6). In the 1990s some radical theorists returned to macro-analyses of the relationship between crime, criminal justice and late modernity or consumer society, in combination with interpretive cultural analysis (Taylor 1999; Hall, Winlow and Ancrum 2008; Hall 2011). There have also been vigorous continuations of radical approaches in certain areas, notably the critical analysis of gender issues by feminist criminologists (Heidensohn and Silvestri 2012).

Since the mid-1970s, mainstream criminology, especially in the USA, has been dominated by pragmatic realism, concerned with 'what works?'. This was initially based on an explicit rejection of 'root cause' theories seeking to explain crime by macro-social causes (Wilson 1975: xv). Causal explanation was not eschewed altogether but pursued at individual (Wilson and Herrnstein 1985), situational or community levels. These are more amenable to policy interventions that do not raise questions of wider social justice or reform.

While realism largely ousted macro-sociology and political economy in studying crime, it was associated with a resurgence of the economics of crime applying Chicago School neoclassical economic models (Becker 1968). There has also been a broader revival of rational choice theories based on an 'economic man' model of the offender, which has had huge influence on government crime-control policies.

SEMINAR QUESTIONS

1 What individual biological and psychological factors have been used to explain criminal behaviour?

2 Are sociological theories of crime too sympathetic to offenders?

3 One of the most controversial statements in modern criminology was the 1960s assertion that 'deviance is not a quality inherent in an act, but a consequence of others' reactions to it'. Assess its significance and validity.

4 What was 'critical' about critical criminology?

5 Assess the sources and the consequences of the variety of 'realist' perspectives that developed after the 1970s.

EXPLAINING CONTEMPORARY CRIME TRENDS: AN ECLECTIC MODEL

As the above review indicates, there are many competing perspectives on the conceptualization, commission and control of crime. Most were formulated as imperialistic explanations whose proponents believed they had found *the* magic bullet for the problem of order. While these grand claims cannot be sustained for any perspective, they do all illuminate aspects of the interlocking processes of crime and control.

The synthesis I propose is unashamedly a 'root cause' theory of the kind that was castigated by 'realists' of both the right and the left. While recognizing the need to find effective short-run policies to alleviate the problems of crime, there remain social 'root causes' that must be addressed.

The ultimate sources of crime lie deep in social structure and culture: they are social injustice and an egoistic ethos, as suggested by many classic theorists, notably Bonger and Merton. There is a mass of evidence demonstrating that inequality and social exclusion are linked to crime.

The inequality–crime link does not excuse those who commit crimes (the canard suggested by conservative critics of social explanations of crime), but it does show that it is necessary to probe the deeper roots of criminality if we are serious about wanting to protect potential victims. Offenders bear responsibility for the harm they do – but all citizens have a responsibility to get tough on crime's ultimate causes: the unjust and amoral societies we live in.

BOX 19.4 INEQUALITY AND CRIME: THE EVIDENCE

In his book *Recession, Crime and Punishment*, Steven Box (1987: 86–90) reviewed seventeen econometric studies probing links between income inequality and crime levels. Theoretically these variables would be expected to be closely associated, because inequality would be likely to produce anomie, motivating property crime in particular. Twelve studies reported that greater inequality was associated with more property crime, but five studies of homicide did not find a link.

More recent work confirms the association between property crime and inequality but shows overwhelming evidence for a link with homicide and violent crime too.

The Equality Trust's 'Income Inequality and Violent Crime' (2011) cites eleven recent studies demonstrating associations between variations in inequality (over time and between different places) and levels of homicide and serious violent crime (for more detail, see also Wilkinson and Pickett 2009: ch. 10).

Danny Dorling's paper 'Prime Suspect' demonstrates vividly how the large increase in homicide in Britain over the last three decades is linked to the surge in inequality and social exclusion that stemmed from the Thatcherite economic policies after 1979 (Dorling 2004).

Crime vs. criminality

It is helpful to distinguish between the concepts of crime and criminality. The latter term has been invoked frequently by coalition government ministers, who described the riots of 2011 as 'sheer criminality' (Theresa May) and 'criminality pure and simple' (David Cameron).

It is more illuminating to see the concepts of 'crime' and 'criminality' as distinct from each other rather than as synonymous. 'Criminality' connotes a *propensity* to produce crime (Currie 2000). Biological and psychological theories have postulated a variety of factors – from body type to genetic predispositions, from low IQ to maternal deprivation – supposedly marking out some individuals as more likely to commit crimes. Macro-social theories such as anomie analyse criminality as the propensity of societies to generate higher or lower levels of crime. The understanding of crime, whether at the macro-level of broad trends or patterns or the micro-level of specific incidents, involves a weaving together of different elements and levels of explanation. It requires recognition *both* of the choices and responsibility of perpetrators, *and* of how these are framed by political economy, social structure and culture.

BOX 19.5 CONSERVATIVE CONCEPTIONS OF 'CRIMINALITY'

Ministers smuggle into the supposedly 'pure and simple' term 'criminality' a conservative theory of crime causation. This attributes crime solely to lack of control, suggesting that firmly reasserting discipline is the effective antidote. This condenses a variety of debates about why control becomes inadequate. It is axiomatic to conservatives that crime is behaviour *chosen* by offenders. Nonetheless they concede that some factors make failure to exercise self-control more likely.

In conservative theories the usual suspects are alleged pathological characteristics of particular cultures, often apparently rooted in supposed biological differences (as in eugenic or socio-biological perspectives). Or they are the malign legacy of an imagined growing liberal dominance of the common culture, as in conservative laments about 'permissiveness' and the 1960s. These claims are grossly limited by their blinkered focus on the single dimension of control. It is like explaining the speed and direction of a car solely in terms of the driver's skill with the brake.

Crime's complex preconditions

Several logically necessary preconditions must be met before a crime can occur: labelling, motive, means, opportunity and the absence of control. The criminological theories discussed earlier all feed into explaining one or more of these conditions.

Apparent shifts in crime rates and patterns are frequently the result of changes in criminal law or in patterns of reporting and recording incidents. In the 1970s, for example, the spread of household contents insurance induced more victims to report burglaries, sparking an apparent surge in crime. Changes in the rules for counting offences in 1998 and 2002 drove up the police-recorded crime rate. *Labelling* may also act as a cause of criminal behaviour itself. Changes in how people treat identified offenders (stigmatization, ostracism, denial of jobs) may contribute to further offending, as may alterations in a convicted person's self-identity. Whether the crime-producing consequences of official reactions to deviance outweigh their crime-control effects is an open empirical question.

Detective fiction, as well as newspaper and 'true crime' stories, usually portray the *motives* driving crime as complex, puzzling, often bizarre, requiring the sensitivity of Dostoevsky or Freud – or at least Agatha Christie or Sherlock Holmes – to unravel. This is because the media focus on extremely unusual, very serious, pathologically violent and sexual cases. Most offences are committed for quite conventional, readily comprehensible reasons, motivated by desires that are widely shared – money, fashionable goods, sex, excitement, thrills, intoxication by alcohol, adrenalin or other drugs. Offenders are driven not by deviant values but by immersion in contemporary consumer culture (Hall, Winlow and Ancrum 2008). The fact that most crime is motivated by mundane aspirations and desires does not mean that understanding motives is unimportant. Social, cultural and economic changes affect the attractions of behaviour labelled as criminal, increasing or decreasing the numbers of people motivated to commit them, as spelled out seminally by the theory of anomie.

As lovers of detective mysteries know, in addition to motive, criminals need *means and opportunity*. The commission of crime requires a variety of personal and technical resources. Changes in political economy, culture, technology and social patterns can expand or contract the *means* of committing crimes. New types of crime become possible, old ones are blocked off, and new ways of committing old offences are created. Innovative means of exchange, from cheques to credit cards and, more recently, the internet, have provided new techniques for the old art of relieving people of their money.

Cyberspace enables many new types of offence and novel ways of committing old offences, such as terrorism, piracy, fraud, identity theft, stalking, sexual offences against children, hacking security codes, racist harassment. The increased speed and extent of travel and communications signified by globalization facilitates a variety of crimes – for example, trafficking in people, drugs, arms, money laundering, terrorism.

Criminal opportunities can be expanded by a proliferation of targets (for example, the spread of car ownership, televisions, videos, DVD players, home PCs, laptops and, more recently, mobile phones, iPods and iPads – each in turn becoming the hottest items for theft). Many studies have charted surges in particular kinds of theft following the development of new 'must-have' consumer goods. For instance, there was a sharp rise in robberies of mobile phones from early 2000 to early 2002 (while thefts of other goods remained roughly static), tracking the rapid rise in ownership.

One further ingredient is necessary before a crime can be committed – *the absence of controls,*

BOX 19.6 MERTON'S ANOMIE THEORY AND CONTEMPORARY CRIME

Durkheim had suggested in the 1890s that rapid social change, such as economic downturns *and* economic upturns, dislocated effective cultural regulation of people's aspirations, releasing anomic dissatisfaction conducive to suicide and other deviance. Merton developed this in a brief but seminal article, offering a framework for explaining variations in deviance between and within societies (Merton 1938). Despite the ritual slaying of caricatures of Merton's analysis in countless textbooks and exam answers over the decades, it remains an illuminating structural social theory of crime (cf. the special issue of *Theoretical Criminology*, 11(1), 2007). Contemporary American versions frequently reduce Merton's structural political economy to social psychology, attributing deviance to a psychic gap between individual aspirations and achievement (Agnew 2006).

Merton's is the classic analysis of how macro-social structures affect variations in motivations to commit crime between cultures and over time. It was first developed in the 1930s to explain why the USA was then the Western world's crime capital. Legitimate opportunities to gain wealth were structurally limited, thereby generating pressures for crime, not automatically, but in cultures that encourage widespread wealth aspirations for all. This was epitomized by the 'American Dream' of the widespread possibility of rising from rags to riches. Cultures that emphasize material and monetary success generate strains towards deviance to achieve this success at *all* levels of society, not least – indeed, perhaps above all – among elites. There is no terminal point for monetary aspirations, and success breeds desire rather than satisfaction. Winning is all that counts. Conceptions of legitimate means get pushed aside: nice guys or gals finish last; losers are zeroes. Cutting corners, coming first, is all that matters, at all levels of society and all times.

These arguments have been used widely to understand contemporary crime patterns (e.g., Young 2003; Messner and Rosenfeld 2006; Reiner 2007). The recent parliamentary expenses scandals, the revelations of the corrupt networks linking politicians, police and press, and, at the other end of the social scale, the 2011 shopping riots are all testimony to the power of this seventy-year-old theory.

formal and informal. A potential burglar, say, may be eager to find a property to burgle, perhaps to feed her children or a habit. Equipped with jemmy and know-how, she comes across a relatively secluded house, milk bottles curdling on the doorstep indicating absent owners, and she spies the flashing LCDs of tempting electronic equipment through the ground floor window. But her progress up the garden path may be arrested by the plod of a patrolling constable's feet or the sound of a siren. Even in the likely event that the strong arm of the law is deployed elsewhere, one final intervention may hold her back. On the shelf she spots a Bible, and she hears the still, small voice of her Sunday School teacher, 'Thou shalt not steal', and goes home for tea and reflection.

Changes in the efficacy of *formal* criminal justice controls will alter the attractions or possibility of crime. The 1990s drop in crime in the USA has been popularly attributed to harder, smarter or simply more policing. 'Crime is down, blame the police', boasted former NYPD Chief Bratton. Others give the credit to tougher punishment, claiming vindication for Michael Howard's 'prison works' slogan. Both claims are vigorously disputed, and the evidence supporting them is dubious, as we will see. The very fact that in the last fifteen years the decline in crime was universal throughout the Western world, despite substantial variations in policing and penal policies in different jurisdictions, calls the parochial assertions of Bratton, Howard

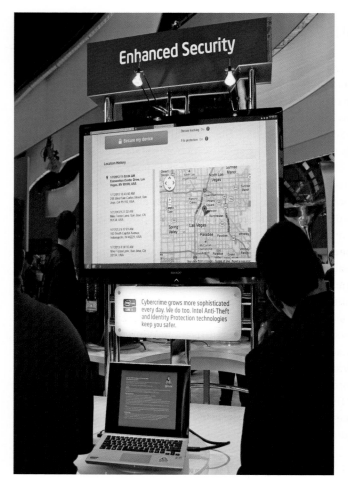

The digital age has offered new means and opportunities for criminality in the form of cybercrime and cyberterrorism. A big business has grown around security technologies which aim to protect from cyber-attacks, which in some cases have hit high-profile targets. (© the JoshMeister/Flickr)

and their ilk into question. Nonetheless external controls do play a part in shaping crime trends.

Informal social controls are also important in interpreting crime trends. The thesis that informal controls – family, school, socialization, community or 'social capital' – are the fundamental basis of order has a long pedigree. However, a major problem facing the common conservative argument that increasing 'permissiveness' caused rising crime is to explain why crime has fallen in recent times despite continuing cultural liberalization.

Multiple causes and crime trends

Crime has complex and multiple causes, so no single-factor accounts (such as the conservative control thesis) can withstand close examination. The analysis in terms of five necessary conditions of crime provides a variety of tools for explaining particular turning points. For example, the explosion of crime in the Thatcher years (confirmed by both police statistics and the British Crime Survey) was attributable above all to the pernicious social effects (rapidly rising inequality and social exclusion) of the introduction of neoliberal economic policies.

The more recent fall in crime remains rather more mysterious, as it is difficult to see any attenuation of 'criminality' (the tendency of society to produce criminals). The right's *bête noir*, 'permissiveness', has continued unabated, as has the economic and social polarization attributable to neoliberal globalization. The most plausible account is the 'security hypothesis': the huge expansion in the use and efficacy of technical crime-prevention techniques, especially car and home security devices (Farrell, Tseloni and Tilley 2011). These have held the lid down on a continuing underlying increase in 'criminality'. The 2011 riots show dramatically what happens when the lid is temporarily lifted. Smart and fair criminal justice can help, but only as first aid. It is necessary to be tough not only on crime but on its underlying causes, which lie way beyond the ambit of cops, courts and corrections, as the conclusion will elaborate.

SEMINAR QUESTIONS

1 To what extent can crime trends be explained by changes in motives, means and opportunities?

2 What part does social control play in understanding crime?

3 Discuss how the recent fall in recorded crime could be explained in terms of the model outlined above.

CONTEMPORARY CRIME TRENDS

Criminal statistics are riddled with pitfalls. Changes in the figures may be the result not of changes in offence levels but of fluctuations in reporting or recording, or in the rules for counting. Substantial steps have been taken in recent decades to alleviate these problems by developing alternative measures.

Any attempt to measure crime is of course bedevilled by the conceptual issues in defining crime. Official crime statistics are part of the administrative processes of the state and are based on a legal conception of crime. Since 1856, crime statistics based on police records have been published by the Home Office. From the early 1980s an additional set of crime statistics has been regularly compiled by the Home Office: the British Crime Survey (BSC), now the Crime Survey for England and Wales (CSEW) (since 2008, Scotland has produced the Scottish Crime and Justice Survey (SCJS), which replaced the Scottish Crime and Victimization Survey; the Northern Ireland Crime Survey (NICS) began operating on a continuous yearly basis in 2005). The CSEW is based on interviews with samples of the population. The Home Office published an annual volume, *Crime in England and Wales* (as well as quarterly updates), of both the police-recorded crime and BSC figures until 1 April 1 2012, when the Office for National Statistics (ONS) took over responsibility for the data.

Problems of interpreting crime statistics: police-recorded crime statistics

Criminologists have long been aware that the official crime statistics suffer from many pitfalls, making interpretation hazardous (Reiner 2007: ch. 3; Maguire 2012). What tabloid newspapers unabashedly call the 'crime rate' is officially labelled as 'crimes recorded by the police' in Home Office/ONS publications. But the question is: How accurately do the police-recorded figures measure crime?

The police statistics are problematic because of the so-called dark figure of unrecorded crime. In a well-worn metaphor, the recorded rate represents only the tip of the iceberg of criminal activity. At issue is what we can learn about the totality from the visible part. There is much evidence that police statistics have been 'supply-side' driven, reflecting the changing exigencies of Home Office policy-makers and police bureaucracies (Taylor 1998). If we could be confident that the recorded rate was representative of the whole, it would at least be a reliable guide to trends and patterns. But the fundamental problem is that the recorded statistics are not only incomplete but biased: some crimes and criminals are more likely to enter the records than others, with clear patterns of class, age, ethnic, gender and area disproportionality.

For an event to be recorded as a crime it must get over two hurdles: 1) it must become known to the police; 2) it must be recorded by them. The 'dark figure' of unrecorded crime arises because many crimes do not get over these hurdles.

Victim surveys show that victims' decisions about whether or not to report property offences turns on a more-or-less explicit cost–benefit assessment. About three-quarters of victims who do not report a crime tell the BCS that this is because the offence was too trivial and that there was no point as the police wouldn't do anything about it. For violent crimes, however, other factors, such as regarding the matter as 'private', or fear of reprisal, are important. Trends in overall reporting are highly sensitive to pragmatic considerations such as the value of property lost, the possibilities of making an insurance claim, and the convenience of reporting (where the nearest police station is, whether crimes can be reported by phone, etc.).

Many crimes do not involve victims who can report them, for a variety of reasons. The victims may not realize the nature of what has happened. They may be children who are aware of their suffering, but not that what was done to them was a crime. They may be adult victims of frauds that are so successful that the victim does not realize that they have been deceived. Many crimes do not have clear individual victims at all. 'Consensual' offences such as drug-taking, and 'vice' offences such as those relating to prostitution, pornography or gambling, may paternalistically be regarded as people harming themselves or others, but the putative victims are willing participants. The 'victim' of other offences, such as tax evasion, pensions mis-selling, insider trading and other financial crimes, public order offences and treason, is the public at large. The common element of these examples is that they come to be known to the police only by chance or through proactive policing work (e.g., surveillance of 'hot spots', undercover work, raids on pubs and clubs for drugs, analysis of financial transactions for fraud or other crimes, searches of travellers at customs). Mapping and measuring the 'dark figure' is problematic, and any estimation can only be tentative.

What surprises many people is that, even if 'known' to them, the police may not record victimizations as crimes. The first British Crime Survey estimated that, in 1981, the police recorded only 62 percent of all crimes reported to them, and 'less than half of those involving violence' (Hough and Mayhew 1983: 12). Recent policy changes have increased the proportion recorded, but only to about 70 percent. Although structured by Home Office counting rules, police officers exercise discretion about whether and how to record crimes reported to them. A Home Office research study that monitored the outcome of calls to the police found only 47 percent of crime allegations were eventually recorded as crimes, although 71 percent of those in which the caller was 'definite' a crime had occurred were recorded (Burrows et al. 2000: ch.5). In 21 percent of cases where a crime was recorded it was classified differently from the initial allegation (ibid.)

Police exercise discretion not to record crimes for reasons varying from legitimate (for example, if there is genuine doubt about the truthfulness or accuracy of a victim's report) to completely corrupt (for example, in return for a bribe). Major revisions of recording procedures, represented by the 1998 Counting Rules and the 2002 National Crime Recording Standard, have aimed *inter alia* to prioritize the victim's perspective. But legal and organizational pressures tend in the opposite direction, as the increasing emphasis on performance measurement makes spinning the figures more desirable. Certainly there continue to be scandals about the deliberate manipulation of statistics (Davies 1999, 2003a, 2003b).

BOX 19.7 TECHNICAL PROBLEMS IN COUNTING CRIMES

Many technical issues affect the validity and reliability of crime statistics. The police are required to record 'notifiable offences', regarded as the most serious. From time to time – most recently in 1998, when common assault and assault on a constable were added – changes are made in the scope of the 'notifiable offences'. However strong the case for this to take account of changing conceptions of seriousness, it introduces problems of comparison between statistics before and after the alteration.

The Home Office tally of 'crimes known to the police' excludes offences recorded by forces such as the British Transport Police or Ministry of Defence Police. Other enforcement agencies, for example HM Revenue and Customs, investigate and prosecute offences. Their cases rarely enter the Home Office statistics.

How many crimes should be counted in particular situations? If an offender attacks a series of targets in a short time (say she or he breaks every window of a number of neighbouring houses), is that one offence or as many as the number of windows? There may also be ambiguity about what offence has occurred. For example, an alleged attempted burglary may exhibit evidence only of criminal damage (a broken window or scratch marks around a lock). Should the recording be guided by the lurid perceptions of the anxious householder or only by the physical signs? There is scope for defining crime up or down according to police convenience. At a more serious level, how many crimes were committed on 11 September 2001 or 7 July 2005? There is no absolutely right or wrong answer to these questions. If the statistics are to be capable of comparison across time and space, however, there must be consistency in the handling of such dilemmas (which is what the Home Office Counting Rules aim at).

Dimensions of the 'dark' figure

To get some sense of the extent to which recorded crime figures are incomplete, it is salutary, if shocking, to consider the following figures on what the Home Office calls the 'attrition rate', the disappearance of cases at different stages of the criminal justice process. Figure 19.1 shows the attrition rate for 1998, as published by the Home Office (it has not been revised since, but earlier versions showed a similar pattern and there is unlikely to have been any substantial change). It starts with a baseline that is described as 'offences committed'. This is taken from the BCS, at best only an estimate of crimes with individual aware victims. Completely absent from this baseline of '100 percent' of 'offences committed' is the truly dark figure of crimes without individual victims capable of reporting the incident in a survey. This includes murder, generally seen as the most serious crime of all. Figure 19.1 shows that officially recorded crime rates, and data on identified offenders, relate to only a very small proportion of all crimes committed.

Recorded crime statistics are not just incomplete, but biased, as demonstrated by a plethora of studies showing the influence of class, gender, ethnicity, age and other dimensions of social inequality on all stages of the criminal justice process. A clear example is provided by table 19.1, which compares the characteristics of people in prison with the general population.

Table 19.1 shows that people in prison are a highly skewed sample of the overall population, as summed up pithily in the title of a critical criminology classic: *The Rich Get Richer and the Poor Get Prison* (Reiman 2004). The prison population is overwhelmingly male, and ethnic minorities are considerably overrepresented. Prisoners are drawn predominantly from the most marginal economic groups in the population: prior to incarceration, most

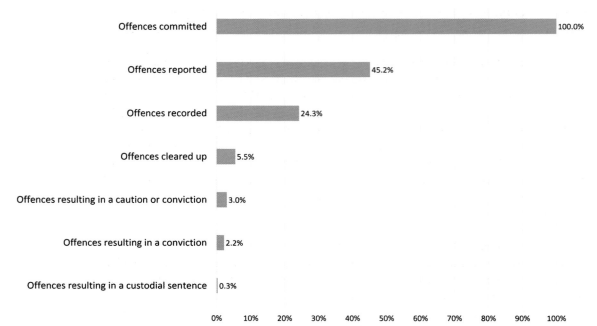

Figure 19.1 Attrition in the criminal justice system

Note: 'Cleared up' relates to cases where the police have some reason to believe they know the identity of the perpetrator.

Source: Barclay and Tavares (1999: 29).

Table 19.1: 'The rich get rich and the poor get prison' (%)		
	General population	**Prison population**
Under 25	16	40
Male	49	96
Ethnic minority	5	25
Semi-/unskilled occupation	18	41
Unemployed	8.7	66
No permanent home	0.3	33
Lived with both parents until 16	83	62
Taken into care as child	2	25
Left school before 16	11	40
Skill levels below average 11-year-old	Numeracy	66
	Reading	52
	Writing	82

Sources: Walmsley (1991); *Social Trends* 33 (2003); Berman (2012).

were either unemployed or employed at the lowest occupational levels. Many were homeless when arrested. They have extremely poor educational backgrounds and histories of family disruption.

The incompleteness and bias of official crime statistics mean that apparent trends and patterns may be quite misleading, with devastating consequences for the assessment of crime trends and for constructing explanations of the sources of criminality from study of the prison population (as so many theories, past and present, have done). A rise in recorded crime, for example, may occur because of increased reporting by victims, and/or more recording by the police of offences reported to them, and/or more successful proactive policing (and vice versa for a fall). The disproportionate representation of the economically marginal and ethnic minorities in the suspect population may be because, for various possible reasons, they commit more crime or because the crimes they do commit are more likely to be recorded and cleared up, or both.

Alternatives to the police statistics

Growing awareness of the limitations and biases of the police-recorded crime statistics has prompted the development of a variety of new measures since the 1960s. Victimization surveys (such as the BCS) are by far the most significant, because they offer an alternative measure of trends over time. They also provide insights into reporting and recording processes that enable better understanding of the police statistics. Other measures, such as self-report studies, can be used to assess the relationship between the characteristics of offending that they reveal and the pattern shown in police and criminal justice statistics. However, they are not usually constructed so as to assess overall trends through time, an exception being the self-reported drug-use questions that have been used by the BCS in recent years. Another innovative measure uses data from hospital accident and emergency departments to assess trends and patterns of injuries sustained as a result of violence (Sivarajasingam et al. 2012). This offers a useful alternative source of data capable of mapping trends in interpersonal violence.

The proliferation of alternative measures is a boon to understanding crime trends and patterns. When the different measures point in the same direction (as they did in the 1980s and early 1990s and have again since the mid-2000s) we can be much more confident that this corresponds to what is happening to offending and victimization. Even when they diverge (as for much of the 1990s and early 2000s) it is possible to understand some of the reasons for this and to make appropriate allowances in interpreting each series of statistics.

The BCS/CSEW, SCJS and NICS are thus valuable additional sources of data but not a definitive calculation of crime rates. We must always bear in mind the issues of whether changes in the police-recorded figures are likely to be a result of changes in victim reporting, local police recording practices, or Home Office and police policy. Similarly, are trends in the BCS/CSEW explicable by changing sample coverage or other methodological problems? There can never be certainty about any of this, but triangulation of different data sources allows more informed attempts at interpretation. In the next section I will try to describe recent trends and patterns in crime, interpreting the statistics with due caution in the light of the many problems.

BOX 19.8 CRIME SURVEYS IN THE UK

The British Crime Survey (BCS) was first conducted in 1981, but its name was changed to the Crime Survey for England and Wales (CSEW) in 2012. The survey used for Scotland is the Scottish Crime and Justice Survey (SCJS) and that for Northern Ireland the Northern Ireland Crime Survey (NICS).

All crime surveys have many limitations, as identified in the first BCS report (Hough and Mayhew 1983: 3–4). Firstly, there are the thorny conceptual issues about how to define crime: what the interviewed 'victim' may see as an assault may be regarded by the supposed aggressor as a playful push.

Secondly, victim surveys can only measure crimes with interviewable victims, so murder, generally seen as the most serious crime of all, cannot be included. Each year the police record well over a quarter of a million thefts from shops, just under half a million burglaries other than from dwellings, and well over 100,000 drug offences. None of these are within the scope of the BCS/CSEW – but they are just a fraction of what is likely to be a huge dark figure of crime that cannot be counted by these surveys.

Thirdly, as with all surveys, there are sampling issues. The BCS regularly conducted over 46,000 interviews in England and Wales until 2012, when the ONS announced a reduction to 35,000 and a name change to the Crime Survey for England and Wales to reflect its actual geographic coverage. The BCS was originally a survey of adults, but since 2006 there have been surveys of victimization in the ten to fifteen age group.

Finally, interviews are only as good as the honesty and memory of respondents. These issues are most acute with the gravest interpersonal offences, especially violent and sex crimes, where willingness to confide in a strange visitor from the Home Office is problematic, although improvements in methodology have been introduced over time.

Trends in crime

The most apparent trends in crime are the spectacular overall rise in recorded offences since the late 1950s and the downturn since the mid-1990s. In the early 1950s the police recorded fewer than half a million offences per annum. By the mid-1970s this had risen to 2 million. The 1980s showed even more staggering rises, with recorded crime peaking in 1992 at over 5.5 million; but by 1997 recorded crime had fallen back to 4.5 million. Major counting rule changes introduced in 1998 and 2002 make comparison of the subsequent figures especially fraught, but on the new rules (which undoubtedly exaggerate the increase) just under 6 million offences were recorded by the police for 2003–4. This has now fallen back again, to 3.8 million in 2011–12.

Contrasting the police-recorded statistics with victim surveys suggests a more complex picture, as shown in figure 19.2, which pinpoints Thatcherite neoliberalism as the accelerant behind a crime explosion in the 1980s and early 1990s, with a sustained decline since 1995 (apart from a brief period of increasing police-recorded crime from 1998 to 2004, owing to counting rule changes). Three distinct phases can be distinguished since the mid-1950s.

Until the 1970s there was no other measurement of trends apart from police statistics. But during the 1970s the General Household Survey began to ask about burglary victimization, and its data showed that most of the increase in recorded burglary was because of more reporting by victims. In the 1970s recorded burglaries doubled, but victimization increased by only 20 percent. Victims reported more burglaries mainly because of the spread of household contents insurance, and it is plausible to infer that this applied to property crimes more generally. So the rise of crime in the heyday of the mixed-economy, welfarist consensus was probably

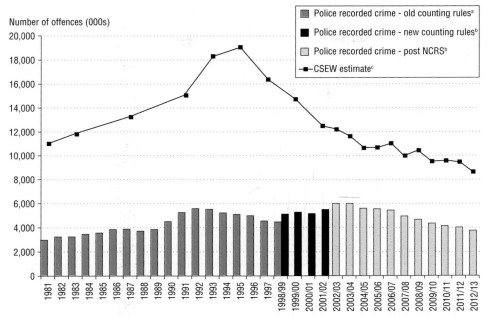

Figure 19.2 Trends in police-recorded crime and BSC/CSEW data, 1981–2012/13

ᵃ Calendar year.
ᵇ Financial year (April to March).
ᶜ Prior to 2001/02, crimes experienced in that calendar year; from 2001/02 onwards, crimes experienced in 12 months prior to interview, based on interviews in that financial year.

Source: ONS (2013a: 6)

substantially less than the recorded statistics suggested – although, no doubt, the first stirrings of consumerism stimulated acquisitiveness and crime. As the growth of consumer credit urged people to 'take the waiting out of wanting' (the slogan for the first 'Access' credit cards), those without legitimate means were tempted to find illicit routes to the must-have glittering prizes.

The British Crime Survey showed huge increases in offending in its first decade, roughly in line with the police statistics. BCS crime rose by 77 percent from 1981 to 1993, while police-recorded crime increased by 111 percent. By both measures, crime rose at an explosive rate during the 1980s and early 1990s. The one clearly booming industry during the decade and a half in which neoliberalism (the 'free' market economics spearheaded by Margaret Thatcher) destroyed Britain's industrial base was crime.

After the early 1990s the trends indicated by the police statistics and the BCS diverged for a decade. The BCS continued to chart a rise until 1995, but the police data fell between 1992 and 1997. Paradoxically, this was because of the extraordinarily high levels of victimization. The police recorded fewer crimes as insurance companies made claiming more onerous, discouraging reporting by victims; and, at the same time, more 'businesslike' managerial accountability for policing implicitly introduced incentives against recording.

After New Labour came to power in 1997, the two measures continued to diverge, but in the opposite direction. BCS-recorded crime has fallen rapidly since 1995 and in 2007–8 was below the level of the first BCS, conducted in 1981. The police-recorded statistics, however,

Number of offences (000s)

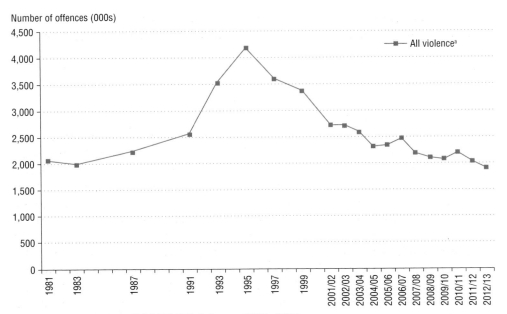

Figure 19.3 Trends in BSC/CSEW violence, 1981–2013
[a] Prior to 2001/02, crimes experienced in that calendar year; from 2001/02 onwards, crimes experienced in 12 months prior to interview, based on interviews in that financial year.

Source: ONS (2013a: 22).

rose from 1998 to 2004, since when they have declined again. This temporary rise in the police-recorded rate was because of the two major changes in police procedures for counting crimes that were discussed earlier.

The dramatic overall fall in BCS and police-recorded crime masked increases in some of the most alarming offences. Murder and other serious crimes of violence have increased in the last thirty years and are now a higher proportion of all crimes than they used to be. Since the 1960s, annual recorded homicides have roughly doubled, although the trend has been downwards in the last few years. The figures for the year ending September 2012 show a 10 percent decline in the number of homicides recorded by the police compared with the previous year (from 607 to 549). The number of homicides had increased from around 300 per year in the early 1960s to over 800 per year in the early years of this century before falling back to late 1970s levels. In 1976, just 5 percent of recorded offences were classified as violent, but by 2007 this had increased to 22 percent. While the proportion of violent crimes has increased, however, the absolute number has fallen.

The next section will analyse the relationship of these trends in crime to the politics of law and order.

SEMINAR QUESTIONS

1 How reliable are official crime statistics as a basis for explaining crime and developing crime-control policies?
2 To what extent have new measures of crime that have been developed in recent years succeeded in overcoming the problems of ascertaining crime trends and patterns?

3 What have been the major trends in crime in the last half-century?

4 Assess the evidence that the criminal justice system is discriminatory with respect to a) race; b) gender; c) class.

LAW AND ORDER: POLITICS AND POLICY

The early 1990s saw a hardening of public and political discourse about both law and order and crime-control policies, initially in the USA and the UK, but eventually in most Western countries. The decline in crime since the 1990s has been commonly attributed to these tougher crime-control policies, notably rising imprisonment, and 'hard cop' tactics such as 'zero tolerance' (the name given by the media to the tactic, in New York and elsewhere, of cracking down on minor street offences). This section will analyse the rise of the politics and culture of 'law and order' and assess its impact on crime control.

David Garland's book *The Culture of Control* (2001) offers a *tour de force* analysis that has deservedly become exceptionally influential. Garland constructed a Foucault-inspired 'history of the present', weaving together many strands of cultural, social, political and economic change. While the changes in crime control result from a complex dialectic of different causes, the growing dominance of neoliberalism in the globalizing political economy of the late twentieth century is arguably *primus inter pares* in understanding what has happened (Reiner 2007).

The origins of the politics of 'law and order' lie in the 1970s. However, since the early 1990s there has been a sharp accentuation of the trend towards harder crime-control discourse and policies, embedding them ever more deeply, despite some counter-trends and resistances. This is not equally prominent in all societies: some jurisdictions have restrained or at least slowed the punitive trend. The variations are closely related to the extent to which different political economies embraced neoliberalism. Nonetheless, those states that have succeeded to date in retaining relatively greater welfarism and social democracy face increasing pressure from global markets and from the hegemony of consumerist culture. This threatens to push them in the direction not only of more neoliberal economic policies but of the more repressive law and order control policies that are their Janus face.

The rise of law and order politics

Until the late 1960s, criminal justice policy had not been a partisan political issue since the early nineteenth century. It did not feature in any party's election manifesto between the Second World War and 1970 (Downes and Morgan 2012). Nor was crime an important issue to the public until the 1970s, at least as registered by opinion polls. Some specific aspects of criminal justice policy *were* politically controversial, notably capital punishment. Particularly spectacular or salacious crimes have always been regular topics of popular fascination. But the overall state of crime was not a widespread cause of concern, nor was criminal justice policy subject to political controversy and conflict.

'Law and order' first became politicized in the USA in the 1960s by the political right, demanding that the law and its front-line troops, the cops, be unleashed. Law and order was a successful campaigning slogan for Richard Nixon in his 1968 presidential election victory, becoming a codeword for race, culture and generational backlash.

The politicization of law and order was heralded in Britain in the 1970 general election, when the Conservative manifesto said that 'the Labour government cannot entirely shrug off responsibility' for rising 'crime and violence'. With hindsight, this was a remarkably genteel opening shot in the coming political war about law and order! Politicization of law and order accelerated under Margaret Thatcher's leadership of the Conservative Party. During the late 1970s, in the build-up to her election victory in 1979, Thatcher blamed the Labour government for rising crime and disorder, pledging a 'ring of steel' to protect people against lawlessness. The Tories' law and order campaign was greatly helped by the emergence of the police as a political lobby, backing up the Conservatives' agenda in a series of advertisements and speeches. According to polls monitoring shifts in public opinion, the issue was a major factor in Thatcher's 1979 election victory.

The party-political gulf on law and order reached its widest point in the mid-1980s. The key conflicts were over the policing of urban disorders and of the miners' strike of 1984–5 (results of the economic and social dislocation engendered by the Thatcher government's monetarist policies), the Police and Criminal Evidence Act 1984, and radical campaigns for democratic police accountability. On all these issues Labour took a civil libertarian stance, attacking the Conservative government for violating the principles of the rule of law. Labour also attacked Conservative law and order policies for increasing social divisions, aggravating rather than reforming the root causes of crime – social inequality and relative deprivation. This position proved to be an electoral liability for Labour. In the 1984 and 1987 general elections the Tories attacked Labour for being 'soft' on crime because of its links with civil liberties, 'permissiveness', trade unionism (associated with disorder), and failure to develop any short-term solutions to bolster public protection.

In the late 1980s signs appeared of a new cross-party consensus on law and order. The Conservatives, concerned about the apparent failure of toughness to stem rising crime, began to emphasize crime prevention, proportionality in penal policy, and value for money (a major Thatcherite theme of course). The new tack culminated in the 1991 Criminal Justice Act. For its part, Labour began to try and repair some of the 'soft on law and order' image that the Tories had foisted on them, culminating in Tony Blair's legendary soundbite 'tough on crime, tough on the causes of crime'. Blair began to tout this in media interviews and articles during 1993, in the wake of the anguish and national soul-searching about crime and moral decline triggered by the tragic murder of Liverpool toddler Jamie Bulger by two young boys. The slogan touched all bases, finely balancing the Left Realist recognition that crime was a serious problem with a more traditional criminological concern with 'causes'. But the main departure was rhetorical: the double whammy of toughness packed into one short, sharp sentence. Since 1993 there has developed a new 'second-order' consensus on the fundamentals of law and order policy – toughness, toughness, toughness – with frenzied partisan conflict on specifics: anything you can do, I can do tougher.

In the early 1990s, Labour began to attack the Tories with some success, pointing to failures of Conservative criminal justice policies. Given the record increases in crime in the 1980s, despite burgeoning expenditure on policing and punishment, this was an open goal – as even Tory cabinet ministers conceded. The Conservative home secretary, Michael Howard, fought back vigorously with his 'prison works' speech to the October 1993 party conference. Nonetheless the game had changed dramatically. Labour was making the political running on what had hitherto been one of the Tories' most secure policy areas.

BOX 19.9 THE CRIME-CONTROL CONSENSUS

The post-1993 crime-control consensus had five core elements.

1 **Crime is public enemy no. 1** Crime and disorder are seen as *the* major threats to society and to individual citizens by both the public and politicians. Many opinion polls have demonstrated that crime (and more recently terrorism) moved to the forefront of public concern from the early 1970s.

2 **Individual not social responsibility for crime** Crime is the fault of offenders, *not* caused by social structural factors. This was expressed most bluntly in 1993 by the then prime minister, John Major – 'Society needs to condemn a little more and understand a little less' – and this was frequently echoed by Tony Blair.

3 **Foregrounding victims v. offenders** The victim has become the iconic centre of discourse about crime, ideal-typically portrayed as totally innocent. Crime discourse and policy are predicated on a zero-sum game: concern for victims precludes understanding – let alone any sympathy for – offenders.

4 **Crime control works** Since the early 1990s can-do optimism has reinvigorated confidence in tough (but smart) policing and penal policy. 'Prison works', as does 'zero tolerance' policing and the 'responsibilization' of citizens to take self-protective measures against victimization. Civil liberties and human rights are at best marginal issues, to be subordinated to crime-control exigencies, and deeper social causes of crime are denied or played down.

5 **High-crime society normalized** Popular culture and routine activities have become increasingly focused on crime risks and the perception that we live in a 'high-crime society'. Crime-prevention techniques have penetrated everyday life, paradoxically enhancing fear rather than security.

1992–3 was a decisive watershed for the politics of law and order. While during the late 1970s and 1980s neoliberal and neoconservative political parties, ideas and policies became dominant in Britain, the USA and most of the Western world, they were fiercely if unsuccessfully contested. On a world scale the New Right's ascendancy was marked by the fall of the Soviet Union in 1989. But what really confirmed the global hegemony of neoliberalism was the acceptance of the fundamentals of its economic and social policy framework by the erstwhile social democratic or New Deal parties of the West. The Clinton Democrats and New Labour, and their embrace of the 'Third Way' – neoliberalism to a cool beat – marked a new, deep consensus, sounding the death-knell of the post-war mixed-economy, Keynesian settlement that the conservative parties had accepted when they returned to power in the early 1950s.

SEMINAR QUESTIONS

1 Why did 'law and order' become a partisan political issue from the 1970s?

2 Discuss whether the 'law and order' discourse and the 'crime-control consensus' make it impossible to follow 'rational' or 'progressive' crime policies.

3 What arguments could be made to challenge the crime-control consensus?

TOUGH ON CRIME? ASSESSING THE IMPACT OF LAW AND ORDER

To what extent, if any, can the 1990s crime drop, in Britain and the USA, be attributed to the politics of law and order – tougher policing and punitiveness? The police have not been slow to claim credit, particularly in the USA, and especially in New York City, with its highly publicized precipitous decline in crime.

Independent research suggests a more complex, indeed enigmatic, picture. Most commentators do not question that substantial declines in crime have occurred in the USA and in Britain, but explaining this is problematic. Indeed, it is precisely the widespread character of the drop in crime that calls into question some of the most popular explanations, in particular 'zero-tolerance' policing. As many analysts have argued, crime fell in most parts of the USA despite the considerable variations in policing styles. While the celebrated New York City drop was especially marked, crime declined to a comparable extent even in cities that did not pursue the same (or indeed any) reform strategy.

The crime drop: blame the cops?

Close analysis of the New York experience itself suggests policing changes, because of their timing, are unlikely to have resulted in most of the falls in homicide and other serious crime. Certainly some of the huge decline in New York City is plausibly because of policing changes, but there is considerable doubt about how much is attributable to the celebrated 'zero-tolerance' aspect. Even the former NYPD Chief Bratton has played down the label of 'zero tolerance' for his reforms. Most analysts see much more rigorous and speedy analysis of crime and stricter local managerial accountability for crime trends, summed up as 'COMPSTAT', as the most important element in the NYPD's success.

The most vigorous arguments for the significance of criminal justice policies on the drop in crime come from a celebrated analysis by the economist Steven Levitt that is the basis for a chapter in his best-selling book *Freakonomics* (2005). This gained huge notoriety for its claim that a major factor was the impact of the legalization of abortion following the 1973 US Supreme Court decision in *Roe* v. *Wade*. Indirectly this argument is really one about how legalized abortion reduced the impoverished and excluded underclass, implicit testimony to the significance of economic and social exclusion – though hopefully more humane programmes can achieve this than what potentially amounts to a form of eugenics.

Levitt also attributed the crime drop to criminal justice factors, notably the expansion of police and prisons. He points out that the 'universality of the drop in crime' militates against its explanation in terms of factors that varied considerably between places, such as police innovation. Levitt attributes 'between one-fifth and one-tenth of the overall decline in crime' (i.e., 5 to 6 percent) to the approximately 14 percent increase in police officers per capita in the USA during the 1990s, supported by other studies calculating that increasing police numbers by 1 percent is associated with a reduction of roughly 30 percent in the crime rate. There is no specification of the causal mechanisms bringing this about, only a taken-for-granted but questionable assumption that a larger police force deters crime and catches more criminals.

Nobody would claim that police have no effect on crime: that disbanding the police or, at the other extreme, saturation policing would make no difference. What is debatable is the impact on crime of the relatively marginal changes in police numbers that are economically or politically feasible. The experimental studies that were the basis for the 'nothing works' pessimism of the 1970s bore this out. As Home Office research argued, this is because of the very small chance that patrolling police officers will encounter crime at all. A 'patrolling policeman in London could expect to pass within 100 yards of a burglary in progress roughly once every eight years – but not necessarily to catch the burglar or even realise that the crime was taking place' (Clarke and Hough 1984: 6–7).

The problem lies not in police ineffectiveness but in the huge number of potential targets of crime, vastly outstretching any conceivable level of police resources. As a 1996 Audit Commission report calculated, a typical patrolling officer has to cover an area with 18,000 inhabitants, 7,500 houses, twenty-three pubs, nine schools, 140 miles of pavement, 85 acres of park or open space and 77 miles of road. Not a happy lot for the poor constable expected to provide meaningful cover for so many possible crime victims.

The response to this from police forces over the last two decades has been the search for new tricks, innovative strategies that, by analysing information and crime patterns, can hopefully target scarce resources at 'hot spots' and prolific offenders so that meaningful prevention and detection become possible. These have contributed to the crime drop, both through more effective protection and better investigative techniques and because the fall in crime levels itself enables a higher proportion of offenders to be detected. Increasing police strength may well have facilitated the adoption of innovative methods. But, for the reasons indicated by the Home Office and the Audit Commission, relatively marginal increases in numbers by themselves are unlikely to have had a significant effect (Reiner 2010: ch.5).

Prison works?

Did prison work, as promised by Michael Howard and his American counterparts? What role has the huge American prison expansion, and the smaller but still historically and comparatively very large imprisonment rise in Britain, played in the crime drop? Comprehensive reviews in both countries (Spelman 2000; Bottoms 2004) show that, while the considerable growth of imprisonment certainly played a part, in conjunction with other social and criminal justice changes, this was achieved at enormous cost economically, but even more in human terms. The scope for further reduction through continuing increases in imprisonment is getting less, and there are other less costly alternative policies that offer more potential.

According to the traditional utilitarian rationale, imprisonment (and other forms of penalty) may work to reduce crime in four possible ways: rehabilitation – interventions enabling the offender to live a law-abiding life; special deterrence – frightening an offender away from future offending; general deterrence – driving off potential offenders by the prospect of punishment; and incapacitation – removing the practical possibility of offending. Some official reviews, notably the Halliday Report, expressed renewed optimism about the prospects of rehabilitation through the use in prison of new techniques such as cognitive behaviour therapy (Home Office 2001). However, subsequent research has had disappointing outcomes (Bottoms 2004: 62). In any case, the prospects of therapeutic techniques succeeding is greater with non-incarcerated offenders. Rehabilitation may work even in prison contexts, but the prospects for successful programmes have been greatly undermined by the remorseless expansion of the last decade. In truth, when Michael Howard spoke of prison working, it was not rehabilitation he had in mind, but deterrence and incapacitation.

Although claims have been made about the special deterrence effects of new tough regimes, these have seldom if ever withstood empirical evaluation. Many believe that more severe punishment reduces crime through general deterrence. On a rational economic actor model, it should follow that raising the cost of crime through increasing penalties would lead to less offending. Nonetheless, most assessments of the empirical research 'conclude that there is little or no consistent evidence that harsher sanctions reduce crime rates in western populations . . . sentence severity has no effect on the level of crime in society' (Doob and Webster 2003: 134). The economic model has a number of flaws: for example, potential offenders may not know of sentencing trends, they are frequently not acting in a rationally calculating way but under the sway of drugs, alcohol, sexual or other excitement; or they may be in such a desperate state (perhaps because of hunger or addiction) that they are willing to take risks. Above all, however, the rational attractions of committing crimes even if penalties are severe may still be considerable, as only a very tiny minority of offences result in an offender being sentenced. The common finding of studies of active offenders is that the prospect of punishment is not prominent in their consciousness. Given the almost infinitesimal chance of being punished for any specific offence, this is far from irrational. Empirical research confirms the old view of the eighteenth-century classical school that the *certainty* of punishment is much more important in deterrence than its severity.

The most plausible link between the massive rise in incarceration and the 1990s drop in crime is in terms of incapacitation. Prisoners cannot victimize the general public while they are behind bars. A Home Office estimate suggested that 'the prison population would have to increase by around 15% for a reduction of crime of 1%' (Home Office 2001: § 1.66). This is based on the self-reported offending of people entering prison in early 2000. The many American studies seeking to evaluate the impact of the rise in imprisonment on crime come to a variety of estimates depending on their particular methodologies, some much higher, some lower (Spelman 2000).

It is hard to deny that the massive increase in imprisonment had some part to play in the crime drop, but this is unlikely to continue. Unless people leave prison less likely to commit crime than when they entered – and the evidence about rehabilitation and special deterrence does not make this plausible – then only by continually jacking up the prison population can incapacitation produce a decline in crime (in a steady state, as many people are leaving as entering prison, and the only difference is who is committing the crimes, not how many crimes are being committed). Even if the prison population continues to rise, however, there are diminishing returns in terms of incapacitation. This is because the offenders caught first are more likely to be serious and prolific ones. Thus, even in purely economic cost–benefit terms, there comes a point (long past already in the most plausible calculations) where prison does not pay from a hard-headed economic cost–benefit perspective, especially compared to putting the equivalent resources into alternative policies such as policing or economic regeneration. Jobs may do better than jail as a way of reducing crime (Spelman 2005).

The most rigorous assessments of the 1990s reduction in crime in America find that socio-economic and demographic changes (particularly the more buoyant labour market, the decline in the high-crime age groups in the population, and shifting drug markets) made

Although crime rates have dropped, public fears of crime remain high. Crime may have become normalized as people expect criminality and increase their use of deterrents, such as bicycle locks. This in itself might explain the drop in crime, but it relies on the fear of crime remaining high. (© Joost De Cock/Flickr)

a significant impact, albeit in conjunction with criminal justice policies (Blumstein and Wallman 2000; Zimring 2006). In Britain too, the success of New Labour in maintaining relatively low levels of unemployment and reducing poverty (but not overall inequality) were key factors. More intelligence-based assessments of risk underlying patterns of policing, prevention and punishment have also played a part. Certainly the marked reductions in the highest volume property crimes such as car crime and burglary owe much to vastly improved prevention practices.

Minding the reassurance gap

While emphasizing that crime overall has been declining, New Labour (and indeed police leaders) have struggled to benefit from this, above all because of the evidence from surveys and from media discussions that public fears have not declined. This has been labelled the 'reassurance gap' by policy-makers and has stimulated a 'reassurance policing' agenda to try to plug it. There may be a rational kernel to the stubborn refusal of public anxiety to decline with the crime rate, beyond blaming the messengers of the sensationalist and bad-news-addicted media. In so far as the decline in crime overall is due to more successful adoption of protective equipment and preventive routines by crime-conscious citizens, rather than any reduction in the root causes of offending, the burden falls above all on potential victims. While prevention tactics, burdensome as they may be, are preferable to victimization, they may reinforce rather than reduce fear by highlighting threats. What is required is reassurance not about crime but about the causes of crime. However, this cannot be provided so long as neoliberalism, the fundamental source of increasing criminality, and of the accentuation of insecurity and law and order solutions by media and political discourse, remains triumphant.

SEMINAR QUESTIONS

1 What impact has the growth of 'law and order' politics had on criminal justice policy?
2 To what extent has a 'culture of control' developed in the USA, Britain and elsewhere?
3 'Crime is down, blame the cops'. Assess the evidence supporting or challenging this boast by former New York Police Chief William Bratton.
4 'Prison works'. What evidence if any confirms the claim of the former Conservative home secretary Michael Howard?
5 How far is the crime drop of recent years evidence of better criminal justice policies?

CONCLUSION

Stories of serious (but fortunately rare) violent crime dominate news bulletins and tabloid headlines, in line with the traditional editorial maxim 'If it bleeds, it leads'. This chapter has sought to probe the complex realities behind the rather simplistic depictions of crime in the media and popular culture. It analysed the multiple meanings of the complex concept of crime and the diverse attempts to explain crime and deviance. A model for understanding trends and patterns in crime and control was distilled from these perspectives.

Despite methodological health warnings about crime statistics, a cautious account of what has happened to crime over the last half century was constructed from them. The rise in offending and the intertwined 'culture of control' were closely related to the rise of neoliberalism in economic policy and governance since the 1970s, with its consequences of huge increases in inequality and social exclusion. The fall in crime that has occurred throughout the Western world since the mid-1990s remains ultimately mysterious. The grand narratives of neither the left nor the right explain it satisfactorily. It was suggested that the considerable advances in security techniques provide the most plausible explanation of the overall crime fall.

As the fundamental drivers of crime have not been tackled, this suggests that criminality, the propensity for a society to generate crime, has not abated, although the lid has been held down on actual offending. On this basis it could be predicted that crime would rise as a consequence of the post-2007 economic crisis (as even the Home Office predicted). At the time of writing, this has not yet happened, although there has been a return of rioting and political protest. But if, as the review in this chapter indicates, political economy is ultimately more powerful than policing and penal policy in shaping crime, current economic trends indicate that the decline in crime may not last. As a T-shirt I bought recently on the Berkeley campus of the University of California (birthplace of the 1960s radical student movement) read: 'No Justice, No Peace'.

SEMINAR QUESTIONS

1 In the light of the arguments and evidence in this chapter, discuss the view that 'criminality, the propensity for a society to generate crime, has not abated, although the lid has been held down on actual offending'.
2 What kinds of criminal justice policies could be adopted on the basis of the slogan 'No justice, No Peace'?

FURTHER READING

▶ There are two texts that provide clear, comprehensive and up-to-date coverage of crime and criminal justice issues: Newburn, T. (2012) *Criminology* (2nd edn, Routledge) is a user-friendly and reliable textbook that is most suitable for introductory courses; Maguire, M., R. Morgan and R. Reiner (eds) (2012) *The Oxford Handbook of Criminology* (5th edn, Oxford University Press) is also comprehensive and up to date, with each chapter written by leading authorities on their specific topics, giving an authoritative review of theory, research and policy issues. It is clearly written but is pitched at a more advanced level.

▶ Reiner, R. (2007) *Law and Order: An Honest Citizen's Guide to Crime and Control* (Polity) shares the same approach as this chapter and offers a critical analysis of contemporary issues and trends, emphasizing the importance of the transition to a neoliberal political economy since the 1970s. It is useful as an introductory overview and final revision aid.

▶ Garland, D. (2001) *The Culture of Control* (Oxford University Press) is the most influential work on contemporary criminal justice trends and a magisterial yet readable account of the fundamental transitions of recent times.

▶ Hall, S., S. Winlow and C. Ancrum (2008) *Criminal Identities and Consumer Culture: Crime, Exclusion and the New Culture of Narcissism* (Willan) is a theoretically sophisticated sociological analysis of crime trends that provides a challenging but insightful perspective on crime and contemporary society.

Section F
Theory and Methods

The final section of the book addresses topics which provide the foundation for all sociology: theory and methodology. Theoretical and methodological issues have been addressed throughout the book in relation to specific topic areas. The concluding section looks more generally at the ways in which theoretical and methodological approaches have developed in the subject as a whole. William Outhwaite (chapter 20) and Martyn Hammersley (chapter 21) offer an overview of historical trends in theory and methods respectively, and they discuss the state of contemporary sociology in relation to these core concerns. Both also address the importance of sociology today with particular reference to the idea of 'public sociology'. Public sociology is concerned with the extent to which sociologists enter into public debate and play a part in developing that debate. Outhwaite frames this issue in terms of the development of 'celebrity theory', in which much of the impact of sociology comes from the reputation and public interventions of particular theorists (for example, Anthony Giddens, Ulrich Beck and Zygmunt Bauman). Hammersley also acknowledges the importance of very influential contemporary theorists, but he discusses public sociology more in the context of sociological claims to be able to produce distinctive and worthwhile knowledge. Nevertheless, both share a belief that sociology can successfully engage with the public and policy-makers in relation to crucial issues (such as environmental concerns or riots and social disorder) and give a strong sense of the pluralism of theoretical and methodological approaches in contemporary sociology, while neither believes that a single, dogmatic theoretical or methodological approach is the best avenue for sociology to pursue. Furthermore, while both acknowledge pluralism and relativism in the subject, neither believes that these make sociology incoherent or lacking in relevance and vitality.

In the sociological theory chapter, Outhwaite discusses the continuing significance of classical theory in sociology and examines attempts to produce a formal sociological theory of the social. He argues that, in the nineteenth century, Marx (even though he did not think of himself as a sociologist) and subsequent Marxists were the first to attempt a thorough formalizing theory of society. In the twentieth century only Talcott Parsons made a similar attempt to produce an all-embracing theoretical study of the social. Much of the classical tradition of sociology (such as that produced by Durkheim and Weber) was much less formalized and consisted more of a series of studies than an integrated theoretical approach. While many theoretical insights were offered by these writers, and attempts were made to formalize some aspects of sociology (for example, in Durkheim's *Rules of Sociological Method*), neither of them completed a fully developed theory which others could follow.

If much classical sociological theory was less than formal, in the late twentieth and early twenty-first century there has been a move towards even more informal theory. Recent sociology has developed with 'weak sociology' but 'strong sociologists', with theory developing through a range of influential celebrity sociologists. For a time, there was a retreat from grand theorizing towards a greater focus on empirical investigation. However, a number of recent theorists have not confined themselves to looking at specific issues but have engaged in 'broad-brush' speculation. These theorists (including Bourdieu, Giddens, Foucault, Beck and Bauman) have been integrated into much contemporary sociological work in a piecemeal fashion. Many sociologists draw upon an eclectic mix of these and other theorists rather than slavishly following any particular approach or perspective.

If sociology which is based upon eclectic and pluralistic theory has become more common, that has not prevented the continuation and development of fracture lines between different schools of thought. For example, debates about agency and structure continue to be important, and all traditional sociological theory has been challenged by post-traditional theories of postmodernism, post-structuralism and social constructionism. The latter fracture is illustrated by Outhwaite in terms of the disputes between Habermas and Lyotard, who represent quite different modern and postmodern theoretical approaches. While postmodernism threatened to undermine traditional theory for a while, Outhwaite is slightly dismissive of it, arguing that 'it's not new and not true'. Certainly, Outhwaite implies that more extreme social constructionist approaches are on the wane while grand (although informal) theory and policy-oriented studies are in the ascendancy. Although he is generally quite positive about trends in theory, Outhwaite does see dangers from a countervailing trend towards narrowly focused and highly empirical work which may limit the relevance of sociology to address big issues. In part, he sees this as resulting from the institutional framework within which sociologists, particularly in the UK, operate. Their careers depend to a considerable extent upon the frequent publication of articles in line with the priorities set through the Research Excellence Framework. While theory is not dead, and grand theory is thriving in some quarters, there is therefore a danger of a retreat from theory into disciplinary specialization.

Somewhat in contrast, Hammersley sees methodology rather than theory as 'the core of sociology' and argues that it is through proceeding in a 'methodologically sound way' that sociologists can 'generate more reliable factual knowledge about the social world than that coming from other sources'. However, just as many contemporary sociologists do not have very strong attachments to one theory, contemporary thinking about methodology often supports mixed methodological approaches and the eclectic use of data. The choice of methodology is still influenced by assumptions about the nature of social reality, and there remain some divisions between those advocating more quantitative or more qualitative approaches. Interpretivism, critical theory and constructionism, along with more 'scientific' approaches, do point towards different methodological stances and the use of different types of data. However, as well as being influenced by 'assumptions about the nature of social phenomena', methodological approaches are just as influenced by factors such as 'the nature of the questions being addressed and the circumstances in which the research must be carried out'. One factor is whether the research intends to use cross-case analysis or within-case analysis, but this doesn't represent a simple divide between using more quantitative or more qualitative data. For example, qualitative comparative analysis can be employed.

Hammersley draws on the 2011 riots as an example of how a whole variety of data and a whole range of methodological approaches have and could be used to study the same phenomenon. He also notes that several theoretical positions can generate explanations about the causes of these riots (for example, Bauman's claim that they could be related to the frustrations of consumers). Hammersley insists that empirical research is necessary to give any credibility to such theorizing. Furthermore, the research may use a variety of methodologies appropriate to the particular questions without any one methodology being seen as inherently superior to all others. It is more important that researchers are open to 'reflecting on the meaning of the concepts being used, the validity threats associated with reliance upon particular forms of data or methods of analysis, and so on'. In other words, they need to be self-critical and should aim for a degree of value neutrality, as advocated by Max Weber. Hammersley's position is different to that of critical sociologists, who see sociology as a means to identifying and combatting injustice and exploitation. For Hammersley, sociological research can certainly be used to inform policies, but sociologists cannot claim any special expertise is deciding what is just and what is unjust. Nevertheless he concludes that, in terms of achieving particular objectives, sociology '*can* provide essential resources to enable sound judgements'.

Both Outhwaite and Hammersley see dangers for contemporary sociology in having too narrow a focus, guarding disciplinary boundaries too rigidly, and in being too closed to alternative theoretical and empirical approaches. They also see distinct dangers in lacking theoretical ambition (in the case of Outhwaite) or being too value-laden or careless about empirical rigour (in the case of Hammersley). But both also believe that sociology remains vital for understanding contemporary social issues, and both welcome the engagement of sociology with wider audiences through 'public sociology'.

20

SOCIOLOGICAL THEORY

formal and informal

WILLIAM OUTHWAITE

CONTENTS

INTRODUCTION

THIS BOOK SHOULD GIVE you a sense of the diversity of sociology. Even with twenty-one chapters, it does not cover anything remotely like the full, rich diversity of the sociological enterprise. Furthermore, most of these chapters draw upon a wide range of theories, and it is evident that a plurality of theories influences contemporary sociologists. Many individual sociologists appear to draw upon an often eclectic mix of theoretical insights. If you are hoping that this chapter will provide a clear sense of the theoretical unity of *the* sociological approach, you will be disappointed. It is still possible, though, to identify clusters of concerns, principles and preoccupations gathered together in something like families of theory which have some resemblances within them but interrelate with others.

These theory families are brought to bear on a number of substantive topics. Marxism, for instance, tends to focus particularly on class. Durkheim wrote a major book of 'pure' theory, his *Rules of Sociological Method*, but he also studied the division of labour, suicide and religion. These three topics, for example, have also been approached from Marxist, Weberian, 'rational choice', 'phenomenological' and ethnomethodological perspectives. Similarly, a single item, such as the term 'class', may be used by a militant Marxist sociologist and by a social statistician with a more descriptive approach. More to the point is the configuration or constellation of concepts within which they locate their use of the term.

Contemporary sociological theory is shaped in part by the continuation of classical traditions such as those of Marx, Durkheim, Simmel or Max Weber, and also by more diffuse lines of influence. If there is one thing which links much classical and contemporary sociology it is a concern with modernity, whether as a framework for analysis or as something to be problematized or deconstructed – as it is in much Marxist, postmodern or postcolonial theory (Wood 1997; Bhambra 2007). The problematization of modernity has been a significant driving force in a good deal of recent sociological theory, adding to the diversity of approaches from which empirical sociology can draw. Does modernity mean critical thinking, freedom, democracy, and so on, or discipline, surveillance, slavery, imperialism and mass warfare – or both? (Wagner 1994, 2012)

As well as having a plurality of theories on which to draw, sociology is a subject with open borders, interrelating in particular with the other social sciences such as social anthropology, political science and international relations. The theory families discussed in this chapter are also to be found in these other social sciences. Sociology has an in-built tendency to 'take over' the domains of the other social sciences, putting political or economic life into a broader social framework. The relation between the social and the *political* is, however, much more fundamental than just between the disciplines which have come to be called sociology and politics or political science, and it deserves special mention at the outset of this chapter.

There is a tendency in social thought to incorporate and subordinate political processes as just one set of social processes among others. The crudest reductive account of the political is in simplified versions of the Marxist theory of base and superstructure, in which legal and political structures (superstructure) arise on the basis of social relations of production (base) and perform an essentially secondary role in relation to them. In periods of social revolution, political structures may retard social change for a time and, conversely, politics may even play a determinant role in revolutionary situations, but by and large the causal influence is from below upwards.

Non-Marxist sociology, too, tends to take a similar view of the political as just one area of human activity, along with work, reproduction, sport, and so on. Some societies, in other words, develop specialized state structures, just as they develop formal education or professional sport.

This approach has a long history. Well before the beginning of the nineteenth century, we see the emergence of a distinction between political phenomena and underlying social processes. Montesquieu had already in 1748 clearly expressed the basic idea that political and legal arrangements depend on broader social processes. In the early nineteenth century Henri de Saint-Simon, although he was closely attentive to political issues (including what we now call European integration), stressed the importance of social and economic processes and played down the role of the political class. Marx gave this approach a materialist spin by stressing the importance of forms of economic production for the rest of social life.

Two challenges to the reductionist conception of legal and political 'superstructures' emerged in the later twentieth century. One was theoretical and is essentially the work of the US sociologist and political scientist Theda Skocpol, with her slogan of 'bringing the state back in'. In a brilliant analysis, published in 1979, of the French, Russian and Chinese revolutions, Skocpol argued that they had to be understood as processes of state collapse as well as of social revolution. The other challenge, a practical one, occurred ten years later, with another set of revolutions which put an end to the Soviet communist bloc; these took different forms in different countries, but essentially involved processes of regime collapse in the face of mostly quite modest popular protest movements. Taken together, these two challenges suggested that the social and the political, society and the state, needed to be seen in a more sophisticated mode of interdependence.

This introduction has stressed the diversity of social theories and the different ways in which they have addressed the fundamental issue of the relation between the social and the political. The rest of this chapter offers a more detailed account of these processes.

SEMINAR QUESTIONS

1   What problems might the diversity of contemporary sociological theories create for the subject?
2   Do disciplinary boundaries help or hinder the study of social life?

THEORY: OLD AND NEW

What do we mean by theory in sociology? I suggest that there are two main answers: one which was dominant in the mid-twentieth century and another which is more common today. We could also describe this contrast as one between 'hard' and 'soft', or strong and weak, but the chronological contrast is less loaded and I think more helpful.

Formal theory and the natural sciences

The old conception is a rather formal one, modelled on the natural sciences, in which theories spell out in precise language the relationships between entities and processes – in this case, social ones – and also often aim ultimately to provide testable predictions. Theories, on this account, are located at different levels. Talcott Parsons (1937, 1951) tried to develop a general theory of social action and later of social systems; another North American functionalist, Robert Merton ([1942] 1957), argued that this needed to be complemented by 'middle-range' theories, such as his own theory of the relationship between anomie and deviance. Finally, there might be theories of specific phenomena, such as the 9/11 terrorist attack in the USA or the urban riots of 2011 in England.

Even in the heyday of this conception, some theorists questioned the viability or usefulness of general social theory. The philosopher Alasdair MacIntyre satirized the conception with the image of a man (it probably would have been a *man*) who tried to develop a general theory of holes.

> There once was a man who aspired to be the author of the general theory of holes. When asked 'What kind of hole – holes dug by children in the sand for amusement, holes dug by gardeners to plant lettuce seedlings, tank traps, holes made by road makers?' he would reply indignantly that he wished for a general theory that would explain all of these. He rejected . . . the – as he saw it – pathetically common-sense view that of the digging of different kinds of holes there are quite different kinds of explanations to be given; 'why then', he would ask, 'do we have the concept of a hole?' (MacIntyre 1971: 260)

In sociology, the radical US sociologist C. Wright Mills (1959a) attacked its polarization between 'grand theory' and 'abstracted empiricism', while most social interactionists were not interested in formal theoretical models, preferring close ethnographic description of social processes.

There was also a philosophical and historical critique of the model of science oriented to laws, prediction and testing. In sociology, anything presented as a 'law' either looked trivial, along the lines of 'if people want something they will probably try to achieve it', or had so many exceptions that it seemed useless. The US historian of science Thomas Kuhn (1962) and, following him, the Hungarian-British philosopher Imre Lakatos (2000) showed that scientists tended not to abandon theories which failed a test unless there was an alternative theory available. Karl Popper, whose model of theory-testing and 'falsification' had been dominant in the mid-twentieth century, could respond that these were just scientists behaving badly, but another line of argument, notably by the US philosopher W. V. O. Quine (1951), suggested that scientific 'facts' or 'observations' were shaped by theories which had to be evaluated as a package.

BOX 20.1 KUHN AND SCIENTIFIC REVOLUTIONS

Kuhn's *The Structure of Scientific Revolutions* (1962) raised questions about why any particular paradigm should be seen as providing the definitive theoretical approach in an area of academic endeavour. Kuhn admitted he used the term 'paradigm' in many different ways, but the two principal ones are *exemplars* (discoveries such as Lavoisier's discovery of oxygen, which act as an inspiration to later researchers) and the *disciplinary matrix* (the frameworks of assumptions, working practices and experimental techniques which are shared by a scientific community). In social thought, Rousseau's attempt to explain the origins of inequality or Durkheim's attempt to explain suicide might count as exemplars.

Kuhn believed, that under conditions of 'normal science', a particular paradigm was accepted with little questioning of the assumptions on which it was based. It was only when anomalies were acknowledged, anomalies that were inexplicable in terms of the paradigm, that science entered a revolutionary state. Ultimately a new paradigm would appear which was able to accommodate the anomalies.

In contrast, sociologists and other social scientists have not been, for the most part, wedded to 'paradigms' in the way Kuhn described in the natural sciences (and the contrast between these varieties of science was what inspired his analysis). In social science a plurality of 'paradigms' has long coexisted. Structural functionalism was dominant in some parts of the world in the middle of the twentieth century (particularly the USA), but even in America sociologists began to switch to a looser conception of theory in the later twentieth century. This conception is closer to literary and cultural theory, where what counts are ways of interpreting texts or broader cultural phenomena and the vocabulary used to describe them. The chosen theory becomes more like a set of tinted glasses, red for Marxism, purple for feminism, green for eco-criticism, and so on, which one can put on temporarily or permanently. It is not, however, possible to use untinted glasses and engage in a completely unmediated way with your object of study.

Formalizing theory: the example of Marxism

If we look at the history of sociology, it seems fairly clear that there is nothing like a systematic formal theory before the second half of the nineteenth century, and this section therefore begins with a discussion of Marxism. Marx's genius was partly that he offered a theory which could be formalized, even if it was not testable in the way later argued for by Karl Popper. Marx provides a model of the way in which value is produced and reproduced in capitalist economies and of the determinant influence of the forces and relations of production, more specifically class relations, on modern societies (and perhaps all societies).

Without going into details here, I suggest that Marxism can best be understood in the categories of realist philosophy of science as developed by Rom Harré and Paul Secord (1972)

BOX 20.2 FUNDAMENTALS OF MARXISM

The following three tweet-sized propositions sum up, in simplified form, a good deal of Marx's sociology.

1   The historical shift from exchange of commodities via money, which Marx represents as C-M-C^1, to the use of money to buy commodities (including, crucially, human labour-power, which produces more value than is paid out in wages) with the aim of making more money (M-C-M^1). (Marx [1867] 1954: vol. 2)
2   'The hand-mill gives you society with the feudal lord; the steam-mill society with the industrial capitalist.' (Marx [1847] 1976: 176)
3   'The history of all societies up to the present is the history of class struggles.' (Marx and Engels [1848] 1968)

These three elements represent the tip of a theoretical iceberg which Engels called historical materialism: Engels distinguished between *historical* materialism (the Marxist theory of history and society, summarized by Marx in his 1959 'Preface to the Critique of Political Economy') and *dialectical* materialism (the underlying philosophy of Marxism).

and Roy Bhaskar ([1975] 1997). Here science is recognized as the attempt to describe and explain entities, structures and mechanisms which may or may not be accessible to perception and whose operation may or may not lead to observable outcomes (since one tendency may counteract another). On this model, scientific laws should be understood as referring to tendencies: the law-like tendency for objects near the Earth's surface to fall to the ground is not refuted by the flight of birds and planes.

This is the point at which Popper ([1957] 1961) attacked Marxism for not exposing itself to decisive testing and possible refutation. A proper scientific theory, for Popper, exposes itself to tests and survives only on licence until the next crucial test. Einstein's general theory of relativity made a precise prediction in 1916, about the position of Mercury in relation to the sun, which was confirmed by observation. So far so good for Einstein. In 2011–12, however, there was a flurry of speculation, this time concerning his special theory of relativity, when it seemed that a particle had travelled from CERN in Geneva to an observation point in Italy at a speed slightly greater than that of light, which if true would falsify Einstein's theory. This was subsequently shown to be an observational error, so the challenge to the paradigm could be safely forgotten.

BOX 20.3 EXAMPLES OF REALISM

A good example of realism is the way the centrifugal force of the Earth's rotation is balanced by its gravitational attraction so that we can jump a metre or so in the air but not much more. In the social world, too, causal tendencies may cancel one another out. An increased tax on alcohol or tobacco will tend to discourage consumption, but increased smuggling may counteract this effect. Often the effects of the underlying processes involved can be seen or measured but the processes themselves cannot. In realist theory, though, they are just as real as physical phenomena which can be directly observed. An unobservable magnetic field may have an effect on iron filings, and many sociologists would argue that class structures determine educational achievement.

The trouble with a theory such as Marxism, according to Popper, is that it does not expose itself to testing in this way. It posits a *tendency* for the rate of profit to fall in capitalist economies, as human labour is replaced by machinery, but produces a set of countervailing tendencies if the rate of profit does not fall over a given period. Again, Marxism suggests that the working class will become radical in capitalist societies, and then wheels out a theory of ideology if it does not and instead adopts religious, nationalistic or other mistaken beliefs. In Popper's view, psychoanalytic theory is similarly defective: if you deny the analyst's interpretation, your denial can be explained away as 'resistance'.

Marx himself, we should note, was hostile to the idea of treating his theories as independent of time and space and concerned more to explain particular processes. It may not be an accident that he never completed the section of *Capital* defining his conception of class, and his best work using the concept is to be found in his accounts of episodes in recent French history. For Marx, theory and applied historical work were inseparable, as was (at least in theory) a connection between theory and practice – something largely abandoned in 'Western Marxism' (Anderson 1976).

There have been many attempts, however, to give Marxism a more formal expression, in the spirit of what I have called formal theory. First, in the 1960s, there was 'structuralist' Marxism in France, in the work of Louis Althusser (1918–1990) and his associates (Althusser [1965] 1969; Althusser et al. [1965] 1975). This focused on a 'structural' and rather static analysis of the relation between economic and political processes in modes of production, leaving the 'transition' from one to another for separate discussion. In a rather different way, analytical Marxism (or, as Gerry Cohen (1978) called it, 'non-bullshit Marxism') was applied to class theory by the US sociologist Erik Olin Wright (b. 1947) (Wright 1997). It was also combined with rational action theory, an approach dominant in economic theory and based on the idea of individuals choosing on the basis of expected (and usually individual) advantage, by the Norwegian philosopher and social scientist Jon Elster (b. 1940) (Elster 1986) and others in a variant known as rational choice Marxism.

I have discussed Marxism at some length because it is only here, I think, that we can

Can Marxism, formulated during late nineteenth-century urbanization and industrialization, explain modern-day sweatshops? (left © Kheel Center/Flickr; right © zakattak/Flickr)

BOX 20.4 RATIONAL CHOICE MARXISM AND SOLIDARISTIC COLLECTIVISM

Explaining solidaristic behaviour such as the formation of trade unions – sometimes called a 'collective action problem' (Dowding 1996) – has always been a challenge for Marxism: How would an alienated and demoralized working class develop a revolutionary consciousness and work together as a collectivity? Rational choice Marxism harnesses self-interest to explain why individuals may find collective action worthwhile. 'The Union makes *us* strong' and thereby increases *my* individual advantage.

see anything like a formal set of theories in classical sociology. Turning to the cluster of sociologists active in the late nineteenth and early twentieth century, we tend to find partial theories, often shaped, as Marxism had been, by a contrast between the modern world of European and North American modernity and what had preceded it in this part of the world and apparently survived for the time being elsewhere. Marx and Engels had drawn a contrast in their *Communist Manifesto* ([1848] 2008: 36–7) between capitalism and what had preceded it:

> The bourgeoisie, historically, has played a most revolutionary part. The bourgeoisie, wherever it has got the upper hand, has put an end to all feudal, patriarchal, idyllic relations. It has pitilessly torn asunder the motley feudal ties that bound man to his 'natural superiors', and has left no other nexus between man and man than naked self-interest, than callous 'cash payment' . . .
>
> The bourgeoisie, during its rule of scarce one hundred years, has created more massive and more colossal productive forces than have all preceding generations together.

In similarly vigorous language, Marx notoriously stressed the long-term benefits of British rule in India and claimed that the developed world showed to the less-developed world 'the image of its own future'. Ideas of social evolution are prevalent in Marx's work, and even more so in that of Engels. It is developed more explicitly in the writing of Marx's contemporary Herbert Spencer (whose grave faces that of Marx in Highgate cemetery in London) and, in the following generation, in the work of Emile Durkheim.

Classical sociology and less formal theory

Marx would probably have responded with an obscenity if anyone had called him a sociologist. (The word 'sociology' had been introduced in the 1830s by Auguste Comte, for whom Marx had no respect at all.) Durkheim, by contrast, was passionately committed to developing sociology as an independent discipline (and planting his students at strategic points in the French academic and intellectual scene). It is therefore not surprising that Durkheim ([1895] 1964) formulated a set of 'rules' of sociological method. His most fundamental rule was that what he called social facts should be treated 'as things': social processes could not be reduced to individual action or individual psychology. He had already made this argument in relation to suicide rates (Durkheim [1897] 1951): these were stable over time and related, he believed, to the ways in which people were integrated into their societies, by religious belief, marriage, and so on. This focus on social integration and social solidarity is central to Durkheim's thought.

He combined it with an evolutionary model of social development: his first major book on the division of labour (Durkheim [1893] 1973) traced the contrast between the 'mechanical solidarity' of what he thought of as simpler societies, in which people mostly did the same things (except perhaps for a division of labour by gender), and the 'organic solidarity' of societies where labour is more specialized and people therefore depend on one another for the provision of goods and services.

This is one of the set of typological contrasts which structure social theory of this period. Max Weber (1904–6) distinguished modern 'rational' capitalism from its earlier, less developed forms, and Ferdinand Tönnies (1855–1936) ([1887] 1957) contrasted *Gemeinschaft* – small-scale community with strong mutual bonds – and *Gesellschaft* – anonymous modern society where relationships are more instrumental.

Durkheim's *Rules of Sociological Method* ([1895] 1964) is a striking and rare example of explicit prescriptions for the emergent science of sociology. Even he, however, did not present a formal theory but rather a set of more detailed studies – of the division of labour, suicide and religion (Durkheim [1912] 1971) – illustrating, like a kaleidoscope, aspects of his model of society.

Max Weber was more ambivalent about identifying himself with sociology and avoided using the word 'society', even in his posthumous main work published under the title *Economy and Society* (Weber [1922] 1992), which is full of references to the fact that he is offering only one view of sociology.

Weber traced the process which he called rationalization, the systematization of religious belief, economic activity and human conduct in general, through a vast range of historical studies, but he would not have thought of presenting it as a *theory*. Having rejected as too speculative evolutionary theories of society, including Marxism, he offered instead a set of categories for analysis, formulated as 'ideal types' to which actual phenomena corresponded more or less closely. Tönnies provides perhaps the best illustration of the typological contrasts which are the main feature of this period of sociology. Community and society as he presents them are ideal types in Max Weber's sense, to which actual societies and patterns of social relations will conform more or less closely. Tönnies is now known almost entirely for his *Community and Society* ([1887] 1957), though he also produced substantial work in criminology and other areas of applied and empirical sociology and an overview of how the different levels of sociology – pure, applied and empirical – related to one another.

For Weber, what Durkheim called 'social facts' should be analysed as consequences of regular forms of human *action*, as described in his four-part typology (discussed in box 20.5). The contrast between Weber and Durkheim introduces us to one of the main structuring oppositions in sociological theory, which I shall discuss in more detail later, and which continues to this day – what has come to be called the action–structure debate. This continues, more recently, between approaches which retain a notion of social structure and those, such as symbolic interactionism, ethnomethodology, social constructionism and (at the 'hard' end of the theoretical spectrum) rational action theory, which reduce structures to action. (Marxist theory displays a microcosm of the same opposition, as we saw above: between the Marxist mainstream, including structuralist Marxism, and rational choice Marxism.)

Durkheim also illustrates an important feature of what we call sociological theory. *The Rules* was an explicitly theoretical text, but his other principal works, on the division of labour, suicide and religion, are also mostly read today for their theoretical principles and their status as

BOX 20.5 WEBER'S TYPOLOGY OF ACTION

Weber distinguished four pure types of action: traditional, affectually or emotionally determined, purposive-rational and value-rational.

Traditional action is based upon customs in a society. People act in a particular way because people have acted that way in the past. An example is putting on dark clothes to attend a funeral. Affectual or emotional actions express feelings, for example cheering if 'your' football team scores. Purposive-rational action is undertaken to achieve a particular goal having taken into account other goals and other possible means. An example of this is deciding not to cheat and to forgo leisure and spend more time revising in order to do better in an exam. Value-rational action is also designed to achieve valued goals but involves less consideration of alternatives. An example might be a risky or even suicidal act of resistance to an occupying army. Real action, Weber stressed, will often be driven by a combination of these.

what Kuhn called exemplars rather than for their substantive or methodological content. If you follow your 'theory' course with a specialist option on deviance or religion, you may find yourself re-reading Durkheim's books, but it will be with a very different focus. Historians of social thought will have a different approach again, aiming to reconstruct the context in which works such as these were produced and received and rejecting the 'presentist' focus on what we *now* consider the most important contributions.

If we look at the opening pages of Max Weber's massive *Economy and Society* (Weber [1922] 1992), we find a set of categories for social analysis and some propositions about how they fit together, but nothing like a theory in a formal sense. Weber does often refer to theories such as the 'materialist interpretation of history', but always to hypotheses to be confronted with real historical material, as he did in his classic essays on 'The Protestant Ethic and the "Spirit" of Capitalism', written in 1904–5. Even if he had lived to something like the same age as his brother Alfred (1868–1958), I doubt if he would have produced a systematic theory. Of the classical theorists of sociology, it is probably Vilfredo Pareto (1848–1923) who came closest to advancing a formal general sociological theory (Pareto 1935: 74). He certainly saw himself as offering 'a sociology that is purely experimental, after the fashion of chemistry, physics, and other such sciences' (ibid.: 6). On the other hand, he turned to sociology partly because he felt formal theories in economics had failed to provide adequate explanations. His own sociological (as opposed to economic) work is now read mainly for his analysis of elites and, sometimes, of ideology.

Taken together, these theorists represent the coming of age of sociology and social theory. In 1883, the year of Marx's death, there were Marx himself, Herbert Spencer (who survived until 1903), Auguste Comte (who had died in 1857) and a host of names which have long since been forgotten, except perhaps as the object of critiques by Max Weber. By 1920, the year of Weber's death, most of the central theorists of what we know as classical sociology had either completed or were well into their work.

Formal theory in the mid-twentieth century

If classical sociology advocated theories that were less formal than those of Marxism, it was in the next generation that the ideal of general and very formalized theory became established, most notably in the USA by Talcott Parsons (1902–1979) (see Holmwood 2006). As Javier Treviño (2001: xxvii) writes: 'The theory that Parsons elaborated . . . was intended to be so general that it would be capable of analyzing and ultimately explaining all the components of human social action.' In *The Structure of Social Action*, Parsons (1937) had argued for a convergence of Pareto, Durkheim and Weber in what he called a voluntaristic theory of social action. After the Second World War, he turned to system theory (Parsons 1951; Parsons, Bales and Shils 1953). Social systems, made up of social roles such as teacher and student or child and parent, interrelate with personality systems based on needs and cultural systems made up of cultural values. Together, these explain the maintenance (and, occasionally, the temporary breakdown) of social order.

In an article of 1960, Parsons spelled out his conception of theory and expressed some optimism about the prospects of eventual empirical verification (Parsons 1960: 482) of these concepts. But his work is better understood as a system of categories (Bershady 1973; Parsons 1978). Bryan Turner (2001a: 91) has usefully traced the different versions of Parsons's theory and its affinities with alternative system models such as Niklas Luhmann's, concluding, however, that Parsons's social system was too systemic and that a defensible modern conception of social systems would have to see them as 'a precarious balance of processes of risk and regulation'. John Holmwood (2006: xlvi), one of Parsons's more sympathetic interpreters, also suggests that 'we might perhaps look for the positive substance of his (or any other) contribution at a lower – and more fallible – level in specific sociological insights about the nature of social life.'

System theory was the main place in which to find a strong conception of theory, but elements of it can also be found in the writings of a number of theorists with a very different orientation, as well as in synoptic works aiming to present other theories in formal terms. A good example of an empirical study aiming to test an existing theory is a classic from the 1960s, the 'Affluent Worker' study by John Goldthorpe, David Lockwood and their colleagues (1968, 1969). This investigation of manual workers in various sites in England aimed to test the theory of 'embourgeoisement' or bourgeoisification: that, as workers became better off, as many had done in the 'thirty glorious years' of capitalism after the Second World War, they would become less politically radical (in the modest sense of voting for social democratic parties such as the British Labour Party) and less militant. The authors concluded that there was little evidence of embourgoisement, though they identified an 'instrumental' attitude towards work as a means to an end – suggesting that such workers might take militant industrial action if their expectations of material reward were frustrated.

In retrospect, what is striking is the vagueness of the theory which the authors were claiming to 'test' and their taking the language of 'testing' too literally. As Mike Savage (2005: 932–3) has argued, their 'deductive' conception of theory meant that, 'Having gathered rich qualitative material, the researchers then explicitly stripped out such materials in favour of more formal analytical strategies when they came to write up their findings.'

Informal theory

What I am calling the new conception of theory dominates the last third of the twentieth century and continues into the present. Whereas the main opposition to system theory had previously been from symbolic interactionism, the revival of social and political theory after 1968 was marked by a more serious engagement with the 'classics' and the canonization of Marx, Weber and Durkheim as the holy trinity who continue to dominate 'classical sociology' in the UK (for an early and influential example, see Giddens 1971). And this was in turn shaped by broader processes of social and political *thought*: in particular the revival of Marxism and the emergence of 'second-wave' feminism (the first wave being in the early decades of the twentieth century), of environmentalism and of responses to anti-colonial and 'Third World' liberation movements. The first and last of these were central to the years around 1968 (Bhambra and Demir 2009), notably in protests against the Vietnam War, while feminist, gay and green politics emerged rather later.

In social and political *theory*, the revival of serious interest in Marxist theory reinforced the appeal of other classical social theorists: Durkheim, Weber, Simmel and others. This in turn led to a revival of interest in their concern to produce broad-spectrum theories of modernity and to the emergence of a cluster of *contemporary* theorists pursuing these issues. There was a shift, in other words, from what we might call a natural scientific model of theory, where each cluster of theories has a set of more or less prominent representatives and a larger penumbra of people doing 'normal science' within those frameworks (functionalism, symbolic interactionism, and so on), to something I would tentatively (and without intending to be rude about it) call 'celebrity social theory' – a shift to what Alan Wolfe (1992) called a field of 'weak sociology' and 'strong sociologists' (see also Bershady 1991). In this model, you typically find:

1   a single theorist developing a personal approach or vision;
2   a cluster of interpreters of the great theorist; and
3   another, often overlapping cluster of people applying that theorist's approach to a substantive topic or set of topics.

A fairly uncontentious list of such theorists would include Zygmunt Bauman, Ulrich Beck, Pierre Bourdieu, Michel Foucault, Anthony Giddens, Jürgen Habermas and Alain Touraine. There are four obvious points to make about these figures. They are all male – something to which I will return later. Secondly, they are all European, reversing the previous predominance of North Americans in the heyday of system theory and symbolic interactionism. (Major figures in the USA, such as Randall Collins or Jeffrey Alexander, have not so far achieved the same global prominence.) Thirdly, unless we count Europe as a single entity, we should note the international character of the theorists on my list: two British (one of Polish origin), three French and two German.

Since this part of the chapter is particularly concerned with the shift from one conception of theory to another, it is worth noting that all of the individuals mentioned, except Bauman and Beck, did at one point offer fairly systematic presentations of their theories. Foucault's *Archaeology of Knowledge* (1969) is an uncompromisingly theoretical defence of the approach he had taken in *The Order of Things* ([1966] 1970). Touraine (1977) also produced a formal theory in *The Self-Production of Society*, as did Bourdieu (1977) in *Outline of a Theory of Practice*. Habermas and Giddens followed, with, respectively, *The Theory of Communicative Action* (1986, 1989a) and *The Constitution of Society* (1984).

It is, however, noticeable, as Peter Wagner (2011: 271) has pointed out, that, with the 'partial exception' of Touraine, none of them pursued this line of theoretical reconstruction. This, he suggests, may be because modern societies have experienced such radical processes of social change that these theories no longer seem relevant. I suspect that the real reason may

BOX 20.6 BECK AND RISK SOCIETY

Beck's concept of risk society (1992) suggests the contrast between the industrial societies of modernity, in which classes compete for a share of social wealth, and a 'second modernity', in which we aim to avoid risks by individual or collective strategies. In risk society, risks tend to be a product of human action rather than natural disasters, and they can affect all social groups regardless of their class. Environmental risks, such as those that result from global warming, are a case in point. Controversially, Beck has claimed that class has become a zombie category. While still alive in sociological literature, it is dead as a powerful source of explanation or understanding in the subject. Collective identities, such as those associated with class and other social divisions, become less important because they are undermined through a process of individualization. For example, because employment is less secure and people change jobs frequently, class solidarity is undermined. Bauman also stresses the fluidity of social relations, a feature of a number of contemporary theories, perhaps most obviously in his notion of liquid modernity. (See below for more discussion of Beck.)

be a more stylistic or methodological one, that such formal models have lost their appeal. Instead, we find a conception which Patrick Baert (2006: 14–24) calls 'representational theory', in which the social world is represented under a broad category such as 'risk' (Beck), 'liquidity' (Bauman), 'habitus and field' (Bourdieu), communicative versus strategic action (Habermas) or 'modernity' (almost everybody). In the case of 'modernity', there is often some prefix such as 'reflexive' or 'second' to distinguish the contemporary variant from a broader understanding of modernity as beginning in Europe and North America around the eighteenth century.

In both sociology and political theory, then, there was a willingness again to engage in broad-brush speculative theory; 'the classics' seemed less like remote ancestors and more like older contemporaries. (Getting to know them better, through detailed biographies and textual analyses, helped in this.) My rather upbeat account of this process should be compared to Peter Wagner's more pessimistic assessment: 'There was some revival of social theorising in the 1960s and 1970s . . . again thriving on a positive intellectual and political climate just as . . . in the late 1800s . . . But again, and to some extent analogous to what happened in the early 1900s, this positive conjuncture has vanished and the intellectual alliances have fallen apart again' (Wagner 2001: 24). This is perhaps too pessimistic. As Stephen Turner (2009) writes, focusing particularly on the US situation,

social theory goes on, both within sociology and, increasingly, outside of it. The same forces that led to the estrangement between social theory and empirical sociology have brought social theory closer to political theory, to such topics as citizenship and such figures as [Hannah] Arendt and [Carl] Schmitt, for example, and to other bodies of thought, such as pragmatism and cultural studies in the humanities.

SEMINAR QUESTIONS

1 Compare the two conceptions of theory discussed above. Should contemporary sociologists attempt more systematic theorizing?

2 Compare Beck's 'risk society' and 'second modernity' with Bauman's 'liquid modernity'.

3   Is the celebrity status of one or more of the sociologists named above justified in terms of their contribution to the understanding of social life?

4   'Today it is possible to pick and mix ideas from different theorists because their ideas are less systematic and therefore not mutually exclusive. In the past, you had to choose one theory or another because they were systematic and directly contradicted one another.' Discuss this statement.

CONTEMPORARY THEORETICAL DIVISIONS

Theories of action and structure

Within this new configuration of theory, we might differentiate between theorists who still take systematic theory and the relation between 'action' and 'structure' as a central concern and those who feel they have moved beyond such considerations. The first category I shall call 'neo-traditionalists'. I do not mean this in a pejorative sense, since I identify myself with them, to varying degrees. Among them I would include Margaret Archer (b. 1943) and Norbert Elias (1897–1990), along with Bourdieu (1930–2002), Giddens (b. 1938), Habermas (b. 1929), Niklas Luhmann (1927–1998) and Alain Touraine (b. 1925). All seven have written systematic works of theory, locating their positions at various points along the action–structure spectrum.

ACTION ⟵————————————————————————⟶ STRUCTURE

Touraine   Giddens; Elias   Bourdieu; Habermas   Archer   Luhmann

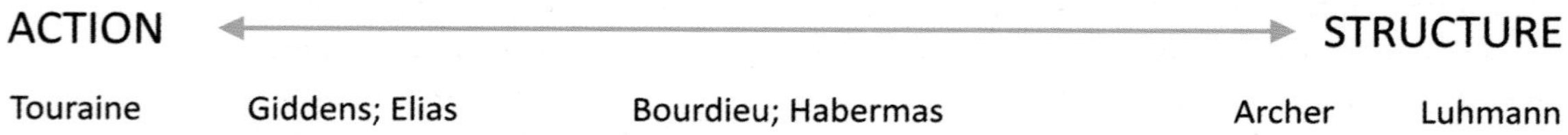

Figure 20.1 Locating theorists on the action–structure spectrum

Touraine is easily located at the action pole. His 'sociology of action' (Touraine 1965) drew on the ideas of the existentialist philosopher Jean-Paul Sartre (1905–1980) and his theory of society (Sartre [1960] 1976) in an explicitly anti-functionalist approach. His concern with what he called the 'production of society' was linked to his rejection of society as a substantive concept and his study of social movements, from the labour movement to feminist, anti-nuclear and regionalist movements and the Polish anti-communist movement Solidarity.

Where Touraine had reacted against Parsons and system theory, Bourdieu reacted against the structuralist social anthropology of Claude Lévi-Strauss (1908–2009), stressing the role of structured action (habitus) in a field. Where structuralism concentrated on the formal oppositions between, for example, kinship categories, Bourdieu was interested in the way actors played within these formal constraints. A football match, we might say, involves not just the opposition between two teams and their positions (forward/back, left/right, etc.) but the players' strategic movements and their 'sense of the game'. (Elias's notion of 'figurations' is similarly focused on images of games and dances. Elias illustrates this, saying: 'no one will imagine a dance as a structure outside of the individuals. Different people may dance the same configurations. Nevertheless, there is no dance without a plurality of reciprocally oriented and dependent individuals' (Elias [1939] 2000: 482). Many readers find Bourdieu's model too rigid and mechanical – a kind of structural variant of rational action theory – but the action theme is at least as strong in his work. His book on language, for example, has the rather formal subtitle 'economy of linguistic exchanges', preserved in the English translation, but the title is the more direct 'what it means to speak' (Bourdieu [1982] 1991).

Giddens's 'structuration theory', despite its name, is closer to the action pole than the work of Bourdieu. He was strongly influenced by the ethnomethodologist Harold Garfinkel's stress on the 'knowledgeability' of social actors, that they should not be seen, as in structural functionalism, as 'cultural dopes' blindly following the promptings of the common value system of society (Garfinkel 1967). Giddens (1984) defines structure in terms of rules and resources, such as the syntax and vocabulary of a language which regulate what we say or write but also make it possible.

Giddens's critics tend to argue that his model has, as John B. Thompson (1989) puts it, 'too much action, too little structure'. Margaret Archer (1982), with a background in system theory, argues that he 'conflates' them in his model of structuration, whereas she differentiates between morphogenesis (the production or transformation of structures) and morphostasis (the preservation of their established state) and insists on their temporal separation. Demographic processes, for example, take time to modify, even by the most drastic interventions such as the Romanian government's ban on abortion in the late 1960s or the Chinese one-child policy. As another example, Archer cites the Cuban government's literacy strategy, where each person who was taught to read was required to teach two others, resulting over time in near universal literacy.

Habermas (1986, 1989a) takes action and structure or, in his terminology, communicative action and system processes as part of a historical trajectory of capitalist modernity, in which traditional practices of what he calls the 'lifeworld' are subjected to rational analysis but also increasingly 'colonized' by formal systems of monetary exchange and bureaucratic administration. The first form of rationalization opens things up to discussion and rethinking; the second closes them down again as they are subjected to the laws of the market or the state administration. Habermas has been accused of taking on board too much of system theory, and also of thinking of the social too much in terms of moral norms – another feature of Parsons's system. Recent Marxist theory, as noted earlier, has its own version of these oppositions, poised between the structuralist Marxism of Althusser (1965) and others and the 'voluntaristic' alternatives of Antonio Gramsci (1971b), 'praxis philosophy', critical theory and 'post-Marxism'.

Finally, I have included Luhmann (1997) in this category because, although he dissolved the category of agency wholly into systems, he was concerned in a quite traditional way with the differentiation of the separate subsystems of society (political, legal, scientific, etc.) and the relations between them: society, in fact 'world society', remained his basic framework.

Non-traditional contemporary theories: the focus on processes

Under this heading I include theories which do not aim at a general account of society but are also not simply 'middle-range' theories of the traditional type (theories of crime and deviance, religion, etc.). They discuss processes which are felt across many different areas of social life but they make no claim to be all-encompassing. For example, Beck's theory of 'risk society', as discussed above, begins with, but is not confined to, environmental risks. It is a theory of 'second modernity': whereas in earlier forms of capitalist modernity the various classes compete for a larger share of social wealth, in risk society we are concerned more with *reducing*

BOX 20.7 HOLLIS AND SMITH: EXPLANATION, UNDERSTANDING, HOLISM AND INDIVIDUALISM

One of the best discussions of these issues is a short book by Martin Hollis and Steve Smith (1991). Their main focus is on the difference between 'understanding' and 'explaining', but this intersects with that between individualism and structural holism. There may be, as Max Weber ([1922] 1992) insisted, an affinity between individualistic approaches and understanding, but it is also possible to take individual behaviour as the mere outcome of causal influences (as in behaviourism) or, conversely, to give primacy to large structures of ideas which have to be understood from the inside (Hollis and Smith 1991: 4–5).

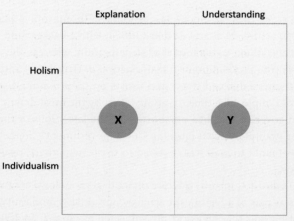

Figure 20.2 Categorizing theory

Source: Hollis and Smith (1991: 5). By permission of Oxford University Press.

X is an actor conceived in the spirit of the scientific tradition, Y the counterpart in the spirit of the interpretive tradition. For both there is a pull in two directions. On the one hand, X and Y are human beings with beliefs and aims, and we are interested in what is in their heads. On the other hand, their situation is structured, and . . . we are interested in the social constraints on their actions.

our share of environmental and other risks (to the extent that this is possible), for example by hiding from crime in 'gated communities' which are air-conditioned, like the cars we drive, to protect us from the pollution to which we are contributing.

Modernity is again a shared theme, as it was in classical sociology, but now with an adjective to distinguish it from the form it took at the last turn of the century. Beck's 'second modernity' is paralleled by Giddens's 'reflexive modernity'. For Habermas, modernity remains an 'incomplete project' of the extension of communicative action and discursive democracy, while for Bauman, who for a time favoured theories of postmodernity, modernity has become 'liquid'.

Bauman, like Beck, has a background in critical theory (Bauman 1976) (and also, in his case, Marxism and hermeneutics (Bauman 1978)), but has focused increasingly on the 'liquidity' of modern social relations of employment, love, and so on. This converges with a stress in the work of both Giddens and Beck on what Beck and Beck-Gersheim (2001) call individualization, linked to the fluidity (Bauman) and unscriptedness (Giddens) of contemporary social roles. Beck and Beck-Gernsheim (2001: 2) define it thus:

> On the one hand, individualization means the disintegration of previously existing social forms – for example, the increasing fragility of such categories as class and social status, gender roles, family, neighbourhood etc. . . . the second aspect of individualization . . . is, simply, that in modern societies new demands are being imposed on individuals. Through the job market, the welfare state and institutions, people are tied into a network of regulations, conditions, provisos . . .

The decisive feature of these modern regulations and guidelines is that, far more than earlier, individuals must, in part, supply them for themselves, import them into their biographies through their own actions. This is one of the areas where their work draws on and intersects with that of Foucault (1977). Giddens (1990: 59) follows Foucault in making surveillance one of the 'institutional dimensions of modernity', along with industrialism, capitalism and military power. Industrialism and capitalism are long-standing categories of sociological analysis, but there are fewer sociological studies of militarism and warfare, which tend to be found in 'international relations'. Although the notion of surveillance has echoes of Max Weber's analysis of self-control in his essays on the Protestant ethic and of Elias's concept of 'affect control', it was Foucault, with his image of the panoptical prison, who put it on the map.

The 1990s saw the beginning of a new body of interdisciplinary social theory: globalization theory. Bauman, Beck, Bourdieu and Giddens all plunged into this new wave. Giddens is an old friend and former Leicester colleague of Martin Albrow, one of the pioneers of globalization theory in the late 1980s (Albrow and King 1990; Albrow 1993, 1997, 2007). Giddens co-founded Polity Press in 1984 with John B. Thompson and David Held, who had also been writing about globalization since 1990 (Held 1990, 1991). Giddens's Reith lectures of 1999 were his first major statement on globalization, but in *Runaway World* he also addressed the very Beckian theme of risk. Beck had published a book on globalization in 1997 (2000b), and Bauman a short and rather gloomy one in 1998. Bourdieu, who by now had moved into a more militant mode marked by the publication of *The Weight of the World* (1999) and what became a series of public interventions ended only by his death in 2002, was even more negative in his response to globalization. Even more so than risk, individualization and surveillance, globalization is an almost ubiquitous topic in contemporary sociology, but it makes no claims to be a comprehensive alternative paradigm in its own right. Rather it simply emphasizes the importance of (what is claimed to be) an enormously important process shaping contemporary society, and sometimes earlier forms of society as well. It has some implications for general theory (particularly in arguing that society or the nation-state can no longer be seen as the 'thing' that sociology focuses its study on) but it should be understood as a particular theory about large-scale social processes rather than a general theory like that of Giddens.

The present century sees Bourdieu's early death from cancer, Giddens's continuation of a political role alongside the production of some policy and political books, Bauman continuing to cultivate his liquid garden, and Habermas and Beck developing their problematization of the nation-state into the areas of cosmopolitan and more specifically European Union politics – and, in Habermas's case, the changing place of religion. The configuration of sociological attention therefore alters, with Bourdieu and Giddens remaining central *theoretical* reference points focused mainly, and in Bourdieu's case necessarily, on their work in the last century, while Bauman's and Beck's current writing continues to build on their previous activity. (Beck had in any case never published a work of 'pure' theory, as the others had done.)

Despite their differences, there are, I think, a set of interlocking intellectual structures which link all of them, to varying degrees. But, despite these intellectual structures assuming enormous influence, they have not been without their critics. Some have suggested that the theme of globalization has been greatly overstated (Hirst and Thompson 1999; Rosenberg 2000); others that the term 'modernity' has not only been overused but is fundamentally problematic (Wood 1997, 1999). Finally, some regret the entire 'continental' direction of sociological theory, seeing it as an unwelcome diversion from a healthier state in the earlier post-war period in which theory operated more as an interpreter of empirical research and less as a would-be legislator for it. Such critics tend to point out that theorists such as Bauman, Beck, Giddens and Habermas (Bourdieu is again an exception) have done little empirical research.

I shall not engage these criticisms in relation to globalization and modernity, but I think that the charge misses the mark in relation to the role of theory. All these thinkers have consistently presented their theoretical models as directing attention to certain phenomena and providing a loose framework for analysis, rather than laying down formal categories in the manner of Parsons or, more recently, Niklas Luhmann. Giddens's structuration theory, for example, is linked only loosely with his substantive analyses of class stratification, state power or globalization (see Baert and Carreira da Silva 2010).

SEMINAR QUESTIONS

1   Compare the role of 'action' and 'structure' in the theories of Giddens and Bourdieu.
2   Is globalization best understood in structural or individual terms?
3   'Sociology is better off with loose frameworks than all-encompassing theory.' Discuss this statement in the light of the work presented here.

POST-TRADITIONAL THEORY

Under this heading I include some theorists whose thought has been shaped by some combination of postmodernism, post-structuralism and social constructionism. This 'family' is far more diverse than those previously discussed, but the theorists mentioned are linked by a more militantly sceptical attitude towards systematic theory than one finds in, for example, Bauman. They are predominantly French: Jean-François Lyotard (1924–1998), Bruno Latour (b. 1947) and Steve Woolgar (b. 1950), Jean Baudrillard (1929–2007) and Michel Maffesoli (b. 1944).

Postmodernity

Lyotard (1979) brought the term postmodernity into sociology, and his analysis of disagreement (Lyotard 1983) contrasts interestingly with Habermas's notion of mutual understanding.

The disagreement between Habermas and Lyotard is not between modern and postmodern conceptions of social scientific theory. I have argued elsewhere (Outhwaite 1999) that the contrast between modernity and postmodernity, as well as that between modernism and

BOX 20.8 HABERMAS AND LYOTARD

Habermas stresses the way communication is oriented to mutual understanding and possible agreement, while Lyotard emphasizes the other side of the coin – the diversity of frameworks and the prevalence of unbridgeable disagreements. For Habermas, modernity is a rational if incomplete project, while for Lyotard the 'grand narratives' of progress are now over, and in their heyday they often led to disastrous experiments such as the pursuit of communism or the 'civilizing mission' of colonialism. Whereas Habermas believes it is essential to uphold universalistic principles if we are to avoid the risks of political irrationalism, Lyotard insists on the diversity of language-games with their own incommensurable rules.

postmodernism, is not particularly useful. In social theory, the idea of formal systems resembling modernist skyscrapers in their massive construction scarcely fits any system except perhaps that of Parsons; even Luhmann's, although he planned it out in advance – his research proposal in 1969 read: 'theory of society; project duration: 30 years; research expenses: none' (Luhmann 1997: 11) – is much more differentiated. 'Social constructionism', which is now often associated with postmodernism, goes back to the classic work of Berger and Luckmann (1967) and to earlier traditions of symbolic interactionism and, also in the 1960s, ethnomethodology. Bauman, as we saw, abandoned postmodernism in favour of his own notion of liquid modernity. Baudrillard continued to defend it, as does Maffesoli (2010a, 2010b). Latour (1991) argues in relation to the history of science that we were never modern anyway; he returns to the theme of modernity, or what he calls 'the modern parenthesis' (now closed), in a recent book (Latour 2013).

If, however, there is something like a postmodern style, sceptical, provocative and debunking, it can be found in different ways in all these thinkers. Postmodern theory in the social sciences began with a critique of 'grand narratives'. In Jean-François Lyotard's classic formulation, 'I would argue that the project of modernity (the realization of universality) has not been forsaken or forgotten but destroyed, "liquidated"'. As Lyotard put it a little earlier, in the book which initiated postmodernism in social theory, *The Postmodern Condition*: 'economic "redeployment" in the current phase of capitalism . . . goes hand in hand with a change in the function of the State . . . What is new in all this is that the old poles of attraction represented by nation-states, parties, professions, institutions, and historical traditions are losing their attraction' (Lyotard 1979: 14).

There are roughly two kinds of postmodern thinkers: those emphasizing scepticism and those celebrating a more playful social world beyond the discipline of modernity. The French-Canadian sociologist Pauline Marie Rosenau (1992) usefully differentiates between these two admittedly overlapping and cross-cutting strands of postmodern thought:

the skeptical post-modernists . . . argue that the post-modern age is one of fragmentation, disintegration, malaise, meaninglessness, a vagueness or even absence of moral parameters and societal chaos . . . the affirmative postmodernists . . . have a more hopeful, optimistic view of the post-modern age . . . They are either open to positive political action (struggle and resistance) or content with the recognition of visionary, celebratory personal nondogmatic projects that range from New Age religion to New Wave life-styles and include a whole spectrum of post-modern social movements. (Rosenau 1992: 15)

Baudrillard (1983) contrasts the static notion of society or the social with a more dynamic, fluid and symbolically mediated notion of sociality. Michel Maffesoli (2010b), in a related approach, has developed the notion of society as sociality, tracing it theoretically back to Simmel and forward to a reflection on subcultural 'neo-tribalism' in modern societies. Sociality is intrinsically (and increasingly) playful, dionysiac and far removed from the Durkheimian severity of more traditional models of society. According to Maffesoli, the emphasis on economics and rationality in much theory left it completely unable to understand this playfulness. In Bryan Turner's (2010) analysis, postmodernism reflects a challenge to the hegemony of bourgeois European culture, and thus has an underlying affinity with the decolonization process and postcolonial critique. Postmodernism occupied a gap left by the inability of Marxism to analyse culture in a postcolonial world.

A second way of differentiating postmodern theory is Zygmunt Bauman's (1997) distinction between theorists *of postmodernity*, who may practise social science according to traditional norms of rigour, and methodologically or stylistically *postmodern* theorists. Bauman himself, whose version of postmodernity, or what he now calls 'light' or 'liquid' modernity, has also always been measured, reflectively analyses the loss of faith in society in quite concrete terms:

> The image of society drew its credibility from the experience of collective constraint – but also from the sense of collective insurance against individual misfortune, brought about by the establishment of collectively sustained welfare provisions, and above all from the sense of the solidity and continuity of shared social institutions . . . all three types of experience – of consistent normative pressure, of protection against the vagaries of individual fate, and of the majestic longevity of a collectively controlled order – began to fade fast in the last decades of the twentieth century and to be replaced by another experience, which no longer suggested a 'company', but rather (to borrow Keith Tester's description) a world that was 'separated from individuals', a world that 'has experientially become increasingly like a seamless web of overlapping institutions with an independent existence'. (Bauman 2005: 137)

Bauman rightly stresses that these institutions have an uncertain life expectancy. This type of institutional change is not a mere by-product of capitalist concentration or globalization. As Richard Sennett (1998) and others have shown, it is explicitly pursued as a management strategy of control. It is here that one can find a more moderate version of postmodern theory, stressing the fragmentation of work relations and other social practices.

The limitations and/or future of postmodernism

What I find problematic about postmodernism is merely that it's not new and not true. Not new, because I do not believe that there is a clear divide between an earlier age, modern or at least pre-postmodern, and a postmodern condition prevailing since the last third of the twentieth century. The shock appeal of postmodern analyses derived largely from this chronological claim, made paradigmatically in Lyotard's (1979) slogan of the *end* of grand narratives. Postmodernism, as it came to be known, was presented as not just a theoretical or meta-theoretical option; it was allegedly underwritten by the movement of the advanced societies themselves towards a postmodern state. In Jean-François

Lyotard's words, quoted earlier, 'I would argue that the project of modernity (the realization of universality) has not been forsaken or forgotten but destroyed, "liquidated"' (1979: 18).

Lyotard himself, however, backed away more or less immediately from this chronological claim, asserting that modern and postmodern elements coexist and suggesting, rather irritatingly, that the postmodern could *precede* the modern as easily as follow it. But chronological postmodernism survived, suggesting that modernism and modernity were passé. As Maffesoli (2010a) put it in an interview, 'I stand by the word "postmodernity" because it shows well that the house is burning.' For Latour (2013), also, 'the touchstone that served to distinguish past from present, to sketch out the modernization front that was ready to encompass the planet by offering an identity to those who felt "modern," has lost all its efficacy.'

On the whole, however, it was the epistemically sceptical variant of postmodernism adopted by what Bauman called postmodern theorists that now survives in a rather undifferentiated cocktail with 'post-structuralism', deconstruction and anti-foundationalism. To say that postmodernism in the sense of epistemic scepticism is not new is hardly news: to say it's not true is not really entering into the spirit of the game (since postmodern theorists generally deny the possibility of truth). But I shall confine myself to the observation that the 'social construction of reality', like W. I. Thomas's much earlier dictum that, 'if men define things as real, they are real in their consequences' (Thomas and Thomas 1928: 572), had been largely assimilated into the mainstream of social scientific discourse, not least in the sociology of scientific knowledge.

As I suggested earlier, we should perhaps resist the appeal of what might be called the postmodern metaphor in the social sciences and scholarship as a whole, in which the modern, the non- or pre-postmodern, is identified with modernist architecture and with its stress on function, order and system. The metaphor is seductive, if one thinks of massive closely argued treatises in philosophy or sociology such as those of Talcott Parsons and sociology's indisputable connections to social policy, social engineering and applied social science (Scott 1998). But this captures only one aspect of philosophy and social theory: there is also a more tentative, questioning, exploratory aspect, which is concerned more with description and understanding than with formal demonstration and explanation, still less with prediction and control. Many of the most influential works have a more ethnographic or essayistic character, such as Goffman's *The Presentation of Self in Everyday Life* (1959) or the more recent work of Beck, Bauman and others.

Latour's Actor-Network Theory deserves separate consideration here. Networks, as Latour, Callon (1986) and their collaborators conceive them, include both human agents, such as fishermen, merchants and consumers of shellfish, and physical objects such as the molluscs themselves and fishing boats. Latour's focus on material objects or, as he now puts it, 'the multiplicity of objects admitted to existence' (Latour 2013: 21) is also one way into a recent preoccupation of utopian and feminist thought with hybrids (Kenshur 1995) and cyborgs (Haraway 1991). For Haraway, 'One important route for reconstructing socialist-feminist politics is through theory and practice addressed to the social relations of science and technology, including crucially the systems of myth and meanings structuring our imaginations. The cyborg is a kind of disassembled and reassembled, postmodern collective and personal self. This is the self feminists must code' (Haraway 1991: 164).

BOX 20.9 TOP TEN SOCIOLOGY BOOKS OF THE TWENTIETH CENTURY?

In the run-up to the International Sociological Association's World Congress of Sociology held in Montreal in 1998, ISA members were asked to list the five books published in the twentieth century which were 'most influential in their work as sociologists'.

Here are the top ten books of the (twentieth) century, numbered in order with percentage scores:

1 Weber, Max: *Economy and Society* (20.9%)
2 Mills, Charles Wright: *The Sociological Imagination* (13.0%)
3 Merton, Robert K.: *Social Theory and Social Structure* (11.4%)
4 Weber, Max: *The Protestant Ethic and the Spirit of Capitalism* (10.3%)
5 Berger, P. L. and Luckmann, T.: *The Social Construction of Reality* (9.9%)
6 Bourdieu, Pierre: *Distinction: A Social Critique of the Judgement of Taste* (9.5%)
7 Elias, Norbert: *The Civilizing Process* (6.6%)
8 Habermas, Jürgen: *The Theory of Communicative Action* (6.4%)
9 Parsons, Talcott: *The Structure of Social Action* (6.2%)
10 Goffman, Erving: *The Presentation of Self in Everyday Life* (5.5%)

The eclectic mix, spanning most of the century, illustrates the wide variety of theoretical approaches that continue to influence contemporary theory.

Whatever one thinks of these developments (as a former colleague once said, 'I wear contact lenses but it doesn't mean I'm a cyborg'), it seems clear that social theory needs to take much more account of the natural world and in particular the biological domain (Moog and Stones 2009). Whether or not the term 'post-human' catches on, this may in the end be the most lasting influence of postmodern thought.

SEMINAR QUESTIONS

1 Do you agree that the distinction between modernity and postmodernity is unhelpful in social theory?
2 Discuss the view that the relativism of postmodern theorists is nothing new and adds little to sociological theory.
3 What aspects of postmodern theory have contributed most to contemporary sociology?

CONCLUSION

The current scene in sociological theory, and social and political thought more broadly, is, then, one where a number of well-established theory families (Marxist, Weberian, Durkheimian, functionalist/system theoretical, rational choice/action, interactionist, social constructionist and ethnomethodological) coexist with more recent approaches. The first three (and, as we shall see, the very strong influence of Simmel) date from the late nineteenth and early twentieth century, the others from the middle of the twentieth century. Simplifying drastically, we might differentiate between the theoretical offspring of Marx (critical theory, structuralist Marxism, Bourdieu (Burawoy 2012) – despite his rejection of Marxism as a formal system – postcolonial theory and some versions of feminism) and those of Max Weber. Here, as well as a number of 'card-carrying' Weberians, such as Günther Roth and Wolfgang Schluchter (1979) in Germany and the USA or Martin Albrow (1990) in Britain, there are strong Weberian influences in Touraine's sociology of action, the blend of economic and social theory in rational choice theory, the stress on state power and violence in some of Giddens's work, and Bauman's 'gardening' metaphor – which corresponds in many ways to Weberian rationalization. The influence of Durkheim is strong in functionalism and system theory and in related political theories of communitarianism (Etzioni 1994); Parsons also drew substantially on Tönnies's distinction between *Gemeinschaft* and *Gesellschaft*. Simmel's influence is probably the most widespread – notably on Bauman, Maffesoli and the sociology of culture as a whole.

All these theorists also have some substantive work to offer, such as Giddens's on the state (1984, 1990) or on self-identity (1991), which readers without a taste for pure theory can latch onto. If this can be summarized in a single word or phrase, such as 'structuration', 'risk', 'liquidity' or 'habitus', so much the better. Once again, Therborn (2000: 42) puts his finger on it:

> It is in this perspective of understanding and discourse, that social labelling, as a way of grasping and conveying the sense of the contemporary world, becomes so central to sociologists of prime-time aspirations. Are we living in post-modernity, or in reflexive modernity, or perhaps in a second modernity, in a risk society or in an event society (*Erlebnisgesellschaft*), in an information society, network society, or maybe in something completely different? (Therborn 2000: 42; see also Baert 2006)

What of the broader scene of social and political thought? Of the 1960s movements, feminist theory has fundamentally reshaped it, though perhaps not really at its core. Turner (2009: 557) suggests that 'movement women did not want into the "boys' club" of theory so much as want deference from it for their views'. Environmental concerns, despite the work of Beck and, more recently, Giddens (2011) and John Urry (2011), have also not achieved the prominence which they deserve. A political identification with liberation movements and 'the wretched of the earth' (Fanon 1965) has fed into postcolonial theory, but this has not really taken root in social and political thought more broadly. It has found a warmer welcome in literary study, where, however, it has often come to mean developing a new angle on European or North American literature rather than exploring that emanating from former colonial territories. Finally, race-critical theory has to some extent displaced the previously dominant approach (at least in British sociology) which avoided the term race and preferred 'ethnicity', but without yet establishing itself as prominently as one might expect, given the importance of such issues in public debate (Lentin 2008).

Is what Quentin Skinner (1985) called the 'return of grand theory' likely to be permanent? First, we need to question how substantial it was. British sociology, for example, as a glance through the journals illustrates, has always resembled an iceberg, with the greater part consisting of substantive and often empirical studies (Heath and Edmondson 1981: 45). The same could I think be shown for political science. Certain processes which predominated in the past thirty-odd years, such as the rediscovery of the classics, may now seem to be essentially complete. Further work will of course continue to be done on them, and journals such as *History of the Human*

Does it make sense to seek grand, formal theories to explain our complex society? Or should sociologists focus on broad themes which can be applied to particular areas of specialism, such as the environment, feminism, race, etc.? (© Jim Pennucci/Flickr)

Sciences and the *Journal of Classical Sociology* provide a natural home for it, but one can expect the emphasis to become increasingly historical and only rarely presentist. There may also be an individual life-cycle effect, as sociologists develop their theory in engagement with classical and contemporary influences and then move on to apply it in increasingly substantive, empirical or policy-oriented studies. Giddens's trajectory seems paradigmatic of this progression, reflecting an impulse to use what he had so thoroughly elaborated. One can expect to find also the kind of process theorized by Durkheim in his book on the division of labour and applied to philosophy by Randall Collins (1998), in which thinkers move out of fields perceived to be overcrowded.

Therborn (2000) suggests a rather different periodization, in which the thinkers whom I have characterized here as theorists of action and structure occupy an intermediate period between a substantially evolutionist and structural-functionalist past and a possible future dominated by nodes of investigation, diverse but linked by what remains a recognizably socio-logical approach (as distinct from an economic or rational choice one). Therborn draws a rather finer-grained distinction than I have done between an emphasis on social antagonism and emancipation, around 1975, and a more open-ended approach to the contingencies of action and structure toward the end of the twentieth century. He also notes (2000: 47) the ongoing tension between scientist and humanistic approaches to sociology, while hoping, as I do, that the 'unhappy marriage' will not lead to divorce.

I referred earlier to Peter Wagner's (2001) pessimistic diagnosis of the 'moment of theory'. From where I sit, the dangers to social and political thought of the formalizations of empiricism on the one hand and rational choice theory on the other are also extremely real. They are reinforced by institutional pressures towards a retreat into disciplinary specialization, driven partly by the intrinsic demands of professionalization in a still expanding academic system (for every job lost in the UK's seriously threatened university sector, hundreds are created in China) and partly by monitoring systems such as the UK's Research Assessment Exercise / Research Excellence Framework (RAE/REF), which, despite paying lip service to interdisciplinarity, are often narrowly focused on the disciplinary 'core' and lead to a sharp, if intellectually unconvincing, differentiation between academic disciplines.

I have addressed these issues elsewhere (Outhwaite 2008), and Michael Burawoy and others have put the issue of 'public sociology' (which of course should include political science and the other social sciences) in the forefront of current debates. For the moment, it is enough to point to the affinity between what I have called celebrity theory and the expectation that theorists will contribute to public debates. 'Diagnosis of the times' is a timely concept, as our times become arguably more and more 'interesting'.

SEMINAR QUESTIONS

1 Should sociology pay so much attention to its 'founding fathers'?
2 What new developments can we expect in sociological theory?
3 Do we still need sociology? If so, why?

FURTHER READING

▶ There are a number of textbooks which provide a readable but thorough review of contemporary theory while including some coverage of 'classic' sociology as well. Among the most useful are Harrington, A. (ed.) (2005) *Modern Social Theory: An Introduction* (Oxford University Press); Baert, P., and F. Carreira da Silva (2010) *Social Theory in the Twentieth Century and Beyond* (2nd edn, Polity); Elliot, A. (2009) *Contemporary Social Theory: An Introduction* (Routledge); Joas, H., and W. Knöbl (2009) *Social Theory: Twenty Introductory Lectures* (Cambridge University Press); and Andersen, H. and L. B. Kaspersen (eds) (1996) *Classical and Modern Social Theory: An Introduction* (Wiley-Blackwell). For a particularly readable critical take on sociology, see Turner, C. (2010) *Investigating Sociological Theory* (Sage).

21

METHODOLOGY

the essence of sociology?

MARTYN HAMMERSLEY

CONTENTS

INTRODUCTION

UNLIKE THE OTHER CHAPTERS in this book, which are concerned with specific concepts and fields in sociology, the topic of this one – methodology – relates to an aspect of *all* sociological work. In general terms, methodology is 'the study of method', of how we should go about an activity; and, in the context of sociology, its main focus is on how sound knowledge about social phenomena can be produced. Most centrally, it is concerned with what sorts of evidence are required, what methods are available (for obtaining the data and for analysing it), and what threats to the validity of conclusions are associated with these methods. However, discussion of these matters spreads out into other important topics as well. Thus, the field of methodology also includes broad questions such those in box 21.1.

BOX 21.1 SOME BROAD METHODOLOGICAL QUESTIONS

- What is the proper goal of sociological research? What function(s) should it serve in society?
- How does it differ from journalism, or even from imaginative literature?
- What sorts of question can sociologists answer effectively? Big issues that face the world or only much more specific questions?
- What is the role of theory in sociological research? And what does the term 'theory' mean in this context?
- How should findings be presented in research reports, and how ought they to be disseminated? In what sorts of public or practical engagement should sociologists be involved?
- How should the products of sociological research be assessed? In terms of what criteria and through what processes?
- What are the characteristics of healthy research communities? How should they be regulated, and by whom?

All these questions are clearly very important. Yet there has often been ambivalence towards methodology among sociologists, and indeed among scholars more generally. On the one hand, there are those who place great emphasis on it, treating close attention to method as essential for the effective production of sociological knowledge. These writers are often very critical of the quality of much research – for example, on the grounds that speculations are put forward as if they were well-grounded conclusions.

For them, methodology is central to the education of social scientists, and in this spirit there have been calls for the general level of methodological knowledge and skills of qualified sociologists to be upgraded, particularly as regards quantitative method.

On the other hand, there are sociologists who have questioned the value of methodology, or the priority given to it. For example, in the first decade of the twentieth century Max Weber declared that there was a 'methodological pestilence' in German social science (cited in Oakes 1975: 13) – in other words, an excessive preoccupation with methodology. He also insisted that 'method is the most sterile thing that exists . . . Method *alone* has never yet created anything' (cited in Bruun and Whimster 2012: xiv). Much later, the American sociologist C. Wright Mills complained about 'the fetishism of method and technique' (Mills 1959a: 224), suggesting that methodological discussion simply 'disturb[s] people who are at work', as well as leading to 'methodological inhibition' (Mills 1959b: 27). And his views would probably be echoed by many sociologists today. Ironically, however, both Weber and Mills made significant contributions to methodology.

Rather than taking disagreement about the value of methodology at face value, we need to recognize that what is being lauded and criticized under this heading can vary considerably (Hammersley 2011: ch. 1). This reflects the fact that there are fundamental divergences in orientation, and in forms of practice, among sociologists; and *the meaning of the term 'methodology' has been caught up in these*. So, when commentators insist on the value of methodology, what they have in mind can vary a great deal – and this is probably even more true when it is being criticized. We therefore need to begin by clarifying the current divisions within sociology, and within social science more generally, that have produced different understandings of, and attitudes towards, methodology.

SOCIOLOGICAL DIVISIONS

Social theory and social research

One broad distinction that is often drawn is between *social theory*, on the one hand, and *empirical social research* or *empirical sociology*, on the other. 'Social theory' is a term that has come to be widely used to refer to general discussions of the character of modern Western societies and/or of the globalized social system of recent times (see Turner 2009). Under this heading a variety of kinds of work are included, from the ideas of 'classical' sociologists such as Marx, Durkheim and Weber about the development of European societies, especially during the eighteenth and nineteenth centuries, to more recent writers concerned with the distinctive nature of late twentieth- and early twenty-first-century society, such as Bauman, Beck, Castells and Giddens (see Elliott and Ray 2003; Scott 2012).

By contrast with social theory, empirical sociology is usually portrayed as focusing on much more specific and relatively concrete issues in contemporary or past society rather than on the whole nature of society (see Oberschall 1965, 1972). It is also seen as requiring the systematic collection and/or analysis of data, in a way that much social theory is not. Here, then, methodology, of a certain kind, is viewed as central.

So, social theorists are often criticized for paying insufficient attention to methodology: it is said that their work lacks conceptual clarity and also that they do not provide sufficient evidence for their claims, or that the evidence they cite is unreliable (see, for example, Abell and Reyniers 2000). On the other side, it is frequently complained that empirical social research neglects the theoretical assumptions on which it relies and that it is overly preoccupied with methodology – in the sense that it restricts itself solely to questions that are amenable to those methods assumed to be scientific. As a result, so the argument goes, it tends to focus on narrow and trivial matters.

The key issue here concerns what is and what is not an adequate contribution to sociological

knowledge; how this can be produced; and what evidence is required in order to provide sufficient support for the knowledge claims that sociologists make. And these are, of course, themselves central methodological topics.

The conflict between social theory and empirical sociology is not the only division that is of significance. There is another important one *within* empirical research: this concerns the *type* of evidence that is required in order to support sociological claims to knowledge, with *quantitative* and *qualitative* approaches frequently being lined up against one another. Thus, a major source of opposition to methodology, especially on the part of qualitative researchers in the past, was that it was viewed as an attempt to impose the requirements of quantitative method on all social research (see Becker 1970). This was connected to general issues about the nature of sociology as a discipline – about whether it is a science and, if it is, what this entails (see, for example, Keat and Urry 1982). More recently, some qualitative researchers have abandoned any commitment to science, emphasizing instead links with the humanities. This has deepened the division between quantitative and qualitative approaches (Hammersley 2012).

In order to consider some of the arguments to be found within the methodological literature today, it will be necessary to sketch the history of this divide between quantitative and qualitative approaches and the philosophical ideas associated with it.

Positivism

If we look at trends in Anglo-American sociological research up until the middle of the twentieth century, we see the gradual rise to dominance of the use of quantitative data and methods, a process that rendered preceding qualitative work marginal. However, during the second half of the twentieth century there was a revival of qualitative approaches, and also of social theory, with these coming to dominate in many parts of the discipline, especially in the UK. But later, from around the beginning of the twenty-first century, there was growing re-emphasis in influential quarters on the importance of quantitative method (MacInnes 2009; Payne and Williams 2011: introduction) and/or on the need to use this as a complement to qualitative work, in the form of what has come to be referred to as *mixed methods research* (Bryman 2008).

Behind the rise of quantitative method in the early twentieth century were influential ideas about what is required for scientific knowledge to be achieved, ideas that are often given the label 'positivism'. This term was invented by the French philosopher Auguste Comte, who also popularized the word 'sociology' (see Scharff 1995). For Comte, sociology was the queen of the sciences, providing the capstone to the body of knowledge that was essential for reforming modern societies. However, probably the most influential version of positivism for twentieth-century social science was a largely separate philosophical development in the 1920s and 1930s that came to be called *logical positivism* or *logical empiricism* (Kolakowski 1972; Hammersley 1995: ch. 1). Here, to a large extent, physics was taken as the methodological exemplar of sound scientific knowledge and of how it can be produced (Halfpenny 1982; Bryant 1985).

Today, the term 'positivism' is almost always used in a negative way to dismiss what the speaker or writer disagrees with. As a result, it has become virtually meaningless – few, if any, social scientists would now refer to themselves as positivists. But, in its original sense within sociology, it generally referred to a philosophical view that treats natural science as the only sound model for inquiry, requiring that sociologists adopt an approach that follows the same logic. Moreover, this logic was frequently conceived as involving statistical inference from observational or experimental data.

BOX 21.2 THE KEY ASSUMPTIONS OF POSITIVISM IN SOCIAL SCIENCE

● Social scientific knowledge consists of probabilistic laws, according to which variation in some outcome variable tends to be produced by variation in one or more other variables.
● In order to discover such laws, the relevant variables must be manipulated or controlled in ways that reveal the relationships among them.
● For this to be done, these variables must be measured through explicit and standardized procedures.
● The whole process should be open to replication, so as to allow checks on its reliability.

Despite the fact that few sociologists today would call themselves positivists, some of the ideas listed in box 21.2 remain influential in many quarters, at least as representing an ideal to be approximated. Partly under the influence of this kind of positivism, quantitative research came to be formulated as a distinctive, self-contained approach, having the characteristics outlined in box 21.3.

BOX 21.3 THE FEATURES OF QUANTITATIVE RESEARCH

● *A commitment to hypothesis-testing* An explicit research design is to be produced at the start of any inquiry which is often aimed at testing some set of closely defined hypotheses. This requires operationalizing key variables – in other words, specifying the data that would be relevant to them – selecting or developing the instruments needed to produce these data and indicating how the latter are to be analysed.
● *The use of numerical data* Data take the form of specific counts of instances belonging to some category, or of rankings or measurements of objects according to the degree to which they possess some feature. Measurement is often treated as superior to counting and ranking, and the ideal is to employ scales similar to those used in natural science, as for example in the measurement of temperature.
● *Procedural objectivity* Counting, ranking and measurement procedures must operate in ways that are 'objective', in the sense that they are standardized – as far as possible eliminating any effect of the social, cultural or personal characteristics of the researcher.
● *Generalization* Samples may be studied with a view to generalizing to some larger population, and statistical techniques can be used to maximize the validity of the generalization and to assess the chances of serious error in this process.
● *Identifying systematic patterns of association* Statistical techniques are also used to describe the patterns found in the data, and perhaps also to test the likelihood that these could have been produced by chance rather than by a systematic causal relationship.
● *Controlling variables* There is usually an attempt to control variables, either 'physically' via experimental method or 'statistically' through cross-case analysis of a large sample or population of cases. In other words, comparison of cases is used to try to separate out, analytically, what effects a causal variable has on a particular type of outcome from the systematic influence of other variables that might impact upon it.

Interpretivism

As noted earlier, a positivist conception of social scientific method dominated sociology to a considerable degree around the middle of the twentieth century, especially in the United States. And, under this influence, the methodological literature tended to focus on the requirements of hypothesis-testing, the details of experimental and survey method, measurement strategies, and techniques of statistical analysis. However, with the rise of qualitative approaches during the second half of the twentieth century, increasing numbers of sociologists came to reject many elements of this conception of empirical sociology. As a result, the content of the methodological literature changed significantly: in particular, it broadened to take in guidance about qualitative methods and also started to include philosophical ideas associated with these that are very different from positivism (Hammersley 2012: ch. 2).

One alternative methodological philosophy that received attention, often labelled *interpretivism*, insists that understanding people's actions, and the social institutions within which these occur, requires a quite different approach from explaining the behaviour of physical objects in the manner of natural science: in particular, it demands a capacity for empathy and/or an ability and a willingness to learn the culture of the people whose behaviour is to be understood. It is argued that very different cultures can be identified as having existed over the course of history even in the same country, as well as across contemporary societies, and that these have shaped people's thoughts, feelings and actions in significant ways. This idea was central to history and anthropology from early on, but it became increasingly influential in sociology too – with the existence of cultural differences *within* large, complex societies being recognized, these relating most obviously to different social classes, genders or ethnic groups but also to variation across more specific local settings.

Critical theory

Another influential philosophy was *critical theory*. By contrast with interpretivism, which treats people's perspectives and actions as expressions of cultures that must be regarded as justified in their own terms, at least for sociological purposes, critical research views culture as ideological, as the product of material factors. In the case of Marxism, for example, it is treated as the product of prevailing, and past, modes of economic production. Moreover, it is argued that ideologies function to preserve current, unjust forms of society. This is why a 'critical' approach is required that challenges the assumptions and legitimacy of dominant ideas – by explaining their origins and their functioning. It is insisted that this is essential if we are truly to understand contemporary society and, even more important, if we are to be able to act effectively so as to change it and bring about a new social order.

Constructionism

I will mention one final set of ideas associated with qualitative research, which came to be influential in the second half of the twentieth century – *constructionism* (Burr 2003). In one form or another, this has had an increasing presence in the methodological literature in recent years. It requires that we think of social phenomena as constituted through the social practices in which people engage – for example, the *discursive strategies* they employ both to provide accounts of themselves and of their world and to produce the various forms of action that make up that world. This perspective contrasts sharply with the idea that people's actions are *caused* by their social backgrounds and/or by the situations they face, a view that is most explicit in positivism but also in practice characterizes much work influenced by interpretivism and critical theory as well. Constructionism has, however, been interpreted in a variety of ways and has led to diverse kinds of work; most notably it has shaped influential forms of qualitative research that operate under the name of *discourse analysis* (Wetherell, Taylor and Yates 2001).

Appealing to philosophical ideas of these kinds, and initially relying especially on interpretivism, qualitative researchers challenged quantitative work, emphasizing some or all of the following:

- the importance of studying what happens in the 'real' world, rather than what happens under experimental conditions or in other circumstances heavily controlled by the researcher, such as in formal, highly structured interviews;
- the need to *observe* what happens rather than to rely solely upon people's accounts in interview or questionnaire responses;
- the requirement that people be allowed to speak in their own terms in interviews, rather than responding to relatively closed questions – this is seen as essential if we are to be able to understand their distinctive perspectives;
- the danger that quantification results in the meaning of central concepts being lost, through their being reduced to the results of measurement procedures;
- the concern that the kind of 'variable analysis' employed by quantitative researchers ignores the complex, contingent and context-sensitive character of social life, and the extent to which actions and outcomes are produced by people *interpreting* situations in diverse ways, and then acting on the basis of these interpretations rather than passively responding to external causes.

The characteristics of qualitative research

Influenced by these arguments, much qualitative research came to have many of the following characteristics.

- *A flexible, 'inductive' or data-driven orientation* Qualitative researchers place more emphasis on *generating* and *developing* descriptions and/or explanations than upon testing pre-defined hypotheses. This means that a flexible research design is adopted rather than one in which a detailed plan is laid out at the start of the research and then 'implemented'. This orientation is also reflected at the stage of analysing data, where the task is to *generate* categories rather than to place data into pre-determined ones. And the categories developed tend to be open-ended in character. In other words, they do not form a mutually exclusive and exhaustive set, at least not at the beginning of the analytic process.
- *Relatively unstructured kinds of data are used* For example, in the case of observation, qualitative researchers watch carefully what is happening and will often try to write concrete fieldnote descriptions in natural language that captures relevant aspects of what is observed and of how events unfold. Alternatively, or as a complement, audio- or video-recording is used, with transcripts being produced on the basis of these. Similarly, in the case of interviews, qualitative research typically involves a relatively unstructured approach, where the aim is to invite informants to talk at length about matters that are

broadly relevant to the research, with the interviewer following up to encourage more elaboration, detail, or exemplification where necessary.

Qualitative researchers may also use documentary data, such as official reports, newspapers and magazines, photographs, maps, diaries, and so on, without seeking to quantify their content in the manner of much 'content analysis' (on which, see Krippendorff 2004). In recent years, there has been a growth in the use of visual data, for example in the form of video, aiming to counter the more common reliance upon text (see Banks 2001; Pink 2007). And this subsequently developed into the idea of multi-modal research, combining text, images and the study of artefacts (Dicks, Soyinka and Coffey 2006).

In addition, there has been increasing use of online material (see Markham 1998; Hine 2000). Digital media have provided researchers with new sorts of data, both textual and visual, as well as new phenomena to investigate, notably online communities of various kinds. These may be studied through observation and participation in these communities and/or by using online methods to elicit information about the online (and perhaps also the offline) lives of people – for example, using email, social networking sites or conferencing to make contact with people and carry out interviews, administer questionnaires, etc.

Qualitative researchers also sometimes *elicit* documentary data – for example, asking people to write diaries, life histories or blogs, or to produce drawings, take photographs, make videos, etc.

- *Subjectivity is seen as unavoidable* There is acceptance, perhaps even celebration, of the fact that data, and inferences from them, are always shaped by the social and personal characteristics of the researcher. It is insisted that it is impossible to eliminate the effect of these, and indeed that they may facilitate insight rather than only leading to error (as typically assumed by positivism). It is sometimes argued that autobiographical reflexivity – the provision of detailed information about the researcher and the research process – can enable readers to discount any effects of the researcher's characteristics, or of how the research was carried out, that might obscure or threaten the validity of the analysis (Hammersley 2004). In short, there is opposition to the notion that research should be a standardized and impersonal process – and often to any requirement that the personal be suppressed in the name of science. However, this does not necessarily imply opposition to the kind of concern with objectivity that requires researchers to assess and try to counter potential threats to the validity of their conclusions.

- *'Natural' settings are studied* Experimental research creates settings, within a laboratory or outside, that are specifically designed to allow control over the causal variable(s) being investigated and to rule out confounding factors. And much non-experimental quantitative research relies upon questionnaires or formal interviews that are structured with the aim of standardizing the stimuli to which respondents are subjected, with the idea that this will render responses comparable. By contrast, most qualitative work investigates what goes on in the ordinary settings in which people live and work and/or uses interviews that are designed to be close in character to ordinary conversations in key respects, minimizing the impact of the researcher. Indeed, there have been debates about whether even unstructured interviews can be used legitimately as a source of data in qualitative inquiry, given that what informants say in these is necessarily influenced by the interviewer's questions and behaviour – so that the data are effectively 'co-constructed' (see Rapley 2001; Potter and Hepburn 2005; Hammersley 2008: ch. 5).

- *A small number of cases are studied* As we saw, much quantitative research, for example in the form of social surveys, investigates large samples in order to generalize to a population and/or to provide enough cases to employ comparative analysis so as to control variables and use statistical analysis. By contrast, qualitative inquiry often involves investigation of a small number of naturally occurring cases, perhaps just one. This stems from an insistence on the need for in-depth examination of each case in order to document its complexity. Closely involved here sometimes is the argument that each feature of a case can be understood only *within the context of that case*, because features will shape one another rather than having pre-determined and fixed characters. There is opposition, then, to the tendency in quantitative research to rely upon data that have been *extracted from their ordinary contexts* – for instance, questionnaire responses whose relationship to people's everyday lives is, at best, uncertain. Furthermore, in-depth investigation of cases allows the checking of interpretations through comparison of data of different kinds – for example, that from observation with that from interviews, or the comparing of accounts from different informants. This is rarely possible in social surveys.

- *Verbal rather than statistical analysis of data* The predominant mode of analysis is verbal description and interpretation, supported by illustrative or evocative examples. Such descriptions are often seen as simultaneously fulfilling the functions of explanation, as for example with the notion of 'thick' or 'theoretical' description (see Geertz 1973; Hammersley 1992: ch. 1, 2008: ch. 3). Nevertheless, qualitative researchers are still frequently concerned with discovering which factors tend to produce some outcome, or what the typical consequences of a particular type of event or action are – though they usually seek to do this through describing in detail the features of a small number of cases, and perhaps changes in these over time. The approach here is quite similar to that employed by historians, who produce narrative accounts of the events leading up to some outcome they are interested in explaining. Qualitative researchers may also compare one or more cases in order to try to assess which of several factors involved seem to play the crucial role in the sort of social processes being investigated, and they may draw more general conclusions from the cases studied about the types of phenomena of which these are instances.

Continuum versus dichotomy

What I have outlined in my discussion above are ideal types of quantitative and qualitative research – in practice there is a continuum here rather than a dichotomy. Much research blends features of the two types and draws on both sorts of data. Indeed, as noted earlier, in recent years this has been explicitly championed by the 'mixed methods' movement. This treats quantitative and qualitative research strategies as complementary. While such combining of methods is by no means new, it became much more influential in the first decade of the twenty-first century, generating textbooks and journals devoted to the topic, and it continues to be influential today. This movement is sometimes criticized on the grounds that it seeks to incorporate qualitative methods into a positivist framework (Giddings and Grant 2006: 59), but there have also been attempts to formulate alternative methodological philosophies that provide a better basis for combining or integrating quantitative and qualitative methods (see Tashakkori and Teddlie 2010: chs 4–7).

Given the history of sociological research methodology over the past 100 years, as sketched briefly above, it is not hard to see why social science now displays great methodological heterogeneity. Indeed, qualitative research itself diversified considerably in the second half of the last century, and has continued to do so, with 'new paradigms' emerging within particular fields, competing and debating with one another. The case of discourse analysis, mentioned earlier, provides an illustration. This category now includes many very different approaches (for example, speech act analysis, Bakhtinian discourse analysis, critical discourse analysis, discursive psychology, Foucault-inspired discourse analysis – the list goes on), with some – such as *conversation analysis* and *critical discourse analysis* – differing very sharply indeed from one another in their assumptions and practices (Wetherell, Taylor and Yates 2001).

In the next two sections I will focus in a little more detail both on the kinds of data and forms of analysis used by sociologists and on the methodological issues associated with them.

SEMINAR QUESTIONS

1 Is social theory methodologically defective? Is empirical research theoretically inadequate?

2 Do the very different assumptions underlying positivism and interpretivism make the two approaches irreconcilable?

3 If a constructionist approach is adopted, does this invalidate other approaches by showing that the data they use are constructed?

4 Would you agree that qualitative methods inevitably get you closer to the social world than quantitative approaches?

5 Is systematic quantitative analysis the only method that can produce reliable generalizations about the social world (if such things are possible)?

DATA

What are data?

The term 'data' is used routinely in the methodological literature and in discussions by sociologists of their work more generally. However, little attention is usually given to what this word means. Of course, researchers know what sorts of things count as sociological data, but they do not generally think much about *why* these count as data or *what it means* for them to be data. A starting point for understanding this is to recognize that the task of any study is to answer a set of questions *to which there is currently no agreed or well-established answer*. This means that any answers that are put forward *must be supported in some way*: both researchers themselves and readers of research reports need to have reason to believe that the answers presented there are true. This is one place where data come in – as resources that enable us to decide what should and should not be believed, *and why*.

In everyday life, all manner of reasons may be given as support for knowledge claims. If I want to know the time of the next train I will usually be prepared to accept what the person in the ticket office tells me, the information in the timetable, or what can be found online about the progress of this train. Similarly, I may well accept the word of a fellow passenger who says 'I've just asked at the ticket office' or 'I've just checked the timetable'. Here it is assumed that other people are sources of information on which we can rely, for the most part. In much the same way, some social science data take the form of testimony: for example, reliance is often placed upon information in documents or upon that supplied by informants in interviews or via questionnaires, *unless there is specific reason to believe that this information is likely to be false* (for instance, that it is very implausible, that the authors or informants have a strong reason to lie, that they did not have reliable access to the relevant information, and so on). At the same time, as we have seen, researchers also often draw on their own observations of what people do. The anthropologist Clifford Geertz (1988) has pointed out how research in anthropology generally involves strong appeals to the fact that the researcher has been present her- or himself in the community written about and therefore has first-hand experience of it. And observation is also central to much sociological research.

So, researchers seek testimony and/or observations relevant to their research questions with a view to developing answers and producing evidence that is convincing not only to them but also to the audiences they intend to address, whether colleagues in the relevant research community or some broader public. However, in the early stages of inquiry, researchers will often not be very sure about what would and would not be relevant data, and collecting data can even lead to changes in the initial research questions and therefore, in turn, in what should count as relevant data. So, data function to indicate possible answers to research questions and serve as a means of testing both whether or not potential answers are convincing and *which* potential answers are most convincing; at the same time, data may also sometimes prompt redirection of the research process.

BOX 21.4 DATA AND THE 2011 RIOTS IN THE UK

As an illustration of the nature and role of data, we can look at investigation of the riots that occurred in London, and some other UK cities, in August 2011. What sort of evidence would be necessary to tell us what form these riots took, why they occurred *when* and *where* they did, why particular sorts of people participated, and so on? To start with, we should note that riots are not usually scheduled events, so that they are not phenomena about which research can normally be planned in advance. Of course, it might still have been possible for a sociologist to have gone out on to the streets soon after the riots began, and one or two did. This allowed the production of direct observational data and the gathering of testimony from those involved at the time, but not usually on the scale possible in a pre-planned piece of research.

One aspect of the task that would have faced any sociologist out on the streets in the riots would have been to document exactly what the various people involved were doing – when and where – which particular buildings were being attacked and by whom, and what this involved (looting, arson, etc). Equally important would be what participants said about what they were doing and why. There would have been uncertainty about where best to observe what was happening at any particular time, however, given that riots are often dispersed and fast-moving events, and difficulty in determining who would be best to talk to. Also, which background features of people would turn out to be relevant may not have been obvious. The list could be endless: gender, social class, ethnicity, level of education, etc., plus more mundane matters such as home area, how they heard about the events, how they got to them, etc. The amount of potentially relevant data is huge, and of course in practical terms it could not all have been collected.

Needless to say, there were media reports produced about what was happening, some by journalists who were out on the streets who interviewed a few of the participants, bystanders and victims – though what appeared in media reports would have been only a selection from this material and would not necessarily be reliable. There were also photographs and video-recordings, plus statements made by politicians and others, as well as many blogs, tweets and chatroom discussions, including by people directly involved in the riots in one way or another or who witnessed them. These materials could be, and were, used by researchers later. There were a number of sociological projects in which people who had been involved in the riots were interviewed after the event, and data were gathered from the court cases that ensued (for examples of research on the riots, see Lewis and Newburn 2011; Reicher and Stott 2011).

An important point that this case illustrates is that there are always constraints on what sorts of data are accessible, and that what is available may not always meet the requirements of producing sound sociological knowledge. Nevertheless, there will often be useable material, even in cases where it is not possible to mount sociological investigations in advance. Moreover, the data will take diverse forms, and what would be relevant will always, to a degree, be uncertain.

Methodological approaches and 'good' data

It is in deciding what sorts of data might be relevant, and what would be necessary, that the conflicting methodological ideas outlined in the previous section play a significant role. Research questions may vary, of course, in terms of whether they seem to require quantitative or qualitative data. Thus, if we are interested in the frequency of some phenomenon – say bullying in schools or drug-taking in prisons – it seems that a count will be required, though even here it is possible that we could rely upon judgements in terms of 'more versus less' rather than precise figures. However, when we are seeking to *explain* bullying or drug-taking, or anything else, the issue of what sorts of data are required is more open to debate. Much will depend, in part, upon what we think a convincing explanation would look like and upon what sort of evidence is likely to be required to develop it and test its likely validity. Someone influenced by positivism would generally take a very different view about these matters than would an interpretivist, a 'critical' researcher or a constructionist – and the latter would also disagree among themselves.

So, judgements about what are data, and what would be *good* data, are likely to vary partly according to the nature of the questions being addressed and the circumstances in which the research must be carried out, but also according to assumptions about the nature of social phenomena, how they can be understood, and what the purpose of this understanding is. Moreover, these assumptions will shape what research questions are addressed, even where what is being investigated is more or less the same topic. So, whereas much work on the riots adopted a broadly interpretive and/or 'critical' approach, there were also researchers who took a more 'positivist' line – for example, seeking to build a mathematical model that would account for why the riots occurred in the places they did and why particular types of people were involved (Baudains, Braithwaite and Johnson 2013; see also Fry 2012 and figure 21.1).

BOX 21.5 METHODOLOGICAL APPROACHES AND THE 2011 RIOTS

In the case of studying the 2011 riots, if we believe that sociological research must be scientific in the manner of positivism, then we would be concerned primarily with counting and measuring key features of the riots: How many people were involved, and across what extent of each city? What were the measureable background characteristics of these people? How serious were the offences, and against whom were they committed? Equally important would be the task of assessing the factors that might have been involved in generating this behaviour, perhaps using statistical analysis to assess their relative causal power.

By contrast, if we believe that sociological research is about explicating the meanings that phenomena have for people, their intentions and motives, or that it requires documenting the ideological character and functioning of these meanings, or that it is about identifying the constitutive processes through which social phenomena are produced, this will lead us in very different directions. For example, in adopting an interpretivist approach, rather than relying upon counts and measurements, the meanings and processes involved will need to be explored: How did those involved in the riots, not just those who might be labelled rioters, define the situations they faced and interpret what was happening? What reasons do they give for their actions, and what discourses do they draw upon in doing this? Here, in-depth interviews with informants are likely to play a key role, along with other kinds of data thought to provide access to these meanings – perhaps including participant observation.

Of course, interpreting these data will often be far from uncontentious. Many questions might be asked: How are we to make sense of what rioters say about what they did and why, what they believe, and so on? Do they not have reasons to lie, for example to avoid prosecution or to minimize the level of any punishment? More fundamentally, any account they give will have been prepared for an audience and so would draw on particular cultural resources and assumptions rather than simply being an expression of their thought processes at the time. Beyond this, would knowledge of their thought processes at the time be all we needed in order to explain their behaviour, or even be necessary? Would participants be aware of the factors that had shaped their behaviour? Do we not sometimes do things for unconscious reasons? Is our behaviour not shaped by cultural and social factors of which we are largely unaware? How these various questions are answered will depend upon the philosophical assumptions on which researchers are operating.

Of course, what are included as data in a research report are somewhat different from the data that the researcher collects during the course of inquiry. For one thing, what appears in any research report is generally only a very small part of the data collected – or, at least, these data will appear only in highly summarized form. In the case of quantitative research, for example, people's answers to a questionnaire will have been turned into numbers, such as tables indicating the frequencies with which particular answers were given by specific categories of people. In the case of qualitative research the data quoted in the report will often amount to

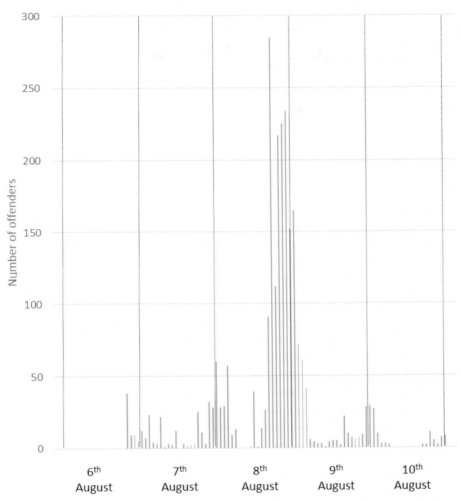

Figure 21.1 Temporal distribution of recorded crime, from police arrest reports, during the 2011 London riots

Note: These data map the temporal patterns of offences recorded by the police, though they do not necessarily provide an accurate picture of the scale of activity on different days during the riots because they also reflect variation in the presence of police and in their gathering of information about offences over those days, their interpretation of what does and does not count as an offence, and so on.

Source: Fry, Davis and Wilson (2012).

brief extracts from fieldnotes and/or transcripts relating to the researcher's observations, to what informants said in interviews or to what was found in documents. Moreover, it will usually have been selected to illustrate and support important analytic points. What this indicates is that a great deal of work goes into turning the data originally collected into evidence that can be used to assess descriptive and explanatory ideas, and only some of these data will then be presented in research reports, in support of the conclusions reached.

It is equally important to note that the target audience for a research report will shape the kind of data presented and *how* they are presented. If the primary audience is fellow researchers, the aim will be to try to offer sufficient evidence of kinds that they are likely to find convincing. And this may be very different from what would persuade policy-makers or members of some other relevant public. Here, rather different kinds of data and forms of presentation may be required. For example, policy-makers are renowned for requiring extremely brief summaries of research findings. An ex-UK government minister reportedly demanded of researchers: 'Don't bore us, get to the "useful answer"' (Reisz 2012; in fact, the article to which this media report refers – Clarke (2012) – does not include this statement, which tells us something important about the media's use of sources).

The process of data and evidence production

Not surprisingly, exactly what is involved in the process of data and evidence production also varies according to the kind of data involved, and this has changed to some degree over the past fifty or sixty years. In the first half of the twentieth century, sociologists relied almost entirely on published documents of various kinds, including official statistics, on people's responses to questions in surveys and, in the case of qualitative research, on fieldnotes written by researchers about what they had observed and about what people had told them. However, with the development of portable audio-recorders in the 1960s it became possible to produce recordings of what was said, rather than researchers having to write down as much as they could at the time and adding in later what they could remember. This development led to a preoccupation on the part of some qualitative researchers with analysing oral discourse in detail, though, as we noted earlier, such discourse analysis came to take diverse forms on the basis of conflicting methodological and theoretical assumptions. In much the same way, the development of portable, relatively cheap video-cameras in the 1980s, and later of digital devices, led to considerable discussion of visual data and of how they should be collected and analysed. Later still, when it became possible to obtain textual and visual data from online sources, attention began to be paid to the methodological and ethical issues these involved. For example, there has been particular concern about the relationship between online and offline identities – What can we infer from what people write or say via various forms of internet communication about their offline lives? (Markham 1998; Markham and Baym 2009).

Another significant change in the data available for sociological research stems from the fact that increasing amounts of material, of many kinds, are now produced not just by national governments but also by commercial and other organizations, much of it being generated directly by the activities of these organizations. This includes patterns of spending monitored by supermarkets, communications logged by telecommunications companies and online service providers, material from consumer surveys, and so on. Some commentators argue that such 'big data' represent a major threat to the existence of sociology, or at least to its claim to have access to distinctive and authoritative forms of data (Savage and Burrows 2007).

Finally, there have been increasing moves to archive the data produced by social scientists and to encourage their 'reuse'. Initially this concentrated upon quantitative data, but in the past twenty years in the UK it has been extended to qualitative data as well. What has been archived includes data from classic sociological studies of the past (Savage 2005) but also much data produced more recently (see, for example, the Timescapes project). Archiving has opened up considerable discussion about the possibilities and problems in reusing data, especially in the case of qualitative material (Heaton 2004; Hammersley 2010).

In addition, changes in the data available have had consequences for the kinds of analysis that are possible. We will look at the task of analysis in the next section.

SEMINAR QUESTIONS

1 Does the necessity of choosing what to use as data mean that research is inevitably shaped by the values of the researcher from the beginning?

2 Can we assess the findings of a sociological study on the basis of the data included in the research report, or is it necessary to evaluate the whole body of data collected?

3 How do different methodological philosophies shape what counts as data?

4 Are social scientists no longer the main producers of the data that they use? If so, what are the implications of this?

FORMS OF ANALYSIS

Specific explanations and general ideas

As suggested earlier, much sociological work focuses on explanatory questions concerned not just with what has occurred but also with *why* it has happened. Furthermore, frequently the declared aim has been to produce more general theoretical knowledge about what are the typical causes and/or consequences of some type of social phenomenon. And, of course, any explanation for some specific occurrence at a particular place and time necessarily draws on general ideas about how events of this kind are normally produced.

There is, then, a mutual relationship between specific explanations for particular events, actions, etc., and general ideas about what factors are key determinants of social phenomena. So, for example, if we look at the sociological accounts provided about the August 2011 riots we find that they frequently appeal to general ideas about why riots, or social unrest more generally, might occur, and about the nature of the wider society – including those found in the social theory literature. Furthermore, the nature of the riots sometimes seems to have been used as evidence for or against the validity of particular general theories.

Within-case and cross-case analysis

In developing and testing sociological explanations there are two basic analytic strategies that are used in both quantitative and qualitative research: these can be referred to as *within-case* and *cross-case* analysis. And, while there is often a tendency to emphasize one or the other in particular studies, they are complementary.

Within-case analysis   Here, sociologists study what has happened, or what is happening, *within cases where the phenomena of interest have occurred or are occurring*. Associations among features within a single case, or sequential patterns over time within the case, may stimulate explanatory ideas and can also be used to check whether a particular candidate explanation is sound, or at least whether it is more convincing than its competitors. Sociologists may

BOX 21.6 EXPLAINING THE 2011 RIOTS

In explaining riots, sociologists have appealed to a range of factors, including:

- material deprivation, both absolute (where people are unable to meet basic needs) and relative (where they lack the resources for participation as full members of society);
- inequitable discrimination in relation to employment, housing, etc.;
- interventions by the police and other authorities – many riots follow such interventions;
- the alienation of some groups from society, so that they have no sense of belonging to a community and/or no feeling that they have some ownership of their surroundings;
- political and cultural marginalization of groups, in that they have no means of peacefully expressing grievances and gaining support for these to be remedied.

If we look at two brief explanatory accounts put forward by sociologists for the 2011 riots, we can see how these factors may be selected from, interpreted and combined in various ways. Here, first of all, is an extract from an account offered by Zygmunt Bauman (2011), a well-known social theorist:

> This was not a rebellion . . . of famished and impoverished people or an oppressed ethnic or religious minority – but a mutiny of defective and disqualified consumers, people offended and humiliated by the display of riches to which they had been denied access. We have all been coerced and seduced to view shopping as the recipe for the good life and the principal solution of all life problems – but then a large part of the population has been prevented from using that recipe.

Here, Bauman specifically rejects any appeal to absolute material deprivation or to political marginalization and relies entirely on a particular interpretation of relative deprivation in order to account for the riots. Another sociologist offered a very different account, specifically challenging that of Bauman:

> Without wanting to say that Zygmunt Bauman's analysis is simplistic . . ., one of the dangers of calling the riots consumer riots is that we bring an individualised notion into this discussion. . . . Many social issues that existed in the 1980s and 1990s have not disappeared – unemployment, inequality, policing. [Let's] not fall into the trap of saying that the riots of today are consumer riots and the riots of 1980s and 2001 were different in that kind of way. (Solomos 2011)

Where Bauman explains the riots as arising from inequalities in access to consumer goods that people have been persuaded they need, Solomos suggests that they resulted from genuine deprivations and inequities in access to goods and resources, as well as from the actions of the police.

There are, then, *many* explanatory factors to which appeal might be made, and these can be formulated and combined in different ways. And, if we look across the whole spectrum of commentary on the 2011 riots, we find a very diverse set of explanations being offered, many of them highlighting factors not even mentioned in the list I presented earlier. Reicher and Stott (2011: preface) indicate the problem that this generates:

> The riots were due to spending cuts, they were due to educational policies, they were due to rap music, black culture, single-parent families, lack of respect, liberal education . . . and the list goes on. . . . How can one explain an event before we really know what that event was? One might as well suggest that the riots happened because of the place of Mars in relation to Venus or because a five-footed calf was born in June. Without evidence, any opinion is equally good or bad.

therefore try to document the *processes* by which the phenomena were produced, the motivations of the people involved that brought them about, and so on. Thus, in the case of the UK riots, sociologists have looked at links between the police shooting that started them off and what followed, in terms of who was involved and when, what accounts they provide of their actions, and so on (see Reicher and Stott 2011: ch. 4). Here the focus is on distinctive patterns of motivation and activity, including perhaps how individuals were mobilized by others and how they responded to what others were doing. There may also be an attempt to trace background patterns within a case over a longer period of time. For example, how did the riots relate to relevant longer-term changes in the areas concerned, previous disturbances there, and so on?

An important issue that arises for within-case analysis is what constitutes a case. As the discussion in box 21.7 indicates, this is by no means always a straightforward matter.

BOX 21.7 DEFINING CONCEPTS – WHAT COUNTS AS A RIOT?

Apparently, the legal definition in the UK is 'the use of unlawful violence on the part of at least twelve persons, in a way which would make "a person of reasonable firmness" afraid for his or her safety', while a sociological definition is 'large-scale public disorder involving violence to property and violent confrontation with the police' (for both definitions, see Jary and Jary 1999: 559). It is also noted that many sociologists believe that the term 'riot' is so loaded, morally and politically, that it is useless for analytic purposes, not least because it takes over 'the viewpoint of the authorities'. As a result, there has instead been a tendency to use 'more neutral' phrases, such as 'urban unrest', 'popular protest' and 'public disorder' (ibid.: 560).

Some care is required, then, both in defining what does and does not count as a riot and in thinking about what this and other terms are being used to depict. For example, should it have been called a riot when members of the Bullingdon Club, a student fraternity at the University of Oxford, went on the rampage in 1986, its members at the time including the current UK prime minister (David Cameron) and the present mayor of London (Boris Johnson) (see Young 2009) – both prominent critics of the rioters in 2011? There may be a tendency for the term 'riot' to be applied selectively in a way that has more to do with who was involved than the actual features of the event, much as crime tends to be defined in ways that ignore a great deal of white-collar crime (Sutherland 1949).

Equally important is the question of how to draw boundaries around particular instances of a *case*. For example, we might treat the UK riots of 2011 as one case to compare with other riots at other times in the UK and elsewhere. However, for other purposes we could treat what went on in each of the different cities affected, or in different parts of each city, in August 2011 as *separate* cases. Thus, the riots began in Tottenham, North London, in response to an incident in which police shot a local man whom they believed to be in possession of a gun and to be involved in organized gang crime. It seems likely that the riot in this place was significantly different, at least at first, from what happened subsequently in other parts of London (see Reicher and Stott 2011: ch. 4). Furthermore, areas of London vary in ways that could be significant for any explanation of the nature of the riots that took place there – for instance, in terms of aggregate profiles as regards the social class and ethnicity of inhabitants, levels of material deprivation, and so on. London also differs from other English cities in these and other respects. Finally, we could treat each individual person involved in the riots as representing a case, so that we are interested in why each of them came to participate and in what role. Given that there are various options here, it is necessary to be clear about how we are defining 'riot' and about what we are counting as a case, and why. And this applies to any other social phenomenon we might be interested in studying.

Investigating what goes on *within* cases can be an extremely fruitful way of developing and testing explanatory and theoretical ideas. However, it will often need to be complemented by the second strategy: *cross-case* analysis.

Cross-case analysis   As the name implies, here the sociologist looks for relevant patterns *across* cases that might indicate what caused the outcome that is of interest. If a particular factor seems to have been associated frequently with the outcome, we might treat this as suggestive evidence that this factor is at least one of its causes. However, it would be foolish immediately to jump to this conclusion or to assume that this factor is its main cause: we should engage in more systematic testing of the hypothesis by examining under what conditions the association appears. In particular, it is necessary to find some means of checking that it is not a chance result or the product of a different causal process from the one assumed.

BOX 21.8 CROSS-CASE ANALYSIS AND THE 2011 RIOTS

In investigating the 2011 riots, we might compare them with other examples of riots, looking for what could be significant commonalities, in terms of the activities involved, where and when they occurred, what types of people participated, what preceded them, and so on (see Waddington, Jobard and King 2009; Reicher and Stott 2011). Or, if we define what occurred in different parts of London and other UK cities as separate riots, we can compare *these* cases. Either way, the aim is to discover whether we can find generic social processes that could be involved in producing riots, perhaps even with the idea that this would enable us to predict them in the future. In cross-case analysis, researchers look for *differences* as well as similarities, so it might be concluded that there are distinct types of riot, or of rioter, that are generated by different sets of factors, so that a first requirement in seeking to explain any particular riot might be to determine what type it is.

Of course, if we were to focus on individual people as cases, we would almost certainly find great differences among those participating even in any single event, in terms of the motivation that seems to have been involved, the external factors stimulating participation, and also in the roles people played. Quantitative researchers using cross-case analysis will often be concerned with whether there was a *predominant* motivational pattern within any particular riot and, if so, how this compares with what was dominant in other riots. However, some qualitative researchers, for example those using life history methods to investigate differences in people's experiences and perspectives, may be more interested in the diversity among individuals involved.

While both quantitative and qualitative researchers can use cross-case analysis, there are differences in how they employ it. Quantitative researchers usually look for patterns of association between relevant factors and the outcome to be explained *across some large population or a sample from it*. They will normally report the frequencies with which each factor co-occurs with the outcome, and they may also examine what happens in cases that are similar as regards other factors thought to have an effect on the outcome, to check that the pattern is a product of the suspected cause. Thus, it might have been possible to carry out sample surveys of people in the main areas affected by the riots, looking for similarities and differences between those who were involved and those who were not, and examining whether these held across variation in, say, gender, ethnicity and social class.

It may also be necessary to try to take account of differences in the causal processes operating at different levels within the cases studied. For instance, if we were interested in the role of police interventions in generating riots, we might want to examine relations between those organizational processes operating at the top of police forces which generate policy guidelines, disciplinary regimes, and so on, and the 'canteen culture' that shapes the actions of police officers 'on the ground'. This would be a staple of much qualitative analysis, but there is also a form of statistical analysis, called *multi-level modelling*, that is concerned precisely with separating out causal processes operating at different levels (see Goldstein 1987).

As we saw, qualitative researchers generally study a smaller number of cases than the samples investigated by survey researchers and will often examine a wider range of features within each of them. Nevertheless, as in quantitative work, there may be a search for patterns of association, though qualitative researchers do not always report the actual frequencies with which the suspected causal factor and the outcome are associated (in other words, the proportion of cases in which they both appear). They too may systematically compare cases so as to control for other factors, in order to get a sense of how strong the relationship is between the

Sociology has as important part to play – as, critically, do sociological methods – in explaining and investigating important public issues, though this is by no means straightforward, as this chapter has demonstrated in relation to the 2011 London riots. (© Beacon/Flickr)

candidate cause and the occurrence of the outcome. In addition, they will frequently explore how *combinations* of factors operate together to bring about the outcome, something which is more difficult to do with the kind of correlational analysis used in much quantitative research (see Byrne and Ragin 2009; Rihoux and Ragin 2009; Cooper et al. 2012). One approach used here is *Qualitative Comparative Analysis* (see Ragin 2008). While this was initially developed in relation to the analysis of qualitative data drawn from a relatively small number of cases, it can also be applied to large, quantitative data sets (see Cooper et al. 2012: ch. 6).

Generally speaking, what sociologists set out to explain relates to important public issues. The 2011 UK riots are a case in point. They were significant events from a variety of perspectives: for example, in terms of the disorder, damage and deaths caused but also perhaps because they signalled underlying social structural problems within UK society that need to be addressed. And they were an issue about which sociologists felt they had authoritative expertise (see Brewer and Wollman 2011). In the final section of this chapter I want to examine one of the broader methodological questions mentioned earlier, concerning the distinctive public function of sociological research.

SEMINAR QUESTIONS

1 Would the definition of a riot used by a researcher influence the credibility of the explanation he or she put forward?

2 Thinking about Bauman's explanation of the 2011 riots as a product of consumer society, suggest how it could be tested using either a within-case or a cross-case analysis.

3 How do you think that the various factors frequently identified as generating riots could be related to one another in determining when and where riots occur?

WHAT IS THE PUBLIC FUNCTION OF SOCIOLOGICAL RESEARCH?

Public sociology

One way of approaching this issue is via debates that have taken place over the past few years around the notion of 'public sociology'. This was advocated by Michael Burawoy in his presidential address to the American Sociological Association in 2005 (Burawoy 2005). While he recognized the value of other types of sociology (he identified 'professional', 'critical' and 'applied' versions as well), he gave primary emphasis to work which engages with current public debates in society and is designed to enter into dialogue with, and serve, lay groups. This idea of public sociology has been widely taken up but also subjected to criticism (see, for example, J. Holmwood 2007; Tittle 2004; Wacquant 2009: afterword).

We can get a sense of what might be involved in public sociology by returning to the issue of predicting and explaining riots. The 2011 riots occurred at a time when there was increasing pressure on the social science research community in the UK, in the face of threatened cuts in funding, to demonstrate the value of its work. A campaign in support of social science had already been started (see the Campaign for Social Science website). Given this, it is perhaps not surprising that, as we saw earlier, there was quite a lot of commentary on the riots by sociologists. While only a small amount of empirical research was carried out on them (notably, Reicher and Stott 2011; Lewis and Newburn 2011; Morrell et al. 2011; Briggs 2012), sociological work had been done on various other broadly similar events that had happened previously, both in England and in other countries (see, for instance, Waddington, Jobard and King 2009). Sociologists had also carried out research on topics related to explanations for the riots, both in the areas concerned and elsewhere – for example, on gangs, on police stop-and-search policies and their effects, etc. In fact, though, the comments on the riots by eminent sociologists did not for the most part draw directly, or at least explicitly, on this evidence. Instead, these commentators tended simply to *apply* general social theories. For example, Bauman's (2011) argument that the rioters were frustrated consumers, reacting to the fact that they did not have the money to buy the goods that advertisers had persuaded them they must have, is a variant of a well-known general sociological theory focused on the concept of anomie (Merton [1942] 1957: chs 6 and 7).

In thinking about the contribution that sociologists make, or could make, to public discussions, we need to consider what would be distinctive about this. The most obvious answer is that sociologists have access to knowledge of social phenomena that is more likely to be reliable than that from other sources. However, as we have seen, producing sociological knowledge is a complex and difficult task, and there are conflicting views among sociologists both about how it should be done and about what would count as success in achieving it. Furthermore, we still need to consider what would be involved in translating sociological knowledge into a form that would be appropriate for the public sphere (see Hammersley 2014: ch. 6).

Research reports clearly need to be tailored to the background understanding and interests of the audience. They need to be translated into terms that are intelligible and of interest to that audience. There are some important issues associated with this process of 'translation': How much simplification is necessary, and at what point does simplification distort the knowledge being presented? How much explanation of sociological concepts to lay audiences is required? How much evidence in support of the explanations presented needs to be provided, and of what kinds? Should it be assumed that audiences ought simply to accept the explanations sociologists offer or do they need to be supplied with the information necessary to assess them critically? To what extent must sociologists engage with public audiences so as to attract attention to their contributions? If they do, again we can ask: How far will this distort the knowledge being presented?

These are challenging questions, but they do not exhaust what needs to be taken into account in thinking about the idea of a public sociology. I have assumed up to this point that the task of the sociologist engaging with publics is simply to disseminate or apply sociological knowledge. But many sociologists today see their role as going beyond this, and this was certainly how Burawoy conceived of public sociology. Like him, many regard themselves as public intellectuals whose role is to counter the ideological explanations that dominate the public sphere, or they believe that they have a responsibility to give 'voice' to those whose views are not normally heard or to promote a particular political cause, for example feminism or anti-racism. This stance is characteristic of sociologists adopting an explicitly 'critical' approach of one kind or another, but of many others too.

Involvement or detachment?

One of the effects of this broader commitment is that much sociological research today does not simply present factual knowledge in the form of descriptions and explanations but also offers evaluations of policies, practices, institutions, etc., and perhaps policy recommendations (positive or negative) as well. For example, Reicher and Stott's study of the 2011 riots was produced very rapidly with the specific intent of making a contribution to the public debate, and what they had in mind was not simply supplying information, though that was certainly part of it. At one point they write:

> As long as [readers] feel, after reading what we have to say, that perhaps the riots were not all about criminality, that they were not entirely mindless and meaningless eruptions, and that policing our streets with baton rounds and water cannons will not provide an answer, then we will have achieved what we set out to do. (Reicher and Stott 2011: preface)

Here the authors see themselves as challenging prevailing evaluations and policies. But a critic might ask: On what basis can sociologists determine what should and should not be regarded as 'criminal' or 'mindless' actions, or determine what are and are not legitimate police tactics? It might be argued that these are matters that involve value judgements, about which there is room for legitimate disagreement – disagreement that sociological research cannot resolve on its own.

In this respect, the debate over public sociology touches on a deep-seated methodological disagreement that has long been present in the discipline and that extends across social science. On one side it has been argued that sociological work must engage with the wider society, whether so as to serve policy goals (for example, to demonstrate 'what works') or to challenge current institutional arrangements (for instance, on the grounds that these reproduce social inequities). Indeed, it is sometimes argued that sociologists have a responsibility to participate directly in the application of their findings in policy-making or practice (Gewirtz and Cribb 2006), or that sociological work should take the form of action research, with sociologists becoming directly involved in political and other forms of activity (on which, see Reason and Bradbury 2001; Levin and Greenwood 2011).

These proposals contrast with the view that sociology is a form of academic inquiry that ought to be largely detached from practical or political concerns, being aimed solely at producing knowledge, albeit knowledge relevant to human beings generally, or even specifically to contemporary policy issues. From this second point of view, research should not be *aimed at* achieving practical or political goals but only at producing worthwhile knowledge. In this context, it might also be argued that the most important immediate audience for any research report is fellow researchers, rather than any wider public, since it is their role to assess the conclusions that can be reliably drawn from it – in the context of related studies. From this perspective, what should be communicated to lay audiences are conclusions validated by the research community – in the form of reviews of all the relevant literature rather than findings from individual studies. This is because the latter are always open to serious question given the threats to validity that are endemic in social inquiry. Furthermore, the value of research findings is seen as lying in their potential role in stimulating and feeding reflection and practical deliberation among policymakers, occupational practitioners of various kinds, citizens, political activists, and others: it should not be judged in terms of 'impact' in some specific direction, whether in terms of 'improving' current policy, undermining the status quo or realizing 'social justice'. (I have put inverted commas around some words in this sentence to signal that their meaning is open to dispute.)

An influential version of this second position was put forward by Max Weber at the beginning of the twentieth century. In effect, he argued that academic social scientists enter into an implicit or explicit contract with society and state, according to which they are given the autonomy to carry out investigations and publish their findings even where these may be judged objectionable – this is what is often referred to as academic freedom (see Russell 1993; Menand 1998). In return, however, they must restrict their focus to matters of fact, rather than setting out to evaluate or criticize social institutions and practices, or seeking to achieve through their work any other goal than the production of knowledge.

This Weberian position is founded on the idea that social research can produce authoritative findings only about factual matters, that it cannot decide value issues. This is because value judgements can appeal to conflicting value principles and always have to be interpreted in relation to particular cases. And it is argued that social science has no distinctive expertise in doing this. Nor is sociological research the only legitimate source of factual evidence: this can come from other disciplines and from practical experience as well. From this point of view, then, public sociology amounts to a form of scientism (in other words, it exceeds the legitimate claim sociology can make to intellectual authority) and might even be seen as a threat to democracy (see Tittle 2004; on Weber's arguments, see Weber 1974; Bruun and Whimster 2012; for my own attempt to develop a position along these lines, see Hammersley 1995, 2002).

Fewer sociologists today than in the past would explicitly adopt this second, Weberian position. Many advocate or practise the first: not only those committed to some version of 'critical' sociology, but also many sociologists engaged in carrying out what is often referred to as applied social research or 'policy science', concerned with supplying information to governments, commercial organizations and interest groups of various kinds.

SEMINAR QUESTIONS

1 To what extent and in what ways can sociology make a distinctive contribution to public debate?

2 Do attempts by sociologists to engage in public debate tend to distort sociological knowledge?

3 Should the point of sociology be to change the social world, not merely to interpret it?

CONCLUSION

In this chapter I have provided a brief outline of some key issues in sociological methodology as a field. I noted how, originally, it had been associated with positivism and quantitative method and was therefore looked upon with suspicion by social theorists and qualitative researchers, but that it broadened considerably over the course of the second half of the twentieth century and into the twenty-first. However, this has made the field much more heterogeneous and has given rise to many disputes. As we have seen, these relate not just to what sort of data to use and how to collect and analyse it, but also to what the purpose of research is and how it should be related to other activities – such as government policy-making or political struggle.

I noted that data have to be worked up into evidence and that there have been significant changes over time in the sorts of data available to sociologists, partly as a result of technological developments. I also examined the two main analytic strategies that sociologists use in seeking to document causal relations: within-case and cross-case analysis. My discussion here indicates the substantial difficulties we face in producing sound knowledge about the social world.

For this reason, and others, in my view methodology is the core of sociology: what is distinctive about the discipline, along with the other social sciences, is that it can usually generate more reliable factual knowledge about the social world than that coming from other sources – or at least it can do this if sociologists go about their task in a methodologically sound way. What this requires is a matter not of rigidly following procedures but rather of approaching the answering of research questions in a thoughtful manner, reflecting on the meaning of the concepts being used, the validity threats associated with reliance upon particular forms of data or methods of analysis, and so on. The production of knowledge about the social world in this way can make an extremely valuable contribution to public debate about policy issues, even if it is not always given due recognition. Moreover, the sociological task is one that is properly restricted to factual description and explanatory knowledge: sociology cannot tell us what is wrong and what should be changed, any more than it can indicate what is right and what ought to be preserved. But it *can* provide essential resources to enable sound judgements to be made about these important matters.

SEMINAR QUESTIONS

1 Do you agree that sociology 'can usually generate more reliable factual knowledge about the social world than that coming from other sources'?

2 Is it more important to be thoughtful and self-critical in conducting research than it is to follow 'rigid' procedures?

3 Discuss the view that it is difficult but not impossible to produce sound knowledge about the social world.

4 Is it true that 'sociology cannot tell us what is wrong and what should be done about it'?

FURTHER READING

▶ Bryman, A. (2012) *Social Research Methods* (4th edn, Oxford University Press). This is a comprehensive and critical guide to commonly used methods, which would be a very useful resource throughout a social science degree and at postgraduate level as well.

▶ Byrne, D. (2002) *Interpreting Quantitative Data* (Sage). This introduces quantitative methods of analysis in a critical way and shows how they can be applied in investigating particular issues.

▶ Hammersley, M. (2012) *What is Qualitative Research?* (Bloomsbury). This provides an overview of the nature of qualitative inquiry – the methodological philosophies that underpin it and some of the debates to be found within it.

Acknowledgements: My thanks go to Roger Gomm and Martin Holborn for comments on and suggestions for this chapter.

REFERENCES

Aarsand, P. A. (2007) 'Computer and video games in family life: the digital divide as a resource in intergenerational interactions', *Childhood*, 14(2).

Abell, P., and D. Reyniers (2000) 'On the failure of social theory', *British Journal of Sociology*, 51(4).

Abel-Smith, B., and P. Townsend (1965) *The Poor and the Poorest* (G. Bell & Sons).

Ackroyd, S., and P. Thompson (1999) *Organizational Misbehaviour* (Sage).

Adam, B. (1990) *Time and Social Theory* (Polity).

Adams, M. (2003) 'The reflexive self and culture: a critique', *British Journal of Sociology*, 54.

Adams, W. M. (2001) *Green Development* (2nd edn, Routledge).

Adkins, L. (2002) *Revisions: Gender and Sexuality in Later Modernity* (Open University Press).

Adkins, L., and B. Skeggs (2004) *Feminism after Bourdieu* (Blackwell).

Adorno, T. (2001) *The Culture Industry: Selected Essays in Mass Culture* (Routledge).

Adorno, T., and M. Horkheimer ([1947] 1997) *Dialectic of Enlightenment* (Verso).

Agamben, G. (2000) *Means without End: Notes on Politics* (University of Minnesota Press).

Agamben, G. (2005) *State of Exception* (University of Chicago Press).

Agassi, J. (1985) *Technology: Philosophical and Social Aspects* (D. Reidel).

agediscrimination.info (2011) 'Hidden age discrimination in the recession, 100,000 over 50 year olds are long term unemployed', www.agediscrimination.info/News/Pages/ItemPage.aspx?Item=517.

Agnew, R. (2006) *Pressured into Crime: An Overview of General Strain Theory* (Oxford University Press).

Agosto, D. E., J. Abbas and R. Naughton (2012) 'Relationships and social rules: teens' social network and other ICT selection practices', *Journal of the American Society for Information Science and Technology*, 63(6).

Aisenbrey, S., and A. E. Fasang (2010) 'New life for old ideas: the "second wave" of sequence analysis bringing the "course" back into the life course', *Sociological Methods and Research*, 38.

Aitchison, C. (2000) 'Young disabled people, leisure and everyday life: reviewing conventional definitions for leisure studies', *Annals of Leisure Research*, 3(1).

Aitchison, C. (2003) *Gender and Leisure: Social and Cultural Perspectives* (Routledge).

Aitchison, C. (2009) 'Exclusive discourses: leisure studies and disability', *Leisure Studies*, 28 (4).

Al Aswany, A. (2011) *On the State of Egypt: What Caused the Revolution* (Canongate).

Albrow, M. (1990) *Max Weber's Construction of Social Theory* (Macmillan).

Albrow, M. (1993) 'Globalization', in W. Outhwaite and T. Bottomore (eds), *The Blackwell Dictionary of Twentieth-Century Social Thought* (Blackwell).

Albrow, M. (1996) *The Global Age: State and Society beyond Modernity* (Polity).

Albrow, M. (1997) *Do Organizations Have Feelings?* (Routledge).

Albrow, M. (2007) 'Unfinished work: the career of a European sociologist', in M. Deflem (ed.), *Sociologists in a Global Age* (Ashgate).

Albrow, M., and E. King (eds) (1990) *Globalization: Knowledge and Society* (Sage).

Alcock, P. (2006) *Understanding Poverty* (3rd edn, Macmillan).

Alexander, J. (1993) 'The return of civil society', *Contemporary Sociology*, 22.

Alexander, J. (2004) 'Toward a theory of cultural trauma', in J. C. Alexander, R. Eyerman, B. Giesen, N. J. Smelser and P. Sztompka (eds), *Cultural Trauma and Collective Identity* (University of California Press).

Alexander, S. (2012) 'Planned economic contraction: the emerging case for degrowth', *Environmental Politics*, 21(3).

Allen, K. (2012) 'Ageism is back as unemployed over-50s struggle to get back into work', *The Observer*, 15 April.

Allen, K., and Y. Taylor (2012) 'Failed femininities and troubled mothers: gender and the riots', *Sociology and the Cuts*, online [registration necessary].

Allen, S. (1971) *New Minorities, Old Conflicts: Asian and West Indian Migrants in Britain* (Random House).

Almack, K. (2008) 'Display work: lesbian parent couples and their families of origin negotiating new kin relationships', *Sociology*, 42(6).

Althusser, L. ([1965] 1969) *For Marx* (Penguin).

Althusser, L. (1972) 'Ideology and the ideological state apparatuses', in B. Cosin (ed.), *Education, Structure and Society* (Penguin).

Althusser, L., with É. Balibar, R. Establet, P. Macherey and J. Rancière ([1965] 1975) *Reading Capital* (New Left Books).

Altnurme, L. (2011) 'Changes in mythic patterns in Estonian religious life stories', *Social Compass*, 58(1).

Alwin, D. F. and R. J. McCammon (2003) 'Generations, cohorts and social change', in J. T. Mortimer and M. J. Shanahan (eds), *Handbook of the Life Course* (Kluwer Academic/ Plenum).

Amoore, L. (ed.) (2005) *The Global Resistance Reader* (Routledge).

Anderson, B. (1983) *Imagined Communities: Reflections on the Origin and Spread of Nationalism* (Verso).

Anderson, B. (2000) *Doing the Dirty Work? The Global Politics of Domestic Labour* (Zed Books).

Anderson, P. (1976) *Considerations on Western Marxism* (Verso).

Andrew, M., J. Eggerling-Boeck, G. D. Sandefur and B. Smith (2007) 'The "inner" side of the transition to adulthood: how young adults see the process of becoming an adult', *Advances in Life Course Research*, 11.

Aneki (2014) 'Richest countries in the world', www.aneki.com/richest.html.

Angell, N. (1914) *The Foundations of International Policy* (Heinemann).

Anthias, F. (1990) 'Race and class revisited – a reconceptualising of race and racisms', *Sociological Review*, 38(1).

Anthony, P. (1978) *Ideology of Work* (Routledge).

Anxo, D., and J. Y. Boulin (2006) 'The organisation of time over the life course: European trends', *European Societies*, 8(2).

Appadurai, A. (1990) 'Disjuncture and difference in the global cultural economy', in M. Featherstone (ed.), *Global Culture: Nationalism, Globalization and Modernity* (Sage).

Appadurai, A. (1998) 'Dead certainty: ethnic violence in the era of globalization', *Public Culture*, 10(2).

Appelbaum, R., and W. I. Robinson (eds) (2005) *Critical Globalization Studies* (Routledge).

Archer, M.S. (1982) 'Morphogenesis versus structuration: on combining structure and action', *British Journal of Sociology*, 33(4).

Archer, M. S. (2003) 'The private life of the social agent: what difference does it make?', in J. Cruickshank (ed.), *Critical Realism: The Difference it Makes* (Routledge).

Arendt, H. (1951) *The Origins of Totalitarianism* (Schocken Books).

Arendt, H. (1965) *On Revolution* (Penguin).

Arendt, H. (1970) *On Violence* (Allen Lane).

Ariès, P. (1960) *Centuries of Childhood* (Penguin).

Arnett, J. (1999) 'Adolescent storm and stress', *American Psychologist*, 54(5).

Arnett, J. (2000) 'Emerging adulthood: a theory of development from the late teens through the twenties', *American Psychologist*, 50(5).

Arnett, J. (2004) *Emerging Adulthood: The Winding Road from Late Teens through the Twenties* (Oxford University Press).

Arnot, M. (2007) 'Education feminism, gender equality and school reform in late twentieth-century England', in R. Teese, S. Lamb and M. Duru-Bellat (eds), *International Studies in Educational Inequality, Theory and Policy*, Vol. 2: *Inequality in Education Systems* (Springer).

Astin, J. A. (1998) 'Why patients use alternative medicine: results of a national survey', *Journal of the American Medical Association*, 279.

Atkinson, A. B. (1985) *How Should We Measure Poverty? Some Conceptual Issues* (ESRC).

Atkinson, W. (2012) *Class Inequality in Austerity Britain: Power, Difference and Suffering* (Palgrave Macmillan).

Attwood, F. (2005) 'What do people do with porn? Qualitative research into the consumption, use and experience of pornography and other sexually explicit material', *Sexuality & Culture*, 9(2).

Audit Commission (2008) *Don't Stop Me Now: Preparing for an Ageing Population*, www.cpa. org.uk/cpa/Dont_Stop_Me_Now.pdf.

Aupers, S. (2005) '"We are all gods": new age in the Netherlands 1960–2000', in E. Senger (ed.), *The Dutch and their Gods: Secularization and Transformation of Religion in the Netherlands since 1950* (Verloren).

Back, L., and V. Ware (2001) *Out of Whiteness: Color, Politics and Culture* (University of Chicago Press).

Bäckman, O., and A. Nilsson (2011) 'Pathways to social exclusion – a life-course study', *European Sociological Review*, 27(1).

Baert, P. (2006) 'Social theory and the social sciences', in G. Delanty (ed.), *Contemporary European Social Theory* (Routledge).

Baert, P., and F. Carreira da Silva (2010) *Social Theory in the Twentieth Century and Beyond* (2nd edn, Polity).

Bagg, S., and D. Voas (2009) 'The triumph of indifference: irreligion in British society', in P. Zuckerman (ed.), *Atheism and Secularity*, Vol. 2: *Global Expressions* (Praeger).

Bailey, C. (1984) *Beyond the Present and the Particular: A Theory of Liberal Education* (Routledge & Kegan Paul).

Baker, S. (2006) *Sustainable Development* (Routledge).

Baker, S., M. Kousis, D. Richardson and S. Young (eds) (1997) *The Politics of Sustainable Development: Theory, Policy and Practice within the European Union* (Routledge).

Balanya, B., A. Doherty, O. Hoedeman, A. Ma'anit and E. Wesselius (2000) *Europe Inc.: Regional and Global Restructuring and the Rise of Corporate Power* (Pluto Press).

Baldamus, W. (1961) *Efficiency and Effort: An Analysis of Industrial Administration* (Tavistock).

Bales, K. (1999) *Disposable People: New Slavery in the Global Economy* (University of California Press).

Bales, K. (2005) *Understanding Global Slavery: A Reader* (University of California Press).

Bales, K., Z. Trodd and A. Kent (2009) *Modern Slavery: The Secret World of 27 Million People* (Oneworld).

Ball, S. J. (2003) *Class Strategies and the Education Market: The Middle-Classes and Social Advantage* (RoutledgeFalmer).

Ball, S. J. (2011) *Politics and Policy Making in Education* (Routledge).

Ballard, K. and M. A. Elston (2005) 'Medicalization: a multi-dimensional concept', *Social Theory and Health*, 3.

Ballard, R. (2006) 'Popular Islam in Northern Pakistan and its reconstruction in urban Britain', in J. Malik and J. Hinnells (eds), *Sufism in the West* (Routledge).

Bandura, A. (2004) 'The role of selective moral disengagement in terrorism and counterterrorism', in F. M. Moghaddam and A. I. Marsella (eds), *Understanding Terrorism: Psychological Roots, Consequences and Interventions* (American Psychological Association Press).

Banerjee, S.B. (2003) 'Who sustains whose development? Sustainable development and the reinvention of nature', *Organization Studies*, 24(1).

Banks, M. (2001) *Visual Methods in Social Research* (Sage).

Banting, K., and W. Kymlicka (eds) (2006) *Multiculturalism and the Welfare State* (Oxford University Press).

Barak, B. R., and L. G. Schiffman (1981) 'Cognitive age: a nonchronological age variable', *Advances in Consumer Research*, 8.

Barber, B., and W. Hirsch (eds) (1962) *The Sociology of Science* (Free Press).

Barclay, G., and C. Tavares (1999) *Digest 4: Information on the Criminal Justice System in England and Wales* (Home Office).

Barker, C. (1997) *Global Television* (Blackwell).

Barker, E. (2004) 'The church without and the god within?', in D. Marinovic, S. Zrinscak and I. Borowkci (eds), *Religion and Patterns of Social Transformation* (Institute for Social Research).

Barnett, J., and N. Adger (2005) 'Security and climate change: towards an improved understanding', Human Security and Climate Change: An International Workshop, Oslo, 21–3 June; available online.

Basso, P. (2003) *Modern Times, Ancient Hours: Working Lives in the Twenty-First Century* (Verso).

Battersby, C. (1998) *The Phenomenal Woman* (Polity).

Baudains, P., A. Braithwaite and S. Johnson (2013) 'Spatial patterns in the 2011 London riots', *Policing*, 7(1).

Baudrillard, J. (1983) *Simulations* (Semiotext(e)).

Bauman, Z. (1976) *Towards a Critical Sociology: An Essay on Common-Sense and Emancipation* (Routledge).

Bauman, Z. (1978) *Hermeneutics and Social Science: Approaches to Understanding* (Hutchinson).

Bauman, Z. (1989) *Modernity and the Holocaust* (Polity).

Bauman, Z. (1997) *Postmodernity and its Discontents* (Polity).

Bauman, Z. (1998a) *Globalization: The Human Consequences* (Polity).

Bauman, Z. (1998b) *Work, Consumption and the New Poor* (Open University Press).

Bauman, Z. (2000) *Liquid Modernity* (Polity).

Bauman, Z. (2001) *The Individualized Society* (Polity).

Bauman, Z. (2002) 'Reconnaissance wars of the planetary frontierland', *Theory, Culture and Society*, 19(4).

Bauman, Z. (2005) 'Chasing elusive society', *International Journal of Politics, Culture and Society*, 18(3).

Bauman, Z. (2006) *Liquid Fear* (Polity).

Bauman, Z. (2011) 'The London riots – on consumerism coming home to roost', *Social Europe Journal*, 9 August; available online.

Bauman, Z. (2012) 'Politics, the good society and "Westphalian sovereignty"', *Social Europe Journal*, 25 May; available online.

BBC (2006a) 'Fragile states risk instability', *BBC News*, 14 September, http://news.bbc.co.uk/1/hi/business/5344866.stm.

BBC (2006b) 'Conflict "wipes out" global aid', *BBC News*, 25 October, http://news.bbc.co.uk/1/hi/uk_politics/6082558.stm.

BBC (2010) 'Q & A: Professor Phil Jones', *BBC News*, 13 February, http://news.bbc.co.uk/1/hi/8511670.stm.

BBC (2013) 'Gender pay gap "at risk of worsening", say campaigners', *BBC News*, 7 November, http://www.bbc.co.uk/news/business-20223264.

Beauvoir, S. de ([1949] 1989) *The Second Sex* (Random House).

Beck, J. (1999) 'Makeover or takeover: the strange death of educational autonomy in neo-liberal England', *British Journal of Sociology of Education*, 20(2).

Beck, U. (1992) *Risk Society: Towards a New Modernity* (Sage).

Beck, U. (1994) 'The reinvention of politics: towards a theory of reflexive modernization', in U. Beck, A. Giddens and S. Lash, *Reflexive Modernization: Politics, Tradition and Aesthetics in the Modern Social Order* (Polity).

Beck, U. (1999) *World Risk Society* (Polity).

Beck, U. (2000a) *The Brave New World of Work* (Polity).

Beck, U. ([1997] 2000b) *What is Globalization?* (Polity).

Beck, U. ([1995] 2002) *Ecological Politics in an Age of Risk* (Polity).

Beck, U. (2006) *Cosmopolitan Vision* (Polity).

Beck, U. (2008) *World at Risk* (Polity).

Beck, U. (2013) 'Why "class" is too soft a category to capture the explosiveness of social inequality at the beginning of the twenty-first century', *British Journal of Sociology*, 64(1).

Beck, U., and E. Beck-Gernsheim (1995) *The Normal Chaos of Love* (Polity).

Beck, U., and E. Beck-Gernsheim (2001) *Individualization: Institutionalized Individualism and its Social and Political Consequences* (Sage).

Beck, U., A. Giddens and S. Lash (1994) *Reflexive Modernization: Politics, Tradition and Aesthetics in the Modern Social Order* (Polity).

Becker, H. S. (1963) *Outsiders* (Free Press).

Becker, H. S. (1967) 'Whose side are we on?', *Social Problems*, 14.

Becker, H. S. (1970) 'On methodology', in H. S. Becker, *Sociological Work* (Aldine).

Beder, S. (1997) *Global Spin: The Corporate Assault on Environmentalism* (Green Books).

Beder, S. (2006a) *Suiting Themselves: How Corporations Drive the Global Agenda* (Earthscan).

Beder, S (2006b) *Free-Market Missionaries: The Corporate Manipulation of Community Values* (Earthscan).

Behe, M. J. (2003) 'Design in the details: the origin of biomolecular machines', in J. A. Campbell and S. C. Meyer (eds), *Darwinism, Design, and Public Education* (Michigan State University Press).

Bell, D. (1973) *The Coming of the Post-Industrial Society: A Venture in Social Forecasting* (Penguin).

Bell, D. (1977) 'The return of the sacred', *British Journal of Sociology*, 28(4).

Bell, M. M. (2011) *An Invitation to Environmental Sociology* (Pine Forge Press).

Bellah, R. N. (1967) 'Civil religion in America', *Journal of the American Academy of Arts and Sciences*, 96(1).

Beller, E., and M. Hout (2006) 'Intergenerational social mobility: the United States in comparative perspective', *The Future of Children*, 16(4).

Bello, W., and S. Rosenfeld (1990) *Dragons in Distress: Asia's Miracle Economies in Crisis* (Penguin).

Belyaev, D. (2011) '"Heterodox religiousness" in today's Russia: results from an empirical study', *Social Compass*, 58(3).

Ben-Eli, M. (2007) 'Defining sustainability', *Resurgence*, 244.

Bengtson, V. L., T. J. Biblarz and R. E. L. Roberts (2002) *How Families Still Matter: A Longitudinal Study of Youth in Two Generations* (Cambridge University Press).

Bennett, R. (2008) 'Middle-aged people are being overwhelmed by their family responsibilities?', *The Times*, 10 December.

Bennett, T., M. Savage, E. Silva, A. Warde, M. Gayo-Cal and D. Wright (2009) *Culture, Class, Distinction* (Routledge).

Benton, T. (1994) *Natural Relations: Ecology, Animal Rights and Social Justice* (Verso).

Benton, T. (ed.) (1996a) *The Greening of Marxism* (Guilford Press).

Benton, T. (1996b) 'Marxism and natural limits: an ecological critique and reconstruction', in T. Benton (ed.), *The Greening of Marxism* (Guilford Press).

Beresford, P., D. Green, R. Lister and K. Woodward (1999) *Poverty First Hand: Poor People Speak for Themselves* (Child Poverty Action Group).

Berger, P. L. (1999) 'The desecularization of the world: a global overview', in P. Berger (ed.), *The Desecularization of the World: Resurgent Religion and World Politics* (Eerdmans).

Berger, P. L., and T. Luckman (1967) *The Social Construction of Reality* (Allen Lane).

Berman, G. (2012) *Prison Population Statistics* (House of Commons Library).

Bernstein, B. (1975) *Class, Codes and Control*, Vol. 3: *Towards a Theory of Educational Transmissions* (Routledge).

Bernstein, B. (2000) *Pedagogy, Symbolic Control and Identity: Theory, Research, Critique* (2nd edn, Rowman & Littlefield).

Bernstein, B. (2009) *Class, Codes and Control*, Vol. 4: *The Structuring of Pedagogic Discourse* (Routledge).

Berry, J. W. (1997) 'Immigration, acculturation, and adaptation', *Applied Psychological International Review*, 46.

Bershady, H. (1973) *Ideology and Social Knowledge* (Blackwell).

Bershady, H. (1991) 'Practice against theory in American sociology', in R. Robertson and B. S. Turner (eds), *Talcott Parsons: Theorist of Modernity* (Sage).

Bhabha, H. (1990) 'The third space', in J. Rutherford (ed.), *Identity, Culture, Difference* (Lawrence & Wishart).

Bhagwati, J. (2004) *In Defence of Globalisation* (Oxford University Press).

Bhambra, G. K. (2007) *Rethinking Modernity* (Palgrave).

Bhambra, G. K., and I. Demir (eds) (2009) *1968 in Retrospect: History, Theory, Alterity* (Palgrave).

Bhaskar, R. ([1975] 1997) *A Realist Theory of Science* (Verso).

Bhattacharya, S. (2003) 'European heatwave caused 35,000 deaths', *New Scientist*, 10 October.

BICC (Bonn International Center for Conversion) (2013) 'BICC's Global Militarization Index (GMI) 2013', http://gmi.bicc.de/index.php?page=ranking-table.

Biggart, A. (2003) *Families and Transitions in Europe: Survey Report of Young Adults in Education and Training Institutions*, Executive Summary, http://cordis.europa.eu/documents/documentlibrary/100124161EN6.pdf.

Biggs, S. (1999) *The Mature Imagination* (Open University Press).

Biggs, S., C. Phillipson, R. Leach and A. Money (2007) 'The mature imagination and consumption strategies: age and generation in the development of a United Kingdom boomer identity', *International Journal of Ageing and Later Life*, 2(2).

Billari, F. C., and A. C. Liefbroer (2010) 'Towards a new pattern of transition to adulthood', *Advances in Life Course Research*, 15(2–3).

Billig, M. (1995) *Banal Nationalism* (Sage).

Birch, S., and D. Allen (2011) 'There will be a-burning and a-looting tonight: the social and political correlates of law breaking', working paper, University of Essex.

Birke, L. (1986) *Women, Feminism and Biology: The Feminist Challenge* (Methuen).

Björnberg, U. (2002) 'Ideology and choice between work and care: Swedish family policy for working parents', *Critical Social Policy*, 22.

Black, R., and H. White (eds) (2006) *Targeting Development: Critical Perspectives on the Millennium Development Goals* (Routledge).

Blacker, T. (2006) 'A generation still trying to grow up', *The Independent*, 7 February.

Blackless, M., A. Charuvastra, A. Derryck, A. Fausto-Sterling, K. Lauzanne and E. Lee (2000) 'How sexually dimorphic are we? Review and synthesis', *American Journal of Human Biology*, 12.

Blanchflower, D. G., and A. J. Oswald (2009) 'The U-shape without controls: a response to Glenn', *Social Science and Medicine*, 69.

Blanden, J., P. Gregg and S. Machin (2005) *Intergenerational Social Mobility in Europe and North America: A Report Supported by the Sutton Trust* (Centre for Economic Performance).

Blane, D., G. Netuvelli and M. Bartley (2007) 'Does quality of life at older ages vary with socio-economic position?', *Sociology*, 41(4).

Blatterer, H. (2007) 'Adulthood: the contemporary redefinition of a social category', *Sociological Research Online*, 12(4).

Blaxter, M. (1990) *Health and Lifestyles* (Tavistock).

Bloch, A., and J. Solomos (2010) *Race and Ethnicity in the 21st Century* (Palgrave).

Bloor, D. ([1976] 1991) *Knowledge and Social Imagery* (Routledge & Kegan Paul).

Bluestone, B., and B. Harrison (1982) *The Deindustrialization of America: Plant Closing, Community Abandonment, and the Dismantling of Basic Industry* (Basic Books).

Blumenthal, P. (2011) 'Obama's revolving door: transparency', 19 June, http://sunlightfoundation.com/blog/2011/01/19/obamas-revolving-door-transparency/.

Blumstein, A., and J. Wallman (eds) (2000) *The Crime Drop in America* (Cambridge University Press).

Bøås, M., and K. M. Jennings (2007) '"Failed states" and "state failure": threats or opportunities?', *Globalizations*, 4(4).

Boden, S. (2006) 'Another day, another demand: how parents and children negotiate consumption matters', *Sociological Research Online*, 11(2).

Boehmer, I. (2005) 'Postcolonial terrorist: the example of Nelson Mandela', *Parallax*, 11(4).

Boffey, D. (2011) 'Lord Lawson's "misleading" climate claims challenged by scientific adviser', *The Guardian*, 27 March.

Bolzan, N. (2005) '"To know them is to love them" but instead fear and loathing: community perceptions of young people', in J. Mason and T. Fattore (eds), *Children Taken Seriously: Theory, Policy and Practice* (Jessica Kingsley).

Bonger, W. ([1916] 1969) *Criminality and Economic Conditions* (Indiana University Press).

Bonnaert, T., and N. Vettenburg (2011) 'Young people's internet use: divided or diversified?', *Childhood*, 18(1).

Booth, C. (1889) *Life and Labour of the People in London* (Williams & Northgate).

Bottero, W. (2011) 'Personal life in the past', in V. May (ed.), *Sociology of Personal Life* (Palgrave Macmillan).

Bottoms, A. (2004) 'Empirical evidence relevant to sentencing frameworks', in A. Bottoms, S. Rex and G. Robinson (eds), *Alternatives to Prison* (Willan).

Boudon, R. (1974) *Education, Opportunity and Social Inequality* (John Wiley).

Boudon, R. (1977) 'Education and social mobility: a structural model', in J. Karabel and A. H. Halsey (eds), *Power and Ideology in Education* (Oxford University Press).

Bourdieu, P. (1977) *Outline of a Theory of Practice* (Cambridge University Press).

Bourdieu, P. ([1979] 1984) *Distinction: A Social Critique of the Judgement of Taste* (Routledge).

Bourdieu, P. ([1982] 1991) *Language and Symbolic Power* (Polity).

Bourdieu, P. (1999) *The Weight of the World* (Polity).

Bourdieu, P. (2001) *Masculine Domination* (Polity).

Bourdieu, P. (2006) 'The forms of capital', in H. Lauder, P. Brown, J. Dillabough and A. H. Halsey (eds), *Education, Globalization, and Social Change* (Oxford University Press).

Bourdieu, P., and J.-C. Passeron (1977) *Reproduction in Education, Society and Culture* (Sage).

Bowles, S., and H. Gintis (1976) *Schooling in Capitalist America* (Routledge & Kegan Paul).

Bowling, A., S. See-Tai, S. Ebrahim, G. Zahava and S. Priya (2005) 'Attributes of age-identity', *Ageing and Society*, 25(4).

Box, S. (1987) *Recession, Crime and Punishment* (Macmillan).

Boykoff, M. T. (2011) *Who Speaks for the Climate? Making Sense of Media Reporting on Climate Change* (Cambridge University Press).

Boykoff, M. T., and J. M. Boykoff (2004) 'Balance as bias: global warming and the US prestige press', *Global Environmental Change*, 14.

Boykoff, M. T., and J. M. Boykoff (2007) 'Climate change and journalistic norms: a case-study of US mass-media coverage', *Geoforum*, 38.

Braddock, J. (2010) 'From lad to 4D man: the ever-changing face of modern masculinity', *The Guardian*, 11 November.

Bradford, K. R. (2011) 'Chauffeur dads: fathers will spend a year of their lives driving children', www.parentdish.co.uk/2011/06/16/chauffeur-dads-fathers-will-spend-a-year-of-their-life-driving/.

Bradley, H. (1989) *Men's Work, Women's Work* (Polity).

Bradshaw, J. (ed.) (1993) *Budget Standards for the United Kingdom* (Avebury).

Bradshaw, J., S. Middleton. A. Davis, N. Oldfield, N. Smith, L. Cusworth and J. Williams (2008) *A Minimum Income Standard for Britain: What People Think* (Joseph Rowntree Foundation).

Brady, D. (2009) *Rich Democracies, Poor People: How Politics Explain Poverty* (Oxford University Press).

Braidotti, R. (1994) *Nomadic Subjects: Embodiment and Sexual Difference in Contemporary Feminist Theory* (Columbia University Press).

Bramham, P., and J. Spink (2009) 'Leeds – becoming a postmodern city', in P. Bramham and S. Wagg (eds), *Sport, Leisure and Culture in the Postmodern City* (Ashgate).

Branigan, T. (2012) 'China's foreign policy is playing catch-up with its new status', *The Guardian*, 22 March.

Brannen, J. (2003) 'Towards a typology of intergenerational relations: continuities and change in families', *Sociological Research Online*, 8(2).

Brannen, J., and A. Nilsen (2005) 'Individualization, choice and structure: a discussion of current trends in sociological analysis', *Sociological Review*, 53(3).

Brannen, J., and A. Nilsen (2006) 'From fatherhood to fathering: transmission and change among British fathers in four-generation families', *Sociology*, 40(2).

Braungart, R., and M. M. Braungart (1986) 'Life course and generational politics', *Annual Review of Sociology*, 1.

Braverman, H. (1974) *Labour and Monopoly Capitalism: The Degradation of Work in the Twentieth Century* (Monthly Review Press).

Brecher, J., J. B. Childs and J. Cutler (eds) (1993) *Global Visions: Beyond the New World Order* (South End Press).

Brewer, J., and H. Wollman (2011) 'Letter from the British Sociological Association', *The Guardian*, 11 August 2011.

Briant, E., G. Philo and N. Watson (2011) *Bad News for Disabled People: How the Newspapers are Reporting Disability* (University of Glasgow).

Brierley, P. (2006) *Pulling Out of the Nosedive* (Christian Research).

Brierley, P. (2010) 'Thoughts on trends in church attendance', 30 September, www.brin.ac.uk/news/2010/thoughts-on-trends-in-church-attendance/.

Briggs, D. (ed.) (2012) *The English Riots of 2011* (Waterside Press).

Brody, D. (1993) *In Labor's Cause: Main Themes on the History of the American Worker* (Oxford University Press).

Broks, P. (2006) *Understanding Popular Science* (Open University Press).

Brooks, A. (1997) *Postfeminisms: Feminisms, Cultural Theory and Cultural Forms* (Routledge).

Brown, C., and H. Lauder (2009) *Social Class and Education: Changes and Challenges*

(University of Bath), http://beyondcurrenthorizons.org.uk/wp-content/uploads/final_lauder_20090202.pdf.

Brown, C. G. (2001) *The Death of Christian Britain: Understanding Secularization 1800–2000* (Routledge).

Brown, O., M. Halle, S. Peña Moreno and S. Winkler (eds) (2007) *Trade, Aid and Security* (Earthscan).

Brown, R. K. (1992) *Understanding Industrial Organizations: Theoretical Perspectives in Industrial Sociology* (Routledge).

Brubaker, R. (2010) 'Charles Tilly as a theorist of nationalism', *American Sociologist*, 41.

Bruce, S. (1996) 'Religion in Britain at the close of the 20th century: a challenge to the silver lining perspective', *Journal of Contemporary Religion*, 11(3).

Bruce, S. (2002) *God is Dead* (Blackwell).

Bruce, S. (2011) *Secularization: In Defence of an Unfashionable Theory* (Oxford University Press).

Brückner, H., and K. U. Mayer (2005) 'De-standardization of the life course: what it might mean? And if it means anything, whether it actually took place?', *Advances in Life Course Research*, 9.

Bruns, A. (2009) *Blogs, Wikipedia, Second life, and Beyond: From Production to Produsage* (Peter Lang).

Bruun, H., and S. Whimster (eds) (2012) *Max Weber: Collected Methodological Writings* (Routledge).

Bruzzi, S. (2005) *Bringing up Daddy: Fatherhood and Masculinity in Post-War Hollywood* (British Film Institute).

Bryant, C. (1985) *Positivism in Social Theory and Research* (Macmillan).

Bryman, A. (2008) 'The end of the paradigm wars?', in P. Alasuutari, J. Brannen and L. Bickman (eds), *Handbook of Social Research* (Sage).

Bryman, A., B. Bytheway, P. Allatt and T. Keil (eds) (1987) *Rethinking the Life Cycle* (Macmillan).

Brynin, M., and A. Guveli (2012) 'Understanding the ethnic pay gap in Britain', *Work, Employment and Society*, 26(4).

Buchman, M. C., and I. Kriesi (2011) 'Transition to adulthood in Europe', *Annual Review of Sociology*, 37.

Buckley, J., H. Haidar and C. Provost (2013) 'How migrants' money makes the world go round', *The Guardian*, 30 January.

Buckner, L., and K. Yeandle (2007) 'Valuing carers: calculating the value of unpaid care', http://circle.leedsac.uk/files/2012/09/valuing-carers.pdf.

Budd, J. (2011) *The Thought of Work* (Cornell University Press).

Budgeon, S. (2006) 'Friendship and formations of sociality in late modernity: the challenge of post-traditional intimacy', *Sociological Research Online*, 11(3).

Bullivant, S. (2012) 'Not so indifferent after all? Self-conscious atheism and the secularisation thesis', *Approaching Religion*, 2(1).

Burawoy, M. (1979) *Manufacturing Consent: Changes in the Labor Process Under Monopoly Capitalism* (University of Chicago Press).

Burawoy, M. (2005) 'For public sociology', *American Sociological Review*, 70.

Burawoy, M. (2012) 'The roots of domination: beyond Bourdieu and Gramsci', *Sociology*, 46(2).

Bures, R. M. (2009) 'Living arrangements over the life course: families in the 21st century', *Journal of Family Issues*, 30.

Burgoyne, C., V. Clarke and M. Burns (2011) 'Money management and views of civil partnership in same-sex couples: results from a UK survey of non-heterosexuals', *Sociological Review*, 59(4).

Burgoyne, C., V. Clarke, J. Reibstein and A. Edmunds (2006) '"All my worldly goods I share with you"? Managing money at the transition to heterosexual marriage', *Sociological Review*, 54(4).

Burn-Murdoch, J. (2012) 'Over-45s more likely to drink every day, survey reveals', *The Guardian*, 8 March.

Burr, V. (2003) *Social Constructionism* (2nd edn, Routledge).

Burrows, J., R. Tarling, A. Mackie, R. Lewis and G. Taylor (2000) *Review of Police Forces' Crime Recording Practices* (Home Office).

Bury, M. (1982) 'Chronic illness as biographical disruption', *Sociology of Health and Illness*, 4.

Bury, M. (2005) *Health and Illness* (Polity).

Butler, J. (1990) *Gender Trouble: Feminism and the Subversion of Identity* (Routledge).

Butler, J. (1993) *Bodies That Matter: On the Discursive Limits of Sex* (Routledge).

Butler, P. (2013) 'Every welfare cut listed: how much a typical family will lose per week', *The Guardian*, 1 April.

Butler, P., A. Topping and S. Boseley (2012) 'Truth about young people and drugs revealed in *Guardian* survey', *The Guardian*, 15 March.

Buzan, B., O. Waever and J. de Wilde (1998) *Security: A New Framework for Analysis* (Lynne Rienner).

Bynner, J. (2005) 'Rethinking the youth phase of the life-course: the case for emerging adulthood?', *Journal of Youth Studies*, 8(4).

Byrne, D., and C. Ragin (eds) (2009) *The Sage Handbook of Case-Based Methods* (Sage).

Bytheway, B. (1995) *Ageism* (Open University Press).

Bywater, M. (2006) 'Baby boomers and the illusion of perpetual youth', *New Statesman*, 30 October.

Cabinet Office (2003) *Ethnic Minorities and the Labour Market: Final Report*, www.guidance-research.org/EG/equal-opps/race/EORE2/EORELPCO.

Cabinet Office (2011) *Opening Doors, Breaking Barriers: A Strategy for Social Mobility*, http://dera.ioe.ac.uk/2369/1/opening-doors-breaking-barriers.pdf.

Cabral, L. (2013) 'BRICS and Africa', *The Guardian*, 26 March.

CACE (Central Advisory Council for Education) (1967) *Children and their Primary Schools* (HMSO) [Plowden Report].

Callon, M. (1986). 'Some elements of a sociology of translation: domestication of the scallops and the fishermen of St Brieuc Bay', in J. Law (ed.), *Power, Action and Belief: A New Sociology of Knowledge* (Routledge & Kegan Paul).

Cameron, D. (2011a) 'PM's speech at Munich security conference', https://www.gov.uk/government/speeches/pms-speech-at-munich-security-conference.

Cameron, D. (2011b) 'Cameron raises stakes in debate on immigration', *The Times*, 14 April.

Campbell, C. (2007) *The Easternisation of the West* (Paradigm).

Carroll, W. (2010) *Corporate Power in a Globalizing World* (Oxford University Press).

Casey, C. (1995) *Work, Self and Society after Industrialism* (Routledge).

Cassen, R., and G. Kingdon (2007) *Tackling Low Educational Achievement* (Joseph Rowntree Foundation).

Castells, M. (1996) *The Rise of the Network Society*, vol.1 (Blackwell).

Castells, M. (1997) *The Power of Identity* (Blackwell).

Castells, M. (2012) *Networks of Outrage and Hope: Social Movements in the Internet Age* (Polity).

Castles, S. (1995) 'How nation-states respond to immigration and ethnic diversity', *New Community*, 21(3).

Castles, S., and M. Miller (2007) *The Age of Migration* (4th edn, Palgrave).

Catton, W. R., Jr. (1998) 'Darwin, Durkheim and mutualism', in L. Freese (ed.), *Advances in Human Ecology* (JAI Press).

Catton, W. R., Jr. (2002) 'Has the Durkheim legacy misled sociology?', in R. E. Dunlap, F. H. Buttel, P. Dickens and A. Gijswijt (eds), *Sociological Theory and the Environment: Classical Foundations, Contemporary Insights* (Rowman & Littlefield).

Catton, W. R., Jr., and R. E. Dunlap (1978) 'Environmental sociology: a new paradigm', *American Sociologist*, 13.

Central Bureau of Statistics, Holland (2009) 'Revised Version: Less Often to Church or Mosque', online.

Centre for Social Justice (2012) *Rethinking Child Poverty* (Centre for Social Justice).

Cesari, J., and S. McLoughlin (eds) (2005) *European Muslims and the Secular State* (Ashgate).

Chamberlain, M. (2006) *Family Love in the Diaspora: Migration and the Anglo-Caribbean Experience* (Transaction).

Chambers, R. (1997) *Whose Reality Counts? Putting the First Last* (ITDG).

Chan, T. W., and J. H. Goldthorpe (2010) 'Social status and cultural consumption', in T. W. Chan (ed.), *Social Status and Cultural Consumption* (Cambridge University Press).

Chant, S. (ed.) (2010) *The International Handbook of Gender and Poverty: Concepts, Research, Policy* (Edward Elgar).

Chanter, T. (2006) *Gender: Key Concepts in Philosophy* (Continuum).

Charmaz, K. (1983) 'Loss of self: a fundamental form of suffering in the chronically ill', *Sociology of Health and Illness*, 5.

Chartered Institute of Public Relations (2005) *Reaching New Heights* (CIPR) [annual review].

Chase, E., and R. Walker (2013) 'The co-construction of shame in the context of poverty: beyond a threat to the social bond', *Sociology*, 47(4).

Chatterjee, P., D. Bailey and N. Aronoff (2001) 'Adolescence and old age in twelve communities', *Journal of Sociology and Social Welfare*, 28(4).

Chatzitheochari, S., and S. Arber (2009) 'Lack of sleep, work and the long hours culture: evidence from the UK time use survey', *Work, Employment and Society*, 32(30).

Chayko, M. (2002) *Connecting: How We Form Social Bonds and Communities in the Internet Age* (State University of New York Press).

Chen, S., and M. Ravallion (2008) 'The developing world is poorer than we thought, but no less successful in the fight against poverty', *World Bank Report*, 26 August; available online.

Chernilo, D. (2007) *A Social Theory of the Nation State: The Political Forms of Modernity Beyond Methodological Nationalism* (Routledge).

Cheung, S. Y., and A. Heath (2007) 'Ethnic penalties in Britain', in A. Heath and S. Y. Cheung (eds), *Unequal Chances: Ethnic Minorities in Western Labour Markets* (Oxford University Press).

Chouhan, K., S. Speeden and U. Qazi (2011) *Experience of Poverty and Ethnicity in London* (Joseph Rowntree Foundation).

Christian Research (2005) *The 2005 English Church Census* (Christian Research).

Christiano, K. J. (2007) 'Assessing modernities: from "pre-" to "post" to "ultra"', in J. A. Beckford and N. J. Demerath (eds), *The Sage Handbook of the Sociology of Religion* (Sage).

CHS (2003) *Human Security Now*, Commission on Human Security; available online.

Church Statistics (2012) *Church Statistics 2010/11*; available online.

Cixous, H. ([1975] 1980) 'Sorties', in E. Marks and I. Courtviron (eds), *New French Feminisms: An Anthology* (University of Massachusetts Press).

Clapp, J., and P. Dauvergne (2005) *Paths to a Green World: The Political Economy of the Global Environment* (MIT Press).

Clark, K., and S. Drinkwater (2007) *Ethnic Minorities in the Labour Market: Dynamics and Diversity* (Joseph Rowntree Foundation).

Clark, L. S., and L. Sywyj (2012) 'Mobile intimacies in the USA among refugee and recent immigrant teens and their parents', *Feminist Media Studies*, 12(4).

Clarke, C. (2012) 'Discussion – the value of educational research', *International Journal for Lesson and Learning Studies*, 1(3).

Clarke, J., and C. Critcher (1985) *The Devil Makes Work: Leisure in Capitalist Britain* (Macmillan).

Clarke, R., and M. Hough (1984) *Crime and Police Effectiveness* (Home Office).

Coburn, D. (2000) 'Income inequality, social cohesion and the health status of populations: the role of neo-liberalism', *Social Science and Medicine*, 51.

Coburn, D. (2009) 'Inequality and health', in L. Panitch and C. Leys (eds), *Morbid Symptoms: Health Under Capitalism* (Merlin Press).

Cohen, G. A. (1978) *Karl Marx's Theory of History: A Defence* (Oxford University Press).

Cohen, P. (2012) *In Our Prime: The Invention of Middle Age* (Scribner).

Cohen, S. (ed.) (1971) *Images of Deviance* (Penguin).

Coleman, J., and L. Hendry (1999) *The Nature of Adolescence* (3rd edn, Routledge).

Coles, B. (1995) *Youth and Social Policy: Youth, Citizenship and Young Careers* (UCL Press).

Colley, L. (1992) *Britons: Forging the Nation, 1707–1837* (Pimlico).

Colley, L. (1999) 'This country is not so special', *New Statesman*, 3 May.

Collier, P. (2007) *The Bottom Billion* (Oxford University Press).

Collier, P., and A. Hoeffler (2004) 'The challenge of reducing the global incidence of civil war', in B. Lomborg (ed.), *Global Crises, Global Solutions* (Cambridge University Press).

Collins, H. M., and R. Evans (2007) *Rethinking Expertise* (University of Chicago Press).

Collins, R. (1979) *The Credential Society: An Historical Sociology of Education and Stratification* (Academic Press).

Collins, R. (1986) *Weberian Sociological Theory* (Cambridge University Press).

Collins, R. (1998) *The Sociology of Philosophies: A Global Theory of Intellectual Change* (Harvard University Press).

Collins, R. (1999) *Macro History: Essays in Sociology of the Long Run* (Stanford University Press).

Collins, R. (2008) *Violence: A Micro-Sociological Theory* (Princeton University Press).

Collinson, P. (2009) 'Truth about our kidult generation', *The Guardian*, 18 April.

Connell, R. W. (1995) *Masculinities* (Polity).

Connell, R. W. (2002) *Gender* (Polity).

Connell, R. W. (2007) *Southern Theory* (Polity).

Conrad, P. (2005) 'The shifting engines of medicalization', *Journal of Health and Social Behaviour*, 46.

Conrad, P. (2007) *The Medicalization of Society* (Johns Hopkins University Press).

Cooke, G. (2008) 'Effacing the face: Botox and the anarchivic archive', *Body and Society*, 14(2).

Coontz, S. (1992) *The Way We Never Were: American Families and the Nostalgia Trap* (Basic Books).

Cooper, B., J. Glaesser, R. Gomm and M. Hammersley (2012) *Challenging the Qualitative–Quantitative Divide* (Continuum).

Corbridge, S. (1998) 'Development ethics: distance, difference, plausibility', *Ethics, Place and Environment*, 1(1).

Cornell, S., and D. Hartmann (2007) *Ethnicity and Race: Making Identities in a Changing World* (2nd edn, Pine Forge Press).

Cornia, G. A. (ed.) (2005) *Inequality, Growth, and Poverty in an Era of Liberalization and Globalization* (Oxford University Press).

Cornia, G. A. and J. Court (2001) *Inequality, Growth and Poverty in the Era of Liberalization and Globalization – A Policy Brief* (UNU/WIDER).

Coupland, D. (1991) *Generation X: Tales for an Accelerated Culture* (St Martin's Press).

Cowen, M. P., and R. W. Shenton (1996) *Doctrines of Development* (Routledge).

Cowie, J. (1999) *Capital Moves: RCA's 70-Year Quest for Cheap Labor* (New Press).

Crawford, H. (2007) *When is a Child not a Child? Asylum, Age Disputes and the Process of Age Assessment* (ILPA).

Crenshaw, M. (2011) *Explaining Terrorism* (Routledge).

Cribb, J., R. Joyce and D. Phillips (2012) *Living Standards, Poverty and Inequality in the UK: 2012* (Institute for Fiscal Studies).

Crockett, A., and D. Voas (2006) 'Generations of decline: religious change in 20th-century Britain', *Journal for the Scientific Study of Religion*, 45(4).

Crompton, R. (2006) *Employment and the Family: The Reconfiguration of Work and Family Life in Contemporary Societies* (Cambridge University Press).

Crompton, R. (2008) *Class and Stratification: An Introduction to Current Debates* (3rd edn, Polity).

Crompton, R., and C. Lyonette (2008) 'Who does the housework? The division of labour within the home', in A. Park, J. Curtice, K. Thomson, M. Philips, M. Johnson and E. Clery (eds), *British Social Attitudes: The 24th Report* (Sage).

Crook, S., J. Pakulski and M. Waters (1992) *Postmodernization: Change in Advanced Society* (Sage).

Crossick, G. (1991) 'From gentlemen to the residuum: languages of social description in Victorian Britain', in P. J. Corfield (ed.), *Langauge, History and Class* (Blackwell).

Crossley, M. (2006) *Contesting Psychiatry: Social Movements in Mental Health* (Routledge).

Crouch, C. (2004) *Post-Democracy* (Polity).

Csikszentmihalyi, M. (1975) *Beyond Boredom and Anxiety: Experiencing Flow in Work and Play* (Jossey Bass).

Cunningham, H. (2006) *The Invention of Childhood* (BBC Books).

Curran, J. (2011) *Media and Democracy* (Routledge).

Curran, J., N. Fenton and D. Freedman (2012) *Misunderstanding the Internet* (Routledge).

Currie, E. (2000) 'Reflections on crime and criminology at the millennium', *Western Criminology Review*, 2(1).

Curtis, P. (2008) 'Free school meals pupils lose out in race for top A-levels', *The Guardian*, 23 November.

Dabakis, M. (1999) *Visualizing Labor: American Sculpture* (Cambridge University Press).

DAC (2008) 'Evaluating conflict prevention and peacebuilding activities', www.oecd.org/development/evaluation/dcdndep/39289596.pdf.

Dalal-Clayton, B., and S. Bass (2002) *Sustainable Development Strategies* (Earthscan).

Dalla Costa, M., and S. James (1972) *The Power of Women and the Subversion of the Community* (Falling Wall Press).

Daly, M. (2011) *Welfare* (Polity).

Daly, M., and M. Leonard (2002) *Against All Odds: Family Life on a Low Income in Ireland* (Institute of Public Administration/Combat Poverty Agency).

Daly, M., and K. Rake (2003) *Gender and the Welfare State: Care, Work and Welfare in Europe and the USA* (Polity).

Daly, M., and H. Silver (2008) 'Social exclusion and social capital: a comparison and critique', *Theory and Society*, 37(6).

Dannefer, D. (2012) 'Enriching the tapestry: expanding the scope of life course concepts', *Journals of Gerontology, Series B, Psychological and Social Sciences*, 67(2).

Davies, K. (2011) 'Friendship and personal Life', in V. May (ed.), *Sociology of Personal Life* (Palgrave).

Davies, N. (1999) 'Watching the detectives: how the police cheat in the fight against crime', *The Guardian*, 18 March.

Davies, N. (2003a) 'Fiddling the figures' *The Guardian*, 11 July.

Davies, N. (2003b) 'Exposing the myth of the falling crime rate', *The Guardian*, 10 July.

Davis, A. (2000) 'Public relations, business news and the reproduction of corporate elite power', *Journalism*, 1(3).

Davis, K. (2008) *Intersectionality as Buzzword* (Pantheon Press).

Davis, R. (2010) 'Does your social class decide if you go to university? Get the full list of colleges', *Guardian Data Blog*, 28 September.

Dawkins, R. (2006a) *Unweaving the Rainbow: Science, Delusion and the Appetite for Wonder* (Penguin).

Dawkins, R. (2006b) *The God Delusion* (Bantam Press).

De Maio, F. (2010) *Health and Social Theory* (Palgrave Macmillan).

De Swaan, A. (1988) *In Care of the State: Health Care, Education and Welfare in Europe and the USA in the Modern Era* (Oxford University Press).

De Vries, G. (2002) 'Transformations in vulnerability', paper given at the International Sociological Association, World Congress of Sociology, Brisbane, 7–13 July.

Dearden, C., J. Goode, G. Whitfield and L. Cox (2010) *Credit and Debt in Low Income Families* (Joseph Rowntree Foundation).

Deery, S., R. Iverson and J. Walsh (2002) 'Work relationships in telephone call centres: understanding emotional exhaustion and employee withdrawal', *Journal of Management Studies*, 39(4).

Deleuze, G., and J. Guattari (1986) *Nomadology: The War Machine* (Semiotext(e)).

Della Porta, D., and M. Diani (1999) *Social Movements: An Introduction* (Blackwell).

Demeritt, D. (1998) 'Science, social constructivism and nature', in B. Braun and N. Castree (eds), *Remaking Reality: Nature at the Millennium* (Routledge).

Dennis, N., F. Henriques and C. Slaughter (1956) *Coal is our Life: An Analysis of a Yorkshire Mining Community* (Eyre & Spottiswoode).

Denzin, N. (1989) *Interpretive Interactionism* (Sage).

Department for Work and Pensions (2013) *Households Below Average Income: An Analysis of the Income Distribution 1994/95–2011/12* (Department for Work and Pensions).

Derber, C. (1998) *Corporation Nation: How Corporations are Taking Over our Lives and What We Can Do About It* (St Martin's Press).

Dermott, E. (2008) *Intimate Fatherhood: A Sociological analysis* (Routledge).

Dermott, E., and J. Seymour (eds) (2011) *Displaying Families: A New Concept for the Sociology of Family Life* (Palgrave Macmillan).

Derrida, J. (1976) *Of Grammatology* (Johns Hopkins University Press).

Devlin, P. (1965) *The Enforcement of Morals* (Oxford University Press).

Diamond, L. (1993) 'The globalization of democracy', in R. O. Slater, B. M. Schutz and S. R. Dorr (eds), *Global Transformation and the Third World* (Lynne Rienner).

Dickens, P. (1996) *Reconstructing Nature: Alienation, Emancipation and the Division of Labour* (Routledge).

Dickens, P. (2002) 'A green Marxism? Labor processes, alienation, and the division of labor', in R. Dunlap, F. H. Buttel, P. Dickens and A. Gijswijt (eds), *Sociological Theory and the Environment: Classical Foundations, Contemporary Insights* (Rowman & Littlefield).

Dickens, P. ([1992] 2004) *Society and Nature: Towards a Green Social Theory* (Harvester Wheatsheaf).

Dicks, B., B. Soyinka and A. Coffey (2006) 'Multimodal ethnography', *Qualitative Research*, 6(1).

Dilley, R. (2007) 'Women and climbing subculture: an exploration of gender identity, bodies and physicality', doctoral dissertation, Leeds Metropolitan University.

Dilley, R., and S. Scraton (2010) 'Women, climbing and serious leisure', *Leisure Studies*, 29(2).

Dinan, W., and D. Miller (2006) 'Transparency in EU decision making, holding corporations to account: why the ETI needs mandatory lobbying disclosure', in T. Spencer and C. McGrath (eds) *Challenge and Response: Essays on Public Affairs and Transparency* (Landmarks).

Dinan, W., and D. Miller (2012) 'Sledgehammers, nuts and rotten apples: reassessing the case for lobbying self-regulation in the United Kingdom', *Interest Groups and Advocacy*, 1(1).

Dobson, R. (2003) 'Half of general practitioners offer patients complementary medicine', *British Medical Journal*, 327.

Dollar, D., and A. Kraay (2001) *Growth is Good for the Poor* (World Bank), http://elibrary. worldbank.org/doi/pdf/10.1596/1813–9450–2587.

Dollar, D., and A. Kraay (2002) 'Spreading the wealth', *Foreign Affairs*, 81(1).

Doob, A., and C. Webster (2003) 'Sentence severity and crime: accepting the null hypothesis', in M. Tonry (ed.), *Crime and Justice 30* (University of Chicago Press).

Doogan, K. (2009) *New Capitalism? The Transformation of Work* (Polity).

Dorling, D. (2004) 'Prime suspect: murder in Britain', in P. Hillyard, C. Pantazis, S. Tombs and D. Gordon (eds), *Beyond Criminology* (Pluto Press).

Dorn, N., and N. South (1989) 'Drugs and leisure, prohibition and pleasure: from subculture to the drugalogue', in C. Rojek (ed.), *Leisure for Leisure: Critical Essays* (Macmillan).

Doucet, A. (2006) '"Estrogen-filled worlds": fathers as primary caregivers and employment', *Sociological Review*, 54(4).

Dowding, K. (1996) *Power* (Open University Press).

Downes, D., and R. Morgan (2012) 'Overtaking on the left? The politics of law and order in the "Big Society"', in M. Maguire, R. Morgan and R. Reiner (eds), *The Oxford Handbook of Criminology* (5th edn, Oxford University Press).

Doyal, L., and I. Gough (1991) *A Theory of Human Need* (Guildford Press).

Doyle, J. (2011) *Mediating Climate Change* (Sage).

Drake, M. S. (2003) 'Representing "old countries": the strategic representation of culture as heritage in the Asia–Europe summit meetings', in S. Lawson (ed.), *Europe and the Asia-Pacific: Culture, Identity and Representations of Region* (Routledge).

Drake M. S. (2007) 'Sociology and new wars in the era of globalization', *Sociology Compass*, 1(2).

Drake, M. S. (2010) *Political Sociology for a Globalizing World* (Polity).

Du Gay, P. (1986) 'Organizing identity: entrepreneurial governance and public management', in S. Hal and P. du Gay (eds), *Questions of Cultural Identity* (Sage).

Du Gay, P. (1996) *Consumption and Identity at Work* (Sage).

Du Gay, P. (2000) *In Praise of Bureaucracy: Weber, Organization, Ethics* (Sage).

Dudley, K. (1994) *The End of the Line: Lost Jobs, New Lives in Postindustrial America* (University of Chicago Press).

Duffield, M. (2007) *Development, Security and Unending War* (Polity).

Dumazedier, J. (1967) *Toward a Society of Leisure* (Free Press).

Dunlap, R. E. (2011) 'The maturation and diversification of environmental sociology: from constructivism and realism to agnosticism and pragmatism', in M. R. Redclift and G. Woodgate (eds), *The International Handbook of Environmental Sociology* (2nd edn, Edward Elgar).

Durkheim, E. ([1897] 1951) *Suicide* (Routledge).

Durkheim, E. (1956) *Education and Sociology* (Free Press).

Durkheim, E. ([1895] 1964) *The Rules of Sociological Method* (Free Press).

Durkheim, E. ([1912] 1971) *The Elementary Forms of the Religious Life* (George Allen & Unwin).

Durkheim, E. ([1893] 1973) *The Division of Labour in Society* (Free Press).

Durkheim, E. (1992) *Professional Ethics and Civic Morals* (Routledge).

Dworkin, A. (1981) *Pornography: Men Possessing Women* (Women's Press).

Dyke, A. H. (2009) *Mosques Made in Britain* (Quilliam Foundation).

Dyke, M., B. Johnston and A. Fuller (2012) 'Approaches to reflexivity: navigating educational and career pathways', *British Journal of Sociology of Education*, 33(6).

Eade, J. (1996) 'Ethnicity and the politics of cultural difference: an agenda for the 1990s?', in T. Ranger, Y. Samad and O. Stuart (eds), *Culture, Identity and Politics* (Avebury).

Eade, J., and D. O'Byrne (eds) (2005) *Global Ethics and Civil Society* (Ashgate).

Easterlin, R. A. (1987) *Birth and Fortune: The Impact of Numbers on Personal Welfare* (2nd edn, University of Chicago Press).

Eberstadt, M. (2009) 'Is pornography the new tobacco?', *Policy Review*, 154.

Eckhardt, W. (1992) *Civilizations, Empires and Wars: A Quantitative History of War* (McFarland).

Eder, K. (1982) 'A new social movement?', *Telos*, 52 (summer).

Eder, K. (1985) 'The "new social movements": moral crusades, political pressure groups, or social movements?', *Social Research*, 52.

Eder, K. (1990) 'The rise of counter-culture movements against modernity: nature as a new field of class struggle', *Theory, Culture and Society*, 7(4).

Eder, K. (1993) *The New Politics of Class: Social Movements and Cultural Dynamics in Advanced Societies* (Sage).

Eder, K. (1996) *The Social Construction of Nature: A Sociology of Ecological Enlightenment* (Sage).

Edgell, S. (2012) *The Sociology of Work: Continuity and Change in Paid and Unpaid Work* (Sage).

Edwards, J. (2000) *Born and Bred: Idioms of Kinship and New Reproductive Technologies in England* (Oxford University Press).

Edwards, R. (1979) *Contested Terrain: The Transformation of the Workplace in the Twentieth Century* (Heinemann).

Ehrenreich, B. (2001) *Nickel and Dimed: On (Not) Getting By in America* (Owl).

Einarsdottir, A. (2011) '"Marriage" and the personal life of same-sex couples', in V. May (ed.), *Sociology of Personal Life* (Palgrave).

Eisenberg, D. M., R. B. Davis, S. L. Ettner, S. Appel, S. Wilkey, M. van Rompay, and R. C. Kessler (1998) 'Trends in alternative medicine use in the United States, 1990–1997', *Journal of the American Medical Association*, 280(18).

Elchardus, M., and W. Smits (2006) 'The persistence of the standardized life cycle', *Time and Society*, 15(2–3).

Elder, G. H. (1974) *Children of the Great Depression* (University of Chicago Press).

Elder, G. H. (1986) 'Military times and turning points in men's lives', *Developmental Psychology*, 22.

Elder, G. H., M. Kirkpatrick Johnson and R. Crosnoe (2003) 'The emergence and development of life course theory', in J. T. Mortimer and M. J. Shanahan (eds), *Handbook of the Life Course* (Kluwer Academic/Plenum).

Elias, A. (2008) 'War and the visual language of flowers', *War, Literature and the Arts*, 20(1–2).

Elias, N. (1982) 'Scientific establishments', in N. Elias, H. Martins and R. Whitley (eds), *Scientific Establishments and Hierarchies* (D. Reidel).

Elias, N. (1997) *The Germans* (Polity).

Elias, N. ([1939] 2000) *The Civilizing Process: Sociogenetic and Psychogenetic Investigations* (Blackwell).

Elias, N., and E. Dunning (2008) *The Quest for Excitement: Sport and Leisure in the Civilizing Process* (2nd edn, University College Dublin Press)

Elliot, L., and D. Atkinson (2008) 'The gods that failed: how blind faith in markets has cost us our future', *The Guardian*, 2 June.

Elliott, A., and L. Ray (eds) (2003) *Key Contemporary Social Theorists* (Blackwell).

Elliott, J. A. (2002) 'Development as improving human welfare and human rights', in V. Desai and R. B. Potter (eds), *The Companion to Development Studies* (Arnold).

Elliott, L. (2004) *The Global Politics of the Environment* (2nd edn, Palgrave).

Elshtain, J. B. (1993) *Public Man, Private Woman: Women in Social and Political Thought* (2nd edn, Princeton University Press).

Elster, J. (1986) *An Introduction to Karl Marx* (Cambridge University Press).

End Child Poverty (2012) *Child Poverty Map*, www.endchildpoverty.org.uk/why-end-child-poverty/poverty-in-your-area.

Engels, F. ([1845] 1987) *The Condition of the Working Class in England of 1845* (Penguin).

Engels, F., C. P. Dutt and J. B. S. Haldane (1940) *Dialectics of Nature* (Lawrence & Wishart).

England, P., E. Schafer and A. Fogarty (2007) 'Hooking up and forming romantic relationships on today's college campuses', in M. Kimmel (ed.), *The Gendered Society Reader* (Oxford University Press).

Epsom, J. (1978) 'The mobile health clinic: a report on the first year's work', in D. Tuckett and J. Kauffert (eds), *Basic Readings in Medical Sociology* (Tavistock).

Equality Trust (2011) 'Income inequality and violent crime', Equality Trust Research Digest, no. 1, https://www.equalitytrust.org.uk/sites/default/files/research-digest-violent-crime-final.pdf.

Erickson, M. (2002) 'Science as a vocation in the 21st century: an empirical study of science researchers', *Max Weber Studies*, 3(1).

Erickson, M. (2005) *Science, Culture and Society: Understanding Science in the 21st Century* (Polity).

Escobar, A. (1995) *Encountering Development: The Making and Unmaking of the Third World* (Princeton University Press).

Esping-Andersen, G. (1990) *The Three Worlds of Welfare Capitalism* (Polity).

Esteva, G. (1992) 'Development', in W. Sachs (ed.), *The Development Dictionary: A Guide to Knowledge as Power* (Zed Books).

Etzioni, A. (1994) *The Spirit of Community: The Reinvention of American Society* (Simon & Schuster).

EU Council of Ministers (1975) *Council Decision of 22 July 1975 concerning a Programme of Pilot Schemes and Studies to Combat Poverty*, 75/458/EEC, OJEC, L 199.

Eurobarometer (2010) *Special Eurobarometer 341: Biotechnology* (European Commission), http://ec.europa.eu/public_opinion/archives/ebs/ebs_341_en.pdf.

European Information Centre for Complementary and Alternative Medicine (EICCAM) (2008) *Brochure*, www.eiccam.eu/portal.html.

European Working Conditions Survey (2010) www.eurofound.europa.eu/surveys/ewcs/2010/.

Eurostat (2008) *Living Conditions in Europe: Data 2003–06*; available online.

Eurostat (2012a) *Population and Social Conditions, Statistics in Focus 9/2012*; available online.

Eurostat (2012b) *Measuring Material Deprivation in the EU*; available online.

Eurostat (2012c) 'Employment statistics', available at http://epp.eurostat.ec.europa.eu/statistics_explained/index.php/Employment_statistics.

Eurostat (2013) *Gender Pay Gap Statistics*; available online.

Evernden, N. (1992) *The Social Creation of Nature* (Johns Hopkins University Press).

Ezzy, D. (2001) *Narrating Unemployment* (Ashgate).

Facchini, C., and M. Rampazi (2009) 'No longer young, not yet old: biographical uncertainty in late-adult temporality', *Time and Society*, 18.

Fairhurst, E. (1998) '"Growing old gracefully as opposed to mutton dressed as lamb": the social construction of recognising older women', in S. Nettleton and J. Watson (eds), *The Body in Everyday Life* (Routledge).

Fanon, F. (1965) *The Wretched of the Earth* (MacGibbon & Kee).

Farrell, G., A. Tseloni and N. Tilley (2011) 'The effectiveness of vehicle security devices and their role in the crime drop', *Criminology and Criminal Justice*, 11(1).

Faulkner, A. (2013) 'Physics geeks brainwashed', *The Sun*, 13 January.

Fausto-Sterling, A. (1992) *Myths of Gender: Biological Theories about Women and Men* (2nd edn, Basic Books).

Fausto-Sterling, A. (2001) *Sexing the Body: Gender Politics in the Constructions of Sexuality* (Basic Books).

Fausto-Sterling, A. (2005) 'The bare bones of sex', *Signs: Journal of Women in Culture and Society*, 30(21).

Favell, A. (2001) 'Migration, mobility and globaloney: metaphors and rhetoric in the sociology of globalisation', *Global Networks*, 1(4).

Featherstone, M. (ed.) (1990) *Global Culture: Nationalism, Globalization and Modernity* (Sage).

Featherstone, M. (1991) 'The body in consumer culture', in M. Featherstone, M. Hepworth and B. S. Turner (eds), *The Body: Social Process and Cultural Theory* (Sage).

Featherstone, M. (2007) *Consumer Culture and Postmodernism* (2nd edn, Sage).

Featherstone, M., and M. Hepworth (1983) 'The midlifestyle of "George and Lynne": notes on a popular strip', *Theory, Culture and Society*, 1(3).

Featherstone, M., and M. Hepworth (1994) 'The mask of ageing and the postmodern life course', in M. Featherstone, M. Hepworth and B. S. Turner (eds), *The Body: Social Process and Cultural Theory* (Sage).

Federici, S. (2004) *Caliban and the Witch: Woman, the Body and Primitive Accumulation* (Autonomedia).

Felstead, A., N. Jewson and S. Walters (2005) *Changing Places of Work* (Palgrave).

Fenton, S. (2010) *Ethnicity* (2nd edn, Polity).

Ferrera, M. (1996) 'The "southern model" of welfare in social Europe', *Journal of European Social Policy*, 6(1).

Ferrill, A. (1985) *The Origins of War: From the Stone Age to Alexander the Great* (Thames & Hudson).

Fevre, R. (2007) 'Employment insecurity and social theory: the power of nightmares', *Work, Employment and Society*, 21(3).

Feyerabend, P. (1978) *Against Method* (Verso).

Field, C. (2010a) 'Belief in a personal God, or God as a life force, 1947–2000', *British Religion in Numbers*, www.brin.ac.uk.

Field, C. (2010b) 'Belief that the New Testament is of divine origin, 1960–1993', *British Religion in Numbers*, www.brin.ac.uk.

Field, C. (2010c) 'Belief in divinity of Jesus Christ, 1957–2008', *British Religion in Numbers*, www.brin.ac.uk.

Field, C. (2010d) 'Muslim opinions and opinions of Muslims: British experiences', *British Religion in Numbers*, www.brin.ac.uk.

Field, C. (2010e) 'Belief in magic: Great Britain, all adults, percentages', *British Religion in Numbers*, www.brin.ac.uk.

Field, C. (2011) 'Young British Muslims since 9/11: a composite attitudinal profile', *Religion, State & Society*, 39(2–3).

Field, C. (2012) 'Religious census 2011 – England and Wales', *British Religion in Numbers*, www.brin.ac.uk.

Field, C. (2013a) 'More census data and other news', *British Religion in Numbers*, www.brin.ac.uk.

Field, C. (2013b) '2011 census detailed characteristics', *British Religion in Numbers*, www.brin.ac.uk.

Field, J. (2008) *Social Capital* (2nd edn, Routledge).

Filinson, R. (2008) 'Age discrimination legislation in the UK: a comparative and gerontological analysis', *Journal of Cross Cultural Gerontology*, 23.

Finch, J. (2007) 'Displaying families', *Sociology*, 41(1).

Finch, J., and J. Mason (2000) *Passing On: Kinship and Inheritance in England* (Routledge).

Fincham, B. (2008) 'Balance is everything: bicycle messengers, work and leisure', *Sociology*, 42(4).

Fine, B. (1999) 'The developmental state is dead – long live social capital?', *Development and Change*, 30.

Fine, R. (2007) *Cosmopolitanism* (Routledge).

Fineman, S. (ed.) (1993) *Emotion in Organizations* (Sage).

Finney, N., and L. Simpson, L (2009) *'Sleepwalking to Segregation'?* (Policy Press).

Firebaugh, G. (2003) *The New Geography of Global Income Inequality* (Harvard University Press).

Firestone, S. (1970) *The Dialectic of Sex* (Farrar, Strauss, Giroux).

Fitzgerald, H., and D. Kirk (2009) 'Identity work: young disabled people, family and sport', *Leisure Studies*, 28(4).

Fitzpatrick, R. (2008) 'Society and changing patterns of disease', in G. Scambler (ed.), *Sociology as Applied to Medicine* (6th edn, W. B. Saunders).

Flatley, J., C. Kershaw, K. Smith, R. Chaplin and D. Moon (eds) (2010) *Crime in England and Wales, 2009–10* (Home Office).

Fleck, L. ([1935] 1979) *Genesis and Development of a Scientific Fact* (University of Chicago Press).

Flint, J. (2010) *Coping Strategies? Agencies, Budgeting and Self-Esteem amongst Low-Income Households* (Joseph Rowntree Foundation).

Foley, C., C. Holzman and S. Wearing (2007) 'Moving beyond conspicuous leisure consumption: adolescent women, mobile phones and public space', *Leisure Studies*, 26(2).

Foong-Khong, Y. (2001) 'Human security: a shotgun approach to alleviating human misery?', *Global Governance*, 7(3).

Foran, J. (2005) *Taking Power: On the Origins of Third World Revolutions* (Cambridge University Press).

Foran, J., D. S. Lane and A. Zivkovic (eds) (2008) *Revolution in the Making of the Modern World* (Routledge).

Ford, R. (2008) 'Is racial prejudice declining in Britain?', *British Journal of Sociology*, 59(4).

Foster, J. B. (2000) *Marx's Ecology: Materialism and Nature* (Monthly Review Press).

Foucault, M. (1969) *The Archaeology of Knowledge* (Routledge).

Foucault, M. ([1966] 1970) *The Order of Things* (Pantheon).

Foucault, M. (1972) *The Archaeology of Knowledge and the Discourse of Language* (Pantheon).

Foucault, M. (1977) *Discipline and Punish: The Birth of the Prison* (Allen Lane).

Foucault, M. (1978) *The History of Sexuality*, Vol. 1: *An Introduction*, trans. Robert Hurley (Pantheon).

Foucault, M. (1980) *Power/Knowledge: Selected Interviews and Other Writings* (Harvester Wheatsheaf).

Foucault. M. (1984) *The Foucault Reader* (Penguin).

Foucault, M. (1991) 'Governmentality', in G. Burchell, C. Gordon and P. Miller (eds), *The Foucault Effect: Studies in Governmentality* (Harvester Wheatsheaf).

Fox, A. (1974) *Beyond Contract: Work, Power and Trust Relations* (Faber).

Fox, N. (1998) 'Postmodernism and "health"', in A. Peterson and C. Waddell (eds), *Health Matters: A Sociology of Illness, Prevention and Care* (Open University Press).

Fox, N. (2012) 'Deleuze and Guatarri', in G. Scambler (ed.), *Contemporary Theorists for Medical Sociology* (Routledge).

Francis, P. (2002) 'Social capital, civil society and social exclusion', in U. Kothari and M. Minogue (eds), *Development Theory and Practice: Critical Perspectives* (Palgrave Macmillan).

Frank, A. G. (1967) *Capitalism and Underdevelopment in Latin America* (Monthly Review Press).

Franklin, B., and J. Horwath (1996) 'The murder of innocence: newspaper reporting of the death of Jamie Bulger', in S. Wagg and J. Pilcher (eds), *Thatcher's Children* (Falmer Press).

Fraser, J. (2001) *White-Collar Sweatshop: The Deterioration of Work and its Rewards in Corporate America* (W. W. Norton).

Fraser, M., and M. Greco (eds) (2005) *The Body: A Reader* (Routledge).

Fraser, N. (1989) *Unruly Practices* (Polity).

Fraser, N. (1990) 'Rethinking the public sphere: a contribution to the critique of actually existing democracy', *Social Text*, 25/26.

Freese, J., J. C. A. Li and L. D. Wade (2003) 'The potential relevance of biology to social inquiry', *Annual Review of Sociology*, 29.

Freidson, E. (1970) *Profession of Medicine* (Dodds, Mead).

Frericks, P., M. Harvey and R. Maier (2010) '"The paradox of the shrinking middle": the central dilemma of European social policy', *Critical Social Policy*, 30(3).

Friedman, A. (1977) *Industry and Labour: Class Struggle and Work and Monopoly Capitalism* (Macmillan).

Friese, C., G. Becker and D. Nachtigall (2008) 'Older motherhood and the changing life course in the era of assisted reproductive technologies', *Journal of Aging Studies*, 22.

Frisk, L., F. Höllinger and P. Åkerbäck (2014) 'Size and structure of the holistic milieu: a comparison of local mapping studies in Austria and Sweden', *Journal of Contemporary Religion*, 29(2).

Frith, M. (2004) 'Baby boomers defiantly refuse to grow old', *The Independent*, 12 July.

Fry, H. (2012) 'Is life really that complex?', *YouTube*.

Fry, H., T. Davis and A. Wilson (2012) *Spatial Analysis Modelling of the London Riots* (UCL Press).

Fryer, P. (1984) *Staying Power: The History of Black People in Britain* (Pluto Press).

Fukuyama, F. (1991) *The End of History and the Last Man* (Free Press).

Fukuyama, F. (2001) 'Social capital, civil society and development', *Third World Quarterly*, 22.

Fuller, E. (2011) *Smoking, Drinking and Drug Use among Young People in England in 2011* (Health and Social Care Information Centre).

Fuller, S. (1997) *Science* (Open University Press).

Fuller, S. (2000) *The Governance of Science: Ideology and the Future of the Open Society* (Open University Press).

Fuller, S. (2006) *The New Sociological Imagination* (Sage).

Fuller, S. (2007) *Science vs. Religion: Intelligent Design and the Problem of Evolution* (Polity).

Furedi, F. (2003) 'Children who won't grow up', www.spiked-online.com/newsite/article/2775#.U9ZiKVIg-Hs.

Furlong, A. (ed.) (2009) *Handbook of Youth and Young Adulthood: New Perspectives and Agendas* (Routledge).

Furlong, A., and F. Cartmel (2007) *Young People and Social Change* (2nd edn, Open University Press).

Galambos, N. L., P. K. Turner and L. C. Tilton-Weaver (2005) 'Chronological age and subjective age in emerging adulthood: the crossover effect', *Journal of Adolescent Research*, 20(5).

Gallup (2009) 'On Darwin's birthday, only 4 in 10 believe in evolution', www.gallup.com/poll/114544/darwin-birthday-believe-evolution.aspx.

Gambetta, D. (2005) 'Can we make sense of suicide missions?', in D. Gambetta (ed.), *Making Sense of Suicide Missions* (Oxford University Press).

Gambetta, D., and S. Hertog (2009) 'Why are there so many engineers among Islamic radicals?', *European Journal of Sociology*, 50(2).

Gamble, A. (1983) *The Free Economy and the Strong State: The Politics of Thatcherism* (Macmillan).

Gamson, W. (1992) *Talking Politics* (Cambridge University Press).

Ganska, H. (2010) 'Cougars ready to pounce', *Sunday Times* [Western Australia], 14 February.

Garfield, E. (1979) *Citation Indexing: Its Theory and Application in Science, Technology, and Humanities* (Wiley).

Garfinkel, H. (1967) *Studies in Ethnomethodology* (Polity).

Garland, D. (2001) *The Culture of Control* (Oxford University Press).

Garner, S. (2010) *Racisms* (Sage).

Gartman, D. (1994) *Auto Opium: A Social History of Automobile Design* (Routledge).

Gatehouse, G. (2012) 'How much will technology boom change Kenya?', *BBC News*, 11 October, www.bbc.co.uk/news/world-africa-19903839.

Gatens, M. (1991) *Feminism and Philosophy: Perspectives on Difference and Equality* (Polity).

Gatens, M. (1996) *Imaginary Bodies: Ethics, Power and Corporeality* (Routledge).

Geaves, R. (ed.) (2013) *Sufism in Britain* (Bloomsbury).

Geertz, C. (1973) *The Interpretation of Cultures* (Basic Books).

Geertz, C. (1988) *Works and Lives: The Anthropologist as Author* (Stanford University Press).

Gellner, E. (1983) *Nations and Nationalism* (Blackwell).

George, V., and I. Howards (1991) *Poverty amidst Affluence: Britain and the United States* (Edward Elgar).

Gewirtz, S., and A. Cribb (2006) 'What to do about values in social research: the case for ethical reflexivity in the sociology of education', *British Journal of Sociology of Education*, 27(2).

Gewirtz, S., S. Ball and R. Bowe (1995) *Markets, Choice, an Equity in Education* (Open University Press).

Giannelli, G. C., L. Mangiavacchi and L. Piccoli (2010) *GDP and the Value of Family Caretaking: How Much Does Europe Care?*, http://ftp.iza.org/dp5046.pdf.

Giddens, A. (1971) *Capitalism and Modern Social Theory* (Cambridge University Press).

Giddens, A. (1984) *The Constitution of Society* (Polity).

Giddens, A. (1985) *The Nation-State and Violence* (Polity).

Giddens, A. (1990) *The Consequences of Modernity* (Polity).

Giddens, A. (1991) *Modernity and Self Identity: Self and Society in the Late Modern Age* (Polity).

Giddens, A. (1992) *The Transformation of Intimacy* (Polity).

Giddens, A. (1994a) 'Living in a post-traditional society', in U. Beck, A. Giddens and S. Lash, *Reflexive Modernization: Politics, Tradition and Aesthetics in the Modern Social Order* (Polity).

Giddens, A. (1994b) *Beyond Left and Right* (Polity).

Giddens, A. (1998) *The Third Way: The Renewal of Social Democracy* (Polity).

Giddens, A. (1999) *Runaway World* (Profile Books).

Giddens, A. (2011) *The Politics of Climate Change* (2nd edn, Polity).

Giddens, A., and P. W. Sutton (2013) *Sociology* (7th edn, Polity).

Giddings, L., and B. Grant (2006) 'Mixed-methods research, positivism dressed in drag?', *Journal of Research in Nursing*, 11(3).

Gilbert, R., and K. Constantine (2005) 'When strength can't last a lifetime', *Men and Masculinities*, 7(4).

Gilding, M. (2010) 'Reflexivity over and above convention: the new orthodoxy in the sociology of personal life, formerly sociology of the family', *British Journal of Sociology*, 61(4).

Gillborn, D., and H. Mirza (2000) *Mapping Race, Class and Gender: A Synthesis of Research Evidence* (Office for Standards in Education).

Gilleard, C., and P. Higgs (2007) 'The third age and the baby boomers: two approaches to the social structuring of later life', *International Journal of Ageing and Later Life*, 2(2).

Gillespie, R. (1991) *Manufacturing Knowledge: A History of the Hawthorne Experiments* (Cambridge University Press).

Gillies, V. (2009) 'Understandings and experiences of involved fathering in the United Kingdom: exploring classed dimensions', *Annals of the American Academy of Political and Social Science*, 624.

Gillis, J. (1996) *A World of their Own Making: Myth, Ritual, and the Quest for Family Values* (Basic Books).

Gillis, S., G. Howie and R. Munford (2007) *Third Wave Feminism: A Critical Exploration* (2nd edn, Palgrave).

Gilroy, P. (1993) *The Black Atlantic: Modernity and Double Consciousness* (Verso).

Gittins, D. (1998) *The Child in Question* (Macmillan).

Glasgow, F. (2003) 'Beware of the baby boomers as retirement time gets further away', *The Independent*, 6 September.

Glasgow Media Group (2000) *Viewing the World: News Content and Audience Studies* (Department for International Development).

Glewwe, P., and G. Hall (1998), 'Are some groups more vulnerable to macroeconomic shocks than others? Hypothesis tests based on the panel data from Peru', *Journal of Development Economics*, 56.

Glyptis, S. (1989) *Leisure and Unemployment* (Open University Press).

Goffman, E. (1959) *The Presentation of Self in Everyday Life* (Doubleday Anchor).

Gold, T. (2011) 'The right has chosen its scapegoat – the single mum. And she will bleed', *The Guardian*, 19 August.

Goldacre, B. (2012) *Big Pharma* (Fourth Estate).

Goldblatt, D. (1996) *Social Theory and the Environment* (Polity).

Goldhagen, D. (2009) *Worse Than War* (Public Affairs).

Goldstein, H. (1987) *Multi-Level Models in Educational and Social Research* (Griffin).

Goldstone, J. A. (1991) *Revolution and Rebellion in the Early Modern World* (University of California Press).

Goldstone, J. A. (2001) 'Toward a fourth generation of revolutionary theory', *Annual Review of Political Science* 4.

Goldstone, J. A. (2011) 'Understanding the revolutions of 2011: weakness and resilience in Middle Eastern autocracies', *Foreign Affairs* (May–June).

Goldthorpe, J. H. (2000) *On Sociology* (Oxford University Press).

Goldthorpe, J. H., D. Lockwood, F. Bechhofer and J. Platt (1968) *The Affluent Worker: Industrial Attitudes and Behaviour* (Cambridge University Press).

Goldthorpe, J. H., D. Lockwood, F. Bechhofer and J. Platt (1969) *The Affluent Worker in the Class Structure* (Cambridge University Press).

Goodhart, D. (2004) 'Discomfort of strangers', *The Guardian*, 24 February.

Goodhart, D. (2006) *Progressive Nationalism* (Demos).

Goodhew, D. (ed.) (2012) *Church Growth in Britain* (Ashgate).

Goodin, R. E. and J. Le Grand (1987) *Not Only the Poor: The Middle Classes and the Welfare State* (Allen & Unwin).

Goodley, D. (2012) 'Dis/entangling critical disability studies', *Disability & Society*, 28(5).

Goodwin, J. (2001) *No Other Way Out: States and Revolutionary Movements, 1945–1991* (Cambridge University Press).

Goodwin, J. (2004) 'What must we explain to explain terrorism?', *Social Movement Studies* 3(2).

Gordon, D., and P. Townsend (eds) (2000) *Breadline Europe: The Measurement of Poverty* (Policy Press).

Gordon, D., J. Mack, S. Lansley, G. Main, S. Nandy, D. Patsios and M. Pomati (2013) 'The impoverishment of the UK', *Poverty and Social Exclusion*, www.poverty.ac.uk/pse-research/pseuk-reports.

Gornick, J. C., and M. K. Meyers (2003) 'Welfare regimes in relation to paid work and care', in J. Z. Giele and E. Holst (eds), *Advances in Life Course Research: Changing Life Patterns in Western Industrial Societies* (Elsevier).

Gorz, A. (1980) *Ecology as Politics* (Pluto Press).

Gorz, A. (1985) *Paths to Paradise: On the Liberation from Work* (Pluto Press).

Gorz, A. (1989) *Critique of Economic Reason* (Verso).

Gorz, A. (1994) *Capitalism, Socialism, Ecology* (Verso).

Gorz, A. (1999) *Reclaiming Work: Beyond the Wage-Based Society* (Polity).

Goudsblom, J. (1989) 'Human history and long-term social processes', in J. Goudsblom, E. Jones and S. Mennell (eds), *Human History and Social Process* (University of Exeter Press).

Goudsblom, J. (1992) *Fire and Civilization* (Allen Lane).

Gouldner, A. (1968) 'The sociologist as partisan: sociology and the welfare state', *American Sociologist*, 3(2).

Graaff, J. (2003) *Poverty and Development* (Oxford University Press).

Graham, S. (2010) *Cities under Siege: The New Military Urbanism* (Verso).

Gramsci, A. (1966) *Passato e presente* (Einaudi).

Gramsci, A. (1971a) *Selections from the Prison Notebooks* (Lawrence & Wishart).

Gramsci, A. (1971b) *The Modern Prince* (International).

Granovetter, M. (1995) *Getting a Job: A Study of Contacts and Careers* (University of Chicago Press).

Green, E., and C. Singleton (2007) 'Mobile selves: gender, ethnicity and mobile phones in the everyday lives of young Pakistani-British men and women', *Information, Communication and Society*, 10(4).

Green, E., S. Hebron and D. Woodward (1990) *Women's Leisure, What Leisure?* (Macmillan).

Green, G. (2009) *The End of Stigma? Changes in the Social Experience of Long-Term Illness* (Routledge).

Green, J. (1998) *The World of the Worker: Labor in Twentieth-Century America* (University of Illinois Press).

Green, L. (2006) 'An unhealthy neglect? Examining the relationship between child health and gender in research and policy', *Critical Social Policy*, 26.

Green, L. (2010) *Understanding the Life Course: Sociological and Psychological Perspectives* (Polity).

Green, L., and V. Grant (2008) 'Gagged grief and beleaguered bereavements: an analysis of multidisciplinary theory relating to same sex partnership bereavement, *Sexualities*, 11(3).

Green, L., W. Parkin and J. Hearn (2001) 'Power', in E. Wilson (ed.), *Organizational Behaviour Reassessed: The Impact of Gender* (Sage).

Green, P., and T. Ward (2012) 'State crime: a dialectical view', in M. Maguire, R. Morgan and R. Reiner (eds), *The Oxford Handbook of Criminology* (5th edn, Oxford University Press).

Greer, C., and R. Reiner (2012) 'Mediated mayhem: media, crime, criminal justice', in M. Maguire, R. Morgan and R. Reiner (eds), *The Oxford Handbook of Criminology* (5th edn, Oxford University Press).

Greer, G. (1970) *The Female Eunuch* (Paladin).

Gregg, B. (2011) *Human Rights as Social Construction* (Cambridge University Press).

Gregory, J., and S. Miller (1998) *Science in Public: Communication, Culture, and Credibility* (Plenum).

Grenfell, M. (ed.) (2012) *Bourdieu: Key Concepts* (2nd edn, Acumen).

Grenier, A. (2007) 'Crossing age and generational boundaries: exploring intergenerational research encounters', *Journal of Social Issues*, 63(4).

Grice, A. (2013) 'Voters "brainwashed by Tory welfare myths", shows new poll', *The Independent*, 4 January.

Griffin, C. (1993) *Representations of Youth: The Study of Youth and Adolescence in Britain and America* (Polity).

Griffin, C. (2001) 'Imagining new narratives of youth research, the "new Europe" and global youth culture', *Childhood*, 8(2).

Griffin, C. (2004) 'Good girls, bad girls: Anglocentrism and diversity in the constitution of contemporary girlhood', in A. Harris (ed.), *All about the Girl: Culture, Power, and Identity* (Routledge).

Griffin, C., F. Measham, K. Moore and S. Riley (2008) 'Social and cultural uses of ketamine, addiction research and theory', *Social and Cultural Uses of Ketamine*, 16(3).

Gross, P. R., and N. Levitt (1994) *Higher Superstition: The Academic Left and its Quarrels with Science* (Johns Hopkins University Press).

Grosz, E. (1994) *Volatile Bodies: Towards a Corporeal Feminism* (Routledge).

Grundmann, R. (1991) 'The ecological challenge to Marxism', *New Left Review*, 187 (May/June).

Grundy, E. (2005) 'Reciprocity in relationships: socio-economic and health influence on intergenerational exchanges between third generation parents and their adult children', *British Journal of Sociology*, 56(2).

Guibernau, M., and D. Goldblatt (2000) 'Identity and nation', in K. Woodward (ed.), *Questioning Identity: Gender, Class, Nation* (Routledge).

Gullette, M. M. (2008) 'What exactly has age got to do with it: my life in critical age studies', *Journal of Aging Studies*, 22.

Gullette, M. M. (2011) *Agewise: Fighting the New Ageism in America* (University of Chicago Press).

Gumbel, P. (2011) 'Black hawk frowns', *Times Higher Education*, 23 June.

Gurr, K. T. (1970) *Why Men Rebel* (Princeton University Press).

Guttmann, A. (1992) *Women's Sports: A History* (Columbia University Press).

Haas, L., and C. P. Hwang (2008) 'The impact of taking parental leave on fathers' participation in childcare and relationships with children: lessons from Sweden', *Community, Work & Family*, 11(1).

Habermas, J. (1981) 'New social movements', *Telos*, 49(fall).

Habermas, J. (1986) *The Theory of Communicative Action*, Vol.1 (Polity).

Habermas, J. (1989a) *The Theory of Communicative Action*, Vol.2 (Polity).

Habermas, J. (1989b) *The Structural Transformation of the Public Sphere* (Polity).

Habermas, J. (1990) *The Philosophical Discourse of Modernity: Twelve Lectures* (Polity).

Habermas, J. (2001) 'The postnational constellation and the future of democracy', in J. Habermas, *The Postnational Constellation: Political Essays* (Polity).

Habermas, J. (2012) *The Crisis of the European Union: A Response* (Polity).

Hage, G. (1998) *White Nation* (Pluto Press).

Hagenaars, A. (1986) *The Perception of Poverty* (North-Holland).

Hager, N., and B. Burton (1999) *Secrets and Lies: The Anatomy of an Anti-Environmental PR Campaign* (Craig Potton).

Hagestad, G. O., and P. Uhlenberg (2005) 'The social separation of old and young: a root of ageism', *Journal of Social Issues*, 61(2).

Hagestad, G. O., and P. Uhlenberg (2006) 'Should we be concerned about age segregation? Some theoretical and empirical explorations', *Research on Aging*, 28.

Hagstrom, W. O. (1965) *The Scientific Community* (Basic Books).

Hakim, C. (2000) *Working-Lifestyle Choices in the 21st Century* (Oxford University Press).

Halberstam, J. (1998) *Female Masculinity* (Duke University Press).

Halford, S., and P. Leonard (2006) *Negotiating Gendered Identities at Work: Place, Space and Time* (Palgrave).

Halfpenny, P. (1982) *Positivism and Sociology* (Allen & Unwin).

Hall, G. S. (1904) *Adolescence: its Psychology and its Relation to Physiology, Anthropology, Sociology, Sex, Crime, Religion and Education* (Appleton).

Hall, S. (1991) 'Old and new identities, old and new ethnicities', in A. D. King (ed.), *Culture, Globalization and the World-System* (Macmillan).

Hall, S. (1992a) 'The question of cultural identity', in S. Hall, D. Held and T. McGrew (eds), *Modernity and its Futures* (Polity).

Hall, S. (1992b) 'Our mongrel selves', *New Statesman*, 19 June.

Hall, S. (2012) *Theorizing Crime & Deviance* (Sage).

Hall, S., and M. Jacques (eds) (1989) *New Times: The Changing Face of Politics in the 1990s* (Lawrence & Wishart).

Hall, S., and T. Jefferson (eds) (1976) *Resistance through Rituals: Youth Sub-Cultures in Post-War Britain* (Hutchison).

Hall, S., C. Critcher, T. Jefferson, J. Clarke and B. Roberts (1978) *Policing the Crisis* (Macmillan).

Hall, S., S. Winlow and C. Ancrum (2008) *Criminal Identities and Consumer Culture: Crime, Exclusion and the New Culture of Narcissism* (Willan).

Halsey, A. H., A. Heath and J. M. Ridge (1980) *Origins and Destinations: Family, Class, and Education in Modern Britain* (Clarendon Press).

Hamilton, C. (2013) 'No, we should not just "at least do the research"', *Nature*, 496(7444).

Hamilton, K., and J. D. Dixon (2003) 'Measuring the wealth of nations', *Environmental Monitoring and Assessment*, 86(1–2).

Hamlin, C. L. (2002) *Beyond Relativism: Raymond Boudon, Cognitive Rationality and Critical Realism* (Routledge).

Hammersley, M. (1992) *What's Wrong with Ethnography?* (Routledge).

Hammersley, M. (1995) *The Politics of Social Research* (Sage).

Hammersley, M. (2002) *Educational Research, Policymaking and Practice* (Sage).

Hammersley, M. (2004) 'Reflexivity', in M. Lewis-Beck, A. Bryman and T. Liao (eds), *Encyclopedia of Social Science Research Methods* (Sage).

Hammersley, M. (2008) *Questioning Qualitative Inquiry* (Sage).

Hammersley, M. (2010) 'Can we re-use qualitative data via secondary analysis? Notes on some terminological and substantive issues', *Sociological Research Online*, 15(1).

Hammersley, M. (2011) *Methodology: Who Needs It?* (Sage).

Hammersley, M. (2012) *What is Qualitative Research?* (Bloomsbury).

Hammersley. M. (2014) *The Limits of Social Science: Causal Explanation and Value Relevance* (Sage).

Hammond, L. (2011) *Cash and Compassion: The Role of the Somali Diaspora in Relief, Development and Peace-Building* (UNDP).

Hamper, B. (1992) *Rivethead: Tales from the Assembly Line* (Warner Books).

Hannerz, U. (1996) *Transnational Connections: Culture, People, Places* (Routledge).

Hannigan, J. A. (2006) *Environmental Sociology* (2nd edn, Routledge).

Hansard Society (2013) *Audit of Political Engagement 10*; available online.

Hansard Society (2014) *Audit of Political Engagement 11*; available online.

Happer, C., G. Philo and A. Froggatt (2012) *Climate Change and Energy Security: Assessing the Impact of Information and its Delivery on Attitudes and Behaviour* (UK Energy Research Council).

Haraway, D. (1985) 'A manifesto for cyborgs: science technology and socialist feminism in the 1980s', *Socialist Review*, 80.

Haraway, D. (1989) 'The biopolitics of postmodern bodies: determinations of self in immune system discourse', in *differences: A Journal of Feminist Cultural Studies*, 1.

Haraway, D. (1991) *Simians, Cyborgs and Women: The Reinvention of Nature* (Routledge).

Haraway, D. (2000) *How Like a Leaf: An Interview with Thyrza Nichols Goodeve* (Routledge).

Hardey, M. (2002) 'Life beyond the screen: embodiment and identity through the internet', *Sociological Review*, 50(4).

Harding, S. (1991) *Whose Science? Whose Knowledge? Thinking from Women's Lives* (Cornell University Press).

Hardt, M., and A. Negri (2000) *Empire* (Harvard University Press).

Hardy, C. (2012) 'Hysteresis', in M. Grenfell (ed.), *Pierre Bourdieu: Key Concepts* (Acumen).

Hareven, T. (1994) 'Aging and generational relations: a historical and life course perspective', *Annual Review of Sociology*, 20.

Hargreaves, J. (1994) *Sporting Females* (Routledge).

Hargreaves, J. (2000) *Heroines of Sport: The Politics of Difference and Identity* (Routledge).

Hargreaves, J., and P. Vertinsky (eds) (2007) *Physical Culture, Power and the Body* (Routledge).

Harkin, J. (2006) 'The baby boomers are an inspiration to us all', *The Independent*, 21 July.

Harkin, J., and J. Huber (2004) *Eternal Youths: How the Baby Boomers Are Having their Time Again* (Demos).

Harré, R., and P. F. Secord (1972) *The Explanation of Social Behaviour* (Blackwell).

Harriss, J. (2002) *Depoliticizing Development: The World Bank and Social Capital* (Anthem Press).

Harriss, J., and P. de Renzio (1997) '"Missing link" or analytically missing? The concept of social capital: an introductory biographic essay', *Journal of International Development*, 9(7).

Hart, H. (1963) *Law, Liberty and Morality* (Oxford University Press).

Hartigan, J. J. (1997) 'Unpopular culture: the case of white trash', *Cultural Studies*, 11(2).

Hartmann, D., and T. T. Swartz (2007) 'The new adulthood: the transition to adulthood from the perspective of transitioning adults', *Advances In Life Course Research*, 11.

Harvey, D. (1989) *The Condition of Postmodernity* (Blackwell).

Haskey, J. (2005) 'Living arrangements in contemporary Britain: having a partner who lives elsewhere and living apart together (LAT)', *Population Trends*, 122(winter).

Hassan, R. (2011) *Suicide Bombings* (Routledge).

Hatcher, R. (1998) 'Class differentiation: rational choices?', *British Journal of Sociology of Education*, 19(1).

Hawking, S. W., and L. Mlodinow (2011) *The Grand Design* (Bantam).

Hay, C. (2007) *Why We Hate Politics* (Polity).

Hay, C., and D. Marsh (eds) (2001) *Demystifying Globalization* (Palgrave).

Hay, D. (2012) 'The spirituality of adults in Britain: recent research', in P. Heelas (ed.), *Spirituality in the Modern World*, Vol. 1 (Routledge).

Haylett, C. (2001) 'Illegitimate subjects? Abject whites, neoliberal modernisation and middle class multiculturalism', *Environment and Planning D: Society and Space*, 19.

Hayward, K., and J. Young (2012) 'Cultural criminology', in M. Maguire, R. Morgan and R. Reiner (eds), *The Oxford Handbook of Criminology* (5th edn, Oxford University Press).

Hazlehurst, J. (2013) 'Spin masters: how PR is taking over the world', *Management Today*, 1 January.

Heaphy, B. (2011) 'Critical relational displays', in E. Dermott and J. Seymour (eds), *Displaying Families: A New Concept for the Sociology of Family Life* (Palgrave Macmillan).

Hearn, J., D. L. Sheppard, P. Tancred-Sheriff and G. Burrell (eds) (1990) *The Sexuality of Organization* (Sage).

Heath, A., and R. Edmondson (1981) 'Oxbridge sociology: the development of centres of excellence?', in P. Abrams, R. Deem, J. Finch and P. Rock (eds), *Practice and Progress: British Sociology 1950–1980* (Allen & Unwin).

Heath, A., and D. McMahon (2005) 'Social mobility of ethnic minorities', in G. Loury, T. Modood and S. Teles (eds), *Ethnicity, Social Mobility and Public Policy* (Cambridge University Press).

Heath, A., C. Rothon and S. Ali (2010) 'Identity and public opinion', in A. Bloch and J. Solomos (eds), *Race and Ethnicity in the 21st Century* (Palgrave).

Heaton, J. (2004) *Reworking Qualitative Data* (Sage).

Heelas, P. (1996) 'On things not being worse, and the ethic of humanity', in P. Heelas, S. Lasch and P. Morris (eds), *De-Traditionalization: Critical Reflections on Authority and Identity* (Blackwell).

Heelas, P. (2002) 'The spiritual revolution. from "religion" to "spirituality"', in L. Woodhead, P. Fletcher, H. Kawanami and D. Smith (eds), *Religions in the Modern World* (Routledge).

Heelas, P. (2006) 'Nursing spirituality', *Spirituality and Health International*, 7.

Heelas, P. (2007) 'The holistic milieu and spirituality: reflections on Voas and Bruce', in K. Flanagan and P. C. Jupp (eds), *A Sociology of Spirituality* (Ashgate).

Heelas, P. (2008) *Spiritualities of Life* (Blackwell).

Heelas, P. (2012a) 'On making some sense of spirituality', in P. Heelas (ed.), *Spirituality in the Modern World: Within Religious Tradition and Beyond* (Routledge).

Heelas, P. (2012b) 'Theorizing the sacred: the role of the implicit in yearning "away"', *Implicit Religion*, 15(4).

Heelas, P. (2013a) 'CAM: healing the person, spiritual humanism, and the cultivation of humanity', in E. Hense, F. Jespers and P. Nissen (eds), *Present Day Spiritualities* (Brill).

Heelas, P. (2013b) 'On transgressing the secular: spiritualities of life, idealism, vitalism', in S. J. Sutcliffe and I. S. Gilhus (eds), *New Age Spirituality: Rethinking Religion* (Acumen).

Heelas, P. (2013c) 'Transpersonal Pakistan', *International Journal of Transpersonal Studies*, 32(2).

Heelas, P., and D. Houtman (2009) 'RAMP findings and making sense of the "God within each person rather than out there"', *Journal of Contemporary Religion*, 24(1).

Heelas, P., and P. Morris (eds) (1992) *The Values of the Enterprise Culture: The Moral Debate* (Routledge).

Heelas, P., and L. Woodhead (with B. Seel, B. Szerszynski and K. Tusting) (2005) *The Spiritual Revolution* (Blackwell).

HEFCE (Higher Education Funding Council for England) (2012) *Young Participation Rates in Higher Education*, www.hefce.ac.uk/pubs/year/2012/201226/.

Heidensohn, F., and M. Silvestri (2012) 'Gender and crime', in M. Maguire, R. Morgan and R. Reiner (eds) *The Oxford Handbook of Criminology* (5th edn, Oxford University Press).

Heinz, W. R., and H. Kruger (2001) 'Life course: innovations and challenges for social research', *Current Sociology*, 49.

Held, D. (1990) 'Democracy and the global system', *Teoria Politica*, 6(3).

Held, D. (1991) 'Democracy, the nation-state and the global system', *Economy and Society*, 20(2).

Held, D., and A. Kaya (eds) (2007) *Global Inequality* (Polity).

Helm, D. (2012) 'Climate policy: the Kyoto approach has failed', *Nature*, 491(7426).

Henderson, K. A., and M. D. Bialeschki (1991) 'A sense of entitlement to leisure as constraint and empowerment for women', *Leisure Sciences*, 13(1).

Hendry, L. B., M. Kloep and S. Olsson (1998) 'Youth, lifestyles and society: a class issue?', *Childhood*, 5(2).

Hendry, L. B., J. Shucksmith, J. G. Love and A. Glendinning (1993) *Young People's Leisure and Lifestyles* (Routledge).

Henry, S., and M. Lanier (eds) (2001) *What is Crime?* (Rowman & Littlefield).

Herbert, M. (2008) 'Adolescence', in M. Davies (ed.), *The Blackwell Companion to Social Work* (3rd edn, Blackwell).

Herbst, S. (1998) *Reading Public Opinion: How Political Actors view the Democratic Process* (University of Chicago Press).

Herman, E., and N. Chomsky (1988) *Manufacturing Consent* (Pantheon Books).

Herrnstein, R. J., and C. M. Murray (1994) *The Bell Curve: Intelligence and Class Structure in American Life* (Free Press).

Herzlich, C. (1973) *Health and Illness* (Academic Press).

Heywood, C. (2001) *A History of Childhood* (Polity).

Heywood, L., and S. L. Dworkin (2003) *Built to Win: The Female Athlete as Cultural Icon* (University of Minnesota Press).

High, S., and D. Lewis (2007) *Corporate Wasteland: The Landscape and Memory of Deindustrialization* (Cornell University Press).

Hill, A. (2007) 'Baby boomers: broke, ailing and anxious', *The Observer*, 10 June.

Hillcoat-Nalletamby, S., and A. Dharmalingam (2003) 'Mid-life parental support for adult children in New Zealand', *Journal of Sociology*, 39(3).

Hills, J. (2010) *An Anatomy of Economic Inequality in the UK: Report of the National Equality Panel*, http://eprints.lse.ac.uk/28344/1/CASEreport60.pdf.

Hillyard, P., C. Pantazis, S. Tombs and D. Gordon (eds) (2004) *Beyond Criminology: Taking Harm Seriously* (Pluto Press).

Hilpern, K. (2008a) 'Generation game', *The Guardian*, 21 August.

Hilpern, K. (2008b) 'Umbilical cords just got longer', *The Guardian*, 10 September.

Hine, C. (2000) *Virtual Ethnography* (Sage).

Hirst, P. (1997) *From Statism to Pluralism: Democracy, Civil Society and Global Politics* (UCL Press).

Hirst, P. (2001) *War and Power in the 21st Century: The State, Military Conflict and the International System* (Polity).

Hirst, P., and G. Thompson (1999) *Globalization in Question: The International Economy and the possibilities of governance* (2nd edn, Polity).

Hirst, P., G. Thompson and S. Bromley (2009) *Globalization in Question: The International Economy and the Possibilities of Governance* (3rd edn, Polity).

Hislop, J., and S. Arber (2003) 'Sleepers wake! The gendered nature of sleep disruption among mid-life women', *Sociology*, 37(4).

Hjorth, L., and S. S. Lim (2012) 'Mobile intimacy in an age of affective mobile media', *Feminist Media Studies*, 12(4).

Hobbes, T. ([1651] 1968) *Leviathan* (Penguin).

Hobsbawm, E., and T. Ranger (eds) (1983) *The Invention of Tradition* (Cambridge University Press).

Hochschild, A. (1983) *The Managed Heart: Commercialization of Human Feeling* (University of California Press).

Hochschild, A. (1989) *The Second Shift: Working Parents and the Revolution at Home* (Viking Penguin).

Hochschild, A. (2003) *The Commercialization of Intimate Life: Notes from Home and Work* (University of California Press).

Hogarth, T., D. Owen, L. Gambin, C. Hasluck, C. Lyonette and B. Casey (2009) *The Equality Impacts of the Current Recession* (Equality and Human Rights Commission).

Holden, A. (2009) *Religious Cohesion in Times of Conflict* (Continuum).

Holland, J., T. Reynolds and S. Weller (2007) 'Transitions, networks and communities: the significance of social capital in the lives of children and young people', *Journal of Youth Studies*, 10(1).

Holland, S. (2010) *Pole Dancing: Empowerment and Embodiment* (Palgrave Macmillan).

Hollis, M., and S. Smith (1991) *Understanding and Explaining International Relations* (Clarendon Press).

Holmes, M. (2006) 'Love lives at a distance: distance relationships over the life course', *Sociological Research Online*, 11(3).

Holmwood, J. (ed.) (2006) *Talcott Parsons* (Ashgate).

Holmwood, J. (2007) 'Sociology as public discourse and professional practice: a critique of Michael Burawoy', *Sociological Theory*, 25(1).

Holmwood, L. (2007) 'Moira Stuart leaves BBC news amid allegations of ageism', *The Guardian*, 4 October.

Holstein, J. (1990) 'The discourse of age in involuntary commitment proceedings', *Journal of Aging Studies*, 4.

Holton, R. (1998) *Globalization and the Nation-State* (Macmillan).

Holton, R., and B. Turner (1994) 'Debate and pseudo-debate in class analysis: some unpromising aspects of Goldthorpe and Marshall's defence', *Sociology*, 28(3).

Home Office (2001) *Making Punishments Work: Report of a Review of the Sentencing Framework for England and Wales* (Home Office).

hooks, b. (2000) *Where We Stand: Class Matters* (Routledge).

Hopper, P. (2003) *Rebuilding Communities in an Age of Individualism* (Ashgate).

Hopper, P. (2006) *Living with Globalization* (Berg).

Horgan, J. (2003) 'The search for the terrorist personality', in A. Silke (ed.), *Terrorist, Victims and Society* (Wiley).

Hough, D. (2013) *Unemployment by Ethnic Background* (House of Commons Library).

Hough, M., and P. Mayhew (1983) *The British Crime Survey* (Home Office).

Houtman, D., and S. Aupers (2007) 'The spiritual turn and the decline of tradition: the spread of post-Christian spirituality in 14 Western countries, 1981–2000', *Journal for the Scientific Study of Religion*, 46(3).

Houtman, D., and P. Mascini (2002) 'Why do churches become empty, while new age grows?', *Journal for the Scientific Study of Religion*, 41(3).

Howe, P. D. (2009) 'Reflexive ethnography, impairment and the pub', *Leisure Studies*, 28(4).

Howson, A. (2005) *Embodying Gender* (Sage).

HSRP (2005) *Human Security Report 2005: War and Peace in the 21st Century* (Oxford University Press).

Hultsman, W. Z. (2012) 'Couple involvement in serious leisure: examining participation in dog agility', *Leisure Studies*, 31(2).

Huntington, S. P. (1996) *The Clash of Civilizations and the Remaking of World Order* (Simon & Schuster).

Hutchinson, J. (2005) *Nations as Zones of Conflict* (Sage).

Hutchinson, J. (2007) 'Warfare, remembrance and national identity', in A. Leoussi and S. Grosby (eds), *Nationalism and Ethno-Symbolism* (Edinburgh University Press).

Hutchinson, J., and A. Smith (eds) (1994) *Nationalism* (Oxford University Press).

Hyman, R. (1987) 'Strategy or structure? Capital, labour and control', *Work, Employment and Society*, 1(1).

IAAF (International Association of Athletics Federations) (2006) *Gender Verification and Sex Reassignment Policy*, www.iaaf.org.

Iacovou, M., and A. J. Skew (2010) 'Household structure in the EU', *ISER Working Paper*, https://www.iser.essex.ac.uk/publications/working-papers/iser/2010–10.

Ibon Foundation (2007) *The Reality of Aid 2006: Focus on Conflict, Security and Development* (Zed Books).

Ignaas, D., and I. Hoyweghen (2011) 'A new era of medical consumption: medicalization revisited', *Aporia*, 3.

Illich, I. (1975) *Medical Nemesis* (Calder & Boyars).

Illouz, E. (1997) 'Who will care for the caretaker's daughter? Towards a sociology of happiness in the era of reflexive modernity', *Theory, Culture and Society*, 14(4).

Inman, P. (2013) 'China overtakes US in world trade', *The Guardian*, 11 February.

Institute of Physics (2012) *It's Different for Girls*, www.iop.org/education/teacher/support/girls_physics/different/page_61620.html.

IPCC (Intergovernmental Panel on Climate Change) (2007) *Fourth Assessment Synthesis Report*, available online.

IPCC (Intergovernmental Panel on Climate Change) (2013) *Climate Change 2013: The Physical Science Basis. Contribution of Working Group I to the Fifth Assessment Report of the Intergovernmental Panel on Climate Change*, available online.

Irigaray, L. (1985a) *Speculum of the Other Woman* (Cornell University Press).

Irigaray, L. (1985b) *This Sex Which is Not One* (Cornell University Press).

Irving, H. R., and A. R. Giles (2011) 'Examining the child's impacts on single mothers' leisure', *Leisure Studies*, 30(3).

Irwin, A. (2001) *Sociology and the Environment: A Critical Introduction to Society, Nature and Knowledge* (Polity).

ITU (International Telecommunication Union) (2010) *The World in 2010: ICT Facts and Figures*, available online.

Jackson, C., and P. Tinkler (2007) '"Ladettes" and "modern girls": troublesome young femininities', *Sociological Review*, 55(2).

Jackson, M. I. (2010) 'A life course perspective on child health, cognition and occupational skill qualifications in adulthood: evidence from a British cohort', *Social Forces*, 89(1).

Jacob, M. (1994) 'Toward a methodological critique of sustainable development,' *Journal of Developing Areas*, 28.

Jacobs, M. (1990) *Sustainable Development: Greening the Economy* (Fabian Society).

Jacobs, M. (1999) 'Sustainable development as a contested concept', in A. Dobson (ed.), *Fairness and Futurity: Essays on Environmental Sustainability and Social Justice* (Oxford University Press).

Jacques, E. (1965) 'Death and the midlife crisis', *Journal of Psychoanalysis*.

Jacques, M. (2012) 'Why do we continue to ignore China's rise? Arrogance', *The Guardian*, 25 March.

James, A., and P. Curtis (2010) 'Family displays and personal lives', *Sociology*, 44(6).

James, W. ([1902] 1974) *The Varieties of Religious Experience* (Collins).

Jameson, F. (1991) *Postmodernism: or, The Cultural Logic of Late Capitalism* (Verso).

Jamieson, L. (1998) *Intimacy: Personal Relationships in Modern Societies* (Polity).

Jamieson, L. (1999) 'Intimacy transformed? A critical look at the "pure relationship"', *Sociology*, 33(3).

Jamieson, L., M. Anderson, D. McCrone, F. Bechofer, R. Stewart and Y. Li (2002) 'Cohabitation and commitment: partnership plans of young men and women', *Sociological Review*, 50(3).

Janssen, D. F. (2009) 'Life course staging as cultural and subjective practice: review, critique and theoretical possibilities', *Culture and Psychology*, 15.

Jary, D., and J. Jary (1999) *Dictionary of Sociology* (3rd edn, Unwin Hyman).

Jefferson, T. (2008) 'Policing the crisis revisited: the state, masculinity, fear of crime and racism', *Crime, Media, Culture*, 4(1).

Jeffreys, S. (2003) 'Sex tourism: do women do it too?', *Leisure Studies*, 22(3).

Jenkins, H. (2006) *Convergence Culture: Where Old and New Media Collide* (New York University Press).

Jenkins, R. (1997) *Rethinking Ethnicity* (Sage).

Jessop, B. (1990) *State Theory: Putting the Capitalist State in its Place* (Polity).

Jessop, B. (2002) *The Future of the Capitalist State* (Polity).

Jivraj, S. (2012) *How Has Ethnic Diversity Grown 1991–2001–2011?*, ESRC Centre on Dynamics of Ethnicity, www.ethnicity.ac.uk.

Jivraj, S. (2013) *How Can We Count Immigration and Integration?*, ESRC Centre on Dynamics of Ethnicity, www.ethnicity.ac.uk.

Joas, H. (2003) *War and Modernity* (Polity).

Johnston, O., J. Reilly and J. Kremer (2004) 'Women's experiences of appearance concern and body control across the lifespan: challenging accepted wisdom', *Journal of Health Psychology*, 9(3).

Jones, C., and T. Novak (1999) *Poverty, Welfare and the Disciplinary State* (Routledge).

Jones, I. (2000) 'A model of serious leisure identification: the case of football fandom', *Leisure Studies*, 19(4).

Juergensmeyer, M. (2003) *Terror in the Mind of God* (University of California Press).

Juravich, T. (2009) *At the Altar of the Bottom Line: The Degradation of Work in the 21st Century* (University of Massachusetts Press).

Justino, P., J. Litchfield and L. Whitehead (2003) *The Impact of Inequality in Latin America*, www.sussex.ac.uk/Units/PRU/wps/wp21.pdf.

Kagan, M. (2011) '10 essential Twitter stats', http://blog.hubspot.com/blog/tabid/6307/bid/12234/10-Essential-Twitter-Stats-Data.aspx.

Kahn, J. S. (2001) *Modernity and Exclusion* (Sage).

Kaldor, M. (2004) 'Nationalism and globalization', *Nations and Nationalism*, 10(1–2).

Kaldor, M. (2007) *New and Old Wars* (2nd edn, Polity).

Kalyvas, S. (2001) '"New" and "old" civil wars: a valid distinction?', *World Politics*, 54.

Kanigel, R. (1997) *The One Best Way: Fredrick Winslow Taylor and the Enigma of Efficiency* (Abacus).

Kaplinsky, R. (2005) *Globalization, Poverty and Inequality* (Polity).

Kaplinsky, R., D. McCormick and M. Morris (2010) 'Impacts and challenges of a growing relationship between China and sub-Saharan Africa', in V. Padayachee (ed.), *The Political Economy of Africa* (Routledge).

Katwala, S. (2012) 'An island story: Boyle's Olympic opening ceremony was irresistibly British', *OpenDemocracy*, 31 July.

Katz, J. (1988) *Seductions of Crime* (Basic Books).

Keane, J. (1988) *Civil Society and the State* (Verso).

Keane, J. (1999) *Civil Society: Old Images, New Visions* (Polity).

Keat, R., and J. Urry (1982) *Social Theory as Science* (2nd edn, Routledge).

Keith, J. (1990) 'Age in social and cultural context: anthropological perspectives', in R. H. Binstock and L. K. George (eds), *Aging in the Social Sciences* (3rd edn, Academic Press).

Kelly, P. (2003) 'Growing up as risky business? Risks, surveillance and the institutionalised mistrust of youth', *Journal of Youth Studies*, 6(2).

Kempson, E., A. Bryson and K. Rowlingson (1994) *Hard Times? How Poor Families Make Ends Meet* (Policy Studies Institute).

Kenshur, O. (1995) 'The allure of the hybrid: Bruno Latour and the search for a new grand theory', *Annals of the New York Academy of Sciences*, 775.

Kerr, C., J. T. Dunlop, F. H. Harbison and C. A. Myers (1960) *Industrialism and Industrial Man* (Harvard University Press).

Kershaw, I. (2009) *Hitler, the Germans, and the Final Solution* (Yale University Press).

Kessler, S. (1998) *Lessons from the Intersexed* (Rutgers University Press).

Kettley, N. (2006) *Educational Attainment and Society* (Continuum).

Kideckel, D. (2008) *Getting by in Postsocialist Romania: Labor, the Body, and Working-Class Culture* (Indiana University Press).

Kiely, R. (1998) 'Introduction: globalisation, (post-)modernity and the Third World', in R. Kiely and P. Marfleet (eds), *Globalisation and the Third World* (Routledge).

Kiernan, B. (2007) *Blood and Soil* (Yale University Press).

King's Fund (2012) *Long-Term Conditions and Mental Health: The Cost of Co-Morbidities*, available online.

Kintisch, E. (2010) 'Bill Gates funding geoengineering research', *Science*, 26 January.

Kirkup, G., A. Zalevski, T. Maruyama and I. Batool (2010) *Women and Men in Science, Engineering and Technology: The UK Statistics Guide 2010* (UKRC).

Kitzinger, J. (1990) 'Audience understandings of AIDS media messages: a discussion of methods', *Sociology of Health & Illness*, 12(3).

Kitzinger, J. (1993) 'Understanding AIDS: media messages and what people know about acquired immune deficiency syndrome', in J. Eldridge (ed.), *Getting the Message* (Routledge).

Kitzinger, J. (1997) 'Who are you kidding? Children, power and the struggle against sexual abuse', in A. James and A. Prout (eds), *Constructing and Reconstructing Children* (Routledge).

Klein, R. (2006) *The New Politics of the National Health Service: From Creation to Reinvention* (5th edn, Radcliffe).

Kleinman, A. (1985) 'Indigenous systems of healing: questions for professional, popular and folk care', in J. Salmon (ed.), *Alternative Medicines: Popular and Policy Perspectives* (Tavistock).

Klugman, K. (1995) *Inside the Mouse: Work and Play at Disney World* (Duke University Press).

Knowles, E., and H. Evans (2012) *PISA 2009: How Does the Social Attainment Gap in England Compare with Countries Internationally?*, Department for Education; available online.

Kobrin, N. H. (2002) 'A psychoanalytic approach to bin Laden, political violence, and Islamic suicidal terrorism', *Clio's Psyche* 8(4).

Koenig, D. (1995) 'Sustainable development: linking global environmental change to technology cooperation', in O. P. Dwivedi and D. K. Vajpeyi (eds), *Environmental Politics in the Third World: A Comparative Analysis* (Greenwood Press).

Kohli, M. (1986) 'Lest we forget: an historical review of the life course', in W. Marshall (ed.), *Later Life: The Social Psychology of Aging* (Sage).

Kok, J. (2007) 'Principles and prospects of the life course paradigm', *Annales de Demographie Historique*, 1.

Kolakowski, L. (1972) *Positivist Philosophy: From Hume to the Vienna Circle* (Penguin).

Konrad, M. (2003) 'From secrets of life to the life of secrets: tracing genetic knowledge as genealogical ethics in biomedical Britain', *Journal of the Royal Anthropological Institute*, 9(2).

Konrad, M. (2005) *Nameless Relations: Anonymity, Melanesia and Reproductive Gift Exchange Between British Ova Donors and Recipients* (Berghahn Books).

Konstam, V. (2010) *Emerging and Young Adulthood: Multiple Perspectives, Diverse Narratives* (Springer).

Kotarba, J. (2005) 'Rock 'n' roll experiences in middle age', *American Behavioral Scientist*, 48(11).

Kraut, R., M. Patterson, V. Landmark, S. Kiesler, T. Mukopadhyay and W. Scherlis (1998) 'Internet paradox: a social technology that reduces social involvement and psychological well-being', *American Psychologist*, 53(9).

Krekula, C. (2007) 'The intersection of age and gender: reworking gender theory and social gerontology', *Current Sociology*, 55.

Krippendorff, K. (2004) *Content Analysis: An Introduction to its Methodology* (2nd edn, Sage).

Kuhn, T. S. (1962) *The Structure of Scientific Revolutions* (University of Chicago Press).

Kumar, K. (2005) *From Post-Industrial to Post-Modern Society: New Theories of the Contemporary World* (Blackwell).

Kunemund, H. (2006) 'Changing welfare states and the "sandwich generation": increasing burden for the next generation', *International Journal of Ageing and Later Life*, 1(2).

Kuznets, S. (1955) 'Economic growth and income inequality', *American Economic Review*, 45(1).

Kymlicka, W. (2003) 'Immigration, citizenship, multiculturalism: exploring the links', *Political Quarterly*, 74(1).

Lacey, N., and L. Zedner (2012) 'Legal constructions of crime', in M. Maguire, R. Morgan and R. Reiner (eds), *The Oxford Handbook of Criminology* (5th edn, Oxford University Press).

Lachkar, J. (2002) 'The psychological make-up of a suicide bomber', *Journal of Psychohistory* 29.

Lakatos, I. (2000) *For and Against Method: Including Lakatos's Lectures on Scientific Method and the Lakatos–Feyerabend Correspondence* (University of Chicago Press).

Lamont, M. (1991) *Money, Morals and Manners: The Culture of the French and the American Upper Middle Class* (University of Chicago Press).

Landes, D. (1998) *The Wealth and Poverty of Nations* (Little, Brown).

Lane, C. (2011) *A Company of One: Insecurity, Independence, and the New World of White-Collar Unemployment* (Cornell University Press).

Lansley, S. (2006) *Rich Britain: The Rise and Rise of the New Super-Wealthy* (Politico's).

Lansley, S. (2012) *The Costs of Inequality: Why Equality is Essential to Economic Recovery. Three Decades of the Super-Rich and the Economy* (Gibson Square).

Large, J., and T. D. Et Sisk (eds) (2006) *Democracy, Conflict and Human Security* (International IDEA).

Larsen, P. C. and M. von Ins (2010) 'The rate of growth in scientific publication and the decline in coverage provided by Science Citation Index', *Scientometrics*, 84(3).

Lasén, A., and E. Casado (2012) 'Mobile telephony and the remediation of couple intimacy', *Feminist Media Studies*, 12(4).

Lash, S., and J. Urry (1987) *The End of Organized Capitalism* (Polity).

Lash, S., and J. Urry (1994) *Economies of Signs and Space* (Sage).

Laslett, P. (1989) *A Fresh Map of Life: The Emergence of the Third Age* (Weidenfeld & Nicolson).

Latour, B. (1987) *Science in Action* (Harvard University Press).

Latour, B. (1991) *We Have Never Been Modern* (Harvard University Press).

Latour, B. (1996) *Aramis or the Love of Technology* (Harvard University Press).

Latour, B. (2010) *The Making of Law: An Ethnography of the Conseil d'Etat* (Polity).

Latour, B. (2013) *An Inquiry into Modes of Existence* (Harvard University Press).

Latour, B., and S. Woolgar (1979) *Laboratory Life: The Social Construction of Scientific Facts* (Sage).

Lauder, H., P. Brown, J. Dillabough and A. H. Halsey (2006) *Education, Globalization, and Social Change* (Oxford University Press).

Laurance, J. (2012) 'One foot in the rave: middle age drug using rising', *The Independent*, 5 April.

Lawson, N. (2009) *An Appeal to Reason: A Cool Look at Global Warming* (Duckworth).

Le Grand, J., C. Propper and S. Smith (2008) *The Economics of Social Problems* (4th edn, Palgrave).

Lea, J., and J. Young (1984) *What is to Be Done about Law and Order?* (Penguin).

Lee, A. (2011) 'Manufacturer Foxconn makes employees sign "no suicide" pact', *Huffington Post*, 6 May.

Lee, N. (2001) *Childhood and Society: Growing Up in an Age of Uncertainty* (Open University Press).

Legrain, P. (2011) 'Progressives should embrace diversity', in M. McTernan (ed.), *Exploring the Cultural Challenges to Social Democracy* (Policy Network).

Leigh, D., and E. Vulliamy (1997) *Sleaze: The Corruption of Parliament* (Fourth Estate).

Lemert, E. (1967) *Human Deviance* (Prentice Hall).

Lenin, V. I. ([1908] 1967) *Materialism and Empirio-Criticism: Critical Comments on a Reactionary Philosophy* (Progress).

Lenin, V. I. ([1918] 1992) *The State and Revolution* (Penguin).

Lentin, A. (2008) *Racism: A Beginner's Guide* (Oneworld).

Levada Center (2011) 'Religious Faith in Russia', online.

Levecque, K., R. Van Rossem, K. De Boyser, S. Van de Velde and P. Bracke (2011) 'Economic hardship and depression across the life course: the impact of welfare state regimes', *Journal of Health and Social Behavior*, 52.

Levene, M. (2005) *Genocide in the Age of the Nation-State*, vol. 2 (I. B. Tauris).

Levin, M., and D. Greenwood (2011) 'Revitalizing universities by reinventing the social sciences: Bildung and action research', in N. Denzin and Y. Lincoln (eds), *Sage Handbook of Qualitative Research* (4th edn, Sage).

Levitas, R. (1998) *The Inclusive Society? Social Exclusion and New Labour* (Palgrave Macmillan).

Levitt, S. D., and S. J. Dubner (2005) *Freakonomics: A Rogue Economist Explores the Hidden Side of Everything* (HarperCollins).

Levy, A. (2005) *Female Chauvinist Pigs: Women and the Rise of Raunch Culture* (Free Press).

Lewin, I. (1985) *The Jewish Community in Poland* (Philosophical Library).

Lewis, J. (2001) *Constructing Public Opinion* (Columbia University Press).

Lewis, O. (1959) *Five Families: Mexican Case Studies in the Culture of Poverty* (Basic Books).

Lewis, O. (1961) *The Children of Sanchez* (Random House).

Lewis, P., and T. Newburn (2011) *Reading the Riots: Investigating England's Summer of Disorder* (Guardian Books).

Leys, C. (2003) *Market-Driven Politics: Neoliberal Democracy and the Public Interest* (Verso).

Liazos, A. (1972) 'The poverty of the sociology of deviance: nuts, sluts, and preverts', *Social Problems*, 20(1).

Lichterman, P. (1996) *The Search for Political Community* (Cambridge University Press).

Lindley, J., and S. Machin (2013) *The Postgraduate Premium: Revisiting Trends in Social Mobility and Educational Inequalities in Britain and America* (Sutton Trust).

Lister, R. (2003) 'Investing in citizen-workers of the future: transformation in citizenship and the state under New Labour', *Social Policy and Administration*, 37(5).

Lister, R. (2004) *Poverty* (Polity).

Livingstone, S. (2008) 'Taking risky opportunities in youthful content creation: teenagers' use of social networking sites for intimacy, privacy and self-expression', *New Media & Society*, 10(3).

Lloyd M. (2007) *Judith Butler* (Polity).

Lockstone-Binney, L., K. Holmes and T. G. Baum (2010) 'Volunteering and volunteers as leisure: social science perspectives', *Leisure Studies*, 29(4).

Lomborg, B. (2001) *The Skeptical Environmentalist: Measuring the Real State of the World* (Cambridge University Press).

Luhmann, N. (1997) *Theory of Society* (Stanford University Press).

Lukács, G. ([1922] 1971) *History and Class Consciousness: Studies in Marxist Dialectics* (Merlin Press).

Lukes, S. (1969) 'Durkheim's "Individualism and the Intellectuals"', *Political Studies*, 17.

Lukes, S. ([1974] 2005) *Power: A Radical View* (2nd edn, Palgrave Macmillan).

Lunkin, R. (2012) 'I believe – I do not believe', *Kommersant*, online.

Lykke, N. (2012) *A Guide to Intersectional Theory, Methodology and Writing* (Routledge).

Lyon, D., and L. Back (2012) 'Fish and fishmongers in a global city: socio-economy, craft, and social relations on a London market', *Sociological Research Online*, 17(2).

Lyotard, J.-F. (1971) *On the Postmodern Condition* (Manchester University Press).

Lyotard, J.-F. (1979) *The Postmodern Condition: A Report on Knowledge* (University of Minnesota Press).

Lyotard, J.-F. (1983) *The Differend: Phrases in Dispute* (University of Minnesota Press).

McAdams, D. P. (1989) 'The biographical consequences of activism', *American Sociological Review*, 54.

McAuley, R. (2007) *Out of Sight: Crime, Youth and Social Exclusion in Modern Britain* (Willan).

McCauley, C. (2002) 'Psychological issues in understanding terrorism and the response to terrorism', in C. Stout (ed.), *The Psychology of Terrorism: Theoretical Understandings and Perspectives* (Praeger).

McClintock, A. (1995) *Imperial Leather: Race, Gender and Sexuality in the Colonial Context* (Routledge).

McCoombs, M. (2014) *Setting the Agenda: Mass Media and Public Opinion* (2nd edn, Polity).

McCormick, J. (1992) *The Global Environmental Movement: Reclaiming Paradise* (Bellhaven Press).

McDowell, L. (2009) *Working Bodies: Interactive Service Employment and Workplace Identities* (Wiley).

McGrew, A., and N. K. Poku (eds) (2007) *Globalization, Development and Human Security* (Polity).

McGuire, B. (2008) *Seven Years to Save the Planet* (Weidenfeld & Nicolson).

McIlwaine, C. (2002) 'Perspectives on poverty, vulnerability and exclusion', in C. McIlwaine and K. Willis (eds), *Challenges and Change in Middle America* (Pearson).

MacInnes, J. (2009) 'Final report: strategic adviser for quantitative methods: proposals to support and improve the teaching of quantitative research methods at undergraduate level in the UK', www.esrc.ac.uk/_images/undergraduate_quantitative_research_methods_ tcm8–2722.pdf.

McIntosh, I., and S. Punch (2009) '"Barter", "deals", "bribes" and "threats": exploring sibling interactions', *Childhood*, 16.

McIntosh, M. (1996) 'Social anxieties about lone motherhood and ideologies of the family: two sides of the same coin', in E. B. Silva (ed.), *Good Enough Mothering? Feminist Perspectives on Lone Motherhood* (Routledge).

MacIntyre, A. C. (1971) *Against the Self-Images of the Age: Essays on Ideology and Philosophy* (Duckworth).

Mack, J., and S. Lansley (1985) *Poor Britain* (Allen & Unwin).

McKay, J. (2004) 'Crises in Africa, Asia and Latin America: lessons and wider implications', in D. Kingsbury, J. Remenyi, J. McKay and J. Hunt (eds), *Key Issues in Development* (Palgrave).

Mackay, M. (2006) 'Many are turning to plastic surgery to avoid age discrimination at work', *The Independent*, 19 March.

McKee, M., and R. Raine (2011) 'Riots on the streets', *British Medical Journal*, 343.

MacKenzie, D., and J. Wajcman (eds) (1999) *The Social Shaping of Technology* (2nd edn, Open University Press).

McKeown, T. (1979) *The Role of Medicine: Dream, Mirage or Nemesis?* (2nd edn, Blackwell Scientific).

McKibben, B. (1990) *The End of Nature* (Penguin).

MacKinnon, C. (1987) *Feminism Unmodified: Discourses on Life and Law* (Harvard University Press).

Macleod, D. (2008) 'In they swoop to direct their children's careers: the helicopter parents have landed', *The Guardian*, 3 January.

McLuhan, M. (1964) *Understanding Media* (Mentor).

Macmillan, R. (2005) 'The structure of the life course: classic issues and current controversies', *Advances In Life Course Research*, 9.

Macmillan, R. (2007) 'Constructing adulthood: agency and subjectivity in the transition to adulthood', *Advances in Life Course Research*, 11.

Macnaghten, P., and J. Urry (1995) 'Towards a sociology of nature', *Sociology*, 29(2).

Macnaghten, P., and J. Urry (1998) *Contested Natures* (Sage).

McNeil, D. (2000) *Bodywork Therapies for Women: A Guide* (Women's Press).

McNeill, W. H. (1979) *A World History* (Oxford University Press).

Macnicol, J. (2010) *Ageism and Age Discrimination: Some Analytical Issues* (ILC).

McPherson, M., L. Smith-Lovin and J. M. Cook (2001) 'Birds of a feather: homophily in social networks', *Annual Review of Sociology*, 27.

Macpherson, W. (1999) *The Stephen Lawrence Inquiry* (HMSO).

McRobbie, A. (2009) *The Aftermath of Feminism: Gender, Culture and Social Change* (Sage).

Macunevich, D. J. (1999) 'The fortune of one's birth: relative cohort size and youth labor in the United States', *Journal of Economics*, 12.

Madge, N. (2005) *Children These Days* (Policy Press).

Maffesoli, M. (2010a) 'Interview with Michel Maffesoli on postmodernity', *Theory, Culture and Society blog*.

Maffesoli, M. (2010b) *Le Temps revient: formes élémentaires de la postmodernité* (Desclée de Brouwer).

Maguire, M. (2012) 'Criminal statistics and the construction of crime', in M. Maguire, R. Morgan and R. Reiner (eds), *The Oxford Handbook of Criminology* (5th edn, Oxford University Press).

Maleckova, J. (2005) 'Improvised terrorists: stereotype or reality', in T. Bjorgo (ed.), *Root Causes of Terrorism* (Routledge).

Malešević, S. (2010) *The Sociology of War and Violence* (Cambridge University Press).

Malešević, S. (2013a) *Nation-States and Nationalisms* (Polity).

Malešević, S. (2013b) 'Forms of brutality: towards a historical sociology of violence', *European Journal of Social Theory*, 16(3).

Malešević, S., and K. Ryan (2013) 'The disfigured ontology of figurational sociology: Norbert Elias and the question of violence', *Critical Sociology*, 39(2).

Maliepaard, M., M. Lubbers and M. Gijsberts (2010) 'Generational differences in ethnic and religious attachment and their interrelation: a study among Muslim minorities in the Netherlands', *Ethnic and Racial Studies*, 33(3).

Malik, K. (1996) *The Meaning of Race* (Macmillan).

Malik, K. (2008) *Strange Fruit* (Oneworld).

Malik, S., P. Wintour and J. Ball (2012) 'Work experience scheme in disarray as Tesco and other retailers change tack', *The Guardian*, 21 February.

Mann, M. (1986) *The Sources of Social Power I* (Cambridge University Press).

Mann, M. (1988) *War, States and Capitalism* (Blackwell).

Mann, M. (1993) *The Sources of Social Power II* (Cambridge University Press).

Mann, M. (2003) *Incoherent Empire* (Verso).

Mann, M. (2005) *The Dark Side of Democracy: Explaining Ethnic Cleansing* (Cambridge University Press).

Mann, M. (2006) 'The sources of power revisited: a response to criticism', in J. A. Hall and R. Schroder (eds), *An Anatomy of Power: The Social Theory of Michael Mann* (Cambridge University Press).

Mann, M. (2008) 'Infrastructural power revisited', *Studies in Comparative International Development* 43.

Mann, M. (2012) *The Sources of Social Power III* (Cambridge University Press).

Mann, M. (2013) *The Sources of Social Power IV* (Cambridge University Press).

Mannheim, K. (1952) 'The problem of generations', in K. Mannheim, *Essays on the Sociology of Knowledge* (Routledge & Kegan Paul).

Mannheim, K. ([1936] 1960) *Ideology and Utopia: An Introduction to the Sociology of Knowledge* (Routledge & Kegan Paul).

Mansfield, L. (2011) '"Sexercise": working out heterosexuality in Jane Fonda's fitness books', *Leisure Studies*, 30(2).

Marcuse, H. (1964) *One-Dimensional Man: Studies in the Ideology of Advanced Capitalist Society* (Beacon Press).

Markham, A. (1998) *Life Online: Researching Real Experience in Virtual Space* (AltaMira Press).

Markham, A., and N. Baym (eds) (2009) *Internet Inquiry: Conversations about Method* (Sage).

Markoff, J. (1996) *The Abolition of Feudalism* (Pennsylvania State University Press).

Marks, E., and I. de Courtviron (1981) *New French Feminisms: An Anthology* (Schocken Books).

Marmot, M. (2004) *Status Syndrome: How your Social Standing Directly Affects your Health* (Bloomsbury).

Marmot, M. (2010) *Post-2010 Strategic Review of Health Inequalities* (The Marmot Review).

Marmot, M., G. Davey Smith, S. Stansfeld, C. Patel, F. North, I. White, E. Brunner and A. Feeney (1991) 'Health inequalities among British civil servants: the Whitehall II study', *The Lancet*, 337.

Marshall, T. H. (1950) *Citizenship and Social Class and Other Essays* (Cambridge University Press).

Martell, L. (1994) *Ecology and Society: An Introduction* (Polity).

Martell, L. (2010) *The Sociology of Globalization* (Polity).

Marx, K. ([1867] 1954) *Capital*, Vol.1 (Lawrence & Wishart).

Marx, K. ([1847] 1976) *The Poverty of Philosophy* (Lawrence & Wishart).

Marx, K. ([1871] 1988) *The Civil War in France: The Paris Commune* (International).

Marx, K. (1999) *Capital* (Oxford University Press).

Marx, K., and F. Engels ([1845] 1970) *The German Ideology: Part One* (Lawrence & Wishart).

Marx, K., and F. Engels ([1848] 1968) *The Communist Manifesto* (Penguin).

Marx, K., and F. Engels ([1848] 2008) *The Communist Manifesto* (Bantam).

Mason, D. (2000) *Race and Ethnicity in Modern Britain* (2nd edn, Oxford University Press).

Mason, J. (2008) 'Tangible affinities and the real life fascination of kinship', *Sociology*, 42(1).

Mason, J. (2011) 'What it means to be related', in V. May (ed.), *Sociology of Personal Life* (Palgrave Macmillan).

Massey, D. (1994) *Space, Place and Gender* (Polity).

Maton, K., and R. Moore (eds) (2010) *Social Realism, Knowledge and the Sociology of Education* (Continuum).

May, V. (2010) 'Lone motherhood as a category of practice', *Sociological Review*, 58(3).

May, V. (2011) 'Introducing a sociology of personal life', in V. May (ed.), *Sociology of Personal Life* (Palgrave Macmillan).

Mayer, K. U. (2003) 'The sociology of the life course and life span psychology: diverging or converging pathways', in U. M. Staudinger and U. Lindenberger (eds), *Understanding Human Development: Dialogues with Lifespan Psychology* (Kluwer Academic).

Mays, N. (2008) 'Origins and development of the National Health Service', in G. Scambler (ed.), *Sociology as Applied to Medicine* (6th edn, Elsevier).

Mead, G. H. (1934) *Mind, Self and Society* (University of Chicago Press).

Mechanic, D., and E. H. Volkart (1960) 'Illness behavior and medical diagnoses', *Journal of Health and Human Behavior*, 1(2).

Meillassoux, C. (1981) *Maidens, Meal and Money: Capitalism and the Domestic Community* (Cambridge University Press).

Menand, L. (ed.) (1998) *The Future of Academic Freedom* (University of Chicago Press).

Mennell, S. (2007) *The American Civilizing Process* (Polity).

Mennesson, C. (2000) '"Hard women" and "soft" women: the social construction of identity among female boxers', *International Review for the Sociology of Sport*, 35(1).

Merck, M. (2010) 'The question of Caster Semenya', *Radical Philosophy*, March/April.

Merleau-Ponty, M. (1962) *Phenomenology of Perception* (Routledge).

Merrick, J., and M. Chorley (2012) 'Osborne accused over gas lobbyist father-in-law', *The Independent*, 29 July.

Merton, R. K. (1938) 'Social structure and anomie', *American Sociological Review*, 3.

Merton, R. K. ([1942] 1957) *Social Theory and Social Structure* (2nd edn, Free Press).

Merton, R. K. ([1942] 1973) *The Sociology of Science: Theoretical and Empirical Investigations* (University of Chicago Press).

Messner, S., and R. Rosenfeld (2006) *Crime and the American Dream* (4th edn, Wadsworth).

Meyer, A. (2007) 'The moral rhetoric of childhood', *Childhood*, 14.

Meyer, J. (1980) 'The world polity and the authority of the nation-state', in A. Bergeson (ed.), *Studies of the Modern World System* (Academic Press).

Midgley, M. (2001) *Science and Poetry* (Routledge).

Midgley, M. (2010) *The Solitary Self: Darwin and the Selfish Gene* (Acumen).

Milanović, B. (2005) *Worlds Apart: Measuring International and Global Inequality* (Princeton University Press).

Miles, R. (1989) *Racism* (Routledge).

Miles, R. (1993) *Racism after 'Race Relations'* (Routledge).

Miliband, R., and N. Poulantzas (1972) 'The problem of the capitalist state', in R. Blackburn (ed.), *Ideology in Social Science: Readings in Critical Social Theory* (Pantheon Books).

Mill, J. S. ([1859] 1998) *On Liberty* (Oxford University Press).

Millburn, A. (2012) *Fair Access to Professional Careers* (Social Mobility and Child Poverty Commission).

Millennium Ecosystem Assessment (2005) *Living Beyond Our Means: Natural Assets and Human Well-Being* (UNEP).

Miller, D. (1993) 'Official sources and primary definition: the case of Northern Ireland', *Media, Culture and Society*, 15(3).

Miller, D. (1994a) *Don't Mention the War: Northern Ireland, Propaganda and the Media* (Pluto Press).

Miller, D. (1994b) 'Understanding "terrorism": US and British audience interpretations of the televised conflict in Ireland', in M. Aldridge and N. Hewitt (eds), *Controlling Broadcasting: Access, Policy and Practice in North America and Europe* (Manchester University Press).

Miller, D. (1995a) *On Nationality* (Oxford University Press).

Miller, D. (1995b) 'Reflections on British national identity', *New Community*, 21(2).

Miller, D. (1997) 'Dominant ideologies and media power: the case of Northern Ireland', in M. Kelly and B. O'Connor (eds), *Media Audiences in Ireland* (University College Dublin Press).

Miller, D. (1998) 'Promotional strategies and media power', in A. Briggs and P. Cobley (eds), *The Media: An Introduction* (Longman).

Miller, D. (2004a) 'System failure: it's not just the media – the whole political system has failed', *Journal of Public Affairs*, 4(4).

Miller, D. (2004b) 'The propaganda machine', in D. Miller (ed.), *Tell Me Lies: Media and Propaganda in the Attack on Iraq* (Pluto).

Miller, D. (2006) 'Multiculturalism and the welfare state: theoretical reflections', in K. Banting and W. Kymlicka (eds), *Multiculturalism and the Welfare State* (Oxford University Press).

Miller, D. (2008) 'Corporate lobbying's new frontier: from influencing policy-making to shaping public debate', in D. Zinnbauer (ed.), *Global Corruption Report* (Cambridge University Press).

Miller, D., and W. Dinan (2000) 'The rise of the PR industry in Britain 1979–1998', *European Journal of Communication*, 15(1).

Miller, D., and W. Dinan (2003) 'Global public relations and global capitalism', in D. Demers (ed.), *Terrorism, Globalization and Mass Communication* (Marquette Books).

Miller, D., and W. Dinan (2008) 'Journalism, public relations and spin', in K. Wahl-Jorgensen and T. Hanitzsch (eds), *Handbook of Journalism Studies* (Routledge).

Miller, D., and W. Dinan (2009) 'Revolving doors, accountability and transparency: emerging regulatory concerns and policy solutions in the financial crisis', paper prepared for the OECD and the Dutch National Integrity Office organized Global Forum on Public Governance 'Building a Cleaner World: Tools and Good Practices for Fostering a Culture of Integrity', Paris, 4–5 May.

Miller, D., and C. Harkins (2010) 'Corporate strategy and corporate capture: food and alcohol industry and lobbying and public health', *Critical Social Policy*, 30(4).

Miller, D., J. Kitzinger, K. Williams and P. Beharrell (1998) *The Circuit of Mass Communication: Media Strategies, Representation and Audience Reception in the AIDS Crisis* (Sage).

Miller, S. M. (1996) 'The great chain of poverty explanations', in E. Oyen, S. M. Miller and S. A. Samad (eds), *Poverty: A Global Review Handbook of International Poverty Research* (Scandinavian University Press).

Miller, T. (2007) '"Is this what motherhood is all about?" Weaving experiences and discourse through transition to first-time motherhood', *Gender & Society*, 21.

Miller, T. (2010) *Making Sense of Fatherhood: Gender, Caring and Work* (Cambridge University Press).

Miller, T. (2011) 'Falling back into gender? Men's narratives and practices around first-time fatherhood', *Sociology*, 45(6).

Mills, C. W. (1956) *The Power Elite* (Oxford University Press).

Mills, C. W. (1959a) *The Sociological Imagination* (Oxford University Press).

Mills, C. W. (1959b) 'On intellectual craftmanship', in L. Gross (ed.), *Symposium on Sociological Theory* (Row, Peterson).

Minichiello, V., J. Browne and H. Kendig (2000) 'Perceptions and consequences of ageism: views of older people', *Ageing and Society*, 20(3).

Ministry of Health (1944) 'A National Health Service', Cmnd 6502 (HMSO).

Mintel (2001) *Extreme Sports* (Mintel International Group).

Mintel (2003) *Teenage Shopping Habits* (Mintel International Group).

Mitchell, J (1971) *Women's Estate* (Penguin).

Modood, T. (1998) 'Ethnic diversity and racial disadvantage in employment', in T. Blackstone, B. Parekh and P. Sanders (eds), *Race Relations in Britain* (Routledge).

Modood, T (2005) 'Remaking multiculturalism after 7/7, *openDemocracy*, 29 September.

Modood, T. (2013) *Multiculturalism* (2nd edn, Polity).

Modood, T., R. Berthoud, J. Lakey, J. Nazroo, P. Smith, S. Virdee and S. Beishon (1997) *Ethnic Minorities in Britain* (Policy Studies Institute).

Mohan, G., E. Brown, B. Milward and A. B. Zack-Williams (2000) *Structural Adjustment: Theory, Practice and Impacts* (Routledge).

Moi, T. (1999) *What is a Woman? and Other Essays* (Oxford University Press).

Mol, A. (2003) *The Body Multiple: Ontology in Medical Practice* (Duke University Press).

Molgat, M. (2007) 'Do transitions and social structures matter? How "emerging adults" define themselves as adults', *Journal of Youth Studies*, 10(5).

Monbiot, G. (2000) *Captive State: The Corporate Takeover of Britain* (Macmillan).

Moog, S., and R. Stones (eds) (2009) *Nature, Social Relations and Human Needs: Essays in Honour of Ted Benton* (Palgrave).

Moore, K., P. Mason and J. Lewis (2008) *Images of Islam in the UK: The Representation of British Muslims in the National News Print Media, 2000–2008* (Cardiff School of Journalism, Media and Cultural Studies).

Moore, R. (2009) *Sociology of Knowledge and Education* (Continuum).

Moore, R. (2012) 'Social realism and the problem of the problem of knowledge in the sociology of education', *British Journal of Sociology of Education*, 34(3).

Moore, R. (2013) *Basil Bernstein: The Thinker and the Field* (Routledge).

Moore, R., and J. Muller (2002) 'The growth of knowledge and the discursive gap', *British Journal of Sociology of Education*, 23(4).

Morais, A., and P. Neves (2006) 'Teachers as creators of social contexts for scientific education: new approaches for teacher education', in R. Moore, M. Arnot, J. Beck and H. Daniels (eds), *Knowledge, Power and Educational Reform: Applying the Sociology of Basil Bernstein* (Routledge).

Morey, P., and A. Yaqin (2011) *Framing Muslims* (Harvard University Press).

Morgan, D. (1996) *Family Connections* (Polity).

Morgan, D. (2011) *Rethinking Family Practices* (Palgrave Macmillan).

Morgenthau, H. (1948) *Politics among Nations* (Alfred Knopf).

Morgenthau, H. (1951) *In Defense of the National Interest* (Alfred Knopf).

Morley, D., and K. Robins (1995) *Spaces of Identity* (Routledge).

Morrell, G., S. Scott, D. McNeish and S. Webster (2011) *The August Riots in England: Understanding the Involvement of Young People* (National Centre for Social Research).

Morris, L. (1994) *Dangerous Classes: The Underclass and Social Citizenship* (Routledge).

Mount, F. (2004) *Mind the Gap: Class in Britain Now* (Short Books).

Mueller, J. (2004) *The Remnants of War* (Cornell University Press).

Mulcahy, C. M. (2008) 'Ladies of leisure: parks, policy, and the problem of prostitution', *Journal of Unconventional Parks, Tourism & Recreation Research*, 1(1).

Muller, J. (2004) 'Introduction: the possibilities of Basil Bernstein', in J. Muller, B. Davies and A. Morais (eds), *Reading Bernstein, Researching Bernstein* (RoutledgeFalmer).

Mulvey, L. (1975) 'Visual pleasure and narrative cinema', *Screen*, 16(3).

Münkler, H. (2005) *The New Wars* (Polity).

Murphy, R. (1994a) *Rationality and Nature* (Westview Press).

Murphy, R. (1994b) 'The sociological construction of science without nature', *Sociology*, 28(4).

Murphy, R. (1997) *Sociology and Nature: Social Action in Context* (Westview Press).

Murphy, R. (2002) 'Ecological materialism and the sociology of Max Weber', in R. E. Dunlap, F. H. Buttel, P. Dickens and A. Gijswijt (eds), *Sociological Theory and the Environment: Classical Foundations, Contemporary Insights* (Rowman & Littlefield).

Murray, C. A. (1984) *Losing Ground: American Social Policy, 1950–1980* (Basic Books).

Murray, P. (2002) *Disabled Teenagers' Experiences of Access to Inclusive Leisure* (Joseph Rowntree Foundation).

Naess, A. (1973) 'The shallow and the deep, long-range ecology movement', *Inquiry*, 16.

Najam, A., S. Huq and Y. Sokona (2003) 'Climate negotiations beyond Kyoto: developing countries concerns and interests', *Climate Policy*, 3.

Narayan, D., R. Chambers, M. K. Shah and P. Petesch (2000) *Voices of the Poor: Crying Out for Change* (Oxford University Press).

NASA (2012) 'NASA finds 2011 ninth-warmest year on record', www.nasa.gov/topics/earth/features/2011-temps.html.

Nayyar, D. (2003) 'Globalization and development', in H.-J. Chang (ed.) *Rethinking Development Economics* (Anthem Press).

Nead, L. (1988) *Myths of Sexuality: Representations of Women in Victorian Britain* (Blackwell).

Neate, P. (2007) 'Generation X: the slackers who changed the world', *The Independent*, 18 February.

Nederveen Pieterse, J. (2001) *Development Theory* (Sage).

Nederveen Pieterse, J. (2012) 'Global rebalancing: crisis and the East–South turn', in J. Nederveen Pieterse and J. Kim (eds), *Globalization and Development in East Asia* (Routledge).

Negri, A., with R. V. Scelsi (2008) *Goodbye Mr Socialism: Radical Politics in the 21st Century* (Profile Books).

Nelken, David (2012) 'Corporate and white-collar crime', in M. Maguire, R. Morgan and R. Reiner (eds), *The Oxford Handbook of Criminology* (5th edn, Oxford University Press).

Nelkin, Dorothy (2004) 'God talk: confusion between science and religion – posthumous essay', *Science Technology & Human Values*, 29(2).

Nelson, J. (1989) *Sultans of Sleaze: Public Relations and the Media* (Between the Lines).

Neugarten, B. L. (1968) 'Adult personality: towards a psychology of the lifecycle', in B. L. Neugarten (ed.), *Middle Age and Aging: A Reader in Social Psychology* (University of Chicago Press).

Newton, T. (2003) 'Truly embodied sociology: marrying the social and the biological', *Sociological Review*, 51(1).

Nichols, T. (1997) *The Sociology of Industrial Injury* (Mansell).

Nicholson, L. (1986a) 'Interpreting gender', *Signs*, 29(1).

Nicholson, L. (1986b) *Gender and History* (Columbia University Press).

Nickson, D., C. Warhurst and E. Dutton (2005) 'The importance of attitude and appearance in the service encounter in retail and hospitality', *Managing Service Quality*, 15(2).

Nikander, P. (2009) 'Doing change and continuity: age identity and the micro–macro divide', *Ageing and Society*, 29.

Nolan, B., and C. T. Whelan (1996) *Resources, Deprivation and Poverty* (Clarendon Press).

Nordqvist, P. (2012) '"I don't want us to stand out more than we already do": lesbian couples negotiating family connections in donor conception', *Sexualities*, 15(5/6).

Norgaard, K. M. (2011) *Living in Denial: Climate Change, Emotions, and Everyday Life* (MIT Press).

Norton, A., with B. Bird, K. Brock, M. Kakander and C. Turk (2001) *A Rough Guide to PPAS* (Overseas Development Institute).

Novak, M. (1996) 'Concepts of poverty', in E. Oyen, S. M. Miller and S. A. Samad (eds), *Poverty: A Global Review Handbook of International Poverty Research* (Scandinavian University Press).

Nowotny, H., P. Scott and M. Gibbons (2001) *Rethinking Science: Knowledge and the Public in an Age of Uncertainty* (Polity).

Nussbaum, M. (2000) *Women and Human Development: The Capabilities Approach* (Cambridge University Press).

Nussbaum, M. (2013) *Political Emotions: Why Love Matters for Justice* (Harvard University Press).

O'Byrne, D. J. (1997) 'Working-class culture: local community and global conditions', in J. Eade (ed.), *Living the Global City: Globalization as Local Process* (Routledge).

O'Byrne, D. J. (2003) *The Dimensions of Global Citizenship: Political Identity Beyond the Nation-State* (Frank Cass).

O'Byrne, D. J., and A. Hensby (2011) *Theorizing Global Studies* (Palgrave Macmillan).

O'Connor, J. (1998) *Natural Causes: Essays in Ecological Marxism* (Guilford Press).

O'Donnell, M. (2007) 'We need human rights not nationalism "lite": globalization and British solidarity', *Ethnicities*, 7(2).

O'Rand, A. M. (1996) 'The precious and the precocious: understanding cumulative disadvantage and advantage over the life course', *The Gerontologist*, 36(2).

O'Riordan, T. (ed.) (1995) *Environmental Science for Environmental Management* (Longman).

Oakes, G. (1975) 'Introductory essay', in M. Weber, *Roscher and Knies: The Logical Problems of Historical Economics* (Free Press).

Oakley, A. (1972) *Sex, Gender and Society* (Temple Smith).

Oakley, A. (1974a) *Housewife* (Penguin).

Oakley, A. (1974b) *The Sociology of Housework* (Martin Robertson).

Oakley, A. (1980) *Women Confined: Towards a Sociology of Childbirth* (Martin Robertson).

Oakley, A. (1981) *Subject Woman* (Martin Robertson).

Obel, C. (1996) 'Collapsing gender in competitive bodybuilding', *International Review for the Sociology of Sport*, 31(2).

Oberschall, A. (1965) *Empirical Social Research in Germany* (Mouton).

Oberschall, A. (ed.) (1972) *The Establishment of Empirical Sociology* (Harper & Row).

OECD (2008) *Growing Unequal? Income Distribution and Poverty in OECD Countries* (OECD).

OECD (2011) *Doing Better for Families* (OECD).

Ohmae, K. (1990) *The Borderless World: Power and Strategy in the Interlinked Economy* (Collins).

Oliver, M. (1995) *Understanding Disability: From Theory to Practice* (Palgrave Macmillan).

Omi, M., and H. Winant (1994) *Racial Formation in the United States* (2nd edn, Routledge).

ONS (Office for National Statistics) (2006) *The Time Use Survey, 2005: How We Spend Our Time*, available online.

ONS (Office for National Statistics) (2008) *Life Expectancy: Life Expectancy Continues to Rise*, available online.

ONS (Office for National Statistics) (2011) *Trends in Life Expectancy by the National Statistics Socio-Economic Classification 1982–2006*, available online.

ONS (Office for National Statistics) (2012a) *Ethnicity and National Identity in England and Wales 2011*, available online.

ONS (Office for National Statistics) (2012b) *Wealth in Great Britain, Wave 2, 2008–2010*, available online.

ONS (Office for National Statistics) (2013a) *Crime in England and Wales: Statistical Bulletin*, available online.

ONS (Office for National Statistics) (2013b) *Young People Not in Education, Employment or Training (NEET)*, August, www.ons.gov.uk/ons/dcp171778_324364.pdf.

Oreskes, N., and E. M. Conway (2010) *Merchants of Doubt: How a Handful of Scientists Obscured the Truth on Issues from Tobacco Smoke to Global Warming* (Bloomsbury).

Ortner, S. (1974) 'Is female to male as nature to culture?', in M. Z. Rosaldo and L. Lamphere (eds), *Women, Culture and Society* (Stanford University Press).

Osgerby, B. (2004) *Youth Media* (Routledge).

Osgood, D. W., E. M. Foster, C. Flanagan and G. R. Ruth (eds) (2005) *On Your Own Without a Net: The Transition to Adulthood for Vulnerable Populations* (University of Chicago Press).

Otterbein, K. F. (2004) *How War Began* (Texas A&M University Press).

Otto, S. L. (2011) 'Science in America: decline and fall', *New Scientist*, 2836.

Outhwaite, W. (1999) 'The myth of modernist method', *European Journal of Social Theory*, 2(1).

Outhwaite, W. (2008) 'European civil society and the European intellectual: what is, and how does one become, a European intellectual?', in C. Fleck, A. Hess and E. S. Lyon (eds), *Intellectuals and their Publics: Perspectives from the Social Sciences* (Ashgate).

Pahl, J. (1980) 'Patterns of money management within marriage', *Journal of Social Policy*, 9(3).

Pahl, J. (2000) 'Our changing lives', in D. Dench (ed.), *Grandmothers of the Revolution* (HERA Trust with Institute of Community Studies).

Pahl, J. (2005) 'Individualization in couple finances: who pays for the children?', *Social Policy and Society*, 4.

Pahl, R. (1970) *Patterns of Urban Life* (Longman).

Pahl, R., and D. Pevalin (2005) 'Between family and friends: a longitudinal study of friendship choice', *British Journal of Sociology*, 56(3).

Pakulski, J., and M. Waters (1996) *The Death of Class* (Sage).

Pallett, T. V., S. G. B. Roberts and R. I. M. Dunbar (2011) ' Use of social networks and instant messenger does not lead to increased offline network size, or to emotionally closer relationships with offline network members', *Cyberpsychology, Behaviour and Social Networks*, 14(4).

Pape, R. (2005) *Dying to Win: The Strategic Logic of Suicide Terrorism* (Random House).

Parekh, B. (1998) 'Integrating minorities', in T. Blackstone, B. Parekh and P. Sanders (eds), *Race Relations in Britain* (Routledge).

Parekh, B. (2000) *The Future of Multi-Ethnic Britain* (Profile).

Pareto, V. (1935) *The Mind and Society*, Vol. 1: *Non-Logical Conduct* (Harcourt, Brace, Jovanovich).

Paris, R. (2001) 'Human security: paradigm shift or hot air', *International Security*, 26(2).

Parker, S. (1971) *The Future of Work and Leisure* (MacGibbon & Kee).

Parkin, F. (1979) *Marxism and Class Theory* (Tavistock).

Parsons, H. (ed.) (1977) *Marx and Engels on Ecology* (Greenwood Press).

Parsons, T. (1937) *The Structure of Social Action* (Free Press).

Parsons, T. (1951) *The Social System* (Free Press).

Parsons, T. (1960) 'Pattern variables revisited; a response to Robert Dubin', *American Sociological Review*, 25(4).

Parsons, T. (1978) 'A 1974 retrospective perspective', in R. Grathoff (ed.), *The Correspondence of Alfred Schutz and Talcott Parsons: The Theory of Social Action* (Indiana University Press).

Parsons, T., R. F. Bales and E. A. Shils (1953) *Working Papers in the Theory of Action* (Free Press).

Partington, E., S. Partington, L. Fishwick and L. Allin (2005) 'Mid-life nuances and negotiations: narrative maps and the social construction of mid-life in sport and physical activity', *Sport, Education and Society*, 10(1).

Pateman, C. (1988) *The Sexual Contract* (Polity).

Paton, G. (2013) '"Brian Cox effect" leads to surge in demand for physics', *Daily Telegraph*, 11 January.

Payne, G., and M. Williams (2011) *Teaching Quantitative Methods* (Sage).

Peach, C. (2007) 'Muslim population of Europe: a brief overview of demographic trends and socioeconomic integration, with particular reference to Britain', in S. Angenendt, P. M. Barrett, J. Laurence, C. Peach, J. Smith and T. Winter, *Muslim Integration: Challenging Conventional Wisdom in Europe and the United States* (Center for Strategic and International Studies); available online.

Pearce, D., A. Markandya and E. B. Barbier (1989) *Blueprint for a Green Economy* (Earthscan).

Pemberton, S., E. Sutton and E. Fahmy (2013) *A Review of the Qualitative Evidence Relating to the Experience of Poverty and Exclusion* (PSE UK).

Perfect, D. (2013) *Gender Pay Gaps 2012* (EHRC).

Perlin, R. (2011) *Intern Nation: How to Earn Nothing and Learn Little in the Brave New Economy* (Verso).

Peterson, R., and R. Kern (1996) 'Changing highbrow taste: from snob to omnivore', *American Sociological Review*, 61.

Pew Research Center (2010) 'Sufi orders', *Religion and Public Life Project*, available online.

Pew Research Center (2012) '"Nones" on the rise', 9 October, available online.

Phillips, A. (ed.) (1998) *Feminism and Politics* (Oxford University Press).

Phillips, T. (2004) 'Multiculturalism's legacy is "have a nice day" racism', *The Guardian*, 28 May.

Phillipson, C. (2007) 'Understanding the baby boom generation: comparative perspectives', *International Journal of Ageing and Late Life*, 2(2).

Phillipson, C., R. Leach, A. Money and S. Biggs (2008) 'Social and cultural constructions of ageing: the case of the baby boomers', *Sociological Research Online*, 13(3).

Philo, G. (1990) *Seeing and Believing* (Routledge).

Philo, G. (1995) 'Television, politics and the rise of the New Right', in G. Philo (ed.), *Glasgow Media Group Reader*, Vol. 2: *Industry, Economy, War and Politics* (Routledge).

Philo, G. (ed.) (1996) *Media and Mental Distress* (Longman).

Philo, G., and M. Berry (2006) *Israel and Palestine* (Pluto Press).

Philo, G., and M. Berry (2011) *More Bad News from Israel* (Pluto Press).

Philo, G., and D. Miller (2001) *Market Killing* (Longman).

Piachaud, D. (1987) 'Problems in the definition and measurement of poverty', *Journal of Social Policy*, 16 (2).

Picciotto, R., and R. Weaving (eds) (2006) *Security and Development* (Routledge).

Picciotto, R., F. Olonisakin and M. Clarke (2007) *Global Development and Human Security* (Transaction).

Pierce, T. (2009) 'Social anxiety and technology: face-to-face communication versus technological communication among teens', *Computers in Human Behaviour*, 25.

Pigott, R. (2006) 'Religions united in struggling with falling attendance', *The Edge*, 22.

Pilcher, J. (1994) 'Mannheim's sociology of generations: an undervalued legacy', *British Journal of Sociology*, 45(3).

Pilcher, J. (2000) 'Domestic divisions of labour in the twentieth century: "change slow-a-coming"', *Work, Employment and Society*, 14(4).

Pilgrim, D., and A. Rogers (1993) *A Sociology of Mental Health and Illness* (Open University Press).

Pilkington, A. (1984) *Race Relations in Britain* (University Tutorial Press).

Pilkington, A. (2003) *Racial Disadvantage and Ethnic Diversity in Britain* (Palgrave).

Pilkington, A. (2005) 'Social cohesion, racial equality and ethnic diversity', in M. Holborn (ed.), *Developments in Sociology* (Causeway Press).

Pilkington, A. (2007) 'In defence of both multiculturalism and progressive nationalism: a response to Mike O'Donnell', *Ethnicities*, 7(2).

Pilkington, A. (2008a) 'From institutional racism to community cohesion: the changing nature of racial discourse', *Sociological Research Online*, 13(3).

Pilkington, A. (2008b) 'Beyond political correctness?', *International Journal of Interdisciplinary Social Sciences*, 2(4).

Pilkington, A. (2009) 'New Labour and the new integrationism', in A. Pilkington, S. Housee and K. Hylton (eds), *Race(ing) Forward: Transitions in Theorising 'Race' in Education* (Higher Education Academy).

Pilkington, A. (2011) *Institutional Racism in the Academy* (Trentham Books).

Pinch, T. J. (1986) *Confronting Nature: The Sociology of Solar-Neutrino Detection* (D. Reidel).

Pink, S. (2007) *Doing Visual Ethnography: Images, Media and Representation in Research* (2nd edn, Sage).

Pinker, R. (1999) 'Do poverty definitions matter?', in D. Gordon and P. Spicker (eds), *The International Glossary on Poverty* (Zed Books).

Pinker, S. (2011) *The Better Angels of our Nature: The Decline of Violence and its Causes* (Allen Lane).

Pipes, D. (2010) 'Muslims going less to mosques in Europe', *Daniel Pipes*, 31 May, www.danielpipes.org/blog/.

Platt, L. (2005) *Migration and Social Mobility* (Joseph Rowntree Foundation).

Platt, L. (2011) *Understanding Inequalities* (Polity).

Plunkett, J. (2012) 'Miriam O'Reilly: there was seething resentment when I went back to the BBC', *The Guardian*, 25 March.

Poggi, G. (2001) *Forms of Power* (Polity).

Polsky, N. (1967) *Hustlers, Beats and Others* (Penguin).

Pooley, C. J., Turnbull, J., and M. Adams (2005) '". . . Everywhere she went I had to tag along beside her": family, life course and mobility in England since the 1940s', *History of the Family*, 10.

Popper, K. ([1957] 1961) *The Poverty of Historicism* (2nd edn, Routledge).

Potter, J., and A. Hepburn (2005) 'Qualitative interviews in psychology: problems and possibilities', *Qualitative Research in Psychology*, 2(4).

Power, S., and G. Whitty (2006) 'Education and the middle class: a complex but crucial case for the sociology of education', in H. Lauder, P. Brown, J. Dillabough and A. H. Halsey (eds), *Education, Globalization, and Social Change* (Oxford University Press).

Price, J., and M. Shildrick (1999) *Feminist Theory and the Body: A Reader* (Edinburgh University Press).

Provost, C. (2013) 'Migrants' billions put aid in the shade', *The Guardian*, 30 January.

Provost, C., and R. Harris (2013) 'China commits billions in aid to Africa as part of charm offensive', *The Guardian*, 29 April.

Purdam, K., R. Afkhami, A. Crockett and W. Olsen (2007) 'Religion in the UK: an overview of equality statistics and evidence gaps', *Journal of Contemporary Religion*, 22(2).

Putnam, R. D. (2000) *Bowling Alone: The Collapse and Revival of American Community* (Simon & Schuster).

Putnam, R. D. and D. E. Campbell (2010) *American Grace: How Religion Divides and Unites Us* (Simon & Schuster).

Quine, W. V. O. (1951) 'Two dogmas of empiricism', *Philosophical Review*, 60.

Qvortrup, J. (1997) 'A voice for children in statistical and social accounting: a plea for children to be heard', in A. James and A. Prout (eds), *Constructing and Reconstructing Children* (RoutledgeFalmer).

Rabinow, P. (1996) *Making PCR: A Story of Biotechnology* (University of Chicago Press).

Ragin, C. (2008) *Redesigning Social Inquiry* (University of Chicago Press).

Ramesh, R. (2011) 'The child poverty map of Britain', *The Guardian*, 23 February.

Rampino, T., and M. Taylor (2012) *Educational Aspirations and Attitudes over the Business Cycle* (University of Essex, Institute for Economic and Social Research).

Rapley, T. (2001) 'The art(fulness) of open-ended interviewing: some considerations on analyzing interviews', *Qualitative Research*, 1(3).

Raskin, P., T. Banuri, G. Gallopin, P. Gutman, A. Hammond, R. Kates and R. Swart (2002) *Great Transition: The Promise and Lure of the Times Ahead* (Stockholm Environment Institute).

Rata, E. (2012) *The Politics of Knowledge in Education* (Routledge).

Raunig, G. (2007) *Art and Revolution: Transversal Activism in the Long Twentieth Century* (Semiotext(e)).

Ray, L. (2007) *Globalization and Everyday Life* (Routledge).

Ray, L., and M. Reed (eds) (1994) *Organizing Modernity: New Weberian Perspectives on Work, Organization and Society* (Routledge).

Reality of Aid (2006) *2006 Report – Facts and Figures*, www.ccic.ca/_files/en/what_we_do/002_aid_roa_2006_facts_and_figures.pdf.

Reason, P., and H. Bradbury (eds) (2001) *Handbook of Action Research: Participative Inquiry and Practice* (Sage).

Reay, D. (1998) *Class Work: Mother's Involvement in their Children's Primary Schooling* (UCL Press).

Reay, D. (2004) 'Gendering Bourdieu's concept of capitals? Emotional capital, women and social class', in L. Adkins and B. Skeggs (eds), *Feminism after Bourdieu* (Blackwell).

Reay, D. (2005) 'Doing the dirty work of social class? Mothers' work in support of their children's schooling', in M. Glucksmann., L. Pettinger and J. West (eds), *A New Sociology of Work* (Blackwell).

Reay, D., G. Crozier and D. James (2011) *White Middle-Class Identities and Urban Schooling* (Palgrave Macmillan).

Reay, D., M. David and S. J. Ball (2005) *Degrees of Choice: Class, Race and Gender in Higher Education* (Trentham Books).

Redclift, M. R. (2002) 'Sustainable development', in V. Desai and R. B. Potter (eds), *The Companion to Development Studies* (Arnold).

Reicher, S., and C. Stott (2011) *Mad Mobs and Englishmen? Myths and Realities of the 2011 Riots* (Constable & Robinson).

Reiman, J. (2004) *The Rich Get Richer and the Poor Get Prison* (7th edn, Allyn & Bacon).

Reiner, R. (2002) 'Classical social theory and law', in J. Penner, D. Schiff and R. Nobles (eds), *Jurisprudence* (Butterworths).

Reiner, R. (2007) *Law and Order: An Honest Citizen's Guide to Crime and Control* (Polity).

Reiner, R. (2010) *The Politics of the Police* (4th edn, Oxford University Press).

Reiner, R. (2012) 'Political economy, crime and criminal justice', in M. Maguire, R. Morgan and R. Reiner (eds), *The Oxford Handbook of Criminology* (5th edn, Oxford University Press).

Reisz, M. (2012) 'Don't bore us, get to the "useful answer" chorus, says ex-minister', *Times Higher Education*, 19 July.

Rex, J. (1973) *Race, Colonialism and the City* (Routledge & Kegan Paul).

Reynolds, T. (2005) *Caribbean Mothers: Identity and Experience* (Tufnell Press).

Richardson, D. (1997) 'The politics of sustainable development', in S. Baker, M. Kousis, D. Richardson and S. Young (eds), *The Politics of Sustainable Development* (Routledge).

Ricolfi, L. (2005) 'Palestinians 1981–2003', in D. Gambetta (ed.), *Making Sense of Suicide Missions* (Oxford University Press).

Rifkin, J. (1995) *The End of Work: The Decline of the Global Labor Force and the Dawn of the Post-Market Era* (Putnam).

Rihoux, B., and C. Ragin (2009) *Configurational Comparative Methods: Qualitative Comparative Analysis (QCA) and Related Techniques* (Sage).

Ringen, S. (1988) 'Direct and indirect measures of poverty', *Journal of Social Policy*, 17(3).

Ritzer, G. (2000) *The McDonaldization of Society* (Pine Forge Press).

Roberts, K. (1978) *Contemporary Society and the Growth of Leisure* (Longman).

Roberts, K. (1999) *Leisure in Contemporary Society* (CABI).

Roberts, K. (2010) *Sociology of Leisure* (Sociopedia.isa).

Roberts, K. (2012) *Sociology* (Edward Elgar).

Robertson, J. (2002) *Crimes against Humanity* (New Press).

Robertson, R. (1992) *Globalization: Social Theory and Global Culture* (Sage).

Robine, J. M., J. P. Michel and F. R. Herrmann (2007) 'Who will care for the eldest people in our society?', *British Medical Journal*, 334(7593).

Robinson V., and J. Hockey (2011) *Masculinities in Transition* (Palgrave Macmillan).

Rogers, P. (2002) *Losing Control: Global Security in the Twenty-First Century* (Pluto Press).

Rogers, P. P., J. F. Jalal and J. A. Boyd (2008) *An Introduction to Sustainable Development* (Earthscan).

Rogers, R. (2010) 'Internet research: the question of method – a keynote address from the YouTube and the 2008 election cycle in the United States conference', *Journal of Information Technology & Politics*, 7.

Rogovin, M., and M. Frisch (1993) *Portraits in Steel* (Cornell University Press).

Rojek, C. (1985) *Capitalism and Leisure Theory* (Tavistock).

Rojek, C. (1995) *Decentring Leisure* (Sage).

Rojek, C. (2000) *Leisure and Culture* (Palgrave Macmillan).

Rojek, C. (2005) *Leisure Theory: Principles and Practice* (Palgrave Macmillan).

Rojek, C. (2010) *The Labour of Leisure* (Sage).

Roll, J. (1992) *Understanding Poverty: A Guide to the Concepts and Measures* (Family Policy Studies Centre).

Roscigno, V. J., S. Mong, R. Byron and G. Tester (2007) 'Age discrimination, social closure and employment', *Social Forces*, 86(1).

Rose, D., and D. Pevalin (eds) (2003) *A Researcher's Guide to the National Statistics Socioeconomic Classification* (Sage).

Rose, N. (1989) *Governing the Soul: The Shaping of the Private Self* (Routledge).

Rose, N. (2007) 'Beyond medicalization', *The Lancet*, 369.

Rose, N., and P. Miller (1992) 'Political power beyond the state: problematics of government', British Journal of Sociology 43(2).

Rose, S. (1998) *Lifelines: Biology, Freedom, Determinism* (Penguin).

Rose, S., and H. Rose (2005) 'Why we should give up on race', *The Guardian*, 9 April.

Rose, S. O. (1999) 'Cultural analysis and moral discourses: episodes, continuities and transformations', in V. E. Bonnell and L. Hunt (eds), *Beyond the Cultural Turn* (University of California Press).

Rosenau, P. M. (1992) *Post-Modernism and the Social Sciences: Insights, Inroads, and Intrusions* (Princeton University Press).

Rosenberg, J. (2000) *The Follies of Globalization Theory* (Verso).

Roseneil, S., and S. Budgeon (2004) 'Beyond the conventional family: intimacy, care and community in the 21st century', *Current Sociology*, 52(2).

Rosier, K. B. and D. A. Kinney (2005) 'Introduction to volume 11: historical and contemporary pressures on children's freedom', in D. A. Kinney and K. B. Rosier (eds), *Sociological Studies of Children and Youth*, vol. 11 (JAI/Elsevier).

Rostow, W. (1960) *The Stages of Economic Growth: A Non-Communist Manifesto* (Cambridge University Press).

Roth, G., and Schluchter, W. (1979) *Max Weber's Vision of History: Ethics and Methods* (University of California Press).

Rowbotham, S. (1973) *Woman's Consciousness, Man's World* (Penguin).

Rowbotham, S. (1974) *Hidden from History: 300 years of Women's Oppression and the Fight against it* (Pluto Press).

Rowe, D., and R. Lynch (2012) 'Play and work in the city', *Annals of Leisure Research*, 15(2).

Rowell, A. (1996) *Green Backlash: Global Subversion of the Environmental Movement* (Routledge).

Rowntree, B. S. (1901) *Poverty: A Study of Town Life* (Macmillan).

Rowntree, B. S. (1941) *Poverty and Progress: A Second Social Survey of York* (Longman).

Roy, D. (1973) 'Banana time', in G. Salaman and K. Thompson (eds), *People and Organizations* (Longman).

RT News (2013) 'Islam could be dominant UK religion in 10 years – census analysis', 17 May, http://rt.com/news/christianity-decline-uk-islam-rise-405/.

Russell, C. (1993) *Academic Freedom* (Routledge).

Ryan-Flood, R. (2009) *Lesbian Motherhood: Gender, Families and Sexual Citizenship* (Palgrave Macmillan).

Sachs, W. (ed.) (1992) *The Development Dictionary* (Zed Books).

Sagan, C. (1996) *The Demon-Haunted World: Science as a Candle in the Dark* (Ballantine Books).

Sageman, M. (2004) *Understanding Terror Networks* (University of Pennsylvania Press).

Sageman, M. (2008) *Leaderless Jihad: Terror Networks in the Twenty-First Century* (University of Pennsylvania Press).

Said, E. W. (2003) *Orientalism* (25th anniversary edn, Penguin).

Saith, A. (2006) 'From universal values to millennium development goals: lost in translation', *Development and Change*, 37(6).

Salaman, G. (1974) *Community and Occupation: An Exploration of Work/ Leisure Relationships* (Cambridge University Press).

Salib, E. (2003) 'Suicide terrorism: a case of folie à plusieurs?', *British Journal of Psychiatry* 182.

Sampsell-Willmann, K. (2009) *Lewis Hine as Social Critic* (University Press of Mississippi).

Sandford, S. (2011) 'Sex: a transdisciplinary concept', *Radical Philosophy*, 165(Jan/Feb).

SAPRI (2004) *Structural Adjustment: The SAPRI Report* (Zed Books).

Sapsted, D. (2010) 'UK poll finds profound anti-Muslim sentiment', *The National*, 15 January.

Sartre, J.-P. ([1960] 1976) *Critique of Dialectical Reason* (New Left Books).

Sassen, S. (2006) *Territory, Authority, Rights: From Medieval to Global Assemblages* (Princeton University Press).

Savage, M. (2000) *Class Analysis and Social Transformation* (Open University Press).

Savage, M. (2005) 'Revisiting classic qualitative studies', *Forum: Qualitative Social Research*, 6(1).

Savage, M., and R. Burrows (2007) 'The coming crisis of empirical sociology', *Sociology*, 41(5).

Savage, M., J. Barlow, P. Dickens and T. Feilding (1992) *Property, Bureaucracy and Culture: Middle-Class Formation in Contemporary Britain* (Routledge).

Savage, M., F. Devine, N. Cunningham, M. Taylor, Y. Li, J. Hjellbrekke, B. Le Roux, S. Friedman and A. Miles (2013) 'A new model of social class: findings from the BBC's great British class survey experiment', *Sociology*, 47(2).

Sawchuk, K., and B. Crow (2012) '"I'm G-mom on the phone"', *Feminist Media Studies*, 12(4).

Sayer, A. (2005) *The Moral Significance of Class* (Cambridge University Press).

Scambler, A., G. Scambler and D. Craig (1981) 'Kinship and friendship networks and women's demand for primary care', *Journal of the Royal College of General Practitioners*, 26.

Scambler, G. (2002) *Health and Social Change: A Critical Theory* (Open University Press).

Scambler, G. (2012) 'Health inequalities', *Sociology of Health and Illness*, 34(1).

Scambler, G., and A. Hopkins (1986) '"Being epileptic": coming to terms with stigma', *Sociology of Health and Illness*, 8.

Scambler, G., and D. Kelleher (2006) 'New social and health movements: issues of representation and change', *Critical Public Health*, 16.

Schafer, M. H. (2009) 'Parental death and subjective age: indelible imprints from early in the life course', *Sociological Inquiry*, 79(1).

Schafer, M. H., and T. Shippee (2010) 'Age identity in context', *Social Psychology Quarterly*, 73(3).

Schaffer, G. (2008) *Racial Science and British Society, 1930–62* (Palgrave).

Scharff, R. (1995) *Comte after Positivism* (Cambridge University Press).

Scherger, S. (2009) 'Cultural practices, age and the life course', *Cultural Trends*, 18(1).

Schifferes, S. (2007) 'Globalisation shakes the world', *BBC News*, 21 January, http://news.bbc.co.uk/1/hi/business/6279679.stm.

Schlesinger, P. (1991) *Media, State and Nation* (Sage).

Schlesinger, P., D. Miller and W. Dinan (2001) *Open Scotland? Journalists, Spin Doctors and Lobbyists* (Polygon).

Schor, J. (1991) *The Overworked American: The Unexpected Decline of Leisure* (Basic Books).

Schur, E. (1965) *Crimes without Victims* (Prentice Hall).

Schutz, A. (1967) *Phenomenology of the Social World* (Northwestern University Press).

Schwaiger, L. (2006) 'To be forever young: towards reframing corporeal subjectivity in maturity', *International Journal of Ageing and Later Life*, 1(1).

Schwartz, B. (2004) *The Paradox of Choice: Why More is Less* (HarperCollins).

Schwartz, C. (2010) 'Interview: the "shadow elite", Wikileaks and living in a "dangerous era"', *Radio Free Europe/Radio Liberty*, 16 August.

Scott, E., A. London and K. Edin (2000) 'Looking to the future: welfare reliant women talk about their job aspirations in the context of welfare reform', *Journal of Social Issues*, 56(4).

Scott, J. (2012) *Sociological Theory* (2nd edn, Edward Elgar).

Scott, J. C. (1998) *Seeing Like a State. How Certain Schemes to Improve the Human Condition Have Failed* (Yale University Press).

Scott, J. W. (1988) 'Gender: a useful category of historical analysis', in J. W. Scott, *Gender and the Politics of History* (Columbia University Press).

Scott-Samuel, A. (2012) 'Where the NHS is heading', *The Guardian*, 20 January.

Scraton, S. (1994) 'The changing world of women and leisure: feminism, "post-feminism" and leisure', *Leisure Studies*, 13(4).

Scraton, S., and P. Bramham (1998) 'Leisure in the postmodern city', in M. Haralambos (ed.), *Developments in Sociology* (Causeway Press).

Scraton, S., and B. Watson (1998) 'Gendered cities: women and public leisure space in the postmodern city', *Leisure Studies*, 17(2).

Scraton, S., K. Fasting, G. Pfister and A. Bunnel (1999) 'It's still a man's game? The experiences of top-level women footballers', *International Review for the Sociology of Sport*, 34(2).

Segal, L. (1994) *Straight Sex: The Politics of Pleasure* (Virago).

Segal, L. (1999) *Why Feminism?* (Polity).

Segal, L. (2007) *Making Trouble: Life and Politics* (Serpent's Tail Press).

Seigrist, J. (2009) 'Unfair exchange and health: social bases of stress-related diseases', *Social Theory and Health*, 7.

Selbin, E. (2010) *Revolution, Rebellion, Resistance* (Zed Books).

Sen, A. (1983) 'Poor, relatively speaking', *Oxford Economic Papers*, 35(2).

Sen, A. (1985) *Commodities and Capabilities* (North-Holland).

Sen, A. (1992) *Inequality Re-examined* (Oxford University Press).

Sen, A. (2001) *Development as Freedom* (Oxford University Press).

Sennett, R. (1998) *The Corrosion of Character: The Personal Consequences of Work in the New Capitalism* (W. W. Norton).

Settersten, R. A. (2007) 'Social relationships in the new demographic regime: potentials and risks reconsidered', *Advances in Life Course Research*, 12.

Settersten, R. A. (2009) '"It takes two to tango": the uneasy dance between life-course sociology and life span psychology', *Advances in Life Course Research*, 14(12).

Shanahan, M. J., E. Porfeli and J. Mortimer (2005) 'Subjective age identity and the transition to adulthood: when does one become an adult?', in R. A. Settersen, F. Furstenberg and R. G. Rumbaut (eds), *On the Frontier of Adulthood: Theory, Research and Public Policy* (University of Chicago Press).

Shaw, A. (2000) *Kinship and Continuity: Pakistani Families in Britain* (Routledge).

Shaw, M. (2003) *War and Genocide* (Polity).

Shaw, M. (2005) *The New Western Way of War* (Polity).

Shaw, M. (2007) *What is Genocide?* (Polity).

Shaw, S. M. (1999) 'Men's leisure and women's lives: the impact of pornography on women', *Leisure Studies*, 18(3).

Shepherd, J. (2009) 'The grade class: private pupils widen lead over state schools', *The Guardian*, 21 August.

Shilling, C. (2012) *The Body and Social Theory* (3rd edn, Sage).

Shils, E. (1967) 'The sanctity of life', *Encounter*, January.

Shirani, F., and C. Henwood (2011) 'Taking one day at a time: temporal experiences in the context of unexpected life course transitions', *Time and Society*, 20.

Shlaim, A. (2000) *The Iron Wall: Israel and the Arab World* (Penguin).

Shove, E. (2003) *Comfort, Cleanliness and Convenience: The Social Organization of Normality* (Berg).

Shove, E., and N. Spurling (eds) (2013) *Sustainable Practice: Social Theory and Climate Change* (Routledge).

Shulman, B. (2003) *The Betrayal of Work: How Low-Wage Jobs Fail 30 Million Americans* (Free Press).

Sial, S. (2008) 'Exploring the mindset of the British-Pakistani community: the socio-cultural and religious context', *Conflict and Peace Studies*, 1(1).

Silverstein, K. (1998) *Washington on $10 Million a Day: How Lobbyists Plunder the Nation* (Common Courage Press).

Simmel, G. ([1909] 1997) 'Fundamental religious ideas and modern science: an inquiry', in G. Simmel, *Essays on Religion* (Yale University Press).

Simmel, G. ([1911] 1997) 'The problem of religion today', in G. Simmel, *Essays on Religion* (Yale University Press).

Simmel, G. ([1917] 1976) 'The crisis of culture', in P. A. Lawrence (ed.) *George Simmel: Sociologist and European* (Thomas Nelson).

Simmel, G. (1965) 'The poor', *Social Problems*, 13.

Simon, J. L. (1981) *The Ultimate Resource* (Princeton University Press).

Singh-Manoux, A., J. E. Ferrie, T. Chandola and M. Marmot (2004) 'Socio-economic trajectories across the life course and health outcomes in midlife: evidence for the accumulation hypothesis', *International Journal of Epidemiology*, 33(5).

Sisjord, M. K., and E. Kristiansen (2009) 'Elite women wrestlers' muscles: physical strength and social burden', *International Review for the Sociology of Sport*, 44(2–3).

Sismondo, S. (2004) *An Introduction to Science and Technology Studies* (Blackwell).

Sivarajasingam, V., J. P. Wells, S. Moore, P. Morgan and J. Shepherd (2012) *Trends in Violence in England and Wales 2011: An Accident and Emergency Perspective*, Cardiff University Violence & Society Research Group, www.vrg.cf.ac.uk/nvit/NVIT_2011.pdf.

Skeggs, B. (1997) *Formations of Class and Gender: Becoming Respectable* (Sage).

Skeggs, B. (2004) *Class, Self and Culture* (Routledge).

Skeggs, B. (2009) 'The moral economy of person production: the class relations of self-performance on "reality" television', *Sociological Review*, 57(4).

Skeggs, B. (2011) 'Imagining personhood differently: person value and autonomist working class value practices', *Sociolocical Review*, 59(3).

Skeggs, B., and V. Loveday (2012) 'Struggles for value: value practices, injustice, judgment, affect and the idea of class', *British Journal of Sociology*, 63(3).

Skeggs, B., and H. Wood (2011) 'Turning it on is a class act: immediated object relations with the television', *Media, Culture and Society*, 33(6).

Skeggs, B., and H. Wood (2012) *Reacting to Reality Television: Performance, Audience and Value* (Routledge).

Skinner, Q. (ed.) (1985) *The Return of Grand Theory in the Human Sciences* (Cambridge University Press).

Sklair, L. (2000) *The Transnational Capitalist Class* (Blackwell).

Sklair, L. (2002) *Globalization: Capitalism and its Alternatives* (Oxford University Press).

Skocpol, T. (1979) *States and Social Revolutions: A Comparative Analysis of France, Russia, and China* (Cambridge University Press).

Skribis, Z., and I. Woodward (2013) *Cosmopolitanism: Uses of the Idea* (Sage).

Smart, C. (2007a) 'Same sex couples and marriage: negotiating relational landscapes with families and friends', *Sociological Review*, 55(4).

Smart, C. (2007b) *Personal Life: New Directions in Sociological Thinking* (Polity).

Smart, C. (2009) 'Family secrets: law and understandings of openness in everyday relationships', *Journal of Social Policy*, 38(4).

Smart, C. (2011) 'Close relationships and personal life', in V. May (ed.), *Sociology of Personal Life* (Palgrave Macmillan).

Smart, C., K. Davies, B. Heaphy and J. Mason (2012) 'Difficult friendships and ontological insecurity', *Sociological Review*, 60(1).

Smith, A. ([1776] 1999) *The Wealth of Nations* (Penguin).

Smith, A., M. Thurston and K. Green (2011) 'Propinquity, sociability and excitement: exploring the normalisation of sensible drug use among 15–16-year-olds in north-west England and north-east Wales', *Journal of Youth Studies*, 14(3).

Smith, A. D. (1986) *The Ethnic Origin of Nations* (Blackwell).

Smith, A. D. (1995) 'The formation of national identity', in H. Harris (ed.), *Identity* (Oxford University Press).

Smith, P. (2005) *Why War? The Cultural Logic of Iraq, the Gulf War, and Suez* (University of Chicago Press).

Smith, P. (2008) 'Meaning and military power: moving on from Foucault', *Journal of Power*, 1(3).

Smith, S. C. (2005) *Ending Global Poverty: A Guide to What Works* (Palgrave Macmillan).

Smith, T. W. (2009) *Religious Change around the World*, University of Chicago National Opinion Research Center, http://news.uchicago.edu/static/newsengine/pdf/religionsurvey_20091023.pdf.

Smith, T. W. (2012) *Beliefs about God across Time and Countries*, University of Chicago National Opinion Research Center, www.norc.org/PDFs/Beliefs_about_God_Report.pdf.

Smith Maguire, J. (2008) 'Leisure and the obligation of self-work: an examination of the fitness field', *Leisure Studies*, 27(1).

Snow, J. (2000) 'Journalism, the techno revolution, and the art of disinformation', Hetherington Memorial Lecture, Stirling Media Research Institute, Stirling University, 1 November, www-fms.stir.ac.uk/WebProp/Hetherington/2000Snow.htm.

Sokal, A. (1996) 'Transgressing the boundaries; towards a transformative hermeneutics of quantum gravity', *Social Text*, 46–67.

Sokal, A., and J. Bricmont (1998) *Intellectual Impostures: Postmodern Philosophers' Abuse of Science* (Profile Books).

Solomos, J. (2011) 'The riots: not so "pure and simple" to explain', *Network: The Magazine of the British Sociological Association*, no. 109(winter).

Somerville, W. (2007) *Immigration under New Labour* (Policy Press).

Song, M. (2008) 'Does "race" matter? A study of "mixed race" siblings' identifications', *Sociological Review*, 58(2).

Sorokin, P. (1942) 'The cause and factors of war and peace', American Historical Association, Report 3: 83–95.

Sosteric, M. (1996) 'Subjectivity and the labour process: a case study in the restaurant industry', *Work, Employment and Society*, 10(2).

Soto, A. (1992) 'The global environment: a Southern perspective', *International Journal*, 47(4).

Spelman, E. V. (1988) *Inessential Woman* (Beacon Press).

Spelman, W. (2000) 'The limited importance of prison expansion', in A. Blumstein and J. Wallman (eds), *The Crime Drop in America* (Cambridge University Press).

Spelman, W. (2005) 'Jobs or jails? The crime drop in Texas', *Journal of Policy Analysis and Management*, 24(1).

Spencer, H. (1874) *The Study of Sociology* (Henry S. King).

Spencer, H., and S. Andreski (1972) *Herbert Spencer: Structure, Function and Evolution* (Nelson).

Spencer, I. (1997) *British Immigration Policy since 1939* (Routledge).

Spencer, L., and R. Pahl (2006) *Rethinking Friendship: Hidden Solidarities Today* (Princeton University Press).

Spencer, S. (2011) *The Migration Debate* (Policy Press).

Spicker, P. (1993) *Poverty and Social Security Concepts and Principles* (Routledge).

Spivak, G. C. (1988) *Can the Subaltern Speak?* (Macmillan).

Stacey, J. (1991) *Brave New Families: Stories of Domestic Upheaval in Late Twentieth Century America* (Basic Books).

Stainton Rogers, W., R. Stainton Rogers, J. Vyrost and L. Lovas (2004) 'Worlds apart: young people's aspirations in a changing Europe', in J. Roche., S. Tucker., R. Thomson and R. Flynn (eds), *Youth in Society* (2nd edn, Sage).

Standing, G. (2011) *The Precariat: The New Dangerous Class* (Bloomsbury).

Stanley, L., and S. Wise (1984) *Breaking Out: Feminist Consciousness and Feminist Research* (Routledge).

Stanworth, M. (1984) 'Women and class analysis: a reply to Goldthorpe', *Sociology*, 18(2).

Stauber, J. C., and S. Rampton (1995) *Toxic Sludge is Good for You: Lies, Damn Lies and the Public Relations Industry* (Common Courage Press).

Stauber, J. C., and S. Rampton (2001) *Trust Us, We're Experts* (Jeremy P. Tarcher).

Stebbins, R. A. (1992) 'The costs and rewards in barbershop singing', *Leisure Studies*, 11(2).

Stebbins, R. A. (2005) 'Choice and experiential definitions of leisure', *Leisure Sciences*, 27(4).

Stebbins, R. A. (2007) *Serious Leisure: A Perspective for our Time* (Aldine Transaction).

Stebbins, R. A., C. Rojek and A. M. Sullivan (2006) 'Editorial: deviant leisure', *Loisir*, 30(1).

Stedman Jones, G. (1971) *Outcast: A Study in the Relationship between Classes in Victorian Society* (Clarendon Press).

Stein, B. (2006) 'In class warfare, guess which class is winning', *New York Times*, 26 November.

Steinmetz, G. (1999) *State/Culture: State-Formation after the Cultural Turn* (Cornell University Press).

Stepan, N. (1990) 'Race and gender: the role of analogy in science', in T. Goldberg (ed.), *The Anatomy of Racism* (University of Minnesota Press).

Stephen, D. E., and P. Squires (2004) '"They're still children and entitled to be children": problematising the institutionalised mistrust of marginalised youth', *Journal of Youth Studies*, 7(3).

Stewart, A. (2001) *Theories of Power and Domination: The Politics of Empowerment in Late Modernity* (Sage).

Stewart, H., and L. Elliott (2013) 'Nicholas Stern: "I got it wrong on climate change – it's far, far worse"', *The Guardian*, 26 January.

Stiglitz, J. E. (2003) 'Globalization and development', in D. Held and M. Koenig-Archibugi (eds), *Taming Globalization* (Polity).

Storm, I. (2009) 'Halfway to heaven: four types of fuzzy fidelity in Europe', *Journal for the Scientific Study of Religion*, 48(4).

Strand, G. (2008) 'Keyword: evil: Google's addiction to cheap electricity', *Harper's Magazine*, March.

Strangleman, T. (2004) 'Ways of (not) seeing work: the visual as a blind spot in WES?', *Work, Employment and Society*, 18(1).

Strangleman, T. (2007) 'The nostalgia for permanence at work? The end of work and its commentators', *Sociological Review*, 55(1).

Strangleman, T. (2008) 'Representations of labour: visual sociology and work', *Sociological Compass*, 2(4).

Strauch, B. (2010) *The Secret Life of the Grown-Up Brain: The Surprising Talents of the Middle Aged Mind* (Viking Penguin).

Strenger, C. (2009) 'Sosein: active self-acceptance in midlife', *Journal of Humanistic Psychology*, 49(1).

Strong, P. (1979) 'Sociological imperialism and the profession of medicine: a critical analysis of the thesis of medical imperialism', *Social Science and Medicine*, 13A.

Stuckler, D., and S. Basu (2011) 'Evaluating the health burden of chronic diseases', in D. Stuckler and K. Siegel (eds), *Sick Societies: Responding to the Global Challenge of Chronic Disease* (Oxford University Press).

Sullivan, O. (2000) 'The division of domestic labour: twenty years of change?', *Sociology*, 34(3).

Surette, R. (2011) *Media, Crime and Criminal Justice: Images and Realities* (4th edn, Wadsworth).

Sutherland, E. H. (1949) *White Collar Crime* (Holt, Rinehart & Winston).

Sutton, P. W. (2004) *Nature, Environment and Society* (Palgrave Macmillan).

Sutton Trust (2010) *The Educational Backgrounds of Members of Parliament in 2010*, www.suttontrust.com/public/documents/2MPs_educational_backgrounds_2010_A.pdf.

Takemi, K., M. Jimba, S. Ishii, Y. Katsuma and Y. Nakamura (2008) 'Human security approach for global health', *The Lancet*, 372.

Tashakkori, A., and C. Teddlie (eds) (2010) *Handbook of Mixed Methods in Social and Behavioral Research* (2nd edn, Sage).

Taylor, C. (1991) *The Ethics of Authenticity* (Harvard University Press).

Taylor, C. (2007) *A Secular Age* (Harvard University Press).

Taylor, H. (1998) 'Rising crime: the political economy of criminal statistics since the 1850s', *Economic History Review*, 51(3).

Taylor, I. (1999) *Crime in Context* (Polity).

Taylor, I., P. Walton and J. Young (1973) *The New Criminology* (Routledge & Kegan Paul).

Taylor, I., P. Walton and J. Young (eds) (1975) *Critical Criminology* (Routledge & Kegan Paul).

Taylor, Y. (2009) *Lesbian and Gay Parenting* (Palgrave Macmillan).

Taylor, Y., and S. Hines (2012) *Sexualities: Past Reflections, Future Directions* (Palgrave Macmillan).

Temkin, O. (1945) *The Falling Sickness* (Johns Hopkins University Press).

Tester, K. (1991) *Animals and Society: The Humanity of Animal Rights* (Routledge).

Theos (2013) 'The spirit of things unseen: beliefs in post-religious Britain', Theos Think Tank, available online.

Therborn, G. (2000) 'At the birth of second century sociology: times of reflexivity, spaces of identity, nodes of knowledge', *British Journal of Sociology*, 51(1).

Thoburn, N. (2002) 'Difference in Marx: the lumpenproletariat and the proletarian unnameable', *Economy and Society*, 31(3).

Thomas, A. (2000) 'Development as practice in a liberal capitalist world', *Journal of International Development*, 12(6).

Thomas, C. (2012) 'Theorising disability and chronic illness: where next for perspectives in medical sociology?', *Social Theory and Health*, 10.

Thomas, K. (1984) *Man and the Natural World: Changing Attitudes in England 1500–1800* (Penguin).

Thomas, W. I., and D. S. Thomas (1928) *The Child in America: Behavior Problems and Programs* (Alfred A. Knopf).

Thompson, G., O. Hawkins, A. Dar and M. Taylor (2012) *Olympic Britain: Social and Economic Change since the 1908 and 1948 London Games* (House of Commons Library).

Thompson, G. F. (2007) 'Global inequality, the "great divergence" and supranational regionalization', in D. Held and A. Kaya (eds), *Global Inequality* (Polity).

Thompson, J. B. (1989) 'The theory of structuration', in D. Held and J. B. Thompson (eds),

Social Theory of Modern Societies: Anthony Giddens and his Critics (Cambridge University Press).

Thompson, P., and D. McHugh (1995) *Work Organizations: A Critical Introduction* (Macmillan).

Threadgold, S. (2011) 'Should I pitch my tent on the middle ground? On "middling tendency", Beck and inequality in youth sociology', *Journal of Youth Studies*, 14(4).

Tilly, C. (1985) 'War making and state making as organized crime', in P. Evans, D. Rueschemeyer and T. Skocpol (eds), *Bringing the State Back In* (Cambridge University Press).

Tilly, C. (1992) *Coercion, Capital and European States* (Blackwell).

Tilly, C. (1994) *Social Revolutions in the Modern World* (Cambridge University Press).

Tilly, C. (1996) *European Revolutions: 1492–1992* (Blackwell).

Tiryakian, E. A. (1999) 'War: the covered side of modernity', *International Sociology*, 14(4).

Tittle, C. (2004) 'The arrogance of public sociology', *Social Forces*, 82(4).

Tolstoy, L. ([1882] 2008) *A Confession* (Penguin).

Tomlinson, J. (1999) *Globalization and Culture* (Polity).

Tönnies, F. ([1887] 1957) *Community and Society* (Harper & Row).

Toothman, E. L., and A. E. Barrett (2011) 'Mapping midlife: an examination of social factors shaping conceptions of the timing of middle age', *Advances in Life Course Research*, 16.

Tornstam, L. (2006) 'The complexity of ageism: a proposed typology', *International Journal of Ageing and Later Life*, 1(1).

Toumey, C. (2006) 'Science and democracy', *Nature Nanotechnology* 1(1).

Touraine, A. (1965) *Sociologie de l'action* (Seuil).

Touraine, A. (1977) *The Self-Production of Society* (University of Chicago Press).

Townsend, P. (1979) *Poverty in the United Kingdom: A Survey of Household Resources and Standards of Living* (Allen Lane).

Townsend, P. (1993) *The International Analysis of Poverty* (Harvester Wheatsheaf).

Toynbee, P. (2003) *Hard Work: Life in Low Pay Britain* (Bloomsbury).

Trethewey, A. (2001) 'Reproducing and resisting the master narrative of decline', *Management Communication Quarterly*, 15(2).

Treviño, J. (ed.) (2001) *Talcott Parsons Today: His Theory and Legacy in Contemporary Sociology* (Rowman & Littlefield).

Tulle, E. (2008) 'The ageing body and the ontology of ageing: athletic competence in later life', *Body and Society*, 14(3).

Tunstall, J. (1962) *The Fishermen: The Sociology of an Extreme Occupation* (MacGibbon & Kee).

Tunstall, J. (1964) *The Advertising Man in London Advertising Agencies* (Chapman & Hall).

Turkle, S. (2011) *Alone Together: Why We Expect More from Technology and Less from Each Other* (Basic Books).

Turner, B. S. (1984) *The Body and Society: Explorations in Social Theory* (Blackwell).

Turner, B. S. (1993) 'Outline of a theory of human rights', *Sociology*, 27(3).

Turner, B. S. (2001a) 'Social systems and complexity theory', in J. Treviño (ed.), *Talcott Parsons Today: His Theory and Legacy in Contemporary Sociology* (Rowman & Littlefield).

Turner, B. S. (2001b) 'The erosion of citizenship', *British Journal of Sociology*, 52(2).

Turner, B. S. (2006a) 'Global sociology and the nature of rights', *Societies without Borders*, 1.

Turner, B. S. (2006b) *Vulnerability and Human Rights* (Pennsylvania University Press).

Turner, B. S. (ed.) (2009) *The New Blackwell Companion to Social Theory* (Blackwell).

Turner, C. (2010) *Sociological Theory and the Art of Living* (Sage).

Turner, J. H. (1996) 'The evolution of emotions in humans: Darwinian–Durkheimian analysis', *Journal for the Theory of Social Behaviour*, 26(1).

Turner, J. H. (1999) 'Toward a general sociological theory of emotions', *Journal for the Theory of Social Behaviour*, 29(2).

Turner, S. (2009) 'The future of social theory', in B. S. Turner (ed.), *The New Blackwell Companion to Social Theory* (Blackwell).

Twigg, J. (2007) 'Clothing, age and the body: a critical review', *Ageing and Society*, 27.

UKRC (2010) *Women and Men in Science, Engineering and Technology: The UK Statistics Guide 2010* (UKRC).

UNDP (1994) *Human Development Report, 1994* (Oxford University Press).

UNDP (2001) *Human Development Report, 2001: Promoting Linkages* (Oxford University Press).

UNDP (2002) *Human Development Report, 2002: Deepening Democracy in a Fragmented World* (Oxford University Press).

UNDP (2005) *Human Development Report, 2005: International Cooperation at a Crossroads* (United Nations).

UNDP (2013) *Human Development Report, 2013: The Rise of the South* (United Nations).

UN-Habitat (2003) *The Challenge of Slums: Global Report on Human Settlements 2003* (Earthscan).

United Nations (1995) *The Copenhagen Declaration and Programme of Action* (United Nations).

United Nations (2005) *Report on the World Social Situation 2005: The Inequality Predicament* (United Nations).

United Nations (2010) 'Women in politics 2010 map', www.unwomen.org/en/digital-library/publications/2010/1/women-in-politics-2010-map.

UNMDG (2005) *UN Millennium Development Goals* (United Nations).

UNMDG (2009) *The Millennium Development Goals Report 2009* (United Nations).

Urry, J. (2000) *Sociology beyond Societies: Mobilities for the Twenty-First Century* (Routledge).

Urry, J. (2011) *Climate Change and Society* (Polity).

Vajja, A., and H. White (2008) 'Can the World Bank build social capital? The experience of social funds in Malawi and Zambia', *Development and Change*, 44(8).

Van den Bosch, K. (2001) *Identifying the Poor Using Subjective and Consensual Methods* (Ashgate).

Van Dijck, J. (2009) 'Users like you? Theorizing agency in user-generated content', *Media, Culture, and Society*, 31.

Veblen, T. (1899) *The Theory of the Leisure Class: An Economic Study of Institutions* (Macmillan).

Veit-Wilson, J. (1998) *Setting Adequacy Standards: How Governments Define Minimum Incomes* (Policy Press).

Vertigans, S. (2011) *The Sociology of Terrorism* (Routledge).

Vertovec, S. (2007) 'Super-diversity and its implications', *Journal of Ethnic and Racial Studies*, 30(6).

Vertovec, S., and S. Wessendorf (2010) *The Multiculturalism Backlash* (Routledge).

Victoroff, J. (2005) 'The mind of the terrorist: a review and critique of psychological approaches', *Journal of Conflict Resolution*, 49(1).

Vincent, J. (2003) *Old Age* (Routledge).

Virchow, R. ([1848] 1985) *Collected Essays on Public Health and Epidemiology* (Science History).

Visram, R. (2002) *Asians in Britain* (Pluto Press).

Voas, D. (2009) 'The rise and fall of fuzzy fidelity in Europe', *European Sociological Review*, 25(2).

Voas, D., and S. Bruce (2007) 'The spiritual revolution: another false dawn for the sacred', in K. Flanagan and P. C. Jupp (eds), *A Sociology of Spirituality* (Ashgate).

Voas, D., and A. Crockett (2005) 'Religion in Britain: neither believing nor belonging', *Sociology*, 39(1).

Voas, D., and S. Doebler (2011) 'Secularization in Europe: religious change between and within birth cohorts', *Religion and Society in Central and Eastern Europe*, 4(1).

Voas, D., and F. Fleischmann (2012) 'Islam moves west: religious change in the first and second generations', *Annual Review of Sociology*, 38.

Voas, D., and R. Ling (2010) 'Religion in Britain and the United States', in A. Park, J. Curtice, K. Thomson, M. Phillips, E. Clery and S. Butt (eds), *British Social Attitudes: The 26th Report* (Sage).

Voas, D., and S. McAndrew (2012) 'Three puzzles of non-religion in Britain', *Journal of Contemporary Religion*, 27(1).

Vogler, C., M. Brockmann and R. Wiggins (2006) 'Intimate relationships and changing patterns of money management at the beginning of the twenty-first century', *British Journal of Sociology*, 57(3).

Vogler, C., C. Lyonette and R. Wiggins (2008) 'Money, power and spending decisions in intimate relationships', *Sociological Review*, 56(1).

Wacquant, L. (2009) *Prisons of Poverty* (University of Minnesota Press).

Waddington, D., F. Jobard and M. King (eds) (2009) *Rioting in the UK and France: A Comparative Analysis* (Willan).

Wade, R. H. (2003) 'The disturbing rise in poverty and inequality: is it all a "big lie"?', in D. Held and M. Koenig-Archibugi (eds), *Taming Globalization* (Polity).

Wade, R. H., and M. Wolf (2003) 'Are global poverty and inequality getting worse?', in D. Held and A. McGrew (eds), *The Global Transformations Reader* (2nd edn, Polity).

Wadsworth, M., W. Butterfield and R. Blaney (1971) *Health and Sickness: The Choice of Treatment* (Tavistock).

Wagner, P. (1994) *A Sociology of Modernity: Liberty and Discipline* (Routledge).

Wagner, P. (2001) *A History and Theory of the Social Sciences* (Sage).

Wagner, P. (2011) 'Handlung, Institution, Kritik: Materialien zur immer noch notwendigen Erneuerung der Gesellschaftstheorie', *Soziologische Revue*, 34.

Wagner, P. (2012) *Modernity: Understanding the Present* (Polity).

Wajcman, J. (2004) *TechnoFeminism* (Polity).

Walby, S. (1986) *Patriarchy at Work* (Polity).

Walkerdine, V. (2012) 'Shame on you! Intergenerational trauma and working-class femininity on reality television', in H. Wood and B. Skeggs (eds), *Real Class: Reality Television and Class* (Palgrave).

Walkerdine, V., and H. Lucey (2001) *Growing Up Girl: Psychosocial Explorations of Gender and Class* (Palgrave).

Wallerstein, I. (1979) *The Capitalist World Economy* (Cambridge University Press).

Wallerstein, I. (1990) 'Culture as the ideological battleground of the modern world-system', in M. Featherstone (ed.), *Global Culture: Nationalism, Globalization and Modernity* (Sage).

Wallerstein, I. (1991) *Unthinking Social Science: The Limits of Nineteenth-Century Paradigms* (Polity).

Wallerstein, I. (2006) *European Universalism: The Rhetoric of Power* (New Press).

Walmsley, R. (1991) *The National Prison Survey* (Home Office).

Walsemann, K. M., A. T. Geronimus and G. C. Gee (2008) 'Accumulating disadvantage over the life course: evidence from a longitudinal study investigating the relationship between educational advantage in youth and health in middle age', *Research on Aging*, 30.

Walter, N. (2010) *Living Dolls: The Return of Sexism* (Virago).

Walters, S. (2012) *Ethnicity, Race and Education* (Continuum).

Walzer, M. (ed.) (1995) *Toward a Global Civil Society* (Berghahn Books).

Wamsley, K. B., and G. Pfister (2005) 'Olympic men and women: the politics of gender in the modern games', in K. Young and K. B. Wamsley (eds), *Global Olympics: Historical and Social Studies of the Modern Games* (Elsevier).

Ward, L. (2005) 'Flexible work rights failing middle-aged women', *The Guardian*, 19 February.

Warde, A., M. Tomlinson and A. McMeekin (2000) *Expanding Tastes? Cultural Omnivorousness and Social Change in the UK* (CRIC, University of Manchester).

Warhurst, C., and D. Nickson (2007) 'Employee experience of aesthetic labour in retail and hospitality', *Work, Employment and Society*, 21(1).

Waters, M. (1996) 'Human rights and the univeralisation of interests: towards a social constructionist approach', *Sociology* 30(3).

Waters, M. (2001) *Globalization* (2nd edn, Routledge).

Watson, B., and A. Ratna (2011) 'Bollywood in the park: thinking intersectionally about public leisure space', *Leisure/Loisir*, 35(1).

Watson, B., and S. Scraton (2001) 'Confronting whiteness? Researching the leisure lives of South Asian mothers', *Journal of Gender Studies*, 10(3).

Watson, B., and S. Scraton (2013) 'Leisure studies and intersectionality', *Leisure Studies*, 32(1).

WCED (World Commission on Environment and Development) (1987) *Our Common Future* (Oxford University Press).

Wearing, B. (1998) *Leisure and Feminist Theory* (Sage).

Wearing, S. L., M. McDonald and M. Wearing (2012) 'Consumer culture, the mobilisation of the narcissistic self and adolescent deviant behaviour', *Leisure Studies*, 31(1).

Webb, J. (2006) *Organizations, Identities and the Self* (Palgrave).

Weber, M. ([1919] 1946) 'Politics as a vocation', in *From Max Weber: Essays in Sociology*, ed. H. H. Gerth and C. W. Mills (Oxford University Press).

Weber, M. (1974) *Max Weber on Universities* (University of Chicago Press).

Weber, M. ([1905] 1985) *The Protestant Ethic and the Spirit of Capitalism* (Unwin).

Weber, M. ([1922] 1992) *Economy and Society* (University of California Press).

Weber, M. (1995) *Russian Revolutions* (Polity).

Weber, M. (1997) 'What is an ethnic group?', in M. Guibernau and J. Rex (eds), *The Ethnicity Reader* (Polity).

Weber, M. ([1919] 2007) 'Science as a vocation', in *From Max Weber: Essays in Sociology*, ed. H. H. Gerth and C. W. Mills (Routledge).

Webster, A. (1991) *Science, Technology and Society: New Directions* (Macmillan).

Webster, S., D. Simpson, R. MacDonald, R. Abbas, M. Cieslik, T. Shildrick and M. Simpson (2004) *Poor Transitions: Social Exclusions and Young Adults* (Policy Press).

Wedel, J. (2011) *The Shadow Elite: How the World's New Powerbrokers Undermine Democracy, Government and the Free Market* (Basic Books).

Weeks, J., B. Heaphy and C. Donovan (2001) *Same Sex Intimacies: Families of Choice and Other Life Experiments* (Routledge).

Weiner, B. (ed.) (1985) *Just a Bunch of Girls: Feminist Approaches to Schooling* (Open University Press).

Wells, A. (2006) 'NOP poll of British Muslims', *UK Polling Report*, August 8, http://ukpoll ingreport.co.uk/blog/archives/291.

Wells, K. (2005) 'Strange practices: children's discourses on transgressive unknowns in urban public space', *Childhood*, 12(4).

Wells, M., and K. J. Mitchell (2008) 'How do high-risk youth use the internet? Characteristics and implications for prevention', *Child Maltreatment*, 13(3).

Werbner, P. (2013) 'Everyday multiculturalism: theorising the difference between "intersectionality" and "multiple identities"', *Ethnicities*, 13(4).

West, P. (2005) *The Poverty of Multiculturalism* (Civitas).

West, P. C. (1985) 'Max Weber's human ecology of the historical sciences', in V. Murvar (ed.), *Theory of Liberty, Legitimacy and Power: New Directions in the Intellectual and Scientific Legacy of Max Weber* (Routledge & Kegan Paul).

Westerhof, G. J., A. E. Barrett and N. Steverink (2003) 'Forever young: a comparison of age identities in the United States and Germany', *Research on Aging*, 25(4).

Weston, K. (1991) *Families We Choose: Lesbians, Gays and Kinship* (Columbia University Press).

Wetherell, M., S. Taylor and S. Yates (eds) (2001) *Discourse Theory and Practice* (Sage).

Wheaton, B (ed.) (2004) *Understanding Lifestyle Sports: Consumption, Identity and Difference* (Routledge).

Whitehead, J. M. (2003) 'Summary report of findings of the project on indicators of academic performance', *Cambridge University Reporter*, 133.

Whitford, M. (1991) *Luce Irigaray: Philosophy of the Feminine* (Routledge).

Whitham, G. (2012) *Child Poverty in 2012: It Shouldn't Happen Here*, www.savethechildren. org.uk.

Widmer, E. D., and G. Ritschard (2009) 'The de-standardisation of the life course: are men and women equal?', *Advances in Life Course Research*, 14.

Wiesmann, D. (2006) *2006 Global Hunger Index: A Basis for Cross-Country Comparisons*, www. ifpri.org/publication/2006-global-hunger-index.

Wilding, R. (2006) '"Virtual" intimacies? Families communicating across transnational contexts', *Global Networks: A Journal of Transnational Affairs*, 6(2).

Wilkinson, R. (1996) *Unhealthy Societies: The Afflictions of Inequality* (Routledge).

Wilkinson, R., and M. Marmot (2003) *Social Determinants of Health* (2nd edn, World Health Organization).

Wilkinson, R., and K. Pickett (2009) *The Spirit Level: Why More Equal Societies Almost Always Do Better* (Allen Lane).

Willetts, D. (2010) *The Pinch: How the Baby Boomers Took their Children's Future – and Why They should Give it Back* (Atlantic Books).

Williams, D. J. (2009) 'Deviant leisure: rethinking "the good, the bad, and the ugly"', *Leisure Sciences*, 31.

Williams, F. (2004) *Rethinking Families* (Calouste Gulbenkian Foundation).

Williams, G. (1955) 'The definition of crime', *Current Legal Problems*, 8(1).

Williams, G. (1984) 'The genesis of chronic illness: narrative reconstruction', *Sociology of Health and Illness*, 6.

Williams, S., and S. Williams (2005) 'Space invaders: the negotiation of teenage boundaries through the mobile phone', *Sociological Review*, 53(2).

Wilson, A. R. (2007) 'With friends like these: the liberalization of queer family policy', *Critical Social Policy*, 27(1).

Wilson, E. (2010) 'Billions pour in for India's insulated superclass', *The Observer*, 9 May.

Wilson, J. Q. (1975) *Thinking about Crime* (Vintage).

Wilson, J. Q., and R. Herrnstein (1985) *Crime and Human Nature* (Simon & Schuster).

Wilson, W. J. (1987) *The Truly Disadvantaged: The Inner City, the Underclass and Public Policy* (University of Chicago Press).

Wimmer, A., and N. Glick-Schiller (2002) 'Methodological nationalism and beyond: nation-state building, migration and the social sciences', *Global Networks*, 2(4).

Winlow, S., and S. Hall (2006) *Violent Night: Urban Leisure and Contemporary Culture* (Berg).

Wisor, S. (2012) *Measuring Global Poverty: Toward a Pro-Poor Approach* (Palgrave Macmillan).

Witz, A. (2000) '"Whose body matters?" Feminist sociology and the corporeal turn in sociology and feminism', *Body and Society*, 6.

Witz, A., C. Warhurst and D. Nickson (2003) 'The labour of aesthetics and the aesthetics of organization', *Organization* 10(1).

Wolf, M. (2000) 'The big lie of global inequality', *Financial Times*, 8 February.

Wolf, M. (2004) *Why Globalization Works* (Yale University Press).

Wolfe, A. (1992) 'Weak sociology/strong sociologists: consequences and contradictions of a field in turmoil', *Social Research*, 59(4).

Wolkowitz, C. (2006) *Bodies at Work* (Sage).

Wood, E. M. (1997) 'Modernity, postmodernity or capitalism?', *Review of International Political Economy*, 4(3).

Wood, E. M. (1999) *The Origin of Capitalism* (Monthly Review Press).

Wood, M., J. Hales, S. Purdon, T. Sejersen and O. Hayllar (2009) A Test for Racial Discrimination in Recruitment Practice in British Cities (Department for Work and Pensions), www.natcen.ac.uk/media/20541/test-for-racial-discrimination.pdf.

Wood, P. H. N. (1980) 'The language of disablement: a glossary relating to disease and its consequences', *International Journal of Rehabilitation Medicine*, 2(2).

Woodhead, L. (2013) 'Restoring religion to the public square: faith's role in civil society', *The Tablet*, 28 January.

Woodhead, M. (1997) 'Psychology and the cultural construction of children's needs', in A. James and A. Prout (eds), *Constructing and Reconstructing Children* (RoutledgeFalmer).

Woodiwiss, A. (2005) *Human Rights* (Routledge).

Woodward, K. (ed.) (1997) *Identity and Difference* (Sage).

Woodward, K. (2006) *Boxing, Masculinity and Identity: The 'I' of the Tiger* (Routledge).

Woodward, K. (2009a) *Embodied Sporting Practices: Regulating and Regulatory Bodies* (Palgrave).

Woodward, K. (2009b) 'Bodies on the margins: regulating bodies, regulatory bodies', *Leisure Studies*, 28(2).

Woodward, K. (2011) *The Short Guide to Gender* (Policy Press).

Woodward, K. (2012a) *Sex Power and the Games* (Palgrave).

Woodward, K. (2012b) *Planet Sport* (Routledge).

Woodward, K. (2012c) *Sporting Times* (Palgrave).

Woodward, K. (2014) *Globalizing Boxing* (Bloomsbury Academic).

Woodward, K., and S. Woodward (2009) *Why Feminism Matters: Feminism Lost and Found* (Palgrave Macmillan).

World Bank (2005) *World Development Report 2005: A Better Investment Climate for Everyone* (World Bank).

World Bank (2006) *World Development Report 2006: Equity and Development* (World Bank).

World Bank (2011) *World Development Report 2011: Conflict, Security and Development Overview* (World Bank).

World Bank (2012a) 'World Bank sees progress against extreme poverty, but flags vulnerabilities', World Bank News & Broadcast, available online.

World Bank (2012b) *Information and Communications for Development 2012: Maximizing Mobile* (World Bank).

World Bank (2013) 'Poverty headcount ratio at $1.25 a day (PPP) (% of population)', http://data.worldbank.org/indicator/SI.POV.DDAY.

Worsley, P. (1964) *The Third World* (Weidenfeld & Nicolson).

Wright, E. O. (1997) *Class Counts: Comparative Studies in Class Analysis* (Cambridge University Press).

Wright, J., and G. Clarke (1999) 'Sport, the media and the construction of compulsory heterosexuality', *International Review for the Sociology of Sport*, 34(3).

Wright, S. (ed.) (1994) *Anthropology of Organizations* (Routledge).

Wriston, W. (1992) *The Twilight of Sovereignty* (Scribner).

Yearley, S. (1991) *The Green Case: A Sociology of Environmental Issues, Arguments and Politics* (HarperCollins Academic).

Yearley, S. (2005) *Making Sense of Science: Understanding the Social Study of Science* (Sage).

Yeo, E. (1993) *The Contest of Social Science in Britain: Relations and Representations of Gender and Class* (Rivers Oram Press).

Young, I. M. (2005) *On Female Body Experience: 'Throwing Like a Girl' and Other Essays* (Oxford University Press).

Young, J. (1986) 'The failure of criminology: the need for a radical realism', in R. Matthews and J. Young (eds), *Confronting Crime* (Sage).

Young, J. (2003) 'Merton with energy, Katz with structure: the sociology of vindictiveness and the criminology of transgression', *Theoretical Criminology*, 7.

Young, M. F. D. (ed.) (1971) *Knowledge and Control: New Directions for the Sociology of Education* (Collier Macmillan).

Young, M. F. D. (2008) *Bringing Knowledge Back In: From Social Constructivism to Social Realism in the Sociology of Education* (Routledge).

Young, T. (2009) 'Let me tell you the secret behind the Bullingdon posturing of David and Boris: Oxford contemporary looks behind that decadent image', *Daily Mail*, 23 July.

Younge, G. (2010) *Who Are We – and Should it Matter in the 21st Century?* (Viking).

Zelizer, V. A. (1985) *Pricing the Priceless Child: Changing the Social Value of Children* (Basic Books).

Zelizer, V. A. (2005) *The Purchase of Intimacy* (Princeton University Press).

Zimring, F. (2006) *The Great American Crime Decline* (Oxford University Press).

Žižek, S. (1996) 'Invisible ideology: political violence between fiction and fantasy', *Journal of Political Ideologies*, 1(1).

Žižek, S. (2005) 'Against human rights', *New Left Review*, 34.

Zola, I. (1972) 'Medicine as an institution of social control', *Sociological Review*, 20.

Zola, I. (1973) 'Pathways to the doctor: from person to patient', *Social Science and Medicine*, 7.

Zuckerman, H., and J. R. Cole (1975) 'Women in American science', *Minerva*, 13(1).

Zuckerman, P. (2012) 'Contrasting irreligious orientations: atheism and secularity in the USA and Scandinavia', *Approaching Religion*, 2(1).

INDEX